Lecture Notes in Computer Science   14006

Founding Editors

Gerhard Goos
Juris Hartmanis

Editorial Board Members

The series Lecture Notes in Computer Science (LNCS), including its subseries Lecture Notes in Artificial Intelligence (LNAI) and Lecture Notes in Bioinformatics (LNBI), has established itself as a medium for the publication of new developments in computer science and information technology research, teaching, and education.

LNCS enjoys close cooperation with the computer science R & D community, the series counts many renowned academics among its volume editors and paper authors, and collaborates with prestigious societies. Its mission is to serve this international community by providing an invaluable service, mainly focused on the publication of conference and workshop proceedings and postproceedings. LNCS commenced publication in 1973.

Carmit Hazay · Martijn Stam
Editors

Advances in Cryptology – EUROCRYPT 2023

42nd Annual International Conference on the Theory
and Applications of Cryptographic Techniques
Lyon, France, April 23–27, 2023
Proceedings, Part III

 Springer

Editors
Carmit Hazay 🆔
Bar-Ilan University
Ramat Gan, Israel

Martijn Stam 🆔
Simula UiB
Bergen, Norway

ISSN 0302-9743   ISSN 1611-3349 (electronic)
Lecture Notes in Computer Science
ISBN 978-3-031-30619-8   ISBN 978-3-031-30620-4 (eBook)
https://doi.org/10.1007/978-3-031-30620-4

This Springer imprint is published by the registered company Springer Nature Switzerland AG
The registered company address is: Gewerbestrasse 11, 6330 Cham, Switzerland

Preface

The 42nd Annual International Conference on the Theory and Applications of Cryptographic Techniques, Eurocrypt 2023, was held in Lyon, France between April 23–27 under the auspices of the International Association for Cryptologic Research. The conference had a record number of 415 submissions, out of which 109 were accepted.

Preparation for the academic aspects of the conference started in earnest well over a year ago, with the selection of a program committee, consisting of 79 regular members and six area chairs. The area chairs played an important part in enabling a high-quality review process; their role was expanded considerably from last year and, for the first time, properly formalized. Each area chair was in charge of moderating the discussions of the papers assigned under their area, guiding PC members and reviewers to consensus where possible, and helping us in making final decisions. We created six areas and assigned the following area chairs: Ran Canetti for Theoretical Foundations; Rosario Gennaro for Public Key Primitives with Advanced Functionalities; Tibor Jager for Classic Public Key Cryptography; Marc Joye for Secure and Efficient Implementation, Cryptographic Engineering, and Real-World Cryptography; Gregor Leander for Symmetric Cryptology; and finally Arpita Patra for Multi-party Computation and Zero-Knowledge.

Prior to the submission deadline, PC members were introduced to the reviewing process; for this purpose we created a slide deck that explained what we expected from everyone involved in the process and how PC members could use the reviewing system (HotCRP) used by us. An important aspect of the reviewing process is the reviewing form, which we modified based on the Crypto'22 form as designed by Yevgeniy Dodis and Tom Shrimpton. As is customary for IACR general conferences, the reviewing process was two-sided anonymous.

Out of the 415 submissions, four were desk rejected due to violations of the Call for Papers (non-anonymous submission or significant deviations from the submission format). For the remaining submissions, the review process proceeded in two stages. In the first stage, every paper was reviewed by at least three reviewers. For 109 papers a clear, negative consensus emerged and an early reject decision was reached and communicated to the authors on the 8th of December 2022. This initial phase of early rejections allowed the program committee to concentrate on the delicate task of selecting a program amongst the more promising submissions, while simultaneously offering the authors of the rejected papers the opportunity to take advantage of the early, full feedback to improve their work for a future occasion.

The remaining 302 papers progressed to an interactive discussion phase, which was open for two weeks (ending slightly before the Christmas break). During this period, the authors had access to their reviews (apart from some PC only fields) and were asked to address questions and requests for clarifications explicitly formulated in the reviews. It gave authors and reviewers the opportunity to communicate directly (yet anonymously) with each other during several rounds of interaction. For some papers, the multiple rounds helped in clarifying both the reviewers' questions and the authors' responses.

For a smaller subset of papers, a second interactive discussion phase took place in the beginning of January allowing authors to respond to new, relevant insights by the PC. Eventually, 109 papers were selected for the program.

The best paper award was granted to the paper "An Efficient Key Recovery Attack on SIDH" by Wouter Castryck and Thomas Decru for presenting the first efficient key recovery attack against the Supersingular Isogeny Diffie-Hellman (SIDH) problem. Two further, related papers were invited to the Journal of Cryptology: "Breaking SIDH in Polynomial Time" by Damien Robert and "A Direct Key Recovery Attack on SIDH" by Luciano Maino, Chloe Martindale, Lorenz Panny, Giacomo Pope and Benjamin Wesolowski.

Accepted papers written exclusively by researchers who were within four years of PhD graduation at the time of submission were eligible for the Early Career Best Paper Award. There were a number of strong candidates and the paper "Worst-Case Subexponential Attacks on PRGs of Constant Degree or Constant Locality" by Akın Ünal was awarded this honor.

The program further included two invited talks: Guy Rothblum opened the program with his talk on "Indistinguishable Predictions and Multi-group Fair Learning" (an extended abstract of his talk appears in these proceedings) and later during the conference Vadim Lyubashevsky gave a talk on "Lattice Cryptography: What Happened and What's Next".

First and foremost, we would like to thank Kevin McCurley and Kay McKelly for their tireless efforts in the background, making the whole process so much smoother for us to run. Thanks also to our previous co-chairs Orr Dunkelman, Stefan Dziembowski, Yevgeniy Dodis, Thomas Shrimpton, Shweta Agrawal and Dongdai Lin for sharing the lessons they learned and allowing us to build on their foundations. We thank Guy and Vadim for accepting to give two excellent invited talks. Of course, no program can be selected without submissions, so we thank both the authors of accepted papers, as well as those whose papers did not make it (we sincerely hope that, notwithstanding the disappointing outcome, you found the reviews and interaction constructive). The reviewing was led by our PC members, who often engaged expert subreviewers to write high-quality, insightful reviews and engage directly in the discussions, and we are grateful to both our PC members and the subreviewers. As the IACR's general conferences grow from year to year, a very special thank you to our area chairs, our job would frankly not have been possible without Ran, Rosario, Tibor, Marc, Gregor, and Arpita's tireless efforts leading the individual papers' discussions. And, last but not least, we would like to thank the general chairs: Damien Stehlé, Alain Passelègue, and Benjamin Wesolowski who worked very hard to make this conference happen.

April 2023   Carmit Hazay
                                                                                Martijn Stam

Organization

General Co-chairs

Damien Stehlé   ENS de Lyon and Institut Universitaire de France, France
Alain Passelègue   Inria, France
Benjamin Wesolowski   CNRS and ENS de Lyon, France

Program Co-chairs

Carmit Hazay   Bar-Ilan University, Israel
Martijn Stam   Simula UiB, Norway

Area Chairs

Ran Canetti   Boston University, USA
(for Theoretical Foundations)

Rosario Gennaro   Protocol Labs and CUNY, USA
(for Public Key Primitives with Advanced Functionalities)

Tibor Jager   University of Wuppertal, Germany
(for Classic Public Key Cryptography)

Marc Joye   Zama, France
(for Secure and Efficient Implementation, Cryptographic Engineering, and Real-World Cryptography)

Gregor Leander   Ruhr-Universität Bochum, Germany
(for Symmetric Cryptology)

Arpita Patra   Google and IISc Bangalore, India
(for Multi-party Computation and Zero-Knowledge)

Program Committee

Masayuki Abe	NTT Social Informatics Laboratories and Kyoto University, Japan
Adi Akavia	University of Haifa, Israel
Prabhanjan Ananth	UC Santa Barbara, USA
Gilad Asharov	Bar-Ilan University, Israel
Marshall Ball	New York University, USA
Christof Beierle	Ruhr University Bochum, Germany
Mihir Bellare	UC San Diego, USA
Tim Beyne	KU Leuven, Belgium
Andrej Bogdanov	Chinese University of Hong Kong, China
Xavier Bonnetain	Inria, France
Joppe Bos	NXP Semiconductors, Belgium
Chris Brzuska	Aalto University, Finland
Ignacio Cascudo	IMDEA Software Institute, Spain
Nishanth Chandran	Microsoft Research India, India
Chitchanok Chuengsatiansup	The University of Melbourne, Australia
Michele Ciampi	The University of Edinburgh, UK
Ran Cohen	Reichman University, Israel
Jean-Sébastien Coron	University of Luxembourg, Luxembourg
Bernardo David	IT University of Copenhagen, Denmark
Christoph Dobraunig	Intel Labs, Intel Corporation, Hillsboro, USA
Léo Ducas	CWI Amsterdam and Leiden University, Netherlands
Maria Eichlseder	Graz University of Technology, Austria
Pooya Farshim	IOHK and Durham University, UK
Serge Fehr	CWI Amsterdam and Leiden University, Netherlands
Dario Fiore	IMDEA Software Institute, Spain
Pierre-Alain Fouque	Université Rennes 1 and Institut Universitaire de France, France
Steven Galbraith	University of Auckland, New Zealand
Chaya Ganesh	IISc Bangalore, India
Si Gao	Huawei Technologies Co., Ltd., China
Daniel Genkin	GeorgiaTech, USA
Craig Gentry	TripleBlind, USA
Benedikt Gierlichs	KU Leuven, Belgium
Rishab Goyal	UW-Madison, USA
Vipul Goyal	NTT Research and CMU, USA
Viet Tung Hoang	Florida State University, USA
Andreas Hülsing	Eindhoven University of Technology, Netherlands

Antoine Joux   CISPA, Helmholtz Center for Cybersecurity,
                                 Germany
Karen Klein   ETH Zurich, Switzerland
Markulf Kohlweiss   University of Edinburgh and IOHK, UK
Jooyoung Lee   KAIST, Korea
Gaëtan Leurent   Inria, France
Shengli Liu   Shanghai Jiao Tong University, China
Yunwen Liu   Cryptape Technology Co., Ltd., China
Stefan Lucks   Bauhaus-Universität Weimar, Germany
Hemanta Maji   Purdue, USA
Alexander May   Ruhr University Bochum, Germany
Nele Mentens   Leiden University, Netherlands and KU Leuven,
                                 Belgium
Tal Moran   Reichman University, Israel
Michael Naehrig   Microsoft Research, USA
Ngoc Khanh Nguyen   EPFL, Switzerland
Emmanuela Orsini   Bocconi University, Italy and KU Leuven,
                                 Belgium
Jiaxin Pan   NTNU, Norway
Omkant Pandey   Stony Brook University, USA
Anat Paskin-Cherniavsky   Ariel University, Israel
Chris Peikert   University of Michigan and Algorand, Inc., USA
Léo Perrin   Inria, France
Giuseppe Persiano   Università di Salerno, Italy
Thomas Peters   UCLouvain, Belgium
Christophe Petit   Université libre de Bruxelles, Belgium and
                                 University of Birmingham, UK
Krzysztof Pietrzak   ISTA, Austria
Bertram Poettering   IBM Research Europe – Zurich, Switzerland
Bart Preneel   KU Leuven, Belgium
Divya Ravi   Aarhus University, Denmark
Christian Rechberger   TU Graz, Austria
Ron Rothblum   Technion, Israel
Carla Ràfols   Universitat Pompeu Fabra, Spain
Paul Rösler   FAU Erlangen-Nürnberg, Germany
Yu Sasaki   NTT Social Informatics Laboratories, NIST
                                 Associate, Japan
Dominique Schröder   FAU Erlangen-Nürnberg, Germany
Omri Shmueli   Tel Aviv University, Israel
Janno Siim   Simula UiB, Norway
Daniel Slamanig   AIT Austrian Institute of Technology, Austria
Yifan Song   Tsinghua University, China

Qiang Tang	The University of Sydney, Australia
Serge Vaudenay	EPFL, Switzerland
Fernando Virdia	Intel Labs, Switzerland
Meiqin Wang	Shandong University, China
Mor Weiss	Bar-Ilan University, Israel
David Wu	UT Austin, USA

Additional Reviewers

Behzad Abdolmaleki	Katharina Boudgoust
Damiano Abram	Christina Boura
Hamza Abusalah	Zvika Brakerski
Leo Ackermann	Lennart Braun
Amit Agarwal	Marek Broll
Ghous Amjad	Ileana Buhan
Benny Applebaum	Matteo Campanelli
Gal Arnon	Federico Canale
Thomas Attema	Anne Canteaut
Benedikt Auerbach	Gaëtan Cassiers
Lukas Aumayr	Wouter Castryck
Gennaro Avitabile	Pyrros Chaidos
Melissa Azouaoui	André Chailloux
Saikrishna Badrinarayanan	T.-H. Hubert Chan
Karim Baghery	Anirudh Chandramouli
Kunpeng Bai	Rohit Chatterjee
Shi Bai	Hao Chen
David Balbás	Long Chen
Manuel Barbosa	Mingjie Chen
Khashayar Barooti	Yanbo Chen
James Bartusek	Yanlin Chen
Andrea Basso	Yilei Chen
Balthazar Bauer	Yu Long Chen
Carsten Baum	Wei Cheng
Michiel van Beirendonck	Céline Chevalier
Josh Benaloh	James Chiang
Fabrice Benhamouda	Wonhee Cho
Ward Beullens	Wonseok Choi
Amit Singh Bhati	Wutichai Chongchitmate
Ritam Bhaumik	Hien Chu
Alexander Bienstock	Valerio Cini
Alexander Block	Christine Cloostermans
Jonathan Bootle	Andrea Coladangelo
Cecilia Boschini	Daniel Collins

Sandro Coretti-Drayton
Craig Costello
Elizabeth Crites
Miguel Cueto Noval
Jan-Pieter D'Anvers
Sourav Das
Alex Davidson
Gabrielle De Micheli
Cyprien Delpech de Saint Guilhem
Patrick Derbez
Lalita Devadas
Siemen Dhooghe
Jesus Diaz
Khue Do
Jelle Don
Rafael Dowsley
Avijit Dutta
Sébastien Duval
Christoph Egger
Tariq Elahi
Lynn Engelberts
Felix Engelmann
Muhammed F. Esgin
Thomas Espitau
Andre Esser
Simona Etinski
Prastudy Fauzi
Patrick Felke
Hanwen Feng
Rex Fernando
Tako Boris Fouotsa
Danilo Francati
Sapir Freizeit
Paul Frixons
Rachit Garg
Sanjam Garg
Aymeric Genêt
Marios Georgiou
Satrajit Ghosh
Niv Gilboa
Valerie Gilchrist
Emanuele Giunta
Aarushi Goel
Eli Goldin
Junqing Gong

Alonso González
Lorenzo Grassi
Jiaxin Guan
Zichen Gui
Aurore Guillevic
Aditya Gulati
Aldo Gunsing
Chun Guo
Divya Gupta
Felix Günther
Hosein Hadipour
Mohammad Hajiabadi
Shai Halevi
Peter Hall
Shuai Han
Patrick Harasser
David Heath
Lena Heimberger
Alexandra Henzinger
Julia Hesse
Minki Hhan
Dennis Hofheinz
Maya-Iggy van Hoof
Sam Hopkins
Akinori Hosoyamada
Kristina Hostáková
Martha Norberg Hovd
Yu-Hsuan Huang
Loïs Huguenin-Dumittan
Kathrin Hövelmanns
Yuval Ishai
Muhammad Ishaq
Tetsu Iwata
Michael John Jacobson, Jr.
Aayush Jain
Samuel Jaques
Jinhyuck Jeong
Corentin Jeudy
Ashwin Jha
Mingming Jiang
Zhengzhong Jin
Thomas Johansson
David Joseph
Daniel Jost
Fatih Kaleoglu

Novak Kaluderovic
Chethan Kamath
Shuichi Katsumata
Marcel Keller
John Kelsey
Erin Kenney
Hamidreza Khorasgani
Hamidreza Khoshakhlagh
Seongkwang Kim
Elena Kirshanova
Fuyuki Kitagawa
Bor de Kock
Konrad Kohbrok
Lisa Kohl
Sebastian Kolby
Dimitris Kolonelos
Ilan Komargodski
Yashvanth Kondi
Venkata Koppula
Alexis Korb
Matthias Krause
Hugo Krawczyk
Toomas Krips
Mike Kudinov
Péter Kutas
Thijs Laarhoven
Yi-Fu Lai
Baptiste Lambin
Nathalie Lang
Abel Laval
Laurens Le Jeune
Byeonghak Lee
Changmin Lee
Eysa Lee
Seunghoon Lee
Sihyun Lee
Dominik Leichtle
Jannis Leuther
Shai Levin
Chaoyun Li
Yanan Li
Yiming Li
Xiao Liang
Jyun-Jie Liao
Benoît Libert

Wei-Kai Lin
Yao-Ting Lin
Helger Lipmaa
Eik List
Fukang Liu
Jiahui Liu
Qipeng Liu
Xiangyu Liu
Chen-Da Liu-Zhang
Satya Lokam
Alex Lombardi
Patrick Longa
George Lu
Jinyu Lu
Xianhui Lu
Yuan Lu
Zhenliang Lu
Ji Luo
You Lyu
Reinhard Lüftenegger
Urmila Mahadev
Mohammad Mahmoody
Mohammad Mahzoun
Christian Majenz
Nikolaos Makriyannis
Varun Maram
Laurane Marco
Ange Martinelli
Daniel Masny
Noam Mazor
Matthias Meijers
Fredrik Meisingseth
Florian Mendel
Bart Mennink
Simon-Philipp Merz
Tony Metger
Pierre Meyer
Brice Minaud
Kazuhiko Minematsu
Victor Mollimard
Tomoyuki Morimae
Nicky Mouha
Tamer Mour
Marcel Nageler
Mridul Nandi

María Naya-Plasencia
Patrick Neumann
Hai Nguyen
Ky Nguyen
Phong Q. Nguyen
Ryo Nishimaki
Olga Nissenbaum
Anca Nitulescu
Ariel Nof
Julian Nowakowski
Adam O'Neill
Sai Lakshmi Bhavana Obbattu
Miyako Ohkubo
Eran Omri
Claudio Orlandi
Michele Orrù
Elisabeth Oswald
Omer Paneth
Guillermo Pascual-Perez
Kenneth G. Paterson
Sikhar Patranabis
Alice Pellet-Mary
Maxime Plancon
Antigoni Polychroniadou
Alexander Poremba
Bernardo Portela
Eamonn Postlethwaite
Emmanuel Prouff
Kirthivaasan Puniamurthy
Octavio Pérez Kempner
Luowen Qian
Tian Qiu
Willy Quach
Håvard Raddum
Srinivasan Raghuraman
Justin Raizes
Sebastian Ramacher
Hugues Randriambololona
Shahram Rasoolzadeh
Simon Rastikian
Joost Renes
Nicolas Resch
Alfredo Rial Duran
Doreen Riepel
Silvia Ritsch

Melissa Rossi
Mike Rosulek
Yann Rotella
Lawrence Roy
Roozbeh Sarenche
Amirreza Sarencheh
Pratik Sarkar
Arish Sateesan
Christian Schaffner
Carl Richard Theodor Schneider
Markus Schofnegger
Peter Scholl
André Schrottenloher
Gregor Seiler
Sruthi Sekar
Nicolas Sendrier
Meghna Sengupta
Jinrui Sha
Akash Shah
Siamak Shahandashti
Moni Shahar
Shahed Sharif
Laura Shea
Abhi Shelat
Yaobin Shen
Sina Shiehian
Jad Silbak
Alice Silverberg
Luisa Siniscalchi
Tomer Solomon
Karl Southern
Nicholas Spooner
Sriram Sridhar
Srivatsan Sridhar
Akshayaram Srinivasan
François-Xavier Standaert
Uri Stemmer
Lukas Stennes
Patrick Steuer
Christoph Striecks
Patrick Struck
Chao Sun
Erkan Tairi
Akira Takahashi
Abdullah Talayhan

Titouan Tanguy
Stefano Tessaro
Emmanuel Thomé
Sri AravindaKrishnan Thyagarajan
Yan Bo Ti
Mehdi Tibouchi
Tyge Tiessen
Bénédikt Tran
Andreas Trügler
Daniel Tschudi
Aleksei Udovenko
Jonathan Ullman
Dominique Unruh
Vinod Vaikuntanathan
Daniele Venturi
Michiel Verbauwhede
Javier Verbel
Gilles Villard
Mikhail Volkhov
Satyanarayana Vusirikala
Benedikt Wagner
Roman Walch
Hendrik Waldner
Alexandre Wallet
Michael Walter
Mingyuan Wang
Yuyu Wang
Florian Weber
Hoeteck Wee
Puwen Wei
Charlotte Weitkaemper

Weiqiang Wen
Benjamin Wesolowski
Daniel Wichs
Wessel van Woerden
Ke Wu
Keita Xagawa
Hanshen Xiao
Jiayu Xu
Yingfei Yan
Xiuyu Ye
Kevin Yeo
Eylon Yogev
Albert Yu
Aaram Yun
Alexandros Zacharakis
Thomas Zacharias
Michal Zajac
Greg Zaverucha
Runzhi Zeng
Cong Zhang
Lei Zhang
Ren Zhang
Xinrui Zhang
Yuqing Zhao
Yu Zhou
Dionysis Zindros
Giorgos Zirdelis
Lukas Zobernig
Arne Tobias Ødegaard
Morten Øygarden

Sponsoring Institutions

- Platinum Sponsor: Université Rennes 1 and PEPR Quantique, Zama
- Gold Sponsor: Apple, Cryptolab, ENS de Lyon, ENS PSL, Huawei, Sandbox AQ, Thales, TII
- Silver Sponsor: Algorand Foundation, ANSSI, AWS, PQShield
- Bronze Sponsor: Cosmian, CryptoExperts, CryptoNext Security, IBM, Idemia, Inria, LIP

Contents – Part III

Differential Privacy

A Theory of Composition for Differential Obliviousness

Mingxun Zhou[1]([📧]), Elaine Shi[1], T.-H. Hubert Chan[2], and Shir Maimon[3]

[1] Carnegie Mellon University, Pittsburgh, USA
mingxunz@andrew.cmu.edu, runting@cs.cmu.edu
[2] The University of Hong Kong, Pokfulam, Hong Kong
hubert@cs.hku.hk
[3] Cornell University, Ithaca, USA
shir@cs.cornell.edu

Abstract. Differential obliviousness (DO) is a privacy notion which guarantees that the access patterns of a program satisfies differential privacy. Differential obliviousness was studied in a sequence of recent works as a relaxation of full obliviousness. Earlier works showed that DO not only allows us to circumvent the logarithmic-overhead barrier of fully oblivious algorithms, in many cases, it also allows us to achieve polynomial speedup over full obliviousness, since it avoids "padding to the worst-case" behavior of fully oblivious algorithms.

Despite the promises of differential obliviousness (DO), a significant barrier that hinders its broad application is the lack of composability. In particular, when we apply one DO algorithm to the output of another DO algorithm, the composed algorithm may no longer be DO (with reasonable parameters). Specifically, the outputs of the first DO algorithm on two neighboring inputs may no longer be neighboring, and thus we cannot directly benefit from the DO guarantee of the second algorithm.

In this work, we are the first to explore a theory of composition for differentially oblivious algorithms. We propose a refinement of the DO notion called (ϵ, δ)-neighbor-preserving-DO, or (ϵ, δ)-NPDO for short, and we prove that our new notion indeed provides nice compositional guarantees. In this way, the algorithm designer can easily track the privacy loss when composing multiple DO algorithms.

We give several example applications to showcase the power and expressiveness of our new NPDO notion. One of these examples is a result of independent interest: we use the compositional framework to prove an optimal privacy amplification theorem for the differentially oblivious shuffle model. In other words, we show that for a class of distributed differentially private mechanisms in the shuffle-model, one can replace the perfectly secure shuffler with a DO shuffler, and nonetheless enjoy almost the same privacy amplification enabled by a shuffler.

Randomized order. This paper subsumes part of the results in an unpublished manuscript [73] written by a subset of the authors. Full version of this paper: [74].

Supplementary Information The online version contains supplementary material available at https://doi.org/10.1007/978-3-031-30620-4_1.

© International Association for Cryptologic Research 2023
C. Hazay and M. Stam (Eds.): EUROCRYPT 2023, LNCS 14006, pp. 3–34, 2023.
https://doi.org/10.1007/978-3-031-30620-4_1

1   Introduction

It is well-known that access patterns to even encrypted or secret-shared data can leak sensitive information [15,46,47,50,52,60]. Initiated by Goldreich and Ostrovsky [42,43], *oblivious* algorithms is a line of work that aims to provably obfuscate a program's access patterns without incurring too much slowdown. In particular, *obliviousness* (also referred to as *full obliviousness*) requires that a program's access patterns be indistinguishable for any two inputs. It is well-known that oblivious algorithms have broad applications, including in multi-party computation [44,55], secure processors [54,57,59,63,69], secure outsourcing [67,72], databases [6,28,35], blockchains [16], and so on. In the past decade, our community have significantly improved the efficiency of oblivious algorithms [65,68,70], leading to large-scale real-world adoption such as Signal's private contact discovery [25]. However, as we discuss below, in some applications, the overhead of full obliviousness may still be unacceptable.

Differential Obliviousness (DO), defined by Chan, Chung, Maggs, and Shi [17], is relaxed notion of access pattern privacy. DO requires that the program's access patterns satisfy only differential privacy (DP) [30], as opposed to a simulation-based notion like in full obliviousness [42,43,65]. Recent works [10, 12,17,24,45] explored DO and showed how DO can allow us to circumvent fundamental performance barriers pertaining to full obliviousness:

- Chan et al. [17] showed a fundamental separation in terms of efficiency between DO and full obliviousness. Specifically, for a class of common tasks such as compaction, merging, and range query data structures, while full obliviousness is inherently subject to at least $\Omega(\log N)$ multiplicative overhead [3,36,51,53] (in comparison with the insecure baseline), using DO allows us to reduce the overhead to only $O(\log \log N)$ where N denotes the data size.
- Not only does DO allow us to overcome the logarithmic barrier for fully oblivious algorithms, another important aspect that is sometime overlooked is that DO allows us to overcome the "worst-case barrier" of fully oblivious algorithms [24], which leads to *polynomial* speedup over full obliviousness in many applications. Specifically, to achieve full obliviousness, we must pad the running time and output length to the worst case over all possible inputs (of some fixed length), whereas DO algorithms may reveal the *noisy* running time or output length. In many real-world scenarios such as database joins [24], the common case enjoys much shorter runtime and output length than the worst case. For exactly this reason, there is an entire line of work that focuses on designing algorithms optimized for the common rather than the worst case [64]. In such cases, prior works showed that DO can achieve polynomial speedup over any fully oblivious algorithm [17,24]!

Basic DO does NOT Lend to Composition. Given the promises of DO, we would like to apply DO to more applications. Unfortunately, the status quo of DO hinders its broad applicability due to the lack of *compositional* guarantees. When designing algorithms, it is customary to compose several algorithmic building blocks together. In such cases, it would be nice to say that the composed algorithm also satisfies DO with reasonable parameters as long as the underlying algorithmic building blocks also satisfy DO. Similarly, in some applications, we may need to apply a DO algorithm to the outcome of another (e.g., the SQL database application below). In such cases, we also want to be able to track the privacy loss over time. While the original full obliviousness notion indeed allows such composition, unfortunately, the standard DO notion [17] does not!

As an explicit example of composition, imagine that we want to build a differentially oblivious database supporting SQL queries. Consider the following natural SQL query where we want to select entries from a table which in itself is the result of a previous `Select` operation[1]:

```
Select (id, position) from
    (Select (id, dept, position) from Employees where salary > 200K)
where dept = "CS"
```

To support this query in a differentially oblivious manner, the most natural idea is to use the DO stable compaction algorithm of Chan et al. [17] to realize each `Select` operator. In stable compaction, we obtain an input array where each element is either a *real* element or a *filler*, and we want to output an array containing all the *real* elements of the input and preserving the order they appear in the input. Unfortunately, this approach completely fails since Chan et al. [17]'s DO compaction algorithm does NOT compose.

To understand why, we will introduce some basic notation. Let $M : \mathcal{X} \to \mathcal{Y}$ denote an algorithm, which takes in an input $x \in \mathcal{X}$, and produces an output $y \in \mathcal{Y}$. Consider some neighboring notion $\sim_{\mathcal{X}}$ defined over the input domain $\mathcal{X}$. For example, let $x, x' \in \mathcal{X}$ be two input arrays/tables where each entry corresponds to an individual user. One example is Hamming-distance neighboring: we say that $x \sim_{\mathcal{X}} x'$ iff the Hamming distance of x and x' is at most 1—this is also the neighboring notion adopted by the DO compaction algorithm of Chan et al. [17]. The standard DO notion requires the following.

Definition 1.1 (Basic differential obliviousness [17]). *We say that an algorithm* M *satisfies* (ϵ, δ)*-DO w.r.t. some symmetric relation* $\sim_{\mathcal{X}}$ *iff for any* $x, x' \in \mathcal{X}$ *such that* $x \sim_{\mathcal{X}} x'$, *for any subset* S,

$$\Pr[\mathsf{View}^M(x) \in S] \leq e^{\epsilon} \cdot \Pr[\mathsf{View}^M(x') \in S] + \delta, \tag{1}$$

where $\mathsf{View}^M(x)$ *is a random variable denoting the the memory access patterns observed when running the algorithm* M *over the input* x.

Now, imagine that we have two DO mechanisms $M_1 : \mathcal{X}_1 \to \mathcal{X}_2$ and $M_2 : \mathcal{X}_2 \to \mathcal{Y}$ (e.g., think of M_1 and M_2 as Chan et al.'s DO compaction algorithm). We want to apply M_2 to the output of M_1, and hope that the composed mechanism $M_2 \circ M_1(\cdot)$ satisfies DO. By the DO definition, we know that M_2 offers indistinguishability for two *neighboring* inputs from $\mathcal{X}_2$. Now, consider two neighboring inputs $x \sim_{\mathcal{X}_1} x'$ from $\mathcal{X}_1$, and consider running the mechanism M_1

---

[1] Here we write the two `Select` statements in a single query for convenience, In practice, it could be that the first `Select` query is interactively issued and its result stored as a temporary table, and then the second `Select` query is interactively issued.

over x and x', respectively. Unfortunately, the basic DO notion (of M_1) does *not* guarantee that the outputs $M_1(x)$ and $M_1(x')$ are also neighboring. Therefore, we may not be able to benefit from the DO property of M_2!

We stress that this is not just a deficiency of the basic DO definition. Natural designs of DO algorithms often do not guarantee that the outputs obtained from two neighboring inputs must be neighboring too. For example, consider the stable compaction algorithm of Chan et al. [17]. Given two input arrays $x = (1, 2, \perp, 3, 4)$ and $x' = (\perp, 2, \perp, 3, 4)$ with Hamming distance 1 where $\perp$ denotes a filler, the compacted outputs will be $(1, 2, 3, 4)$ and $(2, 3, 4)$, respectively. The outputs have Hamming distance more than 1. While the outputs have large Hamming distance, the edit distance is only one—unfortunately, Chan et al.'s compaction algorithm provides privacy only for Hamming-distance neighboring and the guarantees do not generalize to edit-distance neighboring.

DP Composition Theorems do not Work for DO. Since DO is essentially DP applied to the memory access patterns, a natural question is: *can we simply use DP composition theorems to reason about the composition DO mechanisms?* The answer is *no* because DP composition and composition of DO mechanisms are of different nature. In DP composition, we have multiple mechanisms $M_1, \ldots, M_k$ where M_i satisfies (ϵ_i, δ_i)-DP. The basic DP composition theorem says that the composed mechanism $M(x) := (M_1(x), \ldots, M_k(x))$ satisfies $(\sum_{i=1}^{k} \epsilon_i, \sum_{i=1}^{k} \delta_i)$-DP. Here, all these mechanisms are applied to the *same input* x. In DO composition, we want to apply M_2 to the *output* of of M_1 instead. More generally, if there are k DO mechanisms $M_1, \ldots, M_k$, we want to know whether the composed mechanism $M_k \circ M_{k-1} \circ \ldots, \circ M_1(x) = M_k(M_{k-1}(\ldots M_1(x)))$ is also DO.

Given the status quo, we ask the following natural question:

Can we have suitable and useful refinements of differential obliviousness (DO) that lend to composition?

1.1 Main Contribution: A Theory of Composition for Differential Obliviousness

We are the first to initiate a formal exploration of the composability of differential obliviousness. In this sense, we make an important conceptual contribution: by laying the groundwork for the composition of DO algorithms. We hope that our work can allow DO to have wider applicability.

A New, Composable DO Notion. Our first contribution is to introduce a new, composable DO notion called *Neighbor-Preserving Differential Obliviousness (NPDO)* that can be viewed as a strengthening of the basic DO by Chan et al. [17]. Our NPDO notion is composition friendly in the following senses:

C1. If M_1 satisfies (ϵ_1, δ_1)-NPDO, and M_2 satisfies (ϵ_2, δ_2)-DO (the basic version), then the composed mechanism $M_2 \circ M_1$ satisfies $(\epsilon_1 + \epsilon_2, \delta_1 + \delta_2)$-DO.

C2. If M_1 satisfies (ϵ_1, δ_1)-NPDO, and M_2 satisfies (ϵ_2, δ_2)-NPDO, then the composed mechanism $M_2 \circ M_1$ satisfies $(\epsilon_1 + \epsilon_2, \delta_1 + \delta_2)$-NPDO.

In the above, the first property allows us to apply any basic-DO algorithm M_2 to the output of an NPDO algorithm M_1, and the composed algorithm $M_2 \circ M_1$

would satisfy basic DO. The second property allows us to perform composition repeatedly. In particular, if both M_1 and M_2 are NPDO, then the composed algorithm $M_2 \circ M_1$ also satisfies NPDO, i.e., it can be further composed with other DO or NPDO algorithms.

Finding the right notion turned out to be non-trivial. We want to capture the intuition that "the algorithm should produce neighboring outputs for neighboring inputs". However, it is not obvious how to formally capture this idea of "neighbor-preserving" especially when the outputs of the DO algorithm may be randomized. Indeed, naïve ways to define "neighbor-preserving" turned out to be too stringent and preclude many natural and interesting algorithms (see Sect. 3.1). We instead suggest a more general version that allows us to capture a probabilistic notion of neighbor-preserving. More specifically, our NPDO notion requires that when one applies the algorithm M on two neighboring inputs x and x', the *joint distribution* of the adversary's view and the output must be distributionally close in some technical sense, where *closeness is parametrized by some output neighboring relation*. The formal definition is presented below:

Definition 1.2 $((\epsilon, \delta)$-NPDO). *We say that an algorithm* $M : \mathcal{X} \to \mathcal{Y}$ *with view space* $\mathcal{V}$ *satisfies* (ϵ, δ)-*NPDO w.r.t. input relation* $\sim_{\mathcal{X}}$ *and output relation* $\sim_{\mathcal{Y}}$, *if for any* $x, x' \in \mathcal{X}$ *such that* $x \sim_{\mathcal{X}} x'$, *for any subset* $S \subseteq \mathcal{V} \times \mathcal{Y}$,

$$\Pr[\mathsf{Exec}^M(x) \in S] \leq e^\epsilon \cdot \Pr[\mathsf{Exec}^M(x') \in \mathcal{N}(S)] + \delta.$$

In the above, $\mathsf{Exec}^M(x)$ *samples a random execution of* M *on the input* x, *and returns the view (i.e., access patterns) as well as the algorithm's output. Further, the notation* $\mathcal{N}(S)$, *i.e., the neighboring set of* S, *is defined as follows:*

$$\mathcal{N}(S) = \{(v, y) | \exists (v, y') \in S \ s.t. \ y \sim_{\mathcal{Y}} y'\}$$

Expressiveness of Our Notion. We give various natural examples to demonstrate the expressiveness and power of our notion. We believe that our NPDO notion is indeed the right notion, given the simplicity in form and its broad applicability. Besides the motivating SQL database example mentioned earlier in this section, other notable examples include the design of a differentially oblivious subsampling algorithm, a stable compaction algorithm that is DO w.r.t. edit distance, and finally, proving an optimal privacy amplification theorem in the differentially oblivious shuffle model. Since the last application is of independent interest even as a standalone result, we will discuss the context and the implications of this result separately in Sect. 1.2.

Proof of Composition Theorem. Our second contribution is to prove the composition theorem:

Theorem 1.3 (Composition theorem). *The aforementioned compositional properties C1 and C2 hold, as long as the algorithm* M_1's *view space and output space are finite or countably infinite.*

The proof of the composition theorem is rather non-trivial. A key step in the proof is to show the following equivalence (see Lemma 4.1). An algorithm

M : $\mathcal{X} \to \mathcal{Y}$ (with at most countably infinite view space $\mathcal{V}$ and output space $\mathcal{Y}$) satisfies (ϵ, δ)-NPDO w.r.t. $\sim_{\mathcal{X}}$ and $\sim_{\mathcal{Y}}$, *if and only if* for any neighboring inputs $x \sim_{\mathcal{X}} x'$, there exists an (ϵ, δ)-matching between the the probability spaces of the random variables $\mathsf{Exec}^{\mathsf{M}}(x) \in \mathcal{V} \times \mathcal{Y}$ and $\mathsf{Exec}^{\mathsf{M}}(x') \in \mathcal{V} \times \mathcal{Y}$. In an (ϵ, δ)-matching, imagine that we have a (possibly countably infinitely large) bipartite graph where one side has the sources, and the other side has the destinations. Both sources and destinations come from the space $\mathcal{V} \times \mathcal{Y}$. If there is an edge of weight w between some source and some destination, we may imagine that the source wants to send w amount of commodity to the destination. Now, each source $(v, y) \in \mathcal{V} \times \mathcal{Y}$ produces an amount of commodity equal to $\Pr\left[\mathsf{Exec}^{\mathsf{M}}(x) = (v, y)\right]$, and each destination (v, y') can receive at most $e^{\epsilon} \cdot \Pr\left[\mathsf{Exec}^{\mathsf{M}}(x') = (v, y')\right]$ amount of commodity. Furthermore, a source (v, y) can be matched with a desitination (v', y') only if they are neighboring, i.e., $v = v'$ and $y \sim_{\mathcal{Y}} y'$. We want to find a matching such that all but δ amount of commodity is delivered to the destinations. To prove this key equivalence lemma, we are inspired by techniques used to prove the Hall's marriage theorem [48,49]. Once we prove the key equivalence lemma, we then rely on it to prove the composition theorem.

In the main body, we primarily focus on proving the composition theorem for *statistical* notions of DO. In Appendix A of the full version [74], we further extend our composition theorem to support suitable, *computational* notions of differential obliviousness as well.

Finally, in our composition theorem, we assume that the view and output spaces of M_1 are at most countably infinitely large. This assumption is reasonable given that we primarily focus on the standard word-RAM model of execution. It is indeed an interesting open question whether we can remove this restriction and prove the composition theorem for uncountably large view and output spaces— this is useful if we consider RAM machines that can handle real arithmetic. In Appendix C of the full version [74], we discuss the additional technicalities that one might encounter if we wish to remove the countable restriction.

1.2   Additional Result: Optimal Privacy Amplification in the DO-Shuffle Model

As an application of our composition framework, we use it to prove an optimal privacy amplification theorem in the differentially oblivious shuffle (DO-shuffle) model. Since this result can be of independent interest on its own, we explain the motivation and context below.

Background: Privacy Amplification in the Shuffle Model. To understand the DO-shuffle model, let us first review some background on the so-called shuffle model. Imagine that a set of clients each hold some private data, and an *untrusted* server wants to perform some analytics over the union of the clients' data, while preserving each individual client's privacy. Specifically, we want to guarantee that for two neighboring input configurations of the clients denoted $\mathbf{x}$ and $\mathbf{x}'$ respectively, the distributions of the server's view are "close".

The shuffle model, first proposed by Bittau et al. [11] in an empirical work, has become a popular model for implementing distributed differentially private mechanisms. The model assumes the existence of a trusted shuffler that takes the union of all clients' messages, randomly permutes them, and presents the shuffled result to the server. The server then performs some computation and outputs the analytics result. The trusted shuffler guarantees that the server can only see the union of all messages, without knowing the source of an individual message. Numerous earlier works [8,22,23,39,40] have shown that the shuffle model often enables differentially private mechanisms whose utility approximates the best known algorithms in the *central model* (where the server is trusted and we only need privacy on the outcome of the analytics). Moreover, several works have shown that the trusted shuffler can be efficiently implemented either using trusted hardware [11] or using cryptographic protocols [1,2,9,14,20,21,26,27, 29,34,38,61,62,66,75]. This makes the shuffle model a compelling approach not just in theory, but also in practical applications such as federated learning [41].

A particular useful type of theorem in the shuffle model is called a privacy amplification theorem, which we explain below. Henceforth, let $\mathcal{R}(x_i)$ be some differentially private mechanism each client i applies to randomize its own private input x_i (often called a *locally differentially private (LDP)* randomizer). Roughly speaking, a privacy amplification theorem makes a statement of the following nature where $\mathcal{S}(\cdot)$ denotes the shuffler that outputs a random permutation of the inputs: if each client's LDP mechanism $\mathcal{R}$ consumes ϵ_0 privacy budget, then shuffler's outcome $\mathcal{S}(\mathcal{R}(x_1), \ldots, \mathcal{R}(x_n))$ satisfies (ϵ, δ)-DP for $\epsilon = \epsilon(\epsilon_0, \delta) \ll \epsilon_0$, i.e., privacy is amplified for the overall shuffle-model mechanism. A line of work [8,23,33] focused on proving privacy amplification theorems for the shuffle model, culminating in the recent work by Feldman et al. [37], who proved a privacy amplification theorem for any LDP mechanism with optimal parameters.

Connection Between the Shuffle Model and Our DO Composition Framework. We realize that the shuffle model can be expressed with our DO composition framework. Consider a composed mechanism $\mathsf{S} \circ \mathsf{M}_1$. $\mathsf{M}_1 : \mathcal{X}^n \to \mathcal{Y}^n$ is a local randomization mechanism that takes n clients' inputs $(x_1, \ldots, x_n)$ and outputs the message sequence $(y_1, \ldots, y_n)$ where $y_i = \mathcal{R}(x_i)$. $\mathsf{S} : \mathcal{Y}^n \to \mathcal{Y}^n$ is a shuffling mechanism that takes a message sequence $(y_1, \ldots, y_n)$ and outputs a random permutation of the sequence. All computation in M_1 are done by the clients locally, so we define $\mathsf{View}^{\mathsf{M}_1} := \emptyset$. We define the view in S as exactly its output: the random permutation. Then, the view of the server in the shuffle model is exactly the same as the view of the adversary in $\mathsf{S} \circ \mathsf{M}_1$. Thus, (ϵ, δ)-shuffle-DP guarantee can be expressed by $\mathsf{S} \circ \mathsf{M}_1$ being (ϵ, δ)-DO w.r.t the input neighboring notion $\sim_\mathcal{X}$ where $\mathbf{x} \sim_\mathcal{X} \mathbf{x}'$ iff the Hamming distance is at most 1.

Can We Replace the Shuffler with a DO-shuffler? A couple very recent works [5,13,45] have suggested a relaxed shuffler model called the *differentially oblivious shuffle* model (or *DO-shuffle model* for short). Unlike the traditional shuffle model which provides full anonymity on the clients' messages, the DO-shuffle model permutes the clients' messages but possibly allowing some differentially private leakage. More concretely, a DO-shuffle protocol guarantees that for two *neighboring* input vectors $\mathbf{x}_H$ and $\mathbf{x}'_H$ corresponding to the set of honest parties, the adversary's views in the protocol execution are computationally or statistically close. The recent works by Gordon et al. [45] and Bünz et al. [13] both show that the relaxed DO-shuffle can be asymptotically more efficient to cryptographically realize than a fully anonymous shuffle. It would therefore be desirable to use a DO-shuffler as a drop-in replacement of the perfectly secure shuffle. This raises a couple very natural questions:

– *If we were to replace the shuffler in shuffle-model differentially private mechanisms with a DO-shuffler, can we still get comparable privacy-utility tradeoff?*
– *More specifically, can we prove an optimal privacy amplification theorem for the DO-shuffle model, matching the parameters of Feldman et al. [37]?*

The pioneering work of Gordon et al. [45] was the first to explore how to use a DO shuffler to design distributed differentially private mechanisms. Gordon et al. [45] showed two novel results. First, they prove an optimal privacy amplification theorem for the randomized response mechanism in the DO-shuffle model, with parameters that tightly match the shuffle-model counterpart. Next, they generalize their first result, and prove a privacy amplification theorem for any local differentially private (LDP) mechanism—however, this more general result is *non-optimal*, since they rely on the non-optimal shuffle-model amplification theorem from Balle et al. [8].

Our Results. We prove a privacy amplification theorem for *any LDP mechanism* that achieves *optimal* parameters, tightly matching Feldman et al. [37]'s privacy amplification parameters for the shuffle model. This result improves work of Gordon et al. [45] in the following senses: 1) we asymptotically improve their privacy amplification theorem for any general LDP mechanism; and 2) their privacy amplification theorem for the specific randomized response mechanism can be viewed as a special case of our general theorem. More interestingly, we can prove our result fully under our DO composition framework. The curx of the proof is to show that the local randomization mechanism M_1 is (ϵ, δ)-NPDO w.r.t the output neighboring notion being exactly the DO-shuffler's input neighboring notion. Then, when M_1 composes with an (ϵ_1, δ_1)-DO shuffler, the composed mechanism will be $(\epsilon + \epsilon_1, \delta + \delta_1)$-DO.

Below, we give a more formal statement of our result. Let Φ denote a DO-shuffling protocol. Given an LDP-randomizer $\mathcal{R}(\cdot)$, we use the notation $\Pi(x_1, \ldots, x_n) := \Phi(\mathcal{R}(x_1), \ldots, \mathcal{R}(x_n))$ to denote the composed protocol where each of the n parties first applies the local randomizer $\mathcal{R}(\cdot)$ to its own private data, and then invokes an instance of the DO-shuffling protocol Φ on the outcome $\mathcal{R}(x_i)$.

Theorem 1.4 (Optimal privacy amplification for any LDP mechanism in the DO-shuffle model). *Suppose $\epsilon_0 \leq \log\left(\frac{n}{16\log(2/\delta)}\right)$. Given n copies of an ϵ_0-LDP randomizer $\mathcal{R}$ and an (ϵ_1, δ_1)-DO shuffler Φ resilient to t corrupted parties, the composed protocol $\Pi(x_1, \ldots, x_n) := \Phi(\mathcal{R}(x_1), \ldots, \mathcal{R}(x_n))$ is $(\epsilon + \epsilon_1, \delta + \delta_1)$-DO against up to t corrupted parties where*

$$\epsilon = O\left(\frac{(1 - e^{\epsilon_0})e^{\epsilon_0/2}\sqrt{\log(1/\delta)}}{\sqrt{n-t}}\right).$$

Furthermore, if the DO-shuffler satisfies computational (or statistical, resp.) DO, then the composed protocol satisfies computation (or statistical, resp.) DO.

Further, if the underlying DO-shuffle protocol satisfies semi-honest security [5,45], then the composed protocol is also secure in a semi-honest corruption model. Similarly, if the underlying DO-shuffle satisfies malicious security (e.g., [5,13]), then the composed protocol is also secure in a malicious model.

2 Model and Preliminaries

2.1 Model of Computation

We consider a standard Random Access Machine (RAM) model of computation. We use the standard word-RAM model where the word size is logarithmic in the space. We assume that addition, multiplication, and boolean operations on words can be done in constant time. We also assume that sampling from truncated geometric distributions can be done in constant time[2]. We assume that the adversary can observe the memory access patterns of the algorithm, including which locations are read or written and in which time steps. The adversary cannot see the contents of the memory tape themselves, which also means that the adversary cannot see the contents of the input and output.

Format of Input and Output Tape. We explain the format of the input and output tape—the modeling technicalities are without loss of generality, and matter if we want to mask the true input and output lengths.

In the most general model, *the algorithm may or may not be able to observe the input and output length, depending on the algorithm*. More specifically, we may assume that the input is written on an input tape—the input tape itself has *unbounded* length and the *actual length of the input is written on some dedicated location*, e.g., address 0, of the input tape. The algorithm can read address 0 to learn the actual input length. During the execution, the algorithm *may read a random number of extraneous locations* on the input tape, such that the adversary may not be able to observe the exact input length. We assume that every extraneous location on the input tape stores a filler symbol $\perp$.

---

[2] Based on Appendix B of [24], we can obliviously sample a truncated geometric variable in expected time of $O(\frac{1}{\epsilon}\log\frac{1}{\delta})$. Further, we can sample M truncated geometric variables in time $O((M/\epsilon)\log(1/\delta))$ with probability $1 - \mathsf{negl}(M)$. Our algorithms described in Sect. 5 only need to sample $\frac{\epsilon L}{(\log^2 L \log(1/\delta))} + O(1)$ truncated geometrics. Therefore, all our runtime bounds(i.e., Theorem 5.2 and Theorem 5.6) hold in expectation and with high probability without assuming sampling in constant time.

The algorithm must write the output on an output tape. Again, the algorithm, may *write a random number of extraneous locations* on the output tape. For example, if the actual output length is m, the algorithm may actually write $m' > m$ locations on the output tape where m' is a random variable, to mask the true output length. To indicate the actual output length, the algorithm can write the actual output length m on some dedicated location of the output tape. By doing so, the adversary may not be able to observe the exact output length.

2.2   Preliminaries

Mathematical Tools. We introduce some basic mathematical tools.

Definition 2.1 (Symmetric geometric distribution). *Let $\alpha > 1$. The symmetric geometric distribution* $\mathsf{Geom}(\alpha)$ *takes integer values such that the probability mass function at k is* $\frac{\alpha-1}{\alpha+1} \cdot \alpha^{-|k|}$.

In designing DO algorithms, we often pad the true output length with random fillers such that the adversary observes a randomized output length. Below, we define a shifted and truncated geometric distribution which is often used to sample the number of fillers used for padding. In particular, this distribution always gives non-negative and bounded random variables.

Definition 2.2 (Shifted and truncated geometric distribution). *Let $\epsilon > 0$ and $\delta \in (0, 1)$ and $\Delta \geq 1$. Let k_0 be the smallest positive integer such that* $\Pr[|\mathsf{Geom}(e^{\frac{\epsilon}{\Delta}})| \geq k_0] \leq \delta$, *where* $k_0 = \frac{\Delta}{\epsilon} \ln \frac{2}{\delta} + O(1)$. *The shifted and truncated geometric distribution* $\mathcal{G}(\epsilon, \delta, \Delta)$ *has support* $[0, 2(k_0 + \Delta - 1)]$, *and is defined as:*

$$\min\{\max\{0, k_0 + \Delta - 1 + \mathsf{Geom}(e^\epsilon)\}, 2(k_0 + \Delta - 1)\}$$

For the special case $\Delta = 1$, we write $\mathcal{G}(\epsilon, \delta) := \mathcal{G}(\epsilon, \delta, 1)$.

Common Distance Notions. We will also use a couple common distance notions in our examples, including Hamming distance and edit distance.

Definition 2.3 (Hamming distance neighboring $\sim_H$). *We say that two arrays x, x' are neighboring by the Hamming distance iff 1) they have the same length; and 2) they differ in at most one position.*

Definition 2.4 (Edit distance neighboring $\sim_E$). *We say that two arrays x, x' are neighboring by the edit distance iff x' can be obtained from x through either one insertion, one deletion, or one substitution. Note that x and x' need not have the same length.*

Notations for Randomized Execution. Given randomized mechanisms $\mathsf{M}_1 : \mathcal{X} \to \mathcal{Y}$ and $\mathsf{M}_2 : \mathcal{Y} \times \mathcal{Z}$, the composed mechanism $\mathsf{M}_2 \circ \mathsf{M}_1 : \mathcal{X} \to \mathcal{Z}$ works as follows: for input $x \in \mathcal{X}$, we first apply $\mathsf{M}_1(x)$ to produce an intermediate $y \in \mathcal{Y}$, and then we apply $\mathsf{M}_2(y)$.

Henceforth, given an algorithm $\mathsf{M} : \mathcal{X} \to \mathcal{Y}$, and an input $x \in \mathcal{X}$, we often use the following random variables:

- The random variable $\mathsf{View}^{\mathsf{M}}(x) : \mathcal{X} \to \mathcal{V}$ denotes the memory access patterns (also called the **view**) observed by the adversary when M receives the input x, where $\mathcal{V}$ is the view space for M.
- The notation $\mathsf{Exec}^{\mathsf{M}}(x) : \mathcal{X} \to \mathcal{V} \times \mathcal{Y}$ is a random variable that outputs the view and the output over a random execution of $\mathsf{M}(x)$.

3   A Composition Framework for DO

In this section, we explore what kind of DO notions are composition-friendly. As a warmup, we first suggest a simple notion called strongly neighbor-preserving (or strongly NP for short), and show that any DO algorithm that is strongly NP lends to composition. The strong NP notion, however, is too stringent. We then propose a more general notion called (ϵ, δ)-neighbor-preserving differential obliviousness or (ϵ, δ)-NPDO for short, which captures a probabilistically approximate notion of neighbor-preserving. We then present our main composition theorem which states that any algorithm that satisfies NPDO lends to composition. Along the way, we give several simple motivating examples to demonstrate the usefulness our compositional framework.

3.1   Strongly Neighbor-Preserving

Definition and Composition Theorem. Earlier, in Sect. 1, we argued why basic DO algorithms do not lend to composition, because neighboring inputs may lead to very dissimilar outputs. One (somewhat imprecise) intuition is the following: if a DO mechanism is additionally *neighbor-preserving*, i.e., neighboring inputs lead to neighboring outputs, then it should lend to composition.

We first define strongly neighbor-preserving that running the algorithm over two neighboring inputs produces neighboring outputs with probability 1.

Definition 3.1 (Strongly neighbor-preserving). *We say that a randomized algorithm* $\mathsf{M} : \mathcal{X} \to \mathcal{Y}$ *is strongly neighbor-preserving w.r.t.* $\sim_{\mathcal{X}}$ *and* $\sim_{\mathcal{Y}}$, *iff for any two inputs* $x, x' \in \mathcal{X}$ *such that* $x \sim_{\mathcal{X}} x'$,

$$\Pr[y \leftarrow \mathsf{M}(x), y' \leftarrow \mathsf{M}(x') : y \sim_{\mathcal{Y}} y'] = 1.$$

We can prove that if an algorithm satisfies both DO and strongly neighbor-preserving, then it is composable, formally stated below.

Theorem 3.2 (Strongly neighbor-preserving + DO gives composition). *Suppose that* $\mathsf{M}_1 : \mathcal{X} \to \mathcal{Y}$ *is* (ϵ_1, δ_1)-*DO w.r.t.* $\sim_{\mathcal{X}}$ *and strongly neighbor-preserving w.r.t.* $\sim_{\mathcal{X}}$ *and* $\sim_{\mathcal{Y}}$, *and moreover, suppose that* $\mathsf{M}_2 : \mathcal{Y} \to \mathcal{Z}$ *is* (ϵ_2, δ_2)-*DO w.r.t.* $\sim_{\mathcal{Y}}$, *then* $\mathsf{M}_2 \circ \mathsf{M}_1$ *satisfies* $(\epsilon_1 + \epsilon_2, \delta_1 + \delta_2)$-*DO w.r.t.* $\sim_{\mathcal{X}}$.

Furthermore, if M_2 *is additionally strongly neighbor-preserving w.r.t.* $\sim_{\mathcal{Y}}$ *and* $\sim_{\mathcal{Z}}$, *then* $\mathsf{M}_2 \circ \mathsf{M}_1$ *is also strongly neighbor-preserving w.r.t.* $\sim_{\mathcal{X}}$ *and* $\sim_{\mathcal{Z}}$.

Proof. Later in Lemma 3.7 of Sect. 3.4, we will prove that (ϵ_1, δ_1)-DO plus strongly neighbor-preserving is a special case of our more general notion (ϵ_1, δ_1)-NPDO. In this sense, this composition theorem can be viewed as a special case of our main composition theorem for NPDO (Theorem 3.6).

Composition Examples

Example 1. Recall that in Sect. 1, we gave a natural SQL database example that required applying one compaction algorithm on the output of another compaction algorithm. We pointed out that two sequential instances of Chan et al.'s DO compaction algorithm [17] do not give (tight) composable guarantees. In Example 1, we will see that if we replace the second instance with a modification of the compaction algorithm such that it is DO w.r.t. edit distance (as opposed to Hamming distance), the two instances would compose nicely.

Specifically, let M_1 be Chan et al.'s DO compaction algorithm [17]. Recall that the algorithm receives an input array where each element is either a *real* element or a *filler*, and outputs an array containing all the real elements in the input and preserving the order they appear in the input. M_1 is (ϵ_1, δ_1)-DO w.r.t. $\sim_H$ (i.e., Hamming distance). Now, suppose we can construct another compaction algorithm denoted M_2 that is (ϵ_2, δ_2)-DO w.r.t. to $\sim_E$ (i.e., *edit* distance). How to construct such an M_2 while preserving efficiency turns out to be non-trivial, and we defer the construction to Sect. 5—interestingly, designing M_2 itself demonstrates the usefulness of our composition framework, too.

Observe that given a fixed input array x, the output of $M_1(x)$ must be an ordered list of real elements contained in x plus an appropriate number of fillers, and the total length of the output[3] is the same as the input x. Thus, for any neighboring inputs $x \sim_H x'$, it must be that $M_1(x) \sim_E M_2(x')$. Therefore, we conclude that M_1 is strongly neighbor-preserving w.r.t. the input relation $\sim_H$ and the output relation $\sim_E$. Applying Theorem 3.2, we conclude that the composed mechanism $M_2 \circ M_1$ satisfies $(\epsilon_1 + \epsilon_2, \delta_1 + \delta_2)$-DO.

Example 2. Let M_1 be an algorithm that merges two sorted input arrays (x_0, x_1), where each element in the input array has a payload besides the sort-key. Suppose that M_1 satisfies (ϵ_1, δ_1) differential obliviousness w.r.t. $\overset{2}{\sim}_E$, i.e., two inputs (x_0, x_1) and (x_0', x_1') are considered neighboring iff for $b \in \{0,1\}$, $|x_b| = |x_b'|$, and x_b and x_b' have edit distance at most 2 (i.e., $x_b \overset{2}{\sim}_E x_b'$). Such an DO merge algorithm was proposed by Chan et al. [17], and moreover, their algorithm always outputs an array whose length is the sum of the input arrays. Notice that for neighboring inputs, M_1 always produces outputs that have edit distance at most 4.

Let M_2 be a stable tight compaction algorithm that selects elements from the input array whose payload string satisfies a certain predicate (e.g., entries corresponding to students in the computer science department). Suppose that M_2 satisfies (ϵ_2, δ_2)-DO w.r.t. $\overset{4}{\sim}_E$, i.e., where neighboring inputs are those with edit distance at most 4—such an M_2 is described in Sect. 5.

By Theorem 3.2, we conclude that the composed mechanism $M_2 \circ M_1$ satisfies $(\epsilon_1 + \epsilon_2, \delta_1 + \delta_2)$-DO w.r.t. $\overset{2}{\sim}_E$.

---

[3] Even though the algorithm M_1 itself is randomized, the output of M_1 is deterministic and unique given the input.

Remark 3.3 (Capturing k-neighboring relations). Recall that our strongly neighbor-preserving definition (i.e., Definition 3.1) is parametrized with the input and output relations. Example 2 is used to illustrate the case when the these input/output relations are parametrized with a k-neighboring notion (rather than 1-neighboring)—this shows the generality of the approach. For example, later in Sect. 5, we will construct an efficient stable compaction algorithm that is (ϵ, δ)-DO w.r.t. to $\overset{1}{\sim}_E$ neighboring. Applying the standard group privacy theorem of differential privacy [32], we can get a compaction algorithm that is $(4\epsilon, 4e^{4\epsilon}\delta)$-DO w.r.t. to $\overset{4}{\sim}_E$ neighboring.

Limitations. The strong neighbor-preserving requirement (i.e., Definition 3.1) is natural and directly captures our intuition that if a DO mechanism maps neighboring inputs to neighboring outputs, then it is composable. The strongly neighbor-preserving requirement is often suitable when the output computed by the algorithm is deterministic (i.e., uniquely determined by the inputs), even though the algorithm itself may be randomized, like Examples 1 and 2.

However, the strongly neighbor-preserving requirement may be too stringent especially when the output of the algorithm may be randomized. For example, consider the following DO subsampling algorithm.

Example 3. We consider the task of subsampling, which is widely used in private data analytics [7,71]: given an input array x, we want to sample each entry with probability p, and generate a new array with only the sampled elements. Consider a subsampling algorithm where n denotes the length of the input array x:

1. Call $\mathsf{M}_1(x) := \mathsf{InPlaceSample}(x)$ which is defined as follows: Scan the input array x. For each real element encountered, append it to the output tape with probability p and append a filler element otherwise. For each filler element encountered, just append a filler to the output tape.
2. Apply M_2, a compaction algorithm that is (ϵ', δ')-DO w.r.t. $\sim_H$ to the output of the above step.

We want to prove that the above algorithm satisfies DO w.r.t. $\sim_H$ through composition—intuitively, this should be true. In particular, the first subroutine $\mathsf{M}_1 := \mathsf{InPlaceSample}$ has deterministic access patterns. We explicitly denote $\mathsf{M}_1(\cdot; \rho)$ to fix the random tape ρ consumed by M_1. For any fixed random tape ρ, and any neighboring inputs $x \sim_H x'$, $\mathsf{M}_1(x; \rho)$ and $\mathsf{M}_1(x'; \rho)$ output two arrays with Hamming distance 1. Therefore, intuitively, as long as the compaction algorithm in the second step is (ϵ', δ')-DO w.r.t. Hamming distance, the entire subsampling algorithm should be (ϵ', δ')-DO as well. Unfortunately, we cannot directly use strong neighbor-preserving to prove this composition here, since a random execution of $\mathsf{M}_1(x)$ and a random execution of $\mathsf{M}_1(x')$ are not guaranteed to always output Hamming-distance-neighboring outputs—it depends on which subset of elements are selected.

This motivates us to relax the strongly neighbor-preserving to make it more general, such that our compositional framework can be more expressive. However, before we do so, we introduce another more general example, Example 4, which is a variation of Example 3. Specifically, in Example 3, although the output of $M_1 :=$ InPlaceSample is randomized, the view of M_1 is deterministic. In Example 4, both the view and the output of the first algorithm are randomized.

Example 4. The main difference between Examples 3 and 4 is that Example 4 aims to have a subsampling algorithm that is DO w.r.t. *edit distance*, whereas Example 3 aims to be DO w.r.t. *Hamming distance*. To achieve this, in Example 4, we need to mask the true length of the input and output by reading/writing a random number of extraneous locations on the input tape, Further, the compaction algorithm we call must now be DO w.r.t. edit distance too. The detailed algorithm is described below. The key differences are highlighted by underlining.

1. Call $M_1(x) :=$ InPlaceSample$_{\epsilon,\delta}(x)$ which is defined as follows:
   - Sample $r \xleftarrow{\$} \mathcal{G}(\epsilon, \delta, \Delta = 1)$, let $n' = n + r$ be the noisy input length.
   - Scan $\underline{n'}$ locations on the input tape. For each real element encountered, append it to the output tape with probability p and append a filler element otherwise. For each filler encountered, append a filler to the output tape.
   - The output array is defined to be the first n elements of the output tape. Write down its length n at a fixed dedicated location on the output tape.
2. Apply M_2, a compaction algorithm that is (ϵ', δ')-DO w.r.t. $\sim_E$ to the output of the above step, i.e., the compaction algorithm treats the output tape of M_1 as its own input tape.

We later prove that Examples 3 and 4 satisfy DO with our new framework.

3.2 (ϵ, δ)-Neighbor-Preserving Differential Obliviousness (NPDO)

Recognizing the limitations of strongly neighbor-preserving (Definition 3.1), we would like to make the compositional framework more general. In particular, the above Examples 3 and 4 can serve as simple motivating examples.

Given a mechanism M whose view space is $\mathcal{V}$ and output space is $\mathcal{Y}$, given some symmetric relation $\sim_\mathcal{Y}$ over the output space, and given a set $S \subseteq \mathcal{V} \times \mathcal{Y}$, we define the following notation for denoting **neighbor sets**:

$$\mathcal{N}(S) := \{(v, y') | \exists (v, y) \in S \text{ s.t. } y' \sim_\mathcal{Y} y\}$$

Definition 3.4 ((ϵ, δ)-NPDO). *Given a mechanism* M $: \mathcal{X} \to \mathcal{Y}$ *with view space* $\mathcal{V}$, *we say that it satisfies* (ϵ, δ)-*neighbor-preserving differential obliviousness, or* (ϵ, δ)-*NPDO for short, w.r.t. symmetric relations* $\sim_\mathcal{X}$ *and* $\sim_\mathcal{Y}$, *respectively, iff for all* $x \sim_\mathcal{X} x'$, *for every* $S \subseteq \mathcal{V} \times \mathcal{Y}$,

$$\Pr[\mathsf{Exec}^\mathsf{M}(x) \in S] \leq e^\epsilon \cdot \Pr[\mathsf{Exec}^\mathsf{M}(x') \in \mathcal{N}(S)] + \delta. \tag{2}$$

Our NPDO definition looks similar in form as the standard differential privacy notion, with some important observations: 1) the notion is defined over the Cartesian product of the view and the output of the mechanism, which is important for composition to hold; 2) on the right-hand-side of Definition 2, we consider the probability of $M(x')$ landing in the *neighboring* set $\mathcal{N}(S)$ on a neighboring input $x' \sim_{\mathcal{X}} x$—this is important for capturing a probabilistic notion of neighbor-preserving.

It is not hard to see that if an algorithm satisfies (ϵ, δ)-NPDO, it must satisfy (ϵ, δ)-DO, as stated in the following theorem.

Theorem 3.5. *Suppose that* $M : \mathcal{X} \to \mathcal{Y}$ *satisfies* (ϵ, δ)-*NPDO w.r.t.* $\mathcal{X}$ *and* $\mathcal{Y}$. *Then,* M *satisfies* (ϵ, δ)-*DO w.r.t.* $\mathcal{X}$.

The proof is deferred to Appendix B.1 of the full version [74].

3.3 Main Composition Theorem

One main technical contribution of our paper is to prove a composition theorem for our NPDO notion, as stated below.

Theorem 3.6 (Main composition theorem). *Suppose that an algorithm* $M_1 : \mathcal{X} \to \mathcal{Y}$ *satisfies* (ϵ_1, δ_1)-*NPDO w.r.t.* $\sim_{\mathcal{X}}$ *and* $\sim_{\mathcal{Y}}$. *Further, suppose that the algorithm* M_1*'s view space* $\mathcal{V}$ *and the output space* $\mathcal{Y}$ *are finite or countably infinite. Then, the following composition statements hold:*

1. *Suppose that* $M_2 : \mathcal{Y} \to \mathcal{Z}$ *satisfies* (ϵ_2, δ_2)-*DO w.r.t.* $\sim_{\mathcal{Y}}$. *Then, the composed mechanism* $M_2 \circ M_1 : \mathcal{X} \to \mathcal{Z}$ *satisfies* $(\epsilon_1 + \epsilon_2, \delta_1 + \delta_2)$-*DO.*
2. *Suppose that* $M_2 : \mathcal{Y} \to \mathcal{Z}$ *satisfies* (ϵ_2, δ_2)-*NPDO w.r.t.* $\sim_{\mathcal{Y}}$ *and* $\sim_{\mathcal{Z}}$. *Then, the composed mechanism* $M_2 \circ M_1 : \mathcal{X} \to \mathcal{Z}$ *satisfies* $(\epsilon_1 + \epsilon_2, \delta_1 + \delta_2)$-*NPDO.*

The proof of Theorem 3.6 is presented in Sect. 4. We can use Theorem 3.6 to prove that the algorithms in the earlier Examples 1 to 4 satisfy DO. Before doing so, let us first introduce some helpful tools for proving an algorithm NPDO.

3.4 Helpful Tools for Proving NPDO

To use our main composition theorem, we need to prove that some algorithm satisfies NPDO. The following lemmas provide helpful tools for this purpose.

Strongly NP + DO $\Longrightarrow$ NPDO. First, it is not hard to see that if an algorithm satisfies the earlier strongly neighbor-preserving notion (Definition 3.1) as well as DO, then it also satisfies NPDO as stated below:

Lemma 3.7 (Strongly NP and DO imply NPDO). *Suppose that an algorithm* $M : \mathcal{X} \to \mathcal{Y}$ *is strongly neighbor-preserving w.r.t.* $\sim_{\mathcal{X}}$ *and* $\sim_{\mathcal{Y}}$, *as well as* (ϵ, δ)-*DO w.r.t.* $\sim_{\mathcal{X}}$. *Then,* M *satisfies* (ϵ, δ)-*NPDO.*

The proof is deferred to Appendix B.1 of the full version [74].

(ϵ, δ)-**NP.** Next, we define another notion that captures the idea of "probabilistically approximate neighbor-preserving" called (ϵ, δ)-neighbor-preserving, or (ϵ, δ)-NP for short. We show that if an algorithm satisfies (ϵ, δ)-NP as well as (ϵ', δ')-DO, then it also satisfies $(\epsilon + \epsilon', \delta + \delta')$-NPDO.

Definition 3.8 $((\epsilon, \delta)$-NP). *Given a mechanism* $\mathsf{M} : \mathcal{X} \to \mathcal{Y}$ *whose view space is* $\mathcal{V}$, *we say that it satisfies* (ϵ, δ)*-neighbor-preserving, or* (ϵ, δ)*-NP for short, w.r.t.* $\sim_{\mathcal{X}}$ *and* $\sim_{\mathcal{Y}}$, *iff for all* $x \sim_{\mathcal{X}} x'$, *for every view* $v^* \in \mathcal{V}$ *that happens with non-zero probability in* $\mathsf{Exec}^{\mathsf{M}}(x)$ *as well as* $\mathsf{Exec}^{\mathsf{M}}(x')$, *for every* $Y \subseteq \mathcal{Y}$,

$$\Pr[(v, y) \leftarrow \mathsf{Exec}^{\mathsf{M}}(x) : y \in Y \,|\, v = v^*]$$
$$\leq e^{\epsilon} \cdot \Pr[(v', y') \leftarrow \mathsf{Exec}^{\mathsf{M}}(x') : y' \in \mathcal{N}(Y) \,|\, v' = v^*] + \delta \quad (3)$$

where $\mathcal{N}(Y)$ *contains all* y' *such that* $y' \sim_{\mathcal{Y}} y$ *for all* $y \in Y$.

Intuitively, (ϵ, δ)-NP requires that *conditioned on any view*, the algorithm, on neighboring inputs, must output probabilistically approximately close outputs.

Lemma 3.9 $((\epsilon, \delta)$-NP and DO imply NPDO). *Suppose that an algorithm* $\mathsf{M} : \mathcal{X} \to \mathcal{Y}$ *is* (ϵ_1, δ_1)*-DO and* (ϵ_2, δ_2)*-neighbor-preserving w.r.t.* $\sim_{\mathcal{X}}$ *and* $\sim_{\mathcal{Y}}$. *Then,* M *satisfies* $(\epsilon_1 + \epsilon_2, \delta_1 + \delta_2)$*-NPDO w.r.t* $\sim_{\mathcal{X}}$ *and* $\sim_{\mathcal{Y}}$.

The proof is deferred to Appendix B.1 of the full version [74].

3.5 Our Composition Theorem in Action

Using the simple motivating examples introduced so far, we can see our composition theorems in action.

Examples 1 and 2. As mentioned earlier, the first algorithm M_1 in either Example 1 or Example 2 satisfies strongly neighbor-preserving as well as (ϵ_1, δ_1)-DO. Therefore, they can be viewed as a special case of (ϵ, δ)-NPDO. Since M_2 in Example 1 or 2 satisfies (ϵ_2, δ_2)-DO, by our main composition theorem, we immediately reach the conclusion that the composed algorithm $\mathsf{M}_2 \circ \mathsf{M}_1$ satisfies $(\epsilon_1 + \epsilon_2, \delta_1 + \delta_2)$-DO.

Example 3. We can use Theorem 3.6 to prove that the subsampling algorithm of Example 3 satisfies (ϵ', δ')-DO w.r.t. $\sim_H$. To accomplish this, it suffices to show that the first algorithm, $\mathsf{M}_1 := \mathsf{InPlaceSample}$, satisfies $(0,0)$-NPDO w.r.t. $\sim_H$ and $\sim_H$. Observe that in Example 3, two inputs are neighboring if their Hamming distance is at most 1, which implies that neighboring inputs must have the same length. Also, M_1 always generates a deterministic view that depends only on the length of the input. Therefore, to prove that $\mathsf{M}_1(x)$ satisfies $(0,0)$-NPDO, it suffices to show that for any pair of neighboring inputs $x \sim_H x'$, for any subset of outputs $Y \subseteq \mathcal{Y}$ where $\mathcal{Y}$ is the output space of M_1,

$$\Pr[\mathsf{M}_1(x) \in Y] \leq \Pr[\mathsf{M}_1(x') \in \mathcal{N}(Y)], \quad (4)$$

where $\mathcal{N}(Y)$ denotes the set of all output arrays that are neighboring to some array in Y. Observe also that for any possible output y of $\mathsf{M}_1(x)$, let ρ be the random coins used for subsampling that led to the result y, then, if the same random coins ρ is encountered in an execution of $\mathsf{M}_1(x')$ on some neighboring $x' \sim_H x$, the outcome must be neighboring to y. Therefore, Eq. (4) holds.

Example 4. Similarly, we can use Theorem 3.6 to prove that the subsampling algorithm of Example 4 satisfies $(\epsilon + \epsilon', \delta + \delta')$-DO w.r.t. $\sim_E$. By Theorem 3.6, it suffices to show that the $\mathsf{M}_1 := \mathsf{InPlaceSample}_{\epsilon,\delta}$ algorithm in Example 4 satisfies (ϵ, δ)-NPDO w.r.t. $\sim_E$ being both of the input and output neighboring notion. Recall that M_1 pads the input array with a random number of elements, such that the noisy length is n'. Then, it simply scans through the n' elements and either writes down the element if it is a real element and has been sampled, or writes down $\bot$. To show that M_1 satisfies (ϵ, δ)-NPDO, we will prove that M_1 satisfies $(0,0)$-NP and (ϵ, δ)-DO, respectively, and then the conclusion follows from Lemma 3.9. It is easy to prove that M_1 satisfies (ϵ, δ)-DO. To see this, observe that the view depends only on the noisy input length where the noise is sampled according to a truncated geometric distribution.

Therefore, we focus on showing that M_1 satisfies $(0,0)$-NP. Observe that in M_1, the random coins that determine the view and those that determine the output are independent. Therefore, it suffices to show that for any $x \sim_E x'$, for any $Y \subseteq \mathcal{Y}$ where $\mathcal{Y}$ is the output space of M_1,

$$\Pr[\mathsf{M}_1(x) \in Y] \leq \Pr[\mathsf{M}_1(x') \in \mathcal{N}(Y)].$$

Since $x \sim_E x'$, there can be at most one element in x that is not in x' (e.g., the element that is added or modified in x), and vice versa. Henceforth, we use $\mathsf{Common}(x, x')$ to denote the list of common elements that appear both in x and x'. Let $G(Y)$ be the event that there exists some $y \in Y$, such that the elements in $\mathsf{Common}(x, x')$ receive the same sampling decision as in y. We also say that $G(Y)$ represents the event that $\mathsf{Common}(x, x')$ receive coins compatible with Y. Therefore, we have that

$$\Pr[\mathsf{M}_1(x) \in Y] \leq \Pr[\mathsf{M}_1(x) : G(Y)] \leq \Pr[\mathsf{M}_1(x') \in \mathcal{N}(Y)].$$

In the above, the second inequality holds since conditioned on $\mathsf{Common}(x, x')$ receiving coins compatible with Y in a random execution of $\mathsf{M}_1(x')$, the outcome must be neighboring to some element in Y with probability 1.

Additional Applications. Later in Sect. 5, we use our composition framework to design a differentially oblivious stable compaction algorithm w.r.t. the edit distance—this building block was needed in Examples 1, 2, 4. Last but not the least, in Sect. 6, we use our composition framework to prove an optimal privacy amplification theorem for the DO-shuffle model.

4   Proof of Main Composition Theorem

In this section, we shall prove our main composition theorem, that is, Theorem 3.6. A key stepping stone is the following equivalence lemma.

Lemma 4.1 (Equivalence of (ϵ, δ)-NPDO and existence of an (ϵ, δ)-matching). *Assume the axiom of choice. Given a finite or countable infinite sample space Ω and a symmetric relation $\sim$ on Ω, consider two random variables $A, B \in \Omega$. The following statements are equivalent:*

1. For every $S \subseteq \Omega$, $\Pr[A \in S] \le e^{\epsilon} \cdot \Pr[B \in \mathcal{N}(S)] + \delta$, where the neighbor set $\mathcal{N}(S)$ is defined as $\mathcal{N}(S) := \{b \in \Omega | \exists a \in S, a \sim b\}$.
2. There exists an (ϵ, δ)-matching $w : \Omega \times \Omega \to [0, 1]$ satisfying the following conditions:
    (a) For all $a, b \in \Omega$, $w(a, b) > 0$ only if $a \sim b$;
    (b) For all $a \in \Omega$, $\sum_{b \in \Omega, b \sim a} w(a, b) \le \Pr[A = a]$;
    (c) For all $b \in \Omega$, $\sum_{a \in \Omega, a \sim b} w(a, b) \le e^{\epsilon} \cdot \Pr[B = b]$;
    (d) $\sum_{a, b \in \Omega} w(a, b) \ge 1 - \delta$.

Graph Interpretation. Lemma 4.1 has a similar flavor as the Hall's theorem for bipartite graphs. The Hall's theorem says that if for each subset S of one component of a bipartitie graph, the size of its neighbor set satisfies $|\mathcal{N}(S)| \ge |S|$, then we can find a perfect matching in the graph. The proof of Lemma 4.1 is also inspired by the proof of the Hall's theorem.

We think of a bipartite graph where vertices on the left and right both come from the set Ω, and $w(a, b)$ defines the weight on edge (a, b). Imagine that each vertex $a \in \Omega$ on the left is factory that produces $\Pr[A = a]$ amount of produce, and each vertex $b \in \Omega$ on the right is a warehouse that can store up to $e^{\epsilon} \cdot \Pr[B = b]$ amount of produce. Condition (a) says that a factory is only allowed to route its produce to neighboring warehouses. The function w effectively defines a fractional flow such that almost all, i.e., $1 - \delta$ amount of produce is routed to some warehouse, and moreover, none of the warehouses exceed their capacity. For this reason, we also call w an (ϵ, δ)-**matching**. The full proof of Lemma 4.1 is deferred to Appendix B.2 of the full version [74]. Below, we prove our main composition theorem assuming that Lemma 4.1 holds.

Proof (Proof of Theorem 3.6). We directly prove the more general case when $\mathsf{M_2}$ is (ϵ_2, δ_2)-NPDO. When $\mathsf{M_2}$ is only (ϵ_2, δ_2)-DO, we can prove $\mathsf{M_2} \circ \mathsf{M_1}$ is $(\epsilon_1 + \epsilon_2, \delta_1 + \delta_2)$-DO with nearly the same argument.

Fix any neighboring input x, x'. By Lemma 4.1, there exists an (ϵ_1, δ_1)-matching $w : (\mathcal{V}_1 \times \mathcal{Y}) \times (\mathcal{V}_1 \times \mathcal{Y}) \to [0, 1]$ w.r.t the natural neighbor notion $\sim$ in the product space $\mathcal{V}_1 \times \mathcal{Y}$: $(v_1, y) \sim (v'_1, y')$ when $v_1 = v'_1$ and $y \sim_y y'$. We want to prove that, for any subset $S \subseteq \mathcal{V}_1 \times \mathcal{V}_2 \times \mathcal{Z}$,

$$\Pr[\mathsf{Exec}^{\mathsf{M_2} \circ \mathsf{M_1}}(x) \in S] \le e^{\epsilon_1 + \epsilon_2} \Pr[\mathsf{Exec}^{\mathsf{M_2} \circ \mathsf{M_1}}(x') \in \mathcal{N}(S)] + \delta_1 + \delta_2.$$

Define the partial set $S_{v_1} := \{(v_2, z) | \exists (v_1, v_2, z) \in S\}$ for any $v_1 \in \mathcal{V}_1$. Then,

$\Pr[\mathsf{Exec}^{\mathsf{M_2} \circ \mathsf{M_1}}(x) \in S]$

$$= \sum_{(v_1, y) \in \mathcal{V}_1 \times \mathcal{Y}} \Pr[\mathsf{Exec}^{\mathsf{M_1}}(x) = (v_1, y)] \cdot \Pr[\mathsf{Exec}^{\mathsf{M_2}}(y) \in S_{v_1}]$$

(Use condition (a), (b) and (d) of the matching)

$$\le \sum_{(v_1, y) \in \mathcal{V}_1 \times \mathcal{Y}, y' \sim_y y} w((v_1, y), (v_1, y')) \cdot \Pr[\mathsf{Exec}^{\mathsf{M_2}}(y) \in S_{v_1}] + \delta_1$$

$$\leq \sum_{(v_1,y) \in \mathcal{V}_1 \times \mathcal{Y}, y' \sim_{\mathcal{Y}} y} w\left((v_1,y),(v_1,y')\right) \cdot \left(e^{\epsilon_2} \Pr[\mathsf{Exec}^{M_2}(y') \in \mathcal{N}(S_{v_1})] + \delta_2\right) + \delta_1$$

(Use condition (b) of the matching)

$$\leq \sum_{(v_1,y) \in \mathcal{V}_1 \times \mathcal{Y}, y' \sim_{\mathcal{Y}} y} w\left((v_1,y),(v_1,y')\right) \cdot \left(e^{\epsilon_2} \Pr[\mathsf{Exec}^{M_2}(y') \in \mathcal{N}(S_{v_1})]\right) + \delta_2 + \delta_1$$

(Use condition (c) of the matching)

$$\leq \sum_{(v_1,y') \in \mathcal{V}_1 \times \mathcal{Y}} e^{\epsilon_1} \Pr[\mathsf{Exec}^{M_1}(x') = (v_1,y')] \cdot \left(e^{\epsilon_2} \Pr[\mathsf{Exec}^{M_2}(y') \in \mathcal{N}(S_{v_1})]\right) + \delta_2 + \delta_1$$

$$= e^{\epsilon_1 + \epsilon_2} \Pr[\mathsf{Exec}^{M_2 \circ M_1}(x') \in \mathcal{N}(S)] + \delta_2 + \delta_1.$$

5 Application: DO Compaction w.r.t. Edit Distance

Earlier in our Examples 1, 2, and 4, we assumed a stable compaction algorithm that is differentially oblivious w.r.t. the *edit* distance. Chan et al. [17] showed how to construct a stable compaction algorithm that is (ϵ, δ)-DO w.r.t. the *Hamming* distance [17], taking $O(n(\log \log n + \log \log \frac{1}{\delta}))$ time to compact an array of size n (assuming that ϵ is a constant). However, we are not aware of any straight-forward way to modify their algorithm to work for edit distance. Another naïve approach is to use oblivious sorting directly but this would incur $\Theta(n \log n)$ run-time which is asymptotically worse. In this section, we fill in this missing piece that is needed by Examples 1, 2, and 4. We will describe a stable compaction algorithm that works for edit distance and it preserves the runtime of Chan et al. [17]. Intriguingly, the design of our new compaction algorithm turns out to be a great example that demonstrates the power of our compositional framework.

5.1 Additional Preliminaries

Stable Compaction. Recall that in stable compaction, we are given an input array which is written on an input tape. Some elements in the input array are *real* elements, and others are *fillers*. We want to output an array that contains only the real elements, and they must appear in the same order as the input array. We assume that the input array is written on the input tape, and its true length is written on some designated location on the input tape. The algorithm should write the output array to an output tape, and the true length of the output array should be written to some dedicated location on the output array.

Stable Oblivious Sorting. Suppose we are given an input array I containing a list of m elements with a key attached to each element. Earlier works [18,53] showed how to oblivious sort the array according to the keys in $O(m \log m)$ runtime while maintaining the stable property: the elements will be ordered by their relative order in the original array when their keys are the same.

Differentially Private Prefix Sum. Given an input array I containing a list of m integers, we want to its prefix sums. We say that two inputs I, and I' are neighboring iff 1) they have the same length and 2) they differ in at most one position j, and $|I[j] - I'[j]| \leq 1$. Earlier works [19,31] showed how to construct a prefix sum mechanism that satisfies (ϵ, δ)-differential privacy, and moreover, the mechanism satisfies the following properties: 1) The access patterns (i.e., view) of the algorithm depend only on the input length; 2) The additive error is upper bounded by $O\left(\frac{1}{\epsilon}(\log|I|)^{1.5} \log\frac{1}{\delta}\right)$ with probability 1.

5.2   Roadmap and Intuition

Our algorithm Compact is the composition of the following two algorithms, i.e., Compact$(\cdot)$ = CompactBin $\circ$ RandBin$(\cdot)$. Suppose we can prove that RandBin is (ϵ_1, δ_1)-NPDO and prove that CompactBin is (ϵ_2, δ_2)-NPDO, we have Compact is $(\epsilon_1 + \epsilon_2, \delta_1 + \delta_2)$-NPDO due to our main composition Theorem 3.6.

1. RandBin: Given an input array I containing real elements and fillers, and whose true length is stored in a dedicated location on the input tape, RandBin outputs a list of B bins denoted $(\mathsf{Bin}_i^{(Z)} : i \in [B])$, each of capacity Z. Each bin contains a random number of real elements and the rest are fillers. Furthermore, the ordered list of all real elements in all bins is the same as the ordered list of real elements in the input. The algorithm should output the parameters B and Z to some dedicated location on the output tape.
2. CompactBin: Given a list of B bins denoted $(\mathsf{Bin}_i^{(Z)} : i \in [B])$ each of capacity Z, where the parameters B and Z are stored in some dedicated location on the input tape, the CompactBin algorithm outputs a compacted array containing only the real elements in the input bins, and preserving the same order they appear in the input bins. The algorithm outputs the true output length to some dedicated location on the output tape.

In short, RandBin is a pre-processing step that takes the input array and converts it into bin format, and CompactBin takes the bin representation, and performs the actual compaction. The informal intuition is as follows. From earlier work [17], we know how to construct an efficient DO stable compaction algorithm for Hamming distance. However, in our case, we have two inputs I and I' that have *edit* distance 1. The difficulty with edit distance is when I is obtained by inserting an extra element into I' at position j, the two inputs I and I' will differ in *every* position after j. Our idea is to leverage RandBin to "probabilistically localize" this difference caused by a single insertion operation. In particular, if some bin representation occurs for input I with some probability p, we want that under the neighboring input I', with probability close to p, we should encounter a similar bin representation where the difference is localized to only one or two bins. If we can accomplish this, then hopefully we can adapt ideas that worked for Hamming distaince [17] to compact the resulting bin representation.

Below, we will define an appropriate neighboring notion $\sim_B$ on the bin representation. We want to show that the RandBin pre-processing step satisfies NPDO w.r.t. the input relation $\sim_E$ and output relation $\sim_B$ for the bin representation. Further, we want to show that CompactBin satisfies NPDO w.r.t. $\sim_B$ and $\sim_H$. Then, the composed algorithm should be NPDO by our composition theorem.

Neighboring Relation for Bin Representation $\sim_B$. Specifically, the neighboring relation $\sim_B$ is defined as below. Two lists of bins $(\mathsf{Bin}_i^{(Z)} : i \in [B])$ and $(\mathsf{Bin}_i'^{(Z')} : i \in [B'])$ are said to be neighboring, iff the following all hold:

- they have compatible dimensions, i.e., $B = B'$ and $Z = Z'$;
- After removing all fillers and concatenating the real elements in the list of bins, the resulting outcomes have edit distance at most one;
- There are at most *two* bins that have different bin loads (defined to be the number of real elements in the bin), further, for both of them, the difference in load is at most one.

5.3   RandBin Algorithm

We now describe the RandBin algorithm, which preprocesses the input array into a bin representation.

$\underline{\mathsf{RandBin}^{\epsilon,\delta}(I)}$:   // *Let* $\epsilon_1 = \epsilon_2 = \epsilon_3 = \frac{\epsilon}{3}$, *and* $\delta_1 = \delta_2 = \delta_3 = \frac{\delta}{3}$.

- Sample $G \xleftarrow{\$} \mathcal{G}(\epsilon_1, \delta_1)$. Let $L = |I| + G$ be the noisy input length. Let $s = \frac{15}{\epsilon} \log^2 L \log \frac{1}{\delta}$ be an upper bound on the support of $\mathcal{G}(\epsilon_2, \delta_2)$ and also the additive error of $\mathsf{PrefixSum}^{\epsilon_3, \delta_3}$ on at most L integers. Let the maximum bin load be $Z = 2s$ and $B = \lceil \frac{2L}{Z} \rceil + 1$ be the number of bins.
- For $i = 1$ to B, let $\rho_i \xleftarrow{\$} s + \mathcal{G}(\epsilon_2, \delta_2) \in [\frac{Z}{2} \ldots Z]$. Let $\boldsymbol{\rho} := (\rho_1, \rho_2, \ldots, \rho_B)$.
- Let $\mathbf{cnt} := \mathsf{PrefixSum}^{\epsilon_3, \delta_3}(\boldsymbol{\rho}) \in \mathbb{Z}^B$. Let $\mathbf{Buf} := \emptyset$ be a working buffer.
- For $i = 1$ to B:
  - fetch the unvisited elements in the input array up to index[a] $\mathsf{cnt}[i] + s$ and add them to Buf; mark them as visited.
  - if the current length of Buf is less than Z, append enough fillers such that its length is at least Z;
  - perform stable oblivious sorting on Buf such that the first Z positions contains only the real elements coming from the first $\sum_{j \leq i} \rho_i$ positions in the input and fillers; all remaining elements are moved to the end of Buf.
  - pop the first Z elements of Buf to Bin_i.
  - perform stable oblivious sorting on Buf to move all the fillers to the end, if necessary, truncate Buf such that its length is at most $2s$.
- Output the bin representation $(\mathsf{Bin}_i^{(Z)} : i \in [B])$, and store the parameters B and Z in some dedicated location on the output tape.

---

[a] We may assume that any location in the input array beyond the original length $|I|$ is occupied by a filler.

Roughly speaking, the RandBin algorithm generates a list of random counts $\rho := (\rho_1, \ldots, \rho_B)$. Then, all real elements contained in the first ρ_1 positions of the input are moved into Bin_1, all real elements contained in the next ρ_2 positions of the input are moved into Bin_2, and so on. To guarantee differential obliviousness, the algorithm cannot directly reveal the vector ρ—instead, it reveals only the noisy prefix sum of ρ. Specifically, we apply an (ϵ_3, δ_3)-differentially private prefix sum algorithm to the vector y, i.e., $\text{cnt} := \text{PrefixSum}^{\epsilon_3, \delta_3}(Y)$. In other words, $\text{cnt}[i]$ stores a noisy version of $\sum_{j \leq i} \rho_i$, and it is guaranteed that the estimation error is at most s. Now, in each step i of the algorithm, we want to populate Bin_i. To do so, we simply fetch the next batch of elements in the input array up to position $\text{cnt}[i]$ into a poly-logarithmically sized working buffer Buf. Buf also contains previously fetched elements that have not been placed into any bin yet. We can now obliviously sort Buf to create the next Bin_i. At the end of each step i, it is guaranteed that there are at most $2s$ real elements remaining in Buf. Therefore, we can obliviously sort Buf and compact its length to $2s$. This makes sure that Buf is always poly-logarithmic in size. Finally, to make the algorithm secure, we also need to mask the true input length, and we can accomplish this by adding a truncated geometric random noise to the true length, and revealing only the noisy length. Note that the number of bins B is a random variable that depends only on the noisy input length.

Theorem 5.1. *The* RandBin *algorithm always outputs the correct bin representation: For all $i \in [B]$, all real elements from $I\left[\sum_{j<i} \rho_j + 1\right]$ to $I\left[\sum_{j \leq i} \rho_j\right]$ are moved to Bin_i. Also, all real elements in the input array are moved to the bins.*

Theorem 5.2. *Assuming $|I| \geq \frac{c}{\epsilon} \log \frac{1}{\delta}$ for any fix constant c,* RandBin *has a worst-case runtime of $O\left(|I| \left(\log \log |I| + \log \frac{1}{\epsilon} + \log \log \frac{1}{\delta}\right)\right)$.*

Theorem 5.3. RandBin *is (ϵ, δ)-NPDO w.r.t. the input neighboring notion $\sim_E$ and the output neighboring notion $\sim_B$.*

The above theorems' proofs are in Appendix B.3 of the full version [74].

5.4   CompactBin Algorithm

We now describe the CompactBin algorithm which takes in a bin representation, outputs a compacted array, and writes the true length of the output to some dedicated location on the output tape.

$\mathsf{CompactBin}^{\epsilon,\delta}\left(\left(\mathsf{Bin}_i^{(Z)} : i \in [B]\right)\right)$:   // Let $\epsilon_1 = \frac{\epsilon}{2}$, $\delta_1 = \frac{\delta}{2(1+e^{\epsilon_1})}$.

- Let $s = \frac{4}{\epsilon_1} \log^2 B \log \frac{2}{\delta_1}$, be an upper bound of the additive error of (ϵ_1, δ_1)-differentially private prefix sums on at most B integers.
- Let $R := (R_i : i \in [B])$, where R_i is the number of real elements in Bin_i. Call cnt $:= \mathsf{PrefixSum}^{\epsilon_1,\delta_1}(R)$.
- Let Buf and the output array be initially empty. For $i = 1$ to B:
  - Read the i-th bin and append it to the end of Buf.
  - Perform stable oblivious sorting on Buf such that all real elements are moved to the front.
  - Let L be the current length of the output array. Remove an appropriate number of elements from the beginning of Buf and append them to the output array, such that the output array has length exactly $\max(\mathsf{cnt}[i] - s, L)$.
  - Truncate Buf if necessary such that its length is at most $2s$.
- Append Buf to the end of the output array. Write the true output length $\sum_{i \in [B]} R_i$ to some dedicated location on the output tape.

To gain some intuition, basically in each step i, the CompactBin algorithm reads the next bin i, and tries to copy the real elements in bin i to the end of the output array. To achieve differential obliviousness, the algorithm cannot reveal the true number of real elements inside each bin. Therefore, it calls a differentially private prefix sum mechanism to compute an array cnt$[1 : B]$ where cnt$[i]$ is an estimate of the number of real elements contained in the first i bins. The prefix sum algorithm guarantees that the estimation error is upper bounded by s. Therefore, at the end of the i-th step, the algorithm should have written exactly cnt$[i] - s$ number of real elements to the output array. To accomplish this, the algorithm makes use of a temporary working buffer Buf that is used to store the real elements that have been fetched from the input bins but have not been appended to the output array. It guarantees that at the end of each step, there are at most $2s$ real elements leftover in Buf.

Theorem 5.4. *With probability 1, the output of* CompactBin *includes all the real elements from the B input bins with their order preserved and the filler elements in the output array only appear after the last real element.*

Theorem 5.5. CompactBin$^{\epsilon,\delta}$ *is (ϵ, δ)-NPDO w.r.t. the input neighboring relation $\sim_B$ and output neighboring relation $\sim_E$.*

Theorem 5.6. CompactBin *has a worst-case runtime of $O(B(Z+s)\log(Z+s))$.*

The theorems' proofs are deferred to Appendix B.3 of the full version [74].

From the RandBin algorithm, $BZ = O(|I|)$, $Z = \Theta(s)$, and $s = O(\frac{1}{\epsilon} \log^2 |I| \log \frac{1}{\delta})$. By Theorem 5.2 and Theorem 5.6, the following corollary holds:

Corollary 5.7. *Assuming $|I| \geq \frac{c}{\epsilon} \log \frac{1}{\delta}$ for any fix constant c, then the full compaction algorithm* Compact$^{\epsilon,\delta} := $ CompactBin$^{\epsilon/2,\delta/2} \circ$ RandBin$^{\epsilon/2,\delta/2}$ *has a worst-case runtime of $O\left(|I|\left(\log\log|I| + \log\frac{1}{\epsilon} + \log\log\frac{1}{\delta}\right)\right)$.*

6   Application: Optimal Privacy Amplification in the Differentially Oblivious Shuffle Model

In this section, we use our composition framework to prove a privacy amplification theorem for the differentially oblivious shuffle (DO-shuffle) model.

Background. Consider a distributed setting with n clients and an untrusted server who wants to learn some statistics of the clients' private data. To achieve this, the differential privacy literature proposed two models for achieving this. In the *local model*, each client adds some noise to its own data by running an ϵ_0-locally differentially private (LDP) mechanism, and sends the noisy result the server. The server then computes the desired statistics using each client's noisy input. In the local model, the server's view satisfies ϵ_0-DP.

Some more recent works [22,23,39,40] considered a new model called the *shuffle model*. In this model, we assume that a trusted shuffler can shuffle all of the clients' messages, and the server only sees the permuted messages (without learning the permutation). Interestingly, earlier works [22,23,39,40] showed that the shuffle model can *amplify* privacy. In particular, suppose each client still runs an ϵ_0-locally differentially private (LDP) mechanism before sending the noisy outcomes to the shuffler, then the server's view would satisfy (ϵ, δ)-DP where ϵ can be much smaller than ϵ_0. Notably, the recent work of Feldman et al. [37] proved optimal parameters for privacy amplification in a perfectly secure shuffle model, that is, it can achieve (ϵ, δ)-DP with any $\delta > 0$ and $\epsilon = O\left((1 - e^{-\epsilon_0})e^{\epsilon_0/2}\sqrt{\frac{\log(1/\delta)}{n}}\right)$. In this section, our goal is to show that the *perfectly secure* shuffle in privacy amplification can be replaced with a much weaker, (ϵ, δ)-*differentially oblivious* shuffle, without degrading the amplification guarantees (except for extra ϵ and δ additive factors that arise from the differentially oblivious shuffler itself).

To benefit from the shuffle model, we need to realize the shuffle either using trusted hardware or through a cryptographic protocol. Some recent works [5, 13,45] showed that it may be asymptotically more efficient to realize a relaxed shuffler that satisfies differential obliviousness than a perfectly secure shuffler. Therefore, a natural question is whether we can also enjoy the same degree of privacy amplification with a differentially oblivious shuffler rather than a perfectly secure shuffler. We explore this question in the remainder of this section.

6.1   Definitions

Suppose that the server and the clients jointly execute a protocol to realize a shuffler. The syntax of a shuffle protocol is defined below.

Definition 6.1 (Syntax of a shuffle protocol). *A protocol between a server and n clients each with some input from $\mathcal{X}$ is said to be a shuffle protocol, iff under an honest execution, the server outputs a random permutation of the clients' inputs.*

Before defining security, we need to define the adversary's capabilities and the view of the adversary. We assume that an adversary $\mathcal{A}$ may control up to t clients as well as the server, we define the random variable $\mathsf{View}^{\mathcal{A}}(\mathbf{x}_H)$ to mean the view of the adversary during an execution where the honest clients' inputs are $\mathbf{x}_H \in \mathcal{X}^{n-t}$. The view of the adversary $\mathcal{A}$ should include whatever the adversary can observe during the execution. Specifically, the view include the server's output, all messages sent and received by the corrupted clients and the server. Further, the view may include any additional information the adversary can observe. For example, if the adversary can observe honest-to-honest communication (e.g., a network adversary), then, the view should also include the honest-to-honest communication. For a protocol secure in the *semi-honest* model, we assume that the corrupt players will honestly follow the protocol. For the protocol secure in the *malicious* model, we assume that the corrupt players can send arbitrary messages and the adversary $\mathcal{A}$ controls the messages sent by corrupt players.

Remark 6.2. Different DO-shuffle protocols may provide security guarantees under differing adversarial power. For example, of Gordon et al. [45] assumes a semi-honest adversary cannot observe honest-to-honest communication, whereas Bünz et al. [13] assumes a malicious adversary who can observe the entire network communication. Our privacy amplification theorem does not care about the exact modeling choice made by the underlying DO-shuffle protocol, and the composed DO-shuffle-model mechanism essentially inherits the same assumptions as the underlying DO-shuffle.

Next, we define the notion of differential obliviousness for a shuffle protocol. We first need to define what neighboring means.

Neighboring by Swapping. Given some set $\mathcal{D}$ and two vectors $\mathbf{y}, \mathbf{y}' \in \mathcal{D}^m$, we say that $\mathbf{y} \sim_S \mathbf{y}'$, iff either $\mathbf{y} = \mathbf{y}'$, or $\mathbf{y}'$ can be obtained from $\mathbf{y}$ by swapping the values of two coordinates.

Definition 6.3 (Differential obliviousness of a shuffle protocol). *A shuffle protocol is said to satisfy statistical (ϵ, δ)-differential obliviousness in the presence of $t \leq n$ corruptions, iff the following holds: for any adversary $\mathcal{A}$ controlling the server and at most t clients, for any two honest input configurations $\mathbf{y}_H, \mathbf{y}'_H \in \mathcal{Y}^{n-t}$ such that $\mathbf{y}_H \sim_S \mathbf{y}'_H$, for any subset $S \subseteq \mathcal{V}$ where $\mathcal{V}$ denotes the view space, it holds that*

$$\Pr\left[\mathsf{View}^{\mathcal{A}}(\mathbf{y}_H) \in S\right] \leq e^{\epsilon} \cdot \Pr\left[\mathsf{View}^{\mathcal{A}}(\mathbf{y}'_H) \in S\right] + \delta$$

If we set $\epsilon = 0$ and $\delta = 0$, the above notion becomes equivalent to the security of a perfectly secure shuffle.

We next define a computational variant of the DO notion, since some known DO shuffler instantiations enjoy computational security [5,13,45].

Definition 6.4 (Computational DO for a shuffle protocol). *A shuffle protocol Φ is said to satisfy computational (ϵ, δ)-differential obliviousness in the presence of $t \leq n$ corruptions, iff for any non-uniform probabilistic polynomial-time (p.p.t.) adversary $\mathcal{A}$ controlling the server and at most t clients, for any two neighboring honest input configurations $\mathbf{y}_H \sim_S \mathbf{y}'_H$, it holds that*

$$\Pr\left[\mathsf{Expt}^{\mathcal{A}}(1^{\lambda}, \mathbf{y}_H) = 1\right] \leq e^{\epsilon} \cdot \Pr\left[\mathsf{Expt}^{\mathcal{A}}(1^{\lambda}, \mathbf{y}'_H) = 1\right] + \delta$$

where $\mathsf{Expt}^{\mathcal{A}}(1^{\lambda}, \mathbf{y})$ is the randomized experiment where we execute the protocol using security parameter λ and interacting with the adversary $\mathcal{A}$, and at the end we output whatever $\mathcal{A}$ outputs.

Next, we define the notion of a locally differentially private (LDP) mechanism. The main privacy amplification theorem we want to prove in this section asks the following question: if each client computes its message by applying an ϵ_0-LDP mechanism to its private input, and then a DO shuffler shuffles all clients' messages before revealing the shuffled result to the server, can we prove that the server's view satisfies (ϵ, δ)-DP where ϵ is much smaller than ϵ_0?

Definition 6.5 (ϵ_0-LDP mechanism). *$\mathcal{R} : \mathcal{X} \to \mathcal{Y}$ is an ϵ_0-LDP mechanism if for any $x, x' \in \mathcal{X}$ and any subset $S \subseteq \mathcal{Y}$, $\Pr[\mathcal{R}(x) \in S] \leq e^{\epsilon_0} \Pr[\mathcal{R}(x') \in S]$.*

6.2   Privacy Amplification in the DO-Shuffle Model

We formally restate Theorem 1.4 when the DO-shuffler Φ statisfies statistical DO as the following theorem. In Appendix A.1 of the full version [74], we will extend our composition framework to support the case when the DO-shuffler satisfies computational differential obliviousness (Definition 6.4).

Theorem 6.6. *Let $\mathcal{R} : \mathcal{X} \to \mathcal{Y}$ be an ϵ_0-LDP mechanism to be run by each client over its private input. Suppose $\mathcal{A}$ is an adversary controlling the server and at most t clients. Let Φ be a statistical (ϵ_1, δ_1)-DO shuffling protocol. Define the random experiment $\mathsf{Expt}^{\mathcal{A}}(x_1, \ldots, x_n)$ as the following where each $x_i \in \mathcal{X}$ denotes the private input of client $i \in [n]$:*

1. *Each honest client i treats the output of $\mathcal{R}(x_i)$ as the input in the next step;*
2. *Execute the DO-shuffling protocol Φ with the presence of the adversary $\mathcal{A}$ and let $\mathcal{A}$ also observe the outcome of the shuffling.*
3. *Output whatever $\mathcal{A}$ outputs.*

Let $\mathbf{x} = (x_1, \ldots, x_n) \in \mathcal{X}^n$ and $\mathbf{x}' = (x'_1, \ldots, x'_n) \in \mathcal{X}^n$ be any two neighboring input configurations that differ in at most one client's input. For any $\delta > 0$ that $\epsilon_0 \leq \log\left(\frac{n-t}{16 \log(2/\delta)}\right)$, we have that

$$\Pr\left[\mathsf{Expt}^{\mathcal{A}}(\mathbf{x}) = 1\right] \leq e^{\epsilon + \epsilon_1} \cdot \Pr\left[\mathsf{Expt}^{\mathcal{A}}(\mathbf{x}') = 1\right] + \delta + \delta_1$$

for $\epsilon = O\left((1 - e^{-\epsilon_0})e^{\epsilon_0/2}\sqrt{\frac{\log(1/\delta)}{n-t}}\right)$.

Since we want to use our composition framework to prove optimal privacy amplification in the DO-shuffle model, we can define the first and second mechanism M_1 and M_2 as follows:

- The first mechanism $M_1 : \mathcal{X}^n \to \mathcal{Y}^n$ is where the n clients each apply the ϵ_0-LDP mechanism $\mathcal{R} : \mathcal{X} \to \mathcal{Y}$ to their private data, respectively. The mechanism generates no view observable by the adversary, and moreover, its output is the concatenation of all clients' outputs.
- The second mechanism $M_2 : \mathcal{Y}^n \to \mathcal{Y}^n$ is the DO-shuffler itself. Here, the view of the adversary is its view in the DO-shuffle protocol, and the output is the shuffled outcome. In the main body, we shall first assume that M_2 satisfies *statistical* differential obliviousness (Definition 6.3).

It is easy to see that the adversary has the same view in the composed mechanism $M_2 \circ M_1$ and in the random experiment described in Theorem 6.6. So we only need to prove that $M_2 \circ M_1$ is $(\epsilon + \epsilon_1, \delta + \delta_1)$-DO. The crux is to show that M_1 satisfies (ϵ, δ)-NPDO when at most t clients are corrupted, as more formally stated in the following lemma:

Lemma 6.7. *Suppose* $\epsilon_0 \leq \log\left(\frac{n-t}{16\log(2/\delta)}\right)$. *The above mechanism* M_1 *satisfies* (ϵ, δ)-*NPDO w.r.t. the input relation* $\sim_H$, *(i.e., two vectors are neighboring if they have the same length and differ in at most one position) and the output relation* $\sim_S$ *(i.e., neighboring by swapping).*

We can directly apply our composition theorem (Theorem 3.6) and Lemma 6.7 to get the desired result. The proof is in Appendix B.4 of the full version [74].

Acknowledgments. This work is in part supported by a grant from ONR, a gift from Cisco, NSF awards under grant numbers CIF-1705007, 2128519 and 2044679, and a Packard Fellowship. The work is also supported by DARPA SIEVE research program. T-H. Hubert Chan was partially supported by the Hong Kong RGC under the grants 17201220, 17202121 and 17203122.

References

1. Abe, M.: Mix-networks on permutation networks. In: Lam, K.-Y., Okamoto, E., Xing, C. (eds.) ASIACRYPT 1999. LNCS, vol. 1716, pp. 258–273. Springer, Heidelberg (1999). https://doi.org/10.1007/978-3-540-48000-6_21
2. Abraham, I., Pinkas, B., Yanai, A.: Blinder - scalable, robust anonymous committed broadcast. In: Ligatti, J., Ou, X., Katz, J., Vigna, G. (eds.) ACM CCS 2020, pp. 1233–1252. ACM Press, November 2020. https://doi.org/10.1145/3372297.3417261
3. Afshani, P., Freksen, C.B., Kamma, L., Larsen, K.G.: Lower bounds for multiplication via network coding. In: Baier, C., Chatzigiannakis, I., Flocchini, P., Leonardi, S. (eds.) ICALP 2019. LIPIcs, vol. 132, pp. 10:1–10:12. Schloss Dagstuhl, July 2019. https://doi.org/10.4230/LIPIcs.ICALP.2019.10
4. Aharoni, R., Berger, E., Georgakopoulos, A., Perlstein, A., Sprüssel, P.: The max-flow min-cut theorem for countable networks. J. Combin. Theory Ser. B **101**(1), 1–17 (2011). https://doi.org/10.1016/j.jctb.2010.08.002

5. Ando, M., Lysyanskaya, A., Upfal, E.: Practical and provably secure onion routing. In: Chatzigiannakis, I., Kaklamanis, C., Marx, D., Sannella, D. (eds.) ICALP 2018. LIPIcs, vol. 107, pp. 144:1–144:14. Schloss Dagstuhl, July 2018. https://doi.org/10.4230/LIPIcs.ICALP.2018.144
6. Arasu, A., Kaushik, R.: Oblivious query processing. In: Proc. 17th International Conference on Database Theory (ICDT), Athens, Greece, March 24–28, 2014. pp. 26–37. OpenProceedings.org (2014). https://doi.org/10.5441/002/icdt.2014.07
7. Balle, B., Barthe, G., Gaboardi, M.: Privacy amplification by subsampling: tight analyses via couplings and divergences. In: NeurIPS (2018). https://doi.org/10.5555/3327345.3327525
8. Balle, B., Bell, J., Gascón, A., Nissim, K.: The privacy blanket of the shuffle model. In: Boldyreva, A., Micciancio, D. (eds.) CRYPTO 2019. LNCS, vol. 11693, pp. 638–667. Springer, Cham (2019). https://doi.org/10.1007/978-3-030-26951-7_22
9. Bayer, S., Groth, J.: Efficient zero-knowledge argument for correctness of a shuffle. In: Pointcheval, D., Johansson, T. (eds.) EUROCRYPT 2012. LNCS, vol. 7237, pp. 263–280. Springer, Heidelberg (2012). https://doi.org/10.1007/978-3-642-29011-4_17
10. Beimel, A., Nissim, K., Zaheri, M.: Exploring differential obliviousness. In: Approx/Random. LIPIcs, vol. 145, pp. 65:1–65:20 (2019). https://doi.org/10.4230/LIPIcs.APPROX-RANDOM.2019.65, https://doi.org/10.4230/LIPIcs.APPROX-RANDOM.2019.65
11. Bittau, A., et al.: Prochlo: strong privacy for analytics in the crowd. In: SOSP, New York, NY, USA, pp. 441–459. Association for Computing Machinery (2017). https://doi.org/10.1145/3132747.3132769
12. Bogatov, D., Kellaris, G., Kollios, G., Nissim, K., O'Neill, A.: εpsolute: Efficiently querying databases while providing differential privacy. In: Vigna, G., Shi, E. (eds.) ACM CCS 2021, pp. 2262–2276. ACM Press, November 2021. https://doi.org/10.1145/3460120.3484786
13. Bünz, B., Hu, Y., Matsuo, S., Shi, E.: Non-interactive differentially anonymous router. Cryptology ePrint Archive, Report 2021/1242 (2021). https://eprint.iacr.org/2021/1242
14. Camenisch, J., Lysyanskaya, A.: A formal treatment of onion routing. In: Shoup, V. (ed.) CRYPTO 2005. LNCS, vol. 3621, pp. 169–187. Springer, Heidelberg (2005). https://doi.org/10.1007/11535218_11
15. Cash, D., Grubbs, P., Perry, J., Ristenpart, T.: Leakage-abuse attacks against searchable encryption. In: Ray, I., Li, N., Kruegel, C. (eds.) ACM CCS 2015, pp. 668–679. ACM Press, October 2015. https://doi.org/10.1145/2810103.2813700
16. Cecchetti, E., Zhang, F., Ji, Y., Kosba, A.E., Juels, A., Shi, E.: Solidus: confidential distributed ledger transactions via PVORM. In: Thuraisingham, B.M., Evans, D., Malkin, T., Xu, D. (eds.) ACM CCS 2017. pp. 701–717. ACM Press, October/November 2017. https://doi.org/10.1145/3133956.3134010
17. Chan, T.H.H., Chung, K.M., Maggs, B.M., Shi, E.: Foundations of differentially oblivious algorithms. In: Chan, T.M. (ed.) 30th SODA, pp. 2448–2467. ACM-SIAM, January 2019. https://doi.org/10.1137/1.9781611975482.150
18. Chan, T.H.H., Guo, Y., Lin, W.K., Shi, E.: Cache-oblivious and data-oblivious sorting and applications. In: Czumaj, A. (ed.) 29th SODA, pp. 2201–2220. ACM-SIAM, January 2018. https://doi.org/10.1137/1.9781611975031.143
19. Hubert Chan, T.-H., Shi, E., Song, D.: Private and continual release of statistics. In: Abramsky, S., Gavoille, C., Kirchner, C., Meyer auf der Heide, F., Spirakis, P.G. (eds.) ICALP 2010. LNCS, vol. 6199, pp. 405–417. Springer, Heidelberg (2010). https://doi.org/10.1007/978-3-642-14162-1_34

20. Chaum, D.: The dining cryptographers problem: *Unconditional sender and recipient untraceability.* J. Cryptol. **1**(1), 65–75 (1988). https://doi.org/10.1007/BF00206326

21. Chaum, D.L.: Untraceable electronic mail, return addresses, and digital pseudonyms. Commun. ACM **24**(2), 84–90 (1981). https://doi.org/10.1145/358549.358563

22. Cheu, A.: Differential privacy in the shuffle model: a survey of separations. arXiv preprint arXiv:2107.11839 (2021). https://doi.org/10.48550/arXiv.2107.11839

23. Cheu, A., Smith, A., Ullman, J., Zeber, D., Zhilyaev, M.: Distributed differential privacy via shuffling. In: Ishai, Y., Rijmen, V. (eds.) EUROCRYPT 2019. LNCS, vol. 11476, pp. 375–403. Springer, Cham (2019). https://doi.org/10.1007/978-3-030-17653-2_13

24. Chu, S., Zhuo, D., Shi, E., Chan, T.H.: Differentially oblivious database joins: Overcoming the worst-case curse of fully oblivious algorithms. In: Tessaro, S. (ed.) ITC (2021). https://doi.org/10.4230/LIPIcs.ITC.2021.19

25. Connell, G.: Technology deep dive: Building a faster oram layer for enclaves. https://signal.org/blog/building-faster-oram/

26. Corrigan-Gibbs, H., Boneh, D., Mazières, D.: Riposte: an anonymous messaging system handling millions of users. In: 2015 IEEE Symposium on Security and Privacy, pp. 321–338. IEEE Computer Society Press, May 2015. https://doi.org/10.1109/SP.2015.27

27. Corrigan-Gibbs, H., Ford, B.: Dissent: accountable anonymous group messaging. In: Al-Shaer, E., Keromytis, A.D., Shmatikov, V. (eds.) ACM CCS 2010, pp. 340–350. ACM Press, October 2010. https://doi.org/10.1145/1866307.1866346

28. Crooks, N., Burke, M., Cecchetti, E., Harel, S., Agarwal, R., Alvisi, L.: Obladi: oblivious serializable transactions in the cloud. In: 13th USENIX Symposium on Operating Systems Design and Implementation, OSDI 2018, Carlsbad, CA, USA, October 8–10, 2018. pp. 727–743. USENIX Association (2018). https://doi.org/10.5555/3291168.3291222

29. Degabriele, J.P., Stam, M.: Untagging tor: a formal treatment of onion encryption. In: Nielsen, J.B., Rijmen, V. (eds.) EUROCRYPT 2018. LNCS, vol. 10822, pp. 259–293. Springer, Cham (2018). https://doi.org/10.1007/978-3-319-78372-7_9

30. Dwork, C., McSherry, F., Nissim, K., Smith, A.: Calibrating noise to sensitivity in private data analysis. In: Halevi, S., Rabin, T. (eds.) TCC 2006. LNCS, vol. 3876, pp. 265–284. Springer, Heidelberg (2006). https://doi.org/10.1007/11681878_14

31. Dwork, C., Naor, M., Pitassi, T., Rothblum, G.N.: Differential privacy under continual observation. In: Schulman, L.J. (ed.) 42nd ACM STOC, pp. 715–724. ACM Press, June 2010. https://doi.org/10.1145/1806689.1806787

32. Dwork, C., Roth, A.: The algorithmic foundations of differential privacy. Found. Trends Theor. Comput. Sci. **9**(3–4), 211–407 (2014). https://doi.org/10.1561/0400000042

33. Erlingsson, Ú., Feldman, V., Mironov, I., Raghunathan, A., Talwar, K., Thakurta, A.: Amplification by shuffling: From local to central differential privacy via anonymity. In: Chan, T.M. (ed.) 30th SODA, pp. 2468–2479. ACM-SIAM, January 2019. https://doi.org/10.1137/1.9781611975482.151

34. Eskandarian, S., Boneh, D.: Clarion: Anonymous communication from multiparty shuffling protocols. Cryptology ePrint Archive, Report 2021/1514 (2021). https://eprint.iacr.org/2021/1514

35. Eskandarian, S., Zaharia, M.: Oblidb: oblivious query processing for secure databases. Proc. VLDB Endow. **13**(2), 169–183 (2019). https://doi.org/10.14778/3364324.3364331

36. Farhadi, A., Hajiaghayi, M., Larsen, K.G., Shi, E.: Lower bounds for external memory integer sorting via network coding. In: Charikar, M., Cohen, E. (eds.) 51st ACM STOC, pp. 997–1008. ACM Press, June 2019. https://doi.org/10.1145/3313276.3316337

37. Feldman, V., McMillan, A., Talwar, K.: Hiding among the clones: a simple and nearly optimal analysis of privacy amplification by shuffling. In: FOCS (2021). https://doi.org/10.1109/FOCS52979.2021.00096

38. Gertner, Y., Ishai, Y., Kushilevitz, E., Malkin, T.: Protecting data privacy in private information retrieval schemes. JCSS (2000). https://doi.org/10.1145/276698.276723

39. Ghazi, B., Golowich, N., Kumar, R., Pagh, R., Velingker, A.: On the power of multiple anonymous messages: frequency estimation and selection in the shuffle model of differential privacy. In: Canteaut, A., Standaert, F.X. (eds.) EUROCRYPT 2021, Part III. LNCS, vol. 12698, pp. 463–488. Springer, Heidelberg (2021). https://doi.org/10.1007/978-3-030-77883-5_16

40. Ghazi, B., Kumar, R., Manurangsi, P., Pagh, R.: Private counting from anonymous messages: Near-optimal accuracy with vanishing communication overhead (2021). https://doi.org/10.48550/ARXIV.2106.04247

41. Girgis, A.M., Data, D., Diggavi, S., Kairouz, P., Suresh, A.T.: Shuffled model of federated learning: privacy, accuracy and communication trade-offs. IEEE J. Sel. Areas Inf. Theory **2**(1), 464–478 (2021). https://doi.org/10.1109/JSAIT.2021.3056102

42. Goldreich, O.: Towards a theory of software protection and simulation by oblivious RAMs. In: Aho, A. (ed.) 19th ACM STOC. pp. 182–194. ACM Press, May 1987. https://doi.org/10.1145/28395.28416

43. Goldreich, O., Ostrovsky, R.: Software protection and simulation on oblivious rams. J. ACM **43**(3), 431–473 (1996). https://doi.org/10.1145/233551.233553

44. Gordon, S.D., Katz, J., Kolesnikov, V., Krell, F., Malkin, T., Raykova, M., Vahlis, Y.: Secure two-party computation in sublinear (amortized) time. In: Yu, T., Danezis, G., Gligor, V.D. (eds.) ACM CCS 2012, pp. 513–524. ACM Press, October 2012. https://doi.org/10.1145/2382196.2382251

45. Gordon, S.D., Katz, J., Liang, M., Xu, J.: Spreading the privacy blanket: - differentially oblivious shuffling for differential privacy. In: Ateniese, G., Venturi, D. (eds.) ACNS 22. LNCS, vol. 13269, pp. 501–520. Springer, Heidelberg, June 2022. https://doi.org/10.1007/978-3-031-09234-3_25

46. Grubbs, P., Lacharité, M.S., Minaud, B., Paterson, K.G.: Learning to reconstruct: Statistical learning theory and encrypted database attacks. In: 2019 IEEE Symposium on Security and Privacy, pp. 1067–1083. IEEE Computer Society Press, May 2019. https://doi.org/10.1109/SP.2019.00030

47. Grubbs, P., McPherson, R., Naveed, M., Ristenpart, T., Shmatikov, V.: Breaking web applications built on top of encrypted data. In: Weippl, E.R., Katzenbeisser, S., Kruegel, C., Myers, A.C., Halevi, S. (eds.) ACM CCS 2016, pp. 1353–1364. ACM Press, October 2016. https://doi.org/10.1145/2976749.2978351

48. Hall, P.: On representatives of subsets. J. Lond. Math. Soc. **1**(1), 26–30 (1935). https://doi.org/10.1112/jlms/s1-10.37.26

49. Hall, M., Jr.: Distinct representatives of subsets. Bull. Am. Math. Soc. **54**(10), 922–926 (1948). https://doi.org/10.1090/S0002-9904-1948-09098-X

50. Islam, M.S., Kuzu, M., Kantarcioglu, M.: Access pattern disclosure on searchable encryption: Ramification, attack and mitigation. In: NDSS 2012. The Internet Society, February 2012

51. Jacob, R., Larsen, K.G., Nielsen, J.B.: Lower bounds for oblivious data structures. In: Chan, T.M. (ed.) 30th SODA, pp. 2439–2447. ACM-SIAM, Jan 2019. https://doi.org/10.1137/1.9781611975482.149
52. Kellaris, G., Kollios, G., Nissim, K., O'Neill, A.: Generic attacks on secure outsourced databases. In: Weippl, E.R., Katzenbeisser, S., Kruegel, C., Myers, A.C., Halevi, S. (eds.) ACM CCS 2016. pp. 1329–1340. ACM Press, October 2016. https://doi.org/10.1145/2976749.2978386
53. Lin, W.K., Shi, E., Xie, T.: Can we overcome the n log n barrier for oblivious sorting? In: Chan, T.M. (ed.) 30th SODA, pp. 2419–2438. ACM-SIAM, January 2019. https://doi.org/10.1137/1.9781611975482.148
54. Liu, C., Hicks, M., Harris, A., Tiwari, M., Maas, M., Shi, E.: Ghostrider: a hardware-software system for memory trace oblivious computation. In: ASPLOS (2015). https://doi.org/10.1145/2694344.2694385
55. Liu, C., Wang, X.S., Nayak, K., Huang, Y., Shi, E.: ObliVM: a programming framework for secure computation. In: 2015 IEEE Symposium on Security and Privacy, pp. 359–376. IEEE Computer Society Press, May 2015. https://doi.org/10.1109/SP.2015.29
56. Lochbihler, A.: A mechanized proof of the max-flow min-cut theorem for countable networks with applications to probability theory. Journal of Automated Reasoning, pp. 1–26 (2022). https://doi.org/10.1007/s10817-022-09616-4
57. Maas, M., et al.: PHANTOM: practical oblivious computation in a secure processor. In: Sadeghi, A.R., Gligor, V.D., Yung, M. (eds.) ACM CCS 2013, pp. 311–324. ACM Press, November 2013. https://doi.org/10.1145/2508859.2516692
58. Mironov, I., Pandey, O., Reingold, O., Vadhan, S.: Computational differential privacy. In: Halevi, S. (ed.) CRYPTO 2009. LNCS, vol. 5677, pp. 126–142. Springer, Heidelberg (2009). https://doi.org/10.1007/978-3-642-03356-8_8
59. Mishra, P., Poddar, R., Chen, J., Chiesa, A., Popa, R.A.: Oblix: An efficient oblivious search index. In: 2018 IEEE Symposium on Security and Privacy, pp. 279–296. IEEE Computer Society Press, May 2018. https://doi.org/10.1109/SP.2018.00045
60. Naveed, M., Kamara, S., Wright, C.V.: Inference attacks on property-preserving encrypted databases. In: Ray, I., Li, N., Kruegel, C. (eds.) ACM CCS 2015, pp. 644–655. ACM Press, October 2015. https://doi.org/10.1145/2810103.2813651
61. Ostrovsky, R., Shoup, V.: Private information storage (extended abstract). In: 29th ACM STOC, pp. 294–303. ACM Press, May 1997. https://doi.org/10.1145/258533.258606
62. Reed, M., Syverson, P., Goldschlag, D.: Anonymous connections and onion routing. IEEE J. Sel. Areas Commun. **16**(4), 482–494 (1998). https://doi.org/10.1109/49.668972
63. Ren, L., Yu, X., Fletcher, C.W., van Dijk, M., Devadas, S.: Design space exploration and optimization of path oblivious RAM in secure processors. In: ISCA, pp. 571–582 (2013). https://doi.org/10.1145/2485922.2485971
64. Roughgarden, T.: Beyond the Worst-Case Analysis of Algorithms. Cambridge University Press (2020). https://doi.org/10.1017/9781108637435
65. Shi, E., Chan, T.-H.H., Stefanov, E., Li, M.: Oblivious RAM with $O((\log N)^3)$ worst-case cost. In: Lee, D.H., Wang, X. (eds.) ASIACRYPT 2011. LNCS, vol. 7073, pp. 197–214. Springer, Heidelberg (2011). https://doi.org/10.1007/978-3-642-25385-0_11
66. Shi, E., Wu, K.: Non-interactive anonymous router. In: Canteaut, A., Standaert, F.-X. (eds.) EUROCRYPT 2021. LNCS, vol. 12698, pp. 489–520. Springer, Cham (2021). https://doi.org/10.1007/978-3-030-77883-5_17

67. Stefanov, E., Shi, E.: ObliviStore: high performance oblivious cloud storage. In: 2013 IEEE Symposium on Security and Privacy. pp. 253–267. IEEE Computer Society Press, May 2013. https://doi.org/10.1109/SP.2013.25

68. Stefanov, E., et al.: Path ORAM: an extremely simple oblivious RAM protocol. In: Sadeghi, A.R., Gligor, V.D., Yung, M. (eds.) ACM CCS 2013, pp. 299–310. ACM Press, November 2013. https://doi.org/10.1145/2508859.2516660

69. Tinoco, A., Gao, S., Shi, E.: EnigMap: Signal should use oblivious algorithms for private contact discovery. Cryptology ePrint Archive, Report 2022/1083 (2022). https://eprint.iacr.org/2022/1083

70. Wang, X., Chan, T.H.H., Shi, E.: Circuit ORAM: On tightness of the Goldreich-Ostrovsky lower bound. In: Ray, I., Li, N., Kruegel, C. (eds.) ACM CCS 2015, pp. 850–861. ACM Press, October 2015. https://doi.org/10.1145/2810103.2813634

71. Wang, Y.X., Balle, B., Kasiviswanathan, S.: Subsampled rényi differential privacy and analytical moments accountant. J. Privacy Confident. 10(2) (2021). https://doi.org/10.29012/jpc.723

72. Williams, P., Sion, R., Tomescu, A.: PrivateFS: a parallel oblivious file system. In: Yu, T., Danezis, G., Gligor, V.D. (eds.) ACM CCS 2012, pp. 977–988. ACM Press, October 2012. https://doi.org/10.1145/2382196.2382299

73. Zhou, M., Shi, E.: The power of the differentially oblivious shuffle in distributed privacy mechanisms. Cryptology ePrint Archive, Report 2022/177 (2022). https://eprint.iacr.org/2022/177

74. Zhou, M., Shi, E., Chan, T.H.H., Maimon, S.: A theory of composition for differential obliviousness. Cryptology ePrint Archive, Report 2022/1357 (2022). https://eprint.iacr.org/2022/1357

75. Zhuang, L., Zhou, F., Zhao, B.Y., Rowstron, A.: Cashmere: Resilient anonymous routing. In: NSDI (2005). https://doi.org/10.5555/1251203.1251225

On Differential Privacy and Adaptive Data Analysis with Bounded Space

Itai Dinur[1]([✉]), Uri Stemmer[2,3], David P. Woodruff[4], and Samson Zhou[5,6]

[1] Ben-Gurion University, Be'er Sheva, Israel
dinuri@bgu.ac.il
[2] Tel Aviv University, Tel Aviv-Yafo, Israel
u@uri.co.il
[3] Google Research, Tel Aviv-Yafo, Israel
[4] Carnegie Mellon University, Pittsburgh, USA
dwoodruf@andrew.cmu.edu
[5] UC Berkeley, Berkeley, USA
[6] Rice University, Houston, USA

Abstract. We study the space complexity of the two related fields of *differential privacy* and *adaptive data analysis*. Specifically,

1. Under standard cryptographic assumptions, we show that there exists a problem P that requires exponentially more space to be solved efficiently with differential privacy, compared to the space needed without privacy. To the best of our knowledge, this is the first separation between the space complexity of private and non-private algorithms.
2. The line of work on adaptive data analysis focuses on understanding the number of *samples* needed for answering a sequence of adaptive queries. We revisit previous lower bounds at a foundational level, and show that they are a consequence of a space bottleneck rather than a sampling bottleneck.

To obtain our results, we define and construct an encryption scheme with multiple keys that is built to withstand a limited amount of key leakage in a very particular way.

1 Introduction

Query-to-communication lifting theorems allow translating lower bounds on the *query complexity* of a given function f to lower bounds on the *communication complexity* of a related function $\hat{f}$. Starting from the seminal work of Raz and McKenzie [31], several such lifting theorems were presented, and applied, to obtain new communication complexity lower bounds in various settings.

In the domain of cryptography, related results have been obtained, where the starting point is a lower bound on the *query complexity* of an adversary solving a cryptanalytic problem in an idealized model, such as the random oracle model [4].

The full version of this paper is available at https://eprint.iacr.org/2023/171.

C. Hazay and M. Stam (Eds.): EUROCRYPT 2023, LNCS 14006, pp. 35–65, 2023.
https://doi.org/10.1007/978-3-031-30620-4_2

The query complexity lower bound is then lifted to a *query-space* lower bound for a non-uniform (preprocessing) adversary solving the same problem [11,12,37].

Building on ideas developed in these lines of work, we present a new technique for translating sampling lower bounds to space lower bounds for problems in the context of *differential privacy* and *adaptive data analysis*. Before presenting our results, we motivate our settings.

1.1   Differential Privacy

Differential privacy [16] is a mathematical definition for privacy that aims to enable statistical analyses of datasets while providing strong guarantees that individual-level information does not leak. Informally, an algorithm that analyzes data satisfies differential privacy if it is robust in the sense that its outcome distribution does not depend "too much" on any single data point. Formally,

Definition 1.1 ([16]). *Let $\mathcal{A} : X^* \to Y$ be a randomized algorithm whose input is a dataset $D \in X^*$. Algorithm $\mathcal{A}$ is (ε, δ)-differentially private (DP) if for any two datasets D, D' that differ on one point (such datasets are called* neighboring*) and for any outcome set $F \subseteq Y$ it holds that $\Pr[\mathcal{A}(D) \in F] \leq e^\varepsilon \cdot \Pr[\mathcal{A}(D') \in F] + \delta$.*

To interpret the definition, let D be a dataset containing n data points, each of which represents the information of one individual. Suppose that Alice knows all but one of these data points (say Bob's data point). Now suppose that we compute $z \leftarrow \mathcal{A}(D)$, and give z to Alice. If $\mathcal{A}$ is differentially private, then Alice learns very little about Bob's data point, because z would have been distributed roughly the same no matter what Bob's data point is.

Over the last few years, we have witnessed an explosion of research on differential privacy in various settings. In particular, a fruitful line of work has focused on designing differentially private algorithms with small *space* complexity, mainly in streaming settings. These works show many *positive* results and present differentially private algorithms with small space complexity for various problems. In fact, some of these works show that classical streaming algorithms are differentially private essentially *as is*. For example, Blocki et al. [5] show that the Johnson-Lindenstrauss transform itself preserves differential privacy, and Smith et al. [32] show this for the classical Flajolet-Martin Sketch.

In light of these positive results, one might think that algorithms with small space are particularly suitable for differential privacy, because these algorithms are not keeping too much information about the input to begin with.

Question 1.2. *Does differential privacy require more space?*

Our Results for Differential Privacy With bounded Space. We answer Question 1.2 in the affirmative, i.e., we show that differential privacy *may require more space*. To this end, we come up with a problem that can be solved using a small amount of space without privacy, but requires a large amount of space to be solved with privacy. As a first step, let us examine the following toy problem, which provides *some* answer to the above question.

A Toy Problem. Recall that F_2 (the second frequency moment of a stream) estimation with multiplicative approximation error $1 + \alpha$ has an $\Omega(1/\alpha^2)$ space lower bound [38]. This immediately shows a separation for the problem of "output either the last element of the stream or a $(1 + \alpha)$-approximation to the F_2 value of the stream". In the non-private setting, the last element can be output using space independent of α, but in the private setting the algorithm is forced to (privately) estimate F_2 and thus use at least $1/\alpha^2$ space. Of course, we could replace F_2 with other tasks that have a large space lower bound in the standard non-private model.

We deem this toy problem non-interesting because, at a high level, our goal is to show that there are cases where computing something privately requires a lot more space than computing "the same thing" non-privately. In the toy problem, however, the private and non-private algorithms are arguably *not* computing "the same thing". To reconcile this issue, we will focus on problems that are defined by a *function* (ranging over some metric space), and the desired task would be to approximate the value of this function. Note that this formulation disqualifies the toy problem from being a valid answer to Question 1.2, and that with this formulation there is a formal sense in which every algorithm for solving the task must compute (or approximate) "the same thing".

Let us make our setting more precise. In order to simplify the presentation, instead of studying the streaming model, we focus on the following computation model.[1] Consider an algorithm that is instantiated on a dataset D and then aims to answer a query with respect to D. We say that such an algorithm has space s if, before it gets the query, it shrinks D to a *summary* z containing at most s bits. Then, when obtaining the query, the algorithm answers it using only the summary z (without additional access to the original dataset D). Formally, we consider problems that are defined by a function $P : X^* \times Q \to M$, where X is the data domain, Q is a family of possible queries, and M is a metric space.

Definition 1.3. *We say that $\mathcal{A} = (\mathcal{A}_1, \mathcal{A}_2)$ solves a problem $P : X^* \times Q \to M$ with space complexity s, sample complexity n, error α, and confidence β if*

1. *$\mathcal{A}_1 : X^* \to \{0,1\}^s$ is a preprocessing procedure that takes a dataset D and outputs an s-bit string.*
2. *For every input dataset $D \in X^n$ and every query $q \in Q$ it holds that*

$$\Pr_{\substack{z \leftarrow \mathcal{A}_1(D) \\ a \leftarrow \mathcal{A}_2(z,q)}} [|a - P(D,q)| \leq \alpha] \geq 1 - \beta.$$

We show the following theorem.

Theorem 1.4 (informal). *Let $d \in \mathbb{N}$ be a parameter controlling the size of the problem (specifically, data points from X can be represented using $\mathrm{polylog}(d)$ bits, and queries from Q can be represented using $\mathrm{poly}(d)$ bits). There exists a problem $P : X^* \times Q \to M$ such that the following holds.*

---

[1] We remark, however, that all of our results extend to the streaming setting. See Remark 3.3.

1. *P can be solved non-privately using* polylog(d) *bits of space.*
   % See Lemma 3.2 for the formal statement.
2. *P can be solved privately using sample and space complexity* $\tilde{O}(\sqrt{d})$.
   % See Lemma 3.4 for the formal statement.
3. *Assuming the existence of a sub-exponentially secure symmetric-key encryption scheme, every computationally-efficient differentially-private algorithm $\mathcal{A}$ for solving P must have space complexity $\tilde{\Omega}(\sqrt{d})$, even if its sample complexity is a large polynomial in d. Furthermore, this holds even if $\mathcal{A}$ is only required to be* computationally *differentially private (namely, the adversary we build against $\mathcal{A}$ is computationally efficient).*
   % See Corollary 3.13 for the formal statement.

Note that this is an exponential separation (in d) between the non-private space complexity and the private space complexity. We emphasize that the hardness of privately solving P does not come from not having enough samples. Indeed, by Item 2, $\tilde{O}(\sqrt{d})$ samples suffice for privately solving this problem. However, Item 3 states that unless the algorithm has large space, then it cannot privately solve this problem *even if it has many more samples than needed.*

To the best of our knowledge, this is the first result that separates the space complexity of private and non-private algorithms. Admittedly, the problem P we define to prove the above theorem is somewhat unnatural. In contrast, our negative results for adaptive data analysis (to be surveyed next) are for the canonical problem studied in the literature.

1.2   Adaptive Data Analysis

Consider a data analyst interested in testing a specific research hypothesis. The analyst acquires relevant data, evaluates the hypothesis, and (say) learns that it is false. Based on the findings, the analyst now decides on a second hypothesis to be tested, and evaluates it *on the same data* (acquiring fresh data might be too expensive or even impossible). That is, the analyst chooses the hypotheses *adaptively*, where this choice depends on previous interactions with the data. As a result, the findings are no longer supported by classical statistical theory, which assumes that the tested hypotheses are fixed before the data is gathered, and the analyst runs the risk of overfitting to the data.

Starting with [15], the line of work on *adaptive data analysis (ADA)* aims to design methods for provably guaranteeing statistical validity in such settings. Specifically, the goal is to design a mechanism $\mathcal{A}$ that initially obtains a dataset D containing t i.i.d. samples from some unknown distribution $\mathcal{P}$, and then answers k *adaptively chosen queries* w.r.t. $\mathcal{P}$. Importantly, $\mathcal{A}$'s answers must be accurate w.r.t. the underlying distribution $\mathcal{P}$, and not just w.r.t. the empirical dataset D. The main question here is,

Question 1.5. *How many samples does $\mathcal{A}$ need (i.e., what should t be) in order to support k such adaptive queries?*

As a way of dealing with worst-case analysts, the analyst is assumed to be adversarial in that it tries to cause the mechanism to fail. If a mechanism can maintain utility against such an adversarial analyst, then it maintains utility against any analyst. Formally, the canonical problem pursued by the line of work on ADA is defined as a two-player game between a mechanism $\mathcal{A}$ and an adversary $\mathcal{B}$. See Fig. 1.

---

1. The adversary $\mathcal{B}$ chooses a distribution $\mathcal{P}$ over a data domain X.
2. The mechanism $\mathcal{A}$ obtains a sample $S \sim \mathcal{P}^t$ containing t i.i.d. samples from $\mathcal{P}$.
3. For k rounds $j = 1, 2, \ldots, k$:
   - The adversary chooses a function $h_j : X \to \{-1, 0, 1\}$, possibly as a function of all previous answers given by the mechanism.
   - The mechanism obtains h_j and responds with an answer z_j, which is given to $\mathcal{B}$.

Fig. 1. A two-player game between a mechanism $\mathcal{A}$ and an adversary $\mathcal{B}$.

Definition 1.6 ([15]). *A mechanism $\mathcal{A}$ is (α, β)-accurate for k queries over a domain X using sample size t if for every adversary $\mathcal{B}$ (interacting with $\mathcal{A}$ in the game specified in Fig. 1) it holds that*

$$\Pr\left[\exists j \in [k] \text{ s.t. } |z_j - h_j(\mathcal{P})| > \alpha\right] \le \beta,$$

where $h_j(\mathcal{P}) = \mathbb{E}_{x \sim \mathcal{P}}[h_j(x)]$ is the "true" value of h_j on the underlying distribution $\mathcal{P}$.

Following Dwork et al. [15], this problem has attracted a significant amount of work, most of which is focused on understanding how many *samples* are needed for adaptive data analysis (i.e., focused on Question 1.5). In particular, the following almost matching bounds are known.

Theorem 1.7 ([2,15]). *There exists a computationally efficient mechanism that is $(0.1, 0.1)$-accurate for k queries using sample size $t = \tilde{O}\left(\sqrt{k}\right)$.*

Theorem 1.8 ([24,34], **informal**). *Assuming the existence of one-way functions, every computationally efficient mechanism that is $(0.1, 0.1)$-accurate for k queries must have sample size at least $t = \Omega\left(\sqrt{k}\right)$.*

Our Results for Adaptive Data Analysis with Bounded Space. All prior work on the ADA problem treated it as a *sampling* problem, conveying the message that "adaptive data analysis requires more samples than non adaptive data analysis". In this work we revisit the ADA problem at a foundational level, and ask:

Question 1.9. *Is there a more fundamental bottleneck for the ADA problem than the number of samples?*

Consider a mechanism $\mathcal{A}$ that initially gets the *full description of the underlying distribution* $\mathcal{P}$, but is required to shrink this description into a summary z, whose description length is identical to the description length of t samples from $\mathcal{P}$. (We identify the *space complexity* of $\mathcal{A}$ with the size of z in bits.) Afterwards, $\mathcal{A}$ needs to answer k adaptive queries using z, without additional access to $\mathcal{P}$. Does this give $\mathcal{A}$ more power over a mechanism that only obtains t samples from $\mathcal{P}$?

We show that, in general, the answer is no. Specifically, we show the following theorem.

Theorem 1.10 (informal version of Theorem 4.1). *Assuming the existence of one-way functions, then every computationally efficient mechanism that is $(0.1, 0.1)$-accurate for k queries must have* space complexity *at least* $\Omega\left(\sqrt{k}\right)$.

In fact, in the formal version of this theorem (see Theorem 4.1) we show that the space complexity must be at least $\Omega\left(\sqrt{k}\right)$ times the representation length of domain elements. We view this as a significant strengthening of the previous lower bounds for the ADA problem: it is not that the mechanism did not get enough information about $\mathcal{P}$; it is just that it cannot shrink this information in a way that allows for efficiently answering k adaptive queries. This generalizes the negative results of [24,34], as sampling $t = \sqrt{k}$ points from $\mathcal{P}$ is just one particular way for storing information about $\mathcal{P}$.

1.3   Our Techniques

We obtain our results through a combination of techniques across several research areas including cryptography, privacy, learning theory, communication complexity, and information theory.

Our Techniques: Multi-instance Leakage-Resilient Scheme. The main cryptographic tool we define and construct is a suitable encryption scheme with multiple keys that is built to withstand a certain amount of key leakage in a very particular way. Specifically, the scheme consists of n instances of an underlying encryption scheme with independent keys (each of length λ bits). The keys are initially given to an adversary who shrinks them down to a summary z containing $s \ll n \cdot \lambda$ bits. After this phase, each instance independently sets an additional parameter, which is public but unknown to the adversary in the initial phase. Then, the adversary obtains encryptions of plaintexts under the n keys. We require that given z and the public parameters, the plaintexts encrypted with each key remain computationally hidden, except for a small number of the keys (which depends on s, but not on n).

We call the scheme a *multi-instance leakage-Resilient scheme* (or MILR scheme) to emphasize the fact that although the leakage of the adversary is an arbitrary function of all the n keys, the scheme itself is composed of n instances that are completely independent.

The efficiency of the MILR scheme is measured by two parameters: (1) the number of keys under which encryptions are (potentially) insecure, and (2) the loss in the security parameter λ. The scheme we construct is optimal in both parameters up to a multiplicative constant factor. First, encryptions remain hidden for all but $O\left(\frac{s}{\lambda}\right)$ of the keys. This is essentially optimal, as the adversary can define z to store the first $\frac{s}{\lambda}$ keys. Second, we lose a constant factor in the security parameter λ. An additional advantage of our construction is that its internal parameters do not depend on s. If we did allow such a dependency, then in some settings (particularly when $s \leq o(n \cdot \lambda)$) it would be possible to fine-tune the scheme to obtain a multiplicative $1 + o(1)$ loss in the efficiency parameters, but this has little impact on our application.

Our construction is arguably the most natural one. To encrypt a plaintext with a λ-bit key after the initial phase, we first apply an extractor (with the public parameter as a seed) to hash it down to a smaller key, which is used to encrypt the plaintext with the underlying encryption scheme.

The MILR scheme is related to schemes developed in the area of leakage-resilient cryptography (cf., [10,19,20,26,27,30,33]) where the basic technique of randomness extraction is commonly used. However, leakage-resilient cryptography mainly deals with resilience of cryptosystems to side-channel attacks, whereas our model is not designed to formalize security against such attacks and has several properties that are uncommon in this domain (such as protecting independent multiple instances of an encryption scheme in a way that inherently makes some of them insecure). Consequently, the advanced cryptosytems developed in the area of leakage-resilient cryptography are either unsuitable, overly complex, or inefficient for our purposes.

Despite the simplicity of our construction, our proof that it achieves the claimed security property against leakage is somewhat technical. We stress that we do not rely on hardness assumptions for specific problems, nor assume that the underlying encryption scheme has special properties such as resilience to related-key attacks. Instead, our proof is based on the pre-sampling technique introduced by Unruh [37] to prove security of cryptosystems against non-uniform adversaries in the random oracle model. This technique has been recently refined and optimized in [11,12,14] based on tools developed in the area of communication complexity [22,28]. The fact that we use the technique to prove security in a computational (rather than information-theoretic) setting seems to require the assumption that the underlying encryption scheme is secure against non-uniform adversaries (albeit this is considered a standard assumption).

Our Techniques: Privacy Requires More Space. We design a problem that can be solved non-privately with very small space complexity, but requires a large space complexity with privacy. To achieve this, we lift a known negative result on the *sample* complexity of privately solving a specific problem to obtain a *space* lower bound for a related problem. The problem we start with, for which there exists a sampling lower bound, is the so-called *1-way marginals* problem with parameter d. In this problem, our input is a dataset $D \in (\{0,1\}^d)^*$ containing a collection of binary vectors, each of length d. Our goal is to output a vector $\vec{a} \in [0,1]^d$ that approximates the *average* of the input vectors to within small L_∞ error, say to within error $1/10$. That is, we want vector $\vec{a} \in [0,1]^d$ to satisfy:
$$\left\| \vec{a} - \tfrac{1}{|D|} \sum_{\vec{x} \in D} \vec{x} \right\|_\infty \leq \tfrac{1}{10}.$$
We say that an algorithm for this problem has *sample complexity* n if, for every input dataset of size n, it outputs a good solution with probability at least 0.9. One of the most fundamental results in the literature of differential privacy shows that this problem requires a large dataset:

Theorem 1.11 ([9], informal). *Every differentially private algorithm for solving the 1-way marginal problem with parameter d must have sample complexity* $n = \Omega(\sqrt{d})$.

To lift this sampling lower bound into a space lower bound, we consider a problem in which the input dataset contains n keys $\vec{x} = (x_1, \ldots, x_n)$ (sampled from our MILR scheme). The algorithm must then shrink this dataset into a summary z containing s bits. Afterwards, the algorithm gets a "query" that is specified by a collection of n ciphertexts, each of which is an encryption of a d-bit vector. The desired task is to approximate the average of the *plaintext* input vectors. Intuitively, if the algorithm has space $s \ll \sqrt{d}$, then by the properties of our MILR scheme, it can decrypt at most $\approx s \ll \sqrt{d}$ of these d-bit vectors, and is hence trying to solve the 1-way marginal problem with fewer than $\sqrt{d}$ samples. We show that this argument can be formalized to obtain a contradiction.

Our Techniques: ADA Is About Space. As we mentioned, Hardt and Ullman [24] and Steinke and Ullman [34] showed that the ADA problem requires a large *sample* complexity (see Theorem 1.8). Specifically, they showed that there exists a computationally efficient adversary that causes every efficient mechanism to fail in answering adaptive queries. Recall that the ADA game (see Fig. 1) begins with the adversary choosing the underlying distribution.

We lift the negative result of [24,34] to a *space* lower bound. To achieve this, we design an alternative adversary that first samples a large collection of *keys* for our MILR scheme, and then defines the target distribution to be uniform on these sampled keys. Recall that in our setting, the mechanism gets an exact description of this target distribution and afterwards it must shrink this description into s bits. However, by the properties of our MILR scheme, this means that the mechanism would only be able to decrypt ciphertexts that correspond to at most $\approx s/\lambda$ of the keys. We then show that the adversary of [24,34] can be simulated under these conditions, where the "input sample" from their setting corresponds to the collection of indices of keys for which the mechanism can decrypt ciphertexts.

1.4 Applications to Communication Complexity

Finally, our arguments also provide distributional one-way communication complexity lower bounds, which are useful when the goal is to compute a relation with a very low success probability. To the best of our knowledge, existing query-to-communication lifting theorems, e.g., [22,23,31] do not consider the problems and input distributions that we consider here. Roughly speaking, we show that if any sampling based protocol for computing a function f requires k samples $(a_1, b_1), \ldots, (a_k, b_k)$, where $a_i \in \{0,1\}^t$ for each $i \in [k]$, then any one-way protocol that computes $f(A, B)$ in this setting must use $\Omega(kt)$ communication.

More precisely, in the two-player one-way communication game, inputs A and B are given to Alice and Bob, respectively, and the goal is for Alice to send a minimal amount of information to Bob, so that Bob can compute $f(A, B)$ for some predetermined function f. The communication cost of a protocol Π is the size of the largest message in bits sent from Alice across all possible inputs A and the (randomized) communication complexity is the minimum communication cost of a protocol that succeeds with probability at least $\frac{2}{3}$. In the distributional setting, A and B are further drawn from a known underlying distribution.

In our distributional setting, suppose Alice has m independent and uniform numbers $a_1, \ldots, a_m$ so that either $a_i \in GF(p)$ for all $i \in [m]$ or $a_i \in GF(2^t)$ for sufficiently large t for all $i \in [m]$ and suppose Bob has m independent and uniform numbers $b_1, \ldots, b_m$ from the same field, either $GF(p)$ or $GF(2^t)$. Then for any function $f(\langle a_1, b_1 \rangle, \ldots, \langle a_m, b_m \rangle)$, where the dot products are taken over $GF(2)$ or $f(a_1 \cdot b_1, \ldots, a_m \cdot b_m)$, where the products are taken over $GF(p)$, has the property that the randomized one-way communication complexity of computing f with probability σ is the same as the number of samples from $a_1, \ldots, a_m$ that Alice needs to send Bob to compute f with probability $\sigma - \varepsilon$. It is easy to prove sampling lower bounds for many of these problems, sum as $\sum_i a_i \cdot b_i \pmod{p}$ or $\text{MAJ}(\langle a_1, b_1 \rangle, \ldots, \langle a_m, b_m \rangle)$, and this immediately translates into communication complexity lower bounds. The main intuition for our overall lower bound argument is that the numbers $b_1, \ldots, b_m$ can be viewed as the hash functions that Bob has and thus we can apply a variant of the leftover hash lemma if Bob only has a small subset of these numbers. See the full version of this work for the details.

1.5 Related Works

Dwork et al. [17] used *traitor-tracing schemes* to prove computational sampling lower bounds for differential privacy. Their results were extended by Ullman [36], who used *fingerprinting codes* to construct a novel traitor-tracing scheme and to obtain stronger computational sampling lower bounds for differential privacy. Ullman's construction can be viewed as an encrypted variant of the 1-way marginal problem. Bun et al. [8] and Alon et al. [1] showed that there are trivial learning tasks that require asymptotically more samples to solve with differential privacy (compared to the non-private sample complexity). These results are fundamentally different than ours, as they are about sampling rather than space. Feldman [21] and Brown et al. [7] showed that there are learning problems for which every *near optimal* learning algorithm (obtaining near optimal error w.r.t. to the number of input *samples* it takes) must memorize a large portion of its input data. These works do not directly address the *additional* space required for preserving privacy. See the full version for additional related works.

1.6   Paper Structure

The rest of the paper is structured as follows. The MILR scheme is defined in Sect. 2. Our results for differential privacy and adaptive data analysis are described in Sects. 3 and 4, respectively. We construct our MILR scheme in Sect. 5, and prove its security in Sect. 6. Some of the technical details from these sections are deferred to the full version of this work.

2   Multi-instance Leakage-Resilient Scheme

We define a *multi-instance leakage-resilient scheme* (or MILR scheme) to be a tuple of efficient algorithms (Gen, Param, Enc, Dec) with the following syntax:

- Gen is a randomized algorithm that takes as input a security parameter λ and outputs a λ-bit secret key. Formally, $x \leftarrow \text{Gen}(1^\lambda)$.
- Param is a randomized algorithm that takes as input a security parameter λ and outputs a $\text{poly}(\lambda)$-bit public parameter. Formally, $p \leftarrow \text{Param}(1^\lambda)$.
- Enc is a randomized algorithm that takes as input a secret key x, a public parameter p, and a message $m \in \{0,1\}$, and outputs a ciphertext $c \in \{0,1\}^{\text{poly}(\lambda)}$. Formally, $c \leftarrow \text{Enc}(x, p, m)$.
- Dec is a deterministic algorithm that takes as input a secret key x, a public parameter p, and a ciphertext c, and outputs a decrypted message m'. If the ciphertext c was an encryption of m under the key x with the parameter p, then $m' = m$. Formally, if $c \leftarrow \text{Enc}(x, p, m)$, then $\text{Dec}(x, p, c) = m$ with probability 1.

To define the security of an MILR scheme, let $n \in \mathbb{N}$, let $\vec{x} = (x_1, \ldots, x_n)$ be a vector of keys, and let $\vec{p} = (p_1, \ldots, p_n)$ be a vector of public parameters (set once for each scheme by invoking Param). Let $J \subseteq [n]$ be a subset, referred to as the "hidden coordinates". Now consider a pair of oracles $\mathcal{E}_1(\vec{x}, \vec{p}, J, \cdot, \cdot)$ and $\mathcal{E}_0(\vec{x}, \vec{p}, J, \cdot, \cdot)$ with the following properties.

1. $\mathcal{E}_1(\vec{x}, \vec{p}, J, \cdot, \cdot)$ takes as input an index of a key $j \in [n]$ and a message m, and returns $\text{Enc}(x_j, p_j, m)$.
2. $\mathcal{E}_0(\vec{x}, \vec{p}, J, \cdot, \cdot)$ takes the same inputs. If $j \in J$ then the outcome is $\text{Enc}(x_j, p_j, 0)$, and otherwise the outcome is $\text{Enc}(x_j, p_j, m)$.

Definition 2.1. *Let λ be a security parameter. Let $\Gamma : \mathbb{R} \to \mathbb{R}$ and $\overline{\tau} : \mathbb{R}^2 \to \mathbb{R}$ be real-valued functions. An MILR scheme* (Gen, Param, Enc, Dec) *is $(\Gamma, \overline{\tau})$-secure against space bounded preprocessing adversaries if the following holds.*

(1) **Multi semantic security:** *For every $n = \text{poly}(\Gamma(\lambda))$ and every $\text{poly}(\Gamma(\lambda))$-time adversary $\mathcal{B}$ there exists a negligible function negl such that*

$$\left| \Pr_{\vec{x},\vec{p},\mathcal{B},\text{Enc}} \left[\mathcal{B}^{\mathcal{E}_0(\vec{x},\vec{p},[n],\cdot,\cdot)}(\vec{p}) = 1 \right] - \Pr_{\vec{x},\vec{p},\mathcal{B},\text{Enc}} \left[\mathcal{B}^{\mathcal{E}_1(\vec{x},\vec{p},[n],\cdot,\cdot)}(\vec{p}) = 1 \right] \right| \leq \text{negl}(\Gamma(\lambda)).$$

That is, a computationally bounded adversary that gets the public parameters, but not the keys, cannot tell whether it is interacting with $\mathcal{E}_0$ or with $\mathcal{E}_1$.

(2) **Multi-security against a bounded preprocessing adversary:** *For every $n = \text{poly}(\Gamma(\lambda))$, every $s \leq n \cdot \lambda$, and every preprocessing procedure $F : \left(\{0,1\}^\lambda \right)^n \to \{0,1\}^s$ (possibly randomized), there exists a random function $J = J(F, \vec{x}, z, \vec{p}) \subseteq [n]$ that given a collection of keys $\vec{x}$ and public parameters $\vec{p}$, and an element $z \leftarrow F(\vec{x})$, returns a subset of size $|J| \geq \tau := n - \overline{\tau}(\lambda, s)$ such that for every $\text{poly}(\Gamma(\lambda))$-time algorithm $\mathcal{B}$ there exists a negligible function negl satisfying*

$$\left| \Pr_{\substack{\vec{x},\vec{p},\mathcal{B},\text{Enc} \\ z \leftarrow F(\vec{x}) \\ J \leftarrow J(F,\vec{x},z,\vec{p})}} \left[\mathcal{B}^{\mathcal{E}_0(\vec{x},\vec{p},J,\cdot,\cdot)}(z,\vec{p}) = 1 \right] - \Pr_{\substack{\vec{x},\vec{p},\mathcal{B},\text{Enc} \\ z \leftarrow F(\vec{x}) \\ J \leftarrow J(F,\vec{x},z,\vec{p})}} \left[\mathcal{B}^{\mathcal{E}_1(\vec{x},\vec{p},J,\cdot,\cdot)}(z,\vec{p}) = 1 \right] \right| \leq \text{negl}(\Gamma(\lambda)).$$

That is, even if s bits of our n keys were leaked (computed by the preprocessing function F operating on the keys), then still encryptions w.r.t. the keys of J are computationally indistinguishable.

Remark 2.2. *When Γ is the identity function, we simply say that the scheme is $\overline{\tau}$-secure. Note that in this case, security holds against all adversaries with runtime polynomial in the security parameter λ. We will further assume the existence of a sub-exponentially secure encryption scheme. By that we mean that there exists a constant $\nu > 0$ such that the scheme is $(\Gamma, \overline{\tau})$-secure for $\Gamma(\lambda) = 2^{\lambda^\nu}$. That is, we assume the existence of a scheme in which security holds against all adversaries with runtime polynomial in 2^{λ^ν}.*

In Sects. 5 and 6 we show the following theorem.

Theorem 2.3. *Let $\Omega(\lambda) \leq \Gamma(\lambda) \leq 2^{o(\lambda)}$. If there exists a $\Gamma(\lambda)$-secure encryption scheme against non-uniform adversaries then there exists an MILR scheme that is $(\Gamma(\lambda), \overline{\tau})$-secure against space bounded non-uniform preprocessing adversaries, where $\overline{\tau}(\lambda, s) = \frac{2s}{\lambda} + 4$.*

3 Space Hardness for Differential Privacy

Consider an algorithm that is instantiated on a dataset D and then aims to answer a query w.r.t. D. We say that such an algorithm has space s if, before it gets the query, it shrinks D to a *summary* z containing at most s bits. Then, when obtaining the query, the algorithm answers it using only the summary z (without additional access to the original dataset D).

Let (Gen, Param, Enc, Dec) be an MILR scheme with security parameter λ. In the (λ, d)-decoded average (DA) problem with sample complexity n, the input dataset contains n keys, that is $D = (x_1, \ldots, x_n) \in \left(\{0,1\}^\lambda\right)^n$. A query $q = ((p_1, c_1), \ldots, (p_n, c_n))$ is specified using n pairs (p_i, c_i) where p_i is a public parameter and c_i is a ciphertext, which is an encryption of a binary vector of length d. The goal is to release a vector $\vec{a} = (a_1, \ldots, a_d) \in [0,1]^d$ that approximates the "decrypted average vector (dav)", defined as $\mathrm{dav}_q(D) = \frac{1}{n} \sum_{i=1}^n \mathrm{Dec}(x_i, p_i, c_i)$.

Definition 3.1. *Let $\mathcal{A} = (\mathcal{A}_1, \mathcal{A}_2)$ be an algorithm where $\mathcal{A}_1 : \left(\{0,1\}^\lambda\right)^n \to \{0,1\}^s$ is the preprocessing procedure that summarizes a dataset of n keys into s bits, and where $\mathcal{A}_2$ is the "response algorithm" that gets the outcome of $\mathcal{A}_1(D)$ and a query q. We say that $\mathcal{A}$ solves the DA problem if with probability at least $9/10$ the output is a vector $\vec{a}$ satisfying $\|\vec{a} - \mathrm{dav}_q(D)\|_\infty \le \frac{1}{10}$.*

Without privacy considerations, the DA problem is almost trivial. Specifically,

Lemma 3.2. *The (λ, d)-DA problem can be solved efficiently using space $s = O\left(\lambda \log(d)\right)$.*

Proof. The preprocessing algorithm $\mathcal{A}_1$ samples $O(\log d)$ of the input keys. Algorithm $\mathcal{A}_2$ then gets the query q and estimates the dav vector using the sampled keys. The lemma then follows by the Chernoff bound.

Remark 3.3. *As we mentioned, to simplify the presentation, in our computational model we identify the space complexity of algorithm $\mathcal{A} = (\mathcal{A}_1, \mathcal{A}_2)$ with the size of the output of algorithm $\mathcal{A}_1$. We remark, however, that our separation extends to a streaming model where both $\mathcal{A}_1$ and $\mathcal{A}_2$ are required to have small space. To see this, note that algorithm $\mathcal{A}_1$ in the above proof already has small space (and not just small output length), as it merely samples $O(\log d)$ keys from its input dataset. We now analyze the space complexity of $\mathcal{A}_2$, when it reads the query q in a streaming fashion. Recall that the query q contains n public parameters $p_1, \ldots, p_n$ and n ciphertexts $c_1, \ldots, c_n$, where each c_i is an encryption of a d-bit vector, call it $y_i \in \{0,1\}^d$. To allow $\mathcal{A}_2$ to read q using small space, we order it as follows: $q = (p_1, \ldots, p_n), (c_{1,1}, \ldots, c_{n,1}), \ldots, (c_{1,d}, \ldots, c_{n,d}) \triangleq q_0 \circ q_1 \circ \cdots \circ q_d$. Here $c_{i,j} = \mathrm{Enc}(x_i, p_i, y_i[j])$ is an encryption of the jth bit of y_i using key x_i and public parameter p_i. Note that the first part of the stream, q_0, contains the public parameters, and then every part q_j contains encryptions of the jth bit of each of the n input vectors. With this ordering of the query, algorithm $\mathcal{A}_2$ begins by reading q_0 and storing the $O(\log d)$ public parameters corresponding to the keys that were stored by $\mathcal{A}_1$. Then, for every $j \in [d]$, when reading q_j, algorithm $\mathcal{A}_2$*

estimates the average of the jth coordinate using the sampled keys. Algorithm $\mathcal{A}_2$ then outputs this estimated value, and proceeds to the next coordinate. This can be implemented using space complexity $\mathrm{poly}(\lambda \log(d))$.

So, without privacy constraints, the DA problem can be solved using small space. We now show that, assuming that the input dataset is large enough, the DA problem can easily be solved with differential privacy using *large* space. Specifically,

Lemma 3.4. *There is a computationally efficient (ε, δ)-differentially private algorithm that solves the (λ, d)-DA problem using space $s = O\left(\frac{1}{\varepsilon} \cdot \sqrt{d \cdot \log(\frac{1}{\delta})} \cdot \lambda \cdot \log d\right)$, provided that the size of the input dataset satisfies $n = \Omega(s)$ (large enough).*

Proof. The preprocessing algorithm $\mathcal{A}_1$ samples $\approx \sqrt{d}$ of the keys. By standard composition theorems for differential privacy [18], this suffices for the response algorithm $\mathcal{A}_2$ to privately approximate each of the d coordinates of the target vector.

Thus the DA problem can be solved non-privately using small space, and it can be solved privately using large space. Our next goal is to show that large space is indeed necessary to solve this problem privately. Before showing that, we introduce several additional preliminaries on computational differential privacy and on fingerprinting codes.

3.1 Preliminaries on Computational Differential Privacy and Fingerprinting Codes

Computational differential privacy was defined by Beimel et al [3] and Mironov et al. [29]. Let $\mathcal{A}$ be a randomized algorithm (mechanism) that operates on datasets. Computational differential privacy is defined via a two player game between a *challenger* and an adversary, running a pair of algorithms (Q, T). The game begins with the adversary Q choosing a pair of neighboring datasets (D_0, D_1) of size n each, as well as an arbitrary string r (which we think of as representing its internal state). Then the challenger samples a bit b and applies $\mathcal{A}(D_b)$ to obtain an outcome a. Then $T(r, \cdot)$ is applied on a and tries to guess b. Formally,

Definition 3.5. *Let λ be a security parameter, let ε be a constant, and let $\delta : \mathbb{R} \to \mathbb{R}$ be a function. A randomized algorithm $\mathcal{A} : X^* \to Y$ is (ε, δ)-computationally differentially private (CDP) if for every $n = \mathrm{poly}(\lambda)$ and every non-uniform $\mathrm{poly}(\lambda)$-time adversary (Q, T) there exists a negligible function negl such that*

$$\Pr_{\substack{(r,D_0,D_1)\leftarrow Q \\ \mathcal{A},T}}[T(r, \mathcal{A}(D_0)) = 1] \leq e^{\varepsilon} \cdot \Pr_{\substack{(r,D_0,D_1)\leftarrow Q \\ \mathcal{A},T}}[T(r, \mathcal{A}(D_1)) = 1] + \delta(n) + \mathrm{negl}(\lambda).$$

Definition 3.6. *Let ε be a constant and let $\delta = \delta(\lambda)$ be a function. Given two probability ensembles $\mathcal{X} = \{X_\lambda\}_{\lambda \in \mathbb{N}}$ and $\mathcal{Y} = \{Y_\lambda\}_{\lambda \in \mathbb{N}}$ we write $\mathcal{X} \approx_{\varepsilon, \delta} \mathcal{Y}$ if for* *every non-uniform probabilistic polynomial-time distinguisher D there exists a negligible function* negl *such that* $\Pr_{x \leftarrow X_\lambda}[D(x) = 1] \le e^\varepsilon \cdot \Pr_{y \leftarrow Y_\lambda}[D(y) = 1] + \delta(\lambda) + \text{negl}(\lambda)$, *and vice versa.*

We recall the concept of *fingerprinting codes*, which was introduced by Boneh and Shaw [6] as a cryptographic tool for watermarking digital content. Starting from the work of Bun, Ullman, and Vadhan [9], fingerprinting codes have played a key role in proving lower bounds for differential privacy in various settings.

A (collusion-resistant) fingerprinting code is a scheme for distributing codewords $w_1, \cdots, w_n$ to n users that can be uniquely traced back to each user. Moreover, if a group of (at most k) users combines its codewords into a pirate codeword $\hat{w}$, then the pirate codeword can still be traced back to one of the users who contributed to it. Of course, without any assumption on how the pirates can produce their combined codeword, no secure tracing is possible. To this end, the pirates are constrained according to a *marking assumption*, which asserts that the combined codeword must agree with at least one of the "real" codewords in each position. Namely, at an index j where $w_i[j] = b$ for every $i \in [n]$, the pirates are constrained to output $\hat{w}$ with $\hat{w}[j] = b$ as well.[2]

Definition 3.7 ([6,35]). *A k-collusion resilient fingerprinting code of length d for n users with failure probability γ, or (n, d, k, γ)-FPC in short, is a pair of random variables $C \in \{0,1\}^{n \times d}$ and* Trace $: \{0,1\}^d \to 2^{[n]}$ *such that the following holds. For all adversaries $P : \{0,1\}^{k \times d} \to \{0,1\}^d$ and $S \subseteq [n]$ with $|S| = k$,*

$$\Pr_{C, \text{Trace}, P} [(\forall 1 \le j \le d \; \exists i \in [n] \; s.t. \; P(C_S)[j] = c_i[j]) \wedge (\text{Trace}(P(C_S)) = \emptyset)] \le \gamma,$$

and

$$\Pr_{C, \text{Trace}, P} [\text{Trace}(P(C_S)) \cap ([n] \setminus S) \ne \emptyset] \le \gamma,$$

where C_S contains the rows of C given by S.

Remark 3.8. *As mentioned, the condition $\{\forall 1 \le j \le d \; \exists i \in [n] \; s.t. \; P(C_S)[j] = c_i[j]\}$ is called the "marking assumption". The second condition is called the "small probability of false accusation". Hence, if the adversary P guarantees that its output satisfies the marking assumption, then with probability at least $1 - 2\gamma$ it holds that algorithm* Trace *outputs an index $i \in S$.*

Theorem 3.9 ([6,34,35]). *For every $1 \le k \le n$ there is a k-collusion-resilient fingerprinting code of length $d = O(k^2 \cdot \log n)$ for n users with failure probability $\gamma = \frac{1}{n^2}$ and an efficiently computable* Trace *function.*

We remark that there exist both adaptive and non-adaptive constructions of fingerprinting codes with the guarantees of Theorem 3.9; we use the non-adaptive variant.

---

[2] We follow the formulation of the marking assumption as given by [34], which is a bit different than the commonly considered one.

3.2 A Negative Result for the DA Problem

Our main negative result for space bounded differentially private algorithms is the following.

Theorem 3.10. *Let* $\Pi = (\text{Gen}, \text{Param}, \text{Enc}, \text{Dec})$ *be an MILR scheme with security parameter* λ *that is* $(\Gamma, \overline{\tau})$-*secure against space bounded preprocessing adversaries. Let* $d \leq \text{poly}(\Gamma(\lambda))$ *and* $n \leq \text{poly}(\Gamma(\lambda))$ *be functions of* λ. *Let* ε *be a constant and let* $\delta \leq \frac{1}{4n(e^\varepsilon+1)} = \Theta(\frac{1}{n})$. *For every* $\text{poly}(\Gamma(\lambda))$-*time* (ε, δ)-*CDP algorithm for the* (λ, d)-*DA problem with sample complexity* n *and space complexity* s *it holds that* $\overline{\tau}(\lambda, s) = \Omega\left(\sqrt{\frac{d}{\log n}}\right)$.

Proof. Let $\mathcal{A} = (\mathcal{A}_1, \mathcal{A}_2)$ be a $\text{poly}(\Gamma(\lambda))$-time CDP algorithm for the (λ, d)-DA problem using sample complexity $n = \text{poly}(\Gamma(\lambda))$ and space complexity s. Denote $\overline{\tau} = \overline{\tau}(\lambda, s)$, and assume towards a contradiction that $\overline{\tau} = O\left(\sqrt{\frac{d}{\log n}}\right)$ (small enough). We construct the following adversary $\mathcal{B}$ to an $(n+1, d, \overline{\tau}, \frac{1}{n^2})$-FPC (such a code is guaranteed to exist by Theorem 3.9 and by the contradictory assumption).

1. The input is n codewords $w_1, \ldots, w_n \in \{0, 1\}^d$.
2. Sample n keys $x_1, \ldots, x_n \sim \text{Gen}(1^\lambda)$.
3. Let $z \leftarrow \mathcal{A}_1(x_1, \ldots, x_n)$.
4. Sample n public parameters $p_1, \ldots, p_n \sim \text{Param}(1^\lambda)$.
5. For $i \in [n]$ let $c_i \leftarrow \text{Enc}(x_i, p_i, w_i)$.
6. Let $\vec{a} \leftarrow \mathcal{A}_2(z, (p_1, c_1), \ldots, (p_n, c_n))$.
7. Output $\vec{a}$, after rounding its coordinates to $\{0, 1\}$.

We think of $\mathcal{B}$ as an adversary to an FPC, and indeed, its input is a collection of codewords and its output is a binary vector of length d. Observe that if $\mathcal{A}$ solves the DA problem (i.e., approximates the decrypted average vector), then for every coordinate, the outcome of $\mathcal{B}$ must agree with at least one of the input codewords, namely, it satisfies the marking assumption (see Remark 3.8).

Remark 3.11. *Before we proceed with the formal proof, we give an overview of its structure (this remark can be ignored, and is not needed for the formal proof). Informally, we will show that*

(1) Algorithm $\mathcal{B}$ *is computationally differentially private w.r.t. the collection of codewords (even though our assumption on* $\mathcal{A}$ *is that it is private w.r.t. the keys).*

(2) Leveraging the properties of the MILR scheme, we will show that $\mathcal{B}$ *must effectively ignore most of its inputs, except for at most* $\overline{\tau}$ *codewords. This means that* $\mathcal{B}$ *is effectively an FPC adversary that operates on only* $\overline{\tau}$ *codewords (rather than the* n *codewords it obtains as input).*

(3) A known result in the literature of differential privacy (starting from [9]) is that a successful FPC adversary cannot be differentially private, because this would contradict the fact that the tracing algorithm is able to recover one of its input points. Our gain here comes from the fact that $\mathcal{B}$ only uses (effectively) $\overline{\tau}$ codewords, and hence, in order to get a contradiction, it suffices to use an FPC with a much shorter codeword-length (only $\approx \overline{\tau}^2$ instead of $\approx n^2$). This will mean that the hardness of the DA problem depends on the space of $\mathcal{A}$ (which controls $\overline{\tau}$) rather than the size of the input (which is n).

Recall that $\mathcal{A} = (\mathcal{A}_1, \mathcal{A}_2)$ is computationally differentially private w.r.t. the *keys*. We first show that $\mathcal{B}$ is computationally differentially private w.r.t. the *codewords*. To this end, let Q be an adversary (as in Definition 3.5) that outputs a pair of neighboring datasets $(\vec{w}, \vec{w'})$, each containing n codewords, together with a state r. Given $(\vec{w}, \vec{w'})$, we write $\ell = \ell(\vec{w}, \vec{w'}) \subseteq [n]$ to denote the index on which $\vec{w}, \vec{w'}$ differ. We also write x_0 to denote another key, independent of the keys $x_1, \ldots, x_n$ sampled by algorithm $\mathcal{B}$. By the privacy guarantees of algorithm $\mathcal{A}$ and by the semantic security of the encryption scheme (see Definition 2.1) we have that

$$
\begin{aligned}
&\langle r, \mathcal{B}(\vec{w}) \rangle \equiv \\
&\equiv \langle r, \mathcal{A}_2\left(\mathcal{A}_1(x_1, \ldots, x_\ell, \ldots, x_n), \vec{p}, \mathrm{Enc}(x_1, p_1, w_1), \ldots, \mathrm{Enc}(x_\ell, p_\ell, w_\ell), \ldots, \mathrm{Enc}(x_n, p_n, w_n)\right) \rangle \\
&\approx_{(\varepsilon, \delta)} \langle r, \mathcal{A}_2\left(\mathcal{A}_1(x_1, \ldots, x_0, \ldots, x_n), \vec{p}, \mathrm{Enc}(x_1, p_1, w_1), \ldots, \mathrm{Enc}(x_\ell, p_\ell, w_\ell), \ldots, \mathrm{Enc}(x_n, p_n, w_n)\right) \rangle \\
&\equiv_c \langle r, \mathcal{A}_2\left(\mathcal{A}_1(x_1, \ldots, x_0, \ldots, x_n), \vec{p}, \mathrm{Enc}(x_1, p_1, w_1), \ldots, \mathrm{Enc}(x_\ell, p_\ell, w'_\ell), \ldots, \mathrm{Enc}(x_n, p_n, w_n)\right) \rangle \\
&\approx_{(\varepsilon, \delta)} \langle r, \mathcal{A}_2\left(\mathcal{A}_1(x_1, \ldots, x_\ell, \ldots, x_n), \vec{p}, \mathrm{Enc}(x_1, p_1, w_1), \ldots, \mathrm{Enc}(x_\ell, p_\ell, w'_\ell), \ldots, \mathrm{Enc}(x_n, p_n, w_n)\right) \rangle \\
&\equiv \langle r, \mathcal{B}(\vec{w'}) \rangle.
\end{aligned}
$$

So algorithm $\mathcal{B}$ is $(2\varepsilon, (e^\varepsilon + 1)\delta)$-computationally differentially private. Now consider the following variant of algorithm $\mathcal{B}$, denoted as $\hat{\mathcal{B}}$. The modifications from $\mathcal{B}$ are marked in red.

1. The input is n codewords $w_1, \ldots, w_n \in \{0,1\}^d$.
2. Sample n keys $x_1, \ldots, x_n \sim \mathrm{Gen}(1^\lambda)$.
3. Let $z \leftarrow \mathcal{A}_1(x_1, \ldots, x_n)$.
4. Sample n public parameters $p_1, \ldots, p_n \sim \mathrm{Param}(1^\lambda)$.
5. Let $J \leftarrow J(\mathcal{A}_1, \vec{x}, z, \vec{p}) \subseteq [n]$ be the subset of coordinates guaranteed to exist by Definition 2.1, of size $|J| = n - \overline{\tau}$.
6. For $i \in J$ let $c_i \leftarrow \mathrm{Enc}(x_i, p_i, 0)$.
7. For $i \in [n] \setminus J$ let $c_i \leftarrow \mathrm{Enc}(x_i, p_i, w_i)$.
8. Let $\vec{a} \leftarrow \mathcal{A}_2(z, (p_1, c_1), \ldots, (p_n, c_n))$.
9. Output $\vec{a}$, after rounding its coordinates to $\{0,1\}$.

Remark 3.12. *Observe that algorithm $\hat{\mathcal{B}}$ is not necessarily computationally efficient, since computing $J(\mathcal{A}_1, \vec{x}, z, \vec{p})$ might not be efficient. Nevertheless, as we next show, this still suffices to obtain a contradiction and complete the proof of the lower bound. Specifically, we will show that $\hat{\mathcal{B}}$ is computationally differentially private (w.r.t. the codewords) and that it is a successful adversary to the FPC. This will lead to a contradiction, even if $\hat{\mathcal{B}}$ itself is a non-efficient mechanism.*

We now show that, by the multi-security of the MILR scheme (see Definition 2.1), the outcome distributions of $\mathcal{B}$ and $\hat{\mathcal{B}}$ are computationally indistinguishable. Specifically, we want to show that for every efficient adversary (Q, T), as in Definition 3.5, it holds that

$$| \Pr[T(r, \mathcal{B}(\vec{w})) = 1] - \Pr[T(r, \hat{\mathcal{B}}(\vec{w})) = 1]| \leq \mathrm{negl}(\Gamma(\lambda)).$$

Note that here both expressions are with the same dataset $\vec{w}$ (without the neighboring dataset $\vec{w}'$). To show this, consider the following algorithm, denoted as $\mathcal{W}$, which we view as an adversary to the MILR scheme. This algorithm has only oracle access to encryptions, via an oracle $\mathcal{E}$.

1. The input of $\mathcal{W}$ is n codewords $w_1, \ldots, w_n \in \{0, 1\}^d$, an element z (supposedly computed by $\mathcal{A}_1$), and a collection of n public parameters $p_1, \ldots, p_n$.
2. For $i \in [n]$ let $c_i \leftarrow \mathcal{E}(i, w_i)$.
3. Let $\vec{a} \leftarrow \mathcal{A}_2(z, (p_1, c_1), \ldots, (p_n, c_n))$.
4. Output $\vec{a}$, after rounding its coordinates to $\{0, 1\}$.

Now by the multi-security of the MILR scheme we have

$$\left| \Pr_{Q,T,\mathcal{B}}[T(r, \mathcal{B}(\vec{w})) = 1] - \Pr_{Q,T,\mathcal{B}}[T(r, \hat{\mathcal{B}}(\vec{w})) = 1] \right|$$

$$= \left| \Pr_{\substack{\vec{x},\vec{p},\mathcal{W},Q,T,\mathrm{Enc} \\ z \leftarrow \mathcal{A}_1(\vec{x}) \\ J \leftarrow J(\mathcal{A}_1,\vec{x},z,\vec{p})}}[Q(r, \mathcal{W}^{\mathcal{E}_1(\vec{x},\vec{p},J,\cdot,\cdot)}(\vec{w}, z, \vec{p})) = 1] \right.$$

$$\left. - \Pr_{\substack{\vec{x},\vec{p},\mathcal{W},Q,T,\mathrm{Enc} \\ z \leftarrow \mathcal{A}_1(\vec{x}) \\ J \leftarrow J(\mathcal{A}_1,\vec{x},z,\vec{p})}}[Q(r, \mathcal{W}^{\mathcal{E}_0(\vec{x},\vec{p},J,\cdot,\cdot)}(\vec{w}, z, \vec{p})) = 1] \right|$$

$$\leq \mathrm{negl}(\Gamma(\lambda)).$$

So we have that $\hat{\mathcal{B}} \equiv_c \mathcal{B}$ and we have that $\mathcal{B}$ is $(2\varepsilon, (e^\varepsilon + 1)\delta)$-computationally differentially private. Hence, algorithm $\hat{\mathcal{B}}$ is also $(2\varepsilon, (e^\varepsilon + 1)\delta)$-computationally differentially private (w.r.t. the input codewords). Observe that algorithm $\hat{\mathcal{B}}$ ignores all but $N - |J| = \overline{\tau}$ of the codewords, and furthermore, the choice of which codewords to ignore is independent of the codewords themselves. Now consider the following thought experiment.

1. Sample a codebook $w_0, w_1, \ldots, w_n$ for the fingerprinting code.
2. Run $\hat{\mathcal{B}}$ on $(w_1, \ldots, w_n)$.
3. Run Trace on the outcome of $\hat{\mathcal{B}}$ and return its output.

As $\hat{\mathcal{B}}$ ignores all but $\overline{\tau}$ codewords, by the properties of the FPC, with probability at least $1 - \frac{1}{n^2} \geq \frac{1}{2}$ the outcome of Trace is a coordinate of a codeword that $\hat{\mathcal{B}}$ did not ignore, and in particular, it is a coordinate between 1 and n. Therefore, there must exist a coordinate $i^* \neq 0$ that is output by this thought experiment with probability at least $\frac{1}{2n}$. Now consider the following modified thought experiment.

1. Sample a codebook $w_0, w_1, \ldots, w_n$ for the fingerprinting code.
2. Run $\hat{\mathcal{B}}$ on $(w_1, \ldots, w_{i^*-1}, w_0, w_{i^*+1}, \ldots, w_n)$.
3. Run Trace on the outcome of $\hat{\mathcal{B}}$ and return its output.

As $\hat{\mathcal{B}}$ is computationally differentially private and as Trace is an efficient algorithm, the probability of outputting i^* in this second thought experiment is roughly the same as in the previous thought experiment, specifically, at least

$$e^{-2\varepsilon} \left(\frac{1}{2n} - (e^\varepsilon + 1)\delta - \mathrm{negl}(\Gamma(\lambda)) \right) \geq e^{-2\varepsilon} \left(\frac{1}{4n} - \mathrm{negl}(\Gamma(\lambda)) \right) = \Omega\left(\frac{1}{n}\right).$$

However, by the guarantees of the FPC (small probability of false accusation), in the second experiment the probability of outputting i^* should be at most $\frac{1}{n^2}$. This is a contradiction to the existence of algorithm $\mathcal{A}$.

The following corollary follows by instantiating Theorem 3.10 with our MILR scheme, as specified in Theorem 2.3.

Corollary 3.13. *Let $\Omega(\lambda) \leq \Gamma(\lambda) \leq 2^{o(\lambda)}$, and let $d \leq \mathrm{poly}(\Gamma(\lambda))$. If there exists a $\Gamma(\lambda)$-secure encryption scheme against non-uniform adversaries then there exists an MILR scheme such that the corresponding (λ, d)-DA problem requires large space to be solved privately. Specifically, let $n \leq \mathrm{poly}(\Gamma(\lambda))$, let ε be a constant, and let $\delta \leq \frac{1}{4n(e^\varepsilon+1)} = \Theta(\frac{1}{n})$. Every $\mathrm{poly}(\Gamma(\lambda))$-time (ε, δ)-CDP algorithm for the (λ, d)-DA problem with sample complexity n must have space complexity $s = \Omega\left(\lambda \cdot \sqrt{\frac{d}{\log n}}\right)$.*

4   Space Hardness for Adaptive Data Analysis (ADA)

Consider a mechanism that first gets as input a sample containing t i.i.d. samples from some underlying (unknown) distribution $\mathcal{D}$, and then answers k *adaptively chosen* statistical queries w.r.t. $\mathcal{D}$. Importantly, the answers must be accurate

---

Algorithm 1. AdaptiveGameSpace($\mathcal{A} = (\mathcal{A}_1, \mathcal{A}_2), \mathcal{B}, s, k$)

---

1. The adversary $\mathcal{B}$ chooses a distribution $\mathcal{D}$ over a domain $\mathcal{X}$.
2. The mechanism $\mathcal{A}_1$ gets $\mathcal{D}$ and summarizes it into s bits, denoted as z.
3. The mechanism $\mathcal{A}_2$ is instantiated with z.
4. For round $i = 1, 2, \ldots, k$:
    (a) The adversary $\mathcal{B}$ specifies a query $q_i : \mathcal{X} \to \{-1, 0, 1\}$
    (b) The mechanism $\mathcal{A}_2$ obtains q_i and responds with an answer $a_i \in [-1, 1]$
    (c) a_i is given to $\mathcal{A}$
5. The outcome of the game is one if $\exists i$ s.t. $|a_i - \mathbb{E}_{y \sim \mathcal{D}}[q_i(y)]| > 1/10$, and zero otherwise.

---

w.r.t. the underlying distribution and not just w.r.t. the empirical sample. The challenge here is that as the queries are being chosen adaptively, the interaction might quickly lead to *overfitting*, i.e., result in answers that are only accurate w.r.t. the empirical sample and not w.r.t. the underlying distribution. This fundamental problem, which we refer to as the ADA problem, was introduced by Dwork et al. [15] who connected it to differential privacy and showed that differential privacy can be used as a countermeasure against overfitting. Intuitively, overfitting happens when answers reveal properties that are specific to the input sample, rather than to the general population, and this is exactly what differential privacy aims to protect against.

Hardt, Steinke, and Ullman [24,34] showed negative results for the ADA problem. Specifically, they showed that given t samples, it is computationally hard to answer more than $k = O(t^2)$ adaptive queries. We show that the hardness of the ADA problem is actually more fundamental; it is, in fact, a result of a space bottleneck rather than a sampling bottleneck. Informally, we show that the same hardness result continues to hold even if in the preprocessing stage the mechanism is given the full description of the underlying distribution $\mathcal{D}$, and is then required to store only a limited amount of information about it (an amount that equals the representation length of t samples from $\mathcal{D}$). So it is not that the mechanism did not get enough information about $\mathcal{D}$; it is just that it cannot shrink this information in a way that supports t^2 adaptive queries. This generalizes the negative results of [24,34], as sampling t points from $\mathcal{D}$ is just one particular way of trying to store information about $\mathcal{D}$.

Consider AdaptiveGameSpace, where the mechanism initially gets the full description of the underlying distribution, but it must shrink it into an s-bit summary z. To emphasize that the mechanism does not have additional access to the underlying distribution, we think about it as two mechanisms $\mathcal{A} = (\mathcal{A}_1, \mathcal{A}_2)$ where $\mathcal{A}_1$ computes the summary z and where $\mathcal{A}_2$ answers queries given z. We consider $s = |z|$ as the space complexity of such a mechanism $\mathcal{A}$.

Our main theorem in the context of the ADA problem is the following.

Theorem 4.1. *Let $\Omega(\lambda) \leq \Gamma(\lambda) \leq 2^{o(\lambda)}$, and let $k \leq \mathrm{poly}(\Gamma(\lambda))$. If there exists a $\Gamma(\lambda)$-secure encryption scheme against non-uniform adversaries then there exists a $\mathrm{poly}(\Gamma(\lambda))$-time adversary $\mathcal{B}$ such that the following holds. Let $\mathcal{A}=(\mathcal{A}_1, \mathcal{A}_2)$ be a $\mathrm{poly}(\Gamma(\lambda))$-time mechanism with space complexity $s \leq O\left(\lambda \cdot \sqrt{k}\right)$ (small enough). Then, $\Pr[\texttt{AdaptiveGameSpace}(\mathcal{A}, \mathcal{B}, s, k) = 1] > \frac{2}{3}$.*

Furthermore, the underlying distribution defined by the adversary $\mathcal{B}$ can be fully described using $O(\sqrt{k} \cdot \lambda)$ bits, it is sampleable in $\mathrm{poly}(\Gamma(\lambda))$-time, and elements sampled from this distribution can be represented using $O(\lambda + \log(k))$ bits.

In a sense, the "furtheremore" part of the theorem shows that the distribution chosen by our adversary is not too complex. Specifically, our negative result continues to hold even if the space of the mechanism is *linear* in the full description length of the underlying distribution (in a way that allows for efficiently sampling it). If the space of the mechanism was just a constant times bigger, it could store the full description of the underlying distribution and answer an unbounded number of adaptive queries. The formal proof of Theorem 4.1 is deferred to the full version of this work. Here we only provide an informal (and overly simplified) proof sketch.

4.1 Informal Proof Sketch

Let k denote the number of queries that the adversary makes. Our task is to show that there is an adversary that fails every efficient mechanism $\mathcal{A}_{\mathrm{space}}$ that plays in `AdaptiveGameSpace`, provided that it uses space $s \ll \sqrt{k}$. What we know from [24,34] is that there is an adversary $\mathcal{B}_{\mathrm{sample}}$ that fails every efficient mechanism that plays in the standard ADA game (the game specified in Fig. 1), provided that its sample complexity is $t \ll \sqrt{k}$. We design an adversary $\mathcal{B}_{\mathrm{space}}$ that plays in `AdaptiveGameSpace` in a way that emulates $\mathcal{B}_{\mathrm{sample}}$. We now elaborate on the key points in the construction of $\mathcal{B}_{\mathrm{space}}$, and their connection to $\mathcal{B}_{\mathrm{sample}}$.

Recall that both games begin with the adversary specifying the underlying distribution. A useful fact about the adversary $\mathcal{B}_{\mathrm{sample}}$ (from [24,34]) is that the distribution it specifies is uniform on a small set of points of size $n = \Theta(t)$ (these n points are unknown to the mechanism that $\mathcal{B}_{\mathrm{sample}}$ plays against). Our adversary, $\mathcal{B}_{\mathrm{space}}$, first samples n independent keys $(x_1, \ldots, x_n)$ from our MILR scheme, and then defines the target distribution $\mathcal{D}_{\mathrm{space}}$ to be uniform over the set $\{(j, x_j)\}_{j \in [n]}$. Recall that in `AdaptiveGameSpace` this target distribution is given to the mechanism $\mathcal{A}_{\mathrm{space}}$, who must shrink it into a summary z containing s bits. After this stage, by the security of our MILR scheme, there should exist a large set $J \subseteq [n]$ of size $|J| = n - \overline{\tau}$ corresponding to keys uncompromised by $\mathcal{A}_{\mathrm{space}}$. Denote $I = [n] \setminus J$.

Our adversary $\mathcal{B}_{\mathrm{space}}$ now emulates $\mathcal{B}_{\mathrm{sample}}$ as follows. First, let $\mathcal{D}_{\mathrm{sample}}$ denote the target distribution chosen by $\mathcal{B}_{\mathrm{sample}}$, and let $m_1, \ldots, m_n$ denote its support. Our adversary then samples n public parameters $p_1, \ldots, p_n$, and encrypts every point in the support m_j using its corresponding key and public parameter. Specifically, $c_j \leftarrow \text{Enc}(x_j, p_j, m_j)$. % This is an over-simplification. For technical reasons, the actual construction is somewhat different.

Now, for every query q specified by $\mathcal{B}_{\text{sample}}$, our adversary outputs the query f_q defined by $f_q(j, x) = q(\text{Dec}(x, p_j, c_j))$. Our adversary then obtains an answer a from the mechanism $\mathcal{A}_{\text{space}}$, and feeds a to $\mathcal{B}_{\text{sample}}$. Observe that the "true" value of f_q w.r.t. $\mathcal{D}_{\text{space}}$ is the same as the "true" value of q w.r.t. $\mathcal{D}_{\text{sample}}$. Therefore, if $\mathcal{A}_{\text{space}}$ maintains accuracy in this game against our adversary $\mathcal{B}_{\text{space}}$, then in the emulation that $\mathcal{B}_{\text{space}}$ runs internally we have that $\mathcal{B}_{\text{space}}$ maintains utility against $\mathcal{B}_{\text{sample}}$. Intuitively, we would like to say that this leads to a contradiction, since $\mathcal{B}_{\text{sample}}$ fails every efficient mechanism it plays against. But this is not accurate, because $\mathcal{B}_{\text{space}}$ saw the full description of the target distribution $\mathcal{D}_{\text{sample}}$, and $\mathcal{B}_{\text{sample}}$ only fools mechanisms that get to see at most t *samples* from this target distribution.

To overcome this, we consider the following modified variant of our adversary, called $\widehat{\mathcal{B}}_{\text{space}}$. The modification is that $\widehat{\mathcal{B}}_{\text{space}}$ does not get to see the full description of $\mathcal{D}_{\text{sample}}$. Instead it only gets to see points from the support of $\mathcal{D}_{\text{sample}}$ that correspond to indices in the set $I = [n] \setminus J$. Then, when generating the ciphertexts c_j, the modified adversary $\widehat{\mathcal{B}}_{\text{space}}$ encrypts zeroes instead of points m_j which it is missing. By the security of our MILR scheme, the mechanism $\mathcal{A}_{\text{space}}$ cannot notice this modification, and hence, assuming that it maintains accuracy against our original adversary $\mathcal{B}_{\text{space}}$ then it also maintains accuracy against our modified adversary $\widehat{\mathcal{B}}_{\text{space}}$. As before, this means that $\widehat{\mathcal{B}}_{\text{space}}$ maintains accuracy against the emulated $\mathcal{B}_{\text{sample}}$. Intuitively, this leads to a contradiction, as $\widehat{\mathcal{B}}_{\text{space}}$ is using only $\overline{\tau} \leq t$ points from the target distribution $\mathcal{D}_{\text{sample}}$.

We stress that this proof sketch is over-simplified and inaccurate. In particular, the following two technical issues need to be addressed: (1) It is true that $\widehat{\mathcal{B}}_{\text{space}}$ uses only $\overline{\tau}$ points from the support of the target distribution $\mathcal{D}_{\text{sample}}$, but these points are not necessarily *sampled* from $\mathcal{D}_{\text{sample}}$; and (2) The modified adversary $\widehat{\mathcal{B}}_{\text{space}}$ is not computationally efficient because computing the set J is not efficient. We address these issues, and other informalities made herein, in the full version of this work.

5   Construction of an MILR Scheme from a Semantically Secure Encryption Scheme

Construction. Let $\lambda' \leq \lambda$ be such that $\lambda = \text{poly}(\lambda')$. Given an encryption scheme $\Pi' = (\text{Gen}', \text{Enc}', \text{Dec}')$ such that $\text{Gen}'(1^{\lambda'})$ outputs a key uniformly distributed on $\{0, 1\}^{\lambda'}$ (i.e., $x' \leftarrow_R \{0, 1\}^{\lambda'}$), we construct an MILR scheme $\Pi = (\text{Gen}, \text{Param}, \text{Enc}, \text{Dec})$ as follows:

- Gen: On input 1^λ, return $x \leftarrow_R \{0,1\}^\lambda$.
- Param: On input 1^λ, let $\mathcal{G}$ be a family of universal hash functions with domain $\{0,1\}^\lambda$ and range $\{0,1\}^{\lambda'}$. Return (a description of) $g \leftarrow_R \mathcal{G}$.
- Enc: On input (x,p,m), parse $g := p$ (as a description of a hash function), let $x' = g(x)$ and return $\mathrm{Enc}'(x',m)$.
- Dec: On input (x,p,c), parse $g := p$, let $x' = g(x)$ and return $\mathrm{Dec}'(x',c)$.

Using a standard construction of a universal hash function family, all the algorithms run in time polynomial in λ. Moreover, if $c \leftarrow \mathrm{Enc}(x,p,m)$, then $\mathrm{Dec}(x,p,c) = m$ with probability 1 (as this holds for Enc' and Dec').

The following two theorems (corresponding to the two security properties in Definition 2.1) establish the security of Π and prove Theorem 2.3.

Theorem 5.1 (Multi semantic security). *Let $\Omega(\lambda) \leq \Gamma(\lambda) \leq 2^{o(\lambda)}$ and $\lambda' = 0.1\lambda$. If Π' is $\Gamma(\lambda')$-secure against uniform (resp. non-uniform) adversaries, then Π is $\Gamma(\lambda)$-secure against uniform (resp. non-uniform) adversaries.*

Theorem 5.2 (Multi-security against bounded preprocessing adversaries). *Let $\Omega(\lambda) \leq \Gamma(\lambda) \leq 2^{o(\lambda)}$, $\lambda' = 0.1\lambda$ (as in Theorem 5.1). If Π' is $\Gamma(\lambda')$-secure against non-uniform adversaries then Π is $(\Gamma(\lambda), \overline{\tau})$-secure against space bounded non-uniform preprocessing adversaries, where $\overline{\tau}(\lambda, s) = \frac{2s}{\lambda} + 4$.*

Remark 5.3. *Since $\Gamma(\lambda) \leq 2^{o(\lambda)}$ and $\lambda' = 0.1\lambda$, then $\mathrm{poly}(\Gamma(\lambda')) = \mathrm{poly}(\Gamma(\lambda))$. Therefore, for the sake of simplicity, we analyze the runtime and advantage of all adversaries (including those that run against Π') as functions of λ.*

The proof of Theorem 5.1 is given in the full version of this work. We prove Theorem 5.2 in Sect. 6.

6 Multi-security Against a Bounded Preprocessing Adversary

In this section we prove Theorem 5.2. The proof requires specific definitions and notation, defined below.

6.1 Preliminaries

Notation. Given a sequence of elements $X = (X_1, \ldots, X_n)$ and a subset $I \subseteq [n]$, we denote by X_I the sequence composed of elements with coordinates in I.

For a random variable X, denote its min-entropy by $H_\infty(X)$. For random variables X, Y with the same range, denote by $\Delta(X, Y)$ the statistical distance of their distributions. We say that X and Y are γ-close if $\Delta(X, Y) \leq \gamma$. We use the notation $X \leftarrow_R \mathcal{X}$ to indicate that the random variable X is chosen uniformly at random from the set $\mathcal{X}$.

Dense and Bit-Fixing Sources. We will use the following definition (see [12, Definition 1]).

Definition 6.1. *An $(n, 2^\lambda)$-source is a random variable X with range $(\{0, 1\}^\lambda)^n$. A source is called*

- *$(1 - \delta)$-dense if for every subset $I \subseteq [n]$, $H_\infty(X_I) \geq (1 - \delta) \cdot |I| \cdot \lambda$,*
- *$(k, 1 - \delta)$-dense if it is fixed on at most k coordinates and is $(1 - \delta)$-dense on the rest,*
- *k-bit-fixing if it is fixed on at most k coordinates and uniform on the rest.*

Namely, the min-entropy of every subset of entries of a $(1 - \delta)$-dense source is at most a fraction of δ less than what it would be for a uniformly random one.

6.2 Key Leakage Lemma

Let $X = (X_1, \dots, X_n) \in (\{0, 1\}^\lambda)^n$ be a random variable for n keys of Π chosen independently and uniformly at random. Let $Z := F(X)$ be a random variable for the leakage of the adversary. For $z \in \{0, 1\}^s$, let X_z be the random variable chosen from the distribution of X conditioned on $F(X) = z$.

We denote $G := (G_1, \dots, G_n)$ and $G(X) := (G_1(X_1), \dots, G_n(X_n))$ the random variable for the hash functions (public parameters) of Π. We will use similar notation for sequences of different lengths (which will be clear from the context).

The proof of Theorem 5.2 is based on the lemma below (proved in Sect. 6.4), which analyzes the joint distribution $(G, Z, G(X))$.

Lemma 6.2. *Let $F : (\{0, 1\}^\lambda)^n \to \{0, 1\}^s$ be an arbitrary function, $X = (X_1, \dots, X_n) \leftarrow_R (\{0, 1\}^\lambda)^n$ and denote $Z := F(X)$. Let $\mathcal{G}$ be a family of universal hash functions with domain $\{0, 1\}^\lambda$ and range $\{0, 1\}^{\lambda'}$ and let $G \leftarrow_R (\mathcal{G})^n$. Let $\delta > 0, \gamma > 0, s' > s$ be parameters such that $(1 - \delta)\lambda > \lambda' + \log n + 1$.*

Then, there exists a family $V_{G,Z} = \{V_{\vec{g},z}\}_{\vec{g} \in (\mathcal{G})^n, z \in \{0,1\}^s}$ of convex combinations $V_{\vec{g},z}$ of k-bit-fixing $(n, 2^{\lambda'})$-sources for $k = \frac{s' + \log 1/\gamma}{\delta \cdot \lambda}$ such that

$$\Delta[(G, Z, G(X)), (G, Z, V_{G,Z})] \leq \sqrt{2^{-(1-\delta)\lambda + \lambda' + \log n}} + \gamma + 2^{s-s'}.$$

We obtain the following corollary (which implies the parameters of Theorem 5.2).

Corollary 6.3. *In the setting of Lemma 6.2, assuming $n < 2^{0.15\lambda}$ and sufficiently large λ, the parameters $s' = s + \lambda, \lambda' = 0.1\lambda, \delta = 0.5, \gamma = 2^{-\lambda}$ give*

$$\Delta[(G, Z, G(X)), (G, Z, V_{G,Z})] \leq 2^{-0.1\lambda}, \quad \text{and} \quad k = \frac{2s}{\lambda} + 4.$$

Proof. Set $s' = s + \lambda$, $\lambda' = 0.1\lambda$, $\delta = 0.5, \gamma = 2^{-\lambda}$. Then, for sufficiently large λ, $(1 - \delta)\lambda = 0.5\lambda > 0.1\lambda + 0.15\lambda + 1 > \lambda' + \log n + 1$ (and the condition of Lemma 6.2 holds). We therefore have (for sufficiently large λ):
$\Delta[(G, Z, G(X)), (G, Z, V_{G,z})] \leq \sqrt{2^{-(1-\delta)\lambda+\lambda'+\log n}} + \gamma + 2^{s-s'} = \sqrt{2^{-0.4\lambda+\log n}} + 2^{-\lambda} + 2^{-\lambda} \leq 2^{-0.1\lambda}$, and $k = \frac{s'+\log 1/\gamma}{\delta\cdot\lambda} = \frac{s+\lambda+\lambda}{0.5\cdot\lambda} = \frac{2s}{\lambda} + 4$.

6.3   The Proof of Theorem 5.2

Using Lemma 6.2 to Prove Theorem 5.2. Before proving Theorem 5.2, we explain why Lemma 6.2 is needed and how it used in the proof.

It is easy to prove some weaker statements than Lemma 6.2, but these do not seem to be sufficient for building the MILR scheme (i.e., proving Theorem 5.2). For example, one can easily prove that with high probability, given the leakage z and hash functions $\vec{g}$, there is a large subset of (hashed) keys such that each one of them is almost uniformly distributed. However, the adversary could have knowledge of various relations between the keys of this subset and it is not clear how to prove security without making assumptions about the resistance of the encryption scheme against related-key attacks.

Moreover, consider a stronger statement, which asserts that with high probability, given the leakage z and hash functions $\vec{g}$, there is a large subset of (hashed) keys that are jointly uniformly distributed. We claim that even this stronger statement may not be sufficient to prove security, since it does not consider the remaining keys outside of the subset. In particular, consider a scenario in which the adversary is able to recover some weak keys outside of the subset. Given this extra knowledge and the leakage z, the original subset of keys may no longer be distributed uniformly (and may suffer from a significant entropy loss).

Lemma 6.2 essentially asserts that there is a subset of keys that is almost jointly uniformly distributed even if we give the adversary $z, \vec{g}$ and all the remaining keys. More specifically, given the hash functions $\vec{g}$ and the leakage z, according to the lemma, the distribution of the hashed keys $\vec{g}(X)$ is (close to) a convex combinations $V_{\vec{g},z}$ of k-bit-fixing sources. In the proof of Theorem 5.2 we will fix such a k-bit-fixing source by giving the adversary k hashed keys (we will do this carefully, making sure that the adversary's advantage does not change significantly). Since the remaining hashed keys are uniformly distributed from the adversary's view, security with respect to these keys follows from the semantic security of the underlying encryption scheme.

Proof (Proof of Theorem 5.2). Fix a preprecessing procedure F and let λ be sufficiently large, $n < 2^{0.15\lambda}$. By Lemma 6.2 (with parameters set in Corollary 6.3), there exists a family $V_{G,Z}$ of convex combinations $V_{\vec{g},z}$ of k-bit-fixing $(n, 2^{\lambda'})$-sources for $k = \frac{2s}{\lambda} + 4$ such that $\Delta[(G, Z, G(X)), (G, Z, V_{G,z})] \leq 2^{-0.1\lambda}$.

Sampling the Index Set J and Simplifying the Distribution. We first define how the oracles $\mathcal{E}_0$ and $\mathcal{E}_1$ in Definition 2.1 sample J. The random variable J is naturally defined when sampling the random variables $(G, Z, V_{G,Z})$: given $\vec{g} \in (\mathcal{G})^n, z \in \{0,1\}^s$, sample a k-bit-fixing source in the convex combination $V_{\vec{g},z}$

(according to its weight) and let J be the set of (at least) $n-k$ indices that are not fixed. This defines a joint distribution on the random variables $(G, Z, V_{G,Z}, J)$. Another way to sample from this distribution is to first sample the variables $(G, Z, V_{G,Z})$ and then sample J according to its marginal distribution. This defines a randomized procedure for sampling J. Although the oracles do not sample $(G, Z, V_{G,Z})$, we reuse the same sampling procedure for sampling J given the sample $(\vec{g}, z, \vec{g}(\vec{x}))$ (if the sample $(\vec{g}, z, \vec{g}(\vec{x}))$ is not in the support of the distribution of $(G, Z, V_{G,Z})$, define $J = [n]$).

Consider a poly$(\Gamma(\lambda))$-time algorithm $\mathcal{B}$. As encryption queries of $\mathcal{B}$ to $\mathcal{E}_0$ and $\mathcal{E}_1$ are answered with the hash keys $\vec{g}(\vec{x})$, then given $\vec{g}(\vec{x})$, the interaction of $\mathcal{B}$ with $\mathcal{E}_0$ and $\mathcal{E}_1$ no longer depends on $\vec{x}$. Therefore, for $t = 0, 1$ we define $\mathcal{E}_t^{(1)}(\vec{g}(\vec{x}), \vec{g}, J, \cdot, \cdot)$ that simulates the interaction of $\mathcal{E}_t(\vec{x}, \vec{g}, J, \cdot, \cdot)$ with $\mathcal{B}$. Instead of sampling $\vec{x}$, the oracles directly sample $(\vec{g}, z, \vec{g}(\vec{x}), J)$ according to their joint distribution before the interaction with $\mathcal{B}$. To simplify notation, we denote this joint distribution by $\mathcal{D}_1$. Denote

$$\text{Adv}_{\mathcal{B}}(\lambda) =$$

$$\left| \Pr_{\substack{\mathcal{B}, \text{Enc} \\ (\vec{g}, z, \vec{g}(\vec{x}), J) \leftarrow \mathcal{D}_1}} \left[\mathcal{B}^{\mathcal{E}_0^{(1)}(\vec{g}(\vec{x}), \vec{g}, J, \cdot, \cdot)}(z, \vec{g}) = 1 \right] - \Pr_{\substack{\mathcal{B}, \text{Enc} \\ (\vec{g}, z, \vec{g}(\vec{x}), J) \leftarrow \mathcal{D}_1}} \left[\mathcal{B}^{\mathcal{E}_1^{(1)}(\vec{g}(\vec{x}), \vec{g}, J, \cdot, \cdot)}(z, \vec{g}) = 1 \right] \right|.$$

It remains to prove that $\text{Adv}_{\mathcal{B}}(\lambda) \leq \text{negl}(\Gamma(\lambda))$.

Using Lemma 6.2 to switch to a family of convex combinations of bit-fixing sources. We have

$$\Delta[(G, Z, G(X)), J), (G, Z, V_{G,Z}, J)] \leq \Delta[(G, Z, G(X)), (G, Z, V_{G,Z})] \leq 2^{-0.1\lambda},$$

where the first inequality follows by the data processing inequality, since J is computed by applying the same function to the three variables of both distributions, and the second inequality is by Corollary 6.3. Hence, for $t = 0, 1$ we replace $\mathcal{E}_t^{(1)}$ that samples from $\mathcal{D}_1$ with $\mathcal{E}_t^{(2)}$ that samples from the joint distribution of $(G, Z, V_{G,Z}, J)$, which we denote by $\mathcal{D}_2$. Since $\mathcal{B}$ and Enc use independent randomness, by the triangle inequality, the total penalty is at most $2 \cdot 2^{-0.1\lambda}$, namely

$$\left| \Pr_{\substack{\mathcal{B}, \text{Enc} \\ (\vec{g}, z, \vec{y}, J) \leftarrow \mathcal{D}_2}} \left[\mathcal{B}^{\mathcal{E}_0^{(2)}(\vec{y}, \vec{g}, J, \cdot, \cdot)}(z, \vec{g}) = 1 \right] - \Pr_{\substack{\mathcal{B}, \text{Enc} \\ (\vec{g}, z, \vec{y}, J) \leftarrow \mathcal{D}_2}} \left[\mathcal{B}^{\mathcal{E}_1^{(2)}(\vec{y}, \vec{g}, J, \cdot, \cdot)}(z, \vec{g}) = 1 \right] \right| \geq$$
$$\text{Adv}_{\mathcal{B}}(\lambda) - 2^{-0.1\lambda + 1},$$

where we denote a sample from $\mathcal{D}_2$ by $(\vec{g}, z, \vec{y}, J)$.

Giving the Adversary Additional Input. Consider a (potentially) more powerful poly$(\Gamma(\lambda))$-time algorithm $\mathcal{B}_1$ against Π whose input consists of $(z, \vec{g}, J, \vec{y}_{\bar{J}})$, where $\bar{J} = [n] \setminus J$. Namely, in addition to $(z, \vec{g})$ the input also consists of J, as well as the hashed keys $\vec{y}_{\overline{J}} \in \left(\{0,1\}^{\lambda'} \right)^{n-|J|}$ (note that these parameters define a $|\overline{J}|$-bit-fixing source). We denote $in = (z, \vec{g}, J, \vec{y}_{\overline{J}})$, and

$$
\mathrm{Adv}_{\mathcal{B}_1}(\lambda) =
$$

$$
\left| \Pr_{\substack{\mathcal{B}_1,\mathrm{Enc} \\ (\vec{g},z,\vec{y},J)\leftarrow \mathcal{D}_2}} \left[\mathcal{B}_1^{\mathcal{E}_0^{(2)}(\vec{y},\vec{g},J,\cdot,\cdot)}(in) = 1 \right] - \Pr_{\substack{\mathcal{B}_1,\mathrm{Enc} \\ (\vec{g},z,\vec{y},J)\leftarrow \mathcal{D}_2}} \left[\mathcal{B}_1^{\mathcal{E}_1^{(2)}(\vec{y},\vec{g},J,\cdot,\cdot)}(in) = 1 \right] \right|.
$$

Next, we prove that for any such $\mathrm{poly}(\Gamma(\lambda))$-time algorithm $\mathcal{B}_1$, $\mathrm{Adv}_{\mathcal{B}_1}(\lambda) \leq \mathrm{negl}(\Gamma(\lambda))$. As any algorithm $\mathcal{B}$ with input $(z, \vec{g})$ can be simulated by an algorithm $\mathcal{B}_1$ with input in and similar runtime, this implies that $\mathrm{Adv}_{\mathcal{B}}(\lambda) - 2^{-0.1\lambda+1} \leq \mathrm{negl}(\Gamma(\lambda))$ and hence $\mathrm{Adv}_{\mathcal{B}}(\lambda) \leq \mathrm{negl}(\Gamma(\lambda))$, concluding the proof.

Fixing the Adversary's Input. Since both $\mathcal{E}_0^{(2)}$ and $\mathcal{E}_1^{(2)}$ sample the input of $\mathcal{B}_1$ from the same distribution, by an averaging argument, there exists an input $in^* = in_{\lambda}^* = (z^*, \vec{g}^*, J^*, \vec{y^*}_{\overline{J^*}})$ such that the advantage of $\mathcal{B}_1$ remains at least as large when fixing the input to in^* and sampling from $\mathcal{D}_2$ conditioned on in^*. Note that given in^* sampling from $\mathcal{D}_2$ reduces to sampling from the $|J^*|$-bit-fixing source defined by $(\overline{J^*}, \vec{y^*}_{\overline{J^*}})$, i.e., selecting $\vec{w} \leftarrow_R (\{0,1\}^{\lambda'})^{|J^*|}$. Therefore,

$$
\left| \Pr_{\substack{\mathcal{B}_1,\mathrm{Enc} \\ \vec{w}\leftarrow_R(\{0,1\}^{\lambda'})^{|J^*|}}} \left[\mathcal{B}_1^{\mathcal{E}_0^{(2)}(in^*,\vec{w},\cdot,\cdot)}(in^*) = 1 \right] - \Pr_{\substack{\mathcal{B}_1,\mathrm{Enc} \\ \vec{w}\leftarrow_R(\{0,1\}^{\lambda'})^{|J^*|}}} \left[\mathcal{B}_1^{\mathcal{E}_1^{(2)}(in^*,\vec{w},\cdot,\cdot)}(in^*) = 1 \right] \right| \geq
$$

$\mathrm{Adv}_{\mathcal{B}_1}(\lambda).$

Reducing the Security of Π with Preprocessing from the (Multi-instance) Security of Π'. We now use $\mathcal{B}_1$ to define a non-uniform $\mathrm{poly}(\Gamma(\lambda))$-time adversary $\mathcal{B}_2$ (with no preprocessing) that runs against $|J^*|$ instances of Π' and has advantage at least $\mathrm{Adv}_{\mathcal{B}_1}(\lambda)$. By the semantic security of Π' and a hybrid argument (similarly to the proof of Theorem 5.1), this implies that $\mathrm{Adv}_{\mathcal{B}_1}(\lambda) \leq \mathrm{negl}(\Gamma(\lambda))$, concluding the proof.

The adversary $\mathcal{B}_2$ is given in Algorithm 2. Note that $\mathcal{B}_2$ perfectly simulates the oracles of $\mathcal{B}_1$ given the input in^*, and hence its advantage is at least $\mathrm{Adv}_{\mathcal{B}_1}(\lambda)$ as claimed. Finally, it runs in time $\mathrm{poly}(\Gamma(\lambda))$.

6.4   Proof of Lemma 6.2

Proof Overview. We first prove in Lemma 6.4 that $G = (G_1, \ldots, G_t)$ (for some $t \in [n]$) is a good extractor, assuming its input $Y = (Y_1, \ldots, Y_t)$ is $(1 - \delta)$-dense, namely, it has sufficient min-entropy for each subset of coordinates (see Lemma 6.4 for the exact statement). Specifically, we prove that $(G, G(Y))$ is statistically close to (G, U), where U is uniformly distributed over $(\{0,1\}^{\lambda'})^t$. The proof is by a variant of the leftover hash lemma [25] where a sequence of hash functions $(G_1, \ldots, G_t)$ are applied locally to each block of the input (instead of

Algorithm 2. $\mathcal{B}_2^{\mathcal{E}_{(\cdot)}^{(3)}(\vec{x}',[|J^*|],\cdot,\cdot)}()$

Setting: $\mathcal{B}_2$ is a non-uniform adversary that runs against $|J^*|$ instances of Π' (defined by $\mathcal{E}_{(\cdot)}^{(3)}$). It gets $in^* = in_\lambda^* = (z^*, \vec{g}^*, J^*, \vec{y^*}_{\overline{J^*}})$ as advice. $\mathcal{B}_2$ has access to $\mathcal{B}_1^{\mathcal{E}_{(\cdot)}^{(2)}(in^*,\vec{w},\cdot,\cdot)}(in^*)$, which runs against Π.

1. $\mathcal{B}_2$ gives in^* to $\mathcal{B}_1$ as input.
2. $\mathcal{B}_2$ answers each query (j,m) of $\mathcal{B}_1$ as follows:
   - If $j \in \overline{J^*}$, $\mathcal{B}_2$ uses the advice string in^* (which contains $\vec{y^*}_j$) to compute the answer $\text{Enc}'(\vec{y^*}_j, m)$ and gives it to $\mathcal{B}_1$.
   - If $j \in J^*$, $\mathcal{B}_2$ translates the query (j,m) to (j',m), where $j' \in [|J^*|]$ is obtained by mapping j to J^* (ignoring indices in $\overline{J^*}$). $\mathcal{B}_2$ then queries its oracle with (j',m) and forwards the answer to $\mathcal{B}_1$.
3. $\mathcal{B}_2$ outputs the same output as $\mathcal{B}_1$.

---

applying a single hash function to the entire input). We note that a related lemma was proved in [22, Lem. 13] in a different setting of communication complexity. Our variant is applicable to a different (mostly wider) range of parameters (such as various values of δ and the number of bits extracted, $t \cdot \lambda'$) that is relevant in our setting. Additional (somewhat less related) results were presented in [13,14].

The remainder of the proof is deferred to the full version of this work, and is somewhat similar to [12, Lem. 1].

Block-Wise Extraction from Dense Sources.

Lemma 6.4 *Let* $Y = (Y_1, \dots, Y_t) \in (\{0,1\}^\lambda)^t$ *be a* $(t, 2^\lambda)$*-source that is* $(1-\delta)$*-dense for* $0 < \delta < 1$*. Let* $\mathcal{G}$ *be a family of universal hash functions with domain* $\{0,1\}^\lambda$ *and range* $\{0,1\}^{\lambda'}$*. Then, for* $G \leftarrow_R (\mathcal{G})^t$ *and* $U \leftarrow_R (\{0,1\}^{\lambda'})^t$*,*

$$\Delta[(G, G(Y)), (G, U)] \leq \sqrt{2^{-(1-\delta)\lambda + \lambda' + \log t}},$$

assuming that $(1-\delta)\lambda > \lambda' + \log t + 1$*.*

Proof. Let $d := \log |\mathcal{G}|$. For a random variable Q, and Q' an independent copy of Q, we denote by $Col[Q] = \Pr[Q = Q']$ the collision probability of Q. We have

$$Col[(G, G(Y))] = \Pr_{G,Y,G',Y'}[(G, G(Y')) = (G', G'(Y'))]$$

$$= \Pr_{G,G'}[G = G'] \cdot \Pr_{G,Y,Y'}[G(Y) = G(Y')] = 2^{-t \cdot d} \cdot \Pr_{G,Y,Y'}[G(Y) = G(Y')]. \quad (1)$$

For sequences $Y_1, \dots, Y_t, Y_1', \dots, Y_t'$, define $C = |\{i \mid Y_i = Y_i'\}|$. We now upper bound the expression $\Pr[C = c]$.

Recall that Y is a $(1-\delta)$-dense source, i.e., for every subset $I \subseteq [t]$, $H_\infty(Y_I) \geq (1-\delta) \cdot |I| \cdot \lambda$. Fix a subset $I \subseteq [t]$ such that $|I| = c$. Then,

$$\Pr[Y_I = Y_I'] = \sum_{y_I \in (\{0,1\}^\lambda)^c} (\Pr[Y_I = y_I])^2$$

$$\leq \max_{y_I}\{\Pr[Y_I = y_I]\} \cdot \sum_{y_I \in (\{0,1\}^\lambda)^c} \Pr[Y_I = y_I] \leq 2^{-(1-\delta)\cdot c\cdot\lambda}.$$

Therefore,

$$\Pr[C = c] \leq \sum_{\{I \subseteq [t] | |I|=c\}} \Pr[Y_I = Y_I'] \leq \binom{t}{c} \cdot 2^{-(1-\delta)\cdot c\cdot\lambda} \tag{2}$$

$$\leq t^c \cdot 2^{-(1-\delta)\cdot c\cdot\lambda} = 2^{c\cdot(-(1-\delta)\lambda+\log t)}.$$

We have

$$\Pr_{G,Y,Y'}[G(Y) = G(Y')] = \sum_{c=0}^{t} \Pr_{Y,Y'}[C = c] \cdot \Pr_{G,Y,Y'}[G(Y) = G(Y') \mid C = c].$$

For each coordinate i such that $Y_i \neq Y_i'$, $\Pr_{G_i}(G_i(Y_i) = G_i(Y_i')) = 2^{-\lambda'}$ as G_i is selected uniformly from a family of universal hash functions. Since $G = (G_1, \ldots, G_t)$ contains t independent copies selected uniformly from $\mathcal{G}$,

$$\Pr_{G}[G(Y) = G(Y') \mid C = c] = 2^{-\lambda'\cdot(t-c)}.$$

Hence, using (2) we obtain

$$\Pr_{G,Y,Y'}[G(Y) = G(Y')] = \sum_{c=0}^{t} \Pr[C = c] \cdot 2^{-\lambda'\cdot(t-c)}$$

$$\leq \sum_{c=0}^{t} 2^{c\cdot(-(1-\delta)\lambda+\log t)} \cdot 2^{-\lambda'\cdot(t-c)} = 2^{-\lambda'\cdot t} \cdot \sum_{c=0}^{t} 2^{-c\cdot((1-\delta)\lambda-\lambda'-\log t)}$$

$$= 2^{-\lambda'\cdot t} \cdot \left(1 + \sum_{c=1}^{t} 2^{-c\cdot((1-\delta)\lambda-\lambda'-\log t)}\right) \leq 2^{-\lambda'\cdot t} \cdot (1 + 2^{-(1-\delta)\lambda+\lambda'+\log t+1}),$$

where the last inequality uses the assumption that $(1 - \delta)\lambda > \lambda' + \log t + 1$.

Treating distributions as vectors over $\{0,1\}^{t\cdot d+t\cdot\lambda'}$ (and abusing notation), we plug the above expression into (1) and deduce

$$\|(G, G(Y)) - (G, U)\|_2^2 = Col[(G, G(Y))] - 2^{-t\cdot d-t\cdot\lambda'} \leq$$

$$2^{-t\cdot d-t\cdot\lambda'} \cdot (1 + 2^{-(1-\delta)\lambda+\lambda'+\log t+1}) - 2^{-t\cdot d-t\cdot\lambda'} = 2^{-t\cdot d-t\cdot n'-(1-\delta)\lambda+\lambda'+\log t+1}.$$

Finally, using the Cauchy-Schwarz inequality, we conclude

$$\Delta[(G, G(Y)), (G, U)] \leq 1/2 \cdot \sqrt{2^{t \cdot d + t \cdot \lambda'}} \cdot \|(G, G(Y)) - (G, U)\|_2$$

$$\leq 1/2 \cdot \sqrt{2^{t \cdot d + t \cdot \lambda'}} \cdot \sqrt{2^{-t \cdot d - \lambda' \cdot t - (1-\delta)\lambda + \lambda' + \log t + 1}} < \sqrt{2^{-(1-\delta)\lambda + \lambda' + \log t}}.$$

Acknowledgements. Itai Dinur was partially supported by the Israel Science Foundation (grant 1903/20) and by the European Research Council under the ERC starting grant agreement no. 757731 (LightCrypt). Uri Stemmer was partially supported by the Israel Science Foundation (grant 1871/19) and by Len Blavatnik and the Blavatnik Family foundation. Work done in part while David P. Woodruff was visiting Google Research and Samson Zhou was at Carnegie Mellon University. They were also supported by a Simons Investigator Award and by the National Science Foundation under Grant No. CCF-1815840.

References

1. Alon, N., Livni, R., Malliaris, M., Moran, S.: Private PAC learning implies finite littlestone dimension. In: STOC, pp. 852–860. ACM (2019). https://doi.org/10.1145/3313276.3316312
2. Bassily, R., Nissim, K., Smith, A.D., Steinke, T., Stemmer, U., Ullman, J.R.: Algorithmic stability for adaptive data analysis. SIAM J. Comput. **50**(3) (2021). https://doi.org/10.1137/16M1103646
3. Beimel, A., Nissim, K., Omri, E.: Distributed private data analysis: simultaneously solving how and what. In: Wagner, D. (ed.) CRYPTO 2008. LNCS, vol. 5157, pp. 451–468. Springer, Heidelberg (2008). https://doi.org/10.1007/978-3-540-85174-5_25
4. Bellare, M., Rogaway, P.: Random oracles are practical: a paradigm for designing efficient protocols. In: Denning, D.E., Pyle, R., Ganesan, R., Sandhu, R.S., Ashby, V. (eds.) CCS 1993, pp. 62–73. ACM (1993). https://doi.org/10.1145/168588.168596
5. Blocki, J., Blum, A., Datta, A., Sheffet, O.: The Johnson-Lindenstrauss transform itself preserves differential privacy. In: FOCS, pp. 410–419. IEEE Computer Society (2012). https://doi.org/10.1109/FOCS.2012.67
6. Boneh, D., Shaw, J.: Collusion-secure fingerprinting for digital data. IEEE Trans. Inf. Theory **44**(5), 1897–1905 (1998). https://doi.org/10.1109/18.705568
7. Brown, G., Bun, M., Feldman, V., Smith, A., Talwar, K.: When is memorization of irrelevant training data necessary for high-accuracy learning? In: Proceedings of the 53rd Annual ACM SIGACT Symposium on Theory of Computing, pp. 123–132 (2021). https://doi.org/10.1145/3406325.3451131
8. Bun, M., Nissim, K., Stemmer, U., Vadhan, S.P.: Differentially private release and learning of threshold functions. In: FOCS, pp. 634–649. IEEE Computer Society (2015). https://doi.org/10.1109/FOCS.2015.45
9. Bun, M., Ullman, J.R., Vadhan, S.P.: Fingerprinting codes and the price of approximate differential privacy. In: STOC, pp. 1–10. ACM (2014). https://doi.org/10.1145/2591796.2591877
10. Canetti, R., Dodis, Y., Halevi, S., Kushilevitz, E., Sahai, A.: Exposure-resilient functions and all-or-nothing transforms. In: Preneel, B. (ed.) EUROCRYPT 2000. LNCS, vol. 1807, pp. 453–469. Springer, Heidelberg (2000). https://doi.org/10.1007/3-540-45539-6_33

11. Coretti, S., Dodis, Y., Guo, S.: Non-uniform bounds in the random-permutation, ideal-cipher, and generic-group models. In: Shacham, H., Boldyreva, A. (eds.) CRYPTO 2018. LNCS, vol. 10991, pp. 693–721. Springer, Cham (2018). https://doi.org/10.1007/978-3-319-96884-1_23

12. Coretti, S., Dodis, Y., Guo, S., Steinberger, J.: Random oracles and non-uniformity. In: Nielsen, J.B., Rijmen, V. (eds.) EUROCRYPT 2018. LNCS, vol. 10820, pp. 227–258. Springer, Cham (2018). https://doi.org/10.1007/978-3-319-78381-9_9

13. Dai, W., Tessaro, S., Zhang, X.: Super-linear time-memory trade-offs for symmetric encryption. In: Pass, R., Pietrzak, K. (eds.) TCC 2020. LNCS, vol. 12552, pp. 335–365. Springer, Cham (2020). https://doi.org/10.1007/978-3-030-64381-2_12

14. Dodis, Y., Farshim, P., Mazaheri, S., Tessaro, S.: Towards defeating backdoored random oracles: indifferentiability with bounded adaptivity. In: Pass, R., Pietrzak, K. (eds.) TCC 2020. LNCS, vol. 12552, pp. 241–273. Springer, Cham (2020). https://doi.org/10.1007/978-3-030-64381-2_9

15. Dwork, C., Feldman, V., Hardt, M., Pitassi, T., Reingold, O., Roth, A.L.: Preserving statistical validity in adaptive data analysis. In: Proceedings of the Forty-Seventh Annual ACM Symposium on Theory of Computing, pp. 117–126 (2015)

16. Dwork, C., McSherry, F., Nissim, K., Smith, A.: Calibrating noise to sensitivity in private data analysis. J. Priv. Confidentiality **7**(3), 17–51 (2016). https://doi.org/10.29012/jpc.v7i3.405

17. Dwork, C., Naor, M., Reingold, O., Rothblum, G.N., Vadhan, S.: On the complexity of differentially private data release: efficient algorithms and hardness results. In: Proceedings of the Forty-First Annual ACM Symposium on Theory of Computing, pp. 381–390 (2009). https://doi.org/10.1145/1536414.1536467

18. Dwork, C., Rothblum, G.N., Vadhan, S.P.: Boosting and differential privacy. In: FOCS, pp. 51–60. IEEE Computer Society (2010). https://doi.org/10.1109/FOCS.2010.12

19. Dziembowski, S.: Intrusion-resilience via the bounded-storage model. In: Halevi, S., Rabin, T. (eds.) TCC 2006. LNCS, vol. 3876, pp. 207–224. Springer, Heidelberg (2006). https://doi.org/10.1007/11681878_11

20. Dziembowski, S., Pietrzak, K.: Leakage-resilient cryptography. In: FOCS 2008, pp. 293–302. IEEE Computer Society (2008). https://doi.org/10.1109/FOCS.2008.56

21. Feldman, V.: Does learning require memorization? A short tale about a long tail. In: Proceedings of the 52nd Annual ACM SIGACT Symposium on Theory of Computing, pp. 954–959 (2020). https://doi.org/10.1145/3357713.3384290

22. Göös, M., Lovett, S., Meka, R., Watson, T., Zuckerman, D.: Rectangles are nonnegative juntas. In: Servedio, R.A., Rubinfeld, R. (eds.) STOC 2015, pp. 257–266. ACM (2015). https://doi.org/10.1145/2746539.2746596

23. Göös, M., Pitassi, T., Watson, T.: Deterministic communication vs. partition number. In: 2015 IEEE 56th Annual Symposium on Foundations of Computer Science, pp. 1077–1088. IEEE (2015). https://doi.org/10.1109/FOCS.2015.70

24. Hardt, M., Ullman, J.R.: Preventing false discovery in interactive data analysis is hard. In: FOCS, pp. 454–463. IEEE Computer Society (2014). https://doi.org/10.1109/FOCS.2014.55

25. Håstad, J., Impagliazzo, R., Levin, L.A., Luby, M.: A pseudorandom generator from any one-way function. SIAM J. Comput. **28**(4), 1364–1396 (1999). https://doi.org/10.1137/S0097539793244708

26. Hazay, C., López-Alt, A., Wee, H., Wichs, D.: Leakage-resilient cryptography from minimal assumptions. J. Cryptol. **29**(3), 514–551 (2015). https://doi.org/10.1007/s00145-015-9200-x

27. Kalai, Y.T., Reyzin, L.: A survey of leakage-resilient cryptography. In: Goldreich, O. (ed.) Providing Sound Foundations for Cryptography: On the Work of Shafi Goldwasser and Silvio Micali, pp. 727–794. ACM (2019). https://doi.org/10.1145/3335741.3335768

28. Kothari, P.K., Meka, R., Raghavendra, P.: Approximating rectangles by juntas and weakly-exponential lower bounds for LP relaxations of CSPs. In: Hatami, H., McKenzie, P., King, V. (eds.) STOC 2017, pp. 590–603. ACM (2017). https://doi.org/10.1145/3055399.3055438

29. Mironov, I., Pandey, O., Reingold, O., Vadhan, S.P.: Computational differential privacy. In: Halevi, S. (ed.) CRYPTO 2009. LNCS, vol. 5677, pp. 126–142. Springer, Heidelberg (2009). https://doi.org/10.1007/978-3-642-03356-8_8

30. Pietrzak, K.: A leakage-resilient mode of operation. In: Joux, A. (ed.) EUROCRYPT 2009. LNCS, vol. 5479, pp. 462–482. Springer, Heidelberg (2009). https://doi.org/10.1007/978-3-642-01001-9_27

31. Raz, R., McKenzie, P.: Separation of the monotone NC hierarchy. Comb. **19**(3), 403–435 (1999). https://doi.org/10.1007/s004930050062

32. Smith, A.D., Song, S., Thakurta, A.: The Flajolet-Martin sketch itself preserves differential privacy: private counting with minimal space. In: NeurIPS (2020). https://doi.org/10.5555/3495724.3497365

33. Standaert, F., Pereira, O., Yu, Y., Quisquater, J., Yung, M., Oswald, E.: Leakage resilient cryptography in practice. In: Sadeghi, A., Naccache, D. (eds.) Towards Hardware-Intrinsic Security - Foundations and Practice. Information Security and Cryptography, pp. 99–134. Springer, Heidelberg (2010). https://doi.org/10.1007/978-3-642-14452-3_5

34. Steinke, T., Ullman, J.R.: Interactive fingerprinting codes and the hardness of preventing false discovery. In: COLT. JMLR Workshop and Conference Proceedings, vol. 40, pp. 1588–1628. JMLR.org (2015)

35. Tardos, G.: Optimal probabilistic fingerprint codes. J. ACM (JACM) **55**(2), 1–24 (2008). https://doi.org/10.1145/1346330.1346335

36. Ullman, J.: Answering $n^{2+o(1)}$ counting queries with differential privacy is hard. In: Proceedings of the Forty-Fifth Annual ACM Symposium on Theory of Computing, pp. 361–370 (2013). https://doi.org/10.1145/2488608.2488653

37. Unruh, D.: Random oracles and auxiliary input. In: Menezes, A. (ed.) CRYPTO 2007. LNCS, vol. 4622, pp. 205–223. Springer, Heidelberg (2007). https://doi.org/10.1007/978-3-540-74143-5_12

38. Woodruff, D.P.: Optimal space lower bounds for all frequency moments. In: Munro, J.I. (ed.) Proceedings of the Fifteenth Annual ACM-SIAM Symposium on Discrete Algorithms, SODA 2004, New Orleans, Louisiana, USA, 11–14 January 2004, pp. 167–175. SIAM (2004). https://doi.org/10.5555/982792.982817

Compromise-Resilient Cryptographic Primitives

Deniable Authentication When Signing Keys Leak

Suvradip Chakraborty[1], Dennis Hofheinz[2], Ueli Maurer[2],
and Guilherme Rito[2]($\boxtimes$)

[1] Visa Research, Palo Alto, USA
suvradip1111@gmail.com
[2] Department of Computer Science, ETH Zurich, Zürich, Switzerland
{hofheinz,maurer,gteixeir}@inf.ethz.ch

Abstract. Deniable Authentication is a highly desirable property for secure messaging protocols: it allows a sender Alice to authentically transmit messages to a designated receiver Bob in such a way that only Bob gets convinced that Alice indeed sent these messages. In particular, it guarantees that even if Bob tries to convince a (non-designated) party Judy that Alice sent some message, and even if Bob gives Judy his own secret key, Judy will not be convinced: as far as Judy knows, *Bob could be making it all up!*

In this paper we study Deniable Authentication in the setting where Judy can additionally obtain Alice's secret key. Informally, we want that knowledge of Alice's secret key does not help Judy in learning whether Alice sent any messages, even if Bob does not have Alice's secret key and even if Bob cooperates with Judy by giving her his own secret key. This stronger flavor of Deniable Authentication was not considered before and is particularly relevant for Off-The-Record Group Messaging as it gives users stronger deniability guarantees.

Our main contribution is a scalable "MDRS-PKE" (Multi-Designated Receiver Signed Public Key Encryption) scheme—a technical formalization of Deniable Authentication that is particularly useful for secure messaging for its confidentiality guarantees—that provides this stronger deniability guarantee. At its core lie new MDVS (Multi-Designated Verifier Signature) and PKEBC (Public Key Encryption for Broadcast) scheme constructions: our MDVS is not only secure with respect to the new deniability notions, but it is also the first to be tightly secure under standard assumptions; our PKEBC—which is also of independent interest—is the first with ciphertext sizes and encryption and decryption times that grow only linearly in the number of receivers. This is a significant improvement upon the construction given by Maurer et al. (EUROCRYPT '22), where ciphertext sizes and encryption and decryption times are quadratic in the number of receivers.

All of the work was done while author was at ETH Zurich.

C. Hazay and M. Stam (Eds.): EUROCRYPT 2023, LNCS 14006, pp. 69–100, 2023.
https://doi.org/10.1007/978-3-031-30620-4_3

1   Introduction

Motivation. More than 3 billion people currently use messaging apps.[1] Naturally, there is a demand for *secure* messaging which guarantees, e.g., the secrecy of the transmitted contents, or the authenticity of senders. For point-to-point connections, combining standard cryptographic building blocks (like digital signature, public-key, and secret-key encryption schemes) may be sufficient. However, in particular for *group messaging* (in which groups of users communicate in a group chat), additional security properties are desirable. For instance, group members may want to be sure that all members receive the *same* messages (a property that, surprisingly, is not captured by traditional broadcast encryption definitions [7]).

Another security property that is generally desirable in messaging is *deniability*. Intuitively, it should be possible for a sender to deny having sent a message, or for a receiver to deny having received a particular message. Achieving deniability is even more challenging when considering that users may store copies of received (or even sent) messages on their communication device.

Here, we focus on a relatively mild (but still technically quite challenging) variant of deniability: "Off-The-Record" (OTR) messaging. Informally, with OTR security, received ciphertexts can be simulated, in the sense that it is easy to come up with ciphertexts for arbitrary messages that *look* as if they had been sent by a particular sender. In this sense, OTR security guarantees that third parties cannot be convinced of group-internal interactions. Of course, even OTR is relatively difficult to achieve, and becomes even harder so in the group messaging setting.

MDRS-PKE Schemes. When translating desirable properties of such group messaging protocols into suitable cryptographic primitives (with associated properties), we end up with "Multi-Designated Receiver Signed Public Key Encryption" (MDRS-PKE, [15]). Informally, these protocols function like signed versions of broadcast encryption schemes with additional integrity properties (that guarantee, e.g., that all receivers receive the same message). A little more formally, MDRS-PKE schemes work in a public-key infrastructure, and guarantee the following:

Syntax: A sender can prepare a single broadcast ciphertext c for a set $\mathcal{R}$ of intended receivers. Any intended receiver in $\mathcal{R}$ can decrypt c to retrieve the identity pk_S of the sender S, the encrypted message m, and the set $\mathcal{R}$.

Consistency: Not even a maliciously created c should decrypt to different sender identities, messages, or receiver sets for different intended receivers. Furthermore, if one receiver decrypts to $(\mathrm{pk}_S, m, \mathcal{R})$, then all receivers in $\mathcal{R}$ obtain the same $(\mathrm{pk}_S, m, \mathcal{R})$.

Unforgeability: Nobody except S can produce a ciphertext that decrypts to sender identity pk_S for any receiver.

Anonymity: c does not reveal the sender S or the set $\mathcal{R}$ of intended receivers (only its size $|\mathcal{R}|$).

---

[1] https://www.businessofapps.com/data/messaging-app-market/.

Confidentiality: c does not reveal the encrypted message (only its length $|m|$).

Off-The-Record: Plausible-looking ciphertexts c can be simulated by any (subset of) intended receivers of that ciphertext. Intuitively, this guarantees that receivers cannot convince a third party of a received encrypted message.

MDRS-PKE is a complex primitive, and appears to require specific, case-tailored primitives to realize it. For instance, the combination of a *group* of designated receivers and the simulation properties required by OTR prevent the use of ordinary designated-verifier signatures (or even MACs) [5].

Fortunately, [15] shows how to construct MDRS-PKE schemes from a combination of suitable variants of signature and broadcast encryption schemes. Specifically, they require the following:

- A type of signature scheme called "Multi-Designated Verifier Signature" (MDVS [4,5,11]) with suitable consistency, unforgeability, and OTR properties. (Here, "OTR" means that valid-looking signatures can be simulated by designated receivers.) State-of-the-art MDVS constructions [5] exist from algebraic assumptions (like the combination of Diffie-Hellman and Paillier-like assumptions), and also from generic primitives (like the combination of non-interactive key exchange (NIKE), non-interactive zero-knowledge (NIZK), and a few other standard primitives).
- A type of broadcast encryption scheme called "Public-Key Encryption for Broadcast" (PKEBC [15]) that essentially has all the properties of an MDRS-PKE scheme except for authenticity. PKEBC schemes can be instantiated from a combination of public-key encryption, NIZKs, and commitments.

The Current Situation. In summary, we do have tools that give meaningful security and privacy guarantees for group messaging even in face of corruptions. The current state of the art [5,15] leaves a few questions unanswered, however:

Limited deniability guarantees. The deniability (technically: OTR) guarantees given by the combination of [5,15] are limited to the case where the secret keys of honest senders remain secret. In particular, simulated ciphertexts are only proven to look plausible when the corresponding sender key is unknown. However, current deniability notions do not provide any guarantees if an honest sender is forced (or blackmailed) to give away its secret key, in which case the sender might not be able to plausibly deny having sent a message.

Limited unforgeability guarantees. The MDVS constructions and analyses from [5] show unforgeability only in a setting in which an adversary has no verification oracle. (Intuitively, in such designated-verifier settings, signatures are not publicly verifiable, and hence typically adversaries are given access to an explicit verification oracle [13,18]). This is undesirable, in particular because a constructive modeling of MDVS schemes [14] requires such a verification oracle. As a result, the resulting combined MDRS-PKE scheme from [5,15] suffers from a similarly weak unforgeability guarantee.[2]

Limited scalability. The combined MDRS-PKE construction of [5,15] has ciphertexts whose sizes are *quadratic* in the number of receivers. This is clearly undesirable for large groups. Furthermore, while the generic transformation of [15] itself is tightly secure, i.e., gives security guarantees that do not incur a loss in the number of parties or ciphertexts, the underlying primitives from [5,15] are not known to be. In particular, the (known) security guarantees of the final scheme degrade in the number of ciphertexts and users.

Gaps in some proofs. Unfortunately, some of the proofs in [5] appear incomplete. (See [3, Appendix C] for details.)

Our Contribution. In this work, we construct a MDRS-PKE scheme that

- enjoys strong deniability guarantees (i.e. a strong OTR notion that takes into account leaked sender secret keys),
- likewise enjoys strong unforgeability properties (that take into account adversaries with a verification oracle),
- is scalable, in the sense that ciphertext sizes, encryption and decryption times are linear in the number of receivers, and we can prove it tightly secure based on primitives for which tightly secure instantiations are known.

Like [15], our MDRS-PKE scheme is based upon suitable MDVS and PKEBC schemes. In fact, we use the same generic MDRS-PKE construction as [15], but for more secure and more efficient MDVS and PKEBC schemes (that we also provide). In particular, we provide

- a conceptually simple MDVS scheme that achieves strong OTR and strong unforgeability guarantees (as explained above),
- a PKEBC scheme for which ciphertext sizes, and both encryption and decryption times only grow linearly with the number of receivers.

Both of these schemes can be proven tightly secure from primitives that have tightly secure instantiations from standard computational assumptions. In particular, unlike [5], we avoid the use of non-interactive key exchange, a primitive which is known to be difficult to prove tightly secure [2,10].

---

[2] It should be noted that this shortcoming appears to have gone unnoticed. In particular, [15] explicitly define and assume MDVS schemes that are unforgeable in the presence of a verification oracle, while [5] simply do not prove this property about their MDVS schemes. Technically speaking, this means the transformation of [15] cannot be directly applied to the MDVS schemes from [5]. However, it is easy to see that the results from [15] carry over to "weakly unforgeable" (in the above sense) MDVS schemes, such that the result is simply a weakly unforgeable MDRS-PKE scheme.

2   Technical Overview

We now give an overview of the techniques used to construct our MDRS-PKE scheme. As aforementioned, our scheme is tightly secure under adaptive corruptions and satisfies the new (stronger) OTR notion considered in this paper. The main building blocks of our construction are: 1. a new MDVS scheme construction satisfying (the MDVS analogous of) the new OTR security notion which is tightly secure under adaptive corruptions; and 2. a new PKEBC scheme construction with linear-size ciphertexts, and linear-time encryption and decryption which is also tightly secure under adaptive corruptions. By following (a straightforward generalization of) the transformation given in [15] we then obtain the intended MDRS-PKE scheme. It is worth noting that, since the MDRS-PKE construction given in [15] uses the PKEBC scheme to encrypt a message whose size is already linear in the number of receivers, it is not sufficient for the underlying PKEBC scheme to have ciphertext sizes, encryption and decryption times that grow linearly with the number of receivers *times* the size of the message: it is necessary for the PKEBC's ciphertext sizes, encryption and decryption times to grow linearly with the number of receivers *plus* the size of the message. This is exactly what we achieve: when instantiated with our new MDVS and PKEBC constructions, the MDRS-PKE construction given in [15] yields the first (MDRS-PKE) scheme that satisfies the new stronger OTR notion, that has ciphertext size, encryption and decryption times that grow linearly with the number of receivers, and that is tightly secure under adaptive corruptions.

2.1   MDVS Construction

We now give an overview of our MDVS scheme construction. As a first step we consider the case of a single verifier and show how to construct a Designated Verifier Signature (DVS) scheme. This already conveys the main technical ideas of our construction. Then we discuss how to generalize the DVS to the case of multiple verifiers (MDVS), and, finally, we explain how to achieve tight security under adaptive corruptions. The building blocks of all our (M)DVS constructions are an IND-CPA secure PKE scheme, a One-Way Function (OWF) F and a Simulation-Sound (SS) NIZK.

The DVS Scheme. Our signature scheme is of the following form: the public parameters pp consist of a public key pk of the PKE scheme, and a *Common Reference String* crs of the NIZK argument system. The secret signing key ssk is a pre-image x_S of the OWF F and the signer's public key spk is the corresponding image (i.e. $spk = y_S = F(x_S)$). A verifier's key-pair is similar, except that it additionally includes a PKE key pair (pk_V, sk_V): the verifier's secret key vsk consists of a pre-image x_V of F together with the PKE secret key sk_V; the verifier's public key vpk are the corresponding public keys, i.e. $vpk = (pk_V, y_V := F(x_V))$. To sign a message m (using $ssk = x_S$, and $vpk = (pk_V, y_V)$), we first generate two ciphertexts, c and c_{pp}: c encrypts the bit 1 under the verifier's public key pk_V (the role of this will be clear soon); c_{pp} encrypts the tuple $(m, 1, ssk)$ under the public key pk included in the public parameters

pp. Finally, we generate a NIZK proof π that binds the ciphertexts together: π proves that both c_{pp} and c are well-formed and encrypt the same bit b, and that if $b = 1$ then c_{pp} encrypts a pre-image (under F) of either y_S or y_V. The signature σ then consists of the tuple (c_{pp}, c, π). To verify a signature the receiver first verifies the NIZK proof π and then decrypts ciphertext c using its PKE secret key sk_V; the signature is valid if π is a valid NIZK proof and the decryption of c is 1.

Simulating a signature works as follows: 1. for the case of a dishonest verifier, to simulate a signature one proceeds just like an honest signer would to generate a signature, the only difference being that c_{pp}, instead of encrypting x_S—the pre-image of the signer's public key—encrypts x_V—the pre-image of the verifier's public key; 2. if the verifier is honest, one forges a signature by having c be an encryption of 0 under the verifier's public PKE key pk_V, c_{pp} be an encryption of the triple $(m, 0, 0)$, and π be a NIZK proof. Note that, thanks to the NIZK relation we consider, in both cases one can compute a valid NIZK proof π: in the first case this is possible because c_{pp} encrypts a pre-image of the verifier's secret key; for the latter case this is possible because c is an encryption of 0.

To understand why the DVS scheme sketched above is unforgeable note first that if both the sender and the verifier are honest, by the one-wayness of F the adversary does not know a pre-image of neither $F(x_S)$ nor $F(x_V)$. On a high level the proof proceeds as follows: we begin by changing both the public parameter's crs and each signature's NIZK proof by simulated ones. We, next, further modify the signatures the adversary sees by making c_{pp} be an encryption of a "0" string—possible by the IND-CPA security of the underlying PKE scheme. Note that at this point all the adversary sees is independent of both $ssk = x_S$ and $vsk = x_V$.[3] Now suppose the adversary manages to come up with a forgery (c_{pp}^*, c^*, π^*) corresponding to some message m^* whose signature it has never seen: if the forgery is valid then on one hand c^* is encryption of bit 1 and on the other hand π^* is a valid NIZK proof; by (simulation) soundness this means that c_{pp}^* encrypts a pre-image of either y_S or y_V. However, at this point we can use the PKE secret key corresponding to the public parameter's public key to extract the pre-image, contradicting the one-wayness of F.

Understanding why the scheme sketched above satisfies the (stronger) OTR property is more involved (and refer the reader to the full version [3] for details). For simplicity, below we consider a weaker OTR notion—one where the adversary is not given access to a signature verification oracle: 1. If the verifier is dishonest the only differences between real and simulated signatures are that in the first case c_{pp} encrypts x_S and the NIZK proof π is generated using x_S as (part of the) witness, whereas in the latter case c_{pp} encrypts x_V and π is generated using x_V. If an adversary were able to distinguish real signatures from simulated ones then it would be either breaking the IND-CPA security of the underlying PKE scheme, or the Zero-Knowledge security of the NIZK (or both). 2. If the verifier is honest the differences between real signatures and simulated ones are that in the first

---

[3] Here, independent is in the sense that all the adversary sees only depends on $y_S :=$ $F(x_S)$ and $y_V := F(x_V)$, but not on any pre-image of y_S or y_V.

case c_{pp} encrypts x_S, c is an encryption of 1 and π is generated using x_S, while in a simulated signature c_{pp} encrypts a "0" string, c is an encryption of 0 and π is no longer generated using a pre-image of neither y_S nor y_V. So, if an adversary were be able to distinguish real and simulated signatures then it could break the IND-CPA security of the underlying PKE scheme—since it could distinguish either the c_{pp} or the c ciphertexts—or could break the Zero-Knowledge of the NIZK.

Generalizing for Multiple Verifiers. We now discuss how to extend the previous construction to the case of multiple designated verifiers. The main difference is that we additionally need to guarantee consistency—meaning that either all honest verifiers accept a signature, or they all reject.

Signatures in our MDVS construction consist of a vector of ciphertexts $\vec{c} = (c_1, \cdots, c_n)$ (one per receiver) and a ciphertext c_{pp}. Each ciphertext c_i is the encryption of a bit b_i under the i-th receiver's public key pk_{V_i}, and the ciphertext c_{pp} is an encryption of the tuple $(m, b_{global}, \vec{\alpha} = (\alpha_1, \cdots, \alpha_n))$, where $\alpha_i = (b_i, x_i)$, under the public parameter's public key pk. Similarly to the DVS construction, signatures also contain a NIZK proof π that not only ensures ciphertexts are well-formed and signatures are unforgeable, but also consistency. In particular, π proves: 1. all ciphertexts in $\vec{c}$ and ciphertext c_{pp} are well-formed—in particular each ciphertext c_i of $\vec{c}$ encrypts the bit b_i that is in the α_i encrypted in c_{pp}; 2. for each verifier, say the i-th, if $b_i = 1$ then the α_i encrypted in c_{pp} contains a pre-image of either y_S—the signer's public key—or y_{V_i}—the i-th verifier's public key—under F (this guarantees unforgeability); and 3. for each i-th verifier, if the value x_i in α_i that is encrypted under c_{pp} is not a pre-image of this verifier's public key y_{V_i} then $b_i = b_{global}$ (this guarantees consistency). Note that, if the verification of the NIZK proof is deterministic, the NIZK's soundness implies that if two verifiers disagree on a signature's validity, one of them is dishonest.

Achieving Tight Security Under Adaptive Corruptions. While the MDVS construction above already satisfies correctness, consistency, unforgeability and OTR, we do not know how to prove it is tightly secure under adaptive corruptions. Our problem is that we do not know how a reduction could know in advance which parties the adversary will corrupt (and thus ask for their secret keys) and which ones it will not. Suppose for example we are reducing an adversary from breaking some security property of the MDVS construction to breaking the IND-CPA game of the underlying PKE scheme, and in particular consider a reduction that simply guesses whether the adversary will corrupt a party P_i: on one hand, if the reduction guesses incorrectly that P_i will be corrupted then it is not taking advantage of the adversary to win the underlying IND-CPA game; on the other hand, if the reduction incorrectly guesses P_i will not be corrupted—in which case it would set P_i's public key to be one output by the underlying IND-CPA game—then we do not know how the reduction could handle a query for the secret key of P_i—and so the reduction would again not be taking advantage of the adversary to win the underlying IND-CPA game. So although one could resort to this guessing technique to prove the security of the MDVS scheme under adaptive corruptions (via a hybrid argument), this leads to a reduction loss that grows linearly with the number of parties.

To void this reduction loss we follow the "two-key" technique already used in the context of tightly secure public-key encryption [1]. In the new scheme, and at a high level, the public key of each party P_i is a pair of public keys—say $(\mathsf{pk}_0, \mathsf{pk}_1)$—from the previous scheme, and its secret key consists of a bit b—picked uniformly at random—and the secret key sk_b corresponding to pk_b. Signatures then consist of c_{pp} as before, a vector of ciphertexts that includes two ciphertexts per verifier—one under each of the verifier's public keys—and the NIZK proof π—which now proves that c_{pp} encrypts a pre-image of one of the public keys of a party (rather than a single one as before). This technique allows to come up with tight security reductions to the underlying building blocks: having the two keys allows, on one hand, to embed challenges in the part of the public key whose corresponding secret key is "forgotten", i.e. pk_{1-b}, where b is the bit in the party's secret key, and on the other hand to handle any possible queries the adversary may make, including ones where the party's secret key is leaked.

2.2 PKEBC Construction

We now give a high level overview of our PKEBC scheme's construction. We first explain how to achieve linear sized ciphertexts and linear time encryption (in the number of receivers), and then move towards making decryption time also linear. (We note that the ciphertext size and both the encryption and decryption times of the only prior PKEBC scheme construction (see [15]) all grow quadratically in the number of receivers.) Since the technique we use to obtain tight security reductions under adaptive corruptions is the same one we used in the MDVS construction, we do not include it in this overview.

As building blocks, we assume an IND-CPA and IK-CPA secure PKE scheme, a Simulation-Sound NIZK and a (one-time) IND-CPA secure Symmetric Encryption (SKE) scheme. The public parameters of our PKEBC schemes are the same as for the MDVS construction—comprising a public key of a PKE scheme and a crs for a NIZK, i.e. $\mathsf{pp} = (\mathsf{pk}, \mathsf{crs})$—and in the two constructions discussed below a PKEBC key-pair is simply a key-pair of the underlying PKE scheme.

Achieving Linear Ciphertext Size and Encryption Time. As we now explain, the main idea to achieve linear ciphertext sizes and encryption time (in the number of receivers) is to use hybrid encryption.

To encrypt a message m to a vector of receiver public keys $\vec{v} = (\mathsf{pk}_1, \ldots, \mathsf{pk}_n)$ we first encrypt $(\vec{v}, m)$ under the public parameters' public key; let c_{pp} denote the resulting ciphertext and r_{pp} the sequence of random bits used for this encryption. Next we generate a symmetric key k for the SKE scheme and for each receiver public key pk_i in $\vec{v}$ we encrypt k under pk_i, resulting in a vector of ciphertexts $(c_1, \ldots, c_n)$. Then we use k to encrypt not only $\vec{v}$ and m, but also r_{pp}; let c_{sym} denote the resulting (symmetric) ciphertext. (Having c_{sym} encrypt $\vec{v}$, m and r_{pp} allows receivers to confirm they obtained the correct vector of receivers and message: since the public parameter's public key is honestly sampled, c_{pp} is a commitment to $(\vec{v}, m)$, and since c_{sym} also encrypts r_{pp}, a receiver can simply recompute c_{pp}; as we will see, this is key to guaranteeing correctness, robustness and consistency.) Finally, we create a NIZK proof π showing that: 1. c_{pp} is an encryption of $(\vec{v}, m)$ under the public parameters' public key using r_{pp} as the sequence of random encryption bits; 2. the symmetric key k was correctly sampled; 3. c_{sym} is an encryption under k of $(r_{pp}, \vec{v}, m)$; and 4. for each ciphertext c_i of $\vec{c}$, c_i is an encryption of k under the i-th public key pk_i of $\vec{v}$. The final ciphertext is then the quadruple $c = (c_{pp}, \vec{c}, c_{sym}, \pi)$. To decrypt a receiver first checks if π is a valid NIZK proof; if π is valid the receiver then starts trying to decrypt each ciphertext $c_i \in \vec{c}$; for each symmetric key k' the receiver obtains from successfully decrypting a ciphertext c_i, the receiver tries decrypting c_{sym}. If the decryption of c_{sym} is successful, returning a triple $(r_{pp}, \vec{v}, m)$, the receiver checks if c_{pp} indeed encrypts $(\vec{v}, m)$ under the public parameters' public key using r_{pp} as the random encryption coins, and if it does the receiver outputs $(\vec{v}, m)$ as the result of decryption. If it does not (or any of the decryption attempts failed) the receiver moves on to the next ciphertext c_j of $\vec{c}$, or returns the special error symbol $\perp$ if there are no more ciphertexts.

It is easy to see that for a vector of receivers $\vec{v}$ and message m both the ciphertext size and the encryption time of the scheme are $O(|\vec{v}| + |m|)$, exactly as we needed. Unfortunately, the scheme *does not* achieve linear time decryption: in the worst case the decryption of each ciphertext $c_i \in \vec{c}$ outputs a valid looking symmetric key k'[4], the decryption of c_{sym} is successful—which, given the size of c_{sym} is linear in the number of receivers, already takes time linear in the number of receivers—but then the triple $(r_{pp}', \vec{v}', m')$ resulting from c_{sym}'s decryption does not match c_{pp}, i.e. c_{pp} is not the encryption of $(\vec{v}', m')$ under the public key of the public parameters, and using r_{pp}' as the random encryption coins. Given the number of ciphertexts of $\vec{c}$ is linear in the number of receivers, the time to decrypt then grows *quadratically* in the number of receivers.

Achieving Linear Decryption Time. To achieve linear time decryption receivers need a fast way of checking if any particular ciphertext $c_j \in \vec{c}$ is really meant for them without having to decrypt c_{sym}, as this already takes linear time in the number of receivers. A first idea is adding, for each receiver, an encryption of a long enough 0 bitstring (and appropriately modifying the NIZK relation): to decrypt, a receiver would then first check if the decryption of this new ciphertext would output back the expected 0 bitstring, and if not the receiver would not have to attempt decrypting the (linear sized) c_{sym} ciphertext. Unfortunately, this approach only works for honestly generated ciphertexts. For instance, consider two key-pairs $(pk, sk), (pk', sk')$ of some arbitrary PKE scheme with $pk \neq pk'$: one cannot assume that an adversarially created encryption of a 0 bitstring under pk does not decrypt, under the non-matching secret key sk', to the same 0 bitstring (and, more generally, to any particular value). This means that a

---

[4] For an arbitrary PKE scheme a receiver cannot *a priori* tell whether a given ciphertext is intended for itself.

dishonest sender could potentially come up with "malformed" ciphertexts that would pass this first check, thus making a receiver have to decrypt the (large) c_{sym} ciphertext and then recompute c_{pp} to ensure consistency.

The way our scheme achieves linear time decryption is by pairing each ciphertext $c_i \in \vec{c}$ with: 1. a commitment to the i-th receiver's public key pk_i; and 2. a ciphertext that encrypts, under pk_i, the random coins used to generate the commitment. More concretely, in our scheme there are three ciphertexts per receiver, i.e. $\vec{c} = (c_1, \ldots, c_n)$ with $c_i = (c_{i,0}, c_{i,1}, c_{i,2})$, where: $c_{i,0}$ is an encryption, under the public parameter's public key, of the i-th receiver's public key pk_i using some sequence of random bits $r_{i,0}$; $c_{i,1}$ is an encryption, under pk_i, of the random coins $r_{i,0}$; and $c_{i,2}$ is an encryption of the SKE key k used to encrypt c_{sym}. As one might note, by appropriately modifying the NIZK statement, we can ensure that receivers no longer need to recompute c_{pp} to confirm they obtained the correct pair $(\vec{v} = (pk_1, \ldots, pk_n), m)$ from the decryption of c_{sym}: first, note that the correctness of the underlying PKE scheme together with the soundness of the NIZK (for the modified NIZK statement) guarantee that ciphertext $c_{j,0}$ of each triple $c_j = (c_{j,0}, c_{j,1}, c_{j,2})$ of $\vec{c}$ binds the triple to a single receiver public key pk_j; second, the PKE scheme's correctness with the NIZK's soundness further imply that ciphertext $c_{j,2}$ of every triple is an encryption of the same symmetric key k under the public key pk_j bound to the triple; third, the SKE's (perfect) correctness again with the NIZK's soundness imply that the decryption of c_{sym} using the aforementioned key k yields the same pair $(\vec{v} = (pk_1, \ldots, pk_n), m)$, where for each $i \in \{1, \ldots, n\}$, the triple $c_i \in \vec{c}$ is bound to the (corresponding) public key $pk_i \in \vec{v}$. Since, as explained above, receivers need not recompute c_{pp}, in the new scheme c_{sym} no longer encrypts the random coins r_{pp}. Furthermore, as each receiver's public key pk_i is already encrypted under the public parameter's public key in $c_{i,0}$, c_{pp} no longer needs to encrypt vector $\vec{v}$; in the new scheme c_{pp} encrypts only the message m.

3   Preliminaries

We denote the arity of a vector $\vec{x}$ by $|\vec{x}|$ and its i-th element by x_i. We write $\alpha \in \vec{x}$ to denote $\exists i \in \{1, \ldots, |\vec{x}|\}$ with $\alpha = x_i$. We write $\mathrm{Set}(\vec{x})$ to denote the set induced by vector $\vec{x}$, i.e. $\mathrm{Set}(\vec{x}) := \{x_i \mid x_i \in \vec{x}\}$.

Throughout the paper we frequently use vectors. We use upper case letters to denote vectors of parties, and lower case letters to denote vectors of artifacts such as public keys, sequences of random coins, etc. Moreover, we use the convention that if $\vec{V}$ is a vector of parties, then $\vec{v}$ denotes $\vec{V}$'s corresponding vector of public keys. For example, for a vector of parties $\vec{V} := (\mathrm{Bob}, \mathrm{Charlie})$, $\vec{v} := (pk_{Bob}, pk_{Charlie})$ is $\vec{V}$'s corresponding vector of public keys. In particular, V_1 is Bob and v_1 is Bob's public key pk_{Bob}, and V_2 is Charlie and v_2 is Charlie's public key $pk_{Charlie}$. More generally, for a vector of parties $\vec{V}$ with corresponding vector of public keys $\vec{v}$, V_i's public key is v_i, for $i \in \{1, \ldots, |\vec{V}|\}$.

4 Multi-designated Verifier Signature Schemes with Enhanced Off-The-Record Security

An MDVS scheme Π is a 6-tuple of Probabilistic Polynomial Time Algorithms (PPTs) $\Pi = (S, G_S, G_V, Sig, Vfy, Forge)$, where:

- S: on input 1^k, generates public parameters pp;
- G_S: on input pp, generates a signer key-pair (spk, ssk);
- G_V: on input pp, generates a verifier key-pair (vpk, vsk);
- Sig: on input $(pp, ssk, \vec{v}, m)$, where ssk is the signer's secret key, $\vec{v}$ is the vector of public verifier keys of the designated verifiers and m is the message, generates a signature σ;
- Vfy: on input $(pp, spk, vsk, \vec{v}, m, \sigma)$, where vsk is a verifier's secret key, Vfy checks if σ is a valid signature on message m with respect to signer's public key spk and vector of verifier public keys $\vec{v}$;
- $Forge$: on input $(pp, spk, \vec{v}, m, \vec{s})$, where spk is the signer's public key, $\vec{v}$ is the vector of the designated verifiers' public keys, $\vec{s}$ is a vector of designated verifiers' secret keys—with $|\vec{s}| = |\vec{v}|$ and where for $i \in \{1, \ldots, |\vec{v}|\}$, either $s_i = \bot$ or s_i is the secret key corresponding to the i-th public key of $\vec{v}$, i.e. v_i—and m is the message, generates a forged signature σ.

In this section we introduce a new (stronger) Off-The-Record security notion for MDVS schemes capturing the setting where the signer's secret key can leak (Definition 4) and give a new construction satisfying this stronger notion.

4.1 Security Notions

Let $\Pi = (S, G_S, G_V, Sig, Vfy, Forge)$ be an MDVS scheme. The MDVS security games ahead have an implicitly defined security parameter k, and provide adversaries with access to the following oracles:

Public Parameter Generation Oracle: $\mathcal{O}_{PP}$
1. On the first call to $\mathcal{O}_{PP}$, compute pp $\leftarrow S(1^k)$; output pp;
2. On subsequent calls, simply output pp.

Signer Key-Pair Generation Oracle: $\mathcal{O}_{SK}(A_i)$
1. On the first call to $\mathcal{O}_{SK}$ on input A_i, compute $(spk_i, ssk_i) \leftarrow G_S(pp)$, and output (spk_i, ssk_i);
2. On subsequent calls, simply output (spk_i, ssk_i).

Verifier Key-Pair Generation Oracle: $\mathcal{O}_{VK}(B_j)$
1. Analogous to the Signer Key-Pair Generation Oracle.

Signer Public-Key Oracle: $\mathcal{O}_{SPK}(A_i)$
1. $(spk_i, ssk_i) \leftarrow \mathcal{O}_{SK}(A_i)$; output spk_i.

Verifier Public-Key Oracle: $\mathcal{O}_{VPK}(B_j)$
1. Analogous to the Signer Public-Key Oracle.

Signing Oracle: $\mathcal{O}_S(A_i, \vec{V}, m)$
1. $(spk_i, ssk_i) \leftarrow \mathcal{O}_{SK}(A_i)$;
2. $\vec{v} = (\mathcal{O}_{VPK}(V_1), \ldots, \mathcal{O}_{VPK}(V_{|\vec{v}|}))$;

3. Output $\sigma \leftarrow Sig_{pp}(\mathrm{ssk}_i, \vec{v}, m)$.

Verification Oracle: $\mathcal{O}_V(A_i, B_j, \vec{V}, m, \sigma)$

1. $\mathrm{spk}_i \leftarrow \mathcal{O}_{SPK}(A_i)$;
2. $\vec{v} = (\mathcal{O}_{VPK}(V_1), \ldots, \mathcal{O}_{VPK}(V_{|\vec{V}|}))$;
3. $(\mathrm{vpk}_j, \mathrm{vsk}_j) \leftarrow \mathcal{O}_{VK}(B_j)$;
4. Output $d \leftarrow Vfy_{pp}(\mathrm{spk}_i, \mathrm{vsk}_j, \vec{v}, m, \sigma)$, where $d \in \{0, 1\}$.

Definition 1 (Correctness). *Game system* $\mathbf{G}^{\mathsf{Corr}}$ *provides an adversary* $\mathbf{A}$ *with access to oracles* $\mathcal{O}_{PP}, \mathcal{O}_{SK}, \mathcal{O}_{VK}, \mathcal{O}_{SPK}, \mathcal{O}_{VPK}, \mathcal{O}_S$ *and* $\mathcal{O}_V$. $\mathbf{A}$ *wins the game if there are two queries* q_S *and* q_V *to* $\mathcal{O}_S$ *and* $\mathcal{O}_V$, *respectively, where* q_S *has input* $(A_i, \vec{V}, m)$ *and* q_V *has input* $(A_i', B_j, \vec{V}', m', \sigma)$, *satisfying* $(A_i, \vec{V}, m) = (A_i', \vec{V}', m')$, $B_j \in \vec{V}$, *the input* σ *in* q_V *is the output of the oracle* $\mathcal{O}_S$ *on query* q_S, *and the output of the oracle* $\mathcal{O}_V$ *on the query* q_V *is* 0. *The advantage of* $\mathbf{A}$ *in winning the Correctness game, denoted* $Adv^{\mathsf{Corr}}(\mathbf{A})$, *is the probability that* $\mathbf{A}$ *wins game* $\mathbf{G}^{\mathsf{Corr}}$ *as described above.*

We say an adversary $\mathbf{A}$ (ε, t)-breaks the (n_V, q_S, q_V)-Correctness of Π if $\mathbf{A}$ runs in time at most t, queries $\mathcal{O}_{VK}, \mathcal{O}_{VPK}, \mathcal{O}_S$ and $\mathcal{O}_V$ on at most n_V different verifiers, makes at most q_S and q_V queries to $\mathcal{O}_S$ and $\mathcal{O}_V$, respectively, and satisfies $Adv^{\mathsf{Corr}}(\mathbf{A}) \geq \varepsilon$.

Definition 2 (Consistency). *Game* $\mathbf{G}^{\mathsf{Cons}}$ *provides an adversary* $\mathbf{A}$ *with access to oracles* $\mathcal{O}_{PP}, \mathcal{O}_{SK}, \mathcal{O}_{VK}, \mathcal{O}_{SPK}, \mathcal{O}_{VPK}, \mathcal{O}_S$ *and* $\mathcal{O}_V$. *We say that* $\mathbf{A}$ *wins the game if it queries* $\mathcal{O}_V$ *on inputs* $(A_i, B_j, \vec{V}, m, \sigma)$ *and* $(A_i', B_j', \vec{V}', m', \sigma')$ *with* $(A_i, \vec{V}, m, \sigma) = (A_i', \vec{V}', m', \sigma')$ *and where* $\{B_j, B_j'\} \subseteq \vec{V}$, *the outputs of the two queries differ, and there is no* $\mathcal{O}_{VK}$ *query on either* B_j *or* B_j'. *The advantage of* $\mathbf{A}$ *in winning the Consistency game, denoted* $Adv^{\mathsf{Cons}}(\mathbf{A})$, *is the probability that* $\mathbf{A}$ *wins game* $\mathbf{G}^{\mathsf{Cons}}$ *as described above.*

An adversary $\mathbf{A}$ (ε, t)-breaks the (n_V, q_V)-Consistency of Π if $\mathbf{A}$ runs in time at most t, queries $\mathcal{O}_{VK}, \mathcal{O}_{VPK}, \mathcal{O}_S$ and $\mathcal{O}_V$ on at most n_V different verifiers, makes at most q_V queries to $\mathcal{O}_V$ and satisfies $Adv^{\mathsf{Cons}}(\mathbf{A}) \geq \varepsilon$.

Definition 3 (Unforgeability). *Game system* $\mathbf{G}^{\mathsf{Unforg}}$ *provides an adversary* $\mathbf{A}$ *with access to oracles* $\mathcal{O}_{PP}, \mathcal{O}_{SK}, \mathcal{O}_{VK}, \mathcal{O}_{SPK}, \mathcal{O}_{VPK}, \mathcal{O}_S$ *and* $\mathcal{O}_V$. $\mathbf{A}$ *wins if it makes a query* $\mathcal{O}_V(A_i^*, B_j^*, \vec{V}^*, m^*, \sigma^*)$ *with* $B_j^* \in \vec{V}^*$ *that outputs* 1, *for every query* $\mathcal{O}_S(A_i', \vec{V}', m')$, $(A_i^*, \vec{V}^*, m^*) \neq (A_i', \vec{V}', m')$, *and there is no* $\mathcal{O}_{SK}$ *query on* A_i^* *nor* $\mathcal{O}_{VK}$ *query on* B_j^*. *The advantage of* $\mathbf{A}$ *in winning the Unforgeability game is the probability that* $\mathbf{A}$ *wins* $\mathbf{G}^{\mathsf{Unforg}}$, *and is denoted* $Adv^{\mathsf{Unforg}}(\mathbf{A})$.

An adversary $\mathbf{A}$ (ε, t)-breaks the (n_S, n_V, q_S, q_V)-Unforgeability of Π if $\mathbf{A}$ runs in time at most t, queries $\mathcal{O}_{SK}, \mathcal{O}_{SPK}, \mathcal{O}_S$ and $\mathcal{O}_V$ on at most n_S different signers, $\mathcal{O}_{VK}, \mathcal{O}_{VPK}, \mathcal{O}_S$ and $\mathcal{O}_V$ on at most n_V different verifiers, makes at most q_S and q_V queries to $\mathcal{O}_S$ and $\mathcal{O}_V$, respectively, and satisfies $Adv^{\mathsf{Unforg}}(\mathbf{A}) \geq \varepsilon$.

4.1.1 New Off-The-Record Security Notion

We now present the new enhanced off-the-record security notion for MDVS schemes. As already mentioned, the main difference between our new notion and the existing one (see [5,15]) is that in our new notion the adversary can query for the secret key of any sender (and still win the game). This is reflected in Definition 4 in that there is no restriction on which signer secret keys an adversary may query.

The off-the-record security notion defines two game systems, $\mathbf{G}_0^{\mathsf{OTR}}$ and $\mathbf{G}_1^{\mathsf{OTR}}$, which provide adversaries with access to an additional oracle $\mathcal{O}_{Challenge}$ whose behavior varies depending on the underlying game system:

Challenge Oracle: $\mathcal{O}_{Challenge}(\mathtt{type} \in \{\mathtt{sig}, \mathtt{sim}\}, A_i, \vec{V}, m, \mathcal{C})$
For game system $\mathbf{G}_{\mathsf{b}}^{\mathsf{OTR}}$, the oracle behaves as follows:
1. $(\mathrm{spk}_i, \mathrm{ssk}_i) \leftarrow \mathcal{O}_{SK}(A_i)$;
2. Let $\vec{v} = (v_1, \ldots, v_{|\vec{V}|})$ and $\vec{s} = (s_1, \ldots, s_{|\vec{V}|})$, where, for $i \in \{1, \ldots, |\vec{V}|\}$:
$$- (v_i, s_i) = \begin{cases} \mathcal{O}_{VK}(V_i) & \text{if } V_i \in \mathcal{C} \\ (\mathcal{O}_{VPK}(V_i), \perp) & \text{otherwise}; \end{cases}$$
3. $(\sigma_0, \sigma_1) \leftarrow (\Pi.Sig_{\mathsf{pp}}(\mathrm{ssk}_i, \vec{v}, m), \Pi.Forge_{\mathsf{pp}}(\mathrm{spk}_i, \vec{v}, m, \vec{s}))$;
4. If $\mathsf{b} = 0$, output σ_0 if $\mathtt{type} = \mathtt{sig}$ and σ_1 if $\mathtt{type} = \mathtt{sim}$; otherwise, if $\mathsf{b} = 1$, output σ_1.

Definition 4 (Off-The-Record). *For* $\mathsf{b} \in \{0,1\}$, *game* $\mathbf{G}_{\mathsf{b}}^{\mathsf{OTR}}$ *provides an adversary* $\mathbf{A}$ *with access to oracles* $\mathcal{O}_{PP}, \mathcal{O}_{SK}, \mathcal{O}_{VK}, \mathcal{O}_{SPK}, \mathcal{O}_{VPK}, \mathcal{O}_V$ *and* $\mathcal{O}_{Challenge}$. *We say that* $\mathbf{A}$ *wins the game if it outputs a guess bit* b' *with* $b' = \mathbf{b}$, *and for every query* $\mathcal{O}_{Challenge}(\mathtt{type}, A_i, \vec{V}, m, \mathcal{C})$: 1. $\mathcal{C} \subseteq Set(\vec{V})$; 2. there is no query $\mathcal{O}_{VK}(B_j)$ with $B_j \in Set(\vec{V}) \setminus \mathcal{C}$; 3. letting σ be the output of the $\mathcal{O}_{Challenge}$ query above, there is no query $\mathcal{O}_V(A_i, B_j, \vec{V}, m, \sigma)$ with $B_j \in \vec{V}$. *The advantage of* $\mathbf{A}$ *in winning the Off-The-Record security game is*

$$Adv^{\mathsf{OTR}}(\mathbf{A}) := \left| \Pr[\mathbf{A}\mathbf{G}_0^{\mathsf{OTR}} = \mathtt{win}] + \Pr[\mathbf{A}\mathbf{G}_1^{\mathsf{OTR}} = \mathtt{win}] - 1 \right|.$$

An adversary $\mathbf{A}$ (ε, t)-breaks the (n_V, d_S, q_S, q_V)-Off-The-Record security of Π if $\mathbf{A}$ runs in time at most t, queries $\mathcal{O}_{VK}, \mathcal{O}_{VPK}, \mathcal{O}_V$ and $\mathcal{O}_{Challenge}$ on at most n_V different verifiers, makes at most q_S and q_V queries to $\mathcal{O}_{Challenge}$ and $\mathcal{O}_V$, respectively, with the sum of the verifier vectors' lengths input to $\mathcal{O}_{Challenge}$ being at most d_S, and satisfies $Adv^{\mathsf{OTR}}(\mathbf{A}) \geq \varepsilon$. We say that Π is

$$(\varepsilon_{\mathsf{Corr}}, \varepsilon_{\mathsf{Cons}}, \varepsilon_{\mathsf{Unforg}}, \varepsilon_{\mathsf{OTR}}, t, n_S, n_V, d_S, q_S, q_V)\text{-secure}$$

if there is no adversary $\mathbf{A}$ that: 1. $(\varepsilon_{\mathsf{Corr}}, t)$-breaks Π's (n_V, q_S, q_V)-Correctness; 2. $(\varepsilon_{\mathsf{Cons}}, t)$-breaks Π's (n_V, q_V)-Consistency; 3. $(\varepsilon_{\mathsf{Unforg}}, t)$-breaks Π's (n_S, n_V, q_S, q_V)-Unforgeability; or 4. $(\varepsilon_{\mathsf{OTR}}, t)$-breaks Π's (n_V, d_S, q_S, q_V)-Off-The-Record.

4.2 DVS Construction

We present our MDVS construction incrementally.[5] We begin by giving a construction of a (single verifier) DVS scheme (see Algorithm 1) that is Correct

---

[5] We only prove the security of the final MDVS construction given in Sect. 4.4.

(Definition 1), Unforgeable (Definition 3) and Off-The-Record (Definition 4); next, we generalize it into an MDVS scheme (which has to additionally satisfy consistency); finally, we use a technique first introduced by Bader et al. in [1] to make the scheme tightly secure under adaptive corruptions. The building blocks for all our constructions are a NIZK scheme $\Pi_{\text{NIZK}} = (G, P, V, S := (S_G, S_P))$, a PKE scheme $\Pi_{\text{PKE}} = (G, E, D)$, and a One Way Function $\Pi_{\text{OWF}} = (S, F)$.

For modularity, rather than introducing a single language/relation for the NIZK scheme used by our constructions, we will introduce different relations and then define the relation/language for our constructions as the intersection of these relations. For example, in Algorithm 1 we consider the language induced by a relation $R_{\text{DVS}} := R_{\text{DVS-Match}} \cap R_{\text{DVS-Unforg}}$, where

- $R_{\text{DVS-Match}} := \Big\{ ((\text{pk}_{\text{pp}}, \text{spk}, \text{vpk}, m, c, c_{\text{pp}}), (a, b, r, r_{\text{pp}})) \mid$

$$\Big(c_{\text{pp}} = \Pi_{\text{PKE}}.E_{\text{pk}_{\text{pp}}}((m, b, a); r_{\text{pp}}) \Big) \wedge (c = \Pi_{\text{PKE}}.E_{\text{vpk.pk}}(b; r)) \Big\};$$

- $R_{\text{DVS-Unforg}} := \Big\{ ((\text{pk}_{\text{pp}}, \text{spk}, \text{vpk}, m, c, c_{\text{pp}}), (a, b, r, r_{\text{pp}})) \mid$

$$(b = 1) \rightarrow (\Pi_{\text{OWF}}.F(a) \in \{\text{spk}.y, \text{vpk}.y\}) \Big\}.$$

The corresponding language is then defined as $L_{\text{DVS}} := \{(\text{pk}_{\text{pp}}, \text{spk}, \text{vpk}, m, c, c_{\text{pp}}) \mid \exists (a, b, r, r_{\text{pp}}) : ((\text{pk}_{\text{pp}}, \text{spk}, \text{vpk}, m, c, c_{\text{pp}}), (a, b, r, r_{\text{pp}})) \in R_{\text{DVS}}\}$.

In our scheme a signature consists of two ciphertexts, c and c_{pp}, together with a NIZK proof p which is the key for guaranteeing signature unforgeability. Informally, Π_{NIZK}'s soundness guarantees that, on one hand, since $R_{\text{DVS}} \subseteq R_{\text{DVS-Match}}$, ciphertexts c_{pp} and c encrypt the same bit b, and on the other hand, since $R_{\text{DVS}} \subseteq R_{\text{DVS-Unforg}}$, if this bit b is 1 (in which case the signature verification succeeds), c_{pp} encrypts either the signer's or the verifier's secret key.

4.3   A Conceptually Simple MDVS Construction

We now show how to generalize the DVS scheme from before into an MDVS scheme. Our MDVS scheme construction is defined in Algorithm 2 and is analogous to the DVS scheme from before, but adapted to the multi-verifier case. The main difference is that MDVS schemes need to guarantee consistency.

Algorithm 1. DVS scheme construction $\Pi_{\mathrm{DVS}} = (S, G_S, G_V, Sig, Vfy, Forge)$.

$S(1^k)$
   $(\mathrm{pk}, \mathrm{sk}) \leftarrow \Pi_{\mathrm{PKE}}.G(1^k)$
   return $\mathrm{pp} := (1^k, \mathrm{crs} \leftarrow \Pi_{\mathrm{NIZK}}.G(1^k), \mathrm{pk})$

$G_S(\mathrm{pp})$
   $x \leftarrow \Pi_{\mathrm{OWF}}.S(1^k)$
   return $(\mathrm{spk} := \Pi_{\mathrm{OWF}}.F(x), \mathrm{ssk} := (\mathrm{spk}, x))$

$G_V(\mathrm{pp})$
   $(\mathrm{pk}, \mathrm{sk}) \leftarrow \Pi_{\mathrm{PKE}}.G(1^k)$
   $x \leftarrow \Pi_{\mathrm{OWF}}.S(1^k)$
   return $(\mathrm{vpk} := (\Pi_{\mathrm{OWF}}.F(x), \mathrm{pk}), \mathrm{vsk} := (\mathrm{vpk}, \mathrm{sk}, x))$

$Sig_{\mathrm{pp}}(\mathrm{ssk}, \mathrm{vpk}, m)$
   $c \leftarrow \Pi_{\mathrm{PKE}}.E_{\mathrm{vpk.pk}}(1; r)$
   $c_{\mathrm{pp}} \leftarrow \Pi_{\mathrm{PKE}}.E_{\mathrm{pp.pk}}((m, 1, \mathrm{ssk}.x); r_{\mathrm{pp}})$
   $p \leftarrow \Pi_{\mathrm{NIZK}}.P_{\mathrm{crs}}((\mathrm{pp.pk}, \mathrm{spk}, \mathrm{vpk}, m, c, c_{\mathrm{pp}}) \in L_{\mathrm{DVS}}, (\mathrm{ssk}.x, 1, r, r_{\mathrm{pp}}))$
   return $\sigma := (p, c, c_{\mathrm{pp}})$

$Vfy_{\mathrm{pp}}(\mathrm{spk}, \mathrm{vsk}, m, \sigma := (p, c, c_{\mathrm{pp}}))$
   $b \leftarrow \Pi_{\mathrm{NIZK}}.V_{\mathrm{crs}}((\mathrm{pp.pk}, \mathrm{spk}, \mathrm{vpk}, m, c, c_{\mathrm{pp}}) \in L_{\mathrm{DVS}}, p)$
   return $b \wedge \Pi_{\mathrm{PKE}}.D_{\mathrm{vsk.sk}}(c)$

$Forge_{\mathrm{pp}}(\mathrm{spk}, \mathrm{vpk}, m, \mathrm{vsk})$
   if $\mathrm{vsk} \neq \perp$ **then**   ▷ Forge using verifier's secret key.
      $c \leftarrow \Pi_{\mathrm{PKE}}.E_{\mathrm{vpk.pk}}(1; r)$
      $c_{\mathrm{pp}} \leftarrow \Pi_{\mathrm{PKE}}.E_{\mathrm{pp.pk}}((m, 1, \mathrm{vsk}.x); r_{\mathrm{pp}})$
      $p \leftarrow \Pi_{\mathrm{NIZK}}.P_{\mathrm{crs}}((\mathrm{pp.pk}, \mathrm{spk}, \mathrm{vpk}, m, c, c_{\mathrm{pp}}) \in L_{\mathrm{DVS}}, (\mathrm{vsk}.x, 1, r, r_{\mathrm{pp}}))$
   else   ▷ Forge without using verifier's secret key.
      $c \leftarrow \Pi_{\mathrm{PKE}}.E_{\mathrm{vpk.pk}}(0; r)$
      $c_{\mathrm{pp}} \leftarrow \Pi_{\mathrm{PKE}}.E_{\mathrm{pp.pk}}((m, 0, 0); r_{\mathrm{pp}})$
      $p \leftarrow \Pi_{\mathrm{NIZK}}.P_{\mathrm{crs}}((\mathrm{pp.pk}, \mathrm{spk}, \mathrm{vpk}, m, c, c_{\mathrm{pp}}) \in L_{\mathrm{DVS}}, (0, 0, r, r_{\mathrm{pp}}))$
   return $\sigma := (p, c, c_{\mathrm{pp}})$

In the following, let $\vec{\alpha} := ((b_1, a_1), \ldots, (b_{|\vec{\alpha}|}, a_{|\vec{\alpha}|}))$; we assume for simplicity that all vectors have matching lengths, i.e. $|\vec{v}| = |\vec{c}| = |\vec{\alpha}|$.

- $R_{\mathrm{MDVS^{static}\text{-}Match}} := \Big\{ ((\mathrm{pk}_{\mathrm{pp}}, \mathrm{spk}, \vec{v}, m, \vec{c}, c_{\mathrm{pp}}), (\vec{\alpha}, \vec{r}, r_{\mathrm{pp}}, b)) :$

$$\Big[c_{\mathrm{pp}} = \Pi_{\mathrm{PKE}}.E_{\mathrm{pk}_{\mathrm{pp}}}((m, b, \vec{\alpha}); r_{\mathrm{pp}}) \Big] \wedge \Big[\bigwedge_{i \in \{1, \ldots, |\vec{v}|\}} (c_i = \Pi_{\mathrm{PKE}}.E_{v_i.\mathrm{pk}}(b_i; r_i)) \Big] \Big\}$$

- $R_{\mathrm{MDVS^{static}\text{-}Unforg}} := \Big\{ ((\mathrm{pk}_{\mathrm{pp}}, \mathrm{spk}, \vec{v}, m, \vec{c}, c_{\mathrm{pp}}), (\vec{\alpha}, \vec{r}, r_{\mathrm{pp}}, b)) :$

$$\bigwedge_{i \in \{1, \ldots, |\vec{v}|\}} \Big((b_i = 1) \rightarrow (\Pi_{\mathrm{OWF}}.F(a_i) \in \{\mathrm{spk}.y, v_i.y\}) \Big) \Big\}$$

- $R_{\mathrm{MDVS^{static}\text{-}Cons}} := \Big\{ ((\mathrm{pk}_{\mathrm{pp}}, \mathrm{spk}, \vec{v}, m, \vec{c}, c_{\mathrm{pp}}), (\vec{\alpha}, \vec{r}, r_{\mathrm{pp}}, b)) :$

$$\bigwedge_{i \in \{1, \ldots, |\vec{v}|\}} ((\Pi_{\mathrm{OWF}}.F(a_i) \neq v_i.y) \rightarrow (b_i = b)) \Big\}.$$

Similarly to R_{DVS}, and for the sake of modularity, we define relation $R_{\text{MDVS}^{\text{static}}}$ as $R_{\text{MDVS}^{\text{static}}} := R_{\text{MDVS}^{\text{static}}\text{-Match}} \cap R_{\text{MDVS}^{\text{static}}\text{-Unforg}} \cap R_{\text{MDVS}^{\text{static}}\text{-Cons}}$. In Algorithm 2, we consider the respective induced language $L_{\text{MDVS}^{\text{static}}} := \{(\text{pk}_{\text{pp}}, \text{spk}, \vec{v}, m, \vec{c}, c_{\text{pp}}) \mid \exists (\vec{\alpha}, \vec{r}, r_{\text{pp}}, b) : ((\text{pk}_{\text{pp}}, \text{spk}, \vec{v}, m, \vec{c}, c_{\text{pp}}), (\vec{\alpha}, \vec{r}, r_{\text{pp}}, b)) \in R_{\text{MDVS}^{\text{static}}}\}$.

Note that, since $R_{\text{MDVS}^{\text{static}}} \subseteq R_{\text{MDVS}^{\text{static}}\text{-Match}} \cap R_{\text{MDVS}^{\text{static}}\text{-Unforg}}$, Π_{NIZK}'s soundness guarantees that if for any $i \in \{1, \ldots, |\vec{v}|\}$, c_i is an encryption of 1, then c_{pp} contains either the signer's secret key or the i-th verifier's secret key. Similarly, since $R_{\text{MDVS}^{\text{static}}} \subseteq R_{\text{MDVS}^{\text{static}}\text{-Match}} \cap R_{\text{MDVS}^{\text{static}}\text{-Cons}}$, Π_{NIZK}'s soundness implies that every designated verifier B_j whose secret key is not in c_{pp}'s underlying plaintext will agree on whether the signature is valid.

4.4 Achieving Tight Security Under Adaptive Corruptions

We now show how to transform the MDVS scheme from before into one that is tightly secure under adaptive corruptions. The main challenge here is finding a way to embed the challenges from the security games of the underlying PKE and OWF building blocks into the reductions (in such a way that the reduction is tight on the security of the underlying building blocks) while still being able to answer queries for the secret keys of signers and/or verifiers. To achieve this, we rely on a technique that was first introduced in [1]. Essentially, for each party two key-pairs are now sampled; the party's public key are the public keys of each of the underlying key-pairs, and the secret key is the secret key of one (and only one) of these key-pairs. This allows answering secret key queries by the adversary while still being able to embed challenges from the underlying security games into reductions.

Let $\vec{\alpha} := ((b_1, a_1), \ldots, (b_{|\vec{\alpha}|}, a_{|\vec{\alpha}|}))$; in the following, vectors are assumed to have matching lengths:

- $R_{\text{MDVS}^{\text{adap}}\text{-Match}} := \Big\{ ((\text{pp.pk}, \text{spk}, \vec{v}, m, \vec{c}, c_{\text{pp}}), (\vec{\alpha}, \vec{r}, r_{\text{pp}}, b)) :$

$(c_{\text{pp}} = \Pi_{\text{PKE}}.E_{\text{pp.pk}}((m, b, \vec{\alpha}); r_{\text{pp}})) \bigwedge$

$\left[\bigwedge_{i \in \{1, \ldots, |\vec{v}|\}} ((c_{i,0} = \Pi_{\text{PKE}}.E_{v_i.\text{pk}_0}(b_i; r_{i,0})) \wedge (c_{i,1} = \Pi_{\text{PKE}}.E_{v_i.\text{pk}_1}(b_i; r_{i,1}))) \right] \Big\}$

- $R_{\text{MDVS}^{\text{adap}}\text{-Unforg}} := \Big\{ ((\text{pp.pk}, \text{spk}, \vec{v}, m, \vec{c}, c_{\text{pp}}), (\vec{\alpha}, \vec{r}, r_{\text{pp}}, b)) :$

$\bigwedge_{i \in \{1, \ldots, |\vec{\alpha}|\}} \Big((b_i = 1) \to (\Pi_{\text{OWF}}.F(a_i) \in \{\text{spk}.y_0, \text{spk}.y_1, v_i.y_0, v_i.y_1\}) \Big) \Big\}$

- $R_{\text{MDVS}^{\text{adap}}\text{-Cons}} := \Big\{ ((\text{pp.pk}, \text{spk}, \vec{v}, m, \vec{c}, c_{\text{pp}}), (\vec{\alpha}, \vec{r}, r_{\text{pp}}, b)) :$

$\bigwedge_{i \in \{1, \ldots, |\vec{\alpha}|\}} \Big((\Pi_{\text{OWF}}.F(a_i) \notin \{v_i.y_0, v_i.y_1\}) \to (b_i = b) \Big) \Big\}.$

Algorithm 2. $\Pi_{\mathrm{MDVS}}^{\mathrm{stat}}$.

$S(1^k)$
    $(\mathrm{pk}, \mathrm{sk}) \leftarrow \Pi_{\mathrm{PKE}}.G(1^k)$
    return $\mathrm{pp} := (1^k, \mathrm{crs} \leftarrow \Pi_{\mathrm{NIZK}}.G(1^k), \mathrm{pk})$

$G_S(\mathrm{pp})$
    $x \leftarrow \Pi_{\mathrm{OWF}}.S(1^k)$
    return $(\mathrm{spk} := \Pi_{\mathrm{OWF}}.F(x), \mathrm{ssk} := (\mathrm{spk}, x))$

$G_V(\mathrm{pp})$
    $(\mathrm{pk}, \mathrm{sk}) \leftarrow \Pi_{\mathrm{PKE}}.G(1^k)$
    $x \leftarrow \Pi_{\mathrm{OWF}}.S(1^k)$
    return $(\mathrm{vpk} := (\Pi_{\mathrm{OWF}}.F(x), \mathrm{pk}), \mathrm{vsk} := (\mathrm{vpk}, \mathrm{sk}, x))$

$Sig_{\mathrm{pp}}(\mathrm{ssk}, \vec{v} := (\mathrm{vpk}_1, \ldots, \mathrm{vpk}_{|\vec{v}|}), m)$
    for each $i \in \{1, \ldots, |\vec{v}|\}$ **do**
        $c_i \leftarrow \Pi_{\mathrm{PKE}}.E_{v_i.\mathrm{pk}}(1; r_i)$
    $(\vec{c}, \vec{r}) \leftarrow ((c_1, \ldots, c_{|\vec{v}|}), (r_1, \ldots, r_{|\vec{v}|}))$
    $\vec{\alpha} \leftarrow (\alpha_1 := (1, \mathrm{ssk}.x), \ldots, \alpha_{|\vec{v}|} := (1, \mathrm{ssk}.x))$
    $c_{\mathrm{pp}} \leftarrow \Pi_{\mathrm{PKE}}.E_{\mathrm{pp}.\mathrm{pk}}((m, 1, \vec{\alpha}); r_{\mathrm{pp}})$
    $p \leftarrow \Pi_{\mathrm{NIZK}}.P_{\mathrm{crs}}((\mathrm{pp}.\mathrm{pk}, \mathrm{spk}, \vec{v}, m, \vec{c}, c_{\mathrm{pp}}) \in L_{\mathrm{MDVS^{static}}}, (\vec{\alpha}, \vec{r}, r_{\mathrm{pp}}, 1))$
    return $\sigma := (p, \vec{c}, c_{\mathrm{pp}})$

$Vfy_{\mathrm{pp}}(\mathrm{spk}, \mathrm{vsk}, \vec{v}, m, \sigma := (p, \vec{c}, c_{\mathrm{pp}}))$
    if $\Pi_{\mathrm{NIZK}}.V_{\mathrm{crs}}((\mathrm{pp}.\mathrm{pk}, \mathrm{spk}, \vec{v}, m, \vec{c}, c_{\mathrm{pp}}) \in L_{\mathrm{MDVS^{static}}}, p) = 1$ **then**
        for $i = 1, \ldots, |\vec{v}|$ **do**
            if $\mathrm{vsk}.\mathrm{vpk} = v_i$ **then**
                return $\Pi_{\mathrm{PKE}}.D_{\mathrm{vsk}.\mathrm{sk}}(c_i)$
    return 0

$Forge_{\mathrm{pp}}(\mathrm{spk}, \vec{v}, m, \vec{s} := (\mathrm{vsk}_1, \ldots, \mathrm{vsk}_{|\vec{v}|}))$
    for each $i \in \{1, \ldots, |\vec{v}|\}$ **do**
        if $s_i \neq \perp$ **then**
            $c_i \leftarrow \Pi_{\mathrm{PKE}}.E_{v_i.\mathrm{pk}}(1; r_i)$
            $\alpha_i \leftarrow (1, s_i.x)$
        else
            $c_i \leftarrow \Pi_{\mathrm{PKE}}.E_{v_i.\mathrm{pk}}(0; r_i)$
            $\alpha_i \leftarrow (0, 0)$
    $(\vec{c}, \vec{r}) \leftarrow ((c_1, \ldots, c_{|\vec{v}|}), (r_1, \ldots, r_{|\vec{v}|}))$
    $\vec{\alpha} \leftarrow (\alpha_1, \ldots, \alpha_{|\vec{v}|})$
    $c_{\mathrm{pp}} \leftarrow \Pi_{\mathrm{PKE}}.E_{\mathrm{pp}.\mathrm{pk}}((m, 0, \vec{\alpha}); r_{\mathrm{pp}})$
    $p \leftarrow \Pi_{\mathrm{NIZK}}.P_{\mathrm{crs}}((\mathrm{pp}.\mathrm{pk}, \mathrm{spk}, \vec{v}, m, \vec{c}, c_{\mathrm{pp}}) \in L_{\mathrm{MDVS^{static}}}, (\vec{\alpha}, \vec{r}, r_{\mathrm{pp}}, 0))$
    return $\sigma := (p, \vec{c}, c_{\mathrm{pp}})$

As in Sect. 4.3, we define $R_{\mathrm{MDVS^{adap}}} := R_{\mathrm{MDVS^{adap}\text{-}Match}} \cap R_{\mathrm{MDVS^{adap}\text{-}Unforg}} \cap R_{\mathrm{MDVS^{adap}\text{-}Cons}}$; in Algorithm 3, we consider the language $L_{\mathrm{MDVS^{adap}}}$ that is induced by $R_{\mathrm{MDVS^{adap}}}$, which is defined as: $L_{\mathrm{MDVS^{adap}}} := \{(\mathrm{pp}.\mathrm{pk}, \mathrm{spk}, \vec{v}, m, \vec{c}, c_{\mathrm{pp}}) \mid \exists (\vec{\alpha}, \vec{r}, r_{\mathrm{pp}}, b) : ((\mathrm{pp}.\mathrm{pk}, \mathrm{spk}, \vec{v}, m, \vec{c}, c_{\mathrm{pp}}), (\vec{\alpha}, \vec{r}, r_{\mathrm{pp}}, b)) \in R_{\mathrm{MDVS^{adap}}}\}$.

4.4.1 Security Analysis of $\Pi_{\mathrm{MDVS}}^{\mathrm{adap}}$

The theorem below gives an informal summary of our construction's security properties. See [3] for the formal security theorems and the corresponding full proofs.

Theorem 1 (Informal). *If Π_{PKE} is correct and tightly multi-user and multi-challenge IND-CPA and IK-CPA secure under non-adaptive corruptions, Π_{NIZK} is complete, sound, tightly multi-statement adaptive zero-knowledge and tightly*

Algorithm 3. The $\Pi_{\mathrm{MDVS}}^{\mathrm{adap}}$ MDVS scheme.

$S(1^k)$
  $(\mathsf{pk}, \mathsf{sk}) \leftarrow \Pi_{\mathrm{PKE}}.G(1^k)$
  return $\mathsf{pp} := (1^k, \mathsf{crs} \leftarrow \Pi_{\mathrm{NIZK}}.G(1^k), \mathsf{pk})$

$G_S(\mathsf{pp})$
  $(x_0, x_1) \leftarrow (\Pi_{\mathrm{OWF}}.S(1^k), \Pi_{\mathrm{OWF}}.S(1^k))$
  $(y_0, y_1) \leftarrow (\Pi_{\mathrm{OWF}}.F(x_0), \Pi_{\mathrm{OWF}}.F(x_1))$
  $b \leftarrow RandomCoin$
  return $(\mathsf{spk} := (y_0, y_1), \mathsf{ssk} := (\mathsf{spk}, x := x_b))$

$G_V(\mathsf{pp})$
  $((\mathsf{pk}_0, \mathsf{sk}_0), (\mathsf{pk}_1, \mathsf{sk}_1)) \leftarrow (\Pi_{\mathrm{PKE}}.G(1^k), \Pi_{\mathrm{PKE}}.G(1^k))$
  $(x_0, x_1) \leftarrow (\Pi_{\mathrm{OWF}}.S(1^k), \Pi_{\mathrm{OWF}}.S(1^k))$
  $(y_0, y_1) \leftarrow (\Pi_{\mathrm{OWF}}.F(x_0), \Pi_{\mathrm{OWF}}.F(x_1))$
  $b \leftarrow RandomCoin$
  return $(\mathsf{vpk} := (\mathsf{pk}_0, y_0, \mathsf{pk}_1, y_1), \mathsf{vsk} := (\mathsf{vpk}, b, \mathsf{sk} := \mathsf{sk}_b, x := x_b))$

$Sig_{\mathsf{pp}}(\mathsf{ssk}, \vec{v} := (\mathsf{vpk}_1, \dots, \mathsf{vpk}_{|\vec{v}|}), m)$
  for each $i \in \{1, \dots, |\vec{v}|\}$ do
    $(c_{i,0}, c_{i,1}) \leftarrow (\Pi_{\mathrm{PKE}}.E_{v_i.\mathsf{pk}_0}(1; r_{i,0}), \Pi_{\mathrm{PKE}}.E_{v_i.\mathsf{pk}_1}(1; r_{i,1}))$
  $(\vec{c}, \vec{r}) \leftarrow (((c_{1,0}, c_{1,1}), \dots, (c_{|\vec{v}|,0}, c_{|\vec{v}|,1})), ((r_{1,0}, r_{1,1}), \dots, (r_{|\vec{v}|,0}, r_{|\vec{v}|,1})))$
  $\vec{\alpha} \leftarrow (\alpha_1 := (1, \mathsf{ssk}.x), \dots, \alpha_{|\vec{v}|} := (1, \mathsf{ssk}.x))$
  $c_{\mathsf{pp}} \leftarrow \Pi_{\mathrm{PKE}}.E_{\mathsf{pp}.\mathsf{pk}}((m, 1, \vec{\alpha}); r_{\mathsf{pp}})$
  $p \leftarrow \Pi_{\mathrm{NIZK}}.P_{\mathsf{crs}}((\mathsf{pp}.\mathsf{pk}, \mathsf{spk}, \vec{v}, m, \vec{c}, c_{\mathsf{pp}}) \in L_{\mathrm{MDVS}^{\mathrm{adap}}}, (\vec{\alpha}, \vec{r}, r_{\mathsf{pp}}, 1))$
  return $\sigma := (p, \vec{c}, c_{\mathsf{pp}})$

$Vfy_{\mathsf{pp}}(\mathsf{spk}, \mathsf{vsk}, \vec{v}, m, \sigma := (p, \vec{c}, c_{\mathsf{pp}}))$
  if $\Pi_{\mathrm{NIZK}}.V_{\mathsf{crs}}((\mathsf{pp}.\mathsf{pk}, \mathsf{spk}, \vec{v}, m, \vec{c}, c_{\mathsf{pp}}) \in L_{\mathrm{MDVS}^{\mathrm{adap}}}, p) = 1$ then
    for $i = 1, \dots, |\vec{v}|$ do
      if $\mathsf{vsk}.\mathsf{vpk} = v_i$ then
        return $\Pi_{\mathrm{PKE}}.D_{\mathsf{vsk}.\mathsf{sk}}(c_{i,\mathsf{vsk}.b})$
  return 0

$Forge_{\mathsf{pp}}(\mathsf{spk}, \vec{v}, m, \vec{s} := (\mathsf{vsk}_1, \dots, \mathsf{vsk}_{|\vec{v}|}))$
  for each $i \in \{1, \dots, |\vec{v}|\}$ do
    if $s_i \neq \bot$ then
      $(c_{i,0}, c_{i,1}) \leftarrow (\Pi_{\mathrm{PKE}}.E_{v_i.\mathsf{pk}_0}(1; r_{i,0}), \Pi_{\mathrm{PKE}}.E_{v_i.\mathsf{pk}_1}(1; r_{i,1}))$
      $\alpha_i := (1, s_i.x)$
    else
      $(c_{i,0}, c_{i,1}) \leftarrow (\Pi_{\mathrm{PKE}}.E_{v_i.\mathsf{pk}_0}(0; r_{i,0}), \Pi_{\mathrm{PKE}}.E_{v_i.\mathsf{pk}_1}(0; r_{i,1}))$
      $\alpha_i := (0, 0)$
  $(\vec{c}, \vec{r}) \leftarrow (((c_{1,0}, c_{1,1}), \dots, (c_{|\vec{v}|,0}, c_{|\vec{v}|,1})), ((r_{1,0}, r_{1,1}), \dots, (r_{|\vec{v}|,0}, r_{|\vec{v}|,1})))$
  $\vec{\alpha} \leftarrow (\alpha_1, \dots, \alpha_{|\vec{v}|})$
  $c_{\mathsf{pp}} \leftarrow \Pi_{\mathrm{PKE}}.E_{\mathsf{pp}.\mathsf{pk}}((m, 0, \vec{\alpha}); r_{\mathsf{pp}})$
  $p \leftarrow \Pi_{\mathrm{NIZK}}.P_{\mathsf{crs}}((\mathsf{pp}.\mathsf{pk}, \mathsf{spk}, \vec{v}, m, \vec{c}, c_{\mathsf{pp}}) \in L_{\mathrm{MDVS}^{\mathrm{adap}}}, (\vec{\alpha}, \vec{r}, r_{\mathsf{pp}}, 0))$
  return $\sigma := (p, \vec{c}, c_{\mathsf{pp}})$

---

multi-statement simulation sound, and Π_{OWF} *is tightly multi-instance secure under* non-adaptive *corruptions, then* $\Pi_{\mathrm{MDVS}}^{\mathrm{adap}}$ *is:*

1. *tightly correct;*
2. *tightly consistent under adaptive corruptions;*
3. *tightly unforgeable under adaptive corruptions; and*
4. *tightly off-the-record under adaptive corruptions.*

4.4.2 On Efficiently Instantiating the NIZK Relations

All the relations we consider consist of checking a number of equations over a pairing-friendly group, when implemented with suitably algebraic primitives.

(For instance, we can use ElGamal [6] as the PKE scheme, and a pairing with one fixed input as the One Way Function). Then, we can use a simulation-sound variant of Groth-Sahai proofs [8,9] as a compatible NIZK scheme to prove these relations. This yields proofs that are only linear-sized in the number of witness variables and equations. Of course, this will result in an unoptimized solution that may not be quite practical yet.

5   PKEBC Scheme with Linear Ciphertext Size and Decryption Time

A PKEBC scheme Π is a quadruple $\Pi = (S, G, E, D)$ of PPTs, where:

- S: on input 1^k, generates public parameters pp;
- G: on input pp, generates a receiver key-pair (pk, sk);
- E: on input $(\text{pp}, \vec{v}, m)$, where $\vec{v}$ is a vector of public keys of the intended receivers and m is the message, generates a ciphertext c;
- D: on input $(\text{pp}, \text{sk}, c)$, where sk is the receiver's secret key, D decrypts c using sk, and outputs the decrypted receiver-vector/message pair $(\vec{v}, m)$ (or $\perp$ if the ciphertext did not decrypt correctly).

In this section we introduce new security notions capturing the security of PKEBC schemes under adaptive corruptions and give a new construction of a PKEBC scheme that not only is tightly secure under these stronger notions, but also for which both the ciphertext size and the decryption time only grow linearly with the number of receivers.

5.1   Security Notions for Adaptive Corruptions

The security notions we now introduce are a strengthening of the original ones introduced by Maurer et al. in [15], but capturing the security of PKEBC schemes under adaptive corruptions. More concretely, in the Correctness, Robustness and Consistency notions adversaries are now allowed to query for the secret keys of any receiver and still win the game; in the (IND + IK)-CCA-2^{adap} security games— a combination of the original IND-CCA-2 and IK-CCA-2 security notions [15] capturing adaptive corruptions—adversaries can now corrupt parties adaptively. (Our (IND + IK)-CCA-2^{adap} security notion can also be interpreted as a variant of the notion introduced by Lee et al. in [12]—which captures the IND-CCA-2 security of PKE schemes under adaptive corruptions—but adapted for PKEBC schemes and also capturing anonymity).

We now introduce some oracles that the game systems ahead provide to the adversaries. In the following, consider a PKEBC scheme $\Pi = (S, G, E, D)$ with message space $\mathcal{M}$. The oracles below are defined for a game-system with (an implicitly defined) security parameter k:

Public Parameters Oracle: $\mathcal{O}_{PP}$
    1. On the first call, compute and store pp $\leftarrow S(1^k)$; output pp;

2. On subsequent calls, output the previously generated pp.

Secret Key Generation Oracle: $\mathcal{O}_{SK}(B_j)$

1. If $\mathcal{O}_{SK}$ was queried on B_j before, simply look up and return the previously generated key for B_j;
2. Otherwise, store $(\mathrm{pk}_j, \mathrm{sk}_j) \leftarrow G(\mathrm{pp})$ as B_j's key-pair, and output $(\mathrm{pk}_j, \mathrm{sk}_j)$.

Public Key Generation Oracle: $\mathcal{O}_{PK}(B_j)$

1. $(\mathrm{pk}_j, \mathrm{sk}_j) \leftarrow \mathcal{O}_{SK}(B_j)$;
2. Output pk_j.

Encryption Oracle: $\mathcal{O}_E(\vec{V}, m)$

1. $\vec{v} \leftarrow (\mathcal{O}_{PK}(V_1), \ldots, \mathcal{O}_{PK}(V_{|\vec{V}|}))$;
2. Create and output a fresh encryption $c \leftarrow E_{\mathrm{pp},\vec{v}}(m)$.

Decryption Oracle: $\mathcal{O}_D(B_j, c)$

1. Query $\mathcal{O}_{SK}(B_j)$ to obtain the corresponding secret-key sk_j;
2. Decrypt c using sk_j, $(\vec{v}, m) \leftarrow D_{\mathrm{pp},\mathrm{sk}_j}(c)$, and then output the resulting receivers-message pair $(\vec{v}, m)$, or $\perp$ (if $(\vec{v}, m) = \perp$, i.e. the ciphertext is not valid with respect to B_j's secret key).

Definition 5 (Correctness). *Game* $\mathbf{G}^{\mathsf{Corr}}$ *provides an adversary* $\mathbf{A}$ *with access to oracles* $\mathcal{O}_{PP}, \mathcal{O}_{SK}, \mathcal{O}_{PK}, \mathcal{O}_E$ *and* $\mathcal{O}_D$. $\mathbf{A}$ *wins the game if there are two queries* q_E *and* q_D *to* $\mathcal{O}_E$ *and* $\mathcal{O}_D$, *respectively, where* q_E *has input* $(\vec{V}, m)$ *and* q_D *has input* (B_j, c), *satisfying* $B_j \in \vec{V}$, *the input* c *in* q_D *is the output of* q_E, *and the output of* q_D *is either* $\perp$ *or* $(\vec{v}', m')$ *with* $(\vec{v}, m) \neq (\vec{v}', m')$. *The advantage of* $\mathbf{A}$ *in winning the Correctness game, denoted* $Adv^{\mathsf{Corr}}(\mathbf{A})$, *is the probability that* $\mathbf{A}$ *wins game* $\mathbf{G}^{\mathsf{Corr}}$ *as described above.*

An adversary $\mathbf{A}$ $(\varepsilon_{\mathsf{Corr}}, t)$-breaks the (n, d_E, q_E, q_D)-Correctness of a PKEBC scheme Π if $\mathbf{A}$ runs in time at most t, queries $\mathcal{O}_{SK}, \mathcal{O}_{PK}, \mathcal{O}_E$ and $\mathcal{O}_D$ on at most n different parties, makes at most q_E and q_D queries to $\mathcal{O}_E$ and $\mathcal{O}_D$, respectively, with the sum of lengths of the party vectors input to $\mathcal{O}_E$ being at most d_E, and satisfies $Adv^{\mathsf{Corr}}(\mathbf{A}) \geq \varepsilon_{\mathsf{Corr}}$.

Definition 6 (Robustness). *Game* $\mathbf{G}^{\mathsf{Rob}}$ *provides an adversary* $\mathbf{A}$ *with access to oracles* $\mathcal{O}_{PP}, \mathcal{O}_{SK}, \mathcal{O}_{PK}, \mathcal{O}_E$ *and* $\mathcal{O}_D$. $\mathbf{A}$ *wins the game if there are two queries* q_E *and* q_D *to* $\mathcal{O}_E$ *and* $\mathcal{O}_D$, *respectively, where* q_E *has input* $(\vec{V}, m)$ *and* q_D *has input* (B_j, c), *satisfying* $B_j \notin \vec{V}$, *the input* c *in* q_D *is the output of* q_E, *and the output of* q_D *is* $(\vec{v}', m')$ *with* $(\vec{v}', m') \neq \perp$. *The advantage of* $\mathbf{A}$ *in winning the Robustness game is the probability that* $\mathbf{A}$ *wins game* $\mathbf{G}^{\mathsf{Rob}}$ *as described above, and is denoted* $Adv^{\mathsf{Rob}}(\mathbf{A})$.

An adversary $\mathbf{A}$ $(\varepsilon_{\mathsf{Rob}}, t)$-breaks the Robustness of a PKEBC scheme Π if $\mathbf{A}$ runs in time at most t and satisfies $Adv^{\mathsf{Rob}}(\mathbf{A}) \geq \varepsilon_{\mathsf{Rob}}$.

Definition 7 (Consistency). *Game* $\mathbf{G}^{\mathsf{Cons}}$ *provides an adversary* $\mathbf{A}$ *with access to oracles* $\mathcal{O}_{PP}, \mathcal{O}_{SK}, \mathcal{O}_{PK}$ *and* $\mathcal{O}_D$. $\mathbf{A}$ *wins the game if there is a ciphertext* c *such that* $\mathcal{O}_D$ *is queried on inputs* (B_i, c) *and* (B_j, c) *for some* B_i *and* B_j *(possibly with* $B_i = B_j$*), query* $\mathcal{O}_D(B_i, c)$ *outputs some* $(\vec{v}, m)$ *satisfying* $(\vec{v}, m) \neq$

$\perp$ with $\mathtt{pk}_j \in \vec{v}$ (where $\mathtt{pk}_j$ is B_j's public key), and query $\mathcal{O}_D(B_j, c)$ does not output $(\vec{v}, m)$. The advantage of $\mathbf{A}$ in winning the Consistency game is denoted $Adv^{\mathsf{Cons}}(\mathbf{A})$ and corresponds to the probability that $\mathbf{A}$ wins game $\mathbf{G}^{\mathsf{Cons}}$.

We say that an adversary $\mathbf{A}$ ($\varepsilon_{\mathsf{Cons}}, t$)-breaks the (n, q_D)-Consistency of Π if $\mathbf{A}$ runs in time at most t, queries $\mathcal{O}_{SK}$, $\mathcal{O}_{PK}$ and $\mathcal{O}_D$ on at most n different parties, makes at most q_D queries to $\mathcal{O}_D$ and satisfies $Adv^{\mathsf{Cons}}(\mathbf{A}) \geq \varepsilon_{\mathsf{Cons}}$.

Below we present the definition of $(\mathsf{IND} + \mathsf{IK})\text{-}\mathsf{CCA\text{-}2}^{\mathsf{adap}}$ security. This notion is a combination of the original IND-CCA-2 and IK-CCA-2 security notions introduced in [15] that captures adaptive security (i.e. the adversary is allowed to corrupt parties adaptively). The games defined by this definition provide adversaries with access to the oracles $\mathcal{O}_{PP}$, $\mathcal{O}_{SK}$ and $\mathcal{O}_{PK}$ defined above, as well as to oracles $\mathcal{O}_E$ and $\mathcal{O}_D$ defined below:

Encryption Oracle: $\mathcal{O}_E((\vec{V}_0, m_0), (\vec{V}_1, m_1))$
1. For game system $\mathbf{G}_{\mathsf{b}}^{(\mathsf{IND}+\mathsf{IK})\text{-}\mathsf{CCA\text{-}2}^{\mathsf{adap}}}$, encrypt m_{b} under $\vec{v}_{\mathsf{b}}$, the vector of public keys corresponding to $\vec{V}_{\mathsf{b}}$; output c.

Decryption Oracle: $\mathcal{O}_D(B_j, c)$
1. If c was the output of some query to $\mathcal{O}_E$, output $\mathtt{test}$;
2. Otherwise, compute and output $(\vec{v}, m) \leftarrow D_{\mathsf{pp},\mathsf{sk}_j}(c)$, where sk_j is B_j's secret key.

Definition 8 $((\mathsf{IND} + \mathsf{IK})\text{-}\mathsf{CCA\text{-}2}^{\mathsf{adap}}$ **Security).** *For* $\mathsf{b} \in \{0, 1\}$, *game system* $\mathbf{G}_{\mathsf{b}}^{(\mathsf{IND}+\mathsf{IK})\text{-}\mathsf{CCA\text{-}2}^{\mathsf{adap}}}$ *provides an adversary* $\mathbf{A}$ *with access to oracles* $\mathcal{O}_{PP}$, $\mathcal{O}_{SK}$, $\mathcal{O}_{PK}$, $\mathcal{O}_E$ *and* $\mathcal{O}_D$. $\mathbf{A}$ *wins the game if it outputs a guess bit* b' *satisfying* $b' = \mathsf{b}$ *and for every query* $\mathcal{O}_E((\vec{V}_0, m_0), (\vec{V}_1, m_1))$: 1. $\left|\vec{V}_0\right| = \left|\vec{V}_1\right|$; 2. $|m_0| = |m_1|$; and 3. *there is no query to* $\mathcal{O}_{SK}$ *on any* $B_j \in Set(\vec{V}_0) \cup Set(\vec{V}_1)$ *at any point during the game. We define the advantage of* $\mathbf{A}$ *in winning the* $(\mathsf{IND} + \mathsf{IK})\text{-}\mathsf{CCA\text{-}2}^{\mathsf{adap}}$ *game as*

$$Adv^{(\mathsf{IND}+\mathsf{IK})\text{-}\mathsf{CCA\text{-}2}^{\mathsf{adap}}}(\mathbf{A}) :=$$
$$\left| \Pr[\mathbf{AG}_0^{(\mathsf{IND}+\mathsf{IK})\text{-}\mathsf{CCA\text{-}2}^{\mathsf{adap}}} = \mathtt{win}] + \Pr[\mathbf{AG}_1^{(\mathsf{IND}+\mathsf{IK})\text{-}\mathsf{CCA\text{-}2}^{\mathsf{adap}}} = \mathtt{win}] - 1 \right|.$$

We say that an adversary $\mathbf{A}$ (ε, t)-breaks the (n, d_E, q_E, q_D)-$(\mathsf{IND} + \mathsf{IK})$-$\mathsf{CCA\text{-}2}^{\mathsf{adap}}$ security of Π if $\mathbf{A}$ runs in time at most t, queries the oracles it has access to on at most n different parties, makes at most q_E and q_D queries to oracles $\mathcal{O}_E$ and $\mathcal{O}_D$, respectively, with the sum of lengths of all the party vectors input to $\mathcal{O}_E$ being at most d_E, and satisfies $Adv^{(\mathsf{IND}+\mathsf{IK})\text{-}\mathsf{CCA\text{-}2}^{\mathsf{adap}}}(\mathbf{A}) \geq \varepsilon$. Finally, we say that Π is

$$(\varepsilon_{\mathsf{Corr}}, \varepsilon_{\mathsf{Rob}}, \varepsilon_{\mathsf{Cons}}, \varepsilon_{(\mathsf{IND}+\mathsf{IK})\text{-}\mathsf{CCA\text{-}2}^{\mathsf{adap}}}, t, n, d_E, q_E, q_D, \mathsf{adap})\text{-secure},$$

if there is no adversary $\mathbf{A}$ that: 1. $(\varepsilon_{\mathsf{Corr}}, t)$-breaks Π's (n, d_E, q_E, q_D)-Correctness; 2. $(\varepsilon_{\mathsf{Rob}}, t)$-breaks Π's Robustness; 3. $(\varepsilon_{\mathsf{Cons}}, t)$-breaks Π's (n, q_D)-Consistency; or 4. $(\varepsilon_{(\mathsf{IND}+\mathsf{IK})\text{-}\mathsf{CCA\text{-}2}^{\mathsf{adap}}}, t)$-breaks Π's (n, d_E, q_E, q_D)-$(\mathsf{IND} + \mathsf{IK})$-$\mathsf{CCA\text{-}2}^{\mathsf{adap}}$ security.

5.2 Achieving Linear Ciphertext Size

As before, we present our PKEBC construction incrementally (and only prove the security of the final PKEBC construction given Sect. 5.4). Our first PKEBC scheme is defined in Algorithm 4. Like Maurer et al.'s scheme [15], our construction is a generalization of Naor-Yung's PKE scheme for multiple receivers (see [17]). However, while Maurer et al.'s scheme encrypts, for each receiver, the vector of all receivers' public keys plus the message—leading not only to quadratic sized ciphertexts but also to quadratic encryption and decryption time—our scheme instead relies on a SKE scheme Π_{SKE} to encrypt the vector of all receivers plus the message under a key k that is then encrypted under each receiver's public key, resembling the hybrid encryption technique [19]. Furthermore, while Maurer et al.'s construction relies on a binding commitment scheme in order to achieve consistency, our scheme instead uses a PKE scheme: note that as long as a PKE key-pair $(\mathrm{pk}, \mathrm{sk})$ is sampled honestly, by the correctness of the PKE scheme, the encryption of any message m under pk also works as a commitment to m.[6] The building blocks of this first scheme consist of a PKE scheme $\Pi_{\mathrm{PKE}} = (G, E, D)$, a SKE scheme $\Pi_{\mathrm{SKE}} = (G, E, D)$ and a NIZK scheme $\Pi_{\mathrm{NIZK}} = (G, P, V, S := (S_G, S_P))$. In the following, vectors are assumed to have matching lengths; consider relation $R_{\mathrm{PKEBC^{lin\text{-}ctxt}}}$ defined as

$$R_{\mathrm{PKEBC^{lin\text{-}ctxt}}} := \Big\{ ((1^k, \mathrm{pk}_{\mathrm{pp}}, c_{\mathrm{pp}}, \vec{c}, c_{\mathrm{sym}}), (\vec{v}, m, r_{\mathrm{pp}}, \vec{r}, r_{\mathrm{sym}}, r_{\mathrm{sym}}')) : \tag{5.1}$$

$$(k_{\mathrm{sym}} = \Pi_{\mathrm{SKE}}.G(1^k; r_{\mathrm{sym}})) \wedge (c_{\mathrm{sym}} = \Pi_{\mathrm{SKE}}.E(k_{\mathrm{sym}}, (r_{\mathrm{pp}}, \vec{v}, m); r_{\mathrm{sym}}')) \wedge$$

$$\left[\bigwedge_{j \in \{1, \dots, |\vec{c}|\}} (c_j = \Pi_{\mathrm{PKE}}.E_{v_j}(k_{\mathrm{sym}}; r_j)) \right] \wedge (c_{\mathrm{pp}} = \Pi_{\mathrm{PKE}}.E_{\mathrm{pk}_{\mathrm{pp}}}((\vec{v}, m); r_{\mathrm{pp}})) \Big\}.$$

In Algorithm 4, we consider the language $L_{\mathrm{PKEBC^{lin\text{-}ctxt}}}$ that is induced by relation $R_{\mathrm{PKEBC^{lin\text{-}ctxt}}}$: $L_{\mathrm{PKEBC^{lin\text{-}ctxt}}} := \{ (1^k, \mathrm{pk}_{\mathrm{pp}}, c_{\mathrm{pp}}, \vec{c}, c_{\mathrm{sym}}) \mid \exists (\vec{v}, m, r_{\mathrm{pp}}, \vec{r}, r_{\mathrm{sym}}, r_{\mathrm{sym}}') : ((1^k, \mathrm{pk}_{\mathrm{pp}}, c_{\mathrm{pp}}, \vec{c}, c_{\mathrm{sym}}), (\vec{v}, m, r_{\mathrm{pp}}, \vec{r}, r_{\mathrm{sym}}, r_{\mathrm{sym}}')) \in R_{\mathrm{PKEBC^{lin\text{-}ctxt}}} \}$.

5.3 Achieving Linear Time Decryption

As discussed in Sect. 2.2, while the scheme given in Sect. 5.2 already achieves linear size ciphertexts and linear time encryption, it does not achieve linear time decryption. We now show how to modify $\Pi_{\mathrm{PKEBC}}^{\mathrm{lin\text{-}ctxt}}$ to achieve linear time decryption. The new scheme, denoted $\Pi_{\mathrm{PKEBC}}^{\mathrm{lin\text{-}dec}}$, is defined in Algorithm 5, and uses the same building blocks as $\Pi_{\mathrm{PKEBC}}^{\mathrm{lin\text{-}ctxt}}$. In the following, vectors are assumed to have matching lengths; furthermore, to simplify the definition of the relations below, we introduce the following predicate:

---

[6] At a more technical level, replacing the binding commitment scheme of Maurer et al.'s PKEBC construction by a PKE scheme also serves the purpose of allowing the (IND + IK)-CCA-2 security reductions to handle decryption queries.

Algorithm 4. Construction of PKEBC scheme $\Pi_{\text{PKEBC}}^{\text{lin-ctxt}} = (S, G, E, D)$.

$S(1^k)$
 $(\text{pk}, \text{sk}) \leftarrow \Pi_{\text{PKE}}.G(1^k)$
 $\textbf{return } \text{pp} := (1^k, \text{crs} \leftarrow \Pi_{\text{NIZK}}.G(1^k), \text{pk})$

$G(\text{pp})$
 $(\text{pk}', \text{sk}') \leftarrow \Pi_{\text{PKE}}.G(1^k)$
 $\textbf{return } (\text{pk} := \text{pk}', \text{sk} := (\text{pk}, \text{sk}'))$

$E_{\text{pp}}(\vec{v} := (\text{pk}_1, \dots, \text{pk}_{|\vec{v}|}), m)$
 $c_{\text{pp}} \leftarrow \Pi_{\text{PKE}}.E_{\text{pp.pk}}((\vec{v}, m); r_{\text{pp}})$
 $k_{\text{sym}} \leftarrow \Pi_{\text{SKE}}.G(1^k; r_{\text{sym}})$
 $c_{\text{sym}} \leftarrow \Pi_{\text{SKE}}.E_{k_{\text{sym}}}((r_{\text{pp}}, \vec{v}, m); r_{\text{sym}}')$
 $\textbf{for each } j \in \{1, \dots, |\vec{v}|\} \textbf{ do}$
  $c_j \leftarrow \Pi_{\text{PKE}}.E_{v_j}(k_{\text{sym}}; r_j)$
 $(\vec{r}, \vec{c}) := ((r_1, \dots, r_{|\vec{v}|}), (c_1, \dots, c_{|\vec{v}|}))$
 $p \leftarrow \Pi_{\text{NIZK}}.P_{\text{crs}}((1^k, \text{pp.pk}, c_{\text{pp}}, \vec{c}, c_{\text{sym}}) \in L_{\text{PKEBC}^{\text{lin-ctxt}}}, (\vec{v}, m, r_{\text{pp}}, \vec{r}, r_{\text{sym}}, r_{\text{sym}}'))$
 $\textbf{return } (p, c_{\text{pp}}, \vec{c}, c_{\text{sym}})$

$D_{\text{pp}}(\text{sk}, c := (p, c_{\text{pp}}, \vec{c}, c_{\text{sym}}))$
 $\textbf{if } \Pi_{\text{NIZK}}.V_{\text{crs}}((1^k, \text{pp.pk}, c_{\text{pp}}, \vec{c}, c_{\text{sym}}) \in L_{\text{PKEBC}^{\text{lin-ctxt}}}, p) = \textbf{valid then}$
  $\textbf{for } j = 1, \dots, |\vec{c}| \textbf{ do}$
   $k_{\text{sym}} \leftarrow \Pi_{\text{PKE}}.D_{\text{sk.sk}'}(c_j)$
   $(r_{\text{pp}}, \vec{v}, m) \leftarrow \Pi_{\text{SKE}}.D_{k_{\text{sym}}}(c_{\text{sym}})$
   $\textbf{if } (r_{\text{pp}}, \vec{v}, m) \neq \bot \wedge \text{sk.pk} = v_j \textbf{ then}$
    $\textbf{if } c_{\text{pp}} = \Pi_{\text{PKE}}.E_{\text{pp.pk}}((\vec{v}, m); r_{\text{pp}}) \textbf{ then}$
     $\textbf{return } (\vec{v}, m)$
 $\textbf{return } \bot$

$$\text{CtxtMatch}(\text{pk}, \text{pk}', r_0, r_1, r_2, \alpha, k, c_0, c_1, c_2) := ((c_0, c_1, c_2) \tag{5.2}$$
$$= (\Pi_{\text{PKE}}.E_{\text{pk}}(\alpha; r_0), \Pi_{\text{PKE}}.E_{\text{pk}'}(r_0; r_1), \Pi_{\text{PKE}}.E_{\text{pk}'}(k; r_2))).$$

Consider relation $R_{\text{PKEBC}^{\text{lin-dec}}}$ defined as

$$R_{\text{PKEBC}^{\text{lin-dec}}} := \Big\{ ((1^k, \text{pk}_{\text{pp}}, c_{\text{pp}}, \vec{c}, c_{\text{sym}}), (\vec{v}, m, r_{\text{pp}}, \vec{r}, r_{\text{sym}}, r_{\text{sym}}')) : \tag{5.3}$$

$$(k_{\text{sym}} = \Pi_{\text{SKE}}.G(1^k; r_{\text{sym}})) \wedge (c_{\text{sym}} = \Pi_{\text{SKE}}.E(k_{\text{sym}}, (\vec{v}, m); r_{\text{sym}}'))$$

$$\wedge \left[\bigwedge_{j \in \{1, \dots, |\vec{c}|\}} \text{CtxtMatch}(\text{pk}_{\text{pp}}, v_j, r_{j,0}, r_{j,1}, r_{j,2}, v_j, k_{\text{sym}}, c_{j,0}, c_{j,1}, c_{j,2}) \right]$$

$$\wedge (c_{\text{pp}} = \Pi_{\text{PKE}}.E_{\text{pk}_{\text{pp}}}(m; r_{\text{pp}})) \Big\}.$$

In Algorithm 5, we consider the language $L_{\text{PKEBC}^{\text{lin-dec}}}$ that is induced by relation $R_{\text{PKEBC}^{\text{lin-dec}}}$: $L_{\text{PKEBC}^{\text{lin-dec}}} := \{(1^k, \text{pk}_{\text{pp}}, c_{\text{pp}}, \vec{c}, c_{\text{sym}}) \mid \exists (\vec{v}, m, r_{\text{pp}}, \vec{r}, r_{\text{sym}}, r_{\text{sym}}') : ((1^k, \text{pk}_{\text{pp}}, c_{\text{pp}}, \vec{c}, c_{\text{sym}}), (\vec{v}, m, r_{\text{pp}}, \vec{r}, r_{\text{sym}}, r_{\text{sym}}')) \in R_{\text{PKEBC}^{\text{lin-dec}}}\}$.

5.4 Achieving Tight Security Under Adaptive Corruptions

Finally, we modify $\Pi_{\text{PKEBC}}^{\text{lin-dec}}$ to get a PKEBC scheme that is tightly security under adaptive corruptions. Informally, we use the same two-key technique that we used

Algorithm 5. Construction of PKEBC scheme $\Pi_{\text{PKEBC}}^{\text{lin-dec}}$.

$S(1^k)$
    $(\text{pk}, \text{sk}) \leftarrow \Pi_{\text{PKE}}.G(1^k)$
    $\textbf{return } \text{pp} := (1^k, \text{crs} \leftarrow \Pi_{\text{NIZK}}.G(1^k), \text{pk})$

$G(\text{pp})$
    $(\text{pk}', \text{sk}') \leftarrow \Pi_{\text{PKE}}.G(1^k)$
    $\textbf{return } (\text{pk} := \text{pk}', \text{sk} := (\text{pk}, \text{sk}'))$

$E_{\text{pp}}(\vec{v} := (\text{pk}_1, \dots, \text{pk}_{|\vec{v}|}), m)$
    $c_{\text{pp}} \leftarrow \Pi_{\text{PKE}}.E_{\text{pp.pk}}(m; r_{\text{pp}})$
    $k_{\text{sym}} \leftarrow \Pi_{\text{SKE}}.G(1^k; r_{\text{sym}})$
    $c_{\text{sym}} \leftarrow \Pi_{\text{SKE}}.E_{k_{\text{sym}}}((\vec{v}, m); r_{\text{sym}}')$
    $\textbf{for each } j \in \{1, \dots, |\vec{v}|\} \textbf{ do}$
        $(c_{j,0}, c_{j,1}, c_{j,2}) \leftarrow (\Pi_{\text{PKE}}.E_{\text{pp.pk}}(v_j; r_{j,0}), \Pi_{\text{PKE}}.E_{v_j}(r_{j,0}; r_{j,1}), \Pi_{\text{PKE}}.E_{v_j}(k_{\text{sym}}; r_{j,2}))$
    $\vec{r} := ((r_{1,0}, r_{1,1}, r_{1,2}), \dots, (r_{|\vec{v}|,0}, r_{|\vec{v}|,1}, r_{|\vec{v}|,2}))$
    $\vec{c} := ((c_{1,0}, c_{1,1}, c_{1,2}), \dots, (c_{|\vec{v}|,0}, c_{|\vec{v}|,1}, c_{|\vec{v}|,2}))$
    $p \leftarrow \Pi_{\text{NIZK}}.P_{\text{crs}}((1^k, \text{pp.pk}, c_{\text{pp}}, \vec{c}, c_{\text{sym}}) \in L_{\text{PKEBC}^{\text{lin-dec}}}, (\vec{v}, m, r_{\text{pp}}, \vec{r}, r_{\text{sym}}, r_{\text{sym}}'))$
    $\textbf{return } (p, c_{\text{pp}}, \vec{c}, c_{\text{sym}})$

$D_{\text{pp}}(\text{sk}, c := (p, c_{\text{pp}}, \vec{c}, c_{\text{sym}}))$
    $\textbf{if } \Pi_{\text{NIZK}}.V_{\text{crs}}((1^k, \text{pp.pk}, c_{\text{pp}}, \vec{c}, c_{\text{sym}}) \in L_{\text{PKEBC}^{\text{lin-dec}}}, p) = \texttt{valid then}$
        $\textbf{for } j = 1, \dots, |\vec{c}| \textbf{ do}$
            $r \leftarrow \Pi_{\text{PKE}}.D_{\text{sk.sk}'}(c_{j,1})$
            $\textbf{if } r \neq \bot \wedge \Pi_{\text{PKE}}.E_{\text{pp.pk}}(\text{sk.pk}; r) = c_{j,0} \textbf{ then}$
                $k_{\text{sym}} \leftarrow \Pi_{\text{PKE}}.D_{\text{sk.sk}'}(c_{j,2})$
                $\textbf{return } \Pi_{\text{SKE}}.D_{k_{\text{sym}}}(c_{\text{sym}})$
    $\textbf{return } \bot$

---

for our MDVS scheme construction [1,17]. In other words, in our scheme each party generates two key-pairs, $(\text{pk}_0, \text{sk}_0)$ and $(\text{pk}_1, \text{sk}_1)$, and then discards one of the secret keys sk_b picked uniformly at random. The new scheme is denoted $\Pi_{\text{PKEBC}}^{\text{adap}}$ and is defined in Algorithm 6. Similarly to $\Pi_{\text{PKEBC}}^{\text{lin-dec}}$, $\Pi_{\text{PKEBC}}^{\text{adap}}$ uses the same building blocks as $\Pi_{\text{PKEBC}}^{\text{lin-ctxt}}$. Consider relation $R_{\text{PKEBC}^{\text{adap}}}$ defined as

$$R_{\text{PKEBC}^{\text{adap}}} := \left\{ ((1^k, \text{pk}_{\text{pp}}, c_{\text{pp}}, \vec{c}, c_{\text{sym}}), (\vec{v}, m, r_{\text{pp}}, \vec{r}, r_{\text{sym}}, r_{\text{sym}}')) \mid \right. \tag{5.4}$$

$$(k_{\text{sym}} = \Pi_{\text{SKE}}.G(1^k; r_{\text{sym}})) \wedge (c_{\text{sym}} = \Pi_{\text{SKE}}.E(k_{\text{sym}}, (\vec{v}, m); r_{\text{sym}}'))$$

$$\wedge (c_{\text{pp}} = \Pi_{\text{PKE}}.E_{\text{pk}_{\text{pp}}}(m; r_{\text{pp}})) \wedge [\bigwedge_{j \in \{1, \dots, |\vec{c}|\}, \, b \in \{0,1\}}$$

$$\left. \text{CtxtMatch}(\text{pk}_{\text{pp}}, v_j.\text{pk}_b, r_{j,0}, r_{j,b,1}, r_{j,b,2}, v_j, k_{\text{sym}}, c_{j,0}, c_{j,b,1}, c_{j,b,2})] \right\},$$

where CtxtMatch is as in Eq. 5.2. In Algorithm 6, we consider the following language: $L_{\text{PKEBC}^{\text{adap}}} := \{(1^k, \text{pk}_{\text{pp}}, c_{\text{pp}}, \vec{c}, c_{\text{sym}}) \mid \exists (\vec{v}, m, r_{\text{pp}}, \vec{r}, r_{\text{sym}}, r_{\text{sym}}') : ((1^k, \text{pk}_{\text{pp}}, c_{\text{pp}}, \vec{c}, c_{\text{sym}}), (\vec{v}, m, r_{\text{pp}}, \vec{r}, r_{\text{sym}}, r_{\text{sym}}')) \in R_{\text{PKEBC}^{\text{adap}}}\}$.

5.4.1 Security Analysis of $\Pi_{\text{PKEBC}}^{\text{adap}}$

The following theorem gives an informal overview of the security properties of

Algorithm 6. Construction $\Pi_{\text{PKEBC}}^{\text{adap}}$.

$S(1^k)$
   $(\text{pk}, \text{sk}) \leftarrow \Pi_{\text{PKE}}.G(1^k)$
   $\text{return } \text{pp} := (1^k, \text{crs} \leftarrow \Pi_{\text{NIZK}}.G(1^k), \text{pk})$

$G(\text{pp})$
   $(\text{pk}_0, \text{sk}_0) \leftarrow \Pi_{\text{PKE}}.G(1^k)$
   $(\text{pk}_1, \text{sk}_1) \leftarrow \Pi_{\text{PKE}}.G(1^k)$
   $b \leftarrow RandomCoin$
   $\text{return } (\text{pk} := (\text{pk}_0, \text{pk}_1), \text{sk} := (\text{pk}, b, \text{sk}_b))$

$E_{\text{pp}}(\vec{v} := (\text{pk}_1, \ldots, \text{pk}_{|\vec{v}|}), m)$
   $c_{\text{pp}} \leftarrow \Pi_{\text{PKE}}.E_{\text{pp.pk}}(m; r_{\text{pp}})$
   $k_{\text{sym}} \leftarrow \Pi_{\text{SKE}}.G(1^k; r_{\text{sym}})$
   $c_{\text{sym}} \leftarrow \Pi_{\text{SKE}}.E_{k_{\text{sym}}}((\vec{v}, m); r_{\text{sym}}')$
   $\text{for each } j \in \{1, \ldots, |\vec{v}|\} \text{ do}$
      $c_{j,0} \leftarrow \Pi_{\text{PKE}}.E_{\text{pp.pk}}(v_j; r_{j,0})$
      $\text{for each } b \in \{0, 1\} \text{ do}$
         $(c_{j,b,1}, c_{j,b,2}) \leftarrow (\Pi_{\text{PKE}}.E_{v_j.\text{pk}_b}(r_{j,0}; r_{j,b,1}), \Pi_{\text{PKE}}.E_{v_j.\text{pk}_b}(k_{\text{sym}}; r_{j,b,2}))$
      $(r_j, c_j) \leftarrow ((r_{j,0}, r_{j,0,1}, r_{j,0,2}, r_{j,1,1}, r_{j,1,2}), (c_{j,0}, c_{j,0,1}, c_{j,0,2}, c_{j,1,1}, c_{j,1,2}))$
   $(\vec{r}, \vec{c}) := ((r_1, \ldots, r_{|\vec{v}|}), (c_1, \ldots, c_{|\vec{v}|}))$
   $p \leftarrow \Pi_{\text{NIZK}}.P_{\text{crs}}((1^k, \text{pp.pk}, c_{\text{pp}}, \vec{c}, c_{\text{sym}}) \in L_{\text{PKEBC}^{\text{adap}}}, (\vec{v}, m, r_{\text{pp}}, \vec{r}, r_{\text{sym}}, r_{\text{sym}}'))$
   $\text{return } (p, c_{\text{pp}}, \vec{c}, c_{\text{sym}})$

$D_{\text{pp}}(\text{sk}, c := (p, c_{\text{pp}}, \vec{c}, c_{\text{sym}}))$
   $\text{if } \Pi_{\text{NIZK}}.V_{\text{crs}}((1^k, \text{pp.pk}, c_{\text{pp}}, \vec{c}, c_{\text{sym}}) \in L_{\text{PKEBC}^{\text{adap}}}, p) = \text{valid then}$
      $\text{for } j = 1, \ldots, |\vec{c}| \text{ do}$
         $r \leftarrow \Pi_{\text{PKE}}.D_{\text{sk.sk}}(c_{j,\text{sk}.b,1})$
         $\text{if } r \neq \perp \wedge \Pi_{\text{PKE}}.E_{\text{pp.pk}}(\text{sk.pk}; r) = c_{j,0} \text{ then}$
            $k_{\text{sym}} \leftarrow \Pi_{\text{PKE}}.D_{\text{sk.sk}}(c_{j,\text{sk}.b,2})$
            $\text{return } \Pi_{\text{SKE}}.D_{k_{\text{sym}}}(c_{\text{sym}})$

   $\text{return } \perp$

---

our PKEBC scheme construction. See [3] for the formal security theorems and the corresponding full proofs.

Theorem 2 (Informal). *If Π_{PKE} is correct and tightly multi-user and multi-challenge* IND-CPA *and* IK-CPA *secure under* non-adaptive *corruptions, Π_{NIZK} is complete, sound, tightly multi-statement adaptive zero-knowledge and tightly multi-statement simulation sound, and Π_{SKE} is correct and tightly multi-instance* IND-CPA *secure, then $\Pi_{\text{PKEBC}}^{\text{adap}}$ is:*

1. *tightly correct;*
2. *tightly robust;*
3. *tightly consistent; and*
4. *tightly* (IND + IK)-CCA-2^{adap} *secure under adaptive corruptions.*

6 Multi-designated Receiver Signed Public Key Encryption Schemes

An MDRS-PKE scheme is a 6-tuple of PPTs $\Pi = (S, G_S, G_R, E, D, Forge)$, where:

- S: on input 1^k, generates public parameters pp;
- G_S: on input pp, generates a sender key-pair (spk, ssk);
- G_R: on input pp, generates a receiver key-pair (rpk, rsk);
- E: on input $(\text{pp}, \text{ssk}, \vec{v}, m)$, where ssk is the secret sending key, $\vec{v}$ is a vector of public keys of the intended receivers, and m is the message, generates a ciphertext c;
- D: on input $(\text{pp}, \text{rsk}, c)$, where rsk is the receiver's secret key, D decrypts c using rsk, obtaining a triple sender/receiver-vector/message $(\text{spk}, \vec{v}, m)$ (or $\perp$ if decryption fails) which it then outputs;
- $Forge$: on input $(\text{pp}, \text{spk}, \vec{v}, m, \vec{s})$, where spk is the sender's public key, $\vec{v}$ is a vector of public keys of the intended receivers, m is the message and $\vec{s}$ is a vector of designated receivers' secret keys—with $|\vec{s}| = |\vec{v}|$ and where for $i \in \{1, \dots, |\vec{v}|\}$, either $s_i = \perp$ or s_i is the secret key corresponding to the i-th public key of $\vec{v}$, i.e. v_i—generates a ciphertext c.

Analogously to Sect. 4, in this section we introduce new (stronger) security notions for MDRS-PKE schemes (see Definitions 12 and 13). Then, we briefly describe how one use the MDVS and PKEBC constructions from before to obtain an MDRS-PKE scheme with the desired properties (by following the construction given by Maurer et al. in [15]), and argue why the scheme is secure with respect to our new stronger MDRS-PKE security notions.

6.1 Security Notions

Below we state the notions of Correctness, Consistency, Unforgeability, $(\text{IND} + \text{IK})\text{-CCA-2}^{\text{adap}}$ and Off-The-Record for MDRS-PKE schemes. Analogously to the new MDVS Off-The-Record security notion we introduced in Sect. 4.1 (Definition 4), the $(\text{IND} + \text{IK})\text{-CCA-2}^{\text{adap}}$ and Off-The-Record security notions we now present (Definitions 12 and 13, respectively), allow the adversary to obtain the sender's secret key; and analogously to the new PKEBC security notions we introduced in Sect. 5.1 (in particular Definition 8), our new MDRS-PKE security notions capture the setting where the adversary can adaptively corrupt parties (see Definition 12). The security notions we now present are thus an enhancement over the original ones given in [15].

Let $\Pi = (S, G_S, G_V, E, D, Forge)$ be an MDRS-PKE scheme with message space $\mathcal{M}$. The oracles below are defined for a game-system with (an implicitly defined) security parameter k:

Public Parameter Generation Oracle: $\mathcal{O}_{PP}$
1. On the first call, compute $\text{pp} \leftarrow S(1^k)$; output pp;
2. On subsequent calls, simply output pp.

Sender Key-Pair Oracle: $\mathcal{O}_{SK}(A_i)$
1. On the first call on input A_i, compute and store $(\text{spk}_i, \text{ssk}_i) \leftarrow G_S(\text{pp})$; output $(\text{spk}_i, \text{ssk}_i)$;
2. On subsequent calls, simply output $(\text{spk}_i, \text{ssk}_i)$.

Receiver Key-Pair Oracle: $\mathcal{O}_{RK}(B_j)$

1. Analogous to the Sender Key-Pair Oracle.

Sender Public-Key Oracle: $\mathcal{O}_{SPK}(A_i)$

   1. $(\mathrm{spk}_i, \mathrm{ssk}_i) \leftarrow \mathcal{O}_{SK}(A_i)$; output spk_i.

Receiver Public-Key Oracle: $\mathcal{O}_{RPK}(B_j)$

   1. Analogous to the Sender Public-Key Oracle.

Encryption Oracle: $\mathcal{O}_E(A_i, \vec{V}, m)$

   1. $(\mathrm{spk}_i, \mathrm{ssk}_i) \leftarrow \mathcal{O}_{SK}(A_i)$;

   2. $\vec{v} \leftarrow (\mathcal{O}_{RPK}(V_1), \ldots, \mathcal{O}_{RPK}(V_{|\vec{V}|}))$;

   3. Output $c \leftarrow E_{\mathrm{pp}}(\mathrm{ssk}_i, \vec{v}, m)$.

Decryption Oracle: $\mathcal{O}_D(B_j, c)$

   1. $(\mathrm{rpk}_j, \mathrm{rsk}_j) \leftarrow \mathcal{O}_{RK}(B_j)$;

   2. Output $(\mathrm{spk}, \vec{v} := (\mathrm{rpk}_1, \ldots, \mathrm{rpk}_{|\vec{v}|}), m) \leftarrow D_{\mathrm{pp}}(\mathrm{rsk}_j, c)$.

Definition 9 (Correctness). *Game system* $\mathbf{G}^{\mathsf{Corr}}$ *provides an adversary* $\mathbf{A}$ *with access to oracles* $\mathcal{O}_{PP}, \mathcal{O}_{SK}, \mathcal{O}_{RK}, \mathcal{O}_{SPK}, \mathcal{O}_{RPK}, \mathcal{O}_E$ *and* $\mathcal{O}_D$. $\mathbf{A}$ *wins the game if there are two queries* q_E *and* q_D *to* $\mathcal{O}_E$ *and* $\mathcal{O}_D$, *respectively, where* q_E *has input* $(A_i, \vec{V}, m)$ *and* q_D *has input* (B_j, c), *satisfying* $B_j \in \vec{V}$, *the input* c *in* q_D *is the output of* q_E, *the output of* q_D *is* $(\mathrm{spk}_i', \vec{v}', m')$ *with* $(\mathrm{spk}_i', \vec{v}', m') = \perp$ *or* $(\mathrm{spk}_i', \vec{v}', m') \neq (\mathrm{spk}_i, \vec{v}, m)$—*where* spk_i *is* A_i's *public key and* $\vec{v}$ *is the corresponding vector of public keys of the parties of* $\vec{V}$. *The advantage of* $\mathbf{A}$ *in winning the Correctness game, denoted* $Adv^{\mathsf{Corr}}(\mathbf{A})$, *is the probability that* $\mathbf{A}$ *wins game* $\mathbf{G}^{\mathsf{Corr}}$ *as described above.*

Definition 10 (Consistency). *Game system* $\mathbf{G}^{\mathsf{Cons}}$ *provides an adversary* $\mathbf{A}$ *with access to oracles* $\mathcal{O}_{PP}, \mathcal{O}_{SK}, \mathcal{O}_{RK}, \mathcal{O}_{SPK}, \mathcal{O}_{RPK}, \mathcal{O}_E$ *and* $\mathcal{O}_D$. $\mathbf{A}$ *wins the game if there is a ciphertext* c *such that* $\mathcal{O}_D$ *is queried on inputs* (B_i, c) *and* (B_j, c) *for some* B_i *and* B_j *(possibly with* $B_i = B_j$), *there is no prior query on either* B_i *or* B_j *to* $\mathcal{O}_{RK}$, *query* $\mathcal{O}_D(B_i, c)$ *outputs some* $(\mathrm{spk}_l, \vec{v}, m)$ *satisfying* $(\mathrm{spk}_l, \vec{v}, m) \neq \perp$, spk_l *is some party* A_l's *public sender key (i.e.* $\mathcal{O}_{SPK}(A_l) = \mathrm{spk}_l$) *and* $\mathrm{rpk}_j \in \vec{v}$ *(where* rpk_j *is* B_j's *public key), and query* $\mathcal{O}_D(B_j, c)$ *does not output the same triple* $(\mathrm{spk}_l, \vec{v}, m)$. *The advantage of* $\mathbf{A}$ *in winning the Consistency game is denoted* $Adv^{\mathsf{Cons}}(\mathbf{A})$ *and corresponds to the probability that* $\mathbf{A}$ *wins game* $\mathbf{G}^{\mathsf{Cons}}$ *as described above.*

Definition 11 (Unforgeability). *Game system* $\mathbf{G}^{\mathsf{Unforg}}$ *provides an adversary* $\mathbf{A}$ *with access to oracles* $\mathcal{O}_{PP}, \mathcal{O}_{SK}, \mathcal{O}_{RK}, \mathcal{O}_{SPK}, \mathcal{O}_{RPK}, \mathcal{O}_E$ *and* $\mathcal{O}_D$. *We say that* $\mathbf{A}$ *wins the game if there is a query* q *to* $\mathcal{O}_D$ *on an input* (B_j, c) *that outputs* $(\mathrm{spk}_i, \vec{v}, m) \neq \perp$ *with* spk_i *being some party* A_i's *sender public key (i.e.* $\mathcal{O}_{SPK}(A_i) = \mathrm{spk}_i$), *there was no query* $\mathcal{O}_E(A_i, \vec{V}, m)$ *where* $\vec{V}$ *is the vector of parties with corresponding public keys* $\vec{v}$, $\mathcal{O}_{SK}$ *was not queried on input* A_i, *and* $\mathcal{O}_{RK}$ *was not queried on input* B_j. *The advantage of* $\mathbf{A}$ *in winning the Unforgeability game is the probability that* $\mathbf{A}$ *wins game* $\mathbf{G}^{\mathsf{Unforg}}$ *as described above, and is denoted* $Adv^{\mathsf{Unforg}}(\mathbf{A})$.

We say that an adversary $\mathbf{A}$ (ε, t)-breaks the $(n_S, n_R, d_E, q_E, q_D)$-Correctness, Consistency, or Unforgeability of Π if $\mathbf{A}$ runs in time at most

t, queries $\mathcal{O}_{SK}$, $\mathcal{O}_{SPK}$, $\mathcal{O}_E$ and $\mathcal{O}_D$ on at most n_S different senders, queries $\mathcal{O}_{RK}$, $\mathcal{O}_{RPK}$, $\mathcal{O}_E$ and $\mathcal{O}_D$ on at most n_R different receivers, makes at most q_E and q_D queries to $\mathcal{O}_E$ and $\mathcal{O}_D$, respectively, with the sum of lengths of the party vectors input to $\mathcal{O}_E$ being at most d_E, and **A**'s advantage in winning the (corresponding) security game is at least ε.

6.1.1　New $(\mathsf{IND} + \mathsf{IK})$-$\mathsf{CCA}$-$2^{\mathsf{adap}}$ and Off-The-Record Notions

Analogously to Sect. 4.1.1, in this section we present the new enhanced OTR and $(\mathsf{IND} + \mathsf{IK})$-$\mathsf{CCA}$-$2^{\mathsf{adap}}$ security notions for MDRS-PKE schemes. As already mentioned, the main difference between our new notions and existing ones (see [15]) is that in our new notions the adversary can query for the secret key of any sender (see Definitions 12 and 13) and can corrupt parties adaptively.

The games defined by these notions provide adversaries with access to the oracles from before as well as to the oracles $\mathcal{O}_E$ and $\mathcal{O}_D$ defined below:

Encryption Oracle: $\mathcal{O}_E((A_{i,0}, \vec{V}_0, m_0), (A_{i,1}, \vec{V}_1, m_1))$
1. For game system $\mathbf{G}_\mathbf{b}^{(\mathsf{IND}+\mathsf{IK})\text{-}\mathsf{CCA}\text{-}2^{adap}}$, encrypt $m_\mathbf{b}$ under $\mathtt{ssk}_{i,\mathbf{b}}$ ($A_{i,\mathbf{b}}$'s sender secret key) and $\vec{v_\mathbf{b}}$ ($\vec{V_\mathbf{b}}$'s corresponding vector of receiver public keys); output c.

Decryption Oracle: $\mathcal{O}_D(B_j, c)$
1. If c was the output of some query to $\mathcal{O}_E$, output $\mathtt{test}$;
2. Otherwise, compute $(\mathtt{spk}_i, \vec{v}, m) \leftarrow D_{\mathtt{pp},\mathtt{sk}_j}(c)$, where $\mathtt{sk}_j$ is B_j's secret key; output $(\mathtt{spk}_i, \vec{v}, m)$.

Definition 12. $((\mathsf{IND} + \mathsf{IK})$-$\mathsf{CCA}$-$2^{adap}$ *Security*). *For* $\mathbf{b} \in \{0,1\}$, *game system* $\mathbf{G}_\mathbf{b}^{(\mathsf{IND}+\mathsf{IK})\text{-}\mathsf{CCA}\text{-}2^{adap}}$ *provides an adversary* **A** *with access to oracles* $\mathcal{O}_{PP}$, $\mathcal{O}_{SK}$, $\mathcal{O}_{RK}$, $\mathcal{O}_{SPK}$, $\mathcal{O}_{RPK}$, $\mathcal{O}_E$ *and* $\mathcal{O}_D$. **A** *wins the game if it outputs a guess bit* b' *with* $b' = \mathbf{b}$ *and for every query* $\mathcal{O}_E((A_{i,0}, \vec{V}_0, m_0), (A_{i,1}, \vec{V}_1, m_1))$: *1.* $|m_0| = |m_1|$; *2.* $\left|\vec{V}_0\right| = \left|\vec{V}_1\right|$; *and 3. there is no query to* $\mathcal{O}_{RK}$ *on any* $B_j \in Set(\vec{V}_0) \cup Set(\vec{V}_1)$ *at any point during the game. We define the advantage of* **A** *in winning the* $(\mathsf{IND} + \mathsf{IK})$-$\mathsf{CCA}$-$2^{adap}$ *game as*

$$Adv^{(\mathsf{IND}+\mathsf{IK})\text{-}\mathsf{CCA}\text{-}2^{adap}}(\mathbf{A}) :=$$
$$\left| \Pr[\mathbf{AG}_0^{(\mathsf{IND}+\mathsf{IK})\text{-}\mathsf{CCA}\text{-}2^{adap}} = \mathtt{win}] + \Pr[\mathbf{AG}_1^{(\mathsf{IND}+\mathsf{IK})\text{-}\mathsf{CCA}\text{-}2^{adap}} = \mathtt{win}] - 1 \right|.$$

An adversary **A** (ε, t)-breaks the (n_R, d_E, q_E, q_D)-$(\mathsf{IND} + \mathsf{IK})$-$\mathsf{CCA}$-$2^{adap}$ security of Π if **A** runs in time at most t, queries $\mathcal{O}_{RK}$, $\mathcal{O}_{RPK}$, $\mathcal{O}_E$ and $\mathcal{O}_D$ on at most n_R different receivers, makes at most q_E and q_D queries to $\mathcal{O}_E$ and $\mathcal{O}_D$, respectively, with the sum of lengths of the party vectors input to $\mathcal{O}_E$ being at most d_E, and satisfies $Adv^{(\mathsf{IND}+\mathsf{IK})\text{-}\mathsf{CCA}\text{-}2^{adap}}(\mathbf{A}) \geq \varepsilon$.

The following notion defines two game systems, $\mathbf{G}_0^{\mathsf{OTR}}$ and $\mathbf{G}_1^{\mathsf{OTR}}$, which provide adversaries with access to an oracle $\mathcal{O}_E$, whose behavior varies depending on the underlying game system. For $\mathbf{b} \in \{0,1\}$, $\mathcal{O}_E$ behaves as follows:

Encryption Oracle: $\mathcal{O}_E(\text{type} \in \{\text{sig}, \text{sim}\}, A_i, \vec{V}, m, \mathcal{C})$
For game system $\mathbf{G}_{\mathbf{b}}^{\text{OTR}}$, the oracle behaves as follows:

1. Let $\vec{v} = (v_1, \ldots, v_{|\vec{V}|})$ and $\vec{s} = (s_1, \ldots, s_{|\vec{V}|})$, where, for $i \in \{1, \ldots, |\vec{V}|\}$:

$$- (v_i, s_i) = \begin{cases} \mathcal{O}_{RK}(V_i) & \text{if } V_i \in \mathcal{C} \\ (\mathcal{O}_{RPK}(V_i), \bot) & \text{otherwise}; \end{cases}$$

2. $(c_0, c_1) \leftarrow (\Pi.E_{\text{pp}}(\text{ssk}_i, \vec{v}, m), \Pi.Forge_{\text{pp}}(\text{spk}_i, \vec{v}, m, \vec{s}))$;
3. If $\mathbf{b} = 0$, output c_0 if $\text{type} = \text{sig}$ and c_1 if $\text{type} = \text{sim}$; otherwise, if $\mathbf{b} = 1$, output c_1.

Definition 13 (Off-The-Record). *For $\mathbf{b} \in \{0,1\}$, game system $\mathbf{G}_{\mathbf{b}}^{\text{OTR}}$ provides an adversary $\mathbf{A}$ with access to oracles $\mathcal{O}_{PP}$, $\mathcal{O}_{SK}$, $\mathcal{O}_{RK}$, $\mathcal{O}_{SPK}$, $\mathcal{O}_{RPK}$, $\mathcal{O}_E$ and $\mathcal{O}_D$. $\mathbf{A}$ wins the game if it outputs a guess bit b' with $b' = \mathbf{b}$ and for every query $(\text{type}, A_i, \vec{V}, m, \mathcal{C})$ to $\mathcal{O}_E$, and letting c be the output of $\mathcal{O}_E$, all of the following hold: 1. $\mathcal{C} \subseteq Set(\vec{V})$; 2. for every query B_j to $\mathcal{O}_{VK}$, $B_j \notin Set(\vec{V}) \setminus \mathcal{C}$; 3. for all queries $\mathcal{O}_D(B_j, c')$, $c' \neq c$. $\mathbf{A}$'s advantage in winning the Off-The-Record security game is*

$$Adv^{\text{OTR}}(\mathbf{A}) := \left| \Pr[\mathbf{AG}_0^{\text{OTR}} = \text{win}] + \Pr[\mathbf{AG}_1^{\text{OTR}} = \text{win}] - 1 \right|.$$

We say that an adversary $\mathbf{A}$ $(\varepsilon_{\text{OTR}}, t)$-breaks the $(n_S, n_R, d_E, q_E, q_D)$-Off-The-Record security of Π if $\mathbf{A}$ runs in time at most t, queries $\mathcal{O}_{SK}$, $\mathcal{O}_{SPK}$, $\mathcal{O}_E$ and $\mathcal{O}_D$ on at most n_S different senders, queries $\mathcal{O}_{RK}$, $\mathcal{O}_{RPK}$, $\mathcal{O}_E$ and $\mathcal{O}_D$ on at most n_R different receivers, makes at most q_E and q_D queries to $\mathcal{O}_E$ and $\mathcal{O}_D$, respectively, with the sum of lengths of the party vectors input to $\mathcal{O}_E$ being at most d_E, and satisfies $Adv^{\text{OTR}}(\mathbf{A}) \geq \varepsilon_{\text{OTR}}$. Finally, we say that Π is

$$(\varepsilon_{\text{Corr}}, \varepsilon_{\text{Cons}}, \varepsilon_{\text{Unforg}}, \varepsilon_{(\text{IND}+\text{IK})\text{-CCA-2}^{\text{adap}}}, \varepsilon_{\text{OTR}},$$

$$t, n_S, n_R, d_E, q_E, q_D)\text{-secure},$$

if no adversary $\mathbf{A}$: 1. $(\varepsilon_{\text{Corr}}, t)$-breaks the $(n_S, n_R, d_E, q_E, q_D)$-Correctness of Π; 2. $(\varepsilon_{\text{Cons}}, t)$-breaks the $(n_S, n_R, d_E, q_E, q_D)$-Consistency of Π; 3. $(\varepsilon_{\text{Unforg}}, t)$-breaks the $(n_S, n_R, d_E, q_E, q_D)$-Unforgeability of Π; 4. $(\varepsilon_{(\text{IND}+\text{IK})\text{-CCA-2}^{\text{adap}}}, t)$-breaks the (n_R, d_E, q_E, q_D)-(IND + IK)-CCA-2^{adap} security of Π; or 5. $(\varepsilon_{\text{OTR}}, t)$-breaks the $(n_S, n_R, d_E, q_E, q_D)$-Off-The-Record security of Π.

6.2   Construction of MDRS-PKE with Short Ciphertexts

Maurer et al. give a black-box construction of an MDRS-PKE scheme from a PKEBC scheme and an MDVS scheme [15]. At a high level, the construction [15, Algorithm 2] essentially relies on the MDVS scheme to sign messages, and on the PKEBC scheme to encrypt the message, the signature and all relevant public keys. More concretely, in their construction a sender key-pair consists of an MDVS signer key-pair, whereas a receiver key-pair consists of an MDVS verifier key-pair and a PKEBC key-pair. To encrypt a message m, a signer first uses its MDVS signer key-pair to generate a signature σ on both m and the vector of PKEBC public keys of the intended receivers, and then uses the PKEBC scheme to encrypt its own MDVS signer public key, the MDVS verifier public key of each receiver, the message m and the signature σ; the resulting MDRS-PKE ciphertext is the one output by the PKEBC scheme. Conversely, to decrypt an MDRS-PKE ciphertext, a receiver first decrypts the PKEBC ciphertext, obtaining not only the vector of PKEBC public keys of the receivers, but also a signer's MDVS public key (of the sender), a vector of MDVS verifier public keys (of each of the receivers), a message m, and an MDVS signature σ; then, it uses its MDVS secret verification key to check if σ is a valid MDVS signature on the message m and the vector of PKEBC public keys obtained from decryption, and with respect to all the MDVS public keys obtained from decrypting the PKEBC ciphertext.

Security of the Resulting MDRS-PKE *Scheme.* In contrast to the MDRS-PKE security notions considered in this paper, the original notions introduced in [15] do not capture the setting where the adversary is given access to the secret keys of signers (see [15, Definitions 9, 10 and 11]). Yet, as noted by the authors, on one hand the IND-CCA-2 and IK-CCA-2 security proofs of the MDRS-PKE construction (see [16, Sections H.2 and H.3]) actually prove the scheme's security with respect to the stronger IND-CCA-2 and IK-CCA-2 security notions where the adversary is given access to any sender secret keys. On the other hand, and as is even noted by the authors in [15, Remark 11], if one would assume the underlying MDVS scheme satisfies the stronger off-the-record notion we consider in this paper—wherein the adversary is given access to the sender's secret key, see Definition 4—then the resulting MDRS-PKE scheme also satisfies the corresponding stronger off-the-record notion (that we also consider in this paper, see Definition 13).

Regarding adaptive security, note that the only security notions from [15] where the adversary cannot adaptively corrupt parties are the IND-CCA-2 and IK-CCA-2 security notions (see [15, Definitions 9 and 10]). Yet, the MDRS-PKE construction's IND-CCA-2 security proof (see [16, Section H.2]) is a trivial reduction to the IND-CCA-2 security of the underlying PKEBC scheme, and the IK-CCA-2 security proof (see [16, Section H.3]) is also a trivial reduction, but to both the IND-CCA-2 and IK-CCA-2 security of the underlying PKEBC scheme (this is necessary since the PKEBC is used to encrypt the MDVS public keys of the involved parties). It is then rather straightforward to see that the IND-CCA-2 and IK-CCA-2 security proofs from [16] can be trivially adapted for the case of adaptive corruptions, as long as one assumes that the underlying PKEBC scheme is also secure with respect to adaptive corruptions. In fact, and since, as one may note, we consider the joint $(\mathsf{IND} + \mathsf{IK})\text{-CCA-2}^{\mathsf{adap}}$ security notions (see Definitions 8 and 12) that capture both $\mathsf{IND\text{-}CCA\text{-}2}^{\mathsf{adap}}$ and $\mathsf{IK\text{-}CCA\text{-}2}^{\mathsf{adap}}$, the MDRS-PKE scheme's $(\mathsf{IND} + \mathsf{IK})\text{-CCA-2}^{\mathsf{adap}}$ security proof becomes even simpler: it essentially becomes a one to one reduction to the $(\mathsf{IND} + \mathsf{IK})\text{-CCA-2}^{\mathsf{adap}}$ security of the underlying PKEBC scheme.

References

1. Bader, C., Hofheinz, D., Jager, T., Kiltz, E., Li, Y.: Tightly-secure authenticated key exchange. In: Dodis, Y., Nielsen, J.B. (eds.) TCC 2015, Part I. LNCS, vol. 9014, pp. 629–658. Springer, Heidelberg (2015). https://doi.org/10.1007/978-3-662-46494-6_26

2. Bader, C., Jager, T., Li, Y., Schäge, S.: On the impossibility of tight cryptographic reductions. In: Fischlin, M., Coron, J.S. (eds.) EUROCRYPT 2016, Part II. LNCS, vol. 9666, pp. 273–304. Springer, Heidelberg (2016). https://doi.org/10.1007/978-3-662-49896-5_10

3. Chakraborty, S., Hofheinz, D., Maurer, U., Rito, G.: Deniable authentication when signing keys leak. Cryptology ePrint Archive, Report 2023/213 (2023). https://eprint.iacr.org/2023/213

4. Chaum, D.: Designated confirmer signatures. In: Santis, A.D. (ed.) EUROCRYPT 1994. LNCS, vol. 950, pp. 86–91. Springer, Heidelberg (1995). https://doi.org/10.1007/BFb0053427

5. Damgård, I., Haagh, H., Mercer, R., Nitulescu, A., Orlandi, C., Yakoubov, S.: Stronger security and constructions of multi-designated verifier signatures. In: Pass, R., Pietrzak, K. (eds.) TCC 2020, Part II. LNCS, vol. 12551, pp. 229–260. Springer, Cham (2020). https://doi.org/10.1007/978-3-030-64378-2_9

6. ElGamal, T.: A public key cryptosystem and a signature scheme based on discrete logarithms. In: Blakley, G.R., Chaum, D. (eds.) CRYPTO 1984. LNCS, vol. 196, pp. 10–18. Springer, Heidelberg (1985). https://doi.org/10.1007/3-540-39568-7_2

7. Fiat, A., Naor, M.: Broadcast encryption. In: Stinson, D.R. (ed.) CRYPTO 1993. LNCS, vol. 773, pp. 480–491. Springer, Heidelberg (1994). https://doi.org/10.1007/3-540-48329-2_40

8. Groth, J.: Simulation-sound NIZK proofs for a practical language and constant size group signatures. In: Lai, X., Chen, K. (eds.) ASIACRYPT 2006. LNCS, vol. 4284, pp. 444–459. Springer, Heidelberg (2006). https://doi.org/10.1007/11935230_29

9. Groth, J., Sahai, A.: Efficient non-interactive proof systems for bilinear groups. In: Smart, N.P. (ed.) EUROCRYPT 2008. LNCS, vol. 4965, pp. 415–432. Springer, Heidelberg (2008). https://doi.org/10.1007/978-3-540-78967-3_24

10. Hesse, J., Hofheinz, D., Kohl, L.: On tightly secure non-interactive key exchange. In: Shacham, H., Boldyreva, A. (eds.) CRYPTO 2018, Part II. LNCS, vol. 10992, pp. 65–94. Springer, Cham (2018). https://doi.org/10.1007/978-3-319-96881-0_3

11. Jakobsson, M., Sako, K., Impagliazzo, R.: Designated verifier proofs and their applications. In: Maurer, U.M. (ed.) EUROCRYPT 1996. LNCS, vol. 1070, pp. 143–154. Springer, Heidelberg (1996). https://doi.org/10.1007/3-540-68339-9_13

12. Lee, Y., Lee, D.H., Park, J.H.: Tightly CCA-secure encryption scheme in a multi-user setting with corruptions. Designs Codes Cryptogr. 88(11), 2433–2452 (2020). https://doi.org/10.1007/s10623-020-00794-z

13. Lombardi, A., Quach, W., Rothblum, R.D., Wichs, D., Wu, D.J.: New constructions of reusable designated-verifier NIZKs. In: Boldyreva, A., Micciancio, D. (eds.) CRYPTO 2019, Part III. LNCS, vol. 11694, pp. 670–700. Springer, Cham (2019). https://doi.org/10.1007/978-3-030-26954-8_22

14. Maurer, U., Portmann, C., Rito, G.: Giving an adversary guarantees (or: how to model designated verifier signatures in a composable framework). In: Tibouchi, M., Wang, H. (eds.) ASIACRYPT 2021, Part III. LNCS, vol. 13092, pp. 189–219. Springer, Cham (2021). https://doi.org/10.1007/978-3-030-92078-4_7

15. Maurer, U., Portmann, C., Rito, G.: Multi-designated receiver signed public key encryption. In: Dunkelman, O., Dziembowski, S. (eds.) EUROCRYPT 2022, Part II. LNCS, vol. 13276, pp. 644–673. Springer, Heidelberg (2022). https://doi.org/10.1007/978-3-031-07085-3_22

16. Maurer, U., Portmann, C., Rito, G.: Multi-designated receiver signed public key encryption. Cryptology ePrint Archive, Report 2022/256 (2022). https://eprint.iacr.org/2022/256

17. Naor, M., Yung, M.: Public-key cryptosystems provably secure against chosen ciphertext attacks. In: 22nd ACM STOC, pp. 427–437. ACM Press (1990). https://doi.org/10.1145/100216.100273

18. Quach, W., Rothblum, R.D., Wichs, D.: Reusable designated-verifier NIZKs for all NP from CDH. In: Ishai, Y., Rijmen, V. (eds.) EUROCRYPT 2019, Part II. LNCS, vol. 11477, pp. 593–621. Springer, Cham (2019). https://doi.org/10.1007/978-3-030-17656-3_21

19. Shoup, V.: Using hash functions as a hedge against chosen ciphertext attack. In: Preneel, B. (ed.) EUROCRYPT 2000. LNCS, vol. 1807, pp. 275–288. Springer, Heidelberg (2000). https://doi.org/10.1007/3-540-45539-6_19

Let Attackers Program Ideal Models: Modularity and Composability for Adaptive Compromise

Joseph Jaeger (✉) (ID)

School of Cybersecurity and Privacy, Georgia Institute of Technology, Atlanta, USA
josephjaeger@gatech.edu
https://cc.gatech.edu/~josephjaeger/

Abstract. We show that the adaptive compromise security definitions of Jaeger and Tyagi (Crypto '20) cannot be applied in several natural use-cases. These include proving multi-user security from single-user security, the security of the cascade PRF, and the security of schemes sharing the same ideal primitive. We provide new variants of the definitions and show that they resolve these issues with composition. Extending these definitions to the asymmetric settings, we establish the security of the modular KEM/DEM and Fujisaki-Okamoto approaches to public key encryption in the full adaptive compromise setting. This allows instantiations which are more efficient and standard than prior constructions.

Keywords: Adaptive security · Ideal models · Selective-opening attacks

1 Introduction

Definitions lie at the heart of modern cryptography. They allow us to mathematically specify what should be achieved by a scheme in practice and give modular, proof-based analyses to ensure these properties are achieved. Studying and understanding definitions is fundamental to the field of cryptography.

There are multiple desiderata to consider when giving a security definition for a primitive including: (i) Is it philosophically sound? Does it meaningfully model the uses and goals of a primitive in the real world? (ii) Is it sufficiently strong? Can we prove that this security notion will imply security of higher-level protocols constructed from the primitive? (iii) Is it sufficiently weak? Can we prove that schemes which "should be" secure satisfy the definition?[1]

In this work, we consider a set of definitions recently introduced by Jaeger and Tyagi [23] for the security of encryption schemes and pseudorandom functions in the "adaptive compromise" setting. They gave several examples of

---

[1] More nuanced versions of (ii) and (iii) ask not just whether these proofs are possible, but also how easy they are to write. Definitions which are difficult to work with can result in proof errors or cryptographers only loosely sketching their proofs (potentially hiding errors).

© International Association for Cryptologic Research 2023
C. Hazay and M. Stam (Eds.): EUROCRYPT 2023, LNCS 14006, pp. 101–131, 2023.
https://doi.org/10.1007/978-3-031-30620-4_4

schemes achieving their definitions as well as higher-level protocols which can be proven secure based on sub-primitives achieving their definitions, thereby evidencing that their definitions achieve desiderata (ii) and (iii). We provide counter-evidence. There are natural goals and constructions for which their definitions fail with respect to (ii) and (iii).[2]

As an example, it does not seem to be possible to prove that single-user restrictions of their definitions implies the full multi-user versions. Across a wide variety of definitions, the notion of multi-user security that is considered "correct" follows from single-user security by a straightforward hybrid argument. Thus, whether this holds for a definition might be considered a sort of litmus test. A definition for which this is not possible should be examined carefully to understand why. Having done so, we propose new variants of Jaeger and Tyagi's definitions and show that they resolve these shortcomings, while preserving the positive qualities of the original definitions.

1.1   Adaptive Compromise and SIM-AC Security

Before discussing our contributions, let us first briefly recall the adaptive compromise setting broadly and the specific SIM-AC definitions of Jaeger and Tyagi (simulation security under adaptive compromise). Roughly speaking, the adaptive compromise setting captures times when there are multiple users of a system, each of whom have their own secrets. An attacker then interacts with these users and based on these interactions may adaptively decide to steal some of the secrets. In applications of these definitions, this description may be somewhat metaphorical. For example, in the searchable encryption scheme of CJJJKR [14] the "users" are keywords, each of which are assigned a secret key. The "stealing" of keys occurs because to perform a search for a particular keyword, the protocol shares the keyword's secret key. The adaptive compromise setting is widely studied in cryptography and is associated with a variety of terms including (but not limited to) adaptive corruption/compromise/security [23,26], non-committing encryption [10,12,13,25], and selective-opening attacks [6,7,9,18,19,21].

Jaeger and Tyagi's work was motivated by various papers that ran into adaptive compromise issues for symmetric encryption or PRFs and had addressed the issues by fixing particular uses of random oracles acting like PRFs. They observed that these works all technically required the same detail-intensive random oracle analysis (which was usually omitted or incorrect). To address this, they introduced their SIM-AC definitions which allow one to abstract away this detail-intensive analysis as something that need only be done once at the lowest levels of analysis. They showed that these notions were achieved by standard efficient schemes in appropriate ideal models, and sufficed for proving the security of their motivating higher-level applications. Broadly their definitions were online-simulator based definitions in which the attacker tries to distinguish between a

---

[2] The examples for which (iii) fails are "intermediate-level" proofs where both the assumption and desired result use their definitions. Arguably then, it is only with respect to (ii) that these definitions have issues.

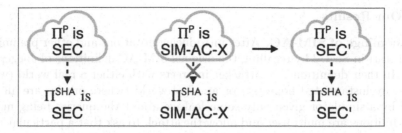

Fig. 1. Left: Typically one proves a scheme Π achieves a security notion with random oracle P, then heuristically assumes it is SEC secure with a particular hash function (e.g. SHA-384). **Middle and Right:** A scheme Π *cannot* be SIM-AC-X secure with any standard model hash function [23,25]. Instead, one uses SIM-AC-X security of Π^P as an intermediate step to showing that Π^P achieves some security notion SEC'. Then one heuristically assumes Π^{SHA} is SEC' secure.

real world where they interact with the honest algorithms of the scheme and an ideal world where the simulator provides responses for every oracle query (including ideal primitive queries). Security requires that for every adversary there is a simulator whose responses it cannot distinguish from the real world.

Notably these definitions were defined explicitly for use only with ideal primitives because techniques of Nielsen [25] show that such definitions cannot be achieved in the standard model. Arguably this causes issues with desiderata (i). Consider a scheme Π^H which expects access to a hash function H. In practice, the might be deployed with the hash function SHA-384 (giving Π^{SHA}) under the hope that it achieves some security notion SEC. Towards justifying this the scheme may be analyzed when the hash function is replaced with a random oracle P (giving Π^P). If Π^P is shown to be SEC secure, this may be taken as heuristic evidence that Π^{SHA} will be SEC secure. However, this clearly cannot be the case for SEC–SIM-AC-X from the aforementioned result that SIM-AC notions cannot be achieved in the standard model.

From our perspective, the "correct" interpretation is that the SIM-AC definitions are intentionally chosen to be overly strong so that (in ideal models) they imply any other security property SEC' one desires. Suppose SEC' is plausibly achievable in the standard model and one proves that SIM-AC-X security implies SEC' security. Then a proof that Π^P is SIM-AC-X secure can be viewed as part of a longer ideal model proof that it achieves SEC'. Then the proof can act as heuristic evidence that Π^{SHA} is a standard model scheme achieving SEC'. We represent this pictorially in Fig. 1.

A similar viewpoint can be taken to proving that a particular hash function construction is indifferentiable from a random oracle. It is trivial to show that no standard model hash function can achieve this. However, analyzing indifferentiability in ideal models still serves as a convenient intermediate notion for heuristically justifying the use of the hash function in some contexts.

1.2   Our Results

Shortcomings of SIM-AC. After introducing notations and other preliminaries, we start in Sect. 3 by recalling the original SIM-AC definitions of Jaeger and Tyagi. In their definitions, an attacker interacts with either a real world (where oracles are instantiated honestly) or an ideal world (where oracles are all simulated by a simulator given only some leakage about the queries being made). The definitions are multi-user and allow the attack to ask that a particular users secrets be revealed at any time. Then, in the ideal world, the simulator is given all of the suppressed information about prior queries and must produce a consistent key, lest it be discovered. In the ideal world, the simulator completely controls the responses of the ideal primitive.

We evidence some shortcomings of these definitions, in that they are seemingly unable to prove some very natural results.[3] One example, which came up in their own work, is that their definitions cannot be used for proofs wherein the ideal object is used multiple times within a protocol (whether by multiple different sub-primitives or repeated use of the same sub-primitive). For example, in the searchable encryption construction of CJJJKR [14] the same random oracle was shared across encryption and a PRF, but for the analysis done by Jaeger and Tyagi they were forced to use different primitives for the two uses. One can generically solve this problem via oracle cloning [5], but we find this unsatisfactory. A good definitional framework should allow us to capture when uses of ideal primitives don't require domain separation techniques. Furthermore, while domain separation is relatively fast and efficient for random oracles, we are generally interested in the use of a variety of ideal primitives and it is much less clear how to do oracle cloning efficiently with something like an ideal cipher.

Similar and even more subtle issues arise in some "standard" results that one would expect to hold with a "good" definition. One would expect that it should be possible to prove secure the cascade construction of a PRF [4,17] which iteratively applies a smaller PRF, as well as to prove that for most security notions single-user security implies multi-user security. The cascade construction underlies several other construction PRFs including AMAC, HMAC, and NMAC [1–3]. These (and other) issues all stem from a common cause. In SIM-AC, the simulator completely controls and replaces the ideal primitive. As such the definition is not robust to proofs which require multiple different applications of security with respect to the same ideal primitive.

New Definition, SIM*-AC. Motivated by these shortcomings, in Sect. 4 we propose new variants of these definitions, which we term SIM*-AC. Our new definitions match the prior SIM-AC definitions, but make three crucial modifications. The first is that rather having complete control of the ideal primitive, we give the simulator access to an oracle for querying the primitive and which

---

[3] We use "seemingly" here and similar phrasing elsewhere because, while we have deeply considered these problems and do not see how SIM-AC could be used to prove these results, we do not have any explicit counterexamples showing it is impossible.

additionally provides the special power of being able to give an input-output pair which the primitive will program itself to be consistent with, if possible. This modification means that applications of SIM*-AC in a proof will leave the ideal primitive around for use in further proof steps. However, these future steps can run into issues where the simulator is supposed to have programmed the ideal primitive, but a reduction attacker who wants to run the simulator internally has no way of forcing other parties to use a programmed ideal primitive. This issue is resolved by our second modification which *gives the adversary the ability to program the ideal primitive.* The final modification is aimed at proofs which require a polynomial number of hybrids and, as such, the reduction adversary needs to depend on the simulator so that it can properly simulate internal hybrids. We simply reverse the order of quantification so that a universal simulator is quantified before a specific attacker.

After the introduction of the new definitions we show by example that the modifications suffice to write the proofs we identified as seemingly not possible with the original SIM-AC definitions. Namely, we prove that for all of our SIM*-AC definitions (with one exception) single-user security implies multi-user security[4] and that the cascade construction of a large-domain PRF from a small-domain PRF is secure. Both proofs are hybrid arguments which conceptually resemble such proofs for most standard indistinguishability-based security notions. For going from single-user to multi-user the hybrid is over how many of the users will be honestly run versus emulated by a copy of the single-user simulator. For the cascade construction (which is a generalization of the GGM construction of a PRF from a PRG), we think of there being an underlying tree structure imposed on the internal values of the computation. The proof performs a hybrid over how many layers of the tree are honestly run versus emulated by a multi-user simulator for the underlying PRF. Using multi-user security allows us to hybrid one layer at a time, rather than having hybrid over each node individually.

Asymmetric Encryption. The SIM-AC definitions focus on symmetric primitives (encryption and PRFs) because this is what was required by their applications. However, adaptive compromise has been studied in detail for public-key encryption, so it is natural to ask how a SIM*-AC notion for public key encryption would work. We do so in Sect. 5, providing a definition that captures the compromise of receiver secret decryption keys and sender randomness. The resulting definition roughly matches the SIM-FULL definition of Camensich, Lehmann, Neven, and Samelin [12].[5] In their work, they showed that SIM-FULL was stronger than various prior adaptive compromise definitions [11,18] and equivalent to a new universal composability definition they introduce.

Casting this definition in SIM*-AC language provides benefits. Where CLNS constructed one particular secure encryption scheme from one-way trapdoor permutations, the broader context of SIM*-AC style definitions allows us to

---

[4] The exception is key-private security which is meaningless with only a single user.
[5] Their definition is basically a SIM-AC-CCA (not SIM*-AC) definition with labels and using a random oracle.

follow the example of Jaeger and Tyagi by giving modular analysis. In particular, we introduce SIM*-AC definitions for key-encapsulation mechanisms (KEM), then show the KEM/DEM approach [15] allows one to combine a KEM with a symmetric encryption scheme to construct public-key encryption. We consider one version of the Fujisaki-Okamoto transformation [16] (as modularized by Hofheinz, Hövelmanns, and Kiltz [20]) to show that it can lift a KEM satisfying a one-wayness security notion to a KEM satisfying our full SIM*-AC-CCA notion. Thereby we have a more general collection of different options how to construct a public-key encryption scheme secure against adaptive compromise. We can instantiate this with well-studied and standardized schemes, improving efficiency because our analysis allows the use of block-cipher based symmetric encryption for the DEM.

An interesting comparison point for our KEM/DEM analysis is the work of Heuer and Poettering [19] who also looked at the KEM/DEM construction. They proved a weaker offline-simulation notion of security for public key encryption by making a particular concrete assumption about the DEM being constructed from a blockcipher and having to have a particular simulatable form.

New Definition, Old Results. Jaeger and Tyagi showed a number positive results in their original work. These include that random oracles and ideal ciphers make SIM-AC-PRF secure function families, that various constructions of symmetric encryption achieve SIM-AC security when their underlying function families are SIM-AC-PRF secure, and that higher-level protocols can be proven secure assuming the SIM-AC security of their constituent elements. It would be rather disappointing if our switch to SIM*-AC security required us to re-prove all of these results from scratch.

In Sect. 6, we dedicate the end of our paper to showing that these results hold with SIM*-AC security. We roughly divide these pre-existing results into three categories: low-level results (constructing basic SIM-AC primitives directly from ideal primitives), intermediate-level results (using one notion of SIM-AC to achieve another), and high-level results (proving secure some non-SIM-AC protocol). For each we discuss how the existing result can be seen, possibly with minor modification to the proof, to hold for SIM*-AC security. In some cases we can get minor improvements along the way, such as allowing the proof to handle when a single ideal primitive is shared between multiple schemes.

2   Preliminaries

Pseudocode Notation. We define security notions using pseudocode-based games. The pseudocode "Require bool" is shorthand for "If not bool then return $\perp$". If S is a set, then $x \leftarrow_\$ S$ sets x equal to a uniformly random element of S. The notation $x_{(.)} \leftarrow_\$ S$ means that each x_u will be sampled according to $x_u \leftarrow_\$ S$ the first time it is accessed.

The notation $y \leftarrow_\$ A(x_1, x_2, \cdots : \sigma)$ denotes the (randomized) execution of A with state σ. Deterministic execution uses $\leftarrow$. The state σ is passed by reference, so changes that A makes to σ are maintained after A's execution. All other inputs are passed by value. For given $x_1, x_2, \ldots$ and σ we let $[A(x_1, x_2, \cdots : \sigma)]$ denote the set of possible outputs of A given these inputs.

The symbol $\perp$ is used to indicate rejection or uninitialized variables. The symbol $\diamond$ is used as a return value by functions that do not need to return anything. Unless specified otherwise, these values are assumed not to be contained in sets. Algorithms and oracles will typically assume their input is from a particular domain (e.g. the message space of an encryption scheme). We implicitly assume adversaries never provide them with input not in these domains.

A list T of length $n \in \mathbb{N}$ specifies an ordered sequence of elements $T[1], T[2], \ldots, T[n]$. The operation $T.\mathsf{add}(x)$ appends x to this list by setting $T[n+1] \leftarrow x$, so T is now of length $n + 1$. We let $|T|$ denote the length of T. In pseudocode lists are assumed to be initialized empty (i.e. have length 0). An empty list or table is denoted by $[\cdot]$. We sometimes use set notation with a list. For example, $x \in T$ is true if $x = T[i]$ for any $1 \leq i \leq |T|$. The loop "For $x \in T$" is defined to be looping "For $i = 1, \ldots, |T|$" and defining $x \leftarrow T[i]$ in each iteration.

If T is a list of tuples (x, y) then we index into T like a table where $T\langle x \rangle$ is the y value of the last tuple in the list with first component x (or is $\perp$ if no such tuple exists). By $T.\mathsf{add}(x, y)$ we mean $T.\mathsf{add}((x, y))$.

We use an asymptotic formalism with security parameter λ. A function f is negligible if for all polynomials p there exists a $\lambda_p \in \mathbb{N}$ such that $f(\lambda) \leq 1/p(\lambda)$ for all $\lambda \geq \lambda_p$. We say it is super-polynomial if $1/f$ is negligible and super-logarithmic if 2^f is super-polynomial.

Suppose $\mathrm{G}_x^{\mathsf{sec}}$ is a game that samples a uniformly random bit b, runs an adversary which guesses bit b', and then returns the boolean $(b = b')$. Then for $d \in \{0, 1\}$, we let $\mathrm{G}_{x,d}^{\mathsf{sec}}$ be the game with b hardcoded to have value d and which outputs the boolean $(b' = 1)$. Standard conditional probability calculations give that $2\Pr[\mathrm{G}_x^{\mathsf{sec}}] - 1 = \Pr[\mathrm{G}_{x,1}^{\mathsf{sec}}] - \Pr[\mathrm{G}_{x,0}^{\mathsf{sec}}]$.

Ideal Primitives. Most of the definitions we consider are dependent on ideal primitives such as random oracles or ideal ciphers, so we require a careful formalization of them. An ideal primitive P specifies (for each $\lambda \in \mathbb{N}$) a distibution $\mathcal{P}_\lambda$ over functions $f : \mathcal{K}_\lambda \times \mathcal{D}_\lambda \to \mathcal{R}_\lambda$. When needed to avoid ambiguity we write $\mathsf{P}.\mathcal{P}_\lambda$, $\mathsf{P}.\mathcal{K}_\lambda$, $\mathsf{P}.\mathcal{D}_\lambda$, and $\mathsf{P}.\mathcal{R}_\lambda$. In the P ideal model, $f \leftarrow\!\!{\scriptstyle\$}\ \mathcal{P}_\lambda$ is sampled at the beginning of any security game and algorithms are given oracle access to f.

It is often important that oracle access to an ideal primitive can be efficiently simulated despite the fact that each $f \in \mathcal{P}_\lambda$ is typically exponential in size. This is referred to as lazy sampling, which we notate using an algorithm $\mathsf{P}.\mathsf{Ls}$. We will think of f as being (partially) specified by a table σ_P indexed by $\mathcal{K}_\lambda \times \mathcal{D}_\lambda$. Then the evaluation algorithm has syntax $y \leftarrow\!\!{\scriptstyle\$}\ \mathsf{P}.\mathsf{Ls}(1^\lambda, k, x : \sigma_\mathsf{P})$. If $\sigma_\mathsf{P}[k, x] = \perp$, it samples $\sigma_\mathsf{P}[k, x]$ according to the appropriate distribution conditioned on the current value of σ_P.[6] Then it outputs $\sigma_\mathsf{P}[k, x]$. We sometimes use A^P as shorthand for giving algorithm A oracle access to $\mathsf{P}.\mathsf{Ls}(1^\lambda, \cdot, \cdot : \sigma_\mathsf{P})$.

---

[6] Concretely, this is the distribution induced by sampling $f \leftarrow\!\!{\scriptstyle\$}\ \mathcal{P}_\lambda$ subject to $f(k', x') = \sigma[k', x']$ wherever the latter is not $\perp$ and assigning $\sigma_\mathsf{P}[k, x] \leftarrow f(k, x)$.

The standard model is captured by the primitive P_{sm} for which $\mathcal{P}_\lambda$ always returns the function f defined exactly by $f(\varepsilon, \varepsilon) = \varepsilon$. A random oracle P_{rom} is captured by $\mathcal{P}_\lambda$'s output being uniform over the set of all functions $f : \mathcal{K}_\lambda \times \mathcal{D}_\lambda \to \mathcal{R}_\lambda$. An ideal injection P_{inj} is captured by letting $\mathcal{K}_\lambda$ consist of tuples $(\circ, k)$ for $\circ \in \{+, -\}$. Then $\mathcal{P}_\lambda$ returns a uniform f for which $f((+, k), \cdot)$ is an injection with inverse $f((-, k), \cdot)$ (we define inverse functions to output $\diamond$ on input a value not in the image of the original function). An ideal cipher P_{icm} is an ideal injection for which $f((+, k), \cdot)$ is a bijection on the finite set $\mathcal{D}_\lambda = \mathcal{R}_\lambda$. Standard techniques allow Ls to be efficiently evaluated for such functions.

Cryptographic schemes may be constructed from multiple underlying cryptographic schemes, each expecting its own ideal primitive. Let P' and P'' be ideal primitives. We define $\mathsf{P} = \mathsf{P}' \times \mathsf{P}''$ via the following algorithms.

$\mathsf{P}.\mathsf{Init}(1^\lambda)$	$\mathsf{P}.\mathsf{Ls}(1^\lambda, k, x : \sigma_\mathsf{P})$
$\sigma_{\mathsf{P}'} \leftarrow_\$ \mathsf{P}'.\mathsf{Init}(1^\lambda)$	$(\sigma_{\mathsf{P}'}, \sigma_{\mathsf{P}''}) \leftarrow \sigma_\mathsf{P}$
$\sigma_{\mathsf{P}''} \leftarrow_\$ \mathsf{P}''.\mathsf{Init}(1^\lambda)$	$(d, k) \leftarrow k$
Return $(\sigma_{\mathsf{P}'}, \sigma_{\mathsf{P}''})$	If $d = 1$ then $y \leftarrow_\$ \mathsf{P}'.\mathsf{Ls}(1^\lambda, k, x : \sigma_{\mathsf{P}'})$
	If $d = 2$ then $y \leftarrow_\$ \mathsf{P}''.\mathsf{Ls}(1^\lambda, k, x : \sigma_{\mathsf{P}''})$
	$\sigma_\mathsf{P} \leftarrow (\sigma_{\mathsf{P}'}, \sigma_{\mathsf{P}''})$
	Return y

In other words, $\mathsf{P}.\mathcal{P}_\lambda$ samples $f' \leftarrow_\$ \mathsf{P}'.\mathcal{P}_\lambda$ and $f'' \leftarrow_\$ \mathsf{P}''.\mathcal{P}_\lambda$, then defines f by $f((1, k), x) = f'(k, x)$ and $f((2, k), x) = f''(k, x)$.

Programming Ideal Primitives. For our new security notions we need to make explicit a notion of "programming" an ideal model. By this we mean allowing some third party to define the output of ideal model on inputs that have not previously been queried. Let σ_P be a table indexed by $\mathcal{K}_\lambda \times \mathcal{D}_\lambda$ and let $(k, x, y) \in \mathcal{K}_\lambda \times \mathcal{D}_\lambda \times \mathcal{R}_\lambda$. We say that σ_P is compatible with (k, x, y), denoted $\sigma_\mathsf{P} \heartsuit (k, x, y)$ if there exists $f \in \mathcal{P}_\lambda$ such that (i) $\sigma_\mathsf{P}[k', x'] = f(k', x')$ wherever $\sigma_\mathsf{P}[k', x'] \neq \bot$ and (ii) $f(k, x) = y$. Then we allow programming of an ideal model P using the algorithm $\mathsf{P}.\mathsf{Prog}$ defined as follows.

$$\frac{\mathsf{P}.\mathsf{Prog}(1^\lambda, k, x, y : \sigma_\mathsf{P})}{\text{If } \sigma_\mathsf{P} \heartsuit (k, x, y) \text{ then } \sigma_\mathsf{P}[k, x] \leftarrow y}$$
$$\text{Return } \diamond$$

This ensures that P cannot be redefined on an input where it was already defined and that an ideal injection cannot be made to have inconsistent inverses.

Our careful formalizing of ideal primitives in terms of functions, particularly in requiring that $\mathsf{P}.\mathsf{Prog}$ maintain consistency, is important for avoiding subtle issues in later proofs. This formalization ensures that a deterministic algorithm with oracle access to P always gives consistent outputs even if P is programmed between executions. Correctness of a scheme with access to P (e.g. that decryption inverts encryption) is maintained even if P is programmed between executions of different algorithms. Without these properties it would be difficult to avoid erroneous proofs that implicitly assumed them during typically "straight-forward" proof steps.

This is not without cost. The requirement for consistency in programming has the potential to introduce subtle errors elsewhere in proofs by implicitly assuming an attempt to program an oracle worked, when in fact it failed because of inconsistency. Additionally, the act of honestly querying the ideal primitive can be detected by a programming adversary who attempts to program at that point and then checks if they succeed in this programming. We believe this cost to be worthwhile because in the analyses we have considered, the places that could cause such proof errors would anyway need to be analyzed carefully to avoid other errors if we were using a more permission notion of programming.

For generality, we allow the use of non-programmable ideal primitives in games that allow programming. This is captured by defining P.Prog to immediately return $\diamond$. When we quantify over an arbitrary ideal primitive, we allow it to be programmable or non-programmable (or the combination of multiple ideal primitives – some programmable, some not). When we discuss a specific ideal primitive, we mean the programmable version unless specified otherwise.

Syntax for Cryptographic Primitives. We assume familiarity with (randomized) symmetric encryption, asymmetric encryption, function families (e.g. PRFs), and key encapsulation mechanisms. We use the following syntax.

Symmetric encryption	Asymmetric encryption
$k \leftarrow_{\$} \mathsf{SE.Kg}(1^\lambda)$	$(ek, dk) \leftarrow_{\$} \mathsf{PKE.Kg}(1^\lambda)$
$c \leftarrow_{\$} \mathsf{SE.Enc}^\mathsf{P}(1^\lambda, k, m)$	$c \leftarrow_{\$} \mathsf{PKE.Enc}^\mathsf{P}(1^\lambda, ek, m)$
$m \leftarrow \mathsf{SE.Dec}^\mathsf{P}(1^\lambda, k, c)$	$m \leftarrow \mathsf{PKE.Dec}^\mathsf{P}(1^\lambda, dk, c)$

Function Family	Key Encapsulation Mechanism
$k \leftarrow_{\$} \mathsf{F.Kg}^\mathsf{P}(1^\lambda)$	$(ek, dk) \leftarrow_{\$} \mathsf{KEM.Kg}(1^\lambda)$
$y \leftarrow \mathsf{F.Ev}^\mathsf{P}(1^\lambda, k, x)$	$(c, k) \leftarrow_{\$} \mathsf{KEM.Encaps}^\mathsf{P}(1^\lambda, ek)$
$x \leftarrow \mathsf{F.Inv}^\mathsf{P}(1^\lambda, k, y)$	$k \leftarrow \mathsf{KEM.Decaps}^\mathsf{P}(1^\lambda, dk, c)$

A family of functions F only has inverse algorithm F.Inv if it is a blockcipher. For simplicity, we assume perfect correctness which holds for all $f \in \mathsf{P}.\mathcal{P}_\lambda$. We will make careful note of where proofs make use of this correctness. To use notions of imperfect correctness in these proofs, one must choose an imperfect correctness notion that is "robust" to the ideal primitive being programmable.

We additionally will sometimes assume a notion we call *query consistency* which requires that if c is produced by encryption/encapsulation, then decrypting/decapsulating c with the correct key only makes ideal primitive queries that were also made by encryption/encapsulation. This ensures that any querying of the ideal primitive while decrypting/decapsulating an honest ciphertext cannot be detected by a programming adversary.

3   SIM-AC Definitions and Their Shortcomings

We start by recalling the definitions that Jaeger and Tyagi [23] introduced for the simulation security of symmetric encryption or pseudorandom functions under adaptive compromise. Jaeger and Tyagi showed that these definition were achieved by very natural encryption/PRF constructions in the random oracle or ideal cipher model and that they moreover sufficed for proving the security of higher-level constructions (e.g. searchable encryption schemes, asymmetric password-authenticated key exchange, and self-revocable encrypted cloud storage). In this section, we will identify ways in which these definitions fall short. Namely, that there are other natural encryption/PRF constructions and high-level construction which cannot be proven secure using these definitions.[7]

3.1   SIM-AC Definitions

All of the SIM-AC definitions have a common structure; they measure the ability of an adversary to distinguish between a "real" and a "simulated" world. In the real world, the adversary interacts with multiple "users" that honestly execute the algorithms of scheme. The adversary has access to an exposure oracle which it can query to be given the secret keys of any users it chooses. Finally, the adversary has oracle access to the ideal primitive algorithm P.Ls. In the ideal world, the output of *all* of these oracles is provided instead by a simulator S. For the definition to be meaningful, the behavior of the simulator when responding to queries for "unexposed" users is restricted in some manner. (For example, the simulator may be required to return a uniformly random string or may only be given partial information about what the query was).

Pseudorandom Function Security. We start with the notion of SIM-AC-PRF security for a function family F. It is captured by the game $G^{sim-ac-prf}_{F,S,P,\mathcal{A}_{prf}}$ shown in Fig. 2. The variable X is used to track which users have been exposed, so X_u is true when the user has been exposed. The game hardcodes that random values are returned for evaluation queries to unexposed users in the simulated world. Inputs and outputs to evaluation are stored in the table T_u which is given to S when u is exposed.

We define $\mathsf{Adv}^{sim-ac-prf}_{F,S,P,\mathcal{A}_{prf}}(\lambda) = 2\Pr[G^{sim-ac-prf}_{F,S,P,\mathcal{A}_{prf}}(\lambda)] - 1$ and say that F is SIM-AC-PRF secure with P if for all PPT $\mathcal{A}_{prf}$ there exists a PPT S such that $\mathsf{Adv}^{sim-ac-prf}_{F,S,P,\mathcal{A}_{prf}}(\cdot)$ is negligible. Intuitively, this definition captures that the outputs of F_k look random to an adversary until they expose k.

Encryption Definitions. Next we recall the SIM-AC security notions for a symmetric encryption scheme SE. Consider the game $G^{sim-ac-cca}_{SE,S,P,\mathcal{A}_{cca}}(\lambda)$ shown in Fig. 2. During encryption queries for unexposed users, the simulator is only told

---

[7] Technically, we do not show that these proofs are impossible. We show why the "natural" proofs fail and informally argue why it seems difficult to find other proofs.

Game $G_{F,S,P,\mathcal{A}_{prf}}^{sim-ac-prf}(\lambda)$

$k_{(\cdot)} \leftarrow\!\!{\scriptstyle\$}\ \mathsf{F.Kg}(1^\lambda)$
$\sigma_\mathsf{P} \leftarrow\!\!{\scriptstyle\$}\ \mathsf{P.Init}(1^\lambda)$
$\sigma \leftarrow\!\!{\scriptstyle\$}\ \mathsf{S.Init}(1^\lambda)$
$b \leftarrow\!\!{\scriptstyle\$}\ \{0,1\}$
$b' \leftarrow\!\!{\scriptstyle\$}\ \mathcal{A}_{prf}^{\mathrm{Ev},\mathrm{Exp},\mathrm{Prim}}(1^\lambda)$
Return $(b = b')$

$\underline{\mathrm{Prim}(k,x)}$
$y_1 \leftarrow\!\!{\scriptstyle\$}\ \mathsf{P.Ls}(1^\lambda,k,x:\sigma_\mathsf{P})$
$y_0 \leftarrow\!\!{\scriptstyle\$}\ \mathsf{S.Ls}(1^\lambda,k,x:\sigma)$
Return y_b

Game $G_{SE,S,P,\mathcal{A}_{cca}}^{sim-ac-cca}(\lambda)$

$k_{(\cdot)} \leftarrow\!\!{\scriptstyle\$}\ \mathsf{SE.Kg}(1^\lambda)$
$\sigma_\mathsf{P} \leftarrow\!\!{\scriptstyle\$}\ \mathsf{P.Init}(1^\lambda)$
$\sigma \leftarrow\!\!{\scriptstyle\$}\ \mathsf{S.Init}(1^\lambda)$
$b \leftarrow\!\!{\scriptstyle\$}\ \{0,1\}$
$b' \leftarrow\!\!{\scriptstyle\$}\ \mathcal{A}_{cca}^{\mathrm{Enc},\mathrm{Dec},\mathrm{Exp},\mathrm{Prim}}(1^\lambda)$
Return $(b = b')$

$\underline{\mathrm{Prim}(k,x)}$
$y_1 \leftarrow\!\!{\scriptstyle\$}\ \mathsf{P.Ls}(1^\lambda,k,x:\sigma_\mathsf{P})$
$y_0 \leftarrow\!\!{\scriptstyle\$}\ \mathsf{S.Ls}(1^\lambda,k,x:\sigma)$
Return y_b

$\underline{\mathrm{Ev}(u,x)}$
If $T_u[x] \neq \perp$ then return $T_u[x]$
$y_1 \leftarrow \mathsf{F.Ev}^\mathsf{P}(1^\lambda,k_u,x)$
If X_u then $y_0 \leftarrow\!\!{\scriptstyle\$}\ \mathsf{S.Ev}(1^\lambda,u,x:\sigma)$
Else $y_0 \leftarrow\!\!{\scriptstyle\$}\ \mathsf{F.Out}(\lambda)$
$T_u[x] \leftarrow y_b$
Return y_b

$\underline{\mathrm{Exp}(u)}$
$k_1' \leftarrow k_u$
$k_0' \leftarrow\!\!{\scriptstyle\$}\ \mathsf{S.Exp}(1^\lambda,u,T_u:\sigma)$
$X_u \leftarrow$ true
Return k_b'

$\underline{\mathrm{Enc}(u,m)}$
If not X_u then $\ell \leftarrow |m|$ else $\ell \leftarrow m$
$c_1 \leftarrow\!\!{\scriptstyle\$}\ \mathsf{SE.Enc}^\mathsf{P}(1^\lambda,k_u,m)$
$c_0 \leftarrow\!\!{\scriptstyle\$}\ \mathsf{S.Enc}(1^\lambda,u,\ell:\sigma)$
$M_u.\mathsf{add}(c_b,m)$; Return c_b

$\underline{\mathrm{Dec}(u,c)}$
If $M_u c \neq \perp$ then return $M_u c$
$m_1 \leftarrow \mathsf{SE.Dec}^\mathsf{P}(1^\lambda,k_u,c)$
$m_0 \leftarrow\!\!{\scriptstyle\$}\ \mathsf{S.Dec}(1^\lambda,u,c:\sigma)$
Return m_b

$\underline{\mathrm{Exp}(u)}$
$k_1' \leftarrow k_u$; $k_0' \leftarrow\!\!{\scriptstyle\$}\ \mathsf{S.Exp}(1^\lambda,u,M_u:\sigma)$
$X_u \leftarrow$ true; Return k_b'

Fig. 2. Games defining SIM-AC-PRF security of F and SIM-AC-CCA security of SE.

the length of the message m. The list M_u stores the messages queried to user u and ciphertexts returned. It is given to the simulator when that user is exposed. If the attacker forwards challenge ciphertexts from encryption to decryption, this list is used to respond appropriately.

We define $\mathrm{Adv}_{SE,S,P,\mathcal{A}_{cca}}^{sim-ac-cca}(\lambda) = 2\Pr[G_{SE,S,P,\mathcal{A}_{cca}}^{sim-ac-cca}(\lambda)] - 1$ and say SE is SIM-AC-CCA secure with P if for all PPT $\mathcal{A}_{cca}$ there exists a PPT S such that $\mathrm{Adv}_{SE,S,P,\mathcal{A}_{cca}}^{sim-ac-cca}(\cdot)$ is negligible. Intuitively, this definition captures that an adversary learns nothing (other than the length) about a message m encrypted with a key k until they expose k. For chosen-plaintext security we restrict attention to attackers that never query decryption. We then write the superscript sim-ac-cpa.

Stronger notions of security are captured by requiring that S be chosen from some restricted set. Key-private security (SIM-AC-KP) requires that the CPA simulator respond to encryption queries for un-exposed users using an algorithm $\mathsf{S.Enc}_1(1^\lambda,\ell:\sigma)$ which *is not* given u as input. Indistinguishable from random security (SIM-AC-\$) requires that the CPA simulator respond to encryption queries for un-exposed users by sampling c from a set $\mathsf{S.Out}(\lambda,\ell)$. Authenticated encryption security (SIM-AC-AE) requires that the CCA simulator respond to encryption queries as in SIM-AC-$ security and to decryption queries for un-exposed users with $\perp$.

Simplifying Assumptions. Jaeger and Tyagi observed the following simplify-ing assumptions (copied almost verbatim from [23]) for their SIM-AC definitions.

- If an oracle is deterministic in the real world we can assume that the adversary never repeats a query to this oracle or that the simulator always provides the same output to repeated queries.
- We can assume the adversary never makes a query to a user it has already exposed or that for such queries the simulator just runs the code of the real world (replacing calls to P with calls to S.Ls).
- We can assume the adversary always queries with $u \in [u_\lambda] = \{1, 2, \ldots, u_\lambda\}$ for some polynomial $u_{(\cdot)}$ or that the simulator is agnostic to the particular strings used to reference users.
- We can assume that adversaries never make queries that fail "Require" state-ments. (All requirements of oracles will be efficiently computable given the transcripts of queries the adversary has made).

Looking ahead, we will be able to make the analogous assumptions for the new definitions introduced in this paper. These assumptions are convenient for prov-ing that a scheme satisfies a given SIM-AC definition of security. The fact that these assumptions are not hardcoded into the security game is convenient when proving the security of a higher-level construction assuming that constituent schemes satisfy some SIM-AC security notion.

3.2   Shortcomings of SIM-AC

Now that we have introduced SIM-AC security notions we can discuss ways that they fall short of being able to establish the results we would like.

Multiple Schemes with the Same P. Suppose a higher-level protocol is con-structed from multiple underlying schemes satisfying SIM-AC security notions. We generally will not be able to prove the security of the protocol if the underly-ing schemes make use of the same P.[8] Performing a SIM-AC reduction with the first scheme will replace the entirety of P with some S.Ls. With P being gone, the security of the second scheme with respect to P is of no use.

As a toy example, we might consider function families F_0 and F_1. Even assum-ing they are both SIM-AC-PRF secure with P, it seems impossible to prove F is SIM-AC-PRF secure where $F.Ev^P(1^\lambda, (k_0, k_1), (b, x)) = F_b.Ev^P(1^\lambda, k_b, x)$. Sev-eral of Jaeger and Tyagi's proofs were restricted by this and had to assume underlying schemes used distinct ideal primitives.

---

[8] Note this is the more general result, as we could let $P = P_1 \times P_2 \times \ldots$ and have the i-th scheme using P only actually query P_i.

Multiple Uses of the Same Scheme. Suppose a higher-level protocol is constructed from an underlying scheme satisfying a SIM-AC security notion and that this scheme is used in several distinct ways in the protocol.

If it's not possible to write a careful reduction that covers all of the uses of the scheme at once, then we run into a similar issue as the above. The first application of the scheme's SIM-AC security will replace its ideal primitive with a simulator, preventing us from applying its security again.

As a toy example, we might consider a function family F. Even assuming F is SIM-AC-PRF secure with P, it seems impossible to prove that F′ is SIM-AC-PRF secure where $F'.\mathsf{Ev}^P(1^\lambda, k, (x_0, x_1)) = F.\mathsf{Ev}^P(1^\lambda, F.\mathsf{Ev}^P(1^\lambda, k, x_0), x_1)$.

One of Jaeger and Tyagi's proofs (for their Theorem D.1) almost ran into issue with this. However, they seemingly got "lucky" in that for that particular proof they were able to use just plain PRF security for the first use of the underlying function family.

Single-user Security Implies Multi-user Security. With most "standard" security notions (e.g. PRF, IND-CPA, IND-CCA) single-user security implies multi-user security. These results are proven by a "hybrid proof" wherein the single-user attacker picks a user u at random. It externally simulates u with its own oracle, internally simulates all "prior" users as in the $b = 0$ world, and internally simulates all "later" users as in the $b = 1$ world.

We run into issue if we try to write an analogous proof for SIM-AC definitions. Note that simulating the $b = 0$ world for some users requires the attacker to run the given single-user simulator. This creates a circular dependency as in SIM-AC the simulator is allowed to depend on the adversary.

Even if we changed the order of quantification, we would still run into issues. Each instance of the single-user simulator expects to already have complete control of the ideal primitive. This makes it unclear what ideal primitive oracle the single-user adversary should provide the multi-user adversary it runs internally. Because of these issues, Jaeger and Tyagi directly consider multi-user SIM-AC definitions and do not discuss single-user variants thereof.

It may seem strange to consider "adaptive compromise" in a single-user setting. Do expose queries make sense where there is only one user to be exposed? It is useful to first observe that multi-user SIM-AC notions would be unchanged if we required that the attacker expose all users before halting. Crucially, these definitions use "online" simulators that are forced to commit to simulated ciphertexts (without knowledge of the encrypted message) for users that will later be exposed (at which time the simulator is told the messages).

4 SIM*-AC Security

We saw in the previous section some ways in which SIM-AC security definitions cannot be used for proving results which intuitively "should" be possible to prove with a "good" security defintion. In this section, we will introduce a related class of security definitions which we notate by SIM*-AC. These new definition will strengthen the power of the attacker and weaken the power of the simulator. This allows proving the results that were a challenge for the prior definitions, while still maintaining the value of the prior definitions. In particular, the results previously shown by Jaeger and Tyagi with SIM-AC can be shown to hold with SIM*-AC, while requiring minimal modifications to the proofs. We discuss the details of this in Sect. 6.

Motivating the New Definition. The starting place for our new definitions partially goes back to the original explicit proposal of random oracles by Bellare and Rogaway [8]. Therein, their definition of zero knowledge in the random oracle model requires that the (offline) simulator's final outputs includes the list of points at which it would like the random oracle to have given values. At all other points, the oracle is sampled at random. Wee [28] built on this, considering different levels of how the simulator controls the random oracle and showing that zero-knowledge proofs are closed under sequential composition when the random oracle is explicitly programmable (or non-programmable). Sequential composition fails in the "fully programmable" model as applying the simulator for the first round of execution replaces the random oracle completely, at which point we cannot use it to reason about further rounds.

There is a second subtle detail allowing sequential composition proof to go though with polynomially many rounds. It is important that (part of) the adversary was quantified *after* the simulator. The proof followed a hybrid argument wherein rounds of zero knowledge are switched from real to simulated, one at a time. To apply security for a particular round, the attacker must simulate the other (real and simulated) rounds. For a constant number of rounds, we could fix the attacker for the first round, be given its simulator, use the simulator in the attacker for the second round, be given its simulator, and so on. When the number of rounds is polynomial, we cannot fix an attacker for each round. Instead a single attacker must work for all rounds, which requires knowing the simulator ahead of time so it can properly emulate simulated rounds.

To resolve the issues identified with composition and hybrid arguments for SIM-AC we will restrict the simulator to explicitly program the ideal primitive and require a universal simulator that works for all attackers. However, this still is not enough! The zero knowledge composition discussed above is importantly "sequential" in an "offline simulation" setting. The simulator runs once in isolation, then provides its output to the attacker which runs in isolation. The attacker has complete control over all code executing with it, so can perfectly emulate the programmed random oracle. In an "online simulation" setting like SIM-AC, the attacker runs in parallel with the honest scheme algorithms or the simulator. Our proofs would run into issues when attackers internally run copies of the simulator which wants to program the random oracle, but the attacker is then unable to force the honest scheme algorithms or simulator it does not control to use this modified random oracle. We resolve this issue by expanding the power of the adversary and giving it the capacity to program the ideal primitive.[9] We use the prefix SIM*-AC for the definitions we write in this style.

Summarizing, in our SIM*-AC definitions simulators and adversaries can access an oracle PPRIM which allows them to evaluate *or explicitly program* the ideal primitive. Schemes are still restricted to not program the ideal primitive. This is a restriction on the simulator and strengthening of the attacker. Because of the programmability of P we must write the code so that S is only run in the ideal world and SE is only run in the real world.

Comparisons to Prior Definitions. Through this sequence of ideas we have reached the same general structure of random oracle modeling proposed by Camenisch, Drijvers, Gagliardoni, Lehmann, and Neven [10]. Their work is in the universal composability (UC) setting where they consider several models for global random oracles. In one, simulators and adversaries can explicitly program the random oracle. They show it allows security proofs that very efficient and natural random oracle-based constructions of several primitives satisfy the desired security. Our work generalizes this any ideal primitive (not just random oracles) and considers its application outside the universal composability framework. That UC and SIM-AC work well with a similar programmability notion is, in hindsight, natural as they both consider *online* simulation.

Our SIM*-AC definitions as not strictly better for cryptographers than the SIM-AC definitions of Jaeger and Tyagi [23]. One benefit of their work was the ease with which existing results could be ported to the SIM-AC setting (e.g. replacing IND-CPA in a proof with SIM-AC-CPA). This holds to some extent with the new SIM*-AC definitions as well, but proofs do occasionally run into additional difficulties because of fragilities caused by the programming of the oracle. Overall we believe that this cost is worth the benefits provided by our new definitions being able to show natural and desirable results that are seemingly out of reach of plain SIM-AC.

High-Level Remarks. There is value in incorporating this explicit programming capacity for adversaries even into non-simulation definitions. Consider the construction of some high-level system making use of multiple underlying schemes that use the same ideal primitive, some for SIM*-AC security and some for non-simulation security notions. (See, e.g., the searchable encryption proof in [23] that involved the standard notion of PRF security in addition to SIM-AC-PRF/KPA security). If the proof requires use of the non-simulation security notion *after* a SIM*-AC notion has already been applied, this will only be possible if the attacker can program the ideal primitive in the non-simulation notion.

Allowing the adversary to program the ideal primitive is *strange*. It does not seem to capture anything about reality, despite the fact that we allow the adversary to do this programming even in the "real world". However, this ability

---

[9] We would have run into similar issues had their hybrid tried to switch rounds to simulated from first to last, rather than the last to first approach they took.

Game $G^{\text{sim}^*\text{-ac-prf}}_{F,S,P,\mathcal{A}_{\text{prf}}}(\lambda)$	$\text{Ev}(u,x)$

$k_{(\cdot)} \leftarrow\!\!\$ \, F.\text{Kg}(1^\lambda)$
 $\sigma_P \leftarrow\!\!\$ \, P.\text{Init}(1^\lambda)$
 $\sigma \leftarrow\!\!\$ \, S.\text{Init}(1^\lambda)$
 $b \leftarrow\!\!\$ \, \{0,1\}$
 $b' \leftarrow\!\!\$ \, \mathcal{A}_{\text{prf}}^{\text{Ev},\text{Exp},\text{PPRIM}}(1^\lambda)$
 Return $(b = b')$
	If $T_u[x] \neq \bot$ then return $T_u[x]$
	 If $b = 1$ then $y \leftarrow F.\text{Ev}^P(1^\lambda, k_u, x)$
	 If $b = 0$ then
	    If X_u then $y \leftarrow S.\text{Ev}^{\text{PPRIM}}(1^\lambda, u, x : \sigma)$
	    Else $y \leftarrow\!\!\$ \, F.\text{Out}(\lambda)$
	 $T_u[x] \leftarrow y$
	 Return y

$\text{PPRIM}(\text{Op}, k, x, y)$	$\text{Exp}(u)$
Require $\text{Op} \in \{\text{Ls}, \text{Prog}\}$ $y \leftarrow\!\!\$ \, P.\text{Op}(1^\lambda, k, x, y : \sigma_P)$ Return y	If $b = 1$ then $k' \leftarrow k_u$ If $b = 0$ then $k' \leftarrow\!\!\$ \, S.\text{Exp}^{\text{PPRIM}}(1^\lambda, u, T_u : \sigma)$ $X_u \leftarrow \text{true}$; Return k'
Game $G^{\text{sim}^*\text{-ac-cca}}_{SE,S,P,\mathcal{A}_{\text{cca}}}(\lambda)$	$\text{Enc}(u,m)$
$k_{(\cdot)} \leftarrow\!\!\$ \, SE.\text{Kg}(1^\lambda)$ $\sigma_P \leftarrow\!\!\$ \, P.\text{Init}(1^\lambda)$ $\sigma \leftarrow\!\!\$ \, S.\text{Init}(1^\lambda)$ $b \leftarrow\!\!\$ \, \{0,1\}$ $b' \leftarrow\!\!\$ \, \mathcal{A}_{\text{cca}}^{\text{Enc},\text{Dec},\text{Exp},\text{PPRIM}}(1^\lambda)$ Return $(b = b')$	If not X_u then $\ell \leftarrow |m|$ else $\ell \leftarrow m$ If $b = 1$ then $c \leftarrow\!\!\$ \, SE.\text{Enc}^P(1^\lambda, k_u, m)$ If $b = 0$ then $c \leftarrow\!\!\$ \, S.\text{Enc}^{\text{PPRIM}}(1^\lambda, u, \ell : \sigma)$ $M_u.\text{add}(c, m)$; Return c
	$\text{Dec}(u,c)$
$\text{PPRIM}(\text{Op}, k, x, y)$	If $M_u c \neq \bot$ then return $M_u c$ If $b = 1$ then $m \leftarrow SE.\text{Dec}^P(1^\lambda, k_u, c)$ If $b = 0$ then $m \leftarrow\!\!\$ \, S.\text{Dec}^{\text{PPRIM}}(1^\lambda, u, c : \sigma)$ Return m
Require $\text{Op} \in \{\text{Ls}, \text{Prog}\}$ $y \leftarrow\!\!\$ \, P.\text{Op}(1^\lambda, k, x, y : \sigma_P)$ Return y	$\text{Exp}(u)$
	If $b = 1$ then $k' \leftarrow k_u$ If $b = 0$ then $k' \leftarrow\!\!\$ \, S.\text{Exp}^{\text{PPRIM}}(1^\lambda, u, M_u : \sigma)$ $X_u \leftarrow \text{true}$; Return k'

Fig. 3. Games defining SIM*-AC-PRF security of F and SIM*-AC-CCA security of SE. We use highlighting to indicate where the definitions differ from SIM-AC versions.

will be crucial to how we can use this new definition to prove the results that we were unable to with the original SIM-AC definitions. We can view this in the same paradigm we discussed for SIM-AC-style definitions in general; there is value in studying very strong definitions which exploit ideal primitives beyond how they can reasonably be thought to capture something about reality because these notions can then serve as intermediate steps for proving (in the ideal model) that the scheme satisfies other more "reasonable" security notions.

4.1   SIM*-AC Definitions

Pseudorandom Function Security. We start with PRF security for a function family F. Our new definition is captured by the game $G^{\text{sim}^*\text{-ac-prf}}_{F,S,P,\mathcal{A}_{\text{prf}}}$ shown in Fig. 3. It differs from $G^{\text{sim-ac-prf}}_{F,S,P,\mathcal{A}_{\text{prf}}}$ as described above; namely, $\mathcal{A}_{\text{prf}}$ is given oracle

PPRIM which uses P in both the real and simulated world.[10] In the simulated world, S is also given PPRIM to query and program P. Note that the scheme algorithm F.Ev is still given access only to P.Ls and not to P.Prog.

We define $\mathsf{Adv}^{\mathsf{sim}^*\text{-}\mathsf{ac}\text{-}\mathsf{prf}}_{\mathsf{F},\mathsf{S},\mathsf{P},\mathcal{A}_{\mathsf{prf}}}(\lambda) = 2\Pr[\mathsf{G}^{\mathsf{sim}^*\text{-}\mathsf{ac}\text{-}\mathsf{prf}}_{\mathsf{F},\mathsf{S},\mathsf{P},\mathcal{A}_{\mathsf{prf}}}(\lambda)] - 1$ and say that F is SIM*-AC-PRF secure with P if there exists a PPT S such that for all PPT $\mathcal{A}_{\mathsf{prf}}$, the advantage function $\mathsf{Adv}^{\mathsf{sim}^*\text{-}\mathsf{ac}\text{-}\mathsf{prf}}_{\mathsf{F},\mathsf{S},\mathsf{P},\mathcal{A}_{\mathsf{prf}}}(\cdot)$ is negligible. Note here that we quantified the simulator before the adversary, unlike in SIM-AC-PRF security where the simulator is allowed to depend on the adversary. This strengthens the definition and is necessary for some of our positive results, but for some of our results the weaker quantification will suffice. We say F is wSIM*-AC-PRF secure with P if for all PPT $\mathcal{A}_{\mathsf{prf}}$ there exists a PPT S such that $\mathsf{Adv}^{\mathsf{sim}^*\text{-}\mathsf{ac}\text{-}\mathsf{prf}}_{\mathsf{F},\mathsf{S},\mathsf{P},\mathcal{A}_{\mathsf{prf}}}(\cdot)$ is negligible.

Encryption Definitions. The SIM*-AC-CCA security of an encryption scheme SE is similarly captured by the game $\mathsf{G}^{\mathsf{sim}^*\text{-}\mathsf{ac}\text{-}\mathsf{cca}}$ defined in Fig. 3 which modifies the SIM-AC game to have the attacker and simulator both use PPRIM. We define $\mathsf{Adv}^{\mathsf{sim}^*\text{-}\mathsf{ac}\text{-}\mathsf{cca}}_{\mathsf{SE},\mathsf{S},\mathsf{P},\mathcal{A}_{\mathsf{cca}}}(\lambda) = 2\Pr[\mathsf{G}^{\mathsf{sim}^*\text{-}\mathsf{ac}\text{-}\mathsf{cca}}_{\mathsf{SE},\mathsf{S},\mathsf{P},\mathcal{A}_{\mathsf{cca}}}(\lambda)] - 1$ and say SE is SIM*-AC-CCA secure with P if there exists a PPT S such that for all PPT $\mathcal{A}_{\mathsf{cca}}$, the advantage function $\mathsf{Adv}^{\mathsf{sim}^*\text{-}\mathsf{ac}\text{-}\mathsf{cca}}_{\mathsf{SE},\mathsf{S},\mathsf{P},\mathcal{A}_{\mathsf{cca}}}(\cdot)$ is negligible. wSIM*-AC-CCA is captured by quantifying the simulator after the adversary.

Chosen-plaintext security is captured by restricting attention to attackers that do not query decryption. We then write sim*-ac-cpa in superscripts. SIM*-AC-X and wSIM*-AC-X security for $X \in \{\mathsf{KPA}, \$, \mathsf{AE}\}$ security are defined by restricting the behavior of the simulator appropriately.

4.2 Single-user Security Implies Multi-user Security

As with SIM-AC security, we can capture single-user SIM*-AC security by requiring that all of the attacker's oracle queries use the same value of u. The following theorem captures that single-user SIM*-AC-CPA security implies multi-user security. The result would also hold with SIM*-AC-X security for any $X \in \{\mathsf{PRF}, \mathsf{CCA}, \$, \mathsf{AC}\}$, via the same proof technique. If *does not* hold for $X = \mathsf{KP}$. We will discuss why in more detail after the proof.

Theorem 1. *Single-user SIM*-AC-CPA security implies multi-user SIM*-AC-CPA security.*

This proof follows using the ideas from a fairly standard single-user to multi-user proof via a hybrid argument. Given a single-user simulator S_1 and multi-user adversary $\mathcal{A}$, we define single-user $\mathcal{A}_1$ to pick a random t and respond to queries with $u < t$ by encrypting honestly, with $u = t$ using its own encryption oracle, and with $u > t$ using a copy of S_1 specific for that user. The multi-user simulator we construct runs multiple independent copies of the single-user simulator – one

---

[10] Here we are using a notational convention that an algorithm given more inputs than it expects will ignore any extra inputs, so $\mathsf{P}.\mathsf{Ls}(1^\lambda, k, x, y : \sigma_{\mathsf{P}})$ is equivalent to $\mathsf{P}.\mathsf{Ls}(1^\lambda, k, x : \sigma_{\mathsf{P}})$.

for each user. Note that this proof critically requires all three of the changes we used to derive SIM*-AC from SIM-AC: (i) the simulator needs to be quantified before the adversary so that $\mathcal{A}_1$ can run S_1, (ii) the simulator must not have full control of the ideal primitives output so there is no ambiguity in which "copy" of the simulator run by $\mathcal{A}_1$ should get to respond to primitive queries, and (iii) the adversary must be able to program the ideal primitive so that $\mathcal{A}_1$ is able to correctly control the primitive when running copies of S_1.

Proof. Let SE be single-user SIM*-AC-CPA secure with P and S_1 be the simulator that is guaranteed to exist. We show that SE is SIM*-AC-CPA secure with P via the following simulator which runs independent copies of S_1 for each user.

S.Init(1^λ)	S.Enc$^{\mathrm{PPRIM}}(1^\lambda, u, \ell : \sigma_{(.)})$	S.Exp$^{\mathrm{PPRIM}}(1^\lambda, u, M_u : \sigma_{(.)})$
$\sigma_{(.)} \leftarrow\!\!\$ \ S_1.\mathrm{Init}(1^\lambda)$	$c \leftarrow\!\!\$ \ S_1.\mathrm{Enc}^{\mathrm{PPRIM}}(1^\lambda, u, \ell : \sigma_u)$	$k \leftarrow\!\!\$ \ S_1.\mathrm{Exp}^{\mathrm{PPRIM}}(1^\lambda, u, M_u : \sigma_u)$
Return $\sigma_{(.)}$	Return c	Return k

Let $\mathcal{A}$ be a SIM*-AC-CPA adversary. It will be notationally convenient to assume that it only queries users with identifiers $u \in [u_\lambda] = \{1, \ldots, u_\lambda\}$ where $u_{(.)}$ is a polynomial. This assumption is without loss of generality.

Hybrid $H_i(\lambda)$, $0 \le i \le u_\lambda$	Enc(u, m)	Exp(u)
For $u \in [u_\lambda]$ do	If $u \le i$ then $d \leftarrow 0$	If $u \le i$ then $d \leftarrow 0$
$\quad k_u \leftarrow\!\!\$ \ \mathrm{SE.Kg}(1^\lambda)$	Else $d \leftarrow 1$	Else $d \leftarrow 1$
$\quad \sigma_u \leftarrow\!\!\$ \ S_1.\mathrm{Init}(1^\lambda)$	$c \leftarrow \mathrm{Enc}_d(u, m)$	$k \leftarrow \mathrm{Exp}_d(u)$
$\sigma_P \leftarrow\!\!\$ \ \mathrm{P.Init}(1^\lambda)$	Return c	Return k
$b' \leftarrow\!\!\$ \ \mathcal{A}^{\mathrm{Enc, Exp, PPrim}}(1^\lambda)$		
Return $(b' = 1)$		

Enc$_d(u, m)$	Exp$_d(u)$
If not X_u then $\ell \leftarrow |m|$ else $\ell \leftarrow m$	If $d = 1$ then $k \leftarrow k_u$
If $d = 1$ then $c \leftarrow\!\!\$ \ \mathrm{SE.Enc}^P(1^\lambda, k_u, m)$	Else $\quad k \leftarrow\!\!\$ \ S_1.\mathrm{Exp}^{\mathrm{PPRIM}}(1^\lambda, u, M_u$:
Else $c \leftarrow\!\!\$ \ S_1.\mathrm{Enc}^{\mathrm{PPRIM}}(1^\lambda, u, \ell : \sigma_u)$	$\sigma_u)$
$M_u.\mathrm{add}(c, m)$	$X_u \leftarrow \mathrm{true}$
Return c	Return k

Adversary $\mathcal{A}_1^{\mathrm{Enc, Exp, PPRIM}}(\lambda)$	EncSim(u, m)
For $u \in [u_\lambda]$ do	If $u < t$ then $c \leftarrow \mathrm{Enc}_0(u, m)$
$\quad k_u \leftarrow\!\!\$ \ \mathrm{SE.Kg}(1^\lambda)$	Else if $u = t$ then $c \leftarrow \mathrm{Enc}(u, m)$
$\quad \sigma_u \leftarrow\!\!\$ \ S_1.\mathrm{Init}(1^\lambda)$	Else $c \leftarrow \mathrm{Enc}_1(u, m)$
$t \leftarrow\!\!\$ \ \{1, \ldots, u_\lambda\}$	Return c
$b' \leftarrow\!\!\$ \ \mathcal{A}^{\mathrm{EncSim, ExpSim, PPRIM}}(1^\lambda)$	ExpSim(u)
Return b'	If $u < t$ then $k \leftarrow \mathrm{Exp}_0(u)$
	Else if $u = t$ then $k \leftarrow \mathrm{Exp}(u)$
Enc$_d(u, m)$, Exp$_d(u)$	Else $k \leftarrow \mathrm{Exp}_1(u)$
//Unchanged from above	Return k

Fig. 4. Hybrids and adversary showing single-user security implies multi-user.

Now, consider the hybrid games H_i for $i = 0, \ldots, u_\lambda$ defined in Fig. 4. For $u \le i$, the game uses ENC_0 and EXP_0 to respond to encryption and exposure queries as in the $b = 0$ simulated world of $G^{\text{sim}^*\text{-ac-cpa}}$ using S. Otherwise, it uses ENC_1 and EXP_1 to respond as in the $b = 1$ real world. Each hybrid game returns true whenever $\mathcal{A}$ outputs 1. When $i = u_\lambda$, it always holds that $u \le i$ so this game is identical to the $b = 0$ simulated world (except that the output boolean is flipped). In the other extreme, when $i = 0$, it never holds that $u \le i$ so this game is identical to the $b = 1$ real world. Then (by standard conditional probability calculation) we have

$$\text{Adv}^{\text{sim}^*\text{-ac-cpa}}_{\text{SE,S,P,}\mathcal{A}}(\lambda) = \Pr[H_0] - \Pr[H_{u_\lambda}] = \sum_{i=1}^{u_\lambda} \Pr[H_{i-1}] - \Pr[H_i].$$

We construct a single-user adversary $\mathcal{A}_1$ that obtains advantage $1/u_\lambda$ times the above. It samples an index $t \in \{1, \ldots, u_\lambda\}$ at random. Then it runs $\mathcal{A}$, simulating their oracle queries. When $u < t$, it responds as in the simulated world of $G^{\text{ep-sim-ac-cpa}}$ using S_1. When $u = t$ it forwards the query to its own oracle. Otherwise, it responds to ENC and EXP queries as in the real world. Let b denote the bit in the game $\mathcal{A}_1$ is being run in and t be the random value picked by $\mathcal{A}_1$. Then in the view of $\mathcal{A}$, the oracles for the first $t - b$ users are simulated and the rest are real – this is identical to its view in the hybrid game H_{t-b}.

Then the following calculations complete the proof.

$$\text{Adv}^{\text{sim}^*\text{-ac-cpa}}_{\text{SE,S}_1\text{,P,}\mathcal{A}_1}(\lambda) = \mathbf{E}_t[\Pr[H_{t-1}]] - \mathbf{E}_t[\Pr[H_{t-0}]]$$

$$= (1/u_\lambda) \sum_{t=1}^{u_\lambda} \Pr[H_{t-1}] - (1/u_\lambda) \sum_{t=1}^{u_\lambda} \Pr[H_t]$$

$$= (1/u_\lambda) \sum_{i=1}^{u_\lambda} \Pr[H_{i-1}] - \Pr[H_i]$$

$$= (1/u_\lambda)\text{Adv}^{\text{sim}^*\text{-ac-cpa}}_{\text{SE,S,P,}\mathcal{A}}(\lambda).$$

Here $\mathbf{E}_t$ denotes expectation over $t \twoheadleftarrow \{1, \ldots, u_\lambda\}$.   □

We can note in the above proof that for $\mathcal{A}_1$ to be able to correctly run ENC_0 and EXP_0 it needed to run S_1. This means that we needed the stronger quantification where the adversary can depend on the simulator and that the adversary needed to have the ability to program the random oracle.

Key-Private Security. Among the various SIM*-AC security notions we consider here, the only variant for which single-user security does not imply multi-user security is SIM*-AC-KPA security. Here, the simulator may not make use of its input u when replying to encryption queries for un-exposed users (beyond checking if they are exposed). Note that in the hybrid argument above, the multi-user simulator S uses the user identifier u to decide which state σ_u to use. Hence this is incompatible with SIM*-AC-KPA security. Taking a step back, we can notice that this issue with the proof is unsurprising and inherent. The issue is that that single-user SIM*-AC-KPA does not meaningfully capture any notion of key-privacy because the restriction on the simulator's behavior is trivially achievable when the attacker will only every query a single user. This is nicely captured by the following result.

Theorem 2. *Single-user SIM*-AC-KPA security is equivalent to SIM*-AC-CPA security, which is weaker than SIM*-AC-KPA security.*

Proof (Sketch). Note that single-user SIM*-AC-KPA security implies single-user SIM*-AC-CPA security trivially. Then, by Theorem 1 this implies SIM*-AC-CPA security. In the other direction, we can create a single-user SIM*-AC-KPA simulator from a SIM*-AC-CPA simulator by always running the latter on, say, $u = 1$. Hence the first claim of the theorem holds.

We can see that SIM*-AC-CPA security is weaker than SIM*-AC-KPA security by constructing a contrived scheme. Given some scheme SE, we define a new scheme which adds a random bit d to its keys and then appends d to every ciphertext produced. It is straightforward to show this new scheme is SIM*-AC-CPA secure if SE was, but that is not SIM*-AC-KPA secure.   □

4.3   Cascade Construction

If $F : F.K \times F.Inp \to F.K$ is a function family and n is a polynomial, then the n-cascade construction $F^n : F.K \times F.Inp^n \to F.K$ is defined by the evaluation algorithm $F^n.Ev(1^\lambda, k_0, x)$ which computes $k_i \leftarrow F.Ev(1^\lambda, k_{i-1}, x_i)$ for $i = 1, \ldots, n(\lambda)$ and then outputs $k_{n(\lambda)}$. Here x_i denotes the i-th entry of vector x. This is a "domain extension" technique for building a PRF with a large domain from one with a small domain. It was originally defined and analyzed in [4].[11] F^n generalizes the GGM construction of a PRF from a PRG [17]. It underlies several other constructions of PRFs including AMAC, HMAC, and NMAC [1–3].

Theorem 3. *If F is SIM*-AC-PRF secure with P, then F^n is as well.*

The proof of this result is given in the full version. Intuitively, we can think of the possible keys generated by F^n existing in a tree structure. Our proof does a hybrid argument over the layers of the tree where we one at a time switch the layers to being simulated. The simulator for a given layer treats all of the keys at its layer as being multiple F "users". This proof requires the "strong" quantification, the simulator to not completely replacing the ideal primitive, and the adversary having the ability to program the ideal primitive so that it can internally run the simulator for layers that have been switched already.

Jaeger and Tyagi [23, ePrint, p.22-23] said, "It is often useful to construct a PRF H with large input domains from a PRF F with smaller input domains [...]

---

[11] Technically, they considered a more general construction where the number of iterations was not a priori fixed and so the adversary was restricted to make only prefix-free queries. Our proof would extend to this setting as well.

one can often [use our techniques] to lift a PRF security proof for H to a SIM-AC-PRF security proof for H whenever F is SIM-AC-PRF secure." The cascade construction is one choice of H for which this is *not* possible with SIM-AC, but becomes possible with SIM*-AC.

5 Asymmetric Encryption

In this section, we provide our treatment for the security of asymmetric cryptographic primitives against adaptive compromise. We start by providing our security definitions for public-key encryption (PKEs) and key-encapsulation mechanisms (KEMs). Then we discuss how our definitions compare to prior definitions, in particular those of Camensich, Lehmann, Neven, and Samelin [12]. We show that the KEM/DEM approach to constructing a PKE scheme works with these definitions and that standard ways of constructing CPA/CCA secure KEMs from one-way secure primitives and a random oracle are secure.

5.1 Definitions

Public-Key Encryption. The SIM*-AC-CCA security of a public-key encryption scheme PKE is captured by the game $G^{sim^*-ac-cca}$ shown in Fig. 5. It differs from the SIM*-AC-CCA definition for symmetric encryption (Fig. 2) in that it introduces an encryption key oracle (EK) that the adversary can call to learn the public encryption key for a user and it has oracles for two different kinds of exposure. The receiver exposure oracle (REXP) is like the exposure oracles from prior games, returning a user's secret decryption key. The sender exposure oracle (SEXP) allows the attacker to ask for the randomness underlying the ciphertexts that were returned by encryption.

We define $\mathsf{Adv}^{sim^*-ac-cca}_{PKE,S,P,\mathcal{A}_{cca}}(\lambda) = 2\Pr[G^{sim^*-ac-cca}_{PKE,S,P,\mathcal{A}_{cca}}(\lambda)] - 1$ and say PKE is SIM*-AC-CCA secure with P if there exists a PPT S such that for all PPT $\mathcal{A}_{cca}$, the advantage function $\mathsf{Adv}^{sim^*-ac-cca}_{PKE,S,P,\mathcal{A}_{cca}}(\cdot)$ is negligible. wSIM*-AC-CCA is captured by quantifying the simulator after the adversary. We capture xSIM*-AC-CPA by ignoring the decryption oracle. Security considering only compromise of the receiver/sender can be captured by ignoring the appropriate oracle. Then we write SIM*-rAC or SIM*-sAC.

Key Encapsulation Mechanism. We also give definitions for key encapsulation mechanisms (KEM). Our SIM*-AC definitions are highly analogous to the corresponding public-key encryption definition. They are formally specified by the game $G^{sim-ac-cca}$ shown in Fig. 5. Therein, the ENC and DEC oracles have been replaced with ENCAPS and DECAPS oracles. The encapsulation oracle returns a ciphertext along with the corresponding encapsulated key. In the ideal world, the simulator provides the ciphertext and the encapsulated key is chosen at random from the key space by the game for unexposed users.

We define $\mathsf{Adv}^{sim^*-ac-cca}_{KEM,S,P,\mathcal{A}_{cpa}}(\lambda)$ and the notions xSIM*-yAC-X for $x \in \{\varepsilon, w\}$, $y \in \{\varepsilon, r, s\}$, and $X \in \{CCA, CPA\}$ as for PKE.

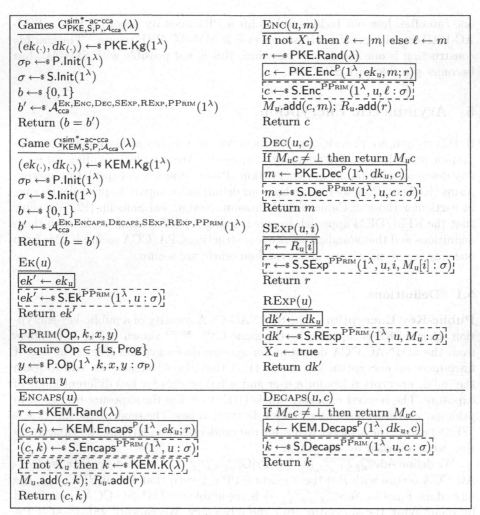

Fig. 5. Games defining the SIM*-AC-CCA security of PKE and KEM. Solid-boxed code is only executed if $b = 1$. Dash-boxed code is only executed if $b = 0$.

5.2   Comparison to SIM-FULL Definition

The definition we have arrived at is similar to the FULL-SIM security definition for PKE introduced by Camensich, Lehmann, Neven, and Samelin (CLNS) [12]. We quickly summarize the differences. There are two dimensions in which their definition is strong than ours. First, their definition considers PKE with labels, while we have decided not consider labels. Labels can easily be added. Likely, the best way to incorporate labels in constructions would be to use a symmetric encryption scheme that accepts associated data as part of the KEM/DEM transform (discussed momentarily). Second, in FULL-SIM the randomness used by key generation is revealed rather than the decryption key. SIM-AC* can be used to reason over this case by simply modify the scheme to use said randomness as its decryption key (and recompute the actual decryption key during decryption).

Our definition strengthens theirs in several dimension. Theirs is more closely analogous to SIM-AC than SIM*-AC as the simulator is given complete control of the random oracle, the adversary is not able to modify it, and the "weak" quantification is used. Resultantly, their single-user definition is seemingly unable to prove that a corresponding multi-user definition holds.

We are not restrictive in the type of ideal primitive considered. CLNS considered only one specific construction in which they basically used a trapdoor permutation generator as a KEM and then hand-crafted a symmetric encryption scheme using a random oracle.[12] We will momentarily show that the task of building SIM*-AC secure PKE can be broken down into constructing KEMs and symmetric encryption. This is modular, allowing numerous instantiation and in particular, allowing the symmetric encryption to be instantiated by well-studied and standardized schemes based on blockciphers rather than using less efficient hash functions throughout.

CLNS showed that SIM-FULL implied a variety of prior definitions considering compromise scenarios for PKE. These implications will carry over to our definition as well. We explore the relationship between SIM*-AC CCA, SIM-FULL, and these other definitions more formally in the full version. Further, CLNS considered a UC secure notion and proved it to be essentially equivalent to SIM-FULL. Camenisch, Drijvers, Gagliardoni, Lehmann, and Nevin [10] considered this in the UC programmable random oracle model, proving the same construction secure. Likely SIM*-AC-CCA is equivalent to this notion and so our result will give modular, standard, efficient instantiations of UC secure public key encryption secure under adaptive compromise.

5.3   KEM/DEM Hybrid Encryption

A common technique for building public key encryption is KEM/DEM hybrid encryption in which a key encapsulation mechanism produces a key which is

---

[12] Speaking loosely, they basically use a random input to the trapdoor permutation as a "symmetric key" with which they perform counter mode encryption, using the random oracle as a pseudorandom function and then perform a MAC over all of the relevant variables, again using the random oracle as a pseudorandom function.

then used to encrypt the message with a symmetric encryption scheme (i.e. "data encapsulation mechanism"). This was proven secure by Cramer and Shoup [15].

Let KEM be a key encapsulation mechanism and SE be a symmetric encryption scheme (i.e. data encapsulation mechanism) where SE.Kg samples uniformly from KEM.K. We denote the KEM/DEM scheme as KD[KEM, SE] and provide the algorithms KD.Enc and KD.Dec below, where we assume KEM and SE expect access to ideal primitive P. Then KD expects access to P. It key generation algorithm is defined by KD[KEM, SE].Kg = KEM.Kg.

$\underline{\text{KD}[\text{KEM}, \text{SE}].\text{Enc}^P(1^\lambda, ek, m)}$	$\underline{\text{KD}[\text{KEM}, \text{SE}].\text{Dec}^P(1^\lambda, dk, c)}$
$(c_{\text{KEM}}, k) \leftarrow_\$ \text{KEM}.\text{Encaps}^P(1^\lambda, ek)$	$(c_{\text{KEM}}, c_{\text{SE}}) \leftarrow c$
$c_{\text{SE}} \leftarrow_\$ \text{SE}.\text{Enc}^P(1^\lambda, k, m)$	$k \leftarrow \text{KEM}.\text{Decaps}^P(1^\lambda, dk, c_{\text{KEM}})$
$c \leftarrow (c_{\text{KEM}}, c_{\text{SE}})$	$m \leftarrow \text{SE}.\text{Dec}^P(1^\lambda, k, c_{\text{SE}})$
Return c	Return m

It is assumed that SE.Dec immediately halts and returns $\perp$ if $k = \perp$. Next, we show that given the appropriate adaptive compromise security for the underlying KEM scheme and encryption scheme, the composed KEM/DEM scheme is also secure against adaptive compromise.

Exposure of encryption randomness is not captured by our definitions for symmetric encryption. Rather than introduce a new security definition, in these cases we restrict attention to *coin extractable* schemes for which there exists an algorithm SE.CExt which always satisfies $\text{SE}.\text{CExt}^P(1^\lambda, k, \text{SE}.\text{Enc}^P(1^\lambda, k, m; r)) = r$. We are not aware of any practically deployed schemes which do not satisfy this. For technical reasons, we assume that SE.CExt is query consistent by which we mean that it does not make any ideal primitive queries that were not made by the execution of SE.Enc that produced its input.

Theorem 4. *Let* $x \in \{\varepsilon, w\}$, $y \in \{\varepsilon, r, s\}$, *and* $X \in \{CPA, CCA\}$. *If* KEM *is xSIM*-yAC-X secure with* P *and* SE *is xSIM*-AC-X secure with* P *(and coin extractable if* $y \in \{\varepsilon, s\}$*), then* KD[KEM, SE] *is xSIM*-yAC-X secure with* P.

In fact, for the DEM we need only "single-challenge" security wherein the attacker makes at most one encryption query per user. This allows the use of deterministic DEMs. The proof of this result is given in the full version. The general flow of the proof is what one would expect, first we replace honest use of the KEM with simulated use that outputs uniformly random keys. We think of the i-th key generated for user u as correspond to a DEM user (u, i) and replace the DEM with simulation.

5.4   Hashed KEM

We consider a simple, standard way to construct a CPA secure KEM from a one-way secure KEM and a random oracle. Conceptually, this construction follows from the CPA secure PKE scheme considered in [8]. Let KEM be a key encapsulation mechanism. Then the hashed KEM scheme which outputs the hash of a key generated by KEM is denoted as HKEM[KEM]. Its algorithms are defined as follows. Its key generation algorithm is defined by HKEM[KEM].Kg = KEM.Kg.

$$\frac{\mathsf{HKEM[KEM].Encaps}^{\mathsf{P}\times\mathsf{P_{rom}}}(1^\lambda, ek)}{(c, k_{\mathsf{KEM}}) \leftarrow\!\!\!{}^\$ \, \mathsf{KEM.Encaps}^{\mathsf{P}}(1^\lambda, ek)}$$
$$k \leftarrow \mathsf{P_{rom}}(k_{\mathsf{KEM}}, \varepsilon); \text{ Return } (c, k)$$

$$\frac{\mathsf{HKEM[KEM].Decaps}^{\mathsf{P}\times\mathsf{P_{rom}}}(1^\lambda, dk, c)}{k_{\mathsf{KEM}} \leftarrow \mathsf{KEM.Decaps}^{\mathsf{P}}(1^\lambda, dk, c)}$$
$$k \leftarrow \mathsf{P_{rom}}(k_{\mathsf{KEM}}, \varepsilon); \text{ Return } k$$

If the KEM expects access to P, then HKEM expects access to $\mathsf{P}\times\mathsf{P_{rom}}$. Note that the random oracle must be "new" and cannot be queried by KEM. This is necessary as the KEM could otherwise query the random oracle on the key it will output and include that as part of the ciphertext. Note that one can use oracle cloning [5], to create multiple random oracles from a single random oracle.

Intuitively, CPA security is achieved if the attacker cannot predict k_{KEM} and query it to the random oracle, i.e., as long as the KEM is one-way secure.

Theorem 5. *If* KEM *is* OW^* *secure with* P, *then* HKEM[KEM] *is* SIM^*-AC-CPA *secure with respect to* $\mathsf{P}\times\mathsf{P_{rom}}$.

The full proof (and the formal definition of OW^*) are given in the full version. The proof works as one would expect. The simulator produces ciphertexts by using KEM honestly. On exposures, it returns the keys/randomness it used and attempts to reprogram the random oracle to map keys encapsulated by KEM to the keys that were randomly sampled by the encapsulation oracle.

5.5 Fujisaki-Okamoto Transform

Finally, we consider a way to construct a CCA secure KEM from a one-way secure KEM. In particular, we look at part of one version of the Fujisaki-Okamoto transformation [16]. We work from the modular treatment of Hofheinz, Hövelmanns, and Kiltz [20] (HHK), in particular showing that the transformation which they refer to as $\mathsf{U}^{\not{\perp}}$ achieves SIM^*-AC-CCA security. This should extend to the other variants as well, but have focused on one for simplicity. Slightly corrected versions of HHK's proofs can be found in [22, Sec. 2.1-2.2].

Let KEM be a key encapsulation mechanism and F be a function family. Then we consider the scheme $\mathsf{U}^{\not{\perp}}[\mathsf{KEM}, \mathsf{F}]$ defined as follows. The key generation algorithm $\mathsf{U}^{\not{\perp}}[\mathsf{KEM}, \mathsf{F}].\mathsf{Kg}$ generates keys $(ek, dk) \leftarrow\!\!\!{}^\$ \, \mathsf{KEM.Kg}(1^\lambda)$ and $fk \leftarrow\!\!\!{}^\$ \, \mathsf{F.Kg}(1^\lambda)$, then outputs $(ek, (dk, fk))$.

$$\frac{\mathsf{U}^{\not{\perp}}[\mathsf{KEM}, \mathsf{F}].\mathsf{Encaps}^{\mathsf{P}\times\mathsf{P_{rom}}}(1^\lambda, ek)}{(c, k_{\mathsf{KEM}}) \leftarrow\!\!\!{}^\$ \, \mathsf{KEM.Encaps}^{\mathsf{P}}(1^\lambda, ek)}$$
$$k \leftarrow \mathsf{P_{rom}}(k_{\mathsf{KEM}}, c); \text{ Return } (c, k)$$

$$\frac{\mathsf{U}^{\not{\perp}}[\mathsf{KEM}, \mathsf{F}].\mathsf{Decaps}^{\mathsf{P}\times\mathsf{P_{rom}}}(1^\lambda, (dk, fk), c)}{k_{\mathsf{KEM}} \leftarrow \mathsf{KEM.Decaps}^{\mathsf{P}}(1^\lambda, dk, c)}$$
$$\text{If } k_{\mathsf{KEM}} \neq \bot \text{ then } k \leftarrow \mathsf{P_{rom}}(k_{\mathsf{KEM}}, c)$$
$$\text{Else } k \leftarrow \mathsf{F.Ev}^{\mathsf{P}\times\mathsf{P_{rom}}}(1^\lambda, fk, c)$$
$$\text{Return } k$$

Here $\mathsf{U}^{\not{\perp}}[\mathsf{KEM}, \mathsf{F}].\mathsf{K}(\lambda) = \mathsf{F.Out}(\lambda) = \mathsf{P_{rom}}.\mathcal{R}_\lambda$. Note that if KEM expects access to P, then $\mathsf{U}^{\not{\perp}}[\mathsf{KEM}, \mathsf{F}]$ expects access to $\mathsf{P}\times\mathsf{P_{rom}}$. We allow F to have access to $\mathsf{P}\times\mathsf{P_{rom}}$. It is important that KEM not have access to the random oracle used by the transform (otherwise it could, for example, ensure that it always produces output for which the first bit of $\mathsf{P_{rom}}(k_{\mathsf{KEM}}, c)$ is 0 and thus distinguishable from random).

However, our results show there is no issue with F having access to the same random oracle used by $U^{\not\perp}$. Indeed, HHK actually used the specific construction $F.Ev(1^\lambda, fk, c) = P_{rom}(fk, c)$. Considering an arbitrary F is more general. We emphasize the proof with this generality only works because we are using our new SIM*-AC security definitions. Moreover, given that caveat, this supports Jaeger and Tyagi's motivation for introducing SIM-AC definitions because this modularity allows our proof to avoid the details of the random oracle analysis required to prove that $P_{rom}(k_{KEM}, c)$ is secure.

Additionally HHK use a public-key encryption scheme applied to a random message in place of KEM. Again, $U^{\not\perp}[KEM, F]$ is a generalization of this as the security they assume of the encryption scheme implies that the KEM obtained by encrypting a randome message satisfies the security we require.

They showed that the construction is IND-CCA secure as long as the underlying scheme achieves a variant of one-way security which provides to the attacker a plaintext checking oracle which decrypts a given ciphertext and returns a boolean indicating whether the result is the same as a given message. We show the same for our security definition.

Theorem 6. *If* KEM *is OW*-PCA secure with* P *and* F *is SIM*-AC-PRF secure with* $P \times P_{rom}$, *then* $U^{\not\perp}[KEM, F]$ *is SIM*-AC-CCA secure with* $P \times P_{rom}$.

HHK gave a transform T which transforms a OW secure PKE scheme into a OW-PCA secure PKE scheme. Interpreting this as a KEM in the natural manner gives a OW-PCA secure KEM.

6   Recovering Prior Results

Finally, we conclude by showing that the positive results Jaeger and Tyagi [23] established regarding various notions of SIM-AC security also hold with respect to our analogous SIM*-AC notions. For this, we divide the results of Jaeger and Tyagi into three general categories. This first category covers results where (non-SIM-AC) security of some "high-level" construction is shown assuming its constituent elements satisfy SIM-AC security. The second category covers results where SIM-AC security of some "intermediate-level" construction is shown assuming its constituent elements satisfy SIM-AC security. The final category covers results where SIM-AC security of some "low-level" primitive is shown by direct ideal model analysis.

6.1   High-Level Proofs

The first category is the easiest in which to replace SIM-AC with SIM*-AC. In particular Jaeger and Tyagi showed: (1) SIM-AC-CPA secure encryption suffices for a version of the OPAQUE password-authenticated key exchange protocol of Jarecki, et al. [24] (because the latter was proven secure assuming "equivocable encryption" which is a weaker notion than SIM-AC-CPA security), (2) SIM-AC-PRF secure PRFs and SIM-AC-KP secure encryption suffice for a searchable symmetric encryption scheme of Cash, et al. [14], and (3) SIM-AC-CPA secure encryption suffices for the self-revocable cloud storage scheme of Tyagi, et al. [27]. We can recover these results with wSIM*-AC in place of SIM-AC by noting that our new notion is strictly stronger.

Lemma 1. *For* X $\in$ {PRF, CPA, KPA, $\$$, CCA, AE}, *wSIM*-AC-X security implies SIM-AC-X security. The converse does not hold.*

This result follows from the fact that wSIM*-AC security strengthens adversaries (by allowing them to program the ideal primitive) and weakens simulators (by restricting them to explicitly program the ideal primitive rather than having complete control of it). For the converse, note that a SIM*-AC adversary can, e.g., break the one-way function or collision-resistance security of a random oracle by programming it appropriately. Hence, one can modify a SIM-AC secure scheme to be trivially insecure (e.g. reveal its secret key) when a collision in the random oracle is known. SIM-AC security will be maintained, but the modified scheme will not be SIM*-AC secure.

In each of the searchable symmetric encryption and BurnBox proof, Jaeger and Tyagi had to assume that the constituent elements each used separate ideal primitives. Using SIM*-AC definitions we could reproduce these results without the assumption of separate ideal primitives using the proof modifications we discussion for intermediate-level proofs.

6.2   Intermediate-Level Proofs

In the second category, Jaeger and Tyagi gave security results for several encryption schemes. There is no general way to prove that these result carry over from SIM-AC to SIM*-AC security notions.[13] However, by examining the details of the proofs used for each of these result we can see that we are in luck. In each, the ideal primitive was used as a black-box. Constructed SIM-AC reduction adversaries provided the given SIM-AC adversaries with direct access to their own PRIM oracle. The S.Ls algorithm of any constructed SIM-AC simulators S just ran the corresponding algorithms of the given SIM-AC simulators.

As such, modifying these proofs for SIM*-AC (or wSIM*-AC) requires only syntactic change to treat the ideal primitive as a black-box. Reduction adversaries provide their given adversaries with direct access to PPRIM. Rather than having a S.Ls algorithm, SIM*-AC simulators will provide their given underlying simulators with direct access to PPRIM. Otherwise the analysis follows as given.

In fact, in places where multiple SIM-AC primitive had to use separate ideal primitives, this black-box use of the primitives allow them to share the same primitive for SIM*-AC security without any extra effort.

Moreover, the only way in which constructed simulators depended on adversaries was through dependance on given simulators for the constituent algorithms (which were allowed to depend on the adversary per SIM-AC security). As such,

---

[13] This follows from the counter-example described above where we construct a scheme which is trivially insecure if a collision in the random oracle is known.

there is no issue when using the order of quantification required for SIM-AC rather than wSIM*-AC security. Hence the following results hold.

Lemma 2. *Let $x \in \{\varepsilon, w\}$. Then the following hold.*

- *If SE is xSIM*-AC-CPA and INT-CTXT* secure with P, then SE is xSIM*-AC-CCA secure with P.*
- *If SE is xSIM*-AC-CPA secure with P and F is UF-CMA* secure with P, then (SE, F) encrypt-then-mac is xSIM*-AC-CCA secure with P.*
- *If SE[·] is IND-AC-EXT secure and F is xSIM*-AC-PRF secure with P, then SE[F] is xSIM*-AC-$ secure with P.*

This last result covers modes of operation such as counter (CTR), cipher-block chaining (CBC), cipher feedback (CFB), and output feedback (OFB) mode.

The asterisks added to INT-CTXT and UF-CMA indicate that we need these security notions to hold *even for adversaries who are able to program the ideal primitive.* We note, for example, that UF-CMA* security is implied by SIM*-AC-PRF security. We similarly expect that schemes which are known to achieve INT-CTXT security when constructed from a PRF secure function family can be shown by essentially the same proof to achieve INT-CTXT* security when using a SIM*-AC-PRF secure function family.

6.3   Low-Level Proofs

For the third category, Jaeger and Tyagi used information theoretic analysis to show that random oracles are SIM-AC-PRF secure, ideal ciphers are SIM-AC-PRF secure, and the ideal encryption model [27] is SIM-AC-AE secure.[14]

To re-establish these results one technically would have to re-write the proofs. We will sketch how to modify the SIM-AC proofs for the first two of these.

Lemma 3. *Random oracles are SIM*-AC-PRF secure (assuming $|\mathcal{K}_\lambda|$ is super-polynomial) and ideal ciphers are SIM*-AC-PRF secure (assuming $|\mathcal{K}_\lambda|$ and $|\mathcal{D}_\lambda|$ are super-polynomial).*

The simulators given for both work by honestly simulating the ideal primitive except whenever a new users is exposed they sample the key at random and then program the primitive to be consistent with the random values returned by earlier evaluation queries. This can done with the more restricted SIM*-AC syntax for simulators. These simulators do not depend on the chosen adversary.

If $\mathsf{F} : \mathcal{K}_\lambda \times \mathcal{D}_\lambda \to \mathcal{R}_\lambda$, their analysis showed that

$$\mathsf{Adv}^{\mathsf{sim}^*\text{-}\mathsf{ac\text{-}prf}}_{\mathsf{F}, \mathsf{S}_{\mathsf{prf}}, \mathsf{P}_{\mathsf{rom}}, \mathcal{A}}(\lambda) \leq \frac{u_\lambda^2}{2|\mathcal{K}_\lambda|} + \frac{u_\lambda p_\lambda}{2|\mathcal{K}_\lambda|} \text{ and}$$

$$\mathsf{Adv}^{\mathsf{sim}^*\text{-}\mathsf{ac\text{-}prf}}_{\mathsf{F}, \mathsf{S}_{\mathsf{prf}}, \mathsf{P}_{\mathsf{icm}}, \mathcal{A}}(\lambda) \leq \frac{u_\lambda^2}{2|\mathcal{K}_\lambda|} + \frac{u_\lambda p_\lambda}{2|\mathcal{K}_\lambda|} + \frac{q_\lambda^2}{2|\mathcal{D}_\lambda|}.$$

---

[14] The last of these is a slight "cheat" as the ideal encryption model does not satisfy their (or our) definitions of what an ideal primitive is.

Here u is the number of distinct users $\mathcal{A}$ interacts with, p is the number of ideal primitive queries it makes, and q is the number of evaluation queries it makes. Each summand represents a bound of the probability that a bad event occurs which could let an adversary distinguish the real and simulated worlds. The first corresponds to distinct users choosing the same random key. The second corresponds to the attacker making an ideal primitive query with an unexposed user's key. The third corresponds to random outputs of Ev colliding. A useful proof flow for this would introduce a notion of SIM*-AC-PRP security then prove that it is achieved by an ideal cipher and equivalent to SIM*-AC-PRF security up to the birthday bound. We sketch this in the full version.

For SIM*-AC-PRF/PRP security of these constructions the only additional bad event we could have to analyze is the probability that the attacker happening to make an ideal model *programming* query using an unexposed user's key. If p'_λ denotes the number of programming queries the attacker makes, this just adds an additional term of $0.5 u_\lambda p'_\lambda / |\mathcal{K}_\lambda|$ to either bound. Alternatively, we could leave the bound unchanged and redefine p_λ to include programming queries as well.

Acknowledgement. We thank Nirvan Tyagi for their collaboration on [23], early drafts of which considered asymmetric encryption. Some definitions and results in Sect. 5 grew out of discussions about those drafts.

References

1. Bellare, M.: New proofs for NMAC and HMAC: security without collision-resistance. In: Dwork, C. (ed.) CRYPTO 2006. LNCS, vol. 4117, pp. 602–619. Springer, Heidelberg (2006). https://doi.org/10.1007/11818175_36
2. Bellare, M., Bernstein, D.J., Tessaro, S.: Hash-function based PRFs: AMAC and its multi-user security. In: Fischlin, M., Coron, J.-S. (eds.) EUROCRYPT 2016. LNCS, vol. 9665, pp. 566–595. Springer, Heidelberg (2016). https://doi.org/10.1007/978-3-662-49890-3_22
3. Bellare, M., Canetti, R., Krawczyk, H.: Keying hash functions for message authentication. In: Koblitz, N. (ed.) CRYPTO 1996. LNCS, vol. 1109, pp. 1–15. Springer, Heidelberg (1996). https://doi.org/10.1007/3-540-68697-5_1
4. Bellare, M., Canetti, R., Krawczyk, H.: Pseudorandom functions revisited: the cascade construction and its concrete security. In: 37th FOCS, Burlington, Vermont, pp. 514–523. IEEE Computer Society Press (1996). https://doi.org/10.1109/SFCS.1996.548510
5. Bellare, M., Davis, H., Günther, F.: Separate your domains: NIST PQC KEMs, oracle cloning and read-only indifferentiability. In: Canteaut, A., Ishai, Y. (eds.) EUROCRYPT 2020. LNCS, vol. 12106, pp. 3–32. Springer, Cham (2020). https://doi.org/10.1007/978-3-030-45724-2_1
6. Bellare, M., Dowsley, R., Waters, B., Yilek, S.: Standard security does not imply security against selective-opening. In: Pointcheval, D., Johansson, T. (eds.) EUROCRYPT 2012. LNCS, vol. 7237, pp. 645–662. Springer, Heidelberg (2012). https://doi.org/10.1007/978-3-642-29011-4_38
7. Bellare, M., Hofheinz, D., Yilek, S.: Possibility and impossibility results for encryption and commitment secure under selective opening. In: Joux, A. (ed.) EUROCRYPT 2009. LNCS, vol. 5479, pp. 1–35. Springer, Heidelberg (2009). https://doi.org/10.1007/978-3-642-01001-9_1

8. Bellare, M., Rogaway, P.: Random oracles are practical: a paradigm for designing efficient protocols. In: Denning, D.E., Pyle, R., Ganesan, R., Sandhu, R.S., Ashby, V. (eds.) ACM CCS 1993, Fairfax, Virginia, USA, pp. 62–73. ACM Press (1993). https://doi.org/10.1145/168588.168596

9. Böhl, F., Hofheinz, D., Kraschewski, D.: On definitions of selective opening security. In: Fischlin, M., Buchmann, J., Manulis, M. (eds.) PKC 2012. LNCS, vol. 7293, pp. 522–539. Springer, Heidelberg (2012). https://doi.org/10.1007/978-3-642-30057-8_31

10. Camenisch, J., Drijvers, M., Gagliardoni, T., Lehmann, A., Neven, G.: The wonderful world of global random oracles. In: Nielsen, J.B., Rijmen, V. (eds.) EUROCRYPT 2018. LNCS, vol. 10820, pp. 280–312. Springer, Cham (2018). https://doi.org/10.1007/978-3-319-78381-9_11

11. Camenisch, J., Lehmann, A., Neven, G., Samelin, K.: Virtual smart cards: how to sign with a password and a server. In: Zikas, V., De Prisco, R. (eds.) SCN 2016. LNCS, vol. 9841, pp. 353–371. Springer, Cham (2016). https://doi.org/10.1007/978-3-319-44618-9_19

12. Camenisch, J., Lehmann, A., Neven, G., Samelin, K.: UC-secure non-interactive public-key encryption. In: Köpf, B., Chong, S. (eds.) CSF 2017 Computer Security Foundations Symposium, Santa Barbara, CA, USA, pp. 217–233. IEEE Computer Society Press (2017). https://doi.org/10.1109/CSF.2017.14

13. Canetti, R., Feige, U., Goldreich, O., Naor, M.: Adaptively secure multi-party computation. In: 28th ACM STOC, Philadelphia, PA, USA, pp. 639–648. ACM Press (1996). https://doi.org/10.1145/237814.238015

14. Cash, D., et al.: Dynamic searchable encryption in very-large databases: data structures and implementation. In: NDSS 2014, San Diego, CA, USA. The Internet Society (2014)

15. Cramer, R., Shoup, V.: Design and analysis of practical public-key encryption schemes secure against adaptive chosen ciphertext attack. SIAM J. Comput. 33(1), 167–226 (2003)

16. Fujisaki, E., Okamoto, T.: Secure integration of asymmetric and symmetric encryption schemes. J. Cryptol. 26(1), 80–101 (2011). https://doi.org/10.1007/s00145-011-9114-1

17. Goldreich, O., Goldwasser, S., Micali, S.: How to construct random functions. J. ACM 33(4), 792–807 (1986)

18. Hazay, C., Patra, A., Warinschi, B.: Selective opening security for receivers. In: Iwata, T., Cheon, J.H. (eds.) ASIACRYPT 2015. LNCS, vol. 9452, pp. 443–469. Springer, Heidelberg (2015). https://doi.org/10.1007/978-3-662-48797-6_19

19. Heuer, F., Poettering, B.: Selective opening security from simulatable data encapsulation. In: Cheon, J.H., Takagi, T. (eds.) ASIACRYPT 2016. LNCS, vol. 10032, pp. 248–277. Springer, Heidelberg (2016). https://doi.org/10.1007/978-3-662-53890-6_9

20. Hofheinz, D., Hövelmanns, K., Kiltz, E.: A modular analysis of the Fujisaki-Okamoto transformation. In: Kalai, Y., Reyzin, L. (eds.) TCC 2017. LNCS, vol. 10677, pp. 341–371. Springer, Cham (2017). https://doi.org/10.1007/978-3-319-70500-2_12

21. Hofheinz, D., Rao, V., Wichs, D.: Standard security does not imply indistinguishability under selective opening. In: Hirt, M., Smith, A. (eds.) TCC 2016. LNCS, vol. 9986, pp. 121–145. Springer, Heidelberg (2016). https://doi.org/10.1007/978-3-662-53644-5_5

22. Hövelmanns, K.: Generic constructions of quantum-resistant cryptosystems. Ph.D. thesis, Dissertation, Bochum, Ruhr-Universität Bochum, 2020 (2021). https://doi.org/10.13154/294-7758
23. Jaeger, J., Tyagi, N.: Handling adaptive compromise for practical encryption schemes. In: Micciancio, D., Ristenpart, T. (eds.) CRYPTO 2020. LNCS, vol. 12170, pp. 3–32. Springer, Cham (2020). https://doi.org/10.1007/978-3-030-56784-2_1
24. Jarecki, S., Krawczyk, H., Xu, J.: OPAQUE: an asymmetric PAKE protocol secure against pre-computation attacks. In: Nielsen, J.B., Rijmen, V. (eds.) EUROCRYPT 2018. LNCS, vol. 10822, pp. 456–486. Springer, Cham (2018). https://doi.org/10.1007/978-3-319-78372-7_15
25. Nielsen, J.B.: Separating random oracle proofs from complexity theoretic proofs: the non-committing encryption case. In: Yung, M. (ed.) CRYPTO 2002. LNCS, vol. 2442, pp. 111–126. Springer, Heidelberg (2002). https://doi.org/10.1007/3-540-45708-9_8
26. Panjwani, S.: Tackling adaptive corruptions in multicast encryption protocols. In: Vadhan, S.P. (ed.) TCC 2007. LNCS, vol. 4392, pp. 21–40. Springer, Heidelberg (2007). https://doi.org/10.1007/978-3-540-70936-7_2
27. Tyagi, N., Mughees, M.H., Ristenpart, T., Miers, I.: BurnBox: self-revocable encryption in a world of compelled access. In: Enck, W., Felt, A.P. (eds.) USENIX Security 2018, pp. 445–461. USENIX Association, Baltimore, MD, USA (2018)
28. Wee, H.: Zero knowledge in the random oracle model, revisited. In: Matsui, M. (ed.) ASIACRYPT 2009. LNCS, vol. 5912, pp. 417–434. Springer, Heidelberg (2009). https://doi.org/10.1007/978-3-642-10366-7_25

Almost Tight Multi-user Security Under Adaptive Corruptions & Leakages in the Standard Model

Shuai Han[1,2] , Shengli Liu[1,2,3](✉) , and Dawu Gu[1]

[1] School of Electronic Information and Electrical Engineering, Shanghai Jiao Tong University, Shanghai 200240, China
{dalen17,slliu,dwgu}@sjtu.edu.cn
[2] State Key Laboratory of Cryptology, P.O. Box 5159, Beijing 100878, China
[3] Westone Cryptologic Research Center, Beijing 100070, China

Abstract. In this paper, we consider tight multi-user security under adaptive corruptions, where the adversary can adaptively corrupt some users and obtain their secret keys. We propose generic constructions for a bunch of primitives, and the instantiations from the matrix decisional Diffie-Hellman (MDDH) assumptions yield the following schemes:

(1) the first digital signature (SIG) scheme achieving almost tight *strong* EUF-CMA security in the multi-user setting with adaptive corruptions in the standard model;

(2) the first public-key encryption (PKE) scheme achieving almost tight IND-CCA security in the multi-user multi-challenge setting with adaptive corruptions in the standard model;

(3) the first signcryption (SC) scheme achieving almost tight privacy and authenticity under CCA attacks in the multi-user multi-challenge setting with adaptive corruptions in the standard model.

As byproducts, our SIG and SC naturally derive the first strongly secure message authentication code (MAC) and the first authenticated encryption (AE) schemes achieving almost tight multi-user security under adaptive corruptions in the standard model. We further optimize constructions of SC, MAC and AE to admit better efficiency.

Furthermore, we consider key leakages besides corruptions, as a natural strengthening of tight multi-user security under adaptive corruptions. This security considers a more natural and more complete "all-or-*part*-or-nothing" setting, where secret keys of users are either fully exposed to adversary ("all"), or completely hidden to adversary ("nothing"), or *partially* leaked to adversary ("part"), and it protects the uncorrupted users even with bounded key leakages. All our schemes additionally support bounded key leakages and enjoy full compactness. This yields the first SIG, PKE, SC, MAC, AE schemes achieving almost tight multi-user security under both adaptive corruptions and leakages.

1 Introduction

Cryptography aims to provide two fundamental security guarantees: privacy and authenticity. Centered around privacy and authenticity, a variety of cryptographic primitives are developed, including public-key encryption (PKE), symmetric encryption (SE), digital signature (SIG), message authentication code (MAC)

© International Association for Cryptologic Research 2023
C. Hazay and M. Stam (Eds.): EUROCRYPT 2023, LNCS 14006, pp. 132–162, 2023.
https://doi.org/10.1007/978-3-031-30620-4_5

(MAC), signcryption (SC), authenticated encryption (AE), etc. To rigorously define security notions for these primitives, proper security models have to be set up according to their working environments and the adversaries' attacking abilities. Along the path of proving security, PKE and SE are defined with indistinguishability under chosen plaintext/ciphertext attacks (IND-CPA/CCA), SIG and MAC are defined with existential unforgeability under chosen message attacks (EUF-CMA), and SC and AE with both privacy (Priv) and authenticity (Auth). To prove a specific primitive construction achieves the security goals, the most important technique is security reduction. Roughly speaking, a security reduction establishes a link from an adversary $\mathcal{A}$ against the security of a primitive to another adversary $\mathcal{B}$ solving a well-studied computationally hard problem, such as the decisional Diffie-Hellman (DDH) and learning with errors (LWE) problems, with approximately the same running time. The ratio of $\mathcal{A}$'s advantage $\epsilon_{\mathcal{A}}$ to $\mathcal{B}$'s advantage $\epsilon_{\mathcal{B}}$ is defined as the loss factor $\ell := \epsilon_{\mathcal{A}}/\epsilon_{\mathcal{B}}$, which measures the quality of the security reduction.[1] If ℓ is a small constant, we call the reduction *tight*. Tight security is more desirable than non-tight one, since it enables a theoretically-sound instantiation without the need to compensate a security loss by increasing key lengths or group sizes, and allows universal key-length recommendations for applications. Many works (e.g., [10,15,16,18,22,26]) also consider the tightness notion called *almost tight*, where ℓ depends at most linearly (or even better, logarithmically) on the security parameter λ. For ease of exposition, we will use the term "tight" to denote "(almost) tight" as conventionally did [15,16,18,22,26], but we will detail the security loss in the security theorems and scheme comparisons to reflect almost tightness.

Tight Multi-user Security Under Adaptive Corruptions (MU^c). Cryptographic primitives are usually deployed in multi-user settings. But most of the security models for the primitives only consider single user. This is acceptable, since single-user security generally implies multi-user security via a security reduction called hybrid argument. But the price is a large loss factor ℓ at least nQ, where n is the number of users and Q the number of instances per user [6]. Considering billions of users and trillions of running instances over Internet, the security loss ℓ can be as large as 2^{60}. Such a large loss factor does hurt and has to be taken into account in the security parameter configuration during the deployment of primitives over Internet. To avoid a large loss factor that varies with the number of users and/or the number of target instances, many works [15,16,21] (to name a few) focus on primitive design with tight multi-user security.

Compared with a single-user setting, a multi-user environment becomes more involved and leaves more opportunities to adversaries implementing new attacks. An important attack is *key corruption* in that the adversary takes full control of some users and of course their keys. This happens since some adversary may snatch secrets from some user by system hacking or from key exposure due to

---

[1] Strictly speaking, the loss factor is defined as $\ell := (\epsilon_{\mathcal{A}}/\epsilon_{\mathcal{B}}) \cdot (\mathbf{T}(\mathcal{B})/\mathbf{T}(\mathcal{A}))$, where $\mathbf{T}(\mathcal{A})$ and $\mathbf{T}(\mathcal{B})$ denote the running time of $\mathcal{A}$ and $\mathcal{B}$, respectively. For reductions where $\mathbf{T}(\mathcal{A})$ and $\mathbf{T}(\mathcal{B})$ are approximately the same (as in many related works and also in this work), the loss factor can be simplified to $\epsilon_{\mathcal{A}}/\epsilon_{\mathcal{B}}$.

the user's bad key management. Therefore, it is reasonable for us to consider Multi-User security under corruptions, which we denote MU^c or more precisely MU^c-XX with notion XX depending on the primitive.[2] The existing works on MU^c indicates that pursuing tight MU^c security is not easy, as shown below.

Technical Difficulties in Achieving Tight MU^c Security. As pointed out in [12,18], there is a seemingly paradoxical technical problem needing to be addressed for proving tight MU^c-CMA security of SIG. On the one hand, the security reduction algorithm has to know the signing keys of *all* users so that it can successfully answer adversary's adaptive corruption query without resorting to a guessing strategy. On the other hand, the reduction algorithm should also be able to extract an answer to the underlying computationally hard problem from the adversary's forged signature. However, if the reduction knows all the signing keys, it should be able to forge a signature by itself without the adversary.

There exist similar technical problems in achieving tight MU^c security for other primitives. For example, to achieve tight MU^c-CPA/CCA security for PKE, the security reduction algorithm has to know the secret keys of *all* users to avoid the loss factor incurred by a guessing strategy. On the other hand, it should also be able to extract an answer from the adversary's guessing of challenge bit. This seems to lead to a similar paradox since the reduction can decrypt the challenge ciphertexts to learn the challenge bit by itself if it knows all the secret keys.

Impossibility Results on Tight MU^c Security. In fact, there is a line of research which showed impossibility results on tight MU^c security for a class of PKE, SIG, MAC and AE schemes that meet certain conditions.

- **PKE.** Bader et al. [5] proved that there exists no tight security reduction from MU^c-CPA/CCA security of PKE to non-interactive assumptions, if the relation between public key and secret key is "unique" or "re-randomizable".
- **SIG.** The above impossibility result for PKE also applies to MU^c-CMA security of SIG, except that the relation is defined for the verification key and signing key [5]. Alternatively, if the signing algorithm is a deterministic one, there exists no tight security reduction from MU^c-CMA security of SIG to bounded-round assumptions [30].
- **MAC.** Morgan et al. [30] showed that if MAC is a deterministic one, then there exists no tight security reduction from MU^c-CMA security of MAC to bounded-round assumptions.
- **AE.** Jager et al. [23] proved that if AE satisfies a minimal key uniqueness, any reasonable reduction from MU^c to single-user security is not tight.

These impossibility results indicate that it is not an easy job to obtain tight MU^c Security. However, it does not eliminate all hopes as long as we can find ways bypassing the conditions leading to the impossibility results.

---

[2] For primitives like PKE, SC, AE, we also consider Multi-User Multi-Challenge security under corruptions to capture multiple challenge ciphertexts, denoted by $MUMC^c$.

Possibility Results on Tight MU^c Security. There are very few constructions in the literature proved to have tight MU^c security, even in the Random Oracle (RO) model.

– **PKE.** To the best of our knowledge, only one PKE scheme in [27] is proved to be tightly multi-user multi-challenge CCA secure under adaptive corruptions (MUMC^c-CCA). Its security proof relies on the RO model.
– **SIG.** Gjøsteen and Jager [17] and Pan and Wagner [33] proposed tightly MU^c-CMA secure SIG schemes in the RO model. Bader et al. [4] constructed a tightly MU^c-CMA secure SIG scheme in the standard model. Its tree-based component makes the signature non-compact. Recently, Han et al. [18] designed a new MU^c-CMA secure SIG in the standard model. Their scheme enjoys compact signature while having non-compact public parameters (consisting of over a thousand group elements).

It is more desirable to pursue *strong* MU^c-CMA security of SIG, which even guarantees the hardness for adversary to forge a new signature for an already signed message, thus additionally ensuring "non-malleablility" of signatures. Strongly MU^c-CMA secure SIG has important applications in building more complex primitives such as SC [3] and authenticated key exchange (AKE) [12], where it can help SC to achieve ciphertext integrity (authenticity) [7] and AKE to achieve strong notion of "matching conversations" security [8] (see more discussions in [12]). One may want to resort to the Generalized Boneh-Shen-Waters (GBSW) transform [35] to convert a (non-strongly) secure SIG scheme to a strongly secure one, with the help of chameleon hash functions. However, the GBSW transform was originally proposed in the single-user setting, and was recently extended to the multi-user setting in [28], but without the consideration of corruptions. As noted in [28], it seems difficult to show that the GBSW transform also works under corruptions and preserves the tightness, i.e., converting a tightly MU^c-CMA secure SIG scheme to a tightly and strongly MU^c-CMA secure one. The reason is, the resulting SIG scheme contains the trapdoor of chameleon hash in its secret key, thus corruption of secret key means revealing of trapdoor, which is not supported by the security of chameleon hash [28].

Up to now, only one SIG scheme in a recent work [12] is proved to have tight strong MU^c-CMA security, based on the RO model.
– **SignCryption(SC).** In [9], Bellare and Stepanovs defined multi-user security for SC to cover both insider and outsider security. Their security notions are essentially multi-user CCA security under adaptive corruptions which considers both privacy (MUMC^c-Priv) and authenticity (MUMC^c-Auth). They also designed a SC scheme with security proved in the RO model.
– **MAC and AE.** Note that SIG naturally implies a MAC scheme and SC implies an AE scheme. As far as we know there is no approach to tight MU^c-CMA security other than derived from SIG. Similar statement holds for AE.

Up to now, there exists no PKE scheme achieving tight MUMC^c-CCA security, no SIG and MAC achieving tight strong MU^c-CMA security, and no SC and AE achieving tight MUMC^c-Priv & Auth in the standard model. The challenges are:

Can we fill the aforementioned blanks on tight MU^c *security in the standard model? Can we step even forward by considering tight multi-user security under not only adaptive corruptions but also key leakages?*

1.1 Our Contributions

We propose generic constructions for a bunch of primitives and prove their tight multi-user security under adaptive corruptions and key leakages.

- We propose generic constructions of SIG, PKE, SC, MAC, AE and prove their MU^c security with tight security reductions. The instantiations yield the following concrete schemes from the matrix DDH (MDDH) assumptions [14] (which corresponds to the standard DDH, k-Linear assumptions under different parameters) over asymmetric pairing groups *in the standard model*:
  - the first PKE scheme achieving almost tight MUMC^c-CCA security;
  - the first SIG scheme achieving almost tight *strong* MU^c-CMA security;
  - the first SC scheme achieving almost tight MUMC^c-Priv&Auth security;
  - the first MAC scheme achieving almost tight *strong* MU^c-CMVA security;
  - the first AE scheme achieving almost tight MUMC^c-Priv&Auth security.

  Moreover, all our schemes are *fully compact*, i.e., all the parameters, keys, signatures, ciphertexts consist of only a constant number of group elements.
- We formalize stronger multi-user security notions for the primitives under not only adaptive corruptions but also *key leakages*, denoted by $\mathrm{MU}^{c\&l}$. In addition to MU^c, the $\mathrm{MU}^{c\&l}$ security protects the uncorrupted users even if adversary also obtains bounded leakage information on their secret keys.

  Key leakage [2,32] is closely related to corruption, especially in the multi-user setting, and $\mathrm{MU}^{c\&l}$ is a natural strengthening of MU^c. The reason is as follows. Existing MU^c security considers an "all-or-nothing" setting, where secret keys of users are either fully exposed to adversary ("all") or completely hidden to adversary ("nothing"), and it protects the uncorrupted users. In realistic environments, there would naturally be users whose secret keys are only partially leaked to adversary ("part"). These users sit in a situation that is neither "all" nor "nothing". The new $\mathrm{MU}^{c\&l}$ security additionally takes into account the security of these users. Hence the new $\mathrm{MU}^{c\&l}$ security considers a more natural and more complete setting of "all-or-*part*-or-nothing".

  Thanks to the leakage resilience property of the building blocks, the almost tight MU^c security of all our SIG, PKE, SC, MAC, AE schemes can be further strengthened to support key leakage, thus achieving almost tight $\mathrm{MU}^{c\&l}$ security.
- At the heart of our constructions is new technical tool called *Publicly-Verifiable Quasi-Adaptive Hash Proof System* and a set of new properties for it. These, together with our novel tight proof strategies for handling corruptions, help us circumvent the seemingly paradoxical technical problems.

We refer to Table 1 and Table 2 for comparisons of our SIG and PKE with known schemes, respectively.

In summary, our work shows that almost tight MU^c security (and even together with full compactness) for SIG, PKE, SC, MAC and AE are achievable in the *standard model*. Moreover, our MDDH-based schemes support bounded key leakages as well, thus our work also provides the *first* schemes achieving almost tight $MU^{c\&l}$ security, no matter in the standard model or RO model.

Table 1. Comparison of signature (SIG) schemes that have (almost) tight MU-CMA security under adaptive corruptions (MU^c-CMA). The column **Standard Model** shows whether the security is proved in the standard model. The column **Strong Security** shows whether the scheme is proved *strongly* existentially unforgeable. The column **Corruption?** asks whether the security is proved in the presence of adaptive corruptions. The column **Leakage?** asks whether the security is proved additionally in the presence of key leakages, and if so, a *leakage rate* (defined as the ratio of leakage amount to secret key size) is presented. The column **Full Compactness** shows whether the scheme is fully compact (i.e., all the public parameters pp, verification key vk, signing key sk and signature σ consist of only a constant number of group elements or lattice vectors), and if not, the non-compact part is presented. The column **Security Loss** shows the security loss factor of the reductions, where λ denotes the security parameter. The column **Assumption** shows the computational assumption on which the security is based.

SIG Scheme	Standard Model	Strong Security	Corruption?	Leakage?	Full Compactness	Security Loss	Assumption
BHJKL [4,21]	✓	–	✓	–	✗ (non-compact σ)	$O(1)$	MDDH
GJ [17]	✗	–	✓	–	✓	$O(1)$	DDH
DGJL [12]	✗	✓	✓	–	✓	$O(1)$	DDH or ϕ-Hiding
HJKLPRS [18]	✓	✗	✓	–	✗ (non-compact pp)	$O(\lambda)$	MDDH
PW [33]	✗	–	✓	–	✗ (non-compact vk)	$O(1)$	LWE
Our SIG$_{\mathsf{MDDH}}$	✓	✓	✓	✓ ($\frac{1}{6} - o(1)$)	✓	$O(\log \lambda)$	MDDH

Table 2. Comparison of public-key encryption (PKE) schemes that have (almost) tight MUMC-CCA security under adaptive corruptions ($MUMC^c$-CCA) *or* key leakages. The columns have similar meanings as those in Table 1.

PKE Scheme	Standard Model	Corruption?	Leakage?	Full Compactness	Security Loss	Assumption
HLLG [20]	✓	–	✓ ($\frac{1}{18} - o(1)$)	✓	$O(\log \lambda)$	MDDH
LLP [27]	✗	✓	–	✓	$O(1)$	CDH
Our PKE$_{\mathsf{MDDH}}$	✓	✓	✓ ($\frac{1}{3} - o(1)$)	✓	$O(\log \lambda)$	MDDH

2 Technical Overview

In this section, we provide a technical overview of our results. We show the main ideas in our generic constructions of SIG and PKE, and give a high-level overview of their tight MU^c security proofs in Subsect. 2.1 and Subsect. 2.2, respectively.

We describe our SC, MAC and AE constructions and how to optimize them in Subsect. 2.3. Then in Subsect. 2.4, we explain the instantiations from the MDDH assumptions and explain why our aforementioned constructions support key leakage and achieve tight $\mathsf{MU}^{c\&l}$ security. Finally, in Subsect. 2.5, we compare our technique with existing techniques for tight MU^c security.

2.1   Our SIG: Technical Overview

Our starting point is a useful tool called Quasi-Adaptive Hash Proof System (QA-HPS), which was proposed by Han et al. [20] for achieving tight leakage resilient security of PKE. QA-HPS generalizes HPS [11] with a collection $\mathscr{L} = \{\mathcal{L}_\rho\}_\rho$ of NP-languages ($\mathcal{L}_\rho \subseteq \mathcal{X}$) and a family of projection functions $\alpha_{(\cdot)}$. The projection key is determined by $pk := \alpha_\rho(sk)$, hence depends on language $\mathcal{L}_\rho$. Meanwhile, QA-HPS has two ways of computing the hash value $\Lambda_{sk}(x)$: the public evaluation $\mathsf{Pub}(pk, x, w)$ for the instance $x \in \mathcal{L}_\rho$ with witness w, and the private evaluation $\mathsf{Priv}(sk, x)$ for $x \in \mathcal{X}$. Its correctness requires $\mathsf{Pub}(pk, x, w) = \mathsf{Priv}(sk, x) = \Lambda_{sk}(x)$ for $x \in \mathcal{L}_\rho$. Moreover, the subset membership problem (SMP) asks the computational indistinguishability of $x \leftarrow_\$ \mathcal{L}_\rho$ and $x \leftarrow_\$ \mathcal{X}$.

Another technical tool is Quasi-Adaptive Non-Interactive Zero-Knowledge argument (QA-NIZK) proposed by Jutla and Roy [24], where the common reference string crs depends on language $\mathcal{L}_\rho$. For tag-based QA-NIZK [25], there are two ways of generating a proof π for $x \in \mathcal{L}_\rho$ w.r.t. tag τ: $\mathsf{Prove}(\mathsf{crs}, \tau, x, w)$ using a witness w for $x \in \mathcal{L}_\rho$, and the simulator $\mathsf{Sim}(\mathsf{crs}, \mathsf{td}_{\mathsf{crs}}, \tau, x)$ using a trapdoor $\mathsf{td}_{\mathsf{crs}}$. With $\mathsf{Vrfy}_{\mathsf{NIZK}}(\mathsf{crs}, \tau, x, \pi)$, one can verify whether π is a valid proof. Perfect zero-knowledge requires that the proofs generated by Prove and Sim are identically distributed. Besides, unbounded simulation-soundness (USS) [1,22,34] stipulates that a PPT adversary cannot prove a false statement $x \notin \mathcal{L}_\rho$, even if it can obtain multiple simulated proofs for instances not necessarily in $\mathcal{L}_\rho$.

QA-HPS and HPS have found wide applications in designing PKE [11], MAC [13], etc. However, there are rarely applications in building SIG schemes, mainly because the designated-verifier style inherent in (QA)HPS is insufficient to support public verification of SIG. To fill the gap, we propose a new tool.

Publicly-Verifiable QA-HPS. The core technical tool underlying our SIG construction is a *Publicly-Verifiable* variant of QA-HPS, or PV-QA-HPS in short, which enables public verification of hash values with an extra verification key. We introduce a verification key generation function $\nu(\cdot)$ to compute verification key $vk := \nu(sk)$, and a verification algorithm $\mathsf{Vrfy}_{\mathsf{HPS}}(vk, x, hv)$ to check whether an element hv equals the hash value $\Lambda_{sk}(x)$ of x with the help of vk.

We also define two important properties for PV-QA-HPS, which play essential roles in the tight security reduction of our SIG.

- **Verification soundness**. It is a computational property requiring that, given all secret/verification key pairs $\{(sk_i, vk_i)\}_{i \in [n]}$, it is hard for any PPT adversary to come up with an index $i^* \in [n]$, an instance $x^* \in \mathcal{X}$ and a hash value hv^* which is false but passes the verification w.r.t. key pair (sk_{i^*}, vk_{i^*}), i.e., $hv^* \neq \Lambda_{sk_{i^*}}(x^*)$ but $\mathsf{Vrfy}_{\mathsf{HPS}}(vk_{i^*}, x^*, hv^*) = 1$.

- $\langle \mathscr{L}_0, \mathscr{L} \rangle$-**One-Time(OT)-extracting.** It is a statistical property parameterized by two language collections $\mathscr{L}_0 = \{\mathcal{L}_{\rho_0}\}_{\rho_0}$ and $\mathscr{L} = \{\mathcal{L}_\rho\}_\rho$. It demands that the hash value $\Lambda_{sk}(x^*)$ for any $x^* \in \mathcal{L}_\rho \in \mathscr{L}$ retains a large enough min-entropy, even conditioned on the verification key $vk = \nu(sk)$ and the projection key $pk_{\rho_0} = \alpha_{\rho_0}(sk)$ w.r.t. language $\mathcal{L}_{\rho_0} \in \mathscr{L}_0$. This min-entropy makes sure that any (unbounded) adversary is unable to guess the correct hash value $\Lambda_{sk}(x^*)$, except with a negligible probability.

Our SIG from PV-QA-HPS and QA-NIZK. The building blocks for our SIG construction consists of a PV-QA-HPS scheme $\mathsf{PVQAHPS} = (\alpha_{(\cdot)}, \nu(\cdot), \mathsf{Pub}, \mathsf{Priv}, \mathsf{Vrfy}_{\mathsf{HPS}})$ for both language $\mathcal{L}_\rho \in \mathscr{L}$ and language $\mathcal{L}_{\rho_0} \in \mathscr{L}_0{}^3$, a tag-based $\mathsf{QANIZK} = (\mathsf{Prove}, \mathsf{Vrfy}_{\mathsf{NIZK}}, \mathsf{Sim})$ for $\mathcal{L}_\rho$ and a collision-resistant hash function H. The signing and verification keys of SIG are just the secret key sk and verification key $vk = \nu(sk)$ of PVQAHPS. The signature for message m is [4]

$$\sigma := (\ x \leftarrow_s \mathcal{L}_\rho, \ d := \mathsf{Priv}(sk, x), \ \pi := \mathsf{Prove}(\mathsf{crs}, \tau, x, w) \ ), \text{ with } \tau := H(vk, m).$$

The verification of SIG checks $\mathsf{Vrfy}_{\mathsf{HPS}}(vk, x, d) = 1$ and $\mathsf{Vrfy}_{\mathsf{NIZK}}(\mathsf{crs}, \tau, x, \pi) = 1$.

In the strong MU^c-CMA security model, adversary $\mathcal{A}$ adaptively issues user-message pairs (i, m) to the signing oracle and obtains valid signatures σ. It can also issue corruption queries and get the corresponding signing keys. $\mathcal{A}$ tries to output a fresh and valid forgery $(i^*, m^*, \sigma^*) \notin \{(i, m, \sigma)\}$ for an uncorrupted user i^*.

Our tight strong MU^c-CMA security proof goes with three steps. See also Fig. 1 for a graphical high-level overview.

Step 1. Switch language from $\mathcal{L}_\rho$ to $\mathcal{L}_{\rho_0}$ for signing queries. Through signing queries, $\mathcal{A}$ obtains a bunch of tuples $(i, m, \sigma = (x, d, \pi))$, where σ is a valid signature of m under sk_i.

- According to the perfect zero-knowledge of QANIZK, the computation of π by Prove can be replaced by Sim without any witness of $x \in \mathcal{L}_\rho$.
- By the hardness of (multi-fold) SMP, the samplings of all x can be changed from $x \leftarrow_s \mathcal{L}_\rho$ to $x \leftarrow_s \mathcal{L}_{\rho_0}$.
- For $x \in \mathcal{L}_{\rho_0}$ with witness w, $d := \mathsf{Priv}(sk_i, x) = \mathsf{Pub}(\alpha_{\rho_0}(sk_i), x, w)$. So

$$\sigma = (\ x \leftarrow_s \mathcal{L}_{\rho_0}, \ d := \mathsf{Pub}(\alpha_{\rho_0}(sk_i), x, w), \pi := \mathsf{Sim}(\mathsf{crs}, \mathsf{td}_{\mathsf{crs}}, \tau, x) \ ).$$

Now $\alpha_{\rho_0}(sk_i)$ (out of the whole sk_i) suffices for generating σ.

Step 2. Restrict language from $\mathcal{X}$ to $\mathcal{L}_\rho$ in the forgery. $\mathcal{A}$'s forgery $(i^*, m^*, \sigma^* = (x^*, d^*, \pi^*))$ is successful if it is fresh and passes the validity check $\mathsf{Vrfy}_{\mathsf{HPS}}(vk_{i^*}, x^*, d^*) = 1 \land \mathsf{Vrfy}_{\mathsf{NIZK}}(\mathsf{crs}, \tau^*, x^*, \pi^*) = 1$ with $\tau^* := H(vk_{i^*}, m^*)$.

---

[3] This means that PVQAHPS works correctly both for $x \in \mathcal{L}_\rho$ with $pk = \alpha_\rho(sk)$ and $x \in \mathcal{L}_{\rho_0}$ with $pk = \alpha_{\rho_0}(sk)$.

[4] Here ρ is part of the public parameters of SIG and is chosen from the language collection $\mathscr{L}$ by the setup algorithm of SIG, while w is a witness for $x \in \mathcal{L}_\rho$ and is picked along with $x \leftarrow_s \mathcal{L}_\rho$ by the signing algorithm of SIG.

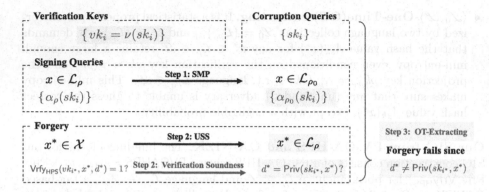

Fig. 1. The high-level overview of our proof strategy for tight strong MU^c-CMA security of SIG. The black arrows illustrate language switches, and the blue arrows as well as the blue brace show the applications of quasi-adaptive properties. (Color figure online)

- By the verification soundness of PVQAHPS, the check of $\mathsf{Vrfy}_{\mathsf{HPS}}(vk_{i^*}, x^*, d^*) = 1$ can be replaced by $d^* = \mathsf{Priv}(sk_{i^*}, x^*)$.
- The USS property of QANIZK makes sure that $x^* \in \mathcal{L}_\rho$ in the forgery, except with a negligible probability.

Strategy for corruptions in reductions. Note that in the above two steps, when reducing to SMP or QANIZK, the reduction algorithms can choose all users' signing keys themselves. As for the verification soundness of PVQAHPS, the reduction algorithm gets all users' signing keys from its own challenger. Therefore, all of them are able to handle $\mathcal{A}$'s adaptive corruption queries.

Step 3. $\mathcal{A}$'s **forgery fails due to the** $\langle \mathscr{L}_0, \mathscr{L} \rangle$-**OT-extracting property.** Now all information about sk_{i^*} that $\mathcal{A}$ learns from the signing queries is limited to the projection key $\alpha_{\rho_0}(sk_{i^*})$ on language $\mathcal{L}_{\rho_0}$. On the other hand, x^* in $\mathcal{A}$'s forgery is restricted in $\mathcal{L}_\rho$ and $\mathcal{A}$ wins only if $d^* = \mathsf{Priv}(sk_{i^*}, x^*)$. By the $\langle \mathscr{L}_0, \mathscr{L} \rangle$-OT-extracting property of PVQAHPS, $\mathcal{A}$ hardly succeeds.

How We Circumvent the Seemingly Paradoxical Technical Problem. Now we conclude how we circumvent the paradoxical technical problem for achieving tight strong MU^c-CMA security of SIG: our proof goes with a constant number of computationally indistinguishable changes to arrive at a final game where the technical problem has turned into a statistical one.

(1) All the reduction algorithms to computational properties or problems possess the signing keys of all users to handle adaptive corruption queries.
(2) After arriving at a statistical problem ($\langle \mathscr{L}_0, \mathscr{L} \rangle$-OT-extracting property), it is hard for the adversary to forge valid signature information-theoretically.

How We Circumvent the Existing Impossibility Results. Below we explain how we circumvent the impossibility results on tight MU^c security. Recall that the impossibility results apply to a SIG scheme when the relation between the verification key and the signing key is "unique" or "re-randomizable" [5], or the signing algorithm is a deterministic one [30].

Firstly, the signing algorithm of our SIG is not a deterministic one since it samples a random element x from $\mathcal{L}_\rho$ with witness w.

Next, we show that the relation between the verification key $vk = \nu(sk)$ and the signing key sk of our SIG is neither "unique" nor "re-randomizable", by the properties we defined for PV-QA-HPS.

- The relation is not "unique" due to the statistical $\langle \mathcal{L}_0, \mathcal{L} \rangle$-OT-extracting property of PV-QA-HPS. Suppose, towards a contradiction, that the relation is unique, then an (unbounded) adversary can uniquely determine sk from $\nu(sk)$, and thus break the property easily by computing $hv^* = \Lambda_s k(x^*)$ for any $x^* \in \mathcal{L}_\rho$.
- The relation is not "re-randomizable" due to the verification soundness property of PV-QA-HPS. Suppose, towards a contradiction, that the relation is re-randomizable, then for any user $i^* \in [n]$, an adversary can resample another sk'_{i^*} from vk_{i^*} and sk_{i^*}, such that $vk_{i^*} = \nu(sk_{i^*}) = \nu(sk'_{i^*})$. Then the adversary picks x^* from $\mathcal{X}$ uniformly, computes $hv^* = \Lambda_{sk'_{i^*}}(x^*)$ using sk'_{i^*}, and outputs (i^*, x^*, hv^*). On the one hand, since vk_{i^*} is also the verification key of sk'_{i^*}, i.e., $vk_{i^*} = \nu(sk'_{i^*})$, hv^* passes the verification w.r.t. vk_{i^*}, i.e., $\mathsf{Vrfy}_{\mathsf{HPS}}(vk_{i^*}, x^*, hv^*) = 1$. On the other hand, we have $sk'_{i^*} \neq sk_{i^*}$ with high probability ($\geq 1/2$, by the fact that the relation between vk and sk is not unique, as shown above), thus $hv^* = \Lambda_{sk'_{i^*}}(x^*) \neq \Lambda_{sk_{i^*}}(x^*)$ with high probability. Consequently, the adversary breaks the verification soundness with high probability.

Of course, being neither "unique" nor "re-randomizable" nor "deterministic" is only a necessary condition for tight MU^c security. To achieve tight MU^c security, the cooperation of PV-QA-HPS and QA-NIZK in the design of our SIG as well as the nice properties of PV-QA-HPS play the most important roles.

2.2   Our PKE: Technical Overview

Our PKE is built upon the recent work [20], where the concept of QA-HPS was proposed to construct PKE with tight leakage resilient security. That tight security heavily relies on two statistical properties of QA-HPS: key-switching and universal. Intuitively, $\langle \mathcal{L}, \mathcal{L}_0 \rangle$-key-switching requires that conditioned on a projection key $\alpha_\rho(sk)$ w.r.t. language $\mathcal{L}_\rho \in \mathcal{L}$, the projection key $\alpha_{\rho_0}(sk)$ w.r.t. language $\mathcal{L}_{\rho_0} \in \mathcal{L}_0$ can be switched to $\alpha_{\rho_0}(sk')$ for an independent key sk'.

The PKE in [20] makes use of three QA-HPS schemes, one for masking the message and the other two for proving the well-formedness of ciphertext. As far as we understand, it is hard to prove the tight security of their PKE under adaptive corruptions, since their proof strategy that increases the entropy in secret keys gradually does not work in the presence of corruptions.

To support corruptions in the tight security, (1) we define *new properties* for QA-HPS, (2) we use *another approach*: QA-HPS with new properties to mask the message and QA-NIZK to prove the well-formedness of ciphertext, and (3) we develop a *new proof strategy* to achieve tight $\mathsf{MUMC^c\text{-}CCA}$ security.

QA-HPS with New Properties. We define two new properties for QA-HPS.

- **Multi-language multi-fold SMP.** This new type of SMP asks the computational indistinguishability of $(x_{i,j} \leftarrow_{\$} \mathcal{L}_\rho)_{i\in[n],j\in[Q]}$ and $(x_{i,j} \leftarrow_{\$} \mathcal{L}_{\rho_0^{(i)}})_{i\in[n],j\in[Q]}$, where $\mathcal{L}_\rho \in \mathscr{L}$, and $\mathcal{L}_{\rho_0^{(1)}}, ..., \mathcal{L}_{\rho_0^{(n)}} \in \mathscr{L}_0$ are n independent languages chosen from $\mathscr{L}_0$. Jumping ahead, this new SMP enables us to switch the language $\mathcal{L}_\rho$ to different languages $\{\mathcal{L}_{\rho_0^{(i)}}\}_{i\in[n]}$ for different users in our tight proof.

- $\mathscr{L}_0$**-Multi-key multi-extracting.** It demands the pseudorandomness of multiple hash values $\{\Lambda_{sk_i}(x_j)\}_{i\in[n],j\in[Q]}$ of multiple instances $x_1, ..., x_Q \in \mathcal{L}_{\rho_0}$ under uniformly and independently chosen keys $sk_1, ..., sk_n$.

Our PKE from QA-HPS with New Properties and QA-NIZK. The secret and public keys of PKE are just the secret key sk and projection key $pk = \alpha_\rho(sk)$ of QA-HPS for language $\mathcal{L}_\rho$. The ciphertext for plaintext m is

$$c := (x \leftarrow_{\$} \mathcal{L}_\rho, \; d := \mathsf{Pub}(pk,x,w) + m, \; \pi := \mathsf{Prove}(\mathsf{crs},\tau,x,w)), \; \text{with } \tau := H(pk,d).$$

The decryption of $c = (x,d,\pi)$ checks whether $\mathsf{Vrfy}_{\mathsf{NIZK}}(\mathsf{crs},\tau,x,\pi) = 1$ and recovers $m := d - \mathsf{Priv}(sk,x)$ after a successful check.

It is interesting to note that our PKE shares a similar design with our SIG. However, their tight proofs are quite different.

In the $\mathsf{MUMC^c\text{-}CCA}$ security model, adversary $\mathcal{A}$ adaptively issues encryption queries (i^*, m_0, m_1) to encryption oracle and obtains challenge ciphertexts $c^* = (x^*, d^*, \pi^*)$ that encrypts m_β under pk_{i^*}, where $\beta \leftarrow_{\$} \{0,1\}$ is the challenge bit. It can issue corruption queries and get the corresponding secret keys, and issue decryption queries $(i, c = (x,d,\pi))$ and obtain the decryption of c under sk_i. Finally $\mathcal{A}$ outputs a guessing bit β' and wins if $\beta' = \beta$.

Our tight $\mathsf{MUMC^c\text{-}CCA}$ security proof goes with five steps. See also Fig. 2 for a graphical high-level overview.

Step 1. Switch language from $\mathcal{L}_\rho$ to $\{\mathcal{L}_{\rho_0^{(i^*)}}\}_{i^*\in[n]}$ for encryption queries.

Through encryption queries (i^*, m_0, m_1), $\mathcal{A}$ obtains multiple challenge ciphertexts $c^* = (x^*, d^*, \pi^*)$.

- According to the perfect zero-knowledge of QANIZK, the computation of π^* by Prove can be replaced by Sim without any witness of $x^* \in \mathcal{L}_\rho$.
- By the correctness of QAHPS, the computation of d^* by Pub can be replaced by $d^* := \mathsf{Priv}(sk_{i^*}, x^*) + m_\beta$, without any witness of $x^* \in \mathcal{L}_\rho$.
- By the new multi-language multi-fold SMP, for each user i^*, the samplings of all x^* can be changed from $x^* \leftarrow_{\$} \mathcal{L}_\rho$ to $x^* \leftarrow_{\$} \mathcal{L}_{\rho_0^{(i^*)}}$.
- For each user i^*, since $x^* \in \mathcal{L}_{\rho_0^{(i^*)}}$ with witness w^*, we have $d^* := \mathsf{Priv}(sk_{i^*}, x^*) + m_\beta = \mathsf{Pub}(\alpha_{\rho_0^{(i^*)}}(sk_{i^*}), x^*, w^*) + m_\beta$. Hence

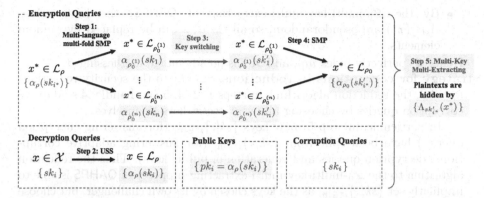

Fig. 2. The high-level overview of our proof strategy for tight MUMC^c-CCA security of PKE. The black arrows illustrate language switches, and the blue arrows as well as the blue brace show the applications of quasi-adaptive properties. (Color figure online)

$$c^* := \left(x^* \leftarrow_{\!\$} \mathcal{L}_{\rho_0^{(i^*)}}, \ d^* := \mathsf{Pub}(\alpha_{\rho_0^{(i^*)}}(sk_{i^*}), x^*, w^*) + m_\beta, \ \pi^* := \mathsf{Sim}(\mathsf{crs}, \mathsf{td}_{\mathsf{crs}}, \tau^*, x^*) \right).$$

Now $\{\alpha_{\rho_0^{(i^*)}}(sk_{i^*})\}_{i^* \in [n]}$ (out of whole $\{sk_{i^*}\}_{i^* \in [n]}$) suffices for generating c^*.

Step 2. Restrict language from $\mathcal{X}$ to $\mathcal{L}_\rho$ for decryption queries. For query $(i, c = (x, d, \pi))$, $\mathcal{A}$ obtains $m := d - \mathsf{Priv}(sk_i, x)$ if $\mathsf{Vrfy}_{\mathsf{NIZK}}(\mathsf{crs}, \tau, x, \pi) = 1$.

- The USS property of QANIZK makes sure that $\mathcal{A}$ obtains m only if $x \in \mathcal{L}_\rho$ in the decryption query, except with a negligible probability.

Hence $\mathcal{A}$ learns only $\{\alpha_\rho(sk_i)\}_{i \in [n]}$ (out of $\{sk_i\}_{i \in [n]}$) from decryption queries.

Step 3. Switch $\{sk_{i^*}\}_{i^* \in [n]}$ to new keys $\{sk'_{i^*}\}_{i^* \in [n]}$ for encryption queries. Note that to avoid trivial attacks, $\mathcal{A}$ is not allowed to corrupt those users i^* for which $\mathcal{A}$ issues encryption queries. Thus for such users i^*, after the first two steps, $\mathcal{A}$'s information about sk_{i^*} can be summarized by $\alpha_\rho(sk_{i^*})$ (involved in public keys and decryption oracle) and $\alpha_{\rho_0^{(i^*)}}(sk_{i^*})$ (involved in encryption oracle).

- According to the $\langle \mathscr{L}, \mathscr{L}_0 \rangle$-key-switching property of QAHPS, $\alpha_{\rho_0^{(i^*)}}(sk_{i^*})$ can be switched to $\alpha_{\rho_0^{(i^*)}}(sk'_{i^*})$ to compute d^* for encryption queries, with sk'_{i^*} uniformly and independently chosen.

Though there are n switches, it does not lead to a loose security reduction, since key-switching is a statistical property of QAHPS.

As a result, new independent secret keys $\{sk'_{i^*}\}_{i^* \in [n]}$ are split from the original $\{sk_{i^*}\}_{i^* \in [n]}$, and are only used for answering encryption queries.

Step 4. Switch languages $\{\mathcal{L}_{\rho_0^{(i^*)}}\}_{i^* \in [n]}$ to $\mathcal{L}_{\rho_0}$ for encryption queries. The argument is similar to step 1. As a result, the computation of $d^* := \mathsf{Pub}(\alpha_{\rho_0^{(i^*)}}(sk'_{i^*}), x^*, w^*) + m_\beta$ is changed to $d^* := \mathsf{Pub}(\alpha_{\rho_0}(sk'_{i^*}), x^*, w^*) + m_\beta$, which is equivalent to $d^* := \Lambda_{sk'_{i^*}}(x^*) + m_\beta$.

Step 5. Plaintexts m_β are perfectly hidden due to the $\mathscr{L}_0$-multi-key-multi-extracting property. Note that the new keys $\{sk'_{i^*}\}_{i^* \in [n]}$ are uniform and only used for computing $d^* := \Lambda_{sk'_{i^*}}(x^*) + m_\beta$.

- By the $\mathscr{L}_0$-multi-key-multi-extracting of QAHPS, the hash values $\Lambda_{sk'_{i*}}(x^*)$ are pseudorandom, so all the d^*'s can be replaced by random elements.

Hence d^* perfectly hides m_β, and $\mathcal{A}$ has no advantage in guessing β.

Strategy for corruptions in reductions. Similar to the security reductions for SIG, the reduction algorithms in steps 1, 2, 4, 5 can handle $\mathcal{A}$'s adaptive corruption queries by choosing all users' secret keys themselves.

In particular, in step 5, new keys $\{sk'_{i*}\}_{i*\in[n]}$ (for answering encryption queries) have been split from $\{sk_{i*}\}_{i*\in[n]}$ (for answering adaptive corruptions, decryption queries and generation of public keys). Thus the reduction algorithm to the $\mathscr{L}_0$-multi-key-multi-extracting property of QAHPS is able to implicitly set $\{sk'_{i*}\}_{i*\in[n]}$ as the keys chosen by its own challenger, but choose $\{sk_{i*}\}_{i*\in[n]}$ itself to deal with $\mathcal{A}$'s adaptive corruption queries.

How We Circumvent the Seemingly Paradoxical Technical Problem. Now we conclude how we circumvent the paradoxical technical problem for achieving tight MUMC^c-CCA security of PKE: our proof goes with a constant number of computationally indistinguishable changes, as well as n statistical changes, to arrive at a final game where the challenge ciphertexts are no longer generated by the users' real secret keys.

(1) All the reduction algorithms to computational properties or problems possess the secret keys of all users to handle adaptive corruption queries.
(2) With n statistical changes ($\langle\mathscr{L},\mathscr{L}_0\rangle$-key-switching), new and independent secret keys (for generating challenge ciphertexts) have been split from real secret keys (for corruption and other queries), ready for the final game.
(3) In the final game, the reduction algorithm (for $\mathscr{L}_0$-multi-key-multi-extracting) can embed its challenge instances in the new secret keys to randomize challenge ciphertexts, and sample the real secret keys itself to handle adaptive corruption queries from the adversary.

How We Circumvent the Existing Impossibility Results. Recall that the impossibility results apply to a PKE scheme when the relation between the public key and the secret key is "unique" or "re-randomizable" [5]. For reasons similar to our SIG (as shown in Subsect. 2.1), we can show that the relation between the public key $pk = \alpha_\rho(sk)$ and the secret key sk of our PKE is neither "unique" nor "re-randomizable", by the new properties we defined for QA-HPS.

2.3 Our SC, MAC and AE: Technical Overview

Our SC. There are a variety of constructions for building SignCryption (SC) from SIG and PKE, encompassing "Encrypt-then-Sign", "Sign-then-Encrypt", "Encrypt-and-Sign", etc. [3,9]. However, there is no SC available with tight MUMC^c-Priv&Auth (multi-user multi-challenge CCA privacy and authenticity under corruptions) in the standard model. As far as we see, this is mainly due to the missing of tightly *strongly* MU^c secure SIG and tightly MU^c secure PKE.

Our SIG and PKE constructions fill the blank and immediately lead to tightly MUMC^c-Priv&Auth secure SC.

Moreover, we can optimize the SC construction by taking advantage of the similar structures and compatible underlying building blocks of our SIG and PKE. In our optimized construction of SC, we integrate the ciphertext of PKE and signature of SIG in a more efficient way of reusing the instance $x \in \mathcal{L}_\rho$ and the proof π of QANIZK, and the signcryption of message m is now given by

$$c := (x \leftarrow_\$ \mathcal{L}_\rho, \ d := \mathsf{Pub}(pk_r, x, w) + m, \ \widetilde{d} := \mathsf{Priv}(\widetilde{sk}_s, x), \ \pi := \mathsf{Prove}(\mathsf{crs}, \tau, x, w)),$$

where $\tau := H(\widetilde{vk}_s, pk_r, d, \widetilde{d})$, pk_r is receiver's public (encryption) key and $\widetilde{sk}_s$ sender's secret (signing) key. The tight MUMC^c-Priv&Auth security of our SC can be proved similar to the tight MU^c security of PKE and SIG.

Our MAC and AE. A SIG scheme is itself a MAC scheme and a SC scheme is an AE scheme, when taking the secret key as the symmetric key. Therefore, our SIG and SC constructions immediately lead to a strongly MU^c-CMA secure MAC and MUMC^c-Priv&Auth secure AE. However, we can do more about MAC since it does not need public verification. We provide a more efficient MAC following our SIG construction but replacing the building block PVQAHPS by QAHPS with new properties. Furthermore, the security of MAC can also be improved to an even stronger notion, namely strong MU^c-CMVA security, which considers *chosen verification attacks* as well [13] in addition to strong MU^c-CMA.

2.4   Instantiations from MDDH Assumptions and Leakage Resilience

Instantiations. We instantiate PV-QA-HPS and QA-HPS with new properties from the MDDH assumptions. The associated language collections $\mathscr{L}$ and $\mathscr{L}_0$ are independently generated linear subspaces [25]. The instantiations stem from the DDH-based HPS proposed by Cramer and Shoup [11], and rely on pairing groups to accomplish public verifiability of PV-QA-HPS, inspired by [25]. We provide tight security proofs for the properties of PV-QA-HPS and QA-HPS based on MDDH. Below we give a high-level overview of our PV-QA-HPS instantiation. We rely on an asymmetric pairing group $(\mathbb{G}_1, \mathbb{G}_2, \mathbb{G}_T, e)$ of prime order p with $e : \mathbb{G}_1 \times \mathbb{G}_2 \longrightarrow \mathbb{G}_T$. We use implicit representation of group elements [14], namely, using $[\cdot]_1, [\cdot]_2, [\cdot]_T$ to denote component-wise exponentiations in respective groups $\mathbb{G}_1, \mathbb{G}_2, \mathbb{G}_T$.

- Let us start with the Cramer-Shoup HPS [11]. We describe the MDDH-based generalized version with $k \geq 1$ the MDDH parameter ($k = 1$ corresponds to the original DDH-based version). The hashing key is $sk = \mathbf{K} \in \mathbb{Z}_p^{(k+1) \times (2k+1)}$ and the projection key is $pk = [\mathbf{KA}]_1$ on a linear subspace language $\mathcal{L}_\rho = \mathsf{Span}([\mathbf{A}]_1) = \{ [\mathbf{c}]_1 | \exists \ \mathbf{w} \in \mathbb{Z}_p^k, \text{ s.t. } [\mathbf{c}]_1 = [\mathbf{Aw}]_1 \}$ with $\rho = [\mathbf{A}]_1 \in \mathbb{G}_1^{(2k+1) \times k}$. For an instance $[\mathbf{c}]_1 = [\mathbf{Aw}]_1 \in \mathcal{L}_\rho$, the HPS hash value is given by $[\boldsymbol{hv}]_1 =$

  (private evaluation) $\mathbf{K} \cdot [\mathbf{c}]_1 = [\mathbf{KA}]_1 \cdot \mathbf{w}$ (public evaluation).

- To support public verification, we resort to pairing technique, inspired by the Kiltz-Wee QA-NIZK [25]. We use $vk = [\mathbf{K}^\top \mathbf{B}]_2$ as the verification key with matrix $[\mathbf{B}]_2 \in \mathbb{G}_2^{(k+1) \times k}$ defined by the MDDH assumption. Then, the correctness of hash value $[hv]_1 \overset{?}{=} [\mathbf{Kc}]_1$ can be verified publicly via pairing:

$$e([hv^\top]_1, [\mathbf{B}]_2) \overset{?}{=} e([\mathbf{c}^\top]_1, [\mathbf{K}^\top \mathbf{B}]_2) \quad (= [(\mathbf{Kc})^\top \mathbf{B}]_T).$$

Verification soundness. This is tightly implied by the Kernal Matrix DH (KerMDH) assumption [31], which in turn is implied by the MDDH assumption [31]. If the adversary is able to produce an incorrect hash value $[hv]_1 \neq [\mathbf{Kc}]_1$ but passes the public verification $e([hv^\top]_1, [\mathbf{B}]_2) = e([\mathbf{c}^\top]_1, [\mathbf{K}^\top \mathbf{B}]_2)$, then $[hv - \mathbf{Kc}]_1$ is a non-zero element such that $e([(hv - \mathbf{Kc})^\top]_1, [\mathbf{B}]_2) = [\mathbf{0}]_T$, resulting in a solution to the KerMDH problem defined by $[\mathbf{B}]_2$.

$\langle \mathscr{L}_0, \mathscr{L} \rangle$-**OT-extracting.** This holds information-theoretically, where $\mathscr{L}_{\rho_0} = \mathsf{Span}([\mathbf{A}_0]_1) \in \mathscr{L}_0$ and $\mathscr{L}_\rho = \mathsf{Span}([\mathbf{A}]_1) \in \mathscr{L}$ with $\rho_0 = [\mathbf{A}_0]_1 \in \mathbb{G}_1^{(2k+1) \times k}$ chosen independently of $\rho = [\mathbf{A}]_1$. Note that $\mathbf{A}_0$ is $(2k+1)$ by k, $\mathbf{B}$ is $(k+1)$ by k, and $sk = \mathbf{K}$ is $(k+1)$ by $(2k+1)$ matrices. Given the projection key $pk_{\rho_0} = [\mathbf{K A}_0]_1$ w.r.t. $\mathscr{L}_{\rho_0}$ and $vk = [\mathbf{K}^\top \mathbf{B}]_2$, the hashing key $sk = \mathbf{K}$ reserves entropy in its projection on the kernel of $\mathbf{A}_0$ and $\mathbf{B}$. Then for any (non-zero) instance $[\mathbf{c}]_1 \in \mathscr{L}_\rho = \mathsf{Span}([\mathbf{A}]_1)$, $[\mathbf{c}]_1$ is outside $\mathscr{L}_{\rho_0} = \mathsf{Span}([\mathbf{A}_0]_1)$, thus the reserved entropy of $sk = \mathbf{K}$ is transmitted to the hash value $[\mathbf{Kc}]_1$ so that the adversary can hardly guess $[\mathbf{Kc}]_1$ correctly. This holds even if some extra (bounded) information of $sk = \mathbf{K}$ is leaked to the adversary.

The instantiation of tag-based QA-NIZK can be adapted from the QA-NIZK scheme proposed by Abe et al. [1], which has tight USS based on MDDH.

According to our generic constructions, the instantiations of PV-QA-HPS, QA-HPS and tag-based QA-NIZK result in concrete SIG, PKE, SC, MAC, AE schemes with tight MU^c security from MDDH in the standard model.

Leakage Resilience. Note that HPS is intrinsically leakage resilient [32]. The leakage resilience can naturally extend to QA-HPS [20], and also to PV-QA-HPS. More precisely, we define leakage-resilient-$\langle \mathscr{L}_0, \mathscr{L} \rangle$-OT-extracting property for PV-QA-HPS (cf. Sect. 4) and adopt the leakage-resilient-$\langle \mathscr{L}, \mathscr{L}_0 \rangle$-key-switching for QA-HPS defined in [20], which are met by our MDDH-based instantiations. This shows that all our SIG, PKE, SC, MAC, AE schemes not only have tight MU^c security but also support key leakage, thus achieving tight $\mathsf{MU}^{c\&l}$ security.

The tight $\mathsf{MU}^{c\&l}$ security protects our schemes from key leakages on the uncorrupted users besides adaptive corruptions. When used in the construction of more advanced protocols, the applications of our tightly $\mathsf{MU}^{c\&l}$ secure primitives may also improve the security of the protocols to be leakage resilient ones. For instance, we can always make a drop-in replacement of the tightly MU^c secure SIG with our tightly $\mathsf{MU}^{c\&l}$ secure SIG in the construction of tightly secure authenticated key exchange (AKE) protocols [4,18,29] where the signing key of SIG serves as the long-term secret key of AKE, and the resulting AKEs readily augment their tight security with leakage-resilience.

Moreover, our tightly $\mathsf{MUMC}^{c\&l}$-CCA secure PKE scheme has essential improvements in terms of leakage resilience beyond corruptions, compared with the tightly leakage-resilient CCA-secure PKE scheme in [20]. See Table 2. Concretely, (1) our leakage rate is $\frac{1}{3} - o(1)$ while theirs is $\frac{1}{18} - o(1)$; (2) our multi-user leakage model is stronger than theirs, since their model [20, Appendix A.1] does not allow any leakage queries to any user after the very first encryption query to *any* user, while our model allows leakage queries for any particular user until the first encryption query to *that* user (cf. Definition 16 in Subsect. 6.1). Informally speaking, our PKE achieves the stronger multi-user leakage resilience mainly due to the introduction of *multi-language multi-fold SMP*, which helps to switch $\mathcal{L}_\rho$ to different and *independently chosen* languages $\{\mathcal{L}_{\rho_0^{(i)}}\}$ for different users, thus the leakages w.r.t. different users can be handled independently.

2.5 Comparison with Existing Techniques for Tight MU^c Security

Most existing works on tight MU^c security [4,12,17,27] designed their schemes in a *"double encryption/signing"* fashion (the only exception is [18]), and the secret key of their schemes consists of only one key (say sk_0) out of two possible keys (say sk_0, sk_1). For example, in [4,27], their PKE encrypts plaintext by running a "sub-encryption procedure" twice (possibly in a correlated way), resulting in a ciphertext containing two "sub-ciphertexts" of the plaintext, and there are two decryption ways according to which possible key (sk_0 or sk_1) is used. In their tight MU^c security proofs, the reduction algorithms always possess the real secret keys (sk_0) of all users, while embed the challenges in the other possible keys (sk_1). With this strategy, their reductions can handle adaptive corruptions.

In contrast, all our constructions are different from the "double encryption/signing" design. For example, it is hard to split the ciphertext of our PKE to two "sub-ciphertexts". So the proof strategy in [4,12,17,27] does not apply.

We develop two different novel proof strategies for tight strong MU^c-CMA security of SIG and tight MUMC^c-CCA security of PKE (cf. Fig. 1 and Fig. 2), respectively. At a high level, we do not "double" the secret key by construction, but "split" the key during our tight proofs, which can be summarized as first "switch the languages for different oracles" then "apply quasi-adaptive properties" (such as $\langle \mathcal{L}_0, \mathcal{L} \rangle$-OT-extracting, $\langle \mathcal{L}, \mathcal{L}_0 \rangle$-Key-switching, $\mathcal{L}_0$-Multi-key multi-extracting).

3 Preliminaries

Notations. Let $\lambda \in \mathbb{N}$ denote the security parameter throughout the paper, and all algorithms, distributions, functions and adversaries take 1^λ as an implicit input. Let $\emptyset$ denote the empty set. If x is defined by y or the value of y is assigned to x, we write $x := y$. For $n \in \mathbb{N}$, define $[n] := \{1, 2, ..., n\}$. For a set $\mathcal{X}$, denote by $x \leftarrow_\$ \mathcal{X}$ the procedure of sampling x from $\mathcal{X}$ uniformly at random. If $\mathcal{D}$ is distribution, $x \leftarrow_\$ \mathcal{D}$ means that x is sampled according to $\mathcal{D}$. All our algorithms are probabilistic unless stated otherwise. We use $y \leftarrow_\$ \mathcal{A}(x)$ to define the random variable y obtained by executing algorithm $\mathcal{A}$ on input x. We use $y \in \mathcal{A}(x)$ to indicate that y lies in the support of $\mathcal{A}(x)$. If $\mathcal{A}$ is deterministic we write $y \leftarrow \mathcal{A}(x)$. We also use $y \leftarrow \mathcal{A}(x; r)$ to make explicit the random coins r used in the probabilistic computation. Denote by $\mathbf{T}(\mathcal{A})$ the running time of $\mathcal{A}$. "PPT" abbreviates probabilistic polynomial-time. Denote by poly some polynomial function and negl some negligible function.

The syntax of signature (SIG), public-key encryption (PKE) and the definition of collision-resistant hash functions are presented in the full version [19].

3.1   Language Distribution

We formalize a collection of NP-languages as a language distribution.

Definition 1 (Language Distribution). *A language distribution $\mathscr{L}$ is a probability distribution that outputs a language parameter ρ as well as a trapdoor td in polynomial time. The language parameter ρ publicly defines an NP-language $\mathcal{L}_\rho \subseteq \mathcal{X}_\rho$. For simplicity, we assume that the universe $\mathcal{X}_\rho$ is the same for all parameters ρ output by all distributions $\mathscr{L}$, and denoted by $\mathcal{X}$. The trapdoor td is required to contain enough information for efficiently deciding whether an instance $x \in \mathcal{X}$ is in $\mathcal{L}_\rho$. We require that there are PPT algorithms for sampling $x \leftarrow_s \mathcal{L}_\rho$ uniformly together with a witness w and sampling $x \leftarrow_s \mathcal{X}$ uniformly.*

A language distribution is associated with a subset membership problem (SMP), which asks whether an element is uniformly chosen from $\mathcal{L}_\rho$ or $\mathcal{X}$. SMP can be extended to multi-fold SMP by considering multiple elements.

Definition 2 (SMP). *The subset membership problem (SMP) related to a language distribution $\mathscr{L}$ is hard, if for any PPT adversary $\mathcal{A}$, it holds that $\mathsf{Adv}^{\mathsf{smp}}_{\mathscr{L},\mathcal{A}}(\lambda) := |\Pr[\mathcal{A}(\rho, x) = 1] - \Pr[\mathcal{A}(\rho, x') = 1]| \leq \mathsf{negl}(\lambda)$, where the probability is over $(\rho, td) \leftarrow_s \mathscr{L}$, $x \leftarrow_s \mathcal{L}_\rho$ and $x' \leftarrow_s \mathcal{X}$.*

Definition 3 (Multi-fold SMP). *The multi-fold SMP related to a language distribution $\mathscr{L}$ is hard, if for any PPT adversary $\mathcal{A}$ and any polynomial $Q = \mathsf{poly}(\lambda)$, it holds that $\mathsf{Adv}^{\mathsf{msmp}}_{\mathscr{L},\mathcal{A},Q}(\lambda) := |\Pr[\mathcal{A}(\rho, \{x_j\}_{j\in[Q]}) = 1] - \Pr[\mathcal{A}(\rho, \{x'_j\}_{j\in[Q]}) = 1]| \leq \mathsf{negl}(\lambda)$, where $(\rho, td) \leftarrow_s \mathscr{L}$, $x_1, ..., x_Q \leftarrow_s \mathcal{L}_\rho$ and $x'_1, ..., x'_Q \leftarrow_s \mathcal{X}$.*

3.2   Quasi-Adaptive Hash Proof System

Hash proof system (HPS) was proposed by Cramer and Shoup [11], and turned out to be a powerful tool in a wide range of applications. Han et al. [20] generalized HPS in a quasi-adaptive setting, termed as *Quasi-Adaptive HPS* (QA-HPS), by allowing the projection key to depend on the specific language $\mathcal{L}_\rho$ for which hash values are computed. We give the definition of QA-HPS according to [20].

Definition 4 (QA-HPS). *A quasi-adaptive hash proof system (QA-HPS) scheme* $\mathsf{QAHPS} = (\mathsf{Setup}_{\mathsf{HPS}}, \alpha_{(\cdot)}, \mathsf{Pub}, \mathsf{Priv})$ *for a language distribution $\mathscr{L}$ consists of four PPT algorithms:*

- $pp_{HPS} \leftarrow_\$ Setup_{HPS}$: *The setup algorithm outputs a public parameter* pp_{HPS}, *which implicitly defines a hashing key space* $\mathcal{SK}$, *a hash value space* $\mathcal{HV}$, *and a family of hash functions* $\Lambda_{(\cdot)} : \mathcal{X} \longrightarrow \mathcal{HV}$ *indexed by hashing keys* $sk \in \mathcal{SK}$, *where* $\mathcal{X}$ *is the universe for languages output by* $\mathcal{L}$.
  We require that $\Lambda_{(\cdot)}$ *is efficiently computable and there are PPT algorithms for sampling* $sk \leftarrow_\$ \mathcal{SK}$ *uniformly and sampling* $hv \leftarrow_\$ \mathcal{HV}$ *uniformly. We require* pp_{HPS} *to be an implicit input of other algorithms.*
- $pk_\rho \leftarrow \alpha_\rho(sk)$: *Taking as input a hashing key* $sk \in \mathcal{SK}$, *the projection algorithm indexed by language parameter* ρ *outputs a projection key* pk_ρ.
- $hv \leftarrow Pub(pk_\rho, x, w)$: *Taking as input a projection key* $pk_\rho = \alpha_\rho(sk)$ *specified by* ρ, *an instance* $x \in \mathcal{L}_\rho$ *and a witness* w *for* $x \in \mathcal{L}_\rho$, *the public evaluation algorithm outputs a hash value* $hv = \Lambda_{sk}(x) \in \mathcal{HV}$.
- $hv \leftarrow Priv(sk, x)$: *Taking as input a hashing key* sk *and an instance* $x \in \mathcal{X}$, *the private evaluation algorithm outputs a hash value* $hv = \Lambda_{sk}(x) \in \mathcal{HV}$.

Correctness requires that for all $(\rho, td) \in \mathcal{L}$, $pp_{HPS} \in Setup_{HPS}$, $sk \in \mathcal{SK}$, $x \in \mathcal{L}_\rho$ *with witness* w, $pk_\rho := \alpha_\rho(sk)$, *it holds that* $Pub(pk_\rho, x, w) = \Lambda_{sk}(x) = Priv(sk, x)$.

We can naturally define QA-HPS for two language distributions $\mathcal{L}$ and $\mathcal{L}_0$, by requiring correctness to hold not only for language parameters ρ output by $\mathcal{L}$, but also for language parameters ρ_0 output by $\mathcal{L}_0$.

We recall a statistical property of QA-HPS from [20], parameterized by $\kappa \in \mathbb{N}$ and two language distributions $\mathcal{L}, \mathcal{L}_0$, called κ-*leakage-resilient(LR)-*$\langle \mathcal{L}, \mathcal{L}_0 \rangle$-*key-switching.* Informally speaking, it stipulates that in the presence of a projection key $\alpha_\rho(sk)$ w.r.t. a language parameter ρ output by $\mathcal{L}$ and given κ bits leakage information about sk, the projection key $\alpha_{\rho_0}(sk)$ w.r.t. another language parameter ρ_0 output by $\mathcal{L}_0$ can be switched to $\alpha_{\rho_0}(sk')$ for an independent sk'.

Definition 5 (κ-**LR-**$\langle \mathcal{L}, \mathcal{L}_0 \rangle$-**Key-Switching of QA-HPS).** *Let* $\kappa = \kappa(\lambda) \subset \mathbb{N}$, *and let* $\mathcal{L}$ *and* $\mathcal{L}_0$ *be a pair of language distributions. A QA-HPS scheme* QAHPS *for* $\mathcal{L}$ *supports* κ-LR-$\langle \mathcal{L}, \mathcal{L}_0 \rangle$-*key-switching, if for any (possibly unbounded) adversary* $\mathcal{A}$, *it holds that* $\epsilon_{QAHPS,\mathcal{A},\kappa}^{lr-\langle \mathcal{L}, \mathcal{L}_0 \rangle-ks}(\lambda) := | \Pr[Exp_{QAHPS,\mathcal{A},\kappa}^{lr-\langle \mathcal{L}, \mathcal{L}_0 \rangle-ks} \Rightarrow 1] - \frac{1}{2} | \leq negl(\lambda)$, *where the experiment* $Exp_{QAHPS,\mathcal{A},\kappa}^{lr-\langle \mathcal{L}, \mathcal{L}_0 \rangle-ks}$ *is specified in Fig. 3.*

3.3   Tag-Based Quasi-Adaptive Non-Interactive Zero-Knowledge

Quasi-Adaptive Non-Interactive Zero-Knowledge argument (QA-NIZK) was proposed by Jutla and Roy [24], where the common reference string (CRS) may depend on the specific language $\mathcal{L}_\rho$ for which proofs are generated. We present the formal definition of QA-NIZK in its *tag-based* variant following [25].

Definition 6 (Tag-based   QA-NIZK). *A tag-based quasi-adaptive non-interactive zero-knowledge scheme* QANIZK $=$ (Setup$_{NIZK}$, CRSGen, Prove, Vrfy$_{NIZK}$, Sim) *for a language distribution* $\mathcal{L}$ *with tag space* $\mathcal{T}$ *consists of five PPT algorithms:*

$\mathsf{Exp}^{\mathsf{lr}\text{-}\langle\mathscr{L},\mathscr{L}_0\rangle\text{-}\mathsf{ks}}_{\mathsf{QAHPS},\mathcal{A},\kappa}$:	$\mathcal{O}_{\mathrm{LEAK}}(L)$: //at most κ leakage bits in total
$\mathsf{pp}_{\mathsf{HPS}} \leftarrow_\$ \mathsf{Setup}_{\mathsf{HPS}}, \ (\rho,td) \leftarrow_\$ \mathscr{L}, \ (\rho_0,td_0) \leftarrow_\$ \mathscr{L}_0$	If $\mathsf{chal} = \mathbf{true}$: Return $\perp$
$sk, sk' \leftarrow_\$ \mathcal{SK}$	Return $L(sk)$
$b \leftarrow_\$ \{0,1\}$ //Challenge bit	$\mathcal{O}_{\mathrm{CHAL}}()$: //one query
$\mathsf{chal} := \mathbf{false}$	$\mathsf{chal} := \mathbf{true}$
$b' \leftarrow_\$ \mathcal{A}^{\mathcal{O}_{\mathrm{LEAK}}(\cdot),\mathcal{O}_{\mathrm{CHAL}}()}(\mathsf{pp}_{\mathsf{HPS}}, \rho, \alpha_\rho(sk))$	If $b = 0$: Return $(\rho_0, \alpha_{\rho_0}(sk))$;
If $b' = b$: Return 1; Else: Return 0	Else $b = 1$: Return $(\rho_0, \alpha_{\rho_0}(sk'))$

Fig. 3. The κ-LR-$\langle\mathscr{L},\mathscr{L}_0\rangle$-Key-Switching experiment $\mathsf{Exp}^{\mathsf{lr}\text{-}\langle\mathscr{L},\mathscr{L}_0\rangle\text{-}\mathsf{ks}}_{\mathsf{QAHPS},\mathcal{A},\kappa}$ for QAHPS.

- $\mathsf{pp}_{\mathsf{NIZK}} \leftarrow_\$ \mathsf{Setup}_{\mathsf{NIZK}}$: *The setup algorithm outputs a public parameter* $\mathsf{pp}_{\mathsf{NIZK}}$, *which serves as an implicit input of other algorithms.*
- $(\mathsf{crs}, \mathsf{td}_{\mathsf{crs}}) \leftarrow_\$ \mathsf{CRSGen}(\rho)$: *Taking as input a language parameter* ρ, *the CRS generation algorithm outputs a common reference string (CRS)* crs *and a simulation trapdoor* $\mathsf{td}_{\mathsf{crs}}$.
- $\pi \leftarrow_\$ \mathsf{Prove}(\mathsf{crs}, \tau, x, w)$: *Taking as input* crs, *a tag* $\tau \in \mathcal{T}$, $x \in \mathcal{L}_\rho$ *and a witness* w *for* $x \in \mathcal{L}_\rho$, *the proof generation algorithm outputs a proof* π.
- $0/1 \leftarrow \mathsf{Vrfy}_{\mathsf{NIZK}}(\mathsf{crs}, \tau, x, \pi)$: *Taking as input* crs, *a tag* $\tau \in \mathcal{T}$, $x \in \mathcal{X}$ *and a proof* π, *the deterministic verification algorithm outputs a bit indicating whether* π *is a valid proof.*
- $\pi \leftarrow_\$ \mathsf{Sim}(\mathsf{crs}, \mathsf{td}_{\mathsf{crs}}, \tau, x)$: *Taking as input* crs, *a simulation trapdoor* $\mathsf{td}_{\mathsf{crs}}$, *a tag* $\tau \in \mathcal{T}$ *and* $x \in \mathcal{X}$, *the simulation algorithm outputs a simulated proof* π.

Perfect completeness requires that for all $(\rho, td) \in \mathscr{L}$, $\mathsf{pp}_{\mathsf{NIZK}} \in \mathsf{Setup}_{\mathsf{NIZK}}$, $(\mathsf{crs}, \mathsf{td}_{\mathsf{crs}}) \in \mathsf{CRSGen}(\rho)$, $\tau \in \mathcal{T}$, $x \in \mathcal{L}_\rho$ *with witness* w, $\pi \in \mathsf{Prove}(\mathsf{crs}, \tau, x, w)$, *it holds that* $\mathsf{Vrfy}_{\mathsf{NIZK}}(\mathsf{crs}, \tau, x, \pi) = 1$.

Perfect zero-knowledge requires that for all $(\rho, td) \in \mathscr{L}$, $\mathsf{pp}_{\mathsf{NIZK}} \in \mathsf{Setup}_{\mathsf{NIZK}}$, $(\mathsf{crs}, \mathsf{td}_{\mathsf{crs}}) \in \mathsf{CRSGen}(\rho)$, $\tau \in \mathcal{T}$, $x \in \mathcal{L}_\rho$ *with witness* w, *the outputs of* $\mathsf{Prove}(\mathsf{crs}, \tau, x, w)$ *and* $\mathsf{Sim}(\mathsf{crs}, \mathsf{td}_{\mathsf{crs}}, \tau, x)$ *are identically distributed, where the probability is over the inner coin tosses of* Prove *and* Sim.

Below we define *Unbounded Simulation-Soundness* (USS) according to [1,22].

Definition 7 (USS of Tag-based QA-NIZK). *A tag-based QA-NIZK scheme* QANIZK *for* $\mathscr{L}$ *has unbounded simulation-soundness (USS), if for any PPT adversary* $\mathcal{A}$, *it holds that* $\mathsf{Adv}^{\mathsf{uss}}_{\mathsf{QANIZK},\mathcal{A}}(\lambda) := \Pr[\mathsf{Exp}^{\mathsf{uss}}_{\mathsf{QANIZK},\mathcal{A}} \Rightarrow 1] \leq \mathsf{negl}(\lambda)$, *where the experiment* $\mathsf{Exp}^{\mathsf{uss}}_{\mathsf{QANIZK},\mathcal{A}}$ *is defined in Fig. 4.*

We note that the above USS definition for tag-based QA-NIZK is stronger than the usual one in [15,25] in two aspects.

- Firstly, $\mathcal{A}$ is given the trapdoor td of the language parameter ρ. Recall that td contains enough information for efficiently deciding whether or not an instance x is in $\mathcal{L}_\rho$. This is stronger than the usual USS, but weaker than the *USS for witness-sampleable distributions* defined in [1,22], where $\mathcal{A}$ essentially samples (ρ, td) itself and provides (ρ, td) to the experiment.
- Secondly, $\mathcal{A}$ is allowed to output a forgery with a reused tag.

$\mathsf{Exp}^{\mathsf{uss}}_{\mathsf{QANIZK},\mathcal{A}}$:	
$(\rho, td) \leftarrow_\$ \mathscr{L}$. $\mathsf{pp}_{\mathsf{NIZK}} \leftarrow_\$ \mathsf{Setup}_{\mathsf{NIZK}}$. $(\mathsf{crs}, \mathsf{td}_{\mathsf{crs}}) \leftarrow_\$ \mathsf{CRSGen}(\rho)$	$\mathcal{O}_{\mathrm{SIM}}(\tau, x)$:
$\mathcal{Q}_{\mathrm{SIM}} := \emptyset$ //Record the simulation queries	$\pi \leftarrow_\$ \mathsf{Sim}(\mathsf{crs}, \mathsf{td}_{\mathsf{crs}}, \tau, x)$
$(\tau^*, x^*, \pi^*) \leftarrow_\$ \mathcal{A}^{\mathcal{O}_{\mathrm{SIM}}(\cdot, \cdot)}(\rho, td, \mathsf{pp}_{\mathsf{NIZK}}, \mathsf{crs})$	$\mathcal{Q}_{\mathrm{SIM}} := \mathcal{Q}_{\mathrm{SIM}} \cup \{(\tau, x, \pi)\}$
If $(x^* \notin \mathcal{L}_\rho) \wedge ((\tau^*, x^*, \pi^*) \notin \mathcal{Q}_{\mathrm{SIM}}) \wedge (\mathsf{Vrfy}_{\mathsf{NIZK}}(\mathsf{crs}, \tau^*, x^*, \pi^*) = 1)$: Return 1;	Return π
Else: Return 0	

Fig. 4. The Unbounded Simulation-Soundness experiment $\mathsf{Exp}^{\mathsf{uss}}_{\mathsf{QANIZK},\mathcal{A}}$ for QANIZK.

In [1], Abe et al. proposed a QA-NIZK scheme with tight USS for witness-sampleable distributions based on the MDDH assumptions. As noted in [1, Subsect. 3.2], their scheme can be easily extended to a tag-based QA-NIZK scheme with tight USS, by using collision-resistant hash functions.

4 Publicly-Verifiable QA-HPS and New Properties

In this section, we propose a new variant of QA-HPS, called *Publicly-Verifiable QA-HPS* (PV-QA-HPS), which additionally enables public verification of hash values with an extra verification key. Then we formalize a set of computational and statistical properties for PV-QA-HPS and QA-HPS serving different applications in subsequent sections.

- For PV-QA-HPS, we define a computational *verification soundness* and statistical properties including *leakage-resilient one-time-extracting (LR-OT extracting)* and *verification key diversity (VK-diversity)*. PV-QA-HPS will be an important building block for SIG in Sect. 5 and these properties help SIG to achieve tight multi-user security under corruptions and leakages.
- For QA-HPS, we define a computational *multi-key-multi-extracting* and a statistical *projection key diversity (PK-diversity)*. We also define a *multi-language multi-fold SMP* for language distributions. QA-HPS will be an important building block for PKE in Sect. 6, and these new properties help PKE to achieve tight multi-user security under corruptions and leakages.

Jumping ahead, we will give instantiations of PV-QA-HPS and QA-HPS based on the matrix DDH (MDDH) assumptions in Sect. 7 and the full version [19].

Firstly, we present the syntax of PV-QA-HPS.

Definition 8 (PV-QA-HPS). *A publicly-verifiable QA-HPS (PV-QA-HPS) scheme* $\mathsf{PVQAHPS} = (\mathsf{Setup}_{\mathsf{HPS}}, \alpha_{(\cdot)}, \nu, \mathsf{Pub}, \mathsf{Priv}, \mathsf{Vrfy}_{\mathsf{HPS}})$ *for a language distribution* $\mathscr{L}$ *consists of six PPT algorithms:*

- $(\mathsf{Setup}_{\mathsf{HPS}}, \alpha_{(\cdot)}, \mathsf{Pub}, \mathsf{Priv})$ *is a QA-HPS scheme for* $\mathscr{L}$ *as per Definition 4.*
- $\mathsf{pp}_{\mathsf{HPS}} \leftarrow_\$ \mathsf{Setup}_{\mathsf{HPS}}$: *It outputs a public parameter* $\mathsf{pp}_{\mathsf{HPS}}$, *which also defines a verification key space* $\mathcal{VK}$ *besides* $(\mathcal{SK}, \mathcal{HV}, \Lambda_{(\cdot)})$ *as per Definition 4.*
- $vk \leftarrow \nu(sk)$: *Taking as input a hashing key* $sk \in \mathcal{SK}$, *the verification key generation algorithm outputs a verification key* $vk \in \mathcal{VK}$.

- $0/1 \leftarrow \mathsf{Vrfy}_{\mathsf{HPS}}(vk, x, hv)$: *Taking as input a verification key $vk = \nu(sk) \in \mathcal{VK}$, an instance $x \in \mathcal{X}$ and a hash value $hv \in \mathcal{HV}$, the deterministic verification algorithm outputs a bit indicating whether $hv = \Lambda_{sk}(x)$ or not.*

Verification completeness requires that for all $(\rho, td) \in \mathscr{L}$, $\mathsf{pp}_{\mathsf{HPS}} \in \mathsf{Setup}_{\mathsf{HPS}}$, $sk \in \mathcal{SK}$, $x \in \mathcal{X}$, $vk := \nu(sk)$ and $hv := \Lambda_{sk}(x)$, it holds $\mathsf{Vrfy}_{\mathsf{HPS}}(vk, x, hv) = 1$.

Remark 1 (Relations between PV-QA-HPS and QA-NIZK). PV-QA-HPS can be viewed as a special kind of Designated-Prover (DP) QA-NIZK [1], but with different properties. The pk_ρ of PV-QA-HPS can be viewed as the proving key of DP-QA-NIZK, sk as the simulation trapdoor and vk as the common reference string (used for verification). With pk_ρ, the prover can prove $x \in \mathcal{L}_\rho$ with the help of a witness w via $hv \leftarrow \mathsf{Pub}(pk_\rho, x, w)$, where the hash value hv can be viewed as a proof for $x \in \mathcal{L}_\rho$. With vk, the verifier can check whether hv is a valid proof for $x \in \mathcal{L}_\rho$ via $\mathsf{Vrfy}_{\mathsf{HPS}}(vk, x, hv)$. Moreover, with sk, the simulator can generate a proof for x without knowing a witness via $hv \leftarrow \mathsf{Priv}(sk, x)$.

Verification completeness of PV-QA-HPS corresponds to the perfect completeness of DP-QA-NIZK. Correctness of (PV-)QA-HPS guarantees $\mathsf{Pub}(pk_\rho, x, w) = \mathsf{Priv}(sk, x)$ for all $x \in \mathcal{L}_\rho$ with witness w, thus corresponding to the perfect zero-knowledge of DP-QA-NIZK.

On the other hand, PV-QA-HPS has its own features. Firstly, it has a projection function $\alpha_\rho(\cdot)$ (which is inherent to HPS) and a verification key generation function $\nu(\cdot)$. Secondly, a set of properties of PV-QA-HPS and QA-HPS are built upon functions $\alpha_\rho(\cdot)$ and/or $\nu(\cdot)$. For instance, the κ-LR-$\langle \mathscr{L}, \mathscr{L}_0 \rangle$-Key-Switching (cf. Definition 5 in Subsect. 3.2) is closely associated with $\alpha_\rho(\cdot)$.

Next we define a computational *verification soundness* for PV-QA-HPS in the setting of multiple keys. Intuitively, it requires that for any (sk, vk) among the multiple key pairs, a PPT adversary cannot find a tuple $(x^* \in \mathcal{X}, hv^*)$ such that $hv^* \neq \Lambda_{sk}(x^*)$ but $\mathsf{Vrfy}_{\mathsf{HPS}}(vk, x^*, hv^*) = 1$, even given all the key pairs.

Definition 9 (Verification Soundness of PV-QA-HPS). *A PV-QA-HPS scheme PVQAHPS for $\mathscr{L}$ has verification soundness, if for any PPT adversary $\mathcal{A}$ and any polynomial $n = \mathsf{poly}(\lambda)$, it holds that $\mathsf{Adv}_{\mathsf{PVQAHPS}, \mathcal{A}, n}^{\mathsf{vrfy\text{-}snd}}(\lambda) := \Pr[\mathsf{Exp}_{\mathsf{PVQAHPS}, \mathcal{A}, n}^{\mathsf{vrfy\text{-}snd}} \Rightarrow 1] \leq \mathsf{negl}(\lambda)$, where $\mathsf{Exp}_{\mathsf{PVQAHPS}, \mathcal{A}, n}^{\mathsf{vrfy\text{-}snd}}$ is defined in Fig. 5.*

We formalize a statistical extracting property for (PV-)QA-HPS, parameterized by $\kappa \in \mathbb{N}$ and two language distributions $\mathscr{L}_0$, $\mathscr{L}$, called κ-*leakage-resilient(LR)-$\langle \mathscr{L}_0, \mathscr{L} \rangle$-one-time(OT)-extracting*. Informally speaking, it demands high min-entropy of $\Lambda_{sk}(x)$ for any $x \in \mathcal{L}_\rho$ with ρ output by $\mathscr{L}$, when sk is uniformly chosen from $\mathcal{SK}$, even in the presence of a projection key $\alpha_{\rho_0}(sk)$ w.r.t. ρ_0 output by $\mathscr{L}_0$ and given κ bits leakage information about sk. For PV-QA-HPS, it requires the property to hold even in the presence of the verification key $\nu(sk)$.

$$\boxed{\begin{array}{l} \mathsf{Exp}^{\mathsf{vrfy\text{-}snd}}_{\mathsf{PVQAHPS},\mathcal{A},n}: \\ \hline \mathsf{pp}_{\mathsf{HPS}} \leftarrow_{\$} \mathsf{Setup}_{\mathsf{HPS}}. \text{ For } i \in [n]: \; sk_i \leftarrow_{\$} \mathcal{SK}, \; vk_i := \nu(sk_i) \\ (i^* \in [n], x^* \in \mathcal{X}, hv^*) \leftarrow_{\$} \mathcal{A}(\mathsf{pp}_{\mathsf{HPS}}, (sk_i, vk_i)_{i \in [n]}) \\ \text{If } (hv^* \neq \varLambda_{sk_{i^*}}(x^*)) \wedge (\mathsf{Vrfy}_{\mathsf{HPS}}(vk_{i^*}, x^*, hv^*) = 1): \text{ Return 1}; \quad \text{Else: Return 0} \end{array}}$$

Fig. 5. Verification Soundness experiment $\mathsf{Exp}^{\mathsf{vrfy\text{-}snd}}_{\mathsf{PVQAHPS},\mathcal{A},n}$ for PVQAHPS.

Definition 10 (κ-LR-$\langle \mathscr{L}_0, \mathscr{L} \rangle$-OT-Extracting of QA-HPS and PV-QA-HPS). *Let $\kappa = \kappa(\lambda) \in \mathbb{N}$, and let $\mathscr{L}_0$ and $\mathscr{L}$ be a pair of language distributions. A (PV-)QA-HPS scheme (PV)QAHPS for $\mathscr{L}$ supports κ-LR-$\langle \mathscr{L}_0, \mathscr{L} \rangle$-OT-extracting, if for any (unbounded) adversary $\mathcal{A}$, it holds that $\epsilon^{\mathsf{lr}\text{-}\langle \mathscr{L}_0, \mathscr{L} \rangle\text{-}\mathsf{otext}}_{\mathsf{(PV)QAHPS},\mathcal{A},\kappa}(\lambda) := \Pr[\mathsf{Exp}^{\mathsf{lr}\text{-}\langle \mathscr{L}_0, \mathscr{L} \rangle\text{-}\mathsf{otext}}_{\mathsf{(PV)QAHPS},\mathcal{A},\kappa} \Rightarrow 1] \leq \mathsf{negl}(\lambda)$, where $\mathsf{Exp}^{\mathsf{lr}\text{-}\langle \mathscr{L}_0, \mathscr{L} \rangle\text{-}\mathsf{otext}}_{\mathsf{(PV)QAHPS},\mathcal{A},\kappa}$ is defined in Fig. 6.*

$$\boxed{\begin{array}{l|l} \mathsf{Exp}^{\mathsf{lr}\text{-}\langle \mathscr{L}_0, \mathscr{L} \rangle\text{-}\mathsf{otext}}_{\mathsf{(PV)QAHPS},\mathcal{A},\kappa}: & \mathcal{O}_{\mathsf{Leak}}(L): \; /\!/\text{at most } \kappa \text{ leakage} \\ \hline \mathsf{pp}_{\mathsf{HPS}} \leftarrow_{\$} \mathsf{Setup}_{\mathsf{HPS}}. \; (\rho_0, td_0) \leftarrow_{\$} \mathscr{L}_0, (\rho, td) \leftarrow_{\$} \mathscr{L}. \; sk \leftarrow_{\$} \mathcal{SK} & \quad /\!/\text{bits in total} \\ (x^*, hv^*) \leftarrow_{\$} \mathcal{A}^{\mathcal{O}_{\mathsf{Leak}}(\cdot)}(\mathsf{pp}_{\mathsf{HPS}}, \rho_0, \rho, \alpha_{\rho_0}(sk), \boxed{\nu(sk)}) & \quad \text{Return } L(sk) \\ \text{If } (x^* \in \mathcal{L}_\rho) \wedge (hv^* = \varLambda_{sk}(x^*)): \text{ Return 1}; \quad \text{Else: Return 0} & \end{array}}$$

Fig. 6. The κ-LR-$\langle \mathscr{L}_0, \mathscr{L} \rangle$-OT-Extracting experiment $\mathsf{Exp}^{\mathsf{lr}\text{-}\langle \mathscr{L}_0, \mathscr{L} \rangle\text{-}\mathsf{otext}}_{\mathsf{(PV)QAHPS},\mathcal{A},\kappa}$ for QAHPS (without gray part) and Publicly-Verifiable PVQAHPS (with gray part).

Han et al. [20] proposed a computational property for QA-HPS, called $\mathscr{L}_0$-*multi-extracting*, which demands the pseudorandomness of $\varLambda_{sk}(x_j)$ for multiple instances $x_j \in \mathcal{L}_{\rho_0}$ ($j \in [Q]$) with ρ_0 output by $\mathscr{L}_0$, when sk is uniformly chosen from $\mathcal{SK}$. We extend this property in the multi-key setting as follows.

Definition 11 ($\mathscr{L}_0$-Multi-Key-Multi-Extracting of QA-HPS). *A QA-HPS scheme QAHPS for $\mathscr{L}$ supports $\mathscr{L}_0$-multi-key-multi-extracting, if for any PPT $\mathcal{A}$, any polynomial $n = \mathsf{poly}(\lambda)$ and any polynomial $Q = \mathsf{poly}(\lambda)$, it holds*

$$\mathsf{Adv}^{\mathscr{L}_0\text{-}\mathsf{mk\text{-}mext}}_{\mathsf{QAHPS},\mathcal{A},n,Q}(\lambda) := | \Pr[\mathcal{A}(\mathsf{pp}_{\mathsf{HPS}}, \rho_0, \{x_j, \boxed{\{\varLambda_{sk_i}(x_j)\}_{i \in [n]}}\}_{j \in [Q]}) = 1]$$

$$- \Pr[\mathcal{A}(\mathsf{pp}_{\mathsf{HPS}}, \rho_0, \{x_j, \boxed{\{hv_{i,j}\}_{i \in [n]}}\}_{j \in [Q]}) = 1]| \leq \mathsf{negl}(\lambda),$$

where $\mathsf{pp}_{\mathsf{HPS}} \leftarrow_{\$} \mathsf{Setup}_{\mathsf{HPS}}$, $(\rho_0, td_0) \leftarrow_{\$} \mathscr{L}_0$, $sk_1, ..., sk_n \leftarrow_{\$} \mathcal{SK}$, $x_1, ..., x_Q \leftarrow_{\$} \mathcal{L}_{\rho_0}$ *and* $hv_{1,1}, ..., hv_{n,Q} \leftarrow_{\$} \mathcal{HV}$.

We formalize two statistical properties, called *projection key diversity (PK-diversity)* and *verification key diversity (VK-diversity)*, for QA-HPS and PV-QA-HPS respectively. Intuitively, PK-diversity (resp. VK-diversity) expresses statistical collision resistance of projection keys (resp. verification keys) under different hashing keys.

Definition 12 (PK-Diversity of QA-HPS). *A QA-HPS scheme* QAHPS *for* $\mathscr{L}$ *has projection key diversity (PK-diversity), if* $\epsilon_{\mathsf{QAHPS}}^{\mathsf{pk\text{-}div}}(\lambda) := \Pr[\alpha_\rho(sk) = \alpha_\rho(sk')] \leq \mathsf{negl}(\lambda)$, *where* $(\rho, td) \leftarrow_\$ \mathscr{L}$, $\mathsf{pp}_{\mathsf{HPS}} \leftarrow_\$ \mathsf{Setup}_{\mathsf{HPS}}$ *and* $sk, sk' \leftarrow_\$ \mathcal{SK}$.

Definition 13 (VK-Diversity of PV-QA-HPS). *A PV-QA-HPS scheme* PVQAHPS *for* $\mathscr{L}$ *has verification key diversity (VK-diversity), if* $\epsilon_{\mathsf{PVQAHPS}}^{\mathsf{vk\text{-}div}}(\lambda) := \Pr[\nu(sk) = \nu(sk')] \leq \mathsf{negl}(\lambda)$, *where* $\mathsf{pp}_{\mathsf{HPS}} \leftarrow_\$ \mathsf{Setup}_{\mathsf{HPS}}$ *and* $sk, sk' \leftarrow_\$ \mathcal{SK}$.

Finally, we define a *multi-language* multi-fold SMP for language distributions.

Definition 14 (Multi-Language Multi-fold SMP). *The multi-language multi-fold SMP related to* $\mathscr{L}$ *is hard, if for any PPT adversary* $\mathcal{A}$, *any polynomial* $n = \mathsf{poly}(\lambda)$ *and any polynomial* $Q = \mathsf{poly}(\lambda)$, *it holds that* $\mathsf{Adv}_{\mathscr{L},\mathcal{A},n,Q}^{\mathsf{ml\text{-}msmp}}(\lambda) :=$
$| \Pr[\mathcal{A}(\{\rho^{(i)}, \{x_j^{(i)}\}_{j\in[Q]}\}_{i\in[n]}) = 1] - \Pr[\mathcal{A}(\{\rho^{(i)}, \{x_j'^{(i)}\}_{j\in[Q]}\}_{i\in[n]}) = 1]| \leq$
$\mathsf{negl}(\lambda)$, *where for each* $i \in [n]$, $(\rho^{(i)}, td^{(i)}) \leftarrow_\$ \mathscr{L}$, $x_1^{(i)}, ..., x_Q^{(i)} \leftarrow_\$ \mathcal{L}_{\rho^{(i)}}$, $x_1'^{(i)}, ..., x_Q'^{(i)} \leftarrow_\$ \mathcal{X}$.

Multi-language multi-fold SMP can generally be reduced to SMP with a security loss of nQ with n the number of languages and Q the number of folds per language. For some language distributions, such as those for linear subspaces based on the MDDH assumptions (cf. the full version [19]), the hardness of multi-language multi-fold SMP can be tightly reduced to that of SMP.

5   SIG with Tight Strong MU$^{\mathsf{c\&l}}$-CMA Security

In this section, we present digital signature (SIG) schemes with tight strong MU$^{\mathsf{c\&l}}$-CMA security, by using Publicly-Verifiable QA-HPS (PV-QA-NIZK) formalized in Sect. 4 as a central building block.

In Subsect. 5.1, we define the strong MU$^{\mathsf{c\&l}}$-CMA security of SIG. Then in Subsect. 5.2, we present our generic construction of SIG.

5.1   Definition of Strong MU$^{\mathsf{c\&l}}$-CMA Security

In [4], Bader et al. defined existential unforgeability for digital signatures under chosen-message attacks (CMA) in a Multi-User setting with adaptive corruptions of secret keys (MU^{c}-CMA). Here we extend it to MU$^{\mathsf{c\&l}}$-CMA, which considers existential unforgeability under not only chosen-message attacks and adaptive corruptions but also key leakages in the multi-user setting. Moreover, *strong* MU$^{\mathsf{c\&l}}$-CMA requires that the adversary cannot even forge a new signature for a message that it has ever queried. Below we present the definition of strong MU$^{\mathsf{c\&l}}$-CMA and the non-strong version can be easily adapted accordingly.

Definition 15 (Strong MU$^{\mathsf{c\&l}}$-CMA Security for SIG). *Let* $\kappa = \kappa(\lambda) \in \mathbb{N}$. *A signature scheme* SIG = $(\mathsf{Setup}_{\mathsf{SIG}}, \mathsf{Gen}, \mathsf{Sign}, \mathsf{Vrfy}_{\mathsf{SIG}})$ *is strongly* MU$^{\mathsf{c\&l}}$-CMA *secure under* κ *bits leakage per user, if for any PPT adversary* $\mathcal{A}$ *and any polynomial* n, *it holds that* $\mathsf{Adv}_{\mathsf{SIG},\mathcal{A},n,\kappa}^{\mathsf{s\text{-}cma\text{-}c\&l}}(\lambda) := \Pr[\mathsf{Exp}_{\mathsf{SIG},\mathcal{A},n,\kappa}^{\mathsf{s\text{-}cma\text{-}c\&l}} \Rightarrow 1] \leq \mathsf{negl}(\lambda)$, *where the experiment* $\mathsf{Exp}_{\mathsf{SIG},\mathcal{A},n,\kappa}^{\mathsf{s\text{-}cma\text{-}c\&l}}$ *is defined in Fig. 7.*

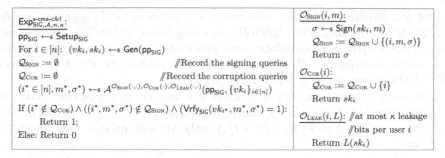

Fig. 7. The strong $\mathsf{MU}^{c\&l}$-CMA security experiment $\mathsf{Exp}^{\text{s-cma-c\&l}}_{\mathsf{SIG},\mathcal{A},n,\kappa}$ for SIG.

5.2 Generic Construction of SIG from PV-QA-HPS and QA-NIZK

We present a generic construction of strongly $\mathsf{MU}^{c\&l}$-CMA secure SIG. Let $\mathcal{M}$ be an arbitrary message space. The underlying building blocks are as follows.

- Two language distributions $\mathscr{L}$ and $\mathscr{L}_0$, both of which have hard SMPs.
- A publicly-verifiable $\mathsf{PVQAHPS} = (\mathsf{Setup}_{\mathsf{HPS}}, \alpha_{(\cdot)}, \nu, \mathsf{Pub}, \mathsf{Priv}, \mathsf{Vrfy}_{\mathsf{HPS}})$ for both $\mathscr{L}$ and $\mathscr{L}_0$, with hashing key space $\mathcal{SK}$ and verification key space $\mathcal{VK}$.
- A tag-based $\mathsf{QANIZK} = (\mathsf{Setup}_{\mathsf{NIZK}}, \mathsf{CRSGen}, \mathsf{Prove}, \mathsf{Vrfy}_{\mathsf{NIZK}}, \mathsf{Sim})$ for $\mathscr{L}$, whose tag space is $\mathcal{T}$.
- A family of collision-resistant hash functions $\mathcal{H} = \{H : \mathcal{VK} \times \mathcal{M} \longrightarrow \mathcal{T}\}$.

Our generic construction of $\mathsf{SIG} = (\mathsf{Setup}_{\mathsf{SIG}}, \mathsf{Gen}, \mathsf{Sign}, \mathsf{Vrfy}_{\mathsf{SIG}})$ is shown in Fig. 8.

$\mathsf{pp}_{\mathsf{SIG}} \leftarrow_s \mathsf{Setup}_{\mathsf{SIG}}$: $(\rho, td) \leftarrow_s \mathscr{L}$. $\mathsf{pp}_{\mathsf{HPS}} \leftarrow_s \mathsf{Setup}_{\mathsf{HPS}}$. $\mathsf{pp}_{\mathsf{NIZK}} \leftarrow_s \mathsf{Setup}_{\mathsf{NIZK}}$. $(\mathsf{crs}, \mathsf{td}_{\mathsf{crs}}) \leftarrow_s \mathsf{CRSGen}(\rho)$. $H \leftarrow_s \mathcal{H}$. Return $\mathsf{pp}_{\mathsf{SIG}} :=$ $\quad (\rho, \mathsf{pp}_{\mathsf{HPS}}, \mathsf{pp}_{\mathsf{NIZK}}, \mathsf{crs}, H)$.	$(vk, sk) \leftarrow_s \mathsf{Gen}(\mathsf{pp}_{\mathsf{SIG}})$: $sk \leftarrow_s \mathcal{SK}$, $vk := \nu(sk)$. Return (vk, sk). $\sigma \leftarrow_s \mathsf{Sign}(sk, m)$: $x \leftarrow_s \mathcal{L}_\rho$ with witness w. $d := \mathsf{Priv}(sk, x)$. $vk := \nu(sk)$. $\tau := H(vk, m) \in \mathcal{T}$. $\pi \leftarrow_s \mathsf{Prove}(\mathsf{crs}, \tau, x, w)$. Return $\sigma := (x, d, \pi)$.	$0/1 \leftarrow \mathsf{Vrfy}_{\mathsf{SIG}}(vk, m, \sigma)$: Parse $\sigma = (x, d, \pi)$. $\tau := H(vk, m) \in \mathcal{T}$. If $\mathsf{Vrfy}_{\mathsf{NIZK}}(\mathsf{crs}, \tau, x, \pi) = 1$ $\quad \wedge \mathsf{Vrfy}_{\mathsf{HPS}}(vk, x, d) = 1$: $\quad$ Return 1. Else: Return 0.

Fig. 8. Generic construction of $\mathsf{SIG} = (\mathsf{Setup}_{\mathsf{SIG}}, \mathsf{Gen}, \mathsf{Sign}, \mathsf{Vrfy}_{\mathsf{SIG}})$ from PVQAHPS, tag-based QANIZK and $\mathcal{H}$. The message space is $\mathcal{M}$.

Correctness of SIG follows directly from the verification completeness of PVQAHPS and the perfect completeness of QANIZK.

Next, we show its strong $\mathsf{MU}^{c\&l}$-CMA security. We stress that the projection key $pk_\rho = \alpha_\rho(sk)$ is not published as part of SIG's verification key, and this is crucial to the security of SIG since otherwise one can publicly generate valid signatures for any message via the Pub algorithm of PVQAHPS by using pk_ρ.

Theorem 1 (Strong $\mathsf{MU}^{c\&l}$-CMA Security of SIG). *Assume that (i) $\mathscr{L}$ and $\mathscr{L}_0$ have hard SMPs, (ii) PVQAHPS is a publicly-verifiable QA-HPS for both*

$\mathscr{L}$ and $\mathscr{L}_0$, having verification soundness, VK-diversity, and supporting κ-LR-$\langle\mathscr{L}_0,\mathscr{L}\rangle$-OT-extracting, (iii) QANIZK is a tag-based QA-NIZK for $\mathscr{L}$, satisfying both perfect zero-knowledge and unbounded simulation-soundness, (iv) $\mathcal{H}$ is collision-resistant. Then the proposed SIG scheme in Fig. 8 is strongly MU$^{c\&l}$-CMA secure under κ bits leakage per user.

Concretely, for any number n of users and any adversary $\mathcal{A}$ who makes at most Q_s times of $\mathcal{O}_{\mathrm{SIGN}}$ queries, there exist adversaries $\mathcal{B}_1, \cdots, \mathcal{B}_6$, such that $\mathbf{T}(\mathcal{B}_1) \approx \cdots \approx \mathbf{T}(\mathcal{B}_5) \approx \mathbf{T}(\mathcal{A}) + (n + Q_s) \cdot \mathsf{poly}(\lambda)$, with $\mathsf{poly}(\lambda)$ independent of $\mathbf{T}(\mathcal{A})$, and

$$\mathsf{Adv}^{\text{s-cma-c\&l}}_{\mathsf{SIG},\mathcal{A},n,\kappa}(\lambda) \leq \mathsf{Adv}^{\text{vrfy-snd}}_{\mathsf{PVQAHPS},\mathcal{B}_1,n}(\lambda) + \mathsf{Adv}^{\text{cr}}_{\mathcal{H},\mathcal{B}_2}(\lambda) + \mathsf{Adv}^{\text{msmp}}_{\mathscr{L},\mathcal{B}_3,Q_s}(\lambda) + \mathsf{Adv}^{\text{msmp}}_{\mathscr{L}_0,\mathcal{B}_4,Q_s}(\lambda)$$
$$+ \mathsf{Adv}^{\text{uss}}_{\mathsf{QANIZK},\mathcal{B}_5}(\lambda) + \tfrac{n(n-1)}{2} \cdot \epsilon^{\text{vk-div}}_{\mathsf{PVQAHPS}}(\lambda) + n \cdot \epsilon^{\text{lr-}\langle\mathscr{L}_0,\mathscr{L}\rangle\text{-otext}}_{\mathsf{PVQAHPS},\mathcal{B}_6,\kappa}(\lambda).$$

We refer to Subsect. 2.1 and Fig. 1 therein for an overview of the proof. Due to space limitations, we postpone the formal proof to the full version [19].

6   PKE with Tight MUMC$^{c\&l}$-CCA Security

In this section, we present public-key encryption (PKE) schemes with tight MUMC$^{c\&l}$-CCA security, by using QA-HPS with new properties formalized in Sect. 4 as a central building block.

In Subsect. 6.1, we define the MUMC$^{c\&l}$-CCA security of PKE. Then in Subsect. 6.2, we present our generic construction of PKE.

6.1   Definition of MUMC$^{c\&l}$-CCA Security

In [27], Lee et al. defined indistinguishability for PKE schemes under chosen-ciphertext attacks (CCA) in a <u>M</u>ulti-<u>U</u>ser <u>M</u>ulti-<u>C</u>hallenge setting with adaptive <u>c</u>orruptions of secret keys (which was originally called MUC$^+$ in [27] and is denoted by MUMC^c-CCA in this paper). Here we extend it to MUMC$^{c\&l}$-CCA, which also takes key <u>l</u>eakages into account. Below we present the formal definition.

Definition 16 (MUMC$^{c\&l}$-CCA Security for PKE). Let $\kappa = \kappa(\lambda) \in \mathbb{N}$. A PKE scheme PKE = (Setup$_{\mathsf{PKE}}$, Gen, Enc, Dec) is MUMC$^{c\&l}$-CCA secure under κ bits leakage per user, if for any PPT adversary $\mathcal{A}$ and any polynomial n, it holds that $\mathsf{Adv}^{\text{cca-c\&l}}_{\mathsf{PKE},\mathcal{A},n,\kappa}(\lambda) := \big| \Pr[\mathsf{Exp}^{\text{cca-c\&l}}_{\mathsf{PKE},\mathcal{A},n,\kappa} \Rightarrow 1] - \tfrac{1}{2} \big| \leq \mathsf{negl}(\lambda)$, where the experiment $\mathsf{Exp}^{\text{cca-c\&l}}_{\mathsf{PKE},\mathcal{A},n,\kappa}$ is defined in Fig. 9.

6.2   Generic Construction of PKE from QA-HPS and QA-NIZK

In this subsection, we present a generic construction of MUMC$^{c\&l}$-CCA secure PKE. The underlying building blocks are as follows.

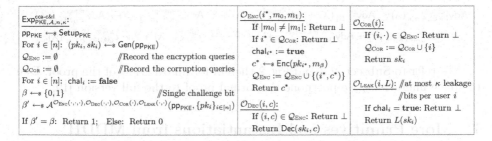

Fig. 9. The $\mathsf{MUMC}^{c\&l}$-CCA security experiment $\mathsf{Exp}^{cca\text{-}c\&l}_{\mathsf{PKE},\mathcal{A},n,\kappa}$ for PKE.

- Two language distributions $\mathscr{L}$ and $\mathscr{L}_0$, both of which have hard SMPs.
- A QAHPS = $(\mathsf{Setup}_{\mathsf{HPS}}, \alpha_{(\cdot)}, \mathsf{Pub}, \mathsf{Priv})$ for both $\mathscr{L}$ and $\mathscr{L}_0$, whose hashing key space is $\mathcal{SK}$, projection key space is $\mathcal{PK}$ and hash value space is $\mathcal{HV}$. We require $\mathcal{HV}$ to be an (additive) group. We stress that QAHPS is not required to be publicly-verifiable.
- A tag-based QANIZK = $(\mathsf{Setup}_{\mathsf{NIZK}}, \mathsf{CRSGen}, \mathsf{Prove}, \mathsf{Vrfy}_{\mathsf{NIZK}}, \mathsf{Sim})$ for $\mathscr{L}$, whose tag space is $\mathcal{T}$.
- A family of collision-resistant hash functions $\mathcal{H} = \{H : \mathcal{PK} \times \mathcal{HV} \longrightarrow \mathcal{T}\}$.

Our generic construction of PKE = $(\mathsf{Setup}_{\mathsf{PKE}}, \mathsf{Gen}, \mathsf{Enc}, \mathsf{Dec})$ is shown in Fig. 10.

	$(pk, sk) \leftarrow_s \mathsf{Gen}(\mathsf{pp}_{\mathsf{PKE}}):$	$m/\bot \leftarrow \mathsf{Dec}(sk, c):$
$\mathsf{pp}_{\mathsf{PKE}} \leftarrow_s \mathsf{Setup}_{\mathsf{PKE}}:$	$sk \leftarrow_s \mathcal{SK},\ pk := \alpha_\rho(sk).$	Parse $c = (x, d, \pi).$
$(\rho, td) \leftarrow_s \mathscr{L}.$	Return $(pk, sk).$	$pk := \alpha_\rho(sk).$
$\mathsf{pp}_{\mathsf{HPS}} \leftarrow_s \mathsf{Setup}_{\mathsf{HPS}}.$		$\tau := H(pk, d) \in \mathcal{T}.$
$\mathsf{pp}_{\mathsf{NIZK}} \leftarrow_s \mathsf{Setup}_{\mathsf{NIZK}}.$	$c \leftarrow_s \mathsf{Enc}(pk, m \in \mathcal{HV}):$	If $\mathsf{Vrfy}_{\mathsf{NIZK}}(\mathsf{crs}, \tau, x, \pi) = 1:$
$(\mathsf{crs}, td_{\mathsf{crs}}) \leftarrow_s \mathsf{CRSGen}(\rho).$	$x \leftarrow_s \mathcal{L}_\rho$ with witness $w.$	$m := d - \mathsf{Priv}(sk, x) \in \mathcal{HV}.$
$H \leftarrow_s \mathcal{H}.$	$d := \mathsf{Pub}(pk, x, w) + m \in \mathcal{HV}.$	Return $m.$
Return $\mathsf{pp}_{\mathsf{PKE}} :=$	$\tau := H(pk, d) \in \mathcal{T}.$	Else: Return $\bot.$
$(\rho, \mathsf{pp}_{\mathsf{HPS}}, \mathsf{pp}_{\mathsf{NIZK}}, \mathsf{crs}, H).$	$\pi \leftarrow_s \mathsf{Prove}(\mathsf{crs}, \tau, x, w).$	
	Return $c := (x, d, \pi).$	

Fig. 10. Generic construction of PKE = $(\mathsf{Setup}_{\mathsf{PKE}}, \mathsf{Gen}, \mathsf{Enc}, \mathsf{Dec})$ from QAHPS, tag-based QANIZK and $\mathcal{H}$. The message space is $\mathcal{M} := \mathcal{HV}$.

Correctness of PKE follows directly from the correctness of QAHPS and the perfect completeness of QANIZK. Next, we show its $\mathsf{MUMC}^{c\&l}$-CCA security.

Theorem 2 ($\mathsf{MUMC}^{c\&l}$-CCA Security of PKE). *Assume that (i) $\mathscr{L}$ and $\mathscr{L}_0$ have hard SMPs, (ii) QAHPS is a QA-HPS for both $\mathscr{L}$ and $\mathscr{L}_0$, having PK-diversity, and supporting both κ-LR-$\langle\mathscr{L}, \mathscr{L}_0\rangle$-key-switching and $\mathscr{L}_0$-multi-key-multi-extracting, (iii) QANIZK is a tag-based QA-NIZK for $\mathscr{L}$, satisfying both perfect zero-knowledge and unbounded simulation-soundness, (iv) $\mathcal{H}$ is collision-resistant. Then the proposed PKE scheme in Fig. 10 is $\mathsf{MUMC}^{c\&l}$-CCA secure under κ bits leakage per user.*

Concretely, for any number n of users and any adversary $\mathcal{A}$ who makes at most Q_e times of $\mathcal{O}_{\mathsf{ENC}}$ queries and Q_d times of $\mathcal{O}_{\mathsf{DEC}}$ queries, there exist adversaries $\mathcal{B}_1, \cdots, \mathcal{B}_7$, such that $\mathbf{T}(\mathcal{B}_1) \approx \cdots \approx \mathbf{T}(\mathcal{B}_6) \approx \mathbf{T}(\mathcal{A}) + (n + Q_e + Q_d) \cdot \mathsf{poly}(\lambda)$, with $\mathsf{poly}(\lambda)$ independent of $\mathbf{T}(\mathcal{A})$, and

$$\mathsf{Adv}^{\mathsf{cca\text{-}c\&l}}_{\mathsf{PKE},\mathcal{A},n,\kappa}(\lambda) \leq \mathsf{Adv}^{\mathsf{cr}}_{\mathcal{H},\mathcal{B}_1}(\lambda) + \mathsf{Adv}^{\mathsf{msmp}}_{\mathscr{L},\mathcal{B}_2,Q_e}(\lambda) + 2 \cdot \mathsf{Adv}^{\mathsf{ml\text{-}msmp}}_{\mathscr{L}_0,\mathcal{B}_3,n,Q_e}(\lambda) + \mathsf{Adv}^{\mathsf{msmp}}_{\mathscr{L},\mathcal{B}_4,Q_e}(\lambda)$$
$$+ \mathsf{Adv}^{\mathsf{uss}}_{\mathsf{QANIZK},\mathcal{B}_5}(\lambda) + \mathsf{Adv}^{\mathscr{L}_0\text{-}\mathsf{mk\text{-}mext}}_{\mathsf{QAHPS},\mathcal{B}_6,n,Q_e}(\lambda) + \frac{n(n-1)}{2} \cdot \epsilon^{\mathsf{pk\text{-}div}}_{\mathsf{QAHPS}}(\lambda) + 2n \cdot \epsilon^{\mathsf{lr\text{-}}(\mathscr{L},\mathscr{L}_0)\text{-}\mathsf{ks}}_{\mathsf{QAHPS},\mathcal{B}_7,\kappa}(\lambda).$$

We refer to Subsect. 2.2 and Fig. 2 therein for an overview of the proof. Due to space limitations, we postpone the formal proof to the full version [19].

7   More Primitives and Instantiations from MDDH

Tightly $MU^{c\&l}$ Secure SC, MAC and AE. Our SIG and PKE immediately lead to direct constructions of tightly $\mathsf{MUMC}^{c\&l}$-Priv&Auth secure SC [3,9]. By fully exploiting the similar and composable components of our SIG and PKE, we can obtain a more efficient SC construction, which is shown in the full version [19]. Since SIG naturally implies MAC and SC implies AE, we can also obtain the constructions of tightly secure MAC and AE. We also give optimized MAC and AE constructions in the full version [19], where PVQAHPS is replaced with QAHPS. Our MAC achieves tight strong $\mathsf{MU}^{c\&l}$-CMVA security, which also considers chosen verification attacks [13] in addition to strong $\mathsf{MU}^{c\&l}$-CMA.

Instantiations from MDDH. We give instantiations of SIG and PKE from the matrix DDH (MDDH) assumptions over asymmetric pairing groups. Our SC, MAC and AE can be similarly instantiated.

Firstly, we instantiate the building blocks needed in our generic constructions (cf. the full version [19]). More precisely, we give concrete instantiations of Publicly-Verifiable QA-HPS (with an overview in Subsect. 2.4) and QA-HPS, built upon the MDDH-based QA-HPS schemes proposed in [20], which are in turn generalizations of the well-known DDH-based HPS scheme proposed by Cramer and Shoup in [11]. Then we instantiate tag-based QA-NIZK with a tag-base variant of the QA-NIZK scheme proposed in [1] that has tight USS based on MDDH, which is recalled in the full version [19] for completeness.

Next we instantiate the generic SIG construction in Sect. 5 with the above building blocks. Let $x \cdot \mathbb{G}$ denote x elements in $\mathbb{G}$. Under MDDH parameters $\ell, k \in \mathbb{N}$ where $\ell \geq 2k + 1$, the MDDH-based SIG scheme $\mathsf{SIG}_{\mathsf{MDDH}}$ has public parameter $\mathsf{pp}_{\mathsf{SIG}} : (5k^2 + 3k + \ell k) \cdot \mathbb{G}_1 + (5k^2 + 4k + 1 + 2\ell k) \cdot \mathbb{G}_2$, verification key $vk : (\ell k) \cdot \mathbb{G}_2$, signing key $sk : \ell(k+1) \cdot \mathbb{Z}_p$, and signature $\sigma : (4k^2 + 4k + 2 + \ell) \cdot \mathbb{G}_1 + (2k^2 + 3k + 1) \cdot \mathbb{G}_2$. By plugging the theorems regarding the tight security of the MDDH-based PV-QA-HPS and QA-NIZK schemes (cf. the full version [19]) into Theorem 1, we have the following corollary showing the tight strong $\mathsf{MU}^{c\&l}$-CMA security of $\mathsf{SIG}_{\mathsf{MDDH}}$ based on the MDDH assumptions (as well as the collision-resistance of hash functions).

Corollary 1 (Tight Strong $\mathsf{MU}^{c\&l}$-CMA Security of $\mathsf{SIG}_{\mathsf{MDDH}}$). *Let $\ell \geq 2k + 1$ and $\kappa \leq \log p - \Omega(\lambda)$. For any number n of users and any adversary $\mathcal{A}$ who makes at most Q_s times of $\mathcal{O}_{\mathrm{SIGN}}$ queries, there exist adversaries $\mathcal{B}_1, \mathcal{B}_2$ and $\mathcal{B}_3$, such that $\mathbf{T}(\mathcal{B}_1) \approx \mathbf{T}(\mathcal{B}_2) \approx \mathbf{T}(\mathcal{B}_3) \approx \mathbf{T}(\mathcal{A}) + (n + Q_s) \cdot \mathsf{poly}(\lambda)$, with $\mathsf{poly}(\lambda)$ independent of $\mathbf{T}(\mathcal{A})$, and*

$$\mathsf{Adv}^{\text{s-cma-c\&l}}_{\mathsf{SIG}_{\mathsf{MDDH}},\mathcal{A},n,\kappa}(\lambda) \leq 2 \cdot \mathsf{Adv}^{\text{cr}}_{\mathcal{H},\mathcal{B}_1}(\lambda) + (4k\lceil \log Q_s \rceil + \ell - k + 6) \cdot \mathsf{Adv}^{\text{mddh}}_{\mathcal{D}_{\ell,k},\mathbb{G}_1,\mathcal{B}_2}(\lambda)$$

$$+ (2\lceil \log Q_s \rceil + 3) \cdot \mathsf{Adv}^{\text{mddh}}_{\mathcal{D}_k,\mathbb{G}_2,\mathcal{B}_3}(\lambda) + \frac{n+2\lceil \log Q_s \rceil Q_s}{p-1} + \frac{n(n-1)}{2} \cdot \frac{1}{p^{k\ell}}.$$

Since $Q_s = \mathsf{poly}(\lambda)$ for PPT adversaries, the security loss is in fact $O(\log Q_s) = O(\log \lambda)$, which is lower than $O(\lambda)$. For $k = 1$ and $\ell = 3$, we get a fully compact SIG scheme with $\mathsf{pp}_{\mathsf{SIG}} : 11 \cdot \mathbb{G}_1 + 16 \cdot \mathbb{G}_2$, $vk : 3 \cdot \mathbb{G}_2$, $sk : 6 \cdot \mathbb{Z}_p$ and $\sigma : 13 \cdot \mathbb{G}_1 + 6 \cdot \mathbb{G}_2$. The resulting SIG scheme has tight strong $\mathsf{MU}^{\text{c\&l}}$-CMA security based on the SXDH assumption (which requires the DDH assumption to hold both in $\mathbb{G}_1$ and $\mathbb{G}_2$), and supports $\kappa = \log p - \Omega(\lambda)$ bits leakage per user. The leakage rate (i.e., $\kappa/$ bit-length of sk) is $\frac{\log p - \Omega(\lambda)}{6 \log p} = \frac{1}{6} - o(1)$ asymptotically as p grows.

We also instantiate the generic PKE construction in Sect. 6. Under MDDH parameters $\ell, k \in \mathbb{N}$ where $\ell \geq 2k + 1$, the MDDH-based PKE scheme $\mathsf{PKE}_{\mathsf{MDDH}}$ has public parameter $\mathsf{pp}_{\mathsf{PKE}} : (5k^2 + 3k + \ell k) \cdot \mathbb{G}_1 + (4k^2 + 3k + 1 + 2\ell k) \cdot \mathbb{G}_2$, public key $pk : k \cdot \mathbb{G}_1$, secret key $sk : \ell \cdot \mathbb{Z}_p$, and ciphertext $c : (4k^2 + 3k + 2 + \ell) \cdot \mathbb{G}_1 + (2k^2 + 3k + 1) \cdot \mathbb{G}_2$. By plugging the theorems regarding the tight security of the MDDH-based QA-HPS and QA-NIZK schemes (cf. the full version [19]) into Theorem 2, we have the following corollary showing the tight $\mathsf{MUMC}^{\text{c\&l}}$-CCA security of $\mathsf{PKE}_{\mathsf{MDDH}}$ based on the MDDH assumptions (as well as the collision-resistance of hash functions).

Corollary 2 (Tight $\mathsf{MUMC}^{\text{c\&l}}$-CCA Security of $\mathsf{PKE}_{\mathsf{MDDH}}$). *Let $\ell \geq 2k + 1$ and $\kappa \leq \log p - \Omega(\lambda)$. For any number n of users and any adversary $\mathcal{A}$ who makes at most Q_e times of $\mathcal{O}_{\mathsf{ENC}}$ queries and Q_d times of $\mathcal{O}_{\mathsf{DEC}}$ queries, there exist adversaries $\mathcal{B}_1, \mathcal{B}_2$ and $\mathcal{B}_3$, such that $\mathbf{T}(\mathcal{B}_1) \approx \mathbf{T}(\mathcal{B}_2) \approx \mathbf{T}(\mathcal{B}_3) \approx \mathbf{T}(\mathcal{A}) + (n + Q_e + Q_d) \cdot \mathsf{poly}(\lambda)$, with $\mathsf{poly}(\lambda)$ independent of $\mathbf{T}(\mathcal{A})$, and*

$$\mathsf{Adv}^{\text{cca-c\&l}}_{\mathsf{PKE}_{\mathsf{MDDH}},\mathcal{A},n,\kappa}(\lambda) \leq 2 \cdot \mathsf{Adv}^{\text{cr}}_{\mathcal{H},\mathcal{B}_1}(\lambda) + (4k\lceil \log Q_e \rceil + \ell - k + 9) \cdot \mathsf{Adv}^{\text{mddh}}_{\mathcal{D}_{\ell,k},\mathbb{G}_1,\mathcal{B}_2}(\lambda)$$

$$+ (2\lceil \log Q_e \rceil + 2) \cdot \mathsf{Adv}^{\text{mddh}}_{\mathcal{D}_k,\mathbb{G}_2,\mathcal{B}_3}(\lambda) + \frac{2n+2\lceil \log Q_e \rceil Q_e}{p-1} + \frac{n(n-1)}{2} \cdot \frac{1}{p^k}.$$

For $k = 1$ and $\ell = 3$, we get a fully compact PKE scheme with $\mathsf{pp}_{\mathsf{PKE}} : 11 \cdot \mathbb{G}_1 + 14 \cdot \mathbb{G}_2$, $pk : 1 \cdot \mathbb{G}_1$, $sk : 3 \cdot \mathbb{Z}_p$ and $c : 12 \cdot \mathbb{G}_1 + 6 \cdot \mathbb{G}_2$. The resulting PKE scheme has tight $\mathsf{MUMC}^{\text{c\&l}}$-CCA security based on the SXDH assumption, and supports $\kappa = \log p - \Omega(\lambda)$ bits leakage per user. The leakage rate is $\frac{\log p - \Omega(\lambda)}{3 \log p} = \frac{1}{3} - o(1)$ asymptotically as p grows.

For an overview, we refer to Table 1 and Table 2 in the introduction.

On Tightness of our MDDH-Based Schemes. Our MDDH-based schemes are the first ones achieving almost tight $\mathsf{MU}^{\text{c}}/\mathsf{MU}^{\text{c\&l}}$ security in the standard model, and the security loss factor is $O(\log \lambda)$.

We stress that all our generic constructions are *fully tightness-preserving*, i.e., the $\mathsf{MU}^{\text{c}}/\mathsf{MU}^{\text{c\&l}}$ securities of the resulting SIG, PKE, SC, MAC, AE schemes are tightly reduced to the security properties of the building blocks PV-QA-HPS, QA-HPS and tag-based QA-NIZK, with constant security loss factors. Moreover, our instantiations of PV-QA-HPS and QA-HPS have fully tight securities, and only the tag-based QA-NIZK instantiation has security loss factor $O(\log \lambda)$. Therefore, our fully tightness-preserving generic constructions leave spaces for even tighter (fully tight) $\mathsf{MU}^c/\mathsf{MU}^{c\&l}$ security, as long as we can find instantiations of tag-based QA-NIZK with tighter security.

On Efficiency of Our MDDH-Based Schemes. Note that all our schemes enjoy *full compactness* (i.e., all the parameters, keys, signatures and ciphertexts consist of only a constant number of group elements). We believe our fully compact schemes are good starts for almost tight $\mathsf{MU}^c/\mathsf{MU}^{c\&l}$ security in the standard model and follow-up work might improve efficiency even further.

Acknowledgment. We would like to thank the reviewers for their helpful comments and valuable suggestions. Shuai Han and Shengli Liu were partially supported by National Natural Science Foundation of China (Grant Nos. 62002223, 61925207), Guangdong Major Project of Basic and Applied Basic Research (2019B030302008), the National Key R&D Program of China under Grant 2022YFB2701500, Shanghai Sailing Program (20YF1421100), Young Elite Scientists Sponsorship Program by China Association for Science and Technology (YESS20200185), and Ant Group through CCF-Ant Research Fund (CCF-AFSG RF20220224). Dawu Gu was partially supported by the National Key R&D Program of China under Grant 2020YFA0712302.

References

1. Abe, M., Jutla, C.S., Ohkubo, M., Pan, J., Roy, A., Wang, Y.: Shorter QA-NIZK and SPS with tighter security. In: Galbraith, S.D., Moriai, S. (eds.) ASIACRYPT 2019. LNCS, vol. 11923, pp. 669–699. Springer, Cham (2019). https://doi.org/10.1007/978-3-030-34618-8_23

2. Akavia, A., Goldwasser, S., Vaikuntanathan, V.: Simultaneous hardcore bits and cryptography against memory attacks. In: Reingold, O. (ed.) TCC 2009. LNCS, vol. 5444, pp. 474–495. Springer, Heidelberg (2009). https://doi.org/10.1007/978-3-642-00457-5_28

3. An, J.H., Dodis, Y., Rabin, T.: On the security of joint signature and encryption. In: Knudsen, L.R. (ed.) EUROCRYPT 2002. LNCS, vol. 2332, pp. 83–107. Springer, Heidelberg (2002). https://doi.org/10.1007/3-540-46035-7_6

4. Bader, C., Hofheinz, D., Jager, T., Kiltz, E., Li, Y.: Tightly-secure authenticated key exchange. In: Dodis, Y., Nielsen, J.B. (eds.) TCC 2015. LNCS, vol. 9014, pp. 629–658. Springer, Heidelberg (2015). https://doi.org/10.1007/978-3-662-46494-6_26

5. Bader, C., Jager, T., Li, Y., Schäge, S.: On the impossibility of tight cryptographic reductions. In: Fischlin, M., Coron, J.-S. (eds.) EUROCRYPT 2016. LNCS, vol. 9666, pp. 273–304. Springer, Heidelberg (2016). https://doi.org/10.1007/978-3-662-49896-5_10

6. Bellare, M., Boldyreva, A., Micali, S.: Public-key encryption in a multi-user setting: security proofs and improvements. In: Preneel, B. (ed.) EUROCRYPT 2000. LNCS, vol. 1807, pp. 259–274. Springer, Heidelberg (2000). https://doi.org/10.1007/3-540-45539-6_18

7. Bellare, M., Namprempre, C.: Authenticated encryption: relations among notions and analysis of the generic composition paradigm. In: Okamoto, T. (ed.) ASIACRYPT 2000. LNCS, vol. 1976, pp. 531–545. Springer, Heidelberg (2000). https://doi.org/10.1007/3-540-44448-3_41

8. Bellare, M., Rogaway, P.: Entity authentication and key distribution. In: Stinson, D.R. (ed.) CRYPTO 1993. LNCS, vol. 773, pp. 232–249. Springer, Heidelberg (1994). https://doi.org/10.1007/3-540-48329-2_21

9. Bellare, M., Stepanovs, I.: Security under message-derived keys: signcryption in iMessage. In: Canteaut, A., Ishai, Y. (eds.) EUROCRYPT 2020. LNCS, vol. 12107, pp. 507–537. Springer, Cham (2020). https://doi.org/10.1007/978-3-030-45727-3_17

10. Chen, J., Wee, H.: Fully, (almost) tightly secure IBE and dual system groups. In: Canetti, R., Garay, J.A. (eds.) CRYPTO 2013. LNCS, vol. 8043, pp. 435–460. Springer, Heidelberg (2013). https://doi.org/10.1007/978-3-642-40084-1_25

11. Cramer, R., Shoup, V.: Universal hash proofs and a paradigm for adaptive chosen ciphertext secure public-key encryption. In: Knudsen, L.R. (ed.) EUROCRYPT 2002. LNCS, vol. 2332, pp. 45–64. Springer, Heidelberg (2002). https://doi.org/10.1007/3-540-46035-7_4

12. Diemert, D., Gellert, K., Jager, T., Lyu, L.: More efficient digital signatures with tight multi-user security. In: Garay, J.A. (ed.) PKC 2021. LNCS, vol. 12711, pp. 1–31. Springer, Cham (2021). https://doi.org/10.1007/978-3-030-75248-4_1

13. Dodis, Y., Kiltz, E., Pietrzak, K., Wichs, D.: Message authentication, revisited. In: Pointcheval, D., Johansson, T. (eds.) EUROCRYPT 2012. LNCS, vol. 7237, pp. 355–374. Springer, Heidelberg (2012). https://doi.org/10.1007/978-3-642-29011-4_22

14. Escala, A., Herold, G., Kiltz, E., Ràfols, C., Villar, J.: An algebraic framework for Diffie-Hellman assumptions. In: Canetti, R., Garay, J.A. (eds.) CRYPTO 2013. LNCS, vol. 8043, pp. 129–147. Springer, Heidelberg (2013). https://doi.org/10.1007/978-3-642-40084-1_8

15. Gay, R., Hofheinz, D., Kiltz, E., Wee, H.: Tightly CCA-secure encryption without pairings. In: Fischlin, M., Coron, J.-S. (eds.) EUROCRYPT 2016. LNCS, vol. 9665, pp. 1–27. Springer, Heidelberg (2016). https://doi.org/10.1007/978-3-662-49890-3_1

16. Gay, R., Hofheinz, D., Kohl, L.: Kurosawa-Desmedt meets tight security. In: Katz, J., Shacham, H. (eds.) CRYPTO 2017. LNCS, vol. 10403, pp. 133–160. Springer, Cham (2017). https://doi.org/10.1007/978-3-319-63697-9_5

17. Gjøsteen, K., Jager, T.: Practical and tightly-secure digital signatures and authenticated key exchange. In: Shacham, H., Boldyreva, A. (eds.) CRYPTO 2018. LNCS, vol. 10992, pp. 95–125. Springer, Cham (2018). https://doi.org/10.1007/978-3-319-96881-0_4

18. Han, S., et al.: Authenticated key exchange and signatures with tight security in the standard model. In: Malkin, T., Peikert, C. (eds.) CRYPTO 2021. LNCS, vol. 12828, pp. 670–700. Springer, Cham (2021). https://doi.org/10.1007/978-3-030-84259-8_23

19. Han, S., Liu, S., Gu, D.: Almost tight multi-user security under adaptive corruptions & leakages in the standard model. Cryptology ePrint Archive, Report 2023/153. https://eprint.iacr.org/2023/153

20. Han, S., Liu, S., Lyu, L., Gu, D.: Tight leakage-resilient CCA-security from quasi-adaptive hash proof system. In: Boldyreva, A., Micciancio, D. (eds.) CRYPTO 2019. LNCS, vol. 11693, pp. 417–447. Springer, Cham (2019). https://doi.org/10.1007/978-3-030-26951-7_15. https://eprint.iacr.org/2019/512

21. Hofheinz, D., Jager, T.: Tightly secure signatures and public-key encryption. In: Safavi-Naini, R., Canetti, R. (eds.) CRYPTO 2012. LNCS, vol. 7417, pp. 590–607. Springer, Heidelberg (2012). https://doi.org/10.1007/978-3-642-32009-5_35

22. Hofheinz, D., Jia, D., Pan, J.: Identity-based encryption tightly secure under chosen-ciphertext attacks. In: Peyrin, T., Galbraith, S. (eds.) ASIACRYPT 2018. LNCS, vol. 11273, pp. 190–220. Springer, Cham (2018). https://doi.org/10.1007/978-3-030-03329-3_7

23. Jager, T., Stam, M., Stanley-Oakes, R., Warinschi, B.: Multi-key authenticated encryption with corruptions: reductions are lossy. In: Kalai, Y., Reyzin, L. (eds.) TCC 2017. LNCS, vol. 10677, pp. 409–441. Springer, Cham (2017). https://doi.org/10.1007/978-3-319-70500-2_14

24. Jutla, C.S., Roy, A.: Shorter quasi-adaptive NIZK proofs for linear subspaces. In: Sako, K., Sarkar, P. (eds.) ASIACRYPT 2013. LNCS, vol. 8269, pp. 1–20. Springer, Heidelberg (2013). https://doi.org/10.1007/978-3-642-42033-7_1

25. Kiltz, E., Wee, H.: Quasi-adaptive NIZK for linear subspaces revisited. In: Oswald, E., Fischlin, M. (eds.) EUROCRYPT 2015. LNCS, vol. 9057, pp. 101–128. Springer, Heidelberg (2015). https://doi.org/10.1007/978-3-662-46803-6_4

26. Langrehr, R., Pan, J.: Tightly secure hierarchical identity-based encryption. In: Lin, D., Sako, K. (eds.) PKC 2019. LNCS, vol. 11442, pp. 436–465. Springer, Cham (2019). https://doi.org/10.1007/978-3-030-17253-4_15

27. Lee, Y., Lee, D.H., Park, J.H.: Tightly CCA-secure encryption scheme in a multi-user setting with corruptions. Des. Codes Crypt. 88(11), 2433–2452 (2020). https://doi.org/10.1007/s10623-020-00794-z

28. Liu, X., Liu, S., Gu, D.: Tightly secure chameleon hash functions in the multi-user setting and their applications. In: Liu, J.K., Cui, H. (eds.) ACISP 2020. LNCS, vol. 12248, pp. 664–673. Springer, Cham (2020). https://doi.org/10.1007/978-3-030-55304-3_36. https://eprint.iacr.org/2022/1258

29. Liu, X., Liu, S., Gu, D., Weng, J.: Two-pass authenticated key exchange with explicit authentication and tight security. In: Moriai, S., Wang, H. (eds.) ASIACRYPT 2020. LNCS, vol. 12492, pp. 785–814. Springer, Cham (2020). https://doi.org/10.1007/978-3-030-64834-3_27

30. Morgan, A., Pass, R., Shi, E.: On the adaptive security of MACs and PRFs. In: Moriai, S., Wang, H. (eds.) ASIACRYPT 2020. LNCS, vol. 12491, pp. 724–753. Springer, Cham (2020). https://doi.org/10.1007/978-3-030-64837-4_24

31. Morillo, P., Ràfols, C., Villar, J.L.: The kernel matrix Diffie-Hellman assumption. In: Cheon, J.H., Takagi, T. (eds.) ASIACRYPT 2016. LNCS, vol. 10031, pp. 729–758. Springer, Heidelberg (2016). https://doi.org/10.1007/978-3-662-53887-6_27

32. Naor, M., Segev, G.: Public-key cryptosystems resilient to key leakage. In: Halevi, S. (ed.) CRYPTO 2009. LNCS, vol. 5677, pp. 18–35. Springer, Heidelberg (2009). https://doi.org/10.1007/978-3-642-03356-8_2

33. Pan, J., Wagner, B.: Lattice-based signatures with tight adaptive corruptions and more. In: Hanaoka, G., Shikata, J., Watanabe, Y. (eds.) PKC 2022. LNCS, vol. 13178, pp. 347–378. Springer, Cham (2022). https://doi.org/10.1007/978-3-030-97131-1_12

34. Sahai, A.: Non-malleable non-interactive zero knowledge and adaptive chosen-ciphertext security. In: FOCS 1999, pp. 543–553 (1999)

35. Steinfeld, R., Pieprzyk, J., Wang, H.: How to strengthen any weakly unforgeable signature into a strongly unforgeable signature. In: Abe, M. (ed.) CT-RSA 2007. LNCS, vol. 4377, pp. 357–371. Springer, Heidelberg (2006). https://doi.org/10.1007/11967668_23

Privately Puncturing PRFs from Lattices: Adaptive Security and Collusion Resistant Pseudorandomness

Rupeng Yang[✉]

Institute of Cybersecurity and Cryptology, School of Computing and Information Technology, University of Wollongong, Wollongong, NSW, Australia
rupengy@uow.edu.au

Abstract. A private puncturable pseudorandom function (PRF) enables one to create a constrained version of a PRF key, which can be used to evaluate the PRF at all but some punctured points. In addition, the constrained key reveals no information about the punctured points and the PRF values on them. Existing constructions of private puncturable PRFs are only proven to be secure against a restricted adversary that must commit to the punctured points before viewing any information. It is an open problem to achieve the more natural adaptive security, where the adversary can make all its choices on-the-fly.

In this work, we solve the problem by constructing an adaptively secure private puncturable PRF from standard lattice assumptions. To achieve this goal, we present a new primitive called explainable hash, which allows one to reprogram the hash function on a given input. The new primitive may find further applications in constructing more cryptographic schemes with adaptive security. Besides, our construction has collusion resistant pseudorandomness, which requires that even given multiple constrained keys, no one could learn the values of the PRF at the punctured points. Private puncturable PRFs with collusion resistant pseudorandomness were only known from multilinear maps or indistinguishability obfuscations in previous works, and we provide the first solution from standard lattice assumptions.

1 Introduction

A constrained pseudorandom function (PRF) [BW13, KPTZ13, BGI14] is a family of PRF [GGM84] that allows one to derive a constrained key for a predicate from a PRF key. The constrained key can be used to evaluate the PRF on inputs satisfying the predicate, but it reveals no information about the PRF values at other points. The latter requirement is denoted as (constrained) pseudorandomness and is the main security property of a constrained PRF. Besides, a constrained PRF is said to be private [BLW17] if the constrained keys also hide the constraint predicates.

As shown in [BW13, KPTZ13, BGI14], private constrained PRFs for the prefix-fixing constraint, where the predicate outputs 1 on inputs starting with a specified string, can be constructed from any one-way function via the GGM

© International Association for Cryptologic Research 2023
C. Hazay and M. Stam (Eds.): EUROCRYPT 2023, LNCS 14006, pp. 163–193, 2023.
https://doi.org/10.1007/978-3-031-30620-4_6

framework [GGM84]. From this framework, we can also construct constrained PRFs for the puncturing constraint (a.k.a. puncturable PRFs), where the predicate outputs 1 on all but some punctured points. This simple construction does not provide privacy, and the first private puncturable PRF is constructed from multilinear maps in [BLW17]. Then in [BKM17], Boneh et al. construct private puncturable PRFs from standard lattice assumptions.

Constrained PRFs for more complicated constraint predicates are also proposed in the literature. In particular, constrained PRFs for circuits are constructed from multilinear maps and indistinguishability obfuscation in [BW13, CRV16] and [BZ14], respectively. Moreover, via using (differing-input) indistinguishability obfuscation, constrained PRFs for Turing machines are presented in [AFP16, AF16, DKW16, DDM17]. Besides, private constrained PRFs for circuits are constructed from indistinguishability obfuscation in [BLW17].

Subsequent works focus on constructing constrained PRFs for general constraints without using heavy tools such as multilinear maps or obfuscations. In [BV15], Brakerski and Vaikuntanathan construct the first constrained PRF for circuits from standard lattice assumptions. Then in [CC17, BTVW17, PS18, CVW18, PS20], lattice-based private constrained PRFs for circuits are provided. Besides, in [Bit17, GHKW17, AMN+18], (private) constrained PRFs are also constructed from Diffie-Hellman type assumptions in traditional groups.

Adaptively Secure (Private) Constrained PRFs. When defining security properties of a (private) constrained PRF, we usually consider an adversary that is able to query some oracles, and the scheme has *adaptive security* if the adversary can query these oracles in an arbitrary order. Most previous (private) constrained PRFs are only proved to have a weaker *selective security*, where the adversary has to query the oracles in some predefined order. To achieve adaptive security generically, one can use complexity leveraging, but this would introduce an exponentially large reduction loss. In addition, the GGM framework based constrained PRFs are proved to have adaptive pseudorandomness in [FKPR14, JKK+17], but the reduction loss is still super-polynomial. Besides, (private) constrained PRFs with adaptive security for various constraints are also proposed in the random oracle model in [BW13, HKKW19, AMN+18].

The first adaptively secure constrained PRF in the standard model with a polynomial reduction loss is given in [HKW15], for the puncturing constraint. In the same setting, adaptively secure constrained PRFs for NC^1 circuits and any polynomial-size circuits are presented in [AMN+19] and [DKN+20], respectively. However, all three constructions need an indistinguishability obfuscation and are not private. Recently, (private) constrained PRFs with adaptive pseudorandomness are also constructed from simple assumptions such as one-way function and standard lattice assumptions in [DKN+20], but the constructions only support constraints that can be implemented by an inner-product predicate and do not have adaptive privacy.

Collusion Resistant (Private) Constrained PRFs. A (private) constrained PRF is *collusion resistant* if its security properties hold against an adversary that sees multiple constrained keys, and in contrast, it is *single-key* secure if it is only secure against an adversary that sees one constrained key. Collusion resistance is generally satisfied by constructions from multilinear maps or indistinguishability obfuscation (e.g., [BW13, BZ14, BLW17]). However, it is quite difficult to achieve it without using these strong primitives. Especially, as shown in [CC17], a private constrained PRF with collusion resistant privacy (for certain constraints) implies indistinguishability obfuscation. Besides, previous constructions of collusion resistant constrained PRFs from standard assumptions [BW13, KPTZ13, BGI14, BFP+15, DKN+20] only support constraints in subclasses of the inner-product predicate, including the prefix-fixing constraint, the left/right predicate, and the $O(1)$-CNF predicate. We refer the readers to [DKN+20] for definitions of these constraints and their relations with the inner-product predicate.

This Work. In this work, we consider private constrained PRFs with adaptive security and collusion resistant pseudorandomness. Both security requirements are necessary for many applications illustrated in [BW13, BZ14, BLW17] and would also be useful in future applications. In addition, to prevent potential security risk (e.g., quantum attacks), we focus on constructions in the standard model from standard lattice assumptions, with a polynomial reduction loss. Existing private constrained PRFs constructed in this "*standard setting*" with either adaptive security or collusion resistant pseudorandomness [BW13, KPTZ13, BGI14, DKN+20] only support constraints that can be implemented by the inner-product predicate. This raises the following natural question:

Can we construct private constrained PRFs with the desired security requirements in the standard setting for beyond inner-product predicates?

To answer the question, we focus on private puncturable PRFs. Note that as demonstrated in [PTW20], in some special cases, constrained PRFs for the inner-product predicate exist, but it is impossible to construct a secure puncturable PRF. Thus, the puncturing constraint *cannot* be implemented by the inner-product predicate. Besides, private puncturable PRFs are useful in constructing many advanced cryptographic primitives, including symmetric deniable encryption [CDNO97], cryptographic watermarking [CHN+16], restricted searchable symmetric encryption [SWP00, BLW17], and distributed point function [GI14, BGI15]. Some of the applications (e.g., collusion resistant watermarking) need a collusion resistant (private) puncturable PRF, and some applications will achieve new desirable features immediately if the employed private puncturable PRF has adaptive security[1]. Moreover, the new security properties might inspire more potential applications. Therefore, it is of both theoretical and practical interest to study private puncturable PRFs with adaptive security and collusion resistance.

---

[1] For example, if we use an adaptively secure private puncturable PRF in the construction of restricted searchable encryption given in [BLW17], the scheme will additionally achieve adaptive security, which allows the database owner to issue restricted search keys on restrictions determined after the system has been put in use.

Table 1: Properties achieved by constrained PRFs that can be instantiated from standard lattice assumptions (including one-way function) in the standard model. For either pseudorandomness or privacy, we use "adaptive" to denote adaptive security and use "selective" to denote selective security. Both the adaptive security and the selective security consider adversaries that can make queries to an evaluation oracle (see Sect. 4.1 for more details), and we use "weak" to denote that the scheme has privacy against a weaker adversary that is not allowed to query the evaluation oracle. Besides, we use the terms 1, $O(1)$, and *poly* to denote that the adversary can obtain 1, constant, and polynomial constrained key(s) when attacking the security properties. For the constraints, "Prefix" denotes the prefix-fixing constraint and "Puncturing" denotes the puncturing constraint. We use "NC^1" and "P/Poly" to denote NC^1 circuits and any polynomial-size circuits. Also, we use "IP" to denote the inner-product predicate and use "$O(1)$-CNF" to denote the $O(1)$-CNF predicate. Note that the predicates Prefix $\subseteq$ $O(1)$-CNF $\subseteq$ IP.

	Pseudorandomness		Privacy		Constraint
[BW13, KPTZ13, BGI14]	selective	*poly*	selective	*poly*	Prefix
[BFP+15]	selective	*poly*	✗	✗	Prefix
[BV15]	selective	1	✗	✗	P/Poly
[BKM17]	selective	1	selective	1	Puncturing
[CC17, CVW18]	selective	1	selective	1	NC^1
[BTVW17, PS18, PS20]	selective	1	selective	1	P/Poly
[DKN+20]	adaptive	$O(1)$	weak	1	$O(1)$-CNF
	adaptive	1	weak	1	IP
This Work	adaptive	*poly*	adaptive	1	Puncturing

1.1 Our Results

In this work, we construct a private puncturable PRF from standard lattice assumptions in the standard model, where the reduction loss is polynomial in the security parameter. The scheme has collusion resistant pseudorandomness against an adaptive adversary. In addition, it has adaptive (single-key) privacy. The latter property (i.e., adaptive privacy) is not achieved in previous construction of private constrained PRFs for any constraint from any assumption in the standard model without using complexity leveraging. We summarize features of our construction and compare it with previous constructions of constrained PRFs in the standard setting in Table 1.

To accomplish our goal, we provide new techniques for constructing adaptively secure and collusion resistant private constrained PRFs. Especially, we present a new primitive called explainable hash and construct it from lattices. The new primitive enables us to upgrade a selectively secure private puncturable PRF to have adaptive security, and it could be applied to construct other adaptively secure cryptographic schemes. We also introduce a new approach to achieve collusion resistance from standard assumptions. The idea is very different from previous methods and would inspire new constructions of collusion resistant constrained PRFs for a wider class of constraints.

1.2   Technical Overview

In this section, we provide an overview of our main techniques for constructing private puncturable PRFs with collusion resistant pseudorandomness and adaptive security. We first describe our main ideas for achieving either adaptive security or collusion resistance. Then we demonstrate how to combine the ideas to construct a private puncturable PRF with both desirable security properties.

On Achieving Adaptive Security. First, we explain how to achieve adaptive security. The adaptive security requires that the adversary cannot break security of the scheme even if it can make queries to a constrain oracle and an evaluation oracle in an arbitrary order, where the constrain oracle returns a constrained key punctured on the submitted set, and the evaluation oracle evaluates the PRF on the submitted input. Here, we consider private 1-*puncturable*[2] PRF with *single-key* security and present a general construction that upgrades a selectively secure scheme to have adaptive security in this setting.[3]

The Difficulty. First, note that it is easy to answer evaluation oracle queries after the constrain oracle query, since the evaluation results can be computed by the constrained key returned to the adversary and will not leak additional information. However, for the evaluation oracle queries before the constrain oracle query, it seems that they must be answered by the original PRF key since the puncture point is still unknown now. Thus, the evaluation results may leak information about the PRF key, which may help the adversary to break security of the scheme. This is the main difficulty for achieving adaptive security.

Our Solution. To overcome the difficulty, we introduce a new primitive called explainable hash function. At a high level, an explainable hash H is an injective keyed function that can reprogram the output on a given input to a predefined value. More precisely, in its security definition, the adversary can first make queries to an evaluation oracle $H(hk, \cdot)$ before viewing the hash key hk, and then it receives hk after submitting a challenge input x^* that is not queried before. Its security requires that the adversary's view in above experiment can be simulated by a simulator, and it is guaranteed that the returned hash key hk satisfies $H(hk, x^*) = u^*$, where u^* is a uniform output sampled in the beginning of the security experiment.[4]

---

[2] A 1-puncturable PRF punctures each PRF key on only one input.

[3] The general construction also works for larger puncture sets if we use a stronger building block in the construction. Looking ahead, this needs an explainable hash that can reprogram the outputs on multiple inputs simultaneously, which is much more difficult to construct (compared to the standard explainable hash constructed in this work).

[4] In the formal definition of explainable hash, the simulator may fail and abort with a non-negligible probability. In this overview, we assume that the simulator always succeeds for simplicity.

Next, let PRF_0 be a private puncturable PRF with selective security, i.e., it is secure against an adversary that can make queries to the evaluation oracle after querying the constrain oracle. Then we show how to construct adaptively secure private puncturable PRF from PRF_0 and an explainable hash H. In our new construction, the PRF key is a PRF key k of PRF_0 and a hash key hk of H. Then, given an input x, the PRF outputs $\mathsf{PRF}_0(k, \mathsf{H}(hk, x))$. Besides, on input a punctured point x^*, the constraining algorithm punctures k on $\mathsf{H}(hk, x^*)$ and outputs the constrained version of k and the hash key hk. Since H is injective, $\mathsf{H}(hk, x) \neq \mathsf{H}(hk, x^*)$ if $x \neq x^*$. Therefore, the constrained key allows one to evaluate the PRF at all points not equal to x^*.

Now, to prove adaptive security (either pseudorandomness or privacy) of the above construction, we can puncture the secret key k on a random string u^* in the beginning and then use this constrained key (denoted as k_{u^*}) and the simulator of H to answer the evaluation oracle queries from the adversary. Next, after receiving the puncture point x^*, we can use the simulator of H to generate a hash key hk s.t. $\mathsf{H}(hk, x^*) = u^*$ and return (k_{u^*}, hk) to the adversary. Adaptive security then comes from security of H and selective security properties of PRF_0.

Constructing Explainable Hash with 1-bit Output. It remains to show how to construct an explainable hash function. We first present a basic construction of (non-injective) explainable hash with 1-bit output. In a nutshell, the construction embeds an admissible hash function [BB04] into a lattice-based PRF using the matrix embedding mechanism given in [BGG+14].

An admissible hash allows one to partition an input space such that for any polynomial-size set $\mathcal{Q}$ of inputs and any input $x^* \notin \mathcal{Q}$, we have

$$\forall x \in \mathcal{Q}, \mathsf{P}(K, x) = 0 \quad \wedge \quad \mathsf{P}(K, x^*) = 1$$

with a non-negligible probability, where P is the partitioning function and K is a random partitioning key. Again, we omit the non-negligible failing probability here and only consider the case that the partitioning succeeds.

To embed the partitioning key $K = (K_1, \ldots, K_N)$ into a matrix $\boldsymbol{A}$, we set

$$\boldsymbol{A} = [\boldsymbol{B}_1 - K_1 \cdot \boldsymbol{G} \mid \ldots \mid \boldsymbol{B}_N - K_N \cdot \boldsymbol{G}]$$

where $\boldsymbol{B}_1, \ldots, \boldsymbol{B}_N \in \mathbb{Z}_q^{n \times m}$ are random matrices and $\boldsymbol{G}$ is the standard powers-of-two gadget matrix [MP12]. Then given the matrix $\boldsymbol{A}$ and an input x (note that the partitioning key K is *not* needed), one can get an encoding of $\mathsf{P}(K, x)$ as

$$\boldsymbol{A}_x = [\boldsymbol{B}_1 \mid \ldots \mid \boldsymbol{B}_N] \cdot \boldsymbol{T} - \mathsf{P}(K, x) \cdot \boldsymbol{G}$$

where $\boldsymbol{T}$ is a low-norm matrix.

Now, we are ready to describe our construction of the explainable hash H_0. The hash key is a random matrix $\boldsymbol{A} \in \mathbb{Z}_q^{n \times m \cdot N}$ and a random vector $\boldsymbol{s} \in \mathbb{Z}_q^n$. Given an input x, the evaluation algorithm first computes $\boldsymbol{A}_x$ from $\boldsymbol{A}$ and x. Then it outputs 0 if

$$\boldsymbol{s}^\mathsf{T} \cdot \boldsymbol{A}_x \cdot \boldsymbol{G}^{-1}(\boldsymbol{v}_1) \in [0, \frac{q}{2}]$$

and outputs 1 otherwise, where $v_1 = (\frac{q-1}{2}, 0, \ldots, 0)^\mathsf{T} \in \mathbb{Z}_q^n$, and $G^{-1}(v_1)$ decomposes each element in v_1 into bits and satisfies $G \cdot G^{-1}(v_1) = v_1$.

Next, we demonstrate how the simulator works. Recall that the simulator will first answer the evaluation oracle queries from an adversary, and then after the adversary submits an input x^*, the simulator needs to output a hash key, which is compatible with the evaluation oracle outputs and can map x^* to a given bit u^*.[5] Inspired by [LST18, DKN+20], we use the lossy mode of A for the simulator. More precisely, let $\bar{n} \ll n$ be an integer, the simulator embeds a random partitioning key K to the matrix A as follows:

$$A = [B_1 - K_1 \cdot G \mid \ldots \mid B_N - K_N \cdot G]$$

where

$$\forall i \in [1, N], \; B_i = \begin{pmatrix} r^\mathsf{T} \cdot \bar{B} \\ \bar{B} \end{pmatrix} \cdot S_i + E_i$$

$$r \xleftarrow{\$} \{0,1\}^{n-1}, \quad \bar{B} \xleftarrow{\$} \mathbb{Z}_q^{(n-1) \times \bar{n}}, \quad \forall i \in [1, N], \; S_i \xleftarrow{\$} \mathbb{Z}_q^{\bar{n} \times m}$$

and E_i is a low-norm noise matrix. Note that A still looks uniform in $\mathbb{Z}_q^{n \times m \cdot N}$ due to the learning with errors (LWE) assumption and the leftover hash lemma. In addition, for any input x, we have

$$A_x = \left[\begin{pmatrix} r^\mathsf{T} \cdot \bar{B} \\ \bar{B} \end{pmatrix} \cdot S_1 + E_1 \mid \ldots \mid \begin{pmatrix} r^\mathsf{T} \cdot \bar{B} \\ \bar{B} \end{pmatrix} \cdot S_N + E_N \right] \cdot T - \mathrm{P}(K, x) \cdot G$$

$$\approx \begin{pmatrix} r^\mathsf{T} \cdot \bar{B} \\ \bar{B} \end{pmatrix} \cdot [S_1 \mid \ldots \mid S_N] \cdot T - \mathrm{P}(K, x) \cdot G$$

The simulator also samples a random vector $s \xleftarrow{\$} \mathbb{Z}_q^n$ and uses the hash key (s, A) to answer the evaluation oracle queries from the adversary. Then given an input x^* and a bit u^*, the simulator computes $u^\dagger = \mathsf{H}_0((s, A), x^*)$. It outputs (s, A) if $u^\dagger = u^*$ and outputs $(s + d, A)$ otherwise, where $d = (-1, r^\mathsf{T})^\mathsf{T}$.

Notice that if the partitioning is successful (i.e., $\mathrm{P}(K, x) = 0$ for all queried x and $\mathrm{P}(K, x^*) = 1$), then for any queried x, we have

$$d^\mathsf{T} \cdot A_x \cdot G^{-1}(v_1) \approx d^\mathsf{T} \cdot \begin{pmatrix} r^\mathsf{T} \cdot \bar{B} \\ \bar{B} \end{pmatrix} \cdot [S_1 \mid \ldots \mid S_N] \cdot T \cdot G^{-1}(v_1) = 0$$

Thus, $\mathsf{H}_0((s, A), x) = \mathsf{H}_0((s+d, A), x)$ for all queried x,[6] and therefore the hash key outputted by the simulator, which is either (s, A) or $(s + d, A)$, is always compatible with its answers to the evaluation oracle. In addition,

$$d^\mathsf{T} \cdot A_{x^*} \cdot G^{-1}(v_1) \approx d^\mathsf{T} \cdot \begin{pmatrix} r^\mathsf{T} \cdot \bar{B} \\ \bar{B} \end{pmatrix} \cdot [S_1 \mid \ldots \mid S_N] \cdot T \cdot G^{-1}(v_1) - d^\mathsf{T} \cdot v_1 = \frac{q-1}{2}$$

---

[5] Here, the adversary cannot view the hash key before submitting x^*, and this allows the simulator to choose a suitable hash key after receiving x^*.

[6] This also relies on the fact that $s^\mathsf{T} \cdot A_x \cdot G^{-1}(v_1)$ is not close to the borders (i.e., 0 and $\frac{q}{2}$), which can be guaranteed by adding an additional random element to it.

Thus, we have $H_0((s, A), x^*) \neq H_0((s + d, A), x^*)$, i.e., if the bit $u^* \neq H_0((s, A), x^*)$, then $u^* = H_0((s + d, A), x^*)$. Therefore the simulator can succeed in mapping x^* to u^*.

Explainable hash with Injectivity. We next describe how to construct injective explainable hash functions from the above (non-injective) explainable hash H_0. The construction runs multiple instances of H_0 and rerandomize the outputs.

More precisely, let l be the length of the inputs, then we define the new hash function as

$$H(HK, x) = (H_0(hk_{i,j}, x) \oplus v_{i,j,x[i]})_{i \in [1,l], j \in [1,L]}$$

where $L = O(l)$ is large enough, $HK = (hk_{i,j}, v_{i,j,0}, v_{i,j,1})_{i \in [1,l], j \in [1,L]}$, and for $i \in [1, l], j \in [1, L]$, $hk_{i,j}$ is a random hash key of H_0 and $v_{i,j,0}, v_{i,j,1}$ are random bits.

For any inputs $x \neq x'$, there exists i s.t. $x[i] \neq x'[i]$. Thus, $v_{i,j,x[i]}$ and $v_{i,j,x'[i]}$ are random and independent bits and therefore, for all $j \in [1, L]$, we have

$$\Pr[H_0(hk_{i,j}, x) \oplus v_{i,j,x[i]} = H_0(hk_{i,j}, x') \oplus v_{i,j,x'[i]}] = \frac{1}{2}$$

This implies that $\Pr[H(HK, x) = H(HK, x')] \leq \frac{1}{2^L}$. Then, as there are at most 2^{2l} possible pairs of distinct inputs (x, x'), we have

$$\Pr[\exists x, x' \text{ s.t. } x \neq x' \wedge H(HK, x) = H(HK, x')] \leq \frac{2^{2l}}{2^L}$$

which can be made negligible for large enough L. That is, with all but negligible probability over the choice of the random hash key, the hash function will be injective. Besides, given an input x^* and a string $u^* \in \{0, 1\}^{l \cdot L}$, the simulator of H can invoke the simulator of H_0 to generate $hk_{i,j}$ satisfying

$$H_0(hk_{i,j}, x^*) = u^*_{i,j} \oplus v_{i,j,x^*[i]}$$

for $i \in [1, l], j \in [1, L]$, and security of the new construction follows.

On Achieving Collision Resistant Pseudorandomness. Next, we describe how to achieve collision resistant pseudorandomness, which requires that given a constrained key punctured on a set $\mathcal{P}_1$ and a constrained key punctured on a set $\mathcal{P}_2$, the adversary cannot learn the PRF value at an input $x \in \mathcal{P}_1 \cap \mathcal{P}_2$[7]. The starting point is a single-key secure private puncturable PRF with special properties. Concretely, we will use the private constrained PRF given in [PS18].

The [PS18] PRF. In a nutshell, the secret key of the PRF is a vector $s \in \mathbb{Z}_q^n$, where $s[1] = 1$ and for $i \in [2, n]$, $s[i]$ is a random element in $\mathbb{Z}_q$. Also, given an input x, the PRF outputs

$$\lfloor \frac{p}{q} \cdot (s^\mathsf{T} \cdot A_x)[1] \rceil$$

---

[7] Note that if $x \notin \mathcal{P}_1 \cap \mathcal{P}_2$, i.e., $x \notin \mathcal{P}_1$ or $x \notin \mathcal{P}_2$, then the PRF value at x can be trivially learned from one of the constrained keys.

where $\boldsymbol{A}_x \in \mathbb{Z}_q^{n \times m}$ is a random matrix determined by x and some public matrices $\boldsymbol{A}_1, \ldots, \boldsymbol{A}_{N+k}$. The constrained key for a constraint predicate C includes a vector

$$\boldsymbol{a}_\mathsf{C} = \boldsymbol{s}^\mathsf{T} \cdot [\boldsymbol{A}_1 + ct_1 \cdot \boldsymbol{G} \mid \ldots \mid \boldsymbol{A}_N + ct_N \cdot \boldsymbol{G}$$
$$\mid \boldsymbol{A}_{N+1} + sk_1 \cdot \boldsymbol{G} \mid \ldots \mid \boldsymbol{A}_{N+k} + sk_k \cdot \boldsymbol{G}] + \boldsymbol{e}^\mathsf{T}$$

and a ciphertext $ct = (ct_1, \ldots, ct_N)$, where ct is the ciphertext that encrypts the constraint C using a fully homomorphic encryption (FHE) scheme, sk is the secret key of the FHE scheme, and $\boldsymbol{e}$ is a low-norm noise vector. Besides, given the constrained key $(\boldsymbol{a}_\mathsf{C}, ct)$ and an input x, the constrained evaluation algorithm first computes

$$\boldsymbol{a}_x \approx (\boldsymbol{s}^\mathsf{T} \cdot \boldsymbol{A}_x)[1] + (1 - \mathsf{C}(x)) \cdot r_x$$

via another version of the matrix embedding technique [BGG+14, GVW15], where r_x is a pseudorandom element in $\mathbb{Z}_q$ determined by x. Then, it rounds $\boldsymbol{a}_x$ to $\mathbb{Z}_p$ and outputs the rounding result. Note that $\boldsymbol{a}_x$ is close to $(\boldsymbol{s}^\mathsf{T} \cdot \boldsymbol{A}_x)[1]$ if $\mathsf{C}(x) = 1$, and is pseudorandom (and thus hides the real PRF value) if $\mathsf{C}(x) = 0$. Then the correctness[8] and the pseudorandomness follow. In addition, its privacy comes from security of the FHE scheme and the LWE assumption, which implies that $\boldsymbol{a}_\mathsf{C}$ is a pseudorandom vector and thus hides sk.

The Difficulty for Achieving Collusion Resistance. In above construction (denoted as PRF_0 here), one can recover the PRF key $\boldsymbol{s}$ from constrained keys for two different constraints $\mathsf{C}^{(1)}$ and $\mathsf{C}^{(2)}$. First, since the constraints are different, the ciphertexts $ct^{(1)}$ and $ct^{(2)}$ that encrypt $\mathsf{C}^{(1)}$ and $\mathsf{C}^{(2)}$ respectively will also be different. That is, there exists i s.t. $ct_i^{(1)} \neq ct_i^{(2)}$ and w.l.o.g., assume that $ct_i^{(1)} = 1$ and $ct_i^{(2)} = 0$. Then, from the constrained keys, one can get

$$(\boldsymbol{s}^\mathsf{T}(\boldsymbol{A}_i + ct_i^{(1)} \cdot \boldsymbol{G}) + \boldsymbol{e}_1^\mathsf{T}) - (\boldsymbol{s}^\mathsf{T}(\boldsymbol{A}_i + ct_i^{(2)} \cdot \boldsymbol{G}) + \boldsymbol{e}_2^\mathsf{T}) = \boldsymbol{s}^\mathsf{T} \cdot \boldsymbol{G} + \boldsymbol{e}^\mathsf{T}$$

from which recovering $\boldsymbol{s}$ is easy. Similar collusion attacks also work for many other lattice-based constrained PRFs (e.g., [BV15, BKM17, BTVW17]).

The First Attempt. To get around the above obstacle and construct collusion resistant τ-puncturable PRFs (i.e., the PRF can be punctured at τ points), our initial idea is to split the PRF key into τ parts and puncture each part on one input.[9] In particular, let $\boldsymbol{t}_1, \ldots, \boldsymbol{t}_\tau$ be τ independent secret keys of PRF_0, then the new PRF key is $(\boldsymbol{t}_1, \ldots, \boldsymbol{t}_\tau)$. Moreover, given an input x, the PRF outputs

$$\sum_{i=1}^{\tau} \mathsf{PRF}_0(\boldsymbol{t}_i, x)$$

---

[8] This also relies on the fact that $(\boldsymbol{s}^\mathsf{T} \cdot \boldsymbol{A}_x)[1]$ is not close to the "rounding border", which can be ensured either by the 1D-SIS assumption [Reg04, BV15, BKM17] or via adding an additional random element to it. In this work, we use the latter method.

[9] A similar idea is also employed in [BKM17] to achieve τ-puncture PRF from 1-puncture PRF. However, as discussed below, we cannot achieve collusion resistance merely from this approach.

and on input a puncture set $\mathcal{P} = \{x_1, \ldots, x_\tau\}$, the constraining algorithm punctures the secret key t_i on x_i and outputs the constrained versions of all t_i.

Now, given two puncture sets $\mathcal{P}^{(1)} = \{x_1^{(1)}, \ldots, x_\tau^{(1)}\}$ and $\mathcal{P}^{(2)} = \{x_1^{(2)}, \ldots, x_\tau^{(2)}\}$ and supposing $x_1^{(1)} = x_1^{(2)} = x_1$, then t_1 is punctured on the same input x_1 in the two constrained keys. Next, by the single-key security of PRF_0, $\mathsf{PRF}_0(t_1, x_1)$ is pseudorandom given the constrained keys, which implies the pseudorandomness of the PRF value at x_1. Note that if $x_2^{(1)} \neq x_2^{(2)}$, then one can still recover t_2 from the constrained keys via the attack described above. Nonetheless, this will not affect security of the t_1 part, since t_1 and t_2 are independent.

The above approach works only if we can assign the "correct" input to each part of the PRF key. Especially, let $x \in \mathcal{P}_1 \cap \mathcal{P}_2$, then we need to assign x (but no other inputs) to the same t_i in both constrained keys. We can ensure that x is assigned to a fixed t_i by using a deterministic function that maps each input into an index in $[1, \tau]$ in the constraining algorithm. However, since the input space is exponentially large, there will be collisions here and we have to puncture t_i also on some other inputs, which will cause the attacks. On the other hand, if we do not use such map, it seems impossible to assign x to the same index i in independent constraining procedures.

Our Solution. To solve this problem, we generate the secret vector t_x for each punctured point x on-the-fly.[10] In more detail, the PRF key of our construction is a PRF key s of PRF_0, and the PRF outputs $\mathsf{PRF}_0(s, x)$ given an input x. Then to puncture s on a set $\mathcal{P} = \{x_1, \ldots, x_\tau\}$, the constraining algorithm first derives t_{x_i}, which is also a PRF key of PRF_0, from x_i via a standard PRF. Then it punctures t_{x_i} on x_i and computes $t_0 = s - \sum_{i=1}^{\tau} t_{x_i}$. The constrained key for $\mathcal{P}$ includes t_0 and the constrained version of each t_{x_i}.

Correctness of PRF_0 guarantees that given a constrained key for $\mathcal{P} = \{x_1, \ldots, x_\tau\}$ and an input $x \notin \mathcal{P}$, one can compute $\mathsf{PRF}_0(t_{x_i}, x)$ and $\mathsf{PRF}_0(t_0, x)$. Then by the key-homomorphism property of PRF_0,[11] we have

$$\mathsf{PRF}_0(t_0, x) + \sum_{i=1}^{\tau} \mathsf{PRF}_0(t_{x_i}, x) = \mathsf{PRF}_0(t_0 + \sum_{i=1}^{\tau} t_{x_i}, x) = \mathsf{PRF}_0(s, x)$$

and the correctness of our new construction follows.

Next, we explain why the construction has collusion resistant pseudorandomness. Given constrained keys for $\mathcal{P}_1$ and $\mathcal{P}_2$, and let $x \in \mathcal{P}_1 \cap \mathcal{P}_2$. Then t_x is punctured on the same input x in both constrained keys. Thus, the adversary cannot learn any information about $\mathsf{PRF}_0(t_x, x)$ from the constrained version of t_x due to the single-key security of PRF_0. We also need to show that other parts

---

[10] As a byproduct, this also leads to puncturable PRFs for puncture sets of unbounded sizes.

[11] The key-homomorphism property requires that $\mathsf{PRF}_0(t_1, x) + \mathsf{PRF}_0(t_2, x) = \mathsf{PRF}_0(t_1 + t_2, x)$. Actually, due to the rounding operation, PRF_0 is only "almost key-homomorphic", i.e., there may exist a small difference between $\mathsf{PRF}_0(t_1, x) + \mathsf{PRF}_0(t_2, x)$ and $\mathsf{PRF}_0(t_1 + t_2, x)$. We close the gap by summing the variables before rounding and then rounding the result to $\mathbb{Z}_p$.

of the constrained keys reveal no information about t_x and $\mathsf{PRF}_0(t_x, x)$. Note that we have

$$t_0^{(1)} + \sum_{x' \in \mathcal{P}_1 \setminus \{x\}} t_{x'} = t_0^{(2)} + \sum_{x' \in \mathcal{P}_2 \setminus \{x\}} t_{x'} = s - t_x$$

where $t_0^{(1)}$ and $t_0^{(2)}$ are the t_0 vectors in the two constrained keys. Since s and t_x are random vectors with the first coordinate set to be 1^{12}, t_x can be masked by s and cannot be learned from other secret vectors, namely, $t_0^{(1)}$, $t_0^{(2)}$ and $t_{x'}$ for $x' \in (\mathcal{P}_1 \cup \mathcal{P}_2) \setminus \{x\}$. As $\mathsf{PRF}_0(t_x, x)$ (and thus $\mathsf{PRF}_0(s, x)$) is pseudorandom for an adversary that sees multiple constrained keys, the collusion resistant pseudorandomness property follows.

The above proof strategy, however, cannot be applied to prove the collusion resistant privacy of our construction. This is because the solution does not provide any protection for an input $x \in (\mathcal{P}_1 \cup \mathcal{P}_2) - (\mathcal{P}_1 \cap \mathcal{P}_2)$, given the constrained keys for $\mathcal{P}_1$ and $\mathcal{P}_2$. Thus, the adversary can still learn these inputs and know if it belongs to $\mathcal{P}_1$ or $\mathcal{P}_2$, from the constrained keys. Therefore, our construction only has 1-key privacy, which is guaranteed by the 1-key privacy of PRF_0.

Remark 1.1. The construction described above is nearly generic. In particular, it can transform a single-key secure private puncturable PRF F into a private puncturable PRF with collusion resistant pseudorandomness if (1) F is key-homomorphic and (2) the distribution of $t_1 + t_2$ is identical to the distribution of t_3, where t_1, t_2, t_3 are PRF keys of F. Although there are no lattice-based private puncturable PRFs satisfying either of the properties, the transform still works for some concrete instantiations (e.g., the one presented in [PS18]) with weaker form of key-homomorphism and suitable PRF key distribution, as we have just shown.

Putting It All Together. We have described a general construction of adaptively secure private 1-puncturable PRF from any selectively secure private 1-puncturable PRF. Also, we have shown how to construct a private puncturable PRF with collusion resistant pseudorandomness from the private puncturable PRF given in [PS18]. Next, we explain how to combine the techniques to get a private puncturable PRF with both adaptive security and collusion resistance.

The construction proceeds in two steps. First, we apply the general construction for achieving adaptive security to the private puncturable PRF from [PS18]. This leads to an adaptively secure private 1-puncturable PRF with single-key security. Note that the new scheme has the same PRF key distribution (excluding the hash key of explainable hash) as the original one, and it is still key-homomorphic (before rounding). So, we can apply our ideas for obtaining collusion resistance to upgrade this scheme to have both adaptive security and collusion resistant pseudorandomness.

---

[12] Recall that both s and t_x are PRF keys of PRF_0.

1.3   Related Work

Constrained PRFs with Additional Features. There are many works constructing (private) constrained PRFs with additional features. For example, in [CRV14,Fuc14,DDM17], constrained PRFs supporting verifiability of evaluation results are constructed. Also, in [BKW17], Boneh et al. present constrained PRFs that allow one to invert the PRF evaluation with a (constrained) key. Besides, in order to construct watermarking schemes for PRFs [CHN+16], (private) puncturable PRFs that support testing of punctured points are proposed in [BLW17,KW17,KW19]. We note that while watermarkable PRFs and puncturable PRFs are highly related, and collusion resistant watermarkable PRFs have been constructed from standard lattice assumptions in [YAYX20], the construction ideas cannot be applied to construct collusion resistant puncturable PRFs.

Private Programmable PRFs. Our notion of explainable hash is close to the notion of private programmable PRF [BLW17], which is a private puncturable PRF that allows one to reprogram the PRF output on a punctured point. It seems that a private programmable PRF with adaptive privacy and injectivity implies an explainable hash. However, existing private programmable PRFs [BLW17,PS18,PS20] only have selective security. On the other hand, a private programmable PRF with adaptive privacy can be constructed from a selectively-secure private programmable PRF and an explainable hash using the techniques provided in this work.

2   Preliminaries

In this section, we give notations and background knowledge that we require.

Notations. We write $negl(\cdot)$ to denote a negligible function, and write $poly(\cdot)$ to denote a polynomial. For integers $a \leq b$, we write $[a, b]$ to denote all integers from a to b. Let s be a string, we use $|s|$ to denote the length of s. For integers $a \leq |s|$, we use $s[a]$ to denote the a-th character of s and for integers $a \leq b \leq |s|$, we use $s[a : b]$ to denote the substring $(s[a], s[a + 1], \ldots, s[b])$. Let $\mathcal{S}$ be a finite set, we use $|\mathcal{S}|$ to denote the size of $\mathcal{S}$, and use $s \xleftarrow{\$} \mathcal{S}$ to denote sampling an element s uniformly from set $\mathcal{S}$. Let $\mathcal{D}$ be a distribution, we use $d \leftarrow \mathcal{D}$ to denote sampling d according to $\mathcal{D}$.

We will use bold lower-case letters to denote vectors, and use bold upper-case letters to denote matrices. All elements in vectors and matrices are integers unless otherwise specified. Let v be a vector of length n, we use $v[i]$ to denote the i-th element of v for $i \in [1, n]$ and use $v[i : j]$ to denote the vector $(v[i], v[i + 1], \ldots, v[j])^{\mathsf{T}}$ for $1 \leq i < j \leq n$. We use $\|v\|_\infty = \max_{i \in [n]} |v[i]|$ to denote the infinity-norm of v. For an m-by-n matrix A, we use $A[i, j]$ to denote the element on the i-th row and the j-th column of A for $i \in [1, m]$ and $j \in [1, n]$.

For any positive integers p, q s.t. $p \leq q$, and for any $y \in \mathbb{Z}_q$, we define $\lfloor y \rceil_p = \lfloor \frac{p}{q} \cdot y \rceil \in \mathbb{Z}_p$. Without loss of generality, we use integers in $[0, q-1]$ (resp. $[0, p-1]$) to represent elements in $\mathbb{Z}_q$ (resp. $\mathbb{Z}_p$).

Discrete Gaussian Distribution. We use D_σ to denote the discrete Gaussian distribution over $\mathbb{Z}$ with standard deviation σ. Let λ be a security parameter, we use $\tilde{D}_\sigma$ to denote the truncated discrete Gaussian distribution over $\mathbb{Z}$, which samples $x \leftarrow D_\sigma$, and then it outputs x if $|x| \leq \lambda \cdot \sigma$ and outputs 0 otherwise. By the following lemma, D_σ and $\tilde{D}_\sigma$ are statistically indistinguishable.

Lemma 2.1 ([Lyu12]). *For any $k > 0$, $\Pr[|z| > k\sigma : z \leftarrow D_\sigma] \leq 2e^{\frac{-k^2}{2}}$.*

Gadget Matrix. For any positive integers n, m, q s.t. $m = n \cdot \lceil \log q \rceil$, we define the gadget matrix $\boldsymbol{G}_{n,q} \in \mathbb{Z}^{n \times m}$ as

$$
\boldsymbol{G}_{n,q} = \begin{bmatrix} 1\ 2\ 4 \ldots 2^{\lceil \log q \rceil - 1} & & & \\ & 1\ 2\ 4 \ldots 2^{\lceil \log q \rceil - 1} & & \\ & & \ddots & \\ & & & 1\ 2\ 4 \ldots 2^{\lceil \log q \rceil - 1} \end{bmatrix}
\tag{1}
$$

For any positive integer l, we also define the inverse function $\boldsymbol{G}_{n,q}^{-1} : \mathbb{Z}_q^{n \times l} \to \{0, 1\}^{m \times l}$ to be a function that decomposes each element $a \in \mathbb{Z}_q$ of a matrix into a column of size $\lceil \log q \rceil$ consisting of the binary representation of a. For any matrix $\boldsymbol{A} \in \mathbb{Z}_q^{n \times l}$, we have

$$
\boldsymbol{G}_{n,q} \cdot \boldsymbol{G}_{n,q}^{-1}(\boldsymbol{A}) = \boldsymbol{A}
$$

The LWE Assumption. We will use the LWE assumption in this paper.

Definition 2.1 (Decision-LWE$_{n,m,q,\chi}$). *Given a random matrix $\boldsymbol{A} \in \mathbb{Z}_q^{m \times n}$, and a vector $\boldsymbol{b} \in \mathbb{Z}_q^m$, where $\boldsymbol{b}$ is generated according to either of the following two cases:*

1. $\boldsymbol{b} = \boldsymbol{A} \cdot \boldsymbol{s} + \boldsymbol{e} \mod q$, where $\boldsymbol{s} \xleftarrow{\$} \mathbb{Z}_q^n$ and $\boldsymbol{e} \leftarrow \chi^m$

2. $\boldsymbol{b} \xleftarrow{\$} \mathbb{Z}_q^m$

distinguish which is the case with non-negligible advantage.

Let $m = poly(n)$, $poly(n) \leq q \leq 2^{poly(n)}$, and $\chi = D_\sigma$ (or $\tilde{D}_\sigma$) be a (truncated) discrete Gaussian error distribution with standard deviation $\sigma \geq O(\sqrt{n})$, then solving the decision-LWE$_{n,m,q,\chi}$ problem is as hard as solving the GapSVP$_\gamma$ problem on arbitrary n-dimensional lattices by a quantum algorithm [Reg05], where $\gamma = \tilde{O}(nq/\sigma)$. In subsequent works [Pei09, BLP+13], classical reductions from LWE to GapSVP are also presented for different parameterizations.

Note that the hardness of the LWE problem depends only on n, q, σ, thus, we write LWE$_{n,m,q,\chi}$ as LWE$_{n,q,\chi}$ for short.

Matrix Embeddings. The matrix embedding technique [BGG+14, GVW15, BV15, BKM17] embeds bits into matrices and then computes circuits on these matrices. Formally, we have the following Lemmas.

Lemma 2.2 ([BGG+14]). *Let* n, m, q, B, d, N *be positive integers that* $m = n \cdot \lceil \log q \rceil$. *Let* $\mathtt{C} : \{0, 1\}^N \rightarrow \{0, 1\}$ *be a depth-d Boolean circuit. Also, let* $s \in \mathbb{Z}_q^n$, $A_0, A_1, \dots, A_N \in \mathbb{Z}_q^{n \times m}$, $x_1, \dots, x_N \in \{0, 1\}$, *and* $a_0, a_1, \dots, a_N \in \mathbb{Z}_q^m$, *where*

$$\|a_0^{\mathsf{T}} - s^{\mathsf{T}}(A_0 + G)\|_\infty \le B \quad \wedge \quad \forall i \in [1, N], \|a_i^{\mathsf{T}} - s^{\mathsf{T}}(A_i + x_i \cdot G)\|_\infty \le B$$

There exists the following two deterministic algorithms:

- $\mathtt{EvalPK}(\mathtt{C}, A_0, \dots, A_N) \rightarrow A_{\mathtt{C}} \in \mathbb{Z}_q^{n \times m}$.
- $\mathtt{EvalCT}(\mathtt{C}, A_0, \dots, A_N, a_0, \dots, a_N, x_1, \dots, x_N) \rightarrow a_{\mathtt{C}} \in \mathbb{Z}_q^m$.

such that for $A_{\mathtt{C}} = \mathtt{EvalPK}(\mathtt{C}, A_0, \dots, A_N)$ *and* $a_{\mathtt{C}} = \mathtt{EvalCT}(\mathtt{C}, A_0, \dots, A_N, a_0, \dots, a_N, x_1, \dots, x_N)$, *we have*

$$\|a_{\mathtt{C}}^{\mathsf{T}} - s^{\mathsf{T}}(A_{\mathtt{C}} + \mathtt{C}(x) \cdot G)\|_\infty \le (m + 2)^d \cdot B$$

Lemma 2.3 ([GVW15]). *Let* n, m, q, B, k *be positive integers that* $m = n \cdot \lceil \log q \rceil$. *Also, let* $s \in \mathbb{Z}_q^n$, $A_1, \dots, A_k, B_1, \dots, B_k \in \mathbb{Z}_q^{n \times m}$, $x_1, \dots, x_k \in \{0, 1\}$, $y_1, \dots, y_k \in \mathbb{Z}_q$, *and* $a_1, \dots, a_k, b_1, \dots, b_k \in \mathbb{Z}_q^m$, *where*

$$\forall i \in [1, k], \|a_i^{\mathsf{T}} - s^{\mathsf{T}}(A_i + x_i \cdot G)\|_\infty \le B \wedge \|b_i^{\mathsf{T}} - s^{\mathsf{T}}(B_i + y_i \cdot G)\|_\infty \le B$$

There exists the following two deterministic algorithms:

- $\mathtt{IPEvalPK}(A_1, \dots, A_k, B_1, \dots, B_k) \rightarrow C_{\mathtt{IP}} \in \mathbb{Z}_q^{n \times m}$.
- $\mathtt{IPEvalCT}(B_1, \dots, B_k, a_1, \dots, a_k, b_1, \dots, b_k, x_1, \dots, x_k) \rightarrow c_{\mathtt{IP}} \in \mathbb{Z}_q^m$.

such that for $C_{\mathtt{IP}} = \mathtt{IPEvalPK}(A_1, \dots, A_k, B_1, \dots, B_k)$ *and* $c_{\mathtt{IP}} = \mathtt{IPEvalCT}(B_1, \dots, B_k, a_1, \dots, a_k, b_1, \dots, b_k, x_1, \dots, x_k)$, *we have*

$$\|c_{\mathtt{IP}}^{\mathsf{T}} - s^{\mathsf{T}}(C_{\mathtt{IP}} + \sum_{i=1}^k x_i \cdot y_i \cdot G)\|_\infty \le k \cdot (m + 1) \cdot B$$

The GSW FHE Scheme. Our construction relies on some specific properties of the GSW FHE scheme:

Lemma 2.4 ([GSW13]). *Let* λ *be the security parameter and* $d = poly(\lambda)$. *Let* n, k, q, c, σ *be positive integers such that* n, σ *are polynomial in* λ, $k = O(n \cdot \lceil \log q \rceil)$, $c = O(n^2 \log^2 q)$, *and* $q > \lambda \cdot \sigma \cdot k^{O(d)}$. *Then there exists a secure FHE scheme* $\mathsf{FHE} = (\mathsf{FHE.KeyGen}, \mathsf{FHE.Enc}, \mathsf{FHE.Dec}, \mathsf{FHE.Eval})$ *for circuits with depth at most d with the following properties, assuming the* $LWE_{n, q, \tilde{D}_\sigma}$ *assumption:*

- *The secret key of* FHE *is in* $\mathbb{Z}_q^k$.
- *The encryption algorithm takes in a message in* $\{0, 1\}$ *and outputs a ciphertext in* $\{0, 1\}^c$.
- *The evaluation algorithm can additionally take as input an integer* $\ell \in [1, \lceil \log q \rceil]$ *and output a ciphertext in* $\{0, 1\}^k$.

- *Given any boolean circuit of depth at most d, the evaluation algorithm can be evaluated by a Boolean circuit of depth at most $D = d \cdot poly(\log \lambda, \log \log q)$.*
- *For any polynomial N, d, any $\ell \in [1, \lceil \log q \rceil]$, any messages $\mu_1, \ldots, \mu_N \in \{0, 1\}$, and any boolean circuit $C : \{0,1\}^N \to \{0,1\}$ of depth at most d, let $(pk, sk) \leftarrow \mathsf{FHE.KeyGen}(1^\lambda, 1^d)$ and for $i \in [1, N]$, let $ct_i \leftarrow \mathsf{FHE.Enc}(pk, \mu_i)$. Also let*

$$ct' \leftarrow \mathsf{Eval}(\ell, C, (ct_1, \ldots, ct_N))$$

$$\nu = \sum_{i=1}^{k} sk[i] \cdot ct'[i] \mod q$$

then we have

$$|\nu - C(\mu_1, \ldots, \mu_N) \cdot 2^{\ell-1}| \leq \lambda \cdot \sigma \cdot k^{O(d)}$$

Admissible Hash. We use the (balanced) admissible hash function [BB04, Jag15] in our construction. The following definition is adapted from the definition given in [Jag15], where we modify the definition of τ in Eq. (3) below.

Definition 2.2. *Let λ be the security parameter. Let l, t be positive integers that are polynomial in λ. Let $\mathsf{H}_{adm} : \{0,1\}^l \to \{0,1\}^t$ be an efficiently computable function. For $K \in \{0, 1, \perp\}^t$, let $\mathsf{P}_K : \{0,1\}^t \to \{0,1\}$ be defined as*

$$\mathsf{P}_K(w) = \begin{cases} 1 & if \ \forall i \in [1, t], K[i] = \perp \ \lor \ K[i] = w[i] \\ 0 & otherwise \end{cases} \tag{2}$$

We say that H_{adm} is a balanced admissible hash function *if for any polynomial Q and non-negligible real value $\delta \in (0, 1]$, there exits a PPT algorithm*

- $\mathsf{AdmSmp}_{Q,\delta}(1^\lambda) \to K$. *On input the security parameter 1^λ, the algorithm outputs $K \in \{0, 1, \perp\}^t$.*

and non-negligible real values γ_{min} and γ_{max} such that for all $x_1, \ldots, x_Q, x^* \in \{0, 1\}^l$ with $x^* \notin \{x_1, \ldots, x_Q\}$[13], we have

$$\gamma_{min} \leq \Pr[\mathsf{P}_K(\mathsf{H}_{adm}(x^*)) = 1 \ \land \ \forall i \in [1, Q], \mathsf{P}_K(\mathsf{H}_{adm}(x_i)) = 0] \leq \gamma_{max}$$

and

$$\tau = \gamma_{min} \cdot \delta - (\gamma_{max} - \gamma_{min}) \tag{3}$$

is a non-negligible positive real value, where the probability is taken over the choice of $K \leftarrow \mathsf{AdmSmp}_{Q,\delta}(1^\lambda)$.

---

[13] We allow $x_i = x_j$ for some distinct $i, j \in [1, Q]$.

The (balanced) admissible hash function presented in [Lys02, FHPS13, Jag15], which are constructed from an error correcting code with suitable minimal distance (see e.g., [SS96, Zém01, Gol08] for explicit constructions of such codes), also satisfy Definition 2.2. We formally state this in Lemma 2.5 and for completeness, we give its proof in the full version.

Lemma 2.5. *Let c be a constant and $t = O(l)$. Let $C : \{0,1\}^l \rightarrow \{0,1\}^t$ be a family of code with minimal distance $c \cdot t$ (i.e., for any distinct $x_1, x_2 \in \{0,1\}^l$, $C(x_1)$ and $C(x_2)$ differ in at least $c \cdot t$ positions). Then C is a balanced admissible hash function defined in Definition 2.2.*

We need to embed the evaluation of P_K into matrices using another form of the matrix embedding technique, and the result can be described by the following lemma.

Lemma 2.6. *Let t be a polynomial in λ. Let $K \in \{0, 1, \perp\}^t$ and let $P_K : \{0, 1\}^t \rightarrow \{0, 1\}$ be the function defined in Eq. (2). For $i \in [1, t]$, let*

$$(K_{i,0}, K_{i,1}) = \begin{cases} (0, 0) & \text{if } K[i] = \perp \\ (1, K[i]) & \text{otherwise} \end{cases}$$

Let n, m, q be positive integers that $m = n \cdot \lceil \log q \rceil$. Also, let $A_{1,0}, A_{1,1}, \ldots, A_{t,0}, A_{t,1}, B_{1,0}, B_{1,1}, \ldots, B_{t,0}, B_{t,1} \in \mathbb{Z}_q^{n \times m}$, where

$$\forall i \in [1, t], \quad A_{i,0} = B_{i,0} - K_{i,0} \cdot G, \quad A_{i,1} = B_{i,1} - K_{i,1} \cdot G$$

There exists the following deterministic algorithm:

- $\text{EvalAdm}(A_{1,0}, A_{1,1}, \ldots, A_{t,0}, A_{t,1}, w) \rightarrow A_P \in \mathbb{Z}_q^{n \times m}$.

such that for any $w \in \{0,1\}^t$ and for $A_P = \text{EvalAdm}(A_{1,0}, A_{1,1}, \ldots, A_{t,0}, A_{t,1}, w)$, there exists $T \in [-m, m]^{2tm \times m}$ satisfying

$$A_P = (B_{1,0}, B_{1,1}, \ldots, B_{t,0}, B_{t,1}) \cdot T - P_K(w) \cdot G$$

3 Explainable Hash Functions

3.1 The Definition

In this section, we provide the definition of explainable hash. Roughly speaking, an explainable hash is an injective function that can generate a hash key mapping a given input to a predefined output and being compatible with previous hash evaluations. Formally, an explainable hash $H = (\text{KeyGen}, \text{Eval})$ with input space $\mathcal{X}$ and output space $\mathcal{U}$ consists of the following probabilistic polynomial-time (PPT) algorithms:

- $\text{KeyGen}(1^\lambda) \rightarrow hk$: On input the security parameter 1^λ, the key generation algorithm outputs the hash key hk.

- Eval$(hk, x) \rightarrow u$: On input the hash key hk and an input $x \in \mathcal{X}$, the deterministic evaluation algorithm outputs an output $u \in \mathcal{U}$.

We require that the hash function is injective for nearly all hash keys.

Definition 3.1 (Injectivity). *Let* $hk \leftarrow \mathsf{KeyGen}(1^\lambda)$, *then the probability that there exist distinct* $x_1, x_2 \in \mathcal{X}$ *s.t.* $\mathsf{Eval}(hk, x_1) = \mathsf{Eval}(hk, x_2)$ *is negligible.*

Besides, its explainability property requires that there exists a simulator that can simulate the hash function evaluation oracle to an adversary, and then after the adversary submits an input, the simulator can generate a hash key that maps this input to a predefined uniform output and is compatible with previous evaluation oracle outputs. Here, we allow the simulator to abort with a non-negligible probability and require that the simulator aborts if and only if the inputs submitted to the evaluation oracle and the final input do not pass a validity check algorithm.

Definition 3.2 (Explainability). *For any polynomial* Q *and non-negligible real value* $\delta \in (0, 1]$, *we first define two algorithms* $(\mathsf{VKeyGen}_{Q,\delta}, \mathsf{Verify}_{Q,\delta})$ *as follows:*

- $\mathsf{VKeyGen}_{Q,\delta}(1^\lambda) \rightarrow vk$: *On input the security parameter* 1^λ, *the verification key generation algorithm outputs the verification key* vk.
- $\mathsf{Verify}_{Q,\delta}(vk, \mathcal{Q}, x^*) \rightarrow \alpha$: *On input the verification key* vk, *a set* $\mathcal{Q} \subset \mathcal{X}$ *s.t.* $|\mathcal{Q}| \leq Q$ *and an input* $x^* \in \mathcal{X}$, *the deterministic verification algorithm outputs a bit* $\alpha \in \{0, 1\}$.

The explainability property has the following two requirements:

- **Abort Probability.** *There exists* Γ_{min}, Γ_{max} *that for any set* $\mathcal{Q} \subset \mathcal{X}$ *s.t.* $|\mathcal{Q}| \leq Q$ *and for any input* $x^* \in \mathcal{X} \backslash \mathcal{Q}$

$$\Gamma_{min} \leq \Pr\left[vk \leftarrow \mathsf{VKeyGen}_{Q,\delta}(1^\lambda) : \mathsf{Verify}_{Q,\delta}(vk, \mathcal{Q}, x^*) = 1\right] \leq \Gamma_{max}$$

and

$$\mathcal{T} = \Gamma_{min} \cdot \delta - (\Gamma_{max} - \Gamma_{min})$$

is a non-negligible positive real value.
- **Indistinguishability.** *There exists a stateful simulator* SIM *such that for any PPT and stateful adversary* $\mathcal{A}$, *we have*

$$|\Pr[\mathsf{ExpReal}_{\mathcal{A}}(1^\lambda) = 1] - \Pr[\mathsf{ExpIdeal}_{\mathcal{A},\mathsf{SIM}}(1^\lambda) = 1]| \leq negl(\lambda)$$

where the experiments ExpReal *and* ExpIdeal *are defined as follows*

$\text{ExpReal}_{\mathcal{A}}(1^\lambda):$

$\quad vk \leftarrow \text{VKeyGen}_{Q,\delta}(1^\lambda);$

$\quad hk \leftarrow \text{KeyGen}(1^\lambda);$

$\quad x^* \leftarrow \mathcal{A}^{\text{Eval}(hk,\cdot)}(1^\lambda);$

$\quad \textit{If } \text{Verify}_{Q,\delta}(vk, \mathcal{Q}, x^*) = 1:$

$\qquad out = (hk, \text{Eval}(hk, x^*));$

$\quad \textit{Otherwise}:$

$\qquad out = \perp;$

$\quad b \leftarrow \mathcal{A}(out);$

$\quad \textit{Output } b;$

$\text{ExpIdeal}_{\mathcal{A},\text{SIM}}(1^\lambda):$

$\quad vk \leftarrow \text{VKeyGen}_{Q,\delta}(1^\lambda);$

$\quad u^* \xleftarrow{\$} \mathcal{U};$

$\quad \text{SIM}(vk, u^*);$

$\quad x^* \leftarrow \mathcal{A}^{\text{SIM}(\cdot)}(1^\lambda);$

$\quad \textit{If } \text{Verify}_{Q,\delta}(vk, \mathcal{Q}, x^*) = 1:$

$\qquad hk \leftarrow \text{SIM}(x^*);$

$\qquad out = (hk, u^*);$

$\quad \textit{Otherwise}:$

$\qquad out = \perp;$

$\quad b \leftarrow \mathcal{A}(out);$

$\quad \textit{Output } b;$

In above experiments, $\mathcal{Q}$ *is the set of inputs submitted to the (simulated) evaluation oracle and we require that (1)* $|\mathcal{Q}| \leq Q$ *and (2)* $x^* \notin \mathcal{Q}$. *In the third step of the experiment* ExpIdeal, *the stateful simulator* SIM *takes as input* (vk, u^*) *and updates its internal state, but it does not output anything in this step.*

3.2   The Construction

In this section, we present our construction of explainable hash. Let λ be the security parameter. Let l, k, t be positive integers that are polynomial in λ such that $k = 4l + \lambda$. Let $\bar{n}, n, m, \sigma, \Sigma$ be positive integers that are polynomial in λ, and let q be a positive odd prime, which satisfy: $m = n \cdot \lceil \log q \rceil$, $n = \bar{n} \cdot \lceil \log q \rceil + \lambda$, $\Sigma = 2tm^3\lambda\sigma$, and $q \geq 2^{l+\omega(\log \lambda)}(4\Sigma + 2)$. Let

$$\mathsf{H}_{adm} : \{0,1\}^l \to \{0,1\}^t$$

be a balanced admissible hash function and let

$$\text{EvalAdm} : (\mathbb{Z}_q^{n \times m})^{2t} \times \{0,1\}^t \to \mathbb{Z}_q^{n \times m}$$

be the algorithm defined in Lemma 2.6. Let $\boldsymbol{G} = \boldsymbol{G}_{n,q}$ and write $\boldsymbol{G}_{n,q}^{-1}$ as $\boldsymbol{G}^{-1}$. Let

$$\boldsymbol{h} = \boldsymbol{G}^{-1}((\frac{q-1}{2}, 0, \ldots, 0)^\mathsf{T}) \in \{0,1\}^m$$

We construct the explainable hash function $\mathsf{H} = (\text{KeyGen}, \text{Eval})$, which has input space $\{0,1\}^l$ and output space $\{0,1\}^{l \cdot k}$ as follows:

- **KeyGen.** On input the security parameter 1^λ, the key generation algorithm samples

$$A_z \overset{\$}{\leftarrow} \mathbb{Z}_q^{n \times m} \qquad \text{for } z \in [1, 2t]$$
$$s_{i,j} \overset{\$}{\leftarrow} \mathbb{Z}_q^n \qquad \text{for } i \in [1, l], j \in [1, k]$$
$$v_{i,j,\iota} \overset{\$}{\leftarrow} \mathbb{Z}_q \qquad \text{for } i \in [1, l], j \in [1, k], \iota \in \{0, 1\}$$

and outputs the hash key

$$hk = ((A_z)_{z \in [1,2t]}, (s_{i,j})_{i \in [1,l], j \in [1,k]}, (v_{i,j,\iota})_{i \in [1,l], j \in [1,k], \iota \in \{0,1\}})$$

- **Eval.** On input the hash key $hk = ((A_z)_{z \in [1,2t]}, (s_{i,j})_{i \in [1,l], j \in [1,k]},$ $(v_{i,j,\iota})_{i \in [1,l], j \in [1,k], \iota \in \{0,1\}})$, and an input $x \in \{0, 1\}^l$, the evaluation algorithm first computes:

$$w = \mathsf{H}_{adm}(x), \quad A_w = \mathsf{EvalAdm}(A_1, \ldots, A_{2t}, w), \quad b_w = A_w \cdot h \mod q$$

Let $u_1, \ldots, u_l$ be k-dimension binary vectors, then for $i \in [1, l]$, $j \in [1, k]$, it computes:

$$y_{i,j} = s_{i,j}^\mathsf{T} \cdot b_w + v_{i,j,x[i]} \mod q$$

and sets

$$u_i[j] = \begin{cases} 0 & \text{if } y_{i,j} \in [0, \frac{q-1}{2}] \\ 1 & \text{otherwise} \end{cases}$$

Finally, it outputs

$$u = (u_1^\mathsf{T}, \ldots, u_l^\mathsf{T})^\mathsf{T}$$

Theorem 3.1. *If H_{adm} is a balanced admissible hash as defined in Definition 2.2, then H is a secure explainable hash assuming the hardness of $\mathrm{LWE}_{\bar{n},q,D_\sigma}$.*

We present proof of Theorem 3.1 in the full version.

Parameters. Next, we give an instantiation for the parameters of H. Security of H relies on the hardness of $\mathrm{LWE}_{\bar{n},q,\tilde{D}_\sigma}$. In addition, we require that

$$q \geq 2^{l+\omega(\log \lambda)} \cdot (4\Sigma + 2) \geq 2^{l+\omega(\log \lambda)} \cdot poly(\lambda) \geq 2^{l+\omega(\log \lambda)}$$

Let $\varepsilon \in (0, 1)$ be a constant real value. We set $\bar{n} = (l + \lambda)^{\frac{1}{\varepsilon}}$ and set $q = 2^{O(l+\lambda)}$. This makes the approximation factor $\gamma = O(\bar{n}q/\sigma)$ of the underlying worst-case lattices problems to be $2^{O(\bar{n}^\varepsilon)}$.

Now, assume that the input length $l = O(\lambda)$, then the output length will be in $O(\lambda^2)$ and the hash key size will be

$$|hk| = 2t \cdot nm\lceil \log q \rceil + lk \cdot n\lceil \log q \rceil + 2lk \cdot \lceil \log q \rceil = O(\lambda^{5+\frac{2}{\varepsilon}})$$

4   Private Puncturable PRFs

4.1   The Definition

In this section, we provide the definition of private puncturable PRF, which is adapted from definitions in previous works (e.g., [BW13, HKW15, BLW17, BKM17, DKN+20]). More precisely, a private puncturable pseudorandom function $\mathsf{PRF} = (\mathsf{KeyGen}, \mathsf{Eval}, \mathsf{Constrain}, \mathsf{ConstrainEval})$ with key space $\mathcal{K}$, input space $\mathcal{X}$, and output space $\mathcal{Y}$ consists of the following four PPT algorithms:

- $\mathsf{KeyGen}(1^\lambda) \to k$: On input the security parameter 1^λ, the key generation algorithm outputs the secret key $k \in \mathcal{K}$.
- $\mathsf{Eval}(k, x) \to y$: On input the secret key $k \in \mathcal{K}$ and an input $x \in \mathcal{X}$, the evaluation algorithm outputs an output $y \in \mathcal{Y}$.
- $\mathsf{Constrain}(k, \mathcal{P}) \to ck$: On input the secret key $k \in \mathcal{K}$ and a polynomial-size set[14] $\mathcal{P} \subset \mathcal{X}$, the constraining algorithm outputs a constrained key ck.
- $\mathsf{ConstrainEval}(ck, x) \to y$: On input the constrained key ck and an input $x \in \mathcal{X}$, the constrained evaluation algorithm outputs an output $y \in \mathcal{Y}$.

Besides, it should satisfy the correctness, pseudorandomness, and privacy properties defined as follows.

Correctness. The correctness of a private puncturable PRF requires that the constrained key can preserve the functionality of the PRF on unpunctured points. In this work, we consider a statistical notion of correctness.

Definition 4.1 (Correctness). *Let $k \leftarrow \mathsf{KeyGen}(1^\lambda)$, then the probability that there exists polynomial-size set $\mathcal{P}^* \subset \mathcal{X}$, input $x^* \in \mathcal{X} \backslash \mathcal{P}^*$, and constrained key $ck \leftarrow \mathsf{Constrain}(k, \mathcal{P}^*)$ satisfying $\mathsf{Eval}(k, x^*) \neq \mathsf{ConstrainEval}(ck, x^*)$ is negligible.*

Pseudorandomness. The pseudorandomness of a private puncturable PRF requires that given a constrained key, the PRF values at the punctured points are pseudorandom. As shown in [BKM17], this property implies the standard pseudorandomness of the PRF.

In this work, we consider adaptive collusion resistant pseudorandomness, i.e., the adversary can make queries to the evaluation oracle and the constrain oracle both before and after seeing the challenge in an adaptive manner, and it can make a priori unbounded number of queries to the constrain oracle.

Definition 4.2 (Pseudorandomness). *For any PPT adversary $\mathcal{A} = (\mathcal{A}_1, \mathcal{A}_2)$, we have*

$$\Pr[b \xleftarrow{\$} \{0,1\}, \mathsf{ExpPR}_{\mathcal{A},b}(1^\lambda) = 1] \leq 1/2 + negl(\lambda)$$

---

[14] We implicitly assume that a set $\mathcal{P}$ is described by listing all elements in $\mathcal{P}$, thus, the puncture set is always of polynomial-size in this paper.

ExpPR$_{\mathcal{A},b}(1^\lambda)$:	ExpPriv$_{\mathcal{A},b}(1^\lambda)$:
1. $k \leftarrow \mathsf{KeyGen}(1^\lambda)$;	1. $k \leftarrow \mathsf{KeyGen}(1^\lambda)$;
2. $(x^*, state) \leftarrow \mathcal{A}_1^{\mathsf{Eval}(k,\cdot),\mathsf{Constrain}(k,\cdot)}(1^\lambda)$;	2. $(\mathcal{P}_0^*, \mathcal{P}_1^*, state) \leftarrow \mathcal{A}_1^{\mathsf{Eval}(k,\cdot)}(1^\lambda)$;
3. $y_0^* = \mathsf{Eval}(k, x^*)$, $y_1^* \xleftarrow{\$} \mathcal{Y}$;	3. $ck^* \leftarrow \mathsf{Constrain}(k, \mathcal{P}_b^*)$;
4. $b' \leftarrow \mathcal{A}_2^{\mathsf{Eval}(k,\cdot),\mathsf{Constrain}(k,\cdot)}(state, y_b^*)$;	4. $b' \leftarrow \mathcal{A}_2^{\mathsf{Eval}(k,\cdot)}(state, ck^*)$;
5. If $b = b'$, output 1; If $b \neq b'$, output 0.	5. Output b';

Fig. 1: The experiments ExpPR and ExpPriv.

where the experiment ExpPR *is defined in Fig. 1. Let* $x_1, \ldots, x_{Q_e}$ *be the inputs submitted to the evaluation oracle* $\mathsf{Eval}(k, \cdot)$ *and let* $\mathcal{P}_1, \ldots, \mathcal{P}_{Q_c}$ *be the sets submitted to the constrain oracle* $\mathsf{Constrain}(k, \cdot)$. *To prevent the adversary from trivially winning in the experiment, we require that:*

$$\forall i \in [1, Q_e], x^* \neq x_i \quad \wedge \quad \forall i \in [1, Q_c], x^* \in \mathcal{P}_i \tag{4}$$

Remark 4.1 (Weak Adaptivity). We say that a private puncturable PRF has *weakly adaptive pseudorandomness* if the adversary $\mathcal{A}_1$ in Definition 4.2 is not allowed to query the constrain oracle.[15]

The following theorem states that weakly adaptive pseudorandomness implies the fully adaptive pseudorandomness defined in Definition 4.2, and we provide the proof of Theorem 4.1 in the full version.

Theorem 4.1. *Let* PRF *be a private puncturable PRF with weakly adaptive pseudorandomness, then it also satisfies the pseudorandomness property defined in Definition 4.2.*

Privacy. The privacy of a private puncturable PRF requires that the constrained key can hide the punctured points. In this work, we consider adaptive 1-key privacy, i.e., the adversary can only obtain 1 constrained key, and it can make queries to the evaluation oracle both before and after seeing the constrained key adaptively.

Definition 4.3 (Privacy). *For any PPT adversary* $\mathcal{A} = (\mathcal{A}_1, \mathcal{A}_2)$, *we have*

$$|\Pr[\mathsf{ExpPriv}_{\mathcal{A},0}(1^\lambda) = 1] - \Pr[\mathsf{ExpPriv}_{\mathcal{A},1}(1^\lambda) = 1]| \leq negl(\lambda)$$

where the experiment ExpPriv *is defined in Fig. 1. Let* $x_1, \ldots, x_{Q_e}$ *be the inputs submitted to the evaluation oracle* $\mathsf{Eval}(k, \cdot)$, *to prevent the adversary from trivially winning in the experiment, we require that:*

$$\forall i \in [1, Q_e], (x_i \in \mathcal{P}_0^* \wedge x_i \in \mathcal{P}_1^*) \vee (x_i \notin \mathcal{P}_0^* \wedge x_i \notin \mathcal{P}_1^*) \tag{5}$$

---

[15] In this setting, $\mathcal{A}_1$ can still make queries to the evaluation oracle, and $\mathcal{A}_2$ can still query the evaluation oracle and the constrain oracle adaptively for a priori unbounded number of times.

Besides, we require that

$$|\mathcal{P}_0^*| = |\mathcal{P}_1^*| \tag{6}$$

Remark 4.2. The requirement of Eq. (6) is *necessary* if $|\mathcal{X}|$ is superpolynomial in λ and we do not have an a priori bound on the sizes of the puncture sets. In particular, assume there exists a private puncturable PRF PRF = (KeyGen, Eval, Constrain, ConstrainEval) that can achieve privacy without requiring Eq. (6). Let x be an arbitrary input, let n be the upper bound on the size of $ck \leftarrow \text{Constrain}(K, \{x\})$, and let $\mathcal{U} \subset \mathcal{X}$ be an arbitrary set with $(n + \lambda)$ inputs. Also, let $\mathcal{P}$ be a random subset of $\mathcal{U}$ and let $ck' \leftarrow \text{Constrain}(K, \mathcal{P})$. Then with all but negligible probability, we have $|ck'| \leq n$ as otherwise, the adversary can distinguish the constrained key for x from the constrained key for $\mathcal{P}$ by comparing the lengths of the constrained keys. In addition, given a constrained key ck', we can test if ck' is punctured on an input $x \in \mathcal{U}$ via checking if $\text{Eval}(K, x) \neq \text{ConstrainEval}(ck', x)$, this will succeed with all but negligible probability due to the correctness and the pseudorandomness of PRF. That is, from PRF, we can construct a mechanism that compresses a random $(n + \lambda)$-bit string[16] into an $(n+1)$-bit code[17] and then recover the input from the code, with all but negligible probability. This is information theoretically impossible.

Remark 4.3. Previous works on puncturable PRFs (e.g., [HKW15, BKM17, PS18]) mainly consider the τ-puncturable PRF, where the sizes of the puncture sets should be equal to (or not greater than) a predefined polynomial τ.[18] One can construct τ-puncturable PRF from our puncturable PRF PRF = (KeyGen, Eval, Constrain, ConstrainEval) as follows:

- KeyGen$'(1^\lambda, 1^\tau)$. Output $k \leftarrow \text{KeyGen}(1^\lambda)$.
- Eval$'(k, x)$. Output $y = \text{Eval}(k, 0\|x)$.
- Constrain$'(k, \mathcal{P})$. Pad $\mathcal{P}' = \{0\|x\}_{x \in \mathcal{P}} \cup \{1\|\bar{x}_i\}_{i \in [\tau - |\mathcal{P}|]}$ and output $ck \leftarrow \text{Constrain}(k, \mathcal{P}')$.
- ConstrainEval$'(ck, x)$. Output $y = \text{ConstrainEval}(ck, 0\|x)$.

where $\bar{x}_i$ are some random inputs and are used to pad the puncture set $\mathcal{P}$. Note that the real input and the dummy inputs for padding $\mathcal{P}$ have different prefix. It is easy to check that correctness, pseudorandomness, and privacy of the new construction follow from the security properties of PRF. Especially, after padding all puncture sets to be of size τ, Eq. (6) in the privacy game will always be satisfied. In contrast, it seems difficult to extend existing constructions of τ-puncturable PRF to be the puncturable PRF defined in this work.

Remark 4.4. A simulation-based definition, which can capture the correctness, pseudorandomness, and privacy in a single definition, is used in [CC17, PS18]. As shown in [CC17], our indistinguishability-based definitions (from Definition 4.1 to Definition 4.3) implies this simulation-based definition.

---

[16] Note that there are $2^{n+\lambda}$ possible subsets of $\mathcal{U}$.

[17] We can use $(n + 1)$-bit strings to represent all strings with length not larger than n.

[18] Since the sizes of the puncture sets are a priori bounded, the restriction described by Eq. (6) is not needed.

4.2   The Construction

In this section, we present our main construction of private puncturable PRF. Our construction can be roughly divided into two steps. In this first step, we construct an adaptively secure private puncturable PRF from the selectively secure private puncturable PRF given in [PS18], and then in the second step, we upgrade the scheme to have collusion resistant pseudorandomness. An overview for how both steps proceed and how to combine the steps is provided in Sect. 1.2, and below we give a concrete construction of private puncturable PRF with both adaptive security and collusion resistant pseudorandomness from scratch.

Let λ be the security parameter. Let $l, L, c, k, n, m, q, p, \varkappa, N, \sigma, \Sigma', \Sigma, d, D$ be positive integers that satisfy:

- l, L, c, k, n, p, σ are polynomial in λ.
- $\varkappa = \lceil \log q \rceil$, $m - n \cdot \varkappa$, and $N = (L + \varkappa) \cdot c$.
- $d = O(\log L) = O(\log \lambda)$.
- $D = d \cdot poly(\log \lambda, \log \log q) = poly(\log \lambda, \log \log q)$.
- $\Sigma' \geq \varkappa \cdot \lambda \cdot \sigma \cdot (k^{O(d)} + k \cdot m^{O(D)})$.
- $\Sigma \geq 2^{\omega(\log \lambda)} \cdot \Sigma'$.
- $q \geq 2^{L + \omega(\log \lambda)} \cdot p \cdot (2\Sigma + 1)$.
- p is an odd prime and q is a power of p.

Let $G = G_{n,q}$ and write $G_{n,q}^{-1}$ as G^{-1}. Let $\mathsf{GS} : \mathcal{R}_{\mathsf{GS}} \to \mathbb{Z}^m$ be an algorithm that takes as input a random string from its randomness space $\mathcal{R}_{\mathsf{GS}}$ and outputs an m-dimension vector e that follows the truncated discrete Gaussian distribution $\tilde{D}_\sigma^m$.

The construction is built on the following building blocks:

- The GSW fully homomorphic encryption scheme FHE = (FHE.KeyGen, FHE.Enc, FHE.Dec, FHE.Eval), where the message space is $\{0,1\}$, the ciphertext space is $\{0,1\}^c$, and the secret key space is $\mathbb{Z}_q^k$. Here, we use $\mathcal{R}_{\mathsf{KeyGen}}$ and $\mathcal{R}_{\mathsf{Enc}}$ to denote the randomness space for the algorithms FHE.KeyGen and FHE.Enc respectively.
- An explainable hash function H = (H.KeyGen, H.Eval) with input space $\{0,1\}^l$ and output space $\{0,1\}^L$.
- A PRF F = (F.KeyGen, F.Eval) with input space $\{0,1\}^L$ and output space $\mathcal{R}_{\mathsf{KeyGen}} \times \mathcal{R}_{\mathsf{Enc}}^{L+\varkappa} \times \mathbb{Z}_q \times \mathbb{Z}_q^{n-1} \times \mathcal{R}_{\mathsf{GS}}^{N+k+1}$.

Besides, for any $u \in \{0,1\}^L$ and $j \in [1, \varkappa]$, we define $\mathsf{eq}_{u,j} : \{0,1\}^L \times \{0,1\}^\varkappa \to \{0,1\}$ of depth d as

$$\mathsf{eq}_{u,j}(u^*, r) = \begin{cases} r[j] & \text{if } u^* = u \\ 0 & \text{otherwise} \end{cases}$$

and for any $u \in \{0,1\}^L$, $j \in [1, \varkappa]$, and $\iota \in [1, k]$, we define $\mathsf{C}_{u,j,\iota} : \{0,1\}^N \to \{0, 1\}$ of depth D as

$$\mathsf{C}_{u,j,\iota}(ct) = \mathsf{FHE.Eval}(j, \mathsf{eq}_{u,j}, ct)[\iota]$$

Let
$$\texttt{EvalPK} : \mathcal{C}_{N,D} \times (\mathbb{Z}_q^{n \times m})^{N+1} \to \mathbb{Z}_q^{n \times m}$$
$$\texttt{EvalCT} : \mathcal{C}_{N,D} \times (\mathbb{Z}_q^{n \times m})^{N+1} \times (\mathbb{Z}_q^m)^{N+1} \times \{0,1\}^N \to \mathbb{Z}_q^m$$

be the algorithms defined in Lemma 2.2, where we use $\mathcal{C}_{N,D}$ to denote the set of polynomial-size circuit from $\{0,1\}^N \to \{0,1\}$ with depth at most D, and let

$$\texttt{IPEvalPK} : (\mathbb{Z}_q^{n \times m})^k \times (\mathbb{Z}_q^{n \times m})^k \to \mathbb{Z}_q^{n \times m}$$
$$\texttt{IPEvalCT} : (\mathbb{Z}_q^{n \times m})^k \times (\mathbb{Z}_q^m)^k \times (\mathbb{Z}_q^m)^k \times \{0,1\}^k \to \mathbb{Z}_q^m$$

be the algorithms defined in Lemma 2.3.

We construct the private puncturable PRF $\texttt{PRF} = (\texttt{KeyGen}, \texttt{Eval}, \texttt{Constrain}, \texttt{ConstrainEval})$ with input space $\{0,1\}^l$ and output space $\mathbb{Z}_p$ as follows:

- **KeyGen.** On input the security parameter 1^λ, the key generation algorithm generates:

$$A_i \xleftarrow{\$} \mathbb{Z}_q^{n \times m} \quad \text{for } i \in [0, N]$$
$$B_i \xleftarrow{\$} \mathbb{Z}_q^{n \times m} \quad \text{for } i \in [1, k]$$
$$\bar{s} \xleftarrow{\$} \mathbb{Z}_q^{n-1} \quad s = (1, \bar{s}^\mathsf{T})^\mathsf{T} \quad v \xleftarrow{\$} \mathbb{Z}_q$$
$$k_\mathsf{H} \leftarrow \mathsf{H.KeyGen}(1^\lambda) \quad k_\mathsf{F} \leftarrow \mathsf{F.KeyGen}(1^\lambda)$$

and outputs the PRF key

$$K = ((A_i)_{i \in [0,N]}, (B_i)_{i \in [1,k]}, s, v, k_\mathsf{H}, k_\mathsf{F})$$

- **Eval.** On input the PRF key $K = ((A_i)_{i \in [0,N]}, (B_i)_{i \in [1,k]}, s, v, k_\mathsf{H}, k_\mathsf{F})$ and an input $x \in \{0,1\}^l$, the evaluation algorithm first computes $u = \mathsf{H.Eval}(k_\mathsf{H}, x)$. Then it computes

$$C_{j,\iota} = \texttt{EvalPK}(\mathsf{C}_{u,j,\iota}, A_0, \ldots, A_N) \quad \text{for } j \in [1, \varkappa], \iota \in [1, k]$$

and

$$D_j = \texttt{IPEvalPK}(C_{j,1}, \ldots, C_{j,k}, B_1, \ldots, B_k) \quad \text{for } j \in [1, \varkappa]$$

Finally, it computes

$$\bar{y} = (\sum_{j=1}^{\varkappa} s^\mathsf{T} \cdot D_j)[1] + v \mod q$$

and outputs

$$y = \lfloor \bar{y} \rfloor_p \mod p$$

- **Constrain.** The constraining algorithm takes as input the PRF key $K = ((A_i)_{i \in [0,N]}, (B_i)_{i \in [1,k]}, s, v, k_\mathsf{H}, k_\mathsf{F})$ and a set $\mathcal{P} \subset \{0,1\}^l$. Let $\mathcal{P} = \{x_1, \ldots, x_{|\mathcal{P}|}\}$, then for $i \in [1, |\mathcal{P}|]$, the constraining algorithm first prepares:

1. $u_i = \mathsf{H.Eval}(k_\mathsf{H}, x_i)$.
2. $(R_{\mathsf{K},i}, (R_{\mathsf{E},i,j})_{j\in[1,L+\varkappa]}, \bar{r}_i, \bar{t}_i, (R_{\mathsf{G},i,j})_{j\in[0,N+k]}) = \mathsf{F.Eval}(k_\mathsf{F}, u_i)$.
3. $t_i = \begin{pmatrix} 1 \\ \bar{t}_i \end{pmatrix}$.
4. $r_i = G_{1,q}^{-1}(\bar{r}_i)$.
5. $(pk_i, sk_i) = \mathsf{FHE.KeyGen}(1^\lambda, 1^d; R_{\mathsf{K},i})$.
6. $e_{i,j} = \mathsf{GS}(R_{\mathsf{G},i,j})$ for $j \in [0, N+k]$.

Next, it computes the ciphertexts

$$ct_{i,j} = \mathsf{FHE.Enc}(pk_i, u_i[j]; R_{\mathsf{E},i,j}) \quad \text{for } j \in [1, L]$$

$$ct_{i,L+j} = \mathsf{FHE.Enc}(pk_i, r_i[j]; R_{\mathsf{E},i,L+j}) \quad \text{for } j \in [1, \varkappa]$$

and encodes the ciphertexts and the secret key into matrices as

$$a_{i,0}^\mathsf{T} = t_i^\mathsf{T} \cdot (A_0 + G) + e_{i,0}^\mathsf{T}$$

$$a_{i,j}^\mathsf{T} = t_i^\mathsf{T} \cdot (A_j + ct_i[j] \cdot G) + e_{i,j}^\mathsf{T} \quad \text{for } j \in [1, N]$$

$$b_{i,j}^\mathsf{T} = t_i^\mathsf{T} \cdot (B_j + sk_i[j] \cdot G) + e_{i,N+j}^\mathsf{T} \quad \text{for } j \in [1, k]$$

where $ct_i = (ct_{i,1}\|\ldots\|ct_{i,L+\varkappa})$.
Besides, it computes

$$t_0 = s - \sum_{i=1}^{|\mathcal{P}|} t_i$$

and generates encodings of 0 as

$$e_{0,0} \leftarrow \tilde{D}_\sigma^m, \quad a_{0,0}^\mathsf{T} = t_0^\mathsf{T} \cdot (A_0 + G) + e_{0,0}^\mathsf{T}$$

$$e_{0,j} \leftarrow \tilde{D}_\sigma^m, \quad a_{0,j}^\mathsf{T} = t_0^\mathsf{T} \cdot (A_j + 0 \cdot G) + e_{0,j}^\mathsf{T} \quad \text{for } j \in [1, N]$$

$$e_{0,N+j} \leftarrow \tilde{D}_\sigma^m, \quad b_{0,j}^\mathsf{T} = t_0^\mathsf{T} \cdot (B_j + 0 \cdot G) + e_{0,N+j}^\mathsf{T} \quad \text{for } j \in [1, k]$$

Finally, the algorithm outputs:

$$CK = ((A_i)_{i\in[0,N]}, (B_i)_{i\in[1,k]}, v, k_\mathsf{H},$$
$$(a_{0,j})_{j\in[0,N]}, (b_{0,j})_{j\in[1,k]},$$
$$\{(a_{i,j})_{j\in[0,N]}, (b_{i,j})_{j\in[1,k]}, ct_i\}_{i\in[1,|\mathcal{P}|]})$$

- $\mathsf{ConstrainEval}$. On input the constrained key $CK = ((A_i)_{i\in[0,N]}, (B_i)_{i\in[1,k]},$ $v, k_\mathsf{H}, (a_{0,j})_{j\in[0,N]}, (b_{0,j})_{j\in[1,k]}, \{(a_{i,j})_{j\in[0,N]}, (b_{i,j})_{j\in[1,k]}, ct_i\}_{i\in[1,P]})$ and an input $x \in \{0,1\}^l$, the constrained evaluation algorithm first computes $u = \mathsf{H.Eval}(k_\mathsf{H}, x)$. Let $ct_0 = 0^N$, then for $i \in [0, P]$, $j \in [1, \varkappa]$, and $\iota \in [1, k]$, the algorithm computes

$$\widetilde{ct}_{i,j,\iota} = \mathsf{C}_{u,j,\iota}(ct_i)$$

$$c_{i,j,\iota} = \mathsf{EvalCT}(\mathsf{C}_{u,j,\iota}, A_0, \ldots, A_N, a_{i,0}, \ldots, a_{i,N}, ct_i)$$

Also, for $i \in [0, P]$ and $j \in [1, \varkappa]$, it computes

$$d_{i,j} = \texttt{IPEvalCT}(\boldsymbol{B}_1, \ldots, \boldsymbol{B}_k, \boldsymbol{c}_{i,j,1}, \ldots, \boldsymbol{c}_{i,j,k}, \boldsymbol{b}_{i,1}, \ldots, \boldsymbol{b}_{i,k}, \widetilde{ct}_{i,j,1}, \ldots, \widetilde{ct}_{i,j,k})$$

Finally, it computes

$$\bar{y} = (\sum_{i=0}^{P} \sum_{j=1}^{\varkappa} d_{i,j})[1] + v \mod q$$

and outputs

$$y = \lfloor \bar{y} \rfloor_p \mod p$$

Theorem 4.2. *If* FHE *is a secure FHE scheme with additional properties defined in Lemma 2.4,* H *is a secure explainable hash function, and* F *is a secure PRF, then* PRF *is a secure private puncturable PRF as defined in Sect. 4.1 assuming the hardness of* $LWE_{n-1,q,\tilde{D}_\sigma}$.

We present proof of Theorem 4.2 in the full version.

Parameters. Next, we give an instantiation for the parameters of PRF. Security of PRF relies on the hardness of $LWE_{n-1,q,\tilde{D}_\sigma}$ and $LWE_{O(k/\lceil \log q \rceil),q,\tilde{D}_\sigma}$, where the latter is required to guarantee the security of FHE. Besides, we require

$$q \geq 2^{L+\omega(\log \lambda)} \cdot p \cdot (2\Sigma + 1) \geq 2^{L+\omega(\log \lambda)} \cdot p \cdot 2^{\omega(\log \lambda)} \cdot \Sigma'$$
$$\geq 2^{L+\omega(\log \lambda)} \cdot p \cdot \varkappa \cdot \lambda \cdot \sigma \cdot (k^{O(d)} + k \cdot m^{O(D)})$$
$$\geq 2^{L+\omega(\log \lambda)} \cdot 2^{poly(\log \lambda, \log \log q)} \geq 2^{L+poly(\log \lambda, \log \log q)}$$

Let $\varepsilon \in (0, 1)$ be a constant real value. We set $k = O(n \cdot \lceil \log q \rceil)$, $n = (L + \lambda)^{\frac{1}{\varepsilon}}$ and $q = 2^{O(L+\lambda)}$. This makes the approximation factor $\gamma = O(nq/\sigma)$ of the underlying worst-case lattices problems to be $2^{O(n^\varepsilon)}$.

Now, assume that the input length and the output length are in $O(\lambda)$, then the size of the PRF key will be

$$|K| = (N+1) \cdot nm\lceil \log q \rceil + k \cdot nm\lceil \log q \rceil + n\lceil \log q \rceil + |k_\mathsf{H}| + |k_\mathsf{F}| = O(\lambda^{10+\frac{8}{\varepsilon}})$$

In addition, assume that the size of the puncture set is constant, then the size of the constrained key will be

$$|CK| = (N+1) \cdot nm\lceil \log q \rceil + k \cdot nm\lceil \log q \rceil + \lceil \log q \rceil + |k_\mathsf{H}| + |\mathcal{P}| \cdot (L+\kappa) \cdot c$$
$$+ (|\mathcal{P}|+1) \cdot ((N+1) \cdot m\lceil \log q \rceil + k \cdot m\lceil \log q \rceil) = O(\lambda^{10+\frac{8}{\varepsilon}})$$

Given the huge key sizes and the large approximation factor of the underlying lattice problems, our construction is far from practical. It is an interesting and challenging open problem to reduce the parameters and construct a practical private puncturable PRF with the desired security properties.

Acknowledgement. We appreciate the anonymous reviewers for their valuable comments.

References

[AF16]   Abusalah, H., Fuchsbauer, G.: Constrained PRFs for unbounded inputs with short keys. In: Manulis, M., Sadeghi, A.-R., Schneider, S. (eds.) ACNS 2016. LNCS, vol. 9696, pp. 445–463. Springer, Cham (2016). https://doi.org/10.1007/978-3-319-39555-5_24

[AFP16] Abusalah, H., Fuchsbauer, G., Pietrzak, K.: Constrained PRFs for unbounded inputs. In: Sako, K. (ed.) CT-RSA 2016. LNCS, vol. 9610, pp. 413–428. Springer, Cham (2016). https://doi.org/10.1007/978-3-319-29485-8_24

[AMN+18] Attrapadung, N., Matsuda, T., Nishimaki, R., Yamada, S., Yamakawa, T.: Constrained PRFs for NC^1 in traditional groups. In: Shacham, H., Boldyreva, A. (eds.) CRYPTO 2018. LNCS, vol. 10992, pp. 543–574. Springer, Cham (2018). https://doi.org/10.1007/978-3-319-96881-0_19

[AMN+19] Attrapadung, N., Matsuda, T., Nishimaki, R., Yamada, S., Yamakawa, T.: Adaptively single-key secure constrained PRFs for NC^1. In: Lin, D., Sako, K. (eds.) PKC 2019. LNCS, vol. 11443, pp. 223–253. Springer, Cham (2019). https://doi.org/10.1007/978-3-030-17259-6_8

[BB04]   Boneh, D., Boyen, X.: Secure identity based encryption without random Oracles. In: Franklin, M. (ed.) CRYPTO 2004. LNCS, vol. 3152, pp. 443–459. Springer, Heidelberg (2004). https://doi.org/10.1007/978-3-540-28628-8_27

[BFP+15] Banerjee, A., Fuchsbauer, G., Peikert, C., Pietrzak, K., Stevens, S.: Key-homomorphic constrained pseudorandom functions. In: Dodis, Y., Nielsen, J.B. (eds.) TCC 2015. LNCS, vol. 9015, pp. 31–60. Springer, Heidelberg (2015). https://doi.org/10.1007/978-3-662-46497-7_2

[BGG+14] Boneh, D., Gentry, C., Gorbunov, S., Halevi, S., Nikolaenko, V., Segev, G., Vaikuntanathan, V., Vinayagamurthy, D.: Fully key-homomorphic encryption, arithmetic circuit ABE and compact garbled circuits. In: Nguyen, P.Q., Oswald, E. (eds.) EUROCRYPT 2014. LNCS, vol. 8441, pp. 533–556. Springer, Heidelberg (2014). https://doi.org/10.1007/978-3-642-55220-5_30

[BGI14] Boyle, E., Goldwasser, S., Ivan, I.: Functional signatures and pseudorandom functions. In: Krawczyk, H. (ed.) PKC 2014. LNCS, vol. 8383, pp. 501–519. Springer, Heidelberg (2014). https://doi.org/10.1007/978-3-642-54631-0_29

[BGI15] Boyle, E., Gilboa, N., Ishai, Y.: Function secret sharing. In: Oswald, E., Fischlin, M. (eds.) EUROCRYPT 2015. LNCS, vol. 9057, pp. 337–367. Springer, Heidelberg (2015). https://doi.org/10.1007/978-3-662-46803-6_12

[Bit17] Bitansky, N.: Verifiable random functions from non-interactive witness-indistinguishable proofs. In: TCC, pp. 567–594. Springer (2017)

[BKM17] Boneh, D., Kim, S., Montgomery, H.: Private puncturable PRFs from standard lattice assumptions. In: Coron, J.-S., Nielsen, J.B. (eds.) EUROCRYPT 2017. LNCS, vol. 10210, pp. 415–445. Springer, Cham (2017). https://doi.org/10.1007/978-3-319-56620-7_15

[BKW17] Boneh, D., Kim, S., Wu, D.J.: Constrained keys for invertible pseudorandom functions. In: Kalai, Y., Reyzin, L. (eds.) TCC 2017. LNCS, vol. 10677, pp. 237–263. Springer, Cham (2017). https://doi.org/10.1007/978-3-319-70500-2_9

[BLP+13] Brakerski, Z., Langlois, A., Peikert, C., Regev, O., Stehlé, D.: Classical hardness of learning with errors. In: STOC, pp. 575–584 (2013)

[BLW17] Boneh, D., Lewi, K., Wu, D.J.: Constraining pseudorandom functions privately. In: Fehr, S. (ed.) PKC 2017. LNCS, vol. 10175, pp. 494–524. Springer, Heidelberg (2017). https://doi.org/10.1007/978-3-662-54388-7_17

[BTVW17] Brakerski, Z., Tsabary, R., Vaikuntanathan, V., Wee, H.: Private constrained PRFs (and More) from LWE. In: Kalai, Y., Reyzin, L. (eds.) TCC 2017. LNCS, vol. 10677, pp. 264–302. Springer, Cham (2017). https://doi.org/10.1007/978-3-319-70500-2_10

[BV15] Brakerski, Z., Vaikuntanathan, V.: Constrained key-homomorphic PRFs from standard lattice assumptions. In: Dodis, Y., Nielsen, J.B. (eds.) TCC 2015. LNCS, vol. 9015, pp. 1–30. Springer, Heidelberg (2015). https://doi.org/10.1007/978-3-662-46497-7_1

[BW13] Boneh, D., Waters, B.: Constrained pseudorandom functions and their applications. In: Sako, K., Sarkar, P. (eds.) ASIACRYPT 2013. LNCS, vol. 8270, pp. 280–300. Springer, Heidelberg (2013). https://doi.org/10.1007/978-3-642-42045-0_15

[BZ14] Boneh, D., Zhandry, M.: Multiparty key exchange, efficient traitor tracing, and more from indistinguishability obfuscation. In: Garay, J.A., Gennaro, R. (eds.) CRYPTO 2014. LNCS, vol. 8616, pp. 480–499. Springer, Heidelberg (2014). https://doi.org/10.1007/978-3-662-44371-2_27

[CC17] Canetti, R., Chen, Y.: Constraint-hiding constrained PRFs for NC^1 from LWE. In: Coron, J.-S., Nielsen, J.B. (eds.) EUROCRYPT 2017. LNCS, vol. 10210, pp. 446–476. Springer, Cham (2017). https://doi.org/10.1007/978-3-319-56620-7_16

[CDNO97] Canetti, R., Dwork, C., Naor, M., Ostrovsky, R.: Deniable encryption. In: Kaliski, B.S. (ed.) CRYPTO 1997. LNCS, vol. 1294, pp. 90–104. Springer, Heidelberg (1997). https://doi.org/10.1007/BFb0052229

[CHN+16] Cohen, A., Holmgren, J., Nishimaki, R., Vaikuntanathan, V., Wichs, D.: Watermarking cryptographic capabilities. In: STOC, pp. 1115–1127 (2016)

[CRV14] Chandran, N., Raghuraman, S., Vinayagamurthy, D.: Constrained pseudorandom functions: verifiable and delegatable. Cryptology ePrint Archive, Report 2014/522 (2014). https://ia.cr/2014/522

[CRV16] Chandran, N., Raghuraman, S., Vinayagamurthy, D.: Reducing depth in constrained PRFs: from bit-fixing to NC^1. In: Cheng, C.-M., Chung, K.-M., Persiano, G., Yang, B.-Y. (eds.) PKC 2016. LNCS, vol. 9615, pp. 359–385. Springer, Heidelberg (2016). https://doi.org/10.1007/978-3-662-49387-8_14

[CVW18] Chen, Y., Vaikuntanathan, V., Wee, H.: GGH15 beyond permutation branching programs: proofs, attacks, and candidates. In: Shacham, H., Boldyreva, A. (eds.) CRYPTO 2018. LNCS, vol. 10992, pp. 577–607. Springer, Cham (2018). https://doi.org/10.1007/978-3-319-96881-0_20

[DDM17] Datta, P., Dutta, R., Mukhopadhyay, S.: Constrained pseudorandom functions for unconstrained inputs revisited: achieving verifiability and key delegation. In: Fehr, S. (ed.) PKC 2017. LNCS, vol. 10175, pp. 463–493. Springer, Heidelberg (2017). https://doi.org/10.1007/978-3-662-54388-7_16

[DKN+20] Davidson, A., Katsumata, S., Nishimaki, R., Yamada, S., Yamakawa, T.: Adaptively secure constrained pseudorandom functions in the standard model. In: Micciancio, D., Ristenpart, T. (eds.) CRYPTO 2020. LNCS, vol. 12170, pp. 559–589. Springer, Cham (2020). https://doi.org/10.1007/978-3-030-56784-2_19

[DKW16] Deshpande, A., Koppula, V., Waters, B.: Constrained pseudorandom functions for unconstrained inputs. In: Fischlin, M., Coron, J.-S. (eds.) EUROCRYPT 2016. LNCS, vol. 9666, pp. 124–153. Springer, Heidelberg (2016). https://doi.org/10.1007/978-3-662-49896-5_5

[FHPS13] Freire, E.S.V., Hofheinz, D., Paterson, K.G., Striecks, C.: Programmable hash functions in the multilinear setting. In: Canetti, R., Garay, J.A. (eds.) CRYPTO 2013. LNCS, vol. 8042, pp. 513–530. Springer, Heidelberg (2013). https://doi.org/10.1007/978-3-642-40041-4_28

[FKPR14] Fuchsbauer, G., Konstantinov, M., Pietrzak, K., Rao, V.: Adaptive security of constrained PRFs. In: Sarkar, P., Iwata, T. (eds.) ASIACRYPT 2014. LNCS, vol. 8874, pp. 82–101. Springer, Heidelberg (2014). https://doi.org/10.1007/978-3-662-45608-8_5

[Fuc14] Fuchsbauer, G.: Constrained verifiable random functions. In: Abdalla, M., De Prisco, R. (eds.) SCN 2014. LNCS, vol. 8642, pp. 95–114. Springer, Cham (2014). https://doi.org/10.1007/978-3-319-10879-7_7

[GGM84] Goldreich, O., Goldwasser, S., Micali, S.: How to construct random functions. In: FOCS, pp. 464–479. IEEE (1984)

[GHKW17] Goyal, R., Hohenberger, S., Koppula, V., Waters, B.: A generic approach to constructing and proving verifiable random functions. In: Kalai, Y., Reyzin, L. (eds.) TCC 2017. LNCS, vol. 10678, pp. 537–566. Springer, Cham (2017). https://doi.org/10.1007/978-3-319-70503-3_18

[GI14] Gilboa, N., Ishai, Y.: Distributed point functions and their applications. In: Nguyen, P.Q., Oswald, E. (eds.) EUROCRYPT 2014. LNCS, vol. 8441, pp. 640–658. Springer, Heidelberg (2014). https://doi.org/10.1007/978-3-642-55220-5_35

[Gol08] Goldreich, O.: Computational complexity: a conceptual perspective. ACM SIGACT News 39(3), 35–39 (2008)

[GSW13] Gentry, C., Sahai, A., Waters, B.: Homomorphic encryption from learning with errors: conceptually-simpler, asymptotically-faster, attribute-based. In: Canetti, R., Garay, J.A. (eds.) CRYPTO 2013. LNCS, vol. 8042, pp. 75–92. Springer, Heidelberg (2013). https://doi.org/10.1007/978-3-642-40041-4_5

[GVW15] Gorbunov, S., Vaikuntanathan, V., Wee, H.: Predicate encryption for circuits from LWE. In: Gennaro, R., Robshaw, M. (eds.) CRYPTO 2015. LNCS, vol. 9216, pp. 503–523. Springer, Heidelberg (2015). https://doi.org/10.1007/978-3-662-48000-7_25

[HKKW19] Hofheinz, D., Kamath, A., Koppula, V., Waters, B.: Adaptively secure constrained pseudorandom functions. In: Goldberg, I., Moore, T. (eds.) FC 2019. LNCS, vol. 11598, pp. 357–376. Springer, Cham (2019). https://doi.org/10.1007/978-3-030-32101-7_22

[HKW15] Hohenberger, S., Koppula, V., Waters, B.: Adaptively secure puncturable pseudorandom functions in the standard model. In: Iwata, T., Cheon, J.H. (eds.) ASIACRYPT 2015. LNCS, vol. 9452, pp. 79–102. Springer, Heidelberg (2015). https://doi.org/10.1007/978-3-662-48797-6_4

[Jag15]   Jager, T.: Verifiable random functions from weaker assumptions. In: Dodis, Y., Nielsen, J.B. (eds.) TCC 2015. LNCS, vol. 9015, pp. 121–143. Springer, Heidelberg (2015). https://doi.org/10.1007/978-3-662-46497-7_5

[JKK+17] Jafargholi, Z., Kamath, C., Klein, K., Komargodski, I., Pietrzak, K., Wichs, D.: Be adaptive, avoid overcommitting. In: Katz, J., Shacham, H. (eds.) CRYPTO 2017. LNCS, vol. 10401, pp. 133–163. Springer, Cham (2017). https://doi.org/10.1007/978-3-319-63688-7_5

[KPTZ13] Kiayias, A., Papadopoulos, S., Triandopoulos, N., Zacharias, T.: Delegatable pseudorandom functions and applications. In: CCS, pp. 669–684. ACM (2013)

[KW17]   Kim, S., Wu, D.J.: Watermarking cryptographic functionalities from standard lattice assumptions. In: Katz, J., Shacham, H. (eds.) CRYPTO 2017. LNCS, vol. 10401, pp. 503–536. Springer, Cham (2017). https://doi.org/10.1007/978-3-319-63688-7_17

[KW19]   Kim, S., Wu, D.J.: Watermarking PRFs from lattices: stronger security via extractable PRFs. In: Boldyreva, A., Micciancio, D. (eds.) CRYPTO 2019. LNCS, vol. 11694, pp. 335–366. Springer, Cham (2019). https://doi.org/10.1007/978-3-030-26954-8_11

[LST18]   Libert, B., Stehlé, D., Titiu, R.: Adaptively secure distributed PRFs from LWE. In: Beimel, A., Dziembowski, S. (eds.) TCC 2018. LNCS, vol. 11240, pp. 391–421. Springer, Cham (2018). https://doi.org/10.1007/978-3-030-03810-6_15

[Lys02]   Lysyanskaya, A.: Unique signatures and verifiable random functions from the DH-DDH separation. In: Yung, M. (ed.) CRYPTO 2002. LNCS, vol. 2442, pp. 597–612. Springer, Heidelberg (2002). https://doi.org/10.1007/3-540-45708-9_38

[Lyu12]   Lyubashevsky, V.: Lattice signatures without trapdoors. In: Pointcheval, D., Johansson, T. (eds.) EUROCRYPT 2012. LNCS, vol. 7237, pp. 738–755. Springer, Heidelberg (2012). https://doi.org/10.1007/978-3-642-29011-4_43

[MP12]   Micciancio, D., Peikert, C.: Trapdoors for lattices: simpler, tighter, faster, smaller. In: Pointcheval, D., Johansson, T. (eds.) EUROCRYPT 2012. LNCS, vol. 7237, pp. 700–718. Springer, Heidelberg (2012). https://doi.org/10.1007/978-3-642-29011-4_41

[Pei09]   Peikert, C.: Public-key cryptosystems from the worst-case shortest vector problem. In: STOC, pp. 333–342 (2009)

[PS18]   Peikert, C., Shiehian, S.: Privately constraining and programming PRFs, the LWE way. In: Abdalla, M., Dahab, R. (eds.) PKC 2018. LNCS, vol. 10770, pp. 675–701. Springer, Cham (2018). https://doi.org/10.1007/978-3-319-76581-5_23

[PS20]   Peikert, C., Shiehian, S.: Constraining and watermarking PRFs from milder assumptions. In: Kiayias, A., Kohlweiss, M., Wallden, P., Zikas, V. (eds.) PKC 2020. LNCS, vol. 12110, pp. 431–461. Springer, Cham (2020). https://doi.org/10.1007/978-3-030-45374-9_15

[PTW20] Peter, N., Tsabary, R., Wee, H.: One-one constrained pseudorandom functions. In: ITC (2020)

[Reg04]   Regev, O.: Lattices in computer science-average case hardness. Lecture Notes for Class (scribe: Elad Verbin) (2004)

[Reg05]   Regev, O.: On lattices, learning with errors, random linear codes, and cryptography. In: STOC, pp. 84–93. ACM (2005)

[SS96]   Sipser, M., Spielman, D.A.: Expander codes. IEEE Trans. Inf. Theory **42**(6), 1710–1722 (1996)

[SWP00] Song, D.X., Wagner, D., Perrig, A.:. Practical techniques for searches on encrypted data. In: S&P, pp. 44–55. IEEE (2000)

[YAYX20] Yang, R., Au, M.H., Yu, Z., Xu, Q.: Collusion resistant watermarkable PRFs from standard assumptions. In: Micciancio, D., Ristenpart, T. (eds.) CRYPTO 2020. LNCS, vol. 12170, pp. 590–620. Springer, Cham (2020). https://doi.org/10.1007/978-3-030-56784-2_20

[Zém01] Zémor, G.: On expander codes. IEEE Trans. Inf. Theory **47**(2), 835–837 (2001)

Constrained Pseudorandom Functions from Homomorphic Secret Sharing

Geoffroy Couteau[1], Pierre Meyer[1,2(✉)], Alain Passelègue[3,4],
and Mahshid Riahinia[4]

[1] Université Paris Cité, CNRS, IRIF, Paris, France
`couteau@irif.fr`
[2] Reichman University, Herzliya, Israel
`pierre.meyer@irif.fr`
[3] Inria, Paris, France
`alain.passelegue@inria.fr`
[4] ENS de Lyon, Laboratoire LIP (U. Lyon, CNRS, ENSL, Inria, UCBL), Paris,
France
`mahshid.riahinia@ens-lyon.fr`

Abstract. We propose and analyze a simple strategy for constructing
1-key constrained pseudorandom functions (CPRFs) from homomorphic
secret sharing. In the process, we obtain the following contributions: first,
we identify desirable properties for the underlying HSS scheme for our
strategy to work. Second, we show that (most of) recent existing HSS
schemes satisfy these properties, leading to instantiations of CPRFs for
various constraints and from various assumptions. Notably, we obtain
the first (1-key selectively secure, private) CPRFs for inner-product and
(1-key selectively secure) CPRFs for NC^1 from the DCR assumption,
and more. Last, we revisit two applications of HSS equipped with these
additional properties to secure computation: we obtain secure computation in the silent preprocessing model with one party being able to
precompute its whole preprocessing material before even knowing the
other party, and we construct one-sided statistically secure computation
with sublinear communication for restricted forms of computation.

1 Introduction

Since their introduction in [21], pseudorandom functions (PRFs) have played a
central role in modern cryptography and numerous extensions have been proposed. Of particular interest is the notion of constrained pseudorandom functions (CPRFs), introduced concurrently in [5,9,25]. Recall that a PRF is a fam-
ily of keyed functions $\{F_k\}_{k\in\mathcal{K}} : \mathcal{X} \to \mathcal{Y}$ such that the input-output behavior of any randomly selected F_k should be computationally indistinguishable
from that of a truly random function with same domain and range (without
any knowledge of k). Constrained pseudorandom functions for a class of constraints $\mathcal{C}$ extend PRFs by allowing to delegate partial evaluation keys ck_C for

© International Association for Cryptologic Research 2023
C. Hazay and M. Stam (Eds.): EUROCRYPT 2023, LNCS 14006, pp. 194–224, 2023.
https://doi.org/10.1007/978-3-031-30620-4_7

any $C : \mathcal{X} \rightarrow \{0,1\} \in \mathcal{C}$, termed constrained keys, generated from the master secret key k as $\mathsf{ck}_C \leftarrow \mathsf{Constrain}(k, C)$. A partial key allows to compute $F_k(x)$ for any input x such that $C(x) = 0$, by running a constrained evaluation algorithm $\mathsf{CEval}(\mathsf{ck}_C, x)$, while preserving pseudorandomness of evaluations on inputs x satisfying $C(x) = 1$[1]. A constrained PRF can further be private, or constraint-hiding, if a constrained key hides the constraint C. Significant efforts have been made to obtain CPRFs for broad classes of constraints from various assumptions in the recent years [2,3,11–13,16,19,23,28]. As of today, CPRFs for simple class of constraints (e.g., point functions or constant-degree CNFs) are known from minimal assumptions (e.g., from one-way functions [19,21]). Yet, constructing CPRFs for broader classes of constraints such as NC^1 has proven notoriously hard. While (private) CPRFs for NC^1 and even $\mathsf{P/poly}$ exist based on the learning with errors assumption (with subexponential modulus-to-noise ratio) [11,12], other families of standard assumptions have so far failed to provide advanced constructions, except for one construction for NC^1 based on an exotic Q-type variant of DDH over the group of quadratic residues modulo a safe prime $q = 2p + 1$, and the DDH assumption [2].

This serious lack of constructions remains when considering simpler classes of constraints such as inner products ($C(x) = 0$ iff $\langle x, y \rangle = 0$ for some fixed vector y), despite the large amount of work on inner-product-based encryption in other contexts (e.g., for attribute-based encryption or functional encryption) and the recent lattice-based CPRF for inner-product [19].

In this work, we draw connections between constrained pseudorandom functions and homomorphic secret sharing (HSS), a notion introduced by Boyle et al. in [8]. One of our main contributions is to construct CPRFs for inner-product as well as for NC^1 via HSS, leading to instantiations from a wide variety of assumptions thanks to the recent developments in HSS [1,27,29]. Before describing in more details our contributions, we briefly remind the definition of HSS. An HSS scheme for a class of functions $\mathcal{F}$ allows to generate a public key pk and two evaluations keys $\mathsf{ek}_0, \mathsf{ek}_1$, such that one can securely share an input x into two shares $(\mathsf{I}_0, \mathsf{I}_1) \leftarrow \mathsf{Input}(\mathsf{pk}, x)$ such that, given one of the two evaluation keys: each share computationally hides x, and it is possible to *homomorphically evaluate* any function $f \in \mathcal{F}$ on the shares of x as $y_b = \mathsf{Eval}(\mathsf{ek}_b, \mathsf{I}_b, f)$, for $b \in \{0,1\}$. Moreover, the resulting shares satisfy $y_1 - y_0 = f(x)$. Since its introduction, HSS has found numerous applications in cryptography and beyond, and notably for (1) low-communication secure computation [8], and for (2) secure computation with *silent* preprocessing [7,27]. In this work, we also revisit the latter applications. Again, we briefly remind them before diving into the details of our contributions. A long-standing problem in secure computation had been to achieve communication smaller than the circuit size (for rich classes of functions). It was first solved via fully-homomorphic encryption (FHE) [20]. To securely compute a function f on their respective private inputs x and y, Alice and Bob can use the following protocol: Alice sends to Bob an FHE encryption of x, and Bob homomorphically

---

[1] The inverse condition is often used (pseudorandomness if $C(x) = 0$ and partial evaluation if $C(x) = 1$). Our choice slightly simplifies our constructions.

computes an encryption of $f(x, y)$ by evaluating $f(\cdot, y)$. He then sends back the result to Alice who can recover $f(x, y)$ by decrypting. Homomorphic secret sharing leads to another solution to this problem, by first having Alice and Bob compute shares of x and y (which is independent of circuit size) and then locally compute shares of $f(x, y)$.

Regarding secure computation in the preprocessing model, a protocol is split in two phases: a first *preprocessing phase* run ahead-of-time (independently of inputs and function to compute) in which Alice and Bob *jointly* generate long, correlated random strings, and a second *online phase* where the actual secure computation takes place. In the latter phase, the former correlated random strings are consumed by a fast, non-cryptographic, information-theoretic secure computation protocol. Homomorphic secret sharing enables secure computation with *silent* preprocessing: a short one-time interaction allows Alice and Bob to generate short keys, from which they can later *locally* (*i.e.*, without any interaction) stretch arbitrarily long correlated (pseudo-)random strings, which are later used in the online phase. Effectively, this pushes almost all the computational overhead of the preprocessing phase to a purely local computation.

1.1   Our Contributions

In this work, we show how to use homomorphic secret sharing schemes towards constructing constrained pseudorandom functions for rich classes of constraints and from new assumptions. Our main contributions are threefold.

Extending HSS Properties. We identify two natural extensions of homomorphic secret sharing, which we term respectively *homomorphic secret sharing with simulatable memory shares* and *staged homomorphic secret sharing*. At a high level, both notions capture the ability to perform some limited form of *programming* of HSS shares, *i.e.*, to construct one of the two HSS shares of an input x before knowing x. It turns out that most of known HSS constructions already achieve these extensions, leading to constructions based on a wide variety of assumptions.

New Constructions of CPRFs. Combining our extensions of HSS with any standard PRF with evaluation in NC^1 (which is known from every assumption implying HSS), we construct: (1) CPRFs for inner-product, starting with any HSS with simulatable memory shares with statistical correctness, and (2) CPRFs for NC^1 starting with any staged HSS with statistical correctness. This leads to the following statement.

Theorem 1 (informal). *Assuming any of the following assumptions:*

- *the DCR assumption,*
- *the hardness of the Joye-Libert encryption scheme,*
- *the DDH and DXDH assumptions over class groups,*
- *the Hard Subgroup Membership assumption over class groups,*
- *the LWE assumption with super-polynomial modulus-to-noise ratio,*

there exist (1-key, selectively secure) private CPRFs for inner product, and (1-key, selectively secure) CPRFs for NC^1.

Our results significantly expand the set of assumptions known to imply CPRFs for rich classes of constraints. In particular, our CPRF for NC^1 from DCR yields the first construction of a CPRF for a rich class of constraints from a well-established standard assumption beyond LWE-based constructions.

Revisiting Applications of HSS to Secure Computation. Equipped with our additional properties for HSS, we revisit two standard applications, namely secure computation with silent preprocessing, and secure computation with sublinear communication, and obtain the following results.

Precomputable Secure Computation with Silent Preprocessing. As described above, secure computation with silent preprocessing requires a short initial interaction before being able to run the heavy local preprocessing. In particular, the parties need to have decided *who* they will execute a secure computation protocol with. In contrast, we show that using staged HSS allows to build a silent preprocessing protocol where one of the parties (say, Alice) can entirely run the heavy offline computation *before she even knows the identity of Bob* (and in particular, before she interacts with Bob). This means that Alice can, at any point, locally generate (her share of) long pseudorandom correlated strings and store them for later use. Then, when she meets someone she wants to securely compute a function with in the future, she can execute the short, one-time interactive protocol (with little communication and computation), and be done with the preprocessing phase. Of course, the other party still needs to execute the heavy offline computation after their interaction[2]. We call this model secure computation with *precomputable* silent preprocessing; it is especially well suited to a client-server setting, where a weak client (Alice) wants to start the bulk of the computation a long time in advance, whereas the powerful server can run the heavy computation after its interaction with the client.

One-Sided Statistically Secure Computation with Sublinear Communication. A core feature of FHE-based sublinear secure computation is that it achieves *one-sided statistical security* when using an FHE scheme with statistical circuit-privacy, since homomorphic evaluation of $f(\cdot, y)$ leaks *statistically* no information about y beyond $f(x, y)$. In other words, Bob's security in the aforementioned protocol holds unconditionally. One-sided statistical security is a desirable security notion and can be achieved quite easily if we do not require sublinear communication, e.g., by using the seminal GMW protocol [22] with a one-sided statistically secure oblivious transfer [26] (to our knowledge, this was first observed in [15]). Yet, as of today, one-sided statistically secure computation with sublinear communication is *only known from FHE*: all HSS-based constructions inherently achieve only computational security for both parties.

---

[2] It is not too hard to see that having *both* parties execute the bulk of the computation prior to interacting (while keeping a non-cryptographic online phase) is impossible.

Using staged HSS, we obtain the first non-FHE-based constructions of one-sided statistically secure protocols with sublinear communication. Concretely, we obtain secure computation for any log log-depth circuits with optimal communication, where x remains statistically hidden, provided that $|x| < |y|/\text{poly}(\lambda)$ (where $\text{poly}(\lambda)$ denotes some fixed polynomial), via a black-box use of staged HSS. We also get secure computation of any layered arithmetic circuit C of size s over a sufficiently large ring $\mathbb{Z}_n$, with sublinear communication $O(s/\log\log s)$ and one-sided statistical security (without any restriction on the statistically protected input size), assuming the Paillier encryption scheme is circular-secure. The latter construction is non-black box and exploits the specific structure of a concrete Paillier-based staged HSS scheme from [27].

2   Technical Overview

2.1   General Strategy

Let us first explain a (partly wrong but insightful) strategy for constructing CPRFs from HSS. Let F denote a pseudorandom function with keyspace $\mathcal{K}$ and domain $\mathcal{X}$, and let $\mathcal{C} : \mathcal{X} \mapsto \{0,1\}$ be a class of constraints. Consider an HSS scheme $\text{HSS} = (\text{Setup}, \text{Input}, \text{Eval})$ for a class of programs $\mathcal{P}$ such that it contains all functions $f_x : (k, C) \mapsto C(x) \cdot F_k(x)$, for all $x \in \mathcal{X}$. Then, we consider the following construction.

- $\text{KeyGen}(1^\lambda, \mathcal{C})$: sample a PRF key $K \xleftarrow{\$} \mathcal{K}$. Run $(\text{pk}, \text{ek}_0, \text{ek}_1) \leftarrow \text{Setup}(1^\lambda)$, $(\text{I}_0^k, \text{I}_1^k) \leftarrow \text{Input}(\text{pk}, k)$, and $(\text{I}_0^C, \text{I}_1^C) \leftarrow \text{Input}(\text{pk}, C)$. Set $\text{pp} \leftarrow \text{pk}$ and $\text{msk} \leftarrow (\text{ek}_0, \text{ek}_1, \text{I}_0^k, \text{I}_1^k, \text{I}_0^C, \text{I}_1^C)$.
- $\text{Constrain}(\text{msk}, C)$: parse msk as $(\text{ek}_0, \text{ek}_1, \text{I}_0^k, \text{I}_1^k, \text{I}_0^C, \text{I}_1^C)$ and output $\text{ck}_C \leftarrow (\text{ek}_1, \text{I}_1^k, \text{I}_1^C)$.
- $\text{Eval}(\text{pp}, \text{msk}, x)$: run $y_0 \leftarrow \text{Eval}(0, \text{ek}_0, \text{I}_0^k, \text{I}_0^C, f_x)$ and output y_0.
- $\text{CEval}(\text{pp}, \text{ck}_C, x)$: run $y_1 \leftarrow \text{Eval}(1, \text{ek}_1, \text{I}_1^k, \text{I}_1^C, f_x)$ and output y_1.

By correctness of the HSS scheme, for any input x, we have $y_1 - y_0 = C(x) \cdot F_k(x)$. Therefore, if $C(x) = 0$, $y_1 = y_0$ i.e. the CEval algorithm outputs the same value as the evaluation with msk. Yet, if $C(x) = 1$, $y_1 = y_0 + F_k(x)$ and y_0 is pseudorandom, even given y_1 (and ck_C).

The problem with the above construction is that the master secret key does depend on the constraint C while it should be independent of it[3]. A way around this issue would be to use an HSS scheme with *programmable input shares*, i.e., a scheme where I_0^C can be generated before knowing C, and the second share I_1^C can be constructed afterwards from I_0^C and C, when the constraint is chosen. Unfortunately, the only known constructions of HSS with such a strong programmability feature rely on powerful primitives such as threshold FHE. As

---

[3] If the key could depend on C, one could just generate two independent PRF keys k_0, k_1 and define the evaluation as $F_{k_{C(x)}}(x)$. Revealing k_0 then allows to compute the evaluation on any x such that $C(x) = 0$ and reveals nothing about the key k_1 used when $C(x) = 1$.

FHE-style constructions of CPRFs for all circuits are already known, this would defeat the purpose of obtaining constructions based on new assumptions. In this work, we identify weaker properties which still suffice to instantiate the above template, yet are achieved by most of known HSS constructions.

2.2 CPRF from HSS with Simulatable Memory Shares

As a start, we propose a first simple solution to circumvent the lack of programmability. This first property already allows to handle simple forms of constraints such as inner-product, and follows from the common design of HSS constructions. We start by providing a high-level description of HSS schemes, which applies to essentially all known HSS constructions (beside FHE-based constructions).

HSS schemes rely on an additively homomorphic encryption scheme with some form of linear decryption. The public key of the HSS scheme is the public key pk of the underlying encryption scheme, and evaluation keys ek_0, ek_1 are additive shares of the underlying secret key s. A scheme uses two types of data: (1) **Input shares** (I_0, I_1) which are generated by running $Input(pk, x)$ on some input x and consist in an encryption of $(x, x \cdot s)$, and (2) **Memory shares** (M_0, M_1) which are typically additive shares of $(x, x \cdot s)$ over $\mathbb{Z}$. Two types of operations are handled: **Additions of memory shares** (simply add the shares as $(x, x \cdot s) + (y, y \cdot s) = (x + y, (x + y) \cdot s))$, and a restricted form of **Multiplication**. Specifically, multiplication can only be performed between an *input share* of some value x and a *memory share* of some value y, and returns a *memory share* of their product $x \cdot y$. Typically, multiplication uses the memory share $(y, y \cdot s)$ to "linearly multiply-and-decrypt" the encryption of $(x, x \cdot s)$, getting some encoding of $(xy, xy \cdot s)$. Then, the encoding is converted into a valid memory share using a specific procedure, which depends on the concrete scheme and is often a form of *distributed discrete logarithm*. We provide more details about multiplication later. Note that one can transform any input share into a memory share of the same value by multiplying it with a memory share of 1. At the end of a computation, each party recovers a memory value consisting in an additive share of $(z, z \cdot s)$, and therefore a share of the result z by dropping the second part. One can evaluate any polynomial-size program following the above restrictions, which precisely corresponds to *restricted multiplication straight-line* (RMS) programs, and encompasses branching programs, NC^1, and more.

HSS with Simulatable Memory Shares. Our starting point is the result of two observations. First, we observe that any HSS following the above structure does in fact allow for a limited form of programming regarding memory values. Indeed, while input shares include a homomorphic encryption of the input (which cannot be generated without knowing the input), *memory shares* are simply additive shares. Thus, we can always *simulate* a memory share of one party before knowing the value to share, by generating a first random share u. The other share is later set to $x - u$ when the actual value x to share is known.

Second, we remark that two parties sharing input shares of some values $(x_1, \ldots, x_n)$ as well as memory shares of a value z can compute memory shares of $z \cdot P(x_1, \ldots, x_n)$ for any RMS program P. The trick is to evaluate all the operations of P "with z in front", i.e. by maintaining as an invariant that any memory share for any value y that should be used in the computation is replaced by a memory share for the value $z \cdot y$. This invariant being preserved by the two RMS operations (addition and multiplication), it is sufficient to guarantee that every memory value satisfies it when created. This is simply done by transforming an input x into a memory value by multiplying it with the memory share of z in order to get a memory share for $z \cdot x$ rather than for x.

CPRF for Linear Constraints. Combining these two observations leads to constructions of constrained PRFs for linear constraints (and in particular for inner-product). Looking back to the construction aforementioned, we just would like to be able to generate I_0^C, the share of C used for evaluation with the master secret key, without knowing the constraint C in advance. We do it by replacing I_0^C by a simulated *memory share* M_0 of the (yet unknown) constraint C. The constrained key for C is then computed from M_0 and C to generate the appropriate memory share M_1 (i.e. setting M_1 such that $M_0 + M_1 = C$).

While this prevents the need for knowing the constraint ahead of time, this comes with a price: we now get a memory share of C rather than an input share, which reduces the set of functions one can evaluate. Still, thanks to our second observation, having a memory share of C and an input share of k allows to compute shares of $C \cdot P(k)$ for any RMS program P. Moreover, given memory shares of multiple C_i's, one can then compute any linear combination of shares $C_i \cdot P(k)$, by summing the latter additive shares. Notably, this allows computing shares of $\langle C, x \rangle \cdot F_k(x)$ as long as the function $k \mapsto F_k(x)$ is an RMS program (assuming F is in NC^1 is sufficient for that purpose).

We just constructed constrained pseudorandom functions for inner-product from any assumption that suffices to construct an HSS scheme for RMS programs satisfying the above conditions. For example, using the recent HSS scheme of [27] yields a CPRF for inner products over $\mathbb{Z}$ (or any integer ring) under the DCR assumption (which also implies PRFs in NC^1). The construction extends immediately to any constant-degree polynomial constraints (by memory-sharing all the coefficients of C). It achieves 1-key selective security, as well as *constraint privacy*. To the best of our knowledge, this is the first construction of (1-key, selective, private) CPRF for inner products that does not rely on LWE.

Security analysis proceeds through a sequence of hybrid games. Recall that the adversary is given a constrained key ck_C of its choice, and access to an evaluation oracle $\mathsf{Eval}(\mathsf{pp}, \mathsf{msk}, \cdot)$. We first modify the evaluation oracle to return $C(x) \cdot F_K(x) + \mathsf{CEval}(\mathsf{pp}, k_C, x)$ on query x. By correctness of the HSS, the adversary's view remains identical to its view in the previous game though the game no longer relies in msk (and in particular now only relies on the evaluation key ek_1 from ck_C). This let us replace the input share I_1 of k in ck_C by an input share of a dummy value, thanks to HSS security. Then, the adversary does no longer have any information about k except in the evaluations, and we can use PRF security to replace evaluations of $F_K(\cdot)$ by truly random values, therefore proving pseudorandomness. Constraint privacy is proven in a similar fashion.

2.3   Handling More Constraints via Staged HSS

While the above already offers enough flexibility to evaluate linear functions (and extensions thereof, such as low-degree polynomials), we still cannot handle general computations like NC^1 circuits. To overcome this limitation, we show by a deeper analysis of known HSS schemes that most of them also achieve some specific, limited form of programmability, which turns out to be sufficient to construct CPRFs for all RMS programs (hence in particular for NC^1).

Concretely, for a vector $\mathbf{u} = (u_1, \ldots, u_\ell)$, our core observation is that it is possible to share $\mathbf{u}$ between parties P_0 and P_1 with two alternate sharing algorithms $(\overline{\mathsf{Input}}_0, \overline{\mathsf{Input}}_1)$ such that: (1) P_0's share of $\mathbf{u}$, obtained from $\overline{\mathsf{Input}}_0$, is *independent* of $\mathbf{u}$ (and can be generated without $\mathbf{u}$), (2) P_0 and P_1 can use specific $\overline{\mathsf{Eval}}_0, \overline{\mathsf{Eval}}_1$ evaluation algorithms to produce memory shares of $P(\mathbf{u})$ for any RMS program P, *provided that P_1 knows $\mathbf{u}$ in the clear*. We call staged-HSS an HSS scheme satisfying the latter properties, as it intuitively allows to split share generation and evaluation in 2 stages: a first *input-independent* stage, corresponding to P_0's view, and a second *input-dependent* stage corresponding to P_1's view.

At first sight, staged-HSS might not seem particularly useful: if P_1 knows $\mathbf{u}$ in the clear, then P_1 can already compute $P(\mathbf{u})$ for any RMS program P. The key observation is that P_0 and P_1 get *memory shares* of $P(\mathbf{u})$, and not just $P(\mathbf{u})$. This memory share can then be combined with the prior observations to let P_0, P_1 compute additive shares of $P(\mathbf{u}) \cdot Q(\mathbf{v})$, for any other RMS program P, Q, given *input shares* of $\mathbf{v}$. Setting $\mathbf{u}$ to be the description of the constraint C, P to be a universal circuit (with input x hardwired) which on input C returns $C(x)$, $\mathbf{v}$ to be a PRF key k, and Q to be the RMS program (with x hardwired) which on input k returns $F_k(x)$, parties P_0 and P_1 can then compute shares of $C(x) \cdot F_k(x)$, with shares of P_0 being independent of C. We can then instantiate our simple aforementioned strategy for constructing CPRFs while circumventing the need for C during KeyGen. As a result, we obtain (1-key selective) CPRFs for RMS programs (and therefore for NC^1) from any staged-HSS, i.e. from a wide variety of assumptions (including DCR [27,29], class groups assumptions, or variants of QR [1,14], and more.). The security analysis is similar to our construction for inner-product, though this new construction is no longer constraint-hiding, since the CEval algorithm now relies on knowing C (i.e. $\mathbf{u}$ above) in clear.

It remains to explain why known HSS schemes are also staged-HSS schemes. To illustrate this, we use the simple ElGamal-based HSS scheme from [8][4]. We assume basic knowledge of ElGamal encryption in what follows. This scheme follows the general structure detailed above by instantiating the additively homomorphic encryption scheme with ElGamal encryption. That is, an *input share* for x is an ElGamal encryption of the pair $(x, x \cdot s)$[5], i.e. a tuple $(c_0, c_0', c_1, c_1') =$

---

[4] This scheme does not yield CPRFs as it does not achieve statistical correctness, but staged-HSS is easily illustrated with it.

[5] Actually of x and $x \cdot s_i$'s for each bit s_i of s.

$(g^{r_0}, h^{r_0} \cdot g^x, g^{r_1}, h^{r_1} \cdot g^{x \cdot s})$ with $s \in \mathbb{Z}_p$ being the secret key, $h = g^s$ being the public key, and $r_0, r_1 \xleftarrow{\$} \mathbb{Z}_p$ encryption randomness[6].

Multiplication between an input share (c_0, c_0', c_1, c_1') of x and a memory share $(\alpha_\sigma, \beta_\sigma)$ of y (which is just an additive share of $(y, y \cdot s)$ over $\mathbb{Z}_p$ owned by party P_σ) is done as follows. First, party P_σ computes $g_\sigma \leftarrow (c_0')^{\alpha_\sigma}/c_0^{\beta_\sigma}$. Observe that $g_0 \cdot g_1 = (c_0')^{\alpha_0 + \alpha_1}/c_0^{\beta_0 + \beta_1} = (g^{sr} \cdot g^x)^y/(g^r)^{sy} = g^{xy}$. Hence, parties get *multiplicative shares* g_0, g_1 of g^{xy}. Doing the same with c_1, c_1' allows to get multiplicative shares of $g^{xy \cdot s}$. Then, an operation termed *distributed discrete logarithm* allows to transform these multiplicative shares of $(g^{xy}, g^{xy \cdot s})$ into additive shares of $(xy, xy \cdot s)$, i.e. memory shares for the value xy, as desired. Despite being at the core of HSS constructions, the details of the distributed discrete logarithm procedure do not matter here. The only important observation is that the $c_i = g^{r_i}$ components of input shares are independent of the input x; only the c_i' components actually depend on x. Furthermore, in the multiplication above, the only place where c_i' is involved is in the computation of $g_\sigma \leftarrow (c_i')^{\alpha_\sigma}/c_i^{\beta_\sigma}$. Now, assume that one of the parties, say, P_1, already knows y in the clear: in this case, one can simply define $\alpha_1 \leftarrow y$ and $\alpha_0 \leftarrow 0$, which form valid additive shares of y. But now, P_0 does no longer need to know c_i' components either, since we now have $g_0 = 1/(c_i)^{\beta_0}$.

2.4   Applications of Staged HSS to Secure Computation

From a different angle, staged HSS allows Alice and Bob, respectively owning private inputs x and y, to securely retrieve, given shares of their joint input (x, y), additive shares of $f(x) \cdot g(y)$ for any RMS programs f, g, and even of any $P(x, y) = \sum_{i=1}^m f_i(x) \cdot g_i(y)$, where the (f_i, g_i) are RMS programs since additive shares can be added.

Secure Computation with Precomputable Silent Preprocessing. In this setting, the goal of the preprocessing phase is to securely distribute *correlated randomness* of a particular form (e.g., random oblivious transfers, vector-OLE, batch-OLE, Beaver triples, authenticated Beaver triples, etc.) which can be seen as special cases of the following general additive correlation: Alice receives random vectors $(\mathbf{r}^A, \mathbf{s}^A)$ and Bob receives random vectors $(\mathbf{r}^B, \mathbf{s}^B)$, such that $\mathbf{s}^A$ and $\mathbf{s}^B$ form additive shares of the tuple $\mathbf{s} = (Q_1(\mathbf{r}^A, \mathbf{r}^B), \cdots, Q_m(\mathbf{r}^A, \mathbf{r}^B))$, where $Q_1, \ldots, Q_m$ are public low-degree polynomials. To *silently* distribute such (pseudorandom) correlations, Alice and Bob can use a generic secure computation protocol to distribute HSS shares of two PRF keys (k_A, k_B) sampled by Alice and Bob respectively. Then, Alice locally defines $\mathbf{r}^A \leftarrow (F_{k_A}(1), \cdots, F_{k_A}(n))$, and Bob does the same with F_{k_B}. Both of them also compute their share $\mathbf{s}^A$ and $\mathbf{s}^B$ by homomorphically evaluating the program P_i for $i \leq m$ with their share of (k_A, k_B), where P_i is defined as:

$$P_i : (k_A, k_B) \to Q_i((F_{k_A}(1), \cdots, F_{k_A}(n)), (F_{k_B}(1), \cdots, F_{k_B}(n))).$$

---

[6] s is encrypted bit-by-bit in the actual construction.

Note that, as long as F is in NC^1 and Q_i is a constant-degree polynomial, P_i remains in NC^1. We now observe that when Q_i is a constant-degree polynomial, the program P_i can always be (publicly) rewritten as

$$P_i(k_A, k_B) = \sum_{j=1}^{M} \alpha_j \cdot \prod_{i \in S_A^j} F_{k_A}(i) \cdot \prod_{i \in S_B^j} F_{k_B}(i) = \sum_{j=1}^{M} f_j(k_A) \cdot g_j(k_B),$$

where S_A^i, S_B^i are public subsets of $[n]$, by writing Q_i in algebraic normal form and separating the component of each monomial depending on whether they are computed using k_A or k_B. Above, each of the f_j, g_j functions belong to NC^1. Therefore, P_i belongs to the class of programs supported by our staged HSS construction. Furthermore, Bob always knows his input k_B in the clear. Therefore, using staged HSS, Alice can generate the HSS shares of k_A together with the *input-independent* share of k_B, and she can locally compute $(\mathbf{r}^A, \mathbf{s}^A)$ entirely from these shares, using the staged evaluation algorithm, and later execute a short interactive update protocol with Bob (with communication and computation *independent* of n and m) to let Bob (with input k_B) obtain the full HSS shares of (k_A, k_B). Therefore, Alice can entirely compute all of her preprocessing material *before she even interacts with Bob* (or knows his identity).

Sublinear Secure Computation with One-Sided Statistical Security. Our last application follows the exact same line as above, further noting that evaluation of $F(x, y) = \sum_i f_i(x) \cdot g_i(y)$ can be performed while statistically protecting one of the two inputs (e.g., x). Moreover, the class of such functions $F(x, y)$ contains in particular all arithmetic circuits (with fan-in 2) of size s and depth $\log \log s$, as in such circuits, every output bit depends on at most $\log s$ inputs, and can therefore be written as a multivariate polynomial in the inputs, with at most s monomials. As a consequence, if there is a secure computation protocol for generating staged HSS shares of inputs x and y with communication $c(|x|, |y|)$, then there exists a protocol for securely computing all circuits of size s and depth $\log \log s$ with $|x| + |y|$ inputs and m outputs with communication $c(|x|, |y|) + 2m$, which is asymptotically optimal. It only remains to find a protocol to securely distribute staged HSS shares with linear communication.

This is not easily done in general, as the standard technique to generate HSS shares with low communication uses *hybrid encryption*: to share an input x, one generate HSS shares of some seed seed (using a generic secure computation protocol), and publishes $x \oplus \mathsf{PRG}(\mathsf{seed})$. Then, the homomorphic evaluation first computes $\mathsf{PRG}(\mathsf{seed})$, unmasks x, and then applies the function. The issue is that this is inherently incompatible with having (one-sided) statistical security. We describe two cases where we can get around this issue:

1. The first way is to use hybrid encryption only on y, for which we just aim to computational security, and to share x using the standard staged HSS sharing algorithm. This yields a one-sided statistically secure protocol for all log log-depth circuits with communication $|y| + |x| \cdot \mathsf{poly}(\lambda) + O(m)$, which is optimal as soon as $|x| < |y| / \mathsf{poly}(\lambda)$. In other terms, if the input to be statistically

protected is polynomially smaller than the other input, we achieve optimal communication.

2. Our second solution relies on a specific construction of staged HSS scheme that relies on the circular security of the Paillier-ElGamal encryption scheme. Here, we manage to leverage the inherent compactness of this specific scheme to get a protocol with optimal communication $|y| + |x| + O(m)$ for arithmetic circuits over a sufficiently large ring (since Paillier encryption is compact only when the values are from a large ring), by designing a tailored low-communication HSS share distribution protocol. By breaking the circuit into log log-depth blocks, this generalizes naturally to a one-sided statistically secure protocol with *sublinear* communication $O(s/\log\log s)$ for any layered arithmetic circuits[7] over a sufficiently large field.

3   Preliminaries

We use λ to denote the security parameter. For a natural integer $n \in \mathbb{N}$, the set $\{0, 1, \ldots, n-1\}$ is denoted by $[n]$. We mostly use bold lowercase letters (e.g., $\mathbf{r}$) to denote vectors. For a vector $\mathbf{r} = (r_1, \ldots, r_n)$, the vector $(g^{r_1} \ldots, g^{r_n})$ is sometimes denoted by $g^{\mathbf{r}}$. We write $\mathsf{poly}(\lambda)$ to denote an arbitrary polynomial function. We denote by $\mathsf{negl}(\lambda)$ a negligible function in λ, and PPT stands for probabilistic polynomial-time. For a finite set S, we write $x \xleftarrow{\$} S$ to denote that x is sampled uniformly at random from S. For an algorithm $\mathcal{A}$, we denote by $y \leftarrow \mathcal{A}(x)$ the output y after running $\mathcal{A}$ on input x.

We recall the notion of constrained pseudorandom functions. For simplicity, we focus on selective, 1-key secure, constraint-hiding, constrained pseudorandom functions, which are the main focus of our work, and refer the reader to [4,5,9,25] for the general definitions. Additional definitions related to our assumptions or applications to multi-party computation (MPC), and in particular definition of pseudorandom correlation functions, can be found in the full version.

Definition 1 (Constrained Pseudorandom Functions). Denote by λ a security parameter. A Constrained Pseudorandom Function (CPRF) with domain $\mathcal{X} = \{\mathcal{X}_\lambda\}_{\lambda \in \mathbb{N}}$, key space $\mathcal{K} = \{\mathcal{K}_\lambda\}_{\lambda \in \mathbb{N}}$, and range $\mathcal{Y} = \{\mathcal{Y}_\lambda\}_{\lambda \in \mathbb{N}}$, that supports a class of circuits $\mathcal{C} = \{\mathcal{C}_\lambda\}_{\lambda \in \mathbb{N}}$, where each C_λ has domain $\mathcal{X}_\lambda$ and range $\{0, 1\}$, consists of the following four algorithms:[8]

- $\mathsf{KeyGen}(1^\lambda) \rightarrow (\mathsf{pp}, \mathsf{msk})$: On input the security parameter λ, the master key generation algorithm outputs a public parameter pp and a master secret key $\mathsf{msk} \in \mathcal{K}$.
- $\mathsf{Eval}(\mathsf{pp}, \mathsf{msk}, x) \rightarrow y$: On input the public parameter pp, the master secret key msk, and an input $x \in \mathcal{X}$, the evaluation algorithm outputs a value $y \in \mathcal{Y}$.

---

[7] An arithmetic circuit is layered if its nodes can be partitioned into layers, such that any wire connects adjacent layers.

[8] In the remaining of the paper, we drop the λ subscript when it is clear from context.

- Constrain(msk, C) → ck_C: On input the master secret key msk, and a circuit $C \in \mathcal{C}$, the constrained key generation algorithm outputs a constrained key ck_C.
- CEval(pp, ck_C, x) → y: On input the public parameter pp, a constrained key ck_C, and an input $x \in \mathcal{X}$, the constrained evaluation algorithm outputs a value $y \in \mathcal{Y}$.

Correctness. For any security parameter λ, any constrain $C \in \mathcal{C}$, and any input $x \in \mathcal{X}$ such that $C(x) = 0$, we have:

$$
\Pr\left[\mathsf{Eval}(\mathsf{pp}, \mathsf{msk}, x) \neq \mathsf{CEval}(\mathsf{pp}, \mathsf{ck}_C, x) : \begin{array}{l} \mathsf{pp} \leftarrow \mathsf{Setup}(1^\lambda) \\ \mathsf{msk} \leftarrow \mathsf{KeyGen}(\mathsf{pp}) \\ \mathsf{ck}_C \leftarrow \mathsf{Constrain}(\mathsf{msk}, C) \end{array} \right] \leq \mathsf{negl}(\lambda).
$$

1-Key Selective Security. We say that a CPRF is 1-key selectively secure if the advantage of any PPT adversary $\mathcal{A}$ in the following game is negligible:

- **Selective Choice of Constraint:** The adversary chooses a (single) circuit $C \in \mathcal{C}$ and sends it to the challenger.
- **Setup:** The challenger runs (pp, msk) ← KeyGen(1^λ), initializes a set $S_{\mathsf{eval}} = \varnothing$, and computes $\mathsf{ck}_C \leftarrow$ Constrain(msk, C). The challenger also chooses a random bit $b \xleftarrow{\$} \{0, 1\}$. It sends pp, ck_C to $\mathcal{A}$.
- **Pre-Challenge Evaluation Queries:** $\mathcal{A}$ can adaptively send arbitrary input values $x \in \mathcal{X}$ to chall. The challenger computes $y \leftarrow$ Eval(pp, msk, x) and returns y to $\mathcal{A}$. It also updates $S_{\mathsf{eval}} \leftarrow S_{\mathsf{eval}} \cup \{x\}$.
- **Challenge Phase:** $\mathcal{A}$ sends an input $x^* \in \mathcal{X}$ as its challenge query to chall with the restriction that $x^* \notin S_{\mathsf{eval}}$, and $C(x^*) \neq 0$. If $b = 0$, then chall computes $y^* \leftarrow$ Eval(pp, msk, x^*). If $b = 1$, it picks a random value $y^* \xleftarrow{\$} \mathcal{Y}$. Finally, chall returns y^* to $\mathcal{A}$.
- **Post-Challenge Evaluation Queries:** $\mathcal{A}$ continues the queries as before, with the restriction that it cannot query x^* as an evaluation query.
- **Guess:** $\mathcal{A}$ outputs a bit $b' \in \{0, 1\}$.

1-Key Selective Constraint-Hiding. We say that a CPRF is selectively 1-key constraint-hiding if the advantage of any PPT adversary $\mathcal{A}$ in the following game is negligible:

- **Selective Choice of Constraint:** The adversary chooses a (single) pair of circuits $(C_0, C_1) \in \mathcal{C}$ and sends it to the challenger.
- **Setup:** The challenger runs (pp, msk) ← KeyGen(1^λ), chooses a random bit $b \xleftarrow{\$} \{0, 1\}$, and computes $\mathsf{ck}^* \leftarrow$ Constrain(msk, C_b). It sends pp, ck^* to $\mathcal{A}$.
- **Evaluation Queries:** $\mathcal{A}$ can query evaluations for arbitrary inputs $x \in \mathcal{X}$ to chall, with the restriction that $C_0(x) = C_1(x)$ must hold. The challenger returns $y \leftarrow$ Eval(pp, msk, x) to $\mathcal{A}$.

– **Guess:** $\mathcal{A}$ outputs a bit $b' \in \{0, 1\}$.

In both games, $\mathcal{A}$ wins if $b' = b$ and its advantage is defined as $|2 \cdot \Pr[\mathcal{A} \text{ wins}] - 1|$ where the probability is over the internal coins of $\mathcal{A}$ and of Setup.

4 Homomorphic Secret Sharing and Extensions

The core notion underlying our constructions is homomorphic secret sharing (HSS), introduced by Boyle et al. in [8]. In this section, we remind the standard definition of HSS as well as propose several extensions, in particular defining some special properties that play an important role in our constructions. We further remark that these extensions are easily instantiated using the DCR-based HSS construction from [27].

4.1 Homomorphic Secret Sharing

We start by recalling the standard definition of homomorphic secret sharing, as well as of Restricted Multiplication Straight-line (RMS) programs which is the common model of computation in the context of HSS.

Definition 2 (Homomorphic Secret Sharing). Denote by λ a security parameter. A Homomorphic Secret Sharing (HSS) scheme for a class of programs $\mathcal{P}$ which is defined over a ring $\mathcal{R}$ and has input space $\mathcal{I} \subseteq \mathcal{R}$ consists of three PPT algorithms (Setup, Input, Eval) such that:

- Setup$(1^\lambda) \to (\mathsf{pk}, (\mathsf{ek}_0, \mathsf{ek}_1))$: On input the security parameter λ, the setup algorithm outputs a public key pk and a pair of evaluation keys $(\mathsf{ek}_0, \mathsf{ek}_1)$.
- Input$(\mathsf{pk}, x) \to (\mathsf{I}_0, \mathsf{I}_1)$: On input the public key pk and an input $x \in \mathcal{I}$, the input algorithm outputs a pair of input information $(\mathsf{I}_0, \mathsf{I}_1)$.
- Eval$(\sigma, \mathsf{ek}_\sigma, \mathsf{I}_\sigma = (\mathsf{I}_\sigma^{(1)}, \dots, \mathsf{I}_\sigma^{(\rho)}), P) \to y_\sigma$: On input a party index $\sigma \in \{0, 1\}$, an evaluation key ek_σ, a vector of ρ input values $(\mathsf{I}_\sigma^{(1)}, \dots, \mathsf{I}_\sigma^{(\rho)})$, and a program $P \in \mathcal{P}$, the evaluation algorithm outputs the party σ's corresponding share of the output y_σ.

We require an HSS scheme to satisfy the following two properties:

- **Correctness.** For any security parameter $\lambda \in \mathbb{N}$, and any program $P \in \mathcal{P}$ with input space $\mathcal{I} \subseteq \mathcal{R}$, we have:

$$\Pr\left[y_0 - y_1 = P(x^{(1)}, \dots, x^{(\rho)})\right] \geq 1 - \mathsf{negl}(\lambda),$$

where the probability is taken over $(\mathsf{pk}, (\mathsf{ek}_0, \mathsf{ek}_1)) \leftarrow \mathsf{Setup}(1^\lambda)$, $(\mathsf{I}_0^{(i)}, \mathsf{I}_1^{(i)}) \leftarrow \mathsf{Input}(\mathsf{pk}, x^{(i)})$ for $i \in [\rho]$, and $y_\sigma \leftarrow \mathsf{Eval}(\sigma, \mathsf{ek}_\sigma, (\mathsf{I}_\sigma^{(1)}, \dots, \mathsf{I}_\sigma^{(\rho)}), P)$, for $\sigma \in \{0, 1\}$.

- **Security.** For any PPT adversaries $\mathcal{A}, \mathcal{A}'$, and any bit $\sigma \in \{0,1\}$ the following value should be negligible in λ:

$$
\left| \Pr \left[b' = b : \begin{array}{l} (x_0, x_1, \text{state}) \leftarrow \mathcal{A}(1^\lambda) \\ (\text{pk}, (\text{ek}_0, \text{ek}_1)) \leftarrow \text{Setup}(1^\lambda) \\ b \xleftarrow{\$} \{0,1\} \\ (\text{I}_0, \text{I}_1) \leftarrow \text{Input}(x_b) \\ b' \leftarrow \mathcal{A}'(\text{state}, \text{pk}, \text{ek}_\sigma, \text{I}_\sigma) \end{array} \right] - \frac{1}{2} \right|
$$

We now remind the definition of Restricted Multiplication Straight-line (RMS) programs. RMS programs form a class of programs which encompasses branching programs of polynomial-size and therefore NC^1 circuits. In an RMS program, the multiplication is restricted to happen between an input value and an intermediate value of the computation (so-called "memory" value).

Definition 3 (RMS Programs). An RMS program with magnitude bound B is defined as a sequence of the instructions as follows:

- ConvertInput(I^x) $\rightarrow$ M^x: Loads an input x into memory.
- Add(M^x, M^y) $\rightarrow$ M^{x+y}: Adds two memory values.
- Mul(I^x, M^y) $\rightarrow$ $\text{M}^{x \cdot y}$: Multiplies an input value and a memory value to produce a memory value of their product.
- Output(M^x, n) $\rightarrow$ $x \bmod n$: Outputs a memory value $w.r.t.$ a modulus $n < B$.

4.2 HSS Following the RMS Template

Similarly to [7], we first propose a more specific definition for HSS with additional algorithms that are relevant in the context of RMS programs.

Definition 4 (HSS Following the RMS Template). A homomorphic secret sharing scheme HSS = (Setup, Input, MemGen, Eval) following the RMS template is an HSS scheme as defined in Definition 2 with an additional algorithm MemGen which serves to produce memory values as follows:

- MemGen($\sigma, \text{ek}_\sigma, x$) $\rightarrow$ M_σ: On input a party index $\sigma \in \{0,1\}$, an evaluation key ek_σ, and an input $x \in \mathcal{I}$, the memory generator algorithm outputs a memory value M_σ.

Moreover, the Eval algorithm proceeds with sub-routines following the RMS operations ConvertInput, Add, Mul, Output as follows:

- Eval($\sigma, \text{ek}_\sigma, (\text{I}_\sigma^{(1)}, \ldots, \text{I}_\sigma^{(\rho)}), P$) $\rightarrow$ y_σ: On input a party index $\sigma \in \{0,1\}$, an evaluation key ek_σ, a vector of ρ input values $(\text{I}_\sigma^{(1)}, \ldots, \text{I}_\sigma^{(\rho)})$, and an RMS program P, this algorithm follows the instructions of P and processes them as follows:
    - ConvertInput($\sigma, \text{ek}_\sigma, \text{I}_\sigma^x$) $\rightarrow$ M_σ^x: This algorithm simply uses the MemGen and Mult algorithms as follows:

- Run $\mathsf{MemGen}(\sigma, \mathsf{ek}_\sigma, 1) \to \mathsf{M}_\sigma^1$.
- Run $\mathsf{Mult}(\sigma, \mathsf{ek}_\sigma, \mathsf{I}_\sigma^x, \mathsf{M}_\sigma^1) \to \mathsf{M}_\sigma^x$.

- $\mathsf{Add}(\sigma, \mathsf{ek}_\sigma, \mathsf{M}^x, \mathsf{M}^y) \to \mathsf{M}^{x+y}$: This algorithm directly adds the given memory values of x and y. Namely, $\mathsf{M}_\sigma^{x+y} = \mathsf{M}_\sigma^x + \mathsf{M}_\sigma^y$.
- $\mathsf{Mul}(\sigma, \mathsf{ek}_\sigma, \mathsf{I}^x, \mathsf{M}^y) \to \mathsf{M}^{x \cdot y}$: It multiplies an input value I_x and a memory value M_y and outputs a memory value of $x \cdot y$. The template does not impose any non-black box requirement on this algorithm.
- $\mathsf{Output}(\sigma, \mathsf{M}^x, n) \to x \bmod n$: It uses M^x to output $x_\sigma \bmod n$.

Correctness and security properties are defined as in Definition 2, and we further require the following property:

Additively Homomorphic Memory. The memory values generated in HSS should be additively homomorphic. Meaning that for any two $x, y \in \mathcal{I}$ and any party index $\sigma \in \{0, 1\}$, it holds that

$$\mathsf{M}_\sigma^x + \mathsf{M}_\sigma^y = \mathsf{M}_\sigma^{x+y},$$

where $\mathsf{M}_\sigma^z \leftarrow \mathsf{MemGen}(\sigma, \mathsf{ek}_\sigma, z)$, for $z \in \{x, y\}$, and $(\mathsf{pk}, (\mathsf{ek}_0, \mathsf{ek}_1)) \leftarrow \mathsf{Setup}(1^\lambda)$. Throughout this work, we may refer to memory values satisfying this property as "valid" memory values.

4.3   Extended Evaluation and Simulatable Memory Values

Any HSS following the RMS template as defined above satisfies the following lemma, which states that one can evaluate share of $z \cdot P(x^{(1)}, \ldots, x^{(\rho)})$ using only a memory value of z (instead of an input value) together with the input values of the rest of variables $(x^{(1)}, \ldots, x^{(\rho)})$. This lemma plays a central role in our CPRF constructions.

Lemma 1. *Let* $\mathsf{HSS} = (\mathsf{Setup}, \mathsf{Input}, \mathsf{MemGen}, \mathsf{Eval})$ *be an HSS scheme following the RMS template. There exists an extended evaluation algorithm* $\mathsf{ExtEval}$:

- $\mathsf{ExtEval}(\sigma, \mathsf{ek}_\sigma, \mathsf{M}_\sigma, (\mathsf{I}_\sigma^{(1)}, \ldots, \mathsf{I}_\sigma^{(\rho)}), P) \to y_\sigma$: *On input a party index* $\sigma \in \{0, 1\}$, *an evaluation key* ek_σ, *a single memory value* M_σ, *a vector of* ρ *input values* $(\mathsf{I}_\sigma^{(1)}, \ldots, \mathsf{I}_\sigma^{(\rho)})$, *and an RMS program* P, *return a value* y_σ *such that the following holds.*

For any security parameter $\lambda \in \mathbb{N}$ *and any RMS program* P, *we have:*

$$\Pr\left[y_0 - y_1 = z \cdot P(x^{(1)}, \ldots, x^{(\rho)})\right] \geq 1 - \mathsf{negl}(\lambda), \tag{1}$$

where the probability is taken of the choice of $(\mathsf{pk}, (\mathsf{ek}_0, \mathsf{ek}_1)) \leftarrow \mathsf{Setup}(1^\lambda)$, $(\mathsf{I}_0^{(i)}, \mathsf{I}_1^{(i)}) \leftarrow \mathsf{Input}(\mathsf{pk}, x^{(i)})$, $\mathsf{M}_\sigma \leftarrow \mathsf{MemGen}(\sigma, \mathsf{ek}_\sigma, z)$, *and* $y_\sigma \leftarrow \mathsf{ExtEval}(\sigma, \mathsf{ek}_\sigma, \mathsf{M}_\sigma, (\mathsf{I}_\sigma^{(1)}, \ldots, \mathsf{I}_\sigma^{(\rho)}), P)$, *for* $\sigma \in \{0, 1\}, i \in [\rho]$.

The proof of the above lemma is detailed in the the full version of the paper. It essentially consists in recursively incorporating the memory value M_σ using the standard Eval algorithm by first multiplying inputs with it.

We now introduce an additional property termed *simulatable memory values*. Here, we require that for an input $x \in \mathcal{I}$, the memory value of one of the two parties can be generated ahead of time and without the knowledge of x using a simulation algorithm, while the other memory value can be generated given the pre-computed first memory value and the exact value of x. This simulation should not affect the correctness of ExtEval.

Definition 5 (HSS with Simulatable Memory Values). Let HSS = (Setup, Input, MemGen, Eval) be an HSS following the RMS template as per Definition 4, with input space $\mathcal{I}$ over the ring $\mathcal{R}$. We say that HSS is simulatable with respect to its memory values if there exist algorithms Sim_0 and Sim_1 such that

- $\mathsf{Sim}_0(1^\lambda) \to M_0$: on input the security parameter λ outputs a memory value M_0.
- $\mathsf{Sim}_1(M_0, z, (\mathsf{ek}_0, \mathsf{ek}_1)) \to M_1$: on input a memory value M_0, an element $z \in \mathcal{I}$, and two encoding keys $(\mathsf{ek}_0, \mathsf{ek}_1)$ outputs a memory value M_1.

We also require the two following properties:

Simulation Correctness. For any $\lambda \in \mathbb{N}$ and any $z \in \mathcal{I}$, the above correctness condition (Eq. 1) still holds when the memory value is simulated, i.e. when $M_0 \leftarrow \mathsf{Sim}_0(1^\lambda)$ and $M_1 \leftarrow \mathsf{Sim}_1(M_0, z, (\mathsf{ek}_0, \mathsf{ek}_1))$.

Simulation Security. It should be computationally hard to distinguish the two memory values obtained via the simulation algorithms. That is, for any $\lambda \in \mathbb{N}$ and any $z \in \mathcal{I}$, we have $(z, M_0) \approx_c (z, M_1)$ for any $(\mathsf{pk}, (\mathsf{ek}_0, \mathsf{ek}_1)) \leftarrow \mathsf{Setup}(1^\lambda)$, $M_0 \leftarrow \mathsf{Sim}_0(1^\lambda)$, and $M_1 \leftarrow \mathsf{Sim}_1(M, z, (\mathsf{ek}_0, \mathsf{ek}_1))$.

4.4 Staged Homomorphic Secret Sharing

Finally, we define a new notion termed staged-HSS which is merely extending the idea of HSS with simulatable memory values to the case where we require the possibility of input values to be simulatable as well.

Definition 6 (staged-HSS). Let HSS = (Setup, MemGen, Input, Eval) be an HSS scheme following the RMS template, with input space $\mathcal{I}$ over the ring $\mathcal{R}$. We say it is a staged-HSS if there exist additional algorithms $(\overline{\mathsf{Input}}_0, \overline{\mathsf{Input}}_1)$, and $(\overline{\mathsf{Eval}}_0, \overline{\mathsf{Eval}}_1)$ such that:

- $\overline{\mathsf{Input}}_0(\mathsf{pk}) \to (\bar{\mathsf{I}}_0, \mathsf{aux})$: On input a public key pk, return a value $\bar{\mathsf{I}}_0$ and an auxiliary output aux.
- $\overline{\mathsf{Input}}_1(\mathsf{pk}, x, \mathsf{aux}, (\mathsf{ek}_0, \mathsf{ek}_1)) \to \bar{\mathsf{I}}_1$: On input a public key pk, an input $x \in \mathcal{I}$, an auxiliary input aux, and two encoding keys $(\mathsf{ek}_0, \mathsf{ek}_1)$, return a value $\bar{\mathsf{I}}_1$.

- $\overline{\mathsf{Eval}}_0(\mathsf{ek}_0, (\bar{\mathsf{I}}_0^{(1)}, \ldots, \bar{\mathsf{I}}_0^{(\rho)}), P) \to \mathsf{M}_0$: On input an evaluation key ek_0, a vector of ρ input values $(\bar{\mathsf{I}}_0^{(1)}, \ldots, \bar{\mathsf{I}}_0^{(\rho)})$, and a program P, return a memory value M_0.
- $\overline{\mathsf{Eval}}_1(\mathsf{ek}_1, (\bar{\mathsf{I}}_1^{(1)}, \ldots, \bar{\mathsf{I}}_1^{(\rho)}), (x^{(1)}, \ldots, x^{(\rho)}), P) \to \mathsf{M}_1$: On input an evaluation key ek_1, a vector of ρ input values $(x^{(1)}, \ldots, x^{(\rho)})$ as well as $(\bar{\mathsf{I}}_1^{(1)}, \ldots, \bar{\mathsf{I}}_1^{(\rho)})$, and a program P, return a memory value M_1.

We further require the two following properties:

Correctness. We would like the outputs of $\overline{\mathsf{Eval}}_0$ and $\overline{\mathsf{Eval}}_1$ to be usable within the extended evaluation algorithm ExtEval (Lemma 1). Formally, for any $\lambda \in \mathbb{N}$ and any two RMS programs $P, Q \in \mathcal{P}$, it should hold that

$$\Pr[y_0 - y_1 = P(z^{(1)}, \ldots, z^{(\ell)}) \cdot Q(x^{(1)}, \ldots, x^{(\rho)})] \geq 1 - \mathsf{negl}(\lambda),$$

where $(\mathsf{pk}, (\mathsf{ek}_0, \mathsf{ek}_1)) \leftarrow \mathsf{Setup}(1^\lambda)$, $(\mathsf{I}_0^{x^{(i)}}, \mathsf{I}_1^{x^{(i)}}) \leftarrow \mathsf{Input}(\mathsf{pk}, x^{(i)})$, for all $i \in [\rho]$, $(\bar{\mathsf{I}}_0^{z^{(i)}}, \mathsf{aux}^{(i)}) \leftarrow \overline{\mathsf{Input}}_0(\mathsf{pk})$ and $\bar{\mathsf{I}}_1^{z^{(i)}} \leftarrow \overline{\mathsf{Input}}_1(\mathsf{pk}, z^{(i)}, \mathsf{aux}^{(i)}, (\mathsf{ek}_0, \mathsf{ek}_1))$, for all $i \in [\ell]$, $\mathsf{M}_0 \leftarrow \overline{\mathsf{Eval}}_0(\mathsf{ek}_0, (\bar{\mathsf{I}}_0^{z^{(1)}}, \ldots, \bar{\mathsf{I}}_0^{z^{(\ell)}}), P)$, $\mathsf{M}_1 \leftarrow \overline{\mathsf{Eval}}_1(\mathsf{ek}_1, (\bar{\mathsf{I}}_1^{z^{(1)}}, \ldots, \bar{\mathsf{I}}_1^{z^{(\ell)}}), (z^{(1)}, \ldots, z^{(\ell)}), P)$, and $y_\sigma \leftarrow \mathsf{ExtEval}(\sigma, \mathsf{ek}_\sigma, (\mathsf{M}_\sigma, \mathsf{I}_\sigma^{x^{(1)}}, \ldots, \mathsf{I}_\sigma^{x^{(\rho)}}), Q)$, for $\sigma \in \{0, 1\}$.

Security. The output of $\overline{\mathsf{Input}}_1$ and Input should be computationally indistinguishable. Formally, for any $\lambda \in \mathbb{N}$, and any $x \in \mathcal{I}$, the two following distributions should be computationally indistinguishable:

$$\left\{ \bar{\mathsf{I}}_1 : \begin{array}{l} (\mathsf{pk}, (\mathsf{ek}_0, \mathsf{ek}_1)) \leftarrow \mathsf{Setup}(1^\lambda) \\ (\bar{\mathsf{I}}_0, \mathsf{aux}) \leftarrow \overline{\mathsf{Input}}_0(\mathsf{pk}) \\ \bar{\mathsf{I}}_1 \leftarrow \overline{\mathsf{Input}}_1(\mathsf{pk}, x, \mathsf{aux}, (\mathsf{ek}_0, \mathsf{ek}_1)) \end{array} \right\} \overset{c}{\approx} \left\{ \mathsf{I}_1 : \begin{array}{l} (\mathsf{pk}, (\mathsf{ek}_0, \mathsf{ek}_1)) \leftarrow \mathsf{Setup}(1^\lambda), \\ (\mathsf{I}_0, \mathsf{I}_1) \leftarrow \mathsf{Input}(\mathsf{pk}, x) \end{array} \right\}.$$

Theorem 2. *Assuming the hardness of* DCR, *there exists HSS scheme following the RMS template which generates simulatable memory values, as well as staged-HSS scheme for the class of RMS programs.*

The above theorem follows from the HSS scheme introduced by Orlandi, Scholl, and Yakoubov in [27] that supports the class of RMS programs and works under the DCR assumption. In the full version of the paper, we show that it satisfies the properties of all the three introduced variants.

5   Constrained Pseudorandom Functions

We now present our two transformations from homomorphic secret sharing to constrained pseudorandom functions.

5.1   CPRF for Inner-Product from HSS

Our first construction is a 1-key selectively secure constrained pseudorandom function for inner-product. The space input is $\mathcal{R}^n$ for some ring $\mathcal{R}$ and $n > 0$, and a constraint is defined by a vector $\mathbf{z} \in \mathcal{R}^n$. A constrained key for a vector $\mathbf{z}$ allows to compute the PRF evaluation on input $\mathbf{x} \in \mathcal{R}^n$ if and only if $\langle \mathbf{z}, \mathbf{x} \rangle = 0$. Specifically, the class of constraints is $\{C_{\mathbf{z}} \mid \mathbf{z} \in \mathcal{R}^n\}$ where the circuit $C_{\mathbf{z}} : \mathcal{R}^n \to \{0,1\}$ is defined as $C_{\mathbf{z}}(\mathbf{x}) = 0$ if $\langle \mathbf{z}, \mathbf{x} \rangle = 0$, else 1.

The intuition behind our construction is that the master secret key and the constrained key (for a vector $\mathbf{z}$) are used to compute, via HSS, a share of $\langle \mathbf{x}, \mathbf{z} \rangle \cdot F_k(\mathbf{x})$, where k is a PRF key encoded via the HSS scheme. Then, if $\langle \mathbf{x}, \mathbf{z} \rangle = 0$, the two evaluations produce substractive shares of 0, i.e. equal shares, while if $\langle \mathbf{x}, \mathbf{z} \rangle \neq 0$, the shares differ by (a non-zero multiple of) $F_k(\mathbf{x})$. By the security of HSS, the PRF key k remains hidden to the constrained key owner, hence the actual PRF evaluation (the value of the share computed from the master secret key) is pseudorandom even given the value of the second share (which can be computed from the constrained key).

Before diving into our construction, we generalize Lemma 1, stating that not only one can produce shares of any evaluation of the form $z \cdot P(\mathbf{x})$ given a memory value for z and encoding of $\mathbf{x}$, but of any linear combination $\sum_i \alpha^{(i)} z^{(i)} \cdot P(\mathbf{x})$ with known coefficients given memory values for multiple $z^{(i)}$'s, i.e. for $\langle \mathbf{z}, \boldsymbol{\alpha} \rangle$ for a known vector $\boldsymbol{\alpha} = (\alpha^{(1)}, \ldots, \alpha^{(\ell)})$.

Corollary 1. *Let* $\mathsf{HSS} = (\mathsf{Setup}, \mathsf{Input}, \mathsf{MemGen}, \mathsf{Eval})$ *be an HSS scheme following the RMS template. There exists an extended evaluation algorithm* $\mathsf{LinExtEval}$:

- $\mathsf{LinExtEval}(\sigma, \mathsf{ek}_\sigma, (\mathsf{M}_\sigma^{(1)}, \ldots, \mathsf{M}_\sigma^{(\ell)}), (\mathsf{I}_\sigma^{(1)}, \ldots, \mathsf{I}_\sigma^{(\rho)}), (\alpha^{(1)}, \ldots, \alpha^{(\ell)}), P) \to y_\sigma$:
  On input a party index $\sigma \in \{0,1\}$, *an evaluation key* ek_σ, *a vector of* ℓ *memory values* $\mathsf{M}_\sigma^{(1)}, \ldots, \mathsf{M}_\sigma^{(\ell)}$, *a vector of* ρ *input values* $(\mathsf{I}_\sigma^{(1)}, \ldots, \mathsf{I}_\sigma^{(\rho)})$, *a vector of* ℓ *ring elements* $\alpha^{(1)}, \ldots, \alpha^{(\ell)}$, *and an RMS program* P, *this algorithm outputs a value* y_σ *such that the following holds.*

For any security parameter $\lambda \in \mathbb{N}$, *any* $\alpha^{(i)} \in \mathcal{R}$ *for* $i \in [\ell]$, *and any RMS program* P, *we have:*

$$\Pr\left[y_0 - y_1 = \left(\sum_{i=1}^{\ell} \alpha^{(i)} \cdot z^{(i)} \right) \cdot P(x^{(1)}, \ldots, x^{(\rho)}) \right] \geq 1 - \mathsf{negl}(\lambda),$$

where the probability is taken over the choice of $(\mathsf{pk}, (\mathsf{ek}_0, \mathsf{ek}_1)) \leftarrow \mathsf{Setup}(1^\lambda)$, $(\mathsf{I}_0^{(i)}, \mathsf{I}_1^{(i)}) \leftarrow \mathsf{Input}(\mathsf{pk}, x^{(i)})$, $\mathsf{M}_\sigma^{(j)} \leftarrow \mathsf{MemGen}(\sigma, \mathsf{ek}_\sigma, z^{(j)})$, *and over the shares* $y_\sigma \leftarrow \mathsf{LinExtEval}(\sigma, \mathsf{ek}_\sigma, (\mathsf{M}_\sigma^{(1)}, \ldots, \mathsf{M}_\sigma^{(\ell)}), (\mathsf{I}_\sigma^{(1)}, \ldots, \mathsf{I}_\sigma^{(\rho)}), (\alpha^{(1)}, \ldots, \alpha^{(\ell)}), P)$, *with* $\sigma \in \{0,1\}, j \in [\ell], i \in [\rho]$.

The proof of the above statement follows from Lemma 1 by linearly combining the substractive shares obtained by applying $\mathsf{ExtEval}$ with each memory value.

For a PRF $F : \mathcal{K} \times \mathcal{R}^n \to \mathcal{Y}$ with domain $\mathcal{R}^n$ and for $\mathbf{x} \in \mathcal{R}^n$, we denote by $F_\bullet(\mathbf{x}) : \mathcal{K} \to \mathcal{Y}$ the function that maps $k \in \mathcal{K}$ to $F_k(\mathbf{x})$.

We now have all the ingredients for our first construction.

Construction 1. (CPRF for IP from HSS). Let $F : \mathcal{K} \times \mathcal{R}^n \to \mathcal{Y}$ be a PRF with evaluation in NC^1. Let $\mathsf{HSS} = (\mathsf{Setup}, \mathsf{Input}, \mathsf{MemGen}, \mathsf{Eval})$ be a homomorphic secret sharing following the RMS template with simulatable memory values. We design $(\mathsf{KeyGen}, \mathsf{Eval}, \mathsf{Constrain}, \mathsf{CEval})$ as follows:

$\underline{\mathsf{KeyGen}(1^\lambda):}$

1. $(\mathsf{pk}, (\mathsf{ek}_0, \mathsf{ek}_1)) \xleftarrow{\$} \mathsf{Setup}(1^\lambda)$.
2. Sample $k \xleftarrow{\$} \mathcal{K}$ for F
3. Run $(\mathsf{I}_0, \mathsf{I}_1) \leftarrow \mathsf{Input}(\mathsf{pk}, k)$.
4. For $i \in \{1, \ldots, n\}$:
   $\mathsf{M}_0^i \leftarrow \mathsf{Sim}_0(1^\lambda)$.
5. $\mathsf{msk} \leftarrow$
   $((\mathsf{ek}_0, \mathsf{I}_0, (\mathsf{M}_0^i)_{i \in [n]}), (\mathsf{ek}_1, \mathsf{I}_1))$
6. Output $\mathsf{pp} = \mathsf{pk}$ and msk.

$\underline{\mathsf{Eval}(\mathsf{pp}, \mathsf{msk}, \mathbf{x}):}$

1. Parse msk as
   $((\mathsf{ek}_0, \mathsf{I}_0, (\mathsf{M}_0^i)_{i \in [n]}), (\mathsf{ek}_1, \mathsf{I}_1))$.
2. Compute $y_0 \leftarrow$
   $\mathsf{LinExtEval}(0, \mathsf{ek}_0, (\mathsf{M}_0^i)_{i \in [n]}, \mathsf{I}_0, \mathbf{x}, F_\bullet(\mathbf{x}))$.
3. Output y_0.

$\underline{\mathsf{Constrain}(\mathsf{msk}, \mathbf{z}):}$

1. Parse msk as
   $((\mathsf{ek}_0, \mathsf{I}_0, (\mathsf{M}_0^i)_{i \in [n]}), (\mathsf{ek}_1, \mathsf{I}_1))$
2. Parse $\mathbf{z} = (z_1, \ldots, z_n)$.
3. For $i \in \{1, \ldots, n\}$:
   $\mathsf{M}_1^i \leftarrow$
   $\mathsf{Sim}_1(\mathsf{M}_0^i, z_i, (\mathsf{ek}_0, \mathsf{ek}_1))$
4. Return $\mathsf{ck}_\mathbf{z} =$
   $(\mathsf{ek}_1, \mathsf{I}_1, (\mathsf{M}_1^i)_{i \in [n]})$.

$\underline{\mathsf{CEval}(\mathsf{pp}, \mathsf{ck}_\mathbf{z}, \mathbf{x}):}$

1. Parse $\mathsf{ck}_\mathbf{z} = (\mathsf{ek}_1, \mathsf{I}_1, (\mathsf{M}_1^i)_{i \in [n]})$.
2. Compute $y_1 \leftarrow$
   $\mathsf{LinExtEval}(1, \mathsf{ek}_1, (\mathsf{M}_1^i)_{i \in [n]}, \mathsf{I}_1, \mathbf{x}, F_\bullet(\mathbf{x}))$.
3. Output y_1.

Theorem 3. *Assuming F is a secure PRF with evaluation in NC^1 and HSS is a secure HSS scheme following the RMS template with simulatable memory values, then Construction 1 is a selective 1-key, constraint-hiding, secure CPRF for inner-product.*

The proof of Theorem 3 is detailed in the full version of our paper.

Remark 1. In the above construction, we require the PRF range $\mathcal{Y}$ to be such that F is pseudorandom on $\mathbb{Z}_n$, for a fixed $n < B$, where B is the magnitude bound of the RMS programs that the HSS scheme used in the construction supports. We need to then reduce the outputs of the HSS evaluation algorithm modulo n by inputting n as the modulus to algorithm Output (See Definition 4). This is used in the security proof to ensure that masking with a pseudorandom value over $\mathcal{Y}$ causes the output to be pseudorandom.

Corollary 2. *There exist 1-key selectively-secure, constraint-hiding constrained pseudorandom functions for inner-product assuming the hardness of DCR.*

5.2   CPRF for NC^1 from HSS

We now describe CPRF for the class of NC^1 constraints. We consider the representation of an NC^1 circuit C with input size $n = \mathsf{poly}(\lambda)$ and depth $d =$

$\mathcal{O}(\log n)$ to be a bit string $(C_1, \ldots, C_z) \in \{0,1\}^z$, where $z = \mathsf{poly}(n)$ is the description size. Also, we denote the universal circuit by $U(\cdot, \cdot)$ that on input a circuit $C \in \{0,1\}^z$ and $x = (x_1, \ldots, x_n) \in \{0,1\}^n$, outputs $U(C, x) = C(x)$. Due to the work of Cooks and Hoover [17], we know that there exists a universal circuit that correctly computes any NC^1 circuit and is itself an NC^1 circuit.

The strategy for our construction is similar as for inner-product. We aim to obtain substractive shares $U(C, x) \cdot F_k(x)$ via the (standard and constrained) evaluation algorithms, where F is a pseudorandom function with evaluation in NC^1, C denotes the constraint, and U denotes the above universal circuit.

A crucial point is that the master secret key should allow to compute such a share for any input x independently of the constraint C. Hence, we have to find a way to replace the encoding of C that is given to the evaluator by oblivious values that guarantee the correctness. In the inner-product case, where we want shares of $\langle \mathbf{x}, \mathbf{z} \rangle \cdot F_k(\mathbf{x})$, we used simulated memory values as the independent share of the undetermined constraint $\mathbf{z}$, and programmed the constrained key to guarantee correctness according to the constraint vector $\mathbf{z}$. However, this technique cannot be applied to the case of NC^1 constraints as we are dealing with non-linear evaluations.

The idea is again to use staged-HSS. We first compute a memory for $U(C, x)$ using $\overline{\mathsf{Eval}}_0$ and $\overline{\mathsf{Eval}}_1$. Then, this memory value is used in the $\mathsf{ExtEval}$ algorithm from Lemma 1 to compute a share of $U(C, x) \cdot F_k(x)$ additionally using an encoding of k.

The important point here, is that inputs of $\overline{\mathsf{Eval}}_0$ can be sampled obliviously using $(\bar{\mathsf{I}}_0, \mathsf{aux}) \leftarrow \overline{\mathsf{Input}}_0(\mathsf{pk})$, and therefore can be sampled during Setup without the knowledge of the constraint C. Yet, when computing the constrained key for C, the master key owner can use the full knowledge of C as well as auxiliary information generated during Setup to appropriately compute memory values for the i-th bit C_i of the description of C, using $\bar{\mathsf{I}}_1 \leftarrow \overline{\mathsf{Input}}_1(\mathsf{pk}, C_i, \mathsf{aux}, (\mathsf{ek}_0, \mathsf{ek}_1))$. The correctness of staged-HSS then guarantees the correctness of evaluations, while its security plays a role in the security proof to remove the need for both evaluation keys when computing $\bar{\mathsf{I}}_1$, therefore allowing to rely on HSS security to remove the information about the underlying PRF key k.

We now detail our construction. For any $x \in \{0,1\}^n$, we denote by $U(\cdot, x)$ the circuit that maps $C \in \{0,1\}^z$ to $U(C, x) = C(x) \in \{0,1\}$.

Construction 2 (CPRF for NC^1 from HSS). Let $F : \mathcal{K} \times \{0,1\}^n \to \mathcal{Y}$ be a pseudorandom function with evaluation in NC^1, where $\mathcal{Y}$ is a finite cyclic group. Let $\mathsf{HSS} = (\mathsf{Setup}, \mathsf{MemGen}, \mathsf{Input}, \mathsf{Eval})$ be a staged homomorphic secret sharing scheme and denote by $(\overline{\mathsf{Input}}_0, \overline{\mathsf{Input}}_1)$, and $(\overline{\mathsf{Eval}}_0, \overline{\mathsf{Eval}}_1)$ the additional algorithms defined in Definition 6. Let $\mathsf{ExtEval}$ be the modified evaluation algorithm as in Lemma 1. We construct a constrained pseudorandom function that supports NC^1 constraints as follows:

- $\mathsf{KeyGen}(1^\lambda)$:
  - Run $(\mathsf{pk}, (\mathsf{ek}_0, \mathsf{ek}_1)) \leftarrow \mathsf{Setup}(1^\lambda)$.
  - Choose a random key $k \xleftarrow{\$} \mathcal{K}$ for F and compute $(\mathsf{I}_0, \mathsf{I}_1) \leftarrow \mathsf{Input}(\mathsf{pk}, k)$.

- For $i \in \{1, \ldots, z\}$, compute $(\bar{\mathsf{I}}_0^{(i)}, \mathsf{aux}^{(i)}) \leftarrow \overline{\mathsf{Input}}_0(\mathsf{pk})$.
- Output $\mathsf{pp} = \mathsf{pk}$, and $\mathsf{msk} = ((\mathsf{ek}_0, \mathsf{ek}_1, \mathsf{I}_0, \mathsf{I}_1), (\bar{\mathsf{I}}_0^{(1)}, \mathsf{aux}^{(1)}, \ldots, \bar{\mathsf{I}}_0^{(z)}, \mathsf{aux}^{(z)}))$.

- $\mathsf{Eval}(\mathsf{pp}, \mathsf{msk}, x)$:
  - Parse $\mathsf{pp} = \mathsf{pk}$, and $\mathsf{msk} = ((\mathsf{ek}_0, \mathsf{ek}_1, \mathsf{I}_0, \mathsf{I}_1), (\bar{\mathsf{I}}_0^{(1)}, \mathsf{aux}^{(1)}, \ldots, \bar{\mathsf{I}}_0^{(z)}, \mathsf{aux}^{(z)}))$.
  - Run $\mathsf{M}_0 \leftarrow \overline{\mathsf{Eval}}_0(\mathsf{ek}_0, (\bar{\mathsf{I}}_0^{(1)}, \ldots, \bar{\mathsf{I}}_0^{(z)}), U(\cdot, x))$. Here, $\bar{\mathsf{I}}_0^{(i)}$ represents the input value of C_i for $i \in \{1, \ldots, z\}$.
  - Run $y_0 \leftarrow \mathsf{ExtEval}(0, \mathsf{ek}_0, \mathsf{M}_0, \mathsf{I}_0, F_\bullet(x))$. Here, M_0 denotes the memory value of $U(C, x)$, and I_0 denotes the input value of k.
  - Output y_0.

- $\mathsf{Constrain}(\mathsf{msk}, C)$:
  - Parse $\mathsf{msk} = ((\mathsf{ek}_0, \mathsf{ek}_1, \mathsf{I}_0, \mathsf{I}_1), (\bar{\mathsf{I}}_0^{(1)}, \mathsf{aux}^{(1)}, \ldots, \bar{\mathsf{I}}_0^{(z)}, \mathsf{aux}^{(z)}))$, and $C = (C_1, \ldots, C_z) \in \{0, 1\}^z$.
  - For $i \in \{1, \ldots, z\}$, run $\bar{\mathsf{I}}_1^{(i)} \leftarrow \overline{\mathsf{Input}}_1(\mathsf{pk}, C_i, \mathsf{aux}^{(i)}, (\mathsf{ek}_0, \mathsf{ek}_1))$.
  - Output $\mathsf{ck}_C = (\mathsf{ek}_1, \mathsf{I}_1, (\bar{\mathsf{I}}_1^{(1)}, \ldots, \bar{\mathsf{I}}_1^{(z)}), C)$.

- $\mathsf{CEval}(\mathsf{pp}, \mathsf{ck}_C, x)$:
  - Parse $\mathsf{ck}_C = (\mathsf{ek}_1, \mathsf{I}_1, (\bar{\mathsf{I}}_1^{(1)}, \ldots, \bar{\mathsf{I}}_1^{(z)}), C)$.
  - Run $\mathsf{M}_1 \leftarrow \overline{\mathsf{Eval}}_1(\mathsf{ek}_1, (\bar{\mathsf{I}}_1^{(1)}, \ldots, \bar{\mathsf{I}}_1^{(z)}), (C^{(1)}, \ldots, C^{(z)}), U(\cdot, x))$.
  - Run $y_1 \leftarrow \mathsf{ExtEval}(1, \mathsf{ek}_1, \mathsf{M}_1, \mathsf{I}_1, F_\bullet(x))$.
  - Output y_1.

Theorem 4. *Assuming F is a secure pseudorandom function with evaluation in NC^1 and HSS is a secure staged-HSS scheme, Construction 2 is a selective 1-key secure constrained pseudorandom function for NC^1.*

We refer the reader to the full version of our paper for the proof of Theorem 4.

Remark 2. We note that the above construction is not constraint-hiding, since the constrained evaluation algorithm relies on the knowledge of the constraint.

Corollary 3. *Assuming the DCR assumption holds, there exist 1-key selectively-secure constrained pseudorandom functions for NC^1 constraints.*

Remark 3 (Other Instantiations). Although not explicitly detailed in this work, our transformations from HSS to CPRF works using either of the schemes from [10] based on the Learning With Errors (LWE) assumption with super-polynomial modulus, from [1] based on the hardness of Joye-Libert encryption scheme, from [1] based on the Decisional Diffie-Hellman (DDH) and Decisional Cross-Group Diffie-Hellman (DXDH) assumptions over class groups, or from [14] based on the Hard Subgroup Membership (HSM) assumption over class groups. All of the above HSS schemes follow the same outline as the DCR-based scheme of [27] when generating input and memory values. More precisely, input values are ciphertexts computed using a PKE scheme, and in all of the mentioned schemes, the used encryption tool generates ciphertexts that contain a separate part as a commitment to the encryption randomness which is independent of the underlying plaintext. This feature makes it feasible to generalize these schemes into staged-HSS schemes and then use it to construct CPRF for NC^1 constraints. These schemes also allow simulation of memory values which enables using the scheme to construct CPRF for inner-product constraints. This holds since a valid memory value of these schemes is a subtractive share of a secret vector dependent on the secret key of the used PKE, thus one share can be sampled obliviously and the other one can be correctly computed given the secret vector.

Also, using HSS with only polynomial correctness (e.g., the DDH-based scheme of [8]) still yields CPRFs for *polynomial-size* domain. This leads to constructions of *poly-size domain* private CPRFs for inner-products and CPRFs for NC^1 from DDH, and from LWE with polynomial modulus-to-noise ratio.

6   Applications to Secure Multiparty Computation

In this section, we explore the applications of staged-HSS (defined in Sect. 4) to secure computation. We first show how using staged-HSS allows constructing a secure two-party computation protocol with *precomputable* silent preprocessing. In this model, one party can perform all of the heavy preprocessing, not only before the inputs are selected (which can be already achieved by "non-staged" HSS for RMS programs) but also before knowing the identity of the other party. Next, we show that the DCR-based construction of staged-HSS (provided in the full version) can be used to obtain sublinear-communication secure two-party computation with *one-sided statistical security*. Our proposal follows the same outline as [8] where the authors showed how HSS for RMS programs yields secure computation with sublinear communication. Definitions and proofs for this section can be found in the full version.

We start by introducing the notion of *precomputability* for pseudorandom correlation functions. Informally, precomputability enables the first party to generate its key locally before knowing anything about the second party. The second party's key is then (securely) computed as a function of the first key.

In the absence of some form of trusted setup, dishonest-majority secure computation requires computational assumptions. A popular paradigm (used for instance in [18,24]) is to first have the parties jointly execute a precomputation phase which is independent of their inputs or the function they want to compute, in order to distribute correlated randomness, and afterwards, use the computed correlated randomness in an information-theoretic online phase to perform the secure computation. Heuristically, this online phase, which is free of any expensive cryptographic operations, can be made highly efficient. The generation of the correlated randomness in the precomputation phase can be done via a *pseudorandom correlation generator* (PCG) [6] or a *pseudorandom correlation function* (PCF), whose seeds (in the case of PCG), or keys (in the case of PCF) are generated using generic (computationally secure) MPC protocol.

Using a precomputable PCF allows the parties to perform the following three-phase MPC protocol: (1) Alice samples her PCF key, and can perform the expensive PCF evaluation with her key offline to recover her share of the correlated randomness; (2) Alice and Bob use generic secure computation to generate Bob's key, which then allows Bob to evaluate the PCF with his key and recover his share of the correlated randomness; (3) Alice and Bob perform the information-theoretic phase online, using their correlated randomness. This allows Alice to perform the brunt of her computation offline, before any interaction with Bob. This offline phase can be viewed as "party-independent" precomputation, which is more general than input-independence.

Definition 7 (Precomputable Pseudorandom Correlation Function).
Let $\mathcal{Y}$ be a reverse-sampleable correlation with output lengths $\ell_0(\lambda), \ell_1(\lambda)$ and let $\lambda \leq n(\lambda) \leq \mathsf{poly}(\lambda)$ be its input length. We say that a pseudorandom correlation function (PCF.Gen, PCF.Eval) is *precomputable* if the description of PCF.Gen contains the descriptions of two algorithms $(\mathsf{PCF.Gen}_0, \mathsf{PCF.Gen}_1)$ such that

- $\mathsf{PCF.Gen}_0(1^\lambda)$: On input the security parameter λ, returns a key k_0 and auxiliary output aux.
- $\mathsf{PCF.Gen}_1(1^\lambda, k_0, \mathsf{aux})$: On input the security parameter λ, a key k_0, and an auxiliary input aux, outputs a key k_1.

We also require the following property to hold:

Precomputability. For any security parameter $\lambda \in \mathbb{N}$, the two following distributions are computationally indistinguishable:

$$\left\{ (k_0, k_1) \colon (k_0, k_1) \leftarrow \mathsf{PCF.Gen}(1^\lambda) \right\} \overset{c}{\approx} \left\{ (k_0, k_1) \colon \begin{matrix} (k_0, \mathsf{aux}) \leftarrow \mathsf{PCF.Gen}_0(1^\lambda) \\ k_1 \leftarrow \mathsf{PCF.Gen}_1(1^\lambda, k_0, \mathsf{aux}) \end{matrix} \right\}.$$

Below, we provide a construction of precomputable PCF for OLE correlations from staged-HSS, and using a pseudorandom function. Given an input, first, each party samples a PRF key and sets the first half of the correlated pair to be the value of the PRF on the input. Next, to generate the additive shares of the product of these two values, they use staged-HSS. Here, we require the staged-HSS scheme to generate shares that are individually pseudorandom given the input, and in Lemma 2 we show that this can be assumed without loss of generality. This is because the property "pseudorandom $\mathcal{R}$-OLE-correlated outputs" for a PCF, which can be seen as a form of *correctness* property, essentially requires that the PCF outputs not only valid OLE tuples but also pseudorandom ones from the view of an external adversary.

Lemma 2 (HSS with Pseudorandom Outputs). *Denote by $\mathcal{P}$ a class of programs defined over a ring $\mathcal{R}$, with input space $\mathcal{I} \subseteq \mathcal{R}$. Assuming the existence of one-way functions, any HSS scheme for $\mathcal{P}$ can be modified in such a way that each output share is pseudorandom to an external adversary given only the input (but neither input share).*

Formally, assuming the existence of an HSS scheme $\mathsf{HSS} = (\mathsf{Setup}, \mathsf{Input}, \mathsf{Eval}, \mathsf{Rec})$ for $\mathcal{P}$, there exists an HSS scheme $\mathsf{HSS}' = (\mathsf{Setup}', \mathsf{Input}', \mathsf{Eval}', \mathsf{Rec}')$ for $\mathcal{P}$ such that:

$\forall \sigma \in \{0,1\}, \forall (P : \mathcal{R} \to \mathcal{Y}) \in \mathcal{P}, \forall x \in \mathcal{R}:$

$$\left\{ (x, y_\sigma): \begin{array}{c} (\mathsf{pk}, (\mathsf{ek}_0, \mathsf{ek}_1)) \leftarrow \mathsf{Setup}'(1^\lambda) \\ (\mathsf{I}_0, \mathsf{I}_1) \leftarrow \mathsf{Input}'(x) \\ y_\sigma \leftarrow \mathsf{Eval}'(\sigma, \mathsf{ek}_\sigma, I_\sigma, P) \end{array} \right\} \overset{c}{\approx} \{(x, r): r \overset{\$}{\leftarrow} \mathcal{Y}\}.$$

Moreover, if HSS *has additive reconstruction, then so does* HSS$'$, *and if* HSS *is a staged-HSS scheme, then* HSS$'$ *is also a staged-HSS.*

The proof of Lemma 2 uses a trick which is standard in the HSS literature, which we sketch here and expand upon in the full version of the paper: a PRF key (the same for both parties) is added to the HSS keys, which is used at evaluation time to "mask" the output shares. Because both parties use the same mask, they can simply remove it before reconstruction and correctness is preserved. Moreover, the HSS shares are pseudorandom from the point of view of an external adversary who does not know the PRF key.

Construction 3 (Precomputable & Programmable PCF for OLE). Let $F : \mathcal{K} \times \mathcal{I} \to \mathcal{Y}$ be a pseudorandom function with evaluation in NC^1, where $\mathcal{I}, \mathcal{Y}$ are finite rings. Let HSS $=$ (Setup, MemGen, Input, Eval) be a staged-homomorphic secret sharing scheme and denote by $(\overline{\mathsf{Input}}_0, \overline{\mathsf{Input}}_1)$, and $(\overline{\mathsf{Eval}}_0, \overline{\mathsf{Eval}}_1)$ the additional algorithms defined in Definition 6. Let ExtEval be the modified evaluation algorithm as in Lemma 1. Our PCF works as follows:

- PCF.Gen(1^λ):
  - Run $(k_0, \mathsf{aux}) \leftarrow \mathsf{PCF.Gen}_0(1^\lambda)$.
  - Run $k_1 \leftarrow \mathsf{PCF.Gen}_1(1^\lambda, k_0, \mathsf{aux})$.
  - Output (k_0, k_1).
- PCF.Gen$_0$(1^λ):
  - Run $(\mathsf{pk}, \mathsf{ek}_0, \mathsf{ek}_1) \leftarrow \mathsf{HSS.Setup}(1^\lambda)$.
  - Sample $k_{\mathsf{prf}}^{(0)} \overset{\$}{\leftarrow} \mathcal{K}$, and compute $(\mathsf{I}_0, \mathsf{I}_1) \leftarrow \mathsf{HSS.Input}(\mathsf{pk}, k_{\mathsf{prf}}^{(0)})$.
  - Run $(\overline{\mathsf{I}}_0, \mathsf{aux}') \leftarrow \mathsf{HSS.\overline{Input}}_0(\mathsf{pk})$.
  - Output $k_0 = (\mathsf{ek}_0, \mathsf{I}_0, \overline{\mathsf{I}}_0, k_{\mathsf{prf}}^{(0)})$, and $\mathsf{aux} = (\mathsf{aux}', \mathsf{ek}_1, \mathsf{I}_1)$.
- PCF.Gen$_1$($1^\lambda, k_0, \mathsf{aux}$):
  - Parse $k_0 = (\mathsf{ek}_0, \mathsf{I}_0, \overline{\mathsf{I}}_0, k_{\mathsf{prf}}^{(0)})$, and $\mathsf{aux} = (\mathsf{aux}', \mathsf{ek}_1, \mathsf{I}_1)$.
  - Sample $k_{\mathsf{prf}}^{(1)} \overset{\$}{\leftarrow} \mathcal{K}$, and compute $\overline{\mathsf{I}}_1 \leftarrow \mathsf{HSS.\overline{Input}}_1(\mathsf{pk}, k_{\mathsf{prf}}^{(1)}, \mathsf{aux}')$.
  - Output $k_1 = (\mathsf{ek}_1, \overline{\mathsf{I}}_1, \mathsf{I}_1, k_{\mathsf{prf}}^{(1)})$.
- PCF.Eval($\sigma, k_\sigma, \mathbf{x}$):
  - Parse $k_\sigma = (\mathsf{ek}_\sigma, \mathsf{I}_\sigma, \overline{\mathsf{I}}_\sigma, k_{\mathsf{prf}}^{(\sigma)})$.
  - If $\sigma = 0$, then
    * Run $\mathsf{M}_\sigma \leftarrow \mathsf{HSS.\overline{Eval}}_0(\mathsf{ek}_\sigma, \overline{\mathsf{I}}_\sigma, F_\bullet(\mathbf{x}))$.
    Else if $\sigma = 1$,
    * Run $\mathsf{M}_\sigma \leftarrow \mathsf{HSS.\overline{Eval}}_1(\mathsf{ek}_\sigma, \overline{\mathsf{I}}_\sigma, k_{\mathsf{prf}}^{(\sigma)}, F_\bullet(\mathbf{x}))$.
  - Run $y_\sigma \leftarrow \mathsf{HSS.ExtEval}(\mathsf{ek}_\sigma, (\mathsf{M}_\sigma, \mathsf{I}_\sigma), F_\times(\mathbf{x}))$, with $F_\times(\mathbf{x})$ defined as $F_\times(\mathbf{x}): (k^{(0)}, k^{(1)}) \mapsto F_{k^{(0)}}(\mathbf{x}) \cdot F_{k^{(1)}}(\mathbf{x})$.
  - Output $(F_{k_{\mathsf{prf}}^{(\sigma)}}(\mathbf{x}), y_\sigma)$.

Theorem 5. *Let $\mathcal{R}$ be a finite ring. Assuming F is a secure pseudorandom function with evaluation in NC^1 and HSS is a secure staged-HSS scheme, Construction 3 is a two-party precomputable PCF for OLE correlations over $\mathcal{R}$. Furthermore, this PCF is programmable.*

The proof of Theorem 5 is provided in the full version of the paper. By combining Theorems 5 and 2, we get Corollary 4.

Corollary 4 (Precomputable PCF for $\mathcal{R}$-OLEfrom DCR). *Assuming the DCR assumption holds, there exists a two-party precomputable pseudorandom correlation function (as per Definition 7) for the $\mathcal{R}$-OLE correlation.*

Corollary 5 (From OLE to Low-Degree Correlations). *Assuming the existence of (one-way functions and of) staged-HSS supporting the class of RMS programs, there exists a two-party precomputable PCF (Definition 7) for low-degree correlations (c.f. full version). In particular, such a PCF exists under the DCR assumption.*

6.1   Sublinear Computation with One-Sided Statistical Security

Most constructions of two-party HSS for super-constant depth circuits can be used in a non black-box way to build two-party secure computation with an amount of communication which is sublinear in (or even independent of) the circuit-size: if the input share generation algorithm is simple enough to be securely distributed with low communication, the parties need to only run the evaluation algorithm locally, then reconstruct the output.

In the $\mathcal{F}^{\mathsf{HSS}}_{\mathsf{update}}$-Hybrid Model. The main component (apart from the HSS scheme itself) in building sublinear secure computation from HSS is the low-communication distributed share generation. When using staged-HSS, the first party can simply sample its share locally, so the hard part is updating the second party so they can receive their share too. We formalize this task in Fig. 1 as the ideal functionality $\mathcal{F}^{\mathsf{HSS}}_{\mathsf{update}}$. We prove in Lemma 3 that there exists sublinear two-party secure computation, provided this step can be performed with one-sided statistical security and with low-enough communication.

Functionality $\mathcal{F}^{\mathsf{HSS}}_{\mathsf{update}}$

The functionality is parameterized with a staged-HSS scheme staged-HSS = (staged-HSS.Setup, staged-HSS.Input, staged-HSS.MemGen, staged-HSS.Eval).

Input: Wait to receive $(\mathsf{share}, \mathsf{staged\text{-}HSS.pk}, \bar{\mathsf{I}}_0, \mathsf{aux})$ from P_0 and (input, x_1) from P_1.

Output: Compute $\bar{\mathsf{I}}_1 \leftarrow \mathsf{staged\text{-}HSS.\overline{Input}}_1(\mathsf{staged\text{-}HSS.pk}, x_1, \mathsf{aux})$, and output $(\mathsf{staged\text{-}HSS.pk}, \bar{\mathsf{I}}_1)$ to P_1.

Fig. 1. Ideal functionality $\mathcal{F}^{\mathsf{HSS}}_{\mathsf{update}}$, parameterized by a staged-HSS scheme, for generating the second input share given the first, precomputed, one.

Protocol Π_C

Parties: Alice and Bob
Parameters: The protocol is parameterized with:

- $C\colon \mathbb{F}^{n_0} \times \mathbb{F}^{n_1} \to \mathbb{F}^m$ is an arithmetic circuit over finite field $\mathbb{F}$.
- HSS = (HSS.Setup, HSS.Input, HSS.MemGen, HSS.Eval) is a staged-HSS scheme with pseudorandom shares supporting the class of RMS programs over $\mathbb{F}$ (seen as a ring). We denote the staged input and evaluation algorithms by (HSS.$\overline{\text{Input}}_0$, HSS.$\overline{\text{Input}}_1$) and (HSS.$\overline{\text{Eval}}_0$, HSS.$\overline{\text{Eval}}_1$). Let HSS.ExtEval be defined as in Lemma 1.
- $F(\cdot, \cdot)$ is a PRF in NC^1 with domain $\{0,1\}^\lambda$, key space $\{0,1\}^\lambda$, and range $\mathbb{F}^{n_1}$.

Hybrid Model: The protocol is defined in the $\mathcal{F}_{\text{update}}^{\text{HSS}}$-hybrid model.
Input: Alice holds $x_0 \in \mathbb{F}^{n_0}$ and Bob holds $x_1 \in \mathbb{F}^{n_1}$.
The Protocol:

Alice's precomputation phase. Alice does the following:
1. $K \xleftarrow{\$} \{0,1\}^\lambda$
2. (HSS.pk, ek_0, ek_1) $\leftarrow$ HSS.Setup(1^λ)
3. ($\bar{\mathsf{I}}_0$, aux) $\leftarrow$ HSS.$\overline{\text{Input}}_0$(HSS.pk)
4. (I_0, I_1) $\leftarrow$ HSS.Input(1^λ, K)
5. $\alpha \xleftarrow{\$} \{0,1\}^\lambda$, $c_{\text{in}} \leftarrow x_0 + F(K, \alpha)$, and $r_{\text{out}} \xleftarrow{\$} \mathbb{F}^m$
6. $M_0 \leftarrow$ HSS.$\overline{\text{Eval}}$(ek_0, $\bar{\mathsf{I}}_0$, $F(\cdot, \alpha)$)
7. $y_0 \leftarrow$ HSS.ExtEval(ek_0, (M_0, I_0), $f_{\alpha, c_{\text{in}}}$),
   where $f_{\alpha, c_{\text{in}}}\colon (X, Y) \mapsto C(c_{\text{in}} - F(X, \alpha), Y)$

Online phase.
8. Alice sends (ek_1, I_1, c_{in}, α, r_{out}) to Bob, who waits to receive it.
9. Alice sends (**share**, HSS.pk, $\bar{\mathsf{I}}_0$, aux) to $\mathcal{F}_{\text{update}}^{\text{HSS}}$;
   Bob sends (**input**, x_1) to $\mathcal{F}_{\text{update}}^{\text{HSS}}$, and waits to receive (HSS.pk, $\bar{\mathsf{I}}_1$) from $\mathcal{F}_{\text{update}}^{\text{HSS}}$.

Bob's computation phase. Bob does the following:
1. $M_1 \leftarrow$ HSS.$\overline{\text{Eval}}$(ek_1, $\bar{\mathsf{I}}_1$, $F(\cdot, \alpha)$)
2. $y_1 \leftarrow$ HSS.ExtEval(ek_1, (M_1, I_1), $f_{\alpha, c_{\text{in}}}$),
   where $f_{\alpha, c_{\text{in}}}\colon (X, Y) \mapsto C(c_{\text{in}} - F(X, \alpha), Y)$

Output phase. Alice outputs $y_0' \leftarrow y_0 + r_{\text{out}}$; Bob outputs $y_1' \leftarrow y_1 - r_{\text{out}}$.

Fig. 2. (Sublinear) Secure Two-Party Computation with One-Sided Statistical Security from staged-HSS Supporting the Class of RMS Programs.

Lemma 3 (Secure Computation with One-Sided Statistical Security in the $\mathcal{F}_{\text{update}}^{\text{HSS}}$-hybrid model). *Let $C\colon \mathbb{F}^{n_0} \times \mathbb{F}^{n_1} \to \mathbb{F}^m$ be an arithmetic circuit* *over a finite field* $\mathbb{F}$. *Let* staged-HSS *be a staged-HSS scheme with pseudorandom shares supporting the class of RMS programs over* $\mathbb{F}$ *(seen as a ring).*

The protocol Π_C *provided in Fig. 2 UC-securely implements the two-party functionality* $\mathcal{F}_{\mathsf{SFE}}(C)$ *in the* $\mathcal{F}_{\mathsf{update}}^{\mathsf{HSS}}$-*hybrid model, against a passive adversary statically corrupting at most one of the parties, with perfect security against Alice, and computational security against Bob. The protocol uses* $\lambda^{\mathcal{O}(1)} + (n_1 + m) \cdot \log|\mathbb{F}|$ *bits of communication.*

Instantiating $\mathcal{F}_{\mathsf{update}}^{\mathsf{HSS}}$ **Under DCR.** We now show how to instantiate $\mathcal{F}_{\mathsf{update}}^{\mathsf{HSS}}$ for construction of staged-HSS from DCR (see the full version). This instantiation is non black-box in the HSS scheme, and uses a combination of the Paillier-ElGamal encryption scheme, which is provably semantically secure under DCR, and oblivious linear evaluation (OLE) with one-sided statistical security, which is known from DCR.

Functionality $\mathcal{F}_{\mathsf{OLE}}$

The functionality $\mathcal{F}_{\mathsf{OLE}}$ for (batch) oblivious linear evaluation is parameterized by a finite field $\mathbb{F}$, and interacts with two parties P_0 and P_1.

Input: Wait to receive $(\mathtt{input}, 0, \mathbf{u} = (u_1, \ldots, u_s))$ (where $u_1, \ldots, u_s \in \mathbb{F}$) from P_0 and $(\mathtt{input}, 1, \mathbf{v} = (v_1, \ldots, v_t))$ (where $v_1, \ldots, v_t \in \mathbb{F}$) from P_1.
Output: Compute $\mathbf{z} \leftarrow (u_i \cdot v_j)_{i \in [s], j \in [t]}$, sample $\mathbf{z}_0 \xleftarrow{\$} \mathbb{F}^{s \cdot t}$, set $\mathbf{z}_1 \leftarrow \mathbf{z} - \mathbf{z}_0$; Output $\mathbf{z}_\sigma$ to P_σ for $\sigma \in \{0, 1\}$.

Fig. 3. Ideal functionality $\mathcal{F}_{\mathsf{OLE}}$ for (batch) oblivious linear evaluation.

Protocol $\Pi_{\mathsf{update}}^{\mathsf{HSS}}$

Parties: Alice and Bob.
Parameters: $\mathbb{F}_{2^\lambda}$ is an exponential-size finite field; n_1 is an input size. staged-HSS is the staged-HSS scheme inspired by [27] using Paillier-ElGamal under DCR (see the full version). The Paillier-ElGamal cryptosystem itself is parameterized by GenPQ, an algorithm that on input 1^λ, generates $(N = p \cdot q, p, q)$, where p and q are $\ell(\lambda)$-bit primes where $\ell \colon \mathbb{N}^* \to \mathbb{N}^*$ is a function such that $\forall \kappa \in \mathbb{N}^*, \ell(\kappa) \geq 1.5\kappa$. $B_{\mathsf{sk}} := 2^{2\ell(\lambda) - 2\log|\mathbb{F}|}$ is the base for the decomposition of the secret key into digits; $s := 2\ell(\lambda) + 2\log|\mathbb{F}|$ is the number of cyphertexts needed to encrypt the secret key; $t := \lceil n_1 \frac{\log|\mathbb{F}|}{2\ell(\lambda)} \rceil$.
Hybrid Model: The protocol is defined in the $\mathcal{F}_{\mathsf{OLE}}$-hybrid model.
Input: Alice holds $(\mathsf{HSS.pk}, \bar{I}_0, \mathsf{aux})$ and Bob holds $x_1 = (x_1^{(1)}, \ldots, x_1^{(t)}) \in \mathcal{R}^{n_1} \approx [N]^t$.
The Protocol:

1. Alice does the following:
   - Parse HSS.pk = $(\mathsf{pk_{PaillierEG}}, D^{(0)}, \ldots, D^{(s-1)})$
     // $D^{(j)}$ is a Paillier-ElGamal encryption under pk of the jth digit of the secret key in base B_{sk}
   - Parse $\bar{I}_0 = (\mathsf{ct_{ind}}, (\mathsf{ct}_{\mathsf{ind}}^{(i,j)})_{(i,j)\in[t]\times[s+1]})$
     // $\mathsf{ct_{ind}}$ is of the form g^r, and $\mathsf{ct}_{\mathsf{ind}}^{(i,j)}$ is of the form $g^{r_{i,j}}$
   - Parse aux $= (g^r, \mathsf{pk}_{\mathsf{PaillierEG}}^r, (g^{r_{i,j}})_{(i,j)\in[t]\times[s+1]}, (\mathsf{pk}_{\mathsf{PaillierEG}}^{r_{i,j}})_{(i,j)\in[t]\times[s+1]})$
     // $\mathsf{pk_{PaillierEG}} = g^{\mathsf{sk_{PaillierEG}}} \bmod N^2$
2. Alice sends $(N, \mathsf{pk_{PaillierEG}}, \mathsf{ct_{ind}})$ to Bob
3. Alice sends $(\mathbf{input}, 0, (1\|d))$ to $\mathcal{F}_{\mathsf{OLE}}$ and waits to receive $\mathbf{y}^{(0)} = (y_{i,j}^{(0)})_{(i,j)\in[t]\times[s+1]}$;
   Bob sends $(\mathbf{input}, 1, x_1)$ to $\mathcal{F}_{\mathsf{OLE}}$ and waits to receive $\mathbf{y}^{(1)} = (y_{i,j}^{(1)})_{(i,j)\in[t]\times[s+1]}$.
   // Adding the digit 1 to the secret key d condenses the notations of the encryption of the input alone, and those of the input times each digit of the secret key, as $x \cdot (1, d_0, \ldots, d_{s-1}) = (x, x \cdot d_0, \ldots, x \cdot d_{s-1})$.
4. Alice does the following:
   For each $(i,j) \in [t] \times [s+1]$, $c_{i,j} \leftarrow (1+N)^{y_{i,j}^{(0)}} \cdot h^{r_{i,j}}$
5. Alice sends $\mathbf{c} = (c_{i,j})_{(i,j)\in[t]\times[s+1]}$ to Bob, who waits to receive it.
6. Bob sets $\mathsf{ct_{dep}} \leftarrow (c_{i,j} \cdot (1+N)^{y_{i,j}^{(1)}})_{(i,j)\in[t]\times[s+1]}$ and outputs $\bar{I}_1 \leftarrow (\mathsf{ct_{ind}}, \mathsf{ct_{dep}})$.

Fig. 4. Protocol for securely realizing $\mathcal{F}_{\mathsf{update}}^{\mathsf{HSS}}$ under the circular security of the Paillier-ElGamal cryptosystem.

Lemma 4 (Instantiating Lemma 3 under DCR). *Let* HSS *be the staged-HSS scheme inspired by [27] using Paillier-ElGamal (see the full version). Assuming the DCR assumption holds, the protocol $\Pi_{\mathsf{update}}^{\mathsf{HSS}}$ provided in Fig. 4 UC-securely implements the two-party functionality $\mathcal{F}_{\mathsf{update}}^{\mathsf{HSS}}$ in the $\mathcal{F}_{\mathsf{OLE}}$-hybrid model, against a passive adversary statically corrupting at most one of the parties, with perfect security against Alice and Bob. The protocol uses $\mathcal{O}(\lambda \cdot n_1)$ bits of communication.*

We then obtain our final claim.

Theorem 6 (Computation for NC^1 with Circuit-Independent-Communication and One-Sided Statistical Security from Circular Security of Paillier-ElGamal). *Let C be an RMS program with $n = n_0 + n_1$ inputs and m outputs over $\mathbb{F}_{2^\lambda}$. Assuming DCR and the circular security of the Paillier-ElGamal encryption scheme, there exists a protocol that UC-securely implements the two-party functionality $\mathcal{F}_{\mathsf{SFE}}(C)$, against a passive adversary that statically corrupts at most one of the parties, with perfect security against a corrupted Alice, and computational security against a corrupted Bob. The protocol uses $\lambda^{\mathcal{O}(1)} + \mathcal{O}((n+m) \cdot \log|\mathbb{F}|)$ bits of communication.*

Acknowledgments. We thank the anonymous reviewers of Eurocrypt 2023. Geoffroy Couteau was supported by the French ANR SCENE (ANR-20-CE39-0001) and the PEPR Cyber France 2030 programme (ANR-22-PECY-0003). Pierre Meyer was supported by ERC Project HSS (852952). Alain Passelègue and Mahshid Riahinia were supported by the French ANR RAGE project (ANR-20-CE48-0011) and the PEPR Cyber France 2030 programme (ANR-22-PECY-0003).

References

1. Abram, D., Damgård, I., Orlandi, C., Scholl, P.: An algebraic framework for silent preprocessing with trustless setup and active security. In: Dodis, Y., Shrimpton, T. (eds.) CRYPTO 2022. LNCS, vol. 13510, pp. 421–452. Springer, Heidelberg (2022). https://doi.org/10.1007/978-3-031-15985-5_15

2. Attrapadung, N., Matsuda, T., Nishimaki, R., Yamada, S., Yamakawa, T.: Constrained PRFs for NC^1 in traditional groups. In: Shacham, H., Boldyreva, A. (eds.) CRYPTO 2018. LNCS, vol. 10992, pp. 543–574. Springer, Cham (2018). https://doi.org/10.1007/978-3-319-96881-0_19

3. Banerjee, A., Fuchsbauer, G., Peikert, C., Pietrzak, K., Stevens, S.: Key-homomorphic constrained pseudorandom functions. In: Dodis, Y., Nielsen, J.B. (eds.) TCC 2015. LNCS, vol. 9015, pp. 31–60. Springer, Heidelberg (2015). https://doi.org/10.1007/978-3-662-46497-7_2

4. Boneh, D., Lewi, K., Wu, D.J.: Constraining pseudorandom functions privately. In: Fehr, S. (ed.) PKC 2017. LNCS, vol. 10175, pp. 494–524. Springer, Heidelberg (2017). https://doi.org/10.1007/978-3-662-54388-7_17

5. Boneh, D., Waters, B.: Constrained pseudorandom functions and their applications. In: Sako, K., Sarkar, P. (eds.) ASIACRYPT 2013. LNCS, vol. 8270, pp. 280–300. Springer, Heidelberg (2013). https://doi.org/10.1007/978-3-642-42045-0_15

6. Boyle, E., Couteau, G., Gilboa, N., Ishai, Y., Kohl, L., Scholl, P.: Efficient pseudorandom correlation generators: silent OT extension and more. In: Boldyreva, A., Micciancio, D. (eds.) CRYPTO 2019. LNCS, vol. 11694, pp. 489–518. Springer, Cham (2019). https://doi.org/10.1007/978-3-030-26954-8_16

7. Boyle, E., Couteau, G., Gilboa, N., Ishai, Y., Orrù, M.: Homomorphic secret sharing: optimizations and applications. In: Thuraisingham, B.M., Evans, D., Malkin, T., Xu, D. (eds.) ACM CCS 2017, pp. 2105–2122. ACM Press (2017). https://doi.org/10.1145/3133956.3134107

8. Boyle, E., Gilboa, N., Ishai, Y.: Breaking the circuit size barrier for secure computation under DDH. In: Robshaw, M., Katz, J. (eds.) CRYPTO 2016. LNCS, vol. 9814, pp. 509–539. Springer, Heidelberg (2016). https://doi.org/10.1007/978-3-662-53018-4_19

9. Boyle, E., Goldwasser, S., Ivan, I.: Functional signatures and pseudorandom functions. In: Krawczyk, H. (ed.) PKC 2014. LNCS, vol. 8383, pp. 501–519. Springer, Heidelberg (2014). https://doi.org/10.1007/978-3-642-54631-0_29

10. Boyle, E., Kohl, L., Scholl, P.: Homomorphic secret sharing from lattices without FHE. In: Ishai, Y., Rijmen, V. (eds.) EUROCRYPT 2019. LNCS, vol. 11477, pp. 3–33. Springer, Cham (2019). https://doi.org/10.1007/978-3-030-17656-3_1

11. Brakerski, Z., Tsabary, R., Vaikuntanathan, V., Wee, H.: Private constrained PRFs (and More) from LWE. In: Kalai, Y., Reyzin, L. (eds.) TCC 2017. LNCS, vol. 10677, pp. 264–302. Springer, Cham (2017). https://doi.org/10.1007/978-3-319-70500-2_10

12. Brakerski, Z., Vaikuntanathan, V.: Constrained key-homomorphic PRFs from standard lattice assumptions. In: Dodis, Y., Nielsen, J.B. (eds.) TCC 2015. LNCS, vol. 9015, pp. 1–30. Springer, Heidelberg (2015). https://doi.org/10.1007/978-3-662-46497-7_1

13. Canetti, R., Chen, Y.: Constraint-hiding constrained PRFs for NC^1 from LWE. In: Coron, J.-S., Nielsen, J.B. (eds.) EUROCRYPT 2017. LNCS, vol. 10210, pp. 446–476. Springer, Cham (2017). https://doi.org/10.1007/978-3-319-56620-7_16

14. Castagnos, G., Laguillaumie, F., Tucker, I.: Threshold linearly homomorphic encryption on $z/2^k z$. Cryptology ePrint Archive (2022)

15. Chaum, D.: The spymasters double-agent problem. In: Brassard, G. (ed.) CRYPTO 1989. LNCS, vol. 435, pp. 591–602. Springer, New York (1990). https://doi.org/10.1007/0-387-34805-0_52

16. Chen, Y., Vaikuntanathan, V., Wee, H.: GGH15 beyond permutation branching programs: proofs, attacks, and candidates. In: Shacham, H., Boldyreva, A. (eds.) CRYPTO 2018. LNCS, vol. 10992, pp. 577–607. Springer, Cham (2018). https://doi.org/10.1007/978-3-319-96881-0_20

17. Cook, S.A., Hoover, H.J.: A depth-universal circuit. SIAM J. Comput. **14**(4), 833–839 (1985)

18. Damgård, I., Pastro, V., Smart, N., Zakarias, S.: Multiparty computation from somewhat homomorphic encryption. In: Safavi-Naini, R., Canetti, R. (eds.) CRYPTO 2012. LNCS, vol. 7417, pp. 643–662. Springer, Heidelberg (2012). https://doi.org/10.1007/978-3-642-32009-5_38

19. Davidson, A., Katsumata, S., Nishimaki, R., Yamada, S., Yamakawa, T.: Adaptively secure constrained pseudorandom functions in the standard model. In: Micciancio, D., Ristenpart, T. (eds.) CRYPTO 2020. LNCS, vol. 12170, pp. 559–589. Springer, Cham (2020). https://doi.org/10.1007/978-3-030-56784-2_19

20. Gentry, C.: Fully homomorphic encryption using ideal lattices. In: Mitzenmacher, M. (ed.) 41st ACM STOC, pp. 169–178. ACM Press (2009). https://doi.org/10.1145/1536414.1536440

21. Goldreich, O., Goldwasser, S., Micali, S.: How to construct random functions (extended abstract). In: 25th FOCS, pp. 464–479. IEEE Computer Society Press (1984). https://doi.org/10.1109/SFCS.1984.715949

22. Goldreich, O., Micali, S., Wigderson, A.: How to play any mental game or a completeness theorem for protocols with honest majority. In: Aho, A. (ed.) 19th ACM STOC, pp. 218–229. ACM Press (1987). https://doi.org/10.1145/28395.28420

23. Hofheinz, D., Kamath, A., Koppula, V., Waters, B.: Adaptively secure constrained pseudorandom functions. In: Goldberg, I., Moore, T. (eds.) FC 2019. LNCS, vol. 11598, pp. 357–376. Springer, Cham (2019). https://doi.org/10.1007/978-3-030-32101-7_22

24. Ishai, Y., Prabhakaran, M., Sahai, A.: Founding cryptography on oblivious transfer – efficiently. In: Wagner, D. (ed.) CRYPTO 2008. LNCS, vol. 5157, pp. 572–591. Springer, Heidelberg (2008). https://doi.org/10.1007/978-3-540-85174-5_32

25. Kiayias, A., Papadopoulos, S., Triandopoulos, N., Zacharias, T.: Delegatable pseudorandom functions and applications. In: Sadeghi, A.R., Gligor, V.D., Yung, M. (eds.) ACM CCS 2013, pp. 669–684. ACM Press (2013). https://doi.org/10.1145/2508859.2516668

26. Naor, M., Pinkas, B.: Efficient oblivious transfer protocols. In: Kosaraju, S.R. (ed.) 12th SODA, pp. 448–457. ACM-SIAM (2001)

27. Orlandi, C., Scholl, P., Yakoubov, S.: The rise of paillier: homomorphic secret sharing and public-key silent OT. In: Canteaut, A., Standaert, F.-X. (eds.) EURO-CRYPT 2021. LNCS, vol. 12696, pp. 678–708. Springer, Cham (2021). https://doi.org/10.1007/978-3-030-77870-5_24

28. Peikert, C., Shiehian, S.: Privately constraining and programming PRFs, the LWE Way. In: Abdalla, M., Dahab, R. (eds.) PKC 2018. LNCS, vol. 10770, pp. 675–701. Springer, Cham (2018). https://doi.org/10.1007/978-3-319-76581-5_23

29. Roy, L., Singh, J.: Large message homomorphic secret sharing from DCR and applications. In: Malkin, T., Peikert, C. (eds.) CRYPTO 2021. LNCS, vol. 12827, pp. 687–717. Springer, Cham (2021). https://doi.org/10.1007/978-3-030-84252-9_23

Advanced Public Key Primitives

Efficient FHEW Bootstrapping with Small Evaluation Keys, and Applications to Threshold Homomorphic Encryption

Yongwoo Lee[1]([⊠])[ID], Daniele Micciancio[2][ID], Andrey Kim[1][ID], Rakyong Choi[1][ID], Maxim Deryabin[1][ID], Jieun Eom[1][ID], and Donghoon Yoo[1][ID]

[1] Samsung Advanced Institute of Technology, Suwon, Republic of Korea
{yw0803.lee,andrey.kim,rakyong.choi,max.deriabin,jieun.eom}@samsung.com,
donghoon.yoo@desilo.ai
[2] University of California, San Diego, USA
daniele@cs.ucsd.edu

Abstract. There are two competing approaches to bootstrap the FHEW fully homomorphic encryption scheme (Ducas and Micciancio, Eurocrypt 2015) and its variants: the original AP/FHEW method, which supports arbitrary secret key distributions, and the improved GINX/TFHE method, which uses much smaller evaluation keys, but is directly applicable only to binary secret keys, restricting the scheme's applicability.

In this paper, we present a new bootstrapping procedure for FHEW-like encryption schemes that achieves the best features of both methods: support for arbitrary secret key distributions at no additional runtime costs, while using small evaluation keys. (Support for arbitrary secret keys is critical in a number of important applications, like threshold and some multi-key homomorphic encryption schemes.) As an added benefit, our new bootstrapping procedure results in smaller noise growth than both AP and GINX, regardless of the key distribution.

Our improvements are both theoretically significant (offering asymptotic savings, up to a $O(\log n)$ multiplicative factor, either on the running time or public evaluation key size), and practically relevant. For example, for a concrete 128-bit target security level, we show how to decrease the evaluation key size of the best previously known scheme by more than 30%, while also slightly reducing the running time. We demonstrate the practicality of the proposed methods by building a prototype implementation within the PALISADE/OpenFHE open-source homomorphic encryption library. We provide optimized parameter sets and implementation results showing that the proposed algorithm has the best performance among all known FHEW bootstrapping methods in terms of runtime and key size. We illustrate the benefits of our method by sketching a simple construction of threshold homomorphic encryption based on FHEW.

Keywords: Automorphism · Blind Rotation · Bootstrapping · Fully Homomorphic Encryption (FHE) · Threshold Homomorphic Encryption

© International Association for Cryptologic Research 2023
C. Hazay and M. Stam (Eds.): EUROCRYPT 2023, LNCS 14006, pp. 227–256, 2023.
https://doi.org/10.1007/978-3-031-30620-4_8

1 Introduction

The FHEW fully homomorphic encryption scheme [24] and its TFHE variant [21] are the best-known methods to perform bit-level homomorphic computations on encrypted data. There are two competing approaches to bootstrap FHEW-like Fully Homomorphic Encryption (FHE) schemes [21,24,38]: the AP bootstrapping method (originally proposed by Alperin-Sheriff and Peikert [2] and efficiently instantiated in the ring setting by the FHEW cryptosystem [24]), and the GINX method (originally proposed by Gama et al. [26] and adapted to the ring setting by the TFHE scheme [21].) A detailed comparison between the two methods is presented in [38], which concludes that the AP/FHEW method [2,24] is faster when LWE (Learning With Errors) secret keys follow the Gaussian (or uniform) distribution, while the (ring) GINX/TFHE method [21,26] has the lead for the special case of *binary* LWE secret keys. For the crossover point of ternary keys, [38] still recommends GINX bootstrapping due to its much lower memory (bootstrapping key) requirements. Very recently, [8,30] further improved GINX bootstrapping for ternary secrets by reducing the computation by half. (In our comparison, we refer to this optimized scheme as GINX*.) Besides the smaller running times, a big attraction of using GINX bootstrapping (with binary or ternary keys, as implemented by [21,38]) is its lower memory footprint, which is substantially smaller than the AP method.

Efficiency aside, the use of secret keys with large entries is still interesting for both theoretical and practical reasons. On the theoretical side, the foundation of lattice cryptography only offers solid support for Gaussian keys with relatively large entries, of the order of $O(\sqrt{n})$ [35,43], where n is the secret vector dimension serving as a security parameter. The use of smaller keys (e.g., with binary coefficients) has also received a substantial amount of theoretical attention [11,13,27,32,36,37]. However, the current state of the art, provided by [36][1], only shows that LWE with binary secrets can be proved as hard as standard LWE (with uniform or gaussian secrets) at the cost of increasing the secret dimension by a factor $O(\log q)$ and the error rate by a factor $O(\sqrt{n})$. So, motivated by practical considerations (limiting error growth during homomorphic computation, and the efficient implementation of GINX bootstrapping), these theoretical results supporting binary secrets are typically ignored, and parameters are set based on the best currently known attacks.[2] For fairness, this is also the approach followed in this paper when comparing our work to previous schemes that benefit from the use of binary secrets.

A more compelling motivation to use larger secret keys in practice is offered by *threshold* (lattice-based, homomorphic) encryption [4,6]. Threshold cryptog-

---

[1] The more recent work [11] provides more general results for arbitrary "entropic" distributions, but does not improve the reduction for binary secrets.

[2] This has become quite common for uniformly random binary secrets, and their use is now included in practical tools, like the lattice estimator of [1]. However, for extreme parameter settings (e.g., sparse keys or a very large number of samples), using binary keys is still a source of concern, as they weaken the security of the LWE problem [3,18], and their use is generally discouraged.

raphy offers a method to distribute a secret key s among a set of participants, say $P_1, \ldots, P_k$, each holding a share s_i of the secret key, in such a way that they can collaboratively decrypt messages. Still, if a subset of parties is corrupted and their secret shares s_i are made available to an adversary, ciphertexts retain their security. So, threshold cryptography eliminates the single point of failure associated with the secret key and ensures that encrypted data remains secure unless collaboratively decrypted by all parties.

The use of threshold cryptography is particularly attractive in the setting of homomorphic computation, as it requires modifications only to the key generation and decryption procedures. A threshold encryption scheme still has a *single public key* p (under which all messages can be encrypted by different parties) and *evaluation key* (used to perform homomorphic computations on ciphertexts.) In other words, applications of threshold Homomorphic Encryption (HE) support the same, simple workflow of standard (single party) HE: all data owners encrypt their data under a single public key p, and send their encrypted data to a single server that securely performs the encrypted computation, leading to a final encrypted result. Only at this point, the protocol requires interaction with multiple decryption servers (each holding a secret share s_i) to recover the final result. So, by only increasing the cost of decryption (and only by a modest amount, see below), threshold cryptography guarantees the security of all data (encrypted under a common public key p), even against the servers holding the decryption key (as long as they are not all corrupted.[3])

Lattices (and the LWE problem) provide a very convenient setting to implement threshold cryptography, as the public key ($p \approx a \cdot s$) is defined as a (noisy) linear function of the secret key s, for a random, publicly known value a. (See next section for a more formal definition of the LWE function.) So, distributed (shared) key generation can be easily implemented by having each party choose a local public-secret key pair ($p_i \approx a \cdot s_i, s_i$) individually (without any interaction), and then setting the public key to the sum $p = p_1 + \cdots + p_k$ of the local public keys. It is immediate to see that this is a valid public key corresponding to the secret key $s = s_1 + \cdots + s_k$ implicitly shared by all parties. In fact, this is how keys are generated in [6] (using uniformly random s_i) and [4] (using an arbitrary LWE key generation algorithm for each s_i.) Decryption can also easily be implemented[4] by decrypting a ciphertext c using the individual secret key shares and then adding up the partial decryptions. So, key generation and decryption are minimally interactive.[5] We remark that the threshold schemes [4,6] predate FHEW-like HE ([6] does not explicitly provide any homomorphic computation capability, and [4] is a BGV-type encryption scheme.) However, the same prin-

---

[3] As standard in HE, we consider security against passive adversaries, in which case the security threshold can be set to $k - 1$.

[4] This requires some care, adding noise to the partial decryptions to avoid information leakage, as already done in [4,6]. In this paper, we focus on the distributed key generation and homomorphic computation stages, which are the most relevant to FHE bootstrapping.

[5] HE also requires the generation of public evaluation keys, which introduces some additional complications, and is discussed below.

ciples apply to virtually any LWE-based encryption scheme, including those considered in this paper. Now comes a critical observation: even if the local key shares s_i have binary coefficients, their sum s (used by homomorphic computations and bootstrapping) is no longer binary and has coefficients potentially as large as k, the number of parties participating in the shared decryption protocol. Depending on the application, this number can be quite high, requiring similarly large secret keys. (E.g., see [17] for an application of lattice-based threshold (additively) HE with as many as 1000 parties.)

The FHEW-like cryptosystems with either AP or GINX bootstrapping are the most attractive methods for bit-level homomorphic computations.[6] But when ported to the threshold cryptography setting (with its correspondingly larger secrets), FHEW-like encryption presents the user with a difficult choice between

- the AP bootstrapping method of [2,24], with its fast performance (essentially independent of the secret key size) but very large evaluation keys, and
- the GINX bootstrapping method and its variants [21,26,29,38], with much smaller evaluation keys, but substantially larger running time due to the use of large secret keys.

A related class of applications to "multi-key HE" is discussed later on. So, one may ask the question: is it possible to design a bootstrapping procedure that offers the advantages of both methods, i.e., fast bootstrapping with arbitrarily distributed secret keys and small public evaluation keys?

1.1   Our Results

We answer the above question in the affirmative, designing a new bootstrapping procedure that supports the use of arbitrary secret key distributions without any performance penalty (similar to AP/FHEW bootstrapping) while keeping the attractive small size of GINX/TFHE bootstrapping keys. In fact, we even improve upon the performance of the best previously known scheme (with binary secrets), both in terms of key size and running time. For example, for the simple case of a (single user) gate bootstrapping operation at a 128-bit target security level, we improve upon previous schemes by reducing the evaluation key size by 30% (from 20 MB to 14 MB) while also slightly reducing the running time. (See Sect. 5 for details.) The impact of our bootstrapping method becomes significant with larger keys or a moderately large number of threshold decryption servers. Our method offers the additional advantage of reducing the amount of noise introduced during bootstrapping, even for the case of binary keys that are the most favorable to GINX so far. The improvements over previous methods are both theoretical (reducing either the running time or memory requirement of previous bootstrapping procedure by factors as high as $O(\log n)$, depending on the size of the secret keys/threshold group size), and practical. We verified our

---

[6] Other methods oriented towards arithmetics on integer or approximations to real/complex numbers like [12,19] offer advantages for a complementary set of applications, but are not within the scope of our paper.

theoretical results and the practicality of the proposed method with experiments, performed using a prototype implementation within the PALISADE/OpenFHE open-source homomorphic encryption library [5, 41].

1.2 Techniques

The main operation underlying both AP and GINX bootstrapping is the evaluation of a so-called "blind rotation". This operation takes some polynomial f_0 as an input and "rotates" it by some value encrypted within a given LWE ciphertext $(\vec{\alpha} = (\alpha_0, \dots, \alpha_{n-1}), \beta)$ using secret key $\vec{s} = (s_0, \dots, s_{n-1})$. (See Sect. 2 for more details.)

Starting with the encryption $\mathsf{RLWE}(f_0)$ of a polynomial f_0, previous blind rotation algorithms work as follows: at step i, given an encryption $\mathsf{RLWE}(f_{i-1})$ of a polynomial $f_{i-1}(X) = f_0 \cdot X^{\sum_{j \leq i-1} \alpha_j s_j}$, homomorphically compute $\mathsf{RLWE}(f_i)$ of an updated polynomial $f_i = f_{i-1} \cdot X^{\alpha_i \cdot s_i} = f_0 \cdot X^{\sum_{j \leq i} \alpha_j s_j}$, using a publicly known constant α_i (part of the input LWE ciphertext) and an encryption[7] $E(s_i)$ of a secret key coordinate s_i. After repeating this step n times, we obtain the encryption of $\mathsf{RLWE}(f_0 \cdot X^{\langle \vec{\alpha}, \vec{s} \rangle})$, which is a negacyclic rotation of f_0 by $\langle \vec{\alpha}, \vec{s} \rangle$ positions. The difference between the two bootstrapping procedures is that

- AP works by including in the evaluation key encryptions $E(\alpha \cdot s_i)$ for all possible values of α and then using α_i as a selector to pick one of them. This allows using arbitrary keys s_i with no impact on the running time, but also requires large evaluation keys due to the need to store multiple encryptions $E(\alpha \cdot s_i)$ for every secret key element s_i.[8]
- GINX on the other hand works by assuming $s_i \in \{0, 1\}$ is a single bit, and using $E(s_i)$ as a selector between the original ciphertext $\mathsf{RLWE}(f_{i-1})$ and a modified one $\mathsf{RLWE}(f_{i-1} \cdot X^{\alpha_i})$, using a homomorphic "MUX" gate. This only requires a single encryption $E(s_i)$ for each key element, but it is directly applicable only to binary secrets. Larger secrets can be handled in a number of ways, but not without a cost either in terms of key size or computation time. For example, [38] shows how to handle k-bit secrets by increasing both the evaluation key size and the bootstrapping running time, each by a factor k. A different tradeoff is given in [29], which incurs a smaller increase in running time (for small values of k) but at the cost of increasing the key size by an exponential factor $2^k - 1$. Both methods also result in higher bootstrapping noise.

In this paper, we present new techniques and optimizations to perform blind rotations using ring automorphisms and key switching. In its most basic form, the idea is the following: given $\mathsf{RLWE}(f_{i-1}(X))$, one can first apply a ring

---

[7] Under a typically different scheme $E(\cdot)$, used when generating the evaluation key.
[8] The method also offers storage memory trade-offs, decomposing a into a sequence of smaller "digits", but the same remarks apply.

autormorphsim[9] $\psi_{1/\alpha_i}(\cdot)$ where $\psi_a(\boldsymbol{h}) := \boldsymbol{h}(X^a)$. This gives an encryption of $\boldsymbol{f}_{i-1}(\alpha^{-1})$. Next, we homomorphically multiply the ciphertext by X^{s_i}, to get an encryption of $\boldsymbol{f}_{i-1}(\alpha^{-1}) \cdot X^{s_i}$. Finally, we apply the ring automorphism $\psi_{\alpha_i}(\cdot)$ to get an encryption of $\boldsymbol{f}_{i-1}(X) \cdot X^{\alpha_i s_i}$. After repeating this process n times, we obtain the encryption of $\mathsf{RLWE}(\boldsymbol{f}_0 \cdot X^{\langle \vec{\alpha}, \vec{s} \rangle})$.

The idea of using automorphisms is not new. For example, it was already used in a different context by Halevi and Shoup [28] to implement linear transformations and permutation networks in the (BGV-based) HElib library. Directly related to our use is the work of Bonnoron et al. (following a suggestion of Micciancio [7, Footnote 6]), which first used automorphisms to reduce the key size of a variant of the FHEW cryptosystem, in a way that is essentially the same as in the basic algorithm presented in our paper, but with some crucial technical differences. Specifically, in [7] the method is applied to the product of two cyclic polynomial rings of prime order, while we apply it to a single power-of-two cyclotomic ring, which is more practical but also more challenging. In fact, in prime-order cyclic rings, automorphisms ψ_α exist for any (nontrivial) value of α, making their application in [7] rather strightforward. However, in the power-of-two cyclotomic setting (as used by FHEW and our paper), automorphisms ψ_α exist only for odd values of α, and we need to develop new techniques to deal (efficiently) with even values of α. It should also be noted that [7] investigates a nontrivial extension of FHEW (to large gates with multi-bit inputs and outputs), resulting in much higher running times. By comparison, our work focuses on the simpler setting of homomorphic computations with small (binary) gates, and uses several algorithmic ideas which make the application of the automorphisms based method more practical and efficient than [7].

The basic algorithm based on automorphisms can be improved in a number of ways. For example, as already mentioned in [7], automorphisms from different steps can be composed together and replaced by a single automorphism. Other optimizations, specific to our paper, revolve around the technical difficulty that in a power-of-two cyclotomic automorphisms ψ_α exist only for *odd* coefficients while bootstrapping requires multiplication by both even and odd values of α. Moreover, the resulting methods require a substantial number of "automorphism keys", to perform the required key switching after each application of ψ_a. We further improve the performance of the algorithm by introducing a new blind rotation strategy that reorders the secret key elements $s_1, \ldots, s_n$. Instead of iterating over the s_i (homomorphically multiplying by s_i), and the applying automorphism $\psi_{\alpha_i/\alpha_{i+1}}$ at each step, we iteratively apply a fixed automorphism ψ_g (where g generates a large subgroup $\mathbb{Z}_q^*$). This alone produces rotations $\boldsymbol{f}_0 \cdot X^{g^i}$ for all possible values of $g^i \in \mathbb{Z}_q^*$. Then, we intersperse the homomorphic multiplications by the secret key elements s_j when g^i is the correct value of α_j. The final result is $\mathsf{RLWE}(\boldsymbol{f}_0 \cdot X^{\langle \vec{\alpha}, \vec{s} \rangle})$ as desired, but using only a single automorphism key corresponding to the generator g. Notice how our proposed

---

[9] The automorphism ψ_a alone maps an encryption under $z(X)$ to an encryption under modified key $z(X^a)$. Then, key-switching is used to turn this into an encryption under the original key $z(X)$.

method is applicable to arbitrary keys, and its performance is independent of the range of the secret coordinates s_i.

The possibility of reducing the key size by reordering the operations is one of the ideas already suggested in [7, Appendix F], but without filling in many important technical implementation details, and offering only a heuristic estimate of the potential memory savings. Fully developing the idea into a concrete algorithm, and providing a rigorous performance analysis as well as an implementation and experimental evaluation, is one of the main contributions of our work. In fact, in the intuitive explanation of the technique given above we omitted several important technicalities:

- The coefficients α_i are arbitrary integers in $\mathbb{Z}_q$, while automorphisms exist only for invertible $\alpha \in \mathbb{Z}_q^*$.
- The multiplicative group $\mathbb{Z}_q^*$ is not cyclic, but factors as the product of two groups of size $q/4$ and 2.
- In order to run over all of $\mathbb{Z}_q^*$, the automorphism g needs to be applied $O(q)$ times, but we would like the computation to take only $O(n)$ steps, independently of q.

The algorithms presented in our paper address all these difficulties and introduce further optimizations, which we analyze both in terms of worst-case and average-case complexity. As a result, our final algorithm achieves the best performance among all the known blind rotation techniques for FHEW-like cryptosystems both in terms of running time and key size.

Remark 1. In practice, one can use Torus LWE or other similar structures over Ring LWE as demonstrated in [21]. To compare all bootstrapping methods observed in the same environment, we will use only Ring LWE in this paper following [38]. We note that it is straightforward to apply Torus LWE to each of the observed methods as it has shown in [21] for GINX.

1.3 Applications to Threshold and Multi-key FHE

As described earlier, the linear properties of LWE allow to easily build threshold public-key encryption schemes: each party locally generates a key pair $p_i \approx a \cdot s_i$, and the public key $p = p_1 + \cdots + p_k$ can be set to the sum of the individual public keys. Things are more complex for threshold *FHE*. This is because, beside a public encryption key p, one needs to generate an *evaluation key*, which is essentially an encryption $E_p(s)$ of the secret key $s = s_1 + \cdots + s_k$ under the public key p. Naturally, this can be done using generic techniques from secure multiparty computation, with each party holding s_i as a local input, and common input p. However, this would not be quite practical. In fact, [4] gives specialized protocols to compute the evaluation key, but the method is specific to the BGV encryption scheme underlying their protocol. So, an interesting question is if a similar specialized evaluation key generation protocol can be designed for the threshold version of FHEW-like HE schemes. We observe that this is indeed possible, again using the linear homomorphic properties of lattice-based encryption. Specifically, after generating the global public key p, parties can encrypt their own secret shares $E_p(s_i)$ under it. Since all the shares are encrypted under a common public key, they can be added up, resulting in a HE $\sum_i E_p(s_i) = E_p(\sum_i s_i) = E_p(s)$ of the global secret key.[10]

Our blind rotation techniques also require the generation of switching keys to be used in conjunction with the ring automorphisms ψ_a. Again, a specialized distributed key generation algorithm can be built using the linearity of LWE encryption *and* the automorphisms. More in detail, in order to apply the automorphism ψ_a to a ciphertext, one needs to generate an encryption of the permuted secret key $E_p(\psi_a(s))$. Using the linearity of ψ_a, this can be achieved by having each party computing the encryption $E_p(\psi_a(s_i))$ of a permuted key share, and then combining these ciphertexts into $\sum_i E_p(\psi_a(s_i)) = E_p(\sum_i \psi_a(s_i)) = E_p(\psi_a(\sum_i s_i)) = E_p(\psi_a(s))$. The difference with standard (non-threshold) key generation, is that when the evaluation key is computed by a single party, the switching key $E_p(\psi_a(s))$ can be computed using a more efficient (and less noisy) private key version of LWE encryption $E_s(\psi_a(s))$. Here, in order to distribute the computation among parties that only have shares s_i of the secret key, encryption is performed using the common public key p.

Another potential application of our techniques is *Multi-Key* HE. This is a generalization of HE where messages can be encrypted under independently generated public keys $p_1, \ldots, p_k$, and still allow to perform joint computations on them. Naturally, decrypting the final result requires knowledge of all relevant secret keys $s_1, \ldots, s_k$. So, this is similar to threshold encryption, but with the difference that $p_1, \ldots, p_k$ are not combined in advance into a single public key p, and the set of keys can be chosen dynamically. GSW-based (e.g., FHEW-like) multi-key HE schemes were proposed in a sequence of works [14,16,23,40,42]. These schemes typically work by combining ciphertexts encrypted under different keys into a "multi-ciphertext", corresponding to the concatenation of the keys. Since the secret (decryption) key is also a concatenation, if the individual keys s_i are binary (as is the case for example in [16]), their concatenation is also binary, and one can make direct use of the efficient GINX bootstrapping for binary keys. However, these concatenated "multi-ciphertexts" are much longer than simple RLWE encryption, and the cost of bootstrapping (compared to the single key setting) is even higher than GINX with large keys. (Specifically, it grows linearly with the number of parties, rather than logarithmically.) Recently, [45] have proposed a multi-key HE scheme with compact ciphertexts. Interestingly, this compact scheme combines the individual secret keys by taking their sum. So, it requires an efficient bootstrapping method with non-binary keys. Similar to the threshold encryption setting, our techniques can be applied to speed up bootstrapping while keeping a small evaluation key.

---

[10] Calculation of $\sum_i E_p(s_i)$ proposed in this paper is done by the products of RGSW ciphertexts encrypting secret shares (see Sect. 6.).

1.4   Other Important Related Works

Besides bootstrapping of FHEW/TFHE, blind rotation is a useful tool to evaluate arbitrary functions in HE. For example, the Cheon-Kim-Kim-Song (CKKS) scheme [19] is efficient in the evaluation of complex numbers, but it only supports addition and multiplication. Thus, the ReLU and comparison functions, which are important components of neural networks, are evaluated using blind rotation in [9,22,33,34] as they are not represented as polynomials in real numbers. Also, a generalized bootstrapping for all the RLWE-based HE schemes including CKKS, Brakerski-Gentry-Vaikuntanathan(BGV) [12], and Brakerski/Fan-Vercauteren (BFV) [10,25], was proposed using blind rotation in [30].

1.5   Organization

The rest of the paper is organized as follows. The basic lattice-based HE and the previous blind rotation techniques are presented in Sect. 2. In Sect. 3, a new blind rotation algorithm and its variants are proposed. The theoretical analysis and comparison to prior works are given in Sect. 4 and the implementation results are given in Sect. 5. In Sect. 6, a threshold HE scheme based on our proposed blind rotation is described as a possible application. Finally, we conclude with remarks in Sect. 7.

2   Preliminaries

Let N be a power of two. We denote the $2N$-th cyclotomic ring by $\mathcal{R} := \mathbb{Z}[X]/(X^N + 1)$ and its quotient ring by $\mathcal{R}_Q := \mathcal{R}/Q\mathcal{R}$. Ring elements in $\mathcal{R}$ are indicated in bold, e.g. $\boldsymbol{a} = \boldsymbol{a}(X)$. For two vectors $\vec{a}$ and $\vec{b}$, we denote their inner product by $\langle \vec{a}, \vec{b} \rangle$. We denote a vector of ones of length n by $\vec{1}_n$. All logarithms are base 2 unless otherwise indicated. We write the floor, ceiling and round functions as $\lfloor \cdot \rfloor$, $\lceil \cdot \rceil$ and $\lfloor \cdot \rceil$, respectively. For $q \in \mathbb{Z}$ and $q > 1$, we identify the ring $\mathbb{Z}_q$ with $[-q/2, q/2)$ as the representative interval, and for $x \in \mathbb{Z}$ we denote the centered remainder of x modulo q by $[x]_q \in \mathbb{Z}_q$. We extend these notations to elements of $\mathcal{R}$ by applying them coefficient-wise. We use $\boldsymbol{a} \leftarrow$ S to denote uniform sampling from the set S. We denote sampling according to a distribution χ by $\boldsymbol{a} \leftarrow \chi$.

2.1   Basic Lattice-Based Encryption

For positive integers q and n, basic LWE encryption of $m \in \mathbb{Z}_q$ under the secret key $\vec{s} \leftarrow \chi_{\text{key}}$ is defined as

$$\mathsf{LWE}_{q,\vec{s}}(m) = (\vec{\alpha}, \beta) = (\vec{\alpha}, -\langle \vec{\alpha}, \vec{s} \rangle + e + m) \in \mathbb{Z}_q^{n+1},$$

where $\vec{\alpha} \leftarrow \mathbb{Z}_q^n$ and error $e \leftarrow \chi_{\text{err}}$. We occasionally drop subscripts q and $\vec{s}$ when they are obvious from the context.

For a positive integer Q and a power of two N, basic RLWE encryption of $m \in \mathcal{R}$ under the secret key $z \leftarrow \chi_{\text{key}}$ is defined as

$$\text{RLWE}_{Q,z}(m) := (a, -a \cdot z + e + m) \in \mathcal{R}_Q^2,$$

where $a \leftarrow \mathcal{R}_Q$, and $e_i \leftarrow \chi_{\text{err}}$ for each coefficient e_i of e where $i \in [0, N-1]$. As with LWE, we will occasionally drop subscripts Q and z.

We say that $(t_0, \cdots, t_{d_g-1})$ is a gadget decomposition of $t \in \mathcal{R}_Q$ if $t = \sum_{i=0}^{d_g-1} g_i \cdot t_i$ where $\vec{g} = (g_0, \ldots, g_{d_g-1})$ is a gadget vector, and $\|t_i\|_\infty < B_g$. We adapt the definitions of RLWE' and RGSW from [38]. For a gadget vector $\vec{g}$, we define $\text{RLWE}_z'(m)$ and $\text{RGSW}_z(m)$ as follows

$$\text{RLWE}_z'(m) := \left(\text{RLWE}_z(g_0 \cdot m), \text{RLWE}_z(g_1 \cdot m), \cdots, \text{RLWE}_z(g_{d_g-1} \cdot m)\right) \in \mathcal{R}_Q^{2d}$$

$$\text{RGSW}_z(m) := \left(\text{RLWE}_z'(z \cdot m), \text{RLWE}_z'(m)\right) \in \mathcal{R}_Q^{2 \times 2d}.$$

The scalar multiplication between an element in $\mathcal{R}_Q$ and RLWE' ciphertext

$$\odot : \mathcal{R}_Q \times \text{RLWE}' \rightarrow \text{RLWE}$$

is defined as

$$t \odot \text{RLWE}_z'(m) = \langle (t_0, \cdots, t_{d_g-1}), \left(\text{RLWE}_z(g_0 \cdot m), \cdots, \text{RLWE}_z(g_{d_g-1} \cdot m)\right)\rangle$$

$$= \sum_{i=0}^{d_g-1} t_i \cdot \text{RLWE}_z(g_i \cdot m) = \text{RLWE}_z \left(\sum_{i=0}^{d_g-1} g_i \cdot t_i \cdot m\right)$$

$$= \text{RLWE}_z(t \cdot m) \in \mathcal{R}_Q^2,$$

For each error e_i in $\text{RLWE}_z(g_i \cdot m)$, the error after multiplication is equal to $\sum_{i=0}^{d_g-1} t_i \cdot e_i$ which is small if t_i and e_i are small.

The multiplication between RLWE and RGSW ciphertexts

$$\circledast : \text{RLWE} \times \text{RGSW} \rightarrow \text{RLWE}$$

is defined as

$$\text{RLWE}_z(m_1) \circledast \text{RGSW}_z(m_2) = (a, b) \circledast \left(\text{RLWE}_z'(z \cdot m_2), \text{RLWE}_z'(m_2)\right)$$

$$= a \odot \text{RLWE}_z'(z \cdot m_2) + b \odot \text{RLWE}_z'(m_2)$$

$$= \text{RLWE}_z(a \cdot z \cdot m_2) + \text{RLWE}_z(b \cdot m_2)$$

$$= \text{RLWE}_z(m_1 \cdot m_2 + e_1 \cdot m_2) \in \mathcal{R}_Q^2.$$

This result represents an RLWE encryption of the product $m_1 \cdot m_2$ with an additional error term $e_1 \cdot m_2$. In order to have $\text{RLWE}_z(m_1) \circledast \text{RGSW}_z(m_2) \approx \text{RLWE}_z(m_1 \cdot m_2)$, it is necessary to make the error term $e_1 \cdot m_2$ small. This can be achieved by using monomials $m_2 = \pm X^v$ as messages. The multiplication between RLWE $\circledast$ RGSW is naturally extended to $\text{RGSW}_z(m_1) \circledast \text{RGSW}_z(m_2) \approx \text{RGSW}_z(m_1 \cdot m_2)$.

Remark 2. We note that for gadget vector $\vec{g} = (1, B_g, \ldots, B_g^{d_g-1})$, we can ignore t_0 without a disadvantage and reduce runtime and key size. The error introduced by $\odot$ is $d_g N \frac{B_g^2}{12} \sigma^2$, where σ^2 is error variance of a fresh ciphertext. The error variance of $\sum_{i=1}^{d_g-1} t_i \cdot \mathsf{RLWE}_z(g_i \cdot m) = \mathsf{RLWE}_z\left(\sum_{i=1}^{d_g-1} g_i \cdot t_i \cdot m\right)$ is $(d_g - 1)N\frac{B_g^2}{12}\sigma^2 + \mathsf{Var}(t_0 \cdot m)$, where $\mathsf{Var}(\gamma)$ is the variance of random variable γ. Thus, it has less or equal error as long as $\mathsf{Var}(m) \leq \sigma^2$, but saves one RLWE in RLWE' and one NTT in $\odot$. This is similar to *approximate gadget decomposition* proposed in [21].

Public-key Lattice-based Encryption. If an encryption of zero $\mathsf{pk}_z^{\mathsf{RLWE}} = \mathsf{RLWE}_z(0) = (a, -a\cdot z + e)$ is given as a public key, then the public-key encryption can be done as

$$\mathsf{Enc}^{\mathsf{RLWE}}(m; \mathsf{pk}_z^{\mathsf{RLWE}}) := v \cdot \mathsf{pk}_z^{\mathsf{RLWE}} + (e_0, m + e_1) = \mathsf{RLWE}_z(m),$$

where $v \leftarrow \chi_{\mathbf{key}}$, and $e_0, e_1 \leftarrow \chi_{\mathbf{err}}$.

We also can find encryption of $z \cdot m$ without the knowledge of z by slightly modifying the public key encryption (with the same amount of noise) as follows:

$$\mathsf{Enc}'^{\mathsf{RLWE}}(m; \mathsf{pk}_z^{\mathsf{RLWE}}) := v \cdot \mathsf{pk}_z^{\mathsf{RLWE}} + (m + e_0, e_1) = \mathsf{RLWE}_z(zm).$$

Using $\mathsf{Enc}^{\mathsf{RLWE}}$ one can generate RLWE' ciphertexts, and also can generate RGSW ciphertexts together with $\mathsf{Enc}'^{\mathsf{RLWE}}$ under the secret z.

Key Switching in RLWE The key switching operation converts a ciphertext $\mathsf{RLWE}_{z_1}(m)$ encrypted under a secret key z_1 to a ciphertext $\mathsf{RLWE}_{z_2}(m)$ encrypted by a new secret key z_2. There are different variants of the key switching technique and readers can refer to the literature (e.g., see [31]) for details. We focus on the BV key switching method [15]:

- $\mathsf{KSGen}(z_1, z_2)$: Outputs $\mathsf{swk} = \mathsf{RLWE}'_{z_2}(z_1)$.
- $\mathsf{KS}_{z_1 \to z_2}(\mathsf{RLWE}_{z_1}(m), \mathsf{swk})$: Given $\mathsf{RLWE}_{z_1}(m) = (a, b)$, it outputs

$$\mathsf{RLWE}_{z_2}(m) = a \odot \mathsf{RLWE}'_{z_2}(z_1) + (0, b) \pmod{Q}.$$

$\mathsf{RLWE}'_{z_2}(z_1)$ generated by KSGen is a public switching key. The key switching error is equal to the error of $\mathcal{R} \odot \mathsf{RLWE}'$ multiplication.

Automorphisms in RLWE. In order to perform some operations in HE, we use the automorphisms of $\mathcal{R}$. There are N automorphisms $\psi_t : \mathcal{R} \to \mathcal{R}$ given by $a(X) \mapsto a(X^t)$ for $t \in \mathbb{Z}_{2N}^*$. We naturally extend ψ_t to $\mathcal{R}^2$ to apply the automorphism on a RLWE ciphertext. Automorphisms are applied using the following procedures which make use of a special set of switching keys $\mathsf{ak}_t = \mathsf{RLWE}_{z(X)}(z(X^t))$:

- $\mathsf{EvalAuto}_t(\mathsf{RLWE}_z(m), \mathsf{ak}_t)$: Given $\mathsf{RLWE}_z(m(X)) = (a(X), b(X))$ and switching key ak_t, apply ψ_t to $a(X)$ and $b(X)$ to obtain $(a(X^t), b(X^t))$, which is an RLWE encryption of $m(X^t)$ under the secret key $z(X^t)$. Then apply the key switching function $\mathsf{KS}_{z(X^t) \to z(X)}$ on the $\mathsf{RLWE}_{z(X^t)}(m(X^t))$ ciphertext, to produce the final output ciphertext $\mathsf{RLWE}_{z(X)}(m(X^t))$.

We note that ψ is a permutation on the coefficients of the elements of $\mathcal{R}$, which is easily calculated. ψ_t does not introduce additional error as an automorphism ψ_t is a norm-preserving map.

2.2   FHEW-Like Bootstrapping

We briefly explain FHEW-like bootstrapping for NAND gates [24,38]. FHEW-like NAND gate bootstrapping starts with two $\mathsf{LWE}_{q,\vec{s}}$ ciphertexts with a small modulus q and adds them (HomNAND). After blind rotation and extraction procedures, we obtain an $\mathsf{LWE}_{Q,\vec{z}}$ encryption of the result with a higher ciphertext modulus Q. Using a sequence of modulus and key switchings we get back to an $\mathsf{LWE}_{q,\vec{s}}$ ciphertext. The bootstrapping procedure is shown in Fig. 1. We focus on the blind rotation part and refer to [38] for more details on other parts of FHEW-like bootstrapping.

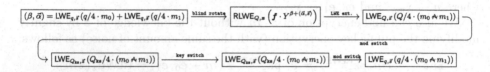

Fig. 1. NAND gate bootstrapping procedure of FHEW scheme [24,38]

Blind Rotation. Blind rotation is an operation that multiplies a given ring element $\boldsymbol{f} \in \mathcal{R}_Q$ by a monomial Y^u, where the exponent $u = \beta + \langle \vec{\alpha}, \vec{s} \rangle \in \mathbb{Z}_q$ is given by an LWE ciphertext $(\vec{\alpha}, \beta) \in \mathbb{Z}_q^{n+1}$ encrypted under a secret key $\vec{s} \in \mathbb{Z}_q^n$. The output of the blind rotation is an RLWE encryption of $\boldsymbol{f} \cdot Y^u$, where q is small in practice ($q \approx 2^{10}$ in [21,24] and $q \approx 2^{12}$ in [30]). The operation is called "blind rotation" because it rotates the coefficients of $\boldsymbol{f}$ negacyclically, by an amount u which is provided in encrypted form. A formal definition is given below.

Definition 1 (Blind Rotation). *For $q|2N$, let $Y = X^{\frac{2N}{q}}$. A blind rotation is an algorithm which takes as input a ring element $\boldsymbol{f} \in \mathcal{R}_Q$, an $\mathsf{LWE}_{q,\vec{s}}$ ciphertext $(\vec{\alpha}, \beta) \in \mathbb{Z}_q^{n+1}$, and blind rotation keys $\mathfrak{brk}_{z,\vec{s}}$ corresponding to secrets z and $\vec{s}$, and outputs an RLWE ciphertext*

$$\mathsf{RLWE}_{Q,z} \left(\boldsymbol{f} \cdot Y^{\beta + \langle \vec{\alpha}, \vec{s} \rangle} \right) \in \mathcal{R}_Q^2.$$

Two different blind rotation algorithms were proposed in [21,24]. Following [38], we refer to the two algorithms as "AP blind rotation" and "GINX blind rotation" respectively, as they are optimized ring versions of two bootstrapping procedures (for general LWE) originally proposed in [2] (AP) and [26] (GINX). Both methods rely on the properties of RGSW ciphertexts described above.

AP Blind Rotation. In AP blind rotation [2,24], the blind rotation keys are generated for each element $s_i \in \mathbb{Z}_q$ of the secret $\vec{s}$ as

$$\mathrm{brk}^{AP} = \{\mathrm{brk}_{i,j,v} = \mathrm{RGSW}_z(Y^{vB_r^j s_i})\}_{i,j,v}$$

for $i \in [0, n-1]$, $j \in [0, \log_{B_r}(q) - 1]$, and $v \in \mathbb{Z}_{B_r}$. In the algorithm, acc is initialized to the trivial encryption $\mathrm{acc} = \mathrm{RLWE}_{Q,z}(f \cdot Y^\beta) = (0, f \cdot Y^\beta)$. Then, for each $i \in [0, n-1]$, α_i is decomposed in base B_r as $\alpha_i = \sum_{j=0}^{\log_{B_r}(q)-1} \alpha_{i,j} B_r^j$ and acc is updated sequentially for all $\alpha_{i,j}$ as

$$\mathrm{acc} \leftarrow \mathrm{acc} \circledast \mathrm{RGSW}_z(Y^{\alpha_{i,j} B_r^j s_i}).$$

The full procedure of AP blind rotation is described in Algorithm 1.

Algorithm 1. Blind Rotation: AP [2,24]

1: **procedure** BLINDROTATEAP($f, (\vec{\alpha}, \beta), \{\mathrm{brk}_{i,j,v} = \mathrm{RGSW}_z(Y^{vB_r^j s_i})\}_{i,j,v}$)
2:     $\mathrm{acc} \leftarrow (0, f \cdot Y^\beta)$
3:     **for** $(i = 0; i < n; i = i + 1)$ **do**
4:         **for** $(j = 0; j < \log_{B_r}(q); j = j + 1)$ **do**
5:             $\alpha_{i,j} = \lfloor \alpha_i / B_r^j \rfloor \pmod{B_r}$
6:             $\mathrm{acc} \leftarrow \mathrm{acc} \circledast \mathrm{brk}_{i,j,\alpha_{i,j}}$
7: **return** $\mathrm{acc} = \mathrm{RlWE}_z(f \cdot Y^u)$

AP blind rotation supports all types of secret key distributions and provides a useful tradeoff between space and computational complexity based on the choice of the base $B_r \geq 2$. Greater B_r allows performing computations faster at the cost of storing more rotation keys, while smaller B_r reduces storage overhead but increases computational time.

GINX Blind Rotation. GINX blind rotation [21,26] is more efficient than AP when the secret key $\vec{s}$ is set to a binary or ternary vector, but its performance degrades when using larger secret keys [38]. In the general case, each secret key element $s_i \in \mathbb{Z}_q$, $i \in [0, N-1]$, is expressed as subset-sum $s_i = \sum_{j=0}^{|U|-1} u_j \cdot s_{i,j}$ where $s_{i,j} \in \{0,1\}$ and $U \subset \mathbb{Z}_q$ is an appropriately chosen subset of $\mathbb{Z}_q$. To express arbitrary elements of $\mathbb{Z}_q$ one can use $U = \{1, 2, 4, \ldots, 2^{k-1}\}$. But one can also use $U = \{1\}$ and $U = \{1, -1\}$ for binary and ternary secrets, respectively [38]. Using this notation for any fixed set U, the blind rotation key is generated as

$$\text{brk}^{GINX} = \{\text{brk}_{i,j} = \text{RGSW}_z(s_{i,j})\}$$

where $i = 0, \ldots, n - 1$ and $j = 0, \ldots, |U| - 1$. In the algorithm, acc is initiated to $\text{acc} = \text{RLWE}_{Q,z}(f \cdot Y^\beta) = (0, f \cdot Y^\beta)$ and updated as

$$\text{acc} \leftarrow \text{acc} + (Y^{\alpha_i u_j} - 1) \cdot (\text{acc} \circledast \text{RGSW}_z(s_{i,j})).$$

If $s_{i,j} = 0$, the second addendum is ignored since it gives an encryption of 0 and the value stored by the accumulator stays the same. If $s_{i,j} = 1$, then $\text{acc} \circledast \text{RGSW}_z(1)$ is equal to acc and the accumulator is updated to $Y^{\alpha_i u_j} \cdot \text{acc}$. Repeating this procedure for all $j \in [0, |U| - 1]$ results in $Y^{\alpha_i s_i} \cdot \text{acc}$. The full procedure for GINX blind rotation is described in Algorithm 2.

Algorithm 2. Blind Rotation: GINX [21,26,38]

1: **procedure** BLINDROTATEGINX($f, (\vec{\alpha}, \beta), \{\text{brk}_{i,j} = \text{RGSW}_z(s_{i,j}) \mid s_i = \sum s_{i,j} u_j\}$)
2:     $\text{acc} \leftarrow (0, f \cdot Y^\beta)$
3:     **for** $(i = 0; i < n; i = i + 1)$ **do**
4:         **for** $(j = 0; j < |U|; j = j + 1)$ **do**
5:             $\text{acc} \leftarrow \text{acc} + (Y^{\alpha_i u_j} - 1) \cdot (\text{acc} \circledast \text{brk}_{i,j})$
6: **return** $\text{acc} = \text{RLWE}_z(f \cdot Y^u)$

It is easy to see that for the small U this procedure may be efficient in both key size and running time. However, the running time and storage overhead grow significantly with larger secret key distributions. GINX blind rotation is more efficient than AP for secret keys $\vec{s}$ chosen from small distributions such as binary or ternary secret keys; but less efficient for general key size.

There is another optimization of GINX to remove the second loop in Algorithm 2 in such a way that it has about half of the computations and the same key size and error for ternary keys. However, it is only optimized for ternary keys [8,30] and cannot be efficiently extended to larger keys. A variant of GINX was proposed in [29], which is a generalization of methods in [38] and [30], however, using binary and ternary secrets is suggested as they are the most efficient.

3   New Blind Rotation Techniques

In this section, we present new blind rotation algorithms which improve on previous methods [2,20,21,24,26,29,38] in terms of running time, public key size, or both. Our algorithms update an accumulator ciphertext acc initialized to $\text{acc} = (0, f') = \text{RLWE}(f')$, holding the encryption of a ring element f' related to f, to be specified. The accumulator is updated through a sequence of RLWE $\circledast$ RGSW products, where RLWE holds the value of the accumulator acc, and RGSW is an auxiliary ciphertext brk_i holding a secret key element s_i.

Unlike previous techniques, our algorithms do not substitute multiplication in the exponent by series of additions (i.e. RLWE ⊛ RGSW products) but make use of ring automorphisms ψ_t and their associated switching keys ak_t instead.

For brevity, we first describe a core blind rotation algorithm for the case where $q = 2N$ and all α_i are odd since ψ_t is only defined for odd t, and then provide its variants and optimizations for other cases.

3.1   The Core Blind Rotation Algorithm

We recall that the goal of the algorithm is to rotate the accumulator by $Y^{\langle \vec{\alpha}, \vec{s} \rangle} = Y^{\sum_i \alpha_i s_i}$, where $\sum_i \alpha_i s_i$ is computed modulo $q = 2N$. For $N \geq 8$ the group $\mathbb{Z}_{2N}^*$ is isomorphic to $\mathbb{Z}_{N/2} \otimes \mathbb{Z}_2$ with generators $\{g, -1\}$ (e.g., $g = 5$) and every $t \in \mathbb{Z}_{2N}^*$ can be written as $\pm g^k$ where $k \in \mathbb{Z}_{N/2}$. Let $\alpha_i = \pm g^{k_i} \pmod{2N}$ for $i = 0, \ldots, n-1$. Let $I_\ell^+ = \{i : \alpha_i = g^\ell\}$ and $I_\ell^- = \{i : \alpha_i = -g^\ell\}$, for $\ell \in [0, N/2-1]$. Using the fact that $g^{N/2} = 1 \pmod{2N}$ we have the following decomposition

$$\textstyle\sum_i \alpha_i s_i = \left(\sum_{j \in I_0^+} s_j + \cdots + g \left(\sum_{j \in I_{N/2-1}^+} s_j - g \left(\sum_{j \in I_0^-} s_j + \cdots + g \left(\sum_{j \in I_{N/2-1}^-} s_j \right) \right) \right) \right) \pmod{2N}.$$

Denote $\mathsf{brk}_j := \mathsf{RGSW}_z(X^{s_j})$. Given an initial ciphertext $\mathsf{acc} = \mathsf{RLWE}_z^0(f'(X))$, we first multiply it by brk_j for all $j \in I_{N/2-1}^-$, then apply automorphism $\mathsf{EvalAuto}_g$ to acc and obtain

$$\mathsf{acc} = \mathsf{RLWE}_z \left(f'(X^g) \cdot X^{g \cdot \sum_{j \in I_{N/2-1}^-} s_j} \right).$$

Then we multiply the accumulator by brk_j for $j \in I_{N/2-2}^-$ and again apply automorphism $\mathsf{EvalAuto}_g$ to acc. This process is repeated for both I_ℓ^- and I_ℓ^+ for all $\ell = N/2 - 1, ..., 0$. However, at the $(N/2)$th step (i.e., after multiplication by I_0^-) we apply the automorphism $\mathsf{EvalAuto}_{-g}$ instead of $\mathsf{EvalAuto}_g$, and (as an optimization) we skip the multiplication by the set I_0^+. The final result is

$$\mathsf{acc} = \mathsf{RLWE}_z \left(f' \left(X^{-g^{(N/2)-1}} \right) \cdot X^{\sum_i \alpha_i s_i} \right).$$

If we set $f'(X) = f(X^{-g}) \cdot X^{-g\beta}$, this equals $\mathsf{acc} = \mathsf{RLWE}_z \left(f(X) \cdot X^{\beta + \langle \vec{\alpha}, \vec{s} \rangle} \right)$. During the computation, we use n keys brk_i for $i \in [0, n-1]$ and two automorphism keys ak_g and ak_{-g}. The algorithm performs two types of homomorphic operations: RLWE⊛RGSW multiplications and key switching for automorphisms. The number of RLWE ⊛ RGSW multiplications is n, and the number of automorphisms is $N - 1$. We can reduce the number of automorphisms when some of the $I_\ell^\pm$ are empty because the automorphisms between them can be composed and replaced by a single automorphism application. However, this requires storing a large number of automorphism keys $\mathsf{ak}_{\pm g^u}$ for all possible values of u. Instead, for efficiency purposes, we store only a small number of keys $\{\mathsf{ak}_{g^u}\}_{u \in [1,w]}$ for some parameter w which we call the *window size*. The full algorithm is provided in Algorithm 3. We will see in Sect. 4 that with a quite small window size we can achieve essentially the same improvement as when storing keys for all N possible automorphisms.

Algorithm 3. Core Blind Rotation Sub Algorithm for odd α_i

1: **procedure** BLINDROTATECORE$\left(\text{acc}, \vec{\alpha}, \{\text{brk}_i\}_{i\in[0,n-1]}, \{\text{ak}_{g^u}\}_{u\in[1,w]}, \text{ak}_{-g}\right)$
2: $\quad v \leftarrow 0$
3: $\quad$ **for** $(\ell = N/2 - 1; \ell > 0; \ell = \ell - 1)$ **do**
4: $\quad\quad$ **for** $j \in I_\ell^-$ **do**
5: $\quad\quad\quad$ acc $\leftarrow$ acc $\circledast$ brk$_j$
6: $\quad\quad$ $v \leftarrow v + 1$
7: $\quad\quad$ **if** $(I_{\ell-1}^- \neq \emptyset$ or $v = w$ or $l = 1)$ **then**
8: $\quad\quad\quad$ acc $\leftarrow$ EvalAuto$_{g^v}$(acc, ak$_{g^v}$)
9: $\quad\quad\quad$ $v \leftarrow 0$
10: $\quad$ **for** $j \in I_0^-$ **do**
11: $\quad\quad$ acc $\leftarrow$ acc $\circledast$ brk$_j$
12: $\quad$ acc $\leftarrow$ EvalAuto$_{-g}$(acc, ak$_{-g}$)
13: $\quad$ **for** $(\ell = N/2 - 1; \ell > 0; \ell = \ell - 1)$ **do**
14: $\quad\quad$ **for** $j \in I_\ell^+$ **do**
15: $\quad\quad\quad$ acc $\leftarrow$ acc $\circledast$ brk$_j$
16: $\quad\quad$ $v \leftarrow v + 1$
17: $\quad\quad$ **if** $(I_{\ell-1}^+ \neq \emptyset$ or $v = w$ or $l = 1)$ **then**
18: $\quad\quad\quad$ acc $\leftarrow$ EvalAuto$_{g^v}$(acc, ak$_{g^v}$)
19: $\quad\quad\quad$ $v \leftarrow 0$
20: $\quad$ **for** $j \in I_0^+$ **do**
21: $\quad\quad$ acc $\leftarrow$ acc $\circledast$ brk$_j$
22: **return** acc

3.2 Dealing with Even α_i

We provide several solutions to overcome the issue with even α_i.

Memory Efficient Algorithm. One solution is to set $\omega_i = \alpha_i - 1$ if α_i is even and $\omega_i = \alpha_i$ if α_i is odd. Now we can apply the core blind rotation algorithm for the vector $\vec{\omega}$ and obtain RLWE $\left(f \cdot X^{\beta + \langle \vec{\omega}, \vec{s} \rangle}\right)$. Then we repeatedly multiply brk$_i$ for each even α_i. This algorithm requires $n/2$ additional RGSW multiplications on average. If we store one additional key brk$_{\text{nsum}} := \text{RGSW}(X^{-\sum_i s_i})$, and in case of the number of even α_i is greater than $n/2$, we initially multiply acc by brk$_{\text{nsum}} := \text{RGSW}(X^{-\sum_i s_i})$, and update $\alpha_i \leftarrow \alpha_i + 1$. This will make the number of odd α_i to be greater than half, mitigating the worst case. The full algorithm is provided in Algorithm 4.

Computation Efficient Algorithm. We can get rid of additional multiplications for even α_i in the previous solution by using auxiliary blind rotation keys brk$_i^* := \text{RGSW}(X^{s_i + s_{i+1}})$, for $i \in [0, n-2]$. The idea is to find odd α_i' such that $\sum_i \alpha_i s_i = \sum_i \alpha_i' s_i'$, where s_i' is either equal to s_i or to $s_i + s_{i+1}$. First, we assume that α_0 is odd and set $\alpha_0' = \alpha_0$, otherwise, we initially multiply the accumulator by brk$_{\text{nsum}}$ and update $\alpha_i \leftarrow \alpha_i + 1$. Then at each step i, assuming (by induction) that α_i' is odd, we consider two cases, depending on the parity of α_{i+1}. If α_{i+1}

Algorithm 4. Memory Efficient Blind Rotation Algorithm, $q = 2N$

1: **procedure** BLINDROTATEME$\left(\boldsymbol{f}, \vec{\alpha}, \beta, \{\text{brk}_i\}_{i \in [0,n-1]}, \text{brk}_{\text{nsum}}, \{\text{ak}_{g^u}\}_{u \in [1,w]}, \text{ak}_{-g} \right)$

2:    $\text{acc} \leftarrow (0, \boldsymbol{f}\left(X^{-g} \right) \cdot X^{-g\beta})$

3:    **if** number of even α_i is $> n/2$ **then**

4:        $\text{acc} \leftarrow \text{acc} \circledast \text{brk}_{\text{nsum}}$

5:        $\vec{\alpha} \leftarrow \vec{\alpha} + \vec{1}_n \pmod{2N}$

6:    **for** $(i = 0; i < n; i = i + 1)$ **do**

7:        **if** α_i is even **then**

8:            $\omega_i \leftarrow \alpha_i - 1 \pmod{2N}$

9:        **else**

10:           $\omega_i \leftarrow \alpha_i$

11:   $\text{acc} \leftarrow \text{BlindRotateCore}(\text{acc}, \vec{\omega}, \{\text{brk}_i\}, \{\text{ak}_{g^u}\}, \text{ak}_{-g})$

12:   **for** $(i = 0; i < n; i = i + 1)$ **do**

13:       **if** α_i is even **then**

14:           $\text{acc} \leftarrow \text{acc} \circledast \text{brk}_i$

15: **return** $\text{acc} = \text{RLWE}_z \left(\boldsymbol{f}(X) \cdot X^{\beta + \langle \vec{\alpha}, \vec{s} \rangle} \right)$

---

is odd, we set $s_i' = s_i$ and $\alpha_{i+1}' = \alpha_{i+1}$. Otherwise, we set $s_i' = s_i + s_{i+1}$ and balance this by setting $\alpha_{i+1}' = \alpha_{i+1} - \alpha_i$. In either case, the value of α_{i+1}' is odd, preserving the inductive hypothesis, and we may move to the next iteration. For the last iteration we always set $s_{n-1}' = s_{n-1}$. Note that during the process we do not need to know the values s_i, we only have the information of whether $s_i' = s_i$ or $s_i' = s_i + s_{i+1}$. The full algorithm is provided in Algorithm 5.

Algorithm 5. Computation Efficient Blind Rotation Algorithm, $q = 2N$

1: **procedure** BLINDROTATECE$\left(\boldsymbol{f}, (\vec{\alpha}, \beta), \{\text{brk}_i\}_{i \in [0,n-1]}, \{\text{brk}_i^*\}_{i \in [0,n-2]}, \right.$
   $\text{brk}_{\text{nsum}}, \{\text{ak}_{g^u}\}_{u \in [1,w]}, \text{ak}_{-g}$

2:    $\text{acc} \leftarrow (0, \boldsymbol{f}\left(X^{-g} \right) \cdot X^{-g\beta})$

3:    **if** α_0 is even **then**

4:        $\text{acc} \leftarrow \text{acc} \circledast \text{brk}_{\text{nsum}}$

5:        $\vec{\alpha} \leftarrow \vec{\alpha} + \vec{1}_n \pmod{2N}$

6:    Find odd $\alpha_i' : \sum_i \alpha_i s_i = \sum_i \alpha_i' s_i'$

7:    **for** $(i = 0; i < n; i = i + 1)$ **do**

8:        **if** $s_i' = s_i$ **then**

9:            $\text{brk}_i' \leftarrow \text{brk}_i$

10:       **else**

11:           $\text{brk}_i' \leftarrow \text{brk}_i^*$

12:   $\text{acc} \leftarrow \text{BlindRotateCore}(\text{acc}, \vec{\alpha}', \{\text{brk}_i'\}, \{\text{ak}_{g^u}\}, \text{ak}_{-g})$

13: **return** $\text{acc} = \text{RLWE}_z \left(\boldsymbol{f}(X) \cdot X^{\beta + \langle \vec{\alpha}, \vec{s} \rangle} \right)$

Case $q = N$. In FHEW-like cryptosystems [21,24,38], commonly the blind rotation input LWE ciphertext $(\vec{\alpha}, \beta)$ has a modulus $q < 2N$. The use of $q <$

Algorithm 6. Blind Rotation Algorithm, $q = N$

1: **procedure** BLINDROTATEOPTIM$\left(f, \vec{\alpha}, \beta, \{\mathrm{brk}_i\}_{i \in [0,n-1]}, \mathrm{brk}_{\mathrm{nsum}}, \{\mathrm{ak}_{g^u}\}_{u \in [1,w]}, \mathrm{ak}_{-g}\right)$

2:    $\mathrm{acc} \leftarrow \left(0, f\left(X^{-g}\right) \cdot X^{-2g\beta}\right)$

3:    $\mathrm{acc} \leftarrow \mathrm{acc} \circledast \mathrm{brk}_{\mathrm{nsum}}$

4:    $\vec{\alpha}' \leftarrow 2\vec{\alpha} + \vec{1}_n \pmod{2N}$

5:    $\mathrm{acc} \leftarrow \mathrm{BlindRotateCore}(\mathrm{acc}, \vec{\alpha}', \{\mathrm{brk}_i\}, \{\mathrm{ak}_{g^u}\}, \mathrm{ak}_{-g})$

6: **return** $\mathrm{acc} = \mathrm{RLWE}_z\left(f(X) \cdot X^{2(\beta + \langle \vec{\alpha}, \vec{s} \rangle)}\right)$

$2N$ helps decrease the key size of AP-style bootstrapping. The size of q affects the decryption failure of LWE ciphertexts. However in practice, in the most interesting case, we can achieve $q = N$ with a negligible probability of decryption failure.

For our case we raise the modulus from N to $2N$, by multiplying the ciphertext $(\vec{\alpha}, \beta)$ by factor 2, resulting $(2\vec{\alpha}, 2\beta)$ with all even $2\alpha_i$. We initially multiply acc by $\mathrm{brk}_{\mathrm{nsum}}$ to make all $2\alpha_i + 1$ to be odd. The full algorithm is provided in Algorithm 6.

3.3 Improved FHEW Scheme and Removal of $\mathrm{brk}_{\mathrm{nsum}}$

As was mentioned in [24] we can reduce the noise and number of key switching operations in FHEW-like bootstrapping, by swapping some operations in the procedure in Fig. 1. We start with a ciphertext with a higher modulus Q rather than q and do modulus switching to q right before the blind rotation. (See Fig. 2.)

Fig. 2. NAND gate bootstrapping procedure of FHEW scheme. We start from $\mathrm{LWE}_{Q,\vec{z}}$ and switch to $\mathrm{LWE}_{q,\vec{s}}$ before blind rotation. We refer [38] for other gates.

Here we propose a trick which we call *round-to-odd* to get all-odd LWE ciphertext during modulus reduction so that $\mathrm{brk}_{\mathrm{nsum}}$ in Algorithm 6 becomes unnecessary. Thus, the round-to-odd gives advantages in runtime, key size, and noise growth regarding multiplication of $\mathrm{brk}_{\mathrm{nsum}}$. For ciphertext $(\vec{\alpha}', \beta') = \mathrm{LWE}_{Q_{\mathrm{ks}}}(Q_{\mathrm{ks}}/4 \cdot m)$, the modulus reduction is defined as

$$\left(\vec{\alpha} = \left\lfloor \frac{q}{Q_{\mathrm{ks}}} \cdot \vec{\alpha}' \right\rceil, \beta = \left\lfloor \frac{q}{Q_{\mathrm{ks}}} \cdot \beta' \right\rceil \right) = \mathrm{LWE}_q(q/4 \cdot m).$$

We modify the rounding operation to round-to-odd, $\lfloor x \rceil_{\mathrm{odd}}$, which returns the nearest odd integer for the given input x. In addition, if x is closer to zero than

---

Algorithm 7. Blind Rotation Algorithm with Round-to-odd Input, $q = 2N$

1: **procedure** BLINDROTATEROUNDTOODD$\left(\boldsymbol{f}, \vec{\alpha}, \beta, \{\text{brk}_i\}_{i \in [0, n-1]}, \{\text{ak}_{g^u}\}_{u \in [1, w]}, \text{ak}_{-g}\right)$
   ▷ $\vec{\alpha}, \beta$ are all odd
2:    acc $\leftarrow \left(0, \boldsymbol{f}\left(X^{-g}\right) \cdot X^{-g\beta}\right)$
3:    acc $\leftarrow$ BlindRotateCore(acc, $\vec{\alpha}, \{\text{brk}_i\}, \{\text{ak}_{g^u}\}, \text{ak}_{-g}$)
4: **return** acc $= \text{RLWE}_z\left(\boldsymbol{f}(X) \cdot X^{\beta + \langle \vec{\alpha}, \vec{s} \rangle}\right)$

---

any other odd number (i.e., 1), it returns zero. Then the new modulus reduction is defined as

$$\left(\vec{\alpha} = \left\lfloor \frac{2N}{Q_{\text{ks}}} \cdot \vec{\alpha}' \right\rceil_{\text{odd}}, \beta = \left\lfloor \frac{2N}{Q_{\text{ks}}} \cdot \beta' \right\rceil_{\text{odd}}\right) = \text{LWE}_{2N}(q/4 \cdot m),$$

which gives an LWE ciphertext of modulus $2N$ with all-odd coefficients. We note that the modulus reduction error by round-to-odd is equivalent to modulus switching to N. The blind rotation algorithm for the round-to-odd trick case is provided in Algorithm 7.

4   Analysis

In this section, we analyze our new blind rotation technique and compare it to the prior art. We analyze blind rotation separately from the full FHEW scheme since blind rotation is a useful tool in a number of other applications, e.g., the homomorphic evaluation of non-polynomial functions [33,34] and CKKS/BGV/BFV bootstrapping [30].

4.1   Analysis of the Number of Automorphisms

We focus on the number of automorphisms for Algorithm 3. First notice that the number of non-empty $I_\ell^\pm$ is always at most $\min(N, n)$ just because there are a total of N sets, and their union has size n, i.e., the total number of terms $\alpha_i s_i$. Moreover, it can be less than n if some of the s_i have the same coefficient α_i. We evaluate the average number of non-empty $I_\ell^\pm$ under the standard assumption that the LWE coefficients α_i are random and independent.[11] Assume without loss of generality that all α_i are odd, as enforced by our algorithms. Each fixed set $I_\ell^\pm$ is empty if all α_i do not belong to it. Since the α_i are uniform and independent, this happens with probability $(1 - 1/N)^n \approx e^{-n/N}$. Therefore $I_\ell^\pm$ is non-empty with probability $1 - (1 - 1/N)^n \approx 1 - e^{-n/N}$, and, by linearity of expectation, the expected number of nonempty sets is $N(1 - (1 - 1/N)^n) \approx N(1 - e^{-n/N})$.

---

[11] This is certainly true for freshly encrypted messages, as the α_i are chosen uniformly at random by the encryption algorithm. But it is reasonable to expect this to be true even when the ciphertext is the result of a homomorphic computation.

Counting the number of non-empty sets $I_\ell^\pm$ is useful to estimate the number of automorphism applications performed by our algorithm because the automorphisms between non-empty sets are composed and replaced by a small number of automorphisms with keys in $\{\mathtt{ak}_{g^u}\}_{u \in [1,w]}$ for a given window size w. Let k be the number of non-empty sets $I_\ell^\pm$, be it either $\min(N,n)$ in the worst case, or $k = N(1 - e^{-n/N})$ on average. Let $v_1, \ldots, v_k$ be the exponents of the k automorphisms g^{v_i} that need to be applied after each non-empty set. Write each exponent as $v_i = v_i' + w \cdot v_i''$ where $v_i' = v_i \bmod w \in \{1, \ldots, w-1\}$, and $v_i'' = \lfloor v_i'/w \rfloor$. (In case v_i is a multiple of w, the v_i' part can be omitted altogether.) In Algorithm 3, the v_i applications of the basic automorphism g (following multiplication by the ith set $I_\ell^\pm$) are replaced by one application of automorphism $g^{v_i'}$ and v_i'' applications of automorphism g^w. So, the number of automorphism applications of type $g^{v_i'}$ is κ, for some $\kappa \le k$.[12] In order to bound the number of applications of automorphism g^w, we use the fact that the sum $\sum_i v_i$ is bounded by N. Therefore, $\sum_i v_i''$ is at most $\frac{N-\kappa}{w}$. In summary, by storing w automorphism keys $\{\mathtt{ak}_{g^u}\}_{u \in [1,w]}$, we can reduce the number of automorphism applications to $\kappa + \frac{N-\kappa}{w} = (1 - 1/w)\kappa + (1/w)N \le (1 - 1/w)k + (1/w)N$. We always have $n \le N$, and in the worst case, we have $k \le n$. So the total number of automorphism applications is always bounded by $(1 - 1/w)n + (1/w)N$. On average, using $k \approx N(1 - e^{-n/N})$, the expected number of automorphism applications reduces to $N(1 - (1 - 1/w) \cdot e^{-n/N})$.

4.2   Complexity, Key Size, and Error Analysis

The comparison of computational complexity, key size, and error are given in Table 1. In order to facilitate the comparison of all blind rotation algorithms, we measure their time complexity in terms of the number of $\mathcal{R} \odot \mathsf{RLWE}'$ products they perform, as the cost of these operations dominates the total running time. Each $\mathsf{RLWE} \circledast \mathsf{RGSW}$ product requires two $\odot$ multiplications, while key switching is performed with a single $\odot$ multiplication. So, both $\circledast$ products and key switching operations are easily expressed in terms of $\odot$ products. We note that the operation $\odot$ can be considered as an abstraction of a basic operation for FHEW and its torus variant TFHE [21]. Another common measure of complexity used in previous works on FHEW-like HE is the number of NTT/FFT performed by the algorithms. We note that one can easily convert the number of $\odot$ products to the number of NTT as each $\odot$ requires precisely $(d_g + 1)$ NTT operations, where d_g is the number of elements of a gadget vector. We note that $\odot$ requires d_g NTT operations if approximate gadget decomposition is used.

Similarly, we compare the memory requirement of all blind rotation algorithms using the total number of RLWE' ciphertexts required by the blind rotation key. The blind rotation keys for all methods consist of several RGSW and RLWE' ciphertexts. In turn, each RGSW is composed of two RLWE' ciphertexts. For the sake of brevity, "blind rotation key size" refers to the size of both $\mathtt{brk}$

---

[12] κ will be less than k if some of the v_i' are 0.

and ak in this section. This can be translated into a traditional "bit size" simply noting that each RLWE' ciphertext requires roughly $2d_gN\log Q$-bit of space (or $2(d_g - 1)N\log Q$-bit with approximate gadget decomposition.)

We also note that in our analysis and implementation we use approximate gadget decomposition described in Remark 2. Approximate gadget decomposition does not introduce additional error but reduces runtime and key size for all analyzed blind rotation techniques. One can find the counterparts for exact gadget decomposition by simply substituting $d_g - 1$ with d_g in the equations.

We use an approach from [24,38] to estimate the variance σ^2_{acc} from the blind rotation procedure. The total error for algorithms using blind rotation such as FHEW/TFHE bootstrapping [21,24,38] and amortized FHEW bootstrapping [39], can be easily estimated using this value. The error variance introduced by a single $\odot$ operation is equal to $d_gN\frac{B_g^2}{12}\sigma^2$, where B_g and d_g are parameters for gadget decomposition used in $\odot$ multiplication. For the sake of brevity we denote $\sigma^2_\odot := d_gN\frac{B_g^2}{12}\sigma^2$.

In AP and our algorithms, each $\circledast$ is performed by RGSW encrypting the monomial, and thus introduces an additive error with variance $2\cdot\sigma^2_\odot$. The automorphism operation due to key switching introduces an additive error with variance $\sigma^2_\odot$. Thus the variance σ^2_{acc} can be estimated as $\sigma^2_\odot$ multiplied by the number of $\odot$ operations. In the GINX and GINX* variants, due to the preprocessing of RGSW ciphertexts before $\circledast$ multiplications, each $\circledast$ introduces an additive error with variance $4\cdot\sigma^2_\odot$ and $8\cdot\sigma^2_\odot$, respectively.

We note that the parameters for the FHEW scheme in Sect. 5 are selected following this theoretical analysis. However, the fact that one technique has a smaller complexity expression than another in this theoretical analysis does not necessarily mean that it will show a better runtime in practice, because of the use of different parameter sets required to achieve a target security level. For example, binary GINX has the smallest expression representing the abstract key size and runtime in this analysis. But in practice, our new blind rotation algorithm outperforms binary GINX because of the following two reasons. First, our blind rotation has less noise growth compared to binary GINX, allowing a smaller parameter set to be used. Second, we can achieve the same security level with a smaller n by using Gaussian secrets at no cost in performance.

5   Implementation

In this section, we present the implementation results of our new blind rotation algorithm as applied to FHEW bootstrapping. For our implementation, we use Algorithm 6 optimized by reducing the number of automorphisms, which gives the best performance. We compare it to the AP and GINX blind rotation techniques. According to the theoretical analysis presented in the previous section, similar results will be achieved for TFHE [21] by using floating-point operations and DFTs instead of operations over finite rings and NTTs, respectively for each discussed blind rotation technique.

Table 1. Complexity, key size, and error variance of each blind rotation technique. Key size (# keys) is the number of RLWE′ ciphertexts, and computational complexity (# mult) is the number of $\mathcal{R} \odot$ RLWE′. The parameter w is a small integer, typically a small constant independent of n. The parameter $|U|$ depends on the secret key size and can be as large as $\log n$ for gaussian secrets following the error distribution.

Method	# keys	# mult	$\sigma_{\mathrm{acc}}^2/\sigma_\odot^2$
AP [2,24]	$2d_r(B_r-1)n$	$2d_r\left(1-\frac{1}{B_r}\right)n$	$2d_r\left(1-\frac{1}{B_r}\right)n$
GINX [21,26,38]	$2\|U\|n$	$2\|U\|n$	$4\|U\|n$
GINX* [8,30]	$4n$	$2n$	$8n$
Ours (Algorithm 4)	$2n+w+3$	$3n+\frac{w-1}{w}\kappa+\frac{N}{w}$	$3n+\frac{w-1}{w}\kappa+\frac{N}{w}$
Ours (Algorithm 5)	$4n+w+1$	$2n+\frac{w-1}{w}\kappa+\frac{N}{w}+2$	$2n+\frac{w-1}{w}\kappa+\frac{N}{w}+2$
Ours (Algorithm 6)	$2n+w+3$	$2n+\frac{w-1}{w}\kappa+\frac{N}{w}+2$	$2n+\frac{w-1}{w}\kappa+\frac{N}{w}+2$
Ours (Algorithm 7)	$2n+w+1$	$2n+\frac{w-1}{w}\kappa+\frac{N}{w}$	$2n+\frac{w-1}{w}\kappa+\frac{N}{w}$

5.1   Parameter Sets

The full procedure for FHEW bootstrapping is presented in Fig. 2. Using the unique characteristics of each blind rotation technique and the choice of secret key distribution, in Table 2 we provide optimized parameter sets for FHEW schemes with AP, GINX, and our new technique. Following to [24], we choose the best parameters to have the smallest key size and runtime while keeping the gate bootstrapping (NAND) failure probability below 2^{-32}. According to these criteria, we propose new 128-bit secure parameter sets 128_Ours/AP, 128_tGINX, and 128_bGINX for Ours/AP with Gaussian secrets, GINX* with ternary secrets, and GINX with binary secrets, respectively. For comparison purposes, Table 2 also provides optimized parameters for AP and GINX from previous works which have smaller security considering the latest cryptoanalysis. The security is estimated using the lattice estimator (commit 09e235) [1]

Table 2. Optimized parameter sets for FHEW schemes. Error variance is 3.2 and for TFHE, we put error variance instead of q and Q as it is defined over Torus.

Parameter set	key	n	q	N	Q	Q_{ks}	d_g	d_{ks}	$\lambda_{\min}$
128_Ours/AP	$\sigma=3.2$	458	1024	1024	2^{28}	2^{14}	3	2	128.2
128_tGINX	ternary	531	2048	1024	2^{26}	2^{14}	4	2	128.5
128_bGINX	binary	571	2048	1024	2^{25}	2^{14}	4	2	128.1
STD128_OPT [38]	ternary	502	1024	1024	2^{27}	2^{14}	4	2	121.0
TFHE [44]	binary	630	$\sigma=2^{-15}$	1024	$\sigma=2^{-25}$	–	3	2	115.11

Let σ_{ms1}^2, σ_{ks}^2, and σ_{ms2}^2 denote the error variances introduced by modulus switching from Q to Q_{ks}, key switching from $\vec{z}$ to $\vec{s}$, and modulus switching from Q_{ks} to q, respectively. $\mathrm{LWE}_{q,\vec{s}}(q/4 \cdot m)$ has the greatest noise, whose variance is

$$\varsigma^2 = \frac{q^2}{Q^2}\cdot 2\sigma_{\mathrm{acc}}^2 + \frac{q^2}{Q_{\mathrm{ks}}^2}\left(\sigma_{\mathrm{ks}}^2+\sigma_{\mathrm{ms1}}^2\right)+\sigma_{\mathrm{ms2}}^2.$$

Similar to [24] we estimate

$$\sigma_{\mathrm{ms}1}^2 = \frac{\|\vec{z}\|^2 + 1}{12}, \sigma_{\mathrm{ks}}^2 = \sigma^2 N d_{\mathrm{ks}}, \sigma_{\mathrm{ms}2}^2 = \frac{\|\vec{s}\|^2 + 1}{12}.$$

We assume $\|\vec{z}\| \leq \sqrt{N/2}$ and $\|\vec{s}\| \leq \sqrt{n/2}$ for binary or ternary secrets [24], and $\|\vec{z}\| = \sqrt{N\sigma^2}$ and $\|\vec{s}\| = \sqrt{n\sigma^2}$ for Gaussian secrets. The decryption fails when the noise of $\mathsf{LWE}_{q,\vec{s}}(q/4 \cdot m)$ exceeds $q/8$, and thus the decryption failure probability per NAND is given by $1 - \mathrm{erf}(\frac{q/8}{\sqrt{2}\varsigma})$.

Table 3. Bootstrapping failure probability of each blind rotation method. The failure probability of Algorithm 7 is estimated for the worst case, i.e., the number of automorphism is $(1 - 1/w)n + (1/w)N$.

Parameter set	Algorithm 7	AP	GINX*	GINX-binary
128_Ours/AP	$2^{-85.68}$	$2^{-77.74}$	x	x
128_tGINX	$2^{-113.02}$	$2^{-105.56}$	$2^{-93.84}$	x
128_bGINX	$2^{-90.53}$	$2^{-79.82}$	x	$2^{-79.82}$
STD128_OPT [38]	$2^{-111.35}$	$2^{-108.87}$	$2^{-104.38}$	x
TFHE [44]	$2^{-77.49}$	$2^{-58.63}$	x	$2^{-58.63}$

Table 3 provides the estimated bootstrapping failure probability $1 - \mathrm{erf}(\frac{q/8}{\sqrt{2}\varsigma})$. It shows that among all the existing methods, the proposed blind rotation has the least error. As our blind rotation and AP take advantage of smaller q, we replaced $q = 1024$ in this table. In this estimate, we set $w = 10$.

5.2 Runtime Results

In order to provide a fair comparison of bootstrapping algorithms, we have implemented all of them using identical libraries and computing environments. The evaluation environment is PALISADE v.1.11.5 on Intel(R) Xeon(R) Gold 6240 CPU @ 2.60 GHz, running Ubuntu 20.04.3 LTS. We compiled with clang 12 and the following CMake flags: NATIVE_SIZE = 32, WITH_OPENMP = OFF, WITH_NATIVEOPT = ON.

Table 4. Timing results (average of 400, $w = 10$ for our method), blind rotation key size, and failure probability for FHEW bootstrapping (NAND gate)

Parameter set	Method	Runtime [ms]	Key size [MB]	Fail. prob
128_Ours/AP	Algorithm 7	**80.1**	**12.67**	$2^{-85.68}$
128_Ours/AP	AP	127.8	776.45	$2^{-77.74}$
128_tGINX	GINX*	89.7	40.45	$2^{-93.84}$
128_bGINX	GINX	84.1	20.91	$2^{-79.82}$

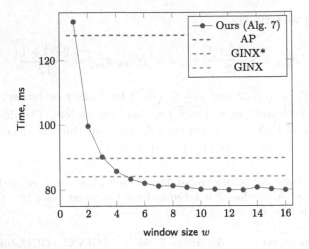

Fig. 3. Bootstrapping performance results of Algorithm 7 method for different window sizes

Table 4 shows runtime results and blind rotation key size for NAND gate evaluation of FHEW. We provide experimental results for different parameter sets for binary, ternary, and Gaussian secret key distributions. This table demonstrates that the proposed algorithm with the parameter set 128_Ours/AP has the best performance. The impact of different window sizes is demonstrated in Fig. 5.2 where runtime results for NAND gate evaluation of FHEW are presented depending on the window size w. With $w \geq 10$, the running time of the proposed blind rotation technique is approximately the same. This is consistent with our complexity analysis in Sect. 3.

6   Applications to Threshold Homomorphic Encryption

In this section, we outline a threshold HE scheme which takes advantage of the proposed blind rotation technique. The simple structure of our blind rotation keys gives us an instinctive design of FHEW-like threshold HE with the approach proposed in [4].

Following the basic concept described in Sect. 1.3, to enable threshold HE using the FHEW scheme, we define the algorithms for distributed evaluation key generation. Each participant j has the secret keys $\vec{s}_j$ for LWE encryption and z_j for RLWE encryption, where $j \in J$ and J denotes the set of participants. The common secret keys are defined as $\vec{s}_* = \sum_{j \in J} \vec{s}_j$ and $z_* = \sum_{j \in J} z_j$.

6.1   Distributed Generation of Evaluation Keys

The distributed generation of evaluation key for threshold version of Algorithm 3 explained in this section is naturally extended to other proposed variants by simple modifications. We omit a description of the LWE switching key which is not the main interest of this paper and is straightforward.

Public Key Generation. The public key for implicit secret keys $z_* = \sum_{j \in J} z_j$ is generated by the following procedures [4].

– Each participant $j \in J$ independently generates their own secrets $\vec{s}_j$ and z_j.
– Given common random string a_{crs}, each participant calculates $b_j = -a_{crs} \cdot z_j + e_j$ and shares them to other participants, where $e_j \leftarrow \chi_{err}$.
– The public key is generated as $pk_{z_*}^{RLWE} = (a_{crs}, \sum_{j \in J} b_j)$.

Generation of Automorphism Keys. The generation of automorphism keys consists of the following two stages.

– Using the shared public key $pk_{z_*}^{RLWE}$, each participant generates encryptions $ak_{j,i}^{Thr} = RLWE'_{z_*}(z_j(X^i))$ as

$$ak_{j,i}^{Thr} := \left(Enc^{RLWE}(B_g^0 \cdot z_j(X^i)), \ldots, Enc^{RLWE}(B_g^{d_g-1} \cdot z_j(X^i)) \right)$$

for each i, where $\vec{B}_g = (B_g^0, B_g^1, \ldots, B_g^{d_g-1})$ is a gadget vector. The error for encryption is sampled from χ_{smenc}, which is a special distribution for a large error to "smudge out" small differences in distributions [4], we denote its variance by σ_{smenc}^2 in the later analysis. Next, each participant sends $ak_{j,i}^{Thr}$ to the computing party.

– The computing party generates automorphism keys ak_i^{Thr} as follows

$$ak_i^{Thr} := \sum_{j \in J} ak_{j,i}^{Thr} = \sum_{j \in J} RLWE'_{z_*}(z_j(X^i)) = RLWE'_{z_*}(z_*(X^i)) .$$

Generation of Blind Rotation Keys. The difference from the generation of the automorphism keys is that the sum of components $s_{j,i}$ is done in the exponent. Hence, the merging is done by RGSW $\circledast$ RGSW multiplications, instead of additions.

– Each participant generates the partial encryption $brk_{j,i}^{Thr} = RGSW_{z_*}(X^{s_{j,i}})$ for $i \in [0, n-1]$, where $s_{j,i}$ is the i-th component of $\vec{s}_j$. We can generate the RGSW key using the following equation:

$$brk_{j,i}^{Thr} := \left(RLWE'_{z_*}(z_* \cdot X^{s_{j,i}}), RLWE'_{z_*}(X^{s_{j,i}}) \right) .$$

Then, each party sends $brk_{j,i}^{Thr}$ to the computing party.
– The computing party calculates $brk_i^{Thr} = RGSW_{z_*}(X^{s_{*,i}})$ for $i \in [0, n-1]$ using the following equation (note that the error is additive.):

$$brk_i^{Thr} := \prod_{j \in J} brk_{j,i}^{Thr} = \prod_{j \in J} RGSW_{z_*}(X^{s_{j,i}}) = RGSW_{z_*}(X^{s_{*,i}}).$$

Any party can use these keys to perform secure computations without revealing the secrets of any participants, including the binary gate evaluation [24] using the proposed blind rotation technique.

6.2   Performance Analysis

Computational Complexity and Key Size. Following the above evaluation key generation, the computing party finds the evaluation keys:

$$
\begin{cases}
\mathsf{brk}_i^{Thr} = \mathsf{RGSW}_{z_*}\left(X^{s_{*,i}}\right), & i \in [0, n-1] \\
\mathsf{ak}_u^{Thr} = \mathsf{RLWE}'_{z_*}\left(z_*(X^{g^u})\right), & u \in [1, w] \\
\mathsf{ak}_{-1}^{Thr} = \mathsf{RLWE}'_{z_*}\left(z_*(X^{-g})\right)
\end{cases}
$$

The computation of blind rotation and the structure of the keys are the same as in Algorithm 3, so the computational complexity and key size are the same as in Table 1 in terms of the number of $\odot$ multiplications (computational complexity) and RLWE' ciphertexts (key size). In other words, the number of participants does not affect asymptotic computational complexity and key size. This implies that the proposed blind rotation is preferable for threshold HE as it takes advantage of fast evaluation and the small key size regardless of the number of participants. In practice, a larger parameter is required due to larger error introduced by distributed key generation.

Error Analysis. This analysis is similar to Sect. 4, except for the fact that ak and brk now have higher error variance. The variance of $\mathsf{pk}_{z_*}^{\mathsf{RLWE}}$ error e_{pk} is equal to $k\sigma^2$ as it is the sum of errors e_j of all parties. The error of each $\mathsf{RGSW}_z(X^{s_{j,i}})$ is equal to $v \cdot e_{\mathsf{pk}} + e_0 \cdot z_* + e_1$. Hence, the error variance is given as $\sigma_{\mathsf{fresh}}^2 \leq \frac{2N}{3}|J| \cdot \sigma^2 + (\|z_*\|_2 + 1) \cdot \sigma_{\mathsf{smenc}}^2$. The blind rotation key $\mathsf{RGSW}_z(X^{s_i})$ is obtained by consecutive multiplication of $\mathsf{RGSW} \circledast \mathsf{RGSW}$ and introduces additive error, whose variance is equal to $\sigma_{\mathsf{brk}}^2 = 2|J| d_g N \frac{B_g^2}{12} \cdot \sigma_{\mathsf{fresh}}^2$. For automorphism keys, again each $\mathsf{RLWE}'_z(z_j(X^t))$ has the error of variance $\sigma_{\mathsf{fresh}}^2$. Thus the error of $\mathsf{RLWE}'_z(z(X^t))$ is equal to $\sigma_{\mathsf{ak}}^2 = |J| \cdot \sigma_{\mathsf{fresh}}^2$.

The worst-case total variance after blind rotation in Algorithm 7 can be estimated as

$$
\sigma_{\mathsf{acc}}^2 = d_g N \frac{B_g^2}{12} \cdot \left(2n \cdot \sigma_{\mathsf{brk}}^2 + \left(\kappa + \frac{N - \kappa}{w} \right) \cdot \sigma_{\mathsf{ak}}^2 \right).
$$

The blind rotation algorithm for AP can be also extended in a similar way, whose blind rotation keys are $\mathsf{RGSW}_{z_*}(Y^{vB_r^t s_{*,i}})$ for $i \in [0, n-1]$, $t \in [0, d_r - 1]$, and $v \in \mathbb{Z}_{B_r}$. Then, the error after AP blind rotation is

$$
\sigma_{\mathsf{acc}}^2 = d_g N \frac{B_g^2}{12} \cdot \left(2d_r \left(1 - \frac{1}{B_r} \right) n \cdot \sigma_{\mathsf{brk}}^2 \right).
$$

Since σ_{brk} is much greater than σ_{ak} (it is same as σ in non-threshold setting), the error difference between our technique and AP variant becomes bigger in threshold setting. The parameters for FHEW-like HE are error-sensitive and our algorithm produces the least blind rotation error (which enables to use smaller parameters). Thus, it is more favorable in threshold HE.

7   Conclusion

A new blind rotation technique for homomorphic encryption is proposed with several variants which provide tradeoffs between key size and complexity. The proposed method offers the best of both previous AP and GINX bootstrapping simultaneously and further improves on them. We demonstrated that our method is better than both approaches in terms of running time and evaluation key size. It offers the additional advantage of reducing the amount of noise introduced during blind rotation, even for the case of the binary key that is the most favorable to GINX.

We also showed a simple threshold HE scheme based on FHEW. This scheme takes advantage of the proposed blind rotation technique since it requires computations under secret keys with distributions wider than binary or ternary. Our analysis showed that the performance and key size could be kept relatively low with increasing the number of participants, unlike GINX. This is an important property for the distributed computation settings. This demonstrates the high potential of FHEW-like schemes in different applications where the secret key distribution is wider than binary or ternary. In addition, it would be of great interest to apply our technique to schemes of other structures such as NTRU and Torus variants of bootstrappings as further work.

Acknowledgments. This work was supported by the Samsung Electronics co. ltd., Samsung Advanced Institute of Technology.

References

1. Albrecht, M., Player, R., Scott, S.: On the concrete hardness of learning with errors. J. Math. Cryptol. **9**(3), 169–203 (2015). https://doi.org/10.1515/jmc-2015-0016
2. Alperin-Sheriff, J., Peikert, C.: Faster bootstrapping with polynomial error. In: Garay, J.A., Gennaro, R. (eds.) CRYPTO 2014. LNCS, vol. 8616, pp. 297–314. Springer, Heidelberg (2014). https://doi.org/10.1007/978-3-662-44371-2_17
3. Arora, S., Ge, R.: New algorithms for learning in presence of errors. In: Aceto, L., Henzinger, M., Sgall, J. (eds.) ICALP 2011. LNCS, vol. 6755, pp. 403–415. Springer, Heidelberg (2011). https://doi.org/10.1007/978-3-642-22006-7_34
4. Asharov, G., Jain, A., López-Alt, A., Tromer, E., Vaikuntanathan, V., Wichs, D.: Multiparty computation with low communication, computation and interaction via threshold FHE. In: Pointcheval, D., Johansson, T. (eds.) EUROCRYPT 2012. LNCS, vol. 7237, pp. 483–501. Springer, Heidelberg (2012). https://doi.org/10.1007/978-3-642-29011-4_29
5. Badawi, A.A., Bet al.: Openfhe: open-source fully homomorphic encryption library. Cryptology ePrint Archive, Paper 2022/915 (2022). https://eprint.iacr.org/2022/915, https://www.openfhe.org
6. Bendlin, R., Damgård, I.: Threshold decryption and zero-knowledge proofs for lattice-based cryptosystems. In: Micciancio, D. (ed.) TCC 2010. LNCS, vol. 5978, pp. 201–218. Springer, Heidelberg (2010). https://doi.org/10.1007/978-3-642-11799-2_13

7. Bonnoron, G., Ducas, L., Fillinger, M.: Large FHE gates from tensored homomorphic accumulator. In: Joux, A., Nitaj, A., Rachidi, T. (eds.) AFRICACRYPT 2018. LNCS, vol. 10831, pp. 217–251. Springer, Cham (2018). https://doi.org/10.1007/978-3-319-89339-6_13

8. Bonte, C., Iliashenko, I., Park, J., Pereira, H.V.L., Smart, N.P.: FINAL: faster FHE instantiated with NTRU and LWE. In: Agrawal, S., Lin, D. (eds.) Advances in Cryptology – ASIACRYPT 2022. ASIACRYPT 2022. LNCS, vol. 13792, pp. 188–215. Springer, Cham (2022). https://doi.org/10.1007/978-3-031-22966-4_7

9. Boura, C., Gama, N., Georgieva, M., Jetchev, D.: Chimera: combining Ring-LWE-based fully homomorphic encryption schemes. J. Math. Cryptol. 14(1), 316–338 (2020). https://doi.org/10.1515/jmc-2019-0026

10. Brakerski, Z.: Fully homomorphic encryption without modulus switching from classical GapSVP. In: Safavi-Naini, R., Canetti, R. (eds.) CRYPTO 2012. LNCS, vol. 7417, pp. 868–886. Springer, Heidelberg (2012). https://doi.org/10.1007/978-3-642-32009-5_50

11. Brakerski, Z., Döttling, N.: Hardness of LWE on general entropic distributions. In: Canteaut, A., Ishai, Y. (eds.) EUROCRYPT 2020. LNCS, vol. 12106, pp. 551–575. Springer, Cham (2020). https://doi.org/10.1007/978-3-030-45724-2_19

12. Brakerski, Z., Gentry, C., Vaikuntanathan, V.: (Leveled) Fully homomorphic encryption without bootstrapping. ACM Trans. Comput. Theory (TOCT) 6(3), 1–36 (2014). https://doi.org/10.1145/2633600

13. Brakerski, Z., Langlois, A., Peikert, C., Regev, O., Stehlé, D.: Classical hardness of learning with errors. In: Proceedings of the forty-fifth annual ACM symposium on Theory of computing, pp. 575–584 (2013). https://doi.org/10.1145/2488608.2488680

14. Brakerski, Z., Perlman, R.: Lattice-based fully dynamic multi-key FHE with short ciphertexts. In: Robshaw, M., Katz, J. (eds.) CRYPTO 2016. LNCS, vol. 9814, pp. 190–213. Springer, Heidelberg (2016). https://doi.org/10.1007/978-3-662-53018-4_8

15. Brakerski, Z., Vaikuntanathan, V.: Fully homomorphic encryption from Ring-LWE and security for key dependent messages. In: Rogaway, P. (ed.) CRYPTO 2011. LNCS, vol. 6841, pp. 505–524. Springer, Heidelberg (2011). https://doi.org/10.1007/978-3-642-22792-9_29

16. Chen, H., Chillotti, I., Song, Y.: Multi-key homomorphic encryption from TFHE. In: Galbraith, S.D., Moriai, S. (eds.) ASIACRYPT 2019. LNCS, vol. 11922, pp. 446–472. Springer, Cham (2019). https://doi.org/10.1007/978-3-030-34621-8_16

17. Chen, M., et al.: Diogenes: lightweight scalable RSA modulus generation with a dishonest majority. In: 2021 IEEE Symposium on Security and Privacy (S&P), pp. 590–607. IEEE (2021). https://doi.org/10.1109/sp40001.2021.00025

18. Cheon, J.H., Hhan, M., Hong, S., Son, Y.: A hybrid of dual and meet-in-the-middle attack on sparse and ternary secret LWE. IEEE Access (2019). https://doi.org/10.1109/access.2019.2925425

19. Cheon, J.H., Kim, A., Kim, M., Song, Y.: Homomorphic encryption for arithmetic of approximate numbers. In: Takagi, T., Peyrin, T. (eds.) ASIACRYPT 2017. LNCS, vol. 10624, pp. 409–437. Springer, Cham (2017). https://doi.org/10.1007/978-3-319-70694-8_15

20. Chillotti, I., Gama, N., Georgieva, M., Izabachène, M.: Faster packed homomorphic operations and efficient circuit bootstrapping for TFHE. In: Takagi, T., Peyrin, T. (eds.) ASIACRYPT 2017. LNCS, vol. 10624, pp. 377–408. Springer, Cham (2017). https://doi.org/10.1007/978-3-319-70694-8_14

21. Chillotti, I., Gama, N., Georgieva, M., Izabachène, M.: TFHE: fast fully homomorphic encryption over the torus. J. Cryptol. **33**(1), 34–91 (2019). https://doi.org/10.1007/s00145-019-09319-x
22. Chillotti, I., Joye, M., Paillier, P.: Programmable bootstrapping enables efficient homomorphic inference of deep neural networks. In: Dolev, S., Margalit, O., Pinkas, B., Schwarzmann, A. (eds.) CSCML 2021. LNCS, vol. 12716, pp. 1–19. Springer, Cham (2021). https://doi.org/10.1007/978-3-030-78086-9_1
23. Clear, M., McGoldrick, C.: Multi-identity and multi-key leveled FHE from learning with errors. In: Gennaro, R., Robshaw, M. (eds.) CRYPTO 2015. LNCS, vol. 9216, pp. 630–656. Springer, Heidelberg (2015). https://doi.org/10.1007/978-3-662-48000-7_31
24. Ducas, L., Micciancio, D.: FHEW: bootstrapping homomorphic encryption in less than a second. In: Oswald, E., Fischlin, M. (eds.) EUROCRYPT 2015. LNCS, vol. 9056, pp. 617–640. Springer, Heidelberg (2015). https://doi.org/10.1007/978-3-662-46800-5_24
25. Fan, J., Vercauteren, F.: Somewhat practical fully homomorphic encryption. IACR Cryptol. ePrint Arch. **2012/144** (2012). https://eprint.iacr.org/2012/144
26. Gama, N., Izabachène, M., Nguyen, P.Q., Xie, X.: Structural lattice reduction: generalized worst-case to average-case reductions and homomorphic cryptosystems. In: Fischlin, M., Coron, J.-S. (eds.) EUROCRYPT 2016. LNCS, vol. 9666, pp. 528–558. Springer, Heidelberg (2016). https://doi.org/10.1007/978-3-662-49896-5_19
27. Goldwasser, S., Kalai, Y.T., Peikert, C., Vaikuntanathan, V.: Robustness of the learning with errors assumption. In: Innovations in Computer Science - ICS 2010, pp. 230–240. Tsinghua University Press (2010). http://conference.iiis.tsinghua.edu.cn/ICS2010/content/papers/19.html
28. Halevi, S., Shoup, V.: Faster homomorphic linear transformations in HElib. In: Shacham, H., Boldyreva, A. (eds.) CRYPTO 2018. LNCS, vol. 10991, pp. 93–120. Springer, Cham (2018). https://doi.org/10.1007/978-3-319-96884-1_4
29. Joye, M., Paillier, P.: Blind rotation in fully homomorphic encryption with extended keys. In: Dolev, S., Katz, J., Meisels, A. (eds.) Cyber Security, Cryptology, and Machine Learning. CSCML 2022. LNCS, vol. 13301, pp. 1–18. Springer, Cham (2022). https://doi.org/10.1007/978-3-031-07689-3_1
30. Kim, A., et al.: General bootstrapping approach for RLWE-based homomorphic encryption. Cryptol. ePrint Arch. **2021/691** (2021). https://eprint.iacr.org/2021/691
31. Kim, A., Polyakov, Y., Zucca, V.: Revisiting homomorphic encryption schemes for finite fields. In: Tibouchi, M., Wang, H. (eds.) ASIACRYPT 2021. LNCS, vol. 13092, pp. 608–639. Springer, Cham (2021). https://doi.org/10.1007/978-3-030-92078-4_21
32. Kirchner, P., Fouque, P.-A.: An improved BKW algorithm for LWE with applications to cryptography and lattices. In: Gennaro, R., Robshaw, M. (eds.) CRYPTO 2015. LNCS, vol. 9215, pp. 43–62. Springer, Heidelberg (2015). https://doi.org/10.1007/978-3-662-47989-6_3
33. Liu, Z., Micciancio, D., Polyakov, Y.: Large-precision homomorphic sign evaluation using FHEW/TFHE bootstrapping. In: Agrawal, S., Lin, D. (eds.) Advances in Cryptology – ASIACRYPT 2022. ASIACRYPT 2022. LNCS, vol. 13792, pp. 130–160. Springer, Cham (2022). https://doi.org/10.1007/978-3-031-22966-4_5
34. Lu, W.J., Huang, Z., Hong, C., Ma, Y., Qu, H.: PEGASUS: bridging polynomial and non-polynomial evaluations in homomorphic encryption. In: 2021 IEEE symposium on Security and Privacy (S&P), pp. 1057–1073. IEEE (2021). https://doi.org/10.1109/sp40001.2021.00043

35. Lyubashevsky, V., Peikert, C., Regev, O.: On ideal lattices and learning with errors over rings. J. ACM (JACM) **60**(6), 1–35 (2013). https://doi.org/10.1145/2535925
36. Micciancio, D.: On the hardness of learning with errors with binary secrets. Theory Comput. **14**(1), 1–17 (2018). https://doi.org/10.4086/toc.2018.v014a013
37. Micciancio, D., Peikert, C.: Hardness of SIS and LWE with small parameters. In: Canetti, R., Garay, J.A. (eds.) CRYPTO 2013. LNCS, vol. 8042, pp. 21–39. Springer, Heidelberg (2013). https://doi.org/10.1007/978-3-642-40041-4_2
38. Micciancio, D., Polyakov, Y.: Bootstrapping in FHEW-like cryptosystems. In: WAHC 2021, pp. 17–28. ACM (2021). https://doi.org/10.1145/3474366.3486924
39. Miccianco, D., Sorrell, J.: Ring packing and amortized FHEW bootstrapping. In: 45th International Colloquium on Automata, Languages, and Programming. Schloss Dagstuhl-Leibniz-Zentrum fuer Informatik (2018). https://doi.org/10.4230/LIPIcs.ICALP.2018.100
40. Mukherjee, P., Wichs, D.: Two round multiparty computation via multi-key FHE. In: Fischlin, M., Coron, J.-S. (eds.) EUROCRYPT 2016. LNCS, vol. 9666, pp. 735–763. Springer, Heidelberg (2016). https://doi.org/10.1007/978-3-662-49896-5_26
41. PALISADE: Lattice Cryptography Library (release 1.11.7), September 2021. https://palisade-crypto.org/
42. Peikert, C., Shiehian, S.: Multi-key FHE from LWE, revisited. In: Hirt, M., Smith, A. (eds.) TCC 2016. LNCS, vol. 9986, pp. 217–238. Springer, Heidelberg (2016). https://doi.org/10.1007/978-3-662-53644-5_9
43. Regev, O.: On lattices, learning with errors, random linear codes, and cryptography. J. ACM (JACM) **56**(6), 1–40 (2009). https://doi.org/10.1145/1060590.1060603
44. TFHE: Fast fully homomorphic encryption library over the torus. https://tfhe.github.io/tfhe/
45. Zhou, T., Zhang, Z., Chen, L., Che, X., Liu, W., Yang, X.: Multi-key fully homomorphic encryption scheme with compact ciphertext. IACR Cryptol. ePrint Arch. **2021/1131** (2021). https://eprint.iacr.org/2021/1131

On Polynomial Functions Modulo p^e and Faster Bootstrapping for Homomorphic Encryption

Robin Geelen[1]([✉]) [ID], Ilia Iliashenko[2] [ID], Jiayi Kang[1] [ID], and Frederik Vercauteren[1] [ID]

[1] imec-COSIC, KU Leuven, Leuven, Belgium
{robin.geelen,jiayi.kang,frederik.vercauteren}@esat.kuleuven.be
[2] CipherMode Labs, Los Angeles, USA
ilia@ciphermode.com

Abstract. In this paper, we perform a systematic study of functions $f : \mathbb{Z}_{p^e} \to \mathbb{Z}_{p^e}$ and categorize those functions that can be represented by a polynomial with integer coefficients. More specifically, we cover the following properties: necessary and sufficient conditions for the existence of an integer polynomial representation; computation of such a representation; and the complete set of equivalent polynomials that represent a given function.

As an application, we use the newly developed theory to speed up bootstrapping for the BGV and BFV homomorphic encryption schemes. The crucial ingredient underlying our improvements is the existence of null polynomials, i.e. non-zero polynomials that evaluate to zero in every point. We exploit the rich algebraic structure of these null polynomials to find better representations of the digit extraction function, which is the main bottleneck in bootstrapping. As such, we obtain sparse polynomials that have 50% fewer coefficients than the original ones. In addition, we propose a new method to decompose digit extraction as a series of polynomial evaluations. This lowers the time complexity from $\mathcal{O}(\sqrt{pe})$ to $\mathcal{O}(\sqrt{p}\sqrt[4]{e})$ for digit extraction modulo p^e, at the cost of a slight increase in multiplicative depth. Overall, our implementation in HElib shows a significant speedup of a factor up to 2.6 over the state-of-the-art.

Keywords: Homomorphic encryption · Bootstrapping · Polyfunctions

1 Introduction

Homomorphic encryption (HE) allows computations on encrypted data without knowledge of the secret key. In the past 15 years, there have been tremendous improvements in HE protocols, both in speed and applicability. In spite of these efforts, homomorphic encryption remains extremely slow compared to unencrypted computations and further speedups are required.

Homomorphic computations are typically realized as arithmetic circuits, i.e. sequences of additions and multiplications that implement a desired functionality. In the lattice-based schemes BGV [6] and BFV [5,10], these operations

© International Association for Cryptologic Research 2023
C. Hazay and M. Stam (Eds.): EUROCRYPT 2023, LNCS 14006, pp. 257–286, 2023.
https://doi.org/10.1007/978-3-031-30620-4_9

are performed over (extensions of) $\mathbb{Z}_{p^e}$, where p is a prime number and e is a positive integer.[1] Functions on $\mathbb{Z}_{p^e}$ have rather interesting properties. First, only a limited class of functions can be described by polynomials with integer coefficients, the so-called *polyfunctions* (short for polynomial functions). Second, the polynomials that represent a given polyfunction are always non-unique and we can therefore try to find the polynomial representation that is most efficient to evaluate homomorphically.

An example application that can benefit from the study of polyfunctions is *bootstrapping* – the ciphertext refreshing procedure that enables unbounded fully homomorphic encryption. This procedure is necessary because lattice-based schemes include a noise term that grows when we evaluate an arithmetic circuit. Bootstrapping reduces the noise back to a lower level, which enables further evaluation of homomorphic additions and multiplications. Since its introduction by Gentry in 2009 [11], the latency and throughput of bootstrapping were improved several orders of magnitude in many subsequent works [8,13,15], but it remains the main bottleneck to achieve fully homomorphic encryption.

1.1 Related Work

Polyfunctions. Research into polyfunctions has a long history. Already in 1921, Kemper [17] studied elementary structures of polyfunctions over $\mathbb{Z}_m$ for a composite integer m. This early research represents polynomials in the monomial basis $\{X^i\}_{i=0,1,\dots}$. However, since the mid-1960s, much of the literature [7,9,16,23] started to use the falling factorial basis $\{X \cdot (X-1) \cdot \dots \cdot (X-i)\}_{i=0,1,\dots}$. The reason for this shift is that the falling factorial polynomials almost directly give rise to non-trivial *null polynomials* (i.e. polynomials that by definition evaluate to zero in every point when interpreted modulo some prime power p^e).

Null polynomials result in equivalent representations of the same polyfunction $f: \mathbb{Z}_{p^e} \to \mathbb{Z}_{p^e}$. Specifically, two polynomials $F(X), H(X) \in \mathbb{Z}[X]$ represent the same function f if and only if their difference $F(X) - H(X)$ is a null polynomial. Equivalently, the set of all possible representations of f is obtained as $F(X) + \mathcal{O}_{p^e}$, where $\mathcal{O}_{p^e}$ is the set of all null polynomials modulo p^e. In other words, there exists a one-to-one correspondence between polyfunctions and collections of equivalent polynomials:

$$\text{polyfunction } f: \mathbb{Z}_{p^e} \to \mathbb{Z}_{p^e} \iff F(X) + \mathcal{O}_{p^e}.$$

Bootstrapping. The first bootstrapping procedure for BGV was proposed by Gentry et al. [13] for encryption of single bits, and improved by subsequent research [1]. The most relevant works for this paper are from Halevi and Shoup [15], and Chen and Han [8]. Halevi and Shoup proposed a bootstrapping

---

[1] Some protocols for secure multi-party computation [3] also work over $\mathbb{Z}_{p^e}$, which makes our study of polyfunctions even more widely applicable. However, improvements in multi-party computation are not the direct focus of this paper.

method that works for the more general plaintext space $\mathbb{Z}_{p^e}$. Their technique relies on a "digit removal" procedure, which involves repeated homomorphic evaluation of the *lifting polynomial* and has degree p^{e-1} in total. Chen and Han introduced an additional *digit extraction polynomial* (sometimes called the *lowest digit retain polynomial*) that has a much lower degree equal to $(p-1) \cdot (e-1) + 1$. Lower degrees are typically favored in homomorphic encryption.

In practice, polynomial evaluations account for most of the computational cost of bootstrapping: in the implementation of HElib, they are altogether $3\times$ to $50\times$ more expensive than all other operations combined [15]. This situation is exactly the same for BGV and BFV, because both schemes have an identical bootstrapping procedure.

1.2 Our Contributions

The aim of this paper is to further develop the theory of polyfunctions with a focus on cryptographic applications. New insights in these polyfunctions allow us to significantly accelerate HE bootstrapping.

Polyfunctions. In the first part of the paper (Sect. 3), we study polyfunctions modulo p^e. This includes the following:

- In Sect. 3.1, we study the complete set of null polynomials modulo p^e (denoted by $\mathcal{O}_{p^e}$) as to obtain the set of all equivalent polyfunction representations. A novel element of our approach is also restricting $\mathcal{O}_{p^e}$ to contain only polynomials of bounded degree. When doing so, the resulting set forms a lattice structure, and we can find small-coefficient representations by solving the closest vector problem in this lattice. This is interesting in homomorphic encryption, because small coefficients lead to less noise growth.
- In Sect. 3.3, we extend Newton interpolation from the real numbers to $\mathbb{Z}_{p^e}$. Our method always returns a polynomial representation of the lowest degree when given a polyfunction as input. When given a function that is not a polyfunction, our method can detect this and returns an error.
- In Sect. 3.5, we discuss several properties of polyfunctions that are especially relevant for HE bootstrapping. In particular, we consider the class of even and odd polyfunctions that satisfy respectively $f(-a) = f(a) \pmod{p^e}$ and $f(-a) = -f(a) \pmod{p^e}$ for $a \in \mathbb{Z}$. We show that each such function can be represented by a sparse polynomial with only even- or odd-exponent terms. Evaluating such a sparse representation is asymptotically cheaper by a factor of $\sqrt{2}$.

Bootstrapping. In the second part of the paper (Sects. 4 and 5), we apply the newly developed theory to speed up BGV and BFV bootstrapping. The most expensive component of bootstrapping, both in degree and execution time, is evaluation of the digit extraction polynomial. In order to accelerate it, we apply the following improvements:

– We propose multiple methods to obtain better representations of the digit extraction function. First, we show that this function is either even or odd, and can therefore be represented as a polynomial with only 50% of the coefficients. Second, we propose a new technique to decompose digit extraction in multiple stages. Let g_e be the digit extraction function modulo p^e, then we write it as $g_e = g_{e,e'} \circ g_{e'}$. In our algorithm, both $g_{e'}$ and $g_{e,e'}$ are evaluated using polynomials of much smaller degree than the direct approach. As a consequence, we lower the time complexity for digit extraction from $\mathcal{O}(\sqrt{pe})$ to $\mathcal{O}(\sqrt{p}\sqrt[4]{e})$, at the cost of $\lceil \log_2 p \rceil$ increase in multiplicative depth.
– In order to fully benefit from the optimized digit extraction polynomials, we revise the digit removal procedure of Chen and Han [8]. Our improved algorithm utilizes the digit extraction polynomial exclusively, without relying on the lifting polynomial. We implemented our new bootstrapping algorithm in HElib, and observe that it is up to 2.6 times faster than the state-of-the-art. Our code is made publicly available.[2]

2 Preliminaries

2.1 Notations

For prime p and integer exponent $e \geqslant 1$, the set of functions from $\mathbb{Z}_{p^e}$ to itself is denoted by $\mathcal{F}_{p^e}$. Moreover, we write the evaluation of a polynomial $F(X)$ at $X = a$ as $F(a)$ or sometimes $F(X)|_{X=a}$.

Let $\nu_p(\cdot)$ denote the *p-adic valuation* function defined as

$$\nu_p(m) = \begin{cases} \max\{k \in \mathbb{N} : p^k \mid m\} & \text{if } m \neq 0 \\ \infty & \text{if } m = 0. \end{cases}$$

It generalizes to the rational numbers as $\nu_p(m/n) = \nu_p(m) - \nu_p(n)$, and we call a rational number *p-integral* if its p-adic valuation is non-negative. Let $\mu(\cdot)$ denote the *Smarandache* function defined as

$$\mu(k) = \min\{i \in \mathbb{N} : k \mid i!\}.$$

Observe that $\nu_p(\cdot)$ and $\mu(\cdot)$ are complementary in some sense. Specifically, it follows directly from the above definitions that $\mu(p^e)$ is the smallest integer for which $\nu_p(\mu(p^e)!) \geqslant e$. A few example instances of $\nu_p(n!)$ and $\mu(p^e)$ for $p = 2$ are listed in Tables 1 and 2.

2.2 Newton Interpolation over $\mathbb{R}$

The Falling Factorial Basis. The Newton interpolation method relies on the so-called *falling factorial polynomials*. Those polynomials are indexed by an integer $i \geqslant 0$ and defined as

$$(X)_i = \prod_{k=0}^{i-1} (X - k) \in \mathbb{Z}[X],$$

---

[2] See https://github.com/KULeuven-COSIC/Bootstrapping_Polyfunctions.

Table 1. Examples of $\nu_2(n!)$

n	1	2	3	4	5	6	7	8	9	10
$\nu_2(n!)$	0	1	1	3	3	4	4	7	7	8

Table 2. Examples of $\mu(2^e)$

e	1	2	3	4	5	6	7	8	9	10
$\mu(2^e)$	2	4	4	6	8	8	8	10	12	12

where by definition we set $(X)_0 = 1$. When reduced modulo p^e, these polynomials exhibit very specific properties that will be studied later in this paper.

Let $\mathbb{P}_n \subseteq \mathbb{Z}[X]$ be the set of polynomials of degree at most n. Obviously, the set $\{X^i \mid 0 \leqslant i \leqslant n\}$ forms a basis for $\mathbb{P}_n$ when seen as a module over $\mathbb{Z}$. We refer to it as the monomial basis. Similarly, also the set $\{(X)_i \mid 0 \leqslant i \leqslant n\}$ forms a basis for $\mathbb{P}_n$, known as the falling factorial basis.

Newton Interpolation. Consider a collection of $n+1$ data points $(i, y_i) \in \mathbb{R}^2$ for $i = 0, \ldots, n$.[3] Using Newton interpolation, we can find a polynomial $F(X)$ of degree at most n that interpolates these data points. Concretely, write the polynomial $F(X) \in \mathbb{R}[X]$ in the format

$$F(X) = c_0 + c_1(X)_1 + c_2(X)_2 + \ldots + c_n(X)_n. \tag{1}$$

Then we can uniquely determine the falling factorial coefficients c_i such that

$$F(i) = y_i, \quad \forall 0 \leqslant i \leqslant n.$$

The coefficients can be computed from forward differences, as introduced in the following definition.

Definition 1. *The i-th forward difference of a function $f \colon \mathbb{R} \to \mathbb{R}$, evaluated at $j \in \mathbb{Z}$, is recursively defined as*

$$\Delta^i f(j) = \begin{cases} f(j) & \text{if } i = 0 \\ \Delta^{i-1} f(j+1) - \Delta^{i-1} f(j) & \text{if } i > 0. \end{cases}$$

We will now apply these forward differences to a polynomial $F(X)$. Note that we slightly abuse notation and consider a polynomial as a function in X. As shown in Fig. 1, the value of $\Delta^i F(X)|_{X=j}$ for $i, j = 0, 1, \ldots, n$ can be derived from Definition 1. Each element in this triangle is defined as $\alpha_{i,j} = \Delta^i F(X)|_{X=j}$, and computed as the difference between the element above and the element above left. We only show rows for $i = 0, \ldots, n$, because all following rows are zero for a polynomial of degree n. This is easily seen by computing

$$\Delta(X)_i = (X+1)X \cdot \ldots \cdot (X-i+2) - X(X-1) \cdot \ldots \cdot (X-i+1)$$
$$= i(X)_{i-1}, \tag{2}$$

---

[3] In a more general version, we could consider the data points (x_i, y_i). For our purpose, however, it is sufficient to choose $x_i = i$.

and using the result in Eq. (1). Note that Eq. (2) is the analogue of taking the derivative of the monomial X^i.

The coefficients of the interpolating polynomial $F(X)$ can now be computed as $c_i = \alpha_{i,0} = \Delta^i F(X)|_{X=0}/i!$. This result is achieved by taking the i-th forward difference of both sides of Eq. (1), and again filling in Eq. (2). This leads to the interpolating polynomial

$$F(X) = \alpha_{0,0} + \alpha_{1,0}(X)_1 + \frac{\alpha_{2,0}}{2!}(X)_2 + \cdots + \frac{\alpha_{n,0}}{n!}(X)_n. \tag{3}$$

Note the analogy with the Taylor series of a function.

Finally, the following relations are useful:

$$\alpha_{0,j} = \sum_{v=0}^{j} \binom{j}{v} \alpha_{v,0}, \tag{4a}$$

$$\alpha_{i,0} = \sum_{v=0}^{i} (-1)^{i+v} \binom{i}{v} \alpha_{0,v}. \tag{4b}$$

These equations establish a relationship between the elements in the first row and the diagonal of Fig. 1.

$$
\begin{array}{llll}
\alpha_{0,0} \ \alpha_{0,1} \ \alpha_{0,2} \ \cdots \ \alpha_{0,n} \\
\quad \alpha_{1,0} \ \alpha_{1,1} \ \cdots \ \alpha_{1,n-1} \\
\qquad \alpha_{2,0} \ \cdots \ \alpha_{2,n-2} \\
\qquad\quad \ddots \quad \vdots \\
\qquad\qquad \alpha_{n,0}
\end{array}
$$

Fig. 1. Evaluation of forward differences with $\alpha_{i,j} = \Delta^i F(X)|_{X=j}$.

The above theory generalizes directly to polynomial rings over any field. However, the subject of this paper is polynomials over $\mathbb{Z}_{p^e}$, which is not a field in general.

2.3   Polyfunctions Modulo p^e

Definition 2. *Let $f \in \mathcal{F}_{p^e}$ be a function from $\mathbb{Z}_{p^e}$ to itself. If there exists a polynomial $F(X) \in \mathbb{Z}[X]$ that satisfies $F(a) = f(a) \pmod{p^e}$ for all $a \in \mathbb{Z}$, then f is a polyfunction modulo p^e and $F(X)$ is a representation of f.*[4]

---

[4] We define the evaluation of a function $f \in \mathcal{F}_{p^e}$ at an integer a in the natural way, by implicitly converting a to its residue class modulo p^e.

As a corollary of the theory in Sect. 2.2, all functions from the field $\mathbb{F}_p$ to itself are polyfunctions. A unique representation of degree less than p is obtained by starting from all data points and applying Newton interpolation. However, the situation is different for functions modulo p^e: first, not all functions are described by integer polynomials modulo p^e, regardless of the degree; second, polyfunctions always have a non-unique representation of the lowest degree due to the existence of *null polynomials* [16,19,21,23].

Null Polynomials Modulo p^e. We define a null polynomial as follows.

Definition 3. *An element $O(X) \in \mathbb{Z}[X]$ is called a* null polynomial modulo p^e *if the function $f \in \mathcal{F}_{p^e}$ that it represents maps every element to zero. In other words, we have that $O(a) = 0 \pmod{p^e}$ for all $a \in \mathbb{Z}$.*

Observe that the evaluation of the falling factorial polynomial $(X)_i$ at *any* integer is divisible by $i!$. Hence it is a null polynomial modulo p^e if $\nu_p(i!) \geqslant e$. Also the other direction holds: if $(X)_i$ is a null polynomial modulo p^e, then evaluating it at $X = i$ gives $(X)_i|_{X=i} = i!$, and therefore $\nu_p(i!) \geqslant e$. Following the notation defined earlier, we find that the smallest possible value of i for which $(X)_i$ is a null polynomial modulo p^e, is equal to $i = \mu(p^e)$.

2.4 Lattices

Definition 4. *The set $\mathcal{L} \subseteq \mathbb{R}^n$ is a* lattice *if there exist $\mathbb{R}$-linearly independent vectors $\mathbf{b}_1, \ldots, \mathbf{b}_k \in \mathbb{R}^n$ such that*

$$\mathcal{L} = \left\{ \sum_{i=1}^k x_i \mathbf{b}_i \mid x_i \in \mathbb{Z} \right\}.$$

The set of vectors $\mathbf{B} = \{\mathbf{b}_1, \ldots, \mathbf{b}_k\}$ constitute a basis, and k is called the rank. A lattice is called q-ary for an integer q if $q\mathbb{Z}^n \subseteq \mathcal{L} \subseteq \mathbb{Z}^n$.

For a lattice vector $\mathbf{v} \in \mathcal{L}$, the length $\|\mathbf{v}\|$ denotes its Euclidean norm (2-norm). We will rely on the closest vector problem (CVP):

Definition 5 (Closest vector problem (exact form)). *Consider a lattice $\mathcal{L} \subseteq \mathbb{R}^n$ and a vector $\mathbf{t} \in \mathbb{R}^n$, CVP asks to recover a lattice vector $\mathbf{v} \in \mathcal{L}$ such that $\|\mathbf{t} - \mathbf{v}\| = \min_{\mathbf{y} \in \mathcal{L}} \|\mathbf{t} - \mathbf{y}\|$.*

Lattices have been studied extensively in cryptography due to the conjectured intractability of certain lattice problems, such as the shortest vector problem (SVP) and the closest vector problem (CVP). The hardness of these problems is used as the security foundation of many cryptosystems, including the BGV and BFV schemes. However, we will use lattices for a different reason, namely the study of polynomial representations with small coefficients.

2.5   Homomorphic Encryption

We are interested in homomorphic encryption schemes that support arithmetic circuits over $\mathbb{Z}_{p^e}$. In the literature, those schemes are known as BGV [6] and BFV [5,10]. Both schemes have the same interface, and only differ from each other in terms of the underlying implementation.

Homomorphic Operations. Next to the usual key generation, encryption and decryption, homomorphic encryption schemes have two extra procedures to evaluate additions and multiplications over the ciphertexts that they encrypt. Both procedures can either take two ciphertexts, or one ciphertext and one plaintext. Moreover, there is one special division operation, which takes a ciphertext that encrypts a message m known to be divisible by p. It outputs a new ciphertext that encrypts m/p, but under plaintext modulus p^{e-1} instead of p^e. This operation fails if the input message is not divisible by p.

Plaintext Batching. BGV and BFV can batch multiple elements of $\mathbb{Z}_{p^e}$ per plaintext [22]. Specifically, the plaintext ring is isomorphic to $\mathbb{Z}_{p^e}^{\ell}$, where addition and multiplication are defined component-wise. Each copy of $\mathbb{Z}_{p^e}$ is called a *plaintext slot*, and can be operated on homomorphically and in parallel. This is sometimes referred to as SIMD operations due to the resemblance in parallel computing architectures.

The above explanation is actually a special case of a more general technique. Given a polynomial $F(X) \in \mathbb{Z}[X]$ that is irreducible modulo p, we can define the Galois ring $E = \mathbb{Z}_{p^e}[X]/(F(X)) \supseteq \mathbb{Z}_{p^e}$. The plaintext rings of BGV and BFV are then isomorphic to E^{ℓ}, again with component-wise addition and multiplication. We refer to this more general version as fully packed slots. If the slots are restricted to encode elements from the subring $\mathbb{Z}_{p^e}$ (like explained above), then they are called sparsely packed.

Bootstrapping. Every HE ciphertext contains a special component called the *noise*. When evaluating homomorphic additions and multiplications, the noise gets larger depending on the complexity of the involved operations. The decryption function removes the noise, but only works correctly if the noise is small enough (depending on the chosen scheme parameters).

To enable circuits that consist of an unlimited number of additions and multiplications, we need a method to reduce the ciphertext noise without decrypting directly. This is achieved via bootstrapping. The idea is to decrypt a ciphertext *homomorphically* by evaluating the scheme's own decryption circuit. This reduces noise and allows further evaluation of additions and multiplications. Bootstrapping comes in two variants: the slots of the encrypted message can either be fully packed or sparsely packed. We refer to the first situation as general bootstrapping, and the second one as thin bootstrapping. Finally, we emphasize that BGV and BFV have an identical bootstrapping procedure. All optimizations for one scheme therefore carry over to the other one immediately.

3   Systematic Study of Polyfunctions

3.1   Null Polynomials

The set of null polynomials modulo p^e can be described in the falling factorial basis. This was already noticed by Singmaster [21] who proved the general
structure of this set. We formulate an adapted version in the following theorem,
where we additionally take into account null polynomials of bounded degree.
Our theorem is proven based on the same outline as Singmaster's proof.

Theorem 1. *A polynomial $O(X) \in \mathbb{Z}[X]$ is a null polynomial modulo p^e of
degree at most n if and only if there exist $a_0, \ldots a_n \in \mathbb{Z}$ such that*

$$O(X) = \sum_{i=0}^{n} a_i \cdot O_i(X), \quad with \quad O_i(X) = p^{\max(e - \nu_p(i!), 0)} \cdot (X)_i. \qquad (5)$$

In this equation, the exponent of p equals 0 if $i \geqslant \mu(p^e)$.

Proof. ($\Leftarrow$) As already pointed out in Sect. 2.3, the evaluation of $(X)_i$ at any
integer is divisible by $p^{\nu_p(i!)}$. Therefore, each term in Eq. (5) evaluated at any
integer is divisible by $p^{\max(e, \nu_p(i!))} \geqslant p^e$. Since each term is a null polynomial
modulo p^e, so is their linear combination.

($\Rightarrow$) We prove the following assertion for $0 \leqslant m \leqslant n + 1$ by applying induction
on m:

$$O(X) = \sum_{i=m}^{n} b_i \cdot (X)_i + \sum_{i=0}^{m-1} a_i \cdot O_i(X), \qquad (6)$$

for some $a_i, b_i \in \mathbb{Z}$.

The base case $m = 0$ is trivial since the second sum is empty, and the first
sum amounts to writing a polynomial in the falling factorial basis. It is therefore
possible to find appropriate constants b_i that satisfy Eq. (6).

Now suppose that Eq. (6) was established for some $m < n + 1$, that is

$$O(X) = b_m \cdot (X)_m + \sum_{i=m+1}^{n} b_i \cdot (X)_i + \sum_{i=0}^{m-1} a_i \cdot O_i(X).$$

Evaluating both sides at $X = m$ gives

$$0 = O(m) = b_m \cdot m! \pmod{p^e}.$$

Taking the p-adic valuation of the right-hand side gives

$$\nu_p(b_m \cdot m!) = \nu_p(b_m) + \nu_p(m!) \geqslant e \implies \nu_p(b_m) \geqslant e - \nu_p(m!).$$

The constants b_i are integers, so it follows that $\nu_p(b_m) \geqslant \max(e - \nu_p(m!), 0)$. We
can therefore write $b_m = a_m \cdot p^{\max(e - \nu_p(m!), 0)}$ for some $a_m \in \mathbb{Z}$, which results in

$$O(X) = \sum_{i=m+1}^{n} b_i \cdot (X)_i + \sum_{i=0}^{m} a_i \cdot O_i(X).$$

This expression replaces m by $m+1$ in Eq. (6) and thereby completes the induction. The final result follows by setting $m = n+1$ in Eq. (6).   □

Corollary 1. *Each null polynomial modulo p^e of degree $n < \mu(p^e)$ is divisible by $p^{e-\nu_p(n!)}$, where divisibility is defined in the polynomial ring $\mathbb{Z}[X]$. Therefore, all monic null polynomials have degree at least $\mu(p^e)$.*

Corollary 2. *The set of all null polynomials modulo p^e is obtained directly from Theorem 1 by allowing an arbitrarily large (but finite) degree n.*

The Null Lattice. Adopting the notation from Eq. (5), the set of null polynomials of degree at most n is given by

$$\mathcal{O}_{p^e}^{(n)} = \left\{ \sum_{i=0}^{n} a_i \cdot O_i(X) \mid a_i \in \mathbb{Z} \right\} \subseteq \mathbb{P}_n.$$

When considering polynomials as coefficient vectors, it can easily be seen that the above set forms a p^e-ary lattice with basis vectors $O_i(X)$. For convenience of notation, we will not make a difference between polynomials and lattice vectors: the set $\mathcal{O}_{p^e}^{(n)}$ inherits all properties from Sect. 2.4, including the norm.

3.2   Cosets of Equivalent Polynomials

A representation $F(X)$ of a polyfunction f is never unique. That is, given a null polynomial $O(X)$, we can construct an equivalent polynomial $H(X) = F(X) + O(X)$ that represents the same polyfunction. The set of all representations of a polyfunction forms the coset $F(X) + \mathcal{O}_{p^e}$. Moreover, the set of all representations of degree at most n forms the coset $F(X) + \mathcal{O}_{p^e}^{(n)}$ (assuming that $\deg(F) \leqslant n$).

As explained in Sect. 2.3, $(X)_{\mu(p^e)}$ is a monic null polynomial modulo p^e, which implies that we can always divide by it (using Euclidean division) to obtain a representation of degree less than $\mu(p^e)$. This proves the following lemma.

Lemma 1 (Small degree representation [16]). *Each polyfunction $f \in \mathcal{F}_{p^e}$ has a representation of degree strictly less than $\mu(p^e)$.*

Although Euclidean division always returns a representation of degree less than $\mu(p^e)$, it is not necessarily minimized. In order to guarantee the lowest possible degree, one has to consecutively divide by $O_i(X)$ for $i = \mu(p^e), \ldots, 0$. This leads to the canonical representation of Keller and Olson [16].

Theorem 2 (Canonical representation [16]). *Let $f \in \mathcal{F}_{p^e}$ be a polyfunction, then there exists a unique canonical representation*

$$F(X) = \sum_{i=0}^{\mu(p^e)-1} c_i (X)_i$$

with $0 \leqslant c_i < p^{e-\nu_p(i!)}$.

From Theorem 2, we can compute the number of canonical representations, which is equal to the number of polyfunctions modulo p^e. This is done by adding the total number of possibilities for the coefficients c_i, which gives

$$\text{vol}\left(\mathcal{O}_{p^e}^{(\mu(p^e)-1)}\right) = \exp_p\left(\sum_{k=0}^{\mu(p^e)-1} e - \nu_p(k!)\right) = \exp_p\left(\sum_{k=1}^e \mu(p^k)\right), \quad (7)$$

where $\text{vol}(\cdot)$ denotes the volume of a lattice and $\exp_p(\cdot)$ the exponential function with base p. The first equality highlights the one-to-one correspondence between polyfunctions and equivalent representations of degree less than $\mu(p^e)$, obtained as cosets modulo the null lattice. The second equality was proven by Specker et al. [23] and not repeated here for brevity.

Note that, although a canonical representative can be chosen in a unique manner, it is not necessarily the most convenient polynomial to evaluate homomorphically. Later we study the digit extraction polynomial in FHE bootstrapping, where we take a different representative than the canonical choice.

Finally, we compare the number of functions in $\mathcal{F}_{p^e}$ to the number of polyfunctions from Eq. (7). Since a function is uniquely determined by its input-output pairs, the total number of functions equals $(p^e)^{p^e} = p^{e \cdot p^e}$. This expression is typically much larger than Eq. (7) for $e \geqslant 2$, so only very few functions are representable by polynomials.

Example 1. There are $2^{8 \cdot 2^8} \approx 10^{617}$ functions in $\mathcal{F}_{2^8}$, while only $2^{50} \approx 10^{15}$ of them are polyfunctions as computed from Eq. (7).

3.3 Existence of Polynomial Representation

In this section, we examine whether a given function $f \in \mathcal{F}_{p^e}$ is a polyfunction or not. We extend the Newton interpolation method to functions modulo p^e, and return a representation of the lowest degree if f is a polyfunction.

Consider a function $f \in \mathcal{F}_{p^e}$ that is defined by p^e data points $(i, f(i)) \in \mathbb{Z}_{p^e}^2$ for $i = 0, \ldots, p^e - 1$. We will now use *reduced* forward differences, which are similar to the regular forward difference defined earlier, but include an extra reduction modulo p^e in the set $\{0, \ldots, p^e - 1\}$.

Definition 6. *The* reduced i-th forward difference *of a function $f \in \mathcal{F}_{p^e}$, evaluated at $j \in \mathbb{Z}$, is defined as*

$$\overline{\Delta^i} f(j) = \Delta^i f(j) \pmod{p^e}.$$

The values $\overline{\Delta^i} f(j)$ for $i = 0, 1, \ldots, \mu(p^e)$ and $j = 0, \ldots, p^e - 1$ can be derived from Definition 6. This is shown in Fig. 2, where $\alpha_{i,j} = \overline{\Delta^i} F(X)|_{X=j}$.

The relations in Sect. 2.2 such as Eqs. (2), (4a), and (4b) still hold modulo p^e. Moreover, we will show later that the interpolating polynomial from Eq. (3) is also valid for polyfunctions over $\mathbb{Z}_{p^e}$.

$$
\begin{array}{ccccccc}
\alpha_{0,0} & \alpha_{0,1} & \alpha_{0,2} & \cdots & \alpha_{0,\mu(p^e)} & \cdots & \alpha_{0,p^e-1} \\
\alpha_{1,0} & \alpha_{1,1} & \cdots & \alpha_{1,\mu(p^e)-1} & \cdots & \alpha_{1,p^e-2} \\
\alpha_{2,0} & \cdots & \alpha_{2,\mu(p^e)-2} & \cdots & \alpha_{2,p^e-3} \\
\ddots & \vdots & & \vdots \\
& \alpha_{\mu(p^e),0} & \cdots & \alpha_{\mu(p^e),p^e-\mu(p^e)-1}
\end{array}
$$

Fig. 2. Evaluation of reduced forward differences with $\alpha_{i,j} = \overline{\Delta^i} F(X)|_{X=j}$.

Polynomial Representation. In order to examine if a function $f \in \mathcal{F}_{p^e}$ is a polyfunction, we introduce a new lemma.

Lemma 2. *Let $F(X) \in \mathbb{Q}[X]$ be a polynomial of degree less than $\mu(p^e)$ with evaluation function f. Then f interpreted modulo p^e is a polyfunction if and only if the coefficients of $F(X)$ are p-integral.*

Proof. ($\Leftarrow$) If the coefficients of $F(X)$ are p-integral, then it can be coerced into $\mathbb{Z}[X]$ by replacing all denominators by their multiplicative inverse modulo p^e.

($\Rightarrow$) Since f is a polyfunction, there exists a representation $H(X) \in \mathbb{Z}[X]$ of degree less than $\mu(p^e)$. The polynomial $O(X) = H(X) - F(X)$ also has degree less than $\mu(p^e)$, and its evaluation function modulo p^e is zero. Writing

$$
O(X) = \sum_{i=0}^{\mu(p^e)-1} \frac{a_i}{b_i} \cdot (X)_i,
$$

where a_i/b_i is a fraction in simplest form, it suffices to prove $\nu_p(b_i) = 0$ for all i.

Assume on the contrary that $\nu_p(b_i) = \max_j\{\nu_p(b_j)\} = c > 0$, then $p^c \cdot O(X)$ can be coerced into a null polynomial modulo p^{c+e}. Since the degree of this null polynomial is strictly less than $\mu(p^e) \leqslant \mu(p^{c+e})$, it follows from Corollary 1 that

$$
p^c \cdot \frac{a_i}{b_i} = 0 \pmod{p}.
$$

From $\nu_p(b_i) = c$, it follows directly that $a_i = 0 \pmod{p}$. Hence both a_i and b_i are divisible by p, which contradicts the fact that a_i/b_i is in its simplest form. □

Remark 1. A polynomial $F(X) \in \mathbb{Q}[X]$ with non-p-integral coefficients can still represent a (poly)function $f \in \mathcal{F}_{p^e}$, for example if its degree is at least $\mu(p^e)$. However, it is not directly possible to evaluate such a function homomorphically.

Now we introduce a simple way to decide whether a given function $f \in \mathcal{F}_{p^e}$ is a polyfunction, relying on the reduced forward differences from Fig. 2.

Theorem 3. *A function $f \in \mathcal{F}_{p^e}$ is a polyfunction if and only if the following two criteria are satisfied:*

1. For all $i < \mu(p^e)$, we have $\nu_p(\alpha_{i,0}) \geqslant \nu_p(i!)$. Note that $\alpha_{i,0}$ are the diagonal elements of Fig. 2.
2. All elements in the last row of Fig. 2 are zero.

Proof. ($\Leftarrow$) Consider the polynomial

$$F(X) = \sum_{i=0}^{p^e-1} \frac{\alpha_{i,0}}{i!} \cdot (X)_i \in \mathbb{Q}[X]. \tag{8}$$

Following Eq. (3), this polynomial interpolates f in all data points. Now we are given that all elements in the last row of Fig. 2 are zero, thus so are all values in the next row (which is not displayed). Hence $\alpha_{i,0} = 0$ for all $i \geqslant \mu(p^e)$. Therefore, we can terminate the summation of Eq. (8) earlier and get

$$F(X) = \sum_{i=0}^{\mu(p^e)-1} \frac{\alpha_{i,0}}{i!} \cdot (X)_i \in \mathbb{Q}[X]. \tag{9}$$

Now it remains to prove that the coefficients of $F(X)$ are p-integral, and then the result follows immediately from Lemma 2. Considering Eq. (9), this is trivial since we are given that $\nu_p(\alpha_{i,0}) \geqslant \nu_p(i!)$ for all $i < \mu(p^e)$.

($\Rightarrow$) If f is a polyfunction, it has a representation $F(X)$ of degree less than $\mu(p^e)$. Hence it follows from Eq. (2) that $\overline{\Delta^{\mu(p^e)}} F(X)$ is zero in every point, which proves the second criterion of the theorem.

Consider again the polynomial of Eq. (9). Following the same line of reasoning as in the first part of this proof, it is a representation of f modulo p^e. According to Lemma 2, we know that $F(X)$ must have p-integral coefficients, which implies $\nu_p(\alpha_{i,0}) \geqslant \nu_p(i!)$ for all $i < \mu(p^e)$. $\qquad\square$

Interestingly, Eq. (9) gives a polynomial representation $F(X)$ obtained by Newton interpolation restricted to $\{0, 1, \ldots, \mu(p^e) - 1\}$, i.e. only information about $f(i)$ for $i < \mu(p^e)$ has been used. Condition 1 of Theorem 3 can be interpreted as restricting the coefficients of $F(X)$ to p-integral values. Condition 2 is a consistency requirement: $F(a) = f(a) \pmod{p^e}$ for each $a \in \{\mu(p^e), \ldots, p^e - 1\}$. Finally, we note that also different interpolation methods could be used.

Corollary 3. *If f is a polyfunction, then Eq. (9) gives a representation of the lowest degree.*

Proof. It was already proven that the polynomial $F(X)$ from Eq. (9) can be coerced into a representation in $\mathbb{Z}[X]$, so it remains to show that its degree is minimal. Suppose that n is the largest integer such that $\alpha_{n,0} \neq 0$, and assume on the contrary that there exists a representation $H(X)$ whose degree is less than n. Then $O(X) = H(X) - F(X)$ is a null polynomial modulo p^e, with leading monomial $(\alpha_{n,0}/n!) \cdot X^n$. It follows from Corollary 1 that

$$\frac{\alpha_{n,0}}{n!} = 0 \pmod{p^{e-\nu_p(n!)}},$$

and thus $\alpha_{n,0} = 0 \pmod{p^e}$, leading to a contradiction. $\qquad\square$

3.4 Bit and Digit Extraction Function

As an example, we apply the previously developed theory to the bit extraction function – a polyfunction that is useful in the part about FHE bootstrapping.

Example 2. Let $g_e \in \mathcal{F}_{2^e}$ be the bit extraction function defined as

$$g_e : \mathbb{Z}_{2^e} \to \mathbb{Z}_{2^e} : a \mapsto a \ (\mathrm{mod}\ 2),$$

where reduction modulo 2 is done in the set $\{0,1\}$. Its forward differences are shown in Fig. 3, which should be closely compared to Fig. 2. The reduced forward differences are computed via reduction modulo 2^e. It can easily be verified in Table 1 that the diagonal elements $\alpha_{i,0} = (-2)^{i-1}$ satisfy $\nu_2(\alpha_{i,0}) \geqslant \nu_2(i!)$, and that all elements on the last row are congruent to zero modulo 2^e. Therefore, the bit extraction function is a polyfunction.

$$
\begin{array}{ccccccc}
0 & 1 & 0 & 1 & 0 & \cdots & 1 & \cdots & 1 \\
& 1 & -1 & 1 & -1 & \cdots & 1 & \cdots & 1 \\
& & -2 & 2 & -2 & \cdots & 2 & \cdots & 2 \\
& & & \ddots & \vdots & & \vdots & & \vdots \\
& & & & (-2)^{i-1} & \cdots & \pm 2^{i-1} & \cdots & 2^{i-1} \\
& & & & & \ddots & \vdots & & \vdots \\
& & & & & & (-2)^{\mu(2^e)-1} & \cdots & 2^{\mu(2^e)-1}
\end{array}
$$

Fig. 3. Forward differences of the bit extraction function.

Following Corollary 3, the polynomial

$$G_e(X) = \sum_{i=1}^{e} \frac{(-2)^{i-1}}{i!} \cdot (X)_i \tag{10}$$

is a representation of g_e of the lowest degree. It follows that there does not exist a bit extraction polynomial of degree less than e. Finally, the complete set of representations is easily obtained as $G_e(X) + \mathcal{O}_{2^e}$.

More generally, we define the digit extraction function modulo p^e for any prime p from its balanced digit decomposition. Denote the balanced digits of $w \in \mathbb{Z}_{p^e}$ by $w_i \in \{-(p-1)/2, \ldots, (p-1)/2\}$ such that

$$w = \sum_{i=0}^{e-1} w_i p^i,$$

then we define the map $g_e \in \mathcal{F}_{p^e}$ as

$$g_e : \mathbb{Z}_{p^e} \to \mathbb{Z}_{p^e} : w \mapsto w_0.$$

Analogously to the previous example, we can show that g_e is a polyfunction and obtain a representation of the lowest degree. In the general case, there does not exist a digit extraction polynomial of degree less than $(p-1)(e-1)+1$. The complete set of representations is obtained by adding $\mathcal{O}_{p^e}$.

3.5   Further Properties of Polyfunctions

Not every function is a polyfunction modulo p^e. For example, the function

$$f(a) = \begin{cases} 1 & \text{if } a = 0 \\ 0 & \text{otherwise} \end{cases}$$

is not a polyfunction for $e > 1$, because it is not *congruence preserving*. More specifically, all polyfunctions satisfy the following lemma.

Lemma 3 (Congruence preservation [7,9,16,17]). *Let f be a polyfunction modulo p^e, then for any $a \in \mathbb{Z}$, we have*

$$f(a + p^k) = f(a) \pmod{p^k}, \quad \forall k \leqslant e. \tag{11}$$

Proof. Let $F(X)$ be a representation of f. Since a polynomial is built from additions and multiplications only, we know that

$$F(a + p^k) = F(a) \pmod{p^k}.$$

Since $p^k \mid p^e$, we can directly replace F by f. This completes the proof.   □

Congruence preservation is not a sufficient condition to be a polyfunction [4]. In Sect. 3.3 – Theorem 3, we derived a necessary and sufficient condition for a function to be a polyfunction based on reduced forward differences [17], which is consistent with the analytical characterization by Carlitz [7] and further leads to a representation of the lowest degree.

We can also give a sufficient but unnecessary condition for a function to be a polyfunction. A function that satisfies

$$f(a + p) = f(a) \pmod{p^e}, \quad \forall a \in \mathbb{Z}, \tag{12}$$

is said to have period p and is always a polyfunction. A representation can be derived as follows.

Lemma 4 (Adapted from [14]). *The polynomial $U(X) = 1 - X^{\varphi(p^e)}$ satisfies the following property modulo p^e:*

$$\forall a \in \mathbb{Z}: U(a) = \begin{cases} 1 & \text{if } p \mid a \\ 0 & \text{otherwise}, \end{cases}$$

where $\varphi(\cdot)$ is Euler's totient function.

A representation for a function f with period p is

$$F(X) = \sum_{k=0}^{p-1} f(k) \cdot U(X - k), \tag{13}$$

from which we can construct the set of complete representations $F(X) + \mathcal{O}_{p^e}$. A well-known example is the digit extraction function.

As shown by the next example, having period p is a sufficient, but not a necessary condition for a function to be a polyfunction.

Example 3. As computed in Example 1, there are $2^{8 \cdot 2^8} \approx 10^{617}$ functions in $\mathcal{F}_{2^8}$, while only $2^{50} \approx 10^{15}$ of them are polyfunctions. From these polyfunctions, only $2^{8 \cdot 2} \approx 10^5$ have period 2.

Even and Odd Polyfunctions. We construct a new lemma to find sparse representations of even and odd polyfunctions.

Lemma 5. *Let $f \in \mathcal{F}_{p^e}$ be an even (resp. odd) polyfunction, that is, $f(-a) = f(a) \pmod{p^e}$ (resp. $f(-a) = -f(a) \pmod{p^e}$) for $a \in \mathbb{Z}$. Moreover, assume that f has a degree-n representation. Then the following holds:*

- *If p is an odd prime, then f has a representation $F(X)$ of degree at most n, which contains only even (resp. odd) exponents.*
- *If $p = 2$, and we consider f modulo p^{e-1} instead of p^e, then it has a representation $F(X)$ of degree at most n, which contains only even (resp. odd) exponents.*

Proof. Consider a representation $H(X) \in \mathbb{Z}[X]$ of f that has degree equal to n. Due to the evenness (resp. oddness) of f, the polynomial $H'(X) = H(-X)$ (resp. $H'(X) = -H(-X)$) is an equivalent representation of f.

Now we consider the integer polynomial

$$F(X) = \frac{H(X) + H'(X)}{2}, \tag{14}$$

which contains only even (resp. odd) exponents and has degree at most n. By evaluating Eq. (14) in any $a \in \mathbb{Z}$, we see that $F(a) = f(a) \pmod{p^e}$ for an odd prime p, and $F(a) = f(a) \pmod{p^{e-1}}$ for $p = 2$. Hence $F(X)$ is also a representation of f, and it can easily be checked that it contains only even (resp. odd) exponents. $\square$

4   Faster Bootstrapping for BGV and BFV

This section explains our improved bootstrapping techniques for BGV and BFV, leveraging the observations from the first part of the paper. Both general and thin bootstrapping involve two important components: the linear transformations and digit removal. We do not propose adaptations to the linear transformations, and leave them unchanged in the implementation. Our improvements are inside the digit removal step, and follow from the polyfunctions theory. Since digit removal is 3× to 50× more expensive than the linear transformations [15], any speedup leads to an almost equal effect in the entire bootstrapping procedure.

4.1 Cost Model

Amdahl's law [2] states that the speedup gained by optimizing a single part of an algorithm is limited to the fraction of time that the improved part is used. In order to accelerate digit removal, we must therefore concentrate on the slowest and most commonly used FHE operations. The true bottleneck of digit removal is *non-scalar multiplication*, i.e. multiplication of two ciphertexts. For an example parameter set with ring dimension $N = 2^{16}$, non-scalar multiplication in HElib is 7× more expensive than its scalar counterpart.

An approach that follows our cost model is the baby-step/giant-step algorithm for evaluating a set of polynomials with scalar coefficients in a common non-scalar point [12, 20]. It can asymptotically evaluate m degree-n polynomials with $2\sqrt{mn}$ non-scalar multiplications. Therefore, our implementation uses this algorithm for polynomial evaluation.

Although not the focus of this paper, digit removal is also costly in terms of multiplicative depth (which is by definition the maximal number of multiplications encountered in each possible input-output path). Our approach accelerates bootstrapping without significantly affecting the multiplicative depth of digit removal. This is achieved by exclusive use of low-degree polynomials.

4.2 Digit Removal Algorithm

The digit removal procedure removes the v least significant digits of its input $w \in \mathbb{Z}_{p^e}$ for a given prime number p and $v < e$. Formally, for odd p, denote the balanced digits of $w \in \mathbb{Z}_{p^e}$ by $w_i \in \{-(p-1)/2, \ldots, (p-1)/2\}$ such that

$$w = \sum_{i=0}^{e-1} w_i p^i.$$

Digit removal is then defined as the map

$$w \mapsto \left\lfloor \frac{w}{p^v} \right\rceil = \sum_{i=v}^{e-1} w_i p^{i-v}.$$

In other words, it consecutively scales and rounds the input. This is necessary in bootstrapping to remove the noise. To evaluate the procedure homomorphically, it is written as a series of polynomial evaluations and divisions.

Note that the balanced digit representation only exists for odd prime numbers. If $p = 2$, we need to consider the digits in $\{0, 1\}$, which causes the output of digit removal to be $\lfloor w/p^v \rfloor$. However, bootstrapping requires a rounding operation instead of flooring. This can be fixed by applying the simple equality $\lfloor x \rceil = \lfloor x + 1/2 \rfloor$ just before digit removal.

Existing Digit Removal Algorithms. Digit removal uses the following notation: we write $w_{i,j}$ for *any* integer of which the least significant digit is w_i, and the next j least significant digits are all zeros. Formally, this means that $w_{i,j} = w_i \pmod{p^{j+1}}$. Moreover, we require two well-known polynomials:

- The *lifting polynomial* $F_e(X) \in \mathbb{Z}[X]$ satisfies $F_e(w_{i,j}) = w_{i,j+1}$ for $j \leqslant e$. In other words, it allows us to compute a valid $w_{i,j+1}$ from any given $w_{i,j}$ by zeroing one extra digit.
- The *digit extraction polynomial* $G_e(X) \in \mathbb{Z}[X]$ satisfies $G_e(w_{i,0}) = w_{i,e-1}$, which allows us to compute a valid $w_{i,e-1}$ from any given $w_{i,0}$ by zeroing $e - 1$ extra digits. In other words, it is a representation of the digit extraction function g_e introduced in Sect. 3.3.

It can be proven that the above polynomials always exist [8]. Their degrees are respectively p and $(e - 1)(p - 1) + 1$.

The high-level idea of digit removal is to use the lifting polynomial and/or digit extraction polynomial to extract the least significant digit of the input w. The result is then subtracted from w and divided by p, and this is repeated until enough digits are removed. A suitable choice of lifting and digit extraction polynomials ensures a low multiplicative depth of the resulting procedure. Digit removal is visualized in the trapezoid of Fig. 4 for an example parameter set of $e = 5$ and $v = 3$. The procedure works as follows:

- We start from $w_{0,0} = w$ in the first row, and then compute the numbers on its right via a series of polynomial evaluations. The choice of polynomials depends on the chosen algorithm, and is explained later.
- In the second row, we first compute $w_{1,0} = (w - w_{0,1})/p$ and then repeat the same procedure from the first row.
- In the last row, we similarly compute $w_{2,0} = ((w - w_{0,2})/p - w_{1,1})/p$ and again repeat the same procedure from the first and second row.
- The result is obtained as $(((w - w_{0,4})/p - w_{1,3})/p) - w_{2,2}/p$. This is omitted from the figure.

In summary, the first digit of each row is computed by subtracting the digits on the same diagonal and dividing by p. All other digits are obtained via a series of polynomial evaluations, starting from the first digit in its row. Finally, the result is obtained by subtracting the last digit of each row from the input and dividing by p.

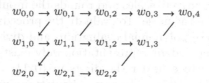

Fig. 4. Visualization of digit removal for $e = 5$ and $v = 3$.

Until now, we have only specified operations *between rows*, which are identical for all methods that we will discuss (including our own). Existing digit removal procedures differ in how they compute digits *within the same row*. Two different methods have been proposed for this: the first one is from Halevi and Shoup [15], and the second one from Chen and Han [8].

Halevi/Shoup Digit Removal. This procedure computes each number in the trapezoid (except for the first one in each row) by applying the lifting polynomial to the number on its left. In other words, we use the identity $w_{i,j+1} = F_e(w_{i,j})$. The cost is dominated by $ev - v(v + 1)/2$ evaluations of the lifting polynomial. The degree of this procedure is roughly p^{e-1}.

Chen/Han Digit Removal. This procedure computes the last number of each row by applying the digit extraction polynomial to the first number of the same row. In other words, we use the identity $w_{i,j} = G_{j+1}(w_{i,0})$. All other digits are computed identical to the Halevi/Shoup procedure; but note that some digits are not used and can therefore be omitted. In the example of Fig. 4, we do not need to compute $w_{0,3}$, $w_{1,2}$ and $w_{2,1}$.

The cost of Chen/Han digit removal is dominated by $v(v - 1)/2$ evaluations of the lifting polynomial and v evaluations of the digit removal polynomial. However, its main advantage is in degree, which is roughly equal to rp^v with $r = e - v$. During bootstrapping, the parameter r represents the precision of the plaintext space, i.e. plaintexts are computed modulo p^r. As such, the Chen/Han procedures has asymptotically lower degree than Halevi/Shoup for high-precision plaintext spaces.

4.3 Faster Digit Removal

In the following sections, we apply five changes to the original Chen/Han digit removal procedure. The first adaptation relates to digit removal itself, and is a better method to evaluate the polynomials of each row. The other improvements follow from polyfunctions theory.

Adapted Row Computation. As already mentioned earlier, digit removal can be analyzed row per row, where Halevi and Shoup take a different approach than Chen and Han. In contrast to both these versions, we propose a method that uses the digit extraction polynomial exclusively, without relying on the lifting polynomial. Specifically, we compute each element of the trapezoid by applying a suitable digit extraction polynomial to the first element in the same row. This has two advantages: firstly, all polynomials can be evaluated *simultaneously* using the baby-step/giant-step technique. Due to the $2\sqrt{mn}$ complexity, this leads to a performance benefit over evaluating all polynomials separately. Secondly, this method works well in conjunction with our next optimization (finding a more efficient representation of the digit extraction polynomial).

In instantiating our method, we need to avoid depth increase of the resulting procedure as much as possible. In particular, we have to be careful with the path along the evaluated circuit of largest depth, referred to as the *critical path*. Any depth increase in the critical path causes a corresponding depth increase in the entire procedure. The critical path of Chen/Han digit removal is depicted in Fig. 5. It runs via the vertical dimension first, because the depth grows linearly there and logarithmically in the horizontal dimension.

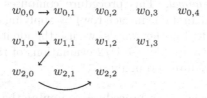

Fig. 5. Critical path of digit removal for $e = 5$ and $v = 3$.

In a first attempt, we can compute each digit as $w_{i,j} \leftarrow G_{j+1}(w_{i,0})$. In some cases, however, we can do better by reusing computed elements. In particular, we can set $w_{i,k} \leftarrow w_{i,j}$ for $k < j$ without affecting correctness; however, also this is not always desirable because it can lead to a depth increase of the digit removal procedure. For example, it is never beneficial to take $w_{i,1} \leftarrow w_{i,j}$ in terms of noise growth, because $w_{i,1}$ lies on the critical path. Our implementation takes the heuristic approach of computing $w_{i,j} \leftarrow G_{j+1}(w_{i,0})$ for each value of $j + 1$ that is a power of 2, and setting $w_{i,j} \leftarrow w_{i,j+1}$ otherwise. This heuristic does not increase the multiplicative depth compared to Chen/Han digit removal.

Even and Odd Functions. The digit extraction function for $p = 2$ is an even function. Following Lemma 5, we can find a representation of degree $e + 1$ or less that contains only even exponents. Specifically, we write the digit extraction polynomial as $G_e(X) = F(X^2)$ for some polynomial $F(X)$ of degree $\lfloor (e + 1)/2 \rfloor$. Such polynomials can be evaluated more efficiently than regular ones by first computing X^2 before applying a standard baby-step/giant-step method. This requires asymptotically $\sqrt{2mn}$ non-scalar multiplications for evaluating m polynomials of degree n.

Similarly to the case above, the digit extraction function for an odd prime p is an odd function. Following Lemma 5, we can find a representation of degree $(e - 1)(p - 1) + 1$ that contains only odd exponents. Specifically, we write the digit extraction polynomial as $G_e(X) = X \cdot F(X^2)$ for some polynomial $F(X)$ of degree $(e - 1)(p - 1)/2$. Such polynomials can be evaluated more efficiently than regular ones, using one the methods of Lee et al. [18]. Their first method omits unused powers of X in the baby-step, and can be evaluated with optimal multiplicative depth. Their second method first evaluates $F(X^2)$ using the strategy from above, and then multiplies by X. This increases the depth by at most one. Both methods require asymptotically $\sqrt{2mn}$ non-scalar multiplications for evaluating m polynomials of degree n. All experiments in Sect. 5 are conducted with the first variant.

Function Composition. We propose a new method to obtain the digit extraction function modulo p^e by decomposing it as $g_e = g_{e,e'} \circ g_{e'}$ for some $e' < e$. In our method, the relevant domain of $g_{e,e'}$ is therefore no longer $\mathbb{Z}$, but rather the range of $g_{e'}$. Our analysis starts from the following definitions.

Definition 7. *Let $f \in \mathcal{F}_{p^e}$ be a function from $\mathbb{Z}_{p^e}$ to itself. If there exists a polynomial $F(X) \in \mathbb{Z}[X]$ that satisfies $F(a) = f(a) \pmod{p^e}$ for all $a \in S \subseteq \mathbb{Z}$, then f is a* polyfunction modulo p^e over S *and $F(X)$ is a* representation *of f.*

Definition 8. *An element $O(X) \in \mathbb{Z}[X]$ is called a* null polynomial modulo p^e over $S \subseteq \mathbb{Z}$ *if the function $f \in \mathcal{F}_{p^e}$ that it represents maps every element from S to zero. In other words, we have that $O(a) = 0 \pmod{p^e}$ for all $a \in S$.*

The inner function $g_{e'}$ can directly be represented as a polynomial in the even or odd representation. For the outer function $g_{e,e'}$, we can use the adapted definitions from above, where we define the set

$$S = \left\{ k + i \cdot p^{e'} : -(p-1)/2 \leqslant k \leqslant (p-1)/2 \text{ and } i \in \mathbb{Z} \right\}. \tag{15}$$

This coincides with the range of $g_{e'}$. For $p = 2$, we slightly need to change the definition of S and allow $0 \leqslant k \leqslant 1$.

Since digit extraction is an idempotent operation, one possible representation of $g_{e,e'}$ is $G_e(X)$. But the domain of $g_{e,e'}$ is restricted to S, so we can find other representations by adding null polynomials that satisfy Definition 8. Therefore, our problem reduces to studying null polynomials over S, which we can construct as follows. Consider

$$H_j(X) = \begin{cases} (X)_j & \text{if } p = 2 \\ \left(X + \frac{p-1}{2}\right)_j & \text{if } p \text{ is an odd prime.} \end{cases} \tag{16}$$

To ease notation, we also write $H(X) = H_p(X)$. Moreover, let

$$(X)_{i,j} = \left(\prod_{k=0}^{i-1} H(X - k \cdot p^{e'}) \right) H_j(X - i \cdot p^{e'}) \tag{17}$$

for $0 \leqslant j < p$. Then we can adapt Theorem 1 as follows.

Theorem 4. *A polynomial $O(X) \in \mathbb{Z}[X]$ is a null polynomial modulo p^e over the set S from Eq. (15) of degree at most n if and only if there exist $a_{i,j} \in \mathbb{Z}$ such that*

$$O(X) = \sum_{0 \leqslant d(i,j) \leqslant n} a_{i,j} \cdot O_{i,j}(X), \quad \text{with} \quad O_{i,j}(X) = p^{\max(e-i\cdot e' - \nu_p(i!), 0)} \cdot (X)_{i,j}.$$

In this equation, the function $d(i,j) = p \cdot i + j$ denotes the degree of $O_{i,j}(X)$. It is also implicitly assumed that $0 \leqslant j < p$.

Proof. ($\Leftarrow$) Evaluating Eq. (17) at any $a \in S$ gives

$$(X)_{i,j}|_{X=a} = \left(\prod_{k=0}^{i-1} H(a - k \cdot p^{e'}) \right) H_j(a - i \cdot p^{e'}). \qquad (18)$$

From the definition of $H(X)$ in Eq. (16) and the restriction to S, it follows that $H(a)$ is divisible by $p^{e'}$. In fact, exactly one factor of $H(X)$ will be divisible by $p^{e'}$ when evaluated at $X = a$. Let $X - q$ be this linear factor where $0 \leqslant q \leqslant 1$ (if $p = 2$) or $-(p-1)/2 \leqslant q \leqslant (p-1)/2$ (if p is odd), then we can set $a - q = \alpha \cdot p^{e'}$ for some α. Equation (18) is then divisible by

$$\prod_{k=0}^{i-1} \left(a - q - k \cdot p^{e'} \right) = \prod_{k=0}^{i-1} \left(\alpha \cdot p^{e'} - k \cdot p^{e'} \right) = p^{i \cdot e'} \cdot (X)_i|_{X=\alpha}.$$

As already pointed out in Sect. 2.3, the evaluation of $(X)_i$ at any integer is divisible by $p^{\nu_p(i!)}$. Hence our result is divisible by $p^{i \cdot e' + \nu_p(i!)}$, and it follows that $O_{i,j}(X)|_{X=a}$ is divisible by $p^{\max(e, i \cdot e' + \nu_p(i!))} \geqslant p^e$. Any $\mathbb{Z}$-linear combination of these $O_{i,j}(X)$ is thus a null polynomial modulo p^e over S.

($\Rightarrow$) We prove the following assertion for $0 \leqslant m \leqslant n + 1$ by applying induction on m:

$$O(X) = \sum_{m \leqslant d(i,j) \leqslant n} b_{i,j} \cdot (X)_{i,j} + \sum_{0 \leqslant d(i,j) < m} a_{i,j} \cdot O_{i,j}(X), \qquad (19)$$

for some $a_{i,j}, b_{i,j} \in \mathbb{Z}$.

The base case $m = 0$ is trivial since the second sum is empty, and the first sum amounts to writing a polynomial in the basis given by $(X)_{i,j}$. It is therefore possible to find appropriate constants $b_{i,j}$ that satisfy Eq. (19).

Now suppose that Eq. (19) was established for some $m < n + 1$, that is

$$O(X) = b_{i',j'} \cdot (X)_{i',j'} + \sum_{m < d(i,j) \leqslant n} b_{i,j} \cdot (X)_{i,j} + \sum_{0 \leqslant d(i,j) < m} a_{i,j} \cdot O_{i,j}(X),$$

with $d(i', j') = m$. Evaluating both sides at $X = a$ with $a = i' \cdot p^{e'} + j'$ (if $p = 2$) or $a = i' \cdot p^{e'} + j' - (p-1)/2$ (if p is odd) gives

$$0 = O(a) = b_{i',j'} \cdot \prod_{k=0}^{i'-1} (X)_p|_{X=(i'-k) \cdot p^{e'} + j'} \cdot (j')! \pmod{p^e}.$$

Taking the p-adic valuation of the right-hand side and following a similar line of reasoning as in the first part of this proof, we get

$$\nu_p \left(b_{i',j'} \cdot \prod_{k=0}^{i'-1} (X)_p|_{X=(i'-k) \cdot p^{e'} + j'} \cdot (j')! \right) = \nu_p(b_{i',j'}) + i' \cdot e' + \nu_p((i')!) \geqslant e.$$

The constants $b_{i',j'}$ are integers, so $\nu_p(b_{i',j'}) \geqslant \max(e - i' \cdot e' - \nu_p((i')!), 0)$. We can therefore write $b_{i',j'} = a_{i',j'} \cdot p^{\max(e-i'\cdot e' - \nu_p((i')!), 0)}$ for some $a_{i',j'} \in \mathbb{Z}$, which results in

$$O(X) = \sum_{m < d(i,j) \leqslant n} b_{i,j} \cdot (X)_{i,j} + \sum_{0 \leqslant d(i,j) \leqslant m} a_{i,j} \cdot O_{i,j}(X).$$

This expression replaces m by $m + 1$ in Eq. (19) and thereby completes the induction. The final result follows by setting $m = n + 1$ in Eq. (19).   □

To study the degree of null polynomials restricted to the set S, we consider an adapted variant of the Smarandache function that takes two inputs:

$$\mu_p(e, e') = \min\{i \in \mathbb{N} : e' \cdot i + \nu_p(i!) \geqslant e\}.$$

Then it is clear that

$$O_{\mu_p(e,e'),0}(X) = \prod_{k=0}^{\mu_p(e,e')-1} H(X - k \cdot p^{c'}) \tag{20}$$

is a monic null polynomial of degree $p \cdot \mu_p(e, e') \approx p \cdot \lceil e/e' \rceil$.

Now we have all ingredients available to find a better representation of $g_{e,e'}$. Starting from $G_e(X)$, we can apply Euclidean division and reduce it modulo the null polynomial of Eq. (20). This results in a representation $G_{e,e'}(X)$ that has degree strictly less than $p \cdot \lceil e/e' \rceil$. This can be much smaller than the degree of $G_e(X)$, which is equal to $(e - 1)(p - 1) + 1$.

For odd primes p, the function $g_{e,e'}$ is odd and we can directly choose $G_{e,e'}(X)$ with only odd-exponent terms. However, if $p = 2$ then $-S \nsubseteq S$, hence $g_{e,e'}$ is not defined for all inputs from $-S$. The function is therefore not even, and we cannot directly choose $G_{e,e'}(X)$ with only even-exponent terms. One possible solution is to allow $-1 \leqslant k \leqslant 1$ in Eq. (15) instead of $0 \leqslant k \leqslant 1$. However, this increases the degree of the polynomial from Eq. (20) by 50%, hence also the degree of the resulting polynomial representation. We did not incorporate this solution in our implementation.

Finally, we note that the set of null polynomials modulo p^e over S of degree bound n still forms a p^e-ary lattice. This lattice is given by

$$\left\{ \sum_{0 \leqslant d(i,j) \leqslant n} a_{i,j} \cdot O_{i,j}(X) \mid a_{i,j} \in \mathbb{Z} \right\} \subseteq \mathbb{P}_n,$$

where the basis vectors are $O_{i,j}(X)$.

Asymptotic Complexities. We now analyze the asymptotic depth and time complexities of our composite approach. Specifically, its depth is bounded by

$$\left\lceil \log_2\left((p - 1) \cdot (e' - 1) + 1\right) \right\rceil + \left\lceil \log_2\left(p \cdot \left\lceil \frac{e}{e'} \right\rceil\right) \right\rceil \approx \lceil \log_2 e \rceil + 2 \cdot \lceil \log_2 p \rceil,$$

counting only non-scalar multiplications. The first term comes from $g_{e'}$ and the second one from $g_{e,e'}$. When compared to the regular $G_e(X)$, there is a depth increase of $\lceil \log_2 p \rceil$. Note that we can also apply function composition multiple times in a row, and then the depth will increase with $\lceil \log_2 p \rceil$ per stage. In terms of scalar multiplications, there is a depth increase of 1 for each stage of function composition. For the sake of noise control, our approach favors a small number of stages and a low value of p.

Performance-wise, we make a difference between scalar and non-scalar multiplications. The baby-step/giant-step technique can asymptotically evaluate a polynomial of degree n with $2\sqrt{n}$ non-scalar and n scalar multiplications. If the polynomial is even or odd, these numbers reduce to respectively $\sqrt{2n}$ and $n/2$. As such, we have the following time complexities for the digit extraction function:

- For $p = 2$, the original method can evaluate the digit extraction polynomial asymptotically with $\sqrt{2e}$ non-scalar and $e/2$ scalar multiplications. Our composite approach reduces this to respectively $\sqrt{2e'} + 2\sqrt{2e/e'}$ and $e'/2 + 2e/e'$. The number of non-scalar multiplications is minimal if $e' = 2\sqrt{e}$, which gives $4\sqrt[4]{e}$ non-scalar and $2\sqrt{e}$ scalar multiplications. Since $p = 2$, this analysis assumes that $G_{e,e'}(X)$ has both even- and odd-exponent terms.
- For larger values of p, the original method can evaluate the digit extraction polynomial asymptotically with $\sqrt{2pe}$ non-scalar and $pe/2$ scalar multiplications. Our composite approach reduces this to respectively $\sqrt{2p}(\sqrt{e'} + \sqrt{e/e'})$ and $(p/2) \cdot (e' + e/e')$. The number of non-scalar multiplications is minimal if $e' = \sqrt{e}$, which gives $2\sqrt{2p}\sqrt[4]{e}$ non-scalar and $p\sqrt{e}$ scalar multiplications. Since $p \neq 2$, this analysis assumes that $G_{e,e'}(X)$ has only odd-exponent terms. Moreover, the degree of $G_e(X)$ is approximated as pe.

In conclusion, our method reduces the number of non-scalar multiplications from $\mathcal{O}(\sqrt{pe})$ to $\mathcal{O}(\sqrt{p}\sqrt[4]{e})$ asymptotically. The number of scalar multiplications are reduced from $\mathcal{O}(pe)$ to $\mathcal{O}(p\sqrt{e})$.

Table 3 shows the number of operations to evaluate digit extraction, comparing the Halevi/Shoup and Chen/Han method to our approach. The even and odd entries represent the standard version (without function composition). The tuples represent the indices (e, e', e'') of the digit extraction function, where e'' is the index of the innermost function and e is the index of the outermost function. It is clear from the table that our composite method works especially well for low p and high e, where the performance benefits can be fully exploited without a significant depth increase. On the other hand, it turns out that even for large values of e (up to 256), splitting in more than 2 stages does not (much) increase performance anymore.

Lattices. Another method to find better polynomial representations is via lattice problems. Given a polynomial $F(X)$ and the null lattice, we can solve the closest vector problem to find a null polynomial $O(X)$ that lies closest to $F(X)$. The representation $F(X) - O(X)$ is then equivalent to the original one, but it has smaller coefficients. This leads to less noise growth in FHE ciphertexts.

Table 3. Non-scalar depth and operation count for the digit extraction function.

p	e	method	depth	#(non-scalar mults)	#(scalar mults)
2	64	H/S	63	63	0
		C/H	6	16	64
		Our even	6	12	32
		(64, 16)	7	9	15
	256	H/S	255	255	0
		C/H	8	33	256
		Our even	8	25	128
		(256, 32)	9	15	31
		(256, 67, 16)	10	13	22
3	64	H/S	126	126	0
		C/H	7	24	127
		Our odd	7	20	64
		(64, 16)	9	16	22
		(64, 25, 8)	10	15	24
	256	H/S	510	510	0
		C/H	9	49	511
		Our odd	9	38	256
		(256, 24)	11	23	40
		(256, 92, 8)	12	21	58

This lattice trick can also be combined with all earlier described techniques. For even or odd functions, we can start from a lattice that only contains even or odd null polynomials. These can be found via simple linear algebra on the original null lattice. For the function composition approach, we can start from the null lattice restricted to the set S as defined earlier.

Example 4. The advantage of using lattices is demonstrated on the bit extraction polynomial. Our method was able to find the following representations for $p = 2$:

- Bit extraction modulo 2^8 can be done with $G_8(X) = 13X^8 - 12X^6$.
- Starting from the result modulo 2^8, bit extraction modulo 2^{25} can be done with $G_{25,8}(X) = 6X^5 - 15X^4 + 10X^3$.

Both polynomials have remarkably small coefficients, since they are defined modulo 2^8 and 2^{25} respectively.

Multivariate Approach. We considered one more strategy to compute better polynomial representations based on multivariate equations. The idea is to write out consecutive digit extraction polynomials in a pattern that minimizes the non-scalar multiplications. This gives a system of non-linear equations, which

Table 4. Recursive evaluation of the bit extraction polynomial.

e	$G_e(X)$
2	X^2
4	$G_2(X)^2$
8	$112 \cdot G_2(X) + (94 \cdot G_2(X) + 121 \cdot G_4(X))^2$
16	$11136 \cdot G_4(X) + (28504 \cdot G_2(X) + 8968 \cdot G_4(X) - G_8(X)) \cdot$ $(15364 \cdot G_4(X) + 14115 \cdot G_8(X))$

can be solved for the coefficients of the digit extraction polynomial. Although this strategy does not generalize to higher parameters, we were able to find bit extraction polynomials for $e \leqslant 16$ that can be evaluated with $\lceil \log_2 e \rceil$ non-scalar multiplications, which is provably minimal. These instances are listed in Table 4.

5   Implementation and Performance

We implemented our new digit removal procedure for the BGV scheme in HElib. For two reasons, we did not implement it for the BFV scheme: firstly, there is no software library that supports BFV bootstrapping; secondly, BGV and BFV are known to be equivalent in terms of bootstrapping, and only differ in some minor implementation details. Therefore, any performance discrepancy would reflect the underlying arithmetic operations and not our improvements.

We give experimental results for general bootstrapping in Table 5 and for thin bootstrapping in Table 6. The tables show capacity (number of bits in the noise) and execution time. The factorization of the parameter m determines the complexity of the linear maps (explained in [15]), but is not relevant for digit removal. The regular plaintext modulus is p^r, which is augmented to p^e during bootstrapping. The function composition method was not used for these tables, since its effect is thoroughly analyzed in Sect. 5.1. All experiments were run on a single-threaded Intel® Core™ i7-6700HQ CPU with 8 GB memory and Ubuntu 22.04.1 LTS installed.

The "improvement" in the last row of Tables 5 and 6 was computed in the amortized sense, i.e. as the ratio

$$\text{improvement} = \frac{\text{old execution time}}{\text{new execution time}} \cdot \frac{\text{new remaining capacity}}{\text{old remaining capacity}}.$$

We achieve a significant improvement for all tested parameter sets, ranging from 1.3× to 2.6×. The speedups are higher for general bootstrapping than for thin bootstrapping. The reason is that the general version requires multiple digit removals, whereas the thin version requires only one. In terms of noise capacity, the advantage also tends to be in our direction. This is likely a consequence of two facts: we replaced the lifting polynomial by the digit extraction polynomial of lower degree; and the coefficients of our polynomials are smaller due to the lattice trick.

5.1 Function Composition

Our implementation also includes the function composition approach, which is asymptotically cheaper for high-precision plaintext spaces (i.e. large values of r and e). We demonstrate its benefit in Table 7 for plaintext moduli up to 2^{59}. For technical reasons (not inherent to the BGV scheme), HElib does not support more than 59 bits of precision, so we could not test with higher values than this. Furthermore, bootstrapping is only supported for $p^e < 2^{30}$ [15], so it is impossible to run bootstrapping with the parameter sets from Table 7. We therefore show the results for digit extraction only. Finally, note that the parameters e and e' have the same meaning as in Sect. 4.3.

Table 5. General bootstrapping in HElib (original/ours).

Cyclotomic index m		$127 \cdot 337$	$101 \cdot 451$	$43 \cdot 757$
Number of slots		2016	1000	2268
Params (p, r, e)		$(2, 8, 15)$	$(17, 4, 6)$	$(127, 2, 4)$
Security level (bits)		81	78	66
Number of digit removals		21	40	14
Capacity (bits)	Initial	1151	1136	1134
	Linear maps	100	147	140
	Digit extract	307/298	541/514	671/712
	Remaining	744/753	448/475	323/282
Execution time (sec)	Linear maps	134	150	290
	Digit extract	2014/743	2665/1879	1407/863
	Total	2248/877	2815/2029	1697/1153
Improvement		2.6×	1.5×	1.3×

The table has four values per column: the original built-in implementation; our standard method without function composition; our method with partial function composition; and our method with full function composition. The third value of each column (partial function composition) is generated by applying function composition to each row of Fig. 5, except for the last one. The motivation for this is as follows. Since the bottom right element of Fig. 5 lies on the critical path, it determines the multiplicative depth of digit removal. Turning this argument around, we can reduce the depth by not applying function composition in the last row. In other words, there is a depth-efficiency trade-off, where function composition favors efficiency and the standard method favors depth.

Table 6. Thin bootstrapping in `HElib` (original/ours).

Cyclotomic index m		$127 \cdot 337$	$101 \cdot 451$	$43 \cdot 757$
Number of slots		2016	1000	2268
Params (p, r, e)		$(2, 8, 15)$	$(17, 4, 6)$	$(127, 2, 4)$
Security level (bits)		81	78	66
Capacity (bits)	Initial	1151	1136	1134
	Linear maps	137	174	164
	Digit extract	267/260	445/435	604/640
	Remaining	747/754	517/527	366/330
Execution time (sec)	Linear maps	35	32	31
	Digit extract	105/35	65/46	101/64
	Total	140/70	97/78	132/95
Improvement		2.0×	1.3×	1.3×

The "speedup" in the last row of Table 7 was computed as the ratio between the original approach and our three methods:

$$\text{speedup} = \frac{\text{old execution time}}{\text{new execution time}}.$$

This cost measure ignores the remaining noise capacity, because we cannot run the full bootstrapping procedure and therefore don't have this number available. Again, we achieve major speedups compared to `HElib`'s built-in digit removal, ranging from 1.6× to 2.8×. Since digit removal is the main bottleneck, bootstrapping would exhibit almost identical speedups.

Table 7. High-precision digit removal in `HElib` (original/our standard method/partial function composition/full function composition).

Cyclotomic index m		42799	63973
Number of slots		2016	2592
Params (p, r, e, e')		$(2, 51, 59, 16)$	$(3, 32, 37, 6)$
Security level (bits)		80	77
Capacity (bits)	Initial	1137	1335
	Digit extract	1049/991/970/1006	1142/1047/1103/1170
Execution time (sec)		180/100/67/64	191/151/124/119
Speedup		1.8×/2.7×/2.8×	1.3×/1.5×/1.6×

6   Conclusion

Although polynomial functions over rings are commonly used in cryptography, their properties are currently not well understood. This paper contributed to the analysis of such polyfunctions, including existence, computation and equivalence of polynomial representations, among other things.

Our theory is directly applicable to FHE bootstrapping: we found sparse representations (either even or odd) for the digit extraction function, which is the bottleneck in bootstrapping; we also proposed a new method to decompose digit extraction into multiple stages, each of which can be evaluated with a polynomial of low degree. Altogether, we observed speedups of up to 2.6× for bootstrapping and up to 2.8× for digit removal, including our function composition approach. Finding the optimal way to evaluate the polynomials during bootstrapping, taking into account both noise growth and execution time, remains an interesting open problem.

Acknowledgements. This material is based upon work supported by the Defense Advanced Research Projects Agency (DARPA) under Contract No. HR0011-21-C-0034. The views, opinions, and/or findings expressed are those of the authors and should not be interpreted as representing the official views or policies of the Department of Defense or the U.S. Government. This work was additionally supported in part by CyberSecurity Research Flanders with reference number VR20192203, and in part by the Research Council KU Leuven grant C14/18/067. Robin Geelen is funded in part by Research Foundation - Flanders (FWO) under a PhD Fellowship fundamental research (project number 1162123N).

References

1. Alperin-Sheriff, J., Peikert, C.: Practical bootstrapping in quasilinear time. In: Canetti, R., Garay, J.A. (eds.) CRYPTO 2013. LNCS, vol. 8042, pp. 1 20. Springer, Heidelberg (2013). https://doi.org/10.1007/978-3-642-40041-4_1
2. Amdahl, G.M.: Validity of the single processor approach to achieving large scale computing capabilities. In: Proceedings of the 18–20 April 1967, Spring Joint Computer Conference, pp. 483 485 (1967)
3. Araki, T., et al.: Generalizing the SPDZ compiler for other protocols. In: Proceedings of the 2018 ACM SIGSAC Conference on Computer and Communications Security, pp. 880–895 (2018)
4. Bhargava, M.: P-orderings and polynomial functions on arbitrary subsets of dedekind rings. Journal für die reine und angewandte Mathematik (Crelles Journal) **1997**(490–491), 101–128 (1997). https://doi.org/10.1515/crll.1997.490.101
5. Brakerski, Z.: Fully homomorphic encryption without modulus switching from classical GapSVP. In: Safavi-Naini, R., Canetti, R. (eds.) CRYPTO 2012. LNCS, vol. 7417, pp. 868–886. Springer, Heidelberg (2012). https://doi.org/10.1007/978-3-642-32009-5_50
6. Brakerski, Z., Gentry, C., Vaikuntanathan, V.: (Leveled) fully homomorphic encryption without bootstrapping. In: Goldwasser, S. (ed.) ITCS 2012: 3rd Innovations in Theoretical Computer Science, pp. 309–325. Association for Computing Machinery, January 2012. https://doi.org/10.1145/2090236.2090262

7. Carlitz, L.: Functions and polynomials (mod p^n). Acta Arith. **9**(1), 67–78 (1964). http://eudml.org/doc/207463
8. Chen, H., Han, K.: Homomorphic lower digits removal and improved FHE bootstrapping. In: Nielsen, J.B., Rijmen, V. (eds.) EUROCRYPT 2018, Part I. LNCS, vol. 10820, pp. 315–337. Springer, Cham (2018). https://doi.org/10.1007/978-3-319-78381-9_12
9. Chen, Z.: On polynomial functions from $\mathbb{Z}_n$ to $\mathbb{Z}_m$. Discret. Math. **137**(1–3), 137–145 (1995)
10. Fan, J., Vercauteren, F.: Somewhat practical fully homomorphic encryption. Cryptology ePrint Archive, Report 2012/144 (2012). http://eprint.iacr.org/2012/144
11. Gentry, C.: Fully homomorphic encryption using ideal lattices. In: Mitzenmacher, M. (ed.) 41st Annual ACM Symposium on Theory of Computing, pp. 169–178. ACM Press (May/June 2009). https://doi.org/10.1145/1536414.1536440
12. Gentry, C., Halevi, S.: Implementing gentry's fully-homomorphic encryption scheme. In: Paterson, K.G. (ed.) EUROCRYPT 2011. LNCS, vol. 6632, pp. 129–148. Springer, Heidelberg (2011). https://doi.org/10.1007/978-3-642-20465-4_9
13. Gentry, C., Halevi, S., Smart, N.P.: Better bootstrapping in fully homomorphic encryption. In: Fischlin, M., Buchmann, J., Manulis, M. (eds.) PKC 2012. LNCS, vol. 7293, pp. 1–16. Springer, Heidelberg (2012). https://doi.org/10.1007/978-3-642-30057-8_1
14. Guha, A., Dukkipati, A.: An algorithmic characterization of polynomial functions over $\mathbb{Z}_{p^n}$. Algorithmica **71**(1), 201–218 (2015)
15. Halevi, S., Shoup, V.: Bootstrapping for helib. J. Cryptol. **34**(1), 1–44 (2021)
16. Keller, G., Olson, F.R.: Counting polynomial functions (mod p^n). Duke Math. J. **35**(4), 835–838 (1968)
17. Kempner, A.J.: Polynomials and their residue systems. Trans. Am. Math. Soc. **22**(2), 240–288 (1921)
18. Lee, J.W., Lee, E., Lee, Y., Kim, Y.S., No, J.S.: Optimal minimax polynomial approximation of modular reduction for bootstrapping of approximate homomorphic encryption. Cryptology ePrint Archive, Paper 2020/552 (2020). https://eprint.iacr.org/archive/2020/552/20200803:084202
19. Li, S.: Null polynomials modulo m. arXiv preprint math/0510217 (2005)
20. Paterson, M.S., Stockmeyer, L.J.: On the number of nonscalar multiplications necessary to evaluate polynomials. SIAM J. Comput. **2**(1), 60–66 (1973)
21. Singmaster, D.: On polynomial functions (mod m). J. Number Theory **6**(5), 345–352 (1974)
22. Smart, N.P., Vercauteren, F.: Fully homomorphic SIMD operations. Des. Codes Cryptogr. **71**(1), 57–81 (2014)
23. Specker, E., Hungerbühler, N., Wasem, M.: The ring of polyfunctions over $\mathbb{Z}/n\mathbb{Z}$ (2021)

Functional Commitments for All Functions, with Transparent Setup and from SIS

Leo de Castro[1] and Chris Peikert[2(✉)] [iD]

[1] EECS, Massachusetts Institute of Technology, Cambridge, USA
[2] Computer Science and Engineering, University of Michigan, Ann Arbor, USA
cpeikert@umich.edu

Abstract. A *functional commitment* scheme enables a user to concisely commit to a function from a specified family, then later concisely and verifiably reveal values of the function at desired inputs. Useful special cases, which have seen applications across cryptography, include vector commitments and polynomial commitments.

To date, functional commitments have been constructed (under falsifiable assumptions) only for functions that are essentially *linear*, with one recent exception that works for arbitrarily complex functions. However, that scheme operates in a strong and non-standard model, requiring an online, trusted authority to generate special keys for any opened function inputs.

In this work, we give the first functional commitment scheme for nonlinear functions—indeed, for *all functions* of any bounded complexity—under a standard setup and a falsifiable assumption. Specifically, the setup is "transparent," requiring only public randomness (and not any trusted entity), and the assumption is the hardness of the standard Short Integer Solution (SIS) lattice problem. Our construction also has other attractive features, including: *stateless updates* via generic composability; excellent *asymptotic efficiency* for the verifier, and also for the committer in important special cases like vector and polynomial commitments, via preprocessing; and *post-quantum security*, since it is based on SIS.

1 Introduction

In a *functional commitment* scheme, a user first commits to a function f from some specified family. Later, the user can *open* the function at one or more desired inputs x_i, generating noninteractive and publicly verifiable *proofs* for the claimed values $y_i = f(x_i)$, which can be checked against the original commitment.[1] In order to be nontrivial, commitments and proofs should be *concise*,

---

L. de Castro and C. Peikert—Some of this work was done while at Algorand, Inc.

[1] Some works consider a dual notion, in which the user commits to some data x and then can open various functions f of it. Our present formulation is a natural one for most specific purposes of interest. Moreover, assuming a sufficiently expressive scheme of either form, its dual notion can be achieved by swapping "code" and "data" using a universal function; see Sect. 4.3 for details.

C. Hazay and M. Stam (Eds.): EUROCRYPT 2023, LNCS 14006, pp. 287–320, 2023.
https://doi.org/10.1007/978-3-031-30620-4_10

i.e., significantly smaller than (i.e., sublinear or better in) the function's representation. The primary security property of interest is *evaluation binding*: a (possibly maliciously generated) commitment should fix some underlying function. That is, it should be infeasible for an attacker to produce a commitment along with valid proofs for two different function values $y \neq y'$ at a single input x (all chosen by the attacker). In this work we will not focus on other security properties like function hiding or zero-knowledge for proofs, since they are often not needed in applications, and when they are needed, they can usually be added using standard techniques.

The notion of functional commitments was first formally defined in [LRY16] to encompass prior notions for specific kinds of functionalities, like vector commitments [LY10, CF13], polynomial commitments [KZG10, PST13, LRY16], and linear commitments [LRY16].[2] These kinds of constructions have had a wealth of applications across cryptography, including verifiable outsourcing of storage [BGV11], authenticated streaming data structures [PSTY13], updateable zero-knowledge sets and databases [MRK03, Lis05], cryptographic accumulators [BdM93], pseudonymous credentials [KZG10], stateless transaction validation in cryptocurrencies [CPSZ18], verifiable secret sharing [CGMA85], content-extraction signatures [SBZ01], proof-carrying data systems, and succinct noninteractive arguments (of knowledge), also known as SNARGs/SNARKs [BFS20, BDFG21].

An important bonus feature of functional commitments, which is needed for several of the above-cited applications, is *(stateless) updateability*. This means that it is possible to concisely update the commitment and proofs for some function f to ones for a related function f', *without needing to know* f. For example, a user—who may or may not be the original committer—may wish to define $f' = f + \delta$ for some "update" function δ, and distribute corresponding updates to existing proofs. This functionality can enable authentication for "streaming" data structures and the like (see, e.g., [PSTY13]).

Beyond Linearity. As noted in [LRY16], there is a simple, generic construction of functional commitments for *arbitrary* functions, which combines an ordinary concise commitment and a SNARG (see also [BNO21]). In turn, SNARGs can be constructed in the random-oracle model, by making a succinct *interactive* argument (e.g., [Kil92, Mic94]) non-interactive via the Fiat–Shamir transform [FS86]. However, in the absence of random oracles, SNARGs are powerful tools whose known constructions are heuristic, since their security cannot be based on any falsifiable assumption via a black-box security reduction [GW11].

Until quite recently, all known functional commitment schemes (without random oracles) from *falsifiable* assumptions were limited to classes of *linearizable* functions, i.e., ones that can be expressed as linear functions of a suitably "preprocessed" input. This includes the recent constructions of [LP20, CFT22, ACL+22]

---

[2] Earlier works [IKO07, BC12] considered similar concepts, but allowing for interaction and private verifier randomness during the commitment and proving phases. Functional commitments require noninteractive commitments and proofs, and public verifiability.

for "semi-sparse" or constant-degree multi-variate polynomials. In particular, a polynomial can be expressed as the (linear) inner product between the vectors of the polynomial's coefficients and the powers of the input; the preprocessing therefore computes these powers.

Recent work [PPS21] overcame this linearizability barrier for the first time. It obtained functional commitments for functions of *any (bounded) complexity* under the standard Short Integer Solution (SIS) assumption, and thereby worst-case lattice assumptions [Ajt96], via techniques from fully homomorphic encryption and commitments [GSW13, GVW15b]. (These homomorphic schemes are not succinct, so they do not immediately yield functional commitments.)

However, the construction from [PPS21] has a major drawback: it operates in a non-standard model that requires an *online trusted authority*. As in other schemes requiring "structured" public parameters, the authority generates such parameters together with a secret "trapdoor" (which can be used to break the scheme's security). But in addition, the authority must remain online to generate *opening keys* for any inputs at which users wish to open their committed functions.[3] So, this model requires a strong trust assumption.

1.1 Our Contributions

Our main contribution resolves the main problem left open by [PPS21]: we construct a functional commitment scheme for *all functions* of a-priori bounded complexity, whose setup needs only an *"unstructured" uniformly random string* (and no trusted authority, online or otherwise), and whose security is based on the standard SIS lattice problem. Such a "transparent" setup of the public parameters is very attractive, because it requires only a public source of trustworthy randomness (which can even be heuristically expanded to the needed size using a cryptographic hash function), and because no entity ever knows a trapdoor that could be use to break the scheme's security.

In particular, we obtain the first constructions, with a standard setup, of polynomial commitments and general linear commitments from standard lattice assumptions (or falsifiable post-quantum assumptions more broadly), and of non-linearizable functional commitments under *any* falsifiable assumption.[4] Moreover, our construction has several other attractive features:

---

[3] The work of [PPS21] actually uses the dual formulation of functional commitments, where data x is committed and then functions f of the data are opened. However, the construction easily adapts to our present formulation of functional commitments.

[4] We caution that some works on polynomial commitment schemes (e.g., [BDFG21]) consider additional requirements, e.g., that the committed function is indeed a polynomial of some bounded degree, or even that openings are proofs of *knowledge* of such a polynomial (which SNARK applications rely upon). These are much stronger properties than originally considered in [KZG10] and in this work, typically requiring strong (often unfalsifiable) assumptions, and our construction does not achieve them. In addition, many works like [BBB+18, VP19, BFS20, BDFG21, Lee21, BNO21, KPV22] allow openings to be *interactive* proofs, then heuristically (and unfalsifiably) make them noninteractive using a random oracle using Fiat–Shamir [FS86]. Our construction is natively noninteractive without any heuristics.

Table 1. Comparison to prior *statelessly updateable* vector commitment schemes for bit vectors of dimension $D = d^h$ (where d, h can be set freely), allowing updates to at most S entries (including the initial commitment). Here 'Setup' is either private coin (i.e., structured random string) or public coin (i.e., transparent, uniformly random string), 'PQ' indicates post-quantum security, $|pp|$ is the public parameter size, $|c|$ is the commitment size, and $|\pi|$ is the proof size. Logarithmic factors in $\log D = h \log d$ and quasi-linear factors in the security parameter are omitted throughout.

Scheme (Assumption)	Setup	PQ	$|pp|$	$|c|$	$|\pi|$
[CF13] (RSA, ECDH)	Private	✗	D, D^2	1	1
[CPSZ18] (q-SBDH)	Private	✗	D	1	1
[PSTY13] (SIS)	Public	✓	$\log^2 S$	$\log S$	$dh \log^2 S$
[PPS21] (SIS)	Private	✓	$d^2 \log S + d \log^2 S$	$\log S$	$h \log^2 S$
Our construction (SIS)	Public	✓	$\log D \log^2 S$	$\log S$	$\log D \log^2 S$

- It is *statelessly updateable* in very general ways, via generic composition properties. In particular, a committed function may be updated additively or multiplicatively, or even generically composed with another function, i.e., outputs of committed functions can be post-processed. The updated commitment and proofs are obtained simply by operating on the original ones according to the update function.
- It *efficiently specializes* to particular functionalities of interest, like vector commitments and polynomial commitments. In these settings and others, the public parameters can first be preprocessed, even by an untrusted party. Then, committing to a function and opening it become relatively fast, highly parallel linear operations (i.e., just one matrix-matrix or even matrix-vector multiplication). Moreover, for vector commitments, the sizes of our commitments and proofs asymptotically beat or essentially match those of prior SIS-based constructions [PSTY13, PPS21] (see Table 1), even though our scheme has simpler opening and verification algorithms (after preprocessing).
- The *verifier is efficient and essentially linear*: it simply checks a single n-dimensional (inhomogeneous) SIS relation, i.e., a short integral solution $\mathbf{S}$ to a linear equation $\mathbf{AS} = \mathbf{Y}$, where the matrices $\mathbf{A}, \mathbf{Y}$ are constructed linearly from the public parameters, the commitment, and the claimed input-output pair. This makes verification highly amenable to recent techniques for proving relations of this kind in zero knowledge, and even succinctly (e.g., [BBC+18, BLS19, LNP22, ACL+22]).
- A variant (using the "context hiding" technique of [GVW15b]) has *(statistical) zero knowledge* commitments and proofs, though with a weaker notion called "target" evaluation binding, which requires the commitment to be generated *honestly*. Zero knowledge means that the commitments and proofs reveal nothing more about the committed function than what is revealed by the provided input-output pairs.

Table 2. Comparison to concurrent works [BCFL22, WW23] that also construct functional commitments for non-linearizable functions, from falsifiable lattice assumptions. For a fair comparison, all quantities are given for the following setting: a two-input circuit $C(\cdot, \cdot)$ of width w is fixed ahead of time, where each input may represent either 'data' or 'code'. Its first input u is committed, then a proof is generated and verified for the evaluation of $C_u(\cdot) := C(u, \cdot)$ at its second input v. Here 'Setup', $|pp|$, $|c|$, and $|\pi|$ are as in Table 1, and T refers to the running time of the operation in the subscript. Dependencies on the security parameter and circuit depth, and poly-logarithmic factors in all parameters, are omitted. In addition, [BCFL22] supports a *sublinear*-time verification, following an input-independent preprocessing step.

Scheme	Assumption (type)	Setup	$|pp|$	$|c|$	$|\pi|$	T_{Commit}	T_{Open}	T_{Verify}
[BCFL22]	Twin-k-M-SIS (new)	Private	w^5	1	1	$|u|$	$|C_u(\cdot)|$	$|C_u(\cdot)|$
[WW23]	BASIS$_{\text{struct}}$ (new)	Private	$|u|^2$	1	1	$|u|^2$	$|C_u(\cdot)|$	$|C_u(\cdot)|$
Construction 2	SIS (standard)	Public	$|v|$	1	$|v|$	$|C_u(\cdot)|$	$|C_u(\cdot)|$	$|v|$

1.2 Concurrent Related Work

We briefly discuss two concurrent works [BCFL22, WW23] that also construct functional commitments from lattice-style assumptions; see Table 2 for a summary. Both of these works require private setup of a *structured random string* (with a trapdoor) by a trusted party—versus our transparent setup—and rely on *new, ad-hoc lattice assumptions*—versus our reliance solely on the standard SIS problem, which has been well studied and is supported by worst-case-hardness theorems [Ajt96, MR04].

Regarding efficiency, their proofs are succinct, whereas ours grow with the size of the opened data, but their runtimes are "dual" to ours in a way that puts a higher burden on the verifier. Specifically, their commitment algorithms' runtimes grow merely with the *size* of the committed data, but their verifiers' runtimes grow with the *function's runtime* (though [BCFL22] also supports sublinear-time verification, after preprocessing that grows with the function's runtime). In our work, this profile is essentially reversed: the committer's runtime grows with the function's runtime (though this can be reduced in many important cases using preprocessing), but the verifier's runtime grows only quasi-linearly with the size of the opened data.

The work of [BCFL22] constructs functional commitments with private setup from a new "twin-k-MSIS" assumption, which extends an assumption recently introduced in [ACL+22]. In this construction, the sizes of some objects grow with the *width* of the function's arithmetic circuit, in addition to the depth. More specifically, the public parameters scale polynomially with the width, the commitment size scales logarithmically with the width, and the proofs scale linearly in the depth.

The work of [WW23] constructs functional commitments with private setup from a new "basis-augmented" SIS-like assumption. As in our work, this construction uses homomorphic techniques from [GSW13, GVW15b], and a variant enjoys zero knowledge (which [WW23] calls "private openings"), but only with the weaker notion of *target* binding that requires the commitment to be honestly generated. In contrast to our work, the new basis-augmented SIS assumption enables succinct proofs (analogously to [PPS21]), and an extension of the public parameters enables *proof aggregation*, which allows multiple proofs (for the same commitment) to be combined into a single, shorter proof that verifies the original collection of openings.

Related Notions. We also mention two other concurrent works [GSW23, KLVW23] that construct primitives that are closely related to functional commitments.

The work of [GSW23] constructs a non-interactive, publicly verifiable *delegation* scheme for committed programs, with private setup from the Learning With Errors (LWE) assumption [Reg05], via non-interactive batch arguments [CJJ21]. In this primitive, a delegator publishes a succinct digest of a program, which can later be used to verify proofs of correctness for input-output pairs, much like in functional commitments. The efficiency requirements are also essentially the same as those for functional commitments, so the two concepts are syntactically interchangeable. However, the security notion considered in [GSW23] assumes that the program digest is *honestly generated*, so it is strictly weaker than (full) evaluation binding for functional commitments, but it does match the weaker notion of target binding. In summary, functional commitments provide an alternative solution to the delegation problem considered in [GSW23].

The work of [KLVW23] constructs SNARGs for *RAM computations*, with private setup from the LWE assumption, via (somewhere-extractable) batch arguments. This primitive concisely commits to a large memory, then proves the output of a RAM program (with that memory) on a small explicit input. This is effectively a functional commitment (in "dual" form) for RAM programs, which, in contrast to the circuit model adopted in this work, can access parts of a large memory *without* having to read all of it as input.

1.3 Technical Overview

Here we summarize our general functional commitment construction and some of its important instantiations. The details are in Sects. 3 and 4, respectively.

Functional Commitment Scheme. At a high level, our functional commitment construction works similarly to the one from [PPS21], but ours does not require an authority or even any structured public parameters. To set the stage, we briefly recall the main ideas from the construction of [PPS21] (adapted so that it commits to functions and opens at inputs).

The public parameters are a uniformly random SIS matrix $\mathbf{A}$, which is generated together with a secret "trapdoor" as in [MP12], along with another uniformly random matrix $\mathbf{C}$ whose width is proportional to the length of a function input. We view $\mathbf{C}$ as a commitment to an *as-yet undetermined* input x, under the fully homomorphic encryption/commitment scheme of [GSW13, GVW15b].

To commit to a function f, one just homomorphically evaluates f on $\mathbf{C}$, resulting in some $\mathbf{C}_f$. Accordingly, we view this as a commitment to the function value $f(x)$, but for an unspecified x.

Recall that opening a committed function at a desired input x requires an authority-generated "opening key" for x. This key is some "short" random coins that open $\mathbf{C}$ as a commitment to x, which the adversary samples using its trapdoor for $\mathbf{A}$. Given these coins, and using the properties of the homomorphic commitment scheme, the committer can track how the coins combine and grow during the homomorphic evaluation of f on $\mathbf{C}$, which results in some fairly short *derived* coins that open $\mathbf{C}_f$ as a commitment to $f(x)$. These coins serve as the proof for the function value $f(x)$. For other inputs x', the authority must generate corresponding opening keys upon request, which, again, are random coins opening $\mathbf{C}$ as a commitment to those x'.

The main challenge in implementing the above strategy is that it is actually *insecure* to equivocate $\mathbf{C}$ as a commitment to two different values—at least *relative to the same "base" matrix* $\mathbf{A}$. The solution given in [PPS21] is as follows: when the authority opens $\mathbf{C}$ as a commitment to x, it does so relative to a "tagged" base matrix $\mathbf{A}_x$ that is derived from $\mathbf{A}$ using x as the tag. This turns out to be secure to do for essentially unlimited values of x. Very importantly, the homomorphic evaluations of functions f on $\mathbf{C}$ do not depend at all on the base matrix, so they can still be computed independent of any specific x.

Our Approach. As already mentioned, our functional commitment scheme works similarly, but does not use an authority or any trapdoored public parameters. Interestingly, we achieve this in a remarkably simple way, by relying on *fewer* features of the underlying homomorphic commitment scheme from [GSW13, GVW15b]. In particular, we do not use any notions of "base" matrices, commitment coins, equivocation, or even committed data at all! We refer to the stripped-down set of features that we do use as a *homomorphic computation* scheme, to reflect the fact that it does not operate on any hidden data. (See Sect. 3.1 for full details.)

In our scheme, the public parameter is just a uniformly random matrix $\mathbf{C}$ as above; there is no longer any trapdoored base matrix $\mathbf{A}$. In contrast to [PPS21], we do not view $\mathbf{C}$ as a commitment to any data, and never open it as such. But to commit to a function f, we still homomorphically evaluate f on $\mathbf{C}$, yielding a commitment $\mathbf{C}_f$. To open the committed function at an input x, we cannot use any opening of $\mathbf{C}$. Instead, we track an "input aware" homomorphic evaluation of f on $\mathbf{C}$, which is "shifted" by (a suitable matrix encoding of) the input x. By the properties of homomorphic computation, the result of this evaluation turns out to be $\mathbf{C}_f$, but similarly shifted by (the encoding of) $f(x)$. Moreover, this evaluation yields a fairly short multiplier matrix that links the shifted $\mathbf{C}$ and $\mathbf{C}_f$ matrices; this multiplier serves as the proof for the function value $f(x)$.

Overall, our functional commitment scheme significantly simplifies the one from [PPS21], by disposing of the trapdoored setup, the online generation of opening keys, and the tracing of commitment randomness, but it otherwise works quite similarly. One additional difference is that in our scheme, the dimension of a proof is linear in the size of the input x (because the proof is left-multiplied by the shifted $\mathbf{C}$ matrix), whereas in [PPS21] the proof dimension is essentially independent of the input size (because the proof is left-multiplied by the trap-doored matrix $\mathbf{A}_x$). This has some implications for proof size and efficiency, but proofs are still concise when the input is smaller than the function description, which is almost always the case in applications.

Instantiations: Key-Value Commitments, Polynomial Commitments, and More. In Sect. 4 we give several concrete instantiations of our general functional commitment scheme, for specific function families of interest. Most of these instantiations fit the following template: we identify a (potentially huge) set of (potentially complex) "basis" functions, and show how to express any member of the family relatively simply in terms of this basis, e.g., as a linear or low-degree combination of not too many basis functions. Using our functional commitment scheme's generic composition properties, this immediately yields a commitment scheme for the family, whose parameters and complexity are mainly determined by the homomorphic implementation of the basis functions. Moreover, if there are not too many basis functions (and similarly, function inputs that might be opened), then commitments to all of them (and their associated openings) can be preprocessed, making the "online" cost of committing (and opening) fairly low. Finally, this approach naturally supports stateless updates, e.g., by other combinations of the basis functions. We next mention some specific examples of this template that we work out in detail.

Bounded-Support Functions. In Sect. 4.1 we consider arbitrary functions of *bounded support* over some potentially huge domain $\mathcal{X}$. We show how bounded-support commitments directly yield commitments to arbitrary *key-value maps* (with a bounded number of keys), a notion introduced in [BBF19] that generalizes and unifies both vector commitments and accumulators (see also [AR20, CEO22]). A suitable basis for bounded-support functions is the set of *point functions* $\mathsf{Eq}_{\bar{x}} \colon \mathcal{X} \to \{0, 1\}$ for $\bar{x} \in \mathcal{X}$, where $\mathsf{Eq}_{\bar{x}}(x)$ is defined to be 1 if $x = \bar{x}$ and 0 otherwise. Any function f of support $\mathrm{supp}(f)$ can be expressed as a linear combination of $|\mathrm{supp}(f)|$ such point functions, as $f(x) = \sum_{\bar{x} \in \mathrm{supp}(f)} f(\bar{x}) \cdot \mathsf{Eq}_{\bar{x}}(x)$.

From the above, we immediately get key-value commitments from any homomorphic implementation of the $\mathsf{Eq}_{\bar{x}}$ functions. We give a (to our knowledge) new, very simple, and low-expansion implementation, which just does $k = \log \mathcal{X}$ homomorphic bit multiplications, scheduled in a certain way. Due to the particular properties of the homomorphic computation scheme, the associated expansion factor is only *linear* in k, which ultimately leads to good SIS parameters.

Polynomials. In Sect. 4.2 we apply the template to obtain commitments for (univariate or multivariate) polynomials of bounded degree. Here the "basis" functions are just the powers of the input variable(s), and each such polynomial can be expressed as a linear combination of these powers (or their products, in the multivariate case). Here the linearity is over the polynomial's coefficient ring, so even if commitments to the powers are precomputed, the "online" commitment procedure does not necessarily consist solely of linear homomorphic operations. However, we show that if the coefficient ring can be embedded as a suitable matrix ring, then the online phase can be made linear, at the expense of sacrificing further multiplicative (but not linear) compositions.

1.4 Future Work

We believe that our work opens many avenues for interesting further research. One exciting direction is to see whether our techniques can pave the way for *succinct noninteractive arguments (of knowledge)* (SNARGs or SNARKs) from lattice assumptions that are simple to state and analyze. Recent work [ACL+22] took a major step forward on lattice-based SNARGs, but under rather complicated and ad-hoc (knowledge) assumptions. Our functional commitments do not directly yield SNARGs because, while a commitment binds the committer to *some function*, it does not guarantee anything about the *form* of that function. In other words, nothing ties the committed function to the computation or relation for which we seek a SNARG. Indeed, SIS-based functional commitments cannot yield a complete solution, because SNARGs for NP cannot be constructed based on any falsifiable assumption, via a black-box security reduction [GW11].

Another direction for future work is to construct *subvector* commitments from standard lattice assumptions. Such commitments allow a user to commit to a vector and then later open any subset of its entries, where for nontriviality the proof size should be sublinear in the size of the subset. Our work does not achieve this because we simply prove and verify each function output independently. However, it seems likely that, due to the simple linear nature of our verifier, multiple proofs could be compressed using amortization techniques for interactive arguments for lattice relations [BBC+18].

Finally, there are a number of technical improvements one could seek for our functional commitment scheme. As mentioned above, the proof size grows at least linearly with the length of the function input, and it would be good to reduce this dependence. (On the other extreme, the proof length in the functional commitment scheme of [PPS21] is essentially independent of the input length, thanks to the online authority.) Another area of potential improvement is in the notion of security achieved. We mainly prove *selective* binding, where the adversary must name the input on which it will attempt to break binding *before* seeing the public parameters. We can immediately obtain the more realistic notion of *adaptive* binding via complexity leveraging, assuming that SIS is hard to break with inverse-subexponential probability $\exp(-\lambda^\varepsilon)$, for some (arbitrarily small) constant $\varepsilon > 0$. However, obtaining adaptive security under a tighter reduction would be welcome.

2   Preliminaries

For any non-negative integer i, denote $[i] = \{1, \ldots, i\}$. For a real vector $\mathbf{v}$, let $\|\mathbf{v}\|_1 := \sum_i |v_i|$ denote its ℓ_1 norm. For a real matrix $\mathbf{V}$, let $\|\mathbf{V}\|_1 := \max_j \|\mathbf{v}_j\|$ denote the maximum $\ell_1$norm of its column vectors $\mathbf{v}_j$. Observe that for any matrices $\mathbf{V}, \mathbf{U}$, we have $\|\mathbf{V}\mathbf{U}\|_1 \leq \|\mathbf{V}\|_1 \cdot \|\mathbf{U}\|_1$ by the triangle inequality.

The *Kronecker product* $\mathbf{A} \otimes \mathbf{B}$, where each of $\mathbf{A}, \mathbf{B}$ is a vector or a matrix, is obtained by replacing each entry $a_{i,j}$ of $\mathbf{A}$ with the block $a_{i,j}\mathbf{B}$. It obeys the *mixed-product* property: $(\mathbf{A} \otimes \mathbf{B})(\mathbf{C} \otimes \mathbf{D}) = (\mathbf{A}\mathbf{C}) \otimes (\mathbf{B}\mathbf{D})$ for any $\mathbf{A}, \mathbf{B}, \mathbf{C}, \mathbf{D}$ having compatible dimensions.

2.1   Short Integer Solution

We briefly recall the Short Integer Solution (SIS) and its hardness based on worst-case lattice problems. Due to the particulars of our constructions and analyses, we define the problem in terms of the ℓ_1 norm, not the ℓ_2 norm (as is more typical). Because the ℓ_1 norm of any vector is at least its ℓ_2 norm, the variant of SIS that uses ℓ_1 is no easier than, and is plausibly even harder than, the one that uses ℓ_2 (for the same norm bound β).

Definition 1. *The normal-form* $SIS_{n,q,m,\beta}$ *problem in the* ℓ_1 *norm is: given a uniformly random matrix* $\mathbf{A} \in \mathbb{Z}_q^{n \times m}$, *find a non-zero integral vector* $\mathbf{z} = (\mathbf{x} \in \mathbb{Z}^m, \mathbf{e} \in \mathbb{Z}^n)$ *such that* $\mathbf{A}\mathbf{x} = \mathbf{e} \pmod{*}q$ *and* $\|\mathbf{z}\|_1 \leq \beta$.

When $q \geq \beta \cdot \tau(n)$ for a sufficiently large $\tau(n) = \tilde{O}(\sqrt{n})$ and m is polynomial in n and $\log q$, solving normal-form $SIS_{n,q,m,\beta}$ (in ℓ_2, and hence also in ℓ_1) is at least as hard as approximating certain worst-case lattice problems on n-dimensional lattices to within a $\beta \cdot \tilde{O}(\sqrt{n})$ factor [Ajt96, MR04, GPV08].

2.2   Functional Commitments

Here we give a general definition of functional commitments and their main security property. In this definition, one *commits to a function* and then can *open it (with proof) at desired inputs*. This is the most natural formulation for our construction (Sect. 3) and most of its instantiations (see Sect. 4), and it naturally generalizes other notions of concise commitments, such as vector and polynomial commitments. However, if desired, the roles of the function and the input can be swapped via the standard technique of using a universal function (see Sect. 4.3).

Definition 2. *A functional commitment scheme for a function family* $\mathcal{F} = \{f \colon \mathcal{X} \to \mathcal{Y}\}$, *where* $\mathcal{X}$ *is a set of* opening inputs *and* $\mathcal{Y}$ *is the space of outputs (and all of* $\mathcal{F}, \mathcal{X}, \mathcal{Y}$ *may depend on the security parameter), is a tuple of algorithms with the following interfaces:*

- Setup(), *given an (implicit) security parameter, outputs public parameters* pp.

- Commit($pp, f \in \mathcal{F}$), *given public parameters pp and a function f, outputs a commitment c_f to f.*
- Open($pp, f, x \in \mathcal{X}$), *given public parameters pp, function f, and an opening input x, outputs a proof $p_{f,x}$ attesting to the value of $f(x)$.*
- Verify($pp, c_f, x \in \mathcal{X}, y \in \mathcal{Y}, p_{f,x}$), *given public parameters pp, some c_f that purportedly commits to some function f, an opening input x, a claimed value y, and a purported proof $p_{f,x}$ that $f(x) = y$, either accepts or rejects.*

The scheme should satisfy the following correctness property: for any $f \in \mathcal{F}$ and $x \in \mathcal{X}$, and for any $pp \leftarrow$ Setup(), $c_f \leftarrow$ Commit(pp, f), and $p_{f,x} \leftarrow$ Open(pp, f, x), Verify($pp, c_f, x, f(x), p_{f,x}$) should accept. For nontriviality, commitments should be concise, i.e., smaller than the representations of functions from the family $\mathcal{F}$.

Definition 3. *For a functional commitment scheme FCS (or more precisely, just its Verify algorithm), the selective-input attack game between an adversary and a challenger is defined as follows:*

1. *The adversary is given the security parameter λ and outputs an opening input $x^* \in \mathcal{X}$ to the challenger.*
2. *The challenger lets $pp \leftarrow$ Setup() and gives pp to the adversary.*
3. *Finally, the adversary outputs a commitment c^* and two value-proof pairs (y_0, p_0) and (y_1, p_1). It wins the game if $y_0 \neq y_1$, and if Verify(pp, c^*, x^*, y_b, p_b) accepts for both $b \in \{0, 1\}$.*

The advantage of an adversary $\mathcal{A}$ in the above game, denoted $\mathbf{Adv}^{sia}_{FCS}(\mathcal{A})$, is the probability that it wins the game (as a function of the security parameter). We say that FCS (or just its Verify algorithm) has (selective) evaluation binding if $\mathbf{Adv}^{sia}_{FCS}(\mathcal{A}) = \mathrm{negl}(\lambda)$ for every probabilistic polynomial-time adversary $\mathcal{A}$.

As explained in Sect. 4, (selective) evaluation binding captures the main security property for prior special cases of functional commitments, e.g., position binding for vector commitments.

Remark 1 (Target security). A weaker notion of security, which is relevant to our zero-knowledge variant construction, is called *target* evaluation binding. Essentially, this says that it is infeasible to prove an incorrect input-output pair relative to an *honestly generated* commitment to a function—even given any randomness used in generating the commitment. (This is sufficient for, e.g., the program-delegation problem considered in [GSW23].) Formally, we consider the following modification of Definition 3:

- After Step 2, the adversary outputs a target function $f^* \in \mathcal{F}$, and the challenger generates a commitment $c^* \leftarrow$ Commit(pp, f^*), which it gives (along with the random coins, if any) to the adversary.
- In Step 3, the adversary outputs a value-proof pair (y^*, p^*), and wins if Verify(pp, c^*, x^*, y^*, p^*) accepts but $y^* \neq f^*(x^*)$.

Remark 2 (Adaptive security). One can strengthen Definition 3 (and its target variant) by changing the attack game so that the adversary does not specify the target opening input x^* until Step 3 (rather than in Step 1, before seeing the public parameters); we call the resulting security notion *adaptive*, or *full*, evaluation binding. Generically, any scheme with selective security also has adaptive security, up to a loose reduction whose advantage is smaller by a factor of $|\mathcal{X}|$, the size of the input space. This follows by the standard technique of complexity leveraging—i.e., initially "guessing" the input x^* that the adversary will eventually choose. Concretely, we can obtain adaptive security for Construction 2 under the assumption that SIS is hard to break with inverse-subexponential probability $\exp(-\lambda^\varepsilon)$, for some (arbitrarily small) constant $\varepsilon > 0$.

3　Functional Commitments from SIS

In this section we construct a very general functional commitment scheme, supporting rich and complex function classes, based on the SIS problem.

3.1　Homomorphic Computation

The heart of our functional commitment scheme is what we call a "homomorphic computation" scheme, which is inherent in the homomorphic encryption scheme of Gentry, Sahai, and Waters (GSW) [GSW13], and was made more explicit in the works of [BV14, AP14, GVW15b], with other useful properties derived in related works like [BGG+14, GVW15a, PS19, PPS21].

Here we lay out a somewhat different perspective that focuses on just those limited properties needed for our purposes, and hence exposes less of the functionality than is used in prior works, making it slightly simpler. In particular, we do not need any explicit notions of encrypted/committed/hidden data, encryption/commitment randomness, or decryption/opening.

Overview. The homomorphic computation scheme operates on matrices $\mathbf{C} \in \mathbb{Z}_q^{n \times W}$ for some fixed q, n and various W. Performing homomorphic operations that correspond to a function f yields a matrix $\mathbf{C}_f \in \mathbb{Z}_q^{n \times W'}$. The key property is that for *any* input x to f,

$$(\mathbf{C} - \mathsf{Rep}(x) \otimes \mathbf{g}^t) \cdot \mathbf{S}_{f,x} = \mathbf{C}_f - \mathsf{Rep}(f(x)) \otimes \mathbf{g}^t \tag{1}$$

for some "short" (and efficiently computable) matrix $\mathbf{S}_{f,x} \in \mathbb{Z}^{W \times W'}$ that can depend on $\mathbf{C}, f, x$. Here Rep outputs a suitable matrix representation of its argument, and $\mathbf{g}$ is a special fixed vector, described next.

The above Kronecker products serve as "robust" matrix encodings using a fixed *gadget* vector $\mathbf{g} \in \mathbb{Z}_q^\ell$, which must come with a corresponding *decomposition* function $\mathbf{g}^{-1} \colon \mathbb{Z}_q \to \mathbb{Z}^\ell$. These are defined so that $\mathbf{g}^{-1}(u) \in \mathbb{Z}^\ell$ is "short" (relative to q) and $\mathbf{g}^t \cdot \mathbf{g}^{-1}(u) = u$, for all $u \in \mathbb{Z}_q$. This naturally extends to $(\mathbf{X} \otimes \mathbf{g}^t) \cdot \mathbf{g}^{-1}(\mathbf{Y}) = \mathbf{X}\mathbf{Y}$ for any $\mathbf{X} \in \mathbb{Z}_q^{n \times d}$ and $\mathbf{Y} \in \mathbb{Z}_q^{d \times d'}$, where $\mathbf{g}^{-1}(\mathbf{Y})$ operates entry-wise, replacing each $y_{i,j}$ with the "short" column vector $\mathbf{g}^{-1}(y_{i,j}) \in \mathbb{Z}^\ell$.

For concreteness, we use the powers-of-two gadget $\mathbf{g} := (1, 2, 4, \ldots, 2^{\ell-1})^t$ for $\ell = \lceil \log_2 q \rceil$, where $\mathbf{g}^{-1} \colon \mathbb{Z}_q \to \{0, 1\}^\ell$ simply outputs the binary representation of (the distinguished representative in $\{0, 1, \ldots, q-1\}$ of) its argument, least-significant bit first. All of what follows straightforwardly generalizes to other choices of gadget, with suitable adjustments to the bounds on "short" objects.

In addition, the decomposition operation $\mathbf{g}^{-1}$ can be *randomized* as in [MP12, AP14]. This can be used for (statistically) *function-hiding* homomorphic computation, using ideas from [BPMW16], but simplified in our setting because only SIS (not LWE) instances need to be re-randomized. Function hiding is used only in the zero-knowledge variant of our functional commitment construction (see Sect. 3.2).

Linear Homomorphisms. We recall the homomorphic operations supporting linear functions. First, for any $\mathbf{X}_1, \mathbf{X}_2 \in \mathbb{Z}_q^{n \times d}$ (for any d) we have

$$([\mathbf{X}_1 \mid \mathbf{X}_2] \otimes \mathbf{g}^t) \cdot \underbrace{\begin{bmatrix} \mathbf{I}_{d\ell} \\ \mathbf{I}_{d\ell} \end{bmatrix}}_{\mathbf{S}_+} = \left([\mathbf{X}_1 \mid \mathbf{X}_2] \cdot \begin{bmatrix} \mathbf{I}_d \\ \mathbf{I}_d \end{bmatrix} \right) \otimes (\mathbf{g}^t \cdot \mathbf{I}_\ell) = (\mathbf{X}_1 + \mathbf{X}_2) \otimes \mathbf{g}^t.$$

This yields the homomorphic operation for addition: given any $\mathbf{C} \in \mathbb{Z}_q^{n \times 2d\ell}$, define $\mathbf{C}_+ := \mathbf{C} \cdot \mathbf{S}_+ \in \mathbb{Z}_q^{n \times d\ell}$. Then for any $\mathbf{X}_1, \mathbf{X}_2 \in \mathbb{Z}_q^{n \times d}$ we have

$$(\mathbf{C} - [\mathbf{X}_1 \mid \mathbf{X}_2] \otimes \mathbf{g}^t) \cdot \mathbf{S}_+ = \mathbf{C}_+ - (\mathbf{X}_1 + \mathbf{X}_2) \otimes \mathbf{g}^t. \tag{2}$$

Note that $\mathbf{S}_+$ is short: $\|\mathbf{S}_+\|_1 = 2$.

Second, recall from above that for any $\mathbf{X} \in \mathbb{Z}_q^{n \times d}$ and $\mathbf{Y} \in \mathbb{Z}_q^{d \times d'}$,

$$(\mathbf{X} \otimes \mathbf{g}^t) \cdot \underbrace{\mathbf{g}^{-1}(\mathbf{Y})}_{\mathbf{S}_{\times \mathbf{Y}}} = \mathbf{X}\mathbf{Y} \in \mathbb{Z}_q^{n \times d'}.$$

This yields homomorphic (right-)multiplication by any fixed matrix $\mathbf{Y}$: given any $\mathbf{C} \in \mathbb{Z}_q^{n \times d\ell}$, define $\mathbf{C}_{\times \mathbf{Y}} := \mathbf{C} \cdot \mathbf{S}_{\times \mathbf{Y}}$. Then for any $\mathbf{X} \in \mathbb{Z}_q^{n \times d}$, we have

$$(\mathbf{C} - \mathbf{X} \otimes \mathbf{g}^t) \cdot \mathbf{S}_{\times \mathbf{Y}} = \mathbf{C}_{\times \mathbf{Y}} - (\mathbf{X}\mathbf{Y}) \otimes \mathbf{g}^t. \tag{3}$$

Note that $\mathbf{S}_{\times \mathbf{Y}}$ is short: $\|\mathbf{S}_{\times \mathbf{Y}}\|_1 \le d\ell$.

Linear Functions Over Finite Fields. For values in the matrix ring $\mathcal{R} = \mathbb{Z}_q^{n \times n}$, the above yields a linearly homomorphic scheme, i.e., one that supports addition and (right-)multiplication by known $\mathcal{R}$-elements. This in turn yields a linearly homomorphic scheme for the finite field $\mathbb{F}_{p^{n'}}$ for any prime p that divides q and any $n' \le n$, using standard encoding and padding techniques. (In summary: $\mathbb{F}_{p^{n'}}$ is an n'-dimensional vector space over $\mathbb{F}_p$, so multiplication by each field element can be represented by a corresponding matrix in $\mathbb{Z}_p^{n' \times n'}$, which can be scaled and padded to $\mathbb{Z}_q^{n \times n}$.)

Multiplicative Homomorphism. To support multiplicative homomorphism, and thereby arbitrary Boolean circuits of bounded size or branching programs, we restrict all the data values to be bits, and represent any $b \in \{0,1\}$ by the scaled identity matrix $b\mathbf{I}_n \in \mathbb{Z}_q^{n \times n}$. This leads to the homomorphic operation for multiplication: given any $\mathbf{C} = [\mathbf{C}_1 \mid \mathbf{C}_2]$ where each $\mathbf{C}_i \in \mathbb{Z}_q^{n \times w}$ for $w = n\ell$, define $\mathbf{C}_\times := \mathbf{C}_1 \cdot \mathbf{g}^{-1}(\mathbf{C}_2) \in \mathbb{Z}_q^{n \times w}$. Then for any $x_1, x_2 \in \{0,1\}$, we have

$$(\mathbf{C} - [x_1\mathbf{I}_n \mid x_2\mathbf{I}_n] \otimes \mathbf{g}^t) \cdot \underbrace{\begin{bmatrix} \mathbf{g}^{-1}(\mathbf{C}_2) \\ x_1\mathbf{I}_w \end{bmatrix}}_{\mathbf{S}_{\times,x_1}} = \mathbf{C}_\times + \mathbf{C}_2 \cdot x_1\mathbf{I}_w - x_1\mathbf{I}_n \cdot \mathbf{C}_2 - (x_2\mathbf{I}_n \otimes \mathbf{g}^t) \cdot (x_1\mathbf{I}_n \otimes \mathbf{I}_\ell)$$

$$= \mathbf{C}_\times - (x_1 x_2)\mathbf{I}_n \otimes \mathbf{g}^t. \tag{4}$$

Note that the multiplier matrix $\mathbf{S}_{\times,x_1}$ is short: $\|\mathbf{S}_{\times,x_1}\|_1 \leq w + 1$. Also note that, unlike above, here the multiplier matrix depends on the initial matrix $\mathbf{C}_2$ as well as one of the input values x_1 (which is not determined at the time of the homomorphic multiplication).

More generally, the asymmetric form of the short multiplier matrix $\mathbf{S}_{\times,x_1}$ means we can perform many sequential multiplications with a short multiplier whose norm bound is only *linear* in the number of operations. Specifically, given any $\mathbf{C} = [\mathbf{C}_1 \mid \cdots \mid \mathbf{C}_k]$ where each $\mathbf{C}_i \in \mathbb{Z}_q^{n \times w}$, define $\mathbf{C}_\times = \mathbf{C}_1 \cdot \mathbf{g}^{-1}(\mathbf{C}_2 \cdot \mathbf{g}^{-1}(\cdots \mathbf{g}^{-1}(\mathbf{C}_k)))$. Then for any $\mathbf{x} \in \{0,1\}^k$, by iteratively applying the above we get a multiplier matrix

$$\mathbf{S}_{\times,\mathbf{x}} = \begin{bmatrix} \mathbf{g}^{-1}(\mathbf{C}_2 \cdot \mathbf{g}^{-1}(\mathbf{C}_3 \cdots \mathbf{g}^{-1}(\mathbf{C}_k))) \\ x_1 \cdot \mathbf{g}^{-1}(\mathbf{C}_3 \cdots \mathbf{g}^{-1}(\mathbf{C}_k)) \\ \vdots \\ x_1 \cdots x_{k-2} \cdot \mathbf{g}^{-1}(\mathbf{C}_k) \\ x_1 \cdots x_{k-1} \cdot \mathbf{I}_w \end{bmatrix} \in \mathbb{Z}^{kw \times w}. \tag{5}$$

Note that $\|\mathbf{S}_{\times,\mathbf{x}}\|_1 \leq (k-1)w + 1$.

Using the above, we can homomorphically evaluate any Boolean circuit f on a given matrix $\mathbf{C}$, by expressing each gate of the circuit algebraically (e.g., x NAND $y = 1 - xy$). Due to Eqs. (2) to (4), the result $\mathbf{C}_f$ satisfies Eq. (1) for any circuit input x, where the multiplier matrix $\mathbf{S}_{f,x}$ is the product of some short multiplier matrices, and hence is somewhat short itself. Similarly, we can homomorphically evaluate *branching programs*, where, as with multiplication of several bits, the asymmetric nature of each step's multiplier matrix means that their product has ℓ_1 norm proportional to the program length.

Summary. We summarize all of the above in the following.

Definition 4. *Define the following function families* $\mathcal{F}_{linear}, \mathcal{F}_{circuit}, \mathcal{F}_{BP}$:

- $\mathcal{F}_{linear}^k = \{f_\mathbf{w} : \mathbb{F}^k \to \mathbb{F} : \mathbf{w} \in \mathbb{F}^k\}$ *is the family of linear functions* $f_\mathbf{w}(\mathbf{x}) := \langle \mathbf{w}, \mathbf{x} \rangle$ *over* $\mathbb{F}$, *where* $\mathbb{F} = \mathbb{F}_{p^{n'}}$ *for any prime* p *that divides* q *and any* $n' \leq n$.

- $\mathcal{F}_{circuit}^{k} = \{f\colon \{0,1\}^{k} \to \{0,1\}\}$ *is the family of functions that are computable by Boolean circuits of some specified depth D (and fan-in two).*
- $\mathcal{F}_{BP}^{k} = \{f\colon \{0,1\}^{k} \to \{0,1\}\}$ *is the family of functions that are computable by branching programs of some specified size S (and some fixed width).*

Remark 3. In the above-defined families, for simplicity we restrict the functions to output a single value (i.e., a field element or bit). This is without loss of generality, because any vector-valued (i.e., multi-output) function of the same complexity can be obtained as the concatenation of the functions that produce each entry of its output vector, and we can commit to and open each such function in parallel. Indeed, our concrete instantiations will use vector-valued functions, which are implicitly handled in this way.

Theorem 1 (Homomorphic computation scheme). *Let $n, q \in \mathbb{N}$ and $D = \{0,1\}$ or $D = \mathbb{F}_{p^{n'}}$ for a prime p that divides q and some $n' \leq n$. There is an efficient deterministic robust matrix encoding for any $\boldsymbol{v} \in D^{d}$, denoted $\boldsymbol{v}^{t} \otimes \boldsymbol{g}^{t} \in \mathbb{Z}_{q}^{n \times dw}$ where $w = n\ell$, and a deterministic polynomial-time homomorphic evaluation algorithm* Eval, *where for any function family $\mathcal{F} = \{f\colon D^{k} \to D\}$ from Definition 4.[5]*

- Eval*'s input in square brackets is optional, and when it is provided, the additional output (also in square brackets) is also produced. The non-optional output is unaffected by whether or not an optional input is provided.*
- Eval$(f \in \mathcal{F}, \mathbf{C} \in \mathbb{Z}_{q}^{n \times kw}[, \boldsymbol{x} \in D^{k}])$ *outputs a matrix $\mathbf{C}_{f} \in \mathbb{Z}_{q}^{n \times w}$ [and an integral matrix $\mathbf{S}_{f,\boldsymbol{x}} \in \mathbb{Z}^{kw \times w}$], where the additional output $\mathbf{S}_{f,\boldsymbol{x}}$ satisfies*

$$(\mathbf{C} - \boldsymbol{x}^{t} \otimes \boldsymbol{g}^{t}) \cdot \mathbf{S}_{f,\boldsymbol{x}} = \mathbf{C}_{f} - f(\boldsymbol{x})^{t} \otimes \boldsymbol{g}^{t}, \tag{6}$$

and
1. *for $\mathcal{F} = \mathcal{F}_{linear}^{k}$, $\|\mathbf{S}_{f,\boldsymbol{x}}\|_{1} \leq kw$; moreover, $\|\mathbf{S}_{f,\boldsymbol{x}}\|_{1} \leq k$ when f is a subset-sum function;*
2. *for $\mathcal{F} = \mathcal{F}_{circuit}^{k}$, $\|\mathbf{S}_{f,\boldsymbol{x}}\|_{1} \leq O(w)^{D}$;*
3. *for $\mathcal{F} = \mathcal{F}_{BP}^{k}$, $\|\mathbf{S}_{f,\boldsymbol{x}}\|_{1} \leq w^{O(1)} \cdot S$.*

Remark 4. The form of Eq. (6) means that Eval is *composable*, i.e., it can be applied to its own outputs, to homomorphically compute on the results of other homomorphic computations. More specifically, we can compute $(\mathbf{C}_{f}[, \mathbf{S}_{f,\boldsymbol{x}}]) =$ Eval$(f, \mathbf{C}[, \boldsymbol{x}])$ then $(\mathbf{C}_{g \circ f}[, \mathbf{S}_{g,f(\boldsymbol{x})}]) = $ Eval$(g, \mathbf{C}_{f}[, f(\boldsymbol{x})])$, where recall that f, g can be vector-valued functions. Then $\mathbf{S}_{f,\boldsymbol{x}}, \mathbf{S}_{g,f(\boldsymbol{x})}$ satisfy the norm bounds corresponding to f, g (respectively), and

$$(\mathbf{C} - \boldsymbol{x}^{t} \otimes \boldsymbol{g}^{t}) \cdot \mathbf{S}_{f,\boldsymbol{x}} \cdot \mathbf{S}_{g,f(\boldsymbol{x})} = (\mathbf{C}_{f} - f(\boldsymbol{x})^{t} \otimes \boldsymbol{g}^{t}) \cdot \mathbf{S}_{g,f(\boldsymbol{x})}$$
$$= \mathbf{C}_{g \circ f} - g(f(\boldsymbol{x}))^{t} \otimes \boldsymbol{g}^{t}.$$

---

[5] More generally, the scheme works for vector-valued (multi-output) functions, following Remark 3.

For notational convenience, we express the above process (hiding the intermediate values) as

$$(\mathbf{C}_{g \circ f}[, \mathbf{S}_{g \circ f, x}]) = \mathsf{Eval}(g \circ f, \mathbf{C}[, x]),$$

where $\mathbf{S}_{g \circ f, x} = \mathbf{S}_{f, x} \cdot \mathbf{S}_{g, f(x)}$.

3.2 Functional Commitment Construction

Our functional commitment scheme is parameterized by a function family $\mathcal{F} = \{f \colon \mathcal{X} \to \mathcal{Y}\}$ and a corresponding norm bound κ, which is used only in verification. Recall from Definition 2 that a user first commits to some function $f \in \mathcal{F}$. Then, for one or more inputs $x \in \mathcal{X}$, the user can generate a proof that $f(x) = y$ for some claimed $y \in \mathcal{Y}$. The main security property of interest (see Definition 3) is essentially that it should be infeasible to generate a (possibly malformed) commitment, an input x, and valid proofs for two different purported function outputs (at x).

Construction 2 (SIS-based functional commitment). Let $n, q \in \mathbb{N}$. Following Theorem 1, let $\mathcal{X}, \mathcal{Y}$ be finite domains where $x \in \mathcal{X}, y \in \mathcal{Y}$ have robust matrix encodings denoted $x^t \otimes \mathbf{g}^t \in \mathbb{Z}_q^{n \times W}, y^t \otimes \mathbf{g}^t \in \mathbb{Z}_q^{n \times W'}$ (respectively), and let Eval be the homomorphic evaluation algorithm. Let $\mathcal{F} = \{f \colon \mathcal{X} \to \mathcal{Y}\}$ be some function family and κ be a corresponding norm bound.[6] Define the following functional commitment scheme for $\mathcal{F}$.

- Setup(): choose uniformly random $\mathbf{C} \leftarrow \mathbb{Z}_q^{n \times W}$ and output it as the public parameter. (Note that this is an "unstructured" random string, so the setup is untrusted.)
- Commit($\mathbf{C}, f \in \mathcal{F}$): output commitment $\mathbf{C}_f = \mathsf{Eval}(f, \mathbf{C}) \in \mathbb{Z}_q^{n \times W'}$.[7]
  [For Boolean functions the commitment can be compressed significantly; see Sect. 3.2 below.]
- Open($\mathbf{C}, f \in \mathcal{F}, x \in \mathcal{X}$): compute $(\mathbf{C}_f, \mathbf{S}_{f,x}) = \mathsf{Eval}(f, \mathbf{C}, x)$, and output proof $\mathbf{S}_{f,x} \in \mathbb{Z}^{W \times W'}$.[8]
  [For Boolean functions the proof can be compressed significantly; see Sect. 3.2 below.]
- Verify$_\kappa(\mathbf{C}, \mathbf{C}^*, x \in \mathcal{X}, y \in \mathcal{Y}, \mathbf{S}^*)$: if $\|\mathbf{S}^*\|_1 \le \kappa$ and

$$(\mathbf{C} - x^t \otimes \mathbf{g}^t) \cdot \mathbf{S}^* = \mathbf{C}^* - y^t \otimes \mathbf{g}^t,$$

then accept; otherwise, reject.

---

[6] The norm bound κ should be set large enough so that the verifier accepts properly generated proofs for all functions in $\mathcal{F}$ (see Lemma 1). Then, n and q should be set so that the SIS problem underlying the scheme's evaluation binding is sufficiently hard (see Theorem 3).

[7] We can make the commitment hide the function f by using *circuit-private* homomorphic computation, such as from [BPMW16], and retaining the randomness for use in opening.

[8] In concert with a function-hiding commitment, we can make the opening reveal nothing more than the single input-output pair $(x, f(x))$ by giving a zero-knowledge proof (of knowledge) of some $\mathbf{S}_{f,x}$ that satisfies the verifier.

Section 3.2 describes a zero-knowledge variant of this construction with the weaker notion of *target* evaluation binding, and sketches the proofs of its security properties.

Complexity. For security (see Theorem 3 and the remark following Definition 1), the modulus q should satisfy $q \geq \kappa \cdot \tau(n)$, or $q \geq k'\kappa \cdot \tau(n)$ for the compressed variant for k'-bit function outputs, for some large enough $\tau(n)$ that can be $\tilde{O}(\sqrt{n})$. Because $\kappa \geq \sqrt{n}$ in any useful instantiation, we can ensure that $\log_2 q = \Theta(\log \kappa)$. Recall that $w = n\ell = n\lceil \log_2 q \rceil$.

The sizes of the scheme's various objects are as follows:

- The public parameter $\mathbf{C}$ is $\approx W \cdot w$ bits, where W is the width of the robust matrix encoding of any input $x \in \mathcal{X}$. Concretely, $W = kw$ when $\mathcal{X} = D^k$ for $D = \{0,1\}$ or $D = \mathbb{F}_{p^{n'}}$ (see Definition 4), so the public parameter is $\approx kw^2$ bits.
- An (uncompressed) commitment $\mathbf{C}_f$ is $\approx W' \cdot w$ bits, where W' is the width of the robust matrix encoding of any output $y \in \mathcal{Y}$, which is $W' = k'w$ when $\mathcal{Y} = D^{k'}$. So, a commitment is $\approx k'w^2$ bits. A compressed commitment for k'-bit function outputs (where $k' \leq n$) is just $\approx w$ bits; see Sect. 3.2 below.
- An (uncompressed) proof $\mathbf{S}_{f,x}$ is $\approx W \cdot W' \cdot \log_2 \kappa$ bits (using a naïve encoding); for a $D^k \to D^{k'}$ function, this is $\approx k \cdot k' \cdot w^2 \cdot \log_2 \kappa$ bits. A compressed proof for k'-bit function outputs (where $k' \leq n$) is just $kw \log_2(k'\kappa)$ bits.

(We can reduce the sizes of all these objects by about a factor of n, using "algebraically structured" lattices and the Ring-SIS problem [Mic02, PR06, LM06].)

The running times of Commit and Open are just those of homomorphic evaluation of the committed function, in the latter case with the known input. The verifier's running time is dominated by a matrix multiplication, or a matrix-vector multiplication for a compressed proof.

Composition, Stateless Updates, and (Outsourced) Precomputation. Because both algorithms Commit, Open are simply the homomorphic evaluation algorithm Eval (with the latter providing the function input x as Eval's optional input), Construction 2 supports function composition in the same way that the homomorphic computation scheme does, as described in Remark 4. We use similar notation $\mathbf{C}_{g \circ f} = \mathsf{Commit}(\mathbf{C}, g \circ f)$ and $\mathbf{S}_{g \circ f, x} = \mathsf{Open}(\mathbf{C}, g \circ f, x)$ to denote this kind of composition. Note that f and g need not come from the same function family. As usual, for correctness we simply need to use an appropriate norm bound κ in verification.

This kind of composition has several beneficial consequences: it enables *stateless updates*, *reuse*, and *(outsourced) precomputation* of commitments and proofs. More specifically, a commitment $\mathbf{C}_f$ to a function f can be updated to a commitment $\mathbf{C}_{g \circ f} = \mathsf{Commit}(\mathbf{C}_f, g)$ to any $g \circ f$, using $\mathbf{C}_f$ and g alone; the original function f is not needed. Similarly, for any x, a proof $\mathbf{S}_{f,x}$ that $f(x) = y$ can be updated to a proof $\mathbf{S}_{g \circ f, x} = \mathbf{S}_{f,x} \cdot \mathsf{Open}(\mathbf{C}_f, g, y)$ that $g(f(x)) = z$, using just $\mathbf{C}_f, g, y$. In addition, commitments and proofs for other functions $g' \circ f$ can be created by reusing $\mathbf{C}_f$ and its proofs $\mathbf{S}_{f,x}$. This enables precomputation, in case a committer does yet not know which of multiple functions with common structure $g_i \circ f$ it will commit to, or which inputs it will open. Finally, this precomputation of commitments and proofs can even be outsourced to an untrusted worker, as long as the client verifies them. Then any commitments and proofs derived (exclusively) from them will verify as well.

Several of our concrete instantiations in Sect. 4 rely on a few specific kinds of compositions. Fix some "base" function f. Then for an "additive update" function δ, the updated function $f' = f + \delta$ obviously satisfies $f'(\bar{x}) = f(\bar{x}) + \delta(\bar{x})$ for all $\bar{x}$. For a "multiplicative update" function c (which can be, but need not be, a constant), the updated function $f' = c \cdot f$ satisfies $f'(\bar{x}) = c(\bar{x}) \cdot f(\bar{x})$ for all $\bar{x}$. Most generally, for a "post-processing update" function g, the updated function $f' = g \circ f$ satisfies $f'(\bar{x}) = g(f(\bar{x}))$ for all $\bar{x}$.

Compression for Binary Functions. For concatenations of any $k' \leq n$ functions with Boolean (or more generally, small integer) outputs, we can significantly reduce the sizes of the commitments and proofs, by a factor of $W' = k'w = k'n\ell$.

Let $\mathbf{e} = (\mathbf{e}_1^t, \mathbf{e}_2^t, \ldots, \mathbf{e}_{k'}^t)^t \otimes \mathbf{g}^{-1}(1) \in \{0,1\}^{k'w}$, where $\mathbf{e}_i \in \mathbb{Z}_q^n$ is the ith standard basis vector, and note that $\|\mathbf{e}\|_1 = k'$. Then any commitment $\mathbf{C}_f \in \mathbb{Z}_q^{n \times W'}$ can be compressed as the single vector $\mathbf{c}_f = \mathbf{C}_f \cdot \mathbf{e} \in \mathbb{Z}_q^n$, and any proof $\mathbf{S}_{f,x} \in \mathbb{Z}^{W \times W'}$ can be replaced by a single vector $\mathbf{s}_{f,x} = \mathbf{S}_{f,x} \cdot \mathbf{e} \in \mathbb{Z}^W$.[9] We then define the compressed verification algorithm $\mathsf{Verify}'_\kappa(\mathbf{C}, \mathbf{c}^*, x, \mathbf{y} \in \{0,1\}^{k'}, \mathbf{s}^*)$ to accept if $\|\mathbf{s}^*\|_1 \leq \kappa' := k'\kappa$ and

$$(\mathbf{C} - x^t \otimes \mathbf{g}^t) \cdot \mathbf{s}^* = \mathbf{c}^* - \binom{\mathbf{y}}{\mathbf{0}}.$$

In brief, this compressed scheme is correct because the uncompressed scheme is, and because $\|\mathbf{s}_{f,x}\|_1 \leq \|\mathbf{S}_{f,x}\|_1 \cdot \|\mathbf{e}\|_1 \leq k'\kappa = \kappa'$ and $(\mathbf{y}^t \otimes \mathbf{I}_n \otimes \mathbf{g}^t) \cdot \mathbf{e} = \binom{\mathbf{y}}{\mathbf{0}}$ by construction of $\mathbf{e}$. See Lemma 1 below for details, and for security see Theorem 3.

Compressed commitments and proofs are no longer generally composable, i.e., they do not support *arbitrary* further homomorphic operations. However, it is straightforward to see that they still are linear homomorphic via small integer combinations, as long as the norm bound used in verification is set appropriately.

Correctness

Lemma 1. *For the values of κ given above, Construction 2 [and its compressed variant for Boolean functions] is a correct functional commitment scheme for the corresponding function family.*

---

[9] In some contexts, compressed commitments and proofs even be computed directly, without first computing uncompressed ones.

Proof. Let $f \in \mathcal{F}$ and $x \in \mathcal{X}$ be arbitrary, and let $\mathbf{C} \leftarrow \mathsf{Setup}()$ and $(\mathbf{C}_f, \mathbf{S}_{f,x}) = \mathsf{Open}(\mathbf{C}, f, x) = \mathsf{Eval}(f, \mathbf{C}, x)$. Note that $\mathbf{C}_f = \mathsf{Commit}(\mathbf{C}, f) = \mathsf{Eval}(f, \mathbf{C})$ by definition of Eval.

We show that $\mathsf{Verify}_\kappa(\mathbf{C}, \mathbf{C}_f, x, f(x), \mathbf{S}_{f,x})$ accepts. By the correctness of Eval (Eq. (6)), we have

$$(\mathbf{C} - x^t \otimes \mathbf{g}^t) \cdot \mathbf{S}_{f,x} = \mathbf{C}_f - f(x)^t \otimes \mathbf{g}^t.$$

In addition, $\|\mathbf{S}_{f,x}\|_1 \le \kappa$ by Theorem 1, so Verify_κ accepts.

For the compressed variant for k'-bit outputs, where $W' = k'w$, the commitment is $\mathbf{c}_f := \mathbf{C}_f \cdot \mathbf{e}$ and proof is $\mathbf{s}_{f,x} := \mathbf{S}_{f,x} \cdot \mathbf{e}$, where $\mathbf{e} \in \{0,1\}^{W'}$ is as defined in Sect. 3.2. Consider $\mathsf{Verify}'_\kappa(\mathbf{C}, \mathbf{c}_f, x, \mathbf{y} = f(x) \in \{0,1\}^{k'}, \mathbf{s}_{f,x})$. Because $f(x)^t \otimes \mathbf{g}^t = \mathbf{y}^t \otimes \mathbf{I}_n \otimes \mathbf{g}^t$ in this setting, we have that

$$(\mathbf{C} - x^t \otimes \mathbf{g}^t) \cdot \mathbf{s}_{f,x} = (\mathbf{C} - x^t \otimes \mathbf{g}^t) \cdot \mathbf{S}_{f,x} \cdot \mathbf{e} = (\mathbf{C}_f - (\mathbf{y}^t \otimes \mathbf{I}_n \otimes \mathbf{g}^t)) \cdot \mathbf{e} = \mathbf{c}_f - \begin{pmatrix} \mathbf{y} \\ \mathbf{0} \end{pmatrix}$$

and $\|\mathbf{s}_{f,x}\|_i \le \|\mathbf{S}_{f,x}\|_1 \cdot \|\mathbf{e}\|_1 \le k'\kappa = \kappa'$, so Verify'_κ accepts. $\square$

Security

Theorem 3. *For any $\kappa > 0$, the Verify_κ algorithm from Construction 2 [and its compressed variant Verify'_κ for k'-bit function outputs, from Sect. 3.2] has selective evaluation binding (Definition 3) if normal-form $\mathsf{SIS}_{n,q,W,\beta}$ in the ℓ_1 norm is hard, where $\beta = 2w\kappa + n$ for finite-field function outputs, and $\beta = 2\kappa + n$ for Boolean function outputs [or for the compressed variant, $\beta = 2k'\kappa + n$].[10]*

More specifically, for any adversary $\mathcal{A}$ against the selective evaluation binding of the scheme, there is a normal-form $\mathsf{SIS}_{n,q,W,\beta}$ adversary $\mathcal{B}$ for which

$$\mathbf{Adv}^{SIS}(\mathcal{B}) \ge \mathbf{Adv}^{sia}(\mathcal{A}),$$

and whose running time is that of $\mathcal{A}$ plus a small polynomial in n.

Proof. Let $\mathcal{A}$ be any adversary that attacks the selective evaluation binding (Definition 3) of Verify_κ [or Verify'_κ]. For the former (non-compressed) version, we assume that the function output is a single finite-field element or bit, and hence $W' = w$, because breaking binding for multi-output functions requires breaking it at some single position.

We construct a reduction $\mathcal{B}$ which, on input $\mathbf{A} \in \mathbb{Z}_q^{n \times W}$, attempts to output a vector $\mathbf{x} \in \mathbb{Z}^W$ such that $\mathbf{A}\mathbf{x} \in \{0, \pm 1\}^n \setminus \{\mathbf{0}\} \subseteq \mathbb{Z}_q^n$ where $\|\mathbf{x}\|_1 \le \beta - n$; note that such an $\mathbf{x}$ is a normal-form SIS solution (in ℓ_1) for $\mathbf{A}$. It operates as follows:

1. Give the security parameter to $\mathcal{A}$ and receive $x^* \in \mathcal{X}$ in return.

---

[10] As mentioned in Sect. 3.2, security for the compressed variant extends to concatenations of k' functions with small integer outputs, where the additive n term in β is replaced by the maximum ℓ_1 norm of the difference between two such output vectors.

2. Let the public parameter $\mathbf{C} := \mathbf{A} + (x^*)^t \otimes \mathbf{g}^t$ and give it to $\mathcal{A}$. Note that this makes $\mathbf{C} - (x^*)^t \otimes \mathbf{g}^t = \mathbf{A}$.

3. $\mathcal{A}$ outputs some $(\mathbf{C}^*, y_0, \mathbf{S}_0, y_1, \mathbf{S}_1)$. If $y_0 = y_1$, abort.
   [For the compressed variant, $\mathcal{A}$ instead outputs some $(\mathbf{c}^*, \mathbf{y}_0, \mathbf{s}_0, \mathbf{y}_1, \mathbf{s}_1)$.]

4. Compute the binary vector $\mathbf{e} = \mathbf{g}^{-1}(\mathbf{Y}^{-1}\mathbf{e}_1) \in \{0,1\}^w$, where $\mathbf{Y} \in \mathbb{Z}_q^{n \times n}$ is the invertible matrix representing multiplication by $y_1 - y_0 \neq 0$ (and $\mathbf{e}_1 \in \mathbb{Z}_q^n$ is the first standard basis vector).
   More specifically, for finite-field outputs, $y_1 - y_0$ is a nonzero field element, hence it corresponds to an invertible $\mathbf{Y} \in \mathbb{Z}_q^{n \times n}$, and $\|\mathbf{e}\|_1 \leq w$. For Boolean functions, $y_0 - y_1 = \pm 1$, and hence corresponds to the invertible matrix $\pm \mathbf{I}_n \in \mathbb{Z}_q^{n \times n}$, so we can use $\mathbf{e} = \pm \mathbf{e}_1$ and hence $\|\mathbf{e}\|_1 = 1$.
   [For the compressed variant, this step is skipped.]

5. Output $\mathbf{x} = (\mathbf{S}_0 - \mathbf{S}_1)\mathbf{e} \in \mathbb{Z}^W$.
   [For the compressed variant, output $\mathbf{x} = \mathbf{s}_0 - \mathbf{s}_1 \in \mathbb{Z}^W$.]

By inspection, it is clear that $\mathcal{B}$ runs in the same time as $\mathcal{A}$, plus a small polynomial. In addition, for any choice of $x^* \in \mathcal{X}$ by $\mathcal{A}$, the public parameter $\mathbf{C}$ is uniformly random (because $\mathbf{A}$ is), as needed.

We now show that if $\mathcal{A}$ successfully breaks selective evaluation binding, then $\mathcal{B}$ outputs an $\mathbf{x}$ such that $\mathbf{A}\mathbf{x} = \mathbf{e}_1 \in \mathbb{Z}_q^n$ and $\|\mathbf{x}\|_1 \leq 2k'\kappa$. In this case, we have $y_0 \neq y_1$; $\|\mathbf{S}_0\|_1, \|\mathbf{S}_1\|_1 \leq \kappa$; and

$$\mathbf{C}^* = \mathbf{A}\mathbf{S}_0 + y_0^t \otimes \mathbf{g}^t = \mathbf{A}\mathbf{S}_1 + y_1^t \otimes \mathbf{g}^t,$$

so $\mathbf{A}(\mathbf{S}_0 - \mathbf{S}_1) = (y_1 - y_0)^t \otimes \mathbf{g}^t$. Therefore,

$$\mathbf{A}\mathbf{x} = \mathbf{A}(\mathbf{S}_0 - \mathbf{S}_1) \cdot \mathbf{e}$$
$$= ((y_1 - y_0)^t \otimes \mathbf{g}^t) \cdot \mathbf{e} = \mathbf{e}_1.$$

Moreover, $\|\mathbf{x}\|_1 = \|(\mathbf{S}_0 - \mathbf{S}_1)_1 \cdot \mathbf{e}\| \leq \|\mathbf{S}_0 - \mathbf{S}_1\|_1 \cdot \|\mathbf{e}\|_1$, which by the triangle inequality is at most $2w\kappa$ for finite-field outputs, and at most 2κ for Boolean outputs, as needed.

For the compressed variant (for functions with binary outputs of length $k' \leq n$), $\mathcal{A}$ instead outputs some $(\mathbf{c}^*, \mathbf{y}_0 \in \{0,1\}^{k'}, \mathbf{s}_0 \in \mathbb{Z}^W, \mathbf{y}_1 \in \{0,1\}^{k'}, \mathbf{s}_1 \in \mathbb{Z}^W)$, and succeeds if $\mathbf{y}_0 \neq \mathbf{y}_1$; $\|\mathbf{s}_0\|_1, \|\mathbf{s}_1\|_1 \leq k'\kappa$; and

$$\mathbf{c}^* = \mathbf{A}\mathbf{s}_0 + \begin{pmatrix} \mathbf{y}_0 \\ \mathbf{0} \end{pmatrix} = \mathbf{A}\mathbf{s}_1 + \begin{pmatrix} \mathbf{y}_1 \\ \mathbf{0} \end{pmatrix}.$$

Since $\mathbf{x} = \mathbf{s}_0 - \mathbf{s}_1$, it immediately follows that

$$\mathbf{A}\mathbf{x} = \mathbf{A}(\mathbf{s}_0 - \mathbf{s}_1) = \begin{pmatrix} \mathbf{y}_1 - \mathbf{y}_0 \\ \mathbf{0} \end{pmatrix} \in \{0, \pm 1\}^n \setminus \{\mathbf{0}\},$$

and $\|\mathbf{x}\|_1 \leq 2k'\kappa$, as needed.

Zero-Knowledge Variant. Using the "context hiding" technique of [GVW15b], Construction 2 for binary functions $f: \{0,1\}^k \rightarrow \{0,1\}$ can be modified to have zero-knowledge commitments and proofs, but a weaker "target" binding property (see Remark 1). We describe this modification and briefly sketch the proofs.

Modified algorithms.

- The Setup algorithm additionally includes a uniformly random $\mathbf{u} \in \mathbb{Z}_q^n$ in the public parameter.
- The Commit algorithm does (statistically) *function-hiding* homomorphic evaluation (which uses a randomized decomposition operation $\mathbf{g}^{-1}$), and retains its random choices for generating proofs.
- The Open algorithm, having computed $\mathbf{S}_{f,x}$ that satisfies Equation (6), treats it as a trapdoor in the sense of [MP12] for a combined matrix $\mathbf{C}_{f,x}$, i.e.,

$$\underbrace{[\mathbf{C} - x^t \otimes \mathbf{g}^t \mid \mathbf{C}_f - (1 - f(x))^t \otimes \mathbf{g}^t]}_{\mathbf{C}_{f,x}} \cdot \begin{bmatrix} \mathbf{S}_{f,x} \\ -\mathbf{I}_{n\ell} \end{bmatrix} = (1 - 2f(x))^t \otimes \mathbf{g}^t = \pm 1^t \otimes \mathbf{g}^t.$$

Using this trapdoor, it randomly samples a Gaussian-distributed integral preimage $\mathbf{s}$ for which $\mathbf{C}_{f,x} \cdot \mathbf{s} = \mathbf{u}$, and outputs $\mathbf{s}$ as the proof.
- The Verify algorithm reconstructs $\mathbf{C}_{f,x}$ using y as the purported value of $f(x)$, and checks that $\mathbf{s}$ is sufficiently short and that $\mathbf{C}_{f,x} \cdot \mathbf{s} = \mathbf{u}$.

Zero Knowledge and Target Binding. The modified scheme has zero-knowledge commitments and proofs: function hiding ensures that $\mathbf{C}_f$ reveals nothing about f (formally, a simulator can return a random "dummy" commitment $\mathbf{C}_f$ instead), while Gaussian preimage sampling ensures that proofs reveal nothing beyond the input-output pairs (formally, a simulator can embed a trapdoor in $\mathbf{C}$ that lets it sample from the desired distribution for any $x, f(x)$; for this it is convenient for x to have one "dummy" coordinate that never changes).

The scheme satisfies *target* evaluation binding (see Remark 1) under a suitable SIS assumption. In brief, the reduction is given a random SIS challenge $\mathbf{A} \in \mathbb{Z}_q^{n \times W}$. It gets x^* from the adversary, and supplies public parameter $\mathbf{C} = \mathbf{A} + (x^*)^t \otimes \mathbf{g}^t = \mathbf{A}$ and $\mathbf{u} = \mathbf{A}\mathbf{r}$ for a (secret) uniformly random $\mathbf{r} \leftarrow \{0, 1\}^W$. It then gets a function f^* from the adversary, and supplies an honestly generated commitment $\mathbf{C}_{f^*}$ (and its underlying randomness); it also computes the associated short multiplier matrix $\mathbf{S}_{f^*, x^*}$ that satisfies Eq. (6). Finally, the adversary (if successful) outputs a sufficiently short proof $\mathbf{s}^*$ for $y^* = 1 - f^*(x^*)$, which satisfies

$$[\mathbf{C} - (x^*)^t \otimes \mathbf{g}^t \mid \mathbf{C}_{f^*} - f^*(x^*)^t \otimes \mathbf{g}^t] \cdot \mathbf{s}^* = [\mathbf{A} \mid \mathbf{A}\mathbf{S}_{f^*, x^*}] \cdot \mathbf{s}^* = \mathbf{u}.$$

Hence $\mathbf{A}([\mathbf{I}_W \mid \mathbf{S}_{f^*, x^*}]\mathbf{s}^* - \mathbf{r}) = \mathbf{0}$, yielding an SIS solution—which is nonzero with high probability, since $\mathbf{r}$ has large min-entropy in the adversary's view.

4 Concrete Instantiations

In this section we present and analyze several important instantiations of our functional commitment scheme from Sect. 3.2. These include commitments to functions of *bounded support* (Sect. 4.1), which encompass vector commitments

(Sect. 4.1), and accumulators (Sect. 4.1); *polynomial commitments* (Sect. 4.2); and commitments to data with openings that reveal functions thereof (Sect. 4.3).

Each instantiation of is obtained by (1) defining an appropriate function family that captures the desired functionality, (2) showing how to efficiently implement it homomorphically using Theorem 1, and (3) analyzing the resulting norm bounds to set the verification threshold κ appropriately (to ensure correctness). Moreover, for all the special-purpose function families, we show how to implement updates via simple compositions, which means the corresponding commitment schemes are statelessly updateable. Finally, we show that the forms of certain function families enable certain optimizations in their corresponding functional commitment schemes.

At a high level, all of our instantiations for specific kinds of functionalities follow a common template. We first identify a (potentially huge) set of "basis" functions, and show how to express the desired functions relatively simply in terms of this basis, e.g., as linear or low-degree combinations. Plugging this into Construction 2 (and using its composition properties) then yields a functional commitment scheme for all functions that have "bounded weight" in terms of the basis. The scheme's running time and associated norm bound is therefore determined mainly by the complexity of the basis functions. Moreover, if there are not too many basis functions (or function inputs), then their commitments (and proofs) can be precomputed, so that the "online" running time is determined by the (low) complexity of the combining operation(s).

4.1 Bounded-Support Commitments

Here we instantiate our general functional commitment scheme (Construction 2) for the general class of functions having *bounded support* over a potentially huge domain. As we show below, vector commitments, accumulators, and a generalization of both called *key-value* commitments [BBF19] can be expressed as special cases of bounded-support commitments. Moreover, all these schemes are statelessly updateable, via composition.

Representing Bounded-Support Functions. Let $f: \mathcal{X} \to \mathcal{Y}$ be a function for some finite $\mathcal{X}, \mathcal{Y}$, where $\mathcal{Y}$ is without loss of generality an additive group with identity element denoted 0, and let $\mathrm{supp}(f) := \{x \in \mathcal{X} : f(x) \neq 0\} \subseteq \mathcal{X}$ denote the support of f. For each $\bar{x} \in \mathcal{X}$, define the "point function" $\mathsf{Eq}_{\bar{x}}: \mathcal{X} \to \{0,1\}$ as

$$\mathsf{Eq}_{\bar{x}}(x) = \begin{cases} 1 & \text{if } x = \bar{x} \\ 0 & \text{otherwise.} \end{cases} \tag{7}$$

Then f can be expressed as a linear combination of the $\mathsf{Eq}_{\bar{x}}$ functions, as

$$f(x) = \sum_{\bar{x} \in \mathcal{X}} \mathsf{Eq}_{\bar{x}}(x) \cdot f(\bar{x}) = \sum_{\bar{x} \in S := \mathrm{supp}(f)} \mathsf{Eq}_{\bar{x}}(x) \cdot f(\bar{x}) = L_{f_S}(\overrightarrow{\mathsf{Eq}}_S(x)), \tag{8}$$

where $\overrightarrow{\mathsf{Eq}}_S(x), f_S$ are respectively the vectors of $\mathsf{Eq}_{\bar{x}}(x), f(\bar{x})$ over all $\bar{x} \in S$, and $L_{f_S}: \{0,1\}^{|S|} \to \mathcal{Y}$ is the linear function that outputs the inner product of its argument with f_S. In summary, we have expressed f as the composition of $\overrightarrow{\mathsf{Eq}}_S$ and L_{f_S}.

Therefore, by the linear homomorphisms given in Sect. 3.1 and the composition properties of the generic functional commitment scheme (see Sect. 3.2), we immediately have the following. (A norm bound $\kappa_{\mathsf{Eq}_\mathcal{X}}$ is derived below.) Similar correctness lemmas can easily be obtained for richer forms of updates (e.g., post-processing of function outputs), with corresponding norm bounds κ.

Lemma 2. *Let $\kappa_{\mathsf{Eq}_\mathcal{X}}$ be a norm bound for which the functional commitment scheme from Construction 2 is correct for function family $\mathcal{F}_{\mathsf{Eq}_\mathcal{X}}$. Then for any $\mathcal{Y} = \mathbb{Z}_q^{n \times d}$, any $s \geq 1$, and any $\kappa \geq s \cdot w \cdot \kappa_{\mathsf{Eq}_\mathcal{X}}$, Construction 2 is a correct functional commitment scheme for any sum of functions $\mathcal{X} \to \mathcal{Y}$ whose total support size is at most s. The same also holds for $\mathcal{Y} = \{0, 1\}$, with the tighter bound $\kappa \geq s \cdot \kappa_{\mathsf{Eq}_\mathcal{X}}$.*

Remark 5 (Optimizations). Note that $\overrightarrow{\mathsf{Eq}}_S$ depends only on the *support* S of f (not its specific values), and L_{f_S} is linear. Together with composition properties of the functional commitment scheme (see Sect. 3.2), these properties allow us to commit to f with a running time, and norm bound, proportional to its support size $|S|$. Moreover, they enable some substantial optimizations. First, if S (or a small enough superset thereof) is known before f itself, then the commitment to $\overrightarrow{\mathsf{Eq}}_S$ can be precomputed, making the "online" commitment to f just a relatively fast linear operation (see Sect. 3.1). Second, and similarly, if a subset $X \subseteq \mathcal{X}$ of potential opening inputs is known in advance, then the openings of $\overrightarrow{\mathsf{Eq}}_S(x)$ for all $x \in X$ can also be precomputed, yielding fast, linear "online" openings of f on these inputs. This precomputation can even be outsourced to an untrusted party, as long as the user verifies the precomputed proofs. Finally, and separately, for functions with binary or small-integer outputs, we can compress commitments and proofs as described in Sect. 3.2.

Instantiating $\mathcal{F}_{\mathsf{Eq}_\mathcal{X}}$. We now describe a particularly simple homomorphic implementation of the family $\mathcal{F}_{\mathsf{Eq}_\mathcal{X}}$, for which the short multiplier matrices satisfy a small polynomial norm bound.

Let $k \geq \lceil \log_2 |\mathcal{X}| \rceil$ be the length of an element of $\mathcal{X}$, represented as a bit string. Each function $\mathsf{Eq}_{\bar{x}} \colon \{0, 1\}^k \to \{0, 1\}$ for $\bar{x} \in \mathcal{X}$ can then be implemented (homomorphically) using bit operations, in the following way: on input $x \in \{0, 1\}^k$, for each $i \in [k]$ let $e_i = x_i$ if $\bar{x}_i = 1$ and $e_i = 1 - x_i$ if $\bar{x}_i = 0$; this represents whether x_i equals $\bar{x}_i$. Then output the product $\prod_{i \in [k]} e_i$. It is clear that this procedure correctly computes $\mathsf{Eq}_{\bar{x}}(x)$. Its homomorphic implementation consists of a fixed pattern of bit flips, which have no effect on the ultimate norm bound (because $\bar{x}$ is fixed, not an input to the function), followed by a homomorphic product of k bits. So, following Eq. (5), the ℓ_1 norm bound associated with the homomorphic evaluation of any member of $\mathcal{F}_{\mathsf{Eq}_\mathcal{X}}$ is

$$\kappa_{\mathsf{Eq}_\mathcal{X}} := (k - 1)w + 1 \leq kw. \tag{9}$$

We remark that the simultaneous (homomorphic) evaluation of *all* $\mathsf{Eq}_{\bar{x}} \in \mathcal{F}_{\mathsf{Eq}_{\mathcal{X}}}$ (i.e., the function $\overrightarrow{\mathsf{Eq}_{\mathcal{X}}}$) can be amortized to save about a $k/2$ factor in the number of (homomorphic) bit multiplications, versus the naïve evaluation of each function individually, which uses $(k-1) \cdot 2^k$ multiplications. On input x, for each $i \in [k]$ we prepare both possible values $x_i, 1 - x_i$ of the bit e_i. Then for $j = k-1, \ldots, 0$, we compute all 2^{k-j} possible partial products $\prod_{i>j} e_i$, by multiplying the previous step's 2^{k-j-1} partial products by the two possible values of e_j.[11] The total number of multiplications used by this method is $4+8+\cdots+2^k \approx 2^{k+1}$. A similar amortized improvement can be obtained for computing openings at all inputs $x \in \mathcal{X}$, for all the functions.

Discussion. It is instructive to consider the structure of the bounded-support scheme's main intermediate matrices, commitments, and proofs in more detail. As above, let k be the length of the bit-string representation of an element of $\mathcal{X}$. The public parameter is a uniformly random $\mathbf{C} \in \mathbb{Z}_q^{n \times kw}$, where recall that $w = n\ell = n\lceil \log_2 q \rceil$. For every $\bar{x} \in \mathcal{X}$, define the commitment $\mathbf{C}_{\bar{x}} = \mathsf{Commit}(\mathbf{C}, \mathsf{Eq}_{\bar{x}}) \in \mathbb{Z}_q^{n \times w}$; together these define the (potentially enormous) matrix $\mathbf{C}_{\mathcal{X}} = [\mathbf{C}_{\bar{x}}]_{\bar{x} \in \mathcal{X}} \in \mathbb{Z}_q^{n \times |\mathcal{X}|w}$. And for every $x, \bar{x} \in \mathcal{X}$, define the "short" proof[12] $\mathbf{S}_{x,\bar{x}} = \mathsf{Open}(\mathbf{C}, \mathsf{Eq}_{\bar{x}}, x) \in \mathbb{Z}^{kw \times w}$, which satisfies

$$(\mathbf{C} - x^t \otimes \mathbf{g}^t) \cdot \mathbf{S}_{x,\bar{x}} = \mathbf{C}_{\bar{x}} - \mathsf{Eq}_{\bar{x}}(x) \otimes \mathbf{I}_n \otimes \mathbf{g}^t.$$

All this can be represented concisely by the single matrix equation

$$\left((\mathbf{I}_{|\mathcal{X}|} \otimes \mathbf{C}) - \mathrm{diag}(x^t \otimes \mathbf{g}^t)_{x \in \mathcal{X}} \right) \cdot (\mathbf{S}_{x,\bar{x}})_{x,\bar{x} \in \mathcal{X}} = (1_{|\mathcal{X}|} \otimes \mathbf{C}_{\mathcal{X}}) - \mathbf{I}_{|\mathcal{X}|} \otimes \mathbf{I}_n \otimes \mathbf{g}^t. \tag{10}$$

As discussed above in Remark 5, any of the matrices $\mathbf{C}_{\bar{x}}, \mathbf{S}_{x,\bar{x}}$ can be precomputed (and verified) in advance, or they can be computed as needed. One can view them as "structured" public parameters for the "online" phase of commitment that depends on the function f.

Now, for a function $f : \mathcal{X} \to \mathcal{Y}$, let $\boldsymbol{f} = (f(\bar{x}))_{\bar{x} \in \mathcal{X}} \in \mathcal{Y}^{|\mathcal{X}|}$ be its "value vector," whose matrix representation is some $\mathbf{F} \in (\mathbb{Z}_q^{n \times n})^{|\mathcal{X}|} = \mathbb{Z}_q^{|\mathcal{X}|n \times n}$. The commitment to f is simply $\mathbf{C}_f = \mathbf{C}_{\mathcal{X}} \cdot \mathbf{S}_{\times \mathbf{F}}$ for the "short" matrix $\mathbf{S}_{\times \mathbf{F}} = \mathbf{g}^{-1}(\mathbf{F} \otimes \mathbf{g}^t) \in \mathbb{Z}^{|\mathcal{X}|w \times w}$ (see Sect. 3.1). Naturally, any blocks of $\mathbf{C}_{\mathcal{X}}$ corresponding to zero outputs of f can be skipped, because the corresponding blocks of $\mathbf{S}_{\times \mathbf{F}}$ are zero; this enables computing $\mathbf{C}_f$ in time roughly proportional to $|\mathrm{supp}(f)|$. Notice that multiplying the right-hand side of Eq. (10) by $\mathbf{S}_{\times \mathbf{F}}$ yields $1_{|\mathcal{X}|} \otimes \mathbf{C}_f - \mathbf{F} \otimes \mathbf{g}^t$, i.e., the xth block is $\mathbf{C}_f$ minus the xth block of $\mathbf{F} \otimes \mathbf{g}^t$, i.e., the robust matrix encoding of $f(x)$. Similarly, the (row) blocks of $(\mathbf{S}_{x,\bar{x}}) \cdot \mathbf{S}_{\times \mathbf{F}}$ are proofs for all inputs $x \in \mathcal{X}$. To verify for a particular x, one just checks these xth blocks against each other using the xth row of the matrix at the left of Eq. (10), which is possible because that matrix is block diagonal.

---

[11] We use decreasing j here simply for consistency with the notation in Sect. 3.1, but any order can work.

[12] For convenience of matrix operations, we have swapped the indices of $\mathbf{S}_{x,\bar{x}}$ from the usual $\mathbf{S}_{f,x}$ form.

Key-Value Commitments. A *key-value map* for a key space $\mathcal{X}$ and a value space $\mathcal{Y}$ is a set of pairs in $\mathcal{X} \times \mathcal{Y}$ whose first entries are mutually distinct, i.e., each key in $\mathcal{X}$ has at most one associated value in $\mathcal{Y}$. In a key-value commitment scheme, a user first commits (concisely) to such a map. Later, the user can (concisely) prove that a given pair $(k, v) \in \mathcal{X} \times \mathcal{Y}$ is in the committed map. The key-binding property says that it is infeasible to prove two different values $v \neq v'$ for the same key. Stateless updateability means that, without needing to know the current contents of the map, the user can add, remove, or change key-value pairs, along with any existing proofs.

Instantiation. We obtain key-value commitments as a special case of bounded-support commitments. We simply represent any key-value map over $\mathcal{X} \times \mathcal{Y}$ as a function $f \colon \mathcal{X} \to \mathcal{Y}$ (and vice-versa) in the natural way, i.e., $f(x) = y$ for each key-value pair (x, y) in the map, and $f(x') = 0$ for all keys $x' \in \mathcal{X}$ that do not have an associated value.[13] Clearly, the support size of f is the number of entries in the map.

We can update (the function representing) a key-value map simply by composing with a suitable update map (function). For example, to insert a key-value pair (k, v) when k does not already have an associated value, or to add v to the existing value for k, we simply add the update function $\delta_{k,v}(x) := v \cdot \mathsf{Eq}_k(x)$. To delete (k, v) from the map, we subtract $\delta_{k,v}(x)$.[14] By Lemma 2, this instantiation works for any initial map and sequence of updates having a bounded total number of keys (with multiplicity). In addition, using the composition properties of the functional commitment scheme, we can perform other kinds of updates on the map, like arbitrary post-processing of its values.

Vector Commitments. A vector commitment scheme for d-dimensional vectors over a message space $\mathcal{M}$ is merely a special case of key-value commitment, where $\mathcal{X} = [d]$ and $\mathcal{Y} = \mathcal{M}$. That is, a vector $\mathbf{m} \subset \mathcal{M}^d$ corresponds to a key-value map consisting of the pairs (i, m_i) for all $i \in [d]$. (Equivalently, the vector $\mathbf{m}$ corresponds to the function $f_{\mathbf{m}} \colon \mathcal{X} \to \mathcal{Y}$ defined as $f_{\mathbf{m}}(i) = m_i$.) Clearly, the support size of any vector is at most the domain size d. As a special case of key-value commitments, the vector commitment scheme supports all the same stateless update operations on the vector entries. Finally, because the index i

---

[13] Note that this makes 0 the implicit 'default' value for all such keys. If we wish to have a distinguished 'undefined' value $\perp$ for such keys, we can replace $\mathcal{Y}$ with a larger group like $\mathcal{Y}' = \mathcal{Y} \times C$ for some nontrivial cycle C, representing each $y \in \mathcal{Y}$ by $(y, 1) \in \mathcal{Y}'$, and letting $\perp$ be represented by the identity element $(0, 0) \in \mathcal{Y}'$. Note that this encoding requires some care regarding updates, because, for example, representing $y - y = 0$ by $(y, 1) - (y, 1) = (0, 0)$ yields $\perp$, not the encoding of $0 \in \mathcal{Y}$. A simple solution is for all insertions and deletions to use 1s in their second components, and for all modifications of existing values to use 0s.

[14] See Footnote 13 for how insertions/deletions can be handled separately from additions/subtractions, when using an encoding that has a distinguished 'undefined' value $\perp$ that is separate from 0.

corresponds to the key, (selective) key binding is equivalent to (selective) position binding for vector commitments, i.e., it should be infeasible to open a vector commitment to two different values at the same index i.

Precomputation. In vector commitments, the domain size $d = |\mathcal{X}|$ is typically considered to be polynomially bounded, so both optimizations described in Remark 5 apply. Specifically, the commitment to $\overrightarrow{\mathsf{Eq}}_{[d]}$ and its openings at every $i \in [d]$ can be precomputed; moreover, this can even be outsourced, as described in Sect. 3.2. Then committing to a vector, and opening it an any position, is just a relatively fast linear combination of these precomputed values. The size of the precomputed data is proportional to $\tilde{O}(d^2)$, which is asymptotically about the same as several prior vector commitments, but here the setup is *untrusted*. The result is a special case of Eq. (10) with $\mathcal{X} = [d]$.

Comparison to Other SIS-Based Vector Commitments. We now briefly compare our vector commitment scheme to prior SIS-based ones [PSTY13, PPS21]. The public parameters for the "base" vector commitment scheme from [PPS21], for d-dimensional vectors of b-bit messages, consist of: uniformly random $\mathbf{C}_j \in \mathbb{Z}_q^{n \times b}$ for each $j \in [d]$, defining $\mathbf{C}_{[d]} = [\mathbf{C}_1 \mid \cdots \mid \mathbf{C}_d] \in \mathbb{Z}_q^{n \times bd}$; a single uniformly random $\mathbf{A} \in \mathbb{Z}_q^{n \times m}$ that for each $i \in [d]$ defines some $\mathbf{A}_i \in \mathbb{Z}_q^{n \times m}$; and for all $i \neq j$, a "short" random matrix $\mathbf{S}_{i,j} \in \mathbb{Z}^{m \times b}$ that satisfies $\mathbf{A}_i \cdot \mathbf{S}_{i,j} = \mathbf{C}_j$. Letting $\mathbf{S}_{i,i} = \mathbf{0}$ for all $i \in [d]$, all this can be represented concisely by the single matrix equation

$$\mathrm{diag}(\mathbf{A}_i)_{i \in [d]} \cdot (\mathbf{S}_{i,j})_{i,j \in [d]} = (\mathbf{1}_d \otimes \mathbf{C}_{[d]}) - \mathrm{diag}(\mathbf{C}_j)_{j \in [d]}. \qquad (11)$$

This has several similarities to Eq. (10), but generating these parameters requires a trusted setup that uses secret randomness (including discrete Gaussian sampling to generate the short $\mathbf{S}_{i,j}$), and the size of the parameters grows at least as d^2, which is prohibitive for even moderate dimensions. By contrast, our setup uses only public randomness, and the size of the public parameter grows only as $\mathrm{poly}(\log d)$. Commitments and proofs in [PPS21] are generated and verified very similarly to what is described following Eq. (10), exploiting the repeated structure of $\mathbf{1}_d \otimes \mathbf{C}_{[d]}$ and the block-diagonal structure of $\mathrm{diag}(\mathbf{A}_i)$.

Finally, the works of [PSTY13, PPS21] also describe specialized Merkle tree-like vector commitments that, unlike ordinary Merkle trees, are statelessly updateable. Asymptotically, our scheme matches or outperforms these in terms of commitment and proof sizes. Moreover, the verifiers from [PSTY13, PPS21] must check a separate short solution to a linear system for *each layer* of their trees, whereas our verifier checks a *single* short solution (of a correspondingly larger dimension). This is a moderate advantage when proving that verification accepts in zero knowledge or with a SNARG, because proving short solutions to linear relations is moderately expensive in these contexts.

Accumulators. A cryptographic *accumulator* [BdM93] is a scheme to concisely commit to a (polynomial-sized) subset of some (possibly huge) universe. This is another special case of key-value commitment, where $\mathcal{X}$ is taken to be the universe and $\mathcal{Y} = \{0, 1\}$. A subset $S \subseteq \mathcal{X}$ corresponds to a key-value map consisting of the pairs $(x, 1)$ for all $x \in S$. (Equivalently, the subset S corresponds to its indicator function $f_S \colon \mathcal{X} \to \{0, 1\}$, defined as $f_S(x) = 1$ if $x \in S$ and $f_S(x) = 0$ otherwise.) Clearly, the number of keys (i.e., support size) is the cardinality of the set. As a special case of key-value commitments, the accumulator supports stateless updates, so elements can be "dynamically" [CL02] added and removed from the committed set. Finally, because keys correspond to universe elements, (selective) key binding is equivalent to set-binding for the accumulator, i.e., it should be infeasible to prove that a value is both in, and not in, the committed set.

4.2   Polynomial Commitments

Here we show how polynomial commitments can be constructed as an instantiation of our general functional commitment scheme, via an analogous approach as for bounded-support commitments, and with similar efficiency and updateability properties. Specifically, we view a polynomial as the composition of a linear function (specified by the coefficients) and a vector of fixed non-linear functions, namely the powers of the input.

Let $\mathcal{R}$ be a finite commutative ring. For an integer $i \geq 0$, define $\mathsf{Pow}_i \colon \mathcal{R} \to \mathcal{R}$ as $\mathsf{Pow}_i(x) = x^i$, and for a positive integer d, define $\overrightarrow{\mathsf{Pow}}_d$ to be the vector of functions Pow_i over $i = 0, \ldots, d - 1$. For any $d \geq 1$ with $k = \lceil \log_2 d \rceil$, we can evaluate $\overrightarrow{\mathsf{Pow}}_d$ by evaluating $\overrightarrow{\mathsf{Pow}}_{2^k}$ recursively, using a depth-k tree of at most 2^k ring multiplications.

Univariate Polynomials. A univariate polynomial $f(x) = \sum_{i=0}^{d-1} f_i \cdot x^i$ of degree less than d over $\mathcal{R}$ can be expressed as the composition of $\overrightarrow{\mathsf{Pow}}_d$ and the $\mathcal{R}$-linear function $L_f(\cdot) :- \langle f, \cdot \rangle$ for the coefficient vector f of f, as

$$f(x) = L_f(\overrightarrow{\mathsf{Pow}}_d(x)).$$

Therefore, we can evaluate f by evaluating $\overrightarrow{\mathsf{Pow}}_d$ in multiplicative depth k, then multiplying the results component-wise with f, then adding the results via a depth-k binary tree of addition operations.[15]

By the composition properties of the generic functional commitment scheme (see Sect. 3.2), we immediately have the following basic, generic instantiation. Similar correctness lemmas can easily be obtained for richer forms of composition, like updating, adding, multiplying, or dividing polynomials. All of this also generalizes to "sparse" polynomials (i.e., ones with a bounded number of nonzero monomials) of potentially huge degree.

---

[15] More generally, the treatment is essentially the same for polynomials whose coefficients come from some $\mathcal{R}$-module.

Lemma 3. *Let $\kappa_{\mathsf{Mul}}, \kappa_{\mathsf{Add}}$ be norm bounds for which the functional commitment from Construction 2 is correct for the multiplication and addition operations in $\mathcal{R}$, respectively. Let $d \geq 1$ be a degree bound and $k = \lceil \log_2 d \rceil$. Then for any $\kappa \geq \kappa_{\mathsf{Mul}}^{k+1} \cdot \kappa_{\mathsf{Add}}^{k}$, Construction 2 is a correct polynomial commitment scheme for polynomials over $\mathcal{R}$ of degree less than d.*

For almost all concrete rings of interest, addition and multiplication are not "natively" supported by the homomorphic operations detailed in Sect. 3.1. Instead, ring operations typically need to be implemented via rich combinations of homomorphic operations on the bit representations of ring elements, and this complexity affects the norm bounds $\kappa_{\mathsf{Mul}}, \kappa_{\mathsf{Add}}$ (as well as the running times of committing and opening). However, for suitable rings like finite fields $\mathbb{F}_{p^{n'}}$, the linear function L_f *can* be implemented "natively" using just the linear homomorphisms from Sect. 3.1, because the coefficients of f are *known*. (See Remark 6 below for further details.)

Remark 6 (Optimizations). Similarly to bounded-support commitments (see Remark 5), the commitment to $\overrightarrow{\mathsf{Pow}}_d$ can be precomputed, making the "online" commitment to f more efficient. Similarly, if a subset $R \subset \mathcal{R}$ of potential opening inputs is known in advance, then the openings of $\overrightarrow{\mathsf{Pow}}_d$ for $x \in R$ can also be precomputed. However, note that this may not make the online computations linear, because ring addition and multiplication (with a known element) may not correspond to linear homomorphic operations.

For a ring that can be embedded into the matrix ring $\mathbb{Z}_q^{n \times n}$, we can further improve the complexity of the "online" phase of committing and opening, making them just *linear* operations, by "flattening" the Pow_i commitments to use the matrix representations of their outputs. This sacrifices the ability to do further *multiplicative* compositions on the powers—but linear combinations, like those needed to commit to a polynomial, are still supported (because the polynomial coefficients are known).

In brief: suppose that for homomorphic computation, the bit representation $\mathsf{bits}(x)$ of any ring element $x \in \mathcal{R}$ is such that each entry of its matrix representation $\mathbf{R} \in \mathbb{Z}_q^{n \times n}$ is some fixed $\mathbb{Z}_q$-linear function of $\mathsf{bits}(x)$. (If not, we can homomorphically convert to such a representation when it is needed.) Then there exists a matrix $\mathbf{M}$ over $\mathbb{Z}_q$ for which $(\mathsf{bits}(r)^t \otimes \mathbf{I}_n) \cdot \mathbf{M} = \mathbf{R}$. So, given a commitment to any function (e.g., Pow_i) that outputs the bit representation of a ring element, we can "flatten" it to a commitment of the same function, but whose output is represented (robustly) in the matrix ring $\mathbb{Z}_q^{n \times n}$. This is done simply by composing the commitment with the linear function given by $\mathbf{M} \otimes \mathbf{g}^t$, i.e., right-multiplying the commitment by the short matrix $\mathbf{S}_{\times \mathbf{M}} = \mathbf{g}^{-1}(\mathbf{M} \otimes \mathbf{g}^t)$.

Multivariate Polynomials. Multivariate polynomials can also be viewed as compositions of Pow functions and a linear function specified by the polynomial's coefficients.

Recall that the *individual degree* of a multivariate polynomial is the maximum degree of any single variable.[16] For a multivariate polynomial with m variables and individual degree less than d, the monomials can be indexed by $D = \{0, \ldots, d-1\}^m$, where each entry of the index is the exponent of the corresponding variable in the monomial. That is, the index $\mathbf{e} \in D$ corresponds to the monomial $\mathsf{Pow}_{\mathbf{e}}(x_1, \ldots, x_m) := x_1^{e_1} \cdots x_m^{e_m}$. Any polynomial $f \colon \mathcal{R}^m \to \mathcal{R}$ on m variables with individual degree less than d can be written as

$$f(x_1, \ldots, x_m) = \sum_{\mathbf{e} \in D} f_{\mathbf{e}} \prod_{i \in [m]} x_i^{e_i} = L_{f_S}(\overrightarrow{\mathsf{Pow}}_S(x_1, \ldots, x_m)),$$

where each coefficient $f_{\mathbf{e}} \in \mathcal{R}$ (many of which may be zero), where $S = \mathrm{supp}(f) := \{\mathbf{e} \in D \colon f_{\mathbf{e}} \neq 0\}$ is the *support* of f; $\boldsymbol{f}_S, \overrightarrow{\mathsf{Pow}}_S$ are the vectors of $f_{\mathbf{e}}, \mathsf{Pow}_{\mathbf{e}}$ over all $\mathbf{e} \in S$ (respectively); and $L_{f_S}(\cdot) := \langle \boldsymbol{f}_S, \cdot \rangle$.

We now discuss the computation of the commitment to $\overrightarrow{\mathsf{Pow}}_S$. By definition, each entry of $\overrightarrow{\mathsf{Pow}}_S$ can be written as the product of *univariate* Pow_i functions, i.e., it has the form $\prod_{i \in [m]} \mathsf{Pow}_{e_i}(x_i)$ for some $\mathbf{e} \in S$. So, we can compute a commitment to $\overrightarrow{\mathsf{Pow}}_S$ by multiplicatively composing commitments to the components of $\overrightarrow{\mathsf{Pow}}_d$. Interestingly, we only need to compute commitments to each $\mathsf{Pow}_{\mathbf{e}}$ *up to permutation*, i.e., we can use the same commitment for any $\mathbf{e}'$ that is a permutation of $\mathbf{e}$. This is simply because upon opening, we can permute the input values appropriately.

4.3   Functional Commitments for Bounded Boolean Functions

In this section, we describe how to commit to *input* data and then open to various *functions* of it. This is the notion of functional commitment originally put forth in [LRY16] and also considered in [PPS21]. The core technique is the standard one of swapping "code" and "data" using a universal evaluator. Let $\mathcal{C} := \{C \colon \mathcal{X} \to \mathcal{Y}\}$ be the family of circuits of depth at most D, and let $U \colon \mathcal{C} \times \mathcal{X} \to \mathcal{Y}$ be a depth-universal circuit for this family, for which $U(C, x) = C(x)$; there exists such a circuit of depth $O(D')$ [CH85]. Define $U_x(\cdot) := U(\cdot, x)$. To commit to an input $x \in \mathcal{X}$, use Construction 2 to commit to the function U_x. We can then open the commitment for a circuit C (implementing a desired function f) in the usual way, by treating C as the input to the committed function. Following Theorem 1, we can use a suitable $\kappa = O(w)^{O(D)}$ for the verification norm bound.

For (constant-width) branching programs of size at most S, we proceed similarly. We first obtain a universal branching program for programs of this size, by applying Barrington's theorem [Bar86] to a certain universal circuit $C_{BP}(B, x)$ that evaluates a given size-S branching program B on a given input x. It can be constructed to have depth $D' = O(\log S)$, because B can be evaluated using

---

[16] Our treatment also adapts straightforwardly to polynomials of bounded *total* degree. We use individual degree because it follows more naturally from the univariate case.

a $\lceil \log_2 S \rceil$-depth tree of multiplications of (constant-dimensional) permutation matrices. Applying Barrington's theorem to C_{BP} then gives a (constant-width) universal branching program of size $4^{D'} = \text{poly}(S)$.

Define $C_x(\cdot) := C_{BP}(\cdot, x)$. To commit to an input x, we simply use Construction 2 to commit to the function C_x. We can then open the commitment for a size-S branching program B (implementing a desired function f) in the usual way, but treating B as the input to the committed function. Following Theorem 1, we can use a suitable $\kappa = w^{O(1)} \cdot \text{poly}(S)$ for the verification norm bound.

Acknowledgments. This material is based upon work supported by NSF Grant No. CCF-2006857 and by DARPA under Agreement No. HR00112020025. Any opinions, findings and conclusions or recommendations expressed in this material are those of the author(s) and do not necessarily reflect the views of the United States Government, the NSF, or DARPA.

References

[ACL+22] Albrecht, M.R., Cini, V., Lai, R.W.F., Malavolta, G., Thyagarajan, S.A.K.: Lattice-based SNARKs: publicly verifiable, preprocessing, and recursively composable. In: Dodis, Y., Shrimpton, T. (eds.) CRYPTO, vol. 13508, pp. 102–132. Springer, Heidelberg (2022). https://doi.org/10.1007/978-3-031-15979-4_4

[Ajt96] Ajtai, M.: Generating hard instances of lattice problems. Quaderni di Matematica **13**, 1–32 (2004). Preliminary version in STOC 1996

[AP14] Alperin-Sheriff, J., Peikert, C.: Faster bootstrapping with polynomial error. In: Garay, J.A., Gennaro, R. (eds.) CRYPTO 2014. LNCS, vol. 8616, pp. 297–314. Springer, Heidelberg (2014). https://doi.org/10.1007/978-3-662-44371-2_17

[AR20] Agrawal, S., Raghuraman, S.: KVaC: key-value commitments for blockchains and beyond. In: Moriai, S., Wang, H. (eds.) ASIACRYPT 2020. LNCS, vol. 12493, pp. 839–869. Springer, Cham (2020). https://doi.org/10.1007/978-3-030-64840-4_28

[Bar86] Barrington, D.A.M.: Bounded-width polynomial-size branching programs recognize exactly those languages in NC^1. J. Comput. Syst. Sci. **38**(1), 150–164 (1989). Preliminary version in STOC 1986

[BBB+18] Bünz, B., Bootle, J., Boneh, D., Poelstra, A., Wuille, P., Maxwell, G.: Bulletproofs: short proofs for confidential transactions and more. In: IEEE Symposium on Security and Privacy, pp. 315–334 (2018)

[BBC+18] Baum, C., Bootle, J., Cerulli, A., del Pino, R., Groth, J., Lyubashevsky, V.: Sub-linear lattice-based zero-knowledge arguments for arithmetic circuits. In: Shacham, H., Boldyreva, A. (eds.) CRYPTO 2018. LNCS, vol. 10992, pp. 669–699. Springer, Cham (2018). https://doi.org/10.1007/978-3-319-96881-0_23

[BBF19] Boneh, D., Bünz, B., Fisch, B.: Batching techniques for accumulators with applications to IOPs and stateless blockchains. In: Boldyreva, A., Micciancio, D. (eds.) CRYPTO 2019. LNCS, vol. 11692, pp. 561–586. Springer, Cham (2019). https://doi.org/10.1007/978-3-030-26948-7_20

[BC12]   Bitansky, N., Chiesa, A.: Succinct arguments from multi-prover interac-
         tive proofs and their efficiency benefits. In: Safavi-Naini, R., Canetti, R.
         (eds.) CRYPTO 2012. LNCS, vol. 7417, pp. 255–272. Springer, Heidelberg
         (2012). https://doi.org/10.1007/978-3-642-32009-5_16
[BCFL22] Balbás, D., Catalano, D., Fiore, D., Lai, R.W.F.: Functional commitments
         for circuits from falsifiable assumptions. Cryptology ePrint Archive, Paper
         2022/1365 (2022). https://eprint.iacr.org/2022/1365
[BDFG21] Boneh, D., Drake, J., Fisch, B., Gabizon, A.: Halo Infinite: proof-carrying
         data from additive polynomial commitments. In: Malkin, T., Peikert, C.
         (eds.) CRYPTO 2021. LNCS, vol. 12825, pp. 649–680. Springer, Cham
         (2021). https://doi.org/10.1007/978-3-030-84242-0_23
[BdM93] Benaloh, J., de Mare, M.: One-way accumulators: a decentralized alter-
         native to digital signatures. In: Helleseth, T. (ed.) EUROCRYPT 1993.
         LNCS, vol. 765, pp. 274–285. Springer, Heidelberg (1994). https://doi.
         org/10.1007/3-540-48285-7_24
[BFS20] Bünz, B., Fisch, B., Szepieniec, A.: Transparent SNARKs from DARK
         compilers. In: Canteaut, A., Ishai, Y. (eds.) EUROCRYPT 2020. LNCS,
         vol. 12105, pp. 677–706. Springer, Cham (2020). https://doi.org/10.1007/
         978-3-030-45721-1_24
[BGG+14] Boneh, D., et al.: Fully key-homomorphic encryption, arithmetic circuit
         ABE and compact garbled circuits. In: Nguyen, P.Q., Oswald, E. (eds.)
         EUROCRYPT 2014. LNCS, vol. 8441, pp. 533–556. Springer, Heidelberg
         (2014). https://doi.org/10.1007/978-3-642-55220-5_30
[BGV11] Benabbas, S., Gennaro, R., Vahlis, Y.: Verifiable delegation of computation
         over large datasets. In: Rogaway, P. (ed.) CRYPTO 2011. LNCS, vol. 6841,
         pp. 111–131. Springer, Heidelberg (2011). https://doi.org/10.1007/978-3-
         642-22792-9_7
[BLS19] Bootle, J., Lyubashevsky, V., Seiler, G.: Algebraic techniques for short(er)
         exact lattice-based zero-knowledge proofs. In: Boldyreva, A., Micciancio,
         D. (eds.) CRYPTO 2019. LNCS, vol. 11692, pp. 176–202. Springer, Cham
         (2019). https://doi.org/10.1007/978-3-030-26948-7_7
[BNO21] Boneh, D., Nguyen, W., Ozdemir, A.: Efficient functional commitments:
         How to commit to a private function. Cryptology ePrint Archive, Paper
         2021/1342 (2021). https://eprint.iacr.org/2021/1342
[BPMW16] Bourse, F., Del Pino, R., Minelli, M., Wee, H.: FHE circuit privacy almost
         for free. In: Robshaw, M., Katz, J. (eds.) CRYPTO 2016. LNCS, vol.
         9815, pp. 62–89. Springer, Heidelberg (2016). https://doi.org/10.1007/
         978-3-662-53008-5_3
[BV14]   Brakerski, Z., Vaikuntanathan, V.: Lattice-based FHE as secure as PKE.
         In: ITCS, pp. 1–12 (2014)
[CEO22] Campanelli, M., Engelmann, F., Orlandi, C.: Zero-knowledge for homo-
         morphic key-value commitments with applications to privacy-preserving
         ledgers. In: Galdi, C., Jarecki, S. (eds.) SCN, vol. 13409, pp. 761–784.
         Springer, Heidelberg (2022). https://doi.org/10.1007/978-3-031-14791-
         3_33
[CF13]   Catalano, D., Fiore, D.: Vector commitments and their applications. In:
         Kurosawa, K., Hanaoka, G. (eds.) PKC 2013. LNCS, vol. 7778, pp. 55–72.
         Springer, Heidelberg (2013). https://doi.org/10.1007/978-3-642-36362-7_5

[CFT22]   Catalano, D., Fiore, D., Tucker, I.: Additive-homomorphic functional commitments and applications to homomorphic signatures. In: Agrawal, S., Lin, D. (eds.) ASIACRYPT, vol. 13794, pp. 159–188. Springer, Heidelberg (2022). https://doi.org/10.1007/978-3-031-22972-5_6

[CGMA85] Chor, B., Goldwasser, S., Micali, S., Awerbuch, B.: Verifiable secret sharing and achieving simultaneity in the presence of faults (extended abstract). In: FOCS, pp. 383–395 (1985)

[CH85]   Cook, S.A., Hoover, H.J.: A depth-universal circuit. SIAM J. Comput. 14(4), 833–839 (1985)

[CJJ21]   Choudhuri, A.R., Jain, A., Jin, Z.: SNARGs for P from LWE. In: FOCS, pp. 68–79 (2021)

[CL02]   Camenisch, J., Lysyanskaya, A.: Dynamic accumulators and application to efficient revocation of anonymous credentials. In: Yung, M. (ed.) CRYPTO 2002. LNCS, vol. 2442, pp. 61–76. Springer, Heidelberg (2002). https://doi.org/10.1007/3-540-45708-9_5

[CPSZ18] Chepurnoy, A., Papamanthou, C., Srinivasan, S., Zhang, Y.: Edrax: a cryptocurrency with stateless transaction validation. Cryptology ePrint Archive, Report 2018/968 (2018). https://eprint.iacr.org/2018/968

[FS86]   Fiat, A., Shamir, A.: How to prove yourself: practical solutions to identification and signature problems. In: Odlyzko, A.M. (ed.) CRYPTO 1986. LNCS, vol. 263, pp. 186–194. Springer, Heidelberg (1987). https://doi.org/10.1007/3-540-47721-7_12

[GPV08]   Gentry, C., Peikert, C., Vaikuntanathan, V.: Trapdoors for hard lattices and new cryptographic constructions. In: STOC, pp. 197–206 (2008)

[GSW13]   Gentry, C., Sahai, A., Waters, B.: Homomorphic encryption from learning with errors: conceptually-simpler, asymptotically-faster, attribute-based. In: Canetti, R., Garay, J.A. (eds.) CRYPTO 2013. LNCS, vol. 8042, pp. 75–92. Springer, Heidelberg (2013). https://doi.org/10.1007/978-3-642-40041-4_5

[GSW23]   Ghosal, R., Sahai, A., Waters, B.: Non-interactive publicly-verifiable delegation of committed programs. In: PKC, pp. 1–42 (2023)

[GVW15a] Gorbunov, S., Vaikuntanathan, V., Wee, H.: Predicate encryption for circuits from LWE. In: Gennaro, R., Robshaw, M. (eds.) CRYPTO 2015. LNCS, vol. 9216, pp. 503–523. Springer, Heidelberg (2015). https://doi.org/10.1007/978-3-662-48000-7_25

[GVW15b] Gorbunov, S., Vaikuntanathan, V., Wichs, D.: Leveled fully homomorphic signatures from standard lattices. In STOC, pp. 469–477 (2015)

[GW11]   Gentry, C., Wichs, D.: Separating succinct non-interactive arguments from all falsifiable assumptions. In: STOC, pp. 99–108 (2011)

[IKO07]   Ishai, Y., Kushilevitz, E., Ostrovsky, R.: Efficient arguments without short PCPs. In: IEEE Conference on Computational Complexity, pp. 278–291 (2007)

[Kil92]   Kilian, J.: A note on efficient zero-knowledge proofs and arguments. In: STOC, pp. 723–732 (1992)

[KLVW23] Kalai, Y.T., Lombardi, A., Vaikuntanathan, V., Wichs, D.: Boosting batch arguments and RAM delegation. In: STOC, pp. 1–45 (2023)

[KPV22]   Kattis, A.A., Panarin, K., Vlasov, A.: RedShift: transparent SNARKs from list polynomial commitments. In: CCS, pp. 1725–1737 (2022)

[KZG10] Kate, A., Zaverucha, G.M., Goldberg, I.: Constant-size commitments to polynomials and their applications. In: Abe, M. (ed.) ASIACRYPT 2010. LNCS, vol. 6477, pp. 177–194. Springer, Heidelberg (2010). https://doi.org/10.1007/978-3-642-17373-8_11

[Lee21] Lee, J.: Dory: efficient, transparent arguments for generalised inner products and polynomial commitments. In: Nissim, K., Waters, B. (eds.) TCC 2021. LNCS, vol. 13043, pp. 1–34. Springer, Cham (2021). https://doi.org/10.1007/978-3-030-90453-1_1

[Lis05] Liskov, M.: Updatable zero-knowledge databases. In: Roy, B. (ed.) ASIACRYPT 2005. LNCS, vol. 3788, pp. 174–198. Springer, Heidelberg (2005). https://doi.org/10.1007/11593447_10

[LM06] Lyubashevsky, V., Micciancio, D.: Generalized compact knapsacks are collision resistant. ICALP 2, 144–155 (2006)

[LNP22] Lyubashevsky, V., Nguyen, N.K., Plançon, M.: Lattice-based zero-knowledge proofs and applications: Shorter, simpler, and more general. In: Dodis, Y., Shrimpton, T. (eds.) CRYPTO, vol. 13508, pp. 71–101. Springer, Heidelberg (2022). https://doi.org/10.1007/978-3-031-15979-4_3

[LP20] Lipmaa, H., Pavlyk, K.: Succinct functional commitment for a large class of arithmetic circuits. In: Moriai, S., Wang, H. (eds.) ASIACRYPT 2020. LNCS, vol. 12493, pp. 686–716. Springer, Cham (2020). https://doi.org/10.1007/978-3-030-64840-4_23

[LRY16] Libert, B., Ramanna, S.C., Yung, M.: Functional commitment schemes: from polynomial commitments to pairing-based accumulators from simple assumptions. In: ICALP, pp. 30:1–30:14 (2016)

[LY10] Libert, B., Yung, M.: Concise mercurial vector commitments and independent zero-knowledge sets with short proofs. In: Micciancio, D. (ed.) TCC 2010. LNCS, vol. 5978, pp. 499–517. Springer, Heidelberg (2010). https://doi.org/10.1007/978-3-642-11799-2_30

[Mic94] Micali, S.: CS proofs. In: FOCS, pp. 436–453 (1994)

[Mic02] Micciancio, D.: Generalized compact knapsacks, cyclic lattices, and efficient one-way functions. Comput. Complex. 16(4), 365–411 (2007). Preliminary version in FOCS 2002

[MP12] Micciancio, D., Peikert, C.: Trapdoors for lattices: simpler, tighter, faster, smaller. In: Pointcheval, D., Johansson, T. (eds.) EUROCRYPT 2012. LNCS, vol. 7237, pp. 700–718. Springer, Heidelberg (2012). https://doi.org/10.1007/978-3-642-29011-4_41

[MR04] Micciancio, D., Regev, O.: Worst-case to average-case reductions based on Gaussian measures. SIAM J. Comput. 37(1), 267–302 (2007). Preliminary version in FOCS 2004

[MRK03] Micali, S., Rabin, M.O., Kilian, J.: Zero-knowledge sets. In: FOCS, pp. 80–91 (2003)

[PPS21] Peikert, C., Pepin, Z., Sharp, C.: Vector and functional commitments from lattices. In: Nissim, K., Waters, B. (eds.) TCC 2021. LNCS, vol. 13044, pp. 480–511. Springer, Cham (2021). https://doi.org/10.1007/978-3-030-90456-2_16

[PR06] Peikert, C., Rosen, A.: Efficient collision-resistant hashing from worst-case assumptions on cyclic lattices. In: Halevi, S., Rabin, T. (eds.) TCC 2006. LNCS, vol. 3876, pp. 145–166. Springer, Heidelberg (2006). https://doi.org/10.1007/11681878_8

[PS19]   Peikert, C., Shiehian, S.: Noninteractive zero knowledge for NP from (plain) learning with errors. In: Boldyreva, A., Micciancio, D. (eds.) CRYPTO 2019. LNCS, vol. 11692, pp. 89–114. Springer, Cham (2019). https://doi.org/10.1007/978-3-030-26948-7_4

[PST13] Papamanthou, C., Shi, E., Tamassia, R.: Signatures of correct computation. In: Sahai, A. (ed.) TCC 2013. LNCS, vol. 7785, pp. 222–242. Springer, Heidelberg (2013). https://doi.org/10.1007/978-3-642-36594-2_13

[PSTY13] Papamanthou, C., Shi, E., Tamassia, R., Yi, K.: Streaming authenticated data structures. In: Johansson, T., Nguyen, P.Q. (eds.) EUROCRYPT 2013. LNCS, vol. 7881, pp. 353–370. Springer, Heidelberg (2013). https://doi.org/10.1007/978-3-642-38348-9_22

[Reg05] Regev, O.: On lattices, learning with errors, random linear codes, and cryptography. J. ACM **56**(6), 1–40 (2009). Preliminary version in STOC 2005

[SBZ01] Steinfeld, R., Bull, L., Zheng, Y.: Content extraction signatures. In: Kim, K. (ed.) ICISC 2001. LNCS, vol. 2288, pp. 285–304. Springer, Heidelberg (2002). https://doi.org/10.1007/3-540-45861-1_22

[VP19]   Vlasov, A., Panarin, K.: Transparent polynomial commitment scheme with polylogarithmic communication complexity. Cryptology ePrint Archive, Paper 2019/1020 (2019). https://eprint.iacr.org/2019/1020

[WW23]   Wee, H., Wu, D.: Succinct vector, polynomial, and functional commitments from lattices. In: EUROCRYPT, pp. 1–55 (2023)

Batch Bootstrapping I:
A New Framework for SIMD Bootstrapping in Polynomial Modulus

Feng-Hao Liu[1] and Han Wang[2,3(✉)]

[1] Florida Atlantic University, Boca Raton, FL, USA
liuf@fau.edu
[2] State Key Laboratory of Information Security, Institute of Information
Engineering, Chinese Academy of Science, Beijing, China
wanghan@iie.ac.cn
[3] School of Cyber Security, University of Chinese Academy of Science, Beijing, China

Abstract. In this series of work, we aim at improving the bootstrapping paradigm for fully homomorphic encryption (FHE). Our main goal is to show that the amortized cost of bootstrapping within a polynomial modulus only requires $\tilde{O}(1)$ FHE multiplications.

To achieve this, we develop substantial algebraic techniques in two papers. Particularly, the first one (this work) proposes a new mathematical framework for batch homomorphic computation that is compatible with the existing bootstrapping methods of AP14/FHEW/TFHE. To show that our overall method requires only a polynomial modulus, we develop a critical algebraic analysis over noise growth, which might be of independent interest. Overall, the framework yields an amortized complexity $\tilde{O}(\lambda^{0.75})$ FHE multiplications, where λ is the security parameter. This improves the prior methods of AP14/FHEW/TFHE, which required $O(\lambda)$ FHE multiplications in amortization.

Developing many substantial new techniques based on the foundation of this work, the sequel (*Bootstrapping II*, Eurocrypt 2023) shows how to further improve the recursive bootstrapping method of MS18 (Micciancio and Sorrell, ICALP 2018), yielding a substantial theoretical improvement that can potentially lead to more practical methods.

1 Introduction

Fully homomorphic encryption (FHE) allows arbitrary computation over ciphertexts without the need to first decrypt it. The concept was first proposed by [34] back to 1978, and soon numerous applications were noticed, albeit no plausible scheme was known. Thirty years later, Gentry [18] proposed the first plausible scheme that supports general homomorphic computation[1], inspiring many follow-up works, (see [36] for a comprehensive listing), with a wide array of optimizations and as well new applications, such as outsourcing computation, multiparty computation, and many others.

---

[1] Homomorphic computation refers to the ability to compute on ciphertexts (encrypted data). A fully homomorphic encryption supports general homomorphic computation, i.e., computation for any arbitrary function.

© International Association for Cryptologic Research 2023
C. Hazay and M. Stam (Eds.): EUROCRYPT 2023, LNCS 14006, pp. 321–352, 2023.
https://doi.org/10.1007/978-3-031-30620-4_11

FHE was initially considered as *theoretical only* as the homomorphic operations were prohibitively expensive. During the past years, many exciting new methods were proposed, e.g., [3,4,12,15,17,21], making substantial steps towards practical realizations. A particularly important progress is the improvement of Gentry's bootstrapping technique, which is currently the only known method to achieve *fully* homomorphic encryption. Originally bootstrapping was extremely impractical, yet after years of efforts, now we can achieve the task within sub-seconds (amortized), e.g., [15,21,28] by even a simple personal computing system. Thus, FHE with bootstrapping can be practical in some applications [21].

Limitations of Current Bootstrapping Techniques. Despite significant progress, there are some fundamental questions unanswered. Below we summarize the two main approaches in the state of the art, and then their deficiencies.

- Bootstrapping BGV. This line was used (and implemented) by the work [3, 19,21]. An advantage of this approach is the support of single instruction multiple data (SIMD) operations, and thus can achieve batch computation that bootstraps multiple ciphertexts per operation. However, the method inherently incurs a super-polynomial error, and thus would require a super-polynomial size modulus (e.g., concretely a 400-bit integer [21]), resulting in large bootstrapping keys and thus large storage to perform the homomorphic computation. Moreover, this would require a stronger assumption (i.e., a super-polynomial modulus-to-noise ratio) of the underlying (Ring)-LWE.
- The AP14/FHEW approach. Bootstrapping within a polynomial size modulus was first achieved by [9], and later improved by AP14 [4], and the ring variant FHEW [17] (with other novel optimizations). With further optimizations [6,13,15,23,28], now bootstrapping a single ciphertext can be computed within 100 ms, with significantly smaller bootstrapping key and memory (compared with the above approach). The methods in this line are modular and thus conceptually simpler, and moreover, can be used to bootstrap *all* currently known (Ring) LWE-based FHE schemes.

  However, all exiting practical methods (in the current libraries) can only bootstrap one single ciphertext per operation, and thus the amortized efficiency does not outperform the above. Particularly, the existing methods [4,6,13,15,17,23, 28] require $O(\lambda)$ FHE multiplications to bootstrap one single (LWE) ciphertext, where λ is the security parameter. Some later works [5,29] tried to mitigate this by new designs built on top of the FHEW, but their techniques have several inherent drawbacks, which limit their potential practicality.

  Specifically, the work [5] cannot batch the computation beyond a logarithmic number of ciphertexts. The work MS18 [29] can bootstrap λ (LWE) ciphertexts using roughly $O(3^{1/\epsilon}\lambda^{1+\epsilon})$ FHE multiplications, for any arbitrary constant $\epsilon > 0$, implying an amortized cost $O(3^{1/\epsilon}\lambda^{\epsilon})$ FHE multiplications per ciphertext. Theoretically, ϵ can be set close to 0, e.g., 0.01, at the cost of a large constant, e.g., 3^{100}, exceeding what can be considered as practical by a large margin. Thus, it is unclear whether MS18 [29] can lead to a practical solution that matches their best theoretical indication.

In this series of works, we aim to achieve *the best of both* by breaking the limitations as above. Our overall goal is to bootstrap λ (LWE) ciphertexts by using only $\tilde{O}(\lambda)$ FHE multiplications, meaning that the amortized cost of bootstrapping is essentially the same as that of the FHE multiplication, up to a factor of $\tilde{O}(1)$. Our goal is summarized by the following statement.

Main Goal. Bootstrapping within a polynomial modulus only requires $\tilde{O}(1)$ FHE multiplications in amortization, with a small hidden constant.

Note: the complexity of existing FHE multiplications in the ring settings (set to the same ring dimension) only differs by a (poly)-logarithmic factor, and thus it is without loss of generality to use the number of "FHE multiplications" as a clean measure of efficiency.

The outcome can consequently improve all the bootstrapping-based FHE for general computation, such as FHEW [17] and TFHE [13], and their applications. This would substantially advance the state of the art research.

1.1 Our Contributions

To achieve this, we present our new techniques in a series of two works – the first (*Batch Bootstrapping I*) focuses on the foundation, i.e., the establishment of a new mathematical framework and noise analysis for batch homomorphic computation. The new framework can improve the FHEW [17] and TFHE [13] bootstrapping methods by a factor of $O(\lambda^{0.25-o(1)})$, implying a new bootstrapping method of amortized cost equal to $\tilde{O}(\lambda^{0.75})$ FHE multiplications.

By using the framework of the first work as a solid foundation, the sequel (*Batch Bootstrapping II*) [24] further develops new critical methods to improve main components of the MS18 [29]. Jointly the two works achieve the main goal as stated above. Below we highlight the significant results of the first work, and then give a preview of the sequel for curious readers.

Significant Results of Bootstrapping I (This Work).

- First, we propose a new algebraic framework that naturally supports the batch homomorphic operations of the AP14/FHEW-like frameworks, e.g., FHEW and TFHE.
- Our next contribution is a new and refined algebraic analysis of the noise growth incurred in our new batch framework. We notice that using the existing existing analysis directly on our framework would result in a super-polynomial noise growth. Thus, our refined analysis is a necessary key to achieve batch bootstrapping within a polynomial modulus.
- Quantitatively, our batch framework allows an explicit batch bootstrapping on FHEW/TFHE with $O(\lambda^{1/4-o(1)})$ slots, where λ denotes the security parameter. This means that we can bootstrap λ (LWE) ciphertexts using $\tilde{O}(\lambda^{1.75})$ FHE multiplications, resulting in the following informal theorem.

Theorem 1.1 (Main Result of this Work, Informal). *Bootstrapping within a polynomial modulus requires $\tilde{O}(\lambda^{0.75})$ FHE multiplications in amortization.*

This result can improve the prior methods of AP14, FHEW and TFHE, which required $O(\lambda)$ FHE multiplications in amortization. We notice that in this series of work (i.e., AP14/FHEW/TFHE), the bootstrapping algorithm only requires workspace for computation (excluding the input and bootstrapping key) roughly $O(1)$ FHE ciphertexts. Thus, our framework yields the first non-trivial batch bootstrapping method that only requires workspace $O(1)$ FHE ciphertexts.

If we allow more workspace (e.g., $O(\lambda)$ FHE ciphertexts) for computation, then the MS18 [29] method provides a more asymptotically efficient bootstrapping, with amortized cost $O(3^{1/\epsilon}\lambda^\epsilon)$ FHE multiplications. As argued however, there is an inherent barrier for a practical realization that matches the best theoretical indication, as it would require to set ϵ close to 0, implying a prohibitively large constant. It is our next target to get rid of the dependency of ϵ in MS18.

A Preview of Bootstrapping II. In our next work [24], we show how to use our batch framework as a key ingredient to improve the MS18 method [29]. Particularly, we apply the technical foundation in this work (along with many new ideas) to the homomorphic Discrete Fourier Transform (DFT) paradigm developed by MS18. The foundation of this work is the crux to achieve our main goal. More details can be found in the sequel [24].

We believe that the new algebraic framework and noise analysis in this work are both important and might find further optimizations and applications. Thus, the foundation can be valuable and deserve its independent merits.

1.2 Technical Overview

Now we present an overview of our new techniques. We first recall the task of bootstrapping and the framework of AP14/FHEW [4,17] and later work TFHE [13,15], who designed an explicit bootstrapping method within a polynomial modulus. Then we discuss why it is inherently incompatible with existing batch computation. Finally, we present our new insights to break the barriers.

Backgrounds and Challenges

Bootstrapping. When we perform homomorphic operations from existing FHE schemes, the noise in the resulting ciphertext would grow with the number of operation, eventually becoming too big for correct decryption. To proceed homomorphic computation, Gentry [18] invented the bootstrapping technique that *refreshes* the noise. Currently, this is the only way to achieve *fully* homomorphic encryption which supports an arbitrary (polynomial) number of operations.

Briefly speaking, the task can be achieved as follow. Given an input ciphertext that encrypts m (i.e., ct, which might contain a large noise) and some evaluation key evk (i.e., some FHE encryption of the secret key Enc(sk)), the goal is to homomorphically compute the decryption function, i.e., $\mathsf{Enc}(\mathsf{Dec}(\mathsf{sk}, \mathsf{ct}))^2$, which by correctness would yield an encryption of m. Suppose the homomorphic decryption only incurs a small noise, then we have achieved the task.

Bootstrapping within a polynomial modulus was first achieved by [9]. However, the method requires to use the Barrington Theorem to convert an NC1 circuit into a polynomial length branching program, and thus does not give an efficient explicit construction. A subsequent work [4] presented the first explicit construction by using the idea of symmetric group, and FHEW [17] showed how to optimize the approach in the ring setting, extending the prior idea to a group of roots of unity. Later on, TFHE [13,15] followed this idea and provided further optimizations, e.g., CMUX, external products, and computation over torus.

As mentioned in [28] that FHEW and TFHE are conceptually the same in the core bootstrapping procedure (with different optimizations and implementation techniques), we refer this approach as the name of the earlier work, i.e., AP14/FHEW framework. This framework in our view, gives a conceptually simple and modular approach. Below we present the high level idea.

The AP14/FHEW Framework. The framework takes input an LWE ciphertext $\mathsf{ct} = (b, a)$ that encrypts m and an evaluation key $\mathsf{evk} = \{\mathsf{BK}_i\}$ where each BK_i is a Ring-GSW ciphertext that encrypts the i-th bit of the secret. Let n, q be the LWE dimension and modulus, N, Q be the Ring-GSW dimension and modulus. Without loss of generality, n, q can be set to small quantities, e.g., $n = O(\lambda)$ and $q = \tilde{O}(\sqrt{n})$, via the dimension reduction and modulus switch [4].[3] We emphasize that $q = \tilde{O}(\sqrt{n})$ is an important setting of parameter. The reader should keep this in mind, and we will further elaborate. Moreover, we notice that the LWE ciphertext has the following structure: $b = sa + e + q/2 \cdot m$, where $m \in \{0, 1\}$ is the message, s is the secret key, and e is some perhaps non-small error. Here we do not need to worry about their actual space, and this presentation is sufficient to illustrate the core idea.

The decryption function can be done in two steps: (1) compute $m' = b - sa \bmod q$, and (2) output $\mathsf{Round}(m')$ for some appropriate rounding function. This function can be computed by a low-depth function, i.e., NC1, but the question is how to compute it *efficiently* with an explicit procedure. And this is the insight of the AP14/FHEW framework as we present next.

Briefly, the approach identifies that the homomorphic decryption should use computation over the root of unity of cyclotomic rings. More specifically, let us consider a commonly used cyclotomic ring R of degree N of a power of 2. In this case, we can think of R as the polynomial ring $R = \mathbb{Z}[X]/(X^N + 1)$, satisfying $X^{2N} = 1$. Suppose $q | N$, $Y = X^{2N/q}$, and one can homomorphically compute *on the exponent* for the first step of linear operation of the

---

[2] More precisely, the computation should be denoted as $\mathsf{Eval}(\mathsf{Dec}(\mathsf{ct}, \cdot), \mathsf{Enc}(\mathsf{sk}))$. By correctness, the output ciphertext should belong to $\mathsf{Enc}(m)$, though perhaps distributed differently from a fresh ciphertext.

[3] The work [4] sets $q = \tilde{O}(\lambda)$. If we use a randomized rounding for the modulus switch, q can be further reduced to $\tilde{O}(\sqrt{n}) = \tilde{O}(\sqrt{\lambda})$.

decryption, i.e., obtain $\mathsf{Enc}(Y^{m'})$ where $m' = b - as$. Then we will have $Y^{m'} = Y^{m' \bmod q}$, as $\{1, Y, Y^2, \ldots, Y^{q-1}\}$ forms a multiplicative (sub)-group of $\{1, X, X^2, \ldots, X^{2N-1}\}$. Then a very simple and efficient extraction procedure can be derived from the work [1,13], computing $\mathsf{Enc}(f(m'))$ given input $\mathsf{Enc}(Y^{m'})$ for *any arbitrary* $f : \mathbb{Z}_q \rightarrow \{0, 1\}$, which includes the non-linear Round function of the decryption procedure. These two insights yield a very efficient bootstrapping that outputs a ciphertext encrypting a single-bit.

Challenge for Batch Computation. As we discuss next, the AP14/FHEW framework is however not compatible with existing batch computation techniques, which heavily rely on the Chinese Remainder Theorem (CRT) decomposition. Roughly speaking, the CRT-based batch method supports computation over some ring R_t that is isomorphic to $\mathbb{Z}_t \times \mathbb{Z}_t \times \cdots \times \mathbb{Z}_t$ for properly chosen modulus t. In this way, we can pack N bits into these N slots, and multiplications and additions over R_t correspond to the component-wise operations over the N slots. This can be used to batch bootstrapping by expressing the decryption function as a boolean circuit as used in prior work [3,21], though the method would incur a super-polynomial noise growth. On the other hand, the CRT slots are intrinsically different from the cyclotomic structure and thus cannot support the AP14/FHEW framework. This is the current major technical barrier.

Our New Techniques. As discussed, to support batch computation over the AP14/FHEW framework, the scheme must support batch homomorphic computation over the subgroup $\{1, Y, Y^2, \ldots, Y^{q-1}\}$. As a high level, we need a math structure that allows the following packing mechanism: let $\boldsymbol{x} = (x_1, \ldots, x_r)$ and $\boldsymbol{y} = (y_1, \ldots, y_r)$ where each vector component resides in a space containing the cyclotomic subgroup. The packing mechanism can pack $\boldsymbol{x}, \boldsymbol{y}$ into some x, y (in some appropriately designed space) such that $x + y$ corresponds to $\boldsymbol{x} + \boldsymbol{y}$, and $x \bullet y$ (for some operation $\bullet$) corresponds to $\boldsymbol{x} \odot \boldsymbol{y}$, where $\odot$ denotes the component-wise multiplication. This mechanism can then be used to perform the AP14/FHEW bootstrapping in a batch way.

To achieve this, this work proposes a new algebraic framework and refined homomorphic methods/analyses for efficient implementations. Particularly, we first describe our new design of for batch computation over the plaintexts, and then show how to do homomorphic computation with a small noise growth. We will point out multiple technical subtleties and challenges, so a straight-forward adoption of the existing noise analysis would not give a satisfactory solution. Our new analytical insights serve as the critical key.

New Batch Plaintext Computation. So now we present our new insights of a new math structure that supports the above property, by using tensor rings in a novel way. To illustrate our ideas, we first present some insightful yet failed attempts that gradually lead to our final construction.

<u>Attempt 1.</u> Let $\mathcal{R}_1 = \mathbb{Z}_q[X]/(X^q + 1)$ be the cyclotomic ring[4], which clearly contains the required subgroup, and $\mathcal{R}_2$ be some linearly disjoint ring with basis $\mathbf{B} = (\mathsf{v}_1, \mathsf{v}_2, \ldots, \mathsf{v}_\rho)$. Then we consider the tensor ring $\mathcal{R} = \mathcal{R}_1 \otimes \mathcal{R}_2$. Intuitively for $r \leq \rho$, we can pack $\boldsymbol{x} = (x_1, \ldots, x_r) \in \mathcal{R}_1^r$ as $x = \sum x_i \mathsf{v}_i$, i.e., each element is put on one basis, and similarly, $\boldsymbol{y} = (y_1, \ldots, y_r) \in \mathcal{R}_1^r$ to $y = \sum y_i \mathsf{v}_i$. Clearly, $x + y$ corresponds $\boldsymbol{x} + \boldsymbol{y}$, but the ring multiplication, i.e., $x \cdot y \in \mathcal{R}_1 \otimes \mathcal{R}_2$, does not correspond to the component-wise multiplication $\boldsymbol{x} \odot \boldsymbol{y}$. This is because there are a lot of uncanceled cross terms $\mathsf{v}_i \cdot \mathsf{v}_j$ when we compute $x \cdot y$.

<u>Attempt 2.</u> To cancel the cross terms, we can use the *dual* basis with the trace function in the following way. Let $\mathcal{R}_2^\vee$ be the dual ring with basis $\mathbf{B}^\vee = (\mathsf{v}_1^\vee, \mathsf{v}_2^\vee, \ldots, \mathsf{v}_\rho^\vee)$, i.e., the dual basis of $\mathbf{B}$. Now we can pack $\boldsymbol{x}$ the same way, i.e., $x = \sum x_i \mathsf{v}_i$, but pack $\boldsymbol{y}$ in the dual space, i.e., $y = \sum y_i \mathsf{v}_i^\vee$. Even though $x \cdot y$ has a lot of cross terms, we notice that $\mathsf{Tr}_{\mathcal{R}/\mathbb{Q}}(x \cdot y) = \sum x_i y_i$, as $\mathsf{Tr}_{\mathcal{R}/\mathbb{Q}}(\mathsf{v}_i \mathsf{v}_j^\vee)$ acts as the Kronecker delta δ_{ij}, which is equal to 1 if $i = j$ or otherwise 0[5]. This method does cancel the cross terms, but it also mixes up the $x_i y_i$'s like the inner product. Thus, this attempt still does not achieve the goal.

<u>Attempt 3.</u> To further separate $x_i y_i$'s, we propose to use a third ring $\mathcal{R}_3$ with basis $\mathbf{W} = (\mathsf{w}_1, \mathsf{w}_2, \ldots, \mathsf{w}_\tau)$ for $\tau > r$. Then we consider the tensor ring $\mathcal{R} = \mathcal{R}_1 \otimes \mathcal{R}_2 \otimes \mathcal{R}_3$. In this setting, we still pack $\boldsymbol{x}$ in the same way, i.e., $x = \sum x_i \mathsf{v}_i$, but $\boldsymbol{y}$ in the space $\mathcal{R}_1 \otimes \mathcal{R}_2^\vee \otimes \mathcal{R}_3$ as $y = \sum y_i \mathsf{v}_i^\vee \mathsf{w}_i$. Interestingly, now we have $w' = \mathsf{Tr}_{\mathcal{R}/\mathcal{R}_1 \otimes \mathcal{R}_3}(xy) = \sum x_i y_i \mathsf{w}_i$, as the trace function (over $\mathcal{R}/\mathcal{R}_1 \otimes \mathcal{R}_3$) would act as δ_{ij} on the term $\mathsf{v}_i \mathsf{v}_j^\vee$ and as a constant function on elements in $\mathcal{R}_1 \otimes \mathcal{R}_3$. Thus, the resulting w' can be viewed as a packed plaintext of $\boldsymbol{x} \odot \boldsymbol{y}$ in $\mathcal{R}_1 \otimes \mathcal{R}_3$. Here a natural question raises – how do we proceed with the computation?

A naive way to achieve this is to introduce a fourth ring $\mathcal{R}_4$, and then pack the next vector, e.g., say $\boldsymbol{z} = (z_1, \ldots, z_r)$ as z in the space $\mathcal{R}_3^\vee \otimes \mathcal{R}_4$, and then compute $w'' = \mathsf{Tr}_{\mathcal{R}/\mathcal{R}_3 \otimes \mathcal{R}_4}(zw')$. However, this way would require to blow up the ring dimension linearly to the number of multiplications. This is clearly unsatisfactory and impractical even in theory.

<u>Final Idea.</u> To tackle the above drawback, we observe that the space can be reused so that the tensor product of three rings, e.g., $\mathcal{R} = \mathcal{R}_1 \otimes \mathcal{R}_2 \otimes \mathcal{R}_3$, is sufficient. Particularly, consider this example where we want to compute $\boldsymbol{x} \otimes \boldsymbol{y} \otimes \boldsymbol{z}$. We can pack $\boldsymbol{x}$ as $\sum x_i \mathsf{v}_i$ and $y = \sum y_i \mathsf{v}_i^\vee \mathsf{w}_i$. Then by using the trace computation, we obtain the intermediate result $w' = \sum x_i y_i \mathsf{w}_i$. Then we can pack $\boldsymbol{z}$ as $z = \sum z_i \mathsf{w}_i^\vee \mathsf{v}_i$, and then compute $w'' = \mathsf{Tr}_{\mathcal{R}/\mathcal{R}_1 \otimes \mathcal{R}_2}(w'z) = \sum x_i y_i z_i \mathsf{v}_i$. Now, w'' is the packed element of $\boldsymbol{x} \odot \boldsymbol{y} \odot \boldsymbol{z}$ in the space $\mathcal{R}_1 \otimes \mathcal{R}_2$. Thus, by alternating between the spaces $\mathcal{R}_1 \otimes \mathcal{R}_2$ and $\mathcal{R}_1 \otimes \mathcal{R}_3$, we can batch plaintext computation

---

[4] The cyclotomic polynomial would be of a different form if q is not a power of two. Here we use this setting for simplicity of exposition, but note that our framework works for general cyclotomic rings.

[5] We abuse the notation in the subscribe by using the rings for simplicity. Precisely, this should be $\mathsf{Tr}_{K/\mathbb{Q}}$ where K is the number field for which $\mathcal{R}$ is its ring of integers.

for any arbitrary number of steps, without further blowing up the ring dimension.

Instantiation. There can be various ways to instantiate the framework. The most intuitive one is to use the decomposability of cyclotomic rings. Particularly, let ξ_m be the m-th root of unity for $m = qpt$ for co-prime factors q, p, t. Then the cyclotomic ring $\mathbb{Z}[\xi_m]$ is isomorphic to the tensor of the three smaller and linearly disjoint cyclotomic rings, i.e., $\mathbb{Z}[\xi_m] \cong \mathbb{Z}[\xi_q] \otimes \mathbb{Z}[\xi_p] \otimes \mathbb{Z}[\xi_t]$. In this case, we can define sub-rings $\mathcal{R}_1, \mathcal{R}_2, \mathcal{R}_3$ as $\mathbb{Z}[\xi_q], \mathbb{Z}[\xi_p], \mathbb{Z}[\xi_t]$, respectively. We notice that the dimension of $\mathcal{R}$ would be $N = \phi(m)$, and the dimensions of the sub-rings would be $\phi(q)$, $\phi(p)$, $\phi(t)$, respectively, where ϕ is the Euler's phi function.

Homomorphic Computation over Batch Plaintexts. Next we present how to perform homomorphic computation over ciphertexts that encrypt the batch plaintexts as above. First we observe that the RGSW supports the computation naturally if we instantiate the scheme in the cyclotomic ring $\mathbb{Z}[\xi_m]$ as above. While the prior analyses of RGSW (e.g., noise growth) focused on the case when m is power-of-two, this work shows that similar analyses would also work in the general cyclotomic rings, by using the toolkits of [26]. However, as we elaborate below, a direct adoption of the analyses would hit several technical challenges, and thus cannot derive a polynomial bound for the noise growth.

Notice that RGSW can be packed the same way as packing the plaintexts. Particularly, given $\mathbf{C}_1, \ldots, \mathbf{C}_r$ that encrypt $(x_1, \ldots, x_r) \in \mathcal{R}_1^r$, $\mathbf{C}' = \sum \mathbf{C}_i v_i$ is an encryption of $x = \sum x_i v_i$. And similarly, we can pack the ciphertexts in the other modes, e.g., $\mathbf{C}' = \sum \mathbf{C}_i v_i^\vee w_i$. As the batch multiplication (for plaintexts) consists of a multiplication followed by a trace computation, homomorphic multiplication would involve a RGSW multiplication followed by a homomorphic trace evaluation. Thus, the task is reduced to how to homomorphically compute the trace function.

Subtle Issue 1. We notice that $\mathsf{Tr}_{\mathcal{R}/\mathcal{R}_1 \otimes \mathcal{R}_3}(x) = \sum_{\sigma \in \mathsf{Gal}(\mathcal{R}/\mathcal{R}_1 \otimes \mathcal{R}_3)}(x)$, i.e., summation over all the automorphisms in the Galois group. Furthermore, homomorphic computation of the automorphism $\sigma()$ can be achieved by the BV key-switch technique [8], roughly of the same complexity of a RGSW homomorphic multiplication. Thus, a naive application of this idea would require $\tau = |\mathsf{Gal}(\mathcal{R}/\mathcal{R}_1 \otimes \mathcal{R}_3)|$ calls to the key-switch methods, meaning roughly τ RGSW homomorphic multiplications. However, this would require complexity as much as computing the individual unpacked homomorphic multiplications separately, meaning that the batch computation does not provide any advantage. Thus, to instantiate a meaningful batch homomorphic multiplication, we must be able to compute the trace homomorphically within $o(\tau)$ RGSW homomorphic multiplications.

While this task is in general difficult, we observe that if $\mathcal{R}_2$ has a tower structure, e.g., $\mathbb{Z}[\xi_\tau]$ for $\tau = 3^d$, then we can compute the homomorphic evaluation by making $O(\log \tau)$ calls to the key-switch algorithm, which is roughly $O(\log \tau)$ RGSW multiplications. Thus under this structure, to compute $\boldsymbol{x} \odot \boldsymbol{y}$ of size $r \lesssim \tau$, we need roughly $O(\log \tau)$ RGSW multiplications to compute in batch, which is significantly better than computing separately (which would require r RGSW multiplications). We notice that this more efficient trace (homomorphic) computation has been explored for cyclotomic rings of two's power [3,11], and this work further extends the result to general cyclotomic rings.

<u>Subtle Issue 2.</u> Another perhaps even more subtle issue is the noise analysis. Consider messages (plaintexts) $\boldsymbol{x} := (x_1, \ldots, x_r)$ and $\boldsymbol{y} := (y_1, \ldots, y_r)$ are packed into $x, y \in \mathcal{R}$, and $\mathbf{C}_x = \mathsf{Enc}(x), \mathbf{C}_y = \mathsf{Enc}(y)$ (in the RGSW form). Then by the asymmetry noise growth property [4], the error of $\mathbf{C}_x \boxdot \mathbf{C}_y$ (where $\boxdot$ denotes RGSW homomorphic multiplication) would roughly be $e_x \sqrt{N} + x e_y$, where N is the dimension of the ring $\mathcal{R}$, e_x and e_y are the noise terms inside $\mathbf{C}_x$ and $\mathbf{C}_y$, respectively. Then the homomorphic trace evaluation would incur a blowup of some multiplicative factor W, which is some fixed polynomial. Thus, the overall noise behavior would be roughly $e_x \mathsf{poly}(\lambda) + x W e_y$.

However, to bootstrap within a polynomial modulus, the AP14/FHEW framework crucially requires that $\|xW\| \leq 1$. In the case of unpacked bit computation, this is true as $x \in \{0, 1\}$ and there is no need to do trace evaluation (so W can be thought as 1). However, in the packed computation of our framework, $\|xW\|$ is inherently greater to 1. Thus, a direct analysis would result in a super-polynomial blow up on noise, implying a super-polynomial modulus.

Even though the general analysis does not work, for our particular batch framework computation, we do identify a beautiful noise characterization if we alternate the multiplications between $\mathcal{R}_1 \otimes \mathcal{R}_2$ and $\mathcal{R}_1 \otimes \mathcal{R}_3$, under a careful algebraic analysis. Below we describe the core insight at a high level and refer curious readers to the proof of Theorem 6.2 for the details.

As we discussed, the W term comes from the trace evaluation, i.e., $\mathsf{Tr}(\cdot)$. If we perform homomorphic multiplications on multiple ciphertexts, then the following term will appear in the noise $- \mathsf{Tr}(x_1 \cdot \mathsf{Tr}(x_2 \cdot \mathsf{Tr}(\ldots \mathsf{Tr}(x_k e)))$, where e is some fresh error, and x_i's are the packed messages. This term will approach W^k for the general case, resulting in an exponential blowup in the noise. However, under the following two conditions: (1) we alternate the trace functions between $\mathcal{R}_1 \otimes \mathcal{R}_2$ and $\mathcal{R}_1 \otimes \mathcal{R}_3$; (2) each x_i is a packing of $(x_{i1}, \ldots, x_{ir})$ where $\|x_{ij}\| = 1$, e.g., a power of some root of unity ξ_q^z, then we can derive a simple and small polynomial upper bound for this term.

This insight can be used to prove that the batch AP14/FHEW bootstrap algorithm only incurs a polynomial error growth under our framework.

Overall – How Many Slots can the Framework Batch. Now we determine how many slots our framework can batch when applying to the AP14/FHEW framework. We can set the tensor ring $\mathbb{Z}[\xi_q] \otimes \mathcal{R}_2 \otimes \mathcal{R}_3$ to perform batch computation of the explicit framework of AP14/FHEW. Let N denote the dimension of the ring $\mathcal{R}$. By setting $n = O(\lambda), q \approx \tilde{O}(\sqrt{n})$ and $\mathcal{R}_2$ roughly of a similar dimension to $\mathcal{R}_3$, we can batch $r = O(\sqrt{N/q})$ slots. Asymptotically, we can set $N = O(n)$, resulting in $r = O(\lambda^{1/4 - o(1)})$.

Thus, we can bootstrap λ LWE ciphertexts, using $O(\lambda/r) = \tilde{O}(\lambda^{1.75})$ FHE multiplications. This proves Theorem 1.1.

Comparison with a Recent Progress. Recently, the work [16] considered batch homomorphic computation, yet only achieved a weaker version of the task. Briefly speaking, [16] is able to bootstrap one LWE input ciphertext, e.g., $\mathsf{Enc}(\mu)$ to ℓ LWE ciphertexts $\mathsf{Enc}(f_1(\mu))$, $\mathsf{Enc}(f_2(\mu)), \ldots, \mathsf{Enc}(f_\ell(\mu))$, for ℓ different functions. However the message space of μ is small, e.g., a bit or $\mathbb{Z}_t$ for some small t, so one cannot squeeze a long string $x \in \{0,1\}^n$ into μ. Moreover, their method does not support batch computing on multiple LWE inputs, whereas our framework does. Thus, our framework has non-trivial advantages.

2 Preliminary

Notations. Denote the set of integers by $\mathbb{Z}$, the set of rational numbers by $\mathbb{Q}$, real numbers by $\mathbb{R}$, and complex numbers by $\mathbb{C}$. Notation log refers to the base-2 logarithm. For a positive $k \in \mathbb{Z}$, let $[k]$ be the set of integers $\{1, ..., k\}$. We denote $[a, b]$ as the set $[a, b] \cap \mathbb{Z}$ for any integers $a \leq b$.

In this work, a vector is always a column vector by default and is denoted by a bold lower-case letter, e.g., $\boldsymbol{x}$. We use x_i to denote the i-th element of $\boldsymbol{x}$. We use $\|\boldsymbol{x}\|_2$ denotes the l_2-norm, i.e., $\|\boldsymbol{x}\|_2 = \sqrt{\sum_i \|x_i\|^2}$ and $\|\boldsymbol{x}\|_\infty$ denotes the l_∞-norm of $\boldsymbol{x}$, i.e., $\|\boldsymbol{x}\| = \max_i \{\|x_i\|\}$. We use bold capital letters to denote matrices. For a matrix $\mathbf{X}$, $\boldsymbol{x}_i$ denotes its i-th column vector without extra instructions, $\mathbf{X}^\top$ denotes the transpose of $\mathbf{X}$, $\|\mathbf{X}\|_2 := \max_i\{\|\boldsymbol{x}_i\|_2\}$, $\|\mathbf{X}\|_\infty := \max_i\{\|\boldsymbol{x}_i\|_\infty\}$. Given some set S, $S^{m \times n}$ denotes the set of all $m \times n$ matrices with entries in S. For matrices $\mathbf{X} \in S^{m \times n_1}$ and $\mathbf{Y} \in S^{m \times n_2}$ over some set S, $[\mathbf{X}\|\mathbf{Y}](\in S^{m \times (n_1+n_2)})$ denotes the concatenation of $\mathbf{X}$ with $\mathbf{Y}$.

For a set A and a probability distribution $\mathcal{P}$, we use $a \leftarrow A$ to denote that a is uniformly chosen from A and $a \leftarrow \mathcal{P}$ to denote that a is chosen according to the distribution $\mathcal{P}$.

2.1 Lattices and Sub-Gaussian Random Variables

Lattices. An n-dimension (full-rank) lattice $\Lambda \subseteq \mathbb{R}^n$ is the set of all integer linear combinations of some set of independent basis vectors $\mathbf{B} = \{\mathsf{b}_1, \ldots, \mathsf{b}_n\} \subseteq \mathbb{R}^n$, $\Lambda = \mathcal{L}(\mathbf{B}) = \{\sum_{i=1}^n z_i \mathsf{b}_i : z_i \in \mathbb{Z}\}$.

Sub-Gaussian. As discussed in [4,17], it is convenient to use the notion of sub-Gaussian to analyze the error growth in the FHE constructions. A sub-gaussian variable X with parameter $\alpha > 0$ satisfies $E[e^{2\pi t X}] \leq e^{\pi \alpha^2/t^2}$, for all $t \in \mathbb{R}$.

- Boundedness: If X is a sub-Gaussian variable with parameter $r > 0$, then $\Pr[|X| \geq t] \leq 2\exp(-\pi t^2/r^2)$.
- Homogeneity: If X is a sub-Gaussian variable with parameter $r > 0$, then cX is sub-gaussian with parameter $c \cdot r$ for any constant $c \geq 0$.
- Pythagorean additivity: If X_1 and X_2 are two sub-Gaussian variables with parameter r_1 and r_2 respectively, then $X_1 + X_2$ is sub-Gaussian with parameter $r_1 + r_2$, or $\sqrt{r_1^2 + r_2^2}$ if the two random variables are independent.

g^{-1} **Algorithm.** This algorithm is used heavily in the research of FHE as we summarize in the following lemma.

Lemma 2.1. *For a given integer q, let $\ell = \lceil \log q \rceil$ and $g = (1, 2, .., 2^{\ell-1})$. Then there is a randomized, efficiently computable algorithm denoted as $g^{-1} : \mathbb{Z}_q \to \mathbb{Z}^\ell$ such that the output of the function, $x \leftarrow g^{-1}(a)$ is sub-gaussian with parameter $O(1)$, satisfying $\langle g, x \rangle = a \mod q$.*

We can extend g^{-1} to the matrix case (using the notation $\mathbf{G}^{-1}(\cdot)$) by applying $g^{-1}(\cdot)$ to each entry of the matrix.

2.2 Algebraic Number Theory Background

We present some necessary background of algebraic number theory. This work heavily uses number fields and their rings of integers, and particularly, we represent a ring element as an algebraic number, instead of a polynomial. This representation gives more algebraic insights for our designs and analyses. Due to space limit, we defer some basic concepts to the full version of this work, and note that more details can be found in the work [26].

Number Fields. This work focuses on number fields as field extension that can be expressed as $K = \mathbb{Q}(\alpha)$, by adjoining some α to $\mathbb{Q}$ where α is a root of some irreducible polynomial $f(x) \in \mathbb{Z}[x]$. Let ξ_m be the m-th root of unity, and $\mathbb{Q}(\xi_m)$ is known as the m-th cyclotomic field. We also use the concept of tensor fields, whose preliminaries are presented in the full version of this paper. Below we present a useful decomposition property of cyclotomic fields.

Lemma 2.2 [26]. *Let $m = \prod_\ell m_\ell$ be the prime-power factorization. Then $K = \mathbb{Q}(\xi_m)$ is isomorphic to the tensor product $\otimes_\ell \mathbb{Q}(\xi_{m_\ell})$, via the bijection $\prod_\ell a_\ell \mapsto \otimes_\ell(a_\ell)$, where each a_ℓ in K_ℓ can be naturally embedded in the field K.*

Geometry of Number Fields. Throughout this work, we use the canonical embedding to define norms for algebraic numbers. As argued in [26], this definition is independent of the representation of the algebraic number and can give us better bounds in the setting of general cyclotomic fields. Due to space limit, we present the details in the full version of this work.

Trace. We notice that the cyclotomic field $K = \mathbb{Q}(\xi_m)$ is a Galois extension over $\mathbb{Q}$, and thus the homomorphisms $\{\sigma_i\}$ are automorphisms that form the Galois group, denoted by $\mathsf{Gal}(K/\mathbb{Q})$. The trace $\mathsf{Tr} = \mathsf{Tr}_{K/\mathbb{Q}} : K \to \mathbb{Q}$ of an element $a \in K$ can be defined as the sum of the embeddings: $\mathsf{Tr}(a) = \sum_i \sigma_i(a) = \sum_{\sigma_i \in \mathsf{Gal}(K/\mathbb{Q})} \sigma_i(a)$. Clearly, the trace is $\mathbb{Q}$-linear, and also notice that $\mathsf{Tr}(a \cdot b) = \langle \sigma(a), \overline{\sigma(b)} \rangle$, so $\mathsf{Tr}(a \cdot b)$ is a symmetric bilinear form akin to the inner product of the embeddings of a and b.

By the Galois theory, there is a bijection between the set of subfields E of K containing $\mathbb{Q}$ and the set of subgroups G of $\mathsf{Gal}(K/\mathbb{Q})$. Thus, for any intermediate subfield E, the Galois group of $\mathsf{Gal}(K/E)$ is also well-defined. Furthermore, we can define the trace function for the intermediate subfields as: $\mathsf{Tr}_{K/E}(a) = \sum_{\sigma \in \mathsf{Gal}(K/E)} \sigma(a)$ for $a \in K$ and $\mathsf{Tr}_{E/\mathbb{Q}}(b) = \sum_{\sigma \in \mathsf{Gal}(E/\mathbb{Q})} \sigma(b)$ for $b \in E$. The trace functions behave well in towers, i.e. for $a \in K$,

$$\mathsf{Tr}_{K/\mathbb{Q}}(a) = \mathsf{Tr}_{E/\mathbb{Q}}(\mathsf{Tr}_{K/E}(a)).$$

Ring of Integers and Ideals. An algebraic integer is an algebraic number whose minimal polynomial over the rationals has integer coefficients. For a number field K, denote its subset of algebraic integers by $\mathcal{O}_K$, which forms a ring, called the ring of integers of K. The norm of any algebraic integer is in $\mathbb{Z}$.

An (integer) ideal $\mathcal{I} \subset \mathcal{O}_K$ is an additive subgroup and for any $x \in K$, $x\mathcal{I} \subset \mathcal{I}$. Every ideal in $\mathcal{O}_K$ is a set of all $\mathbb{Z}$-linear combinations of some basis.

The sum of two ideals $\mathcal{I}, \mathcal{J}$ is the set of all $x + y$ for $x \in \mathcal{I}$, $y \in \mathcal{J}$, and the product ideal $\mathcal{I}\mathcal{J}$ is the ideal generated by terms of xy. A fractional ideal $\mathcal{I} \subset K$ is a set such that $d\mathcal{I} \subset \mathcal{O}_K$ is an integral ideal for some $d \in \mathcal{O}_K$. A fractional ideal $\mathcal{I}$ is invertible if there exists a fractional ideal $\mathcal{J}$ such that $\mathcal{O}_K = \mathcal{I} \cdot \mathcal{J}$, which is unique and denoted as $\mathcal{I}^{-1}$.

Duality. For any lattice $\mathcal{L} \subset K$(i.e. the $\mathbb{Z}$-span of any $\mathbb{Q}$-basis of K), its dual is defined as $\mathcal{L}^\vee = \{x \in K | \mathsf{Tr}(x\mathcal{L}) \subset \mathbb{Z}\}$. Then $\mathcal{L}^\vee$ embeds as the complex conjugate of the dual lattice, which means $\sigma(\mathcal{L}^\vee) = \overline{\sigma(\mathcal{L})^*}$ due to the fact that $\mathsf{Tr}(xy) = \sum_i \sigma_i(x)\sigma_i(y) = \langle \sigma(x), \overline{\sigma(y)} \rangle$. It is easy to check that $\mathcal{L} = (\mathcal{L}^\vee)^\vee$, and that if $\mathcal{L}$ is a fractional ideal, so is the $\mathcal{L}^\vee$.

For any $\mathbb{Q}$-basis $\mathbf{B} = \{\mathsf{b}_j\}$ of K, we denote its dual basis by $\mathbf{B}^\vee = \{\mathsf{b}_j^\vee\}$, which is characterized by $\mathsf{Tr}(\mathsf{b}_i \cdot \mathsf{b}_j^\vee) = \begin{cases} 1, i = j \\ 0, i \neq j \end{cases}$. It is immediate that $(\mathbf{B}^\vee)^\vee = \mathbf{B}$, and if $\mathbf{B}$ is a $\mathbb{Z}$-basis of some fractional ideal $\mathcal{I}$, then $\mathbf{B}^\vee$ is a $\mathbb{Z}$-basis of its dual ideal $\mathcal{I}^\vee$. If $a = \sum a_j \cdot \mathsf{b}_j$ for $a_j \in \mathbb{R}$ is the unique presentation of $a \in K_\mathbb{R}$ in basis $\mathbf{B}$, then $a_j = \mathsf{Tr}(a\mathsf{b}_j^\vee)$. For a fixed $\mathbb{Z}_q$-basis $\{\mathsf{b}_1, ..., \mathsf{b}_n\}$ of $\mathcal{O}_K/q\mathcal{O}_K$, the randomized algorithm $\mathbf{g}^{-1}(\cdot)$ can be extended to the subring of K modulo q, $\mathcal{O}_K/q\mathcal{O}_K$.

Lemma 2.3. *For a given integer q, let $\ell = \lceil \log q \rceil$, $\mathbf{g}^\top = (1, 2, .., 2^{\ell-1})$ and a fixed $\mathbb{Z}_q$-basis $\{\mathsf{b}_1, ..., \mathsf{b}_n\}$ of $\mathcal{O}_K/q\mathcal{O}_K$, then there is a randomized, efficiently computable function $\mathbf{g}^{-1} : \mathcal{O}_K/q\mathcal{O}_K \to \mathcal{O}_K^\ell$, such that the output of the function, $x \leftarrow \mathbf{g}^{-1}(a)$, always satisfies $\langle \mathbf{g}, \mathbf{x} \rangle = a \mod q$.*

In details, if $a = a_1\mathsf{b}_1 + ... + a_n\mathsf{b}_n$ where $a_i \in \mathbb{Z}_q$ and $\mathbf{x}_i \leftarrow \mathbf{g}^{-1}(a_i)$ where the function $\mathbf{g}^{-1}(\cdot)$ is defined in Lemma 2.1, then $\mathbf{x} = \mathbf{x}_1\mathsf{b}_1 + ... + \mathbf{x}_n\mathsf{b}_n$ and each vector $\mathbf{x}_i \in \mathbb{Z}_q^\ell$ is sub-gaussian with parameter $O(1)$.

2.3   Learning with Errors Assumption

The learning with errors (LWE) problem was introduced by Regev [33], which is as hard as several worst-case lattice problems. For the definition of LWE, we need the following distribution $A_{s,\chi}$. If χ is a distribution over $\mathbb{Z}$ and $s \in \mathbb{Z}_q^n$, a sample from the distribution $A_{s,\chi}$ is of the form $(b, \boldsymbol{a}) \in \mathbb{Z}_q \times \mathbb{Z}_q^n$ with $b = \langle \boldsymbol{a}, \boldsymbol{s} \rangle + e$ mod q, where $\boldsymbol{a}$ is chosen from $\mathbb{Z}_q^n$ uniformly and e is chosen from the distribution χ. Now we propose the problem formally in the following definitions.

Definition 2.4 (LWE). Let χ be a distribution over $\mathbb{Z}$, an integer modulus $q \geq 2$. The decision version of LWE, denoted as $\mathsf{LWE}_{n,q,\chi}$, is given m pairs of $(b', \boldsymbol{a}') \in \mathbb{Z}_q \times \mathbb{Z}_q^n$ and decide these pairs are from the uniform distribution or $A_{s,\chi}$.

The ring variant of LWE is the foundation of this work. In the rest of the paper, the special ring $\mathcal{R} = \mathcal{O}_K$ is used by default. We present the definition of RLWE by defining the distribution $A_{s,\chi}$ as follow. Let χ be a distribution over $K_{\mathbb{R}}$ and $s \in \mathcal{R}_q$, and then a sample from $A_{s,\chi}$ is of the form

$$(b = s \cdot a + e \quad \mathrm{mod}\ q\mathcal{R}, a) \in K_{\mathbb{R}}/q \times \mathcal{R}_q,$$

where $a \leftarrow \mathcal{R}_q$ and $e \leftarrow \chi$. Then, the definition of RLWE is presented as follows.

Definition 2.5 (RLWE). For security parameter λ, let $n = n(\lambda)$ be the dimension, $q = q(\lambda) \geq 2$ be an integer modulus, and $\chi = \chi(\lambda)$ be a distribution over $K_{\mathbb{R}}$. The task of decision $\mathsf{RLWE}_{n,q,\chi}$ is, given m pairs of $(b', a') \in K_{\mathbb{R}}/q \times \mathcal{R}_q$, decide whether the pairs are from the uniform distribution or $A_{s,\chi}$.

There is strong evidence showing hardness of LWE e.g., [7,33] and RLWE, e.g., [25,26,32]. These problems have been extensively studied in the NIST's post-quantum standardization process in recent years. Particularly, many plausible candidates are LWE or RLWE-based designs.

Remark 2.6. *In this work, we present the primal version of the RLWE where the secret s lies in the primal ring $\mathcal{R}_q$, where the original RLWE [25] is defined in the dual. Nevertheless, the dual and primal versions are equivalent up to a tweak factor [30], and thus the primal variant is also plausibly as hard. For simplicity of presentation, this work uses secrets in the primal ring by default.*

3   RGSW in General Cyclotomic Rings

In this section, we first revisit the basic RLWE encryption scheme and the FHE scheme GSW [4,20] in the ring settings, denoted as RGSW. The RGSW has been analyzed in power-of-two cyclotomic rings, e.g., [13,17], yet the prior analyses on noise growth crucially relies on the cyclotomic polynomial $\Phi_m(X) = X^{m/2} + 1$, due to some nice properties of the coefficient embedding in such type of rings. However, this work requires to work with RGSW in general cyclotomic rings, where the prior analyses do not carry over directly. To handle this, we re-analyze the noise growth of RGSW by using the techniques of canonical embedding as described in [26], showing that RGSW in general cyclotomic rings behaves basically the same as that in the power-of-two setting.

Important Note. Throughout this work, we use the algebraic representation for ring elements for better mathematical insights.

Below we describe the parameters of the RLWE and RGSW schemes.

- λ: the security parameter.
- $\mathcal{R}$: the m-th cyclotomic ring with degree $N = \phi(m)$.
- Q: the modulus.
- $\mathcal{R}_Q$: the quotient ring $\mathcal{R}/Q\mathcal{R}$.
- $\mathcal{D}$: some error distribution over $\mathcal{R}$.
- ℓ: set $\ell = \lceil \log Q \rceil$.

3.1   RLWE Scheme

We start from the basic symmetric RLWE encryption scheme (in the primal form for simplicity). The scheme contains the following algorithms.

- **KeyGen**(1^λ): Choose randomly $s \leftarrow \mathcal{R}_Q$ and output $\mathsf{sk} := (1, -s)^\top \in \mathcal{R}_Q^2$.
- **Enc**$(\mathsf{sk}, \mu \in \mathcal{R}_t)$: Sample a uniform ring element $a \leftarrow \mathcal{R}_Q$ and a noise $e \leftarrow \mathcal{D}$. The output ciphertext is set as $c := \begin{pmatrix} sa + e \\ a \end{pmatrix} + \begin{pmatrix} \lfloor \frac{Q}{t} \rceil \mu \\ 0 \end{pmatrix} \in \mathcal{R}_Q^2$.

   We call $\lfloor \frac{Q}{t} \rceil \mu$ the encoded message of c and μ the encrypted message of c.
- **Dec**(c, sk): The algorithm outputs an element μ in $\mathcal{R}_t$ as follow:

$$\mu = \lfloor \langle (1, -s), c \rangle \rceil_t := \lfloor t \langle (1, -s), c \rangle / Q \rceil \mod t.$$

We use $\mathsf{RLWE}_s^{t/Q}(\mu)$ to denote the set of all RLWE ciphertexts of encoded message μ under secret s with ciphertext modulus Q and plaintext modulus t. Sometimes, we use $\mathsf{RLWE}_s^Q(\lfloor \frac{Q}{t} \rceil \mu)$ to denote the same set. The latter notion drops the t in the super-script, but presents the whole encoded message in the parentheses.

3.2   RGSW Scheme

Now we present the RGSW scheme, which is basically the same as the work [4] by moving the algebraic structure to the setting of general cyclotomic rings. We notice that it suffices to develop our further results by using the symmetric-key version of RGSW, and thus we just present this version for convenience. The public-key version works analogously.

   We denote the fixed gadget vector as $\boldsymbol{g}^\top = (1, 2, ..., 2^{\ell-1})$, and the gadget matrix is defined as $\mathbf{G} = \boldsymbol{g}^\top \otimes \mathbf{I}_2$. As demonstrated by [4,27], the gadget vector/matrix play a vital role in the homomorphic computation methods. Similar to the RLWE scheme, we present the primal version of RGSW.

- **KeyGen**(1^λ): Choose randomly $s \leftarrow \mathcal{R}_Q$ and set $\mathsf{sk} := (1, -s)^\top \in \mathcal{R}_Q^2$.
- **Enc**$(\mathsf{sk}, \mu \in \mathcal{R})$: Sample a uniform vector $\boldsymbol{a} \leftarrow \mathcal{R}_Q^{2\ell}$ and a noise vector $\boldsymbol{e} \leftarrow \mathcal{D}^{2\ell}$. The ciphertext is set as $\mathbf{C} := \begin{pmatrix} s\boldsymbol{a}^\top + \boldsymbol{e}^\top \\ \boldsymbol{a}^\top \end{pmatrix} + \mu \mathbf{G} \in \mathcal{R}_Q^{2 \times 2\ell}$.

- **Dec(C, sk):** The algorithm outputs an element μ in $\mathcal{R}/2\mathcal{R}$ as follow[6]:

$$\mu = \lfloor \langle (1, -s)^\top, c_{(\ell-1)} \rangle \rceil \mod 2,$$

where $c_{(\ell-1)}$ is the $(\ell-1)$-th column of $\mathbf{C}$.
- **Homomorphic Addition $\mathbf{C}_1 \boxplus \mathbf{C}_2$:** It takes as inputs two RGSW ciphertexts $\mathbf{C}_1$, $\mathbf{C}_2$ under the same secret key sk and outputs $\mathbf{C}_1 \boxplus \mathbf{C}_2 := \mathbf{C}_1 + \mathbf{C}_2$.
- **Homomorphic Multiplication $\mathbf{C}_1 \boxdot \mathbf{C}_2$:** It takes as inputs two RGSW ciphertexts $\mathbf{C}_1$, $\mathbf{C}_2$ under the same secret key sk and outputs the following as the result of homomorphic multiplication: $\mathbf{C}_1 \boxdot \mathbf{C}_2 \leftarrow \mathbf{C}_1 \cdot \mathbf{G}^{-1}(\mathbf{C}_2)$.
  Here $\mathbf{G}^{-1}(\cdot)$ can be either deterministic or randomized. As argued by [4], a randomized instantiation can yield tighter parameters of the noise growth than those derived from the deterministic version. We notice that in the ring setting, a basis needs to be specified when computing $\mathbf{G}^{-1}$.
- **External Product $\mathbf{C}_1 \boxtimes c_2$:** It takes as inputs a RGSW ciphertexts $\mathbf{C}_1$ and a RLWE ciphertext c_2 under the same secret key sk and outputs the following RLWE ciphertext as the result of external product: $\mathbf{C}_1 \boxtimes c_2 \leftarrow \mathbf{C}_1 \cdot g^{-1}(c_2)$.

The IND-CPA security of the above RGSW scheme (for general cyclotomic rings) follows from the RLWE assumption, using the same argument of [4,20]. Therefore, this work focuses on the noise analyses, which are not trivial when porting the results to general cyclotomic rings.

Definition 3.1. *Adapt the notations from the above. Given a ciphertext $\mathbf{C}$ that encrypts message μ under a secret key $\mathsf{sk} = (1, -s)^\top$, we can express as the following relation $\mathsf{sk}^\top \cdot \mathbf{C} = \mu \cdot \mathsf{sk}^\top \cdot \mathbf{G} + e^\top \in \mathcal{R}_Q^m$, for some error vector e. Then define $\mathrm{Err}_\mu(\mathbf{C}) := e^\top = \mathsf{sk}^\top \cdot \mathbf{C} - \mu \cdot \mathsf{sk}^\top \cdot \mathbf{G}$. When the context is clear, we may drop the index μ.*

We use $\mathrm{RGSW}_s^Q(\mu)$ to denote the set of all the RGSW ciphertexts that encrypt μ under secret s in the modulo Q space. If the parameters Q are clear from the context, we would use the abbreviation $\mathrm{RGSW}_s(\mu)$ for simplicity.

Note. The above error function can be defined for RLWE ciphertexts analogously. We do not present another definition to avoid repetition.

Below we present a lemma that summarizes the error behavior of the homomorphic operations. The error behavior in the general cyclotomic rings is similar to that in the case of power-of-two as in the prior work [13,17], yet requires a more refined analysis. Due to the space limit, we describe the statement and defer the proof to the full version of this work.

Lemma 3.2. *For any RGSW ciphertexts $\mathbf{C}_1$, $\mathbf{C}_2$ that encrypt μ_1, μ_2 with the error terms e_1, e_2 respectively, then we have the following.*

- $\mathrm{Err}(\mathbf{C}_1 \boxplus \mathbf{C}_2) = e_1^\top + e_2^\top.$

---

[6] We notice that $\mathcal{R}_2$ is used to denote a second ring in our framework. To avoid notation overloading, we use $\mathcal{R}/2\mathcal{R}$ to denote $\mathcal{R}$ modulo 2.

- $\mathsf{Err}(\mathbf{C}_1 \boxdot \mathbf{C}_2) = \boldsymbol{e}_1^\top \cdot \mathbf{G}^{-1}(\mathbf{C}_2) + \mu_1 \cdot \boldsymbol{e}_2^\top.$

Furthermore, suppose $\mathbf{G}^{-1}$ is sampled with respect to some $\mathbb{Z}$-basis of $\mathcal{R}$, i.e., $\mathbf{B} = \{\mathsf{b}_1, ..., \mathsf{b}_n\}$, such that $\max_{i \in [n]}\{\|\sigma(\mathsf{b}_i)\|_\infty\} \leq 1$ as Lemma 2.3. Then the following facts hold.

- *Denote $\boldsymbol{e}_1^\top \cdot \mathbf{G}^{-1}(\mathbf{C}_2)$ as $\boldsymbol{e}^\top = (e_1, ..., e_{2\ell})$. Then each entry of $\boldsymbol{e}$ is an independent random variable.*
- *$\|\sigma(\boldsymbol{e})\|_\infty$ is upper bounded by a sub-Gaussian variable with parameter $O(r)$, for some real positive $r \leq \sqrt{N \cdot \log Q} \cdot \|\sigma(e_1)\|_\infty$.*

4   New Batch Homomorphic Methods via Tensor Rings

We present our framework for batch (or SIMD) homomorphic computation by using the tensor of linearly disjoint fields (and their rings of integers). Our framework is naturally compatible with the AP14/FHEW/TFHE bootstrapping methods, resulting in more efficient batch bootstrapping mechanisms. We present our new framework for batch plaintext computation, and then show how to perform homomorphically with the framework. In this section, we present in a more abstract and algebraic way, and in Sect. 5 we show instantiations.

4.1   Framework of Batch Plaintext Computation

We first present some math background and then our new framework.

Math Background and Notations. Let $K = K_1 \otimes K_2 \otimes K_3$ be a tensor field of three linearly disjoint fields, and $\mathcal{R}_1, \mathcal{R}_2, \mathcal{R}_3$ be their rings of integers, respectively. It follows that the ring of integers of K (denoted as $\mathcal{R}$) is isomorphic to $\mathcal{R}_1 \otimes \mathcal{R}_2 \otimes \mathcal{R}_3$. Furthermore, we present some useful facts and notations.

- K_{12} and K_{13} denote $K_1 \otimes K_2$ and $K_1 \otimes K_3$, respectively.
- $\mathcal{R}, \mathcal{R}_{12}$ and $\mathcal{R}_{13}$ denote the rings of integers of $K, K_{12},$ and K_{13}, respectively. It is known that $\mathcal{R} \equiv \mathcal{R}_1 \otimes \mathcal{R}_2 \otimes \mathcal{R}_3$, $\mathcal{R}_{12} \equiv \mathcal{R}_1 \otimes \mathcal{R}_2$, and $\mathcal{R}_{13} \equiv \mathcal{R}_1 \otimes \mathcal{R}_3$.
- Let $(\mathsf{v}_1, \mathsf{v}_2, \dots, \mathsf{v}_\rho)$ and $(\mathsf{w}_1, \mathsf{w}_2, \dots, \mathsf{w}_\tau)$ be some $\mathbb{Z}$-bases of $\mathcal{R}_2$ and $\mathcal{R}_3$, respectively, where ρ and τ are the degrees of the rings $\mathcal{R}_2$ and $\mathcal{R}_3$.
- Denote $(\mathsf{v}_1^\vee, \mathsf{v}_2^\vee, \dots, \mathsf{v}_\rho^\vee)$ and $(\mathsf{w}_1^\vee, \mathsf{w}_2^\vee, \dots, \mathsf{w}_\tau^\vee)$ as the corresponding $\mathbb{Z}$-bases of the dual spaces $\mathcal{R}_2^\vee$ and $\mathcal{R}_3^\vee$, respectively.
- Let $r = \min(\rho, \tau)$, the maximal number of slots our method can pack.
- Denote the trace functions (with respect to different underlying subfields) as

$$\mathsf{Tr}_{K/K_{12}} : K \to K_{12} \text{ and } \mathsf{Tr}_{K/K_{13}} : K \to K_{13}$$

Construction. Now we present our plaintext encoding/computation methods.

- **Plaintext Packing.** The algorithm takes input $(x_1, \dots, x_r) \in \mathcal{R}_1^r$, and an index to one of the four modes: (1) "$\mathcal{R}_{12}$", (2) "$\mathcal{R}_{13}$", (3) "$\mathcal{R}_{12} \to \mathcal{R}_{13}$", and (4) "$\mathcal{R}_{13} \to \mathcal{R}_{12}$", and outputs an encoding of the input. The packing algorithm does one of the following, selected by the mode.

- Mode "$\mathcal{R}_{12}$": output $\sum_{i=1}^{r} x_i \cdot \mathsf{v}_i \in \mathcal{R}_{12}$.
- Mode "$\mathcal{R}_{13}$": output $\sum_{i=1}^{r} x_i \cdot \mathsf{w}_i \in \mathcal{R}_{13}$.
- Mode "$\mathcal{R}_{12} \to \mathcal{R}_{13}$": output $\sum_{i=1}^{r} x_i \cdot \mathsf{v}_i^{\vee} \mathsf{w}_i \in \mathcal{R}_1 \otimes \mathcal{R}_2^{\vee} \otimes \mathcal{R}_3$.
- Mode "$\mathcal{R}_{13} \to \mathcal{R}_{12}$": output $\sum_{i=1}^{r} x_i \cdot \mathsf{v}_i \mathsf{w}_i^{\vee} \in \mathcal{R}_1 \otimes \mathcal{R}_2 \otimes \mathcal{R}_3^{\vee}$.

We assume that the packing algorithm will attach an index to its mode.

- **Addition.** The algorithm takes as input two encodings, namely (x, mode_1), (y, mode_2), outputs $(x + y, \mathsf{mode}_1)$ if $\mathsf{mode}_1 = \mathsf{mode}_2$, otherwise $\perp$.
- **Multiplication.** The algorithm takes input two encodings, namely (x, mode_1) and (y, mode_2), and does one of the following, selected by the modes.
  - $\mathsf{mode}_1 = $ "$\mathcal{R}_{12}$" and $\mathsf{mode}_2 = $ "$\mathcal{R}_{12} \to \mathcal{R}_{13}$": output $\mathsf{Tr}_{K/K_{13}}(xy) \in \mathcal{R}_{13}$.
  - $\mathsf{mode}_1 = $ "$\mathcal{R}_{13}$" and $\mathsf{mode}_2 = $ "$\mathcal{R}_{13} \to \mathcal{R}_{12}$": output $\mathsf{Tr}_{K/K_{12}}(xy) \in \mathcal{R}_{12}$.
  - $\mathsf{mode}_1 = $ "$\mathcal{R}_{12} \to \mathcal{R}_{13}$" and $\mathsf{mode}_2 = $ "$\mathcal{R}_{12}$": output $\mathsf{Tr}_{K/K_{13}}(xy) \in \mathcal{R}_{13}$.
  - $\mathsf{mode}_1 = $ "$\mathcal{R}_{13} \to \mathcal{R}_{12}$" and $\mathsf{mode}_2 = $ "$\mathcal{R}_{13}$": output $\mathsf{Tr}_{K/K_{12}}(xy) \in \mathcal{R}_{12}$.
  - Otherwise, output $\perp$.

Correctness of these operations can be easily checked as we summarize in the following theorems. We present the proof in the full version of this work.

Theorem 4.1 (Correctness of Addition). *For any $\boldsymbol{x} = (x_1, \ldots, x_r) \in \mathcal{R}_1^r$ and $\boldsymbol{y} = (y_1, \ldots, y_r) \in \mathcal{R}_1^r$, let x, y be encodings of $\boldsymbol{x}$ and $\boldsymbol{y}$ respectively of the same mode under the plaintext packing. Then $x + y$ is an encoding of $\boldsymbol{x} + \boldsymbol{y}$ of the same mode under the plaintext packing.*

Theorem 4.2 (Correctness of Multiplication). *For any $\boldsymbol{x} = (x_1, \ldots, x_r) \in \mathcal{R}_1^r$ and $\boldsymbol{y} = (y_1, \ldots, y_r) \in \mathcal{R}_1^r$, let x, y be encodings of $\boldsymbol{x}$ and $\boldsymbol{y}$ respectively of modes "$\mathcal{R}_{1b}$" and "$\mathcal{R}_{1b} \to \mathcal{R}_{1f(b)}$" under the plaintext packing for $b \in \{2, 3\}$ and mapping $f(2) = 3$, $f(3) = 2$, and let c be the output of the multiplication algorithm on inputs x, y. Then c is an encoding of $(x_1 y_1, x_2 y_2, \ldots, x_r y_r) \in \mathcal{R}_1^r$, with the mode "$\mathcal{R}_{1f(b)}$" under the plaintext encoding.*

4.2 Homomorphic Encoding and Computation

We now present how to homomorphically perform the batch plaintext computation in the prior section. Here we assume two homomorphic evaluation algorithms, $\mathsf{Eval\text{-}Tr}_{K/K_{12}}(\cdot)$ and $\mathsf{Eval\text{-}Tr}_{K/K_{13}}(\cdot)$, as black-boxes, and will instantiate these algorithms in the next section (i.e., Sect. 4.3). We first describe the syntax of these two algorithms and some other necessary backgrounds.

Homomorphic Eval of Trace. Let $\mathsf{Eval\text{-}Tr}_{K/K_{12}}(\cdot)$ be a homomorphic evaluation algorithm that takes input either a RGSW ciphertext $\mathbf{C} \in \mathsf{RGSW}_s(\mu)$ or a RLWE ciphertext $c \in \mathsf{RLWE}_s(\mu)$, and outputs a RGSW ciphertext $\mathbf{C}' \in \mathsf{RGSW}_s(\mathsf{Tr}_{K/K_{12}}(\mu))$, or respectively a RLWE ciphertext $c' \in \mathsf{RLWE}_s(\mathsf{Tr}_{K/K_{12}}(\mu))$. Importantly, here each entry of the input ciphertext, e.g., $\mathbf{C}$ or c, and the message μ may be in a slightly larger (tensor) ring, i.e.,

$(\mathcal{R}_1 \otimes \mathcal{R}_2^\vee \otimes \mathcal{R}_3)$. The output $\mathbf{C}'$ or c', and the underlying message go back to the original ring $(\mathcal{R}_1 \otimes \mathcal{R}_2 \otimes \mathcal{R}_3)$.

The syntax of $\mathsf{Eval\text{-}Tr}_{K/K_{13}}(\cdot)$ can be defined analogously, so here we omit the statement to avoid repetition.

$\mathbf{G}^{-1}$ for the Dual Spaces. Our homomorphic computation uses $\mathbf{G}^{-1}(\mathbf{C})$ for $\mathbf{C} \in (\mathcal{R}_1 \otimes \mathcal{R}_2^\vee \otimes \mathcal{R}_3)^{2 \times 2\ell}$ or $(\mathcal{R}_1 \otimes \mathcal{R}_2 \otimes \mathcal{R}_3^\vee)^{2 \times 2\ell}$ when computing the homomorphic multiplications, and analogously uses $g^{-1}(c)$ for $c \in (\mathcal{R}_1 \otimes \mathcal{R}_2^\vee \otimes \mathcal{R}_3)^2$ or $\in (\mathcal{R}_1 \otimes \mathcal{R}_2 \otimes \mathcal{R}_3^\vee)^2$ when computing the homomorphic external products. We recall that in the ring/module settings, the function $\mathbf{G}^{-1}$ or g^{-1} is defined with respect to some $\mathbb{Z}$-basis, i.e., express the ring element as integer coefficients with respect to the basis, and then do some (randomized) bit-decomposition. (Ref. Lemma 2.3).

Now we present the homomorphic computation methods corresponding to the plaintext packing/computation in Sect. 4.1.

- RGSW-Pack. The algorithm takes input r RGSW ciphertexts $\mathbf{C}_1, \mathbf{C}_2, \ldots, \mathbf{C}_r \in \mathcal{R}^{2 \times 2\ell}$, where each $\mathbf{C}_i \in \mathsf{RGSW}_s(\mu_i)$ for $\mu_i \in \mathcal{R}_1$, and an index to one of the four modes: (1) "$\mathcal{R}_{12}$", (2) "$\mathcal{R}_{13}$", (3) "$\mathcal{R}_{12} \to \mathcal{R}_{13}$", and (4) "$\mathcal{R}_{13} \to \mathcal{R}_{12}$". The algorithm outputs a packed RGSW ciphertext, by doing one of the following four according to the mode.
  - Mode "$\mathcal{R}_{12}$": output $\sum_{i=1}^r \mathbf{C}_i \cdot \mathsf{v}_i \in \mathcal{R}^{2 \times 2\ell}$.
  - Mode "$\mathcal{R}_{13}$": output $\sum_{i=1}^r \mathbf{C}_i \cdot \mathsf{w}_i \in \mathcal{R}^{2 \times 2\ell}$.
  - Mode "$\mathcal{R}_{12} \to \mathcal{R}_{13}$": output $\sum_{i=1}^r \mathbf{C}_i \cdot \mathsf{v}_i^\vee \mathsf{w}_i \in (\mathcal{R}_1 \otimes \mathcal{R}_2^\vee \otimes \mathcal{R}_3)^{2 \times 2\ell}$.
  - Mode "$\mathcal{R}_{13} \to \mathcal{R}_{12}$": output $\sum_{i=1}^r \mathbf{C}_i \cdot \mathsf{v}_i \mathsf{w}_i^\vee \in (\mathcal{R}_1 \otimes \mathcal{R}_2 \otimes \mathcal{R}_3^\vee)^{2 \times 2\ell}$.

  The packing algorithm attaches the index of its mode in the clear.
- RLWE-Pack. The algorithm takes input r RLWE ciphertexts $c_1, c_2, \ldots, c_r$, where each $c_i \in \mathsf{RLWE}_s(\mu_i)$ for $\mu_i \in \mathcal{R}_1$, and an index to one of the four modes the same as RGSW-packing. The algorithm outputs an encoding of the RLWE ciphertexts.
  - Mode "$\mathcal{R}_{12}$": output $\sum_{i=1}^r c_i \cdot \mathsf{v}_i \in \mathcal{R}^2$.
  - Mode "$\mathcal{R}_{13}$": output $\sum_{i=1}^r c_i \cdot \mathsf{w}_i \in \mathcal{R}^2$.
  - Mode "$\mathcal{R}_{12} \to \mathcal{R}_{13}$": output $\sum_{i=1}^r c_i \cdot \mathsf{v}_i^\vee \mathsf{w}_i \in (\mathcal{R}_1 \otimes \mathcal{R}_2^\vee \otimes \mathcal{R}_3)^2$.
  - Mode "$\mathcal{R}_{13} \to \mathcal{R}_{12}$": output $\sum_{i=1}^r c_i \cdot \mathsf{v}_i \mathsf{w}_i^\vee \in (\mathcal{R}_1 \otimes \mathcal{R}_2 \otimes \mathcal{R}_3^\vee)^2$.

  We assume that the mode is included in the clear.
- Add, (**Addition for RGSW-encodings**). The algorithm takes as input two RGSW-encodings, namely $(\mathbf{C}_1, \mathsf{mode}_1), (\mathbf{C}_2, \mathsf{mode}_2)$, outputs $(\mathbf{C}_1 + \mathbf{C}_2, \mathsf{mode}_1)$ if $\mathsf{mode}_1 = \mathsf{mode}_2$, otherwise $\perp$.
- Add[7], (**Addition for RLWE-encodings**). The algorithm takes as input two RLWE-encodings, namely $(c_1, \mathsf{mode}_1), (c_2, \mathsf{mode}_2)$, outputs $(c_1 + c_2, \mathsf{mode}_1)$ if $\mathsf{mode}_1 = \mathsf{mode}_2$, otherwise $\perp$.
- Mult, (**Homomorphic Product for RGSW-RGSW**). The algorithm takes input two (packed) RGSW ciphertexts, namely $(\mathbf{C}_1, \mathsf{mode}_1)$ and $(\mathbf{C}_2, \mathsf{mode}_2)$, and then computes $\mathbf{C} = \mathbf{C}_1 \cdot \mathbf{G}^{-1}(\mathbf{C}_2)$. Then it outputs as:

---

[7] Here we use the same function name as the above, where the input type specifies which function the call refers to.

- $\text{mode}_1 = \text{``}\mathcal{R}_{12}\text{''}$ and $\text{mode}_2 = \text{``}\mathcal{R}_{12} \to \mathcal{R}_{13}\text{''}$: output $(\text{Eval-Tr}_{K/K_{13}}(\mathbf{C}),$ $\mathcal{R}_{13})$.
- $\text{mode}_1 = \text{``}\mathcal{R}_{13}\text{''}$ and $\text{mode}_2 = \text{``}\mathcal{R}_{13} \to \mathcal{R}_{12}\text{''}$: output $(\text{Eval-Tr}_{K/K_{12}}(\mathbf{C}),$ $\mathcal{R}_{12})$.
- $\text{mode}_1 = \text{``}\mathcal{R}_{12} \to \mathcal{R}_{13}\text{''}$ and $\text{mode}_2 = \text{``}\mathcal{R}_{12}\text{''}$: output $(\text{Eval-Tr}_{K/K_{13}}(\mathbf{C}),$ $\mathcal{R}_{13})$.
- $\text{mode}_1 = \text{``}\mathcal{R}_{13} \to \mathcal{R}_{12}\text{''}$ and $\text{mode}_2 = \text{``}\mathcal{R}_{13}\text{''}$: output $(\text{Eval-Tr}_{K/K_{12}}(\mathbf{C}),$ $\mathcal{R}_{12})$.
- Otherwise, output $\perp$.

- Ext-Prod, **(External Product for RGSW-RLWE).** The algorithm takes inputs a RGSW encoding $(\mathbf{C}_1, \text{mode}_1)$ and a RLWE encoding (c_2, mode_2), and then computes $c = \mathbf{C}_1 \boxtimes c_2 = \mathbf{C}_1 \cdot g^{-1}(c_2)$. Then it outputs according as:
  - $\text{mode}_1 = \text{``}\mathcal{R}_{12}\text{''}$ and $\text{mode}_2 = \text{``}\mathcal{R}_{12} \to \mathcal{R}_{13}\text{''}$: output $\text{Eval-Tr}_{K/K_{13}}(c)$.
  - $\text{mode}_1 = \text{``}\mathcal{R}_{13}\text{''}$ and $\text{mode}_2 = \text{``}\mathcal{R}_{13} \to \mathcal{R}_{12}\text{''}$: output $\text{Eval-Tr}_{K/K_{12}}(c)$.
  - $\text{mode}_1 = \text{``}\mathcal{R}_{12} \to \mathcal{R}_{13}\text{''}$ and $\text{mode}_2 = \text{``}\mathcal{R}_{12}\text{''}$: output $\text{Eval-Tr}_{K/K_{13}}(c)$.
  - $\text{mode}_1 = \text{``}\mathcal{R}_{13} \to \mathcal{R}_{12}\text{''}$ and $\text{mode}_2 = \text{``}\mathcal{R}_{13}\text{''}$: output $\text{Eval-Tr}_{K/K_{12}}(c)$.
  - Otherwise, output $\perp$.

The readers should keep it in mind that the above operations are in $\mathcal{R}_Q$, where the modulo Q is taken implicitly. Next we describe theorems to summarize the correctness and error growth. Detailed proofs appear in the full version.

Theorem 4.3. *Let* $\mathbf{C}_1, \ldots, \mathbf{C}_r$ *be* RGSW *ciphertexts with error terms* $e_1, \ldots, e_r$, *messages* $\mu_1, \ldots, \mu_r \in \mathcal{R}_1$ *and* $\mathbf{C}'_1, \ldots, \mathbf{C}'_r$ *be* RGSW *ciphertexts with error terms* $e'_1, \ldots, e'_r$, *messages* $\mu'_1, \ldots, \mu'_r \in \mathcal{R}_1$. *Denote*

- RGSW-Pack$(\mathbf{C}_1, \ldots, \mathbf{C}_r, \text{``}\mathcal{R}_{12}\text{''})$ *as* $\mathbf{D}$,
- RGSW-Pack$(\mathbf{C}'_1, \ldots, \mathbf{C}'_r, \text{``}\mathcal{R}_{12} \to \mathcal{R}_{13}\text{''})$ *as* $\mathbf{D}'$,
- Mult$(\mathbf{D}', \mathbf{D})$ *as* $\mathbf{F}$,
- *the encrypted messages of the packed ciphertexts* $\mathbf{D}$ *as* $\mu_\mathbf{D}$,
- *the encrypted messages of the packed ciphertexts* $\mathbf{D}'$ *as* $\mu_{\mathbf{D}'}$.

Then, $\mu_\mathbf{D} = \sum_{i=1}^r \mu_i \cdot \mathsf{v}_i$, $\mu_{\mathbf{D}'} = \sum_{i=1}^r \mu'_i \cdot \mathsf{v}_i^\vee \mathsf{w}_i$ *and* $\mathbf{F}$ *is a packed* RGSW *ciphertext encrypting* $\text{Tr}_{K/K_{13}}(\mu_\mathbf{D} \cdot \mu_{\mathbf{D}'})$ *with mode* $\mathcal{R}_{13}$.

Theorem 4.4. *Let* $c_1, \ldots, c_r$ *be* RLWE *ciphertexts with error terms* $e_1, \ldots, e_r$, *messages* $\mu_1, \ldots, \mu_r \in \mathcal{R}_1$ *and* $\mathbf{C}'_1, \ldots, \mathbf{C}'_r$ *be* RGSW *ciphertexts with error terms* $e'_1, \ldots, e'_r$, *messages* $\mu'_1, \ldots, \mu'_r \in \mathcal{R}_1$. *Denote*

- RLWE-Pack$(c_1, \ldots, c_r, \text{``}\mathcal{R}_{12}\text{''})$ *as* d,
- RGSW-Pack$(\mathbf{C}'_1, \ldots, \mathbf{C}'_r, \text{``}\mathcal{R}_{12} \to \mathcal{R}_{13}\text{''})$ *as* $\mathbf{D}'$,
- Ext-Prod$(\mathbf{D}', d)$ *as* f,
- *the encrypted messages of the packed ciphertexts* d *as* μ_d,
- *the encrypted messages of the packed ciphertexts* $\mathbf{D}'$ *as* $\mu_{\mathbf{D}'}$.

Then, $\mu_d = \sum_{i=1}^r \mu_i \cdot \mathsf{v}_i$, $\mu_{\mathbf{D}'} = \sum_{i=1}^r \mu'_i \cdot \mathsf{v}_i^\vee \mathsf{w}_i$ *and* f *is a packed* RLWE *ciphertext encrypting* $\text{Tr}_{K/K_{13}}(\mu_d \cdot \mu_{\mathbf{D}'})$ *with mode* $\mathcal{R}_{13}$.

Assuming that for any x *(in the input domain),* $\text{Err}(\text{Eval-Tr}_{K/K_{13}}(x)) = \text{Tr}_{K/K_{13}}(\text{Err}(x)) + e'$ *for some* e', *whose norm upper bound can be independent of* x, *then we have* $\text{Err}(f) = \text{Tr}_{K/K_{13}}\left(\sum_i e'_i \mathsf{v}_i^\vee \mathsf{w}_i g^{-1}(d) + \mu_{\mathbf{D}'}(e_i \mathsf{v}_i)\right) + e'$.

We notice the above two theorems can be easily adapted to the setting of the modes $\mathcal{R}_{13}$ and $\mathcal{R}_{13} \to \mathcal{R}_{12}$. We omit the statement to avoid repetition.

4.3 Homomorphic Evaluation of the Trace Function

In this section, we present an efficient method for homomorphic evaluation of the trace function, which was used as a black-box in the homomorphic multiplication in the prior subsection. There have been efficient methods studied in the literature, e.g., [3,11,22], in the cyclotomic rings of powers of two, and here we generalize the prior methods to the setting of general cyclotomic rings.

General Method over RLWE Ciphertexts. Suppose E/F is an algebraic extension and the degree $[E : F] = d$, then the function $\mathsf{Tr}_{E/F}$ is the sum of d automorphisms on E that fix every element in F. These d automorphisms form a group, namely the Galois group denoted as $\mathsf{Gal}(E/F)$. Then we can express $\mathsf{Tr}_{E/F}(\cdot) = \sum_{\sigma \in \mathsf{Gal}(E/F)} \sigma(\cdot)$.

The general way to compute homomorphic evaluation of $\mathsf{Tr}_{E/F}$ is to compute homomorphic evaluation of all the σ's in the Galois group, and then sum them up. We notice that homomorphic evaluation of any automorphism σ can be achieved using the classic key-switch technique [8] as follows. We first present the syntax of the key-switch algorithm.

Key-Switch Algorithm. Let KS be the key-switch algorithm (the ring variant of [8]) that takes input a RLWE ciphertext $(b, a) \in \mathsf{RLWE}_s(\mu) \in \mathcal{R}_Q^2$ and an evaluation key $\mathsf{evk}^{(\sigma)}$ and outputs a RLWE ciphertext $(b', a') \in \mathsf{RLWE}_{\sigma(s)}(\mu) \in \mathcal{R}_Q^2$. We present the details of KS in the full version of this work.

Given the evaluation algorithm KS, homomorphic evaluation of Tr can be achieved by the following. Given input $(b, a) \in \mathsf{RLWE}_s(\mu)$ and evaluation keys $\{\mathsf{evk}^\sigma\}_{\sigma \in \mathsf{Gal}(E/F)}$, the algorithm does:

1. For each $\sigma \in \mathsf{Gal}(E/F)$, compute $c_\sigma = (\sigma(b), \sigma(a))$ and set $c'_\sigma = \mathsf{KS}(c_\sigma, \mathsf{evk}^{(\sigma^{-1})})$.
2. Output $\sum_{\sigma \in \mathsf{Gal}(E/F)} c'_\sigma$ as the resulting ciphertext.

It is not hard to check that for each σ, $c_\sigma \in \mathsf{RLWE}_{\sigma(s)}(\sigma(\mu))$, and by correctness of KS, $c'_\sigma \in \mathsf{RLWE}_s(\sigma(\mu))$. Thus, the above is a correct algorithm. Moreover, it requires d calls[8] to the underlying KS algorithm.

More Efficient Evaluation with Algebraic Structures. If there is an intermediate field K between E and F, then we can (homomorphically) compute the trace function more efficiently via the composition property of the trace function. Let $F \subset K \subset E$ be algebraic extensions, $[E : K] = d_1$ and $[K : F] = d_2$, then we have $d = d_1 \cdot d_2$ and $\mathsf{Tr}_{E/F} = \mathsf{Tr}_{K/F} \circ \mathsf{Tr}_{E/K}$. By definition, we have $\mathsf{Tr}_{E/K}(\cdot) = \sum_{\sigma \in \mathsf{Gal}(E/K)} \sigma(\cdot)$, and $\mathsf{Tr}_{K/F}(\cdot) = \sum_{\sigma \in \mathsf{Gal}(K/F)} \sigma(\cdot)$. To compute

---

[8] For small d's, the *Hoistng* technique [22] can be used to improve efficiency.

$\mathsf{Tr}_{E/F}(x)$, we can first compute $x' = \mathsf{Tr}_{E/K}(x)$, and then output $\mathsf{Tr}_{K/F}(x')$. The homomorphic evaluation just computes the basic trace evaluation twice of the cases E/K and K/F. In this way, the algorithm would require only $d_1 + d_2$ calls to the underlying KS. This is more efficient than the basic algorithm applied to the case E/F directly, which would require $d = d_1 \cdot d_2$ calls to the KS.

The Tower Case. The above idea works best in the *tower* case, where there are many intermediate fields between E and F. In the rest, we present an optimized homomorphic evaluation algorithm for $\mathsf{Tr}_{K/K_{13}} : \mathcal{R}_1 \otimes \mathcal{R}_2^\vee \otimes \mathcal{R}_3 \mapsto \mathcal{R}_1 \otimes \mathcal{R}_3$, assuming there are many intermediate fields. We discuss how to instantiate this later in Sect. 5. Note that a homomorphic algorithm for the other case $\mathsf{Tr}_{K/K_{12}}$ can be derived similarly.

Assume the following tower structure: $K_{13} = E_t \subset E_{t-1} \subset \cdots \subset E_1 = K$. Then we can express $\mathsf{Tr}_{K/K_{13}} = \mathsf{Tr}_{E_{t-1}/E_t} \circ \mathsf{Tr}_{E_{t-2}/E_{t-1}} \circ \cdots \circ \mathsf{Tr}_{E_1/E_2}$. We will present how to instantiate this tower structure in the cyclotomic fields in Sect. 5. By using the basic homomorphic evaluation on the cases E_i/E_{i+1}, we can derive a more efficient algorithm.

Before presenting formally the procedure, we notice that there is a technical subtlety – the input RLWE ciphertext is in the dual module, e.g., $(\mathcal{R}_1 \otimes \mathcal{R}_2^\vee \otimes \mathcal{R}_3)^2$, so that we cannot directly apply the above procedure. To tackle this, we first observe that there is an integer P that is invertible under modulo Q, and can map an element in the dual module to a ring element by the multiplication, i.e., (1) $P^{-1} \mod Q$ exists, and (2) for every $x \in \mathcal{R}_1 \otimes \mathcal{R}_2^\vee \otimes \mathcal{R}_3$, $P \cdot x \in \mathcal{R}_1 \otimes \mathcal{R}_2 \otimes \mathcal{R}_3$. In Sect. 5, we show how to set P concretely with detailed instantiations of the required tensor rings. By using this number P, we present a tweaked method in Algorithm 4.1 below.

Algorithm 4.1: (RLWE)-Eval-$\mathsf{Tr}_{K/K_{13}}$ with the tower structure

---

Input   :
- A RLWE ciphertext $(b, a) \in (\mathcal{R}_1 \otimes \mathcal{R}_2^\vee \otimes \mathcal{R}_3)^2$ that encrypts a message $\mu \in \mathcal{R}_1 \otimes \mathcal{R}_2^\vee \otimes \mathcal{R}_3$ under a secret $s \in \mathcal{R}$.
- **Evaluation Key:** $\{\mathsf{evk}^{(\sigma)}\}_{\sigma \in \bigcup_{i \in [t-1]} \mathsf{Gal}(E_i/E_{i+1})}$, and $\mathsf{evk} \in \mathsf{RGSW}_s(P^{-1} \cdot s) \in \mathcal{R}^2$.

Output : A RLWE ciphertext $c \in \mathsf{RLWE}_s(\mathsf{Tr}_{K/K_{13}}(\mu))$.

---

1   Initialize $c = (b, a)$, and set $\bar{a} = P \cdot a$ (interpreted as an element in $\mathcal{R}$) ;
2   Set $c' = (0, \bar{a})$ and compute $d = \mathsf{evk} \boxtimes c'$;   // $d \in \mathsf{RLWE}_s(P^{-1}s \cdot \bar{a}) \in \mathcal{R}^2$;
3   **for** $i = 1$ **to** $t - 1$ **do**
4 | Let $(d_1, d_2) = d$;
5 | Compute $d' = \sum_{\sigma \in \mathsf{Gal}(E_i/E_{i+1})} \mathsf{KS}((\sigma(d_1), \sigma(d_2)), \mathsf{evk}^{(\sigma^{-1})})$;
6 | Set $d = d'$ and $d' = (0, 0)$
7   Return $(\mathsf{Tr}_{K/K_{13}}(b), 0) - d$.   // $d \in \mathsf{RLWE}_s(\mathsf{Tr}_{K/K_{13}}(sa)) \in \mathcal{R}^2$

Remark 4.5. *Here we slightly abuse the notation of the automorphism* $\sigma \in$ $\mathsf{Gal}(E_i/E_{i+1})$ *for simplicity of presentation.*

As the input domain of such σ *is* E_i, *we should not give* $(d_1, d_2) \in \mathcal{R} \subset K$ *(elements of the full ring) as the input to the automorphism. Nevertheless, by the Galois theorem, for any* $\sigma \in \mathsf{Gal}(E_i/E_{i+1})$, *there exists at least one* $\sigma' \in$ $\mathsf{Gal}(K/E_{i+1})$ *such that* $\sigma'|_{E_i} = \sigma$. *In this paper,* σ *refers to (an arbitrary) of such* σ' *who acts identically as* σ *for all inputs in* E_i.

To verify correctness, we first notice that $\mathsf{Tr}_{K/K_{13}}(b) = \mathsf{Tr}_{K/K_{13}}(sa) + \mathsf{Tr}_{K/K_{13}}(e) + \mathsf{Tr}_{K/K_{13}}(\mu) \in \mathcal{R}$. Next, at the end of the for loop (line 6), we can easily check that $d \in \mathsf{RLWE}_s(\mathsf{Tr}_{K/K_{13}}(P^{-1}s\bar{a}))$. Then we have

$$\mathsf{Tr}_{K/K_{13}}(P^{-1}s\bar{a}) = P^{-1}\mathsf{Tr}_{K/K_{13}}(s\bar{a}) = P^{-1}\mathsf{Tr}_{K/K_{13}}(sPa) = \mathsf{Tr}_{K/K_{13}}(sa).$$

Crucially the last equality holds because $\mathsf{Tr}_{K/K_{13}}(sa) \in \mathcal{R}_1 \otimes \mathcal{R}_3$, and $P^{-1} \cdot$ $\mathsf{Tr}_{K/K_{13}}(sPa) = P^{-1} \cdot P \cdot \mathsf{Tr}_{K/K_{13}}(sa) = \mathsf{Tr}_{K/K_{13}}(sa)$ in modulo Q. Then correctness simply follows. As the modulus does not change in the whole procedure, we omit the modulo Q description in the algorithm.

To analyze efficiency, we first denote the degrees as $d_i = [E_i : E_{i+1}]$ for $i \in [t-1]$. Then the above algorithm makes $\sum_{i \in [t-1]} d_i$ calls to the underlying KS algorithm, which is again way more efficient than the basic algorithm applied to the case K/K_{13}, which would require $d = \prod_{i \in [t-1]} d_i$ calls to KS. Moreover, if each $d_i = O(1)$, then the efficient algorithm as above would require $O(\log d)$ calls to the KS, which is significantly better than d calls by the basic approach.

Below we present the noise analysis and defer the proof to the full version.

Theorem 4.6. *Adapt the notations of Algorithm 4.1. Assume that for every* $d \in$ $\mathsf{RLWE}_s(\mu)$, $\mathsf{Err}(\mathsf{KS}(d)) = \mathsf{Err}(d) + e'$ *where* $\|e'\|_\infty$ *is a sub-Gaussian with parameter* B, *and for the initial* d, $\|\mathsf{Err}(d)\|_\infty$ *is also a sub-Gaussian with parameter* B. *Let* c *be the output ciphertext of the algorithm. Then* $\mathsf{Err}(c) = \mathsf{Tr}_{K/K_{13}}(e) + e''$ *where* e *is the noise of the input ciphertext, and* $\|e''\|_\infty$ *is a sub-Gaussian with parameter upper bounded by* $3dB$.

Eval-Tr for RGSW. The Eval-$\mathsf{Tr}_{K/K_{13}}$ algorithm for RLWE ciphertexts can be extended to RGSW ciphertexts. Details are in the full version.

5   Instantiations

In this section, we present how to instantiate all the components used in the abstraction in Sect. 4, so that the parameters can be analyzed concretely. Particularly, we need to instantiate: (1) tensor ring $\mathcal{R} = \mathcal{R}_1 \otimes \mathcal{R}_2 \otimes \mathcal{R}_3$, and (2) good bases of these rings and their duals. Then we can further determine parameters for the noise growth in Theorems 4.3 and 4.4, under the instantiations.

Tensor Fields/Rings. We notice that any cyclotomic field has some nice properties of decomposability, i.e., for $m = q\rho'\tau'$ where q, ρ', τ' are co-prime integers, then $\mathbb{Q}(\xi_m) \cong \mathbb{Q}(\xi_q) \otimes \mathbb{Q}(\xi_{\rho'}) \otimes \mathbb{Q}(\xi_{\tau'})$. Thus, we can use their rings of integers to instantiate our framework. Particularly, we set $\mathcal{R}_1 = \mathbb{Z}[\xi_q]$, $\mathcal{R}_2 = \mathbb{Z}[\xi_{\rho'}]$, and $\mathcal{R}_3 = \mathbb{Z}[\xi_{\tau'}]$. We notice that the tensor ring $\mathcal{R} = \mathcal{R}_1 \otimes \mathcal{R}_2 \otimes \mathcal{R}_3$ has dimension $N = \phi(m)$, $\mathcal{R}_2$ has dimension $\rho = \phi(\rho')$, and $\mathcal{R}_3$ has dimension $\tau = \phi(\tau')$. Moreover, we have $N = \phi(q)\rho\tau$. We notice that the hardness of RLWE scales with N [2,25,31].

To apply the fast trace evaluation as Sect. 4.3, we choose ρ' and τ' as powers of primes, i.e., $\rho' = p_1^{d_1}$ and $\tau' = p_2^{d_2}$, for some small primes p_1, p_2 of constant sizes, e.g., $3, 5$. We notice that for any element $x \in \mathcal{R}_2^\vee$, $\rho'x \in \mathcal{R}_2$, and therefore we can set $P = \rho'$ in Algorithm 4.1. Similarly, we can set $P = \tau'$ for computing (RLWE)-Eval-Tr$_{K/K_{12}}$. As argued before, the homomorphic evaluation of the trace function would need $O(\log \rho')$ or $O(\log \tau')$ calls to the key-switch function (for the RLWE case). To maximize the space utility, we would set $\rho \approx \tau$. For the batch bootstrapping of the AP14/FHEW framework, we set q to be the input LWE modulus, which can be $\tilde{O}(\sqrt{n})$ where n is the LWE dimension.

Bases. We next determine concrete bases for $\mathcal{R}_1, \mathcal{R}_2, \mathcal{R}_3$ (and their dual rings), denoted as $\mathcal{B}_1, \mathcal{B}_2, \mathcal{B}_3$ (and $\mathcal{B}_1^\vee, \mathcal{B}_2^\vee, \mathcal{B}_3^\vee$, respectively).

Particularly, we set $\mathcal{B}_i^\vee$ to be the decoding basis of the work [26] for each $i = 1, 2, 3$. As argued in [26], the primal bases $\mathcal{B}_1, \mathcal{B}_2, \mathcal{B}_3$ are defined as the conjugate of the powerful bases. These bases are "short", and thus would give tighter bounds for our analyses. Below we briefly summarize some nice properties about the decoding bases and their duals from [26].

Lemma 5.1 ([26]). *Let $z = w^e$ be some prime power, $\boldsymbol{d}$ be the decoding basis of $\mathbb{Z}^\vee[\xi_z]$, and $\boldsymbol{b}$ be the dual of $\boldsymbol{d}$. Then for any element $d \in \boldsymbol{d}$, $b \in \boldsymbol{b}$, we have $\|b\|_\infty = 1$ and $\|d\|_\infty \leq 2(w-1)/z$.*

By using our notation in Sect. 4.1, we denote the conjugate of the powerful basis as $\mathcal{B}_2 = \{v_i\}_{i \in [\rho]}$, $\mathcal{B}_3 = \{w_i\}_{i \in [\tau]}$, and the decoding bases (their dual) as $\mathcal{B}_2^\vee = \{v_i^\vee\}_{i \in [\rho]}$, $\mathcal{B}_3^\vee = \{w_i^\vee\}_{i \in [\tau]}$. Then by the above lemma, we have (1) $\|v_i\|_\infty = 1$ and $\|w_i\|_\infty = 1$, and (2) $\|v_i^\vee\|_\infty \leq 2(p_1 - 1)/\rho'$ and $\|w_i^\vee\|_\infty \leq 2(p_2 - 1)/\tau'$.

As we choose q, ρ', τ' to be relatively prime, we can use the individual bases to determine a basis of the tensor ring, i.e., $\mathcal{B}_i \otimes \mathcal{B}_j$ is the powerful basis of $\mathcal{R}_i \otimes \mathcal{R}_j$. Also, we set parameter $r = \min(\rho, \tau)$ as the batch parameter, i.e., the maximal number of slots our method can pack. If we set $\rho \approx \tau$, then $r \approx \sqrt{N/q}$.

Examples. We give some examples of concrete numbers to illustrate the above ideas. Let Q be the RLWE modulus, and σ be the noise parameter (in the absolute value). The RLWE hardness can be estimated by N (the ring dimension) and noise-to-modulus ratio σ/Q (also known as α) from the estimator [2] (Table 1).

Table 1. Some examples of parameters

	m-cyclotomic $= q \times \rho' \times \tau'$	Dim $N = \phi(m)$ $= \phi(q) \times \rho \times \tau$	Batch param r	Modulus Q (approx)	Noise σ	Hardness (in bit)	Input Dim n
Set 1	$251 * 2^3 * 3^2$	$250 * 4 * 6 = 6000$	4	2^{128}	3.2	129.9	500
Set 2	$211 * 3^2 * 7$	$210 * 6 * 6 = 7560$	6	2^{128}	3.2	178.4	500

Note: These examples demonstrate some ideas to set concrete parameters. How to optimize the concrete performance is an interesting future work. The moduli Q's here are approximated at this order. There can be other constraints, e.g., Q and m are co-prime for NTT accelerations.

Key-Switch Instantiation. Our trace evaluation algorithms (both the RLWE and RGSW settings) require to use the key-switch procedure. This can be achieved with existing techniques, e.g., [22]. Details are presented in the full version.

Particularly, by the parameters of the key-switch (in the full version) and Lemma 3.2, we can set $B = \sqrt{N \cdot \log Q} \cdot E$ in Theorem 4.6, where E is the noise bound in the key-switch keys. By using these instantiations applied to Theorem 4.4, we can achieve the following corollary for the external product:

Corollary 5.2. *Adapt the notations of Theorems 4.4. If the errors of the key-switch keys is upper bounded by E, and g^{-1} is with respect to the basis $\mathcal{B}_1 \otimes \mathcal{B}_2 \otimes \mathcal{B}_3$. Then $\|\mathsf{Err}(f)\|_\infty$ is upper bounded by*

$$\frac{2\rho(p_1 - 1)\sqrt{N \log Q}}{\rho'} \sum \|e_i'\|_\infty + \rho\|\mu_{\mathbf{D'}}\| \sum \|e_i\|_\infty + \|e''\|_\infty,$$

where $\|e''\|_\infty$ is a sub-Gaussian with parameter upper bounded by $3\rho'\sqrt{N \log Q}E$.

A similar bound can be derived for the RGSW multiplication of Theorem 4.3 under the instantiation in this section. Details are in the full version.

6   Batch Bootstrapping via Our New Framework

Now we present how to batch the AP14/FHEW bootstrapping [4,13,17] within a polynomial modulus. We first present some background and notations, and then describe how to apply our new batch framework to the bootstrapping procedure.

6.1   Bootstrapping Background

Input. The general bootstrapping algorithm takes an LWE ciphertext $(b, a) \in \mathbb{Z}_q^{1+n}$ as input, where n and q are small, i.e., $n = \widetilde{O}(\lambda)$, $q = \widetilde{O}(\sqrt{\lambda})^9$. Also

---

[9] In the full version of this work, we present how to achieve such a q.

it is without loss of generality to assume the input ciphertexts are encrypted under binary secret vectors. These can be achieved without loss of generality by applying the dimension reduction, modulus switch (the randomized version), and bit-decomposition/power-of-two[10] as described in [4]. We know for any GSW, RLWE, or RGSW ciphertext, we can always publicly extract an LWE ciphertext that encrypts the same message [4]. Therefore, assuming the input to be the LWE form is without loss of generality.

The Batch Setting. Let r be the batch parameter as we instantiate in Sect. 5. Our bootstrapping algorithm takes input r LWE ciphertexts, i.e., $\{(b_i, \boldsymbol{a}_i)\}_{i \in [r]}$, encrypting perhaps different messages under the same secret key $\boldsymbol{s}$.

Output. The output of bootstrapping algorithm is a ciphertext encrypting the same as the input ciphertexts. In the batch setting, the output can be either a packed ciphertext, or r different ciphertexts, encrypting the same message vector. Let N, Q denote the dimension and modulus used by the output ciphertext.

6.2   Batch Bootstrapping

Notations. We use the instantiation in Sect. 5 for the batch framework and present the required parameters in our batch algorithm.

- n: the dimension of the input LWE scheme.
- q: the modulus of the input LWE scheme, set as a prime of size $\tilde{O}(\sqrt{\lambda})$.
- r: the number of slots we can pack, where $r = \min\{\rho, \tau\}$.
- $\boldsymbol{s}$: the secret key of the input LWE ciphertexts.
- $\mathcal{R}$: the underlying ring of the RGSW scheme. We use the instantiation in Sect. 5, i.e., the tensor ring $\mathcal{R} = \mathcal{R}_1 \otimes \mathcal{R}_2 \otimes \mathcal{R}_3$.
- $\mathcal{R}_1$: the first ring is set as $\mathbb{Q}(\xi_q)$.
- $\mathcal{R}_2$: the second ring with dimension $\rho = \phi(\rho')$, $\rho' = p_1^{d_1}$
- $\mathcal{R}_3$: the third ring with dimension $\tau = \phi(\tau')$, $\tau' = p_2^{d_2}$
- Q: the modulus of the RGSW scheme.
- $\boldsymbol{s}'$: the secret of the RGSW scheme.

Auxiliary Algorithm. In Algorithm 6.1 below, we describe a batch blind-rotate (BR) algorithm, which is an SIMD version of FHEW/TFHE blind-rotate of [14,17], under our framework.

---

[10] For any $(\boldsymbol{s}, \boldsymbol{a}) \in \mathbb{Z}_q^n \times \mathbb{Z}_q^n$, $\langle \boldsymbol{s}, \boldsymbol{a} \rangle = \langle \boldsymbol{s}', \boldsymbol{a}' \rangle$ where $\boldsymbol{a}' \in \mathbb{Z}_q^{n \log q}$ is the power-of-two of $\boldsymbol{a}$ and $\boldsymbol{s}' \in \mathbb{Z}_q^{n \log q}$ is the bit-decomposition of $\boldsymbol{s}$. Using this insight, it is without loss of generality to just consider binary secret vectors in the bootstrapping task. Some practical optimizations, e.g., [6,13,17,28] use binary or ternary LWE, so that the secret vector $\boldsymbol{s}$ is set directly to binary or ternary. In this case, there is no need to blow up the dimension of $\boldsymbol{a}$.

Algorithm 6.1: Batch-BR (i.e., Batch Blind Rotate)

Input :
- A packed RLWE ciphertext ACC_0.
- (Partial) **Bootstrapping key:** $\{\mathsf{BK} \in \mathsf{RGSW}_{s'}^Q(s)\}$ where $s \in \{0,1\}$.
- Integers $\{a_i\}_{i \in [r]}$.

Output : A packed RLWE ciphertext.

---

1 **if** *the mode of* ACC_0 *is* "$\mathcal{R}_{12}$" **then**
2 $\quad$ Set $\mathsf{ACC} = \mathsf{Ext\text{-}Prod}((\mathsf{BK} \cdot (\sum_i \xi_q^{a_i} \mathsf{v}_i^{\vee} \mathsf{w}_i) + (\mathsf{G} - \mathsf{BK}) \cdot \sum_i \mathsf{v}_i^{\vee} \mathsf{w}_i,\ "\mathcal{R}_{12} \to$
$\quad\quad \mathcal{R}_{13}"),(\mathsf{ACC}_0, "\mathcal{R}_{12}"))$
3 **else if** *the mode of* ACC_0 *is* "$\mathcal{R}_{13}$" **then**
4 $\quad$ Set $\mathsf{ACC} = \mathsf{Ext\text{-}Prod}((\mathsf{BK} \cdot (\sum_i \xi_q^{a_i} \mathsf{v}_i \mathsf{w}_i^{\vee}) + (\mathsf{G} - \mathsf{BK}) \cdot \sum_i \mathsf{v}_i \mathsf{w}_i^{\vee},\ "\mathcal{R}_{13} \to$
$\quad\quad \mathcal{R}_{12}"),(\mathsf{ACC}_0, "\mathcal{R}_{13}"))$
5 **Return:** ACC

We next present a high level description of what the batch BR algorithm is computing. Suppose the input ACC_0 is a packed ciphertext that encrypts $(\xi_q^{x_1}, \ldots, \xi_q^{x_r})$ under mode "$\mathcal{R}_{12}''$. Then the result of the algorithm will produce a packed ciphertext that encrypts $(\xi_q^{x_1+a_1 s}, \ldots, \xi_q^{x_r+a_r s})$, under mode "$\mathcal{R}_{13}''$. The formal analysis is captured by the following theorem.

Theorem 6.1. *Adapt the notations in Algorithm 6.1. Let the input* ACC_0 *be a packed* RLWE *encrypting* μ *of mode* "$\mathcal{R}_{1b}''$ *for* $b \in \{2,3\}$. *If* $b = 2$, *then the output is a packed* RLWE *ciphertext encrypting* $\mathsf{Tr}_{K/K_{13}}(\mu \cdot \sum_{i \in [r]} \xi_q^{a_i s} \mathsf{v}_i^{\vee} \mathsf{w}_i)$ *of mode* "$\mathcal{R}_{13}$", *or* $\mathsf{Tr}_{K/K_{12}}(\mu \cdot \sum_{i \in [r]} \xi_q^{a_i s} \mathsf{v}_i \mathsf{w}_i^{\vee})$ *of mode* "$\mathcal{R}_{12}$" *if* $b = 3$.

Proof. By symmetry, it suffices to prove the case $b = 2$, and the other case follows analogously. Since $s \in \{0,1\}$, we have $\mathsf{BK} \cdot (\sum_i \xi_q^{a_i} \mathsf{v}_i^{\vee} \mathsf{w}_i) + (\mathsf{G} - \mathsf{BK}) \cdot \sum_i \mathsf{v}_i^{\vee} \mathsf{w}_i \in \mathsf{RGSW}(\sum_{i \in [r]} \xi_q^{a_i s} \mathsf{v}_i^{\vee} \mathsf{w}_i)$. Then by the Theorem 4.4, ACC belongs to $\mathsf{RLWE}(\mathsf{Tr}_{K/K_{13}}(\mu \cdot \sum_{i \in [r]} \xi_q^{a_i s} \mathsf{v}_i^{\vee} \mathsf{w}_i))$.

Batch Bootstrapping. In Algorithm 6.2, we present our final batch bootstrapping algorithm, using the batch BR (Algorithm 6.1) as a subroutine. To analyze the concrete bounds, we use the instantiation in Sect. 5. We recall some basic facts: let $\{\mathsf{v}_i\}_{i \in [\rho]}$, $\{\mathsf{w}_i\}_{i \in [\tau]}$ be the bases of $\mathcal{R}_2$ and $\mathcal{R}_3$. Then we have

1. $\|\mathsf{v}_i\|_\infty = 1$ and $\|\mathsf{w}_i\|_\infty = 1$,
2. $\|\mathsf{v}_i^{\vee}\|_\infty \leq 2(p_1 - 1)/\rho'$ and $\|\mathsf{w}_i^{\vee}\|_\infty \leq 2(p_2 - 1)/\tau'$.

The analysis of Algorithm 6.2 is summarized by the theorem.

Theorem 6.2. *Let* $\boldsymbol{\mu} = (\mu_1, \ldots, \mu_r)$ *be binary messages encrypted in the input* LWE *ciphertexts,* $\{(b_i, \boldsymbol{a}_i)\}_{i \in [r]}$. *Then the algorithm outputs a fresh packed* RLWE *ciphertext* $\boldsymbol{c}$, *either in* $\mathsf{RLWE}_{s'}^Q(\sum \mu_i \mathsf{v}_i)$ *or* $\mathsf{RLWE}_{s'}^Q(\sum \mu_i \mathsf{w}_i)$.

Moreover, $\|\mathsf{Err}(\boldsymbol{c})\|_\infty$ *is bounded by a sub-Gaussian variable with parameter* $O(\gamma)$ *such that* $\gamma \leq nrqN\sqrt{N \log Q}E$, *where* E *is the upper bound (infinity norm of the canonical embedding) of errors in all bootstrapping/evaluation keys.*

Algorithm 6.2: Batch-BTS

Input   :
  - r LWE ciphertexts $(b_i, \boldsymbol{a}_i) = (b_i, a_{i1}, ..., a_{in}) \in \mathsf{LWE_s}(\mu_i)$ for $i \in [r]$.
  - **Bootstrapping key:** $\{\mathsf{BK}_i \in \mathsf{RGSW}_{s'}^{Q'}(s_i)\}_{i \in [n]}$, where s_i is the i-th entry of the common secret $\boldsymbol{s}$ of the LWE ciphertexts, and evk is the evaluation key for the homomorphic trace algorithms.

Output : A packed RLWE ciphertext.

1 Set $\mathsf{ACC}_0 = \mathsf{RLWE\text{-}Pack}((q^{-1}\xi_q^{b_1}, 0), ..., (q^{-1}\xi_q^{b_r}, 0)), \text{``}\mathcal{R}_{12}\text{''})$, where $q^{-1} \in \mathcal{R}_Q$;
2 **for** $k = 1$ **to** n **do**
3 $\quad$ $\mathsf{ACC}_k = \mathsf{Batch\text{-}BR}\left(\mathsf{ACC}_{k-1}, \mathsf{BK}_k \in \mathsf{RGSW}(s_k), \{a_{ik}\}_{i \in [r]}\right)$;
4 Set $\mathsf{test} = \left(\sum_{y \in \mathbb{Z}_q \& \lfloor y \rfloor_2 = 1} \xi_q^{-y}\right)$, $\boldsymbol{d} = (\sum_{i \in [r]} q^{-1}\mathsf{v}_i, 0)$; // $\boldsymbol{d} \in \mathsf{RLWE}_{s'}(q^{-1}\sum_{i \in [r]} \mathsf{v}_i)$;
5 Return $\boldsymbol{c} = \boldsymbol{d} + \mathsf{Eval\text{-}Tr}_{K/K_{23}}(\mathsf{test} \cdot \mathsf{ACC}_n)$.

Proof. We first analyze the correctness. By applying Theorem 6.1 to the for loop in Step 2, we can obtain that ACC_n encrypts $\sum_{i \in [r]} q^{-1} \xi_q^{b_i - \langle \boldsymbol{a}_i, \boldsymbol{s} \rangle} \mathsf{v}_i$, (assuming n is even, which is without loss of generality). Next we use an important fact observed by the work [1] – For any $y = \xi_q^z$, the following equation holds.

$$1 + y + y^2 + \cdots + y^{q-1} = \begin{cases} q & \text{if } z = 0 \mod q \\ 0 & \text{otherwise} \end{cases}.$$

As y is a power of ξ_q, we can further express the equation as $\sum_{0 \le i < q} y^i = 1 + \mathsf{Tr}_{K/K_{23}}(y)$, when q is a prime (which follows by our parameter choice). This corresponds to what step 5 does.

By using this fact, it is easy to verify the following: for any $\xi_q^z, z \in \mathbb{Z}_q$, let $x = \mathsf{test} \cdot (q^{-1}\xi_q^z)$. Then we have $q^{-1} + \mathsf{Tr}_{K/K_{23}}(x) = \begin{cases} 1 & \text{if } \lfloor z \rfloor_2 = 1 \\ 0 & \text{otherwise.} \end{cases} = \lfloor z \rfloor_2$.

By the above equation with our batch computation, the final output of the algorithm would be encrypting $\sum_{i \in [r]} \lfloor b_i - \langle \boldsymbol{a}_i, \boldsymbol{s} \rangle \rfloor_2 \cdot \mathsf{v}_i$. By the correctness of decryption for LWE, the resulting ciphertext belongs to $\mathsf{RLWE}_{s'}^Q(\sum \mu_i \mathsf{v}_i)$. The same analysis works for the case if n is odd, i.e., the resulting ciphertext belongs to $\mathsf{RLWE}_{s'}^Q(\sum \mu_i \mathsf{w}_i)$. Thus, the correctness is proved.

Next we analyze the noise growth. We first analyze the noise of the ACC_n in the for loop and then that of the next stage. By our batch computation framework, we have for $k \in [n]$, $\mathsf{Err}(\mathsf{ACC}_k) = \mathsf{Err}\left(\mathsf{Eval\text{-}Tr}(\mathsf{BK}_k \boxtimes \mathsf{ACC}_{k-1})\right)$. We denote e_k as the $\mathsf{Err}(\mathsf{ACC}_k)$, m_k as the message of BK_k, e_k' as the additive error from the key-switching algorithm in $\mathsf{Eval\text{-}Tr}$. Without loss of generality, we consider that ACC_{k-1} is of the mode "$\mathcal{R}_{12}$", and then identify the recursive relation as following:

$$\begin{aligned} e_k &= e_k' + \mathsf{Tr}_{K/K_{13}}(\mathsf{Err}(\mathsf{BK}_k)\mathbf{G}^{-1}(\mathsf{ACC}_{k-1})) + \mathsf{Tr}_{K/K_{13}}(m_k \cdot e_{k-1}) \\ &= e_k'' + \mathsf{Tr}_{K/K_{13}}(m_k \cdot e_{k-1}), \end{aligned}$$

where $e''_k = e'_k + \mathsf{Tr}_{K/K_{13}}(\mathsf{Err}(\mathsf{BK}_k)\mathbf{G}^{-1}(\mathsf{ACC}_{k-1}))$. We notice that e'_k is *fresh noise* from KS and $\mathsf{Err}(\mathsf{BK}_k)\mathbf{G}^{-1}(\mathsf{ACC}_{k-1})$ is also independent of the recursion index k. Thus, e''_k can also be viewed as *non-accumulating noise* that does not increase over the recursion. Next we further expand the equation and obtain:

$$
\begin{aligned}
e_k &= e''_k + \mathsf{Tr}_{K/K_{13}}(m_k \cdot e_{k-1}) \\
&= e''_k + \mathsf{Tr}_{K/K_{13}}\left(m_k \cdot \left(e''_{k-1} + \mathsf{Tr}_{K/K_{12}}(m_{k-1} \cdot e_{k-2})\right)\right) \\
&= e''_k + \mathsf{Tr}_{K/K_{13}}\left(m_k \cdot e''_{k-1}\right) + \mathsf{Tr}_{K/K_{13}}\left(m_k \cdot \mathsf{Tr}_{K/K_{12}}(m_{k-1} \cdot e_{k-2})\right) \\
&= \widetilde{e}_k + \mathsf{Tr}_{K/K_{13}}\left(m_k \cdot \mathsf{Tr}_{K/K_{12}}(m_{k-1} \cdot e_{k-2})\right),
\end{aligned}
$$

where $\widetilde{e}_k = e''_k + \mathsf{Tr}_{K/K_{13}}\left(m_k \cdot e''_{k-1}\right)$. A similar argument as above shows that $\widetilde{e}_k$ is independent of the recursion index k and thus non-accumulating.

To proceed with the analysis, we first define the following notation. Without loss of generality, we only consider the case where n and k are both even.

Definition 6.3. *Let* $m_k, \ldots, m_1$ *be the packed messages as used in the algorithm, and let* $e \in \mathcal{R}$ *be some input. Define*

$$
T^{2j}(e) = \begin{cases} \mathsf{Tr}_{K/K_{13}}\left(m_k \mathsf{Tr}_{K/K_{12}}(m_{k-1} \cdot e)\right) & \text{for } j = 1 \\ T^{2j-2}\left(\mathsf{Tr}_{K/K_{13}}\left(m_{k-2j+1}\mathsf{Tr}_{K/K_{12}}(m_{k-2j} \cdot e)\right)\right) & \text{for } j \in [2, k/2] \end{cases}.
$$

Then we can unfold the recursive formula and obtain the following expression.

$$
e_k = \widetilde{e}_k + T^2(\widetilde{e}_{k-2}) + T^4(\widetilde{e}_{k-4}) + \cdots + T^k(e_0).
$$

To derive an upper bound for the above, we first prove the following claim:

Claim 6.4. *For* $j \leq k/2$ *and any* $e \in \mathcal{R}$ *such that* $\|e\|_\infty$ *is* B *bounded, then* $\|T^{2j}(e)\|_\infty \leq 4p_1 p_2 r^2 B$.

Proof. We start from the base case $j = 1$. First we can express $e = \sum_{i \in [\rho]} e_i \mathsf{v}_i$ where each $e_i \in \mathcal{R}_{13}$. From our design, we notice that $m_{k-1} = \sum_{i \in [r]} \xi_q^{s_{k-1}} \mathsf{v}_i^\vee \mathsf{w}_i$, and $m_k = \sum_{i \in [r]} \xi_q^{s_k} \mathsf{w}_i^\vee \mathsf{v}_i$. Therefore, $E := \mathsf{Tr}_{K/K_{13}}(m_{k-1} \cdot e) = \sum_{i \in [r]} \xi_q^{s_{k-1}} e_i \mathsf{w}_i$ as the cross terms $\mathsf{v}_i^\vee \mathsf{v}_j$ are all cancelled out by the trace for $i \neq j$. According to our choice of the basis, we have $\|E\|_\infty \leq \rho \cdot \|m_{k-1}\| \cdot \|e\|_\infty \leq \rho \cdot r \cdot 2(p_1 - 1)/\rho' \cdot B \leq 2p_1 r B$. We can further express $E = \sum_{i \in [r]} \xi_q^{s_{k-1}} z_i \mathsf{w}_i$, where each $z_i \in \mathcal{R}_1$. We then use the fact $\|z_i\|_\infty \leq \tau \cdot \|E\|_\infty \cdot \|\mathsf{w}_i^\vee\|_\infty$ as implicitly analyzed in [26]. By plugging the bound of the basis and $\|E\|_\infty$, we have $\|z_i\|_\infty \leq 4p_1 p_2 r B$, for every $i \in [r]$. Then $\mathsf{Tr}_{K/K_{12}}(m_k \cdot \sum_{i \in [r]} \xi_q^{s_{k-1}} z_i \mathsf{w}_i) = \sum_{i \in [r]} \xi_q^{s_k + s_{k-1}} z_i \mathsf{v}_i$. Thus, $\|T^2(e)\|_\infty \leq \sum_{i \in [r]} \|z_i\|_\infty \leq 4p_1 p_2 r^2 B$.

For $j \geq 2$, let $s'_j = \sum_{t \leq j}(s_{k-t+1} + s_{k-t})$. Then we can use the same calculation to obtain $T^{2j}(e) = \sum_{i \in [r]} \xi_q^{s'_{ij}} z_i \mathsf{v}_i$. This means that the coefficient with respect to v_i remains the same but with different phase, i.e., and only the exponent on ξ_q changes but z_i does not. Therefore, $\|T^{2j}(e)\|_\infty \leq 4p_1 p_2 r^2 B$ under the same analysis as above. $\qquad\square$

Next, we can check that each coefficient of $\widetilde{e}_k$ is bounded by a subgaussian with parameter less than $O(r\sqrt{N\log Q} \cdot E)$. Therefore, by setting B as this quantity, the above claim proves that $\|e_k\|_\infty$ is bounded by a subgaussian with parameter less than $O(kr^3\sqrt{N\log Q}E)$ (as p_1, p_2 are constants according to our parameter selection). By plugging $k = n$, we conclude that $\|e_n\|_\infty$ is bounded by a subgaussian with parameter less than $O(nr^3\sqrt{N\log Q}E)$. In Step 4, we further multiply the ACC by the test vector, which at most increase the error by a factor of q. In step 5, we apply another homomorphic trace function Eval-Tr$_{K/K_{23}}()$, which increases the error by at most q. So the final error is bounded by a subgaussian with parameter less than $O(nr^3q^2\sqrt{N\log Q}E) = O(nrqN\sqrt{N\log Q}E)$ and we prove this theorem. $\qquad\square$

Remark 6.5. *We can easily unpack the output* RLWE *ciphertext. If the output* $c \in$ RLWE$_{s'}^Q(\sum \mu_i v_i)$, *then by applying* (RLWE)-Eval-Tr$_{K/K_{13}}$ *to* $v_i^\vee c$, *the result is a* RLWE *ciphertext in* RLWE$_{s'}^Q(\mu_i)$. *The other case can be achieved similarly.*

Remark 6.6. *We notice that the techniques in the analysis of Theorem 6.2 (specifically Claim 6.4) can be used to analyze batch homomorphic computation of branching programs (e.g., [9]) under our framework. In the same way, we can show that our batch framework only incurs a polynomial error growth for computing any constant-width polynomial-depth branching program.*

6.3   Efficiency

Finally, we compare the efficiency of the batch bootstrapping with the sequential non-batch bootstrapping (that can be achieved within a polynomial modulus). We first notice that one call to the non-batch AP14/FHEW framework would require at least $O(n)$ external products, even just counting the step of blind rotate. Thus, to bootstrap r input ciphertexts sequentially, it would require $O(rn)$ external products.

On the other hand, our batch blind-rotate for bootstrapping r input ciphertexts would require $O(n)$ external products and $O(n)$ calls to the homomorphic trace evaluation. We notice that each homomorphic trace evaluation would make $O(\log r)$ calls to the key-switch algorithm, which is roughly equal to $O(\log r)$ external products. The final step of equality test take q queries to the underlying key-switches. Thus, the overall algorithm would require $O(n\log r + q)$ external products to bootstrap r input ciphertexts.

Asymptotic Setting. Now we determine all the parameters in λ as follow. We can set $n = O(\lambda)$, $q = \tilde{O}(\sqrt{n})$, $N = O(n)$, and $r \approx O(\sqrt{N/q}) = O(\lambda^{1/4-o(1)})$ as the AP14/FHEW framework [4,13,17]. By plugging these parameters to the above analysis, our batch algorithm can therefore bootstrap $O(\lambda^{1/4-o(1)})$ input ciphertexts by using $\tilde{O}(\lambda)$ external products, implying the amortized complexity $\tilde{O}(\lambda^{0.75})$ external products per input ciphertext. On the other hand, the non-batch method would require the amortized complexity $O(\lambda)$ external products per input ciphertext.

Our theoretical advances can potentially lead to noticeable practical improvements, as all the components are explicit and have been implemented in the power-of-two's settings. By using the insights of [26], it is possible to port the existing implementations to the general cyclotomic rings, with the same asymptotic computational efficiency. We leave it as an interesting open direction to determine the concrete practical performances of our framework.

Acknowledgement. The authors would like to thank anonymous reviewers for their insightful comments that significantly help improve the presentation. Feng-Hao Liu is supported by NSF CNS-1942400. Han Wang is supported by the National Key R&D Program of China under Grant 2020YFA0712303 and State Key Laboratory of Information Security under Grant TC20221013042.

References

1. Abla, P., Liu, F.-H., Wang, H., Wang, Z.: Ring-based identity based encryption – asymptotically shorter MPK and tighter security. In: Nissim, K., Waters, B. (eds.) TCC 2021. LNCS, vol. 13044, pp. 157–187. Springer, Cham (2021). https://doi. org/10.1007/978-3-030-90456-2_6

2. Albrecht, M.R., et al.: Estimate all the LWE, NTRU schemes! In: Catalano, D., De Prisco, R. (eds.) SCN 2018. LNCS, vol. 11035, pp. 351–367. Springer, Cham (2018). https://doi.org/10.1007/978-3-319-98113-0_19

3. Alperin-Sheriff, J., Peikert, C.: Practical bootstrapping in quasilinear time. In Canetti and Garay [10], pp. 1–20 (2013)

4. Alperin-Sheriff, J., Peikert, C.: Faster bootstrapping with polynomial error. In: Garay, J.A., Gennaro, R. (eds.) CRYPTO 2014. LNCS, vol. 8616, pp. 297–314. Springer, Heidelberg (2014). https://doi.org/10.1007/978-3-662-44371-2_17

5. Bonnoron, G., Ducas, L., Fillinger, M.: Large FHE gates from tensored homomorphic accumulator. In: Joux, A., Nitaj, A., Rachidi, T. (eds.) AFRICACRYPT 2018. LNCS, vol. 10831, pp. 217–251. Springer, Cham (2018). https://doi.org/10. 1007/978-3-319-89339-6_13

6. Bonte, C., Iliashenko, I., Park, J., Pereira, H.V., Smart, N.P.: Smart. FINAL: Faster FHE instantiated with NTRU and LWE. Cryptology ePrint Archive, Report 2022/074 (2022). https://eprint.iacr.org/2022/074

7. Brakerski, Z., Langlois, A., Peikert, C., Regev, O., Stehlé, D.: Classical hardness of learning with errors. In: Boneh, D., Roughgarden, T., Feigenbaum, J. (eds.) 45th ACM STOC, pp. 575–584. ACM Press (2013)

8. Brakerski, Z., Vaikuntanathan, V.: Efficient fully homomorphic encryption from (standard) LWE. In: Ostrovsky, R. (ed.) 52nd FOCS, pp. 97–106. IEEE Computer Society Press (2011)

9. Brakerski, Z., Vaikuntanathan, V.: Lattice-based FHE as secure as PKE. In: Naor, M. (ed.) ITCS 2014, pp. 1–12. ACM (2014)

10. Canetti, R., Garay, J.A. (eds.): LNCS, vol. 8042. Springer, Heidelberg (2013). https://doi.org/10.1007/978-3-642-40041-4

11. Chen, H., Dai, W., Kim, M., Song, Y.: Efficient homomorphic conversion between (ring) LWE ciphertexts. In: Sako, K., Tippenhauer, N.O. (eds.) ACNS 2021. LNCS, vol. 12726, pp. 460–479. Springer, Cham (2021). https://doi.org/10.1007/978-3-030-78372-3_18

12. Cheon, J.H., Kim, A., Kim, M., Song, Y.S.: Homomorphic encryption for arithmetic of approximate numbers. In Takagi and Peyrin [35], pp. 409–437 (2017)
13. Chillotti, I., Gama, N., Georgieva, M., Izabachène, M.: Faster fully homomorphic encryption: bootstrapping in less than 0.1 seconds. In: Cheon, J.H., Takagi, T. (eds.) ASIACRYPT 2016. Part I, volume 10031 of LNCS, pp. 3–33. Springer, Heidelberg (2016)
14. Chillotti, I., Gama, N., Georgieva, M., Izabachène, M.: Faster packed homomorphic operations and efficient circuit bootstrapping for TFHE. In: Takagi and Peyrin [35], pp. 377–408 (2017)
15. Chillotti, I., Gama, N., Georgieva, M., Izabachène, M.: TFHE: fast fully homomorphic encryption over the torus. J. Cryptol. **33**(1), 34–91 (2020)
16. Chillotti, I., Ligier, D., Orfila, J.-B., Tap, S.: Improved programmable bootstrapping with larger precision and efficient arithmetic circuits for TFHE. In: Tibouchi, M., Wang, H. (eds.) ASIACRYPT 2021. LNCS, vol. 13092, pp. 670–699. Springer, Cham (2021). https://doi.org/10.1007/978-3-030-92078-4_23
17. Ducas, L., Micciancio, D.: FHEW: bootstrapping homomorphic encryption in less than a second. In: Oswald, E., Fischlin, M. (eds.) EUROCRYPT 2015. LNCS, vol. 9056, pp. 617–640. Springer, Heidelberg (2015). https://doi.org/10.1007/978-3-662-46800-5_24
18. Gentry, C.: Fully homomorphic encryption using ideal lattices. In: Mitzenmacher, M. (ed.) 41st ACM STOC, pp. 169–178. ACM Press (2009)
19. Gentry, C., Halevi, S., Smart, N.P.: Better bootstrapping in fully homomorphic encryption. In: Fischlin, M., Buchmann, J., Manulis, M. (eds.) PKC 2012. LNCS, vol. 7293, pp. 1–16. Springer, Heidelberg (2012). https://doi.org/10.1007/978-3-642-30057-8_1
20. Gentry, C.,Sahai, A. , Waters, B.: Homomorphic encryption from learning with errors: Conceptually-simpler, asymptotically-faster, attribute-based. In: Canetti and Garay [10], pp. 75–92 (2013)
21. Halevi, S., Shoup, V.: Bootstrapping for HElib. Cryptology ePrint Archive, Report 2014/873 (2014). https://eprint.iacr.org/2014/873
22. Halevi, S., Shoup, V.: Faster homomorphic linear transformations in HElib. In: Shacham, H., Boldyreva, A. (eds.) CRYPTO 2018. LNCS, vol. 10991, pp. 93–120. Springer, Cham (2018). https://doi.org/10.1007/978-3-319-96884-1_4
23. Lee, Y., et al.: Efficient fhew bootstrapping with small evaluation keys, and applications to threshold homomorphic encryption. Cryptology ePrint Archive, Paper 2022/198 (2022). https://eprint.iacr.org/2022/198
24. Liu, F.-H., Wang, H.: Batch bootstrapping II: bootstrapping in polynomial modulus only requires $\tilde{O}(1)$ fhe multiplications in amortization. In: Eurocrypt (2023)
25. Lyubashevsky, V., Peikert, C., Regev, O.: On ideal lattices and learning with errors over rings. In: Gilbert, H. (ed.) EUROCRYPT 2010. LNCS, vol. 6110, pp. 1–23. Springer, Heidelberg (2010). https://doi.org/10.1007/978-3-642-13190-5_1
26. Lyubashevsky, V., Peikert, C., Regev, O.: A toolkit for ring-LWE cryptography. In: Johansson, T., Nguyen, P.Q. (eds.) EUROCRYPT 2013. LNCS, vol. 7881, pp. 35–54. Springer, Heidelberg (2013). https://doi.org/10.1007/978-3-642-38348-9_3

27. Micciancio, D., Peikert, C.: Trapdoors for lattices: simpler, tighter, faster, smaller. In: Pointcheval, D., Johansson, T. (eds.) EUROCRYPT 2012. LNCS, vol. 7237, pp. 700–718. Springer, Heidelberg (2012). https://doi.org/10.1007/978-3-642-29011-4_41

28. Micciancio, D., Polyakov, Y.: Bootstrapping in fhew-like cryptosystems. In: WAHC 2021: Proceedings of the 9th on Workshop on Encrypted Computing & Applied Homomorphic Cryptography, Virtual Event, Korea, 15 November 2021, pp. 17–28. WAHC@ACM (2021)

29. Micciancio, D., Sorrell, J.: Ring packing and amortized FHEW bootstrapping. In: Chatzigiannakis, I., Kaklamanis, C., Marx, D., Sannella, D. (eds.) ICALP 2018, vol. 107 of LIPIcs, pp. 100:1–100:14. Schloss Dagstuhl (2018)

30. Peikert, C.: How (not) to instantiate ring-LWE. In: Zikas, V., De Prisco, R. (eds.) SCN 2016. LNCS, vol. 9841, pp. 411–430. Springer, Cham (2016). https://doi.org/10.1007/978-3-319-44618-9_22

31. Peikert, C., Pepin, Z.: Algebraically structured LWE, revisited. In: Hofheinz, D., Rosen, A. (eds.) TCC 2019. LNCS, vol. 11891, pp. 1–23. Springer, Cham (2019). https://doi.org/10.1007/978-3-030-36030-6_1

32. Peikert, C., Regev, O., Stephens-Davidowitz, N.: Pseudorandomness of ring-LWE for any ring and modulus. In: Hatami, H., McKenzie, P., King, V. (eds.) 49th ACM STOC, pp. 461–473. ACM Press (2017)

33. Regev, O.: On lattices, learning with errors, random linear codes, and cryptography. In: Gabow, H.N., Fagin, R. (eds.) 37th ACM STOC, pp. 84–93. ACM Press (2005)

34. Rivest, R.L., Adleman, L., Dertouzos, M.L.: On data banks and privacy homomorphisms. In: Foundations of Secure Computation (1978)

35. Takagi, T., Peyrin, T. (eds.): LNCS, vol. 10624. Springer, Cham (2017). https://doi.org/10.1007/978-3-319-70694-8

36. Vaikuntanathan, V.: Homomorphic encryption references. https://people.csail.mit.edu/vinodv/FHE/FHE-refs.html

Batch Bootstrapping II:

Bootstrapping in Polynomial Modulus only Requires $\tilde{O}(1)$ FHE Multiplications in Amortization

Feng-Hao Liu[1] and Han Wang[2,3](✉)

[1] Florida Atlantic University, Boca Raton, FL, USA
liuf@fau.edu
[2] State Key Laboratory of Information Security, Institute of Information Engineering, Chinese Academy of Science, Beijing, China
wanghan@iie.ac.cn
[3] School of Cyber Security, University of Chinese Academy of Science, Beijing, China

Abstract. This work continues the exploration of the batch framework proposed in *Batch Bootstrapping I* (Liu and Wang, Eurocrypt 2023). By further designing novel batch homomorphic algorithms based on the batch framework, this work shows how to bootstrap λ LWE input ciphertexts within a polynomial modulus, using $\tilde{O}(\lambda)$ FHE multiplications. This implies an amortized complexity $\tilde{O}(1)$ FHE multiplications per input ciphertext, significantly improving our first work (whose amortized complexity is $\tilde{O}(\lambda^{0.75})$) and the theoretical state of the art MS18 (Micciancio and Sorrell, ICALP 2018), whose amortized complexity is $O(3^{1/\epsilon} \cdot \lambda^\epsilon)$, for any arbitrary constant ϵ.

We believe that all our new homomorphic algorithms might be useful in general applications, and thus can be of independent interests.

1 Introduction

This work is the second work of the Batch Bootstrapping series, aiming to advance the frontier of the Fully homomorphic encryption (FHE). We continue the exploration of the algebraic batch bootstrapping framework of the first work [7], and our particular goal is to prove the following theorem:

Theorem 1.1 (Main Result of this Work, Informal) *Bootstrapping within a polynomial modulus requires $\tilde{O}(1)$ FHE multiplications in amortization.*

Contexts. FHE [5] is a powerful cryptographic tool that allows arbitrary computation over encrypted data, without the secret key. Currently, the only known way to achieve "fully"-HE is via the bootstrapping paradigm, which was originally perceived as *theoretical* only for its large computation overhead. After more than a decade of research and optimizations, there has been significant progress toward more efficient realizations. As major prior results (before the first work) have been summarized in the first work [7], curious readers can find relevant references there, so we do not repeat the presentation.

Below, we just go directly to the point, by staring with what is not achieved in [7], and a comparison with the current state of the art. In this way, the readers can easily identify the "delta", when reading the contributions of this work.

© International Association for Cryptologic Research 2023
C. Hazay and M. Stam (Eds.): EUROCRYPT 2023, LNCS 14006, pp. 353–384, 2023.
https://doi.org/10.1007/978-3-031-30620-4_12

Challenges in the Prior Work. We first present a quick summary of the work [7], and state what was not solved. In Sect. 3, we give a more detailed review of the foundation, based on which, we develop various new homomorphic algorithms to further improve the frontier of the bootstrapping paradigm.

Briefly, the work [7] proposes a new batch framework, allowing single instruction multiple data (SIMD) operations that are compatible with FHEW-like (e.g., [3,4]) bootstrapping methods. The framework allows SIMD computation over $r = O(\lambda^{0.25-o(1)})$ slots, where λ is the security parameter. Applying this to the AP14/FHEW/TFHE methods, we can bootstrap $r = O(\lambda^{0.25-o(1)})$ LWE ciphertexts within a polynomial modulus, using $\tilde{O}(\lambda)$ FHE multiplications, meaning $\tilde{O}(\lambda^{0.75})$ FHE multiplications in amortization. This is an improvement of a factor of $O(r)$ over the prior non-batch methods. We notice that all these methods only require workspace $O(1)$ FHE ciphertext for computation (excluding the input and the bootstrapping keys).

If more workspace for computation is available, the theoretical complexity of the above however, is not better than that of the existing method MS18 [11], whose amortized cost is $O(3^{1/\epsilon} \cdot \lambda^\epsilon)$ FHE multiplications per input ciphertext, where $\epsilon > 0$ is an arbitrary constant. However, the dependency on ϵ posts an undesirable tradeoff between theory and practice – to achieve the best asymptotic complexity, ϵ should approach 0, e.g., 0.01, yet the constant would become prohibitively large, e.g., 3^{100}. Thus, it is not clear whether MS18 can lead to a practical method that matches their best theoretical indication.

Focus of this Work. An obvious open question is whether the tradeoff as stated above is inherent for the MS18 approach [11]. This work shows how to break the technical limitations, by developing various new batch homomorphic algorithms under the batch framework foundation [7]. Below we elaborate.

1.1   Our Contributions

The main result of this work is to prove Theorem 1.1. To achieve this, we first develop several new critical batch homomorphic algorithms based on the batch framework of [7]. These new algorithms play as important building blocks to improve the MS18 method, leading to our main result.

Recall that $r = O(\lambda^{0.25-o(1)})$ denotes the number of slots that the batch framework [7] can support. Using this foundation, we develop significant new batch homomorphic methods as stated below.

- We first propose a new batch vector-matrix multiplication algorithm, computing a vector of dimension w (in the clear) left multiplied by an encrypted matrix of dimension $h \times w$ for $h < r$, using $\tilde{O}(w + r)$ FHE multiplications. Thus, the amortized cost is $\tilde{O}(1 + w/r)$ FHE multiplications per dimension. As a ring multiplication can be expressed as the coefficient vector multiplied by the rotation matrix, our new batch algorithm immediately gives a batch algorithm for multiplying two ring elements of dimension $2d$ with amortized complexity $\tilde{O}(1 + 2d/r)$ FHE multiplications. Particularly, for $2d < r$, the amortized complexity would be $\tilde{O}(1)$ FHE multiplications per dimension. See Sect. 4 for details.

- Next we construct a new batch homomorphic (inverse) Discrete Fourier Transform (DFT) of dimension $2d < r$, with amortized complexity $\tilde{O}(1)$ FHE multiplications per dimension.
  To achieve this, we design three critical subroutines over packed ciphertexts: (1) homomorphic permutation, (2) homomorphic inverse over the exponents, and (3) batch homomorphic anti-cyclic rotation (via (1) + (2)). The batch homomorphic DFT/inverse-DFT can be achieved by using as a key building block the batch homomorphic anti-cyclic rotation. See Sect. 5 for details.
- We show that our batch homomorphic DFT/inverse-DFT is compatible with the recursive optimization of the Nussbaumer Transform. This plays a critical step to get rid of the dependency on ϵ as required by the MS18 framework. See Sect. 6 for details.

Putting these algorithms together, we are able to improve the overall MS18 bootstrapping method and achieve Theorem 1.1. See Sect. 7 for details of the final algorithm. We believe that all the new batch algorithms above can be of independent interests and might find applications in broader scoped of homomorphic computation. Below we present a table to compare results of this work with prior explicit methods (i.e., bootstrapping within a polynomial modulus) (Table 1).

Table 1. Comparison with prior work.

Ref.	Amortized Complexity for Bootstrapping (# of FHE Multiplications per input LWE ciphertext)
[1,3,4]	$O(\lambda)$
[2]	$O(\lambda/\log \lambda)$
[11]	$O(3^{1/\epsilon} \cdot \lambda^\epsilon)$
[7]	$\tilde{O}(\lambda^{0.75})$
This work	$\tilde{O}(1)$

1.2   Technical Overview

We give a quick review of MS18 [11], and then present our new insights to break the technical limitation. We first recall the overall goal below.

The Goal. Let $\{ct_i = (a_i, b_i) \in \mathbb{Z}_q^n \times \mathbb{Z}_q\}_{i \in [n]}$ be n LWE ciphertexts of dimension n, and each $b_i = \langle a_i, s \rangle + e_i + q/2 \cdot m_i$, i.e., an encryption of the bit m_i. The goal is to compute bootstrapping of these n input ciphertexts (given appropriate bootstrapping keys), resulting in $\{ct_i' = (a_i', b_i') \in \mathbb{Z}_q^n \times \mathbb{Z}_q\}_{i \in [n]}$, where each output ct_i' encrypts the same underlying message m_i as ct_i.

The MS18 Framework. To achieve the goal, the MS18 framework does the following high-level steps:

1. First convert the input ciphertexts, i.e., $\{ct_i\}_{i \in [n]}$, into a Ring-LWE ciphertext $(a, b) \in \mathcal{R}_q \times \mathcal{R}_q$ for ring $\mathcal{R}$ of degree n. Namely, $b = as + e + q/2 \cdot m$, where m is a ring element such that $coeffs(m) = (m_1, \ldots, m_n)$, s is a ring element representing the secret key.

2. Let $z = b - as$. Given (a, b) in the clear and appropriate bootstrapping keys that encrypt the secret s, the next step computes n Ring-LWE ciphretexts $d_1, \ldots, d_n$, where each $d_i \in \mathsf{RLWE.Enc}(X^{\mathsf{coeffs}(z)[i]})$. That is, the resulting ciphertexts encrypt the coefficients of z in the exponents.

3. Apply the sample-extraction procedure of [3,4]. As a result, we have $\mathsf{ct}'_i \in \mathsf{LWE.Enc}(\mathsf{Round}(\mathsf{coeffs}(z)[i]))$, where Round is the Ring-LWE decryption rounding procedure.

It is easy to verify correctness of this approach. For complexity, the first and third steps are rather efficient as shown by [11]. The second step is the most computationally heavy one, and requires new techniques of homomorphic computation. The work MS18 [11] shows that this step can be achieved by $O(3^{1/\epsilon} \cdot \lambda^{1+\epsilon})$ FHE (particularly Ring-GSW) multiplications, and thus the amortized complexity is $O(3^{1/\epsilon} \cdot \lambda^{\epsilon})$ FHE multiplications per input LWE ciphertext (by setting $n = O(\lambda)$). This work shows how to further improve the efficiency of Step 2 by designing several new batch methods under the framework of [7].

In order to understand our insights, we need to delve into Step 2. Below we elaborate on this step, and some technical challenges that MS18 [11] faced. Then we present our new insight that breaks all these challenges.

More Details on Step 2. We notice that as long as we can homomorphically compute the coefficients of $w = -as$ in the exponents, i.e., $\tilde{\mathsf{ct}}_i \in \mathsf{RLWE.Enc}(X^{\mathsf{coeffs}(w)[i]})$, then this step can be achieved by additionally multiplying $X^{\mathsf{coeffs}(b)[i]}$ to $\tilde{\mathsf{ct}}_i$. Thus, we focus on how to homomorphically compute w given a in the clear and s encrypted under an appropriate form.

Naively, we can express $\mathsf{coeffs}(w) = \mathsf{Coeffs\text{-}Rot}(a) \cdot \mathsf{coeffs}(s)$ where $\mathsf{Coeffs\text{-}Rot}(a)$ is the anti-cyclic rotation matrix of a and $\mathsf{coeffs}(\cdot)$ denotes the coefficients of the input ring element. Then given bootstrapping keys $\mathsf{BK}_i = \mathsf{RGSW.Enc}(\mathsf{coeffs}(s)[i])$, we can achieve the task by using the FHEW-(like) method on every row of the rotation matrix $\mathsf{Coeffs\text{-}Rot}(a)$. However, this approach does not improve the amortized complexity at all, as it is basically the same as applying the straight-forward method on individual input ciphertexts, separately.

To further improve the complexity, the work MS18 [11] explores nice recursive property from the algebraic ring in a novel way. Below we present some basic high level ideas, and the novel contributions of MS18.

We first recall that currently the most efficient way to compute ring multiplications is via the Fast Fourier Transform (FFT) technique, or its Number Theoretic Transform (NTT) variant as follow. To multiply ring elements a and s, we first convert a and s into the FFT/NTT form $(\tilde{a}_1, \ldots, \tilde{a}_n)$ and $(\tilde{s}_1, \ldots, \tilde{s}_n)$ respectively. Next we do a component-wise multiplication, and then convert the outcome back to the coefficient form using inverse FFT/NTT.

Following this idea, if we can adopt the idea to the homomorphic computation, then we can achieve the Step 2. However, there are several technical subtleties that a direct adoption would not work. Consider the following attempt: let $\mathsf{BK}_i = \mathsf{RGSW.Enc}(X^{\tilde{s}_i})$ be the bootstrapping key, encrypting the FFT/NTT coefficients in the exponents. Then we first homomorphically compute $\mathsf{ct}'_i = \mathsf{RGSW.Enc}(X^{\tilde{s}_i \cdot \tilde{a}_i})$, which can be done via the method of [4]. Finally we compute the inverse-FFT/NTT for the final outcome. This idea seems promising, but would face the following technical barriers.

- The FFT representation needs to work with complex numbers, which is not compatible with the existing FHE schemes, especially for encrypting an element in the exponent.
- The NTT representation would require special property on the modulus q, i.e., $q\mathcal{R}$ fully splits. Such a modulus must be greater to n (and might be even much larger), and thus might not be compatible with FHEW, on which the MS18 framework is based.
- This subtle barrier is identified by the work MS18 [11] – the noise growth of the homomorphic computation based on FHEW would be $O(\lambda^\rho)$ where ρ is the recursive depth of the inverse FFT/NTT step. In order to bootstrap within a polynomial modulus, the recursive depth ρ can only be $O(1)$. As the complexity of (inverse)-FFT/NTT is better for larger recursive depth, this constraint seems to post an inherent barrier of efficiency of homomorphic (inverse)-FFT/NTT. In fact, this is also a major reason why MS18 has the dependency on ϵ.

To tackle the first two challenges as above, one novel technical insight of MS18 [11] is to (recursively) apply the Nussbaumer Transform over the FHEW framework [4], yet the third challenge still remains. This work shows that our new algorithms developed under the batch framework of [7] provide a novel way that solves the third challenge. We next elaborate on the idea of the Nussbaumer Transform, and then our new insights.

Nussbaumer Transform. We describe the high level concept using the algebraic language, which might look different from the description in MS18 [11] (and some other references), but what we state captures exactly the same algorithm. The algebraic presentation would be simpler for distilling its algorithmic ideas, assuming some algebraic number theory backgrounds.

Let $d > 2$ be a power of two, and $\mathbb{Z}[\xi_{2d}]$ be a subring of $\mathbb{Z}[\xi_{d^2}]$ where ξ_m is the m-th root of unity. To multiply $a, s \in \mathbb{Z}[\xi_{d^2}]$, the Nussbaumer Transform does essentially the following steps:

- Convert a, s into $2d$ points in the subring $\mathbb{Z}[\xi_{2d}]$, namely $(\tilde{a}_1, \ldots, \tilde{a}_{2d})$ and $(\tilde{s}_1, \ldots, \tilde{s}_{2d})$ via the Discrete Fourier Transform (DFT).
- Multiply the points in the subring coordinate-wisely, resulting in $(\tilde{z}_1, \ldots, \tilde{z}_{2d})$.
- Convert the result back to $z \in \mathbb{Z}[\xi_{d^2}]$ via the inverse DFT.

The DFT and inverse-DFT require the computation to support operations with the $2d$-th root of unity, i.e., ξ_{2d}, and its powers. Beautifully in the Nussbaumer Transform as above, we have $\xi_{2d} \in \mathbb{Z}[\xi_{2d}] \subset \mathbb{Z}[\xi_{d^2}]$, and thus, this required element and its powers naturally reside in the subring and the ring! This structure naturally supports the DFT/inverse-DFT, solving the first two challenges above.

This idea can be optimized in a recursive way. For example, consider the following tower of subrings: $\mathbb{Z}[\xi_{d^\rho}] \supset \mathbb{Z}[\xi_{d^{\rho-1}}] \supset \cdots \supset \mathbb{Z}[\xi_{d^2}] \supset \mathbb{Z}[\xi_{2d}]$ for $d > 2$ being some power of two. In order to compute ring multiplications over $\mathbb{Z}[\xi_{d^\rho}]$, we can first recursively convert the elements into two vectors, each of $2^\rho \cdot d$ points in $\mathbb{Z}[\xi_{2d}]$. Then we compute the point-wise multiplication over $\mathbb{Z}[\xi_{2d}]$, and finally convert them back to an element in $\mathbb{Z}[\xi_{d^\rho}]$ by the inverse-DFT, recursively.

Now, let us describe the homomorphic version of the above idea, using as example the one-level recursion for simplicity of exposition, i.e., multiplying $a, s \in \mathbb{Z}[\xi_{d^2}]$ as above. The computation consists of the following three high level parts. (1) We can set the bootstrapping key as $\mathsf{BK}_{ij} = \mathsf{RGSW.Enc}(X^{\mathsf{coeffs}(\tilde{s}_i)[j]})$. (2) Then we homomorphically compute $\mathbf{C}_{ij} = \mathsf{RGSW.Enc}(X^{\mathsf{coeffs}(\tilde{z}_i)[j]})$, where $\tilde{z}_i = \tilde{a}_i \cdot \tilde{s}_i \in \mathbb{Z}[\xi_{2d}]$. (3) Finally we apply the homomorphic inverse DFT over these $\mathbf{C}_{ij}$'s as the MS18 method [11], resulting in what we want.

Limitations in MS18. To implement the above high level steps, MS18 however faces several technical challenges.

- First, to multiply elements in the bottom base field $\mathbb{Z}[\xi_{2d}]$, MS18 uses the textbook multiplication[1], whose amortized complexity is roughly $O(d)$ FHE multiplications per dimension.
- For the inverse DFT computation, MS18 also uses the straight-forward multiplication with the inverse-DFT matrix (of dimension $2d$), and similarly, the amortized complexity is roughly $O(d)$ multiplications per dimension.

Analyzing the recursion with the above facts, MS18 can compute multiplication over $\mathbb{Z}[\xi_{d^2}]$ roughly with amortized complexity $O(d)$ FHE multiplications per dimension. As MS18 observed, the recursive depth can be at most $\rho = O(1)$ to maintain a polynomial modulus, because the noise growth is roughly $O(\lambda^\rho)$. This would imply $d = O(\lambda^\epsilon)$, where $\epsilon = O(1/\rho) = O(1)$. Applying the argument recursively, their overall algorithm can achieve the amortized complexity $O(\lambda^\epsilon)$ FHE multiplications per input LWE ciphertext.

Our New Insights. Here we observe – as long as we can improve the amortized complexity of the ring multiplications over $\mathbb{Z}[\xi_{2d}]$ and inverse-DFT of dimension $2d$, we can improve the overall algorithm. Due to the noise growth, we cannot set $d = O(1)$ as it would require a large recursive depth, i.e., $\rho = O(\log \lambda)$. To handle this barrier, we next observe that the batch framework of our first work [7] is exactly the technical tool we need. Even though it can only batch $r = O(\lambda^{0.25-o(1)})$ slots, we can set $r > 2d$ such that the amortized complexity of the sub-ring multiplication over $\mathbb{Z}[\xi_{2d}]$ is small. Similarly, this idea can be applied to the inverse-DFT as well. Particularly, under the batch framework of [7], we develope the following new methods.

---

[1] As this is the bottom base field, no further recursive acceleration can be applied (e.g., Karatsuba or Toom-Cook).

- We design a new homomorphic ring multiplication over $\mathbb{Z}[\xi_{2d}]$, using $\tilde{O}(d + d^2/r)$ FHE multiplications. Thus, the amortized complexity is $\tilde{O}(1)$ FHE multiplications per dimension.
- We design a new homomorphic inverse-DFT with dimension $2d$, with amortized complexity $\tilde{O}(1)$ FHE multiplications per dimension.

Using a similar analysis of MS18 [11], we can then prove that the overall amortized complexity is $\tilde{O}(1)$ FHE multiplications, to bootstrap one input LWE ciphertext, achieving our main result. We notice that to implement the above high level picture requires substantial new design ideas over the batch framework [7]. We elaborate on the details of each piece in the coming sections.

2 Preliminaries

In this section, we present the preliminaries of this work. We note that this work shares a lot of common background with the first work of the series [7], so many basic materials are described verbatim as those in the first work.

Notations. Denote the set of integers by $\mathbb{Z}$, the set of rational numbers by $\mathbb{Q}$, real numbers by $\mathbb{R}$, and complex numbers by $\mathbb{C}$. Notation log refers to the base-2 logarithm. For a positive $k \in \mathbb{Z}$, let $[k]$ be the set of integers $\{1, ..., k\}$. We denote $[a, b]$ as the set $[a, b] \cap \mathbb{Z}$ for any integers $a \leq b$.

In this work, a vector is always a column vector by default and is denoted by a bold lower-case letter, e.g., $\boldsymbol{x}$. We use $\|\boldsymbol{x}\|_2$ denotes the l_2-norm and $\|\boldsymbol{x}\|_\infty$ denotes the l_∞-norm of $\boldsymbol{x}$. We use bold capital letters to denote matrices. For a matrix $\mathbf{X}$, $\mathbf{X}^\top$ denotes the transpose of $\mathbf{X}$. Given some set S, $S^{m \times n}$ denotes the set of all $m \times n$ matrices with entries in S. For matrices $\mathbf{X} \in S^{m \times n_1}$ and $\mathbf{Y} \in S^{m \times n_2}$ over some set S, $[\mathbf{X}\|\mathbf{Y}](\in S^{m \times (n_1+n_2)})$ denotes the concatenation of $\mathbf{X}$ with $\mathbf{Y}$. Let $\mathbf{X}$ be a matrix with even columns a matrix, and denote $\mathbf{X} = (\mathbf{X}^{(1)}\|\mathbf{X}^{(2)})$, where $\mathbf{X}^{(1)}$ is the left half sub-matrix of $\mathbf{X}$ and $\mathbf{X}^{(2)}$ is the right half sub-matrix.

For a set A and a probability distribution $\mathcal{P}$, we use $a \leftarrow A$ to denote that a is uniformly chosen from A and $a \leftarrow \mathcal{P}$ to denote that a is chosen according to the distribution $\mathcal{P}$.

Vector/Matrix Indexing. For vector $\boldsymbol{a}$, we use $\boldsymbol{a}[i]$ to describe the i-th element. Similarly, for matrix $\mathbf{X}$, we use $\mathbf{X}[i, j]$ to index the element in i-th row and j-th column. For an n-dimensional vector $\boldsymbol{a}$, we usually start the index from 1, i.e., $\boldsymbol{a} = (\boldsymbol{a}[1], ..., \boldsymbol{a}[n])$, and set $\boldsymbol{a}[0] = \boldsymbol{a}[n]$. Similarly, for an $n \times m$ matrix $\mathbf{X}$, we usually start the index from $\mathbf{X}[1, 1]$ to $\mathbf{X}[n, m]$, and set $\mathbf{X}[0, j] = \mathbf{X}[n, j]$ and $\mathbf{X}[i, 0] = \mathbf{X}[i, m]$ for general i, j's. For RGSW scheme, we use a bold and upper case variable, e.g., $\mathbf{C}$ to describe a ciphertext as it is a ring matrix. We use $\overrightarrow{\mathbf{C}}$ to describe a vector of ciphertexts, and $\overrightarrow{\mathbf{C}}[j]$ to index the j-th ciphertext. Similar to the previous case, $\overrightarrow{\mathbf{C}}[0] = \overrightarrow{\mathbf{C}}[n]$ indexes the n-th ciphertext where n is the vector dimension.

2.1 Lattices and Sub-Gaussian Random Variables

Lattices. An n-dimension (full-rank) lattice $\Lambda \subseteq \mathbb{R}^n$ is the set of all integer linear combinations of some set of independent basis vectors $\mathbf{B} = \{\mathbf{b}_1, \ldots, \mathbf{b}_n\} \subseteq \mathbb{R}^n$, $\Lambda = \mathcal{L}(\mathbf{B}) = \{\sum_{i=1}^{n} z_i \mathbf{b}_i : z_i \in \mathbb{Z}\}$.

Sub-Gaussian. As discussed in [1,4], it is convenient to use the notion of sub-Gaussian to analyze the error growth in the FHE constructions. A sub-gaussian variable X with parameter $\alpha > 0$ satisfies $E[e^{2\pi tX}] \leq e^{\pi \alpha^2 / t^2}$, for all $t \in \mathbb{R}$.

- Boundedness: If X is a sub-Gaussian variable with parameter $r > 0$, then $\Pr[|X| \geq t] \leq 2\exp(-\pi t^2/r^2)$.
- Homogeneity: If X is a sub-Gaussian variable with parameter $r > 0$, then cX is sub-gaussian with parameter $c \cdot r$ for any constant $c \geq 0$.
- Pythagorean additivity: If X_1 and X_2 are two sub-Gaussian variables with parameter r_1 and r_2 respectively, then $X_1 + X_2$ is sub-Gaussian with parameter $r_1 + r_2$, or $\sqrt{r_1^2 + r_2^2}$ if the two random variables are independent.

g^{-1} **algorithm.** This algorithm is used heavily in the research of FHE as we summarize in the following lemma.

Lemma 2.1. *For a given integer q, let $\ell = \lceil \log q \rceil$ and $\boldsymbol{g} = (1, 2, .., 2^{\ell-1})$. Then there is a randomized, efficiently computable algorithm denoted as $\boldsymbol{g}^{-1} : \mathbb{Z}_q \to \mathbb{Z}^\ell$ such that the output of the function, $\boldsymbol{x} \leftarrow \boldsymbol{g}^{-1}(a)$ is sub-gaussian with parameter $O(1)$, satisfying $\langle \boldsymbol{g}, \boldsymbol{x} \rangle = a \mod q$.*

We can extend $\boldsymbol{g}^{-1}$ to the matrix case (using the notation $\mathbf{G}^{-1}(\cdot)$) by applying $\boldsymbol{g}^{-1}(\cdot)$ to each entry of the matrix.

2.2 Algebraic Number Theory Background

We present some necessary background of algebraic number theory. This work heavily uses number fields and their rings of integers, and particularly, we represent a ring element as an algebraic number, instead of a polynomial. This representation gives more algebraic insights for our designs and analyses. Due to space limit, we defer some basic concepts in the full version of this work, and note that more details can be found in the work [9].

Number Fields. This work focuses on number fields as field extension that can be expressed as $K = \mathbb{Q}(\alpha)$, by adjoining some α to $\mathbb{Q}$ where α is a root of some irreducible polynomial $f(x) \in \mathbb{Z}[x]$. Let ξ_m be the m-th root of unity, and $\mathbb{Q}(\xi_m)$ is known as the m-th cyclotomic field. Suppose $\Phi_m(x)$ is the m-th cyclotomic polynomial, then the $\mathbb{Z}$-ring homomorphism Υ induces an isomorphism of $\mathbb{Z}[x]/\Phi_m(x) \cong \mathbb{Z}[\xi_m]$ as:

$$\Upsilon : \mathbb{Z}[x] \to \mathbb{Z}[\xi_m] \text{ such that } x \mapsto \xi_m.$$

We also use the concept of tensor fields, whose preliminaries are presented in the full version. Below we present a useful decomposition property.

Lemma 2.2. *[9] Let $m = \prod_\ell m_\ell$ be the prime-power factorization. Then $K = \mathbb{Q}(\xi_m)$ is isomorphic to the tensor product $\otimes_\ell \mathbb{Q}(\xi_{m_\ell})$, via the bijection $\prod_\ell a_\ell \mapsto \otimes_\ell(a_\ell)$, where each a_ℓ in K_ℓ can be naturally embedded in the field K.*

Geometry of Number Fields. Throughout this work, we use the canonical embedding to define norms for algebraic numbers. As argued in [9], this definition is independent of the representation of the algebraic number and can give us better bounds in the setting of general cyclotomic fields. Due to space limit, we defer the details to the full version of this work.

Trace, Ring of Integers, and Duality. The first work of this series [7] developed the batch homomorphic computation based heavily on the concepts of the algebraic trace, tensor rings, and their duals. This work builds upon the prior results in a black-box way, so our new results can still be accessible without the mathematical details.

2.3 Learning with Errors Assumption

Our schemes and analyses are based on the learning with errors (LWE) and the ring version RLWE (in general cyclotomic rings) as introduced by [8,12]. We assume that the readers are familiar with these problems, and defer more details to the full version.

2.4 RLWE/RGSW in General Cyclotomic Rings

We present the schemes RLWE [8,9] and RGSW [1,6] in the setting of general cyclotomic rings. As the first work [7] showed, the noise behavior of the homomorphic operations in general cyclotomic rings is similar to that in the setting of power-of-two's, under the analysis of the canonical embedding [8,9]. Below, we describe these schemes with a lemma that summarizes the noise growth.

Below we describe the parameters of the RLWE and RGSW schemes.

- λ: the security parameter.
- $\mathcal{R}$: the m-th cyclotomic ring with degree $N = \phi(m)$.
- Q: the modulus.
- $\mathcal{R}_Q$: the quotient ring $\mathcal{R}/Q\mathcal{R}$.
- $\mathcal{D}$: some error distribution over $\mathcal{R}$.
- ℓ: set $\ell = \lceil \log Q \rceil$ (with respect to some log base).

RLWE Scheme. We describe the basic symmetric RLWE encryption scheme (in the primal form for simplicity). The scheme contains the following algorithms.

- **KeyGen(1^λ):** Choose randomly $s \leftarrow \mathcal{R}_Q$ and output $\mathsf{sk} := (1, -s)^\top \in \mathcal{R}_Q^2$.

- **Enc(sk, $\mu \in \mathcal{R}_t$):** Sample a uniform ring element $a \leftarrow \mathcal{R}_Q$ and a noise $e \leftarrow \mathcal{D}$. The output ciphertext is set as $c := \begin{pmatrix} sa + e \\ a \end{pmatrix} + \begin{pmatrix} \lfloor \frac{Q}{t} \rfloor \mu \\ 0 \end{pmatrix} \in \mathcal{R}_Q^2$.

  We call $\lfloor \frac{Q}{t} \rfloor \mu$ the encoded message of c and μ the encrypted message of c.
- **Dec(c, sk):** The algorithm outputs an element μ in $\mathcal{R}_t$ as follow:

$$\mu = \lfloor \langle (1, -s), c \rangle \rceil_t := \lfloor t \langle (1, -s), c \rangle / Q \rceil \mod t.$$

We use $\mathsf{RLWE}_s^{t/Q}(\mu)$ to denote the set of all RLWE ciphertexts of encoded message μ under secret s with ciphertext modulus Q and plaintext modulus t. Sometimes, we use $\mathsf{RLWE}_s^Q(\lfloor \frac{Q}{t} \rfloor \mu)$ to denote the same set. The latter notion drops the t in the super-script, but presents the whole encoded message in the parentheses.

RGSW Scheme. Now we present the RGSW scheme. We notice that this work suffices to use the symmetric-key version of RGSW, so we just present this for simplicity. The public-key version works analogously.

Denote the fixed gadget vector as $g^\top = (1, 2, ..., 2^{\ell-1})$, and the gadget matrix as $\mathbf{G} = g^\top \otimes \mathbf{I}_2$. As demonstrated by [1,10], the gadget vector/matrix play a vital role in the homomorphic computation methods. Similar to the RLWE scheme above, we present the primal version of RGSW.

- **KeyGen(1^λ):** Choose randomly $s \leftarrow \mathcal{R}_Q$ and set sk $:= (1, -s)^\top \in \mathcal{R}_Q^2$.
- **Enc(sk, $\mu \in \mathcal{R}_2$):** Sample a uniform vector $a \leftarrow \mathcal{R}_Q^{2\ell}$ and a noise vector $e \leftarrow \mathcal{D}^{2\ell}$. The ciphertext is set as $\mathbf{C} := \begin{pmatrix} sa^\top + e^\top \\ a^\top \end{pmatrix} + \mu \mathbf{G} \in \mathcal{R}_Q^{2 \times 2\ell}$.
- **Dec(C, sk):** The algorithm outputs an element μ in $\mathcal{R}_t$ as follow:

$$\mu = \lfloor \langle (1, -s)^\top, c_{(\ell-1)} \rangle \rceil \mod 2,$$

  where $c_{(\ell-1)}$ is the $(\ell-1)$-th column of $\mathbf{C}$.
- **Homomorphic Addition $\mathbf{C}_1 \boxplus \mathbf{C}_2$:** It takes as inputs two RGSW ciphertexts $\mathbf{C}_1, \mathbf{C}_2$ under the same secret key sk and outputs $\mathbf{C}_1 \boxplus \mathbf{C}_2 := \mathbf{C}_1 + \mathbf{C}_2$.
- **Homomorphic Multiplication $\mathbf{C}_1 \boxdot \mathbf{C}_2$:** It takes as inputs two RGSW ciphertexts $\mathbf{C}_1, \mathbf{C}_2$ under the same secret key sk and outputs the following as the result of homomorphic multiplication: $\mathbf{C}_1 \boxdot \mathbf{C}_2 \leftarrow \mathbf{C}_1 \cdot \mathbf{G}^{-1}(\mathbf{C}_2)$. Here $\mathbf{G}^{-1}(\cdot)$ can be either deterministic or randomized. As argued by [1], a randomized instantiation can yield tighter parameters of the noise growth than those derived from the deterministic version. We notice that in the ring setting, a basis needs to be specified when computing $\mathbf{G}^{-1}$.
- **External Product $\mathbf{C}_1 \boxtimes c_2$:** It takes as inputs a RGSW ciphertexts $\mathbf{C}_1$ and a RLWE ciphertext c_2 under the same secret key sk and outputs the following RLWE ciphertext as the result of external product: $\mathbf{C}_1 \boxtimes c_2 \leftarrow \mathbf{C}_1 \cdot g^{-1}(c_2)$.

The IND-CPA security of the above RGSW scheme (for general cyclotomic rings) follows from the RLWE assumption, using the same argument of [1,6]. Below we present some notations for the noise analysis.

Definition 2.3. *Adapt the notations from the above. Given a ciphertext* $\mathbf{C}$ *that encrypts message* μ *under a secret key* $\mathsf{sk} = (1, -s)^\top$, *we can express as the following relation* $\mathsf{sk}^\top \cdot \mathbf{C} = \mu \cdot \mathsf{sk}^\top \cdot \mathbf{G} + e^\top \in \mathcal{R}_Q^m$, *for some error vector* e. *Then define* $\mathsf{Err}_\mu(\mathbf{C}) := e^\top = \mathsf{sk}^\top \cdot \mathbf{C} - \mu \cdot \mathsf{sk}^\top \cdot \mathbf{G}$. *When the context is clear, we may drop the index* μ.

We use $\mathsf{RGSW}_s^Q(\mu)$ *to denote the set of all the RGSW ciphertexts that encrypt* μ *under secret* s *in the modulo* Q *space. If the parameters* Q *are clear from the context, we would use the abbreviation* $\mathsf{RGSW}_s(\mu)$ *for simplicity.*

Note. The above error function can be defined for RLWE ciphertexts analogously. We do not present another definition to avoid repetition.

The following analysis was developed by the prior work of the series [7].

Lemma 2.4. ([7]) *For any RGSW ciphertexts* $\mathbf{C}_1, \mathbf{C}_2$ *that encrypt* μ_1, μ_2 *with the error terms* e_1, e_2 *respectively, then we have the following.*

- $\mathsf{Err}(\mathbf{C}_1 \boxplus \mathbf{C}_2) = e_1^\top + e_2^\top$.
- $\mathsf{Err}(\mathbf{C}_1 \boxdot \mathbf{C}_2) = e_1^\top \cdot \mathbf{G}^{-1}(\mathbf{C}_2) + \mu_1 \cdot e_2^\top$.

Furthermore, suppose $\mathbf{G}^{-1}$ *is sampled with respect to some* $\mathbb{Z}$-*basis of* $\mathcal{R}$, *i.e.,* $\mathbf{B} = \{\mathsf{b}_1, ..., \mathsf{b}_n\}$, *such that for all* $i \in [n]$ $\|\sigma(\mathsf{b}_i)\|_\infty \leq 1$. *Then the following holds.*

- *Denote* $e_1^\top \cdot \mathbf{G}^{-1}(\mathbf{C}_2)$ *as* $e^\top = (e_1, ..., e_{2\ell})$. *Then each entry of* e *is an independent random variable.*
- $\|\sigma(e)\|_\infty$ *is upper bounded by a sub-Gaussian variable with parameter* $O(r)$, *for some real positive* $r \leq \sqrt{N \cdot \log Q} \cdot \|\sigma(e_1)\|_\infty$.

Encrypted Elements in the Exponents. Next we define a notation for RGSW ciphertexts, encrypting integers of a vector in the exponents. This notation will be convenient for the presentation of our new homomorphic algorithms.

Definition 2.5. *Let* ξ_p *be the p-th root of unity which is included in the message space of RGSW. Given an integer vector* $a = (a_0, a_1, \cdots, a_{n-1}) \in \mathbb{Z}^n$, *we denote* $\mathsf{RGSW.EncVec\text{-}Exp}(a)$ *as a vector of ciphertexts, each entry of which is a RGSW ciphertext encrypting* $\xi_q^{a_i}$. *Namely,* $\overrightarrow{\mathbf{C}} = (\mathbf{C}_0, \cdots, \mathbf{C}_{n-1}) \in \mathsf{RGSW.EncVec\text{-}Exp}(a)$, *where each* $\mathbf{C}_i \in \mathsf{RGSW}(\xi_q^{a_i})$.

The parameter ξ_q will be specified in each algorithm that uses $\mathsf{RGSW.EncVec\text{-}Exp}$. Moreover, there exists a homomorphic anti-rotation algorithm $\mathsf{Anti\text{-}Rot}(\cdot, \cdot)$ that on input $\overrightarrow{\mathbf{C}} \in \mathsf{RGSW.EncVec\text{-}Exp}(a)$ and $z \in \mathbb{Z}$ outputs a rotated ciphertext $\overrightarrow{\mathbf{C}}' \in \mathsf{RGSW.EncVec\text{-}Exp}(\mathsf{Anti\text{-}Rot}(a, z))$, where $\mathsf{Anti\text{-}Rot}(a, z)$ is the anti-cyclic rotation of z positions in the plaintext. The error growth is only increased by an additive term e' that is independent of the input ciphertext.

3   Foundation Developed in Batch Bootstrapping I

In this section, we present the framework of batch homomorphic computation of the work [7]. To be rigorous, our presentation uses the math concepts of tensor rings and dual basis. To make it more friendly to the general, we abstract the required homomorphic methods and analyses in a modular way, so that how to apply the framework can be accessible without going into the math details. The main results and algorithms of this work will be presented using the modular abstraction of the homomorphic methods.

Math Background and Notations. Let $K = K_1 \otimes K_2 \otimes K_3$ be a tensor field of three linearly disjoint fields, and $\mathcal{R}_1$, $\mathcal{R}_2$, $\mathcal{R}_3$ be their rings of integers, respectively. It follows that the ring of integers of K (denoted as $\mathcal{R}$) is isomorphic to $\mathcal{R}_1 \otimes \mathcal{R}_2 \otimes \mathcal{R}_3$. Furthermore, we present some useful facts and notations.

- K_{12} and K_{13} denote $K_1 \otimes K_2$ and $K_1 \otimes K_3$, respectively.
- $\mathcal{R}$, $\mathcal{R}_{12}$ and $\mathcal{R}_{13}$ denote the rings of integers of K, K_{12}, and K_{13}, respectively. It is known that $\mathcal{R} \cong \mathcal{R}_1 \otimes \mathcal{R}_2 \otimes \mathcal{R}_3$, $\mathcal{R}_{12} \cong \mathcal{R}_1 \otimes \mathcal{R}_2$, and $\mathcal{R}_{13} \cong \mathcal{R}_1 \otimes \mathcal{R}_3$.
- Let $(\mathsf{v}_1, \mathsf{v}_2, \ldots, \mathsf{v}_\rho)$ and $(\mathsf{w}_1, \mathsf{w}_2, \ldots, \mathsf{w}_\tau)$ be some $\mathbb{Z}$-bases of $\mathcal{R}_2$ and $\mathcal{R}_3$, respectively, where ρ and τ are the degrees of the rings $\mathcal{R}_2$ and $\mathcal{R}_3$.
- Denote $(\mathsf{v}_1^\vee, \mathsf{v}_2^\vee, \ldots, \mathsf{v}_\rho^\vee)$ and $(\mathsf{w}_1^\vee, \mathsf{w}_2^\vee, \ldots, \mathsf{w}_\tau^\vee)$ as the corresponding $\mathbb{Z}$-bases of the dual spaces $\mathcal{R}_2^\vee$ and $\mathcal{R}_3^\vee$, respectively.
- Let $r = \min(\rho, \tau)$, the maximal number of slots our method can pack.
- Denote the trace functions (with respect to different underlying subfields) as

$$\mathsf{Tr}_{K/K_{12}} : K \to K_{12} \text{ and } \mathsf{Tr}_{K/K_{13}} : K \to K_{13}$$

In our instantiation, we set $K := \mathbb{Q}[\xi_{q\rho'\tau'}] \cong \mathbb{Q}[\xi_q] \otimes \mathbb{Q}[\xi_{\rho'}] \otimes \mathbb{Q}[\xi_{\tau'}] := K_1 \otimes K_2 \otimes K_3$, where q is equal to the modulus of input (Ring)-LWE being bootstrapped, ρ' and τ' are powers of some prime numbers of size $O(1)$. Moreover, we have $\rho = \phi(\rho')$ and $\tau = \phi(\tau')$.

3.1   The Framework of Batch Homomorphic Computation

By using the tensor of three rings, the work [7] showed how to batch homomorphic computation as we summarize below.

Message Packing and Operations. First, the message space is the first ring, i.e., $\mathcal{R}_1$, and the other two rings, i.e., $\mathcal{R}_2, \mathcal{R}_3$ are the work rings for computation. Particularly, there are features as following:

1. There are four modes of packing, i.e., mode $\in \{$"$\mathcal{R}_{12}$", "$\mathcal{R}_{13}$", "$\mathcal{R}_{12} \to \mathcal{R}_{13}$", "$\mathcal{R}_{13} \to \mathcal{R}_{12}$"$\}$, where a vector of messages can be packed with respect to.

2. There is an algorithm Pack that on input a vector (of messages) $x = (x_1, \ldots, x_r) \in \mathcal{R}_1^r$ and mode outputs a packed message x. Particularly, if mode $=$ "$\mathcal{R}_{12}$", then $x \in \mathcal{R}_1 \otimes \mathcal{R}_2$; mode $=$ "$\mathcal{R}_{13}$", $x \in \mathcal{R}_1 \otimes \mathcal{R}_3$; mode $=$ "$\mathcal{R}_{12} \rightarrow \mathcal{R}_{13}$", $x \in \mathcal{R}_1 \otimes \mathcal{R}_2^\vee \otimes \mathcal{R}_3$; mode $=$ "$\mathcal{R}_{13} \rightarrow \mathcal{R}_{12}$", $x \in \mathcal{R}_1 \otimes \mathcal{R}_2 \otimes \mathcal{R}_3^\vee$.

3. For any two packed messages (x, mode) and (y, mode) where $x = \text{Pack}(x, \text{mode})$ and $y = \text{Pack}(y, \text{mode})$, $(x + y, \text{mode}) = \text{Pack}((x + y), \text{mode})$.

4. There is a multiplication method that on input two packed messages (x, mode_1) and (y, mode_2), outputs a packed message (z, mode_3) with the following. If $\text{mode}_1 =$ "$\mathcal{R}_{12}$", $\text{mode}_2 =$ "$\mathcal{R}_{12} \rightarrow \mathcal{R}_{13}$" or vice versa, then $\text{mode}_3 =$ "$\mathcal{R}_{13}$". If $\text{mode}_1 =$ "$\mathcal{R}_{13}$", $\text{mode}_2 =$ "$\mathcal{R}_{13} \rightarrow \mathcal{R}_{12}$" or vice versa, then $\text{mode}_3 =$ "$\mathcal{R}_{12}$". For all the other cases, $\text{mode}_3 = \perp$. Moreover, $(z, \text{mode}_3) = \text{Pack}(z, \text{mode}_3)$ where $z = (x_1 y_1, \ldots, x_r y_r)$.

Ciphertext Packing and Operations. For RGSW instantiated over the tensor ring $\mathcal{R}$, the work [7] realizes homomorphic methods for the above plaintext packing and operations. Particularly, we have the following.

1. There is an algorithm RGSW-Pack that on input mode and $\mathbf{C}_1, \ldots, \mathbf{C}_r$ where each $\mathbf{C}_i \in \text{RGSW}(x_i) \in \mathcal{R}^{2 \times 2\ell}$ and $x_i \in \mathcal{R}_1$, outputs a packed ciphertext $(\mathbf{C}, \text{mode})$. The ciphertext $\mathbf{C} \in \mathcal{R}^{2 \times 2\ell}$ or the dual ring (omitting the modulus), depending on mode the same way as Item 2 of the plaintext packing. Importantly, the size of $\mathbf{C}$ is the same as that of each $\mathbf{C}_i$, meaning that the packing method is non-trivial.

2. Let $(\mathbf{C}_x, \text{mode})$ and $(\mathbf{C}_y, \text{mode})$ be two packed ciphertexts of the message vectors $x = (x_1, \ldots, x_r) \in \mathcal{R}_1^r$, $y = (y_1, \ldots, y_r) \in \mathcal{R}_1^r$. Then $(\mathbf{C}_x + \mathbf{C}_y, \text{mode})$ is a packed ciphertext of the message vector $x + y$.

3. Continue from the above notation. There is a non-trivial[2] batch homomorphic algorithm Batch-Mult that on input $(\mathbf{C}_x, \text{mode}_1)$ and $(\mathbf{C}_y, \text{mode}_2)$ outputs $(\mathbf{C}_z, \text{mode}_3)$ where the modes $\text{mode}_1, \text{mode}_2, \text{mode}_3$ follow the relation as described in item 4 of the above plaintext packing. Moreover, $\mathbf{C}_z$ is a packed ciphertext that corresponds to the vector of messages $(x_1 y_1, \ldots, x_r y_r)$.

4. There is an algorithm UnPack that on input a packed ciphertext $(\mathbf{C}_x, \text{mode})$ outputs $\mathbf{C}_1, \ldots, \mathbf{C}_r$ where each $\mathbf{C}_i \in \text{RGSW}(x_i)$ for $x_i \in \mathcal{R}_1$.

Remark 3.1. *In the framework, only two ciphertexts/plaintexts of the modes ("$\mathcal{R}_{12}$" and "$\mathcal{R}_{12} \rightarrow \mathcal{R}_{13}$") or ("$\mathcal{R}_{13}$" and "$\mathcal{R}_{13} \rightarrow \mathcal{R}_{12}$") can be homomorphically multiplied. All the other combinations do not support the multiplication, e.g., if $\mathbf{C}_1$ is mode "$\mathcal{R}_{12}$" and $\mathbf{C}_2$ is mode "$\mathcal{R}_{12}$", then they cannot be multiplied.*

Parameters and Computational Efficiency. The first work [7] showed that the following parameters and computational complexity are feasible. First, we set

---

[2] The term *non-trivial* requires Batch-Mult to be much more efficient than the trivial non-batch computation, i.e., computing r RGSW multiplications separately and then packing the outcomes into one ciphertext.

the first ring as the q-th cyclotomic ring, i.e., $\mathcal{R}_1 = \mathbb{Z}(\xi_q)$, where q the modulus of the input LWE being bootstrapped. Then we set the maximal number of slots as $r = \deg(\mathcal{R}_2/\mathbb{Q}) \approx \deg(\mathcal{R}_3/\mathbb{Q}) = O(\sqrt{N/q})$. Asymptotically, this would be $q = \tilde{O}(\sqrt{\lambda})$, meaning that $r = O(\lambda^{0.25-o(1)})$.

For the (homomorphic) efficiency, the following can be achieved.

- RGSW-Pack requires $O(r)$ RGSW additions.
- Efficiency of the packed addition is the same as that of the RGSW addition.
- Batch-Mult for packed ciphertexts takes $O(\log \lambda)$ number of calls to RGSW multiplications, i.e., $\boxdot$, by setting $\mathcal{R}_2$ and $\mathcal{R}_3$ as cyclotomic rings with a proper tower structure.
  Note: this satisfies the non-trivial requirement as $O(\log \lambda)$ calls of RGSW multiplications are much less than the trivial non-batch method, which requires $r = O(\lambda^{0.25-o(1)})$ RGSW multiplications.
- UnPack takes $O(r)$ RGSW multiplications.

Noise Growth. The noise growth depends on how we choose the basis for $\mathbf{G}^{-1}$ to which the RGSW multiplication is with respect (see Lemma 2.4 for reference). For the case of general cyclotomic rings, the work [7] showed a way to instantiate a short basis (with infinity norms 1 for all elements in the basis) and all the necessary components, leading to the following results:

Theorem 3.2 ([7]) *Let $\mathbf{C}$ be a RGSW ciphertext that encrypts $m \in \mathcal{R}$, and denote $\mathsf{Err}(\mathbf{C}) := (\mathsf{Err}_1(\mathbf{C})\|\mathsf{Err}_2(\mathbf{C}))$, where $\mathsf{Err}_1(\mathbf{C})$ is the first half of the error vector, and $\mathsf{Err}_2(\mathbf{C})$ is the other half. There exists a homomorphic method $\mathsf{Eval\text{-}Tr}_{K/K_{12}}$ that on input $\mathbf{C}$ outputs $\mathbf{C}' \in \mathsf{RGSW}(\mathsf{Tr}_{K/K_{13}}(m))$, satisfying $\mathsf{Err}_1(\mathbf{C}') = \mathsf{Tr}_{K/K_{12}}(\mathsf{Err}_1(\mathbf{C})) + e'$ for some e' that is independent of $\mathbf{C}$. Moreover, $\mathsf{Err}_2(\mathbf{C}') = s \cdot \mathsf{Tr}_{K/K_{12}}(\mathsf{Err}_1(\mathbf{C})) + e''$ for some e'' that is independent of $\mathbf{C}$.*

Theorem 3.3 ([7]) *Let $\mathbf{C}_1, \dots, \mathbf{C}_r$ be RGSW ciphertexts with error terms $e_1, \dots, e_r$, messages $\mu_1, \dots, \mu_r \in \mathcal{R}_1$ and $\mathbf{C}'_1, \dots, \mathbf{C}'_r$ be RGSW ciphertexts with error terms $e'_1, \dots, e'_r$, messages $\mu'_1, \dots, \mu'_r \in \mathcal{R}_1$. Denote*

- RGSW-Pack$(\mathbf{C}_1, \dots, \mathbf{C}_r, \text{``}\mathcal{R}_{12}\text{''})$ *as* $\mathbf{D}$,
- RGSW-Pack$(\mathbf{C}'_1, \dots, \mathbf{C}'_r, \text{``}\mathcal{R}_{12} \to \mathcal{R}_{13}\text{''})$ *as* $\mathbf{D}'$,
- Batch-Mult$(\mathbf{D}', \mathbf{D})$ *as* $\mathbf{F}$,
- *the encrypted messages of the packed ciphertexts $\mathbf{D}$ as $\mu_{\mathbf{D}}$,*
- *the encrypted messages of the packed ciphertexts $\mathbf{D}'$ as $\mu_{\mathbf{D}'}$.*

Then, $\mu_{\mathbf{D}} = \sum_{i=1}^{r} \mu_i \cdot \mathsf{v}_i$, $\mu_{\mathbf{D}'} = \sum_{i=1}^{r} \mu'_i \cdot \mathsf{v}_i^{\vee} \mathsf{w}_i$ and $\mathbf{F}$ is a packed RGSW ciphertext encrypting $\mathsf{Tr}_{K/K_{13}}(\mu_{\mathbf{D}} \cdot \mu_{\mathbf{D}'})$ with mode $\mathcal{R}_{13}$.

Combing Algorithm 3.2, then we have $\mathsf{Err}_1(\mathbf{F}) = \mathsf{Tr}_{K/K_{13}}(\sum_i e'_i \mathsf{v}_i^{\vee} \mathsf{w}_i \mathbf{G}^{-1}(\mathbf{D}^{(1)}) + \mu_{\mathbf{D}'}(e_i^{(1)} \mathsf{v}_i)) + e'$ and $\mathsf{Err}_2(\mathbf{F}) = s \cdot \mathsf{Tr}_{K/K_{13}}(\sum_i e'_i \mathsf{v}_i^{\vee} \mathsf{w}_i \mathbf{G}^{-1}(\mathbf{D}^{(1)}) + \mu_{\mathbf{D}'}(e_i^{(1)} \mathsf{v}_i)) + e''$, where e' and e'' are independent of $\mathbf{C}$.

Corollary 3.4 ([7]) *Adapt the notations of Theorems 3.3. If the errors of the key-switch keys is upper bounded by E, and g^{-1} is with respect to the basis $\mathcal{B}_1 \otimes \mathcal{B}_2 \otimes \mathcal{B}_3$. Denote the error of the output by $\mathsf{Err}(\mathbf{F}) = (e_1^\top \| e_2^\top)$, where e_1 and e_2 are both ℓ-entry vectors. Then $\|\mathsf{Err}_1(\mathbf{F})\|_\infty$ is upper bounded by*

$$\frac{2\rho(p_1 - 1)\sqrt{N \log Q}}{\rho'} \sum \|e_i'\|_\infty + \rho\|\mu_{\mathbf{D}'}\| \sum \|e_i\|_\infty + \|e'\|_\infty,$$

where $\|e'\|_\infty$ is a sub-Gaussian with parameter upper bounded by $3\rho'\sqrt{N \log Q} E$. $\|\mathsf{Err}_2(\mathbf{F})\|_\infty$ is upper bounded by

$$\frac{2\rho(p_1 - 1)\sqrt{N \log Q}\|s\|_\infty}{\rho'} \sum \|e_i'\|_\infty + \rho\|s\|_\infty\|\mu_{\mathbf{D}'}\| \sum \|e_i\|_\infty + \|e''\|_\infty,$$

where $\|e''\|_\infty$ is a sub-Gaussian with parameter upper bounded by $(3\rho'\|s\|_\infty + 2)\sqrt{N \log Q} E$.

4   New Batch Homomorphic Algorithms

Here we present some critical batch homomorphic algorithms, which will be used as building blocks to improve the MS18 method [11]. As discussed in the introduction, an important goal is to design a batch algorithm that gives a better amortized efficiency to compute ring multiplications of the sub-ring $\mathbb{Z}[\xi_{2d}]$.

To achieve this, we first consider a more general setting of batch vector-matrix multiplication of the following form. The input contains:

1. v vectors $\boldsymbol{a}_1 \dots \boldsymbol{a}_v$ where for $k \in [v]$, $\boldsymbol{a}_k \in \{0,1\}^w$;
2. v matrices of ciphertexts $\{\mathbf{C}_{k,(i,j)}\}_{i\in[h],j\in[w],k\in[v]}$, where each $\mathbf{C}_{k,(i,j)} \in \mathsf{RGSW}(\xi_q^{\mathbf{M}_k[i,j]})$ and for each $k \in [v]$, $\mathbf{M}_k$ is a matrix in the domain $\mathbb{Z}_q^{h \times w}$.

Let $\boldsymbol{z}_k = \mathbf{M}_k \cdot \boldsymbol{a}_k \in \mathbb{Z}_q^h$ for $k \in [v]$. The goal is to compute a vector of ciphertext $\overrightarrow{\mathbf{C}} \in \mathsf{RGSW.EncVec\text{-}Exp}(\boldsymbol{z}_1\|\boldsymbol{z}_2\| \dots \|\boldsymbol{z}_v)$, where $\|$ denotes the concatenation.

Even though each input vector $\boldsymbol{a}_i \in \{0,1\}^w$ is just a bit vector, this still suffices to capture general vector-matrix multiplication in $\mathbb{Z}_q$ by using the technique of bit-decomposition and power-of-2. Particularly, any $\mathbf{X} \cdot \boldsymbol{y}$ is equivalent to $\mathbf{X}' \cdot \boldsymbol{y}'$ where $\mathbf{X}'$ is the power-of-2 matrix, i.e., $= \boldsymbol{g}^\top \otimes \mathbf{X}$, and $\boldsymbol{y}' = \mathbf{G}^{-1}(\boldsymbol{y})$ is the bit-decomposition vector. Therefore, this form of homomorphic computation would be sufficient for our later algorithms.

For the naive un-batch homomorphic computation, this would require $v \cdot h \cdot w$ RGSW multiplications. In the next section, we show that suppose the input ciphertext is packed under the batch framework [7], then we can improve the efficiency by using roughly $O(v \cdot h \cdot w/r)$ RGSW multiplications. By using this batch algorithm, we can derive more efficient homomorphic ring multiplications of the sub-ring $\mathbb{Z}[\xi_{2d}]$ and other critical procedures as we will present next.

Note: our further presentation heavily uses indices to vectors and matrices, and thus we would recommend the readers to quickly recall the indexing rules of this work as described in the preliminary (Sect. 2). Consider an example with an n-dimensional vector $\boldsymbol{a}$. We represent it as $(\boldsymbol{a}[1], \boldsymbol{a}[2], \ldots, \boldsymbol{a}[n])$, and for convenience we use $\boldsymbol{a}[0]$ as a reference to $\boldsymbol{a}[n]$ – namely, they are the same variable holding the same value.

4.1 Batch "Vector"-"Encrypted Matrix" Multiplication

Let $\{\mathbf{M}_k\}_{k \in [v]}$ be matrices, each belonging to $\mathbb{Z}_q^{h \times w}$, and $\{\mathbf{C}_{k,(i,j)}\}_{i \in [h], j \in [w], k \in [v]}$ be RGSW ciphertexts as specified as above. Now we consider the following pre-processing of the ciphertexts. In our applications, we assume w to be even, which is without loss of generality. Importantly, for the best amortized efficiency, we require the constraint $hv \leq r$, where r (which can be set to $O(\lambda^{0.25 - o(1)})$) is the number of slots supports by the framework [7]. Intuitively, this means that we have a sufficient number of slots to pack the inputs.

Let $\overrightarrow{\mathbf{C}_{ki}} := (\mathbf{C}_{k,(1,i)}, \mathbf{C}_{k,(2,i)}, \cdots, \mathbf{C}_{k,(h,i)})^{\top}$ as the i-th column vector of $\{\mathbf{C}_{k,(i,j)}\}_{i \in [h], j \in [w]}$. Then the pre-processing step pre-computes the following packed ciphertexts.

Pre-computing $\mathbf{B}_{ki}$'s. We pack the column vectors into mode "$\mathcal{R}_{12} \to \mathcal{R}_{13}$" and mode "$\mathcal{R}_{12} \to \mathcal{R}_{13}$", alternately. Let $\boldsymbol{\eta}_k \in \mathbb{Z}^v$ be the vector with only one 1 in the k-th entry and 0 elsewhere, i.e., $(0, 0, \ldots, 1, 0, \ldots, 0)^{\top}$. Then we compute:

$$\mathbf{B}_{k1} = \mathsf{RGSW\text{-}Pack}(\overrightarrow{\mathbf{C}_{k1}} \otimes \boldsymbol{\eta}_k, \text{``}\mathcal{R}_{12} \to \mathcal{R}_{13}\text{''})$$

$$\mathbf{B}_{k2} = \mathsf{RGSW\text{-}Pack}(\overrightarrow{\mathbf{C}_{k2}} \otimes \boldsymbol{\eta}_k, \text{``}\mathcal{R}_{13} \to \mathcal{R}_{12}\text{''})$$

$$\cdots$$

$$\mathbf{B}_{kw} = \mathsf{RGSW\text{-}Pack}(\overrightarrow{\mathbf{C}_{kw}} \otimes \boldsymbol{\eta}_k, \text{``}\mathcal{R}_{13} \to \mathcal{R}_{12}\text{''})$$

Moreover, we set

$$\mathbf{G}_0 = \mathsf{RGSW\text{-}Pack}(\mathbf{G}, \mathbf{G}, \cdots, \mathbf{G}, \text{``}\mathcal{R}_{13} \to \mathcal{R}_{12}\text{''})$$

$$\mathbf{G}_1 = \mathsf{RGSW\text{-}Pack}(\mathbf{G}, \mathbf{G}, \cdots, \mathbf{G}, \text{``}\mathcal{R}_{12} \to \mathcal{R}_{13}\text{''})$$

Algorithm 4.1: VecMatMult$(\cdot, \cdot)$

Input :
- $a_k \in \{0,1\}^w$, for $k \in [v]$
- a vector of (pre-processed) packed RGSW ciphertext $\{\mathbf{B}_{ki}\}_{i \in [w], k \in [v]}$.

Output : a ciphertext vector $\vec{\mathbf{C}} \in$ RGSW.EncVec-Exp$(z_1 || \cdots || z_v)$, where
$z_k = \mathbf{M}_k \cdot a_k$.

---

1 $\mathrm{ACC}_0 = $ RGSW-Pack$(\mathbf{G}, \mathbf{G}, \cdots, \mathbf{G}, \text{``}\mathcal{R}_{12}\text{''})$;
2 **for** $i = 1$ **to** w **do**
3 $\quad$ $\mathbf{B}_i = \sum_{k \in [v]} \left(a_k[i] \cdot \mathbf{B}_{ki} + (1 - a_k[i]) \cdot \mathbf{G}_{(i \bmod 2)} \right)$;
4 $\quad$ $\mathrm{ACC}_i = $Batch-Mult$(\mathrm{ACC}_{i-1}, \mathbf{B}_i)$;

5 $\vec{\mathbf{C}} = $ UnPack(ACC_w);
6 **Return:** $\vec{\mathbf{C}}$;

Next we present Algorithm 4.1 and Theorem 4.1 to capture the correctness and error growth. As the proof technique is similar to that of [7], due to the space limit, we defer the proof to the full version.

Theorem 4.1 *Algorithm 4.1 satisfies the correctness as required by the input/output specification. Moreover, let s be the secret of the RGSW scheme and E be the upper bound (infinity norm of the canonical embedding) of errors in all evaluation keys and the packed RGSW ciphertexts in $\{\mathbf{B}_{ki}\}$. Then* $\max \|\mathrm{Err}(\vec{\mathbf{C}}[i])\|_\infty$ *is bounded by a sub-Gaussian variable with parameter $O(\gamma)$ such that $\gamma \leq wvr^2\sqrt{N \log Q} \cdot \|s\|_\infty \cdot E$.*

Complexity. The preprocessing step takes wv RGSW-Pack packing, and thus requires $O(wvr)$ RGSW additions. For the online computation, we have $O(wv)$ RGSW additions and w Batch-Mult's in the for loop. Then we compute UnPack(), which is roughly vh Batch-Mult's. We notice that one Batch-Mult is roughly $O(\log \lambda)$ RGSW multiplications. Thus in total, we have $O(wv)$ RGSW additions and $O((w + vh) \log \lambda)$ RGSW multiplications. In amortization, this would be $O(wv/(vh))$ RGSW additions and $O((w+vh) \log \lambda/(vh))$ RGSW multiplications, per dimension (over h) per vector-matrix pair (over v).

4.2 Multiplications Over Small(er) Rings

Now we show how to achieve a batch homomorphic multiplication over $\mathbb{Z}[\xi_{2d}]$ for $2dv < r$ with good amortized complexity, by using the homomorphic method as we developed above. Particularly, let d be a power of two such that $2dv < r$, and $\{a_k\}_{k \in [v]}, \{x_k\}_{k \in [v]}$ be ring elements over $\mathbb{Z}[\xi_{2d}]$. We consider the task of homomorphic computation of $\{a_k x_k\}_{k \in [v]}$ where each $a_k \in \mathbb{Z}[\xi_{2d}]$ is in the clear and $x_k \in \mathbb{Z}[\xi_{2d}]$ is encrypted in some form, as we formalize below.

Task Specifications. Let $\mathbf{X}_k = \mathsf{Coeffs\text{-}Rot}(x_k) \in \mathbb{Z}_q^{2d \times 2d}$ be the anti-cyclic rotation matrix of x_k for $k \in [v]$. Set the power-of-two matrix, i.e., $\mathbf{M}_k = \boldsymbol{g}^\top \otimes \mathbf{X}_k \in \mathbb{Z}_q^{2d \times 2d \log q}$, and generate RGSW ciphertexts $\{\mathbf{C}_{k,(i,j)}\}_{i \in [2d], j \in [2d \log q], k \in [v]}$, each of which encrypts the corresponding entry $\mathbf{M}_k[i,j]$ of $\mathbf{M}_k$. Finally, let $\{\mathbf{B}_{kj}\}_{j \in [2d \log q], k \in [v]}$ be the packed ciphertext as computed in the pre-processing of Sect. 4.1. Now we formally present the task statement:

- **Input:** Let $a_1, \ldots, a_v \in \mathbb{Z}_q[\xi_{2d}]$ and $\{\mathbf{B}_{kj}\}_{j \in [2d \log q], k \in [v]}$ be the packed ciphertexts that represent the pre-processed ciphertext of $x_k \in \mathbb{Z}_q[\xi_{2d}]$.
- **Output:** $(\vec{\mathbf{C}}_1', \vec{\mathbf{C}}_2', \ldots, \vec{\mathbf{C}}_v')$ such that for each $k \in [v]$, $\vec{\mathbf{C}}_k'[i] \in \mathsf{RGSW}(m_k[i])$, $m_k[i] = \xi_q^{z_k[i]}$ and $z_k = \mathsf{coeffs}(a_k \cdot x_k)$.

This task can be achieved easily given Algorithm 4.1 as we present below.

Algorithm 4.2: Multiplications over Small(er) Rings

    Input   : $a_1, \ldots, a_v \in \mathbb{Z}_q[\xi_{2d}]$ and $\{\mathbf{B}_{kj}\}_{j \in [2d \log q], k \in [v]}$ (as specified above).
    Output : $(\vec{\mathbf{C}}_1', \ldots, \vec{\mathbf{C}}_v')$ (as specified above).

1 $a_k' = \boldsymbol{g}^{-1}(\mathsf{coeffs}(a_k))$, for $k \in [v]$;
2 **Return:** $\mathsf{VecMatMult}\left(\{a_k'\}, \{\mathbf{B}_{kj}\}_{k \in [v], j \in [2d \log q]}\right)$ (setting $h = 2d$, $w = 2d \log q$ in Algorithm 4.1).

Theorem 4.2 *The above algorithm satisfies the correctness as required by the input/output specification.*

This theorem simply follows from Theorem 4.1.

Complexity. The complexity of this algorithm follows essentially the same as that of Algorithm 4.1, by setting $h = 2d$, $w = 2d \log q$. Assuming that $d = \lambda^{O(1)}$, $v = \lambda^{O(1)}$, $q = \mathsf{poly}(\lambda)$, then the amortized complexity of the online computation would be $O(\log \lambda)$ RGSW additions, and $O(\log \lambda)$ RGSW multiplications. This can be simplified as $O(\log \lambda) = \tilde{O}(1)$ RGSW multiplications, per dimension (over $2d$) per ring multiplication (over v).

5   Homomorphic DFT/Inverse-DFT

In this section, we consider another form of batch vector-matrix multiplication where the vector is encrypted and the matrix is in the clear yet of some special form, where each entry is a power of a root of unity. By setting the matrix to the DFT (or respectively DFT^{-1}) matrix, this task would immediately give a batch homomorphic DFT/inverse-DFT, which is another important building block of the bootstrapping framework of MS18 [11]. Here we present an efficient batch

DFT/inverse-DFT with dimension $2d < r$ where $r = O(\lambda^{0.25-o(1)})$ is the number of slots that the batch framework can support. Then in Sect. 6, we show that a recursive optimization can be further applied for larger dimensions, e.g., $O(\lambda)$ as required by the bootstrapping. Below we present a detailed formulation.

Setting. Let $m > d$ be two numbers of **powers of two**. Clearly, we have $2d|m$, and thus $\mathbb{Z}[\xi_{2d}]$ is a sub-ring of $\mathbb{Z}[\xi_m]$. Let $\mathbf{M} \in \mathbb{Z}_q[\xi_{2d}]^{2d \times 2d}$ be a matrix where each entry is some power of the $2d$-th root of unity, i.e., each $\mathbf{M}[i,j] = \xi_{2d}^{\delta_{ij}}$ for $\delta_{ij} \in \mathbb{Z}_{2d}$, and let $\boldsymbol{a} \in \mathbb{Z}_q[\xi_m]^{2d}$ be a vector of elements in the ring of the extension field. This task is to homomorphically compute $\mathbf{M} \cdot \boldsymbol{a}$, where $\mathbf{M}$ is in the clear and $\boldsymbol{a}$ is encrypted in some form as specified next.

Basic Facts. We first describe some useful facts in the algebraic number theory. We know that $d' = m/(2d)$ is the degree of field extension $\mathbb{Q}(\xi_m)/\mathbb{Q}(\xi_{2d})$. Then for any $x \in \mathbb{Z}[\xi_m]$, we can uniquely represent x as d' $\mathbb{Z}[\xi_{2d}]$-coefficients (say, $x_0, x_1, \ldots, x_{d'-1} \in \mathbb{Z}[\xi_{2d}]^{d'}$) over some $\mathbb{Q}(\xi_{2d})$-basis of $\mathbb{Q}(\xi_m)$, e.g., $\{1, \xi_m, \xi_m^2, \ldots, \xi_m^{d'-1}\}$, meaning that $x = \sum_{0 \le i < d'} x_i \xi_m^i$. The coefficients can be viewed as a vector space with coefficients in $\mathbb{Z}[\bar{\xi}_{2d}]$, i.e., for any $x' \in \mathbb{Z}[\xi_{2d}]$, we have $x' \cdot x = \sum_{0 \le i < d'} (x' \cdot x_i) \xi_m^i$, whose $\mathbb{Z}[\xi_{2d}]$-coefficients are $(x' x_0, \ldots, x' x_{d'-1})$.

We notice that the matrix $\mathbf{M}$ in the setting suffices to capture the case of DFT/inverse-DFT, as the DFT matrix (of dimension $2d$) can be expressed as

$$\mathbf{M}_{\mathsf{DFT}} = \begin{pmatrix} \xi_{2d}^{1 \cdot 1} & \xi_{2d}^{1 \cdot 1} & \cdots & \xi_{2d}^{1 \cdot 2d} \\ \xi_{2d}^{2 \cdot 1} & \xi_{2d}^{2 \cdot 1} & \cdots & \xi_{2d}^{2 \cdot 2d} \\ & \cdots & & \\ \xi_{2d}^{2d \cdot 1} & \xi_{2d}^{2d \cdot 2} & \cdots & \xi_{2d}^{2d \cdot 2d} \end{pmatrix}.$$

The inverse DFT matrix can be expressed as $\mathbf{M}_{\mathsf{DFT}^{-1}} = (2d)^{-1} \cdot \mathbf{M}_{\mathsf{DFT}}^*$ where $*$ denotes the conjugate. We notice that for the homomorphic DFT^{-1} over the exponent (over $\mathcal{R}_1 = \mathbb{Z}[\xi_q]$), we need that $2d$ to be relatively prime to q, and thus $(2d)^{-1}$ exists when taking modulo q. In our setting, this is not a problem as we can set q to be a prime. For the work [11], they use power-of-two q as required by the FHEW framework [4]. In this case, they would need to change the degree of DFT into 3's powers.

Next we present the details of the task.

Task Specifications. Now we specify how $\boldsymbol{a} = (a_1, \ldots, a_{2d}) \in \mathbb{Z}_q[\xi_m]^{2d}$ is encrypted. For each $i \in [2d]$, we represent $a_i = \sum_{0 \le j < d'} a_{ij} \xi_m^j$ where each $a_{ij} \in \mathbb{Z}[\xi_{2d}]$. Similar to the indexing principle as we used for vectors/matrices, we let $a_{(2d)(j)} = a_{0j}$ and $a_{(i)(d')} = a_{i0}$ for general i, j's. Then we denote $\vec{\mathbf{C}}_{ij} \in \mathsf{RGSW.EncVec\text{-}Exp}(\mathsf{coeffs}(a_{ij}))$ for $i \in [2d], j \in [d']$. Given these ciphertexts, we formally describe the task statement:

- **Input:** (1) $\mathbf{M} \in \mathbb{Z}_q[\xi_{2d}]^{2d \times 2d}$ such that each $\mathbf{M}[i,j] = \xi_{2d}^{\delta_{ij}}$ for $\delta_{ij} \in \mathbb{Z}_{2d}$. (2) $\left\{ \vec{\mathbf{C}}_{ij} \in \mathsf{RGSW.EncVec\text{-}Exp}(\mathsf{coeffs}(a_{ij})) \right\}_{i \in [2d], j \in [d']}$

- **Output:** $\{\overrightarrow{\mathbf{C}}'_{ij}\}_{i\in[2d],j\in[d']}$ such that $\overrightarrow{\mathbf{C}}'_{ij} \in \mathsf{RGSW.EncVec\text{-}Exp}(\mathsf{coeffs}(z_{ij}))$ for each $i \in [2d], j \in [d']$ with the following conditions. Let each $z_i \in \mathbb{Z}_q[\xi_m]$ be the i-th element entry of $\mathbf{M} \cdot \boldsymbol{a}$, i.e., $z_i = \mathbf{M} \cdot \boldsymbol{a}[i] \in \mathbb{Z}_q[\xi_m]$, and $(z_{i0}, \ldots, z_{i(d'-1)}) \in \mathbb{Z}_q[\xi_{2d}]^{d'}$ be its unique coefficient representation with respect to the power basis, i.e., $z_i = \sum_{0 \le j < d'} z_{ij}\xi_{2d}^j$. Note: for convenience, the following two variables are equivalent $z_{id'} := z_{i0}$, as the indexing rule of vectors/matrices.

(*) Importantly, in this section we assume $2d < r$, where r is the number of slots the batch framework supports. Intuitively, this allows us to encrypt all the coefficients of $a_{ij} \in \mathbb{Z}[\xi_{2d}]$ in one packed RGSW cipherext.

5.1 First Attempt

At a first sight, the main task can be achieved by using the prior batch vector-matrix multiplication (Algorithm 4.1). Following this intuition, below we present an attempt that would almost achieve our task, yet would require too many homomorphic additions. Even though unsatisfactory, this attempt still gives insights that lead to our further improvements in the next section. Thus, we still present this algorithm here as a good warm up for the readers.

Recall the following procedure from Sect. 2.4: there is an efficient homomorphic procedure $\mathsf{Anti\text{-}Rot}(\cdot, \cdot)$ that given as inputs $\overrightarrow{\mathbf{C}} \in \mathsf{RGSW.EncVec\text{-}Exp}(\mathsf{coeffs}(z))$ for $z \in \mathbb{Z}[\xi_{2d}]$, and $\delta \in \mathbb{Z}_{2d}$, outputs $\overrightarrow{\mathbf{C}}' \in \mathsf{RGSW.EncVec\text{-}Exp}(\mathsf{coeffs}(z \cdot \xi_{2d}^\delta))$. We notice that in the setting power-of-two, $\mathsf{coeffs}(z \cdot \xi_{2d})$ is an anti-cyclic rotation of $\mathsf{coeffs}(z)$, and this procedure can be computed homomorphically. Next we present the algorithm below.

Algorithm 5.1: Batch Vector-Matrix Mult for Special Matrices

> **Input :**
> - $\mathbf{M} \in \mathbb{Z}_q[\xi_{2d}]^{2d \times 2d}$, where each entry is a power of ξ_{2d};
> - $\left\{\overrightarrow{\mathbf{C}}_{ij} \in \mathsf{RGSW.EncVec\text{-}Exp}(\mathsf{coeffs}(a_{ij}))\right\}_{i\in[2d],j\in[d']}$, as specified above.
>
> **Output :** $\{\overrightarrow{\mathbf{C}}'_{ij}\}_{i\in[2d],j\in[d']}$ as specified above.

---

1 Let $\boldsymbol{v} = (1, 1, \ldots, 1) \in \{0, 1\}^{2d}$ be the all-one vector;
2 **for** $i = 1$ **to** $2d$ **do**
3   **for** $j = 1$ **to** d' **do**
4   **for** $k = 1$ **to** $2d$ **do**
5   set $\overrightarrow{\mathbf{R}}_{kj} = \mathsf{Anti\text{-}Rot}(\overrightarrow{\mathbf{C}}_{kj}, \mathbf{M}[i, k])$;
6   set $\mathbf{D}_{kj} = \mathsf{RGSW\text{-}Pack}(\overrightarrow{\mathbf{R}}_{kj})$ (to the appropriate mode, either "$\mathcal{R}_{12} \to \mathcal{R}_{13}$" or "$\mathcal{R}_{13} \to \mathcal{R}_{12}$") ;
7   Set $\overrightarrow{\mathbf{C}}'_{ij} = \mathsf{VecMatMult}(\boldsymbol{v}, \{\mathbf{D}_{kj}\}_{i\in[2d]})$;

8 **Return:** $\{\overrightarrow{\mathbf{C}}'_{ij}\}_{i\in[2d],j\in[d']}$.

The correctness can be easily verified so we do not present the details. Below we just analyze the complexity and point out a technical subtlety that this algorithm does not satisfy our efficiency requirement.

Complexity Analysis. From the computation, at least the algorithm needs $2dd'$ VecMatMult(), each of which is roughly $2d$ Batch-Mult, and $4d^2d'$ RGSW-Pack. As we analyzed, each Batch-Mult is roughly $O(d\log\lambda)$ RGSW multiplications, and each RGSW-Pack is roughly $O(d)$ RGSW additions. Thus in total this would be $O(d^2d')$ RGSW multiplications and $O(d^3d')$ RGSW additions. In amortization (per ring dimension m and per inverse-DFT dimension $2d$), this would be $\tilde{O}(1)$ RGSW multiplications and $O(d)$ RGSW additions. At first it seems we can neglect the RGSW additions, yet in our parameter setting later, we will require $d = \lambda^{O(1)}$. As a RGSW multiplication is roughly equal to $O(\log\lambda)$ RGSW additions, then the overall amortized complexity will be dominated by the $O(d)$ RGSW additions. This will prevent us from getting the desired efficiency, i.e., overall $\tilde{O}(1)$ RGSW multiplications for bootstrapping, per input ciphertext.

This drawback comes from Step 6, where the above algorithm needs too many calls to RGSW-Pack. At a high level, we need to perform anti-cyclic rotations on the ciphertexts, and then perform the vector-matrix multiplication. The input matrices $\{\mathbf{D}_{kj}\}$ to VecMatMult() need to be packed in the mode of either "$\mathcal{R}_{12} \to \mathcal{R}_{13}$" or "$\mathcal{R}_{13} \to \mathcal{R}_{12}$", but we do not know how to perform homomorphic anti-cyclic rotations over packed ciphertexts of these modes. Therefore, the above method can only perform anti-cyclic rotations on un-packed ciphertexts (Step 5) and then compute different packed ciphertexts (Step 6) for each call of the vector-matrix multiplication (Step 7).

5.2 New Building Blocks

In this section, we present some useful batch homomorphic algorithms, which will be used as major building blocks for our improved method. Particularly, we identify a new batch homomorphic method to compute anti-cyclic rotations for packed ciphertexts of modes "$\mathcal{R}_{12}$" and "$\mathcal{R}_{13}$". Even though this does not solve the challenge described in the prior section[3], later on we will show a new homomorphic method that can incorporate the new homomorphic anti-cyclic algorithm, resulting in the overall improvement.

We now present the task for our new homomorphic method. Let $\boldsymbol{x}$ be some vector, and $\boldsymbol{y}$ be its anti-cyclic rotation, i.e., $\boldsymbol{y} = $ Anti-Rot$(\boldsymbol{x})$. Given input a packed ciphertext $\mathbf{C} \in$ RGSW$(\sum_{i\in[r]} x_i\mathsf{v}_i)$ of mode "$\mathcal{R}_{12}$" (or "$\mathcal{R}_{13}$" respectively), our goal is to compute a packed ciphertext $\mathbf{C} \in$ RGSW$(\sum_{i\in[r]} y_i\mathsf{v}_i)$.

To achieve this, we first consider the following two sub-tasks:

---

[3] Recall that the challenge is to homomorphically rotates batch ciphertexts of modes "$\mathcal{R}_{12} \to \mathcal{R}_{13}$" or "$\mathcal{R}_{13} \to \mathcal{R}_{12}$".

Sub-Task I: Batch Permutation: Given input (1) a permutation $\pi : [r] \rightarrow [r] \in S_r$ where S_r is the symmetric group of degree r, and (2) a packed ciphertext $\mathbf{C} \in \mathsf{RGSW}(\sum_{i \in [r]} x_i \mathsf{v}_i)$ of mode "$\mathcal{R}_{12}$" (or "$\mathcal{R}_{13}$" respectively), the goal is to compute a packed ciphertext $\mathbf{C}' \in \mathsf{RGSW}(\sum_{i \in [r]} x_{\pi(i)} \mathsf{w}_i)$ (or the other mode respectively). This can be achieved by the Algorithm 5.2.

Algorithm 5.2: Batch-Permute$(\cdot, \cdot)$

Input :
- $\mathbf{C}$, a packed RGSW ciphertext encrypting $\sum_{i \in [r]} x_i \mathsf{v}_i$;
- π, a permutation in the symmetric group S_r.

Output : $\mathbf{C}'$, a packed RGSW ciphertext encrypting $\sum x_i \mathsf{w}_{\pi(i)}$.

---

1 Let $\mathbf{C}_\pi = \sum_{i \in [r]} \mathsf{v}_i^\vee \mathsf{w}_{\pi(i)}$, i.e., a packed ciphertext of mode $\mathcal{R}_{12} \rightarrow \mathcal{R}_{13}$;
2 **Return:** $\mathbf{C}' = $ Batch-Mult$(\mathbf{C}, \mathbf{C}_\pi)$.

Sub-Task II: Batch Inverse Automorphism: Given input a packed ciphertext $\mathbf{C} \in \mathsf{RGSW}(\sum_{i \in [r]} \xi_q^{a_i} \mathsf{v}_i)$ of mode "$\mathcal{R}_{12}$" (or "$\mathcal{R}_{13}$" respectively), the goal is to compute a packed ciphertext $\mathbf{C}' \in \mathsf{RGSW}(\sum_{i \in [r]} \xi_q^{-a_i} \mathsf{v}_i)$ (or the other mode respectively). In another word, this is to homomorphically *conjugate* the plaintexts (the $\mathcal{R}_1$ part) while keeping the basis $\{\mathsf{v}_i\}$ intact. The can be achieved by Algorithm 5.3.

Algorithm 5.3: Inv-Auto$(\cdot)$

Input   : $\mathbf{C}$, a packed RGSW ciphertext encrypting $\sum_{i \in [r]} \xi_q^{a_i} \mathsf{v}_i$, i.e., plaintext Pack$(\xi_q^{a_1}, \cdots, \xi_q^{a_r})$ in mode $\mathcal{R}_{12}$;
Output : $\mathbf{C}'$, a packed RGSW ciphertext encrypting $\sum_{i \in [r]} \xi_q^{-a_i} \mathsf{v}_i$, i.e., Pack$(\xi_q^{-a_1}, \cdots, \xi_q^{-a_r})$ in mode $\mathcal{R}_{12}$;

---

1 Let σ be the automorphism of $\mathcal{R}$, satisfying $\xi_q \mapsto \xi_q^{-1}$, $\xi_{\rho'} \mapsto \xi_{\rho'}$ and $\xi_{\tau'} \mapsto \xi_{\tau'}$;
2 Apply σ to each entry of $\mathbf{C}$ and get $\overline{\mathbf{C}}$;
3 **Return:** RGSW-KS$(\overline{\mathbf{C}}, \mathsf{evk}^{(\sigma^{-1})})$

Combining the above two algorithms, we can homomorphically evaluate the homomorphic anti-cyclic rotation over packed ciphertexts as Algorithm 5.4.

Algorithm 5.4: Batch-Anti-Rot$(\cdot,\cdot)$

Input :
- $\mathbf{C}$, a packed RGSW ciphertext encrypting $\sum_{i\in[r]} \xi_q^{a_i} \mathsf{v}_i$, i.e., plaintext $\mathsf{Pack}(\xi_q^{a_1},\cdots,\xi_q^{a_r})$ in mode $\mathcal{R}_{12}$;
- a monomial ξ_q^{δ}.

Output : $\mathbf{C}'$, a packed RGSW ciphertext encrypting
$\sum_{i\in[\delta]} \xi_q^{-a_{r-\delta+i}} \mathsf{w}_i + \sum_{i\in[r-\delta]} \xi_q^{a_i} \mathsf{w}_{i+\delta}$, namely, plaintext is
$\mathsf{Pack}(\xi_q^{-a_{r-\delta+1}},\cdots,\xi_q^{-a_r},\xi_q^{a_1},\cdots,\xi_q^{a_{r-\delta}})$, the anti-cyclic rotation of
the input in mode $\mathcal{R}_{12}$;

---

1 Let π_δ be the *cyclic* rotation that shifts δ;
2 ACC=Batch-Permute$(\mathbf{C},\pi_\delta)$;
3 ACC$'$=Inv-Auto(ACC);
4 ACC$_+$ = Batch-Mult$(\mathrm{ACC}, \sum_{i=\delta+1}^{r} \mathsf{v}_i \cdot \mathsf{w}_i^{\vee})$;
5 ACC$_-$ = Batch-Mult$(\mathrm{ACC}', \sum_{i=1}^{\delta} \mathsf{v}_i \cdot \mathsf{w}_i^{\vee})$;
6 $\mathbf{C}' = \mathrm{ACC}_+ + \mathrm{ACC}_-$;
7 **Return:** $\mathbf{C}'$

Theorem 5.1 *The above algorithm satisfies the correctness as required by the input/output specification.*

The correctness can be easily verified. We do not analyze the noise here. Instead, we analyze the overall noise behavior in our Algorithm 5.5, the improved homomorphic anti-cyclic rotation.

5.3   Our Improved Method

Now we describe our new improved algorithm to achieve the main task of this section, by using the new algorithms in Sect. 5.2 as critical building blocks. We first present some basic ideas for the plaintext computation, and then the homomorphic method.

We use the following (simplified) example to illustrate our core idea. Given $\boldsymbol{b} = (b_1,\ldots,b_{2d}) \in \mathbb{Z}_q[\xi_{2d}]^{2d}$ and $\boldsymbol{x} = (\xi_{2d}^{\delta_1},\ldots,\xi_{2d}^{\delta_{2d}})$, the task is to compute the inner product $\langle \boldsymbol{b}, \boldsymbol{x} \rangle$. In the homomorphic computation, $\boldsymbol{b}$ is encrypted and $\boldsymbol{x}$ is in the clear. At a high level, Algorithm 5.1 performs the computation as: $\sum_{i\in[2d]} \mathsf{coeffs}\left(b_i \cdot \xi_{2d}^{\delta_i}\right)$. Even though the term $\mathsf{coeffs}\left(b_i \cdot \xi_{2d}^{\delta_i}\right)$ can be (homomorphically) computed by using Anti-Rot, i.e., permuting the coefficients and negating some of them properly, the homomorphic algorithm requires to pack the coefficients in every $\mathsf{coeffs}\left(b_i \cdot \xi_{2d}^{\delta_i}\right)$ in mode $\mathcal{R}_{12} \to \mathcal{R}_{13}$ or $\mathcal{R}_{13} \to \mathcal{R}_{12}$, resulting in the undesired $O(d^3 d')$ homomorphic additions. It is unclear whether there is an efficient homomorphic method transforming a ciphertext of $\mathsf{Pack}(\mathsf{coeffs}(b_i))$ into another of $\mathsf{Pack}(\mathsf{Anti\text{-}Rot}(\mathsf{coeffs}(b_i),\xi_{2d}^{\delta_i}))$, under the modes $\mathcal{R}_{12} \to \mathcal{R}_{13}$ or $\mathcal{R}_{13} \to \mathcal{R}_{12}$. It is important to notice that our algorithm in the above section

(Sect. 5.2) can compute the anti-cyclic rotation for ciphertexts of mode $\mathcal{R}_{12}$ or $\mathcal{R}_{13}$ but not $\mathcal{R}_{12} \to \mathcal{R}_{13}$ or $\mathcal{R}_{13} \to \mathcal{R}_{12}$.

To tackle the above challenge, we consider another way of computation. First we observe that the inner product $\langle \boldsymbol{b}, \boldsymbol{x} \rangle$ can be re-expressed as computing g_{2d} recursively as follow: $g_1 = b_1 \cdot \xi_{2d}^{\delta_1 - \delta_2}$, for $1 < j < 2d$, $g_j = (g_{j-1} + b_j) \cdot \xi_{2d}^{\delta_j - \delta_{j+1}}$, $g_{2d} = (g_{2d-1} + b_{2d}) \cdot \xi_{2d}^{\delta_{2d}}$. It is not hard to verify that these two computation methods are equivalent, producing the same value for any $\boldsymbol{b}$ and $\boldsymbol{x}$.

Now, we can homomorphically compute the above sequence using an ACC storing each g_j in mode either $\mathcal{R}_{12}$ or $\mathcal{R}_{13}$. Let consider an example where g_j is stored in mode $\mathcal{R}_{12}$. Now suppose the ciphertexts that encrypt the coefficients of b_{j+1} are packed into mode $\mathcal{R}_{12} \to \mathcal{R}_{13}$. Then we can compute a ciphertext $\mathbf{D}$ of g_{j+1} in mode $\mathcal{R}_{13}$, and then apply the homomorphic Anti-Rot on $\mathbf{D}$ to update the ACC, which works because $\mathbf{D}$ is in mode $\mathcal{R}_{13}$. Proceeding in this way, the final ACC would be a ciphertext that encrypts $g_{2d} = \langle \boldsymbol{b}, \boldsymbol{x} \rangle$. We formalize the idea into Algorithm 5.5.

Algorithm 5.5: RGSW.EncVec-MatMult$(\cdot, \cdot)$

Input :
 1. $\mathbf{M} \in \mathbb{Z}_q[\xi_{2d}]^{2d \times 2d}$ where each entry is a power of ξ_{2d}.
 2. $\left\{ \vec{\mathbf{C}}_{kj} \in \text{RGSW.EncVec-Exp}(\text{coeffs}(a_{kj})) \right\}_{k \in [2d], j \in [d']}$, as above in the task
    specifications.

Output : $\{\vec{\mathbf{C}}'_{ij}\}_{i \in [2d], j \in [d']}$ as required above.

---

1 **for** $j = 1$ to d', $k = 1$ to $2d$ **do**
2 $\quad$ $\mathbf{C}_{kj}$=RGSW-Pack$(\vec{\mathbf{C}}_{kj}, "\mathcal{R}_{1,(3-(k \bmod 2))} \to \mathcal{R}_{1,(2+(k \bmod 2))}")$;
3 Initialize ACC_0=RGSW-Pack$(\mathbf{G}, \cdots, \mathbf{G}, "\mathcal{R}_{12}")$;
4 **for** $i = 1$ to $2d$ **do**
5 $\quad$ **for** $j = 1$ to d' **do**
6 $\quad\quad$ ACC_R=ACC_0;
7 $\quad\quad$ **for** $k = 1$ to $2d - 1$ **do**
8 $\quad\quad\quad$ $\text{ACC}_M = \text{Batch-Mult}(\text{ACC}_R, \mathbf{C}_{kj})$;
9 $\quad\quad\quad$ $\text{ACC}_R = \text{Batch-Anti-Rot}(\text{ACC}_M, \mathbf{M}[i,k]/\mathbf{M}[i,k+1])$;
10 $\quad\quad$ $\text{ACC}_M = \text{Batch-Mult}(\text{ACC}_R, \mathbf{C}_{(2d)j})$;
11 $\quad\quad$ $\text{ACC}_R = \text{Batch-Anti-Rot}(\text{ACC}_M, \mathbf{M}[i, 2d])$;
12 $\quad\quad$ Set $\vec{\mathbf{C}}'_{ij} = \text{UnPack}(\text{ACC}_R)$;

13 **Return:** $\{\vec{\mathbf{C}}'_{ij}\}_{i \in [2d], j \in [d']}$.

Theorem 5.2 summarizes the correctness and error growth. As the proof is similar to that of Theorem 4.1 (though much tedious), due to space limit we defer the proof to the full version.

Theorem 5.2 *The above algorithm satisfies the correctness as required by the main task specification in this section.*

Moreover, let s be the secret of the RGSW scheme and E be the upper bound (infinity norm of the canonical embedding) of errors in all evaluation keys and the packed RGSW ciphertexts in $\left\{\overrightarrow{\mathbf{C}}_{ij}\right\}_{i\in[2d],j\in[d']}$. Then the error of each RGSW ciphertext in $\left\{\overrightarrow{\mathbf{C}}'_{ij}\right\}_{i\in[2d],j\in[d']}$ is bounded by a sub-Gaussian variable with parameter $O(\gamma)$ such that $\gamma \leq dr^3\|s\|\sqrt{N\log Q}E$.

Efficiency. The algorithm makes $O(d'd)$ calls to RGSW-Pack, $O(d^2d')$ calls to Batch-Mult, and $O(dd')$ calls to UnPack. Similar to the prior analysis, this would be upper bounded by $O(d^2d')$ RGSW additions and $\tilde{O}(d^2d')$ RGSW multiplications, which is dominated by $O(d^2d')$ RGSW multiplications. Thus, in amortization (per ring dimension $m = 2dd'$ per inverse-DFT dimension $2d$) the cost would be $\tilde{O}(1)$ RGSW multiplications.

6 Homomorphic DFT^{-1}, Recursively

The multiplication of the DFT/inverse-DFT matrix is a critical step for realizing the recursive DFT/inverse-DFT. In this section, we show how to achieve a homomorphic DFT/inverse-DFT by applying the method in Sect. 5 recursively, via the Nussbaumer Transform as identified by MS18 [11]. First we present the Nussbaumer Transform using the language of algebraic extension, which might give a better intuition than the polynomial representation as used in the work [11].

6.1 Nussbaumer Transform

Let $K \supseteq E \supseteq \mathbb{Q}$ be towers of field extensions, where $K = \mathbb{Q}(\xi_n)$, $E = \mathbb{Q}(\xi_{n'})$ for $n > n'$. Denote $d = n/n'$ be the degree of the field extension K/E, and we assume that $2d \mid n'$, which is required by the DFT framework as we further elaborate later. At a high level, Nussbaumer Transform shows that the multiplication operation (of two elements) in K can be reduced to $2 \cdot d$ multiplications of elements in E in the following way.

First we observe that K is a field extension over E that can be expressed in a polynomial quotient ring with coefficients in E, i.e., $K \cong E[X]/(X^d - \xi_{n'})$, where $\xi_{n'} \in E$ is the n'-th root of unity. Then any two ring elements $a, b \in K$ can be expressed as $a \cong a(X) = a_0 + a_1X + \cdots + a_{d-1}X^{d-1}$ and $b \cong b(X) = b_0 + b_1X + \cdots + b_{d-1}X^{d-1}$, where all the coefficients are in E. In this way, the multiplication of $a \cdot b \in K$ can be computed equivalently as $a(X) \cdot b(X)$ mod $(X^d - \xi_{n'}) \in E[X]/(X^d - \xi_{n'})$.

To compute $a(X) \cdot b(X)$ in the DFT manner, we notice that the $2d$-th root of unity, denoted as $\omega = \xi_{2d}$, would be used. If the underlying coefficients are in $\mathbb{Q}$, then we inherently need to work with complex numbers, which are not compatible with the FHEW-based computation. Interestingly, if the coefficients are in E, then we do have $\omega = \xi_{2d} \in E = \mathbb{Q}(\xi_{n'})$ as long as $2d \mid n'$. Now we can compute DFT-based multiplication with integral coefficients. This is compatible with FHEW as demonstrated by [11], and can be further batched by our framework as we will show in the next section. Now we present the DFT-based multiplication in details.

- Convert $a(X)$ in the DFT representation as $(a(\omega^0), \ldots, a(\omega^{2d-1})) \in E^{2d}$, and similarly $b(X)$ as $(b(\omega^0), \ldots, b(\omega^{2d-1})) \in E^{2d}$.
- Multiply the vectors component-wisely, and obtain $(c(\omega^0), \ldots, c(\omega^{2d-1}))$.
- Convert the resulting vector back to the polynomial $c(X)$ using inverse DFT, and then output $c(X) \mod (X^d - \xi_{n'})$.

We notice that $a(X) \cdot b(X)$ is a polynomial of degree at most $2(d-1) < 2d$, and therefore, can be uniquely interpolated from the DFT representation of $2d$ points. Thus, $c(X) \mod X^d - \xi_{n'}$ would give the correct answer. We notice that there is a natural mapping from $c(X)$ to the ring element in K, namely $c(X) \mapsto c(\xi_n)$, which can be thought as plugging in X with ξ_n.

Recursive Optimizations. This process can be further optimized by recursively computing multiplications in E, as long as there is another intermediate field $E \supset F \supset \mathbb{Q}$. Under this observation, a tower structure would give the best performance for recursion. Particularly, we assume that $n = 2d^\rho$ for some integer $\rho > 1$, and n, d are both two's power, i.e., $d = 2^\delta$, and $n = 2^{\delta\rho+1}$. This allows us to present the recursive optimization in a clean way.

Let DFT_{2d} be an algorithm parameterized by $2d$ and DFT_{2d}^{-1} be the inverse-DFT algorithm parameterized by $2d$. We present these algorithms in Algorithms 6.1 and 6.2. The correctness and efficiency can be easily verified and analyzed. Here our description can help readers get better intuitions of the homomorphic version of the inverse-DFT.

Importantly, these two algorithms are defined for general (recursive) inputs, which can be of varying input lengths. In the first level, DFT_{2d} takes input $a \in \mathbb{Z}[\xi_n]$, and DFT_{2d}^{-1} takes input $\boldsymbol{a} \in \mathbb{Z}[\xi_{2d}]^{(2d)^{\rho-1}}$.

6.2   Homomorphic Evaluation

Now we present the homomorphic algorithm for the recursive inverse-DFT as Aglrotihm 6.3. Here we describe the specifications.

- **Input**: The input contains ciphertext vectors that encrypts $\boldsymbol{a} \in \mathbb{Z}[\xi_{n'}]^{(2d)^{\rho'-1}}$, where $\boldsymbol{a}$ is the input of the plaintext-based algorithm DFT^{-1} as Algorithm 6.2. Specifically, let ρ', n' be two parameters as implicit inputs, indicating which recursive level the algorithm is at. The (explicit) input contains $(2d)^{\rho'-1}$ ciphertext vectors $\left\{ \overrightarrow{\mathbf{C}}_i \right\}_{i \in [(2d)^{\rho'-1}]}$, where each $\overrightarrow{\mathbf{C}}_i \in$ RGSW.EncVec-Exp(coeffs($a[i]$)), meaning that it encrypts all the coefficients of $a[i]$ in the exponents.
- **Output**: Let $a = \mathsf{DFT}^{-1}(\boldsymbol{a}) \in \mathbb{Z}[\xi_{n'd^{\rho'-1}}]$. The output contains a ciphertext vector $\overrightarrow{\mathbf{C}}' \in$ RGSW.EncVec-Exp(coeffs(a)), meaning that it encrypts all the coefficients of a in the exponents.

Algorithm 6.1: DFT_{2d}

Input : $a \in \mathbb{Q}(\xi_{n'})$ for $n' = 2d^{\rho'}$
Output : $a \in \mathbb{Q}(\xi_{2d})^{(2d)^{\rho'-1}}$

1 **if** $n' = 2d$ **then**
2 | **return** a
3 **else**
4 | represent $a \cong a(X) = a_0 + a_1 X + \cdots + a_{d-1} X^{d-1}$, where each $a_i \in \mathbb{Q}(\xi_{n'/d})$;
5 | let $\omega = \xi_{2d} \in \mathbb{Q}(\xi_{n'/d})$;
6 | compute $(a'_0, \ldots, a'_{2d-1}) := (a_0, \ldots, a_{d-1}, 0, \ldots, 0) \cdot \mathsf{M}_{\text{DFT}}$; // $a'_i = a(\omega^i)$
7 | **return** $\left(\text{DFT}_{2d}(a'_1), \ldots, \text{DFT}_{2d}(a'_{2d}) \right)$.

Algorithm 6.2: DFT_{2d}^{-1}

Input : $a \in \mathbb{Q}(\xi_{n'})^{(2d)^{\rho'-1}}$
Output : $a \in \mathbb{Q}(\xi_{n'd^{\rho'-1}})$

1 **if** $\rho' = 1$ **then**
2 | **return:** a;
3 **else**
4 | parse $a = (a_1, \ldots, a_{2d})$ where each $a_i \in \mathbb{Q}(\xi_{n'})^{(2d)^{\rho'-2}}$;
5 | compute $a'_i = \text{DFT}_{2d}^{-1}(a_i)$ for $i \in [2d]$;
6 | compute $(a_1, \ldots, a_{2d}) = (a'_1, \ldots, a'_{2d}) \cdot \mathsf{M}_{\text{DFT}^{-1}}$;
7 | compute $a(X) = a_0 + a_1 X + \cdots + a_{2d-1} X^{2d-1} \mod X^d - \xi_{n'd^{\rho'-2}}$, where we set $a_0 = a_{2d}$;
8 | **return** $a \cong a(X)$ as an element in the extension field $\mathbb{Q}(\xi_{n'd^{\rho'-1}})$.

Before presenting our homomorphic algorithm, we first introduce some useful facts for "change of representation". Let $m \geq 2d$ be two numbers of two's powers. Below, we consider two particular ways to represent a ring element.

- Given ring element $a \in \mathbb{Z}[\xi_m]$, we can express it as a $\mathbb{Z}$-coefficient vector of dimension $m/2$, denoted as $\mathsf{coeffs}(a)$ with respect to the power basis, namely $a \mapsto (a_1, \ldots, a_{m/2}) \in \mathbb{Z}^{m/2}$ such that $a = a_0 + \sum_{i \in [m/2-1]} a_i \xi_m^i$. Using our indexing rule for convenience, we set $a_{m/2}$ as an alias variable of a_0.
- On the other hand, we can also represent a as a $\mathbb{Z}[\xi_{2d}]$-coefficient vector of dimension $m/(2d)$, namely $a \mapsto (a'_1, \ldots, a'_{m/(2d)}) \in \mathbb{Z}[\xi_{2d}]^{m/(2d)}$ such that $a = a'_0 + \sum_{i \in [m/(2d)-1]} a'_i \xi_m^i$. Similarly, we set $a'_{m/(2d)}$ as an alias variable of a'_0. Of course each a'_i can be further expanded by the $\mathbb{Z}$-coefficient representation, namely $a'_i \mapsto (a'_{i1}, \ldots, a'_{id})$ denoted as $\mathsf{coeffs}(a'_i)$.

These two representations are equivalent as they both represent the same ring element. Moreover, the two representations can be mutually converted from one to the other, just by permuting/rearranging the indices. Thus, this also gives an efficient homomorphic method for converting a ciphertext vector $\vec{C}$ that encrypts $(a_1, \ldots, a_{m/2})$, into ciphertext vectors $\{\vec{C}_i\}_{i \in [m/(2d)]}$ where each $\vec{C}_i$ encrypts $\mathsf{coeffs}(a'_i)$, and vice versa. As it just requires to permute the indices, no heavy homomorphic method (even addition) is required.

We can formalize the conversions as the following two algorithms, and their homomorphic variants work analogously.

- Rearr: on input $m \to 2d$, $\mathsf{coeffs}(a) \in \mathbb{Z}^{m/2}$ representing the $\mathbb{Z}$ coefficients of $a \in \mathbb{Z}[\xi_m]$, outputs $\Big(\mathsf{coeffs}(a'_1), \ldots, \mathsf{coeffs}(a'_{m/(2d)})\Big)$;
- Rev-Rearr: on input $2d \to m$, $\Big(\mathsf{coeffs}(a'_1), \ldots, \mathsf{coeffs}(a'_{m/(2d)})\Big)$ representing $(a'_1, \ldots, a'_{m/(2d)}) \in \mathbb{Z}[\xi_{2d}]^{m/(2d)}$, outputs $\mathsf{coeffs}(a) \in \mathbb{Z}^{m/2}$ where $a \in \mathbb{Z}[\xi_m]$.

We notice that it is natural to present our homomorphic inverse-DFT algorithm using the first representation. However, it is more natural to use the second representation for the improved batch homomorphic multiplication of the inverse-DFT matrix as we designed in Algorithm 5.5. Thus, we introduce the above two efficient conversions to glue these two parts together. Additionally, we also define the following notation for convenience.

Definition 6.1 Let $a|b$ be integers. Define sets $S_1, \ldots, S_a$ that equally partition $[b]$ as: $S_1 = [b/a]$, $S_2 = [b/a + 1, 2b/a], \ldots,$ and $S_a = [(a-1)b/a + 1, b]$.

Now we present our new method in Algorithm 6.3 and summarize the result in Theorem 6.2. Due to space limit, we defer the proof to the full version.

Theorem 6.2 *The above algorithm satisfies the correctness as required by the task specification in this section.*

Moreover, let s be the secret of the RGSW scheme and E be the upper bound of errors in all evaluation keys and in all RGSW ciphertexts in $\left\{\vec{C}_{ij}\right\}_{i \in [(2d)^{\rho'-1}], j \in [d']}$. Then the error of each RGSW ciphertext in output is bounded by a sub-Gaussian variable with parameter $O(\gamma)$ such that $\gamma \leq (dr^3 \|s\| N \log Q)^{\rho'} E$.

Complexity. We can show that the amortized complexity of the recursive version is still $\tilde{O}(1)$ RGSW multiplications. Intuitively, if the multiplication of inverse-DFT matrix has $\tilde{O}(1)$ amortized complexity (which is true for our Algorithm 5.5), then we can achieve $\tilde{O}(\rho)$ amortized complexity where ρ is the recursive depth. We will set parameters such that $\rho = O(1)$, and thus the overall amortized complexity matches what we claimed. Below we elaborate.

Let $n = (2d)^\rho$ be the final output (ring) dimension. Similar to the analysis of [11], we first identify that at level i of the recursion, the algorithm makes $(2d)^i$ calls to the RGSW.EncVec-MatMult algorithm, with dimension $m^i = (2d)^{\rho-i-1}$. Thus at this level, each call would be $\tilde{O}(m^i \times 2d) = \tilde{O}((2d)^{\rho-i})$ RGSW multiplications, resulting in a total complexity (at this level) $\tilde{O}((2d)^\rho)$ as the setting of parameters. Thus, in total there would be $\tilde{O}(\rho(2d)^\rho)$ RGSW multiplications. For the case where $\rho = O(1)$, this would be $\tilde{O}((2d)^\rho)$, implying the amortized complexity $\tilde{O}(1)$ RGSW multiplications per dimension.

Algorithm 6.3: Hom-DFT^{-1}

Input   : Integers ρ', n' and ciphertext vectors $\left\{ \overrightarrow{\mathbf{C}}_i \right\}_{i \in [(2d)^{\rho'-1}]}$

Output : A ciphertext vector $\overrightarrow{\mathbf{C}}'$ as specified above.

---

1 **if** $\rho' = 1$ **then**
2 $\quad$ **Return:** $\overrightarrow{\mathbf{C}}$;
3 **else**
4 $\quad$ Let $S_1, \ldots, S_{2d}$ be the sets that equally partition $[(2d)^{\rho'-1}]$;
5 $\quad$ For $i \in [2d]$, compute $\overrightarrow{\mathbf{C}}'_i = \text{Hom-DFT}^{-1}\left(\{\overrightarrow{\mathbf{C}}_j\}_{j \in S_i} \right)$;
6 $\quad$ For $i \in [2d]$, compute $\{\overrightarrow{\mathbf{C}'_{ij}}\}_{j \in [d'']} = \text{Rearr}((2d)^{\rho'-2} \to 2d, \overrightarrow{\mathbf{C}}'_i)$, where
   $\quad$ $d'' = n' d^{\rho'-2} / (2d)$;
7 $\quad$ $\{\overrightarrow{\mathbf{C}''_{ij}}\}_{i \in [2d], j \in [d'']} = \text{RGSW.EncVec-MatMult}(\mathbf{M}_{\text{DFT}^{-1}}, \{\overrightarrow{\mathbf{C}'_{ij}}\}_{i \in [2d], j \in [d'']})$;
8 $\quad$ For $i \in [2d]$, compute $\overrightarrow{\mathbf{C}}''_i = \text{Rev-Rearr}(2d \to (2d)^{\rho'-2}, \{\overrightarrow{\mathbf{C}''_{ij}}\}_{j \in [d'']})$;
9 $\quad$ For $i \in [d+1, 2d]$, $\overrightarrow{\mathbf{C}}''_i = \text{Anti-Rot}(\overrightarrow{\mathbf{C}}''_i, \xi_{n' d^{\rho'-2}})$;
10 $\quad$ **for** $i = 1$ **to** d **do**
11 $\quad\quad$ **for** $j = 1$ **to** $n' d^{\rho'-2}$ **do**
12 $\quad\quad\quad$ $\overrightarrow{\mathbf{C}}''_i[j] = \overrightarrow{\mathbf{C}}''_i[k] \boxdot \overrightarrow{\mathbf{C}}''_{i+d}[k]$;
13 $\quad$ $\overrightarrow{\mathbf{C}}' = \text{Rev-Rearr}((2d)^{\rho'-2} \to (2d)^{\rho'-1}, \{\overrightarrow{\mathbf{C}}''_i\}_{i \in [d]})$;
14 $\quad$ **Return:** $\overrightarrow{\mathbf{C}}'$;

---

7 Putting Things Together – Faster Bootstrapping

Now we present how to use our new batch algorithms in Sects. 4 and 6 to improve MS18 [11], resulting an overall more efficient bootstrapping method.

7.1 MSB Extract and LWE Packing

We recall several building blocks from the literature.

- From [11], there is a conversion algorithm that takes input n LWE ciphertexts (under the same secret key), and outputs $(a, b) \in \text{RLWE}$ with secret $z \in \mathcal{R}$, of dimension n, such that $b - az = \Delta m + e$ where $\text{coeffs}(m)[i]$ corresponds to the i-th message, Δ is some scaling number, e.g., $q/2$, and q is the modulus.
- From [3,4,7,11], there is an algorithm msbExtract that on input $\mathbf{C} \in \text{RGSW}(\xi_q^m)$ outputs an LWE ciphertext $c \in \text{LWE}(f(m))$, where $f(m)$ denotes the most significant bit. Assuming β is the error bound of the input ciphertext, then the error in the resulting ciphertext is bounded by $O(q\beta)$.

7.2 Our Batch Bootstrapping Method

Parameters. Here are the parameters used in our overall bootstrapping.

- N: the ring dimension of RGSW (the bootstrapping keys).
- n: the dimension of input LWE ciphertexts, and number of input ciphertexts. Here we set n to be a power of two.
- q: the input LWE modulus. In the batch framework, $\mathcal{R}_1$ is set to be $\mathbb{Z}[\xi_q]$.
- $2d$: the parameter of DFT/DFT^{-1}. We set d to be a power of two.
- ρ: the depth of the recursive algorithm. We set $n = 2d^\rho$.
- r: the maximal number of slots we can packed in the batch framework of [7].
- v: the number of inputs in Algorithm 4.2. We require $r > 2dv$.

The Bootstrapping Algorithm. We first present how the bootstrapping keys are constructed. Let z be the secret of the RLWE ciphertext derived from packing n input LWE ciphertexts. Let $(z_1, \ldots, z_{(2d)^{\rho-1}}) = \mathsf{DFT}(z)$, $\mathbf{Z}_k = \mathsf{Coeffs\text{-}Rot}(z_k) \in \mathbb{Z}_q^{2d \times 2d}$ be the anti-cyclic rotation matrix of z_k, and the corresponding power-of-two matrix, i.e., $\mathbf{M}_k = \boldsymbol{g}^\top \otimes \mathbf{X}_k \in \mathbb{Z}_q^{2d \times 2d \log q}$. Then we generate RGSW ciphertexts $\{\mathbf{C}_{k,(i,j)}\}_{i \in [2d], j \in [2d \log q], k \in [(2d)^{\rho-1}]}$, each of which encrypts the corresponding entry $\mathbf{M}_k[i,j]$ in the exponents.

Now we equally partition $[(2d)^{\rho-1}]$ into v' sets (ref. Definition 6.1), namely, $U_1, \ldots, U_{v'}$ where $v' = (2d)^{\rho-1}/v$. For each $w \in [v']$, we pack the ciphertexts $\{\mathbf{C}_{k,(i,j)}\}_{i \in [2d], j \in [2d \log q], k \in U_w}$ according to the pre-processing step of Sect. 4.1, obtaining the resulting packed ciphertext as $\{\mathbf{B}_{kj}^{(w)}\}_{w \in [v'], j \in [2d \log q], k \in U_w}$.

Note. The above step uses many indices, which might look overwhelming. Here we remind readers the high level ideas, which would be helpful in understanding what we are doing. Basically, we first encrypt the (power-or-two) rotation matrices of $(z_1, \ldots, z_{(2d)^{\rho-1}})$ in the exponents as $\{\mathbf{C}_{k,(i,j)}\}_{i \in [2d], j \in [2d \log q], k \in [(2d)^{\rho-1}]}$. To compute multiplications over the sub-ring $\mathbb{Z}[\xi_{2d}]$, we would need to pack these ciphertexts according to Algorithm 4.2, particularly the preprocessing steps in Sect. 4.1. Given these packed ciphertexts and ring elements $(x_1, \ldots, x_{(2d)^{\rho-1}}) \in \mathbb{Z}[\xi_{2d}]^{(2d)^{\rho-1}}$, we can homomorphically compute the coefficients $(x_1 z_1, \ldots, x_{(2d)^{\rho-1}} z_{(2d)^{\rho-1}})$ in the exponents, in a batch way using Algorithm 4.2.

Now we present our batch bootstrapping algorithm in Algorithm 7.1, and Theorem 7.1 to summarize the correctness and noise growth. The proof follows from Theorems 4.1 and 6.2 in a straight-forward way.

Theorem 7.1 *Adapt the notations above. If each $(b_i, \boldsymbol{a}_i)$ in the input is an LWE ciphertext encrypting μ_i, then the output are LWE ciphertexts encrypting μ_i respectively.*

Moreover, let s be the secret of the RGSW scheme, E be the upper bound of errors in all evaluation keys and in all RGSW ciphertexts in $\{\mathbf{B}_{kj}^{(i)}\}_{i \in [v'], j \in [2d \log q], k \in U_i}$. Then the error of each LWE ciphertext in output is bounded by a sub-Gaussian variable with parameter $O(\gamma)$ such that $\gamma \leq \sqrt{n} \log q d^\rho r^{3\rho+3} \|s\|^{\rho+1} (N \log Q)^{\rho+1/2} E$.

Algorithm 7.1: Batch Ring Bootstrapping

Input :
- n LWE ciphertexts
- Bootstrapping keys: $\{\mathbf{B}_{kj}^{(i)}\}_{i\in[v'],j\in[2d\log q],k\in U_i}$.

Output : n bootstrapped LWE ciphertexts.

---

1 Convert n LWE ciphertexts into one RLWE ciphertext $(a(\xi_n), b(\xi_n))$ under some
  secret $z(\xi_n)$;
2 $(\overline{a_i})_{i\in[(2d)^{\rho-1}]} \leftarrow \mathsf{DFT}(a)$;
3 **for** $i = 1$ **to** v' **do**
4 $\quad \left\lfloor \ (\vec{\mathbf{C}}_{i1}, \cdots, \vec{\mathbf{C}}_{iv}) = \mathsf{VecMatMult}((\overline{a_i})_{i\in U_i}, \{\mathbf{B}_{kj}^{(i)}\}_{i\in[v'],j\in[2d\log q],k\in U_i})\right.$;
5 Set $\vec{\mathbf{C}}'_{(i-1)v+j} = \vec{\mathbf{C}}_{ij}$, for $i \in [v']$ and $j \in [v]$;
6 $\vec{\mathbf{C}}'' = \mathsf{Hom\text{-}DFT}^{-1}(\vec{\mathbf{C}}'_1, \cdots, \vec{\mathbf{C}}'_{(2d)^{\rho-1}})$;
7 For $i \in [n]$, $\vec{\mathbf{C}}''[i] = \vec{\mathbf{C}}''[i] \cdot \xi_q^{b_i}$;
8 For $i \in [n]$, $(b'_i, a'_i) = \mathsf{msbExtract}(\vec{\mathbf{C}}''[i])$;
9 **Return:** $\{(b'_i, a'_i)\}_{i\in[n]}$.

7.3 Efficiency

To analyze the asymptotic efficiency, we first determine all the parameters in terms of the security parameter λ. Similar to our first work [7], we set $n = O(\lambda)$, $q = \tilde{O}(\sqrt{n})$, $N = O(n)$. In this way, the batch parameter can be set as $r \approx O(\sqrt{N/q}) = O(\lambda^{1/4-o(1)})$. Then we set $d = O(\lambda^{0.2})$, $v = O(\lambda^{0.04})$, satisfying $2dv < r$. Finally, we can set $\rho = 5$, which is $O(1)$, meaning that the noise growth in Theorem 7.1 can be bounded by a fixed polynomial. Moreover, we have $n = 2d^\rho = O(\lambda)$.

By plugging these parameters to the above analysis, now we analyze the efficiency of the overall Algorithm 7.1. It requires $\tilde{O}(2dvv') = O(n)$ RGSW multiplications in the first for loop (Lines 3–4), as analyzed in Sect. 4. The Hom-DFT^{-1} would require $\tilde{O}((2d)^\rho) = \tilde{O}(n)$ RGSW multiplications as analyzed in Sect. 6. The other steps are dominated by these two modules. Thus, the overall complexity is $\tilde{O}(n)$ RGSW multiplications to bootstrap $n = O(\lambda)$ LWE input ciphertexts. In amortization, this would be $\tilde{O}(1)$ RGSW multiplications per input LWE ciphertext as claimed.

Acknowledgement. The authors would like to thank anonymous reviewers for their insightful comments that significantly help improve the presentation. Feng-Hao Liu is supported by NSF CNS-1942400. Han Wang is supported by the National Key R&D Program of China under Grant 2020YFA0712303 and State Key Laboratory of Information Security under Grant TC20221013042.

References

1. Alperin-Sheriff, J., Peikert, C.: Faster bootstrapping with polynomial error. In: Garay, J.A., Gennaro, R. (eds.) CRYPTO 2014. LNCS, vol. 8616, pp. 297–314. Springer, Heidelberg (2014). https://doi.org/10.1007/978-3-662-44371-2_17
2. Bonnoron, G., Ducas, L., Fillinger, M.: Large FHE gates from tensored homomorphic accumulator. In: Joux, A., Nitaj, A., Rachidi, T. (eds.) AFRICACRYPT 2018. LNCS, vol. 10831, pp. 217–251. Springer, Cham (2018). https://doi.org/10.1007/978-3-319-89339-6_13
3. Chillotti, I., Gama, N., Georgieva, M., Izabachène, M.: Faster fully homomorphic encryption: bootstrapping in less than 0.1 seconds. In: Cheon, J.H., Takagi, T. (eds.) ASIACRYPT 2016. LNCS, vol. 10031, pp. 3–33. Springer, Heidelberg (2016). https://doi.org/10.1007/978-3-662-53887-6_1
4. Ducas, L., Micciancio, D.: FHEW: bootstrapping homomorphic encryption in less than a second. In: Oswald, E., Fischlin, M. (eds.) EUROCRYPT 2015. LNCS, vol. 9056, pp. 617–640. Springer, Heidelberg (2015). https://doi.org/10.1007/978-3-662-46800-5_24
5. Gentry, C.: Fully homomorphic encryption using ideal lattices. In: Mitzenmacher, M. (ed.) 41st ACM STOC, pp. 169–178. ACM Press (2009)
6. Gentry, C., Sahai, A., Waters, B.: Homomorphic encryption from learning with errors: conceptually-simpler, asymptotically-faster, attribute-based. In: Canetti, R., Garay, J.A. (eds.) CRYPTO 2013. LNCS, vol. 8042, pp. 75–92. Springer, Heidelberg (2013). https://doi.org/10.1007/978-3-642-40041-4_5
7. Liu, F.-H., Wang, H.: Batch bootstrapping I: a new framework for simd bootstrapping in polynomial modulus. In: Eurocrypt (2023)
8. Lyubashevsky, V., Peikert, C., Regev, O.: On ideal lattices and learning with errors over rings. In: Gilbert, H. (ed.) EUROCRYPT 2010. LNCS, vol. 6110, pp. 1–23. Springer, Heidelberg (2010). https://doi.org/10.1007/978-3-642-13190-5_1
9. Lyubashevsky, V., Peikert, C., Regev, O.: A toolkit for ring-LWE cryptography. In: Johansson, T., Nguyen, P.Q. (eds.) EUROCRYPT 2013. LNCS, vol. 7881, pp. 35–54. Springer, Heidelberg (2013). https://doi.org/10.1007/978-3-642-38348-9_3
10. Micciancio, D., Peikert, C.: Trapdoors for lattices: simpler, tighter, faster, smaller. In: Pointcheval, D., Johansson, T. (eds.) EUROCRYPT 2012. LNCS, vol. 7237, pp. 700–718. Springer, Heidelberg (2012). https://doi.org/10.1007/978-3-642-29011-4_41
11. Micciancio, D., Sorrell, J.: Ring packing and amortized FHEW bootstrapping. In: Chatzigiannakis, I., Kaklamanis, C., Marx, D., Sannella, D. (eds.) ICALP 2018, vol. 107, pp. 100:1–100:14. Schloss Dagstuhl (2018)
12. Regev, O.: On lattices, learning with errors, random linear codes, and cryptography. In: Gabow, H.N., Fagin, R. (eds.) 37th ACM STOC, pp. 84–93. ACM Press (2005)

Succinct Vector, Polynomial, and Functional Commitments from Lattices

Hoeteck Wee[1,2] and David J. Wu[3(✉)]

[1] NTT Research, Sunnyvale, CA, USA
[2] ENS, Paris, France
[3] University of Texas at Austin, Austin, TX, USA
dwu4@cs.utexas.edu

Abstract. Vector commitment schemes allow a user to commit to a vector of values $\mathbf{x} \in \{0,1\}^\ell$ and later, open up the commitment to a specific set of positions. Both the size of the commitment and the size of the opening should be succinct (i.e., polylogarithmic in the length ℓ of the vector). Vector commitments and their generalizations to polynomial commitments and functional commitments are key building blocks for many cryptographic protocols.

We introduce a new framework for constructing non-interactive lattice-based vector commitments and their generalizations. A simple instantiation of our framework yields a new vector commitment scheme from the standard short integer solution (SIS) assumption that supports *private* openings and large messages. We then show how to use our framework to obtain the first succinct *functional* commitment scheme that supports openings with respect to arbitrary bounded-depth Boolean circuits. In this scheme, a user commits to a vector $\mathbf{x} \in \{0,1\}^\ell$, and later on, open the commitment to any function $f(\mathbf{x})$. Both the commitment *and* the opening are non-interactive and succinct: namely, they have size $\mathsf{poly}(\lambda, d, \log \ell)$, where λ is the security parameter and d is the *depth* of the Boolean circuit computing f. Previous constructions of functional commitments could only support constant-degree polynomials, or require a trusted *online* authority, or rely on non-falsifiable assumptions. The security of our functional commitment scheme is based on a new falsifiable family of "basis-augmented" SIS assumptions (BASIS) we introduce in this work.

We also show how to use our vector commitment framework to obtain (1) a polynomial commitment scheme where the user can commit to a polynomial $f \in \mathbb{Z}_q[x]$ and subsequently open the commitment to an evaluation $f(x) \in \mathbb{Z}_q$; and (2) an aggregatable vector (resp., functional) commitment where a user can take a set of openings to multiple indices (resp., function evaluations) and aggregate them into a *single* short opening. Both of these extensions rely on the same BASIS assumption we use to obtain our succinct functional commitment scheme.

1 Introduction

Vector commitment schemes [Mer87, CFM08, LY10, CF13] allow a user to commit to a vector of values $\mathbf{x} \in \{0,1\}^\ell$ and subsequently, open up the commitment to a specific set of positions. Both the commitment and the openings

C. Hazay and M. Stam (Eds.): EUROCRYPT 2023, LNCS 14006, pp. 385–416, 2023.
https://doi.org/10.1007/978-3-031-30620-4_13

should be *succinct* (i.e., have size that scales *polylogarithmically* with the vector length ℓ) and *non-interactive*.[1] There has recently been tremendous interest and progress in the design and application of vector commitments, and even a "Vector Commitment Research Day" [Res22]. Starting from the classic vector commitment scheme of Merkle [Mer87] based on collision-resistant hash functions, we now have a broad range of algebraic constructions from pairing-based assumptions [LY10, KZG10, CF13, LRY16, LM19, TAB+20, GRWZ20] as well as assumptions over groups of unknown order (e.g., RSA groups or class groups) [CF13, LM19, CFG+20, AR20, TXN20]. We refer to [Nit21] for a survey of recent schemes. As a primitive, vector commitment schemes have found numerous applications to verifiable outsourced databases [BGV11, CF13], cryptographic accumulators [CF13], pseudonymous credentials [KZG10], and to blockchain protocols [RMCI17, CPSZ18, BBF19]. Moreover, the generalization of vector commitments to polynomial commitments [KZG10] has emerged as a key building block in many recent (random-oracle) constructions of succinct non-interactive arguments of knowledge (SNARKs) [MBKM19, CHM+20, GWC19, BDFG21, BFS20, COS20] having various appealing properties (e.g., universal or transparent setup, recursive composability, and more).

In this work, we focus on two themes in the study of vector commitments where progress has been more limited: (1) post-quantum constructions based on lattices [PSTY13, LLNW16, PPS21, ACL+22, FSZ22]; and (2) functional commitments, a generalization of vector commitments that supports openings to various functions on the committed values [LRY16, LP20, PPS21, BNO21, ACL+22]. There are good technical reasons for the limited progress on these two fronts. First, many of the techniques developed for vector commitments crucially exploit algebraic structure in pairing and RSA/class groups that do not naturally extend to the lattice setting. Second, pairing and RSA/class groups only support limited homomorphic capabilities.

1.1 Our Results

In this work, we introduce a general framework for constructing lattice-based vector commitments that simultaneously encapsulates recent lattice-based vector commitment schemes [PPS21, ACL+22] and enables us to achieve stronger functionality and security properties. As we describe below, our framework readily generalizes to also yield *polynomial commitments*, *functional commitments*, and *aggregatable commitments* from (falsifiable) lattice-based assumptions.

A New Family of SIS Assumptions. The security of our schemes relies on a new "basis-augmented" family of short integer solution (SIS) assumptions we introduce in this work. We refer to our basis-augmented SIS assumption as the BASIS assumption (Assumption 3.2). The basic version of our assumption (denoted $\mathsf{BASIS_{rand}}$) suffices for constructing standard vector commitments and

---

[1] We discuss interactive commitments (as well as constructions in the random oracle model) in Sect. 1.3.

is implied by the *standard* SIS assumption. The structured version of the assumption (denoted $\mathsf{BASIS}_{\mathsf{struct}}$) we need for our extensions has a similar flavor as the k-SIS-like assumptions introduced in [ACL+22] for constructing lattice-based succinct arguments (c.f., Sect. 6). While the $\mathsf{BASIS}_{\mathsf{struct}}$ assumption is not a standard lattice-based assumption, it is a *falsifiable* assumption [Nao03]. We view our assumption as a "q-type" lattice assumption and at a conceptual level, it shares a similar flavor as the q-type assumptions used in the pairing-based world for constructing vector commitments [CF13] and polynomial commitments [KZG10].

Vector Commitments with Private Opening. An immediate consequence of our framework is a vector commitment scheme that supports *private* openings. In this setting, a user can commit to a vector $\mathbf{x} \in \{0,1\}^\ell$ with a short commitment σ and then open σ to an index-value pair (i, x_i) with a short opening π_i. We say the vector commitment scheme supports private openings if the commitment σ and any collection of openings $\{(i, x_i, \pi_i)\}_{i \in S}$ reveal no additional information about x_j for any $j \notin S$. Notably and in contrast to previous lattice-based vector commitment schemes [PPS21, ACL+22], our scheme also does *not* impose any restrictions on the magnitude of the entries of $\mathbf{x}$ (the vectors can be arbitrary elements of $\mathbb{Z}_q^\ell$ and the commitment as well as the opening are vectors over $\mathbb{Z}_q$). Previous lattice-based schemes [PPS21, ACL+22] require that the components of $\mathbf{x}$ be small and this property was essential for *both* correctness and security.

Our vector commitment scheme has the same efficiency properties as the earlier scheme of Peikert et al. [PPS21] which did not support private openings and was limited to a small message space. Our scheme provides the same functionality (e.g., support for "stateless updates") and like the scheme of [PPS21], security can be based on the *standard* SIS assumption. Thus, relative to [PPS21], our framework achieves private openings and supports a large message space with essentially no overhead.

We could alternatively obtain a lattice-based vector commitment by instantiating Merkle's classic construction [Mer87] with a lattice-based collision-resistant hash function (e.g., Ajtai's hash function from SIS [Ajt96, GGH96]). Our vector commitment scheme improves upon this generic approach in two main ways: (1) we support (bounded) stateless updates like [PPS21] (where a user can update a commitment to a vector $\mathbf{x}$ into a commitment to a vector $\mathbf{x}'$ given only knowledge of the difference $\mathbf{x}' - \mathbf{x}$ and not the entirety of $\mathbf{x}$ or $\mathbf{x}'$); and (2) we can support private openings directly. It is possible to extend Merkle hashing to support private openings via zero-knowledge proofs, but this would either need non-black-box use of cryptography or require interaction, random oracles, or correlation-intractable hash functions [CCH+19, PS19]. More broadly, as we illustrate below, our algebraic scheme serves as a stepping stone for realizing polynomial and functional commitment schemes (for which we crucially exploit *algebraic* structure).

Functional Commitments. A functional commitment [GVW15, LRY16] is a generalization of a vector commitment with the property that given a commitment to an input $\mathbf{x} \in \{0,1\}^\ell$, one can then construct an opening π_f to $y = f(\mathbf{x})$, for some function f. The basic binding property of the commitment scheme says that the adversary cannot come up with openings π_f and π'_f that open σ to different values $y \neq y'$ with respect to the same function f. The efficiency requirements are that the size of the commitment and the opening should be sublinear in both the size of the function f and the length of the input $\mathbf{x}$. Previously, Peikert et al. [PPS21] showed how to construct functional commitments for bounded-depth Boolean circuits in an *online* model where a central *trusted* authority issues opening keys for functions f, with security based on the standard SIS assumption. Albrecht et al. [ACL+22] subsequently showed how to construct functional commitments for constant-degree polynomials from new variants of the SIS assumption in the standard setting without an online authority. Earlier pairing-based functional commitments could only support linear functions [LRY16] or sparse polynomials [LP20]. Functional commitments can also be obtained generically by combining a vanilla vector commitment (e.g., a Merkle tree [Mer87]) with a succinct non-interactive argument of knowledge (for NP). However, existing constructions of SNARKs (for NP) either rely on making non-falsifiable assumptions [GW11] or working in idealized models.

Our vector commitment framework directly yields a succinct functional commitment scheme for all bounded-depth Boolean circuits in the standard offline model without an authority and from falsifiable assumptions. The size of the commitment and the openings are $\mathsf{poly}(\lambda, d, \log \ell)$, where λ is a security parameter, d is the *depth* of the Boolean circuit computing $f \colon \{0,1\}^\ell \to \{0,1\}$, and ℓ is the length of the input. Security relies on the new non-standard, but falsifiable, $\mathsf{BASIS}_{\mathsf{struct}}$ assumption we introduce in this work (with a *sub-exponential* noise bound). Notably, this is the first succinct functional commitment scheme for general circuits from a falsifiable assumption, and answers an open question posed by Peikert et al. [PPS21]. Our construction can be viewed as a *succinct* analog of the homomorphic commitments and signatures introduced by [GSW13, GVW15].[2]

Polynomial Commitments. In a polynomial commitment [KZG10], a user can commit to a polynomial $f \in \mathbb{Z}_q[x]$ over $\mathbb{Z}_q$ and later open to an evaluation $f(x)$ at any point $x \in \mathbb{Z}_q$. A polynomial commitment can be viewed as a succinct commitment to the vector of evaluations of f on all inputs $x \in \mathbb{Z}_q$. While a polynomial commitment can be built from a succinct functional commitment for Boolean circuits, this incurs a $\mathsf{poly}(\log q)$ overhead to encode the polynomial evaluation over $\mathbb{Z}_q$ as a Boolean circuit and also relies on the $\mathsf{BASIS}_{\mathsf{struct}}$ assumption with a *sub-exponential* noise bound. In this work, we show that a simple adaptation of our succinct functional commitments to the setting of linear functions directly gives a polynomial commitment over $\mathbb{Z}_q$. Notably, this construction can be based on our $\mathsf{BASIS}_{\mathsf{struct}}$ assumption with only a *polynomial* noise bound. This is the first polynomial commitment scheme from lattices based on falsifiable assumptions.

An important feature of our framework that enables the direct construction of polynomial commitments is that it natively supports values over $\mathbb{Z}_q$.

---

[2] The homomorphic commitments from [GSW13, GVW15] are *non-succinct*; in particular, the size of the commitment scales *linearly* with the input length ℓ.

Previous lattice-based vector commitments [PPS21, ACL+22] required that the committed value x and the opened value $f(x)$ be "small," and moreover, that the modulus q scale with the norm of the output (i.e., $f(x)$) when computed over the *integers*. This is not suitable when constructing polynomial commitments directly, as the size of $f(x)$ computed over the integers scales with the degree of f. Correspondingly, if the modulus q scales linearly with the degree of f, then the resulting scheme is no longer succinct. The ability to directly work over the entirety of $\mathbb{Z}_q$ is an appealing property of our new framework.

Aggregatable Commitments. A simple modification to our basic vector commitment scheme yields a scheme that supports *aggregation*. We say a vector commitment scheme is aggregatable [BBF19, CFG+20] if given a commitment σ along with a set of openings $\pi_1, \ldots, \pi_t$ to indices $i_1, \ldots, i_t \in [\ell]$ and values $x_{i_1}, \ldots, x_{i_t}$, there is an efficient aggregation algorithm that outputs a short aggregate opening π that validates the full set of values $\{(i_j, x_{i_j})\}_{j \in [t]}$. The requirement is that the size of π scale sublinearly, or better yet, *polylogarithmically* with t. Aggregatable commitments immediately imply subvector commitments [LM19] (i.e., a vector commitment scheme that supports batch openings to a set of indices $S \subseteq [\ell]$). Our framework yields an aggregatable commitment scheme for short messages from the same falsifiable $\mathsf{BASIS}_{\mathsf{struct}}$ assumption used to construct succinct functional commitments. This is the first aggregatable commitment scheme from lattice assumptions *without* relying on general-purpose succinct arguments [ACL+22] or batch arguments [CJJ21, DGKV22], and answers another open question posed by Peikert et al. [PPS21].

A limitation of our aggregatable commitment is that it only satisfies *same-set binding*, which guarantees that for every subset of indices $S \subseteq [\ell]$, the adversary can only open to a single set of values. However, there is still the possibility that an adversary could open the commitment to different sets S and T that are *inconsistent* (i.e., $x_i = 0$ with respect to S while $x_i = 1$ with respect to T).[3] Constructing aggregatable commitments that satisfy the stronger notion of *different-set* binding directly from falsifiable lattice-based assumptions is an interesting open problem.

The same techniques we use to construct aggregatable vector commitments also applies to our succinct functional commitment scheme, and we obtain an aggregatable functional commitment scheme from the same underlying hardness assumption. In this setting, a user can take openings $\pi_1, \ldots, \pi_t$ for function-value pairs $(f_1, y_1), \ldots, (f_t, y_t)$ and aggregate the openings into a single short opening π that validates all t function-value pairs and where the size of the aggregated opening scales polylogarithmically with t.

Summary. Similar to previous lattice-based vector commitments [PPS21, ACL+22], we rely on a *structured* reference string in all of our constructions. We refer to the structured reference string as a common reference string (CRS).

---

[3] Note though that if the commitment is honestly-generated, then same-set binding implies different-set binding; see the full version of this paper [WW22].

To summarize, our new lattice-based vector commitment framework yields the following constructions:

- A vector commitment scheme with private openings based on the *standard* SIS assumption with polynomial noise bound (Corollary 3.6). For vectors of dimension ℓ, the size of the commitment is $O(\lambda(\log \lambda + \log \ell))$ and the size of an opening is $O(\lambda(\log^2 \lambda + \log^2 \ell))$.[4] The size of the CRS is $\ell^2 \cdot \text{poly}(\lambda, \log \ell)$.
- A succinct functional commitment scheme supporting all bounded-depth Boolean circuits from the $\text{BASIS}_{\text{struct}}$ assumption with a sub-exponential noise bound (Corollary 4.3). A variant of this construction supports private openings under a weaker notion of target binding. For both constructions, to support functions on ℓ-bit inputs and computable by Boolean circuits of depth d, the sizes of the commitment and openings are $\text{poly}(\lambda, d, \log \ell)$. The size of the CRS is $\ell^2 \cdot \text{poly}(\lambda, d, \log \ell)$.
- A polynomial commitment (for polynomials of a priori bounded degree) under the $\text{BASIS}_{\text{struct}}$ assumption with a polynomial noise bound. To support polynomials of degree up to d over $\mathbb{Z}_q$ (where $q = \text{poly}(\lambda)$), the sizes of the commitment and openings are $\text{poly}(\lambda, \log d)$. The size of the CRS is $d^2 \cdot \text{poly}(\lambda, \log d)$.
- An aggregatable vector commitment scheme (over a small message space) based on the $\text{BASIS}_{\text{struct}}$ assumption with polynomial noise bound. The sizes of the commitment, openings, and CRS match those above for our vanilla vector commitment.
- An aggregatable functional commitment scheme for all bounded-depth Boolean circuits from the $\text{BASIS}_{\text{struct}}$ assumption used to obtain succinct functional commitments. To support aggregating T openings for functions on ℓ-bit inputs and computable by Boolean circuits of depth d, the sizes of the commitment and opening are $\text{poly}(\lambda, d, \log \ell, \log T)$. The size of the CRS is $(\ell^2 + T) \cdot \text{poly}(\lambda, d, \log \ell, \log T)$. In the random oracle model, we can reduce the CRS size to $\ell^2 \cdot \text{poly}(\lambda, d, \log \ell)$ and support an *arbitrary* polynomial number of aggregations.

1.2 Technical Overview

In this section, we provide a general overview of our new framework for constructing vector commitments from lattices as well as the family of basis-augmented SIS assumptions (BASIS) we use to prove hardness. In the following description, for a matrix $\mathbf{A} \in \mathbb{Z}_q^{n \times m}$ and a target vector $\mathbf{t} \in \mathbb{Z}_q^n$, we write $\mathbf{A}^{-1}(\mathbf{t})$ to denote a random variable $\mathbf{x} \in \mathbb{Z}_q^m$ whose entries are distributed according to a discrete Gaussian conditioned on $\mathbf{A}\mathbf{x} = \mathbf{t}$. Sampling $\mathbf{x} \leftarrow \mathbf{A}^{-1}(\mathbf{t})$ can be done efficiently given a trapdoor for $\mathbf{A}$ [Ajt96, GPV08, AP09, ABB10a, ABB10b, CHKP10, MP12]. Here, we will use the Micciancio-Peikert gadget trapdoors [MP12]; namely, a matrix $\mathbf{R}$ is a gadget trapdoor for $\mathbf{A}$ if $\mathbf{R}$ is short and $\mathbf{A}\mathbf{R} = \mathbf{G}$, where $\mathbf{G} = \mathbf{I}_n \otimes \mathbf{g}^\mathsf{T}$ is the gadget matrix and $\mathbf{g}^\mathsf{T} = [1, 2, \ldots, 2^{\lfloor \log q \rfloor}]$.

---

[4] We note that these bounds match the base construction of Peikert et al. [PPS21]. While [PPS21, Figure 1] reports that their scheme has $O(\log \ell)$-size openings (ignoring the security parameter λ), the construction itself [PPS21, Construction 1] has $O(\log^2 \ell)$-size openings.

A General Framework for Constructing Vector Commitments. We begin by describing a general framework for constructing lattice-based vector commitments that encapsulates the recent schemes from [PPS21, ACL+22]:

- The common reference string (CRS) specifies a collection of ℓ matrices $\mathbf{A}_1, \ldots, \mathbf{A}_\ell \in \mathbb{Z}_q^{n \times m}$ and ℓ vectors $\mathbf{t}_1, \ldots, \mathbf{t}_\ell \in \mathbb{Z}_q^n$ along with some auxiliary input $\mathsf{aux}_\ell := \{\mathbf{A}_i^{-1}(\mathbf{t}_j)\}_{i \neq j}$.
- The commitment to a vector $\mathbf{x} = (x_1, \ldots, x_\ell) \in \{0,1\}^\ell$ is a vector $\mathbf{c} \leftarrow \sum_{i \in [\ell]} x_i \mathbf{t}_i \in \mathbb{Z}_q^n$.
- An opening to index $i \in [\ell]$ and value $x_i \in \{0,1\}$ is a short vector $\mathbf{v}_i \in \mathbb{Z}_q^m$ such that

$$\mathbf{c} = \mathbf{A}_i \mathbf{v}_i + x_i \mathbf{t}_i. \tag{1.1}$$

The honest opening is computed as $\mathbf{v}_i \leftarrow \sum_{j \neq i} x_j \mathbf{A}_i^{-1}(\mathbf{t}_j)$.

Correctness follows by inspection:

$$\mathbf{A}_i \mathbf{v}_i + x_i \mathbf{t}_i = \sum_{j \neq i} x_j \mathbf{A}_i \cdot \mathbf{A}_i^{-1}(\mathbf{t}_j) + x_i \mathbf{t}_i = \sum_{i \in [\ell]} x_i \mathbf{t}_i = \mathbf{c}.$$

For binding, we require that it is hard to find a short vector $\mathbf{z} \in \mathbb{Z}_q^m$ such that $\mathbf{A}_i \mathbf{z} = \mathbf{t}_i$ for any $i \in [\ell]$ given the components in the CRS. Next, we explain how the schemes PPS_1 from [PPS21][5] and MatrixACLMT from [ACL+22][6] fall into this framework.

- In PPS_1, the matrices $\mathbf{A}_i \xleftarrow{\text{R}} \mathbb{Z}_q^{n \times m}$ and vectors $\mathbf{t}_i \xleftarrow{\text{R}} \mathbb{Z}_q^n$ are independent and uniformly random for all $i \in [\ell]$. Binding in turn is based on the standard SIS assumption.
- In MatrixACLMT, they sample uniformly random vectors $\mathbf{u}_i \xleftarrow{\text{R}} \mathbb{Z}_q^n$, a matrix $\mathbf{A} \xleftarrow{\text{R}} \mathbb{Z}_q^{n \times m}$, and invertible matrices $\mathbf{W}_i \xleftarrow{\text{R}} \mathbb{Z}_q^{n \times n}$ for each $i \in [\ell]$. Then, they set $\mathbf{A}_i \leftarrow \mathbf{W}_i \mathbf{A}$, $\mathbf{t}_i \leftarrow \mathbf{W}_i \mathbf{u}_i$. In this case, $\mathbf{A}_i^{-1}(\mathbf{t}_j) = \mathbf{A}^{-1}(\mathbf{W}_i^{-1} \mathbf{W}_j \mathbf{u}_j)$. Binding is based on a new assumption which stipulates that it is hard to find a short vector $\mathbf{z} \in \mathbb{Z}_q^m$ where $\mathbf{A}\mathbf{z} = \mathbf{u}_i$ for any $i \in [\ell]$ given the CRS. The authors of [ACL+22] then show how to leverage the extra structure arising from the correlated $\mathbf{A}_i$'s to obtain a functional commitment scheme for constant-degree polynomials as well as a preprocessing succinct non-interactive argument (SNARG) for NP.

Before describing our approach, we describe two limitations of these instantiations:

---

[5] By PPS_1, we refer to the the base scheme from [PPS21, Construction 1]; they also present a second tree-based scheme that uses PPS_1 as a building block.

[6] The authors of [ACL+22] describe their scheme in the ring setting. We write MatrixACLMT to denote one possible translation from the ring setting to the integer setting. Note that there are other ways to translate their scheme to the integer setting such as sampling $\mathbf{W}_i \xleftarrow{\text{R}} \mathbb{Z}_q^{m \times m}$ and then setting $\mathbf{A}_i \leftarrow \mathbf{A}\mathbf{W}_i$.

- **Small message space:** In both the PPS_1 and the $\mathsf{MatrixACLMT}$ instantiations of this framework, both correctness *and* security require that the entries of the vector $\mathbf{x} = [x_1, \ldots, x_\ell]$ be small. This is because the verification relation is checking that the opening $\mathbf{v}_i = \sum_{j \neq i} x_j \mathbf{A}_i^{-1}(\mathbf{t}_j)$ is small. Thus, correctness requires that each x_j be small. Moreover, in the proof of binding, the reduction algorithm takes a commitment $\mathbf{c}$ along with two openings $(x_i, \mathbf{v}_i)$, $(x_i', \mathbf{v}_i')$ to derive a solution to SIS or a related problem. The existing reductions require that the difference $(x_i - x_i')$ be small (in order to derive a *short* solution).
- **Uniform target vectors.** In both the PPS_1 and $\mathsf{MatrixACLMT}$ constructions, the target vectors $\mathbf{t}_i$ are essentially random vectors. This is important for ensuring that $\mathbf{A}_i^{-1}(\mathbf{t}_j)$ does not leak a trapdoor for $\mathbf{A}_i$, which would immediately break binding. Using structured target vectors could enable additional functionality. For instance, in Remark 6.1, we show that instantiating $\mathsf{MatrixACLMT}$ with structured targets can be used to support functional openings. Unfortunately, this instantiation *also* leaks a trapdoor for $\mathbf{A}_i$, and is insecure.

The approach we take in this work avoids these limitations and allows us to construct vector commitments with a large message space as well as support new capabilities like polynomial and functional openings.

Our Approach. We consider the same verification relation $\mathbf{c} = \mathbf{A}_i \mathbf{v}_i + x_i \mathbf{t}_i$ from Eq. (1.1), but take a completely different approach for computing the commitment $\mathbf{c}$ and the openings $\mathbf{v}_i$: we sample a *random* tuple $(\mathbf{v}_1, \ldots, \mathbf{v}_\ell, \mathbf{c})$ that simultaneously satisfies the verification relation for all $i \in [\ell]$. As in the previous verification relation, we require that the openings $\mathbf{v}_1, \ldots, \mathbf{v}_\ell$ are short. The commitment $\mathbf{c}$ can have large entries. In our particular setting, we write $\mathbf{c}$ as $\mathbf{c} = \mathbf{G}\hat{\mathbf{c}}$ where $\hat{\mathbf{c}} \in \mathbb{Z}_q^m$ is a short vector. Using the gadget matrix $\mathbf{G}$ will be important in the security analysis. Then, Eq. (1.1) corresponds to the relation $\mathbf{G}\hat{\mathbf{c}} = \mathbf{A}_i \mathbf{v}_i + x_i \mathbf{t}_i$, or equivalently, $\mathbf{A}_i \mathbf{v}_i - \mathbf{G}\hat{\mathbf{c}} = -x_i \mathbf{t}_i$ for all $i \in [\ell]$. We can express these ℓ relations as a linear system:

$$\underbrace{\begin{bmatrix} \mathbf{A}_1 & & & -\mathbf{G} \\ & \ddots & & \vdots \\ & & \mathbf{A}_\ell & -\mathbf{G} \end{bmatrix}}_{\mathbf{B}_\ell} \begin{bmatrix} \mathbf{v}_1 \\ \vdots \\ \mathbf{v}_\ell \\ \hat{\mathbf{c}} \end{bmatrix} = \begin{bmatrix} -x_1 \mathbf{t}_1 \\ \vdots \\ -x_\ell \mathbf{t}_\ell \end{bmatrix}. \tag{1.2}$$

Our goal now is to sample a random *short* tuple $(\mathbf{v}_1, \ldots, \mathbf{v}_\ell, \hat{\mathbf{c}})$ that satisfies Eq. (1.2). This can be done by giving out a random trapdoor for the matrix $\mathbf{B}_\ell$:

$$\mathbf{B}_\ell :- \begin{bmatrix} \mathbf{A}_1 & & & -\mathbf{G} \\ & \ddots & & \vdots \\ & & \mathbf{A}_\ell & -\mathbf{G} \end{bmatrix}. \tag{1.3}$$

Using $\mathbf{B}_\ell$, we can sample a random short preimage $(\mathbf{v}_1, \ldots, \mathbf{v}_\ell, \hat{\mathbf{c}})$ satisfying Eq. (1.2). This yields the commitment $\mathbf{c} = \mathbf{G}\hat{\mathbf{c}}$ and the openings $\mathbf{v}_1, \ldots, \mathbf{v}_\ell$. In our construction, we set the target vector $\mathbf{t}_i$ to the first basis vector $\mathbf{e}_1 = [1, 0, \ldots, 0]^{\mathsf{T}}$ for all $i \in [\ell]$. We now make the following observations:

- **Binding:** To argue that the scheme is binding, we require that it is hard to find a short vector $\mathbf{z}$ where $\underline{\mathbf{A}}_i \mathbf{z} = \mathbf{0}$ for any $i \in [\ell]$ even given the (related) matrix $\mathbf{B}_\ell$ and a trapdoor for $\mathbf{B}_\ell$. Here, $\underline{\mathbf{A}}_i$ denotes $\mathbf{A}_i$ with the first row removed. We refer to assumptions of this type as "basis-augmented SIS" (BASIS) assumptions (Assumption 3.2). As we sketch below (and show formally in Theorem 3.4), when $\mathbf{A}_1, \ldots, \mathbf{A}_\ell \xleftarrow{\text{R}} \mathbb{Z}_q^{n \times m}$ are *random*, this instantiation of the BASIS assumption holds under the *standard* SIS assumption. We refer to this instance of the BASIS assumption with random matrices as $\mathsf{BASIS}_{\mathsf{rand}}$. Now, to argue binding, we observe that an adversary that breaks binding is able to come up with an index $i \in [\ell]$, short vectors $\mathbf{v}, \mathbf{v}' \in \mathbb{Z}_q^m$ and values $x, x' \in \mathbb{Z}_q$ such that $\mathbf{c} = \mathbf{A}_i \mathbf{v} + x \mathbf{e}_1 = \mathbf{A}_i \mathbf{v}' + x' \mathbf{e}_1$. This means that

$$\mathbf{A}_i(\mathbf{v} - \mathbf{v}') = (x' - x)\mathbf{e}_1.$$

  As long as $x' - x \neq 0$, $\mathbf{v} - \mathbf{v}' \neq \mathbf{0}$, and so $\mathbf{v} - \mathbf{v}'$ is a SIS solution to $\underline{\mathbf{A}}_i$. Observe that this analysis does not impose *any* restriction on the magnitude of $x' - x$. This means our construction naturally supports committing to arbitrary vectors over $\mathbb{Z}_q$ as opposed to vectors with small entries.[7] We give the formal reduction to the $\mathsf{BASIS}_{\mathsf{rand}}$ assumption in the full version of this paper [WW22].

- **Private openings.** A vector commitment scheme supports private openings if the commitment $\mathbf{c}$ and any collections of openings $\{(i, x_i, \mathbf{v}_i)\}_{i \in S}$ completely hide the values x_j for $j \notin S$. Since we sample the commitment $\mathbf{c}$ and the openings $\mathbf{v}_i$ *jointly* in our approach, it is straightforward to argue (by appealing to properties of discrete Gaussians) that the commitment $\mathbf{c}$ is statistically close to uniform over $\mathbb{Z}_q^n$ and each opening $\mathbf{v}_i$ is statistically close to the distribution $\mathbf{A}_i^{-1}(\mathbf{c} - x_i \mathbf{t}_i)$. Thus our scheme provides *statistically* private openings out of the box.

Taken together, this yields a vector commitment from standard SIS that supports statistically private openings and commitments to arbitrary vectors over $\mathbb{Z}_q^\ell$. We give the full description and analysis in Sect. 3.

Reducing $\mathsf{BASIS}_{\mathsf{rand}}$ *to Standard SIS.* As described above, the binding property of our vector commitment relies on the BASIS assumption, which says that SIS with respect to $\underline{\mathbf{A}}_i$ (i.e., $\mathbf{A}_i$ with the first row removed) is hard even given the related matrix $\mathbf{B}_\ell$ from Eq. (1.3) and a trapdoor for $\mathbf{B}_\ell$. As we show in Theorem 3.4, when the matrices $\mathbf{A}_1, \ldots, \mathbf{A}_\ell \xleftarrow{\text{R}} \mathbb{Z}_q^{n \times m}$ are uniform and independent, this assumption ($\mathsf{BASIS}_{\mathsf{rand}}$) reduces to the *standard* SIS assumption in a straightforward way. Here, we provide a sketch of the reduction. For ease of exposition, we show that SIS with respect to $\mathbf{A}_i$ (as opposed to $\underline{\mathbf{A}}_i$) is hard given a trapdoor

---

[7] As discussed earlier, previous vector commitments [PPS21, ACL+22] based on SIS or its generalizations needed to assume small inputs for *both* correctness and security.

for $\mathbf{B}_\ell$. We also describe the approach for the case $i = 1$, and refer to Theorem 3.4 for the full analysis.

The idea is simple: we set $\mathbf{A}_1$ to be the SIS challenge and sample matrices $\mathbf{A}_2, \ldots, \mathbf{A}_\ell$ together with trapdoors $\mathbf{R}_2, \ldots, \mathbf{R}_\ell$ (i.e., $\mathbf{A}_i \mathbf{R}_i = \mathbf{G}$). Let $\tilde{\mathbf{B}}_\ell$ be $\mathbf{B}_\ell$ with the first column block removed (i.e., the column block containing $\mathbf{A}_1$). Then, using $\mathbf{R}_2, \ldots, \mathbf{R}_\ell$ we can construct a trapdoor $\tilde{\mathbf{R}}_\ell$ for $\tilde{\mathbf{B}}_\ell$ (i.e., $\tilde{\mathbf{B}}_\ell \tilde{\mathbf{R}}_\ell = \mathbf{G}_{n\ell} = \mathbf{I}_{n\ell} \otimes \mathbf{g}^\mathsf{T}$):

$$
\tilde{\mathbf{B}}_\ell = \begin{bmatrix} \mathbf{0} & \cdots & \mathbf{0} & -\mathbf{G} \\ \mathbf{A}_2 & & & -\mathbf{G} \\ & \ddots & & \vdots \\ & & \mathbf{A}_\ell & -\mathbf{G} \end{bmatrix} \quad \text{and} \quad \tilde{\mathbf{R}}_\ell = \begin{bmatrix} -\mathbf{R}_2 & \mathbf{R}_2 & & \\ \vdots & & \ddots & \\ -\mathbf{R}_\ell & & & \mathbf{R}_\ell \\ -\mathbf{I} & \mathbf{0} & \cdots & \mathbf{0} \end{bmatrix}
$$

Using standard trapdoor extension techniques [ABB10a, ABB10b, CHKP10, MP12], we can *extend* $\tilde{\mathbf{R}}_\ell$ to obtain a trapdoor $\mathbf{R}_\ell$ for $\mathbf{B}_\ell$. This yields a BASIS$_\mathsf{rand}$ instance (i.e., comprised of the matrix $\mathbf{A}_1$, the matrix $\mathbf{B}_\ell$, and the trapdoor $\mathbf{R}_\ell$). Thus, an adversary that breaks the BASIS$_\mathsf{rand}$ assumption implies an adversary that breaks SIS (with comparable parameters). We give the formal analysis in Theorem 3.4.

Functional Commitments Using Structured $\mathbf{A}_i$. Instantiating our framework with uniform $\mathbf{A}_i \xleftarrow{\mathsf{R}} \mathbb{Z}_q^{n \times m}$ (as in PPS$_1$), we obtain a vector commitment scheme with private openings and supporting large messages from the standard SIS assumption. If we instead use a structured set of matrices $\mathbf{A}_i$ as in MatrixACLMT, we obtain functional commitments, polynomial commitments, and aggregatable commitments.

We start by describing our functional commitment scheme. Our starting point is to consider the main verification relation from Eq. (1.1) and generalize it in two ways: (1) we replace the matrices $\mathbf{A}_1, \ldots, \mathbf{A}_\ell \in \mathbb{Z}_q^{n \times m}$ with *structured* matrices; and (2) we consider a *matrix* extension of the verification relation. In particular, we first sample $\mathbf{A} \xleftarrow{\mathsf{R}} \mathbb{Z}_q^{n \times m}$. Then, for each $i \in [\ell]$, we sample an invertible matrix $\mathbf{W}_i \xleftarrow{\mathsf{R}} \mathbb{Z}_q^{n \times n}$ and set $\mathbf{A}_i \leftarrow \mathbf{W}_i \mathbf{A}$. We now consider a matrix analog of the verification relation from Eq. (1.1) where each target vector $\mathbf{t}_i$ is replaced with the matrix $\mathbf{W}_i \mathbf{G}$ (this choice will be helpful for supporting *functional* openings). Our matrix verification relation is now

$$
\mathbf{C} = \mathbf{A}_i \mathbf{V}_i + x_i \mathbf{W}_i \mathbf{G}. \tag{1.4}
$$

Our goal now is to sample a tuple $(\mathbf{V}_1, \ldots, \mathbf{V}_\ell, \mathbf{C})$ that satisfy Eq. (1.4) for all $i \in [\ell]$ and where $\mathbf{V}_1, \ldots, \mathbf{V}_\ell \in \mathbb{Z}_q^{m \times m}$ are short. As before, the commitment $\mathbf{C}$ can be large and we specifically define it to be $\mathbf{C} = \mathbf{G}\hat{\mathbf{C}}$, where $\hat{\mathbf{C}} \in \mathbb{Z}_q^{m \times m}$ is short. This way, we can sample $\hat{\mathbf{C}}$ using an analogous trapdoor sampling procedure as before. Specifically, the trapdoor for the same matrix $\mathbf{B}_\ell$ from Eq. (1.3) allows us to jointly sample short openings $\mathbf{V}_1, \ldots, \mathbf{V}_\ell$ along with a matrix $\hat{\mathbf{C}}$ that satisfy Eq. (1.4):

$$\mathbf{B}_\ell \begin{bmatrix} \mathbf{V}_1 \\ \vdots \\ \mathbf{V}_\ell \\ \hat{\mathbf{C}} \end{bmatrix} = \begin{bmatrix} \mathbf{A}_1 & & -\mathbf{G} \\ & \ddots & \vdots \\ & \mathbf{A}_\ell & -\mathbf{G} \end{bmatrix} \cdot \begin{bmatrix} \mathbf{V}_1 \\ \vdots \\ \mathbf{V}_\ell \\ \hat{\mathbf{C}} \end{bmatrix} = \begin{bmatrix} -x_1 \mathbf{W}_1 \mathbf{G} \\ \vdots \\ -x_\ell \mathbf{W}_\ell \mathbf{G} \end{bmatrix}. \quad (1.5)$$

By construction, for all $i \in [\ell]$, we have that $\mathbf{A}_i \mathbf{V}_i - \mathbf{G}\hat{\mathbf{C}} = -x_i \mathbf{W}_i \mathbf{G}$, or equivalently, $\mathbf{C} = \mathbf{G}\hat{\mathbf{C}} = \mathbf{A}_i \mathbf{V}_i + x_i \mathbf{W}_i \mathbf{G}$ and Eq. (1.4) holds. We now show that this directly extends to yield a succinct functional commitment. Since $\mathbf{A}_i = \mathbf{W}_i \mathbf{A}$ and $\mathbf{W}_i$ is invertible, we can rewrite Eq. (1.4) as

$$\mathbf{W}_i^{-1} \mathbf{C} = \mathbf{A} \mathbf{V}_i + x_i \mathbf{G},$$

where $\mathbf{V}_i$ is *short*. Readers familiar with the homomorphic encryption scheme of Gentry et al. [GSW13] or the homomorphic signature scheme of Gorbunov et al. [GVW15] may recognize that $\mathbf{W}_i^{-1} \mathbf{C}$ is an encryption of x_i under randomness $\mathbf{V}_i$ or that $\mathbf{V}_i$ is a signature on x_i under the verification key $\mathbf{W}_i^{-1} \mathbf{C}$. Thus, we can use the same lattice-based homomorphic evaluation machinery [GSW13, BGG+14] to homomorphically compute an opening to $f(\mathbf{x})$ for an arbitrary Boolean circuit $f : \{0,1\}^\ell \to \{0,1\}$.

In slightly more detail, let $\tilde{\mathbf{C}} = [\mathbf{W}_1^{-1} \mathbf{C} \mid \cdots \mid \mathbf{W}_\ell^{-1} \mathbf{C}]$ and $\tilde{\mathbf{V}} = [\mathbf{V}_1 \mid \cdots \mid \mathbf{V}_\ell]$. Then,

$$\mathbf{A}\tilde{\mathbf{V}} = \mathbf{A}[\mathbf{V}_1 \mid \cdots \mid \mathbf{V}_\ell] = [\mathbf{W}_1^{-1} \mathbf{C} - x_1 \mathbf{G} \mid \cdots \mid \mathbf{W}_\ell^{-1} \mathbf{C} - x_\ell \mathbf{G}] = \tilde{\mathbf{C}} - \mathbf{x}^\mathsf{T} \otimes \mathbf{G}.$$

Using the homomorphic evaluation techniques from [GSW13, BGG+14], there exists a short matrix $\mathbf{H}_{\tilde{\mathbf{C}}, f, \mathbf{x}}$ that depends on $\tilde{\mathbf{C}}$, f, and $\mathbf{x}$ such that

$$(\tilde{\mathbf{C}} - \mathbf{x}^\mathsf{T} \otimes \mathbf{G}) \cdot \mathbf{H}_{\tilde{\mathbf{C}}, f, \mathbf{x}} = \tilde{\mathbf{C}}_f - f(\mathbf{x}) \cdot \mathbf{G}, \quad (1.6)$$

where $\tilde{\mathbf{C}}_f$ is a matrix that can be efficiently computed from $\tilde{\mathbf{C}}$ and f. To open $\mathbf{C}$ to a function f, the user computes $\tilde{\mathbf{V}}_f \leftarrow \tilde{\mathbf{V}} \cdot \mathbf{H}_{\tilde{\mathbf{C}}, f, \mathbf{x}}$. To verify a candidate value $y \in \{0,1\}$ with respect to a function f and commitment $\mathbf{C}$, the verifier first computes $\tilde{\mathbf{C}}_f$ from $(\mathbf{C}, \mathbf{W}_1, \ldots, \mathbf{W}_\ell, f)$ and then checks that $\tilde{\mathbf{V}}_f$ is short and moreover,

$$\mathbf{A}\tilde{\mathbf{V}}_f = \tilde{\mathbf{C}}_f - y \cdot \mathbf{G}.$$

For correctness, observe that

$$\mathbf{A}\tilde{\mathbf{V}}_f = \mathbf{A}\tilde{\mathbf{V}}\mathbf{H}_{\tilde{\mathbf{C}}, f, \mathbf{x}} = (\tilde{\mathbf{C}} - \mathbf{x}^\mathsf{T} \otimes \mathbf{G}) \cdot \mathbf{H}_{\tilde{\mathbf{C}}, f, \mathbf{x}} = \tilde{\mathbf{C}}_f - f(\mathbf{x}) \cdot \mathbf{G}.$$

For binding, we require that SIS is hard with respect to $\mathbf{A}$ even given the matrix $\mathbf{B}_\ell$ and a trapdoor for $\mathbf{B}_\ell$. We refer to this instance of the BASIS assumption with structured $\mathbf{A}_i$'s as BASIS$_{\mathsf{struct}}$. Since the matrices $\mathbf{A}_i$ that comprise $\mathbf{B}_\ell$ are now correlated, we do not know how to reduce BASIS$_{\mathsf{struct}}$ to the standard SIS assumption. Nonetheless, BASIS$_{\mathsf{struct}}$ is a falsifiable assumption under which we obtain a succinct functional commitment for all bounded-depth Boolean circuits. This is the first succinct functional commitment for general circuits from a falsifiable assumption. We provide the full description in Sect. 4 and a comparison to previous succinct functional commitments in Table 1.

Functional Commitments with Private Openings. Using the approach from [GVW15] for constructing context-hiding homomorphic signatures [GVW15], we can easily extend our functional commitment scheme above to support *private* openings (i.e., where the commitment $\mathbf{C}$ and the opening $\tilde{\mathbf{V}}_f$ reveals nothing more about the input $\mathbf{x}$ other than the value $f(\mathbf{x})$). We sketch the approach here. Let $\mathbf{C}$ be a commitment to $\mathbf{x}$ and let $\tilde{\mathbf{V}}_f = \tilde{\mathbf{V}} \cdot \mathbf{H}_{\tilde{\mathbf{C}},f,\mathbf{x}}$ be the opening computed as described above. Then, define the matrix $\mathbf{D}_f$ to be

$$\mathbf{D}_f = [\mathbf{A} \mid \tilde{\mathbf{C}}_f + (f(\mathbf{x}) - 1) \cdot \mathbf{G}] = [\mathbf{A} \mid \mathbf{A}\tilde{\mathbf{V}}_f + (2f(\mathbf{x}) - 1) \cdot \mathbf{G}].$$

Since $\tilde{\mathbf{V}}_f$ is short and $2f(\mathbf{x}) - 1 \in \{-1, 1\}$, the matrix $\begin{bmatrix} \tilde{\mathbf{V}}_f \\ -\mathbf{I}_n \end{bmatrix}$ is a trapdoor for $\mathbf{D}_f$. We now include a random target $\mathbf{u} \in \mathbb{Z}_q^n$ as part of the CRS, and define the opening to be a *random* short vector $\mathbf{v}_f$ where $\mathbf{D}_f\mathbf{v}_f = \mathbf{u}$. The honest prover samples $\mathbf{v}_f$ using the trapdoor for $\mathbf{D}_f$ (derived from $\tilde{\mathbf{V}}_f$). To check an opening $\mathbf{v}_f$ is a valid opening to a value $y \in \{0, 1\}$ with respect to a function f and commitment $\mathbf{C}$, the verifier computes $\tilde{\mathbf{C}}_f$ from $(\mathbf{C}, \mathbf{W}_1, \ldots, \mathbf{W}_\ell, f)$ as before, defines the matrix $\mathbf{D}_f = [\mathbf{A} \mid \tilde{\mathbf{C}}_f + (y - 1) \cdot \mathbf{G}]$, and finally, checks that $\mathbf{D}_f\mathbf{v}_f = \mathbf{u}$. To argue that $\mathbf{v}_f$ hides all information about $\mathbf{x}$ other than what is revealed by $f(\mathbf{x})$, observe that the matrix $\mathbf{D}_f$ depends only on $f(\mathbf{x})$ and *not* $\mathbf{x}$. Thus, given a trapdoor for $\mathbf{A}$ (which can be extended into a trapdoor for $\mathbf{D}_f$ for all f), and the value $f(\mathbf{x})$, we can sample a short $\mathbf{v}_f$ such that $\mathbf{D}_f\mathbf{v}_f = \mathbf{u}$ whose distribution is statistically close to the real opening. This latter procedure only depends on $f(\mathbf{x})$ and not $\mathbf{x}$, so hiding follows. While this construction is hiding, we do not know how to show that it is binding; however, it does satisfy the *weaker* notion of *target binding* where binding holds for all honestly-generated commitments. We provide the full details and analysis in the full version of this paper [WW22].

Polynomial Commitments. We can obtain a polynomial commitment over $\mathbb{Z}_q$ via a simple adaptation of our functional commitment. The starting point is to construct a functional commitment scheme for linear functions on $\mathbb{Z}_q^\ell$ (as opposed to a function on the binary domain $\{0, 1\}^\ell$). We first consider linear functions with small coefficients. Let $\mathbf{z} \in \{0, 1\}^\ell$ be a vector and define the linear function $f_{\mathbf{z}}(\mathbf{x}) := \mathbf{z}^\mathsf{T}\mathbf{x}$. We use the same commitment and opening structure as in our functional commitment. Namely, a commitment $\mathbf{C}$ and the openings $\mathbf{V}_1, \ldots, \mathbf{V}_\ell$ for an input $\mathbf{x}$ satisfy $\mathbf{A}\mathbf{V}_i = \mathbf{W}_i^{-1}\mathbf{C} - x_i\mathbf{G}$, where $x_i \in \mathbb{Z}_q$ now. Observe that

$$\underbrace{\sum_{i \in [\ell]} z_i \mathbf{A}\mathbf{V}_i}_{\mathbf{A}\mathbf{V}_{\mathbf{z}}} = \sum_{i \in [\ell]} z_i \mathbf{W}_i^{-1}\mathbf{C} - \sum_{i \in [\ell]} z_i x_i \mathbf{G} = \underbrace{\sum_{i \in [\ell]} z_i \mathbf{W}_i^{-1}\mathbf{C} - \underbrace{(\mathbf{z}^\mathsf{T}\mathbf{x}) \cdot \mathbf{G}}_{f_{\mathbf{z}}(\mathbf{x}) \cdot \mathbf{G}}}_{\tilde{\mathbf{C}}_{\mathbf{z}}}.$$

Thus, $\mathbf{V}_{\mathbf{z}} = \sum_{i \in [\ell]} z_i \mathbf{V}_i$ is an opening to the function $f_{\mathbf{z}}$. Here, we need $\mathbf{z} \in \{0, 1\}^\ell$ to be short so $\mathbf{V}_{\mathbf{z}}$ is short. To extend to arbitrary linear functions over $\mathbb{Z}_q^\ell$ (rather than short ones), we rely on standard binary decomposition and blow

Table 1. Summary of *succinct* functional commitments. For each scheme, we report the size of the CRS as a function of the security parameter λ and the input length ℓ. We say that a scheme supports "fast verification" if after an *input-independent* preprocessing step, the verification running time is sublinear in ℓ. In all schemes, the size of the commitment and the openings are polylogarithmic in the input length ℓ.

Scheme	CRS Size	Function Class	Assumption	Fast Verification
Folklore	$\mathsf{poly}(\lambda, \log \ell)$	Boolean circuits	CRHF + SNARK*	✓
[LRY16]	$O(\ell)$	linear functions	bilinear maps	✓
[PPS21][†]	$s \cdot \mathsf{poly}(\lambda, d)$	depth d Boolean circuits[‡]	SIS	✗
[ACL+22]	$\ell^{2d} \cdot \mathsf{poly}(\lambda)$	degree d polynomials[§]	k-R-ISIS	✓
This work	$\ell^2 \cdot \mathsf{poly}(\lambda, d, \log \ell)$	depth d Boolean circuits	BASIS$_{\mathsf{struct}}$	✗
This work	$\ell^2 \cdot \mathsf{poly}(\lambda, \log \ell)$	linear functions	BASIS$_{\mathsf{struct}}$	✓

* Collision-resistant hash functions (CRHFs) together with a succinct non-interactive argument of knowledge (SNARK).
† This scheme is in a significantly weaker model that requires an *online trusted* authority to issue opening keys.
‡ The Boolean circuit has size at most s.
§ Only supports commitments and openings to *small* values.

up the vector dimension by a factor of $O(\log q)$. Namely, to commit to a vector $\mathbf{x}$, the user now commits to $\mathbf{x} \otimes \mathbf{g}^\mathsf{T}$, and to open to a linear function $f_\mathbf{z}$ where $\mathbf{z} \in \mathbb{Z}_q^n$, the user constructs an opening with respect to $f_{\mathbf{g}^{-1}(\mathbf{z})}$. This yields a functional commitment scheme for linear functions over $\mathbb{Z}_q^\ell$.

As observed by Libert et al. [LRY16], a functional commitment scheme for linear functions over $\mathbb{Z}_q^\ell$ directly implies a polynomial commitment over $\mathbb{Z}_q$ for polynomials of degree up to $d = \ell - 1$. Namely, a commitment to a polynomial $f \in \mathbb{Z}_q[x]$ of degree d is a vector commitment to the coefficients of f. To open the commitment to a point $x \in \mathbb{Z}_q$, the user constructs a linear opening with respect to the evaluation vector $[1, x, x^2, \ldots, x^d]$. For this to work, it is critical that our functional commitment for linear functions over $\mathbb{Z}_q^\ell$ supports committing to and opening to *arbitrary* $\mathbb{Z}_q$ values (and not just *small* values). Thus, we obtain a polynomial commitment scheme where the commitment size and the opening size is $\mathsf{poly}(\lambda, \log d)$. We provide the full details in the full version of this paper [WW22].

Aggregatable Commitments. Another application of using structured matrices $\mathbf{A}_i$ is it immediately gives an aggregatable commitment. As before, we instantiate our framework with $\mathbf{A}_i = \mathbf{W}_i \mathbf{A}$. We also sample target vectors $\mathbf{u}_1, \ldots, \mathbf{u}_\ell \xleftarrow{\text{R}} \mathbb{Z}_q^n$ and include them as part of the CRS. To commit to an input $\mathbf{x} \in \mathbb{Z}_q^\ell$, we sample $(\mathbf{v}_1, \ldots, \mathbf{v}_\ell, \mathbf{c})$ where

$$\mathbf{B}_\ell \begin{bmatrix} \mathbf{v}_1 \\ \vdots \\ \mathbf{v}_\ell \\ \hat{\mathbf{c}} \end{bmatrix} = \begin{bmatrix} \mathbf{A}_1 & & -\mathbf{G} \\ & \ddots & \vdots \\ & \mathbf{A}_\ell & -\mathbf{G} \end{bmatrix} \cdot \begin{bmatrix} \mathbf{v}_1 \\ \vdots \\ \mathbf{v}_\ell \\ \hat{\mathbf{c}} \end{bmatrix} = \begin{bmatrix} -x_1 \mathbf{W}_1 \mathbf{u}_1 \\ \vdots \\ -x_\ell \mathbf{W}_\ell \mathbf{u}_\ell \end{bmatrix}.$$

Let $\mathbf{c} = \mathbf{G}\hat{\mathbf{c}}$. Then, for all $i \in [\ell]$, $\mathbf{A}_i \mathbf{v}_i - \mathbf{c} = -x_i \mathbf{W}_i \mathbf{u}_i$, or equivalently, $\mathbf{W}_i^{-1}\mathbf{c} = \mathbf{A}\mathbf{v}_i + x_i \mathbf{u}_i$. Observe now that this scheme immediately supports aggregation: for any set $S \subseteq [\ell]$,

$$\sum_{i \in S} \mathbf{W}_i^{-1}\mathbf{c} = \mathbf{A} \sum_{i \in S} \mathbf{v}_i - \sum_{i \in S} x_i \mathbf{u}_i.$$

Thus, $\sum_{i \in S} \mathbf{v}_i$ is an opening to all of the indices in S. We show in the full version of this paper [WW22] that under the same $\mathsf{BASIS}_{\mathsf{struct}}$ assumption (i.e., SIS is hard with respect to $\mathbf{A}$ given $\mathbf{B}_\ell$ and a trapdoor for $\mathbf{B}_\ell$), this scheme satisfies "same-set binding." This means no efficient adversary can open a commitment $\mathbf{c}$ to different sets of values $\{(i, x_i)\}_{i \in S}$ and $\{(i, x_i')\}_{i \in S}$ for the *same* set S. Unlike our vector commitment construction, the security of our aggregatable construction only holds when the input vector $\mathbf{x}$ is short (i.e., our reduction to the $\mathsf{BASIS}_{\mathsf{struct}}$ assumption in the full version of this paper [WW22] constructs an SIS solution whose norm scales with the magnitude of the opened values).

Our aggregatable vector commitment scheme does not satisfy the stronger notion of "different-set binding." This means an efficient adversary may be able to construct a commitment $\mathbf{c}$ along with valid openings $\{(i, x_i)\}_{i \in S}$ and $\{(i, x_i')\}_{i \in T}$ to (distinct) sets S and T, respectively, such that $x_i = 0$ and $x_i' = 1$. Indeed in the full version of this paper [WW22], we describe an explicit attack where an adversary can use the trapdoor for $\mathbf{B}_\ell$ to (heuristically) obtain a trapdoor for the matrix $[\mathbf{W}_S^{-1}\mathbf{A} \mid \mathbf{W}_T^{-1}\mathbf{A}]$ whenever $S \neq T$ and where $\mathbf{W}_S = \sum_{i \in S} \mathbf{W}_i^{-1}$ and $\mathbf{W}_T = \sum_{i \in T} \mathbf{W}_i^{-1}$. Knowledge of this trapdoor allows an adversary to construct a valid opening to $\{(i, x_i)\}_{i \in S}$ and $\{(i, x_i')\}_{i \in T}$ for any choice of x_i, x_i'.

Conceptually, our approach for constructing an aggregatable vector commitment scheme is to replace the *fixed* target value $x_i \mathbf{e}_1$ from our basic vector commitment with *random* linear combinations of $\{x_i\}_{i \in S}$ (where the coefficients of the random linear combination are the vectors $\{\mathbf{u}_i\}_{i \in S}$). A similar approach was used for aggregating pairing-based signatures in [BDN18] and for aggregating openings (to constant-degree polynomials) in [ACL+22].

Aggregating Functional Commitments. The same aggregation technique applies to our succinct functional commitment scheme. Recall the functional commitment verification relation from Eq. (1.6): $\mathbf{A}\tilde{\mathbf{V}}_f = \tilde{\mathbf{C}}_f - y \cdot \mathbf{G}$. Here $\tilde{\mathbf{V}}_f$ is the opening, $\tilde{\mathbf{C}}_f$ is a function of the commitment $\mathbf{C}$ and the function f, and y is the value. To support aggregating up to t openings, we include random vectors $\mathbf{u}_1, \ldots, \mathbf{u}_t \xleftarrow{\text{R}} \mathbb{Z}_q^n$ in the CRS. Then, given a collection of openings $(f_1, y_1, \tilde{\mathbf{V}}_1), \ldots, (f_t, y_t, \tilde{\mathbf{V}}_t)$ where the functions $f_1, \ldots, f_t$ are sorted in lexicographic order, we define the aggregate opening to be $\mathbf{v} = \sum_{i \in [t]} \tilde{\mathbf{V}}_i \cdot \mathbf{G}^{-1}(\mathbf{u}_i)$. The new verification relation is then

$$\sum_{i \in [t]} \tilde{\mathbf{C}}_{f_i} \cdot \mathbf{G}^{-1}(\mathbf{u}_i) = \mathbf{A}\mathbf{v} - \sum_{i \in [t]} y_i \mathbf{u}_i.$$

Similar to the case with aggregatable vector commitments, we can argue "same-function binding," where no efficient adversary can open a commitment $\mathbf{C}$ to two different sets of values $(y_1, \ldots, y_t) \neq (y_1', \ldots, y_t')$ with respect to the same set of functions $(f_1, \ldots, f_t)$. We provide the full analysis in the full version of this paper [WW22].

Understanding the BASIS *Assumption.* The BASIS assumptions we introduce in this work enable a number of new constructions of vector commitments and their generalizations. While the basic version BASIS$_{\text{rand}}$ that suffices for vector commitments can be reduced to the standard SIS assumption (Theorem 3.4), the more general version BASIS$_{\text{struct}}$ with structured matrices does not. Nonetheless, the BASIS$_{\text{struct}}$ assumption is still falsifiable and thus, yields the first succinct functional commitments and polynomial commitments from falsifiable lattice assumptions. We invite cryptanalysis of our new family of SIS assumptions and are also optimistic that the assumption as well as our general methodology will be helpful for realizing new lattice-based cryptographic primitives.

In Sect. 6, we compare the BASIS$_{\text{struct}}$ assumption to similar assumptions made in [ACL+22]. We show a close connection between the two families of assumptions. We can also view the BASIS assumptions as a new type of "q-type" assumption in the lattice-based setting (where the size of the assumption grows with the input dimension).

1.3 Related Work and Concurrent Work

Functional commitments have also been extensively studied in the *interactive* model. In these settings, there is typically an *interactive* opening procedure between the committer and the verifier. Ishai et al. [IKO07] introduced interactive functional commitments for linear function, and subsequently, Bitansky and Chiesa [BC12] extended it to interactive functional commitments. In both cases, these were used to construct (interactive) succinct arguments without relying on probabilistically-checkable proofs (PCPs). Alternatively, using PCPs or their generalization to interactive oracle proofs [BCS16], we can also construct a functional commitment from any collision-resistant hash function via Kilian's interactive succinct argument [Kil92], which can then be made non-interactive in the random oracle model [Mic00]. Our focus in this work is on *non-interactive* vector and functional commitments in the plain model (i.e., *without* random oracles).

Concurrent Works. Recently, two concurrent works [dCP23, BCFL22] introduced new constructions of functional commitments. We provide a more detailed comparison with these works in the full version of this paper [WW22].

2 Preliminaries

We write λ to denote the security parameter. For a positive integer $n \in \mathbb{N}$, we write $[n]$ to denote the set $\{1, \ldots, n\}$. For integers $a, b \in \mathbb{N}$, we write $[a, b]$ to denote the set $\{a, a + 1, \ldots, b\}$. For a positive integer $q \in \mathbb{N}$, we write $\mathbb{Z}_q$ to denote the integers modulo q. We use bold uppercase letters to denote matrices (e.g., $\mathbf{A}, \mathbf{B}$) and bold lowercase letters to denote vectors (e.g., $\mathbf{u}, \mathbf{v}$). We use non-boldface letters to refer to their components: $\mathbf{v} = (v_1, \ldots, v_n)$. For matrices $\mathbf{A}_1, \ldots, \mathbf{A}_\ell \in \mathbb{Z}_q^{n \times m}$, we write $\mathrm{diag}(\mathbf{A}_1, \ldots, \mathbf{A}_\ell) \in \mathbb{Z}_q^{n\ell \times m\ell}$ to denote the block diagonal matrix with blocks $\mathbf{A}_1, \ldots, \mathbf{A}_\ell$ along the main diagonal (and 0 elsewhere).

We write $\mathsf{poly}(\lambda)$ to denote a fixed function that is $O(\lambda^c)$ for some $c \in \mathbb{N}$ and $\mathsf{negl}(\lambda)$ to denote a function that is $o(\lambda^{-c})$ for all $c \in \mathbb{N}$. For functions $f = f(\lambda), g = g(\lambda)$, we write $g \geq O(f)$ to denote that there exists a fixed function $f'(\lambda) = O(f)$ such that $g(\lambda) > f'(\lambda)$ for all $\lambda \in \mathbb{N}$. We say an event occurs with overwhelming probability if its complement occurs with negligible probability. An algorithm is efficient if it runs in probabilistic polynomial time in its input length. We say that two families of distributions $\mathcal{D}_1 = \{\mathcal{D}_{1,\lambda}\}_{\lambda \in \mathbb{N}}$ and $\mathcal{D}_2 = \{\mathcal{D}_{2,\lambda}\}_{\lambda \in \mathbb{N}}$ are computationally indistinguishable if no efficient algorithm can distinguish them with non-negligible probability, and we say they are statistically indistinguishable if the statistical distance $\Delta(\mathcal{D}_1, \mathcal{D}_2)$ is bounded by a negligible function $\mathsf{negl}(\lambda)$.

We review additional preliminaries, especially on lattice-based cryptography in the full version of this paper [WW22].

3 Vector Commitments with Private Opening from SIS

In this section, we show how to construct a vector commitment with private openings from the standard SIS assumption. We start by recalling the definition of a vector commitment:

Definition 3.1 (Vector Commitment). *A vector commitment scheme with succinct local openings over a message space $\mathcal{M}$ consists of a tuple of efficient algorithms $\Pi_{\mathsf{VC}} = (\mathsf{Setup}, \mathsf{Commit}, \mathsf{Open}, \mathsf{Verify})$ with the following properties:*

- $\mathsf{Setup}(1^\lambda, 1^\ell) \to \mathsf{crs}$: *On input the security parameter λ and the vector length ℓ, the setup algorithm outputs a common reference string crs.*
- $\mathsf{Commit}(\mathsf{crs}, \mathbf{x}) \to (\sigma, \mathsf{st})$: *On input the common reference string crs and a vector $\mathbf{x} \in \mathcal{M}^\ell$, the commit algorithm outputs a commitment σ and a state st.*
- $\mathsf{Open}(\mathsf{st}, i) \to \pi$: *On input a commitment state st and an index $i \in [\ell]$, the open algorithm outputs an opening π.*
- $\mathsf{Verify}(\mathsf{crs}, \sigma, i, x_i, \pi) \to \{0, 1\}$: *On input the common reference string crs, a commitment σ, an index i, a message $x_i \in \mathcal{M}$, and an opening π, the verification algorithm outputs a bit $b \in \{0, 1\}$.*

We now define several standard properties on vector commitment schemes:

- **Correctness:** *For all security parameters* λ, *vector dimensions* ℓ, *and inputs* $\mathbf{x} = (x_1, \ldots, x_\ell) \in \mathcal{M}^\ell$,

$$\Pr \left[\mathsf{Verify}(\mathsf{crs}, \sigma, i, m_i, \pi) = 1 : \begin{array}{l} \mathsf{crs} \leftarrow \mathsf{Setup}(1^\lambda, 1^\ell); \\ (\sigma, \mathsf{st}) \leftarrow \mathsf{Commit}(\mathsf{crs}, \mathbf{x}); \\ \pi \leftarrow \mathsf{Open}(\mathsf{st}, i) \end{array} \right] = 1 - \mathsf{negl}(\lambda).$$

- **Succinctness:** *The vector commitment scheme is succinct if there exists a universal polynomial* $\mathsf{poly}(\cdot)$ *such that for all* $\lambda \in \mathbb{N}$, $|\sigma| = \mathsf{poly}(\lambda, \log \ell)$ *and* $|\pi| = \mathsf{poly}(\lambda, \log \ell)$ *in the correctness definition.*
- **Binding:** *We say the commitment scheme is statistically binding (resp., computationally binding) if for all polynomials* $\ell = \ell(\lambda)$ *and all adversaries* $\mathcal{A}$ *(resp., efficient adversaries* $\mathcal{A}$*),*

$$\Pr \left[\begin{array}{l} \mathsf{Verify}(\mathsf{crs}, \sigma, i, x_i, \pi) = 1 \\ \text{and } x_i \neq x_i' \text{ and} \\ \mathsf{Verify}(\mathsf{crs}, \sigma, i, x_i', \pi') = 1 \end{array} : \begin{array}{l} \mathsf{crs} \leftarrow \mathsf{Setup}(1^\lambda, 1^\ell); \\ (\sigma, i, (x_i, \pi), (x_i', \pi')) \leftarrow \mathcal{A}(1^\lambda, 1^\ell, \mathsf{crs}) \end{array} \right] = \mathsf{negl}(\lambda).$$

- **Private openings:** *For a vector dimension* ℓ, *an adversary* $\mathcal{A}$, *and a simulator* $\mathcal{S} = (\mathcal{S}_0, \mathcal{S}_1)$, *we define two distributions* $\mathsf{Real}_\mathcal{A}(1^\lambda, 1^\ell)$ *and* $\mathsf{Ideal}_{\mathcal{A}, \mathcal{S}}(1^\lambda, 1^\ell)$ *as follows:*

$\mathsf{Real}_\mathcal{A}(1^\lambda)$:	$\mathsf{Ideal}_{\mathcal{A},\mathcal{S}}(1^\lambda)$:
1. *Give* $\mathsf{crs} \leftarrow \mathsf{Setup}(1^\lambda, 1^\ell)$ *to* $\mathcal{A}$.	1. *Sample* $(\mathsf{crs}, \sigma, \mathsf{st}) \leftarrow \mathcal{S}_0(1^\lambda, 1^\ell)$ *and give* crs *to* $\mathcal{A}$.
2. *Algorithm* $\mathcal{A}$ *outputs an input* $\mathbf{x} \in \mathcal{M}^\ell$.	2. *Algorithm* $\mathcal{A}$ *outputs an input* $\mathbf{x} \in \mathcal{M}^\ell$.
3. *Compute* $(\sigma, \mathsf{st}) \leftarrow \mathsf{Commit}(\mathsf{crs}, \mathbf{x})$ *and give* σ *to* $\mathcal{A}$.	3. *Give* σ *to* $\mathcal{A}$.
4. *Algorithm* $\mathcal{A}$ *outputs an index* $i \in [\ell]$.	4. *Algorithm* $\mathcal{A}$ *outputs an index* $i \in [\ell]$.
5. *Give* $\pi_i \leftarrow \mathsf{Open}(\mathsf{st}, i)$ *to* $\mathcal{A}$.	5. *Compute* $\pi_i \leftarrow \mathcal{S}_1(\mathsf{st}, i, x_i)$ *and give* π_i *to* $\mathcal{A}$.
6. *Algorithm* $\mathcal{A}$ *outputs a bit* $b \in \{0,1\}$ *which is the output of the experiment.*	6. *Algorithm* $\mathcal{A}$ *outputs a bit* $b \in \{0,1\}$ *which is the output of the experiment.*

We say that the vector commitment scheme has statistically (resp., computationally) private openings if for all polynomials $\ell = \ell(\lambda)$ *and adversaries* $\mathcal{A}$ *(resp., efficient adversaries* $\mathcal{A}$*), there exists an efficient simulator* $\mathcal{S} = (\mathcal{S}_0, \mathcal{S}_1)$ *such that* $\mathsf{Real}_\mathcal{A}(1^\lambda, 1^\ell)$ *and* $\mathsf{Ideal}_{\mathcal{A},\mathcal{S}}(1^\lambda, 1^\ell)$ *are statistically (resp., computationally) indistinguishable.*

3.1 The Basis-Augmented SIS (BASIS) Assumption

In this section, we introduce the family of SIS assumptions that we use to build our vector commitment schemes. At a high level, our assumptions assert that the SIS problem is hard with respect to a random matrix $\mathbf{A}$ even given a trapdoor for a matrix $\mathbf{B}$ that is correlated with $\mathbf{A}$. We refer to our family of assumptions as the "basis-augmented SIS" (BASIS) assumption. As we discuss below (Theorem 3.4), some versions of the BASIS assumption can be reduced to the standard SIS assumption. For instance, our first construction of a vector commitments with *private* openings (Construction 3.5) relies on a version that reduces to the standard SIS assumption.

Assumption 3.2 (BASIS Assumption). Let λ be a security parameter and $n = n(\lambda)$, $m = m(\lambda)$, $q = q(\lambda)$, and $\beta = \beta(\lambda)$ be lattice parameters. Let $s = s(\lambda)$ be a Gaussian width parameter. Let Samp be an efficient sampling algorithm that takes as input a security parameter λ and a matrix $\mathbf{A} \in \mathbb{Z}_q^{n \times m}$ and outputs a matrix $\mathbf{B} \in \mathbb{Z}_q^{n' \times m'}$ along with auxiliary input aux. We say that the basis-augmented SIS (BASIS) assumption holds with respect to Samp if for all efficient adversaries $\mathcal{A}$,

$$\Pr\left[\mathbf{Ax} = \mathbf{0} \text{ and } 0 < \|\mathbf{x}\| \leq \beta : \begin{array}{c} \mathbf{A} \xleftarrow{\text{R}} \mathbb{Z}_q^{n \times m}; \\ (\mathbf{B}, \mathsf{aux}) \leftarrow \mathsf{Samp}(1^\lambda, \mathbf{A}), \mathbf{T} \leftarrow \mathbf{B}_s^{-1}(\mathbf{G}_{n'}); \\ \mathbf{x} \leftarrow \mathcal{A}(1^\lambda, \mathbf{A}, \mathbf{B}, \mathbf{T}, \mathsf{aux}) \end{array}\right] = \mathsf{negl}(\lambda).$$

In other words, we require that SIS is hard with respect to $\mathbf{A}$ even given a trapdoor $\mathbf{T}$ for the related matrix $\mathbf{B}$.

Assumption 3.3 (BASIS Assumption Instantiations). Let λ be a security parameter and $n = n(\lambda)$, $m = m(\lambda)$, $q = q(\lambda)$, and $\beta = \beta(\lambda)$ be lattice parameters. Let $s = s(\lambda)$ be a Gaussian width parameter and $\ell = \ell(\lambda)$ be a dimension. We consider two concrete instantiations of the BASIS assumption:

- $\mathsf{BASIS}_{\mathsf{rand}}$: The sampling algorithm $\mathsf{Samp}(1^\lambda, \mathbf{A})$ samples $i^* \xleftarrow{\text{R}} [\ell]$, $\mathbf{A}_i \xleftarrow{\text{R}} \mathbb{Z}_q^{(n+1) \times m}$ for all $i \neq i^*$, $\mathbf{a} \xleftarrow{\text{R}} \mathbb{Z}_q^m$, sets $\mathbf{A}_{i^*} \leftarrow \left[\begin{smallmatrix} \mathbf{a}^\mathsf{T} \\ \mathbf{A} \end{smallmatrix} \right]$, and outputs

$$\mathbf{B}_\ell = \begin{bmatrix} \mathbf{A}_1 & & & -\mathbf{G}_{n+1} \\ & \ddots & & \vdots \\ & & \mathbf{A}_\ell & -\mathbf{G}_{n+1} \end{bmatrix} \quad \text{and} \quad \mathsf{aux} = i^*.$$

  We refer to this assumption as "the BASIS assumption with random matrices."

- $\mathsf{BASIS}_{\mathsf{struct}}$: The sampling algorithm $\mathsf{Samp}(1^\lambda, \mathbf{A})$ samples $\mathbf{W}_i \xleftarrow{\text{R}} \mathbb{Z}_q^{n \times n}$ for all $i \in [\ell]$ and outputs

$$\mathbf{B}_\ell = \begin{bmatrix} \mathbf{W}_1 \mathbf{A} & & & -\mathbf{G}_n \\ & \ddots & & \vdots \\ & & \mathbf{W}_\ell \mathbf{A} & -\mathbf{G}_n \end{bmatrix} \quad \text{and} \quad \mathsf{aux} = (\mathbf{W}_1, \dots, \mathbf{W}_\ell).$$

  This is essentially $\mathsf{BASIS}_{\mathsf{rand}}$ with *structured* matrices $\mathbf{A}_1, \dots, \mathbf{A}_\ell$. We refer to this assumption as "the BASIS assumption with structured matrices."

Each of the above assumptions is parameterized by the tuple of parameters $(n, m, q, \beta, s, \ell)$. Strictly speaking, in both cases above, the auxiliary information aux can be efficiently computed directly from $\mathbf{A}$ and $\mathbf{B}_\ell$, and thus, can be safely omitted. We include them here for notational convenience.

Hardness of $\mathsf{BASIS}_{\mathsf{rand}}$. The $\mathsf{BASIS}_{\mathsf{rand}}$ assumption can be reduced to SIS. We state the theorem below and give the proof in the full version of this paper [WW22].

Theorem 3.4 (Hardness of $\mathsf{BASIS}_{\mathsf{rand}}$). *Let λ be a security parameter and $n = n(\lambda)$, $m = m(\lambda)$, $q = q(\lambda)$, $\beta = \beta(\lambda)$ be lattice parameters. Take any polynomial $\ell = \ell(\lambda)$ and suppose $n \geq \lambda$, $m \geq O(n \log q)$, and $s \geq O(\ell m \log(n\ell))$. Then, under the $\mathsf{SIS}_{n,m,q,\beta}$ assumption, the $\mathsf{BASIS}_{\mathsf{rand}}$ assumption with parameters $(n, m, q, \beta, s, \ell)$ holds.*

3.2 Vector Commitments with Private Opening from SIS

We now show how to construct a vector commitment scheme with statistically private openings from the $\mathsf{BASIS}_{\mathsf{rand}}$ assumption. By Theorem 3.4, we can in turn base hardness on the standard SIS assumption (with polynomial modulus).

Construction 3.5 (Vector Commitments from SIS). Let λ be a security parameter and $n = n(\lambda)$, $m = m(\lambda)$, and $q = q(\lambda)$ be lattice parameters. Let $m' = n(\lceil \log q \rceil + 1)$ and $B = B(\lambda)$ be a bound. Let $s_0 = s_0(\lambda)$, $s_1 = s_1(\lambda)$ be Gaussian width parameters. Let ℓ be the vector dimension. We construct a vector commitment scheme $\Pi_{\mathsf{VC}} = (\mathsf{Setup}, \mathsf{Commit}, \mathsf{Open}, \mathsf{Verify})$ for $\mathbb{Z}_q^\ell$ as follows:

- $\mathsf{Setup}(1^\lambda, 1^\ell)$: On input the security parameter λ and the vector dimension ℓ, the setup algorithm samples $(\mathbf{A}_i, \mathbf{R}_i) \leftarrow \mathsf{TrapGen}(1^n, q, m)$ for each $i \in [\ell]$. Then, it constructs matrices $\mathbf{B}_\ell$ and $\mathbf{R}$ where

$$
\mathbf{B}_\ell = \begin{bmatrix} \mathbf{A}_1 & & -\mathbf{G} \\ & \ddots & & \vdots \\ & & \mathbf{A}_\ell & -\mathbf{G} \end{bmatrix} \quad \text{and} \quad \mathbf{R} = \begin{bmatrix} \mathrm{diag}(\mathbf{R}_1, \ldots, \mathbf{R}_\ell) \\ \mathbf{0}^{m' \times \ell m'} \end{bmatrix}. \tag{3.1}
$$

Finally, the setup algorithm samples $\mathbf{T} \leftarrow \mathsf{SamplePre}(\mathbf{B}_\ell, \mathbf{R}, \mathbf{G}_{n\ell}, s_0)$ and outputs the common reference string $\mathsf{crs} = (\mathbf{A}_1, \ldots, \mathbf{A}_\ell, \mathbf{T})$.

- $\mathsf{Commit}(\mathsf{crs}, \mathbf{x})$: On input the common reference string $\mathsf{crs} = (\mathbf{A}_1, \ldots, \mathbf{A}_\ell, \mathbf{T})$ and a vector $\mathbf{x} \in \mathbb{Z}_q^\ell$, the commit algorithm constructs $\mathbf{B}_\ell$ from $\mathbf{A}_1, \ldots, \mathbf{A}_\ell$ according to Eq. (3.1) and then uses $\mathbf{T}$ to sample

$$
\begin{bmatrix} \mathbf{v}_1 \\ \vdots \\ \mathbf{v}_\ell \\ \hat{\mathbf{c}} \end{bmatrix} \leftarrow \mathsf{SamplePre}(\mathbf{B}_\ell, \mathbf{T}, -\mathbf{x} \otimes \mathbf{e}_1, s_1), \tag{3.2}
$$

where $\mathbf{e}_1 = [1, 0, \ldots, 0]^\mathsf{T} \in \mathbb{Z}_q^m$ is the first standard basis vector. It computes $\mathbf{c} \leftarrow \mathbf{G}\hat{\mathbf{c}} \in \mathbb{Z}_q^n$ and outputs the commitment $\sigma = \mathbf{c}$ and the state $\mathsf{st} = (\mathbf{v}_1, \ldots, \mathbf{v}_\ell)$.

- $\mathsf{Open}(\mathsf{st}, i)$: On input the state $\mathsf{st} = (\mathbf{v}_1, \ldots, \mathbf{v}_\ell)$ and the index $i \in [\ell]$, the opening algorithm outputs $\mathbf{v}_i$.

– Verify(crs, σ, i, x_i, π): On input the common reference string crs = ($\mathbf{A}_1, \ldots, \mathbf{A}_\ell, \mathbf{T}$), a commitment $\sigma = \mathbf{c} \in \mathbb{Z}_q^n$, an index $i \in [\ell]$, a message $x_i \in \mathbb{Z}_q$, and an opening $\pi = \mathbf{v}_i$, the verification algorithm outputs 1 if

$$\|\mathbf{v}_i\| \leq B \quad \text{and} \quad \mathbf{c} = \mathbf{A}_i\mathbf{v}_i + x_i\mathbf{e}_1.$$

Due to space limitations, we defer the formal analysis of Construction 3.5 to the full version of this paper [WW22] and simply state the main result below:

Corollary 3.6 (Vector Commitments with Private Openings from SIS). *Let λ be a security parameter. Then, for all polynomials $\ell = \ell(\lambda)$, under the SIS assumption with a polynomial norm bound $\beta = \mathsf{poly}(\lambda, \ell)$ and a polynomial modulus $q = \mathsf{poly}(\lambda, \ell)$, there exists a vector commitment scheme over $\mathbb{Z}_q^\ell$ that is computationally binding and has statistically private openings. The size of a commitment to a vector $\mathbf{x} \in \mathbb{Z}_q^\ell$ has size $O(\lambda(\log \lambda + \log \ell))$ and the openings have size $O(\lambda(\log^2 \lambda + \log^2 \ell))$. The size of the CRS is $\ell^2 \cdot \mathsf{poly}(\lambda, \log \ell)$.*

Extensions: Linear Homomorphism and Updatability. Similar to the non-private scheme of Peikert et al. [PPS21], our vector commitment scheme is linearly homomorphic and supports stateless updates. We provide more details in the full version of this paper [WW22].

4   Succinct Functional Commitments for Circuits

In this section, we show how to obtain a succinct functional commitment for general circuits from the $\mathsf{BASIS}_{\mathsf{struct}}$ assumption. We consider schemes where the parameters scale with the *depth* of the Boolean circuit. We start with the formal definition:

Definition 4.1 (Succinct Functional Commitment). *Let λ be a security parameter. Let $\mathcal{F} = \{\mathcal{F}_\lambda\}_{\lambda \in \mathbb{N}}$ be a family of functions $f\colon \{0,1\}^\ell \to \{0,1\}$ on inputs of length $\ell = \ell(\lambda)$ and which can be computed by Boolean circuits of depth at most $d = d(\lambda)$. A succinct functional commitment for $\mathcal{F}$ is a tuple of efficient algorithms $\Pi_{\mathsf{FC}} = (\mathsf{Setup}, \mathsf{Commit}, \mathsf{Eval}, \mathsf{Verify})$ with the following properties:*

– $\mathsf{Setup}(1^\lambda, 1^\ell, 1^d) \to \mathsf{crs}$: *On input the security parameter λ, the input length ℓ, and the bound on the circuit depth d, the setup algorithm outputs a common reference string crs.*
– $\mathsf{Commit}(\mathsf{crs}, \mathbf{x}) \to (\sigma, \mathsf{st})$: *On input the common reference string crs and an input $\mathbf{x} \in \{0,1\}^\ell$, the commitment algorithm outputs a commitment σ and a state st.*
– $\mathsf{Eval}(\mathsf{st}, f) \to \pi_f$: *On input a commitment state st and a function $f \in \mathcal{F}$, the evaluation algorithm outputs an opening π_f.*
– $\mathsf{Verify}(\mathsf{crs}, \sigma, f, y, \pi) \to \{0,1\}$: *On input the common reference string crs, a commitment σ, a function $f \in \mathcal{F}$, a value $y \in \{0,1\}$, and an opening π, the verification algorithm outputs a bit $b \in \{0,1\}$.*

We now define several correctness and security properties on the functional commitment scheme:

- **Correctness:** *For all security parameters λ, all functions $f \in \mathcal{F}$, and all inputs $\mathbf{x} \in \{0,1\}^{\ell}$,*

$$
\Pr \left[\text{Verify}(\text{crs}, \sigma, f, f(\mathbf{x}), \pi_f) = 1 : \begin{array}{l} \text{crs} \leftarrow \text{Setup}(1^{\lambda}, 1^{\ell}, 1^d); \\ (\sigma, \text{st}) \leftarrow \text{Commit}(\text{crs}, \mathbf{x}); \\ \pi_f \leftarrow \text{Eval}(\text{st}, f) \end{array} \right] = 1 - \text{negl}(\lambda).
$$

- **Succinctness:** *The functional commitment scheme is succinct if there exists a universal polynomial $\text{poly}(\cdot,\cdot,\cdot)$ such that for all $\lambda \in \mathbb{N}$, $|\sigma| = \text{poly}(\lambda, d, \log \ell)$ and $|\pi_f| = \text{poly}(\lambda, d, \log \ell)$ in the correctness definition.[8]*
- **Binding:** *We say Π_{FC} satisfies statistical (resp., computational) binding if for all adversaries $\mathcal{A}$ (resp., efficient adversaries $\mathcal{A}$),*

$$
\Pr\left[\text{Verify}(\text{crs}, \sigma, f, 0, \pi_0) = 1 = \text{Verify}(\text{crs}, \sigma, f, 1, \pi_1)\right] = \text{negl}(\lambda),
$$

where $\text{crs} \leftarrow \text{Setup}(1^{\lambda}, 1^{\ell}, 1^d)$ and $(\sigma, f, \pi_0, \pi_1) \leftarrow \mathcal{A}(1^{\lambda}, 1^{\ell}, 1^d, \text{crs})$.
- **Private openings:** *For an adversary $\mathcal{A}$ and a simulator $\mathcal{S} = (\mathcal{S}_0, \mathcal{S}_1)$, we start by defining two distributions $\text{Real}_{\mathcal{A}}(1^{\lambda}, 1^{\ell}, 1^d)$ and $\text{Ideal}_{\mathcal{A},\mathcal{S}}(1^{\lambda}, 1^{\ell}, 1^d)$:*

$\text{Real}_{\mathcal{A}}(1^{\lambda}, 1^{\ell}, 1^d)$:	$\text{Ideal}_{\mathcal{A},\mathcal{S}}(1^{\lambda}, 1^{\ell}, 1^d)$:
1. *Give* $\text{crs} \leftarrow \text{Setup}(1^{\lambda}, 1^{\ell}, 1^d)$ *to* $\mathcal{A}$.	1. *Sample* $(\text{crs}, \sigma, \text{st}) \leftarrow \mathcal{S}_0(1^{\lambda}, 1^{\ell}, 1^d)$ *and give* crs *to* $\mathcal{A}$.
2. *Algorithm* $\mathcal{A}$ *outputs an input* $\mathbf{x} \in \{0,1\}^{\ell}$.	2. *Algorithm* $\mathcal{A}$ *outputs an input* $\mathbf{x} \in \{0,1\}^{\ell}$.
3. *Compute* $(\sigma, \text{st}) \leftarrow \text{Commit}(\text{crs}, \mathbf{x})$ *and give* σ *to* $\mathcal{A}$.	3. *Give* σ *to* $\mathcal{A}$.
4. *Algorithm* $\mathcal{A}$ *outputs a function* $f \in \mathcal{F}_{\lambda}$.	4. *Algorithm* $\mathcal{A}$ *outputs a function* $f \in \mathcal{F}_{\lambda}$.
5. *Give* $\pi_f \leftarrow \text{Eval}(\text{st}, f)$ *to* $\mathcal{A}$.	5. *Compute* $\pi_f \leftarrow \mathcal{S}_1(\text{st}, f, f(\mathbf{x}))$ *and give* π_f *to* $\mathcal{A}$.
6. *Algorithm* $\mathcal{A}$ *outputs a bit* $b \in \{0,1\}$ *which is the output of the experiment.*	6. *Algorithm* $\mathcal{A}$ *outputs a bit* $b \in \{0,1\}$ *which is the output of the experiment.*

We say that Π_{FC} has statistical (resp., computational) private openings if for all adversaries $\mathcal{A}$ (resp., efficient adversaries $\mathcal{A}$), there exists an efficient simulator $\mathcal{S} = (\mathcal{S}_0, \mathcal{S}_1)$ such that $\text{Real}_{\mathcal{A}}(1^{\lambda}, 1^{\ell}, 1^d)$ and $\text{Ideal}_{\mathcal{A},\mathcal{S}}(1^{\lambda}, 1^{\ell}, 1^d)$ are statistically (resp., computationally) indistinguishable.

Construction 4.2 (Succinct Functional Commitment). Let λ be a security parameter and $n = n(\lambda)$, $m = m(\lambda)$, and $q = q(\lambda)$ be lattice parameters where q is prime. Let $m' = n(\lceil \log q \rceil + 1)$ and $B = B(\lambda)$ be a bound.

---

[8] We could consider an even stronger notion of succinctness where the size of the commitment and the opening depends polylogarithmically on the *size* of the Boolean circuits computing $\mathcal{F}$. However, like existing (non-succinct) lattice-based homomorphic commitments and signatures [GVW15], the size of the commitment and openings in our construction scale with the *depth* of the computation.

Let $s_0 = s_0(\lambda)$, $s_1 = s_1(\lambda)$ be Gaussian width parameters. Let $\mathcal{F} = \{\mathcal{F}_\lambda\}_{\lambda \in \mathbb{N}}$ be a family of Boolean valued functions $f \colon \{0,1\}^\ell \to \{0,1\}$ where each function $f \colon \{0,1\}^\ell \to \{0,1\}$ is a function on inputs of length $\ell = \ell(\lambda)$ and which can be computed by a Boolean circuit of depth at most $d = d(\lambda)$. We construct a functional commitment $\Pi_{\mathsf{VC}} = (\mathsf{Setup}, \mathsf{Commit}, \mathsf{Open}, \mathsf{Verify})$ for $\mathcal{F}$ as follows:

- $\mathsf{Setup}(1^\lambda, 1^\ell, 1^d)$: On input the security parameter λ, the input length ℓ, and the bound d on the circuit depth, the setup algorithm samples $(\mathbf{A}, \mathbf{R}) \leftarrow \mathsf{TrapGen}(1^n, q, m)$ and for each $i \in [\ell]$, samples an *invertible* matrix $\mathbf{W}_i \xleftarrow{\text{\tiny R}} \mathbb{Z}_q^{n \times n}$. Next, it computes $\tilde{\mathbf{R}}_i \leftarrow \mathbf{R} \mathbf{G}^{-1}(\mathbf{W}_i^{-1}\mathbf{G}) \in \mathbb{Z}_q^{m \times m'}$ for each $i \in [\ell]$ and constructs matrices $\mathbf{B}_\ell$ and $\mathbf{R}$ as follows:

$$\mathbf{B}_\ell = \begin{bmatrix} \mathbf{W}_1\mathbf{A} & & & -\mathbf{G} \\ & \ddots & & \vdots \\ & & \mathbf{W}_\ell\mathbf{A} & -\mathbf{G} \end{bmatrix} \quad \text{and} \quad \tilde{\mathbf{R}} = \begin{bmatrix} \mathrm{diag}(\tilde{\mathbf{R}}_1, \ldots, \tilde{\mathbf{R}}_\ell) \\ \mathbf{0}^{m' \times \ell m'} \end{bmatrix}. \quad (4.1)$$

Finally, the setup algorithm samples $\mathbf{T} \leftarrow \mathsf{SamplePre}(\mathbf{B}_\ell, \tilde{\mathbf{R}}, \mathbf{G}_{n\ell}, s_0)$ and outputs the common reference string $\mathsf{crs} = (\mathbf{A}, \mathbf{W}_1, \ldots, \mathbf{W}_\ell, \mathbf{T})$.

- $\mathsf{Commit}(\mathsf{crs}, \mathbf{x})$: On input the common reference string $\mathsf{crs} = (\mathbf{A}, \mathbf{W}_1, \ldots, \mathbf{W}_\ell, \mathbf{T})$ and a vector $\mathbf{x} \in \{0,1\}^\ell$, the commit algorithm constructs $\mathbf{B}_\ell$ from $\mathbf{A}, \mathbf{W}_1, \ldots, \mathbf{W}_\ell$ according to Eq. (4.1). It then constructs a target matrix

$$\mathbf{U}_{\mathbf{x}} = \begin{bmatrix} -x_1 \mathbf{W}_1 \mathbf{G} \\ \vdots \\ -x_\ell \mathbf{W}_\ell \mathbf{G} \end{bmatrix} \in \mathbb{Z}_q^{n\ell \times m'}. \quad (4.2)$$

It then uses $\mathbf{T}$ to sample a preimage

$$\begin{bmatrix} \mathbf{V}_1 \\ \vdots \\ \mathbf{V}_\ell \\ \hat{\mathbf{C}} \end{bmatrix} \leftarrow \mathsf{SamplePre}(\mathbf{B}_\ell, \mathbf{T}, \mathbf{U}_{\mathbf{x}}, s_1). \quad (4.3)$$

It outputs the commitment $\sigma = \mathbf{C} = \mathbf{G}\hat{\mathbf{C}} \in \mathbb{Z}_q^{n \times m'}$ and the state $\mathsf{st} = (\mathbf{x}, \mathbf{C}, \mathbf{V}_1, \ldots, \mathbf{V}_\ell)$.

- $\mathsf{Eval}(\mathsf{crs}, \mathsf{st}, f)$: On input the common reference string $\mathsf{crs} = (\mathbf{A}, \mathbf{W}_1, \ldots, \mathbf{W}_\ell, \mathbf{T})$, a commitment state $\mathsf{st} = (\mathbf{x}, \mathbf{C}, \mathbf{V}_1, \ldots, \mathbf{V}_\ell)$, and a function $f \colon \{0,1\}^\ell \to \{0,1\}$, the evaluation algorithm sets $\tilde{\mathbf{C}} \leftarrow [\mathbf{W}_1^{-1}\mathbf{C} \mid \cdots \mid \mathbf{W}_\ell^{-1}\mathbf{C}]$, computes $\mathbf{H}_{\tilde{\mathbf{C}}, f, \mathbf{x}} \leftarrow \mathsf{EvalFX}(\tilde{\mathbf{C}}, f, \mathbf{x})$, and outputs the opening $\pi_f = \mathbf{V}_f \leftarrow [\mathbf{V}_1 \mid \cdots \mid \mathbf{V}_\ell] \cdot \mathbf{H}_{\tilde{\mathbf{C}}, f, \mathbf{x}}$.

- $\mathsf{Verify}(\mathsf{crs}, \sigma, f, y, \pi)$: On input the common reference string $\mathsf{crs} = (\mathbf{A}, \mathbf{W}_1, \ldots, \mathbf{W}_\ell, \mathbf{T})$, a commitment $\sigma = \mathbf{C} \in \mathbb{Z}_q^{n \times m'}$, a function $f \colon \{0,1\}^\ell \to \{0,1\}$, a value $y \in \{0,1\}$, and an opening $\pi = \mathbf{V}_f \in \mathbb{Z}_q^{m \times m'}$, the verification algorithm sets $\tilde{\mathbf{C}} \leftarrow [\mathbf{W}_1^{-1}\mathbf{C} \mid \cdots \mid \mathbf{W}_\ell^{-1}\mathbf{C}]$, computes $\tilde{\mathbf{C}}_f \leftarrow \mathsf{EvalF}(\tilde{\mathbf{C}}, f)$ and outputs 1 if

$$\|\mathbf{V}_f\| \le B \quad \text{and} \quad \mathbf{A}\mathbf{V}_f = \tilde{\mathbf{C}}_f - y\mathbf{G}. \quad (4.4)$$

Due to space limitations, we defer the analysis of Construction 4.2 to the full version of this paper [WW22]. We summarize the parameter instantiation below:

Parameter Instantiation. Let λ be a security parameter and $\mathcal{F} = \{\mathcal{F}_\lambda\}_{\lambda \in \mathbb{N}}$ be a family of functions $f\colon \{0,1\}^\ell \to \{0,1\}$ on inputs of length $\ell = \ell(\lambda)$ and which can be computed by Boolean circuits of depth at most $d = d(\lambda)$.

- Let $\varepsilon > 0$ be a constant. We set the lattice dimension $n = d^{1/\varepsilon} \cdot \mathsf{poly}(\lambda)$ and $m = O(n \log q)$.
- We set $s_0 = \tilde{O}(\ell m^2 \log(n\ell))$ and

$$s_1 = \tilde{O}(\ell^{3/2} m^{3/2} \log(n\ell) \cdot s_0) = \tilde{O}(\ell^{5/2} m^{7/2} \log^2(n\ell)) = \tilde{O}(\ell^{5/2} n^{7/2} \log^2(n\ell) \log^{7/2} q).$$

- We set the bound $B = s_1 \cdot \sqrt{\ell m + m'} \cdot (n \log q)^{O(d)} = \ell^3 \log^2 \ell \cdot (n \log q)^{O(d)}$.
- We set the modulus q so that the $\mathsf{BASIS_{struct}}$ assumption holds with parameters $(n, m, q, \beta, s_0, \ell)$, where

$$\beta = 2Bm\sqrt{m'} \log n = \ell^3 \log^2 \ell \cdot (n \log q)^{O(d)} = 2^{\tilde{O}(d)} = 2^{\tilde{O}(n^\varepsilon)},$$

where we write $\tilde{O}(\cdot)$ to suppress polylogarithmic factors in λ, d, ℓ. Note that this also requires that $\mathsf{SIS}_{n,m,q,\beta}$ hold. For instance, we set $q = \beta \cdot \mathsf{poly}(n)$. Then, $\log q = \mathsf{poly}(d, \log \lambda, \log \ell)$. Note that the underlying SIS assumption now relies on a *sub-exponential* noise bound.

With this setting of parameters, we obtain a functional commitment scheme for $\mathcal{F}$ with the following parameter sizes:

- **Commitment size:** A commitment σ to an input $\mathbf{x} \in \{0,1\}^\ell$ consists of a matrix $\sigma = \mathbf{C} \in \mathbb{Z}_q^{n \times m'}$ so

$$|\sigma| = nm' \log q = O(n^2 \log^2 q) = \mathsf{poly}(\lambda, d, \log \ell).$$

- **Opening size:** An opening π to a function f consists of a matrix $\pi = \mathbf{V}_f \in \mathbb{Z}_q^{m \times m'}$. Then,

$$|\pi| = mm' \log q = \mathsf{poly}(\lambda, d, \log \ell).$$

In Remark 4.4, we describe a simple approach to compress the opening to a *vector* instead of a matrix.
- **CRS size:** The CRS consists of $(\mathbf{A}, \mathbf{W}_1, \ldots, \mathbf{W}_\ell, \mathbf{T})$, where $\mathbf{A} \in \mathbb{Z}_q^{n \times m}$, $\mathbf{W}_i \in \mathbb{Z}_q^{n \times n}$, and $\mathbf{T} \in \mathbb{Z}_q^{(\ell m + m') \times \ell m'}$. Thus, the total size of the CRS is

$$|\mathsf{crs}| = nm \log q + \ell n^2 \log q + (\ell m + m')(\ell m') \log q = \ell^2 \cdot \mathsf{poly}(\lambda, d, \log \ell).$$

Thus, Construction 4.2 is a succinct functional commitment scheme for bounded-depth circuits. We summarize the instantiation in the following corollary:

Corollary 4.3 (Succinct Vector Commitment from $\mathsf{BASIS_{struct}}$). *Let λ be a security parameter, and let $\mathcal{F} = \{\mathcal{F}_\lambda\}_{\lambda \in \mathbb{N}}$ be a family of functions $f\colon \{0,1\}^\ell \to \{0,1\}$ on inputs of length $\ell = \ell(\lambda)$ and which can be computed by Boolean circuits of depth at most $d = d(\lambda)$. Under the $\mathsf{BASIS_{struct}}$ assumption with a norm bound $\beta = 2^{\tilde{O}(d)}$ and modulus $q = 2^{\tilde{O}(d)}$, there exists a computationally-binding succinct functional commitment scheme for $\mathcal{F}$. Both the size of the commitment and the opening are $\mathsf{poly}(\lambda, d, \log \ell)$, and the CRS has size $\ell^2 \cdot \mathsf{poly}(\lambda, d, \log \ell)$. Here, $\tilde{O}(\cdot)$ suppresses polylogarithmic factors in λ, d, and ℓ.*

Remark 4.4 (Reducing the Opening Size). An opening π_f to a function f in Construction 4.2 consists of a matrix $\pi_f = \mathbf{V}_f \in \mathbb{Z}_q^{m \times m'}$ where $m, m' = O(n \log q)$. It is easy to adapt Construction 4.2 to obtain slightly shorter openings (i.e., $\pi_f = \mathbf{v}_f \in \mathbb{Z}_q^m$). The idea is simple: we publish a random target vector $\mathbf{u} \xleftarrow{\text{R}} \mathbb{Z}_q^n$ in the CRS and define the new opening to be $\mathbf{v}_f \leftarrow \mathbf{V}_f \mathbf{G}^{-1}(\mathbf{u})$, where $\mathbf{V}_f$ is the original opening from Construction 4.2. The updated verification relation then checks that $\|\mathbf{v}_f\|$ is small and that $\mathbf{A}\mathbf{v}_f = \tilde{\mathbf{C}}\mathbf{G}^{-1}(\mathbf{u}) - y \cdot \mathbf{u}$. We also use this approach to aggregate openings in the full version of this paper [WW22]. However, giving out the "matrix" opening is convenient when specializing our construction to obtain polynomial commitments.

Remark 4.5 (Comparison with [ACL+22]). The authors of [ACL+22] showed how to construct a functional commitment for constant-degree polynomials where the size of the CRS scales exponentially with the *degree* of the polynomial. Our functional commitment scheme (Construction 4.2) supports arbitrary Boolean circuits of bounded depth, and the size of our CRS scales polynomially with the depth of the circuit family. Moreover, security of our construction can be reduced to a function-independent assumption (the $\mathsf{BASIS}_{\mathsf{struct}}$ assumption) whereas the scheme in [ACL+22] relied on a function-dependent assumption. We compare the two types of assumptions in more detail in Sect. 6.

An advantage of the [ACL+22] construction is that if supports *fast* verification with preprocessing. Namely, in their scheme, the verifier can precompute a verification key for a function f, and subsequently, verify openings with respect to f in time that is *polylogarithmic* in the running time of f. In contrast, with our scheme, the verifier has to first homomorphically compute f on the commitment in order to verify. In the full version of this paper [WW22], we show that for the special case of linear functions, we can adapt Construction 4.2 to support fast verification in the preprocessing model.

Remark 4.6 (A Candidate SNARG with Expensive Verification). The authors of [ACL+22] show how to boost their functional commitment for quadratic polynomials to a preprocessing SNARG for NP as follows:

1. First, [ACL+22] applying "sparsification" to their functional commitment scheme. Over the integers, one analog of sparsification is to require the adversary to output a short $\tilde{\mathbf{V}}$ such that $\tilde{\mathbf{A}}\tilde{\mathbf{V}} = \mathbf{D}\mathbf{C}$, where $\mathbf{D} \in \mathbb{Z}_q^{2m \times n}$, where $\tilde{\mathbf{A}} \xleftarrow{\text{R}} \mathbb{Z}_q^{2m \times 2m \log q}$ is a sparsification matrix. The CRS includes short preimages of $\tilde{\mathbf{A}}$ to enable sampling of $\tilde{\mathbf{V}}$.
2. Next, [ACL+22] introduce a knowledge assumption that says that the only way an adversary can produce $\mathbf{C}$ and $\tilde{\mathbf{V}}$ is by computing a short linear combination of the preimages in the CRS (where the coefficients correspond to the committed vector $\mathbf{x}$).
3. To support openings to multiple quadratic polynomials with a succinct opening (i.e., sublinear in the number of openings), [ACL+22] introduces a novel SIS-based technique.

Taken together, [ACL+22] show how to obtain an "extractable" commitment scheme, a notion that is equivalent to a succinct argument of knowledge for satisfiability of quadratic systems. This yields a publicly-verifiable preprocessing SNARG for NP since satisfiability of degree-2 polynomials is NP-complete. Specifically, a proof for a statement x consists of a commitment σ to a satisfying witness w and an opening π of σ to a satisfying assignment to the quadratic constraint system representing the NP relation. By relying on preprocessing (Remark 4.5), the [ACL+22] SNARG has short proofs and fast verification.

We can apply an analogous approach to our functional commitment scheme (Construction 4.2) to obtain a candidate SNARG for NP; our SNARG would have short proofs but an *expensive* verification step (since our functional commitment does not support fast verification in the preprocessing model). We also note that even without sparsification, our construction is still a candidate SNARG: we do not know how to prove soundness of our construction, but at the same time, are not aware of any attacks either. An attack on our candidate SNARG (without sparsification) would be interesting, and we invite cryptanalysis of our candidate.

4.1   Opening to Linear Functions and Applications to Polynomial Commitments

In the full version of this paper [WW22], we describe a variant of Construction 4.2 for the setting of *linear* functions that supports fast verification in the preprocessing model (see Remark 6.1). Moreover, the full version of this paper [WW22] naturally supports linear functions over $\mathbb{Z}_q^\ell$ (as opposed to $\{0,1\}^\ell$) and generalizes to yield a *polynomial commitment* [KZG10]. Unlike [ACL+22], we do *not* require the values in the committed vector or the output of the linear function to be short. Supporting *large* values is necessary for obtaining a succinct polynomial commitment.

4.2   Supporting Private Openings

In the full version of this paper [WW22], we show how to extend Construction 4.2 to additionally support *private* openings. Recall from Definition 4.1 that a functional commitment supports private openings if the commitment σ to an input $\mathbf{x}$ together with an opening π_f with respect to a function f leaks no additional information about $\mathbf{x}$ other than the value $f(\mathbf{x})$. In the context of homomorphic signatures [GVW15], this property is called *context hiding*. We show that the same approach used to achieve context hiding in the setting of homomorphic signatures applies to our setting and yields a succinct functional commitment that supports private openings. However, the transformation does not preserve the binding property on the functional commitments scheme. Nonetheless, we can still show that the scheme satisfies a *weaker* notion of binding called *target binding*, which says that any *honestly-generated* commitment on $\mathbf{x}$ can only be opened to $f(\mathbf{x})$ for any function f. We defer the details to the full version of this paper [WW22].

5   Aggregatable Vector Commitments

In the full version of this paper [WW22], we show how to use the $\mathsf{BASIS}_{\mathsf{struct}}$ assumption to obtain a variant of our SIS-based vector commitment (Construction 3.5) that supports aggregation. Recall that in an aggregatable commitment, one can take a collection of openings $\{(i, \pi_i)\}_{i \in S}$ for a set of $S \subseteq [\ell]$ of indices and aggregate them into a *single* opening π (for the set S) whose size scales sublinearly with the size of S. Aggregatable commitments imply subvector commitments [LM19] which are vector commitments that allow for succinct openings to a set of indices (but do *not* necessarily support aggregating openings).

6   New SIS Assumptions: Relations and Discussion

In this section, we compare our approach of publishing a full trapdoor in the common reference string with the approach of Albrecht et al. [ACL+22] of publishing short preimages in the CRS. While Albrecht et al. formulate their assumption over polynomial rings, their ideas apply equally well in the integer setting. We describe everything over the integers to enable a more direct comparison. We start by recalling the general paradigm for constructing vector commitments from Sect. 1.2 common to our approach and their approach:

- The CRS consists of ℓ matrices $\mathbf{A}_i \in \mathbb{Z}_q^{n \times m}$ and a set of target vectors $\mathbf{t}_i \in \mathbb{Z}_q^n$ for $i \in [\ell]$. The CRS also contains some auxiliary information aux_ℓ that is used to construct commitments and openings.
- An opening $\mathbf{v}_i$ to value x_i at index i with respect to a commitment $\mathbf{c} \in \mathbb{Z}_q^n$ is a short vector $\mathbf{v}_i$ that satisfies $\mathbf{c} = \mathbf{A}_i \mathbf{v}_i - x_i \mathbf{t}_i$.

We now compare the two types of auxiliary information aux_ℓ in our approach (based on the BASIS assumption) and the Albrecht et al. approach (based on variants of the k-ISIS assumption):

(I) **Our approach:** In our approach based on the BASIS assumption, $\mathsf{aux}_\ell = \mathbf{T}$ is a trapdoor $\mathbf{T} \leftarrow \mathbf{B}_\ell^{-1}(\mathbf{G}_{n\ell})$ for the matrix $\mathbf{B}_\ell = [\mathrm{diag}(\mathbf{A}_1, \ldots, \mathbf{A}_\ell) \mid -\mathbf{1}^\ell \otimes \mathbf{G}]$. As shown in Sects. 3 and 4, the trapdoor $\mathbf{T}$ suffices to *jointly* sample commitments $\mathbf{c}$ and openings $\mathbf{v}_1, \ldots, \mathbf{v}_\ell$ that satisfy the verification relation.

(II) **The Albrecht et al. approach:** In the Albrecht et al. [ACL+22] approach, the auxiliary information $\mathsf{aux}_\ell = \{\mathbf{z}_{j,i}\}_{i \neq j}$ consists of a collection of short vectors $\mathbf{z}_{j,i} \leftarrow \mathbf{A}_i^{-1}(\mathbf{t}_j)$. The commitment to a vector $\mathbf{x} \in \{0,1\}^\ell$ is the vector $\mathbf{c} = \sum_{i \in [\ell]} -x_i \mathbf{t}_i$ and the openings are $\mathbf{v}_i = \sum_{j \neq i} -x_j \mathbf{z}_{j,i}$.

We now compare the relative power of these two types of auxiliary information. We refer to the above auxiliary data as "Type I" auxiliary data and "Type II" auxiliary data, respectively.

- When the target vectors $\mathbf{t}_1, \ldots, \mathbf{t}_\ell$ are uniform, we can simulate a CRS with Type II auxiliary data from a CRS with Type I auxiliary data. Namely, given matrices $\mathbf{A}_1, \ldots, \mathbf{A}_\ell$ and the trapdoor $\mathsf{aux}_\ell = \mathbf{T}$ for $\mathbf{B}$, we can sample

$$\begin{bmatrix} \mathbf{z}_{j,1} \\ \vdots \\ \mathbf{z}_{j,\ell} \\ \hat{\mathbf{c}}_j \end{bmatrix} \leftarrow \mathbf{B}_\ell^{-1}(\mathbf{0}),$$

for each $j \in [\ell]$. By construction of $\mathbf{B}_\ell$, for all $j \in [\ell]$, $\mathbf{z}_{j,i} \in \mathbb{Z}_q^m$ is a short vector satisfying $\mathbf{A}_i \mathbf{z}_{j,i} = \mathbf{G}\hat{\mathbf{c}}_j$. The marginal distribution of each $\hat{\mathbf{c}}_j$ is a discrete Gaussian, and $\mathbf{G}\hat{\mathbf{c}}_j$ is uniform over $\mathbb{Z}_q^n$. Thus, we obtain a Type II CRS with matrices $\mathbf{A}_1, \dots, \mathbf{A}_\ell$, target vectors $\mathbf{t}_1 = \mathbf{G}\hat{\mathbf{c}}_1, \dots, \mathbf{t}_\ell = \mathbf{G}\hat{\mathbf{c}}_\ell$, and auxiliary data $\mathsf{aux}_\ell = \{\mathbf{z}_{j,i}\}_{i \neq j}$.

- Next, we show that we can also use Type II auxiliary data to obtain a trapdoor for *sub-matrices* of $\mathbf{B}$. We illustrate this with a concrete example. Suppose we want to obtain a trapdoor for the matrix $\mathbf{B}_k$ (where $k < \ell/m$):

$$\mathbf{B}_k = \begin{bmatrix} \mathbf{A}_1 & & & -\mathbf{G} \\ & \ddots & & \vdots \\ & & \mathbf{A}_k & -\mathbf{G} \end{bmatrix} \in \mathbb{Z}_q^{kn \times (km+m')},$$

where $m' = n(\lfloor \log q \rfloor + 1)$. For $j \neq i$, let $\mathbf{z}_{j,i} \in \mathbb{Z}_q^m$ be short vectors where $\mathbf{A}_i \mathbf{z}_{j,i} = \mathbf{t}_j$ be the vectors in the Type II auxiliary data. For any $j > k$, consider the vector

$$\mathbf{v}_j = \begin{bmatrix} \mathbf{z}_{j,1} \\ \vdots \\ \mathbf{z}_{j,k} \\ \mathbf{G}^{-1}(\mathbf{t}_j) \end{bmatrix} \in \mathbb{Z}_q^{km+m'},$$

Observe that $\mathbf{v}_j$ is short, and moreover $\mathbf{B}_k \mathbf{v}_j = \mathbf{0}$. If $\ell - k > km + m'$, then we can collect $km + m'$ such vectors $\mathbf{v}_j$. Heuristically, if these vectors are linearly independent (over the integers), then this yields a Ajtai-basis for $\mathbf{B}_k$. Thus Type II auxiliary data implies Type I auxiliary data for a slightly smaller dimension $k \approx \ell/m$.

While asking for security given a full trapdoor for the related matrix $\mathbf{B}_\ell$ might seem like a stronger assumption than giving our many short preimages under $\mathbf{A}_1, \dots, \mathbf{A}_\ell$, the above analysis shows that these these two types of auxiliary data have comparable power. Hardness of SIS/ISIS with respect to one type of auxiliary data is comparable to hardness with respect to the other (up to an $O(n \log q)$ loss in the vector dimension ℓ). In fact, the above analysis shows that Type II auxiliary data (with essentially arbitrary target vectors $\mathbf{u}_i$) is already sufficient to construct a trapdoor that yields a Type I auxiliary data for a smaller input dimension. However, the converse is not true, as the trapdoor for $\mathbf{B}_\ell$ seem to only allow sampling preimages of $\mathbf{A}_1, \dots, \mathbf{A}_\ell$ with respect to random target vectors $\mathbf{t}_1, \dots, \mathbf{t}_\ell$. This distinction is important, and as we discuss in Remark 6.1, Type I auxiliary data seem essential to realizing the functional commitment scheme from Sect. 4 (as well as its aggregatable analog in the full version of this paper [WW22]). Other advantages to using a Type I auxiliary data include supporting private openings (Construction 3.5) and commitments to large inputs.

Remark 6.1 (Structured Targets and Functional Commitments). The main verification relation of our functional commitment scheme (Construction 4.2) is $C = A_i V_i + x_i G$ where $A_i = W_i A$. If we consider a Type II auxiliary data for this verification relation, the auxiliary data would contain $A_i^{-1}(G)$, or equivalently, $A^{-1}(W_i^{-1}G)$. However, $A^{-1}(W_i^{-1}G)$ is a trapdoor for A (with tag W_i^{-1}), which trivially breaks security. In contrast, using Type I auxiliary data does not appear to yield a trapdoor for A, and plausibly yields a succinct functional commitment scheme.

6.1   Another View of the $\mathsf{BASIS}_{\mathsf{struct}}$ Assumption

To facilitate cryptanalysis of our new assumption, we provide an equivalent formulation of the $\mathsf{BASIS}_{\mathsf{struct}}$ assumption (Assumption 3.3) underlying our functional, polynomial, and aggregatable commitments. Consider a variant of the $\mathsf{BASIS}_{\mathsf{struct}}$ assumption where T is an Ajtai trapdoor for B (i.e., $T \leftarrow B_s^{-1}(0^{m \times 2m})$). Note that we can efficiently convert between gadget trapdoors and Ajtai trapdoors, up to small polynomial losses in the quality of the trapdoor. It is easy to see that we can re-express $B^{-1}(0^{m \times 2m})$ as $A^{-1}(W_i^{-1}R)$ for all $i \in [\ell]$, and $R \xleftarrow{\text{R}} \mathbb{Z}_q^{n \times 2m}$. Therefore, the $\mathsf{BASIS}_{\mathsf{struct}}$ assumption is equivalent to:

$$\text{SIS is hard with respect to } A \xleftarrow{\text{R}} \mathbb{Z}_q^{n \times m} \text{ given } A^{-1}(W_i^{-1}R)$$
$$\text{for all } i \in [\ell], \text{ where } W_i \xleftarrow{\text{R}} \mathbb{Z}_q^{n \times n} \text{ and } R \xleftarrow{\text{R}} \mathbb{Z}_q^{n \times 2m}.$$

Remark 6.2 (Parameter Choices for the $\mathsf{BASIS}_{\mathsf{struct}}$ assumption). While hardness of the $\mathsf{BASIS}_{\mathsf{rand}}$ assumption can be based on the hardness of the standard SIS assumption, we do not know of an analogous reduction for the $\mathsf{BASIS}_{\mathsf{struct}}$ assumption. When setting parameters for the $\mathsf{BASIS}_{\mathsf{struct}}$ assumption, we use Theorem 3.4 as a guide and consider instantiations where $n \geq \lambda$, $m \geq O(n \log q)$ and $s \geq O(\ell m \log n) = \mathsf{poly}(\lambda, \ell)$. Note that this means the quality of the basis *decreases* with the dimension. For this parameter setting, we are not aware of any concrete attacks on the $\mathsf{BASIS}_{\mathsf{struct}}$ assumption and conjecture that its security is comparable with the hardness of $\mathsf{SIS}_{n,m,q,\beta}$, with a noise bound bound $\beta = \mathsf{poly}(\lambda, \ell)$ that scales with the dimension of the vector (as in Theorem 3.4). In particular, the hardness of the SIS instance decreases with the dimension ℓ (similar to the case with q-type assumptions over groups [Che06]).

Acknowledgments. We thank Jonathan Bootle for helpful conversations about lattice-based SNARKs. D. J. Wu is supported by NSF CNS-2151131, CNS-2140975, a Microsoft Research Faculty Fellowship, and a Google Research Scholar award.

References

[ABB10a] Agrawal, S., Boneh, D., Boyen, X.: Efficient Lattice (H)IBE in the standard model. In: Gilbert, H. (ed.) EUROCRYPT 2010. LNCS, vol. 6110, pp. 553–572. Springer, Heidelberg (2010). https://doi.org/10.1007/978-3-642-13190-5_28

[ABB10b] Agrawal, S., Boneh, D., Boyen, X.: Lattice basis delegation in fixed dimension and shorter-ciphertext hierarchical IBE. In: Rabin, T. (ed.) CRYPTO 2010. LNCS, vol. 6223, pp. 98–115. Springer, Heidelberg (2010). https://doi.org/10.1007/978-3-642-14623-7_6

[ACL+22] Albrecht, M.R., Cini, V., Lai, R.W.F., Malavolta, G., Thyagarajan, S.A.: Lattice-based SNARKs: publicly verifiable, preprocessing, and recursively composable. In: Dodis, Y., Shrimpton, T. (eds.) CRYPTO 2022. LNCS, vol. 13508, pp. 102–132. Springer, Cham (2022). https://doi.org/10.1007/978-3-031-15979-4_4

[Ajt96] Ajtai, M.: Generating hard instances of lattice problems (extended abstract). In: STOC (1996)

[AP09] Alwen, J., Peikert, C.: Generating shorter bases for hard random lattices. In: STACS (2009)

[AR20] Agrawal, S., Raghuraman, S.: KVaC: key-value commitments for blockchains and beyond. In: Moriai, S., Wang, H. (eds.) ASIACRYPT 2020. LNCS, vol. 12493, pp. 839–869. Springer, Cham (2020). https://doi.org/10.1007/978-3-030-64840-4_28

[BBF19] Boneh, D., Bünz, B., Fisch, B.: Batching techniques for accumulators with applications to IOPs and stateless blockchains. In: Boldyreva, A., Micciancio, D. (eds.) CRYPTO 2019. LNCS, vol. 11692, pp. 561–586. Springer, Cham (2019). https://doi.org/10.1007/978-3-030-26948-7_20

[BC12] Bitansky, N., Chiesa, A.: Succinct arguments from multi-prover interactive proofs and their efficiency benefits. In: Safavi-Naini, R., Canetti, R. (eds.) CRYPTO 2012. LNCS, vol. 7417, pp. 255–272. Springer, Heidelberg (2012). https://doi.org/10.1007/978-3-642-32009-5_16

[BCFL22] Balbás, D., Catalano, D., Fiore, D., Lai, R.W.: Functional commitments for circuits from falsifiable assumptions. IACR Cryptol. ePrint Arch. (2022)

[BCS16] Ben-Sasson, E., Chiesa, A., Spooner, N.: Interactive oracle proofs. In: TCC (2016)

[BDFG21] Boneh, D., Drake, J., Fisch, B., Gabizon, A.: Halo infinite: proof-carrying data from additive polynomial commitments. In: Malkin, T., Peikert, C. (eds.) CRYPTO 2021. LNCS, vol. 12825, pp. 649–680. Springer, Cham (2021). https://doi.org/10.1007/978-3-030-84242-0_23

[BDN18] Boneh, D., Drijvers, M., Neven, G.: Compact multi-signatures for smaller blockchains. In: Peyrin, T., Galbraith, S. (eds.) ASIACRYPT 2018. LNCS, vol. 11273, pp. 435–464. Springer, Cham (2018). https://doi.org/10.1007/978-3-030-03329-3_15

[BFS20] Bünz, B., Fisch, B., Szepieniec, A.: Transparent SNARKs from DARK compilers. In: Canteaut, A., Ishai, Y. (eds.) EUROCRYPT 2020. LNCS, vol. 12105, pp. 677–706. Springer, Cham (2020). https://doi.org/10.1007/978-3-030-45721-1_24

[BGG+14] Boneh, D., et al.: Fully key-homomorphic encryption, arithmetic circuit ABE and compact garbled circuits. In: Nguyen, P.Q., Oswald, E. (eds.)

EUROCRYPT 2014. LNCS, vol. 8441, pp. 533–556. Springer, Heidelberg (2014). https://doi.org/10.1007/978-3-642-55220-5_30

[BGV11] Benabbas, S., Gennaro, R., Vahlis, Y.: Verifiable delegation of computation over large datasets. In: Rogaway, P. (ed.) CRYPTO 2011. LNCS, vol. 6841, pp. 111–131. Springer, Heidelberg (2011). https://doi.org/10.1007/978-3-642-22792-9_7

[BNO21] Boneh, D., Nguyen, W., Ozdemir, A.: Efficient functional commitments: how to commit to private functions. IACR Cryptol. ePrint Arch (2021)

[CCH+19] Canetti, R., et al.: Fiat-Shamir: from practice to theory. In: STOC, pp. 1082–1090 (2019)

[CF13] Catalano, D., Fiore, D.: Vector commitments and their applications. In: Kurosawa, K., Hanaoka, G. (eds.) PKC 2013. LNCS, vol. 7778, pp. 55–72. Springer, Heidelberg (2013). https://doi.org/10.1007/978-3-642-36362-7_5

[CFG+20] Campanelli, M., Fiore, D., Greco, N., Kolonelos, D., Nizzardo, L.: Incrementally aggregatable vector commitments and applications to verifiable decentralized storage. In: Moriai, S., Wang, H. (eds.) ASIACRYPT 2020. LNCS, vol. 12492, pp. 3–35. Springer, Cham (2020). https://doi.org/10.1007/978-3-030-64834-3_1

[CFM08] Catalano, D., Fiore, D., Messina, M.: Zero-knowledge sets with short proofs. In: Smart, N. (ed.) EUROCRYPT 2008. LNCS, vol. 4965, pp. 433–450. Springer, Heidelberg (2008). https://doi.org/10.1007/978-3-540-78967-3_25

[Che06] Cheon, J.H.: Security analysis of the strong Diffie-Hellman problem. In: Vaudenay, S. (ed.) EUROCRYPT 2006. LNCS, vol. 4004, pp. 1–11. Springer, Heidelberg (2006). https://doi.org/10.1007/11761679_1

[CHKP10] Cash, D., Hofheinz, D., Kiltz, E., Peikert, C.: Bonsai trees, or how to delegate a lattice basis. In: Gilbert, H. (ed.) EUROCRYPT 2010. LNCS, vol. 6110, pp. 523–552. Springer, Heidelberg (2010). https://doi.org/10.1007/978-3-642-13190-5_27

[CHM+20] Chiesa, A., Hu, Y., Maller, M., Mishra, P., Vesely, N., Ward, N.: Marlin: preprocessing zkSNARKs with universal and updatable SRS. In: Canteaut, A., Ishai, Y. (eds.) EUROCRYPT 2020. LNCS, vol. 12105, pp. 738–768. Springer, Cham (2020). https://doi.org/10.1007/978-3-030-45721-1_26

[CJJ21] Choudhuri, A. R., Jain, A., Jin, Z.: SNARGs for $\mathcal{P}$ from LWE. In: FOCS (2021)

[COS20] Chiesa, A., Ojha, D., Spooner, N.: Fractal: post-quantum and transparent recursive proofs from holography. In: Canteaut, A., Ishai, Y. (eds.) EUROCRYPT 2020. LNCS, vol. 12105, pp. 769–793. Springer, Cham (2020). https://doi.org/10.1007/978-3-030-45721-1_27

[CPSZ18] Chepurnoy, A., Papamanthou, C., Srinivasan, S., Zhang, Y.: EDRAX: a cryptocurrency with stateless transaction validation. IACR Cryptol. ePrint Arch (2018)

[dCP23] de Castro, L., Peikert, C.: Functional commitments for all functions, with transparent setup. In: EUROCRYPT (2023)

[DGKV22] Devadas, L., Goyal, R., Kalai, Y., Vaikuntanathan, V.: Rate-1 non-interactive arguments for batch-NP and applications. IACR Cryptol. ePrint Arch. (2022)

[FSZ22] Fleischhacker, N., Simkin, M., Zhang, Z.: Squirrel: efficient synchronized multi-signatures from lattices. In: ACM CCS (2022)

[GGH96] Goldreich, O., Goldwasser, S., Halevi, S.: Collision-free hashing from lattice problems. IACR Cryptol. ePrint Arch., p. 9 (1996)

[GPV08] Gentry, C., Peikert, C., Vaikuntanathan, V.: Trapdoors for hard lattices and new cryptographic constructions. In: STOC (2008)

[GRWZ20] Gorbunov, S., Reyzin, L., Wee, H., Zhang, Z.: Pointproofs: aggregating proofs for multiple vector commitments. In: ACM CCS (2020)

[GSW13] Gentry, C., Sahai, A., Waters, B.: Homomorphic encryption from learning with errors: conceptually-simpler, asymptotically-faster, attribute-based. In: Canetti, R., Garay, J.A. (eds.) CRYPTO 2013. LNCS, vol. 8042, pp. 75–92. Springer, Heidelberg (2013). https://doi.org/10.1007/978-3-642-40041-4_5

[GVW15] Gorbunov, S., Vaikuntanathan, V., Wichs, D.: Leveled fully homomorphic signatures from standard lattices. In: STOC (2015)

[GW11] Gentry, C., Wichs, D.: Separating succinct non-interactive arguments from all falsifiable assumptions. In: STOC (2011)

[GWC19] Gabizon, A., Williamson, Z.J., Ciobotaru, O.: PLONK: permutations over lagrange-bases for oecumenical noninteractive arguments of knowledge. IACR Cryptol. ePrint Arch. (2019)

[IKO07] Ishai, Y., Kushilevitz, E., Ostrovsky, R.: Efficient arguments without short PCPs. In: CCC (2007)

[Kil92] Kilian, J.: A note on efficient zero-knowledge proofs and arguments (extended abstract). In: STOC (1992)

[KZG10] Kate, A., Zaverucha, G.M., Goldberg, I.: Constant-size commitments to polynomials and their applications. In: Abe, M. (ed.) ASIACRYPT 2010. LNCS, vol. 6477, pp. 177–194. Springer, Heidelberg (2010). https://doi.org/10.1007/978-3-642-17373-8_11

[LLNW16] Libert, B., Ling, S., Nguyen, K., Wang, H.: Zero-knowledge arguments for lattice-based accumulators: logarithmic-size ring signatures and group signatures without trapdoors. In: Fischlin, M., Coron, J.-S. (eds.) EURO-CRYPT 2016. LNCS, vol. 9666, pp. 1–31. Springer, Heidelberg (2016). https://doi.org/10.1007/978-3-662-49896-5_1

[LM19] Lai, R.W.F., Malavolta, G.: Subvector commitments with application to succinct arguments. In: Boldyreva, A., Micciancio, D. (eds.) CRYPTO 2019. LNCS, vol. 11692, pp. 530–560. Springer, Cham (2019). https://doi.org/10.1007/978-3-030-26948-7_19

[LP20] Lipmaa, H., Pavlyk, K.: Succinct functional commitment for a large class of arithmetic circuits. In: Moriai, S., Wang, H. (eds.) ASIACRYPT 2020. LNCS, vol. 12493, pp. 686–716. Springer, Cham (2020). https://doi.org/10.1007/978-3-030-64840-4_23

[LRY16] Libert, B., Ramanna, S.C., Yung, M.: Functional commitment schemes: from polynomial commitments to pairing-based accumulators from simple assumptions. In: ICALP (2016)

[LY10] Libert, B., Yung, M.: Concise mercurial vector commitments and independent zero-knowledge sets with short proofs. In: Micciancio, D. (ed.) TCC 2010. LNCS, vol. 5978, pp. 499–517. Springer, Heidelberg (2010). https://doi.org/10.1007/978-3-642-11799-2_30

[MBKM19] Maller, M., Bowe, S., Kohlweiss, M., Meiklejohn, S.: Sonic: zero-knowledge snarks from linear-size universal and updatable structured reference strings. In: ACM CCS (2019)

[Mer87] Merkle, R.C.: A digital signature based on a conventional encryption function. In: Pomerance, C. (ed.) CRYPTO 1987. LNCS, vol. 293, pp. 369–378. Springer, Heidelberg (1988). https://doi.org/10.1007/3-540-48184-2_32

[Mic00] Micali, S.: Computationally sound proofs. SIAM J. Comput. **30**(4), 1253–1298 (2000)

[MP12] Micciancio, D., Peikert, C.: Trapdoors for lattices: simpler, tighter, faster, smaller. In: Pointcheval, D., Johansson, T. (eds.) EUROCRYPT 2012. LNCS, vol. 7237, pp. 700–718. Springer, Heidelberg (2012). https://doi.org/10.1007/978-3-642-29011-4_41

[Nao03] Naor, M.: On cryptographic assumptions and challenges. In: Boneh, D. (ed.) CRYPTO 2003. LNCS, vol. 2729, pp. 96–109. Springer, Heidelberg (2003). https://doi.org/10.1007/978-3-540-45146-4_6

[Nit21] Nitulescu, A.: SoK: vector commitments (2021). https://www.di.ens.fr/~nitulesc/files/vc-sok.pdf

[PPS21] Peikert, C., Pepin, Z., Sharp, C.: Vector and functional commitments from lattices. In: Nissim, K., Waters, B. (eds.) TCC 2021. LNCS, vol. 13044, pp. 480–511. Springer, Cham (2021). https://doi.org/10.1007/978-3-030-90456-2_16

[PS19] Peikert, C., Shiehian, S.: Noninteractive zero knowledge for NP from (plain) learning with errors. In: Boldyreva, A., Micciancio, D. (eds.) CRYPTO 2019. LNCS, vol. 11692, pp. 89–114. Springer, Cham (2019). https://doi.org/10.1007/978-3-030-26948-7_4

[PSTY13] Papamanthou, C., Shi, E., Tamassia, R., Yi, K.: Streaming authenticated data structures. In: Johansson, T., Nguyen, P.Q. (eds.) EUROCRYPT 2013. LNCS, vol. 7881, pp. 353–370. Springer, Heidelberg (2013). https://doi.org/10.1007/978-3-642-38348-9_22

[Res22] Protocol Labs Research. Vector commitment research day (2022). https://cryptonet.vercel.app/

[RMCI17] Reyzin, L., Meshkov, D., Chepurnoy, A., Ivanov, S.: Improving authenticated dynamic dictionaries, with applications to cryptocurrencies. In: Kiayias, A. (ed.) FC 2017. LNCS, vol. 10322, pp. 376–392. Springer, Cham (2017). https://doi.org/10.1007/978-3-319-70972-7_21

[TAB+20] Tomescu, A., Abraham, I., Buterin, V., Drake, J., Feist, D., Khovratovich, D.: Aggregatable subvector commitments for stateless cryptocurrencies. In: Galdi, C., Kolesnikov, V. (eds.) SCN 2020. LNCS, vol. 12238, pp. 45–64. Springer, Cham (2020). https://doi.org/10.1007/978-3-030-57990-6_3

[TXN20] Tomescu, A., Xia, Y., Newman, Z.: Authenticated dictionaries with cross-incremental proof (dis)aggregation. IACR Cryptol. ePrint Arch. (2020)

[WW22] Wee, H., Wu, D. J.: Succinct vector, polynomial, and functional commitments from lattices. IACR Cryptol. ePrint Arch., p. 1515 (2022)

Efficient Laconic Cryptography from Learning with Errors

Nico Döttling[1], Dimitris Kolonelos[2,3], Russell W. F. Lai[4(✉)], Chuanwei Lin[1],
Giulio Malavolta[5], and Ahmadreza Rahimi[5]

[1] CISPA Helmholtz Center for Information Security, Saarbrücken, Germany
chuanwei.lin@cispa.de
[2] IMDEA Software Institute, Madrid, Spain
dimitris.kolonelos@imdea.org
[3] Universidad Politecnica de Madrid, Madrid, Spain
[4] Aalto University, Espoo, Finland
russell.lai@aalto.fi
[5] Max Planck Institute for Security and Privacy, Bochum, Germany
ahmadreza.rahimi@mpi-sp.org

Abstract. Laconic cryptography is an emerging paradigm that enables cryptographic primitives with sublinear communication complexity in just two messages. In particular, a two-message protocol between Alice and Bob is called *laconic* if its communication and computation complexity are essentially independent of the size of Alice's input. This can be thought of as a dual notion of fully-homomorphic encryption, as it enables "Bob-optimized" protocols. This paradigm has led to tremendous progress in recent years. However, all existing constructions of laconic primitives are considered only of *theoretical interest*: They all rely on non-black-box cryptographic techniques, which are highly impractical.

This work shows that non-black-box techniques are not necessary for basic laconic cryptography primitives. We propose a *completely algebraic* construction of laconic encryption, a notion that we introduce in this work, which serves as the cornerstone of our framework. We prove that the scheme is secure under the standard Learning With Errors assumption (with polynomial modulus-to-noise ratio). We provide proof-of-concept implementations for the first time for laconic primitives, demonstrating the construction is indeed practical: For a database size of 2^{50}, encryption and decryption are in the order of single digit *milliseconds*.

Laconic encryption can be used as a black box to construct other laconic primitives. Specifically, we show how to construct:
- Laconic oblivious transfer
- Registration-based encryption scheme
- Laconic private-set intersection protocol

All of the above have essentially optimal parameters and similar practical efficiency. Furthermore, our laconic encryption can be preprocessed such that the online encryption step is entirely combinatorial and therefore much more efficient. Using similar techniques, we also obtain identity-based encryption with an unbounded identity space and tight security proof (in the standard model).

C. Hazay and M. Stam (Eds.): EUROCRYPT 2023, LNCS 14006, pp. 417–446, 2023.
https://doi.org/10.1007/978-3-031-30620-4_14

1 Introduction

Laconic cryptography [17,20,22,40] is an emerging paradigm to securely compute on large amounts of data in just two messages, while incurring very small communication. Specifically, in the laconic setting the receiver Alice has an input of very large size, whereas we typically think of the sender Bob's input as smaller in size. In the first message, Alice publishes a succinct hash h of her input D, which may be thought of as a large database $D \in \{0,1\}^n$. Such a compressing hash function cannot be unkeyed, therefore laconic protocols also rely on public parameters, which are typically also required to be succinct[1]. Given the hash h, Bob can encrypt his input x with respect to h, obtaining a succinct ciphertext ctxt. Importantly, the workload of Bob should also be independent of n. Such a ciphertext ctxt enables Alice to compute a joint function of her input D and Bob's input x, while Bob has the guarantee that Alice learns nothing but the legitimate function output. The specific choice of the function f computed by such a protocol leads to different laconic primitives:

- In laconic OT [17], Bob's input consists of an index i and two messages m_0 and m_1. The function f is given by $f(D,(i,m_0,m_1)) = (i, m_{D[i]})$, i.e. Alice learns the index i, and if the i-th bit of the database D is 0 she learns m_0, otherwise m_1. The setting of laconic OT typically imposes an additional efficiency requirement concerning Alice. Concretely, we require Alice's second phase to have a runtime essentially independent of n.
- In laconic function evaluation (LFE) [40], Alice's input D is a (large) boolean circuit C, and the function computed by an LFE protocol is $f(C,x) = C(x)$. The construction provided in [40] satisfies a somewhat relaxed succinctness guarantee: While the size of the communication does not scale with the size of the circuit C, it scales polynomially with the depth of C. Furthermore, the runtime of the second phase of Alice scales linearly with the size of C.

Implications. The notion of laconic OT in particular has had broader implications: The core-ideas underlying laconic OT led to a series of constructions of identity-based encryption (IBE) from weaker assumptions [15,18,19,21] and gave rise to the notion of registration-based encryption (RBE) [24,25,33]. These constructions make essential use of the above-mentioned more stringent efficiency-property of the laconic OT constructions they are based on. Consequently, these primitives are not known to be generically constructible from LFE.

Furthermore, the techniques developed in the context of laconic cryptography were key to making progress on a broad range of problems: trapdoor functions from the computational Diffie-Hellman assumption [23], private-information retrieval (PIR) from the decisional Diffie-Hellman assumption [22], two-round multi-party computation protocols from minimal assumptions [8,26,28], adaptively secure garbled circuits [27], laconic conditional disclosure of secrets [20], and laconic private set intersection [3,7].

---

[1] That is, independent or at least sublinear in n.

Reverse Delegation. Laconic cryptography can be seen as enabling *reverse delegation* without requiring additional rounds of communication. In a standard delegation scheme, a user outsources its computation to an untrusted server with the goal of learning the output while keeping its input private. The canonical cryptographic tool that enables delegation is fully-homomorphic encryption (FHE) [29], since it allows the server to perform the computation without knowing the user's input. Reverse delegation allows a user (Bob, in our previous example) to delegate the computation completely to the server (Alice) while also letting her learn the output of the computation and nothing beyond that. For instance, [17] provided a protocol to let Bob reverse-delegate RAM computations to Alice, such that Bob's overhead and the size of the communication scales only with runtime of the RAM program, but not with the size of Alice's (large) input. Likewise, the laconic function evaluation scheme of [40] allows to reverse-delegate circuit computations to Alice, while incurring a communication overhead that only scales with the depth of the circuit.

A Non-blackbox "Barrier" for Practicality. So far, the aforementioned progress in designing new cryptographic primitives has been almost exclusively of *theoretical interest*. In essence, the lack of practicality of these new solutions can be explained by their *non-blackbox* use of underlying cryptographic building blocks. For example, essentially all known constructions of laconic OT involve a re-encryption step, also called *deferred encryption* [15], which gives the receiver Alice the ability to produce ciphertexts under keys that were not known to the sender Bob at the time of encryption. In the above-mentioned constructions, this re-encryption step is implemented using garbled circuits [42] for circuits which perform public-key cryptographic operations. The non-black box use of cryptographic primitives is such a grave source of inefficiency that, to the best of our knowledge, not even the basic laconic OT has ever been implemented as a proof of concept. On a slightly different note, we remark that while the LFE scheme of [40] does not make use of garbled circuits, it relies on a different non-blackbox mechanism based on FHE to bootstrap a weaker notion called attribute-based LFE into fully-fledged LFE.

In summary, the present state of affairs sees laconic cryptography as a powerful theoretical tool for enabling new cryptographic primitives and realizing powerful notions from weaker assumptions. However, the resulting schemes are practically inefficient, thus calling into question the relevance of this framework beyond theoretical feasibility results. Motivated by this gap, we ask:

Can we realize truly efficient laconic cryptography?

Towards a positive resolution to this question, it seems insufficient to optimize existing techniques. Instead, a conceptual reworking of basic laconic primitives will be required.

1.1 Our Results

This work shows that garbled circuits (and other non-black box cryptographic techniques) are not needed to construct laconic cryptography. We establish a new paradigm for constructing *concretely efficient* laconic cryptographic schemes based on the hardness of the standard learning with errors (LWE) problem with a polynomial modulus-to-noise ratio. In contrast to prior works, we show that our schemes are practical with a proof of concept implementation. In the following, we discuss our contributions in more detail.

Laconic Encryption. We propose the notion of *laconic encryption* as the central abstraction of our framework. Laconic encryption allows Alice to construct a binary tree whose leaves are public keys $(\mathsf{pk}_1, \ldots, \mathsf{pk}_n)$ and sends the root of the tree to Bob. Given only the root of the tree and an index ind, Bob can then encrypt a message with respect to $\mathsf{pk}_{\mathsf{ind}}$, which can only be decrypted with the corresponding secret key $\mathsf{sk}_{\mathsf{ind}}$. Such a scheme is called laconic since Alice's message is independent of n, as she only sends the root of the tree.

We then show how to construct laconic encryption *efficiently* and with *(asymptotically) optimal parameters* without relying on garbled circuits or other non-black box cryptographic techniques. At a technical level, our construction relies on the algebraic properties of the SIS-based hash tree. It exploits the gadget matrix to efficiently re-encrypt the message layer-by-layer. In order to demonstrate the security of the scheme, we introduce a new variant of the (ring/module) LWE problem, in which the adversary is also given a leakage on the error. Then we prove that this problem is as hard as the standard (ring/module) LWE problem, with an essentially tight reduction. Our proof relies on spectral analysis of positive definite matrices, a subject of independent interest.

Applications. We show how laconic encryption enables a wide range of laconic cryptographic primitives with minimal overhead. The following constructions use laconic encryption in a black-box sense, and the additional methods required are combinatorial. That is, all of the resulting schemes are *concretely efficient* and have near-optimal parameters. Specifically, we show how to construct:

- **Laconic OT**: As an immediate application of laconic encryption, we construct a laconic OT protocol with essentially optimal parameters.
- **Registration-Based Encryption**: Registration-based encryption (RBE) is a notion recently introduced in [24] to solve the key-escrow problem for identity-based encryption (IBE) while preserving the "encrypt with respect to identity" functionality. Laconic encryption enables the first concretely efficient RBE construction that the size of the public parameters scales *logarithmically* with the number of users.
- **Laconic Private-Set Intersection**: Private-set intersection (PSI) allows Alice and Bob to check whether they have a common item in their database without revealing anything about other items. Laconic encryption allows us to construct an efficient *laconic* PSI protocol where the communication complexity is independent of the size of Alice's database.

Optimizations and Extensions. We explore a number of optimizations and extensions for our laconic encryption construction. First, we show that the encryption algorithm can be *pre-processed*: In an input-independent offline phase, the encryptor can prepare auxiliary information at essentially the same cost as the encryption algorithm. In an online phase, where the message msg and the index ind are known, the encryptor can use the auxiliary information prepared earlier to produce a correctly-formed ciphertext. Importantly, the online phase is entirely combinatorial, and all public-key operations happen in the offline phase.

Second, we explore the possibility of plugging-in different encryption schemes in our construction. Natively, our laconic encryption supports only dual-Regev ciphertexts [30], whereas for some applications it may be desirable to use support other encryption schemes. We show how our scheme can be adapted to support a large class of algorithms, which includes LPN-based encryption [5] and recently NIST-standardized lattice-based schemes [10]. To solve this challenge, we develop a new special-purpose randomized encoding scheme, which may be of independent interest.

Finally, we show that our construction of laconic encryption can be turned into that of identity-based encryption (IBE) [9] with similar efficiency properties. Our IBE is the first scheme that simultaneously achieves: (i) Constant-size public parameters, (ii) an *unbounded* identity space, (iii) a tight proof of (adaptive) security against a standard assumption (specifically, LWE).

Implementation and Benchmark. To demonstrate the practicality of our laconic encryption scheme, we implemented a proof of concept in Go (see the full version for more details). We ran the benchmarks for the scheme with a database size/index space of 2^{50} and achieved encryption and decryption times below 10 ms on a personal computer. We believe these times can be improved using further optimizations, which are beyond the scope of this work.

1.2 Related Work

We mention prior works that study practical variants of laconic cryptographic primitives. In [7] the authors show a variant of laconic private-set intersection that is practically efficient and leads to substantial improvements in real-world protocols. However, the variant that is implemented has a long common reference string, linear in the size of Alice's database D; thus it is not fully laconic.

In [35] the authors propose the notion of registered attribute-based encryption, as an extension of the notion of RBE, and they show a constructions based on bilinear pairings. Compared to our work, their scheme has a long common reference string (in fact, quadratic in n), the runtime of the key generation and registration algorithms is linear in n, and they have an a-priori bound on the number of users. On the flip-side, they achieve the attribute-based functionality, that we do not consider in this work.

Another recent work [31] proposes the first practically efficient registration-based encryption scheme, and shows the first proof of concept implementation. Contrary to this work, their scheme is asymptotically only sublinear in the size of D (specifically, $\sqrt{n}$ as opposed to $\mathsf{polylog}(n)$), and requires an a-priori bound on n. Furthermore, they rely on the hardness of problems over bilinear pairings and thus their scheme is immediately insecure in the quantum settings.

2   Technical Overview

We give a brief overview of the new ideas and the technical innovations introduced in this work. We start by describing the new notion of laconic encryption, how to construct it efficiently from the standard LWE assumptions, and the challenges that arise during the security proofs. Then we outline the new cryptographic schemes that are enabled by this new notion and possible optimizations and extensions. In favor of a more intuitive description, the following outline considers the special case of $\mathbb{Z}$-lattices; however, in the technical sections, we prove all of our statements for the more general $\mathcal{R}$-module settings.

2.1   Laconic Encryption

Before delving into the description of our scheme, we introduce the syntax of laconic encryption, and we recall how prior work (implicitly) addresses the challenges needed to build this notion.

Syntax and Properties. A laconic encryption scheme allows Alice to (iteratively) construct a digest (e.g., via a Merkle hash tree) of public keys $(\mathsf{pk}_1, \ldots, \mathsf{pk}_n)$ where $(\mathsf{pk}_i, \mathsf{sk}_i) \leftarrow \mathsf{KGen}(\mathsf{pp})$ and pp can be thought of as a uniformly random string, which is common to all participants. We denote by st the message that Alice sends to Bob, which consists of the digest (e.g., the root of the Merkle tree). Importantly, the size of pp and st is only polynomial in the security parameter, and in particular, it does not depend on n. On input a message msg and an index $\mathsf{ind} \in [n]$, Bob can then compute a ciphertext $\mathsf{ctxt} \leftarrow \mathsf{Enc}(\mathsf{pp}, \mathsf{st}, \mathsf{ind}, \mathsf{msg})$. Correctness requires that anyone possessing the corresponding secret key can decrypt ctxt, more specifically:

$$\mathsf{msg} = \mathsf{Dec}(\mathsf{sk}_{\mathsf{ind}}, \mathsf{wit}_{\mathsf{ind}}, \mathsf{ctxt})$$

where $\mathsf{wit}_{\mathsf{ind}}$ is some (public) auxiliary information, whose size is logarithmic in n. The reader can think of this information as being the Merkle tree opening, i.e., the root-to-leaf path, of the key $\mathsf{pk}_{\mathsf{ind}}$. For security, we require that if the adversary does not know the secret key associated with index ind (or if no key is added to the tree at that particular index), then:

$$\mathsf{Enc}(\mathsf{pp}, \mathsf{st}, \mathsf{ind}, \mathsf{msg}_0) \approx \mathsf{Enc}(\mathsf{pp}, \mathsf{st}, \mathsf{ind}, \mathsf{msg}_1).$$

In fact, we will require (and prove) a slight strengthening of this property, i.e., that ciphertexts should look pseudorandom to anyone who cannot decrypt them.

Prior Works. To gain some intuition on why constructing laconic encryption is a challenging problem, it is useful to recall how prior works [17] (implicitly) build this cryptographic primitive. Loosely speaking, their main leverage is a construction of a structured two-to-one hash function Hash (which can be constructed from a variety of computational assumptions) that supports an *encryption* functionality. More specifically, given a digest $d \leftarrow \mathsf{Hash}(D)$, Bob can compute a ciphertext $\mathsf{ctxt} \leftarrow \mathsf{Enc}(d, \mathsf{ind}, (\mathsf{msg}_0, \mathsf{msg}_1))$ that allows Alice (who knows the database D) to recover $\mathsf{msg}_{D_{\mathsf{ind}}}$, whereas the message $\mathsf{msg}_{D_{1-\mathsf{ind}}}$ remains computationally hidden. While this looks like a promising start, it should be noted that the hash function is only two-to-one, and therefore the size of the digest d is only half that of the original database D. If one were to naively recurse this scheme, the encryption algorithm would quickly start running in exponential time.

To circumvent the runtime issue, the strategy of [17] is to rely on garbled circuits [42]. More specifically, to boost the compression of the hash function, they define a binary tree of hash values and use garbled circuits to (asymptotically efficiently) implement a re-encryption gadget from one layer to another. Given a digest $d_i \leftarrow \mathsf{Hash}(D_{i+1})$, where $D_{i+1} = (d_{i+1,0}, d_{i+1,1})$ are the digests at a lower layer, the encryption algorithm uses the above procedure to encrypt the *labels* of a garbled circuit, that internally runs the encryption Enc for the layer below. Crucially, the size of the labels is independent of the size of the garbled circuit (except for its input) and therefore this encryption strategy can be recursed without incurring an exponential blow-up. Although this framework achieves asymptotically optimal parameters, it is prohibitively expensive to use garbled circuits for public-key operations. In contrast, our strategy (described below in detail) will bypass this barrier by leveraging the algebraic properties of a particular hash function.

Our Approach. As hinted above, a strategy of constructing laconic encryption is to design a mechanism allowing to "encrypt with respect to a Merkle tree opening", and successfully executing this strategy requires an "encryption-friendly" hash function. Our starting point is the following variant of Ajtai's [2,32] collision-resistant hash function based on the short integer solution (SIS) assumption:

$$f(\mathbf{x}_0, \mathbf{x}_1) := \mathbf{A}_0(-\mathbf{G}^{-1}(\mathbf{x}_0)) + \mathbf{A}_1(-\mathbf{G}^{-1}(\mathbf{x}_1)) \bmod q$$

where $\mathbf{A}_0, \mathbf{A}_1 \in \mathbb{Z}_q^{n \times m}$ are uniformly random matrices with $m \approx n \log q$, $\mathbf{x}_0, \mathbf{x}_1 \in \mathbb{Z}_q^n$ are vectors, and $\mathbf{G}^{-1}$ denote the binary-decomposition operator (so that for any $\mathbf{x} \in \mathbb{Z}_q^n$ we have $\mathbf{G} \cdot \mathbf{G}^{-1}(\mathbf{x}) = \mathbf{x}$). A very similar hash function was used in [36] to build lattice-based Merkle-tree accumulators, ring signatures, and group signatures. At first glance, it may seem that the hash function f is not encryption-friendly since the binary-decomposition operation $\mathbf{G}^{-1}$ is highly non-linear. What enables us to encrypt with respect to a Merkle tree opening is the crucial observation that a hash chain formed by f *induces* a linear relation.

More concretely, consider the Merkle tree built using the hash function f where the node indexed by $\mathsf{str} \in \{0,1\}^*$ is labeled by $\mathbf{y}_{\mathsf{str}}$. Suppose that $\mathbf{u}_{\mathsf{str}} = -\mathbf{G}^{-1}(\mathbf{y}_{\mathsf{str}})$ for each $\mathsf{str} \in \{0,1\}^*$. Closing into the top of the tree, we observe that $(\mathbf{u}_0, \mathbf{u}_1)$ is a short (in fact binary) vector satisfying the linear relation:

$$\begin{pmatrix} \mathbf{A}_0 & \mathbf{A}_1 \\ \mathbf{G} & \mathbf{0} \end{pmatrix} \begin{pmatrix} \mathbf{u}_0 \\ \mathbf{u}_1 \end{pmatrix} = \begin{pmatrix} \mathbf{y}_\epsilon \\ -\mathbf{y}_0 \end{pmatrix} \bmod q.$$

where $\mathbf{y}_\epsilon$ is the node denoting the root of the tree. In other words, the vector $(\mathbf{u}_0, \mathbf{u}_1)$ is a valid solution to the (inhomogeneous) SIS instance

$$\left(\begin{pmatrix} \mathbf{A}_0 \; \mathbf{A}_1 \\ \mathbf{G} \quad \mathbf{0} \end{pmatrix}, \begin{pmatrix} \mathbf{y}_\epsilon \\ -\mathbf{y}_0 \end{pmatrix} \right).$$

Likewise, $(\mathbf{u}_0, \mathbf{u}_1)$ is also a valid solution to the (inhomogeneous) SIS instance

$$\left(\begin{pmatrix} \mathbf{A}_0 \; \mathbf{A}_1 \\ \mathbf{0} \quad \mathbf{G} \end{pmatrix}, \begin{pmatrix} \mathbf{y}_\epsilon \\ -\mathbf{y}_1 \end{pmatrix} \right).$$

Dual-Regev Encryption. It turns out that this structure synergizes remarkably well with the dual-Regev encryption scheme [30]. Recall that in the dual-Regev encryption scheme [30], whose security is based on the standard LWE assumption, a public key is a SIS instance and the corresponding secret key is the SIS solution. Specifically, in the following assume that the matrix $\mathbf{A} = (\mathbf{A}_0 \; \mathbf{A}_1)$ is part of the public parameters. Further assume that $\mathbf{y}_0$ and $\mathbf{y}_1$ are dual-Regev public keys with respect to $\mathbf{A}$. That is, for $b \in \{0,1\}$ we generate $\mathbf{y}_b$ by choosing a uniformly random $\mathbf{w}_b \in \{0,1\}^{2m}$ and set $\mathbf{y}_b = \mathbf{A} \cdot \mathbf{w}_b \bmod q$. Here, $\mathbf{w}_b$ is the secret key corresponding to $\mathbf{y}_b$. By the leftover-hash-lemma [34,41], the $\mathbf{y}_b$ are statistically close to uniform. To encrypt a message msg under $\mathbf{y}_b$, we choose an LWE secret $\mathbf{r}_1$ and compute a ciphertext $(\mathbf{c}_1, d_1)$ via

$$\mathbf{c}_1 \approx \mathbf{r}_1^\mathsf{T} \cdot \mathbf{A} \bmod q,$$
$$d_1 \approx \mathbf{r}_1^\mathsf{T} \cdot \mathbf{y}_b + \mathsf{Encode}(\mathsf{msg}) \bmod q.$$

Here, we use the "$\approx$" notation to omit the LWE error. The function $\mathsf{Encode}(\cdot)$ protects the message msg against small errors, a popular choice is to encode a message bit msg in the most-significant bit, i.e. $\mathsf{Encode}(\cdot) = \frac{q}{2} \cdot \mathsf{msg}$. To decrypt a ciphertext $(\mathbf{c}_1, d_1)$ using a secret key $\mathbf{w}_b$ we compute

$$d_1 - \mathbf{c}_1^\mathsf{T} \cdot \mathbf{w}_b \approx \mathbf{r}_1^\mathsf{T} \cdot \mathbf{y}_b + \mathsf{Encode}(\mathsf{msg}) - \mathbf{r}_1^\mathsf{T} \cdot \underbrace{\mathbf{A} \cdot \mathbf{w}_b}_{=\mathbf{y}_b} = \mathsf{Encode}(\mathsf{msg}) \bmod q,$$

from which the message msg can be efficiently recovered.

Encrypting to Hash Values. Now assume that we are not given $\mathbf{y}_0$ and $\mathbf{y}_1$, but only their hash value

$$\mathbf{y} = \mathbf{A} \cdot \begin{pmatrix} -\mathbf{G}^{-1}(\mathbf{y}_0) \\ -\mathbf{G}^{-1}(\mathbf{y}_1) \end{pmatrix} \bmod q.$$

Our goal is to produce a ciphertext "for the key $\mathbf{y}_b$" given only the hash value $\mathbf{y}$. Towards this goal, let us examine what happens when we generate a dual-Regev encryption scheme with respect to the "public key"

$$\mathsf{pk} := \left(\begin{pmatrix} \mathbf{A}_0 \; \mathbf{A}_1 \\ \mathbf{G} \quad \mathbf{0} \end{pmatrix}, \begin{pmatrix} \mathbf{y} \\ \mathbf{0} \end{pmatrix} \right),$$

Choosing LWE secrets $\mathbf{r}_0$ and $\mathbf{r}_1$ we compute a ciphertext $\mathsf{ctxt} = (\mathbf{c}, d)$ by

$$\mathbf{c}^{\mathsf{T}} \approx (\mathbf{r}_0^{\mathsf{T}}, \mathbf{r}_1^{\mathsf{T}}) \cdot \begin{pmatrix} \mathbf{A}_0\ \mathbf{A}_1 \\ \mathbf{G}\ \ 0 \end{pmatrix} = \mathbf{r}_0^{\mathsf{T}} \cdot \mathbf{A} + \mathbf{r}_1^{\mathsf{T}} \cdot (\mathbf{G}\ 0) \bmod q$$

$$d \approx (\mathbf{r}_0^{\mathsf{T}}, \mathbf{r}_1^{\mathsf{T}}) \cdot \begin{pmatrix} \mathbf{y} \\ 0 \end{pmatrix} + \mathsf{Encode(msg)} = \mathbf{r}_0^{\mathsf{T}} \cdot \mathbf{y} + \mathsf{Encode(msg)} \bmod q.$$

If we "decrypt" the ciphertext using $(\mathbf{u}_0 = -\mathbf{G}^{-1}(\mathbf{y}_0), \mathbf{u}_1 = -\mathbf{G}^{-1}(\mathbf{y}_1))$ as the secret key, we obtain

$$d - \mathbf{c}^{\mathsf{T}} \cdot \begin{pmatrix} \mathbf{u}_0 \\ \mathbf{u}_1 \end{pmatrix} \approx \mathbf{r}_0^{\mathsf{T}} \cdot \mathbf{y} + \mathsf{Encode(msg)} - \underbrace{\mathbf{r}_0^{\mathsf{T}} \cdot (\mathbf{A}_0\ \mathbf{A}_1) \cdot \begin{pmatrix} \mathbf{u}_0 \\ \mathbf{u}_1 \end{pmatrix}}_{=\mathbf{y}} - \underbrace{\mathbf{r}_1^{\mathsf{T}} \cdot (\mathbf{G}\ 0) \cdot \begin{pmatrix} \mathbf{u}_0 \\ \mathbf{u}_1 \end{pmatrix}}_{=-\mathbf{y}_0}$$

$$= \mathbf{r}_1^{\mathsf{T}} \cdot \mathbf{y}_0 + \mathsf{Encode(msg)} \bmod q.$$

Consequently, this "decryption operation" has produced (part of) a ciphertext encrypted under the public key $\mathbf{y}_0$! Analogously, if we use the public key

$$\mathsf{pk} := \left(\begin{pmatrix} \mathbf{A}_0\ \mathbf{A}_1 \\ 0\ \ \mathbf{G} \end{pmatrix}, \begin{pmatrix} \mathbf{y} \\ 0 \end{pmatrix} \right),$$

the above decryption operation would result in a ciphertext component $\mathbf{r}_1^{\mathsf{T}} \cdot \mathbf{y}_1 + \mathsf{Encode(msg)} \bmod q$. Thus, decryption of such ciphertext with $(\mathbf{u}_0 = -\mathbf{G}^{-1}(\mathbf{y}_0), \mathbf{u}_1 = -\mathbf{G}^{-1}(\mathbf{y}_1))$ is effectively a re-encryption to either public key $\mathbf{y}_0$ or $\mathbf{y}_1$.

To make such a ciphertext decryptable under one of the corresponding secret keys, we add an additional ciphertext component $\mathbf{c}_1^{\mathsf{T}} = \mathbf{r}_1^{\mathsf{T}} \cdot \mathbf{A} + \mathbf{e}_1 \bmod q$ to ctxt. Then, a ciphertext ctxt for $\mathbf{y}_b$ comprises of

$$\mathbf{c}^{\mathsf{T}} \approx \mathbf{r}_0^{\mathsf{T}} \cdot \mathbf{A} + \mathbf{r}_1^{\mathsf{T}} \cdot ((1 - b) \cdot \mathbf{G}\ b \cdot \mathbf{G}) \bmod q$$

$$\mathbf{c}_1^{\mathsf{T}} \approx \mathbf{r}_1^{\mathsf{T}} \cdot \mathbf{A} \bmod q$$

$$d \approx \mathbf{r}_0^{\mathsf{T}} \cdot \mathbf{y} + \mathsf{Encode(msg)} \bmod q.$$

Finally, observe that it doesn't matter if the $\mathbf{y}_b$ are actually dual-Regev public keys or itself a hash value, the ciphertext structures are identical! Hence, for a larger tree we can apply this mechanism recursively, which results in one additional ciphertext component $\mathbf{c}_i^{\mathsf{T}} \approx \mathbf{r}_i^{\mathsf{T}} \cdot \mathbf{A} + \mathbf{r}_1^{\mathsf{T}} \cdot ((1 - b_i) \cdot \mathbf{G}\ b_i \cdot \mathbf{G}) \bmod q$ *per level of the tree*, where the b_i define the path through the tree.

Security of the Construction. We will now focus on establishing the security of this construction with the goal of basing security on the LWE assumption. For this purpose, we need to consider the error terms in our construction explicitly. Let $\mathbf{A} = (\mathbf{A}_0\ \mathbf{A}_1)$. A ciphertext $\mathsf{ctxt} = (\mathbf{c}, \mathbf{c}_1, d)$ for $b = 0$ is computed by

$$\mathbf{c}^{\mathsf{T}} = \mathbf{r}_0^{\mathsf{T}} \cdot \mathbf{A} + \mathbf{r}_1^{\mathsf{T}} \cdot (\mathbf{G}\ 0) + \mathbf{e} \bmod q$$

$$\mathbf{c}_1^{\mathsf{T}} = \mathbf{r}_1^{\mathsf{T}} \cdot \mathbf{A} + \mathbf{e}_1 \bmod q$$

$$d = \mathbf{r}_0^{\mathsf{T}} \cdot \mathbf{y} + e^* + \mathsf{Encode(msg)} \bmod q,$$

where $\mathbf{e}$, $\mathbf{e}_1$ and e^* are short error vectors.

On the face of it, this looks almost like a classical LWE encryption. Hence, one might try to reduce security directly to the LWE problem. That is, given LWE samples $(\mathbf{A}, \mathbf{v}^\mathsf{T} = \mathbf{r}_0^\mathsf{T} \cdot \mathbf{A} + \mathbf{e}^\mathsf{T} \bmod q)$ and $(\mathbf{y}, v = \mathbf{r}_0^\mathsf{T} \cdot \mathbf{y} + e^* \bmod q)$ we can simulate a ciphertext by computing

$$\mathbf{c}^\mathsf{T} = \mathbf{v}^\mathsf{T} + \mathbf{r}_1^\mathsf{T} \cdot (\mathbf{G} \; \mathbf{0}) \bmod q$$

$$\mathbf{c}_1^\mathsf{T} = \mathbf{r}_1^\mathsf{T} \cdot \mathbf{A} + \mathbf{e}_1 \bmod q$$

$$d = v + \mathsf{Encode}(\mathsf{msg}) \bmod q.$$

By replacing $\mathbf{v}^\mathsf{T}$ and v by uniformly random values, as per the LWE assumption, the term d now hides msg and security follows.

However, upon closer inspection there is a problem with this approach: The matrix $\mathbf{A}$ and the vector $\mathbf{y}^\mathsf{T}$ are *not* independent from the view of an adversary. Specifically, the adversary knows an explicit relation between $\mathbf{A}$ and $\mathbf{y}^\mathsf{T}$, namely

$$\mathbf{y}^\mathsf{T} = \mathbf{A}_0 \cdot (-\mathbf{G}^{-1}(\mathbf{y}_0)) + \mathbf{A}_0 \cdot (-\mathbf{G}^{-1}(\mathbf{y}_1)) =: \mathbf{A} \cdot \mathbf{z} \bmod q,$$

as $\mathbf{y}_0$ and $\mathbf{y}_1$ are known to the adversary. Here $\mathbf{z} := \begin{pmatrix} -\mathbf{G}^{-1}(\mathbf{y}_0) \\ -\mathbf{G}^{-1}(\mathbf{y}_1) \end{pmatrix}$ is a binary (and thus short) vector (denoted $(\mathbf{u}_0, \mathbf{u}_1)$ above). For this reason, $\mathbf{v}^\mathsf{T} = \mathbf{r}_0^\mathsf{T} \cdot \mathbf{A} + \mathbf{e}^\mathsf{T} \bmod q$ and $v = \mathbf{r}_0^\mathsf{T} \cdot \mathbf{y} + e^* \bmod q$ are easily distinguishable from uniformly random values: It holds that $v - \mathbf{v}^\mathsf{T} \cdot \mathbf{z} = e^* - \mathbf{e}^\mathsf{T} \cdot \mathbf{z} \bmod q$ is short, whereas for uniformly random $\mathbf{v}^\mathsf{T}$ and v this expression is, with high probability, not short.

Drowning Out Correlations. However, there is a fairly routine solution to this issue using a technique called *drowning*. The idea is, given LWE samples $(\mathbf{A}, \mathbf{v}^\mathsf{T} = \mathbf{r}_0^\mathsf{T} \cdot \mathbf{A} + \mathbf{e} \bmod q)$, to *simulate* v from $\mathbf{v}$ and $\mathbf{z}$ by computing it via

$$v \approx \mathbf{v}^\mathsf{T} \cdot \mathbf{z} = (\mathbf{r}_0^\mathsf{T} \cdot \mathbf{A} + \mathbf{e}^\mathsf{T}) \cdot \mathbf{z} = \mathbf{r}_0^\mathsf{T} \cdot \mathbf{A} \cdot \mathbf{z} + \mathbf{e}^\mathsf{T} \cdot \mathbf{z} = \mathbf{r}_0^\mathsf{T} \cdot \mathbf{y} + \mathbf{e}^\mathsf{T} \cdot \mathbf{z} \bmod q.$$

Yet, now the error terms in $\mathbf{v}^\mathsf{T}$ and v are obliviously correlated. To get rid of this correlation, we can opt to *drown* it out: If e^* is chosen from a suitable short distribution which produces super-polynomially larger values than $\mathbf{e}^\mathsf{T} \cdot \mathbf{z}$, then it holds that $\mathbf{e}^\mathsf{T} \cdot \mathbf{z} + e^* \approx_s e^*$, i.e. $\mathbf{e}^\mathsf{T} \cdot \mathbf{z} + e^*$ and e^* are statistically close. Hence, we can simulate v by computing $v = \mathbf{v}^\mathsf{T} \cdot \mathbf{z} + e^* \bmod q$.

Hence, our security proof now proceeds as follows. Given LWE samples $(\mathbf{A}, \mathbf{v}^\mathsf{T} = \mathbf{r}_0^\mathsf{T} \cdot \mathbf{A} + \mathbf{e}^\mathsf{T} \bmod q)$ we can simulate a ciphertext $\mathsf{ctxt} = (\mathbf{c}, \mathbf{c}_1, d)$ by sampling e^* and setting

$$\mathbf{c}^\mathsf{T} = \mathbf{v}^\mathsf{T} + \mathbf{r}_1^\mathsf{T} \cdot (\mathbf{G} \; \mathbf{0}) \bmod q$$

$$\mathbf{c}_1^\mathsf{T} = \mathbf{r}_1^\mathsf{T} \cdot \mathbf{A} + \mathbf{e}_1 \bmod q$$

$$d = \mathbf{v}^\mathsf{T} \cdot \mathbf{z} + e^* + \mathsf{Encode}(\mathsf{msg}) \bmod q.$$

If $(\mathbf{A}, \mathbf{v})$ are well-formed LWE samples, then by the above discussion,

$$d = \mathbf{v}^\mathsf{T} \cdot \mathbf{z} + e^* + \mathsf{Encode}(\mathsf{msg})$$

$$= \mathbf{r}_0^\mathsf{T} \cdot \mathbf{y} + \mathbf{e}^\mathsf{T} \cdot \mathbf{z} + e^* + \mathsf{Encode}(\mathsf{msg})$$

$$\approx_s \mathbf{r}_0^\mathsf{T} \cdot \mathbf{y} + e^* + \mathsf{Encode}(\mathsf{msg}) \bmod q,$$

i.e. such a ctxt $= (\mathbf{c}, \mathbf{c}_1, d)$ is statistically close to a real ciphertext. Under the LWE assumption, we can now replace $\mathbf{v}$ with a uniformly random $\mathbf{v}'$ and get

$$\mathbf{c}^{\mathsf{T}} = \mathbf{v}'^{\mathsf{T}} + \mathbf{r}_1^{\mathsf{T}} \cdot (\mathbf{G}\ \mathbf{0}) \bmod q$$

$$d = \mathbf{v}'^{\mathsf{T}} \cdot \mathbf{z} + e^* + \mathsf{Encode}(\mathsf{msg}) \bmod q.$$

Now, since $\mathbf{v}'$ is uniformly random, we can equivalently choose it by computing $\mathbf{v}'^{\mathsf{T}} = \mathbf{v}''^{\mathsf{T}} - \mathbf{r}_1^{\mathsf{T}}(\mathbf{G}\ \mathbf{0})$, where $\mathbf{v}''$ is also chosen uniformly random. That is, we compute ctxt $= (\mathbf{c}, \mathbf{c}_1, d)$ by

$$\mathbf{c}^{\mathsf{T}} = \mathbf{v}''^{\mathsf{T}}$$

$$\mathbf{c}_1^{\mathsf{T}} = \mathbf{r}_1^{\mathsf{T}} \cdot \mathbf{A} + \mathbf{e}_1 \bmod q$$

$$d = (\mathbf{v}''^{\mathsf{T}} - \mathbf{r}_1^{\mathsf{T}} \cdot (\mathbf{G}\ \mathbf{0})) \cdot \mathbf{z} + e^* + \mathsf{Encode}(\mathsf{msg})$$

$$= \mathbf{v}''^{\mathsf{T}} \cdot \mathbf{z} - \mathbf{r}_1^{\mathsf{T}} \cdot (\mathbf{G}\ \mathbf{0}) \cdot \mathbf{z} + e^* + \mathsf{Encode}(\mathsf{msg})$$

$$= \mathbf{v}''^{\mathsf{T}} \cdot \mathbf{z} + \mathbf{r}_1^{\mathsf{T}} \cdot \mathbf{y}_0 + e^* + \mathsf{Encode}(\mathsf{msg}) \bmod q,$$

as $(\mathbf{G}\ \mathbf{0}) \cdot \mathbf{z} = -\mathbf{y}_0 \bmod q$. Going a step further, we can compute d by $d = \mathbf{v}''^{\mathsf{T}} \cdot \mathbf{z} + d_1 \bmod q$, where $d_1 = \mathbf{r}_1^{\mathsf{T}} \cdot \mathbf{y}_0 + e^* + \mathsf{Encode}(\mathsf{msg}) \bmod q$ is the payload part of an encryption of msg under the public key $\mathbf{y}_0$. In other words, we are now in a situation where we can simulate a ciphertext ctxt $= (\mathbf{c}, \mathbf{c}_1, d)$ given and encryption $(\mathbf{c}_1, d_1)$ of msg under the public key $\mathbf{y}_0$! Hence, we can now immediately appeal to the fact that, from the view of the adversary, $\mathbf{y}_0$ looks indeed uniformly random to argue security: Via the LWE assumption, $(\mathbf{A}, \mathbf{r}_1^{\mathsf{T}} \cdot \mathbf{A} + \mathbf{e}_1 \bmod q)$ and $(\mathbf{y}_0, \mathbf{r}_1^{\mathsf{T}} \cdot \mathbf{y}_0 + e_1^* \bmod q)$ are indistinguishable from uniform. Thus, from the adversary's view d_1 looks uniformly random, and therefore $d = \mathbf{v}''^{\mathsf{T}} \cdot \mathbf{z} + d_1 \bmod q$ also looks uniformly random. In fact, from the adversary's view all ciphertext components look uniformly random and independent.

LWE with Error-Leakage. Drowning is, however, a rather heavy-handed approach that, for all intents and purposes, ruins the LWE parameters. Specifically, to use this approach we need to assume the security of LWE with *superpolynomial modulus-to-noise ratio*. This means, in turn, that the underlying worst-to-average case reduction of LWE [41] reduces LWE to worst-case lattice problems with super-polynomial approximation factors. Moreover, it forces us to use a superpolynomially large modulus q.

We will now look a bit closer at the above drowning step. Specifically, given $\mathbf{z}$ and $\mathbf{v}^{\mathsf{T}} = \mathbf{r}_0^{\mathsf{T}} \cdot \mathbf{A} + \mathbf{e} \bmod q$ we computed

$$v = \mathbf{v}^{\mathsf{T}} \cdot \mathbf{z} + e^* = \mathbf{r}_0^{\mathsf{T}} \cdot \mathbf{A} \cdot \mathbf{z} + \mathbf{e}^{\mathsf{T}} \cdot \mathbf{z} + e^* = \mathbf{r}_0^{\mathsf{T}} \cdot \mathbf{y}_0 + \mathbf{e}^{\mathsf{T}} \cdot \mathbf{z} + e^* \bmod q.$$

Our main observation is the following: If we were somehow given an *advice* $l = -\mathbf{e}^{\mathsf{T}} \cdot \mathbf{z} + e^*$ about $\mathbf{e}$ and e^*, we could use l to *switch* the correlated error term $\mathbf{e}^{\mathsf{T}} \cdot \mathbf{z}$

in $\mathbf{v}^{\mathsf{T}} \cdot \mathbf{z}$ to a fresh and uncorrelated e^*. Namely by computing $v = \mathbf{v}^{\mathsf{T}} \cdot \mathbf{z} + 1 \bmod q$. Then it holds that

$$v = \mathbf{v}^{\mathsf{T}} \cdot \mathbf{z} + 1 = \mathbf{r}_0^{\mathsf{T}} \cdot \mathbf{y}_0 + \mathbf{e}^{\mathsf{T}} \cdot \mathbf{z} - \mathbf{e}^{\mathsf{T}} \cdot \mathbf{z} + e^* = \mathbf{r}_0^{\mathsf{T}} \cdot \mathbf{y}_0 + e^* \bmod q.$$

Thus, such an advice 1 is sufficient to make the security argument in the last paragraph work. Our hope now is that the advice $1 = -\mathbf{e}^{\mathsf{T}} \cdot \mathbf{z} + e^*$ *does not fully reveal* $\mathbf{e}$ and e^*, i.e. that $\mathbf{e}$ and e^* mutually conceal one another, even if the parameters of these error terms are way below the drowning regime.

This motivates the definition of *Learning with Errors with Error-Leakage*, elLWE for short. As the name suggests, in this variant of the LWE problem the adversary gets a *leak* or advice about the LWE error term. To make this definition useful for our purposes, we will allow the leak to depend on the LWE matrix $\mathbf{A}$. Consequently, we will define elLWE similarly to the regular LWE assumption, but via an *interactive experiment*. The security experiment of elLWE is given as follows, where we assume that a modulus q, dimensions n, m and error distributions χ, χ^* are parametrized by the security parameter.

The elLWE Security Experiment:

- In the first step, the experiment chooses a uniformly random matrix $\mathbf{A} \leftarrow_\$ \mathbb{Z}_q^{n \times m}$ and provides $\mathbf{A}$ to the adversary.
- Given the matrix $\mathbf{A}$, the adversary now chooses a *short* vector $\mathbf{z} \in \mathbb{Z}^m$ and provides $\mathbf{z}$ to the experiment.
- The experiment samples $\mathbf{e} \leftarrow_\$ \chi_1$ and $e^* \leftarrow_\$ \chi^*$ and sets $1 = \mathbf{e}^{\mathsf{T}} \cdot \mathbf{z} + e^*$.
- Now the experiment flips a random bit $b \leftarrow_\$ \{0,1\}$. If $b = 0$ it chooses a uniformly random $\mathbf{r} \leftarrow_\$ \mathbb{Z}_q^n$ and sets $\mathbf{v}^{\mathsf{T}} = \mathbf{r}^{\mathsf{T}} \cdot \mathbf{A} + \mathbf{e}^{\mathsf{T}} \bmod q$. If $b = 1$ it chooses $\mathbf{v} \leftarrow_\$ \mathbb{Z}_q^m$ uniformly at random.
- The experiment now provides $(\mathbf{A}, \mathbf{v}, 1)$ to the adversary. The adversary then produces a guess $b' \in \{0,1\}$ for the bit b
- If $b' = b$ the adversary wins, and loses otherwise.

As usual, we say that elLWE is secure if no PPT adversary has non-negligible advantage in this experiment. Now, via the above discussion we can routinely reduce the security of our construction to elLWE.

We remark that the elLWE problem generalizes the *extended LWE problem* [6, 38]. Specifically, in the extended LWE problem the vector $\mathbf{z}$ is chosen at random from a Gaussian distribution instead of adversarially (as in the case of the elLWE problem).

From LWE to elLWE. As an additional technical contribution of this work, we provide a hardness result for elLWE. Specifically, we show that the security of elLWE can be based on *standard LWE with polynomial modulus-to-noise ratio*. In this paragraph, we will sketch the main ideas underlying this result. In a nutshell, the main idea of our approach is to choose the leakage term 1 independent of the LWE error, and then *adjust* the LWE error in such a way that it *conforms* with the leakage. More precisely in the case of Gaussian $\mathbf{e}$ and e^*, we will show the following. There is a (sufficiently wide) Gaussian distribution $\hat{\mathbf{e}}$, such that for every (short) vector $\mathbf{z}$ there is an *efficiently sampleable pair of correlated random variables* $(\mathbf{f_z}, f_\mathbf{z})$ (independent of $\hat{e}$), such that

$$(e^\mathsf{T}, e^\mathsf{T} \cdot \mathbf{z} + e^*) \approx_s (\hat{e}^\mathsf{T} + \mathbf{f_z^\mathsf{T}}, f_\mathbf{z}).$$

In other words, $f_\mathbf{z}$ simulates the leakage $e^\mathsf{T} \cdot \mathbf{z} + e^*$, whereas $\mathbf{f_z}$ can be used to *additively* adjust an independent Gaussian $\hat{e}$ to have the same distribution as e given the leakage $e^\mathsf{T} \cdot \mathbf{z} + e^*$. Equipped with such an efficiently sampleable pair $(\mathbf{f_z}, f_\mathbf{z})$, reducing elLWE to LWE is almost straightforward: Given an LWE instance $(\mathbf{A}, \mathbf{v}^\mathsf{T})$ we run the elLWE adversary on $\mathbf{A}$, who returns $\mathbf{z}$. The reduction now samples $(\mathbf{f_z}, f_\mathbf{z})$, provides $(\mathbf{A}, \mathbf{v}^\mathsf{T} + \mathbf{f_z^\mathsf{T}}, f_\mathbf{z})$ to the adversary, and outputs whatever the adversary outputs.

On one side, if $\mathbf{v}^\mathsf{T}$ is an LWE sample, i.e. $\mathbf{v}^\mathsf{T} = \mathbf{r}^\mathsf{T} \cdot \mathbf{A} + \hat{e} \bmod q$, then

$$(\mathbf{A}, \mathbf{v}^\mathsf{T} + \mathbf{f_z^\mathsf{T}}, f_\mathbf{z}) = (\mathbf{A}, \mathbf{r}^\mathsf{T} \cdot \mathbf{A} + \hat{e} + \mathbf{f_z^\mathsf{T}} \bmod q, f_\mathbf{z})$$
$$\approx_s (\mathbf{A}, \mathbf{r}^\mathsf{T} \cdot \mathbf{A} + e^\mathsf{T} \bmod q, e^\mathsf{T} \cdot \mathbf{z} + e^*),$$

is statistically close to a correctly formed elLWE sample for $b = 0$.

On the other hand, if $\mathbf{v}$ is chosen uniformly random, then $\mathbf{v}' := \mathbf{v} + \mathbf{f_z} \bmod q$ is also uniformly random. Consequently $(\mathbf{A}, \mathbf{v} + \mathbf{f_z} \bmod q, f_\mathbf{z}) \approx_s (\mathbf{A}, \mathbf{v}', e^\mathsf{T}\mathbf{z} + e^*)$, i.e. it is statistically close to an elLWE sample for $b = 1$. The claim follows. Notice that this reduction is *tight*, i.e. it does not (substantially) degrade the adversary's runtime or advantage. Further notice that this reduction is agnostic of the structure of the matrix $\mathbf{A}$ and the secret $\mathbf{r}$. Consequently, it is applicable to any *structured* LWE variant [14].

Constructing the Leakage Simulator. We will now briefly discuss how such a pair $(\mathbf{f_z}, f_\mathbf{z})$ can be constructed. For simplicity, assume that e and $\mathbf{z}$ are scalars, i.e. $\mathbf{e} = e$ and $\mathbf{z} = z$. To further simplify matters, assume first that e and e^* are continuous Gaussians instead of *discrete* Gaussians. In this perspective, $(e, ez + e^*)$ is a pair of *correlated Gaussians*, i.e. a 2-dimensional Gaussian with (possibly) non-diagonal covariance matrix. If $e \sim D_\sigma$ and $e^* \sim D_{\sigma^*}$[2], then a routine calculation shows that the covariance matrix $\mathbf{C}$ of $(e, ez + e^*)$ is

$$\mathbf{C} = \begin{pmatrix} \sigma^2 & \sigma^2 z \\ \sigma^2 z & \sigma^2 z^2 + \sigma^{*2} \end{pmatrix}.$$

Our idea now is, basically speaking, to find an alternative way to represent this distribution. Specifically, we want to alternatively compute $(e, ez + e^*)$ via $(\hat{e} + we^\dagger, e^\dagger)$, where $\hat{e} \sim D_{\hat{\sigma}}$ and $e^\dagger \sim D_{\sigma^\dagger}$ are independent Gaussians and w is fixed (depending on σ, σ^* and z). Again, a routine calculation finds that the covariance matrix $\mathbf{C}'$ of $(\hat{e} + we^\dagger, e^\dagger)$ is

$$\mathbf{C}' = \begin{pmatrix} \hat{\sigma}^2 + \sigma^{\dagger 2} w^2 & \sigma^{\dagger 2} w \\ \sigma^{\dagger 2} w & \sigma^{\dagger 2} \end{pmatrix}.$$

---

[2] We denote the continuous Gaussian distribution with *parameter* σ by D_σ, i.e. the probability density function of D_σ is proportional to $e^{-\pi \frac{x^2}{\sigma^2}}$.

Now, two centered multivariate Gaussians are identically distributed, if and only if they have the same covariance matrix. Consequently, setting $\mathbf{C} = \mathbf{C}'$ and solving for $\hat{\sigma}^2, \sigma^{\dagger 2}$ and w yields

$$\sigma^{\dagger 2} = \sigma^2 z^2 + \sigma^{*2},$$

$$w = \frac{\sigma^2 z}{\sigma^{\dagger 2}} = \frac{\sigma^2 z}{\sigma^2 z^2 + \sigma^{*2}},$$

$$\hat{\sigma}^2 = \sigma^2 - \sigma^{\dagger 2} w^2 = \sigma^2 - \frac{\sigma^4 z^2}{\sigma^2 z^2 + \sigma^{*2}} = \left(1 - \frac{1}{1 + \frac{\sigma^{*2}}{\sigma^2 z^2}}\right) \sigma^2. \tag{1}$$

That is, for these parameters of $\hat{\sigma}, \sigma^{\dagger}$ and w it holds that $(e, ez + e^*) \equiv (\hat{e} + we^{\dagger}, e^{\dagger})$, i.e. the two pairs are identically distributed. Thus, we can define $(\mathbf{f}_z, f_z)$ by $\mathbf{f}_z = we^{\dagger}$ and $f_z = e^{\dagger}$.

Now, recall that in our reduction $\hat{e}$ corresponds to the error-term in the underlying LWE-instance. Thus, we should choose σ^* so as to ensure that $\hat{e} \sim D_{\hat{\sigma}}$ is a sufficiently wide Gaussian, while σ^* should not be too large. A reasonable choice for σ^* (which simplifies calculations) is to choose it such that $\sigma^* \geq \sigma \cdot \beta$, where β is an upper bound for $|z|$ (recall that z is adversarially chosen but short). For this choice of σ^*, it holds by (1) that $\hat{\sigma} \geq \sigma/\sqrt{2}$. In other words, for this parameter choice σ^* is only a factor β bigger than σ, whereas $\hat{\sigma}$ is only a factor $1/\sqrt{2}$ smaller than σ. In essence, this means that the reduction roughly preserves the LWE parameters, up to small factors.

The final piece of our reduction is to make this leakage simulator work for discrete Gaussians instead of continuous Gaussians. For this, we will make use of Peikert's randomized rounding approach [39]. That is, a discrete Gaussian can be computed as the randomized rounding of a continuous Gaussian. This, together with Regev's discrete-to-continuous Gaussian smoothing lemma [41], allows us to adapt the simulator for continuous Gaussians to discrete Gaussians. While the simplified analysis above only uses simple arithmetic, the actual analysis in the full version, while similar in spirit, relies on more involved concepts from singular value analysis to deal with high-dimensional multivariate Gaussians.

2.2 Applications

Laconic OT. As a warm-up application, it is easy to see that laconic encryption immediately implies laconic OT. Alice can construct a binary tree of keys with the following procedure: For each index pair (2ind, 2ind − 1), Alice inserts in the tree a uniformly sampled public key either in the even position if $D_{\mathsf{ind}} = 0$, or in the odd position if $D_{\mathsf{ind}} = 1$. Bob can then simply encrypt msg_0 with respect to the index 2ind and msg_1 with respect to index 2ind − 1. Since Alice is semi-honest, the security of laconic encryption immediately carries over.

Registration-Based Encryption. Laconic Encryption almost implies RBE: Each user ind generates a key-pair and sends her $\mathsf{pk}_{\mathsf{ind}}$ for registration to an (untrusted) Key Curator, which is added to the database $D \leftarrow D \cup \{\mathsf{pk}_i\}$.

Then the digest d (the root of the tree) and the witnesses wit_j of all users are updated accordingly. Encryption and decryption with respect to ind work exactly as in laconic encryption. The crucial caveat is that in RBE, being highly dynamic, it's unrealistic to consider that the users are receiving an updated wit each time a new user registers. Therefore, there is an additional strict efficiency requirement: No user's witness should change more than $\log N$ times throughout the lifetime of the system (N being the total number of users). This requirement minimizes the interaction between a user and the key curator.

Garg et al. [24] achieve this requirement by providing a direct construction based on Merkle trees. In a nutshell, to accumulate the public keys, there are multiple Merkle trees with an increasing number of leaves. A new public key enters a (degenerate) tree that consists of a single leaf. Then, as soon as the number of its leaves is the same with the next tree, the two trees are merged. This means that a tree (and therefore its corresponding paths-witnesses) is changing only when its leaves are doubled. Overall, this translates to $\log N$ number of trees and thus at most $\log N$ number of updates per user's witness. We generalize this idea and show a generic transformation from any laconic encryption scheme to a registration-based encryption scheme. A more detailed overview and a formal description can be found in the full version.

Laconic PSI. We present a semi-honestly secure laconic PSI from laconic encryption. Here the receiver who owns a large database chooses a message for the sender to encrypt, and then it checks whether the ciphertext can be decrypted correctly with respect to the indices registered on the receiver's side.

We first need to have a hash function $H : \{0,1\}^* \mapsto \{0,1\}^\ell$ to map elements into the universe of indices. For simplicity, we assume the sender's set is a singleton set $S_S = \{y\}$. Besides sampling a hash function H, the setup phase is the same as the laconic encryption. Then the receiver constructs a binary tree with the freshly generated public keys with respect to the indices where the elements in S_R are mapped. In the meantime, the receiver generates the witnesses. Then the receiver sends the updated st and a random message msg. Next, the sender encrypts msg with st with respect to the index $H(y)$, and sends the ciphertext ctxt to the receiver. Finally, upon receiving the ciphertext, the receiver will check for all $x_k \in S_R$, whether it holds that $\text{Dec}(\text{sk}_k, \text{wit}_k, \text{ctxt}) = \text{msg}$. If it finds such a k, x_k will be output as the intersection of S_S and S_R. The actual protocol will be obtained by running the above for every element in the sender's set. Correctness and security of this protocol follows from the guarantees of the laconic encryption scheme. For more details, we refer the reader to the full version.

Identity-Based Encryption. We also show that our laconic encryption scheme can be modified to construct an IBE. The basic idea is simple: Instead of constructing a tree of public keys iteratively, the key authority *implicitly* defines an exponentially large tree by sampling the root of the tree at random. The key difference is that now the authority must choose the matrices in the public parameters with a trapdoor. This way, when the user ind wants to register to the system, the authority can provide it with the appropriate root-to-leaf path (which will function as the secret key) by sampling pre-images, starting from the root and all the way down to the corresponding leaf.

Compared with other LWE-based constructions [1,13,16,18,21], our IBE supports an *unbounded* identity space, and has a tight security reduction of *full (adaptive)* security in the standard model. This is achieved with a new simulation strategy that relies on two alternating pairs of matrices $(\mathbf{B}_{0,\text{even}}, \mathbf{B}_{1,\text{even}})$ and $(\mathbf{B}_{0,\text{odd}}, \mathbf{B}_{1,\text{odd}})$, for left and right children and for even and odd layers, respectively. In the security proof, the simulator can "forget" the trapdoor of any one of the four matrices, and it can still issue decryption keys using the remaining trapdoors. This way, one can substitute ciphertext components one-by-one with uniformly sampled vectors. Proceeding until the last layer completes the security proof. A more detailed overview can be found in the full version.

Pre-Processing and Other Extensions. To increase the efficiency of our laconic encryption even further, we also construct a pre-processing variant of our scheme. Informally, the encryption algorithm Enc is split into an offline part (OfflineEnc), which is input-independent, and an online part (OnlineEnc). Crucially, the online algorithm is much more efficient and does not perform any public-key operation. The main observation is that each element of the ciphertext $\mathbf{c}_i$ depends only on *a single bit* of the corresponding index/identity. Thus, we can let the OfflineEnc algorithm computing both possible ciphertexts for each bit of the index (making sure to use the randomness consistently), and output two commitments. The OnlineEnc algorithm is on the other hand given the index ind, so it can complete the encryption by simply revealing the openings of the commitments corresponding to $(\text{ind}_1, \ldots, \text{ind}_\ell)$. As for the message, the OfflineEnc algorithm can simply encrypt a random bit r, and when the message msg is given to the OnlineEnc algorithm, it can simply output $\text{msg} \oplus r$. This way, the OnlineEnc is entirely combinatorial, and all the public-key operation happen in an offline and input-independent phase.

We also explore a number of other extensions of laconic encryption: We describe how we can make the encryption algorithm compatible with other encryption schemes (possibly not even lattice-based), and we present an alternative laconic encryption construction that offers different efficiency trade-offs. We refer the reader to the full version for more details.

3   Preliminaries

Let $(n, p, q) = (n, p, q)(\lambda)$ with $p < q$. Let $m := n \cdot \lceil \log_p q \rceil$. Define the (p, q)-ary gadget matrix

$$\mathbf{G} := \mathbf{I}_n \otimes \left(1 \; p \; \ldots \; p^{\lfloor \log_p q \rfloor} \right)$$

and denote the (balanced) p-ary decomposition by $\mathbf{G}^{-1}(\cdot)$. For a bit $b \in \{0, 1\}$, denote $\bar{b} := 1 - b$.

3.1   Lattices

Let $\mathcal{K} = \mathbb{Q}(\zeta)$ be a cyclotomic field and $\mathcal{R} = \mathbb{Z}[\zeta]$ its ring of integers, where $\zeta \in \mathbb{C}$ is a root of unity. Write $d_{\mathcal{R}}$ for the degree of (the cyclotomic polynomial defining $\mathcal{K}$ and) $\mathcal{R}$. The (infinity) norm $\|\cdot\|$ of an element $a = \sum_{i=0}^{d_{\mathcal{R}}-1} a_i \zeta^i \in \mathcal{R}$ is defined as the norm of its coefficient vector $(a_0, \ldots, a_{d_{\mathcal{R}}-1}) \in \mathbb{Z}^{d_{\mathcal{R}}}$, i.e. $\|a\| = \max_{i=0}^{d_{\mathcal{R}}-1} |a_i|$. For a vector $\mathbf{x} = (x_0, \ldots, x_{m-1}) \in \mathcal{R}^m$, its norm is defined as $\|\mathbf{x}\| := \max_{i=0}^{m-1} \|x_i\|$. For $q \in \mathbb{N}$, write $\mathcal{R}_q := \mathcal{R}/q\mathcal{R}$. Let χ be a distribution over $\mathcal{R}$.

Definition 1 ($\mathsf{LWE}_{\mathcal{R},n,q,\chi}$ Assumption). *Let $\mathcal{R}, n, m, q, \chi$ be parametrised by λ. The (decision) $\mathsf{LWE}_{\mathcal{R},n,m,q,\chi}$ assumption states that for any PPT adversary $\mathcal{A}$*

$$\left| \Pr\left[\mathcal{A}(\mathbf{A}, \mathbf{b}) = 1 \middle| \begin{array}{l} \mathbf{A} \leftarrow_\$ \mathcal{R}_q^{n \times m} \\ \mathbf{s} \leftarrow_\$ \mathcal{R}_q^n \\ \mathbf{e} \leftarrow_\$ \chi^m \\ \mathbf{b}^{\mathsf{T}} = \mathbf{s}^{\mathsf{T}} \cdot \mathbf{A} + \mathbf{e}^{\mathsf{T}} \bmod q \end{array} \right] - \Pr\left[\mathcal{A}(\mathbf{A}, \mathbf{b}) = 1 \middle| \begin{array}{l} \mathbf{A} \leftarrow_\$ \mathcal{R}_q^{n \times m} \\ \mathbf{b} \leftarrow_\$ \mathcal{R}_q^m \end{array} \right] \right|$$
$$\leq \mathsf{negl}(\lambda).$$

The $\mathsf{LWE}_{\mathcal{R},n,q,\chi}$ assumption is said to hold if the $\mathsf{LWE}_{\mathcal{R},n,m,q,\chi}$ assumption holds for all $m = \mathsf{poly}(\lambda)$.

Definition 2 (Discrete Gaussian Distributions). *Let $m \in \mathbb{N}$ and $s > 0$. The discrete Gaussian function over $\mathbb{R}$ with parameter s is defined as $\rho_s(x) := \exp\left(-\pi \frac{|x|^2}{s^2}\right)$ with support $\mathbb{R}$. The discrete Gaussian distribution over $\mathbb{Z}$ with parameter s is defined as $\mathcal{D}_{\mathbb{Z},s}(x) := \frac{\rho_s(x)}{\sum_{x' \in \mathbb{Z}} \rho_s(x')}$ with support $\mathbb{Z}$. The discrete Gaussian distribution over $\mathcal{R}$ with parameter s, denoted by $\mathcal{D}_{\mathcal{R},s}$ is induced by sampling $d_{\mathcal{R}}$ independent samples $x_i \leftarrow_\$ \mathcal{D}_{\mathbb{Z},s}$ and outputing $x = \sum_{i=0}^{d_{\mathcal{R}}-1} x_i \cdot \zeta^i$.*

We recall a version of the leftover hash lemma over cyclotomic rings.

Lemma 1 (Adapted from [11, Lemma 7]). *Let $n = \mathsf{poly}(\lambda)$, $p, q \in \mathbb{N}$, and $m \geq n \cdot \log_p q + \omega(\log \lambda)$. The following distributions are statistically close in λ:*

$$\left\{ (\mathbf{B}, \mathbf{y}) : \begin{array}{l} \mathbf{B} \leftarrow_\$ \mathcal{R}_q^{n \times m} \\ \mathbf{x} \leftarrow_\$ \mathcal{R}_p^m \\ \mathbf{y} := \mathbf{B} \cdot \mathbf{x} \bmod q \end{array} \right\} \quad and \quad \left\{ (\mathbf{B}, \mathbf{y}) : \begin{array}{l} \mathbf{B} \leftarrow_\$ \mathcal{R}_q^{n \times m} \\ \mathbf{y} \leftarrow_\$ \mathcal{R}_p^n \end{array} \right\}.$$

Lemma 2 (Derived from [37, Section 2.4]). *For any $k > 0$,*

$$\Pr[\|u\| > k \cdot s \mid u \leftarrow_\$ \mathcal{D}_{\mathcal{R},s}] < 2 \cdot d_{\mathcal{R}} \cdot \exp(-\pi \cdot k^2).$$

Definition 3 (Ring Expansion Factor). *The expansion factor of $\mathcal{R}$, denoted by $\gamma_{\mathcal{R}}$, is $\gamma_{\mathcal{R}} := \max_{a,b \in \mathcal{R} \setminus \{0\}} \frac{\|a \cdot b\|}{\|a\| \cdot \|b\|}$.*

Proposition 1 ([4]). *If $\mathcal{R}$ is a prime-power cyclotomic ring, then $\gamma_{\mathcal{R}} \leq 2 \deg_{\mathcal{R}}$. If $\mathcal{R}$ is a power-of-2 cyclotomic ring, then $\gamma_{\mathcal{R}} \leq \deg_{\mathcal{R}}$.*

4   Laconic Encryption

4.1   Definition

Definition 4 (Laconic Encryption). *A laconic encryption scheme for message space $\mathcal{M}$ consists of a tuple of PPT algorithms* (Setup, KGen, Upd, Enc, WGen, Dec) *with the following syntax:*

- (pp, st, aux) ← Setup($1^\lambda, 1^\ell$): *The setup algorithm is a randomized algorithm which takes as input the security parameter 1^λ and a length parameter 1^ℓ. It generates the public parameters* pp, *a state* st, *and some auxiliary information* aux.
- (pk, sk) ← KGen(pp): *The key generation algorithm takes as input the public parameters* pp *and outputs a pair of public and secret keys* (pk, sk).
- st′ ← Upd^{aux}(pp, st, ind, pk): *The membership update algorithm, with (read-and-write-)random access to the auxiliary information* aux, *takes as input the public parameters* pp, *the state* st, *an index* ind $\in \{0,1\}^\ell$, *and a public key* pk *(or $\bot$). It outputs updated state* st′.
- ctxt ← Enc(pp, st, ind, msg): *The encryption algorithm is a randomized algorithm which takes as input the public parameters* pp, *the state* st, *an index* ind $\in \{0,1\}^\ell$, *and a message* msg $\in \mathcal{M}$. *It outputs a ciphertext* ctxt.
- wit ← WGen^{aux}(pp, st, ind, pk): *The witness generation algorithm, with (read-)random access to the auxiliary information* aux, *takes as input the public parameters* pp, *the state* st, *an index* ind $\in \{0,1\}^\ell$, *and a public key* pk. *It outputs a (non)-membership witness* wit.
- msg ← Dec(sk, wit, ctxt): *The decryption algorithm takes as input a secret key* sk, *a membership witness* wit, *and a ciphertext* ctxt. *It outputs a message* msg.

Furthermore, there exists $t \in$ poly(λ, ℓ) such that all above algorithms run in time at most $t(\lambda, \ell)$.

Our correctness definition considers a scenario where the public parameters have underdone an arbitrary sequence of updates such that in the latest version a tuple (ind, pk) is registered. In this case, if a message is encrypted with respect to (pp, st, ind, pk), then decrypting the ciphertext with the secret key sk corresponding to pk recovers the message with overwhelming probability.

Definition 5 (Correctness). *A laconic encryption scheme Π is said to be statistically correct if for any (unbounded) algorithm $\mathcal{A}$, any $\ell =$ poly(λ), it holds that*

$$\Pr\left[\text{Correctness}_{\Pi,\mathcal{A}}(1^\lambda, 1^\ell) = 1\right] \geq 1 - \text{negl}(\lambda)$$

where the experiment Correctness$_{\Pi,\mathcal{A}}$ *is defined in Fig. 1.*

Our security definition combines both index and message-hiding. It requires that if each of two adversarially chosen indices $\text{ind}_0, \text{ind}_1$ is either registered by

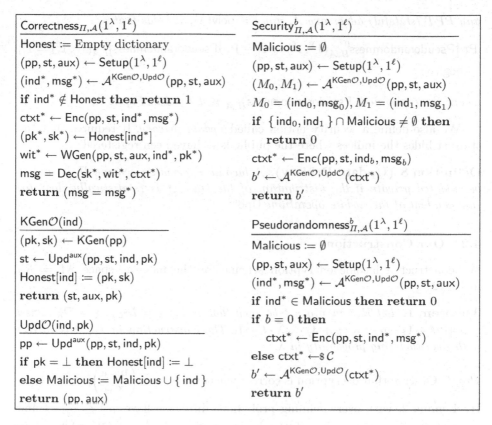

Correctness$_{\Pi,\mathcal{A}}(1^\lambda, 1^\ell)$	Security$^b_{\Pi,\mathcal{A}}(1^\lambda, 1^\ell)$
Honest := Empty dictionary	Malicious := $\emptyset$
$(\mathsf{pp}, \mathsf{st}, \mathsf{aux}) \leftarrow \mathsf{Setup}(1^\lambda, 1^\ell)$	$(\mathsf{pp}, \mathsf{st}, \mathsf{aux}) \leftarrow \mathsf{Setup}(1^\lambda, 1^\ell)$
$(\mathsf{ind}^*, \mathsf{msg}^*) \leftarrow \mathcal{A}^{\mathsf{KGen}\mathcal{O}, \mathsf{Upd}\mathcal{O}}(\mathsf{pp}, \mathsf{st}, \mathsf{aux})$	$(M_0, M_1) \leftarrow \mathcal{A}^{\mathsf{KGen}\mathcal{O}, \mathsf{Upd}\mathcal{O}}(\mathsf{pp}, \mathsf{st}, \mathsf{aux})$
if ind$^* \notin$ Honest **then return** 1	$M_0 = (\mathsf{ind}_0, \mathsf{msg}_0),\ M_1 = (\mathsf{ind}_1, \mathsf{msg}_1)$
$\mathsf{ctxt}^* \leftarrow \mathsf{Enc}(\mathsf{pp}, \mathsf{st}, \mathsf{ind}^*, \mathsf{msg}^*)$	**if** $\{\mathsf{ind}_0, \mathsf{ind}_1\} \cap$ Malicious $\neq \emptyset$ **then**
$(\mathsf{pk}^*, \mathsf{sk}^*) \leftarrow \mathsf{Honest}[\mathsf{ind}^*]$	**return** 0
$\mathsf{wit}^* \leftarrow \mathsf{WGen}(\mathsf{pp}, \mathsf{st}, \mathsf{aux}, \mathsf{ind}^*, \mathsf{pk}^*)$	$\mathsf{ctxt}^* \leftarrow \mathsf{Enc}(\mathsf{pp}, \mathsf{st}, \mathsf{ind}_b, \mathsf{msg}_b)$
$\mathsf{msg} = \mathsf{Dec}(\mathsf{sk}^*, \mathsf{wit}^*, \mathsf{ctxt}^*)$	$b' \leftarrow \mathcal{A}^{\mathsf{KGen}\mathcal{O}, \mathsf{Upd}\mathcal{O}}(\mathsf{ctxt}^*)$
return $(\mathsf{msg} = \mathsf{msg}^*)$	**return** b'

KGen$\mathcal{O}$(ind)	Pseudorandomness$^b_{\Pi,\mathcal{A}}(1^\lambda, 1^\ell)$
$(\mathsf{pk}, \mathsf{sk}) \leftarrow \mathsf{KGen}(\mathsf{pp})$	Malicious := $\emptyset$
$\mathsf{st} \leftarrow \mathsf{Upd}^{\mathsf{aux}}(\mathsf{pp}, \mathsf{st}, \mathsf{ind}, \mathsf{pk})$	$(\mathsf{pp}, \mathsf{st}, \mathsf{aux}) \leftarrow \mathsf{Setup}(1^\lambda, 1^\ell)$
$\mathsf{Honest}[\mathsf{ind}] := (\mathsf{pk}, \mathsf{sk})$	$(\mathsf{ind}^*, \mathsf{msg}^*) \leftarrow \mathcal{A}^{\mathsf{KGen}\mathcal{O}, \mathsf{Upd}\mathcal{O}}(\mathsf{pp}, \mathsf{st}, \mathsf{aux})$
return $(\mathsf{st}, \mathsf{aux}, \mathsf{pk})$	**if** ind$^* \in$ Malicious **then return** 0
	if $b = 0$ **then**
UpdO(ind, pk)	$\mathsf{ctxt}^* \leftarrow \mathsf{Enc}(\mathsf{pp}, \mathsf{st}, \mathsf{ind}^*, \mathsf{msg}^*)$
$\mathsf{pp} \leftarrow \mathsf{Upd}^{\mathsf{aux}}(\mathsf{pp}, \mathsf{st}, \mathsf{ind}, \mathsf{pk})$	**else** $\mathsf{ctxt}^* \leftarrow\!\!\$\ \mathcal{C}$
if $\mathsf{pk} = \perp$ **then** $\mathsf{Honest}[\mathsf{ind}] := \perp$	$b' \leftarrow \mathcal{A}^{\mathsf{KGen}\mathcal{O}, \mathsf{Upd}\mathcal{O}}(\mathsf{ctxt}^*)$
else Malicious := Malicious $\cup \{\mathsf{ind}\}$	**return** b'
return $(\mathsf{pp}, \mathsf{aux})$	

Fig. 1. Correctness, security, pseudorandomness and update privacy experiments for laconic encryption.

an honest party (so that the secret key is unknown to the adversary) or not registered, then for any adversarially chosen messages $\mathsf{msg}_0, \mathsf{msg}_1$ the adversary should not be able to distinguish a ciphertext encrypting msg_0 with respect to ind_0 from that encrypting msg_1 with respect to ind_1.

Definition 6 (Security). *A laconic encryption scheme Π is said to be secure if for any PPT (stateful) adversary $\mathcal{A}$, any $\ell = \mathsf{poly}(\lambda)$, it holds that*

$$|\Pr\left[\mathsf{Security}^0_{\Pi,\mathcal{A}}(1^\lambda, 1^\ell) = 1\right] - \Pr\left[\mathsf{Security}^1_{\Pi,\mathcal{A}}(1^\lambda, 1^\ell) = 1\right]| \leq \mathsf{negl}(\lambda)$$

where the experiment $\mathsf{Security}^b_{\Pi,\mathcal{A}}$ is defined in Fig. 1.

We will further define a slightly stronger security notion called *pseudorandom ciphertexts*. In essence, this property guarantees that if an index ind^* has not been registered, then a ciphertext with respect to ind^* looks pseudorandom.

Definition 7 (Pseudorandom Ciphertexts). *A laconic encryption scheme Π with ciphertext space $\mathcal{C}$ is said to be have pseudorandom ciphertexts if for* *any PPT (stateful) adversary $\mathcal{A}$, any $\ell = \mathsf{poly}(\lambda)$, it holds that*

$$\left|\Pr\left[\mathsf{Pseudorandomness}^0_{\Pi,\mathcal{A}}(1^\lambda, 1^\ell) = 1\right] - \Pr\left[\mathsf{Pseudorandomness}^1_{\Pi,\mathcal{A}}(1^\lambda, 1^\ell) = 1\right]\right|$$
$$\leq \mathsf{negl}(\lambda)$$

where the experiment $\mathsf{Pseudorandomness}^b_{\Pi,\mathcal{A}}$ is defined in Fig. 1.

We also define a security notion called *update privacy*. It requires that the state st hides the indices where the public keys have been registered.

Definition 8 (Update Privacy). *A laconic encryption scheme Π is said to be updated private if the distribution of the state st is (statistically close to) independent of the update operations $\mathsf{Upd}^{\mathsf{aux}}$.*

4.2 Our Construction

We construct a laconic encryption scheme for the message space $\mathcal{M} = \mathcal{R}_2$ in Fig. 2.

Theorem 1. *Let $\mathcal{R}, \ell, m, p, q, s, t$ be such that $s < t$, $\chi = \mathcal{D}_{\mathcal{R},s}$, $\bar{\chi} = \mathcal{D}_{\mathcal{R},t}$, and $q > ((2\ell+1) \cdot m \cdot \gamma_\mathcal{R} \cdot p + 4) \cdot \sqrt{\lambda} \cdot t + 1$. The construction in Fig. 2 is correct with overwhelming probability in λ.*

Proof. Observe that decryption is correct whenever $\left|e - \mathbf{e}^{\mathsf{T}} \cdot \begin{pmatrix} \mathbf{u}_{[\mathsf{ind}]} \\ \mathbf{x}_{\mathsf{ind}} \end{pmatrix}\right| < (q-1)/4$.

By Lemma 2, with overwhelming probability in λ, we have $\|e\| \leq \frac{\sqrt{\lambda}}{2} \cdot t$ and $\|\mathbf{e}\| \leq \frac{\sqrt{\lambda}}{2} \cdot s < \frac{\sqrt{\lambda}}{2} \cdot t$. Since $\begin{pmatrix} \mathbf{u}_{[\mathsf{ind}]} \\ \mathbf{x}_{\mathsf{ind}} \end{pmatrix} \in \mathcal{R}_p^{(2\ell+1)m}$, we have $\left\|\begin{pmatrix} \mathbf{u}_{[\mathsf{ind}]} \\ \mathbf{x}_{\mathsf{ind}} \end{pmatrix}\right\| \leq p/2$.
Combining these facts yields

$$\left\|e - \mathbf{e}^{\mathsf{T}} \cdot \begin{pmatrix} \mathbf{u}_{[\mathsf{ind}]} \\ \mathbf{x}_{\mathsf{ind}} \end{pmatrix}\right\| \leq (2\ell+1) \cdot m \cdot \gamma_\mathcal{R} \cdot \frac{\sqrt{\lambda}}{2} \cdot t \cdot \frac{p}{2} + \sqrt{\lambda} \cdot t < (q-1)/4$$

with overwhelming probability in λ. $\qquad\qquad\square$

Theorem 2. *If $d_\mathcal{R} \geq \lambda$, $m \geq n \cdot \log_p q + \omega(\log \lambda)$, and the $\mathsf{LWE}_{\mathcal{R},n,q,\chi}$ assumption holds, the laconic encryption in Fig. 2 is secure. More specifically, for every PPT adversary $\mathcal{A}$ against the pseudorandom ciphertext security of the construction in Fig. 2, there exist PPT adversaries $\mathcal{A}_1$ against $\mathsf{eILWE}_{\mathcal{R},n,m,1,q,\chi,\bar{\chi},p/2}$, $\mathcal{A}_2$ against $\mathsf{LWE}_{\mathcal{R},n,2m,q,\chi}$ and $\mathcal{A}_3$ against $\mathsf{LWE}_{\mathcal{R},n,m+1,q,\chi}$ such that*

$$\mathsf{adv}(\mathcal{A}) \geq \ell \cdot \mathsf{adv}(\mathcal{A}_1) + \mathsf{adv}(\mathcal{A}_2) + \ell \cdot \mathsf{adv}(\mathcal{A}_3) + |\mathsf{hl}(\lambda)$$

where $|\mathsf{hl}|$ is the statistical distance defined by Lemma 1.

Proof. Denote the construction by Π and write $\mathcal{C} := \mathcal{R}_q^{(2\ell+1)m+1}$ for the ciphertext space. Before we discuss the hybrids, we will briefly analyze the structure of the challenge ciphertext. In the following, let $\mathsf{ind}^* = (\mathsf{ind}_1^*, \ldots, \mathsf{ind}_\ell^*)$,

$\underline{\text{Setup}(1^\lambda)}$

$\mathbf{A}_0, \mathbf{A}_1, \mathbf{B} \leftarrow\!\!{}^\$\ \mathcal{R}_q^{n \times m}$

$\mathbf{y}_\epsilon := \mathbf{y}^* \leftarrow\!\!{}^\$\ \mathcal{R}_q^n$

$\mathcal{T} := \{\epsilon\}$

$\text{pp} := (\mathbf{A}_0, \mathbf{A}_1, \mathbf{B}, \mathbf{y}^*)$

$\text{st} := \mathbf{y}_\epsilon$

$\text{aux} := (\mathcal{T}, \{\mathbf{y}_v\}_{v \in \mathcal{T}})$

$\textbf{return } (\text{pp}, \text{st}, \text{aux})$

$\underline{\text{KGen}(\text{pp})}$

$\mathbf{x} \leftarrow\!\!{}^\$\ \mathcal{R}_p^m$

$\mathbf{y} := \mathbf{B} \cdot \mathbf{x} \bmod q$

$\textbf{return } (\text{pk}, \text{sk}) := (\mathbf{y}, \mathbf{x})$

$\underline{\text{Upd}^{\text{aux}}(\text{pp}, \text{st}, \text{ind}, \text{pk})}$

$\textbf{if } \text{pk} = \bot \textbf{ then}$

$\quad \mathcal{T} := \mathcal{T} \setminus \{\text{ind}\}$

$\textbf{else}$

$\quad \mathcal{T} := \mathcal{T} \cup \{\text{ind}\}$

$\mathbf{y}_{\text{ind}} := \text{pk}$

$\text{st}' \leftarrow \text{TreeUpdate}^{\text{aux}}(\text{pp}, \text{st}, \text{ind})$

$\textbf{return } \text{st}'$

$\underline{\text{Enc}(\text{pp}, \text{st}, \text{ind}, \text{msg})}$

$\mathbf{r}_j \leftarrow\!\!{}^\$\ \mathcal{R}_q^n, \ \forall j \in \{0, \ldots, \ell\}$

$\textbf{for } j = 0, \ldots, \ell - 1 \textbf{ do}$

$\quad \mathbf{e}_j \leftarrow\!\!{}^\$\ \chi^{2m}$

$\quad \mathbf{B}_j := \begin{pmatrix} \mathbf{A}_0 & \mathbf{A}_1 \\ \text{ind}_{j+1} \cdot \mathbf{G} & \overline{\text{ind}}_{j+1} \cdot \mathbf{G} \end{pmatrix}$

$\quad \mathbf{c}_j^{\mathsf{T}} := (\mathbf{r}_j^{\mathsf{T}}, \mathbf{r}_{j+1}^{\mathsf{T}}) \cdot \mathbf{B}_j + \mathbf{e}_j^{\mathsf{T}} \bmod q$

$\mathbf{e}_\ell \leftarrow\!\!{}^\$\ \chi^m, \ e \leftarrow\!\!{}^\$\ \bar{\chi}$

$\mathbf{c}_\ell^{\mathsf{T}} := \mathbf{r}_\ell^{\mathsf{T}} \cdot \mathbf{B} + \mathbf{e}_\ell^{\mathsf{T}} \bmod q$

$d := \mathbf{r}_0^{\mathsf{T}} \cdot \mathbf{y}_\epsilon + e + \lfloor \frac{q}{2} \rfloor \cdot \text{msg} \bmod q$

$\textbf{return } \text{ctxt} := (\mathbf{c}_0, \ldots, \mathbf{c}_\ell, d)$

$\underline{\text{WGen}^{\text{aux}}(\text{pp}, \text{st}, \text{ind}, \text{pk})}$

$\textbf{for } j = \ell - 1, \ldots, 0 \textbf{ do}$

$\quad \mathbf{u}_{\text{ind}_{1:j}\|0} := -\mathbf{G}^{-1}(\mathbf{y}_{\text{ind}_{1:j}\|0})$

$\quad \mathbf{u}_{\text{ind}_{1:j}\|1} := -\mathbf{G}^{-1}(\mathbf{y}_{\text{ind}_{1:j}\|1})$

$\textbf{return } \text{wit} := (\mathbf{u}_{\text{ind}_{1:j}\|0}, \mathbf{u}_{\text{ind}_{1:j}\|1})_{j=0}^{\ell-1}$

$\underline{\text{Dec}(\text{sk}, \text{wit}, \text{ctxt})}$

$\textbf{parse sk as } \mathbf{x}_{\text{ind}}$

$\bar{\mu} := d - \sum_{j=0}^{\ell-1} \mathbf{c}_j^{\mathsf{T}} \cdot \begin{pmatrix} \mathbf{u}_{\text{ind}_{1:j}\|0} \\ \mathbf{u}_{\text{ind}_{1:j}\|1} \end{pmatrix} - \mathbf{c}_\ell^{\mathsf{T}} \cdot \mathbf{x}_{\text{ind}} \bmod q$

$\textbf{if } |\bar{\mu}| < q/4 \textbf{ then return } 0$

$\textbf{else return } 1$

$\underline{\text{TreeUpdate}^{\text{aux}}(\text{pp}, \text{st}, \text{ind})}$

$\textbf{for } j = \ell - 1, \ldots, 0 \textbf{ do}$

$\quad \textbf{if } (\text{ind}_{1:j}\|0) \notin \mathcal{T} \wedge (\text{ind}_{1:j}\|1) \notin \mathcal{T} \textbf{ then} \quad$ // Both children of $\text{ind}_{1:j}$ are unassigned.

$\quad\quad \mathcal{T} := \mathcal{T} \setminus \{\text{ind}_{1:j}\}$

$\quad \textbf{else}$

$\quad\quad \textbf{if } (\text{ind}_{1:j}\|\overline{\text{ind}}_{j+1}) \notin \mathcal{T} \textbf{ then} \quad$ // $\text{ind}_{1:j+1}$ is assigned but its sibling not.

$\quad\quad\quad \mathbf{y}_{\text{ind}_{1:j}\|\overline{\text{ind}}_{j+1}} := \mathbf{y}^*$

$\quad\quad\quad \mathbf{u}_{\text{ind}_{1:j}\|0} := -\mathbf{G}^{-1}(\mathbf{y}_{\text{ind}_{1:j}\|0}), \ \mathbf{u}_{\text{ind}_{1:j}\|1} := -\mathbf{G}^{-1}(\mathbf{y}_{\text{ind}_{1:j}\|1})$

$\quad\quad \mathcal{T} := \mathcal{T} \cup \{\text{ind}_{1:j}\} \quad$ // Assign $\text{ind}_{1:j}$ if any of its children is assigned.

$\quad\quad \mathbf{y}_{\text{ind}_{1:j}} := \mathbf{A}_0 \cdot \mathbf{u}_{\text{ind}_{1:j}\|0} + \mathbf{A}_1 \cdot \mathbf{u}_{\text{ind}_{1:j}\|1} \bmod q$

$\textbf{return } \text{st}$

Fig. 2. Construction of laconic encryption.

and let k be such that $\mathsf{ind}^*_{1:k} = (\mathsf{ind}^*_1, \ldots, \mathsf{ind}^*_k)$ is a *leaf node* in the tree for which the adversary *does not* have a corresponding preimage. Furthermore, we denote $\mathbf{y}^*_i = \mathbf{y}_{\mathsf{ind}^*_{1:i}}$ at the nodes $\mathsf{ind}^*_1, \ldots, \mathsf{ind}^*_{1:k}$. In the following let $\mathsf{ctxt}^* = (\mathbf{c}_0, \ldots, \mathbf{c}_\ell, d)$ be the challenge ciphertext. Consider the following hybrids.

- $\mathcal{H}_0$: Identical to $\mathsf{Pseudorandomness}^0_{\Pi,\mathcal{A}}(1^\lambda, 1^\ell)$. Note that in this hybrid

$$\mathbf{c}^\mathsf{T}_j = \mathbf{r}^\mathsf{T}_j \cdot (\mathbf{A}_0 \ \mathbf{A}_1) + \mathbf{r}^\mathsf{T}_{i+1}(\overline{\mathsf{ind}}_{i+1}\mathbf{G} \ \mathsf{ind}_{i+1}\mathbf{G}) + \mathbf{e}^\mathsf{T}_j \bmod q \ \forall j \in \{0, \ldots, \ell-1\},$$
$$\mathbf{c}^\mathsf{T}_\ell = \mathbf{r}^\mathsf{T}_\ell \cdot \mathbf{B} + \mathbf{e}^\mathsf{T}_\ell \bmod q, \text{ and}$$
$$d = \mathbf{r}^\mathsf{T}_0 \cdot \mathbf{y}^*_0 + e + \lfloor \tfrac{q}{2} \rfloor \cdot \mathsf{msg} \bmod q.$$

- $\mathcal{H}_1$: Compute ctxt^* as follows. Choose $\mathbf{c}_0, \ldots, \mathbf{c}_{k-1} \leftarrow_\$ \mathcal{R}^{2m}_q$ uniformly at random, choose $\mathbf{e}_0, \ldots, \mathbf{e}_{k-1} \leftarrow_\$ \chi^{2m}$, and set

$$d = \sum_{j=0}^{k-1} (\mathbf{c}_j - \mathbf{e}_j)^\mathsf{T} \cdot \mathbf{z}_j + \mathbf{r}^\mathsf{T}_k \cdot \mathbf{y}^*_k + e + \lfloor \tfrac{q}{2} \rfloor \cdot \mathsf{msg} \bmod q,$$

where $\mathbf{z}_j = \begin{pmatrix} \mathbf{u}_{\mathsf{ind}^*_{1:j}\|0} \\ \mathbf{u}_{\mathsf{ind}^*_{1:j}\|1} \end{pmatrix} \in \mathcal{R}^{2m}_p$. Furthermore, compute $\mathbf{c}_k, \ldots, \mathbf{c}_\ell$ as in $\mathcal{H}_0$.

- $\mathcal{H}_2$: In this hybrid we choose $\mathbf{c}_k \leftarrow_\$ \mathcal{R}^{2m}_q$ and $d \leftarrow_\$ \mathcal{R}_q$ uniformly at random.
- $\mathcal{H}_3$: In this hybrid we choose $\mathbf{c}_i \leftarrow_\$ \mathcal{R}^{2m}_q$ uniformly at random for $i = k+1, \ldots, \ell-1$ and $\mathbf{c}_\ell \leftarrow_\$ \mathcal{R}^m_q$ uniformly at random.

Note that in $\mathcal{H}_3$ all ciphertext components are chosen uniformly random. Hence the claim of the theorem follows. We will establish the indistinguishability of successive hybrids via a sequence of lemmata. $\qquad\square$

Lemma 3. *For any PPT adversary $\mathcal{A}$ there exists a PPT adversary $\mathcal{A}_1$ against* $\mathsf{elLWE}_{\mathcal{R},n,m,1,q,\chi,\bar\chi,p/2}$ *such that*

$$|\Pr[\mathcal{H}_0(\mathcal{A}) = 1] - \Pr[\mathcal{H}_1(\mathcal{A}) = 1]| \leq \ell \cdot \mathsf{adv}(\mathcal{A}_1).$$

Proof. To show that $\mathcal{H}_0$ and $\mathcal{H}_1$ are computationally indistinguishable, we define the following sub-hybrids $\mathcal{H}'_0, \ldots, \mathcal{H}'_\ell$ and $\mathcal{H}''_0, \ldots, \mathcal{H}''_\ell$.

- $\mathcal{H}'_i$ (for $i = 0, \ldots, \ell$): $\mathcal{H}'_0$ is identical to $\mathcal{H}_0$ and hybrids $\mathcal{H}'_{>k}$ are identical to $\mathcal{H}_1$. For the middle cases, i.e. $1 \leq i \leq k$, we define hybrid $\mathcal{H}'_i$ so that $\mathbf{c}_0, \ldots, \mathbf{c}_{i-1}$ and d are computed as in $\mathcal{H}_1$, and $\mathbf{c}_i, \ldots, \mathbf{c}_\ell$ are computed as in $\mathcal{H}_0$. Specifically, different from $\mathcal{H}_0$, we choose $\mathbf{c}_0, \ldots, \mathbf{c}_{i-1} \leftarrow_\$ \mathcal{R}^{2m}_q$ uniformly at random, choose $\mathbf{e}_0, \ldots, \mathbf{e}_{i-1} \leftarrow_\$ \chi^{2m}$ and set

$$d = \sum_{j=0}^{i-1} (\mathbf{c}_j - \mathbf{e}_j)^\mathsf{T} \cdot \mathbf{z}_j + \mathbf{r}^\mathsf{T}_i \cdot \mathbf{y}^*_i + e + \lfloor \tfrac{q}{2} \rfloor \cdot \mathsf{msg} \bmod q.$$

– $\mathcal{H}_i''$ (for $i = 1, \ldots, \ell$): If $i > k$, then this hybrid is identical to $\mathcal{H}_i'$. Else ($1 \le i \le k$), $\mathbf{c}_j$ for all $j \in [0 : \ell]\setminus\{i - 1\}$ are computed as in $\mathcal{H}_i'$, and $\mathbf{c}_{i-1}$ is computed as follows. Choose $\hat{\mathbf{c}}_{i-1}$ uniformly at random and set

$$\mathbf{c}_{i-1}^{\mathsf{T}} = \hat{\mathbf{c}}_{i-1}^{\mathsf{T}} + \mathbf{r}_i^{\mathsf{T}} \cdot (\overline{\mathrm{ind}}_i \cdot \mathbf{G} \;\, \mathrm{ind}_i \cdot \mathbf{G}) \bmod q.$$

Furthermore, we set

$$d = \sum_{j=0}^{i-2}(\mathbf{c}_j - \mathbf{e}_j)^{\mathsf{T}} \cdot \mathbf{z}_j + (\hat{\mathbf{c}}_{i-1}^{\mathsf{T}} - \mathbf{e}_{i-1}^{\mathsf{T}}) \cdot \mathbf{z}_{i-1} + e + \lfloor \tfrac{q}{2} \rfloor \cdot \mathsf{msg} \bmod q.$$

First, observe that $\mathcal{H}_i'$ and $\mathcal{H}_i''$ are in fact identically distributed: In $\mathcal{H}_i''$, since $\hat{\mathbf{c}}_{i-1}$ is uniformly and independently distributed, we can equivalently compute it as

$$\hat{\mathbf{c}}_{i-1}^{\mathsf{T}} = \bar{\mathbf{c}}_{i-1}^{\mathsf{T}} - \mathbf{r}_i^{\mathsf{T}} \cdot (\overline{\mathrm{ind}}_i \cdot \mathbf{G} \;\, \mathrm{ind}_i \cdot \mathbf{G})$$

for a uniformly random and independent $\bar{\mathbf{c}}_{i-1}$. This makes $\mathbf{c}_{i-1} = \bar{\mathbf{c}}_{i-1}$ uniformly random, as in $\mathcal{H}_i'$. Substituting the new $\hat{\mathbf{c}}_i$ to the expression of d in $\mathcal{H}_i''$, we have

$$d = \sum_{j=0}^{i-2}(\mathbf{c}_j - \mathbf{e}_j)^{\mathsf{T}} \cdot \mathbf{z}_j + (\hat{\mathbf{c}}_{i-1}^{\mathsf{T}} - \mathbf{e}_{i-1}^{\mathsf{T}}) \cdot \mathbf{z}_{i-1} + e + \lfloor \tfrac{q}{2} \rfloor \cdot \mathsf{msg} \bmod q$$

$$= \sum_{j=0}^{i-2}(\mathbf{c}_j - \mathbf{e}_j)^{\mathsf{T}}\mathbf{z}_j + (\mathbf{c}_{i-1}^{\mathsf{T}} - \mathbf{r}_i^{\mathsf{T}}(\overline{\mathrm{ind}}_i\mathbf{G} \;\, \mathrm{ind}_i\mathbf{G}) - \mathbf{e}_{i-1}^{\mathsf{T}})\mathbf{z}_{i-1} + e + \lfloor \tfrac{q}{2} \rfloor\mathsf{msg} \bmod q$$

$$= \sum_{j=0}^{i-1}(\mathbf{c}_j - \mathbf{e}_j)^{\mathsf{T}} \cdot \mathbf{z}_j - \mathbf{r}_i^{\mathsf{T}} \cdot (\overline{\mathrm{ind}}_i \cdot \mathbf{G} \;\, \mathrm{ind}_i \cdot \mathbf{G}) \cdot \mathbf{z}_{i-1} + e + \lfloor \tfrac{q}{2} \rfloor \cdot \mathsf{msg} \bmod q$$

$$= \sum_{j=0}^{i-1}(\mathbf{c}_j - \mathbf{e}_j)^{\mathsf{T}} \cdot \mathbf{z}_j + \mathbf{r}_i^{\mathsf{T}} \cdot \mathbf{y}_i^* + e + \lfloor \tfrac{q}{2} \rfloor \cdot \mathsf{msg} \bmod q,$$

as in $\mathcal{H}_i'$, where the last equality was due to $(\overline{\mathrm{ind}}_i \cdot \mathbf{G} \;\, \mathrm{ind}_i \cdot \mathbf{G}) \cdot \mathbf{z}_{i-1} = -\mathbf{y}_i^*$.

The main technical part of this proof lies in establishing indistinguishability between hybrids $\mathcal{H}_i'$ and $\mathcal{H}_{i+1}''$ for $i \in \{0, \ldots, \ell - 1\}$. Note that the case $k < i \le \ell - 1$ is trivial since $\mathcal{H}_i'' = \mathcal{H}_i' = \mathcal{H}_1$ for $i > k$. In the following, we focus on the remaining case $0 \le i \le k$. We will show that these two hybrids are indistinguishable under elLWE. Assume towards contradiction that

$$\Pr\left[\mathcal{H}_i'(\mathcal{A}) = 1\right] - \Pr\left[\mathcal{H}_{i+1}''(\mathcal{A}) = 1\right] \ge \epsilon.$$

We will show that this implies a PPT adversary $\mathcal{A}_1'$ against elLWE with advantage ϵ.

The adversary $\mathcal{A}_1'$ is specified as follows. As input it receives a matrix $\mathbf{A} \in \mathcal{R}_q^{n \times 2m}$, and it parses $\mathbf{A}$ as $\mathbf{A} = (\mathbf{A}_0 \;\, \mathbf{A}_1)$ where $\mathbf{A}_0, \mathbf{A}_1 \in \mathcal{R}_q^{n \times m}$. Now $\mathcal{A}_1'$ simulates $\mathcal{H}_i'(\mathcal{A})$ with the matrices $\mathbf{A}_0, \mathbf{A}_1$ thus obtained, until the adversary $\mathcal{A}$ queries the challenge ciphertext. Now it chooses $\mathbf{z}^* = -\mathbf{z}_i$ and sends $\mathbf{z}^*$ to its challenger. Note that $\mathbf{z}^*$ is a legit query as $\|\mathbf{z}^*\| \leq p/2$. Now $\mathcal{A}_1'$ obtaining a leak l and $\mathbf{y}$. Next, it computes the challenge ciphertext as in $\mathcal{H}_i'(\mathcal{A})$, except that it sets

$$\mathbf{c}_i = \mathbf{y} + \mathbf{r}_{i+1} \cdot (\bar{\mathrm{ind}}_{i+1} \cdot \mathbf{G} \ \mathrm{ind}_{i+1} \cdot \mathbf{G}) \bmod q$$

and

$$d = \sum_{j=0}^{i-1} (\mathbf{c}_j - \mathbf{e}_j)^{\mathsf{T}} \mathbf{z}_j - \mathbf{y}^{\mathsf{T}} \cdot \mathbf{z}^* + l + \lfloor \frac{q}{2} \rfloor \cdot \mathsf{msg} \bmod q.$$

Note that the remaining ciphertext components are the same as in $\mathcal{H}_i'(\mathcal{A})$ and $\mathcal{H}_{i+1}''(\mathcal{A})$. From there on, $\mathcal{A}_1'$ continues the simulation of $\mathcal{H}_i'(\mathcal{A})$ and outputs whatever $\mathcal{H}_i'(\mathcal{A})$ outputs.

Now let $b \in \{0, 1\}$ be the challenge bit of the elLWE experiment. We claim that if $b = 0$, then $\mathcal{A}_1'$ faithfully simulates $\mathcal{H}_i'(\mathcal{A})$. On the other hand, we claim that for $b = 1$ the $\mathcal{A}_1'$ faithfully simulates $\mathcal{H}_{i+1}''(\mathcal{A})$. From these two claims it follows that $\mathcal{A}_1'$ has advantage ϵ.

- For $b = 0$, it holds that $\mathbf{y}^{\mathsf{T}} = \mathbf{r}^{\mathsf{T}} \cdot \mathbf{A} + \mathbf{e}^{\mathsf{T}} = \mathbf{r}^{\mathsf{T}} \cdot (\mathbf{A}_0 \ \mathbf{A}_1) + \mathbf{e}^{\mathsf{T}} \bmod q$ and $l = \mathbf{e}^{\mathsf{T}} \cdot \mathbf{z}^* + e = -\mathbf{e}^{\mathsf{T}} \cdot \mathbf{z}_i + e \bmod q$. Renaming $\mathbf{r}$ to $\mathbf{r}_i$ and $\mathbf{e}$ to $\mathbf{e}_i$, it holds that

$$\mathbf{c}_i^{\mathsf{T}} = \mathbf{y}^{\mathsf{T}} + \mathbf{r}_{i+1}^{\mathsf{T}} \cdot (\bar{\mathrm{ind}}_{i+1} \cdot \mathbf{G} \ \mathrm{ind}_{i+1} \cdot \mathbf{G}) \bmod q$$
$$= \mathbf{r}_i^{\mathsf{T}} \cdot (\mathbf{A}_0 \ \mathbf{A}_1) + \mathbf{r}_{i+1}^{\mathsf{T}} \cdot (\bar{\mathrm{ind}}_{i+1} \cdot \mathbf{G} \ \mathrm{ind}_{i+1} \cdot \mathbf{G}) + \mathbf{e}_i^{\mathsf{T}} \bmod q$$

and

$$d = \sum_{j=0}^{i-1} (\mathbf{c}_j - \mathbf{e}_j)^{\mathsf{T}} \cdot \mathbf{z}_j - \mathbf{y}^{\mathsf{T}} \cdot \mathbf{z}^* + l + \lfloor \frac{q}{2} \rfloor \cdot \mathsf{msg} \bmod q \qquad (2)$$

$$= \sum_{j=0}^{i-1} (\mathbf{c}_j - \mathbf{e}_j)^{\mathsf{T}} \cdot \mathbf{z}_j + (\mathbf{r}_i^{\mathsf{T}} \cdot \mathbf{A} + \mathbf{e}_i^{\mathsf{T}}) \cdot \mathbf{z}_i - \mathbf{e}_i^{\mathsf{T}} \mathbf{z}_i + e + \lfloor \frac{q}{2} \rfloor \cdot \mathsf{msg} \bmod q \qquad (3)$$

$$= \sum_{j=0}^{i-1} (\mathbf{c}_j - \mathbf{e}_j)^{\mathsf{T}} \cdot \mathbf{z}_j + \mathbf{r}_i^{\mathsf{T}} \cdot \mathbf{y}_i^* + e + \lfloor \frac{q}{2} \rfloor \cdot \mathsf{msg} \bmod q, \qquad (4)$$

where the last equality holds as $\mathbf{y}_i^* = \mathbf{A}\mathbf{z}_i$. We can conclude that in this case the simulation of $\mathcal{A}_1'$ and $\mathcal{H}_i'(\mathcal{A})$ are identically distributed.
- For $b = 1$, it holds that $\mathbf{y} = \hat{\mathbf{c}}_i$ for a uniformly random $\hat{\mathbf{c}}_i \leftarrow_\$ \mathcal{R}_q^{2m}$ and $l = \mathbf{e}^{\mathsf{T}} \cdot \mathbf{z}^* + e = -\mathbf{e}^{\mathsf{T}} \mathbf{z}_i + e$. It therefore holds that

$$\mathbf{c}_i^{\mathsf{T}} = \mathbf{y}^{\mathsf{T}} + \mathbf{r}_{i+1}^{\mathsf{T}} \cdot (\bar{\mathrm{ind}}_{i+1} \cdot \mathbf{G} \ \mathrm{ind}_{i+1} \cdot \mathbf{G}) \bmod q$$
$$= \hat{\mathbf{c}}_i^{\mathsf{T}} + \mathbf{r}_{i+1}^{\mathsf{T}} \cdot (\bar{\mathrm{ind}}_{i+1} \cdot \mathbf{G} \ \mathrm{ind}_{i+1} \cdot \mathbf{G}) \bmod q$$

and

$$d = \sum_{j=0}^{i-1} (\mathbf{c}_j - \mathbf{e}_j)^\mathsf{T} \cdot \mathbf{z}_j - \mathbf{y}^\mathsf{T} \cdot \mathbf{z}^* + l + \lfloor \frac{q}{2} \rfloor \cdot \mathsf{msg} \bmod q$$

$$= \sum_{j=0}^{i-1} (\mathbf{c}_j - \mathbf{e}_j)^\mathsf{T} \cdot \mathbf{z}_j + \hat{\mathbf{c}}_i^\mathsf{T} \cdot \mathbf{z}_i - \mathbf{e}_i^\mathsf{T} \mathbf{z}_i + e + \lfloor \frac{q}{2} \rfloor \cdot \mathsf{msg} \bmod q$$

$$= \sum_{j=0}^{i-1} (\mathbf{c}_j - \mathbf{e}_j)^\mathsf{T} \cdot \mathbf{z}_j + (\hat{\mathbf{c}}_i^\mathsf{T} - \mathbf{e}_i^\mathsf{T}) \cdot \mathbf{z}_i + e + \lfloor \frac{q}{2} \rfloor \cdot \mathsf{msg} \bmod q.$$

I.e. it holds that in this case the simulation of $\mathcal{A}_1'$ and $\mathcal{H}_{i+1}''(\mathcal{A})$ are identically distributed. □

Lemma 4. *For any PPT adversary $\mathcal{A}$ there exists a PPT adversary $\mathcal{A}_2$ against* $\mathsf{LWE}_{\mathcal{R},n,2m,q,\chi}$ *such that*

$$|\Pr[\mathcal{H}_1(\mathcal{A}) = 1] - \Pr[\mathcal{H}_2(\mathcal{A}) = 1]| \leq \mathsf{adv}(\mathcal{A}_2) + \mathsf{lhl}(\lambda).$$

Proof. In the following we describe the adversary $\mathcal{A}_2$ for the case where $k \neq \ell$, i.e., the challenge identity is not registered. For the case $k = \ell$, the argument is the same, except that we first invoke Lemma 1 to switch the matrix $\mathbf{B}$ to uniformly sampled, which introduces an additive (statistical) term $\mathsf{lhl}(\lambda)$ in the distance between the two hybrids.

$\mathcal{A}_2$ first queries $2m$ LWE samples from its oracle and arranges them in matrix form as $(\mathbf{A}, \mathbf{v})$, this $\mathbf{A}$ is then parsed as $\mathbf{A} = (\mathbf{A}_0 \ \mathbf{A}_1)$ and uses $\mathbf{A}_0$ and $\mathbf{A}_1$ in pp, whereas the vector $\mathbf{v}$ is stored. Next, $\mathcal{A}_2$ queries m LWE samples from its oracle and arranges them in matrix form as $(\mathbf{B}, \mathbf{v}')$, this $\mathbf{B}$ is then used as part of pp. Now $\mathcal{A}_2$ simulates $\mathcal{H}_1$, but whenever a new honest key pk_i^* is generated, $\mathcal{A}_2$ queries its LWE oracle and obtains $(\hat{\mathbf{y}}_i, \hat{v}_i)$, sets $\mathsf{pk}_i = \hat{\mathbf{y}}_i$ and stores $\hat{v}_i$. The challenge ciphertext is generated as follows: Assume the challenge identity ind^* terminates in a public key pk_{i^*}. The challenge ciphertext is computed as in $\mathcal{H}_2(\mathcal{A})$, except that we set

$$d = \sum_{j=0}^{k-1} (\mathbf{u}_j - \mathbf{e}_j)^\mathsf{T} \cdot \mathbf{z}_j + \hat{v}_{i^*} + \lfloor \frac{q}{2} \rfloor \cdot \mathsf{msg} \bmod q$$

and $\mathbf{c}_k^\mathsf{T} = \mathbf{v}$ if $k < \ell$ and $\mathbf{c}_k^\mathsf{T} = \mathbf{v}'$ if $k = \ell$. $\mathcal{A}_2$ then continues simulation of $\mathcal{H}_2(\mathcal{A})$ and outputs whatever $\mathcal{H}_2(\mathcal{A})$ outputs.

First observe that if $(\mathbf{A}, \mathbf{v})$, $(\mathbf{B}, \mathbf{v}')$ and $\{(\hat{\mathbf{y}}_{i^*}, \hat{v}_{i^*})\}$ are LWE samples, i.e. $\mathbf{v} = \mathbf{s}^\mathsf{T} \cdot \mathbf{A} + \mathbf{e}^\mathsf{T} \bmod q$, $(\mathbf{v}')^\mathsf{T} = \mathbf{s}^\mathsf{T} \cdot \mathbf{B} + \hat{\mathbf{e}}^\mathsf{T} \bmod q$ and $\hat{v}_{i^*} = \mathbf{s}^\mathsf{T} \cdot \hat{\mathbf{y}}_{i^*} + \hat{e}_{i^*} \bmod q$, then the simulation of $\mathcal{A}_2$ is identically distributed to $\mathcal{H}_2(\mathcal{A})$. On the other hand, if $\mathbf{c}$, $\mathbf{v}'$ and the $\hat{v}_{i^*}$ are uniformly random and independent, then the simulation of $\mathcal{A}_2$ is identically distributed to $\mathcal{H}_3(\mathcal{A})$. The claim of the lemma follows. □

Lemma 5. *For any PPT adversary $\mathcal{A}$ there exists a PPT adversary $\mathcal{A}_3$ against* $\mathsf{LWE}_{\mathcal{R},n,m+1,q,\chi}$ *such that*

$$|\Pr[\mathcal{H}_2(\mathcal{A}) = 1] - \Pr[\mathcal{H}_3(\mathcal{A}) = 1]| \leq \ell \cdot \mathsf{adv}(\mathcal{A}_3).$$

Proof. Consider the following hybrids $\mathcal{H}_0''', \ldots, \mathcal{H}_\ell'''$, where $\mathcal{H}_0'''$ is identically distributed to $\mathcal{H}_2$, and $\mathcal{H}_\ell'''$ is identically distributed to $\mathcal{H}_3$.

- $\mathcal{H}_{i+1}'''$ (For $i = 0, \ldots, \ell - 1$): Identically distributed to $\mathcal{H}_i$, except that, for $i > k$, $\mathbf{c}_i$ is chosen uniformly at random.

Assume towards contradiction that

$$\Pr\left[\mathcal{H}_{i+1}'''(\mathcal{A}) = 1\right] - \Pr\left[\mathcal{H}_i'''(\mathcal{A}) = 1\right] \geq \epsilon$$

for some $i \in \{0, \ldots, \ell\}$. We will show that this implies a PPT adversary $\mathcal{A}_3$ against $\mathsf{LWE}_{\mathcal{R},n,m,q,\chi}$ with advantage ϵ. The adversary $\mathcal{A}_3$ receives an input $(\mathbf{A}, \mathbf{v})$ and proceeds as follows. $\mathcal{A}_3$ simulates $\mathcal{H}_i'''(\mathcal{A})$, except for the following modifications. First, it uses the matrix $\mathbf{A} = (\mathbf{A}_0 \ \mathbf{A}_1)$ in the public parameters. Next, when the challenge ciphertext is generated, if $i > k$ it sets $\mathbf{c}_i = \mathbf{v}$. $\mathcal{A}_3$ then continues the simulation and outputs whatever its simulation of $\mathcal{H}_{i-1}'''(\mathcal{A})$ outputs.

Now, it follows routinely that if $(\mathbf{A}, \mathbf{v})$ is an LWE sample, i.e. $\mathbf{v}^\mathsf{T} = \mathbf{s}^\mathsf{T} \cdot \mathbf{A} + \mathbf{e}^\mathsf{T} \bmod q$, then the simulation of $\mathcal{A}_3$ is distributed identically to $\mathcal{H}_i'''(\mathcal{A})$. On the other hand, if $\mathbf{v}$ is uniformly random, then the simulation of $\mathcal{A}_3$ is distributed identically to $\mathcal{H}_{i+1}'''(\mathcal{A})$. We can conclude that $\mathcal{A}_3$ has advantage ϵ. □

Update Privacy. There is a simple modification to construction of laconic encryption in Fig. 2 which yields update-privacy. The idea is to make the hash-function $f_{\mathbf{A}_0,\mathbf{A}_1}(\mathbf{y}_0,\mathbf{y}_1) = \mathbf{A}_0 \cdot (-\mathbf{G}^{-1}(\mathbf{y}_0)) + \mathbf{A}_1 \cdot (-\mathbf{G}^{-1}(\mathbf{y}_1))$ randomized such that $f_{\mathbf{A}_0,\mathbf{A}_1}(\mathbf{y}_0,\mathbf{y}_1)$ *statistically hides* $\mathbf{y}_0$ and $\mathbf{y}_1$. This can be achieved by slightly modifying the gadget matrix $\mathbf{G}$ into $\mathbf{G}'$ and making $\mathbf{G}'^{-1}$ randomized[3], and replacing the parameter m with a slightly larger $m' = m + n\log(q)$. Specifically, we set $\mathbf{G}' = (\mathbf{G} \ \mathbf{0}) \in \mathbb{Z}^{n \times m'}$, i.e. we obtain $\mathbf{G}'$ by appending $n\log(q)$ all-zero columns to $\mathbf{G}$. Furthermore, we define $\mathbf{G}'^{-1}(\mathbf{x}) = \begin{pmatrix} \mathbf{G}^{-1}(\mathbf{x}) \\ \mathbf{r} \end{pmatrix}$, where $\mathbf{r} \xleftarrow{\$} \mathcal{R}_2^{2n\log(q)}$ is chosen uniformly at random. Note that it still holds that $\mathbf{G}'\mathbf{G}'^{-1}(\mathbf{x}) = \mathbf{x}$ for all $\mathbf{x} \in \mathcal{R}_q^n$. The modified hash function is now

$$f'(\mathbf{y}_0, \mathbf{y}_1) = \mathbf{A}_0 \cdot (-\mathbf{G}'^{-1}(\mathbf{y}_0)) + \mathbf{A}_1 \cdot (-\mathbf{G}'^{-1}(\mathbf{y}_1)).$$

Now, decomposing $\mathbf{A}_0 = (\mathbf{A}_{0,1} \ \mathbf{A}_{0,2})$ and $\mathbf{A}_1 = (\mathbf{A}_{1,1} \ \mathbf{A}_{1,2})$, where $\mathbf{A}_{0,1}, \mathbf{A}_{1,1} \in \mathcal{R}_q^{n \times m}$ and $\mathbf{A}_{0,2}, \mathbf{A}_{1,2} \in \mathcal{R}_q^{n \times n\log(q)}$, it holds that

$$
\begin{aligned}
f'(\mathbf{y}_0, \mathbf{y}_1) &= \mathbf{A}_0 \cdot (-\mathbf{G}'^{-1}(\mathbf{y}_0)) + \mathbf{A}_1 \cdot (-\mathbf{G}'^{-1}(\mathbf{y}_1)) \\
&= (\mathbf{A}_{0,1} \ \mathbf{A}_{0,2}) \cdot \left(-\begin{pmatrix} \mathbf{G}^{-1}(\mathbf{y}_0) \\ \mathbf{r}_0 \end{pmatrix}\right) + (\mathbf{A}_{1,1} \ \mathbf{A}_{1,2}) \cdot \left(-\begin{pmatrix} \mathbf{G}^{-1}(\mathbf{y}_1) \\ \mathbf{r}_1 \end{pmatrix}\right) \\
&= (\mathbf{A}_{0,1} \ \mathbf{A}_{1,1}) \begin{pmatrix} -\mathbf{G}^{-1}(\mathbf{y}_0) \\ -\mathbf{G}^{-1}(\mathbf{y}_1) \end{pmatrix} \underbrace{- (\mathbf{A}_{0,2} \ \mathbf{A}_{1,2}) \begin{pmatrix} \mathbf{r}_0 \\ \mathbf{r}_1 \end{pmatrix}}_{=:\mathbf{v}}.
\end{aligned}
$$

---

[3] [12] defined a similar notion of *randomized* $\mathbf{G}^{-1}$, *which however samples a discrete gaussian preimage.*

Since the matrix $(\mathbf{A}_{0,2} \ \mathbf{A}_{1,2}) \in \mathcal{R}_q^{n \times 2n \log(q)}$ is chosen uniformly random and $(\mathbf{r}_0, \mathbf{r}_1)$ is uniformly random in $\mathcal{R}_2^{2n \log(q)}$, it holds by the leftover hash lemma (Lemma 1) that $\mathbf{v}$ is 2^{-n}-close to uniform. Consequently, the hash-value $f'(\mathbf{y}_0, \mathbf{y}_1)$ is statistically close to uniform. Hence, update privacy of the modified construction follows. We can conclude the following lemma.

Lemma 6. *The modified construction of Fig. 2 using $\mathbf{G}'$ and the randomized $\mathbf{G}'^{-1}$ is update private.*

Properties and Efficiency. We remark about some properties and efficiency of our construction. The public parameters (initially) consists of three uniformly random matrices $\mathbf{A}_0, \mathbf{A}_1, \mathbf{B} \in \mathcal{R}_q^{n \times m}$ which can be sampled with public coin. Subsequent updates to the public parameters, more specifically to $\mathbf{y}_\epsilon \in \mathcal{R}_q^n$, are deterministic. Suppose we pick q to be linear in ℓ, then the Setup and KGen algorithms run in time logarithmic in ℓ, while the Upd, Enc, WGen, and Dec algorithms run in time quasi-linear in ℓ.

Acknowledgments. Nico Döttling and Chuanwei Lin: Funded by the European Union (ERC, LACONIC, 101041207). Views and opinions expressed are however those of the author(s) only and do not necessarily reflect those of the European Union or the European Research Council. Neither the European Union nor the granting authority can be held responsible for them. Giulio Malavolta and Ahmadreza Rahimi: This work was partially funded by the German Federal Ministry of Education and Research (BMBF) in the course of the 6GEM research hub under grant number 16KISK038 and by the Deutsche Forschungsgemeinschaft (DFG, German Research Foundation) under Germany's Excellence Strategy - EXC 2092 CASA - 390781972. Dimitris Kolonelos: Received funding from projects from the European Research Council (ERC) under the European Union's Horizon 2020 research and innovation program under project PICOCRYPT (grant agreement No. 101001283), from the Spanish Government under project PRODIGY (TED2021-132464B-I00), and from the Madrid Regional Government under project BLOQUES (S2018/TCS-4339). The last two projects are co-funded by European Union EIE, and NextGenerationEU/PRTR funds.

References

1. Agrawal, S., Boneh, D., Boyen, X.: Lattice basis delegation in fixed dimension and shorter-ciphertext hierarchical IBE. In: Rabin, T. (ed.) CRYPTO 2010. LNCS, vol. 6223, pp. 98–115. Springer, Heidelberg (2010). https://doi.org/10.1007/978-3-642-14623-7_6
2. Ajtai, M.: Generating hard instances of lattice problems (extended abstract). In: 28th ACM STOC, pp. 99–108. ACM Press (1996). https://doi.org/10.1145/237814.237838
3. Alamati, N., Branco, P., Döttling, N., Garg, S., Hajiabadi, M., Pu, S.: Laconic private set intersection and applications. In: Nissim, K., Waters, B. (eds.) TCC 2021, Part III. LNCS, vol. 13044, pp. 94–125. Springer, Cham (2021). https://doi.org/10.1007/978-3-030-90456-2_4
4. Albrecht, M.R., Lai, R.W.F.: Subtractive sets over cyclotomic rings. In: Malkin, T., Peikert, C. (eds.) CRYPTO 2021, Part II. LNCS, vol. 12826, pp. 519–548. Springer, Cham (2021). https://doi.org/10.1007/978-3-030-84245-1_18

5. Alekhnovich, M.: More on average case vs approximation complexity. In: 44th FOCS, pp. 298–307. IEEE Computer Society Press (2003). https://doi.org/10.1109/SFCS.2003.1238204

6. Alperin-Sheriff, J., Peikert, C.: Circular and KDM security for identity-based encryption. In: Fischlin, M., Buchmann, J., Manulis, M. (eds.) PKC 2012. LNCS, vol. 7293, pp. 334–352. Springer, Heidelberg (2012). https://doi.org/10.1007/978-3-642-30057-8_20

7. Aranha, D., Lin, C., Orlandi, C., Simkin, M.: Laconic private set-intersection from pairings. Cryptology ePrint Archive, Report 2022/529 (2022). https://eprint.iacr.org/2022/529

8. Benhamouda, F., Lin, H.: k-round multiparty computation from k-round oblivious transfer via garbled interactive circuits. In: Nielsen, J.B., Rijmen, V. (eds.) EUROCRYPT 2018, Part II. LNCS, vol. 10821, pp. 500–532. Springer, Cham (2018). https://doi.org/10.1007/978-3-319-78375-8_17

9. Boneh, D., Franklin, M.: Identity-based encryption from the Weil pairing. In: Kilian, J. (ed.) CRYPTO 2001. LNCS, vol. 2139, pp. 213–229. Springer, Heidelberg (2001). https://doi.org/10.1007/3-540-44647-8_13

10. Bos, J., et al.: CRYSTALS - kyber: a CCA-secure module-lattice-based KEM. Cryptology ePrint Archive, Paper 2017/634 (2017). https://doi.org/10.1109/EuroSP.2018.00032, https://eprint.iacr.org/2017/634

11. Boudgoust, K., Jeudy, C., Roux-Langlois, A., Wen, W.: Towards classical hardness of module-LWE: the linear rank case. In: Moriai, S., Wang, H. (eds.) ASIACRYPT 2020, Part II. LNCS, vol. 12492, pp. 289–317. Springer, Cham (2020). https://doi.org/10.1007/978-3-030-64834-3_10

12. Bourse, F., Del Pino, R., Minelli, M., Wee, H.: FHE circuit privacy almost for free. In: Robshaw, M., Katz, J. (eds.) CRYPTO 2016, Part II. LNCS, vol. 9815, pp. 62–89. Springer, Heidelberg (2016). https://doi.org/10.1007/978-3-662-53008-5_3

13. Boyen, X., Li, Q.: Towards tightly secure lattice short signature and id-based encryption. In: Cheon, J.H., Takagi, T. (eds.) ASIACRYPT 2016, Part II. LNCS, vol. 10032, pp. 404–434. Springer, Heidelberg (2016). https://doi.org/10.1007/978-3-662-53890-6_14

14. Brakerski, Z., Döttling, N.: Lossiness and entropic hardness for ring-LWE. In: Pass, R., Pietrzak, K. (eds.) TCC 2020, Part I. LNCS, vol. 12550, pp. 1–27. Springer, Cham (2020). https://doi.org/10.1007/978-3-030-64375-1_1

15. Brakerski, Z., Lombardi, A., Segev, G., Vaikuntanathan, V.: Anonymous IBE, leakage resilience and circular security from new assumptions. In: Nielsen, J.B., Rijmen, V. (eds.) EUROCRYPT 2018, Part I. LNCS, vol. 10820, pp. 535–564. Springer, Cham (2018). https://doi.org/10.1007/978-3-319-78381-9_20

16. Cash, D., Hofheinz, D., Kiltz, E., Peikert, C.: Bonsai trees, or how to delegate a lattice basis. In: Gilbert, H. (ed.) EUROCRYPT 2010. LNCS, vol. 6110, pp. 523–552. Springer, Heidelberg (2010). https://doi.org/10.1007/978-3-642-13190-5_27

17. Cho, C., Döttling, N., Garg, S., Gupta, D., Miao, P., Polychroniadou, A.: Laconic oblivious transfer and its applications. In: Katz, J., Shacham, H. (eds.) CRYPTO 2017, Part II. LNCS, vol. 10402, pp. 33–65. Springer, Cham (2017). https://doi.org/10.1007/978-3-319-63715-0_2

18. Döttling, N., Garg, S.: From selective IBE to full IBE and selective HIBE. In: Kalai, Y., Reyzin, L. (eds.) TCC 2017, Part I. LNCS, vol. 10677, pp. 372–408. Springer, Cham (2017). https://doi.org/10.1007/978-3-319-70500-2_13

19. Döttling, N., Garg, S.: Identity-based encryption from the Diffie-Hellman assumption. In: Katz, J., Shacham, H. (eds.) CRYPTO 2017, Part I. LNCS, vol. 10401, pp. 537–569. Springer, Cham (2017). https://doi.org/10.1007/978-3-319-63688-7_18

20. Döttling, N., Garg, S., Goyal, V., Malavolta, G.: Laconic conditional disclosure of secrets and applications. In: Zuckerman, D. (ed.) 60th FOCS, pp. 661–685. IEEE Computer Society Press (2019). https://doi.org/10.1109/FOCS.2019.00046

21. Döttling, N., Garg, S., Hajiabadi, M., Masny, D.: New constructions of identity-based and key-dependent message secure encryption schemes. In: Abdalla, M., Dahab, R. (eds.) PKC 2018, Part I. LNCS, vol. 10769, pp. 3–31. Springer, Cham (2018). https://doi.org/10.1007/978-3-319-76578-5_1

22. Döttling, N., Garg, S., Ishai, Y., Malavolta, G., Mour, T., Ostrovsky, R.: Trapdoor hash functions and their applications. In: Boldyreva, A., Micciancio, D. (eds.) CRYPTO 2019, Part III. LNCS, vol. 11694, pp. 3–32. Springer, Cham (2019). https://doi.org/10.1007/978-3-030-26954-8_1

23. Garg, S., Hajiabadi, M.: Trapdoor functions from the computational Diffie-Hellman assumption. In: Shacham, H., Boldyreva, A. (eds.) CRYPTO 2018, Part II. LNCS, vol. 10992, pp. 362–391. Springer, Cham (2018). https://doi.org/10.1007/978-3-319-96881-0_13

24. Garg, S., Hajiabadi, M., Mahmoody, M., Rahimi, A.: Registration-based encryption: removing private-key generator from IBE. In: Beimel, A., Dziembowski, S. (eds.) TCC 2018, Part I. LNCS, vol. 11239, pp. 689–718. Springer, Cham (2018). https://doi.org/10.1007/978-3-030-03807-6_25

25. Garg, S., Hajiabadi, M., Mahmoody, M., Rahimi, A., Sekar, S.: Registration-based encryption from standard assumptions. In: Lin, D., Sako, K. (eds.) PKC 2019, Part II. LNCS, vol. 11443, pp. 63–93. Springer, Cham (2019). https://doi.org/10.1007/978-3-030-17259-6_3

26. Garg, S., Srinivasan, A.: Garbled protocols and two-round MPC from bilinear maps. In: Umans, C. (ed.) 58th FOCS, pp. 588–599. IEEE Computer Society Press (2017). https://doi.org/10.1109/FOCS.2017.60

27. Garg, S., Srinivasan, A.: Adaptively secure garbling with near optimal online complexity. In: Nielsen, J.B., Rijmen, V. (eds.) EUROCRYPT 2018, Part II. LNCS, vol. 10821, pp. 535–565. Springer, Cham (2018). https://doi.org/10.1007/978-3-319-78375-8_18

28. Garg, S., Srinivasan, A.: Two-round multiparty secure computation from minimal assumptions. In: Nielsen, J.B., Rijmen, V. (eds.) EUROCRYPT 2018, Part II. LNCS, vol. 10821, pp. 468–499. Springer, Cham (2018). https://doi.org/10.1007/978-3-319-78375-8_16

29. Gentry, C.: Fully homomorphic encryption using ideal lattices. In: Mitzenmacher, M. (ed.) 41st ACM STOC, pp. 169–178. ACM Press (2009). https://doi.org/10.1145/1536414.1536440

30. Gentry, C., Peikert, C., Vaikuntanathan, V.: Trapdoors for hard lattices and new cryptographic constructions. In: Ladner, R.E., Dwork, C. (eds.) 40th ACM STOC, pp. 197–206. ACM Press (2008). https://doi.org/10.1145/1374376.1374407

31. Glaeser, N., Kolonelos, D., Malavolta, G., Rahimi, A.: Efficient registration-based encryption. Cryptology ePrint Archive, Paper 2022/1505 (2022). https://eprint.iacr.org/2022/1505

32. Goldreich, O., Goldwasser, S., Halevi, S.: Collision-free hashing from lattice problems. Cryptology ePrint Archive, Report 1996/009 (1996). https://eprint.iacr.org/1996/009

33. Goyal, R., Vusirikala, S.: Verifiable registration-based encryption. In: Micciancio, D., Ristenpart, T. (eds.) CRYPTO 2020, Part I. LNCS, vol. 12170, pp. 621–651. Springer, Cham (2020). https://doi.org/10.1007/978-3-030-56784-2_21

34. Håstad, J., Impagliazzo, R., Levin, L.A., Luby, M.: A pseudorandom generator from any one-way function. SIAM J. Comput. 28(4), 1364–1396 (1999)

35. Hohenberger, S., Lu, G., Waters, B., Wu, D.J.: Registered attribute-based encryption. Cryptology ePrint Archive, Paper 2022/1500 (2022). https://eprint.iacr.org/2022/1500

36. Libert, B., Ling, S., Nguyen, K., Wang, H.: Zero-knowledge arguments for lattice-based accumulators: logarithmic-size ring signatures and group signatures without trapdoors. In: Fischlin, M., Coron, J.-S. (eds.) EUROCRYPT 2016, Part II. LNCS, vol. 9666, pp. 1–31. Springer, Heidelberg (2016). https://doi.org/10.1007/978-3-662-49896-5_1

37. Micciancio, D., Peikert, C.: Trapdoors for lattices: simpler, tighter, faster, smaller. In: Pointcheval, D., Johansson, T. (eds.) EUROCRYPT 2012. LNCS, vol. 7237, pp. 700–718. Springer, Heidelberg (2012). https://doi.org/10.1007/978-3-642-29011-4_41

38. O'Neill, A., Peikert, C., Waters, B.: Bi-deniable public-key encryption. In: Rogaway, P. (ed.) CRYPTO 2011. LNCS, vol. 6841, pp. 525–542. Springer, Heidelberg (2011). https://doi.org/10.1007/978-3-642-22792-9_30

39. Peikert, C.: An efficient and parallel Gaussian sampler for lattices. In: Rabin, T. (ed.) CRYPTO 2010. LNCS, vol. 6223, pp. 80–97. Springer, Heidelberg (2010). https://doi.org/10.1007/978-3-642-14623-7_5

40. Quach, W., Wee, H., Wichs, D.: Laconic function evaluation and applications. In: Thorup, M. (ed.) 59th FOCS, pp. 859–870. IEEE Computer Society Press (2018). https://doi.org/10.1109/FOCS.2018.00086

41. Regev, O.: On lattices, learning with errors, random linear codes, and cryptography. In: Gabow, H.N., Fagin, R. (eds.) 37th ACM STOC, pp. 84–93. ACM Press (2005). https://doi.org/10.1145/1060590.1060603

42. Yao, A.C.C.: How to generate and exchange secrets (extended abstract). In: 27th FOCS, pp. 162–167. IEEE Computer Society Press (1986). https://doi.org/10.1109/SFCS.1986.25

Fully Adaptive Decentralized
Multi-Authority ABE

Pratish Datta[1]([✉])[iD], Ilan Komargodski[1,2][iD], and Brent Waters[1,3]

[1] NTT Research, Sunnyvale, CA 94085, USA
`pratish.datta@ntt-research.com`
[2] Hebrew University of Jerusalem, 91904 Jerusalem, Israel
`ilank@cs.huji.ac.il`
[3] University of Texas at Austin, Austin, TX 78712, USA
`bwaters@cs.utexas.edu`

Abstract. Decentralized multi-authority attribute-based encryption (MA-ABE) is a distributed generalization of standard (ciphertext-policy) attribute-based encryption where there is no trusted central authority: any party can become an authority and issue private keys, and there is no requirement for any global coordination other than the creation of an initial set of common reference parameters.

We present the first multi-authority attribute-based encryption schemes that are provably fully-adaptively secure. Namely, our construction is secure against an attacker that may corrupt some of the authorities as well as perform key queries adaptively throughout the life-time of the system. Our main construction relies on a prime order bilinear group where the k-linear assumption holds as well as on a random oracle. Along the way, we present a conceptually simpler construction relying on a composite order bilinear group with standard subgroup decision assumptions as well as on a random oracle.

Prior to this work, there was no construction that could resist adaptive corruptions of authorities, no matter the assumptions used. In fact, we point out that even standard complexity leveraging style arguments do not work in the multi-authority setting.

1 Introduction

Attribute-based encryption schemes [22,41] allow fine-grained access control when accessing encrypted data: Such encryption schemes support decryption keys that allow users that have certain credentials (or attributes) to decrypt certain messages without leaking any additional information. Over the years, the challenge of designing ABE schemes has received tremendous attention resulting in a long sequence of works achieving various trade-offs between expressiveness, efficiency, security, and underlying assumptions.

Multi-Authority Attribute-Based Encryption: In ABE schemes, restricted decryption keys can only be generated and issued by a central authority who possesses the master secret key. Chase [10] introduced the notion of multi-authority

© International Association for Cryptologic Research 2023
C. Hazay and M. Stam (Eds.): EUROCRYPT 2023, LNCS 14006, pp. 447–478, 2023.
https://doi.org/10.1007/978-3-031-30620-4_15

ABE (MA-ABE) which allows multiple parties to play the role of an authority. More precisely, in an MA-ABE, there are multiple authorities which control different attributes and each of them can issue secret keys to users possessing attributes under their control without any interaction with the other authorities in the system. Given a ciphertext generated with respect to some access policy, a user possessing a set of attributes satisfying the access policy can decrypt the ciphertext by pulling the individual secret keys it obtained from the various authorities controlling those attributes.

After few initial attempts [10,11,32,34,35] that had various limitations, Lewko and Waters [30] were able to design the first truly decentralized MA-ABE scheme in which any party can become an authority and there is no requirement for any global coordination other than the creation of an initial trusted setup. In their scheme, a party can simply act as an authority by publishing a public key of its own and issuing private keys to different users that reflect their attributes. Different authorities need not even be aware of each other and they can join the system at any point of time. There is also no bound on the number of attribute authorities that can ever come into play during the lifetime of the system. Their scheme supports all access policies computable by NC^1 circuits. Furthermore, utilizing the powerful dual system technique [45], security is proven assuming a composite order bilinear group with "subgroup decision"-style assumptions and in the random oracle model.

Following Lewko and Waters [30] there were several extensions and improvements. Okamoto and Takashima [38] gave a construction over prime order bilinear groups relying on the decision-linear (DLIN) [7] assumption. Rouselakis and Waters [40] and Ambrona and Gay [2] provided efficiency improvements but provide weaker security guarantees and/or used the less standard q-type assumptions and the generic group model (GGM) respectively. Datta et al. [14] gave the first Learning With Errors (LWE)-based construction supporting a non-trivial class of access policies. All of the above are in the random oracle model. Very recently, Waters, Wee, and Wu [48] gave a construction (for the same class of policies as [14]) whose security can be based in the plain model without random oracles, relying on the recently-introduced evasive LWE assumption [43,49] which is a very strong knowledge type assumption.

Security: The natural MA-ABE security definition requires the usual collusion resistance against unauthorized users with the important difference that now some of the attribute authorities may be corrupted and therefore may collude with the adversarial users. While some constructions support adaptive key queries, *there is no known construction, under any assumption, which supports* **fully adaptive corruption of authorities**. Given the distributed nature of MA-ABE it seems unsatisfying to assume that an attacker commits on a corrupted set of authorities at the beginning of the security game, even before seeing any secret key. Indeed, in reality we do not even expect all attribute authorities to join the system at the same time. Therefore, we argue that the "static corruptions" model that previous works have considered does not capture realistic attack scenarios, and we therefore ask whether it is possible to improve it by supporting adaptive corruption of authorities.

We emphasize that getting fully adaptive security is a well-known gap in existing constructions. Even though the authors of [30] were well versed in sophisticated dual system technique, they (and all followup attempts) got fundamentally stuck in solving this obstacle. More broadly, getting adaptive security is a fundamental area of research in the cryptographic community with many successes over the years (e.g., [3, 21, 26, 33, 47]). Still, this natural question in the MA-ABE domain remained untouched.

Interestingly, this is one of the rare cases where generic complexity leveraging/guessing style arguments fail (even if we are fine with a sub-exponential security loss). Indeed, applying these arguments in our setting results in an exponential loss proportional to the maximum number of authorities per ciphertext. Thus, there needs to be a pre-determined maximum number of authorities per ciphertext limit and then the security parameter needs to be chosen appropriately. Our goal, of course, is to devise a truly decentralized scheme where any party could join as an authority at any point in time and there is no limit to the number of authorities.

1.1 Our Results

We construct the first truly decentralized MA-ABE schemes which is provably secure even when fully adaptive corruption of authorities are allowed, in addition to fully adaptive key queries. Our schemes are based on bilinear groups with standard polynomial hardness assumptions and in the random oracle model. We emphasize that our constructions are the first provably secure schemes against fully adaptive corruptions of authorities *under any assumption*.

We first give a construction based on bilinear groups of composite order with (by now) standard subgroup-decision assumptions, and then give a construction in prime order bilinear groups where the k-Linear (k-Lin) [24, 42] or more generally the matrix Diffie-Hellman (MDDH) [17] holds.

Theorem 1.1 (Informal; see Section 4). *Assume a composite order bilinear group where "standard" subgroup-decision assumptions hold. Then, there is a fully-adaptive MA-ABE scheme in the random oracle model.*

The assumptions that we use in the above theorem have been used multiple times in the past and they were shown to hold in the generic bilinear group model [29–31]. However, we still point out that composite order-based constructions have few drawbacks compared to the more standard prime order setting. First, in prime order groups, we can obtain security under more standard assumptions such as k-LIN or bilinear Diffie-Hellman (BDH) [8] assumption. Second, in prime order groups, we can achieve much more efficient systems for the same security levels [19, 23, 39]. This is because in composite order groups, security typically relies on the hardness of factoring the group order. In turn, this requires the use of large group orders, which results in considerably slower group and pairing operations.

To this end, starting with Freeman [19] and Lewko [27], multiple frameworks and tools have been developed to translate existing composite order group constructions into prime order analogues (see, for example, [1,4,12,13,20,25,36,37]). We use a recent set of tools due to Chen, Gong, Kowalczyk, and Wee [13] (building on [12,20]) and manage to obtain a construction in (asymmetric) bilinear groups of prime order whose security is based on the more standard k-Lin or MDDH assumption.[1]

Theorem 1.2 (Informal; see Section 5). *Assume a prime order bilinear group where the k-Lin or MDDH assumption holds. Then, there is a fully-adaptive MA-ABE scheme in the random oracle model.*

The state of the art MA-ABE constructions are compared in Table 1.

Table 1. State of the Art in Decentralized MA-ABE

Scheme	Access policy	Assumption	Security	Bounded policy size
[2]	NC^1	GGM	adaptive	no
[2]	NC^1	SXDH	selective	no
[30]	NC^1	subgroup decision	adaptive	no
[38]	NC^1	DLin	adaptive	no
[40]	NC^1	q-type	static	no
[14]	DNF	LWE	static	yes
[15]	NC^1	C/D-BDH	static	yes
[48]	DNF	evasive LWE	static	yes
This Work	NC^1	subgroup decision	full	no
This Work	NC^1	k-Lin or MDDH	full	no

In this table, static security requires all of the ciphertexts, secret keys, and corruption queries to be issued by the adversary before the public key of any attribute authority is published, selective security requires the ciphertext and corruption queries to be made upfront while the key queries can be made adaptively, adaptive security requires corruption queries to be issued ahead of time, but all other queries (secret keys and ciphertexts) can be made adaptively, and full security enables all queries, including corruption queries, to be made adaptively. Schemes having a restriction that the maximal size of policies has to be declared during system setup are said to have bounded policy size. All of the works are in the random oracle model except [48]. Lastly, we mention that this table only lists truly decentralized schemes with no trusted centralized authority.

Technical Highlight: As all previous group-based decentralized MA-ABE systems secure against adaptive key queries in the standard model [30,38], we also

---

[1] Our construction is secure based on any choice of k. For instance, setting $k = 1$ we get security under the Symmetric External Diffie-Hellman Assumption (SXDH), and setting $k = 2$ corresponds to security under the DLIN assumption.

use the dual-systems methodology. However, as we explain below, the existing techniques in this space cannot be used to prove fully adaptive security, that is, security against both adaptive key queries and adaptive corruption of attribute authorities. As our main conceptual contribution, we introduce a new technique within this space that allows us to bleed information from one sub-group to another in an unnoticeable way. We call this technique *dual systems with dual sub-systems* and it allows us to undetectably move information between different sub-groups across ciphertexts and key components via a secondary dual sub-system. We believe that this conceptual contribution is of independent interest. See Sect. 2 for details.

2   Technical Overview

This section starts by providing an overview of the notion of MA-ABE schemes and our fully adaptive security definition, followed by an exposition of previous works and why they failed to achieve the fully adaptive security. We then continue with explaining our main new ideas, followed by an overview of the final scheme and its security proof. We decided to provide an extensive and detailed technical overview in order to help in understanding the challenges stemming from the fully adaptive security model and our approach for dealing with them. A reader interested in our constructions can directly refer to Sect. 2.4.1.

2.1   Background on MA-ABE

Our MA-ABE (like all other known MA-ABE schemes) is designed under the assumption that each user in the system has a unique global identifier GID coming from some universe of global identifiers $\mathcal{GID} \subset \{0,1\}^*$. We shall further assume (without loss of generality) that each authority controls just one attribute, and hence we can use the words "authority" and "attribute" interchangeably. (We note that this restriction can be relaxed to support an a priori bounded number of attributes per authority [30].) We denote the authority universe by $\mathcal{AU}$.

Let us recall the syntax of decentralized MA-ABE for NC^1 access policies, which is well known to be realizable by (monotone) linear secret sharing schemes (LSSS) [6,30]. A decentralized MA-ABE scheme consists of 5 procedures GlobalSetup, AuthSetup, KeyGen, Enc, and Dec. The GlobalSetup procedure gets as input the security parameter (in unary encoding) and outputs global public parameters. All of the other procedures depend on these global parameters (we may sometimes not mention them explicitly when they are clear from context). The AuthSetup procedure can be executed by any authority $u \in \mathcal{AU}$ to generate a corresponding public and master secret key pair, $(\mathsf{PK}_u, \mathsf{MSK}_u)$. An authority holding the master secret key MSK_u can then generate a secret key $\mathsf{SK}_{\mathsf{GID},u}$ for a user with global identifier GID. At any point in time, using the public keys $\{\mathsf{PK}_u\}$ of some authorities, one can encrypt a message msg relative to some linear secret sharing policy (M, ρ), where M is the policy matrix and ρ is the function that assigns row indices in the matrix to attributes controlled by those authorities, to get a ciphertext CT. Finally, a user holding a set of secret keys $\{SK_{GID,u}\}$ (relative to the same GID) can decrypt a given ciphertext CT if and only if the attributes corresponding to the secret it possesses "satisfy" the access structure with which the ciphertext was generated. If the MA-ABE scheme is built in the random oracle model as is the case in this paper and in all previous collusion resistant MA-ABE schemes,[2] the existence of a public hash function H mapping the global identifiers in $\mathcal{GID}$ to some appropriate space is considered. This hash function H is generated by GlobalSetup and is modeled as a random oracle in the security proof.

2.2   Fully Adaptive Security

Just like standard ABE, the security of an MA-ABE scheme demands collusion resistance, that is, no group of colluding users, none of whom is individually authorized to decrypt a ciphertext, should be able to decrypt the same when they pull their secret key components together. However, in case of MA-ABE, it is further required that collusion resistance should hold even if some of the attribute authorities collude with the adversarial users and thereby those users can freely obtain secret keys corresponding to the attributes controlled by those corrupt authorities. Decentralized MA-ABE further allows the public and secret keys of the corrupt authorities to be generated in a malicious way and still needs collusion resistance. This is crucial since, in a decentralized MA-ABE scheme, anyone is allowed to act as an attribute authority by generating its public and secret keys locally and independently of everyone else in the system. We are aiming for **fully adaptive security** which is roughly defined by the following game:

- **Global Setup:** The challenger runs GlobalSetup to generate global public parameters.
- **Query Phase I:** The attacker is allowed to adaptively make a polynomial number of queries of the following form:
  1. *Authority Setup Query* : the challenger runs AuthSetup to create a public/master key pair for an authority specified by the adversary.
  2. *Secret Key Query* : the challenger runs KeyGen to create a secret key for a given attribute.
  3. *Authority Master Key Query* : the challenger provides the attacker the master secret key corresponding to some authority of the adversary's choice.
- **Challenge Phase:** The adversary submits two messages msg_0, msg_1, and an access structure along with a set of public keys of authorities involved in the access structure. The authority public keys supplied by the attacker can potentially be malformed, i.e., can fall outside the range of AuthSetup. It gets

---

[2] The very recent construction of Waters, Wee, and Wu [48] is in the plain model, however, as mentioned, it is based on a newly introduced and less standard assumption and achieves the rather weak "static" security definition..

back from the challenger an encryption of one of the messages (chosen at random) with respect to the access structure. It is crucial that the adversary does not hold enough secret keys/authority master keys to decrypt a message that is encrypted with respect to the access structure.

- **Query Phase 2:** Same as in Query Phase 1 (while making sure that the constraint from the challenge phase is not violated).
- **Guess:** The attacker submits a guess for which message underlies the challenge ciphertext.

All previous MA-ABE schemes consider a much weaker definition where the adversary must commit during the Global Setup phase on the set of authorities in the system as well as on the subset of corrupted authorities. Already at that point, the private/public key pairs of all non-corrupt authorities are created by the challenger and the public keys are given to the attacker. (That is, during Query Phase I and II, only queries of form 2 (secret key query) are allowed.) Our fully adaptive definition is much more realistic given the distributed nature of MA-ABE.

2.3 Limitations of Previous Works

As in any ABE scheme, the challenge in MA-ABE is to make it collusion resistant. Usually, ABE schemes achieve collusion resistance by using the system's authority who knows a master secret key to "tie" together different key components representing the different attributes of a user with the help of fresh randomness specific to that user. Such randomization would make the different key components of a user compatible with each other, but not with the parts of a key issued to another user.

In a multi-authority setting, however, we want to satisfy the simultaneous goals of autonomous key generation and collusion resistance. The requirement of autonomous key generation means that standard techniques for key randomization cannot be applied since there is no one party to compile all the pieces together. Furthermore, in a decentralized MA-ABE system each component may come from a different authority, where such authorities have no coordination and are possibly not even aware of each other. To overcome this, all previous decentralized MA-ABE schemes use the output of a public hash function applied on the user's global identity, GID, as the randomness tying together multiple key components issued to a specific user by different authorities.[3]

To see the challenge let us focus on one particular construction due to Lewko and Waters [30]. Although this is the very first truly decentralized MA-ABE scheme, all relevant follow-up works heavily rely on it and therefore suffer from similar problems. The security proof of the [30] construction uses the dual system technique originally developed by Waters [45]. In a dual system, ciphertexts and keys can take on two forms: normal or semi-functional. Semi-functional ciphertexts and keys are not used in the real system, they are only used in the security proof. A normal key can decrypt normal or semi-functional ciphertexts,

---

[3] [48] is an exception; see Footnote 2.

and a normal ciphertext can be decrypted by normal or semi-functional keys. However, when a semi-functional key is used to decrypt a semi-functional ciphertext, decryption will fail. Security for dual systems is proved using a sequence of "indistinguishable" games. The first game is the real security game (with normal ciphertext and keys). In the next game, the ciphertext is semi-functional, while all the keys are normal. For an attacker that makes q secret key requests, we define q games, where in the k-th one, the first k keys are semi-functional while the remaining keys are normal. In game q, all the keys and the challenge ciphertext given to the attacker are semi-functional. Hence, none of the given keys are useful for decrypting the challenge ciphertext.

The proof of [30] follows this high level approach, but inherently relies on the fact that the corrupted authorities are specified in advance. There, towards the end of the proof, all keys are semi-functional and the challenge ciphertext is also semi-functional. The goal in the last hybrid is to move to a game where the semi-functional challenge ciphertext is of a random message (rather than the original message). For this to be indistinguishable, they need to "shut off" the rows in the matrix of the access policy corresponding to the corrupted authorities. This is done by using an information theoretic tool of choosing a vector which is orthogonal to those rows in the challenge ciphertext (such a vector must exist since the corrupted set must be unauthorized). Effectively, this allows them to completely ignore the existence of authority master keys corresponding to those rows, while for the other rows the inexistence of a secret key was already taken care of when they moved to a game where all keys are semi-functional.

This approach clearly fails when authorities can be corrupted adaptively. Technically, it is impossible to "shut off" the rows corresponding to the corrupted authorities since the latter may not be even known at the time the challenge ciphertext is created since authorities may be corrupted *after* the challenge ciphertext is created where the challenger should be able to give the adversary the corresponding master key. However, with the (proof) approach of Lewko and Waters [30] this is impossible since the challenger (at that point) does not even have a properly formed master key for the authority.

A Fundamental Limitation?: At this point it is useful to step back and try to discern whether and why handling corrupted authorities was a foundational problem of [30] and has remained open for more than a decade. Lewko and Waters create an intricate dual system encryption proof that uses two semi-functional subspaces. Their techniques go beyond the prior methods of [28,29] to adapt to the demands of the multi-authority setting. Now the question is the following.

Question: *Is the lack of handling authority corruption mostly an oversight that can be addressed by pushing their techniques a tiny bit further or is there a more fundamental barrier?*

The answer to this question can be distilled by making a quick observation about the Lewko-Waters construction. In their construction all user keys are composed of bilinear group elements. Thus, one can execute a dual system encryption proof by applying subgroup decision or k-linear assumptions (depending on the setting) to change the distribution of such groups over the course of a sequence of games as is typically done.

The authority master secret keys however consist solely of *exponents* over the order of the group. The reason for authority keys being exponents is a consequence of the demands of the multi-authority setting. To bring authority keys into the fold of a dual system encryption proof one would need a plan for changing such keys to some kind of semi-functional form. However, there is no trodden path in the dual system encryption literature for doing this for keys formed solely from exponents. Indeed, none of the hardness assumptions seem to align with this goal at all!

Due to these fundamental barriers, the construction and proof of Lewko and Waters dealt with key queries and corrupted authorities separately. For uncorrupted authorities, the proof handles key generation queries via a dual system encryption. In contrast, corrupted authorities were statically "routed around" in the proof so as to not have important information when needed and thus taken "outside" the dual system encryption proof.

In our work, we will show how to overcome this barrier and bring adaptive corruption of authorities into the fold of a dual system encryption proof. Doing so will require both a novel construction and proof ideas. We shall focus on the composite order construction next as this is where most of the new ideas already come up and it is also much easier to describe. We give an overview of how we port the construction to the prime order setting in Sect. 2.5.

2.4   Overview of Our Approach and Our (Composite Order) Scheme

Looking into the Lewko-Waters [30] MA-ABE scheme and the security proof more closely, we observe that their authority master keys consist of two exponents, namely $\alpha, y \leftarrow \mathbb{Z}_N$ where $N = p_1 p_2 p_3$ is the order of the underlying composite order group. At the final step of their security proof where they transition from a correctly formed semi-functional ciphertext for the challenge message to one for a completely random message, they simulated the exponents α and y based on the instance of the underlying hard problem. As such, they could not hope to give out those keys to the adversary during the security game. In other words, they could not support adaptive corruption of authorities.

In order to resolve this problem, ultimately, we want to come up with a construction and a corresponding proof strategy that never needs to simulate the authority master keys based on instances of underlying hard problems. Towards this end, we first observe that it is due to their scheme design that Lewko-Waters [30] needed to simulate the authority master keys. More specifically, in each ciphertext, the payload is masked with the group element $e(g_1, g_1)^s$ in the target group for random $s \leftarrow \mathbb{Z}_N$. Next, the ciphertext provides secret shares of the masking factor s according to the underlying access policy in the exponent of $e(g_1, g_1)$ and they mask them with α for the corresponding authorities also in the exponent of $e(g_1, g_1)$. This is done to ensure that during decryption, only the shares corresponding to the attributes possessed by the decryptor can be recovered by canceling out the α part with a collection of appropriate secret keys for user GID.

Now, at the final hybrid transition of their security proof, they utilized an assumption similar to decisional bilinear Diffie-Hellman (DBDH) where they simulate s as abc, where $a, b, c \leftarrow \mathbb{Z}_N$ are random exponents and unknown to the simulator. Therefore, the simulator has to embed the term ab within α so that it can simulate the ciphertext components containing the shares of s by canceling out ab in the exponent.

In order to do away with α and transition to a construction and proof technique that do not require simulating the authority master keys, we consider a new element h from the p_1 subgroup in the global public parameters. Instead of relying on the entropy derived from the exponents α corresponding to the authorities/attributes a user does not possess, we would like to rely on the entropy obtained from this new component h to hide the payload (recall that h is a part of the global public parameters and is *not associated* with any attribute authority). Simulating h based on the underlying hard problem would not affect the simulator's ability to give out authority master keys. So, our initial idea is to simply mask the payloads with $e(g_1, h)^s$ for $s \leftarrow \mathbb{Z}_N$. We then provide ElGamal encryptions of the secret shares of the masking factor s under the corresponding authority master keys, which now consist only of the exponents y. More precisely, we include $C_{1,x} = g_1^{\tau_x}, C_{2,x} = g_1^{y_{\rho(x)}\tau_x} g_1^{\sigma_x}$ for all rows x of the associated LSSS access structure $(\boldsymbol{M}, \rho)$.[4] For the user's secret keys, instead of generating it as $g^\alpha \cdot \mathsf{H}(\mathsf{GID})^y$, as in Lewko-Waters construction, we form the secret keys as $(h \cdot \mathsf{H}(\mathsf{GID}))^y$.

The high level idea of the security proof is then to change h from being an element of the p_1 subgroup to being an element of the $p_1 p_2$ subgroup. Then, the factor masking the message would become $e(g_1, h)^s \cdot e(g_2, h)^s$. At this point, we can leverage the entropy of $s \bmod p_2$ to hide the payload in the final game.

Dual Systems with Dual Sub-systems: Unfortunately, the above scheme does not satisfy correctness. This is because, at the time of decryption, while pairing the ciphertext and key components, some additional terms involving the shares of the masking factor s in the exponent of $e(g_1, \mathsf{H}(\mathsf{GID}))$ would remain. In order to cancel out these terms and ensure correctness, we introduce another parallel sub-system where we provide ElGamal encryptions of shares of $-s$ under corresponding authority master keys and provide elements of the form $\mathsf{H}(\mathsf{GID})^y$ as part of the user's secret keys. At the time of decryption, this part will produce $e(g_1, \mathsf{H}(\mathsf{GID}))^{-s}$ that will cancel $e(g_1, \mathsf{H}(\mathsf{GID}))^s$ from the first sub-system.

Now, observe that if the same authority master keys y are used across both the sub-systems, then a user obtaining $(h \cdot \mathsf{H}(\mathsf{GID}))^y$ and $\mathsf{H}(\mathsf{GID})^y$ as parts of its secret key can easily recover h^y which may hamper security. We therefore use two different exponents for the two sub-systems.

Overall, our scheme consists of two sub-systems which we refer to as the "A" sub-system and the "B" sub-system. Accordingly, the master key of an attribute

---

[4] The ρ function maps between rows of the policy matrix $\boldsymbol{M}$ and the index of the associated authorities/attributes.

authority consists of two random exponents $y_A, y_B \leftarrow \mathbb{Z}_N$. The first sub-system deals with encoding the payload and the shares of the masking factor s, whereas the second sub-system works as a shadow system to cancel out some extra terms during decryption to ensure correctness.

Our security proof proceeds as follows. The first step of our proof is to make a ciphertext semi-functional over the p_3 subgroup. The argument relies on two key facts. (1) Any subset of authorities the attacker compromises will not satisfy the access structure. Thus, the corrupted authorities alone are not enough to (information theoretically) determine if the challenge ciphertext is semi-functional. (2) The keys given out by uncorrupted authorities will not have any component in the order p_3 subgroup, thus they will not help out such an attacker (at this step). Put together, this gives a method to leverage the information theoretic steps in order to handle adaptive corruption of authorities. Our approach uses both computational and information theoretic arguments to step between different hybrid experiments. A critical feature of our security proof is that any step that relies on the attacker's keys not satisfying the access structure will be an information theoretic argument, thereby sidestepping issues related to guessing which authorities are corrupted. (There will of course be multiple computational arguments between and setting up the information theoretic ones.) A similar high-level approach of using information regarding what the adversary corrupts only in information theoretic arguments was used in few previous dual system proofs (e.g., [28,29,45]), but here we are able to implement the technique in the (more challenging) distributed setting and enfolding corrupted authorities.

Our approach allows us to establish both semi-functional keys and ciphertexts in a given subspace of the cryptosystem. However, it comes with a big caveat. While the semi-functional argument is established in the p_3 subgroup we had to keep it separate from the ciphertext component blinding the message which lives solely in the p_1 subgroup. At this stage it is therefore unclear that all the work we did will even hide the message at all. Therefore, the next portion of our proof needs to "bleed" the semi-functional portions of the ciphertext into the portions blinding the message. Here again our two sub-system construction crucially comes into play. We will take turns by first bleeding over into one and then into the other.

We call this novel technique as a *dual system with dual sub-systems*. This technique utilizes the semi-functionality within one sub-system to introduce semi-functionality within the other. Then, this will allow us to transform the challenge ciphertext and keys in such a way that the p_2 segment of the special group element h remains information-theoretically hidden to the adversary and so its entropy can then be amplified using a suitable randomness extractor to hide the encrypted message completely.

As we mentioned above, we set the user secret key components for the two sub-system asymmetrically, namely, we multiply the special group element h within the user secret key components that correspond to the first sub-system. But, we do not multiply it within those corresponding to the second sub-system. We crucially leverage this asymmetry in the security proof as follows. We first bleed the semi-functional portions within the p_3 subgroup of the second sub-system into the p_2 subgroup of the same to make the p_2 components semi-functional. After that, we utilize this semi-functionality of the second sub-system to switch the special group element h from being embedded within the user secret key components of the first sub-system to those corresponding to the second sub-system. Once we are done with this step, we then bleed the semi-functional portions within the p_3 subgroup of the first sub-system into the p_2 portions of the same and make the p_2 portions of this sub-system semi-functional. This strategy is crucial since it is not clear how to leverage the dual-system methodology to inject semi-functionality into the p_2 portions of the first sub-system if the group element h is not moved away from this sub-system. At this point, the p_2 segment of the ciphertext component blinding the message becomes completely independent of the p_2 segments of all the other ciphertext and key components. Therefore, we can utilize its entropy to blind the message information-theoretically. For a more detailed overview of our hybrid proof strategy, please refer to Sect. 2.4.2 below.

We once again emphasize that all applications of the dual system methodology so far only dealt with a single system. The two sub-system design is completely new to this work. Also, as we argued above, full security of MA-ABE seems out of reach using standard previously used dual system techniques (since it is not clear how to bleed the semi-functional portions of the ciphertext components into those blinding the message and make the user keys independent of the special group element h within a single system). As is evident from our work, our new technique is useful and we believe that it will find further uses in other contexts related to adaptive security (for example, constructing adaptively secure functional encryption schemes beyond linear functions under standard group-based assumption).

2.4.1   Our Construction

Recall that our scheme relies on bilinear group $\mathbb{G}$ of composite order N which is a product of three primes, that is, $N = p_1 p_2 p_3$ with subgroups $\mathbb{G}_{p_1}, \mathbb{G}_{p_2}$, and $\mathbb{G}_{p_3}$. We also make use of a seeded randomness extractor Ext and let seed be a seed for it. The elements g_1 and h are uniformly random generators of the subgroup $\mathbb{G}_{p_1}$ that along with seed are part of the global parameters GP. H is a global hash function that we model as a random oracle in the security proof.

At a very high level, as is evident from the construction, the encryption algorithm blinds the message msg with the term $\mathrm{Ext}(e(g_1, h)^s, \mathrm{seed})$, where s is a random element in $\mathbb{Z}_N$. The goal in the security proof is to show that given the view of the adversary there is enough entropy left in $e(g_1, h)^s$ so that the message is indeed hidden. There are two secret sharing schemes involved, one of s and the other of $-s$. Let us denote the shares of s with $\sigma_{A,x}$ and the shares of $-s$ with $\sigma_{B,x}$. The decryptor recovers $e(g_1, \mathsf{H}(\mathsf{GID}) \cdot h)^{\sigma_{A,x}}$ and $e(g_1, \mathsf{H}(\mathsf{GID}))^{\sigma_{B,x}}$ by appropriately pairing their keys for attributes and ciphertext components. If the user holds sufficient secret keys to decrypt a ciphertext, the two terms $e(g_1, \mathsf{H}(\mathsf{GID}) \cdot h)^{\sigma_{A,x}}$ and $e(g_1, \mathsf{H}(\mathsf{GID}))^{\sigma_{B,x}}$ can be used to recover $e(g_1, \mathsf{H}(\mathsf{GID}) \cdot$

$h)^s$ and $e(g_1, \mathsf{H}(\mathsf{GID}))^{-s}$ which, if multiplied, give the blinding factor $e(g_1, h)^s$, as necessary.

AuthSetup(GP, u): The algorithm chooses random values $y_{A,u}, y_{B,u} \in \mathbb{Z}_N$ and outputs

$$\mathsf{PK}_u = (g_1^{y_{A,u}}, g_1^{y_{B,u}}) \qquad \mathsf{MSK}_u = (y_{A,u}, y_{B,u}).$$

Enc(GP, msg, (M, ρ), $\{\mathsf{PK}_u\}$): It first chooses a random value $s \leftarrow \mathbb{Z}_N$. It then uses the LSSS access policy[5] (M, ρ) to generate a secret sharing of s where $\sigma_{A,x}$ will be the share for all $x \in [\ell]$, i.e., for all $x \in [\ell]$, let $\sigma_{A,x} = M_x \cdot v_A$, where $v_A \leftarrow \mathbb{Z}_N^d$ is a random vector with s as its first entry and M_x is the xth row of M. It additionally creates another secret sharing of $-s$ with respect to the LSSS access policy (M, ρ) where $\sigma_{B,x}$ is the corresponding share for $\rho(x)$ for all $x \in [\ell]$, i.e., for all $x \in [\ell]$, $\sigma_{B,x} = M_x \cdot v_B$, where $v_B \leftarrow \mathbb{Z}_N^d$ is a random vector with $-s$ as its first entry. The procedure generates the ciphertext as follows: For each row $x \in [\ell]$, it chooses random $r_{A,x}, r_{B,x} \leftarrow \mathbb{Z}_N$ and outputs the ciphertext

$$\mathsf{CT} = ((M, \rho), C, \{C_{1,A,x}, C_{2,A,x}, C_{1,B,x}, C_{2,B,x}\}_{x \in [\ell]}),$$

where

$$C = \mathsf{msg} \oplus \mathsf{Ext}(e(g_1, h)^s, \mathsf{seed}), \qquad C_{1,A,x} = g_1^{r_{A,x}} \qquad C_{2,A,x} = g_1^{y_{A,\rho(x)} r_{A,x}} g_1^{\sigma_{A,x}}$$

$$C_{1,B,x} = g_1^{r_{B,x}} \qquad C_{2,B,x} = g_1^{y_{B,\rho(x)} r_{B,x}} g_1^{\sigma_{B,x}}.$$

KeyGen(GP, GID, MSK_u): The authority attribute u generates a secret key $\mathsf{SK}_{\mathsf{GID},u}$ for GID as $\mathsf{SK}_{\mathsf{GID},u} = (K_{\mathsf{GID},A,u}, K_{\mathsf{GID},B,u})$, where

$$K_{\mathsf{GID},A,u} = (\mathsf{H}(\mathsf{GID}) \cdot h)^{y_{A,u}} \qquad K_{\mathsf{GID},B,u} = (\mathsf{H}(\mathsf{GID}))^{y_{B,u}}.$$

Dec(GP, CT, GID, $\{\mathsf{SK}_{\mathsf{GID},u}\}$): Decryption takes as input the global parameters GP, the hash function H, a ciphertext CT for an LSSS access structure (M, ρ) with $M \in \mathbb{Z}_N^{\ell \times d}$ and $\rho : [\ell] \rightarrow \mathcal{AU}$, the user's global identifier $\mathsf{GID} \in \mathcal{GID}$, and the secret keys $\{\mathsf{SK}_{\mathsf{GID},\rho(x)}\}_{x \in I}$ corresponding to a subset of rows of M with indices $I \subseteq [\ell]$. If $(1, 0, \ldots, 0)$ is *not* in the span of these rows, M_I, then decryption fails. Otherwise, the decryptor finds coefficients $\{w_x \in \mathbb{Z}_N\}_{x \in I}$ such that $(1, 0, \ldots, 0) = \sum_{x \in I} w_x \cdot M_x$.

For all $x \in I$, the decryption algorithm computes:

$$D_{A,x} = e(C_{2,A,x}, \mathsf{H}(\mathsf{GID}) \cdot h) \cdot e(C_{1,A,x}, K_{\mathsf{GID},A,\rho(x)})^{-1} = e(g_1, \mathsf{H}(\mathsf{GID}) \cdot h)^{\sigma_{A,x}}$$

$$D_{B,x} = e(C_{2,B,x}, \mathsf{H}(\mathsf{GID})) \cdot e(C_{1,B,x}, K_{\mathsf{GID},B,\rho(x)})^{-1} = e(g_1, \mathsf{H}(\mathsf{GID}))^{\sigma_{B,x}}.$$

It computes $D = \prod_{x \in I} (D_{A,x} \cdot D_{B,x})^{w_x} = e(g_1, h)^s$ and outputs $C \oplus \mathsf{Ext}(D, \mathsf{seed}) = \mathsf{msg}$. The proposed scheme is correct by inspection; see Sect. 4.3 for details.

---

[5] The access policy (M, ρ) is of the form $M = (M_{x,j})_{\ell \times d} = (M_1, \ldots, M_\ell)^\top \in \mathbb{Z}_N^{\ell \times d}$ and $\rho : [\ell] \rightarrow \mathcal{AU}$. The function ρ associates rows of M to authorities. We assume that ρ is an injective function, that is, an authority/attribute is associated with at most one row of M. This can be extended to a setting where an attribute appears within an access policy for at most a bounded number of times [30, 46].

2.4.2 Our Security Proof

We now dive into a more detailed look at our security proof. We choose to present an overview of the main steps of our proof interleaved with a running commentary on the intuition behind them. Our goal here is to give a reader both a semi-detailed sense of the proof along side the conceptual ideas driving our approach.

Hyb_0 : We start with the real game.

Hyb_1 : Modify the random oracle to return random elements from $\mathbb{G}_{p_1}$. This modification is clearly indistinguishable under the subgroup decision assumption between $\mathbb{G}_{p_1}$ and $\mathbb{G}$.

After this step all user key material is relegated to the $\mathbb{G}_{p_1}$ subgroup. (Recall h was already in $\mathbb{G}_{p_1}$). One important consequence of this is that for any uncorrupted authority u, both the $y_{A,u}$ and $y_{B,u}$ values modulo p_2 and p_3 are *information theoretically* hidden no matter how many keys the attacker requests from the authority u.

Hyb_2 : Add a $\mathbb{G}_{p_3}$ component to each part of the challenge ciphertext. This transition follows from the subgroup decision assumption between $\mathbb{G}_{p_1}$ and $\mathbb{G}_{p_1 p_3}$.

Hyb_3 : We modify the $\mathbb{G}_{p_3}$ components of $C_{2,A,x}, C_{2,B,x}$ to involve shares of independent secrets instead of correlated ones.

This is an information theoretic step relying on two important facts. (1) That the attacker has no information on $y_{A,u}, y_{B,u} (\bmod\ p_3)$ of any uncorrupted authority u per our step in Hyb_1. The fact that $y_{A,u} \bmod p_3$ is hidden (and each authority appears at most once in a ciphertext) means that $C_{2,A,x}$ cannot be distinguished from random in the $\mathbb{G}_{p_3}$ subgroup. Thus, the share is hidden when row x corresponds to an uncorrupted authority u. (2) That the rows of the challenge matrix (M, ρ) associated with the corrupted authorities are unauthorized for decryption. Hence, they are insufficient for learning the value of $s \bmod p_3$.

Critically, this step employs an information theoretic argument and therefore there is no issue to how to properly embed a reduction to a computational assumption in the presence of adaptive corruptions. In general, this is a theme in our whole reduction process. Throughout the proof, we separate the computational and information theoretic arguments. The parts of the argument that relate to what the attacker corrupted is only in the information theoretic pieces where adaptivity is not a problem.

After this step the ciphertext begins to have a somewhat semi-functional form in that the $\mathbb{G}_{p_3}$ subgroups are not correlated in the system A and B halves. However, the effect is currently vacuous as none of the keys "look at" the $\mathbb{G}_{p_3}$ subgroup which vanishes upon pairing the keys and ciphertext.

Hyb_4 : Add a $\mathbb{G}_{p_2}$ component to each part of the challenge ciphertext. This transition follows from the subgroup decision assumption between $\mathbb{G}_{p_1}$ and $\mathbb{G}_{p_1 p_2}$.

Hyb_5 : Modify the random oracle to return random elements from $\mathbb{G}_{p_1 p_3}$. The proof that this change is indistinguishable actually goes through a sequence of sub-hybrids where we change the oracle queries one by one. Intuitively, changing the random oracle output for a certain GID is akin to making the secret key components for GID to be semi-functional. Thus, the proof will need to leverage the fact that the key components acquired by GID do not satisfy the challenge ciphertext access structure. For each GID the proof will first establish this in the $\mathbb{G}_{p_2}$ subgroup to be "temporarily semi-functional", then use this to move it to the "permanent semi-functional" space in $\mathbb{G}_{p_3}$. Finally, undo the work in the $\mathbb{G}_{p_2}$ space to make it available for moving the next GID over.

We consider the following sequence of sub-hybrids for each random oracle query GID_j.

- First modify the random oracle output $\mathsf{H}(\mathsf{GID}_j)$ to be a random element in $\mathbb{G}_{p_1 p_2}$ instead of $\mathbb{G}_{p_1}$. This change is clearly indistinguishable under the subgroup decision assumption between $\mathbb{G}_{p_1}$ and $\mathbb{G}_{p_1 p_2}$.
- Modify the $\mathbb{G}_{p_2}$ components of $C_{2,A,x}, C_{2,B,x}$ to involve shares of independent secrets instead of correlated ones. This is again an information theoretic step which uses the fact that the rows of the challenge matrix (M, ρ) associated with the corrupted authorities *in conjunction* with all those rows for which the adversary requests a secret key for GID_j are unauthorized for decryption. The adaptive corruption of the authority as well as the adaptive key requests for GID_j do not cause any problem.

  We emphasize that since this information theoretic argument is done over the $\mathbb{G}_{p_2}$ subgroup, it does not matter whether the adversary has information about the $\mathbb{G}_{p_3}$ from keys for other global identities. This is the benefit for modifying keys one by one in an isolated subspace.
- Next, modify $\mathsf{H}(\mathsf{GID}_j)$ to be a random element from the whole group $\mathbb{G}$. This transition is indistinguishable under the subgroup decision assumption between $\mathbb{G}_{p_1 p_2}$ and $\mathbb{G}$. The work done so far allows us to simulate this transition using the group elements available in the problem instance.
- Modify the $\mathbb{G}_{p_2}$ components of $C_{2,A,x}, C_{2,B,x}$ to again involve shares of correlated secrets instead of independent ones. This is again an information theoretic step similar to the previous one.
- Change the random oracle output $\mathsf{H}(\mathsf{GID}_j)$ to be a random element in $\mathbb{G}_{p_1 p_3}$ instead of $\mathbb{G}$. This transition is indistinguishable under the subgroup decision assumption between $\mathbb{G}_{p_1}$ and $\mathbb{G}_{p_1 p_2}$.

Note that in the above sequence of sub-hybrids, the $\mathbb{G}_{p_2}$ subgroup is used over and over again to "escort" a value into the $\mathbb{G}_{p_3}$ subgroup. Until this step, this portion of the proof follows closely [30] at a high level although there are differences in the low level details. In particular, unlike [30] which involves a single semi-functional form of the ciphertext, we consider several different semi-functional forms in order to handle a more sophisticated scenario of adaptive authority corruption in addition to the adaptive secret key queries. However, the following steps significantly depart from [30].

Hyb_6 : Sample h from $\mathbb{G}_{p_1 p_2}$ instead of $\mathbb{G}_{p_1}$. The indistinguishability follows from the subgroup decision assumption between $\mathbb{G}_{p_1}$ and $\mathbb{G}_{p_1 p_2}$ In addition, the challenge ciphertext message is now blinded as

$$C = \mathsf{msg}_b \oplus \mathsf{Ext}(e(g_1, h)^s \cdot \boxed{e(g_2, h)^{s''}}, \mathsf{seed})$$

for random s'' and a generator $g_2 \in \mathbb{G}_{p_2}$. At this point the message is blinded in $\mathbb{G}_{p_2}$ while the semi-functional components are established in the $\mathbb{G}_{p_3}$ subgroups for both keys and ciphertexts. We now need to bleed these over into $\mathbb{G}_{p_2}$ to argue the message is hidden.

Hyb_7 : Make the $C_{1,B,x}, C_{2,B,x}$ parts have shares of an independent random secret in $\mathbb{G}_{p_2}$ rather than one correlated to $C_{1,A,x}, C_{2,A,x}$. This is again an information theoretic step which relies on the fact that the rows of the challenge matrix M labeled by the corrupted authorities are unauthorized for decryption.

We now have that the 'B' side of our cryptosystem is complete for our proof with the secret shared on the 'B' side being uncorrelated in the $\mathbb{G}_{p_2}$ component with both the 'A' share and s'' from C. This step is feasible since the keys in our system are created as $\mathsf{H}(\mathsf{GID})^{y_{B,u}}$. In contrast the '$A$' side has keys created as $(\mathsf{H}(\mathsf{GID}) \cdot h)^{y_{A,u}}$. To decouple the $\mathbb{G}_{p_2}$ component of the 'A' side with s'' we must next effectively move the h value from the 'A' side to 'B' side.

Hyb_{10} :[6] Modify the random oracle output for all the global identifiers GID queried by the adversary as $\mathsf{H}(\mathsf{GID}_j) = P_j \cdot h^{-1}$ for the jth random oracle query where P_j is randomly sampled from $\mathbb{G}_{p_1 p_3}$. Once this transition is achieved, we will clearly have $\mathsf{H}(\mathsf{GID}_j) \cdot h = P_j$ for all random oracle queries, i.e., $\mathsf{H}(\mathsf{GID}_j) \cdot h$ involves no $\mathbb{G}_{p_2}$ component. This step is crucial for changing the $\mathbb{G}_{p_2}$ components of $C_{1,A,x}, C_{2,A,x}$ in the subsequent hybrids. This transition is achieved via a sequence of sub-hybrids.

- Modify the jth random oracle query to output random elements from $\mathbb{G}$. The indistinguishability follows from the subgroup decision assumption between $\mathbb{G}_{p_1 p_2}$ and $\mathbb{G}$.
- Modify the jth random oracle query to output $R_j \cdot h^{-1}$ where R_j is randomly sampled from $\mathbb{G}$. Observe that since R_j is uniformly sampled from $\mathbb{G}$, this new form of $\mathsf{H}(\mathsf{GID}_j)$ is actually identical to the one in the previous game.
- Modify the jth random oracle query to output $P_j \cdot h^{-1}$ where P_j is randomly sampled from $\mathbb{G}_{p_1 p_3}$. The indistinguishability follows from the subgroup decision assumption between $\mathbb{G}_{p_1 p_2}$ and $\mathbb{G}$.

Hyb_{11} : Make the $C_{1,A,x}, C_{2,A,x}$ parts have shares of an independent random secret in $\mathbb{G}_{p_2}$. This is again an information theoretic step similar to the previous one of Hyb_6.

---

[6] In our formal proof presented in the full version [16] this is spread out over Hybrids 8–10. We will condense these for this overview and thus skip two numbers of hybrids. We are however not changing the numbers from those in the formal proof for ease of correlation.

Hyb_{12} : Replace C with a random value unrelated to the message. Due to the work done so far, $s'' \bmod p_2$ is information theoretically hidden and so s'' has at least $\log(p_2)$ bits of entropy. The extractor hides the message.

2.5   Porting to Prime Order Groups

As mentioned there have been many works trying to come up with a method to translate existing composite order group constructions into prime order analogues [1,4,12,13,19,20,25,27,36,37]. All of these frameworks are different and have varying levels of simplicity or generality. We use the recent framework of Chen et al. [13] which seems to be the most efficient and (arguably) the simplest to use, and succeed in adapting the construction as well as the proof from the composite order setting to the prime order setting.

This framework, in a high level, shows how to simulate a composite order group and its subgroups using a prime order group while guaranteeing a prime order analogue of various subgroup decision style assumptions. These analogues follow from the standard k-Linear assumption (and more generally, the MDDH assumption [18]). Here, since the translation process is not completely black box and needs to be adapted for the scheme at hand, we need to introduce a few extra technical ideas to handle our specific setting. Specifically, the proof of security of our prime order construction relies not only on subgroup decision style assumptions but also on few information theoretic arguments as well as on the security of a random oracle. Using the framework and making it work on our scheme is fairly technical and systematic; we refer to the technical section for details. Nevertheless, we point out that the high level idea as well as the sequence of hybrids is the same as in the composite order case.

3   Preliminaries

A function $\mathsf{negl} \colon \mathbb{N} \to \mathbb{R}$ is *negligible* if it is asymptotically smaller than any inverse-polynomial function, namely, for every constant $c > 0$ there exists an integer N_c such that $\mathsf{negl}(\lambda) \le \lambda^{-c}$ for all $\lambda > N_c$. We let $[n] = \{1, \ldots, n\}$.

We use bold lower case letters, such as v, to denote vectors and upper-case, such as M, for matrices. We assume all vectors, by default, are column vectors. The ith row of a matrix is denoted M_i and analogously for a set of row indices I, we denote M_I for the sub-matrix of M that consists of the rows M_i for all $i \in I$. For an integer $q \ge 2$, we let $\mathbb{Z}_q$ denote the ring of integers modulo q. We represent $\mathbb{Z}_q$ as integers in the range $(-q/2, q/2]$.

Indistinguishability: Two sequences of random variables $\mathcal{X} = \{\mathcal{X}_\lambda\}_{\lambda \in \mathbb{N}}$ and $\mathcal{Y} = \{\mathcal{Y}_\lambda\}_{\lambda \in \mathbb{N}}$ are *computationally indistinguishable* if for any non-uniform PPT algorithm $\mathcal{A}$ there exists a negligible function $\mathsf{negl}(\cdot)$ such that $|\Pr[\mathcal{A}(1^\lambda, \mathcal{X}_\lambda) = 1] - \Pr[\mathcal{A}(1^\lambda, \mathcal{Y}_\lambda) = 1]| \le \mathsf{negl}(\lambda)$ for all $\lambda \in \mathbb{N}$.

For two distributions $\mathcal{D}$ and $\mathcal{D}'$ over a discrete domain Ω, the statistical distance between $\mathcal{D}$ and $\mathcal{D}'$ is defined as $\mathsf{SD}(\mathcal{D}, \mathcal{D}') = (1/2) \cdot \sum_{\omega \in \Omega} |\mathcal{D}(\omega) - \mathcal{D}'(\omega)|$. A family of distributions $\mathcal{D} = \{\mathcal{D}_\lambda\}_{\lambda \in \mathbb{N}}$ and $\mathcal{D}' = \{\mathcal{D}'_\lambda\}_{\lambda \in \mathbb{N}}$, parameterized by security parameter λ, are said to be *statistically indistinguishable* if there is a negligible function $\mathsf{negl}(\cdot)$ such that $\mathsf{SD}(\mathcal{D}_\lambda, \mathcal{D}'_\lambda) \leq \mathsf{negl}(\lambda)$ for all $\lambda \in \mathbb{N}$.

3.1   Access Structures and Linear Secret Sharing Schemes

Definition 3.1 (Access Structures, [5,6]): Let $\mathbb{U}$ be the attribute universe. An access structure on $\mathbb{U}$ is a collection $\mathbb{A} \subseteq 2^{\mathbb{U}} \setminus \emptyset$ of non-empty sets of attributes. The sets in $\mathbb{A}$ are called the *authorized* sets and the sets not in $\mathbb{A}$ are called the *unauthorized* sets. An access structure is called *monotone* if $\forall B, C \in 2^{\mathbb{U}}$ if $B \in \mathbb{A}$ and $B \subseteq C$, then $C \in \mathbb{A}$.

Definition 3.2 (Linear Secret Sharing Schemes (LSSS), [5,6,30]): Let $q = q(\lambda)$ be a prime and $\mathbb{U}$ the attribute universe. A secret sharing scheme Π with domain of secrets $\mathbb{Z}_q$ for a monotone access structure $\mathbb{A}$ over $\mathbb{U}$, a.k.a. a monotone secret sharing scheme, is a randomized algorithm that on input a secret $z \in \mathbb{Z}_q$ outputs $|\mathbb{U}|$ shares $\mathsf{sh}_1, \ldots, \mathsf{sh}_{|\mathbb{U}|}$ such that for any set $S \in \mathbb{A}$ the shares $\{\mathsf{sh}_i\}_{i \in S}$ determine z and other sets of shares are independent of z (as random variables). A secret sharing scheme Π realizing monotone access structures on $\mathbb{U}$ is linear over $\mathbb{Z}_q$ if

1. The shares of a secret $z \in \mathbb{Z}_q$ for each attribute in $\mathbb{U}$ form a vector over $\mathbb{Z}_q$.
2. For each monotone access structure $\mathbb{A}$ on $\mathbb{U}$, there exists a matrix $\boldsymbol{M} \in \mathbb{Z}_q^{\ell \times s}$, called the share-generating matrix, and a function $\rho \colon [\ell] \to \mathbb{U}$, that labels the rows of $\boldsymbol{M}$ with attributes from $\mathbb{U}$ which satisfy the following: During the generation of the shares, we consider the vector $\boldsymbol{v} = (z, r_2, \ldots, r_s)$, where $r_2, \ldots, r_s \leftarrow \mathbb{Z}_q$. Then the vector of ℓ shares of the secret z according to Π is given by $\boldsymbol{\mu} = \boldsymbol{M}\boldsymbol{v}^\top \in \mathbb{Z}_q^{\ell \times 1}$, where for all $j \in [\ell]$ the share μ_j "belongs" to the attribute $\rho(j)$. We will be referring to the pair $(\boldsymbol{M}, \rho)$ as the LSSS policy of the access structure $\mathbb{A}$.

The correctness and security of a monotone LSSS are formalized in the following: Let S (resp. S') denote an authorized (resp. unauthorized) set of attributes according to some monotone access structure $\mathbb{A}$ and let I (resp. I') be the set of rows of the share generating matrix $\boldsymbol{M}$ of the LSSS policy pair $(\boldsymbol{M}, \rho)$ associated with $\mathbb{A}$ whose labels are in S (resp. S'). For correctness, there exist constants $\{w_i\}_{i \in I}$ in $\mathbb{Z}_q$ such that for any valid shares $\{\boldsymbol{\mu}_i = (\boldsymbol{M}\boldsymbol{v}^\top)_i\}_{i \in I}$ of a secret $z \in \mathbb{Z}_q$ according to Π, it is true that $\sum_{i \in I} w_i \boldsymbol{\mu}_i = z$ (equivalently, $\sum_{i \in I} w_i \boldsymbol{M}_i = (1, \overbrace{0, \ldots, 0}^{s-1})$, where $\boldsymbol{M}_i$ is the ith row of $\boldsymbol{M}$). For soundness, there does not exists any subset I' of the rows of the matrix $\boldsymbol{M}$ and any coefficients $\{w_i\}_{i \in I'}$ for which the above hold.

Remark 3.1 (NC^1 and Monotone LSSS): Consider an access structure $\mathbb{A}$ described by an NC^1 circuit. There is a folklore transformation that converts this circuit to a Boolean formula of logarithmic depth that consists of (fan-in 2) AND, OR, and (fan-in 1) NOT gates. We can further push the NOT gates to the leaves using De Morgan laws, and assume that internal nodes only constitute of OR and AND gates and leaves are labeled either by attributes or by their negations. In other words, we can represent any NC^1 policy over a set of attributes into one described by a monotone Boolean formula of logarithmic depth over the same attributes together with their negations. Lewko and Waters [30] presented a monotone LSSS for access structures described by monotone Boolean formulas. This implies that any NC^1 access policy can be captured by a monotone LSSS.

3.2 Strong Randomness Extractors

The *min-entropy* of a random variable X is $\mathbf{H}_\infty(X) = -\log(\max_x \Pr[X = x])$. A *t-source* is a random variable X with $\mathbf{H}_\infty(X) \geq t$. The *statistical distance* between two random variables X and Y over a finite domain Ω is $\mathbf{SD}(X, Y) = \frac{1}{2}\sum_{\omega \in \Omega}|\Pr[X = \omega] - \Pr[Y = \omega]|$.

Definition 3.3 (Seeded Randomness Extractor, Definition 6.16 [44]): A function Ext : $\Omega \times S \to \Gamma$ is a strong (t, ϵ)-*extractor* if for every t-source X on Ω, $\mathbf{SD}((\mathcal{U}_S, \text{Ext}(X, \mathcal{U}_S)), (\mathcal{U}_S, \mathcal{U}_\Gamma)) < \epsilon$.

Theorem 3.1 (Theorem 6.17 [44]): *For every* $n, t \in \mathbb{N}$ *and* $\epsilon > 0$, *there exists a strong* (t, ϵ)-*extractor* Ext : $\{0, 1\}^n \times \{0, 1\}^d \to \{0, 1\}^m$ *with* $m = t - 2\log(1/\epsilon) - O(1)$ *and* $d = \log(n - t) + 2\log(1/\epsilon) + O(1)$.

3.3 Fully-Adaptive Decentralized MA-ABE for LSSS

A decentralized multi-authority attribute-based encryption (MA-ABE) system MA-ABE = (GlobalSetup, AuthSetup, KeyGen, Enc, Dec) consists of five procedures whose syntax is given below. The supported access structures that we deal with are ones captured by linear secret sharing schemes (LSSS). We denote by $\mathcal{AU}$ the authority universe and by $\mathcal{GID}$ the universe of global identifiers of the users. We denote by $\mathbb{M}$ the supported message space. Additionally, we assume that each authority controls just one attribute, and hence we would use the terms "authority" and "attribute" interchangeably. This definition naturally generalizes to the situation in which each authority can potentially control an arbitrary (bounded or unbounded) number of attributes (see [30,40]).

- GlobalSetup(1^λ) $\mapsto$ GP : The global setup algorithm takes in the security parameter λ in unary representation and outputs the global public parameters GP for the system. We assume that GP includes the descriptions of the universe of attribute authorities $\mathcal{AU}$ and universe of the global identifiers of the users $\mathcal{GID}$. Note that both $\mathcal{AU}$ and $\mathcal{GID}$ are given by $\{0, 1\}^\lambda$ in case there is no bound on the number of authorities and users in the system.
- AuthSetup(GP, u) $\mapsto$ (PK_u, MSK_u) : The authority $u \in \mathcal{AU}$ calls the authority setup algorithm during its initialization with the global parameters GP as input and receives back its public and master secret key pair PK_u, MSK_u.

- KeyGen(GP, GID, MSK$_u$) $\mapsto$ SK$_{\text{GID},u}$: The key generation algorithm takes as input the global parameters GP, a user's global identifier GID $\in \mathcal{GID}$, and a master secret key MSK$_u$ of an authority $u \in \mathcal{AU}$. It outputs a secret key SK$_{\text{GID},u}$ for the user.
- Enc(GP, msg, $(M, \rho), \{$PK$_u\}) \mapsto$ CT : The encryption algorithm takes in the global parameters GP, a message msg $\in \mathbb{M}$, an LSSS access policy (M, ρ) such that M is a matrix over $\mathbb{Z}_N$ and ρ is a row-labeling function that assigns to each row of M an attribute/authority in $\mathcal{AU}$, and the set $\{$PK$_u\}$ of public keys for all the authorities in the range of ρ. It outputs a ciphertext CT. We assume that the ciphertext implicitly contains (M, ρ).
- Dec(GP, CT, $\{$SK$_{\text{GID},u}\}) \mapsto$ msg$'$: The decryption algorithm takes in the global parameters GP, a ciphertext CT generated with respect to some LSSS access policy (M, ρ), and a collection of keys $\{$SK$_{\text{GID},u}\}$ corresponding to user ID-attribute pairs $\{(\text{GID}, u)\}$ possessed by a user with global identifier GID. It outputs a message msg$'$ when the collection of attributes associated with the secret keys $\{$SK$_{\text{GID},u}\}$ satisfies the LSSS access policy (M, ρ), i.e., when the vector $(1, 0, \ldots, 0)$ is contained in the linear span of those rows of M which are mapped by ρ to some attribute/authority $u \in \mathcal{AU}$ such that the secret key SK$_{\text{GID},u}$ is possessed by the user with global identifier GID. Otherwise, decryption fails.

Correctness: An MA-ABE scheme for LSSS-realizable access structures is said to be *correct* if for every $\lambda \in \mathbb{N}$, every message msg $\in \mathbb{M}$, and GID $\in \mathcal{GID}$, every LSSS access policy (M, ρ), and every subset of authorities $U \subseteq \mathcal{AU}$ controlling attributes which satisfy the access structure, it holds that

$$\Pr\left[\text{msg}' = \text{msg} \; \middle| \; \begin{array}{l} \text{GP} \leftarrow \text{GlobalSetup}(1^\lambda) \\ \forall u \in U : \text{PK}_u, \text{MSK}_u \leftarrow \text{AuthSetup}(\text{GP}, u) \\ \forall u \in U : \text{SK}_{\text{GID},u} \leftarrow \text{KeyGen}(\text{GP}, \text{GID}, \text{MSK}_u) \\ \text{CT} \leftarrow \text{Enc}(\text{GP}, \text{msg}, (M, \rho), \{\text{PK}_u\}) \\ \text{msg}' = \text{Dec}(\text{GP}, \text{CT}, \{\text{SK}_{\text{GID},u}\}_{u \in U}) \end{array} \right] = 1.$$

Fully Adaptive Security: We define the fully adaptive (chosen-plaintext) security for a decentralized MA-ABE scheme, namely, we consider a security game where there could be adaptive secret key queries, adaptive authority corruption queries, and adaptive challenge ciphertext query. This is formalized in the following game between a challenger and an attacker. Note that we will consider two types of authority public keys, those which are honestly generated by the challenger and those which are supplied by the attacker itself where the former type of authority keys can be corrupted by the attacker at any point of time during the game and the latter type of authority keys can potentially be malformed.

The game consists of the following phases:

Global Setup: The challenger runs GlobalSetup to generate global public parameters GP and gives it to the attacker.

Query Phase 1: The attacker is allowed to adaptively make a polynomial number of queries of the following types:

- Authority Setup Queries: The attacker request to set up an authority $u \in \mathcal{AU}$ of its choice. If an authority setup query for the same authority u has already been queried before, the challenger aborts. Otherwise, the challenger runs AuthSetup to create a public/master key pair $(\mathsf{PK}_u, \mathsf{MSK}_u)$ for the authority u. The challenger provides PK_u to the attacker and stores $(\mathsf{PK}_u, \mathsf{MSK}_u)$. Note that the challenger does not return the generated public/master key pair to the attacker.
- Secret Key Queries: The attacker makes a secret key query by submitting a pair (GID, u) to the challenger, where $\mathsf{GID} \in \mathcal{GID}$ is a global identifier and $u \in \mathcal{AU}$ is an attribute authority. If an authority setup query for the authority u has not been made already, the challenger aborts. Otherwise, the challenger runs KeyGen using the public/master key pair it already created in response to authority setup query for u and generates a secret key $\mathsf{SK}_{\mathsf{GID},u}$ for (GID, u). The challenger provides $\mathsf{SK}_{\mathsf{GID},u}$ to the attacker.
- Authority Master Key Queries: The attacker requests the master secret key of an authority $u \in \mathcal{AU}$ to the challenger. If an authority setup query for the authority u has not been made previously, the challenger aborts. Otherwise, the challenger provides the attacker the master secret key MSK_u for authority u it created in response to the authority setup query for u.

Challenge Phase: The attacker submits two messages, $\mathsf{msg}_0, \mathsf{msg}_1 \in \mathbb{M}$ and an LSSS access structure (M, ρ). The attacker also submits the public keys $\{\mathsf{PK}_u\}$ for a subset of attribute authorities appearing in the LSSS access structure (M, ρ). The authority public keys $\{\mathsf{PK}_u\}$ supplied by the attacker can potentially be malformed, i.e., can fall outside the range of AuthSetup. The LSSS access structure (M, ρ) and the authority public keys $\{\mathsf{PK}_u\}$ must satisfy the following constraints.

(a) Let $U_{\mathcal{A}}$ denote the set of attribute authorities for which the attacker supplied the authority public keys $\{\mathsf{PK}_u\}$. Also let $U_{\mathcal{B}}$ denote the set of attribute authorities for which the challenger created the master public key pairs in response to the authority setup query of the attacker so far. Then, it is required that $U_{\mathcal{A}} \cap U_{\mathcal{B}} = \emptyset$.

(b) Let V denote the subset of rows of M labeled by the authorities in $U_{\mathcal{A}}$ plus the authorities for which the attacker made a master key query so far. For each global identifier $\mathsf{GID} \in \mathcal{GID}$, let V_{GID} denote the subset of rows of M labeled by authorities u such that the attacker queried a secret key for the pair (GID, u). For each $\mathsf{GID} \in \mathcal{GID}$, it is required that the rows of M labeled by authorities in $V \cup V_{\mathsf{GID}}$ do not span $(1, 0, \ldots, 0)$.

The challenger flips a random coin $b \leftarrow \{0, 1\}$ and generates a ciphertext CT by running the Enc algorithm that encrypts msg_b under the access structure (M, ρ).

Query Phase 2: The attacker is allowed to make all types of queries as in Query Phase 1 as long as they do not violate the constraints Properties (a) and (b) above.

Guess: The attacker must submit a guess b' for b. The attacker wins if $b = b'$.

The advantage of an adversary $\mathcal{A}$ in this game is defined as:

$$\mathsf{Adv}_{\mathcal{A}}^{\mathsf{MA\text{-}ABE,fully\text{-}adaptive}} = |\Pr[b' = b] - 1/2|.$$

Definition 3.4 (Fully adaptive security for MA-ABE for LSSS): An MA-ABE scheme for LSSS-realizable access structures is fully adaptively secure if for any PPT adversary $\mathcal{A}$ there exists a negligible function $\mathsf{negl}(\cdot)$ such that for all $\lambda \in \mathbb{N}$, we have $\mathsf{Adv}_{\mathcal{A}}^{\mathsf{MA\text{-}ABE,fully\text{-}adaptive}} \leq \mathsf{negl}(\lambda)$.

Remark 3.2 (Fully adaptive security of MA-ABE for LSSS in the Random Oracle Model): Similar to [30,38,40], we additionally consider the afore-mentioned notion of fully adaptive security in the random oracle model. In this context, we assume a global hash function H published as part of the global public parameters and accessible by all the parties in the system, including the attacker. In the security proof, we model H as a random function and allow it to be programmed by the challenger. Therefore, in the fully adaptive security game described above, we further let the adversary adaptively submit H-oracle queries to the challenger, along with the key queries it makes both before and after the challenge ciphertext query.

4 Our Composite Order Group MA-ABE Scheme

In Sect. 4.1 we recall composite order bilinear groups. In Sect. 4.2 we give the construction. In Sect. 4.3 we prove correctness of the construction and we give the security proof in the full version [16] The complexity assumptions on which our security proof relies on are basically different types of subgroup decision assumptions and can also be found in the full version.

4.1 Composite Order Bilinear Groups

Our system relies on composite order bilinear groups, which were first defined in [9]. Particularly, we will rely on a bilinear group $\mathbb{G}$ of composite order N which is a product of three primes, that is, $N = p_1 p_2 p_3$. Such a group has unique subgroups of order q for all divisor q of N and we will denote such a subgroup as $\mathbb{G}_q$. Also every element $g \in \mathbb{G}$, can be written (uniquely) as the product of an element of $\mathbb{G}_{p_1}$, an element of $\mathbb{G}_{p_2}$, and an element of $\mathbb{G}_{p_3}$. We refer to these elements as the "$\mathbb{G}_{p_1}$ part of g", the "$\mathbb{G}_{p_2}$ part of g", and the "$\mathbb{G}_{p_3}$ part of g", respectively. We shall assume that there is a procedure $\mathcal{G}(1^\lambda)$ that gets as input a security parameter λ and outputs $\mathsf{G} = (N = p_1 p_2 p_3, \mathbb{G}, \mathbb{G}_T, e)$, where $e\colon \mathbb{G} \times \mathbb{G} \to \mathbb{G}_T$ is a pairing. We assume that the group operations in $\mathbb{G}$ and $\mathbb{G}_T$ as well as the bilinear map e are computable in polynomial time in λ. Further, we assume that e satisfies the following:

1. (Bilinear) $\forall g, h \in \mathbb{G}, a, b \in \mathbb{Z}_N, e(g^a, h^b) = e(g, h)^{ab}$.
2. (Non-degenerate) $\exists g \in \mathbb{G}$ such that $e(g, g)$ has order N in $\mathbb{G}_T$.

4.2 The Construction

Here, we present our MA-ABE for NC^1 construction in composite order bilinear groups. As mentioned, we assume that each authority controls just one attribute, and hence we would use the terms "authority" and "attribute" interchangeably.

GlobalSetup(1^λ): The global setup algorithm takes in the security parameter 1^λ encoded in unary. The procedure first chooses primes p_1, p_2, p_3 and let $N = p_1 p_2 p_3$. Next, it generates a bilinear group $\mathsf{G} = (N, \mathbb{G}, \mathbb{G}_T, e)$ of order N. Let $\mathbb{G}_{p_1}$ be the subgroup of $\mathbb{G}$ of order p_1 and let g_1 and h be uniformly random generators of the subgroup $\mathbb{G}_{p_1}$. We make use of a strong seeded randomness extractor $\mathsf{Ext} : \mathbb{G}_T \times S \to \mathbb{M}$, where $\mathbb{M} \subset \{0,1\}^*$ is the message space and $S \subset \{0,1\}^*$ is the seed space. The algorithm samples a seed $\mathsf{seed} \leftarrow S$. It sets the global parameters $\mathsf{GP} = (\mathsf{G}, g_1, h, \mathsf{seed})$. Furthermore, we make use of a hash function $\mathsf{H} : \{0,1\}^* \to \mathbb{G}$ mapping global identities $\mathsf{GID} \subset \mathcal{GID}$ to elements in $\mathbb{G}$.

AuthSetup($\mathsf{GP}, \mathsf{H}, u$): Given the global parameters GP, the hash function H, and an authority index $u \in \mathcal{AU}$, the algorithm chooses random values $y_{A,u}, y_{B,u} \in \mathbb{Z}_N$ and outputs

$$\mathsf{PK}_u = (P_{A,u} = g_1^{y_{A,u}}, P_{B,u} = g_1^{y_{B,u}}) \qquad \mathsf{MSK}_u = (y_{A,u}, y_{B,u}).$$

Enc($\mathsf{GP}, \mathsf{H}, \mathsf{msg}, (M, \rho), \{\mathsf{PK}_u\}$): The encryption algorithm takes as input the global parameters GP, the hash function H, a message $\mathsf{msg} \in \mathbb{M}$ to encrypt, an LSSS access structure (M, ρ), where $M = (M_{x,j})_{\ell \times d} = (M_1, \ldots, M_\ell)^\top \in \mathbb{Z}_N^{\ell \times d}$ and $\rho : [\ell] \to \mathcal{AU}$, and public keys of the relevant authorities $\{\mathsf{PK}_u\}$. The function ρ associates rows of M to authorities (recall that we assume that each authority controls a single attribute). We assume that ρ is an injective function, that is, an authority/attribute is associated with at most one row of M.

It first chooses a random value $s \leftarrow \mathbb{Z}_N$. It then uses the LSSS access structure (M, ρ) to generate a secret sharing of s where $\sigma_{A,x}$ will be the share for all $x \in [\ell]$, i.e., for all $x \in [\ell]$, let $\sigma_{A,x} = M_x \cdot v_A$, where $v_A \leftarrow \mathbb{Z}_N^d$ is a random vector with s as its first entry and M_x is the xth row of M. It additionally creates another secret sharing of $-s$ with respect to the LSSS access policy (M, ρ) where $\sigma_{B,x}$ is the corresponding share for $\rho(x)$ for all $x \in [\ell]$, i.e., for all $x \in [\ell]$, $\sigma_{B,x} = M_x \cdot v_B$, where $v_B \leftarrow \mathbb{Z}_N^d$ is a random vector with $-s$ as its first entry. The procedure generates the ciphertext as follows: For each row $x \in [\ell]$, it chooses random $r_{A,x}, r_{B,x} \leftarrow \mathbb{Z}_N$ and outputs the ciphertext

$$\mathsf{CT} = ((M, \rho), C, \{C_{1,A,x}, C_{2,A,x}, C_{1,B,x}, C_{2,B,x}\}_{x \in [\ell]}),$$

where

$$C = \mathsf{msg} \oplus \mathsf{Ext}(e(g_1, h)^s, \mathsf{seed}),$$

$$C_{1,A,x} = g_1^{r_{A,x}} \qquad C_{2,A,x} = P_{A,\rho(x)}^{r_{A,x}} g_1^{\sigma_{A,x}} = g_1^{y_{A,\rho(x)} r_{A,x}} g_1^{\sigma_{A,x}}$$

$$C_{1,B,x} = g_1^{r_{B,x}} \qquad C_{2,B,x} = P_{B,\rho(x)}^{r_{B,x}} g_1^{\sigma_{B,x}} = g_1^{y_{B,\rho(x)} r_{B,x}} g_1^{\sigma_{B,x}}.$$

KeyGen(GP, H, GID, MSK$_u$): The key generation algorithm takes as input the global parameters GP, the hash function H, the user's global identifier GID $\in$ $\mathcal{GID}$, and the authority's master secret key MSK$_u$. It generates a secret key SK$_{\text{GID},u}$ for GID as

$$\text{SK}_{\text{GID},u} = (K_{\text{GID},A,u}, K_{\text{GID},B,u})$$

where $K_{\text{GID},A,u} = (\text{H(GID)} \cdot h)^{y_{A,u}}$ and $K_{\text{GID},B,u} = (\text{H(GID)})^{y_{B,u}}$.

Dec(GP, CT, GID, {SK$_{\text{GID},u}$}): Decryption takes as input the global parameters GP, the hash function H, a ciphertext CT for an LSSS access structure (M, ρ) with $M \in \mathbb{Z}_N^{\ell \times d}$ and $\rho : [\ell] \to \mathcal{AU}$ injective, the user's global identifier GID $\in$ $\mathcal{GID}$, and the secret keys {SK$_{\text{GID},u}$}$_{u \in \rho(I)}$ corresponding to a subset of rows of M with indices $I \subseteq [\ell]$. If $(1, 0, \dots, 0)$ is *not* in the span of these rows, M_I, then decryption fails. Otherwise, the decryptor finds $\{w_x \in \mathbb{Z}_N\}_{x \in I}$ such that $(1, 0, \dots, 0) = \sum_{x \in I} w_x \cdot M_x$.

For all $x \in I$, the decryption algorithm first compute:

$$D_{A,x} = e(C_{2,A,x}, \text{H(GID)} \cdot h) \cdot e(C_{1,A,x}, K_{\text{GID},A,\rho(x)})^{-1} = e(g_1, \text{H(GID)} \cdot h)^{\sigma_{A,x}}$$

$$D_{B,x} = e(C_{2,B,x}, \text{H(GID)}) \cdot e(C_{1,B,x}, K_{\text{GID},B,\rho(x)})^{-1} = e(g_1, \text{H(GID)})^{\sigma_{B,x}}$$

Then compute $D = \prod_{x \in I}(D_{A,x} \cdot D_{B,x})^{w_x} = e(g_1, h)^s$. Finally it outputs $C \oplus \text{Ext}(D, \text{seed}) = \text{msg}$.

Remark 4.1 (On GlobalSetup): Similar to all prior decentralized MA-ABE schemes, our proposed schemes utilize a GlobalSetup algorithm that samples a random string ("setup") with a specific structure (i.e., private coin). This setup string needs to be generated only once, can be reused in different sessions, and the randomness used to generate it is never used subsequently so it can be discarded once the setup string is generated.

Theorem 4.1 (Security of Composite-Order MA-ABE Scheme): *The above MA-ABE scheme for NC^1 is fully adaptively secure in the random oracle model assuming the various types of sub-group decision assumptions.*

The proof of correctness of the scheme is presented in Sect. 4.3. The proof of security, i.e., that of Theorem 4.1, is deferred to the full version [16].

4.3 Correctness

Assume that the authorities in {SK$_{\text{GID},u}$} correspond to a qualified set according to the LSSS access structure (M, ρ) associated with CT, that is, the corresponding subset of row indices I corresponds to rows in M that have $(1, 0, \dots, 0)$ in their span.

For each $x \in I$, letting $\rho(x)$ be the corresponding authority,

$$e(C_{2,A,x}, \text{H(GID)} \cdot h) = e(g_1^{y_{A,\rho(x)}r_{A,x}} g_1^{\sigma_{A,x}}, \text{H(GID)} \cdot h)$$
$$= e(g_1^{y_{A,\rho(x)}r_{A,x}}, \text{H(GID)} \cdot h) \cdot e(g_1^{\sigma_{A,x}}, \text{H(GID)} \cdot h)$$
$$= e(g_1, \text{H(GID)} \cdot h)^{y_{A,\rho(x)}r_{A,x}} \cdot e(g_1, \text{H(GID)} \cdot h)^{\sigma_{A,x}}.$$

Also, for each $x \in I$,

$$
\begin{aligned}
e(C_{1,A,x}, K_{\mathsf{GID},A,\rho(x)}) &= e(g_1^{r_{A,x}}, (\mathsf{H}(\mathsf{GID}) \cdot h)^{y_{A,\rho(x)}}) \\
&= e(g_1, \mathsf{H}(\mathsf{GID}) \cdot h)^{y_{A,\rho(x)} r_{A,x}}.
\end{aligned}
$$

Hence,

$$
\begin{aligned}
D_{A,x} &= e(C_{2,A,x}, \mathsf{H}(\mathsf{GID}) \cdot h) \cdot e(C_{1,A,x}, K_{\mathsf{GID},A,\rho(x)})^{-1} \\
&= \frac{e(g_1, \mathsf{H}(\mathsf{GID}) \cdot h)^{y_{A,\rho(x)} r_{A,x}} \cdot e(g_1, \mathsf{H}(\mathsf{GID}) \cdot h)^{\sigma_{A,x}}}{e(g_1, \mathsf{H}(\mathsf{GID}) \cdot h)^{y_{A,\rho(x)} r_{A,x}}} \\
&= e(g_1, \mathsf{H}(\mathsf{GID}) \cdot h)^{\sigma_{A,x}}.
\end{aligned}
$$

Similarly,

$$
\begin{aligned}
D_{B,x} &= e(C_{2,B,x}, \mathsf{H}(\mathsf{GID})) \cdot e(C_{1,B,x}, K_{\mathsf{GID},B,\rho(x)})^{-1} \\
&= \frac{e(g_1, \mathsf{H}(\mathsf{GID}))^{y_{B,\rho(x)} r_{B,x}} \cdot e(g_1, \mathsf{H}(\mathsf{GID}))^{\sigma_{B,x}}}{e(g_1, \mathsf{H}(\mathsf{GID}))^{y_{B,\rho(x)} r_{B,x}}} = e(g_1, \mathsf{H}(\mathsf{GID}))^{\sigma_{B,x}}.
\end{aligned}
$$

We then have

$$
\begin{aligned}
D &= \prod_{x \in I} (D_{A,x} \cdot D_{B,x})^{w_x} \\
&= \prod_{x \in I} (e(g_1, \mathsf{H}(\mathsf{GID}) \cdot h)^{\sigma_{A,x}})^{w_x} \cdot (e(g_1, \mathsf{H}(\mathsf{GID}))^{\sigma_{B,x}})^{w_x} \\
&= \prod_{x \in I} e(g_1, \mathsf{H}(\mathsf{GID}) \cdot h)^{w_x \sigma_{A,x}} \cdot e(g_1, \mathsf{H}(\mathsf{GID}))^{w_x \sigma_{B,x}} \\
&= e(g_1, \mathsf{H}(\mathsf{GID}) \cdot h)^s \cdot e(g_1, \mathsf{H}(\mathsf{GID}))^{-s} = e(g_1, h)^s,
\end{aligned}
$$

where the fourth equality follows since $\sum_{x \in I} w_x \cdot M_x = (1, 0, \ldots, 0)$ and $\sigma_{A,x} = M_x \cdot v_A$ and $\sigma_{B,x} = M_x \cdot v_B$. Thus we have

$$
\begin{aligned}
C \oplus \mathsf{Ext}(D, \mathsf{seed}) &= \mathsf{msg} \oplus \mathsf{Ext}(e(g_1, h)^s, \mathsf{seed}) \oplus \mathsf{Ext}(e(g_1, h)^s, \mathsf{seed}) \\
&= \mathsf{msg}.
\end{aligned}
$$

5 Our Prime Order Group MA-ABE Scheme

In Sect. 5.1 we recall prime order bilinear groups and give the associated notations. In Sect. 5.2 we give the basis structure of the translation framework. Our construction is based on various subspace assumptions derived from the MDDH assumption [13] and can also be found in the full version [16]. In Sect. 5.3 we give the construction. The correctness and security proofs are deferred to the full version.

5.1   Prime Order Bilinear Groups and Associated Notations

Notations: Let A be a matrix over the ring $\mathbb{Z}_q$. We use $\mathsf{span}(A)$ to denote the column span of A, and we use $\mathsf{span}^m(A)$ to denote matrices of width m where each column lies in $\mathsf{span}(A)$; this means $M \leftarrow \mathsf{span}^m(A)$ is a random matrix of width m where each column is chose uniformly from $\mathsf{span}(A)$. We use $\mathsf{basis}(A)$ to denote a basis of $\mathsf{span}(A)$, and we use $(A_1 \parallel A_2)$ to denote the column-wise concatenation of matrices A_1, A_2. We let I be the identity matrix and $\mathbf{0}$ be a zero matrix whose size will be clear from the context.

Fix a security parameter, for any bilinear group parameter $\mathsf{G} = (p, \mathbb{G}_1, \mathbb{G}_2, \mathbb{G}_T, g_1, g_2, e)$ and any $i = 1, 2, T$ with $g_T = e(g_1, g_2)$, we write $[\![M]\!]_i$ for g_i^M where the exponentiation is element-wise. When bracket notation is used, we denote group operations with $\boxplus$, i.e., $[\![M]\!]_i \boxplus [\![N]\!]_i = [\![M + N]\!]_i$ for matrices M, N, and $\boxminus$ as their negatives, i.e., $[\![M]\!]_i \boxminus [\![N]\!]_i = [\![M - N]\!]_i$. Also, we define $N \odot [\![M]\!]_i = [\![NM]\!]_i$ and $[\![M]\!]_i \odot N = [\![MN]\!]_i$. We also slightly abuse notations and use the original pairing notation e to denote the pairing between matrices of group elements as well, i.e., we write $e([\![M]\!]_1, [\![N]\!]_2) = [\![MN]\!]_T$.

Prime Order Bilinear Groups: Let $\mathbb{G}_1, \mathbb{G}_2$ and $\mathbb{G}_T$ be three multiplicative cyclic groups of prime order $p = p(\lambda)$ where the group operations are efficiently computable in the security parameter λ and there is no isomorphism between $\mathbb{G}_1$ and $\mathbb{G}_2$ that can be computed efficiently in λ. Let g_1, g_2 be generators of $\mathbb{G}_1, \mathbb{G}_2$ respectively and $e : \mathbb{G}_1 \times \mathbb{G}_2 \to \mathbb{G}_T$ be an efficiently computable pairing function that satisfies the following properties:

- *Bilinearity*: for all $u \in \mathbb{G}_1, v \in \mathbb{G}_2$ and $a, b \in \mathbb{Z}_p$ it is true that $e(u^a, v^b) = e(u, v)^{ab}$.
- *Non-degeneracy*: $e(g_1, g_2) \neq 1_{\mathbb{G}_T}$, where $1_{\mathbb{G}_T}$ is the identity element of the group $\mathbb{G}_T$.

Let $\mathcal{G}$ be an algorithm that takes as input 1^λ, the unary encoding of the security parameter λ, and outputs the description of an asymmetric bilinear group $\mathsf{G} = (p, \mathbb{G}_1, \mathbb{G}_2, \mathbb{G}_T, g_1, g_2, e)$.

5.2   Composite to Prime Order Translation Framework

We want to simulate composite order groups whose order is the product of three primes. Fix parameters $\ell_1, \ell_2, \ell_3, \ell_W \geq 1$. Pick random

$$A_1 \leftarrow \mathbb{Z}_p^{\ell \times \ell_1}, \ A_2 \leftarrow \mathbb{Z}_p^{\ell \times \ell_2}, \ A_3 \leftarrow \mathbb{Z}_p^{\ell \times \ell_3}$$

where $\ell := \ell_1 + \ell_2 + \ell_3$. Let $(A_1^* \parallel A_2^* \parallel A_3^*)^\top$ denote the inverse of $(A_1 \parallel A_2 \parallel A_3)$, so that $A_i^\top A_i^* = I$ (known as *non-degeneracy*) and $A_i^\top A_j^* = \mathbf{0}$ if $i \neq j$ (known as *orthogonality*).

Correspondence: We have the following correspondence with composite order groups:

$$g_i \mapsto [\![A_i]\!]_1, \qquad\qquad g_i^s \mapsto [\![A_i s]\!]_1$$
$$w \in \mathbb{Z}_N \mapsto W \in \mathbb{Z}_p^{\ell \times \ell_W}, \qquad\qquad g_i^w \mapsto [\![A_i^\top W]\!]_1$$

The following statistical lemma is analogous to the Chinese Remainder Theorem, which tells us that $w \bmod p_2$ is uniformly random given g_1^w, g_3^w, where $w \leftarrow \mathbb{Z}_N$:

Lemma 5.1 (statistical lemma). *With probability $1 - 1/p$ over $A_1, A_2, A_3, A_1^*, A_2^*, A_3^*$, the following two distributions are statistically identical.*

$$\{A_1^\top W, A_3^\top W, \boxed{W}\} \quad and \quad \{A_1^\top W, A_3^\top W, \boxed{W + V^{(2)}}\}$$

where $W \leftarrow \mathbb{Z}_p^{\ell \times \ell_W}$ and $V^{(2)} \leftarrow \mathsf{span}^{\ell_W}(A_2^*)$.

5.3 The Construction

Here, we present our MA-ABE for NC^1 construction in prime order bilinear groups. As mentioned, we assume that each authority controls just one attribute, and hence we would use the terms "authority" and "attribute" interchangeably.

GlobalSetup(1^λ): The global setup algorithm takes in the security parameter 1^λ encoded in unary. The procedure first chooses a prime p. Next it generates a bilinear group $\mathsf{G} = (p, \mathbb{G}_1, \mathbb{G}_2, \mathbb{G}_T, g_1, g_2, e)$ of order p. Let g_1, g_2 be the generators of $\mathbb{G}_1, \mathbb{G}_2$ respectively. We make use of a strong seeded randomness extractor $\mathsf{Ext} : \mathbb{G}_T \times S \to \mathbb{M}$, where $\mathbb{M} \subset \{0,1\}^*$ is the message space and $S \subset \{0,1\}^*$ is the seed space. The algorithm samples a seed $\mathsf{seed} \leftarrow S$. Next, the algorithm samples $A_1, A_2, A_3 \leftarrow \mathbb{Z}_p^{3k \times k}, h \leftarrow \mathbb{Z}_p^k$. Let $(A_1^* \| A_2^* \| A_3^*) = ((A_1 \| A_2 \| A_3)^{-1})^\top$ where $A_1^*, A_2^*, A_3^* \leftarrow \mathbb{Z}_p^{3k \times k}$ such that $A_i^\top A_j^* = I$ if $i = j$, and 0 if $i \neq j$ for all $i, j \in [3]$. It outputs the global parameters as $\mathsf{GP} = (\mathsf{G}, [\![A_1]\!]_1, H = [\![A_1^* h]\!]_2, \mathsf{seed})$.

Furthermore, we assume that all parties has access to the hash function $\mathsf{H} : \{0,1\}^* \to \mathbb{G}_2^{3k}$ mapping global identifiers $\mathsf{GID} \in \mathcal{GID}$ to random vectors in $\mathbb{G}_2^{3k}$, i.e., for all $\mathsf{GID} \in \mathcal{GID}$ we have $\mathsf{H}(\mathsf{GID}) = [\![h_{\mathsf{GID}}]\!]_2$ for some $h_{\mathsf{GID}} \leftarrow \mathbb{Z}_p^{3k}$.

AuthSetup(GP, u): Given the global parameters GP and an authority index $u \in \mathcal{AU}$, the algorithm chooses random matrices $W_{A,u}, W_{B,u} \in \mathbb{Z}_p^{3k \times 3k}$ and outputs

$$\mathsf{PK}_u = (P_{A,u} = W_{A,u}^\top \odot [\![A_1]\!]_1, P_{B,u} = W_{B,u}^\top \odot [\![A_1]\!]_1)$$
$$= ([\![W_{A,u}^\top A_1]\!]_1, [\![W_{B,u}^\top A_1]\!]_1)$$
$$\mathsf{MSK}_u = (W_{A,u}, W_{B,u}).$$

Enc($\mathsf{GP}, \mathsf{msg}, (M, \rho), \{\mathsf{PK}_u\}$): The encryption algorithm takes as input the global parameters GP, a message $\mathsf{msg} \in \mathbb{M}$ to encrypt, an LSSS access structure (M, ρ), where $M = (M_{x,j})_{\ell \times d} = (M_1, \ldots, M_\ell)^\top \in \mathbb{Z}_N^{\ell \times d}$ and $\rho : [\ell] \to \mathcal{AU}$, and public keys of the relevant authorities $\{\mathsf{PK}_u\}$. The function ρ associates rows of M (viewed as column vectors) to authorities (recall that we assume that each authority controls a single attribute). We assume that ρ is an injective function, that is, an authority/attribute is associated with at most one row of M.

It first samples a random vector $\boldsymbol{d} \leftarrow \mathbb{Z}_p^k$ and random matrices $\boldsymbol{U}_A, \boldsymbol{U}_B \leftarrow \mathbb{Z}_p^{3k \times (d-1)}$. The procedure generates the ciphertext as follows: For each row $x \in [\ell]$, it chooses random vectors $\boldsymbol{s}_{A,x}, \boldsymbol{s}_{B,x} \leftarrow \mathbb{Z}_p^k$ and outputs the ciphertext

$$\mathsf{CT} = ((\boldsymbol{M}, \rho), C, \{C_{1,A,x}, C_{2,A,x}, C_{1,B,x}, C_{2,B,x}\}_{x \in [\ell]}),$$

where $C = \mathsf{msg} \oplus \mathsf{Ext}(e([\![\boldsymbol{A}_1 \boldsymbol{d}]\!]_1, H), \mathsf{seed})$, and

$$C_{1,A,x} = [\![\boldsymbol{A}_1]\!]_1 \odot \boldsymbol{s}_{A,x} = [\![\boldsymbol{A}_1 \boldsymbol{s}_{A,x}]\!]_1$$

$$C_{2,A,x} = ([\![\boldsymbol{A}_1]\!]_1 \odot \boldsymbol{d} \,\|\, [\![\boldsymbol{U}_A]\!]_1) \odot \boldsymbol{M}_x + [\![\boldsymbol{W}_{A,\rho(x)}^\top \boldsymbol{A}_1]\!]_1 \odot \boldsymbol{s}_{A,x}$$

$$= \left[\!\left[(\boldsymbol{A}_1 \boldsymbol{d} \,\|\, \boldsymbol{U}_A) \boldsymbol{M}_x + \boldsymbol{W}_{A,\rho(x)}^\top \boldsymbol{A}_1 \boldsymbol{s}_{A,x} \right]\!\right]_1$$

$$C_{1,B,x} = [\![\boldsymbol{A}_1]\!]_1 \odot \boldsymbol{s}_{B,x} = [\![\boldsymbol{A}_1 \boldsymbol{s}_{B,x}]\!]_1$$

$$C_{2,B,x} = ([\![\boldsymbol{A}_1]\!]_1 \odot (-\boldsymbol{d}) \,\|\, [\![\boldsymbol{U}_B]\!]_1) \odot \boldsymbol{M}_x + [\![\boldsymbol{W}_{B,\rho(x)}^\top \boldsymbol{A}_1]\!]_1 \odot \boldsymbol{s}_{B,x}$$

$$= \left[\!\left[(-\boldsymbol{A}_1 \boldsymbol{d} \,\|\, \boldsymbol{U}_B) \boldsymbol{M}_x + \boldsymbol{W}_{B,\rho(x)}^\top \boldsymbol{A}_1 \boldsymbol{s}_{B,x} \right]\!\right]_1.$$

KeyGen(GP, GID, MSK$_u$): The key generation algorithm takes as input the global parameters GP, the user's global identifier $\mathsf{GID} \in \mathcal{GID}$, and the authority's master secret key MSK_u. It generates a secret key $\mathsf{SK}_{\mathsf{GID},u}$ for GID as

$$\mathsf{SK}_{\mathsf{GID},u} = (K_{\mathsf{GID},A,u}, K_{\mathsf{GID},B,u})$$

where

$$K_{\mathsf{GID},A,u} = \boldsymbol{W}_{A,u} \odot (\mathsf{H}(\mathsf{GID}) \cdot H) = [\![\boldsymbol{W}_{A,u} \cdot (\boldsymbol{h}_{\mathsf{GID}} + \boldsymbol{A}_1^* \boldsymbol{h})]\!]_2$$

$$K_{\mathsf{GID},B,u} = \boldsymbol{W}_{B,u} \odot \mathsf{H}(\mathsf{GID}) = [\![\boldsymbol{W}_{B,u} \cdot \boldsymbol{h}_{\mathsf{GID}}]\!]_2$$

Dec(GP, CT, GID, $\{\mathsf{SK}_{\mathsf{GID},u}\}$): Decryption takes as input the global parameters GP, a ciphertext CT for an LSSS access structure $(\boldsymbol{M}, \rho)$ with $\boldsymbol{M} \in \mathbb{Z}_N^{\ell \times d}$ and $\rho : [\ell] \to \mathcal{AU}$ injective, the user's global identifier $\mathsf{GID} \in \mathcal{GID}$, and the secret keys $\{\mathsf{SK}_{\mathsf{GID},u}\}_{u \in \rho(I)}$ corresponding to a subset of rows of $\boldsymbol{M}$ with indices $I \subseteq [\ell]$. If $(1, 0, \ldots, 0)$ is *not* in the span of these rows, $\boldsymbol{M}_I$, then decryption fails. Otherwise, the decryptor finds $\{w_x \in \mathbb{Z}_N\}_{x \in I}$ such that $(1, 0, \ldots, 0) = \sum_{x \in I} w_x \cdot \boldsymbol{M}_x^\top$.

For all $x \in I$, the decryption algorithm first compute:

$$D_{A,x} = e(C_{2,A,x}, [\![\boldsymbol{h}_{\mathsf{GID}} + \boldsymbol{A}_1^* \boldsymbol{h}]\!]_2) e(C_{1,A,x}, K_{\mathsf{GID},A,\rho(x)})^{-1}$$

$$= \left[\!\left[((\boldsymbol{A}_1 \boldsymbol{d} \,\|\, \boldsymbol{U}_A) \boldsymbol{M}_x)^\top \cdot (\boldsymbol{h}_{\mathsf{GID}} + \boldsymbol{A}_1^* \boldsymbol{h}) \right]\!\right]_T$$

$$D_{B,x} = e(C_{2,B,x}, [\![\boldsymbol{h}_{\mathsf{GID}}]\!]_2) e(C_{1,B,x}, K_{\mathsf{GID},B,\rho(x)})^{-1}$$

$$= \left[\!\left[((-\boldsymbol{A}_1 \boldsymbol{d} \,\|\, \boldsymbol{U}_B) \boldsymbol{M}_x)^\top \cdot \boldsymbol{h}_{\mathsf{GID}} \right]\!\right]_T$$

Then compute $D = \prod_{x \in I} (D_{A,x} \cdot D_{B,x})^{w_x} = e([\![\boldsymbol{A}_1 \boldsymbol{d}]\!]_1, H)$. Finally it outputs $C \oplus \mathsf{Ext}(D, \mathsf{seed}) = \mathsf{msg}$.

Theorem 5.1 (Security of Prime-Order MA-ABE Scheme): *Assuming the* MDDH *assumption holds, then all* PPT *adversary has a negligible advantage in breaking the fully adaptive security of the above* MA-ABE *scheme in the random oracle model.*

References

1. Agrawal, S., Chase, M.: A study of pair encodings: predicate encryption in prime order groups. In: Kushilevitz, E., Malkin, T. (eds.) TCC 2016. LNCS, vol. 9563, pp. 259–288. Springer, Heidelberg (2016). https://doi.org/10.1007/978-3-662-49099-0_10

2. Ambrona, M., Gay, R.: Multi-authority ABE, revisited. IACR Cryptology ePrint Archive, Report 2021/1381 (2021). https://eprint.iacr.org/2021/1381

3. Ananth, P., Brakerski, Z., Segev, G., Vaikuntanathan, V.: From selective to adaptive security in functional encryption. In: Gennaro, R., Robshaw, M. (eds.) CRYPTO 2015. LNCS, vol. 9216, pp. 657–677. Springer, Heidelberg (2015). https://doi.org/10.1007/978-3-662-48000-7_32

4. Attrapadung, N.: Dual system encryption framework in prime-order groups via computational pair encodings. In: Cheon, J.H., Takagi, T. (eds.) ASIACRYPT 2016. LNCS, vol. 10032, pp. 591–623. Springer, Heidelberg (2016). https://doi.org/10.1007/978-3-662-53890-6_20

5. Beimel, A.: Secure schemes for secret sharing and key distribution. PhD Thesis, Israel Institute of Technology, Technion, Haifa, Israel (1996). https://technion.primo.exlibrisgroup.com/permalink/972TEC_INST/q1jq5o/alma990021768270203971

6. Benaloh, J., Leichter, J.: Generalized secret sharing and monotone functions. In: Goldwasser, S. (ed.) CRYPTO 1988. LNCS, vol. 403, pp. 27–35. Springer, New York (1990). https://doi.org/10.1007/0-387-34799-2_3

7. Boneh, D., Boyen, X., Shacham, H.: Short group signatures. In: Franklin, M. (ed.) CRYPTO 2004. LNCS, vol. 3152, pp. 41–55. Springer, Heidelberg (2004). https://doi.org/10.1007/978-3-540-28628-8_3

8. Boneh, D., Franklin, M.: Identity-based encryption from the Weil pairing. In: Kilian, J. (ed.) CRYPTO 2001. LNCS, vol. 2139, pp. 213–229. Springer, Heidelberg (2001). https://doi.org/10.1007/3-540-44647-8_13

9. Boneh, D., Goh, E.-J., Nissim, K.: Evaluating 2-DNF formulas on ciphertexts. In: Kilian, J. (ed.) TCC 2005. LNCS, vol. 3378, pp. 325–341. Springer, Heidelberg (2005). https://doi.org/10.1007/978-3-540-30576-7_18

10. Chase, M.: Multi-authority attribute based encryption. In: Vadhan, S.P. (ed.) TCC 2007. LNCS, vol. 4392, pp. 515–534. Springer, Heidelberg (2007). https://doi.org/10.1007/978-3-540-70936-7_28

11. Chase, M., Chow, S.S.M.: Improving privacy and security in multi-authority attribute-based encryption. In: Conference on Computer and Communications Security - CCS, pp. 121–130 (2009). https://doi.org/10.1145/1653662.1653678

12. Chen, J., Gay, R., Wee, H.: Improved dual system ABE in prime-order groups via predicate encodings. In: Oswald, E., Fischlin, M. (eds.) EUROCRYPT 2015. LNCS, vol. 9057, pp. 595–624. Springer, Heidelberg (2015). https://doi.org/10.1007/978-3-662-46803-6_20

13. Chen, J., Gong, J., Kowalczyk, L., Wee, H.: Unbounded ABE via bilinear entropy expansion, revisited. In: Nielsen, J.B., Rijmen, V. (eds.) EUROCRYPT 2018. LNCS, vol. 10820, pp. 503–534. Springer, Cham (2018). https://doi.org/10.1007/978-3-319-78381-9_19

14. Datta, P., Komargodski, I., Waters, B.: Decentralized multi-authority ABE for DNFs from LWE. In: Canteaut, A., Standaert, F.-X. (eds.) EUROCRYPT 2021. LNCS, vol. 12696, pp. 177–209. Springer, Cham (2021). https://doi.org/10.1007/978-3-030-77870-5_7

15. Datta, P., Komargodski, I., Waters, B.: Decentralized multi-authority ABE for NC^1 from Computational-BDH. IACR Cryptol. ePrint Arch., 1325 (2021). https://eprint.iacr.org/2021/1325

16. Datta, P., Komargodski, I., Waters, B.: Fully adaptive decentralized multi-authority ABE. Cryptology ePrint Archive, Paper 2022/1311 (2022). https://eprint.iacr.org/2022/1311

17. Escala, A., Herold, G., Kiltz, E., Ràfols, C., Villar, J.: An algebraic framework for Diffie-Hellman assumptions. In: Canetti, R., Garay, J.A. (eds.) CRYPTO 2013. LNCS, vol. 8043, pp. 129–147. Springer, Heidelberg (2013). https://doi.org/10.1007/978-3-642-40084-1_8

18. Escala, A., Herold, G., Kiltz, E., Ràfols, C., Villar, J.: An algebraic framework for Diffie–Hellman assumptions. J. Cryptol. **30**(1), 242–288 (2015). https://doi.org/10.1007/s00145-015-9220-6

19. Freeman, D.M.: Converting pairing-based cryptosystems from composite-order groups to prime-order groups. In: Gilbert, H. (ed.) EUROCRYPT 2010. LNCS, vol. 6110, pp. 44–61. Springer, Heidelberg (2010). https://doi.org/10.1007/978-3-642-13190-5_3

20. Gong, J., Dong, X., Chen, J., Cao, Z.: Efficient IBE with tight reduction to standard assumption in the multi-challenge setting. In: Cheon, J.H., Takagi, T. (eds.) ASIACRYPT 2016. LNCS, vol. 10032, pp. 624–654. Springer, Heidelberg (2016). https://doi.org/10.1007/978-3-662-53890-6_21

21. Gong, J., Wee, H.: Adaptively secure ABE for DFA from k-lin and more. In: Canteaut, A., Ishai, Y. (eds.) EUROCRYPT 2020. LNCS, vol. 12107, pp. 278–308. Springer, Cham (2020). https://doi.org/10.1007/978-3-030-45727-3_10

22. Goyal, V., Pandey, O., Sahai, A., Waters, B.: Attribute-based encryption for fine-grained access control of encrypted data. In: Conference on Computer and Communications Security - CCS, pp. 89–98. ACM (2006). https://doi.org/10.1145/1180405.1180418

23. Guillevic, A.: Comparing the pairing efficiency over composite-order and prime-order elliptic curves. In: Jacobson, M., Locasto, M., Mohassel, P., Safavi-Naini, R. (eds.) ACNS 2013. LNCS, vol. 7954, pp. 357–372. Springer, Heidelberg (2013). https://doi.org/10.1007/978-3-642-38980-1_22

24. Hofheinz, D., Kiltz, E.: Secure hybrid encryption from weakened key encapsulation. In: Menezes, A. (ed.) CRYPTO 2007. LNCS, vol. 4622, pp. 553–571. Springer, Heidelberg (2007). https://doi.org/10.1007/978-3-540-74143-5_31

25. Kowalczyk, L., Lewko, A.B.: Bilinear entropy expansion from the decisional linear assumption. In: Gennaro, R., Robshaw, M. (eds.) CRYPTO 2015. LNCS, vol. 9216, pp. 524–541. Springer, Heidelberg (2015). https://doi.org/10.1007/978-3-662-48000-7_26

26. Kowalczyk, Lucas, Wee, Hoeteck: compact adaptively secure ABE for NC^1 from k-Lin. J. Cryptol. **33**(3), 954–1002 (2019). https://doi.org/10.1007/s00145-019-09335-x

27. Lewko, A.: Tools for simulating features of composite order bilinear groups in the prime order setting. In: Pointcheval, D., Johansson, T. (eds.) EUROCRYPT 2012. LNCS, vol. 7237, pp. 318–335. Springer, Heidelberg (2012). https://doi.org/10.1007/978-3-642-29011-4_20

28. Lewko, A., Okamoto, T., Sahai, A., Takashima, K., Waters, B.: Fully secure functional encryption: attribute-based encryption and (hierarchical) inner product encryption. In: Gilbert, H. (ed.) EUROCRYPT 2010. LNCS, vol. 6110, pp. 62–91. Springer, Heidelberg (2010). https://doi.org/10.1007/978-3-642-13190-5_4

29. Lewko, A., Waters, B.: New techniques for dual system encryption and fully secure HIBE with short ciphertexts. In: Micciancio, D. (ed.) TCC 2010. LNCS, vol. 5978, pp. 455–479. Springer, Heidelberg (2010). https://doi.org/10.1007/978-3-642-11799-2_27

30. Lewko, A., Waters, B.: Decentralizing attribute-based encryption. In: Paterson, K.G. (ed.) EUROCRYPT 2011. LNCS, vol. 6632, pp. 568–588. Springer, Heidelberg (2011). https://doi.org/10.1007/978-3-642-20465-4_31

31. Lewko, A., Waters, B.: Unbounded HIBE and attribute-based encryption. In: Paterson, K.G. (ed.) EUROCRYPT 2011. LNCS, vol. 6632, pp. 547–567. Springer, Heidelberg (2011). https://doi.org/10.1007/978-3-642-20465-4_30

32. Lin, H., Cao, Z., Liang, X., Shao, J.: Secure threshold multi authority attribute based encryption without a central authority. In: Chowdhury, D.R., Rijmen, V., Das, A. (eds.) INDOCRYPT 2008. LNCS, vol. 5365, pp. 426–436. Springer, Heidelberg (2008). https://doi.org/10.1007/978-3-540-89754-5_33

33. Lin, H., Luo, J.: Compact adaptively secure ABE from k-Lin: Beyond NC^1 and towards NL. In: anteaut, A., Ishai, Y. (eds) Advances in Cryptology - EUROCRYPT 2020, EUROCRYPT 2020. Lecture Notes in Computer Science, vol. 12107, pp. 247–277. Springer, Cham (2020). https://doi.org/10.1007/978-3-030-45727-3_9

34. Müller, S., Katzenbeisser, S., Eckert, C.: Distributed attribute-based encryption. In: Lee, P.J., Cheon, J.H. (eds.) ICISC 2008. LNCS, vol. 5461, pp. 20–36. Springer, Heidelberg (2009). https://doi.org/10.1007/978-3-642-00730-9_2

35. Müller, S., Katzenbeisser, S., Eckert, C.: On multi-authority ciphertext-policy attribute-based encryption. Bull. Korean Math. Soc. **46**, 803–819 (2009). https://doi.org/10.4134/BKMS.2009.46.4.803

36. Okamoto, T., Takashima, K.: Fully secure functional encryption with general relations from the decisional linear assumption. In: Rabin, T. (ed.) CRYPTO 2010. LNCS, vol. 6223, pp. 191–208. Springer, Heidelberg (2010). https://doi.org/10.1007/978-3-642-14623-7_11

37. Okamoto, T., Takashima, K.: Fully secure unbounded inner-product and attribute-based encryption. In: Wang, X., Sako, K. (eds.) ASIACRYPT 2012. LNCS, vol. 7658, pp. 349–366. Springer, Heidelberg (2012). https://doi.org/10.1007/978-3-642-34961-4_22

38. Okamoto, T., Takashima, K.: Decentralized attribute-based encryption and signatures. IEICE Trans. Fundam. Electr. Commun. Comput. Sci. **103-A**(1), 41–73 (2020). https://doi.org/10.1587/transfun.2019CIP0008

39. de la Piedra, A., Venema, M., Alpár, G.: Abe squared: accurately benchmarking efficiency of attribute-based encryption. IACR Cryptology ePrint Archive, Report 2022/038 (2022). https://eprint.iacr.org/2022/038

40. Rouselakis, Y., Waters, B.: Efficient statically-secure large-universe multi-authority attribute-based encryption. In: Böhme, R., Okamoto, T. (eds.) FC 2015. LNCS, vol. 8975, pp. 315–332. Springer, Heidelberg (2015). https://doi.org/10.1007/978-3-662-47854-7_19

41. Sahai, A., Waters, B.: Fuzzy identity-based encryption. In: Cramer, R. (ed.) EURO-CRYPT 2005. LNCS, vol. 3494, pp. 457–473. Springer, Heidelberg (2005). https://doi.org/10.1007/11426639_27

42. Shacham, H.: A cramer-shoup encryption scheme from the linear assumption and from progressively weaker linear variants. IACR Cryptol. ePrint Arch. **2007**, 74 (2007). https://eprint.iacr.org/2007/074

43. Tsabary, R.: Candidate witness encryption from lattice techniques. In: Dodis, Y., Shrimpton, T. (eds.) Advances in Cryptology - CRYPTO 2022, CRYPTO 2022. Lecture Notes in Computer Science, vol. 13507, pp. 535–559. Springer, Cham (2022). https://doi.org/10.1007/978-3-031-15802-5_19

44. Vadhan, S.P.: Pseudorandomness. Found. Trends Theor. Comput. Sci. **7**(1–3), 1–336 (2012). https://doi.org/10.1561/0400000010

45. Waters, B.: Dual system encryption: realizing fully secure IBE and HIBE under simple assumptions. In: Halevi, S. (ed.) CRYPTO 2009. LNCS, vol. 5677, pp. 619–636. Springer, Heidelberg (2009). https://doi.org/10.1007/978-3-642-03356-8_36

46. Waters, B.: Ciphertext-policy attribute-based encryption: an expressive, efficient, and provably secure realization. In: Catalano, D., Fazio, N., Gennaro, R., Nicolosi, A. (eds.) PKC 2011. LNCS, vol. 6571, pp. 53–70. Springer, Heidelberg (2011). https://doi.org/10.1007/978-3-642-19379-8_4

47. Waters, B.: A punctured programming approach to adaptively secure functional encryption. In: Gennaro, R., Robshaw, M. (eds.) CRYPTO 2015. LNCS, vol. 9216, pp. 678–697. Springer, Heidelberg (2015). https://doi.org/10.1007/978-3-662-48000-7_33

48. Waters, B., Wee, H., Wu, D.: Multi-authority ABE from lattices without random oracles. In: Kiltz, E., Vaikuntanathan, V. (eds.) TCC 2022. Lecture Notes in Computer Science, vol. 13747, pp. 651–679. Springer, Cham (2022). https://doi.org/10.1007/978-3-031-22318-1_23

49. Wee, H.: Optimal broadcast encryption and CP-ABE from evasive lattice assumptions. In: Dunkelman, O., Dziembowski, S. (eds.) EUROCRYPT 2022. Lecture Notes in Computer Science, vol. 13276, pp. 217–241. Springer, Cham (2022). https://doi.org/10.1007/978-3-031-07085-3_8

On the Optimal Succinctness and Efficiency of Functional Encryption and Attribute-Based Encryption

Aayush Jain[1]($\boxtimes$), Huijia Lin[2]($\boxtimes$), and Ji Luo[2]($\boxtimes$) (iD)

[1] Carnegie Mellon University, Pittsburgh, USA
`aayushja@andrew.cmu.edu`
[2] Paul G. Allen School of Computer Science & Engineering,
University of Washington, Seattle, USA
`{rachel,luoji}@cs.washington.edu`

Abstract. We investigate the best-possible (asymptotic) efficiency of functional encryption (FE) and attribute-based encryption (ABE) by proving inherent space-time trade-offs and constructing nearly optimal schemes. We consider the general notion of partially hiding functional encryption (PHFE), capturing both FE and ABE, and the most efficient computation model of random-access machine (RAM). In PHFE, a secret key sk_f is associated with a function f, whereas a ciphertext $\mathsf{ct}_x(y)$ is tied to a public input x and encrypts a private input y. Decryption reveals $f(x, y)$ and nothing else about y.

We present the first PHFE for RAM solely based on the necessary assumption of FE for circuits. Significantly improving upon the efficiency of prior schemes, our construction achieves nearly optimal succinctness and computation time:

- Its secret key sk_f is of *constant size* (optimal), independent of the function description length $|f|$, i.e., $|\mathsf{sk}_f| = \mathrm{poly}(\lambda)$.
- Its ciphertext $\mathsf{ct}_x(y)$ is *rate-2* in the private input length $|y|$ (nearly optimal) and *independent* of the public input length $|x|$ (optimal), i.e., $|\mathsf{ct}_x(y)| = 2|y| + \mathrm{poly}(\lambda)$.
- Decryption time is *linear* in the *instance* running time T of the RAM computation, plus the function and public/private input lengths, i.e., $T_{\mathsf{Dec}} = (T + |f| + |x| + |y|)\,\mathrm{poly}(\lambda)$.

As a corollary, we obtain the first ABE with both keys and ciphertexts being constant-size, while enjoying the best-possible decryption time matching the lower bound by Luo [ePrint '22]. We also separately achieve several other optimal ABE subject to the known lower bound.

We study the barriers to further efficiency improvements. We prove the first unconditional space-time trade-offs for (PH-)FE:

- *No* secure (PH-)FE can have $|\mathsf{sk}_f|$ and T_{Dec} *both* sublinear in $|f|$.
- *No* secure PHFE can have $|\mathsf{ct}_x(y)|$ and T_{Dec} *both* sublinear in $|x|$.

Our lower bounds apply even to the weakest secret-key 1-key 1-ciphertext selective schemes. Furthermore, we show a conditional barrier towards the optimal decryption time $T_{\mathsf{Dec}} = T\,\mathrm{poly}(\lambda)$ while keeping linear size dependency — any such (PH-)FE scheme implies doubly efficient private information retrieval (DE-PIR) with linear-size preprocessed database, for which so far there is no candidate.

© International Association for Cryptologic Research 2023
C. Hazay and M. Stam (Eds.): EUROCRYPT 2023, LNCS 14006, pp. 479–510, 2023.
https://doi.org/10.1007/978-3-031-30620-4_16

1 Introduction

Functional encryption (FE) [15,50] and attribute-based encryption (ABE) [34, 52] are powerful enhancement of public-key encryption with many fascinating applications. In this work, we investigate the best-possible efficiency of these primitives, proving inherent space-time trade-offs for FE and presenting nearly optimal constructions of FE and ABE.

To this end, we consider the general notion of partially hiding functional encryption (PHFE) [5,33,38] capturing both FE and ABE. In PHFE, a secret key sk_f is associated with a function f, whereas a ciphertext $\mathsf{ct}_x(y)$ is tied to a public input x and encrypts a private input y. Their decryption recovers the computation output $f(x,y)$. Collusion-resistant (indistinguishability-based) security ensures that given unboundedly (polynomially) many secret keys $\{\mathsf{sk}_{f_q}\}_q$ for different functions $\{f_q\}_q$, ciphertexts $\mathsf{ct}_x(y_0)$ and $\mathsf{ct}_x(y_1)$ tied to the same public input x and encrypting different private inputs y_0, y_1 remain indistinguishable so long as none of the keys separate them by functionality, i.e., $f_q(x,y_0) = f_q(x,y_1)$. Put simply, the only information revealed about the private input y is the outputs $\{f_q(x,y)\}_q$.

Over the past decade, significant progress has been made in establishing the feasibility of (PH-)FE, for various classes of computation, with different levels of efficiency and security, and from different assumptions. However, we are yet to understand the asymptotic optimality and theoretical limits of its efficiency. We ask:

> *What is the best-possible asymptotic efficiency of PHFE?*
> *Are there trade-offs among different aspects of efficiency?*
> *Can we construct optimally efficient PHFE?*

We make progress towards answering the above questions.

For the lower bounds, we prove inherent trade-offs between the size of keys or ciphertexts and the decryption time, and show barriers towards achieving the optimal decryption time.

On the constructive front, we present the first collusion-resistant PHFE for RAM solely based on the necessary assumption of (polynomially secure) collusion-resistant FE for circuits, which in turn can be based on well-studied assumptions [39,40]. Our scheme has nearly minimally sized keys and ciphertexts, and nearly optimal decryption time matching our lower bounds. As a corollary, we obtain the first ABE with both constant-size keys and constant-size ciphertexts, and the best-possible decryption time matching the recently discovered lower bound [48].

By slightly tweaking the construction, we also obtain ABE with linear-size keys and/or ciphertexts and the optimal decryption time subject to the known lower bound.

Dream Efficiency. Before describing our results, we first picture the dream efficiency with respect to three important dimensions. Each dimension has been a consistent research theme across many primitives in cryptography.

Efficient Computation Model. Functions should be represented by random-access machines (RAM), the most efficient computation model subsuming both circuits and Turing machines. RAM is also closer to real-world computers.

We consider a RAM U (fixed[1] at set-up time) with random access to three tapes, a function tape containing f, an input tape containing $x \| y$, and a working tape. It may produce *arbitrarily long* output, e.g., one bit at *every* step. This flexible model captures many natural scenarios, e.g., binary search where the database could be part of f, x, y. It can emulate the evaluation of a circuit C on input (x, y) by putting the circuit description on the function tape. In ciphertext-policy ABE, each ciphertext is tied to a predicate P, which can be captured by setting $x = P$. These examples tell us that any or even all of f, x, y could be long, and we want to optimize the efficiency dependency on their lengths.

Succinctness. Enjoying low communication and storage overhead means having short master public key mpk, secret keys sk_f, and ciphertexts $\mathsf{ct}_x(y)$. At the most basic level, the size of each component should be *polynomial* in the length of the information it is associated with — $|\mathsf{mpk}| = O(1)$,[2] $|\mathsf{sk}_f| = \mathsf{poly}(|f|)$, and $|\mathsf{ct}_x(y)| = \mathsf{poly}(|x|, |y|)$, where $|f|, |x|, |y|$ are the description lengths of f, x, y, respectively — referred to as *polynomial efficiency*.[3] However, there is much to be desired beyond this basic level of efficiency. For instance, linear efficiency means $|\mathsf{sk}_f| = O(|f|)$ and $|\mathsf{ct}| = O(|x| + |y|)$, and rate-1 efficiency means $|\mathsf{sk}_f| = |f| + O(1)$ and $|\mathsf{ct}| = |x| + |y| + O(1)$.

In fact, even smaller parameters are possible. Since (PH-)FE does not aim to hide the function f, it is allowed to put the description of f in the clear in the secret key, and the *non-trivial* part of the secret key may be shorter than f. In this case, the right measure of efficiency should be the size of the non-trivial part (i.e., the overhead), which we now view as *the* secret key. We can aim for secret keys of size *independent* of that of the function — i.e., $|\mathsf{sk}_f| = O(1)$ — referred to as *constant-size* keys. The same observation applies to the public input x tied to the ciphertext and we can hope for ciphertexts of size *independent* of $|x|$ while having optimal, rate-1 dependency on the private input length $|y|$ — i.e., $|\mathsf{ct}_x(y)| = |y| + O(1)$. In summary:

Ideal Succinctness: $|\mathsf{mpk}| = O(1)$, $|\mathsf{sk}_f| = O(1)$, $|\mathsf{ct}_x(y)| = |y| + O(1)$.

Note that the ideal component sizes are completely independent of the running time or the output length of the computation.

---

[1] We can think of U as a universal RAM.

[2] In this introduction, $O(\cdot)$ hides a multiplicative factor of $\mathsf{poly}(\lambda)$.

[3] It may appear that polynomial efficiency is the bare minimum. However, it is possible to consider components whose sizes depend on an upper bound of the length of some information *not* tied to them. Many early schemes are as such, e.g., the FE scheme of [26] has $|\mathsf{mpk}| = O(\mathsf{poly}(\max |y|))$, and the celebrated ABE scheme by [14] has $|\mathsf{mpk}|, |\mathsf{ct}|$ growing polynomially with the maximum depth of the computation. When a scheme requires fixing an upper bound on parameter Z (e.g., input length, depth, or size), it is said to be Z-bounded.

Decryption Time. Decryption is also a RAM computation, $\mathsf{Dec}^{f,x,\mathsf{sk}_f,\mathsf{ct}_x(y)}(\mathsf{mpk})$, which on input mpk and with random access to $f, x, \mathsf{sk}_f, \mathsf{ct}_x(y)$, computes the output $U^{f,x\|y}()$. We want decryption to be efficient, ideally taking time linear in the *instance* running time T of the RAM computation in the clear:

$$\textit{Ideal Decryption Time:} \quad T_{\mathsf{Dec}} = O(T).$$

Organization. In Sect. 1.1, we describe our results. In Sect. 1.2, we present an overview of our techniques. In Sect. 1.3, we discuss the related works. In Sect. 2, we lay out our formulations of succinct garbled RAM and PHFE. In Sect. 3, we formally prove our unconditional lower bounds. Due to the space constraint, we refer the readers to the full version [37] for the complete details on definitions, constructions, applications, and proofs.

1.1 Our Results

The question is whether the dream efficiency is attainable simultaneously in all above three dimensions. Towards understanding this, we present both new constructions and lower bounds.

New PHFE for RAM with Nearly Optimal Succinctness. Starting from selectively and polynomially secure bounded FE for circuits, i.e., all of $|\mathsf{mpk}|$, $|\mathsf{sk}_f|, |\mathsf{ct}(y)|$ are just $\mathrm{poly}(|f|, |y|)$, which in turn can be constructed from three well-studied assumptions [39,40], we construct an adaptively secure (unbounded) PHFE for RAM with nearly optimal succinctness.

Theorem 1 (informal). *Assuming polynomially secure FE for circuits, there exists an adaptively secure PHFE for RAM:*

$$\textit{PHFE Efficiency:} \quad |\mathsf{mpk}| = O(1), \ |\mathsf{sk}_f| = O(1), \ |\mathsf{ct}_x(y)| = 2|y| + O(1),$$
$$T_{\mathsf{Dec}} = O(T + |f| + |x| + |y|).$$

Our construction gives the first collusion-resistant (PH-)FE for RAM, and also the first (PH-)FE for any model of computation (e.g., circuit or TM) with nearly optimal succinctness. The only gap to optimality is that the ciphertext is rate-2 in $|y|$ instead of rate-1. Prior constructions work with either circuits [26,39,40] or Turing machines [1,8,42], except for the recent concurrent and independent work of [3], which also constructs FE for RAM. All of them only achieve polynomial efficiency as summarized in Table 1. We further discuss related works in Sect. 1.3.

As a corollary, we obtain the first ABE for RAM from falsifiable assumptions, and the first for any model of computation with both constant-size keys and constant-size ciphertexts. The only prior construction of ABE for RAM by [31] relies on non-falsifiable assumptions like SNARK and differing-input obfuscation. In terms of succinctness, existing schemes achieve *either* constant-size keys *or* constant-size ciphertexts [9–11,45,46,53–55]. Achieving constant-size keys and ciphertexts *simultaneously* has been an important theoretical open question (see discussion in [45]). The state-of-the-art is summarized in Table 2.

Table 1. Comparison among some (PH-)FE schemes. All rows except this work are FE, and this work is PHFE. C is the circuit. T is the instance running time of TM/RAM. All poly($\cdot$) and O($\cdot$) implicitly contains λ. For assumptions, FE is always for circuits, "sls" means sublinearly succinct, "subexp" means subexponentially secure, and "PK-DE-PIR" means public-key doubly efficient private information retrieval.

reference	functionality	$|\mathsf{sk}|$	$|\mathsf{ct}|$	T_{Dec}	adaptive	assumption
GGHRSW [26]	circuit	poly($|C|$)	poly($|y|$)	poly($|C|$)		$i\mathcal{O}$
KNTY [42]	circuit	poly($|C|$)	poly($|y|$)	poly($|C|$)	✓	1-key sls FE
GWZ [35]	circuit	poly($|C|$)	$|y|+$O(1)	poly($|C|$)		$i\mathcal{O}$
AS [8]	TM	poly($|f|$)	poly($|y|$)	poly($|f|,|y|$)T	✓	$i\mathcal{O}$
AJS [6]	TM	$c|f|+$O(1)	$c|y|+$O(1)	poly($|f|,|y|$)T	✓	subexp $i\mathcal{O}$
AM [1]	TM	poly($|f|$)	O($|y|$)	poly($|f|$)T	✓	FE
KNTY [42]	TM	poly($|f|$)	poly($|y|$)	poly($|f|,|y|$)T		1-key sls FE
ACFQ [3]	RAM	poly($|f|$)	poly($|y|$)	O(T)		PK-DE-PIR & FE
this work	RAM	O(1)	$2|y|+$O(1)	O($T+|f|+|x|+|y|$)	✓	FE

Table 2. Comparison among some KP-ABE schemes. Notations shared with Table 1. ABP means arithmetic branching programs (also using C). For assumptions, "k-Lin" means k-Linear in pairing groups, "GGM" means generic pairing group model, and "$di\mathcal{O}$" means differing-input obfuscation.

reference	functionality	$|\mathsf{sk}|$	$|\mathsf{ct}|$	T_{Dec}	adaptive	assumption
BGGHNSVV [14]	circuit	poly(d)	$|x|$ poly(d)	$|C|$ poly(d)		LWE
LL [46]	ABP	O($|C|\cdot|x|$)	O(1)	O($|C|\cdot|x|$)	✓	k-Lin
LLL [45]	circuit	O(1)	poly(d)	$|C|$ poly(d)	✓	GGM & LWE
GKPVZ [31]	RAM	O(1)	poly($|x|$)	O($T+|f|+|x|$)		SNARK & diO
this work	RAM	O(1)	O(1)	O($T+|f|+|x|$)	✓	FE

Corollary 2 (informal). *Assuming polynomially secure FE for circuits, there exists an adaptively secure key-policy ABE (KP-ABE) for RAM as well as an adaptively secure ciphertext-policy ABE (CP-ABE) for RAM:*

$\underline{\textit{KP-ABE Efficiency:}}$ $|\mathsf{mpk}| =$ O(1), $|\mathsf{sk}_f| =$ O(1), $|\mathsf{ct}_x| =$ O(1),

$\qquad\qquad\qquad T_{\mathsf{Dec}} =$ O($T+|f|+|x|$);

$\underline{\textit{CP-ABE Efficiency:}}$ $|\mathsf{mpk}| =$ O(1), $|\mathsf{sk}_x| =$ O(1), $|\mathsf{ct}_f| =$ O(1),

$\qquad\qquad\qquad T_{\mathsf{Dec}} =$ O($T+|f|+|x|$).

The decryption time of our PHFE and ABE *appears* suboptimal. In addition to the necessary linear dependency on T, it also grows linearly with $|f|,|x|,|y|$. It turns out that *ideal succinctness and ideal decryption time are at conflict.* We prove that under *sublinear* succinctness, the linear dependency of T_{Dec} on $|f|,|x|$ is *inherent*. We also show barriers towards removing the dependency of T_{Dec} on $|y|$ or $|f|,|x|$ while maintaining linear succinctness.

Our PHFE scheme matches the lower bounds and barriers — it is Pareto-optimal with respect to the dependency on $|f|,|x|$. For ABE, our lower bounds and barriers do not apply. Nevertheless, our ABE scheme matches an existing lower bound by [48], which states that any moderately expressive ABE must satisfy $|\mathsf{ct}_x| \cdot T_{\mathsf{Dec}} = \Omega(|x|)$ and $|\mathsf{sk}_f| \cdot T_{\mathsf{Dec}} = \Omega(|f|)$.[4] Given that our scheme has constant-size keys and ciphertexts, its decryption time matches the lower bound of [48], hence it is thus Pareto-optimal. By tweaking the construction, we obtain several other Pareto-optimal ABE schemes:

Theorem 3 (informal). *Assuming polynomially secure FE for circuits, there exist adaptively secure KP-/CP-ABE schemes for RAM:*

$$\underline{KP\text{-}ABE\ Efficiency:} \quad |\mathsf{mpk}| = O(1),\ |\mathsf{sk}_f| = |f|^\alpha + O(1),\ |\mathsf{ct}_x| = |x|^\beta + O(1),$$
$$T_{\mathsf{Dec}} = O(T + |f|^{1-\alpha} + |x|^{1-\beta}).$$

$$\underline{CP\text{-}ABE\ Efficiency:} \quad |\mathsf{mpk}| = O(1),\ |\mathsf{sk}_x| = |x|^\beta + O(1),\ |\mathsf{ct}_f| = |f|^\alpha + O(1),$$
$$T_{\mathsf{Dec}} = O(T + |f|^{1-\alpha} + |x|^{1-\beta}).$$

All four combinations of $\alpha, \beta \in \{0,1\}$ are possible for both KP- and CP-ABE.

Contention Between Succinct Components and Fast Decryption. We now describe our lower bounds in more detail. Consider the efficiency dependency on the lengths of public information f and x. We show that unconditionally, it is impossible to simultaneously achieve key size sublinear in $|f|$ and decryption time sublinear in $|f|$. Similarly, it is impossible to have both ciphertext size and decryption time sublinear in $|x|$. In fact, these trade-offs apply to the weakest secret-key 1-key 1-ciphertext selectively secure PHFE, and the first trade-off with respect to $|f|$ also applies to plain FE. More precisely:

Theorem 5 (informal). *For a secret-key 1-key 1-ciphertext selectively secure moderately expressive PHFE with*

$$|\mathsf{sk}| = O(|f|^\alpha) \quad \text{and} \quad T_{\mathsf{Dec}} = (T + |f|^\beta + |y|)\operatorname{poly}(|x|),$$

it must hold that $\alpha \geq 1$ or $\beta \geq 1$. The same (without x) is true for FE.

Theorem 6 (informal). *For a secret-key 1-key 1-ciphertext selectively secure moderately expressive PHFE with*

$$|\mathsf{ct}| = |x|^\alpha \operatorname{poly}(|y|) \quad \text{and} \quad T_{\mathsf{Dec}} = (T + |f| + |x|^\beta)\operatorname{poly}(|y|),$$

it must hold that $\alpha \geq 1$ or $\beta \geq 1$.

Our PHFE scheme achieves one profile of Pareto-optimality, $\alpha = 0$ and $\beta = 1$.

A natural question that our work leaves open is whether the other Pareto-optimal profile, $\alpha = 1$ and $\beta = 0$ (or even just $\beta < 1$), is attainable. Another question is whether the decryption time must grow with the length of the private input y.

---

[4] The lower bounds apply as long as the ABE scheme supports broadcast encryption. Theorem 14 in [48] is the first trade-off between $|\mathsf{ct}_x|$ and T_{Dec}. Essentially the same proof yields the second trade-off between $|\mathsf{sk}_f|$ and T_{Dec}.

Barriers to Ideal Decryption Time. We illustrate barriers to positive answers to the above two questions. We show that PHFE with decryption time independent of $|y|$, $|x|$, or $|f|$ implies secret-key doubly efficient private information retrieval (SK-DE-PIR) with small preprocessed database.

Theorem 4 (informal). *Suppose a moderately expressive secret-key PHFE with selective security has*

$$|\mathsf{sk}_f| = \ell_{\mathsf{sk}}(\lambda, |f|), \qquad |\mathsf{ct}_x(y)| = \ell_{\mathsf{ct}}(\lambda, |x|, |y|),$$
$$T_{\mathsf{Dec}} = (|f|^{e_f} + |x|^{e_x} + |y|^{e_y}) \operatorname{poly}(T).$$

Then the following hold:

- *If $e_x = 0$, there exists an SK-DE-PIR scheme with preprocessed database size $\ell_{\mathsf{ct}}(N, \operatorname{poly}(\lambda), \lambda)$, where N is the length of the original database. The PHFE only has to be 1-ciphertext secure.*
- *If $e_y = 0$, the SK-DE-PIR preprocessed database will have size $\ell_{\mathsf{ct}}(0, N, \lambda)$. The PHFE only has to be 1-ciphertext secure.*
- *If $e_f = 0$, the SK-DE-PIR preprocessed database will have size $\ell_{\mathsf{sk}}(N, \lambda)$. The PHFE only has to be 1-key secure.*

SK-DE-PIR, introduced by [17,22], allows a client to privately encode a database D into $\widetilde{D}$ while keeping a secret key k. Later, client can outsource the encoded database $\widetilde{D}$ to a remote storage server, and *obliviously* query the database using k hiding the logical access pattern. Different from ORAM, the server never updates the encoded database nor keeps any additional state. Different from PIR, SK-DE-PIR allows the database to be privately encoded in exchange for *double efficiency* — for each query, the complexities of both the client and the server are, ideally, independent of the database size $|D|$, whereas PIR necessarily has server complexity $\Omega(|D|)$. The double efficiency of SK-DE-PIR makes it highly desirable. The initial works [17,22] presented candidate constructions based on a new conjecture that permuted local-decoding queries (for a Reed–Muller code with suitable parameters) are computationally indistinguishable from uniformly random sets of points. More recently, a simple "toy conjecture" inspired by (though formally unrelated to) those SK-DE-PIR schemes has been broken [16]. Very recently, in a concurrent and independent work, Lin, Mook, and Wichs [47] constructed DE-PIR with public preprocessing from the ring-LWE assumption. The most important efficiency metrics of DE-PIR are the preprocessed database size and the complexity per query. None of the existing schemes simultaneously achieve constant complexity per query and linear-size preprocessed database.

Our theorem shows that constructing PHFE with short decryption time entails constructing SK-DE-PIR with preprocessed database size inherited from ciphertext/key size. In particular, a PHFE scheme with decryption time independent of $|y|$ and ciphertext size linear in $|y|$ implies an SK-DE-PIR with preprocessed database of length $O(N)$ and constant complexity per query. Since no such SK-DE-PIR is known even under non-standard assumptions, this represents a barrier towards improving the decryption time dependency on $|y|$ in our PHFE construction.

Succinct Garbled RAM and Constant-Overhead $i\mathcal{O}$. The main tool in our construction of PHFE for RAM is succinct garbled RAM (GRAM). Initiated by [13,21,43], a sequence of works have constructed succinct garbled RAM [2, 19,20,23] based on subexponentially secure FE for circuits and succinct garbled Turing machines [6,7,30,43] based on polynomially secure FE for circuits.

In this work, we formulate a new notion of succinct GRAM (informally described in the technical overview and formally defined in Sect. 2.1) geared for building highly efficient PHFE for RAM, and construct it based on polynomially secure FE for circuits. Our construction has two consequences: *i)* we obtain the first succinct GRAM (our or the standard notion) based on polynomial hardness, as opposed to subexponential hardness as in prior constructions, and *ii)* using $i\mathcal{O}$ for circuits, we obtain $i\mathcal{O}$ for RAM with constant overhead — the size of the obfuscated program is $2|M| + \mathrm{poly}(\lambda, \ell)$, where M is the original RAM and ℓ is the input length. Previously, constant-overhead $i\mathcal{O}$ was only known for Turing machines [6].

1.2 Technical Overview

We start with an overview of our negative results.

Unconditional Lower Bounds. As introduced earlier, we show that it is impossible for a secure PHFE to enjoy sublinear dependency on $|f|$ (resp. $|x|$) simultaneously for $|\mathsf{sk}_f|$ (resp. $|\mathsf{ct}_x(y)|$) and T_{Dec} when T_{Dec} is linear in $T, |x|, |y|$ (resp. $T, |f|, |y|$). We illustrate our ideas of proving the contention between

$$|\mathsf{sk}_f| = O(|f|^\alpha) \quad \text{and} \quad T_{\mathsf{Dec}} = O(T + |f|^\beta + |x| + |y|) \qquad \text{for } \alpha < 1 \text{ and } \beta < 1$$

by exhibiting an efficient adversary breaking the security of PHFE for RAM (polynomial factors in the security parameter are ignored).

Adversarial Function and Strategy. The adversary will selectively request one secret key and one ciphertext. Let $n < N$ be determined later.

- The function f is described by a string $R \in \{0,1\}^N$.
- There is no public input, so $x = \bot$.
- The private input y is either $(I \subseteq [N], w \in \{0,1\}^n)$ or $z \in \{0,1\}^n$, where I is a set containing n indices and w is a one-time pad.

The functionality is simply *reading and XORing* or *outputting as-is*, i.e.,

$$f(x,y) = \begin{cases} R[I] \oplus w, & \text{if } y = (I, w); \\ z, & \text{if } y = z; \end{cases}$$

where $R[I]$ means the n bits of R at the indices in I. Clearly,

$$|f| = O(N), \quad |x| = O(1), \quad |y| = O(n), \quad T = O(n),$$
$$|\mathsf{sk}| = O(N^\alpha), \qquad\qquad\qquad T_{\mathsf{Dec}} = O(n + N^\beta).$$

More precisely, $|y| = O(n \log n)$, but the $\log n$ factor is absorbed by the $\text{poly}(\lambda)$ factor hidden in $O(\cdot)$.

The adversary chooses

key query $\quad f$ with $R \xleftarrow{\$} \{0,1\}^N$,

challenge $\qquad\qquad x \leftarrow \bot, \qquad y_0 \xleftarrow{\$} \text{random}\,(I, w), \qquad y_1 \leftarrow z = R[I] \oplus w.$

By our choice, $f(x, y_0) = R[I] \oplus w = z = f(x, y_1)$, so the challenge is well-formed. Upon receiving sk and ct, the adversary simply runs the decryption algorithm on $(\mathsf{sk}, \mathsf{ct})$ with random access to the function, i.e., R, in the clear. Let $L \subseteq [N]$ be the set of indices in R that is read during decryption:

$$R[I] \oplus w \leftarrow \mathsf{Dec}^{R, x=\bot}(\mathsf{sk}, \mathsf{ct}), \text{ where } \mathsf{Dec} \text{ reads } R[L].$$

The adversary determines that

$$\mathsf{ct} \text{ is an encryption of } \begin{cases} y_0 = (I, w), & \text{if } |L \cap I| \text{ is large}; \\ y_1 = z, & \text{if } |L \cap I| \text{ is small}; \end{cases}$$

where the threshold for *large* and *small* is described below.

Intuition and Toy Proof. The intuition behind the adversary's strategy is simple. Let L_b be the index set L that decryption accessed when decrypting ct encrypting y_b.

- When ct encrypts y_0, decryption must correctly recover $R[I]$ (as the adversary knows w). The decryption algorithm can only obtain information of $R[I]$ either from sk or via accesses to the tape R. Since $R[I]$ contains n bits of information, by setting $|\mathsf{sk}| = O(N^\alpha) \ll n$, decryption must read a *large* portion of information of $R[I]$ from the tape R, implying $|L \cap I|$ is *large*, namely, $\Omega(n)$.
- In contrast, when ct encrypts y_1, observe that the joint distribution of $(R, \mathsf{ct}, \mathsf{sk})$ is independent of I, as w is a one-time pad and completely hides I in $y_1 = R[I] \oplus w$. Therefore, the behavior of Dec is independent of I. Since Dec runs in a short time $O(n + N^\beta) \ll N$, without knowing I, where it reads in R cannot overlap with I for a large portion. Therefore, $|L \cap I|$ is likely to be *small*.

It remains to analyze how large and small $|L \cap I|$ is in the above two cases. Let us first consider a toy proof, under the hypothesis that sk contains no information about $R[I]$ at all. We will remove this hypothesis below. By this hypothesis, when ct encrypts y_0, the decryption algorithm must read the entire $R[I]$ from the tape R and hence $|L \cap I| = n$. When ct encrypts y_1, since the indices L_1 that the decryption algorithm reads from R is independent of I, the intersection size $|L_1 \cap I|$ follows a hypergeometric distribution, and hence

$$\mathbb{E}\big[|L_1 \cap I|\big] \le \frac{T_{\mathsf{Dec}} \cdot n}{N} \ll n. \tag{1}$$

This means the adversary can distinguish when ct encrypts y_0 or y_1 with good probability, and contradicts the security of PHFE.

Removing the Hypothesis. The hypothesis that sk contains no information about $R[I]$ at all may well be false. When it is removed, we can no longer argue that $I \subseteq L_0$, as the adversary may obtain some information of $R[I]$ from sk. Our intuition is $|L_0 \cap I| \geq |I| - |\mathsf{sk}|$, but proving this formally is not trivial as sk may contain arbitrary information of $R[I]$.

We employ a compression argument. The basic idea behind a compression argument is that there is no pair of encoding and decoding algorithms (Encode, Decode), with arbitrarily long shared randomness s, is able to transmit an n-bit random string u (independent of s) from one end to the other, via an encoding v containing less than n bits. Informally,

$$\text{if } \Pr \begin{bmatrix} s \overset{\$}{\leftarrow} \mathcal{D}_s \\ u \overset{\$}{\leftarrow} \{0,1\}^n & : \mathsf{Decode}(s,v) = u \\ v \leftarrow \mathsf{Encode}(s,u) \end{bmatrix} = 1, \quad \text{then } |v| \geq |u|.$$

(Lemma 9 is the formal statement by [24].) We show that if $|L_0 \cap I| < |I| - |\mathsf{sk}|$, then we can design a pair of (Encode, Decode) violating the above information-theoretic bound.

- The shared randomness s is the PHFE randomness and $I, w, R[[N] \setminus I]$.
- To encode $u \in \{0,1\}^n$, the procedure Encode first sets $R[I] = u$. Using s, it then generates a PHFE key sk for R and a ciphertext ct encrypting $y_0 = (I, w)$, runs Dec to obtain the locations L_0 in R that decryption reads. Lastly, it sets the codeword to be $v = (\mathsf{sk}, R[L_0 \cap I])$.
- To decode, Decode regenerates ct using s, and runs Dec to obtain the output $z = R[I] \oplus w$ and recover $u = z \oplus w$. During decryption, Dec queries for locations L_0 in R. Every query is in either $R[[N] \setminus I]$ or $R[L_0 \cap I]$; the former can be answered by finding the right element in s and the latter in v.

Suppose $|L_0 \cap I| < |I| - |\mathsf{sk}|$, then $|v|$ is less than $|I| = |u|$, which contradicts the incompressibility of u. (In the formal proof, we make v fixed-length and suffer from incorrect decoding, hence the statements are probabilistic. See Sect. 3.1 for more details.)

Stepping back, the compression argument shows that $|L_0 \cap I| \geq |I| - |\mathsf{sk}|$. In contrast, by Eq. (1), $|L_1 \cap I| \leq n/2$ with high probability. To show that the adversary can distinguish ct encrypting y_0 or y_1, we can set, e.g., $n = N^{(\alpha+1)/2}$, so that $|\mathsf{sk}| = O(N^\alpha) \ll n$, and $|L_0 \cap I| \geq |I| - |\mathsf{sk}| \geq n/2$. (In the formal proof, N itself is a large poly(λ) to overwhelm poly(λ) factors, which is ignored in this overview.) In summary, any PHFE with both $|\mathsf{sk}|$ sublinear in $|f|$ and T_{Dec} sublinear in $|f|$ (and linear in $T, |x|, |y|$) is insecure.

Technical Barrier Towards Fast Decryption. As described earlier, we show barriers in current techniques against constructing a PHFE scheme with fast decryption. Consider a PHFE scheme whose decryption time is

$$O(T_{\varphi(f,x,y)}^{\beta_T} + |f|^{\beta_f} + |x|^{\beta_x} + |y|^{\beta_y})$$

for constants $\beta_T, \beta_f, \beta_x \beta_y$. We show that even if just one of β_x, β_y, and β_f is zero, then the scheme implies SK-DE-PIR (an informal description of SK-DE-PIR is in the introduction and formal definition in the full version [37]).

To illustrate our main idea, we start by describing this transformation for the case when the decryption is efficient in the length of the public input x, namely when $\beta_x = 0$. The ideas naturally extend to the other cases.

Since the decryption is efficient in $|x|$, as a first attempt, we set $\mathsf{DB} \in \{0,1\}^n$ as x, and y as empty. The client processes the database DB by first sampling $(\mathsf{mpk}, \mathsf{msk})$ for the PHFE scheme and then encodes the database into

$$\widetilde{\mathsf{DB}} = (\mathsf{DB}, \mathsf{ct}_{\mathsf{PHFE}} = \mathsf{PHFE.Enc}(\mathsf{mpk}, (x = \mathsf{DB}, y = \bot)))$$

and sends it over to the server. To look up a location DB_{i_j}, the client can compute a PHFE function key sk_{f_j} for the program f_j that looks up and outputs DB_{i_j} and sends the key as the query to the server.

The server responds to the query by decrypting $\mathsf{ct}_{\mathsf{PHFE}}$ in $\widetilde{\mathsf{DB}}$ using the key sk_{f_j} and with random access to DB, and learns DB_{i_j}. Note that double efficiency requirement is already satisfied. Client only needs to compute a function key sk_{f_j} that can be computed in time polynomial in the description length of f_j, and hence polynomial in λ and $\log n$. On the other hand, due to the supposed efficiency of decryption, the decryption time is polynomial in $T_{f_j(x,y)}, |f_j|, |y|$, which are also polynomial in λ and $\log n$.

While this idea solves the core issue, we have completely missed one important aspect. The scheme reveals the indices $\{i_j\}_j$ to the server as the keys $\{\mathsf{sk}_{f_j}\}_j$ are not guaranteed to hide the function descriptions $\{f_j\}_j$. To resolve this issue, we observe that if we had a function-hiding PHFE scheme, we would have been done. To enable this, we will use similar techniques as used to convert any FE to a function-hiding FE [18]. Namely, we will compute a symmetric-key encryption SKE of the index i (denoted as ctk_1). We will hardwire ctk_1 in the function secret key instead of the index i. The corresponding secret key $\mathsf{SKE.sk}_1$ will be put in the private component y, which will be used to decrypt ctk_1 to learn index i. While this might seem to be enough, we face yet another issue. Learning DB_{i_j} in the clear upon decryption can reveal information about the index i_j to the server. To fix this, the decryption will output an encryption of DB_{i_j} under another secret key $\mathsf{SKE.sk}_2$ of the secret-key encryption scheme. We will put this key in the private input y along with a PRF key to derive randomness to compute the encryption.

$$\widetilde{\mathsf{DB}} = (\mathsf{DB}, \mathsf{ct}_{\mathsf{PHFE}} = \mathsf{PHFE.Enc}(\mathsf{mpk}, (\mathsf{DB}, (\mathsf{SKE.sk}_1, \mathsf{SKE.sk}_2, \mathsf{PRF}.k)))),$$

$$\mathsf{query} = \mathsf{sk}_{f_j} \text{ where } f_j[\mathsf{ckt}_1(i_j), \$]^{\mathsf{DB}, (\mathsf{SKE.sk}_1, \mathsf{SKE.sk}_2, \mathsf{PRF}.k)}$$

$$= \mathsf{SKE}(\mathsf{SKE.sk}_2, \mathsf{DB}_{i_j} \; ; \; \mathsf{PRF}(\mathsf{PRF}.k, \$)).$$

Double efficiency is still preserved. We have increased the complexity of f_j multiplicatively by a polynomial amount (in λ and $\log n$), similarly the size of y is also polynomial in λ to store secret keys of SKE and a PRF key. There are a few more subtleties. To make the proof go through, we need to use the Trojan method in the FE literature [25], which requires another encryption key SKE.sk$_3$ and additional programming.

Overview of Our PHFE for RAM. At a very high level, we use a *succinct garbled RAM (GRAM) scheme* to lift a FE for circuits to a PHFE for RAM. This former can be viewed as a 1-key, 1-ciphertext, secret-key FE for RAM, where succinctness implies that the running time of key generation and encryption is independent of the running time of the RAM computation. The (collusion-resistant) FE for circuits is then used to lift the one-time security to many-time security. This high-level approach first appeared in [8] for building FE for TM. In this work, towards nearly optimally efficient FE for RAM, we first observe that existing definitions and constructions of succinct GRAM [2,13,19–21,23] are insufficient. Therefore, we first formulate a new variant of succinct GRAM, termed *laconic GRAM*, and then construct it using polynomially hard FE for circuit. Along the way, we weaken the assumption underlying succinct GRAM schemes from iO, which requires subexponentially hard FE for circuit, to polynomially-hard FE for circuits.

Let us first review the syntax and security of standard GRAM schemes. They consist of the following algorithms. The encoding algorithm encodes a database D into $\hat{D}$ and outputs a private state τ. The garbling algorithms uses τ to garble a RAM M into $\hat{M}$ and outputs a collection of input labels $\{L_{i,b}\}_{i,b}$. The evaluation algorithm given the garbled RAM $\hat{M}$, a subset of labels L_k corresponding to an input k, and random access to $\hat{D}$, returns the output $M^D(k)$ of the RAM computation. Simulation based security ensures that $\hat{D}, \hat{M}, L_k = \{L_{i,k_i}\}_i$ can be simulated using only the output $M^D(k)$. The efficiency of different algorithms is is described below.

$$(\hat{D}, \tau) \leftarrow \mathsf{Encode}(D) , \quad \hat{M}, \{L_{i,b}\}_{i,b} \leftarrow \mathsf{Garble}(M, \tau) , \quad M^D(k) = \mathsf{Eval}^{\hat{D}}(\hat{M}, L_k)$$

$$|\hat{D}| = |D|\operatorname{poly}(\lambda) , \qquad |\hat{M}| = \operatorname{poly}(\lambda), \qquad\qquad T_{\mathsf{Eval}} = T\operatorname{poly}(|M|, \lambda).$$

We now describe why the standard notion falls short for our purpose of building very efficient FE for RAM and how to address these issues. An informal definition of our succinct GRAM is provided in Fig. 1.

- *many-tape v.s. single-tape*: To start with, we consider RAM computation with multiple tapes $U^{x,y,f}(1)$ instead of a single tape $M^D(k)$.
- *public-tape v.s. private-tape*: Some of the tapes we consider, such as x and f, are public. But standard GRAM only provides a mechanism for encoding private tape, and the encoding is necessarily at least as long as the tape itself. However, optimal succinctness requires the FE ciphertext- and key-size to be independent of $|x|$ and $|f|$. Hence we cannot afford to encode x, f as in standard GRAM. Instead, our new notion of succinct GRAM has a Compress algorithm that compresses the public tapes into hashes/digests h_x and h_f; the Garble algorithm "ties" these hashes to the garbled program $\hat{U}$; and finally Eval makes random access to x and f in the clear directly (just as the decryption algorithm of RAM-FE does).

- *rate-2 encoding v.s. rate-*poly(λ) *encoding of private tape:* Our setting also has private tape, namely y. But optimal succinctness requires concretely efficient, rate-1 or rate-2, encoding of y, whereas standard GRAM allows much worse rate poly(λ). To achieve concretely efficient encoding, we can only encrypt y using a rate-1 encryption scheme. To bind the encryption $\hat{y}$ with a garbled program, we simply treat $\hat{y}$ as yet another public tape just like x, f. In other words, we consider the modified RAM computation $\bar{U}^{x,\hat{y},f}(k) = U^{x,y,f}(1)$, where k is the secret key of the rate-1 encryption. As such, our succinct GRAM only need to handle public tapes.

  In our construction of FE, additional care needs to be taken to ensure that our GRAM security implies that y is hidden. To achieve this, We rely on existing techniques [49], which requires two (rate-1) encryption of y with independent keys so that different security hybrids can invoke the semantic security of different encryption. This is why our FE has rate-2 dependency on $|y|$, instead of rate-1. We omit details in this overview.

- *reusable digests v.s. one-time encoding:* In standard GRAM, the database encoding $\hat{D}$ can only be used, *once*, by a single garbled program $\hat{M}$ generated using the right state τ. The technical cause of the one-time security of $\hat{D}$ is due to the use of ORAM in order to hide the access pattern of M to D; the same ORAM storage $\hat{D}$ cannot be used by multiple garbled programs.[5] The one-time security means that when using succinct GRAM to construct RAM-FE, the decryption of every ciphertext and key pair must generate fresh encoding $\hat{D}$ (and $\hat{M}$). Such fresh encoding can only be generated using the underlying FE for circuit, by encoding D in its key or ciphertext, which would lead to large polynomial dependency on $|D|$.

  Our notion of succinct GRAM compresses the public tapes into hashes $h_x, h_f, h_{\hat{y}}$. For the same reasons, we cannot afford to generate fresh hashes at decryption of every pair of ciphertext and key. Instead, our hashes are *reusable* – they can be tied to multiple garbled programs; this is ensured by the fact that our Garble algorithm does not take any private state from the Compress algorithm. A technical issue we must resolve is how to hide access pattern to the public tapes $x, \hat{y}, f$ since they are not encoded using ORAM, which we discuss later.

- *Difference in decryption time:* The reusability comes at a cost. In our new notion, evaluation time is $(T + |x| + |y| + |f|)\,\text{poly}(\lambda)$ whereas standard GRAM has evaluation time $T\,\text{poly}(|M|, \lambda)$ independent of tape size $|D|$. Nevertheless, our lower bound for RAM-FE implies that the dependency on $|x|, |y|, |f|$ is hard to get around (as our succinct GRAM implies RAM-FE with the same decryption time).

---

[5] This should be distinguished from the scenario of GRAM with persistent database where a sequence of garbled program $(\hat{M}_1, \hat{M}_2, \cdots)^{\hat{D}}$ are executed sequentially with $\hat{D}$. The difference lies in that in sequential execution, each garbled RAM can modify $\hat{D}$ and the changes are kept persistently to the next computation. Here, we are considering the scenario where the unmodified $\hat{D}$ is used by multiple garbled program, which breaks ORAM security.

- *RAM with long outputs v.s. single-bit output:* Standard succinct GRAM handles RAM computation with a single-bit output. To handle RAM with m-bit output, it reduces to creating m instances of garbled RAM, one for each output bit. Under simulation security, the size of the garbled RAM necessarily grows linearly with the output length m.

  In our notion, we require garbling RAM with arbitrarily long outputs, without efficiency degradation in the output length. To do so, we switch to indistinguishability based security instead of simulation security.

Putting the above pieces together, we formulate succinct GRAM as in Fig. 1.

Our Notion of Succinct Garbled RAM

- Compress(τ, D_τ) compresses the τ'th public tape D_τ into a short hash digest$_\tau$ of length poly(λ). It runs in time $O(|D_\tau|)$.
- Garble$(U, \{\text{digest}_\tau\}_{\tau \in [T]})$ outputs a garbled program $\widehat{U}$ tied with hashes of the public tapes, and pairs of labels $\{L_{i,b}\}_{i,b}$. It runs in time poly(λ) (U has constant-size).
- Eval$^{D_1,...,D_T}(U, \{\text{digest}_\tau\}_{\tau \in [T]}, \widehat{U}, L_k)$ returns the (long) output of RAM computation $U^{D_1,...,D_T}(k)$ if $L_k = \{L_{i,k_i}\}_i$. It runs in time $(T + \sum_\tau |D_\tau|)$ poly(λ).
  Security guarantees that for two computations $U^{D_1,...,D_T}(k_0)$ and $U^{D_1,...,D_T}(k_1)$ with different inputs but identical outputs and running time, the distributions of $(\widehat{U}, \{\text{digest}_\tau\}_{\tau \in [T]}, L_{k_0})$ and $(\widehat{U}, \{\text{digest}_\tau\}_{\tau \in [T]}, L_{k_1})$ are indistinguishable. This holds when the tapes $\{D_i\}$ are chosen adaptively dependent on the hashes of previously chosen tapes, before the program U and inputs k_0, k_1 are chosen.

Fig. 1. Our notion of succinct GRAM.

Our Construction of Succinct GRAM. One approach towards constructing succinct GRAM for TM or RAM is starting from a non-succinct GRAM for TM or RAM where the size of the garble program scales with the worst-case time complexity of the TM/RAM U, into one that is succinct. First introduced in [13], this approach uses iO to obfuscate a circuit that on input an index t, outputs the t'th component in the non-succinct GRAM. If every component of the non-succinct GRAM can be locally generated using a small circuit of size poly$(|U|, \lambda)$, then the obfuscated circuit also has size poly$(|U|, \lambda)$ and can be viewed as the succinct garbled program. To prove security, [13] identified that the non-succinct garbling scheme must satisfy another property, articulated later by [7], called *local simulation.* Informally, it requires that the non-succinct garbled scheme is proven secure via a sequence of hybrids, where components of every hybrid garbled program can be locally generated using a small circuit, and in neighboring hybrids, only a few components changes. Beyond succinct garbling, local simulation has also found application in achieving adaptive security [12] of garbling schemes. A sequence of works developed local simulation strategies for garbled circuit [29, 36], TM [7, 30], and RAM [27]. Most notably, the work by Garg and Srinivasan [29] introduced a beautiful pebbling technique for realizing local simulation.

Our construction of succinct GRAM proceeds in steps. First, we use the Garg–Srinivasan [29] pebbling technique to obtain a non-succinct GRAM that has a local simulation proof for, however, weak indistinguishability security called fixed-memory security. Indistinguishability only holds when the two RAM computations have not only identical outputs and running time, but also identical memory access pattern and content. Then by the same approach of [7, 13, 30], we turn it into a succinct GRAM, still with only *fixed-memory security*, relying on iO for polynomial-size domain which is implied by polynomially hard FE for circuits. Many details need to be ironed out in order to realize our new notion of succinct GRAM. For example, prior works [7, 29, 30] deal with single-bit output RAM and can build intermediate security hybrid where the suffix (i.e., the last certain number of steps) of a computation is simulated by hardwiring the single-bit output. In contrast, we directly garble RAM with arbitrarily long outputs. Hardwiring the long output would compromise the local simulation property (since the hybrid garbled program can no longer be locally generated by a small circuit). To avoid this, we build a hybrid GRAM that runs with one input k_0 in the prefix of the computation and with another input k_1 in the suffix (recall that these two inputs produce identical memory). This ensures that the output is always correctly computed, while keeping local simulation. Similar hybrids appeared in [27] for different reasons.

Finally, we lift *fixed-memory security* to full security using punctured PRF and ORAM to protect the memory content and access pattern. One issue is that in our succinct GRAM, the public input tapes $D_1, ..., D_{\mathcal{T}}$ are not encoded using ORAM, and evaluation is given random access to them in the clear. Yet, to ensure security, evaluation must access these tapes in an oblivious way, independent of the input k_0 or k_1. To solve this issue, we consider a modified RAM program U', which has random access to $D_1, ..., D_{\mathcal{T}}$ and additionally a working tape that contains an ORAM storage that initially contains no elements. The program U' starts with linearly scanning every tape D_τ and inserting every element into the ORAM storage. Only after that, it emulates the execution of the original RAM program U; every time U read from/write to a location in tape D_τ, U' accesses the corresponding location on its working tape through ORAM, which hides the access pattern of U. The intuition is that since the access pattern of U' is independent of the input, it suffices to garble it using GRAM with fixed-memory security. Clearly, the running time of U' scales linearly with the total length of all tapes $\sum_\tau |D_\tau|$. This is why the evaluation time of our succinct GRAM is linear in $\sum_\tau |D_\tau|$. Nevertheless, our lower bound shows that this dependency is hard to circumvent. Lastly, we mention that to prove security, one must ensure that the use of ORAM does not hurt local simulation. Fortunately, the techniques by [20] provide a solution.

1.3   Related Works

Our new construction significantly improve upon the efficiency of prior FE and ABE schemes. The state-of-the-art is summarized in Tables 1 and 2. Below, we compare with prior works in more detail.

FE for Circuits. The first construction of collusion-resistant FE for polynomial-size circuits is by [26] and based on $i\mathcal{O}$, which in turn relies on subexponential hardness. Later works [28,41,42,44] improved the assumption from $i\mathcal{O}$ to 1-key FE with sublinearly compact ciphertext, $|\mathsf{ct}(y)| = \mathrm{poly}(|y|)|T_f|^{1-\varepsilon}$, where ε is a positive constant and T_f is the circuit complexity of f. The latter has been recently constructed by [39,40] from the polynomial hardness of three well-studied assumptions. However, these circuit-FE schemes have polynomial efficiency. The only exception is the recent construction by [35], which has rate-1 ciphertext, i.e., $|\mathsf{ct}(y)| = |y| + O(1)$, but still large secret keys $|\mathsf{sk}_f| = \mathrm{poly}(T_f)$.

FE for Turing Machines. Several works constructed FE for Turning machines with arbitrary-length inputs, first from the assumption of iO [8], then from FE for circuits [1], and more recently from 1-key sublinearly compact FE [42] (which implies collusion-resistant FE for circuits). The construction of [8] relies on a 1-key 1-ciphertext secret-key FE for TM, which is essentially a succinct garbling scheme for TM with indistinguishability security. They constructed it by modifying the succinct garbling for TM of [43]. Later, the works of [7,30] improved and simplified the construction of succinct garbling for TM. The work of [42] improved the assumption to the existence of 1-key sublinearly succinct FE, and showed that their garbling scheme can be combined with [8] to obtain FE for TM. On the other hand, the work of [1] presented an alternative direct approach to FE for TM from FE for circuits without going through succinct garbling for TM. Prior constructions of FE for TM [1,8,42] focus more on weakening the underlying assumptions, and only show polynomial efficiency. Examining their schemes, we conclude that they achieve efficiency listed in Table 1.

FE for Bounded-Input RAM. A line of research obtained *bounded-input* $i\mathcal{O}$ for Turing machines [6,30,43] and RAM [2,13,19–21,23]. Plugging these $i\mathcal{O}$ schemes into the construction of [26] yields *bounded-input* FE for TM and RAM. Unfortunately, these schemes are not full-fledged FE for TM or RAM for the following reason: Existing $i\mathcal{O}$ only handles bounded-input TM and RAM in the sense that the obfuscator needs to know the maximum input length max $|y|$ to the TM/RAM f being obfuscated. (Constructing $i\mathcal{O}$ for unbounded input TM/RAM remains a major open question.) Plugging them into [26] yields schemes where the key generation algorithm needs to know the maximum input length max $|y|$, despite that the TM/RAM f could process arbitrarily long inputs. Such FE is said to have *bounded input*. In terms of efficiency, the secret key contains an obfuscated program of size $\mathrm{poly}(|f|, \max|y|)$ when using the RAM-$i\mathcal{O}$ of [20,21], and $\mathrm{poly}(|f|, \max|y|, S)$, where S is the space complexity of f when using the RAM-$i\mathcal{O}$ of [13].

In summary, our construction gives the first full-fledged (PH-)FE scheme for RAM computation with arbitrarily long inputs and outputs, significantly improves the efficiency of prior FE schemes, and matches newly proven lower bounds.

ABE for Circuits and Turing Machines. Since FE implies ABE, the aforementioned FE schemes immediately imply ABE with the same level of efficiency. The literature on ABE focuses on constructing ABE from weaker assumptions, and achieving better efficiency, among others. The celebrated works of [14,32] showed that ABE for *bounded-depth* circuits can be constructed from the learning With errors (LWE) assumption. Parameters of these schemes however depend polynomially on the maximum depth d of the circuits supported, namely, $|\mathsf{mpk}| = \mathrm{poly}(d)$, $|\mathsf{sk}_f| = \mathrm{poly}(d)$, $|\mathsf{ct}(x, m)| = \mathrm{poly}(d)|x|$, and the decryption time is $T_{\mathsf{Dec}} = \mathrm{poly}(d)T$. A recent work [45] improved it to obtain constant-size keys while keeping the sizes of master public key and ciphertext intact, but at the cost of additionally relying on the generic (pairing) group model (GGM). ABE for low-depth computation such as NC^1 or (arithmetic) branching programs can be constructed using pairing groups, where several schemes have either constant-size keys *or* constant-size ciphertexts, but never both [9–11,46,53–55].

The work of [31] constructed ABE for Turing machines and RAM with constant-size secret keys $|\mathsf{sk}_f| = O(1)$, but still large ciphertexts $|\mathsf{ct}_x| = \mathrm{poly}(|x|)$. Their scheme uses SNARK and differing-input $i\mathcal{O}$, which cannot be based on falsifiable assumptions. Another work [4] tries to construct ABE for RAM from LWE, at the cost of making the master public key, secret keys, and ciphertexts all grow polynomially with the maximum running time of the RAM supported, i.e., it is an ABE for bounded-time RAM.

In summary, we give the first ABE for RAM from falsifiable assumptions, simultaneously having constant-size secret keys, constant-size ciphertexts, and the best-possible decryption time matching the known lower bound [48] under the constraint of having constant-size keys and ciphertexts.

Concurrent and Independent Work on FE for RAM. Concurrently and independently of our work, the recent work by Ananth, Chung, Fan, and Qian (ACFQ) [3] also considers the question of FE for RAM. Despite an apparent overlap between both these works, there are many differences. The two works start with different motivations. Our goal is to understand the optimal succinctness and efficiency of PHFE, both constructively and from a lower-bound perspective, whereas ACFQ aims to construct FE for RAM with optimal decryption time $T_{\mathsf{Dec}} = O(T)$. Consequently, the two works obtain mostly complementary results.

First, we prove unconditional trade-offs between the sizes of secret keys/ciphertexts and decryption time; it shows that no PHFE can have both optimal succinctness and optimal decryption time. We then construct PHFE for RAM with (nearly) optimal succinctness, while minimizing the decryption time to the best-possible matching our lower bounds. ACFQ, on the other hand, constructs FE for RAM with optimal decryption time. (They did not attempt to simultaneously minimizing the sizes of secret keys and ciphertexts.)

On the common front, both works show that any (PH-)FE scheme for RAM with optimal decryption time implies SK-DE-PIR. We regard this as a barrier to optimal efficiency due to lack of DE-PIR schemes from well-studied assumptions, whereas in ACFQ, public key version of DE-PIR (PK-DE-PIR) is used as a building block to realizing such PHFE. As a result their scheme relies on ideal obfuscation and a new assumption of permuted puzzles inherited from current candidate PK-DE-PIR, whereas our storage optimal PHFE scheme is based on circuit-FE, which is necessary and can in turn be based on well-studied assumptions.

There are two other major differences in the schemes: Our scheme handles arbitrarily long output, where as ACFQ consider single-bit output. To handle long output, they proposes to generate a separate key for computing each output bit, meaning that the key-size grows linearly with the output length, which could be as long as the running time in many scenarios. Moreover, our scheme achieves adaptive security, whereas that ACFQ scheme is only selectively secure.

In terms of techniques, both works demonstrate that the main bottleneck towards (PH-)FE for RAM is that existing notions of succinct GRAM are insufficient — it needs GRAM with reusable tape encoding. The two works develop different techniques to achieve this: Our construction lets an GRAM instance build fresh ORAM storage at the beginning of every evaluation and hence ORAM is never reused, whereas ACFQ uses PK-DE-PIR which is essentially a reusable ORAM.

2   Preliminaries

We present our formulations of laconic garbled RAM and partially hiding functional encryption, essential for considering the optimal succinctness and efficiency and the lower bounds. The details can be found in the full version [37].

Multi-tape RAM. We consider $\mathcal{T}$-tape RAM for natural number $\mathcal{T}$. Such a machine has $\mathcal{T}$ read-only input tapes and one read/write working tape. Each input tape consists of multiple ℓ_{cell}-bit *cells* indexed by ℓ_{addr}-bit *addresses*. For the working tape, the lengths are ℓ_{CELL} and ℓ_{ADDR}. The machine is also given an ℓ_{in}-bit (short) input that remains constant during one execution, and it maintains an ℓ_{st}-bit internal state. At each step, the machine could produce an optional output bit. We denote an execution of M with input tape contents $D_1, \ldots, D_{\mathcal{T}}$ and short input w by $M^{D_1, \ldots, D_{\mathcal{T}}}(w)$, and write $\text{time}(M, D_1, \ldots, D_{\mathcal{T}}, w)$ and $\text{outS}(M, D_1, \ldots, D_{\mathcal{T}}, w)$ for its running time and its output sequence (a sequence of elements in $\{\perp, 0, 1\}$).

2.1   Laconic Garbled RAM

Our notion of garbling RAM laconically involves two steps. First, a reusable short digest is created for each input tape. The digest has length independent of that of the tape itself and must be computable in linear time. Second, the RAM and the short digests are put together to produce a garbled program and the labels. This procedure runs in time poly-logarithmic in the RAM running time. Given a garbled program and one set of labels (selected by the bits of the short input), the evaluation procedure computes the output sequence in time linear in the RAM running time.

We consider indistinguishability-based security for the short input. The input tape contents can be chosen adaptively, but the short input cannot depend on the garbled program (i.e., selectiveness).

Definition 1 (LGRAM). *Let* $\mathcal{T}$ *be a natural number. A* laconic garbling scheme *for* $\mathcal{T}$*-tape RAM consists of three algorithms:*

- Compress($1^\lambda, 1^{\ell_{\mathrm{cell}}}, 1^{\ell_{\mathrm{addr}}}, \tau, D_\tau$) *takes as input a cell length* ℓ_{cell}, *an address length* ℓ_{addr}, *an input tape index* $\tau \in [\mathcal{T}]$, *and the content of that input tape,* $D_\tau \in (\{0,1\}^{\ell_{\mathrm{cell}}})^{\le 2^{\ell_{\mathrm{addr}}}}$. *It outputs a short digest* digest$_\tau$. *The algorithm runs in time* $|D_\tau| \operatorname{poly}(\lambda, \ell_{\mathrm{cell}}, \ell_{\mathrm{addr}})$ *and its output length is* $\operatorname{poly}(\lambda, \ell_{\mathrm{cell}}, \ell_{\mathrm{addr}})$.
- Garble($1^\lambda, T_{\max}, M, \{\mathrm{digest}_\tau\}_{\tau \in [\mathcal{T}]}$) *takes as input a time bound* $T_{\max} \in \mathbb{N}_+$, *a* $\mathcal{T}$*-tape RAM* M, *and* $\mathcal{T}$ *input tape digests. It outputs a garbled program* $\widehat{M}$ *and* ℓ_{in} *pairs of labels* $\{L_{i,b}\}_{i \in [\ell_{\mathrm{in}}], b \in \{0,1\}}$ *in polynomial time.*
- Eval$^{D_1,\ldots,D_\mathcal{T}}(1^\lambda, T_{\max}, M, \{\mathrm{digest}_\tau\}_{\tau \in [\mathcal{T}]}, \widehat{M}, \{L_i\}_{i \in [\ell_{\mathrm{in}}]})$ *takes as input* $T_{\max}$, M, *the input tape digests,* $\widehat{M}$, *and one set of labels. Given random access to the input tapes, it is supposed to compute the output sequence. The algorithm runs in time*

$$\left(\min\{T_{\max}, \mathrm{time}(M, D_1, \ldots, D_\mathcal{T}, w)\} + \sum_{i=1}^{\mathcal{T}} |D_\tau| \right) \operatorname{poly}(\lambda, |M|, \log T_{\max}),$$

where w *is the short input corresponding to the labels.*

The scheme must be correct, i.e., for all $\lambda, \ell_{\mathrm{in}} \in \mathbb{N}$, $\ell_{\mathrm{cell}}, \ell_{\mathrm{addr}}, T_{\max} \in \mathbb{N}_+$, *input tape contents* $D_1, \ldots, D_\mathcal{T} \in (\{0,1\}^{\ell_{\mathrm{cell}}})^{\le 2^{\ell_{\mathrm{addr}}}}$, *short input* $w \in \{0,1\}^{\ell_{\mathrm{in}}}$, $\mathcal{T}$*-tape RAM* M *such that* $M^{D_1,\ldots,D_\mathcal{T}}(w)$ *halts in time at most* $T_{\max}$,

$$\Pr\left[\begin{array}{c} \mathrm{digest}_\tau \xleftarrow{\$} \mathsf{Compress}(1^\lambda, 1^{\ell_{\mathrm{cell}}}, 1^{\ell_{\mathrm{addr}}}, \tau, D_\tau) \; \forall \tau \in [\mathcal{T}] \\ (\widehat{M}, \{L_{i,b}\}_{i \in [\ell_{\mathrm{in}}], b \in \{0,1\}}) \xleftarrow{\$} \mathsf{Garble}(1^\lambda, T_{\max}, M, \{\mathrm{digest}_\tau\}_{\tau \in [\mathcal{T}]}) \\ \mathsf{Eval}^{D_1,\ldots,D_\mathcal{T}}(1^\lambda, T_{\max}, M, \{\mathrm{digest}_\tau\}_{\tau \in [\mathcal{T}]}, \widehat{M}, \{L_{i,w[i]}\}_{i \in [\ell_{\mathrm{in}}]}) \\ = \mathsf{outS}(M, D_1, \ldots, D_\mathcal{T}, w) \end{array} \right] = 1.$$

Remark 1 (unboundedness). Our notion of LGRAM is *unbounded*, i.e., it is not necessary to know a polynomial upper bound of the instance running time upon garbling. By choosing an exponentially large $T_{\max}$, one garbling works for all polynomial-time computation. In contrast is a *bounded* scheme for all polynomial-time computation, where $T_{\max}$ can be *any* polynomial, but it *must* be a polynomial, hence every garbling is restricted to *some* polynomial time bound upon creation. Unboundedness is reflected in both efficiency and security (below), where $T_{\max}$ is written in binary.

Definition 2 (LGRAM security). *An LGRAM scheme (Definition 1) is* (tape-adaptively, indistinguishability-based) *secure if* $\mathsf{Exp}^0_{\mathrm{LGRAM}} \approx \mathsf{Exp}^1_{\mathrm{LGRAM}}$, *where* $\mathsf{Exp}^\beta_{\mathrm{LGRAM}}(1^\lambda, \mathcal{A})$ *proceeds as follows:*

- **Setup.** Launch $\mathcal{A}(1^\lambda)$ and receive $(1^{\ell_{\mathrm{cell}}}, 1^{\ell_{\mathrm{addr}}})$ from it.
- **Tape Choices.** Repeat this for T rounds. In each round, $\mathcal{A}$ chooses $\tau \in [T]$ and $D_\tau \in (\{0,1\}^{\ell_{\mathrm{cell}}})^{\le 2^{\ell_{\mathrm{addr}}}}$. Upon receiving such choice, run

$$\mathsf{digest}_\tau \xleftarrow{\$} \mathsf{Compress}(1^\lambda, 1^{\ell_{\mathrm{cell}}}, 1^{\ell_{\mathrm{addr}}}, \tau, D_\tau)$$

  and send digest_τ to $\mathcal{A}$.
- **Challenge.** $\mathcal{A}$ chooses an instance running time bound 1^T (in unary), a time bound $T_{\max}$ (in binary), a T-tape RAM M, and two inputs (w_0, w_1). Run

$$(\widehat{M}, \{L_{i,b}\}_{i \in [\ell_{\mathrm{in}}], b \in \{0,1\}}) \xleftarrow{\$} \mathsf{Garble}(1^\lambda, T_{\max}, M, \{\mathsf{digest}_\tau\}_{\tau \in [T]})$$

  and send $(\widehat{M}, \{L_{i,w_\beta[i]}\}_{i \in [\ell_{\mathrm{in}}]})$ to $\mathcal{A}$.
- **Guess.** $\mathcal{A}$ outputs a bit β'. The output of the experiment is β' if all of the following conditions hold:
  - The τ's in all rounds of **Tape Choices** are distinct.
  - Both $M^{D_1,\dots,D_T}(w_0)$ and $M^{D_1,\dots,D_T}(w_1)$ halt in time $T \le \overline{T} \le T_{\max}$ with identical *output sequences* $\mathsf{outS}(\cdots)$.

  Otherwise, the output is set to 0.

Remark 2 (polynomial security). Although $T_{\max}$ can be exponentially large, we only require security for polynomially large *instance* running time, which is captured by the requirement that the adversary must produce 1^T, an upper bound of the instance running time in unary.

2.2 Partially Hiding Functional Encryption and FE for Circuits

We define partially hiding functional encryption with respect to functionality

$$\varphi : F \times X \times Y \to \{\bot\} \cup (\mathbb{N}_+ \times Z),$$

where F, X, Y, Z are the sets of function description, public input, private input, and output, respectively. Each key is associated with some $f \in F$, and each ciphertext encrypts some private input $y \in Y$ and is tied to some public input $x \in X$. The decryptor should be able to recover z if $\varphi(f, x, y) = (T, z)$, in which case T is the time to compute z from f, x, y in the clear and serves as a baseline for decryption efficiency. For security, we only consider f, x, y for which T is polynomially bounded. On the other hand, if $\varphi(f, x, y) = \bot$, we require neither correctness nor security. This can be used to exclude non-halting computation.

Definition 3 (PHFE). *Let* $\Phi = \{\Phi_\lambda\}_{\lambda \in \mathbb{N}}$ *be a sequence of functionality families*

$$\text{with} \quad \varphi : F_\varphi \times X_\varphi \times Y_\varphi \to \{\bot\} \cup (\mathbb{N}_+ \times Z_\varphi) \quad \text{for each } \varphi \in \Phi_\lambda.$$

A partially hiding functional encryption scheme for Φ *consists of four algorithms, with efficiency defined in Definition 4:*

- Setup($1^\lambda, \varphi$) *takes a functionality* $\varphi \in \Phi_\lambda$ *as input, and outputs a pair of master public/secret keys* (mpk, msk).
- KeyGen(1^λ, msk, f) *takes as input* msk *and a function description* $f \in F_\varphi$. *It outputs a secret key* sk_f *for* f.
- Enc(1^λ, mpk, x, y) *takes as input* mpk, *a public input* $x \in X_\varphi$, *and a private input* $y \in Y_\varphi$. *It outputs a ciphertext* ct_x *of* y *tied to* x.
- $\mathsf{Dec}^{f,x,\mathsf{sk}_f,\mathsf{ct}_x}(1^\lambda, \mathsf{mpk})$ *takes* mpk *as input and is given random access to* f, x, $\mathsf{sk}_f, \mathsf{ct}_x$. *It is supposed to compute* z *in* $\varphi(f, x, y) = (T, z)$ *efficiently.*

The scheme must be correct, *i.e., for all* $\lambda \in \mathbb{N}$, $\varphi \in \Phi_\lambda$, $f \in F_\varphi$, $x \in X_\varphi$, $y \in Y_\varphi$ *such that* $\varphi(f, x, y) = (T, z) \neq \bot$, *it holds that*

$$\Pr \left[\begin{array}{c} (\mathsf{mpk}, \mathsf{msk}) \xleftarrow{\$} \mathsf{Setup}(1^\lambda, \varphi) \\ \mathsf{sk}_f \xleftarrow{\$} \mathsf{KeyGen}(1^\lambda, \mathsf{msk}, f) \quad : \quad \mathsf{Dec}^{f,x,\mathsf{sk}_f,\mathsf{ct}_x}(1^\lambda, \mathsf{mpk}) = z \\ \mathsf{ct}_x \xleftarrow{\$} \mathsf{Enc}(1^\lambda, \mathsf{mpk}, x, y) \end{array} \right] = 1.$$

Definition 4 (PHFE efficiency). *The basic efficiency requirements for a PHFE scheme (Definition 3) are as follows:*

- Setup, KeyGen, Enc *are polynomial-time.*
- Dec *runs in time* $\mathrm{poly}(\lambda, |\varphi|, |f|, |x|, |y|, T)$ *if* $\varphi(f, x, y) = (T, z) \neq \bot$.

The following time-efficiency properties are considered:

- *It has* linear-time KeyGen *[resp.* Enc*] if* KeyGen *[resp.* Enc*] runs in time* $|f| \, \mathrm{poly}(\lambda, |\varphi|)$ *[resp.* $(|x| + |y|) \, \mathrm{poly}(\lambda, |\varphi|)$*];*
- *It has* $(T^{e_T} + |f|^{e_f} + |x|^{e_x} + |y|^{e_y})$-time Dec *(for constants* e_T, e_f, e_x, e_y*) if* Dec *runs in time*

$$(T^{e_T} + |f|^{e_f} + |x|^{e_x} + |y|^{e_y}) \, \mathrm{poly}(\lambda, |\varphi|),$$

where $\varphi(M, f, x, y) = (T, z) \neq \bot$. *Furthermore, the scheme has* f-*fast [resp.* x-*fast,* y-*fast]* Dec *if it has* $(T^{e_T} + |f|^{e_f} + |x|^{e_x} + |y|^{e_y})$-*time* Dec *with* $e_f = 0$ *[resp.* $e_x = 0$, $e_y = 0$*].*

The following size-efficiency properties are considered:

- *It is* f-*succinct if* $|\mathsf{sk}_f| = \mathrm{poly}(\lambda, |\varphi|)$, *independent of* $|f|$.
- *It is* x-*succinct if* $|\mathsf{ct}_x| = \mathrm{poly}(\lambda, |\varphi|, |y|)$, *independent of* $|x|$.
- *It has* rate-c ciphertext *for some constant* c *if* $|\mathsf{ct}_x| = c|y| + \mathrm{poly}(\lambda, |\varphi|)$.

Security. We consider adaptive IND-CPA for polynomially bounded T:

Definition 5 (PHFE security). *A PHFE scheme (Definition 3) is* (adaptively) IND-CPA) secure *if* $\mathsf{Exp}^0_{\mathrm{PHFE}} \approx \mathsf{Exp}^1_{\mathrm{PHFE}}$, *where* $\mathsf{Exp}^\beta_{\mathrm{PHFE}}(1^\lambda, \mathcal{A})$ *proceeds as follows:*

- **Setup.** Launch $\mathcal{A}(1^\lambda)$ and receive from it some $\varphi \in \Phi_\lambda$ and 1^T. Run

$$(\mathsf{mpk}, \mathsf{msk}) \xleftarrow{\$} \mathsf{Setup}(1^\lambda, \varphi)$$

and send mpk to $\mathcal{A}$.

- **Query I.** Repeat the following for arbitrarily many rounds determined by $\mathcal{A}$. In each round, $\mathcal{A}$ submits some $f_q \in F_\varphi$. Upon receiving such query, run

$$\mathsf{sk}_q \xleftarrow{\$} \mathsf{KeyGen}(1^\lambda, \mathsf{msk}, f_q)$$

and send sk_q to $\mathcal{A}$.
- **Challenge.** $\mathcal{A}$ submits $x \in X_\varphi$ and $y_0, y_1 \in Y_\varphi$. Upon the challenge, run

$$\mathsf{ct} \xleftarrow{\$} \mathsf{Enc}(1^\lambda, \mathsf{mpk}, x, y_\beta)$$

and send ct to $\mathcal{A}$.
- **Query II.** Same as **Query I**.
- **Guess.** $\mathcal{A}$ outputs a bit β'. The outcome of the experiment is β' if

$$|y_0| = |y_1|,$$
$$\text{and } \varphi(f_q, x, y_0) = \varphi(f_q, x, y_1) = (T_q, z_q) \neq \bot \qquad \text{for all } q,$$
$$\text{and } T_q \leq \overline{T} \qquad \text{for all } q.$$

Otherwise, the outcome is set to 0.

FE for Circuits. As an example, we show how to instantiate Definition 3 into FE for circuits, a building block of our construction (see the full version [37]).

Definition 6 (FE for circuits). *A functional encryption scheme for circuits is a PHFE scheme (Definition 3) for*

$$\Phi = \{\Phi_\lambda\}_{\lambda \in \mathbb{N}}, \qquad \Phi_\lambda = \{\varphi_{\ell,s}\}_{\ell,s \in \mathbb{N}_+},$$
$$\varphi_{\ell,s} : F_{\ell,s} \times X \times Y_\ell \to \{\bot\} \cup (\mathbb{N}_+ \times Z),$$
$$F_{\ell,s} = \{ \text{ circuits of input length } \ell \text{ and size at most } s \},$$
$$X = \{\bot\}, \qquad Y_\ell = \{0,1\}^\ell, \qquad Z = \{0,1\}^*,$$
$$\varphi_{\ell,s}(f, \bot, y) = (1, f(y)),$$

where the functionality $\varphi_{\ell,s}$ is represented by $(1^\ell, 1^s)$.

Remark 3. The first output of $\varphi_{\ell,s}$ is just a placeholder value and all efficiency parameters (Definition 4) are always allowed arbitrary polynomial dependency on λ, ℓ, s by our choice of representing $\varphi_{\ell,s}$ by $(1^\ell, 1^s)$. This is intended as we use FE for circuits as a building block and do not wish to start with too strong a scheme.

2.3 Universal RAM and PHFE for RAM

In this section, we define PHFE for RAM after explaining some rationales behind certain subtleties in our formulation.

To obtain PHFE for RAM, we will employ the standard transformation [51] of using FE for circuits to compute LGRAM. However, in LGRAM (Definition 1), the running time of Garble depends on the machine size. This dependency is inherited by every efficiency parameter of the resultant PHFE for RAM if we associate each key with a RAM. To get rid of this dependency, we fix some universal RAM U of size $\text{poly}(\lambda)^6$ upon setting up the scheme, and associate with each key a piece of code interpreted by U.

The other issue is that LGRAM puts an upper bound on the running time and its incorrectness in case of exceeding the time limit is propagated to the PHFE scheme. We avoid it[7] by defining $\varphi = \bot$ if the running time exceeds some super-polynomial value prescribed upon set-up.

The above explains the intended usage of PHFE for RAM, yet we define it for general machines. Moreover, as an intermediate primitive, we will first consider PHFE for RAM with *bounded private input*, where the private input is simply the short input to the machine:

Definition 7 (PHFE for RAM with bounded private input). *A PHFE scheme for RAM with bounded private input is a PHFE scheme (Definition 3) for*

$$\Phi = \{\Phi_\lambda\}_{\lambda\in\mathbb{N}}, \qquad \Phi_\lambda = \{\varphi_{M,T_{\max}}\}_{M \text{ is a 2-tape RAM and } T_{\max}\in\mathbb{N}_+},$$
$$\varphi_{M,T_{\max}} : F_M \times X_M \times Y_M \rightarrow \{\bot\} \cup (\mathbb{N}_+ \times Z),$$
$$F_M = X_M = (\{0,1\}^{\ell_{\text{cell}}})^{\leq 2^{\ell_{\text{addr}}}}, \qquad Y_M = \{0,1\}^{\ell_{\text{in}}}, \qquad Z = \{\bot, 0, 1\}^*,$$
$$\varphi_{M,T_{\max}}(f, x, y) = \begin{cases} (T, \text{outS}(M, f, x, y)), & \text{if } \text{time}(M, f, x, y) = T \leq T_{\max}; \\ \bot, & \text{otherwise}; \end{cases}$$

where $\varphi_{M,T_{\max}}$ is represented by $(M, T_{\max})$.

In a full-fledged PHFE for RAM, the machine has no short input, and the private input is encoded on a tape:

Definition 8 (full-fledged PHFE for RAM). *A full-fledged PHFE scheme for RAM is a PHFE scheme (Definition 3) for*

$$\Phi = \{\Phi_\lambda\}_{\lambda\in\mathbb{N}}, \qquad \Phi_\lambda = \{\varphi_{M,T_{\max}}\}_{M \text{ is a 2-tape RAM with } \ell_{\text{in}}=0, \text{ and } T_{\max}\in\mathbb{N}_+},$$
$$\varphi_{M,T_{\max}} : F_M \times X_M \times Y_M \rightarrow \{\bot\} \cup (\mathbb{N}_+ \times Z),$$
$$F_M = X_M = Y_M = (\{0,1\}^{\ell_{\text{cell}}})^{\leq 2^{\ell_{\text{addr}}}}, \qquad Z = \{\bot, 0, 1\}^*,$$
$$\varphi_{M,T_{\max}}(f, x, y) = \begin{cases} (T, \text{outS}(M, f, x\|y, \varepsilon)), \\ \qquad \text{if } |x| + |y| \leq 2^{\ell_{\text{addr}}} \text{ and } \text{time}(M, f, x\|y, \varepsilon) = T \leq T_{\max}; \\ \bot, \qquad \text{otherwise}; \end{cases}$$

where ε is the empty string and $\varphi_{M,T_{\max}}$ is represented by $(M, T_{\max})$.

---

[6] U is not the same RAM across different values of λ — its input address length should be $\omega(\log \lambda)$ to accommodate all polynomially long input.

[7] An alternative solution is to blatantly reveal everything if the running time is too large so that correctness in that case can be implemented by executing the machine in the clear. Security is not affected because the adversary is not allowed to choose keys and ciphertexts with super-polynomial instance running time. However, non-halting computation still needs to be handled separately.

Remark 4 (unbounded scheme and polynomial security). When Definitions 3 and 5 are instantiated into PHFE for RAM (Definitions 7 and 8), the scheme is *unbounded*, meaning that $T_{\max}$ can be exponentially large, yet security only holds for polynomially bounded instance running time. This is similar to the case in Sect. 2.1.

3 Efficiency Trade-Offs of PHFE for RAM

We present the unconditional lower bounds. Additional contents about technique barriers can be found in the full version [37].

3.1 Contention Between Storage Overhead and Decryption Time

In this section, we show that it is impossible to achieve

$$|\mathsf{sk}| = O(|f|^\alpha) \quad \text{and} \quad T_{\mathsf{Dec}} = O(T + |f|^\beta + |x| + |y|)$$

simultaneously for a secure PHFE for RAM when $\alpha, \beta < 1$, where polynomial factors in the security parameter are ignored. This leaves us with two candidate optima:

- $\alpha = 0$ and $\beta = 1$ for succinct keys; or
- $\alpha = 1$ and $\beta = 0$ for f-fast decryption.

Similarly, it is impossible to achieve

$$|\mathsf{ct}| = O(|x|^\alpha)\, \mathrm{poly}(|y|) \quad \text{and} \quad T_{\mathsf{Dec}} = O(T + |f| + |x|^\beta + |y|)$$

simultaneously if $\alpha, \beta < 1$, which implies a contention between succinct ciphertexts and x-fast decryption.

Formally, our theorems are slightly stronger than the discussion above:

Theorem 5 (contention of $|f|$-dependency between $|\mathsf{sk}|$ and T_{Dec}; ¶). *For a secure full-fledged PHFE for RAM (Definitions 3, 5, and 8), if*

$$|\mathsf{sk}| \leq |f|^\alpha(\lambda + |\varphi|)^C \quad \text{and} \quad T_{\mathsf{Dec}} \leq (T + |f|^\beta + |y|)(\lambda + |\varphi| + |x|)^C$$

for infinitely many λ, where α, β, C are constants, then $\alpha \geq 1$ or $\beta \geq 1$.

Theorem 6 (contention of $|x|$-dependency between $|\mathsf{ct}|$ and T_{Dec}). *For a secure full-fledged PHFE for RAM (Definitions 3, 5, and 8), if*

$$|\mathsf{ct}| \leq |x|^\alpha(\lambda + |\varphi| + |y|)^C \quad \text{and} \quad T_{\mathsf{Dec}} \leq (T + |f| + |x|^\beta)(\lambda + |\varphi| + |y|)^C$$

for infinitely many λ, where α, β, C are constants, then $\alpha \geq 1$ or $\beta \geq 1$.

We will only prove Theorem 5. The proof of Theorem 6 is similar.

Proof (Theorem 5). Let (Setup, KeyGen, Enc, Dec) be a secure PHFE for RAM. Suppose for contradiction that $\alpha, \beta < 1 - 5\varepsilon$ for some $0 < \varepsilon \leq \frac{1}{5}$. By enlarging C as needed, we could assume $|\varphi| \leq \lambda^C - \lambda - 1$ for all sufficiently large λ, where

$$\varphi = (M_\lambda, 2^\lambda), \quad f = R \in \{0,1\}^{\leq 2^\lambda}, \quad x = \bot,$$

$$y = \begin{cases} (I, w) = (i_1, w[1], \ldots, i_n, w[n]) \in ([2^\lambda] \times \{0,1\})^{\leq 2^\lambda}; \\ z = (\bot, z[1], \ldots, \bot, z[n]) \in (\{\bot\} \times \{0,1\})^{\leq 2^\lambda}; \end{cases}$$

$$M^{f,x\|y}() = \begin{cases} (R[i_1] \oplus w[1], \ldots, R[i_n] \oplus w[n]), & \text{if } y = (I, w); \\ (\quad z[1] \quad, \ldots, \quad z[n] \quad), & \text{if } y = z. \end{cases}$$

Under appropriate encoding and step circuit design, y has exactly n cells and M halts in exactly $(2n+1)$ steps.

We focus on the values of λ (hereafter, "λ with efficiency") such that

$$|\mathsf{sk}| \leq |f|^\alpha(\lambda + |\varphi|)^C \quad \text{and} \quad T_{\mathsf{Dec}} \leq (T + |f|^\beta + |y|)(\lambda + |\varphi| + |x|)^C$$

By setting

$$|R| = N = \lceil \lambda^{(C^2+1)/\varepsilon} \rceil, \quad n = \lfloor N^{1-3\varepsilon} \rfloor,$$

we would have $n < N < 2^\lambda$ for sufficiently large λ. Consider the following adversary $\mathcal{A}$ (Definition 5):

- Upon launching, it computes φ, N, n defined above, sets up the PHFE scheme for φ, and submits 1^{2n+1} as the time bound.
- It samples $R \xleftarrow{\$} \{0,1\}^N$ and requests a key sk for $f = R$.
- It samples $w \xleftarrow{\$} \{0,1\}^n$ and a list I of n distinct random elements from $[N]$, sets

$$z = (R[i_1] \oplus w[1], \ldots, R[i_n] \oplus w[n]).$$

It challenges with

$$x = \bot, \quad y_0 = (I, w), \quad y_1 = z,$$

and obtains a ciphertext ct encrypting either y_0 or y_1.
- It runs $\mathsf{Dec}^{f,x,\mathsf{sk},\mathsf{ct}}(\mathsf{mpk})$ and notes down the list L of indices into $R = f$ where it is read during decryption. $\mathcal{A}$ outputs 1 if and only if

$$|L \cap I| > N^{1-4\varepsilon},$$

where L and I are regarded as sets (unordered and deduplicated) for the intersection operation.

Clearly, $\mathcal{A}$ would be efficient and its challenge would satisfy the constraints of PHFE security for sufficiently large λ. We claim:

Claim 7 (¶). *For sufficiently large λ with efficiency,*

$$\Pr\left[|L \cap I| > N^{1-4\varepsilon} \text{ in } \mathsf{Exp}^0_{\mathrm{PHFE}}\right] \geq \frac{3}{4}.$$

Claim 8 (¶). *For sufficiently large λ with efficiency,*

$$\Pr\left[|L \cap I| > N^{1-4\varepsilon} \text{ in } \mathsf{Exp}^1_{\mathrm{PHFE}}\right] \leq \frac{1}{4}.$$

The two claims together would contradict the security of PHFE, as the advantage of $\mathcal{A}$ would be at least $\frac{1}{2}$ for infinitely many λ. Therefore, $\alpha \geq 1$ or $\beta \geq 1$.   □

To prove Claim 7, we need the following lemma about incompressibility of information:

Lemma 9 ([24]). *Suppose $E : S \times U \to V$ and $D : S \times V \to U$ are functions and S is a distribution over S, then*

$$|V| \geq |U| \cdot \Pr_{\substack{s \overset{\$}{\leftarrow} S \\ u \overset{\$}{\leftarrow} U}} [D(s, E(s, u)) = u].$$

Proof (Claim 7). We use the PHFE scheme to compress a string u of length n. To encode, we embed u into a string R of length N at random locations (i.e., I) and generate a PHFE key for R. The encoding is the key plus some bits in R used during decryption. To decode, run the decryption algorithm. Lemma 9 will generate the following inequality equivalent to the desired one:

$$\Pr\left[|L \cap I| \leq \lfloor N^{1-4\varepsilon}\rfloor \text{ in } \mathsf{Exp}^0_{\mathrm{PHFE}}\right] \leq \frac{1}{4}.$$

Formally, let

$$S = \left\{ \begin{pmatrix} \mathsf{mpk}, \mathsf{msk}, I, w, R', \\ r_{\mathsf{KeyGen}}, r_{\mathsf{Enc}}, r_{\mathsf{Dec}} \end{pmatrix} : \begin{array}{c} (\mathsf{mpk}, \mathsf{msk}) \overset{\$}{\leftarrow} \mathsf{Setup}(\varphi) \\ (I, w) \text{ as how } \mathcal{A} \text{ samples it} \\ R'[i] \overset{\$}{\leftarrow} \{0,1\} \text{ for } i \in [N] \setminus I \\ r_{\mathsf{KeyGen}}, r_{\mathsf{Enc}}, r_{\mathsf{Dec}} \overset{\$}{\leftarrow} \text{ algorithm randomness} \end{array} \right\},$$

$$U = \{0,1\}^n, \qquad V = \{0,1\}^{\lfloor N^{1-4\varepsilon}\rfloor} \times \{0,1\}^{\lfloor N^{1-4\varepsilon}\rfloor}.$$

The encoding procedure $E(s, u)$ works as follows:

– Parse $I = (i_1, \ldots, i_n)$ and set

$$R[i] = \begin{cases} R'[i], & \text{if } i \in [N] \setminus I; \\ u[j], & \text{if } i = i_j. \end{cases}$$

– Run

$$\mathsf{sk} \leftarrow \mathsf{KeyGen}(\mathsf{msk}, R; r_{\mathsf{KeyGen}}),$$
$$\mathsf{ct} \leftarrow \mathsf{Enc}(\mathsf{mpk}, \bot, (I, w); r_{\mathsf{Enc}}),$$
$$u \oplus w \leftarrow \mathsf{Dec}^{R, \bot, \mathsf{sk}, \mathsf{ct}}(\mathsf{mpk}; r_{\mathsf{Dec}}),$$

and note down the list $L = (\ell_1, \dots)$ of indices into R read by Dec.
– Output $v = (v_1, v_2)$ with $v_1, v_2 \in \{0, 1\}^{\lfloor N^{1-4\varepsilon} \rfloor}$ and

$$v_1 = 0^{\lfloor N^{1-4\varepsilon} \rfloor - |\mathsf{sk}| - 1} 1 \| \mathsf{sk},$$

$$v_2[i] = \begin{cases} R[\ell_j], & \text{if } |\{\ell_1, \dots, \ell_{j-1}\} \cap I| = i - 1 \text{ and } |\{\ell_1, \dots, \ell_{j-1}, \ell_j\} \cap I| = i; \\ 0, & \text{if no such } j \text{ exists.} \end{cases}$$

Here, v_1 is a fixed-length encoding of sk and is indeed well-defined since

$$|\mathsf{sk}| \leq |f|^\alpha (\lambda + |\varphi|)^C \leq N^{1-5\varepsilon} \left(\lambda + (\lambda^C - \lambda - 1) \right)^C \leq N^{1-5\varepsilon} \lambda^{C^2} < \lfloor N^{1-4\varepsilon} \rfloor - 1$$

for sufficiently large λ with efficiency. The string v_2 records, *sequentially*, the bits in R at each *distinct* index read by Dec that are part of u and not known from R', for at most $\lfloor N^{1-4\varepsilon} \rfloor$ bits.

The decoding procedure $D(s, v)$ works as follows:

– Run $\mathsf{ct} \leftarrow \mathsf{Enc}(\mathsf{mpk}, \bot, (I, w); r_{\mathsf{Enc}})$.
– Parse $v = (v_1, v_2)$ and recover sk from v_1 as specified in E.
– Initialize j, an index into v_2, by $j \leftarrow 0$, and initialize R by

$$R[i] = \begin{cases} R'[i], & \text{if } i \in [N] \setminus I; \\ \bot, & \text{if } i \in I. \end{cases}$$

Run $z \leftarrow \mathsf{Dec}^{R, \bot, \mathsf{sk}, \mathsf{ct}}(\mathsf{mpk}; r_{\mathsf{Dec}})$ with R filled on the fly. When Dec reads $R[i]$:
  • if $R[i] = \bot$ and $j < \lfloor N^{1-4\varepsilon} \rfloor$, then let $j \leftarrow j + 1$ and set $R[i] \leftarrow v_2[j]$;
  • if $R[i] = \bot$ and $j = \lfloor N^{1-4\varepsilon} \rfloor$, then abort by outputting 0^n;
  • otherwise, $R[i] \neq \bot$, then just proceed without aborting;
  and return $R[i]$ to Dec if not aborting.
– Output $z \oplus w$.

D will fill v_2 into the correct indices of R since the PHFE algorithms are derandomized with the same randomness as in E.

The sampling of s, u and the setting of R in $E(s, u)$ simulate $\mathcal{A}$ in $\mathsf{Exp}^0_{\mathsf{PHFE}}$. If s and u are such that $|L \cap I| \leq \lfloor N^{1-4\varepsilon} \rfloor$ in $E(s, u)$, then D will successfully recover u. By Lemma 9,

$$\Pr \left[|L \cap I| \leq \lfloor N^{1-4\varepsilon} \rfloor \text{ in } \mathsf{Exp}^0_{\mathsf{PHFE}} \right]$$
$$= \Pr_{\substack{s \xleftarrow{\$} S \\ u \xleftarrow{\$} U}} \left[|L \cap I| \leq \lfloor N^{1-4\varepsilon} \rfloor \text{ in } E(s, u) \right]$$
$$\leq \Pr_{\substack{s \xleftarrow{\$} S \\ u \xleftarrow{\$} U}} \left[D(s, E(s, u)) = u \right] \leq \frac{|V|}{|U|} = \frac{2^{2\lfloor N^{1-4\varepsilon} \rfloor}}{2^n} = 2^{2\lfloor N^{1-4\varepsilon} \rfloor - \lfloor N^{1-3\varepsilon} \rfloor} \leq \frac{1}{4}$$

for sufficiently large λ with efficiency. □

Proof (Claim 8). For sufficiently large λ with efficiency,

$$
\begin{aligned}
|L| \leq T_{\mathsf{Dec}} &\leq (T + |f|^\beta + |y|)(\lambda + |\varphi| + |x|)^C \\
&\leq \big((2n+1) + N^{1-5\varepsilon} + n\big)\big(\lambda + (\lambda^C - \lambda - 1) + 1\big)^C \\
&\leq \big(3N^{1-3\varepsilon} + N^{1-5\varepsilon} + 1\big)\lambda^{C^2} \leq N^{1-2\varepsilon}.
\end{aligned}
$$

In $\mathsf{Exp}^1_{\mathsf{PHFE}}$, the input to Dec is independent of I, which only symbolically appears in ct as

$$
y_1 = z = (R[i_1] \oplus w[1], \ldots, R[i_n] \oplus w[n])
$$

and is fully hidden by the one-time pad w. Therefore, the list of indices into R read by Dec (i.e., L) is independent of I. Conditioned on L, the intersection size $|L \cap I|$ follows a hypergeometric distribution. By the law of total expectation,

$$
\mathbb{E}\big[|L \cap I|\big] = \mathbb{E}\Big[\mathbb{E}\big[|L \cap I| \mid L\big]\Big] = \mathbb{E}\left[\frac{|I| \cdot |L|}{N}\right] \leq \frac{N^{1-3\varepsilon} \cdot N^{1-2\varepsilon}}{N} = N^{1-5\varepsilon}
$$

for sufficiently large λ with efficiency, which implies, by Markov's inequality,

$$
\Pr[|L \cap I| > N^{1-4\varepsilon} \text{ in } \mathsf{Exp}^1_{\mathsf{PHFE}}] \leq \frac{\mathbb{E}\big[|L \cap I|\big]}{N^{1-4\varepsilon}} \leq \frac{N^{1-5\varepsilon}}{N^{1-4\varepsilon}} = N^{-\varepsilon} \leq \frac{1}{4}.
$$

$\square$

Acknowledgement. Aayush Jain was supported by departmental funds from CMU Computer Science Department and a gift from CyLab. Huijia Lin and Ji Luo were supported by NSF grants CNS-1936825 (CAREER), CNS-2026774, a JP Morgan AI Research Award, a Cisco Research Award, and a Simons Collaboration on the Theory of Algorithmic Fairness. The views expressed are those of the authors and do not reflect the official policy or position of the funding agencies. The authors thank the anonymous reviewers of Eurocrypt 2023 for their valuable comments.

References

1. Agrawal, S., Maitra, M.: FE and iO for Turing machines from minimal assumptions. In: Beimel, A., Dziembowski, S. (eds.) TCC 2018, Part II. LNCS, vol. 11240, pp. 473–512. Springer, Cham (2018). https://doi.org/10.1007/978-3-030-03810-6_18
2. Ananth, P., Chen, Y.-C., Chung, K.-M., Lin, H., Lin, W.-K.: Delegating RAM computations with adaptive soundness and privacy. In: Hirt, M., Smith, A. (eds.) TCC 2016, Part II. LNCS, vol. 9986, pp. 3–30. Springer, Heidelberg (2016). https://doi.org/10.1007/978-3-662-53644-5_1
3. Ananth, P., Chung, K.M., Fan, X., Qian, L.: Collusion-resistant functional encryption for RAMs. In: Agrawal, S., Lin, D. (eds.) ASIACRYPT 2022, Part I. LNCS, vol. 13791, pp. 160–194. Springer, Heidelberg, December 2022. https://doi.org/10.1007/978-3-031-22963-3_6

4. Ananth, P., Fan, X., Shi, E.: Towards attribute-based encryption for RAMs from LWE: sub-linear decryption, and more. In: Galbraith, S.D., Moriai, S. (eds.) ASIACRYPT 2019, Part I. LNCS, vol. 11921, pp. 112–141. Springer, Cham (2019). https://doi.org/10.1007/978-3-030-34578-5_5

5. Ananth, P., Jain, A., Lin, H., Matt, C., Sahai, A.: Indistinguishability obfuscation without multilinear maps: new paradigms via low degree weak Pseudorandomness and security amplification. In: Boldyreva, A., Micciancio, D. (eds.) CRYPTO 2019, Part III. LNCS, vol. 11694, pp. 284–332. Springer, Cham (2019). https://doi.org/10.1007/978-3-030-26954-8_10

6. Ananth, P., Jain, A., Sahai, A.: Indistinguishability obfuscation for Turing machines: constant overhead and amortization. In: Katz, J., Shacham, H. (eds.) CRYPTO 2017, Part II. LNCS, vol. 10402, pp. 252–279. Springer, Cham (2017). https://doi.org/10.1007/978-3-319-63715-0_9

7. Ananth, P., Lombardi, A.: Succinct garbling schemes from functional encryption through a local simulation paradigm. In: Beimel, A., Dziembowski, S. (eds.) TCC 2018, Part II. LNCS, vol. 11240, pp. 455–472. Springer, Cham (2018). https://doi.org/10.1007/978-3-030-03810-6_17

8. Ananth, P., Sahai, A.: Functional encryption for Turing machines. In: Kushilevitz, E., Malkin, T. (eds.) TCC 2016, Part I. LNCS, vol. 9562, pp. 125–153. Springer, Heidelberg (2016). https://doi.org/10.1007/978-3-662-49096-9_6

9. Attrapadung, N.: Dual system encryption framework in prime-order groups via computational pair encodings. In: Cheon, J.H., Takagi, T. (eds.) ASIACRYPT 2016, Part II. LNCS, vol. 10032, pp. 591–623. Springer, Heidelberg (2016). https://doi.org/10.1007/978-3-662-53890-6_20

10. Attrapadung, N., Libert, B., de Panafieu, E.: Expressive key-policy attribute-based encryption with constant-size ciphertexts. In: Catalano, D., Fazio, N., Gennaro, R., Nicolosi, A. (eds.) PKC 2011. LNCS, vol. 6571, pp. 90–108. Springer, Heidelberg (2011). https://doi.org/10.1007/978-3-642-19379-8_6

11. Attrapadung, N., Tomida, J.: Unbounded dynamic predicate compositions in ABE from standard assumptions. In: Moriai, S., Wang, H. (eds.) ASIACRYPT 2020, Part III. LNCS, vol. 12493, pp. 405–436. Springer, Cham (2020). https://doi.org/10.1007/978-3-030-64840-4_14

12. Bellare, M., Hoang, V.T., Rogaway, P.: Foundations of garbled circuits. In: Yu, T., Danezis, G., Gligor, V.D. (eds.) ACM CCS 2012, pp. 784–796. ACM Press, October 2012. https://doi.org/10.1145/2382196.2382279

13. Bitansky, N., Garg, S., Lin, H., Pass, R., Telang, S.: Succinct randomized encodings and their applications. In: Servedio, R.A., Rubinfeld, R. (eds.) 47th ACM STOC, pp. 439–448. ACM Press, June 2015. https://doi.org/10.1145/2746539.2746574

14. Boneh, D., et al.: Fully key-homomorphic encryption, arithmetic circuit ABE and compact garbled circuits. In: Nguyen, P.Q., Oswald, E. (eds.) EUROCRYPT 2014. LNCS, vol. 8441, pp. 533–556. Springer, Heidelberg (2014). https://doi.org/10.1007/978-3-642-55220-5_30

15. Boneh, D., Sahai, A., Waters, B.: Functional encryption: definitions and challenges. In: Ishai, Y. (ed.) TCC 2011. LNCS, vol. 6597, pp. 253–273. Springer, Heidelberg (2011). https://doi.org/10.1007/978-3-642-19571-6_16

16. Boyle, E., Holmgren, J., Ma, F., Weiss, M.: On the security of doubly efficient PIR. Cryptology ePrint Archive, Report 2021/1113 (2021). https://eprint.iacr.org/2021/1113

17. Boyle, E., Ishai, Y., Pass, R., Wootters, M.: Can we access a database both locally and privately? In: Kalai, Y., Reyzin, L. (eds.) TCC 2017, Part II. LNCS, vol. 10678, pp. 662–693. Springer, Cham (2017). https://doi.org/10.1007/978-3-319-70503-3_22

18. Brakerski, Z., Segev, G.: Function-private functional encryption in the private-key setting. In: Dodis, Y., Nielsen, J.B. (eds.) TCC 2015, Part II. LNCS, vol. 9015, pp. 306–324. Springer, Heidelberg (2015). https://doi.org/10.1007/978-3-662-46497-7_12

19. Canetti, R., Chen, Y., Holmgren, J., Raykova, M.: Adaptive succinct garbled RAM or: how to delegate your database. In: Hirt, M., Smith, A. (eds.) TCC 2016, Part II. LNCS, vol. 9986, pp. 61–90. Springer, Heidelberg (2016). https://doi.org/10.1007/978-3-662-53644-5_3

20. Canetti, R., Holmgren, J.: Fully succinct garbled RAM. In: Sudan, M. (ed.) ITCS 2016, pp. 169–178. ACM, January 2016. https://doi.org/10.1145/2840728.2840765

21. Canetti, R., Holmgren, J., Jain, A., Vaikuntanathan, V.: Succinct garbling and indistinguishability obfuscation for RAM programs. In: Servedio, R.A., Rubinfeld, R. (eds.) 47th ACM STOC, pp. 429–437. ACM Press, June 2015. https://doi.org/10.1145/2746539.2746621

22. Canetti, R., Holmgren, J., Richelson, S.: Towards doubly efficient private information retrieval. In: Kalai, Y., Reyzin, L. (eds.) TCC 2017, Part II. LNCS, vol. 10678, pp. 694–726. Springer, Cham (2017). https://doi.org/10.1007/978-3-319-70503-3_23

23. Chen, Y.C., Chow, S.S.M., Chung, K.M., Lai, R.W.F., Lin, W.K., Zhou, H.S.: Cryptography for parallel RAM from indistinguishability obfuscation. In: Sudan, M. (ed.) ITCS 2016, pp. 179–190. ACM, January 2016. https://doi.org/10.1145/2840728.2840769

24. De, A., Trevisan, L., Tulsiani, M.: Time space tradeoffs for attacks against one-way functions and PRGs. In: Rabin, T. (ed.) CRYPTO 2010. LNCS, vol. 6223, pp. 649–665. Springer, Heidelberg (2010). https://doi.org/10.1007/978-3-642-14623-7_35

25. De Caro, A., Iovino, V., Jain, A., O'Neill, A., Paneth, O., Persiano, G.: On the achievability of simulation-based security for functional encryption. In: Canetti, R., Garay, J.A. (eds.) CRYPTO 2013, Part II. LNCS, vol. 8043, pp. 519–535. Springer, Heidelberg (2013). https://doi.org/10.1007/978-3-642-40084-1_29

26. Garg, S., Gentry, C., Halevi, S., Raykova, M., Sahai, A., Waters, B.: Candidate indistinguishability obfuscation and functional encryption for all circuits. In: 54th FOCS, pp. 40–49. IEEE Computer Society Press, October 2013. https://doi.org/10.1109/FOCS.2013.13

27. Garg, S., Ostrovsky, R., Srinivasan, A.: Adaptive garbled RAM from laconic oblivious transfer. In: Shacham, H., Boldyreva, A. (eds.) CRYPTO 2018, Part III. LNCS, vol. 10993, pp. 515–544. Springer, Cham (2018). https://doi.org/10.1007/978-3-319-96878-0_18

28. Garg, S., Srinivasan, A.: Single-key to multi-key functional encryption with polynomial loss. In: Hirt, M., Smith, A. (eds.) TCC 2016, Part II. LNCS, vol. 9986, pp. 419–442. Springer, Heidelberg (2016). https://doi.org/10.1007/978-3-662-53644-5_16

29. Garg, S., Srinivasan, A.: Adaptively secure garbling with near optimal online complexity. In: Nielsen, J.B., Rijmen, V. (eds.) EUROCRYPT 2018, Part II. LNCS, vol. 10821, pp. 535–565. Springer, Cham (2018). https://doi.org/10.1007/978-3-319-78375-8_18

30. Garg, S., Srinivasan, A.: A simple construction of iO for Turing machines. In: Beimel, A., Dziembowski, S. (eds.) TCC 2018, Part II. LNCS, vol. 11240, pp. 425–454. Springer, Cham (2018). https://doi.org/10.1007/978-3-030-03810-6_16

31. Goldwasser, S., Kalai, Y.T., Popa, R.A., Vaikuntanathan, V., Zeldovich, N.: How to run Turing machines on encrypted data. In: Canetti, R., Garay, J.A. (eds.) CRYPTO 2013, Part II. LNCS, vol. 8043, pp. 536–553. Springer, Heidelberg (2013). https://doi.org/10.1007/978-3-642-40084-1_30

32. Gorbunov, S., Vaikuntanathan, V., Wee, H.: Attribute-based encryption for circuits. In: Boneh, D., Roughgarden, T., Feigenbaum, J. (eds.) 45th ACM STOC, pp. 545–554. ACM Press, June 2013. https://doi.org/10.1145/2488608.2488677

33. Gorbunov, S., Vaikuntanathan, V., Wee, H.: Predicate encryption for circuits from LWE. In: Gennaro, R., Robshaw, M. (eds.) CRYPTO 2015, Part II. LNCS, vol. 9216, pp. 503–523. Springer, Heidelberg (2015). https://doi.org/10.1007/978-3-662-48000-7_25

34. Goyal, V., Pandey, O., Sahai, A., Waters, B.: Attribute-based encryption for fine-grained access control of encrypted data. In: Juels, A., Wright, R.N., De Capitani di Vimercati, S. (eds.) ACM CCS 2006, pp. 89–98. ACM Press, October/November 2006. https://doi.org/10.1145/1180405.1180418. Available as Cryptology ePrint Archive Report 2006/309

35. Guan, J., Wichs, D., Zhandry, M.: Incompressible cryptography. In: Dunkelman, O., Dziembowski, S. (eds.) EUROCRYPT 2022, Part I. LNCS, vol. 13275, pp. 700–730. Springer, Heidelberg, May/June 2022. https://doi.org/10.1007/978-3-031-06944-4_24

36. Hemenway, B., Jafargholi, Z., Ostrovsky, R., Scafuro, A., Wichs, D.: Adaptively secure garbled circuits from one-way functions. In: Robshaw, M., Katz, J. (eds.) CRYPTO 2016, Part III. LNCS, vol. 9816, pp. 149–178. Springer, Heidelberg (2016). https://doi.org/10.1007/978-3-662-53015-3_6

37. Jain, A., Lin, H., Luo, J.: On the optimal succinctness and efficiency of functional encryption and attribute-based encryption. Cryptology ePrint Archive, Report 2022/1317 (2022). https://eprint.iacr.org/2022/1317

38. Jain, A., Lin, H., Matt, C., Sahai, A.: How to leverage hardness of constant-degree expanding polynomials over $\mathbb{R}$ to build $i\mathcal{O}$. In: Ishai, Y., Rijmen, V. (eds.) EUROCRYPT 2019, Part I. LNCS, vol. 11476, pp. 251–281. Springer, Cham (2019). https://doi.org/10.1007/978-3-030-17653-2_9

39. Jain, A., Lin, H., Sahai, A.: Indistinguishability obfuscation from well-founded assumptions. In: Khuller, S., Williams, V.V. (eds.) 53rd ACM STOC, pp. 60–73. ACM Press, June 2021. https://doi.org/10.1145/3406325.3451093

40. Jain, A., Lin, H., Sahai, A.: Indistinguishability obfuscation from LPN over $\mathbb{F}_p$, DLIN, and PRGs in NC^0. In: Dunkelman, O., Dziembowski, S. (eds.) EUROCRYPT 2022, Part I. LNCS, vol. 13275, pp. 670–699. Springer, Heidelberg, May/June 2022. https://doi.org/10.1007/978-3-031-06944-4_23

41. Kitagawa, F., Nishimaki, R., Tanaka, K.: Simple and generic constructions of succinct functional encryption. In: Abdalla, M., Dahab, R. (eds.) PKC 2018, Part II. LNCS, vol. 10770, pp. 187–217. Springer, Cham (2018). https://doi.org/10.1007/978-3-319-76581-5_7

42. Kitagawa, F., Nishimaki, R., Tanaka, K., Yamakawa, T.: Adaptively secure and succinct functional encryption: improving security and efficiency, simultaneously. In: Boldyreva, A., Micciancio, D. (eds.) CRYPTO 2019, Part III. LNCS, vol. 11694, pp. 521–551. Springer, Cham (2019). https://doi.org/10.1007/978-3-030-26954-8_17

43. Koppula, V., Lewko, A.B., Waters, B.: Indistinguishability obfuscation for Turing machines with unbounded memory. In: Servedio, R.A., Rubinfeld, R. (eds.) 47th ACM STOC, pp. 419–428. ACM Press, June 2015. https://doi.org/10.1145/2746539.2746614

44. Li, B., Micciancio, D.: Compactness vs collusion resistance in functional encryption. In: Hirt, M., Smith, A. (eds.) TCC 2016, Part II. LNCS, vol. 9986, pp. 443–468. Springer, Heidelberg (2016). https://doi.org/10.1007/978-3-662-53644-5_17

45. Li, H., Lin, H., Luo, J.: ABE for circuits with constant-size secret keys and adaptive security. In: Kiltz, E., Vaikuntanathan, V. (eds.) TCC 2022, Part I. LNCS, vol. 13747, pp. 680–710. Springer, Heidelberg, November 2022. https://doi.org/10.1007/978-3-031-22318-1_24

46. Lin, H., Luo, J.: Succinct and adaptively secure ABE for ABP from k-Lin. In: Moriai, S., Wang, H. (eds.) ASIACRYPT 2020, Part III. LNCS, vol. 12493, pp. 437–466. Springer, Cham (2020). https://doi.org/10.1007/978-3-030-64840-4_15

47. Lin, W.K., Mook, E., Wichs, D.: Doubly efficient private information retrieval and fully homomorphic RAM computation from ring LWE. Cryptology ePrint Archive, Report 2022/1703 (2022). https://eprint.iacr.org/2022/1703

48. Luo, J.: *Ad hoc* (decentralized) broadcast, trace, and revoke. Cryptology ePrint Archive, Report 2022/925 (2022). https://eprint.iacr.org/2022/925

49. Naor, M., Yogev, E.: Bloom filters in adversarial environments. In: Gennaro, R., Robshaw, M. (eds.) CRYPTO 2015, Part II. LNCS, vol. 9216, pp. 565–584. Springer, Heidelberg (2015). https://doi.org/10.1007/978-3-662-48000-7_28

50. O'Neill, A.: Definitional issues in functional encryption. Cryptology ePrint Archive, Report 2010/556 (2010). https://eprint.iacr.org/2010/556

51. Quach, W., Wee, H., Wichs, D.: Laconic function evaluation and applications. In: Thorup, M. (ed.) 59th FOCS, pp. 859–870. IEEE Computer Society Press, October 2018. https://doi.org/10.1109/FOCS.2018.00086

52. Sahai, A., Waters, B.: Fuzzy identity-based encryption. In: Cramer, R. (ed.) EUROCRYPT 2005. LNCS, vol. 3494, pp. 457–473. Springer, Heidelberg (2005). https://doi.org/10.1007/11426639_27

53. Takashima, K.: Expressive attribute-based encryption with constant-size ciphertexts from the decisional linear assumption. In: Abdalla, M., De Prisco, R. (eds.) SCN 2014. LNCS, vol. 8642, pp. 298–317. Springer, Cham (2014). https://doi.org/10.1007/978-3-319-10879-7_17

54. Yamada, S., Attrapadung, N., Hanaoka, G., Kunihiro, N.: A framework and compact constructions for non-monotonic attribute-based encryption. In: Krawczyk, H. (ed.) PKC 2014. LNCS, vol. 8383, pp. 275–292. Springer, Heidelberg (2014). https://doi.org/10.1007/978-3-642-54631-0_16

55. Zhang, K., et al.: Practical and efficient attribute-based encryption with constant-size ciphertexts in outsourced verifiable computation. In: Chen, X., Wang, X., Huang, X. (eds.) ASIACCS 16, pp. 269–279. ACM Press, May/June 2016

Registered Attribute-Based Encryption

Susan Hohenberger[1]([✉]), George Lu[2], Brent Waters[2,3], and David J. Wu[2]

[1] Johns Hopkins University, Baltimore, MD, USA
dwu4@cs.utexas.edu
[2] University of Texas at Austin, Austin, TX, USA
[3] NTT Research, Sunnyvale, CA, USA

Abstract. Attribute-based encryption (ABE) generalizes public-key encryption and enables fine-grained control to encrypted data. However, ABE upends the traditional trust model of public-key encryption by requiring a single *trusted* authority to issue decryption keys. If an adversary compromises the central authority and exfiltrates its secret key, then the adversary can decrypt *every* ciphertext in the system.

This work introduces registered ABE, a primitive that allows users to generate secret keys on their own and then register the associated public key with a "key curator" along with their attributes. The key curator aggregates the public keys from the different users into a single *compact* master public key. To decrypt, users occasionally need to obtain helper decryption keys from the key curator which they combine with their own secret keys. We require that the size of the aggregated public key, the helper decryption keys, the ciphertexts, as well as the encryption/decryption times to be polylogarithmic in the number of registered users. Moreover, the key curator is entirely *transparent* and maintains no secrets. Registered ABE generalizes the notion of registration-based encryption (RBE) introduced by Garg et al. (TCC 2018), who focused on the simpler setting of identity-based encryption.

We construct a registered ABE scheme that supports an a priori bounded number of users and policies that can be described by a linear secret sharing scheme (e.g., monotone Boolean formulas) from assumptions on composite-order pairing groups. Our approach deviates sharply from previous techniques for constructing RBE and only makes *black-box* use of cryptography. All existing RBE constructions (a weaker notion than registered ABE) rely on heavy non-black-box techniques. The encryption and decryption costs of our construction are comparable to those of vanilla pairing-based ABE. Two limitations of our scheme are that it requires a structured reference string whose size scales quadratically with the number of users (and linearly with the size of the attribute universe) and the running time of registration scales linearly with the number of users.

Finally, as a feasibility result, we construct a registered ABE scheme that supports general policies and an arbitrary number of users from indistinguishability obfuscation and somewhere statistically binding hash functions.

© International Association for Cryptologic Research 2023
C. Hazay and M. Stam (Eds.): EUROCRYPT 2023, LNCS 14006, pp. 511–542, 2023.
https://doi.org/10.1007/978-3-031-30620-4_17

1   Introduction

Attribute-based encryption (ABE) [23,37] extends traditional public-key encryption to enable fine-grained access control to encrypted data. For instance, in a ciphertext-policy ABE, secret keys are associated with attributes, and ciphertexts are associated with decryption policies. A secret key sk_x for an attribute x can decrypt a ciphertext ct_P with policy P only if the attribute satisfies the ciphertext's policy (i.e., $P(x) = 1$). In contrast, with vanilla public-key encryption, decryption is all-or-nothing: if a user has the secret key, she can decrypt *every* ciphertext encrypted under the respective public key and if the user does not know the secret key, she cannot decrypt *any* ciphertext.

While ABE is a versatile cryptographic primitive for enabling fine-grained control to encrypted data, it significantly changes the trust model compared to standard public-key encryption. In an ABE scheme, a central *trusted* authority is required to issue the secret decryption keys associated with each user. Critically, this central authority needs to retain a *long-term* secret key. If the central authority is compromised by an adversary at *any* point, then the adversary gains the ability to decrypt *all* ciphertexts in the system. This makes ABE inherently vulnerable to key exfiltration attacks, and the long-term secret key must be carefully protected for the lifetime of the system. In contrast, with standard public-key encryption, users can generate their *own* public/secret keys, and they do not have to entrust their secret keys to any central party. Public-key encryption do not open users up to a *central* point of failure. The combination of built-in key escrow and vulnerability to key exfiltration is a common impediment to deploying ABE.

Registration-Based Encryption. Garg et al. [18] introduced the notion of registration-based encryption (RBE) to address the key-escrow problem in the setting of identity-based encryption (IBE). In an IBE scheme [6,12,38], secret keys and ciphertexts are associated with identities and decryption succeeds if the identities associated with the secret key and ciphertexts match; an IBE scheme is a special case of ABE for the equality policy. In an RBE scheme, the central authority is replaced by a "key curator." The role of the key curator is *not* to issue secret decryption keys, but instead, to *aggregate* public keys from registered users into a *short* master public key mpk.

In more detail, users in an RBE scheme generate their own public/secret keys (like in traditional public-key encryption), and then register their *public* keys together with their identity with the key curator. The key curator then updates the master public key of the scheme. Like IBE, the master public key can be used to encrypt a message to any identity. If the identity corresponds to that of a registered user, then the user can decrypt the message using their secret key and a *publicly-computable* helper decryption key that binds the user's public key to the current master public key. Since the master public key of the RBE scheme changes whenever new users join the system, users must periodically refresh their helper decryption keys over the lifetime of the system. Note that the helper decryption keys for each user can be computed publicly, and importantly, in an RBE system, the key curator does *not* possess any secret information. The efficiency requirement is that if L users register, then each user only needs to update their decryption key at most $O(\log L)$ times over the lifetime of the system. The size of each update should also be short (i.e., $\mathsf{poly}(\lambda, \log L)$, where λ is a security parameter). In addition, like IBE, the master public key must be short: $|\mathsf{mpk}| \leq \mathsf{poly}(\lambda, \log L)$.

A Challenge: Non-black-Box Use of Cryptography. In recent years, a number of works have constructed registration-based encryption [13, 18–20] from standard assumptions such as CDH, factoring, or LWE assumptions. However, all of the existing constructions make heavy *non-black-box* use of cryptography. Existing constructions either apply indistinguishability obfuscation to a cryptographic hash function [18] or use a hash garbling scheme to traverse a Merkle tree [13, 19, 20]. The latter approach chains together a sequence of garbled circuits (proportional to the length of the identity), where each garbled circuit reads one bit of the input and outputs a set of labels for the next garbled circuit; the final garbled circuit is a garbling of the encryption algorithm for a public-key encryption scheme. The heavy use of non-black-box cryptography in both approaches render existing schemes completely impractical. Even in spite of recent optimization efforts [13], a *single* ciphertext in a system supporting 2 billion users is estimated to be 4.5 *terabytes*.

This Work: Registered ABE. In this work, we introduce a generalization of RBE called registered ABE to address the key escrow problem and remove the need for long-term secret keys in the context of ABE. We introduce a new set of techniques for realizing registered ABE with only *black-box* use of cryptography. Our work extends registration-based encryption in two key ways:

- **Functionality:** Our scheme is attribute-based rather than identity-based, and is capable of supporting any access control policy that can be described by a linear secret sharing scheme (which includes monotone Boolean formulas). This matches the state-of-the-art in pairing-based ABE schemes. We refer to our new primitive as a *registered ABE* scheme. Our scheme includes RBE as a special case if we instantiate the scheme for the class of equality policies. Much like RBE provides a solution to the key-escrow problem for the setting of IBE, registered ABE provides an analogous solution in the setting of ABE.
- **Black-box use of cryptography:** Our construction does not make any non-black-box use of cryptography. The key-generation, encryption, and decryption algorithms in our scheme is comparable to that of existing pairing-based ABE schemes (e.g., [30]). Our approach departs from the hash garbling approach used in all existing constructions of RBE [13, 18–20] and instead, takes an aggregation-based approach that is conceptually similar to those used in the construction of pairing-based vector commitments [8, 29] and batch arguments [41].

We construct a registered ABE scheme from static assumptions on composite-order pairing groups (Assumption 5.2). We rely on the same assumptions as those used previously to construct IBE [31] and ABE [30].

A limitation of our scheme is that it imposes an *a priori* bound L on the number of users in the system, and security relies on a one-time trusted sampling of a common reference string (CRS). We note that this setup only needs to be done *once* and the same CRS can be reused across different systems. The size of the CRS is quadratic in L while the registration time is linear in L. However, the size of the master public key, the size of the helper decryption keys, as well as the encryption and decryption times, all scale polylogarithmically with L. As with standard RBE, the key curator is a deterministic algorithm and does not need to store any secret information. We also note that our scheme is limited to a polynomial-size attribute universe and the size of the CRS, the master public key, and each user's helper decryption key scale linearly with the size of the attribute universe.

While the CRS in our scheme is *structured*[1] and needs to be sampled by a trusted party (or using an MPC protocol), this is the only trusted component in our system. Thereafter, the behavior of the key curator is deterministic and auditable. As long as the adversary does not compromise this *one-time* setup, security holds. This is in contrast to traditional ABE where users must always trust the central authority who holds the *long-term* secret key. If the authority is compromised at *any* point in time and the adversary successfully exfiltrates the authority's secret key, then they gain the ability to decrypt every ciphertext in the system. Thus, even with a structured CRS, the registered ABE model still represents a significant reduction in trust compared to the traditional ABE model.

We summarize our main instantiation with the following (informal) characterization of Corollary 6.2:

Theorem 1.1 (Informal). *Let λ be a security parameter. Let $\mathcal{U}$ be an attribute space and $\mathcal{P}$ be a set of policies that can be described by a linear secret sharing scheme over $\mathcal{U}$. Let L be a bound on the number of users. Then, under reasonable assumptions on a composite-order pairing group, there exists a registered ABE scheme that supports up to L users with attribute universe $\mathcal{U}$ and policy space $\mathcal{P}$ with the following properties:*

- *The size of the CRS and the size of the auxiliary data maintained by the key curator is $L^2 \cdot \mathsf{poly}(\lambda, |\mathcal{U}|, \log L)$.*
- *The running time of key-generation and registration is $L \cdot \mathsf{poly}(\lambda, |\mathcal{U}|, \log L)$.*
- *The size of the master public key and the helper decryption keys are both $|\mathcal{U}| \cdot \mathsf{poly}(\lambda, \log L)$.*
- *The size of a ciphertext is $|P| \cdot \mathsf{poly}(\lambda, \log L)$, where P is the size of the ciphertext policy.*

---

[1] Previous constructions of registration-based encryption [13,18–20] only assumed a *uniform* random string rather than a structured reference string.

Note that only the key-generation, registration, and update algorithms depend on the (long) CRS. The running time of encryption and decryption are all polylog-arithmic in the number of users L.

In addition to the above scheme based on composite-order bilinear maps, we also show how to construct a registered ABE scheme for an *arbitrary* number of users and supporting arbitrary policies (on a super-polynomial size attribute space) using indistinguishability obfuscation [2,3] and somewhere statistically binding hash functions [25]. Coupled with the work of Jain et al. [26,27], this yields a registered ABE scheme from falsifiable assumptions. We view this latter result as primarily a feasibility result for constructing registered ABE schemes capable of supporting general policies and an arbitrary number of users.

1.1 Related Work

Many previous works have explored mechanisms to address the key-escrow lim-itation inherent to IBE and ABE. One approach is based on threshold cryp-tography [6,11,28,35] where the master secret key is secret-shared across mul-tiple independent authorities; this way, no single authority has the ability to decrypt ciphertexts. A similar notion in the setting of ABE is multi-authority ABE [9,10,14,15,32–34,36,40] where anyone can become an authority and issue secret keys corresponding to the set of attributes within their domain. Policies in a multi-authority ABE scheme are in turn formulated with respect to the attributes of one or more authorities. Nonetheless, the keys in threshold and decentralized systems are still issued by entities other than the user, and if a sufficient number of the key-issuing entities are compromised or corrupted, then the schemes no longer ensure confidentiality.

Other techniques have focused on adding accountability to the central author-ity [21,22] or introducing hybrid notions that combine IBE and traditional public-key directories [1]. However, none of these approaches completely elimi-nate the key-escrow problem inherent to notions like IBE and ABE.

Registration-based encryption was first introduced by Garg et al. [18] who also gave a construction from indistinguishability obfuscation and somewhere statistically binding hash functions. They also gave a "weakly-efficient" scheme (where registration runs in time that is polynomial in the number of registered users) from simpler assumptions like CDH or LWE. Subsequently, [18] provided a fully-efficient construction (where registration runs in time that is polyloga-rithmic in the number of registered users) from assumptions like CDH or LWE. Cong et al. [13] subsequently improved the concrete efficiency of their scheme. Goyal and Vusirikala [20] then showed how to augment RBE with protection against malicious key curators. All of these existing constructions (including the *weakly-efficient* ones) rely on non-black-box use of cryptography (e.g., obfusca-tion or hash garbling techniques).

2   Technical Overview

In this work, we construct a ciphertext-policy registered ABE scheme that supports any access policy that can be described by a linear secret sharing scheme (see Sect. 2.1 and Definition 3.2). In the following description, we let $\mathcal{U}$ be the universe of attributes. We will assume that $\mathcal{U}$ is polynomial-size (i.e., we are in the small universe setting). We additionally assume that there is an *a priori* bound L on the maximum number of users that can be registered, and moreover, that there is a (trusted) setup algorithm that samples a common reference string crs that will be used for key-generation, registration, and computing the helper information for decryption. In our setting, we allow the size of the crs to be $\mathsf{poly}(\lambda, L)$. The key curator initializes the master public key mpk to the empty string.

When a user wants to join the system, it first samples a public/secret key-pair (pk, sk). To register, the user provides their public key pk along with their set of attributes $S \subseteq \mathcal{U}$ to the key curator.[2] The key curator then *aggregates* the key into the master public key mpk and produces an updated key mpk′. In addition, the key curator computes a helper decryption key hsk and gives it to the user. In our setting, we allow the key-generation and registration process to be slow (i.e., running in time $\mathsf{poly}(\lambda, L)$).[3] However, the size of the master public key mpk, the secret key sk, and helper decryption key hsk for each user must be short (i.e., $\mathsf{poly}(\lambda, \log L)$). Each time a user registers, the master public key needs to be updated; this means users will need to periodically obtain an updated helper decryption key corresponding to the most recent master public key. As in RBE, we require that over the lifetime of the system, the user only needs to request $O(\log L)$ many updates from the key curator.

In a registered ABE scheme, encryption only requires knowledge of the master public key mpk (and *not* the long common reference string). The encryption algorithm takes in the master public key mpk, the access policy P, and a message μ and outputs a ciphertext ct. In turn, every registered user whose set of attributes S satisfy the policy is able to decrypt using their secret key sk and the helper decryption key hsk. Neither the encryption nor decryption algorithms require knowledge of the crs, and the running time of all of these algorithms scale with $\mathsf{poly}(\lambda, \log L, |P|)$. Notably, in a registered ABE scheme, there is an initial slow *one-time* process for generating and registering keys. Encryption and decryption are both fast (comparable to *standard* ABE).

Slotted Registered ABE. Our construction of registered ABE proceeds in two steps. First, we define and construct an intermediate primitive that we call

---

[2] Just like in RBE, the key curator first verifies the attributes claimed by the user before proceeding. This step is analogous to the checks certificate authorities perform in the public-key infrastructure before issuing a certificate or what the central authority would do in a standard ABE setting before issuing a decryption key. A difference is that the key curator possesses no secret information.

[3] This roughly coincides with the notion of *weak efficiency* in the work of Garg et al. [18].

"slotted registered ABE" (Sect. 4.1). We then show how to compile a slotted registered ABE scheme into a registered ABE scheme (Sect. 6).

In a slotted registered ABE scheme, we specify a *fixed* number of users L at setup, and moreover, each user is associated with a slot index $i \in [L]$. Public keys in a slotted registered ABE scheme are generated with respect to a particular slot. In addition, we replace the registration algorithm with an *aggregation* algorithm that takes as input a collection of L public keys $pk_1, \ldots, pk_L$, one for each slot, along with their associated attribute sets $S_1, \ldots, S_L \subseteq \mathcal{U}$, and outputs the master public key mpk together with the helper decryption keys $hsk_1, \ldots, hsk_L$ associated with each slot. The main difference is that aggregation takes all L keys at once and outputs the master public key (which is then fixed). In contrast, in (non-slotted) registered ABE, the public keys are registered one at a time, and the master public key is updated after each registration. We provide the formal definition of a slotted registered ABE scheme in Sect. 4.1 and show how to construct a slotted registered ABE scheme from assumptions on a composite-order pairing group in Sect. 5. We note that our scheme assumes a polynomial-size attribute universe and the sizes of the master public key and the helper decryption keys scale linearly with the size $|\mathcal{U}|$ of the attribute universe. We provide an overview of our slotted registered ABE scheme in 2.1.

From Slotted Registered ABE to Registered ABE. To go from a slotted registered ABE scheme to a registered ABE scheme, we use a simple "powers-of-two" approach that was also used implicitly in previous constructions [18,19]. Suppose we want to support a maximum of $L = 2^\ell$ users. Our construction uses $\ell + 1$ copies of the slotted registered ABE scheme, where the kth copy is a slotted ABE with exactly 2^k slots (with k ranging from 0 to ℓ). The master public key mpk consists of $\ell + 1$ master public keys $mpk_0, \ldots, mpk_\ell$, one for each of the underlying schemes. Initially, $mpk_k = \perp$ for all k. The first user registers to an empty slot in each of the $\ell + 1$ instances. At this point, the first slotted registered ABE scheme (with 1 slot) is full, and the key curator computes mpk_0 and updates its value in mpk. When subsequent users join the system, they continue to register to the next vacant slot in each of the $\ell + 1$ instances (if one exists). If scheme k fills up (i.e., there is a key associated with each of its 2^k slots), the key curator updates mpk_k in the master public key and then *removes* all of the registered keys from schemes $0, \ldots, k - 1$ (since all of those users' public keys are now aggregated as part of mpk_k).[4] Subsequent registrations will reuse schemes $0, \ldots, k - 1$ since these are no longer full. On every registration, exactly one of the master public keys mpk_k is updated. When this occurs, all of the users who are now registered in the kth scheme will need to obtain a decryption key update from the key curator. By design, this process can only happen at most $\ell + 1 = O(\log L)$ times, so this satisfies the efficiency requirements on the registered ABE scheme. To encrypt a message with respect

---

[4] For ease of notation in the formal description (Sect. 6 Construction 6.1), we do not implement this "clearing out" step explicitly. However, the construction is functionally behaving in this manner.

to $\mathsf{mpk} = (\mathsf{mpk}_0, \ldots, \mathsf{mpk}_\ell)$, the encrypter encrypts the message to each mpk_k to obtain ct_k. The ciphertext is $\mathsf{ct} = (\mathsf{ct}_0, \ldots, \mathsf{ct}_\ell)$. To decrypt, a user who is currently registered in mpk_k takes ct_k and decrypts. Overall this powers-of-two approach incurs $O(\log L)$ overhead on the size of the public parameters, the ciphertext size, and the encryption time compared to the slotted scheme, but now supports efficient updates. We describe and analyze this transformation in Sect. 6 (Construction 6.1). We summarize the properties of our final registered ABE scheme in Corollary 6.2 (and Theorem 1.1).

Registered ABE for Unbounded Users from Obfuscation. Our pairing-based registered ABE construction only supports a bounded number of users. A natural question is whether we can construct registered ABE that supports an *arbitrary* number of users. In 7, we show the feasibility of such a scheme using indistinguishability obfuscation [2,3] and somewhere statistically binding hash functions [25]. Our registered ABE (for arbitrary circuit predicates) is a direct generalization of the RBE scheme of Garg et al. [18] from indistinguishability obfuscation. Here, we describe a slotted version of the scheme. Given a collection of public keys $\mathsf{pk}_1, \ldots, \mathsf{pk}_L$ along with their attribute sets $S_1, \ldots, S_L$, we first construct a Merkle hash tree on values $(\mathsf{pk}_1, S_1), \ldots, (\mathsf{pk}_L, S_L)$. The master public key is the root of the Merkle tree. A ciphertext consists of an obfuscated program that takes as input an index $i \in [L]$, the public key pk_i and its accompanying secret key sk_i, the set of attributes S_i, and a Merkle proof of opening for the value (pk_i, S_i) at index i. The obfuscated program checks that (1) the opening with respect to the hash root (hard-coded) is valid; (2) S_i satisfies the ciphertext policy (also hard-coded); and (3) sk_i is the secret key associated with pk_i. If all of these checks pass, it outputs the message m. This approach directly yields a registered ABE for an arbitrary number of users and which supports general circuit policies. We give the full construction in Sect. 7 (Construction 7.1). We leave the question of constructing registered ABE that supports an unbounded number of users without obfuscation (or without needing non-black-box use of cryptography) as an intriguing open problem.

2.1 Constructing Slotted Registered ABE from Pairings

In this section, we provide a general overview of our slotted registered ABE scheme from composite-order pairing groups. The full construction and analysis are provided in Sect. 5. Together with the slotted-to-full transformation from Sect. 6, we obtain a registered ABE for an a priori bounded number of users.

Composite-Order Pairing Groups. Our construction relies on composite-order pairing groups where the group order N is a product of three primes $N = p_1 p_2 p_3$. Then, a (symmetric) composite-order pairing group consists of two cyclic groups $\mathbb{G}$ and $\mathbb{G}_T$, each of order N. Let g be a generator of $\mathbb{G}$. By the Chinese remainder theorem, we can write $\mathbb{G} \cong \mathbb{G}_1 \times \mathbb{G}_2 \times \mathbb{G}_3$, where $\mathbb{G}_i$ is the subgroup of $\mathbb{G}$ order p_i and is generated by $g_i = g^{N/p_i}$. Additionally, there exists an efficiently-computable, non-degenerate bilinear map $e \colon \mathbb{G} \times \mathbb{G} \to \mathbb{G}_T$ called the *pairing*. For all exponents $a, b \in \mathbb{Z}_N$, we have that $e(g^a, g^b) = e(g, g)^{ab}$. Again by the

Chinese remainder theorem, the subgroups $\mathbb{G}_1, \mathbb{G}_2, \mathbb{G}_3$ are orthogonal: namely $e(g_i, g_j) = 1$ for all $i \neq j$ where $i, j \in \{1, 2, 3\}$.

Linear Secret Sharing Schemes. Like numerous other pairing-based ABE schemes [23,30,32], we design a (ciphertext-policy) ABE scheme that supports access policies which can be described by a linear secret sharing scheme (LSSS). Very briefly, a linear secret sharing scheme is specified by a share-generating matrix $\mathbf{M} \in \mathbb{Z}_N^{K \times n}$, where each row of $\mathbf{M}$ is associated with a distinct attribute $x_1, \ldots, x_K$. We say a set of attributes $\{x_i\}_{i \in S}$ is authorized if and only if there exists a vector $\boldsymbol{\omega}_S \in \mathbb{Z}_N^{|S|}$ such that $\boldsymbol{\omega}_S^\mathsf{T} \mathbf{M}_S = \mathbf{e}_1^\mathsf{T} = [1, 0, \cdots, 0]$, where $\mathbf{M}_S$ is the matrix formed by taking the subset of rows indexed by $S \subseteq [K]$. In other words, the attributes $\{x_i\}_{i \in S}$ satisfy the policy if and only if $\mathbf{e}_1^\mathsf{T}$ is in the row-span of $\mathbf{M}_S$. Given an LSSS matrix $\mathbf{M}$, we can secret share a value $s \in \mathbb{Z}_N$ by sampling $v_2, \ldots, v_n \xleftarrow{\mathsf{R}} \mathbb{Z}_N$, constructing the vector $\mathbf{v} = [s, v_2, \ldots, v_n]^\mathsf{T}$ and computing the vector of shares $\mathbf{u} = \mathbf{M}\mathbf{v} \in \mathbb{Z}_q^K$. The ith component $u_i \in \mathbb{Z}_N$ is the share associated with attribute x_i. Given an authorized set of attributes $\{x_i\}_{i \in S}$ and the subset of shares $\mathbf{u}_S \in \mathbb{Z}_N^{|S|}$ associated with S, reconstructing the secret corresponds to computing $\boldsymbol{\omega}_S^\mathsf{T} \mathbf{u}_S = \boldsymbol{\omega}_S^\mathsf{T} \mathbf{M}_S \mathbf{v} = \mathbf{e}_1^\mathsf{T} \mathbf{v} = s$.

Slotted Registered ABE Overview. In a slotted registered ABE scheme with L slots, users register a public key pk along with a set of attributes $S \subseteq \mathcal{U}$ to a particular slot $i \in [L]$. In our construction, the decryption algorithm implicitly enforces the following two checks:

- **Slot-specific check:** The user possesses a secret key associated with some slot i in the scheme.
- **Attribute-specific check:** The attributes associated with the slot i satisfy the ciphertext policy. In our construction, this check shares a similar structure to the Lewko et al. [30] ciphertext-policy ABE scheme.

Thus, when describing our scheme, we roughly partition the components of the CRS, the master public key, and the ciphertext based on whether they are "slot-specific" or "attribute-specific."

A Single Slot Scheme. We start by describing a simple version of our scheme with just a *single* slot.[5] The single-slot scheme highlights the core components of our construction. Subsequently, we describe how to extend the single-slot scheme into a multi-slot scheme. An important difference between registered ABE and vanilla ABE is the fact that the master public keys in a registered ABE can depend on the set of attributes that have been registered so far. Thus, in the single-slot setting that just supports a single user, the user's attributes are directly embedded into the master public key. Let $\mathcal{U}$ be a (polynomial-size)

---

[5] Note that a single-slot scheme by itself is trivial to construct. We can simply define the master public key to be the public key and set of attributes associated with the slot. However, for describing our construction, it is simpler to first illustrate the mechanics in the single-slot setting and then build up to the full multi-slot construction.

universe of attributes and let $\mathcal{G} = (\mathbb{G}, \mathbb{G}_T, N, g, e)$ be a composite-order pairing group with $N = p_1 p_2 p_3$. We now describe the main components of the scheme:

- The components of the common reference string crs can be partitioned into three general categories:
  - **General components:** The general component is used for blinding the message and linking together the slot-specific and attribute-specific decryption procedures. These components will subsequently be included as part of the master public key. Concretely, we sample exponents $\alpha, \beta \xleftarrow{R} \mathbb{Z}_N$ and include $Z \leftarrow e(g_1, g_1)^\alpha$ and $h \leftarrow g_1^\beta$ in the CRS.
  - **Slot-specific components:** Each slot in the CRS is associated with a set of group elements. In the single-slot setting, we have two elements $A \leftarrow (g_1 g_3)^t$ and $B \leftarrow g_1^\alpha h^t g_3^\tau$, where $t \xleftarrow{R} \mathbb{Z}_N$ is a slot-specific exponent, $\alpha \in \mathbb{Z}_N$ is the "general" exponent from above, and $\tau \xleftarrow{R} \mathbb{Z}_N$ is a blinding factor.
  - **Attribute-specific components:** For each attribute $w \in \mathcal{U}$, the CRS contains a group element $U_w \leftarrow g_1^{u_w}$, where $u_w \xleftarrow{R} \mathbb{Z}_N$ is the attribute-specific exponent associated with w.

  Putting all the pieces together, the CRS in the single-slot setting consists of the following terms:

  $$\mathsf{crs} = \left(\mathcal{G}, g_1, g_3, Z, h, (A, B), \{U_w\}_{w \in \mathcal{U}}\right).$$

- To sample a new public/secret key-pair, the user samples $r \xleftarrow{R} \mathbb{Z}_N$ and sets it as their secret key $\mathsf{sk} = r$. The user sets the public key to be $\mathsf{pk} = T = g_1^r$.
- When the user registers their public key $\mathsf{pk} = T = g_1^r$ along with their set of attributes $S \subseteq \mathcal{U}$, the key curator sets $\hat{T} = T$ and $\hat{U}_w = U_w$ if $w \notin S$ and $\hat{U}_w = 1$ if $w \in S$. The key curator then outputs the master public key

  $$\mathsf{mpk} = \left(\mathcal{G}, g_1, h, Z, \hat{T}, \{\hat{U}_w\}_{w \in \mathcal{U}}\right). \tag{2.1}$$

  As we will see later on, $\hat{T}$ is the attribute-independent key aggregated across all of the slots while $\hat{U}_w$ is the key associated with attribute w aggregated across all of the slots.
- The helper decryption key for the user is just the slot-specific components $A = (g_1 g_3)^t$ and $B = g_1^\alpha h^t g_3^\tau$ from the CRS.
- To encrypt a message $\mu \in \mathbb{G}_T$ to a policy $(\mathbf{M}, \rho)$, where $\mathbf{M} \in \mathbb{Z}_N^{K \times n}$ is the share-generating matrix associated with the policy, and $\rho \colon [K] \to \mathcal{U}$ is an injective row-labeling function that maps the rows of $\mathbf{M}$ onto the particular attribute to which it corresponds, the encrypter samples $s \xleftarrow{R} \mathbb{Z}_N$ and $h_1, h_2 \xleftarrow{R} \mathbb{G}_1$ such that $h_1 h_2 = h$. Namely, h_1 and h_2 function as a secret sharing of h. The ciphertext then consists of the following:
  - **Message-embedding components:** Let $C_1 \leftarrow \mu \cdot Z^s = \mu \cdot e(g_1, g_1)^{\alpha s}$. Let $C_2 \leftarrow g_1^s$.
  - **Attribute-specific component:** Let $\mathbf{v} = [s, v_2, \ldots, v_n]^\top$, where $v_2, \ldots, v_n \xleftarrow{R} \mathbb{Z}_N$. For each $k \in [K]$, set $C_{3,k} \leftarrow h_2^{\mathbf{m}_k^\top \mathbf{v}} \hat{U}_{\rho(k)}^{-s}$. Here $\mathbf{m}_k^\top \in \mathbb{Z}_N^n$ denotes the kth row of $\mathbf{M}$.

- **Slot-specific component:** Set $C_4 \leftarrow h_1^s \hat{T}^{-s}$.

The ciphertext is

$$\mathsf{ct} = \big((\mathbf{M}, \rho), \, C_1, \, C_2, \, \{C_{3,k}\}_{k \in [K]}, \, C_4 \big).$$

Note that if we ignore the slot-specific ciphertext component, then the structure of the ciphertexts in our scheme coincides with those in the ciphertext-policy ABE scheme of Lewko et al. [30].[6] However, once we move beyond the single-slot setting, we will need to introduce additional components into the *aggregated* public key. This leads to a more complex decryption procedure and requires a more intricate security analysis compared to [30]. We discuss some of these details below and refer to Sect. 5 for the complete details.

The decryption algorithm can be decomposed into two main components: the first ensures the user's attributes satisfy the policy, and the second ensures the user's public key is bound to a specific slot. We describe these two steps below:

- **Policy check:** Let $S' = \{k \in [K] : \rho(k) \in S\}$ be the subset of the user's attributes that are associated with the policy $(\mathbf{M}, \rho)$. Suppose S' satisfies the policy $(\mathbf{M}, \rho)$. This means there exists a vector $\omega_{S'} \in \mathbb{Z}_N^{|S'|}$ such that $\omega_{S'}^\top \mathbf{M}_{S'} = \mathbf{e}_1^\top$. Moreover, by construction, $\hat{U}_w = 1$ for all $w \in S'$. In particular, this means that $C_{3,k} = h_2^{\mathbf{m}_k^\top \mathbf{v}}$ for all $k \in S'$. Using $\omega_{S'}$ and $h_2^{\mathbf{m}_k^\top \mathbf{v}}$, the decrypter can compute $h_2^{\omega_{S'}^\top \mathbf{M}_{S'} \mathbf{v}} = h_2^{\mathbf{e}_1^\top \mathbf{v}} = h_2^s$. Finally, the decryption algorithm can pair $A = (g_1 g_3)^t$ with h_2^s to obtain

$$D_{\mathsf{attrib}} = e(h_2^s, A) = e(h_2^s, (g_1 g_3)^t) = e(h_2, g_1)^{st},$$

since $h_2 \in \mathbb{G}_1$. Essentially, the decrypter should only be able to recover $e(h_2, g_1)^{st}$ if its set of attributes satisfy the policy. We note here that if an attribute $\rho(k) \notin S$, then $\hat{U}_{\rho(k)} \neq 1$; this property effectively "prevents" the decrypter from using $C_{3,k}$ during decryption since it would not be able to remove the extra $U_{\rho(k)}^{-s}$ component. The formal security analysis is more delicate and we defer to Sect. 5 for the exact analysis.

- **Slot check:** For the slot component, the decrypter takes its secret key r and computes

$$D_{\mathsf{slot}} = e(C_4, A) \cdot e(C_2, A^r) = e\big(h_1^s g_1^{-sr}, (g_1 g_3)^t\big) \cdot e\big(g_1^s, (g_1 g_3)^{rt}\big)$$
$$= e(h_1, g_1)^{st} \cdot e(g_1, g_1)^{-srt} \cdot e(g_1, g_1)^{srt}$$
$$= e(h_1, g_1)^{st}, \tag{2.2}$$

since $\hat{T} = g_1^r$ and $h_1 \in \mathbb{G}_1$. Essentially, the decrypter should only be able to recover $e(h_1, g_1)^{st}$ if it knows the secret key associated with the slot.

---

[6] The scheme of Lewko et al. [30] also includes a row-specific blinding factor $s_k \xleftarrow{\text{R}} \mathbb{Z}_N$ associated with each row of $\mathbf{M}$. We do not need this additional randomization in our security analysis.

Recall now that h_1 and h_2 are a multiplicative secret sharing of h (i.e., $h_1 h_2 = h$). This means that if both of the policy check and the slot check passes (and in fact, *only* in this case), the decrypter is able to recover $e(h, g_1)^{st}$. This can now be combined with the message-embedding ciphertext components to recover the original message:

$$\frac{C_1 \cdot e(h, g_1)^{st}}{e(C_2, B)} = \frac{\mu \cdot e(g_1, g_1)^{\alpha s} e(h, g_1)^{st}}{e(g_1^s, g_1^{\alpha t} h^t g_3^\tau)} = \frac{\mu \cdot e(g_1, g_1)^{\alpha s} \cdot e(h, g_1)^{st}}{e(g_1, g_1)^{\alpha s} \cdot e(h, g_1)^{st}} = \mu,$$

again using the fact that $h \in \mathbb{G}_1$.

Extending to Multiple Slots via Key Aggregation. To extend to an L-slot scheme, we essentially "concatenate" L *independent* copies of the single-slot scheme in the CRS. Specifically, for each slot $i \in [L]$, the CRS contains a set of slot-specific components and a set of attribute-specific components (in addition to the same set of general components from the single-slot scheme):

- **Slot-specific components:** Sample a slot-specific exponent $t_i \xleftarrow{\text{R}} \mathbb{Z}_N$ and a blinding factor $\tau_i \xleftarrow{\text{R}} \mathbb{Z}_N$, and let $A_i \leftarrow (g_1 g_3)^{t_i}$ and $B_i \leftarrow g_1^\alpha h^{t_i} g_3^{\tau_i}$.
- **Attribute-specific components:** For each attribute $w \in \mathcal{U}$, sample an attribute-specific exponent $u_{i,w} \xleftarrow{\text{R}} \mathbb{Z}_N$ and let $U_{i,w} \leftarrow g_1^{u_{i,w}}$.

The CRS consists of the general components, the slot-specific components, and the attribute-specific components for each of the slots:

$$\mathsf{crs} = \left(\mathcal{G}, g_1, g_3, Z, h, \{(A_i, B_i)\}_{i \in [L]}, \{U_{i,w}\}_{i \in [L], w \in \mathcal{U}}\right).$$

Next, we need a way to *aggregate* the public keys for the different slots into a single *compact* master public key mpk. Let $\{\mathsf{pk}_i\}_{i \in [L]}$ be a collection of public keys where $\mathsf{pk}_i = T_i = g_1^{r_i}$ is the public key associated with slot i. Let $S_i \subseteq \mathcal{U}$ be the set of attributes associated with pk_i. Our aggregation mechanism is simple: the aggregated public key components $\hat{T}, \hat{U}_w$ simply correspond to the *product* of the components associated with each slot:

$$\hat{T} = \prod_{j \in [L]} T_j \quad \text{and} \quad \hat{U}_w = \prod_{j \in [L]: w \notin S_j} U_{j,w}.$$

The structure of the mpk is the same as in Eq. (2.1). Importantly, the size of the master public key is *independent* of the number of slots. The encryption algorithm also remains the same as in the single-slot case.

Cross Term Cancellation for Decryption. When a message is encrypted with respect to an *aggregated* key, the ciphertext components are now a function of the exponents associated with *all* of the slots. However, the decrypter only has a key for a single slot (e.g., r_i), so the decrypter needs additional helper information in order to decrypt. To illustrate this, consider the decryption relation associated with the slot check (Eq. (2.2)). Suppose we are decrypting for slot i (using secret exponent r_i). Then,

$$
\begin{aligned}
D_{\mathsf{slot}} &= e(C_4, A_i) \cdot e(C_2, A_i^{r_i}) \\
&= e(h_1^s \hat{T}^{-s}, (g_1 g_3)^{t_i}) \cdot e(g_1^s, (g_1 g_3)^{r_i t_i}) \\
&= e(h_1, g_1)^{s t_i} \cdot e(g_1, g_1)^{-s r_i t_i} \prod_{j \neq i} e(g_1, g_1)^{-s r_j t_i} \cdot e(g_1, g_1)^{s r_i t_i} \\
&= e(h_1, g_1)^{s t_i} \prod_{j \neq i} e(g_1, g_1)^{-s r_j t_i},
\end{aligned}
\tag{2.3}
$$

using the fact that $\hat{T} = \prod_{j \in [L]} T_j = \prod_{j \in [L]} g_1^{r_j}$. This is the same expression from Eq. (2.2) in the single-slot setting, *except* we have an extra term $\prod_{j \neq i} e(g_1, g_1)^{-s r_j t_i}$ from the slots $j \neq i$. We refer to these terms as the "cross-terms" since they correspond to an interaction between the secret key for slot j with the slot exponent for slot i. We thus require a way to eliminate the cross terms. Here, we take an approach that is often encountered when using pairings for aggregation (e.g., aggregating openings for vector commitments [8,29] or aggregating proofs in the case of batch arguments [41]). The strategy is to have the user for slot i provide the cross-terms $V_{j,i} = A_j^{r_i} = (g_1 g_3)^{r_i t_j}$ for each $j \neq i$ as part of its public key pk_i. Given all of the cross-terms from all of the users, the key curator can compute a helper decryption key component $\hat{V}_i = \prod_{j \neq i} V_{i,j} = \prod_{j \neq i} (g_1 g_3)^{r_j t_i}$ for each slot i. Given $\hat{V}_i$, the decrypter can now compute

$$
e(C_2, \hat{V}_i) = \prod_{j \neq i} e(g_1^s, (g_1 g_3)^{r_j t_i}) = \prod_{j \neq i} e(g_1, g_1)^{s r_j t_i},
$$

which precisely cancels out the extra term in Eq. (2.3). Finally, observe that the additional helper decryption component is just a single group element and is again, *independent* of the number of slots. This means that the size of the master public key, the size of the helper decryption components, as well as the encryption and decryption times are independent of the number of slots. Only the (one-time) key-generation and registration costs scale with the number of slots. We introduce a similar cross-term cancellation approach for the attribute-specific components and refer to Sect. 5.2 for the full description and analysis.

Security Analysis. To prove security of our construction, we follow the dual-system methodology [31,39]. While traditional dual-system proofs modify the distribution of the secret keys and the ciphertexts given out in the security game, in the registered ABE setting, we modify the distribution of the *slot parameters* and the ciphertexts. In more detail, in the security proof, we introduce modified ciphertexts (referred to as "semi-functional ciphertexts") and slot components (referred to as "semi-functional slots"). Keys registered to a semi-functional slot can be used to decrypt normal ciphertexts (i.e., those output by the honest encryption algorithm) and keys registered to a normal slot can be used to decrypt semi-functional ciphertexts. However, a key registered to a semi-functional slot is unable to decrypt a semi-functional ciphertext. The proof then proceeds via a hybrid argument where we first switch the challenge ciphertext from a normal ciphertext to a semi-functional one. Then, we switch the parameters associated with each slot from normal to semi-functional. In the final experiment then, all of the slots are semi-functional, as is the challenge ciphertext. Since keys associated with semi-functional slots cannot be used to decrypt a semi-functional ciphertext, arguing semantic security in the final experiment is straightforward. We give the full proof in Sect. 5. Here, we highlight two of the technical challenges that arise in the proof:

- **Malformed public keys:** In registered ABE, the adversary is allowed to submit *arbitrary* public keys to the key curator. In the security proof (and even for correctness), it will be important that the public keys are well-formed (and in particular, that the cross-terms are properly constructed). To enable this, we introduce a validity-check mechanism that uses the pairing to check that the components of the public key are properly computed. In the security proof, we show that the only public keys an efficient adversary can construct that pass the validity check are those in the support of the honest key-generation algorithm. Note that an alternative approach to rule out malformed public keys is to have users include a non-interactive zero-knowledge proof of knowledge of their public key that certifies well-formedness of the public key. However, doing so generically would either bring in random oracles [16] or require making non-black-box use of cryptography. Hence, we opt for a simpler algebraic mechanism that integrates directly with the rest of our construction.

- **Arguing semantic security.** A standard proof strategy for arguing security of an ABE scheme based on linear secret sharing is to construct a sequence of hybrid experiments such that in the final experiment, the challenge ciphertext *information-theoretically* hides the message by the security of the linear secret sharing scheme. This strategy applies if all of the keys the adversary possesses do *not* satisfy the challenge policy, and indeed, this property is enforced in the standard ABE security experiment. In registered ABE, the scenario is slightly different since there are two possibilities we have to consider:
  - The adversary knows the secret key associated with slot i and the attributes associated with slot i do *not* satisfy the challenge policy; or
  - The adversary does *not* know the secret key associated with slot i. In this case, it could be the case that the attributes associated with slot i do satisfy the challenge policy.

  Handling these two cases requires two different information-theoretic arguments: the first relies on the linear secret sharing scheme while the second relies on the secret key r_i for slot i to be hidden from the view of the adversary. Setting up these information-theoretic arguments requires slightly different distributions on the slot components. Consequently, we rely on two *different* sequence of hybrid experiments to handle the two cases. We refer to the full version of this paper [24] for more details.

We refer to Sect. 5 for the full construction and analysis of our slotted registered ABE scheme.

3   Preliminaries

Throughout this work, we write λ to denote the security parameter. For a positive integer $n \in \mathbb{N}$, we write $[n]$ to denote the set $\{1, \ldots, n\}$, and $[0, n]$ to denote the set $\{0, \ldots, n\}$. We use bold uppercase letters (e.g., $\mathbf{M}$) to denote matrices and bold lowercase letters (e.g., $\mathbf{v}$) to denote vectors. We use non-boldface letters to refer to their components (e.g., $\mathbf{v} = [v_1, \ldots, v_n]$). For a positive integer $N \in \mathbb{N}$, we write $\mathbb{Z}_N$ to denote the integers modulo N.

We write $\mathsf{poly}(\lambda)$ to denote a function that is $O(\lambda^c)$ for some constant $c \in \mathbb{N}$ and $\mathsf{negl}(\lambda)$ to denote a function that is $o(\lambda^{-c})$ for all $c \in \mathbb{N}$. We say that an event occurs with overwhelming probability if its complement occurs with negligible probability. We say an algorithm is efficient if it runs in probabilistic polynomial time in its input length. We say that two families of distributions $\mathcal{D}_1 = \{\mathcal{D}_{1,\lambda}\}_{\lambda \in \mathbb{N}}$ and $\mathcal{D}_2 = \{\mathcal{D}_{2,\lambda}\}_{\lambda \in \mathbb{N}}$ are computationally indistinguishable if no efficient algorithm can distinguish them with non-negligible probability. We say they are statistically indistinguishable if the statistical distance $\Delta(\mathcal{D}_1, \mathcal{D}_2)$ is bounded by a negligible function in λ.

Access Structures and Linear Secret Sharing. We also recall the definition of monotone access structures and linear secret sharing which we will use in this work.

Definition 3.1 (Access Structure [4]). *Let S be a set and let 2^S denote the power set of S (i.e., the set of all subsets of S). An access structure on S is a set $\mathbb{A} \subseteq 2^S \setminus \varnothing$ of non-empty subsets of S. We refer to the elements of $\mathbb{A}$ as the* authorized *sets and those not in $\mathbb{A}$ as the* unauthorized *sets. We say an access structure is* monotone *if for all sets $B, C \in 2^S$, if $B \in \mathbb{A}$ and $B \subseteq C$, then $C \in \mathbb{A}$.*

Definition 3.2 (Linear Secret Sharing Scheme [4]). *Let $\mathcal{P}$ be a set of parties. A linear secret sharing scheme over a ring $\mathbb{Z}_N$ for $\mathcal{P}$ is a pair $(\mathbf{M}, \rho)$, where $\mathbf{M} \in \mathbb{Z}_N^{\ell \times n}$ is a "share-generating" matrix and $\rho \colon [\ell] \to \mathcal{P}$ is a "row-labeling" function. The pair $(\mathbf{M}, \rho)$ satisfy the following properties:*

- **Share generation:** *To share a value $s \in \mathbb{Z}_N$, sample $v_2, \ldots, v_n \xleftarrow{\text{R}} \mathbb{Z}_N$ and define the vector $\mathbf{v} = [s, v_2, \ldots, v_n]^\mathsf{T}$. Then, $\mathbf{u} = \mathbf{M}\mathbf{v}$ is the vector of shares where $u_i \in \mathbb{Z}_N$ belongs to party $\rho(i)$ for each $i \in [\ell]$.*
- **Share reconstruction:** *Let $S \subseteq \mathcal{P}$ be a set of parties and let $I_S = \{i \in [\ell] : \rho(i) \in S\}$ be the row indices associated with S. Let $\mathbf{M}_S \in \mathbb{Z}_N^{|I_S| \times n}$ be the matrix formed by taking the subset of rows in $\mathbf{M}$ that are indexed by I_S. If S is an authorized set of parties, then there exists a vector $\boldsymbol{\omega}_S \in \mathbb{Z}_N^{|I_S|}$ such that $\boldsymbol{\omega}_S^\mathsf{T} \mathbf{M}_S = \mathbf{e}_1^\mathsf{T}$, where $\mathbf{e}_1^\mathsf{T} = [1, 0, \ldots, 0]$ denotes the first elementary basis vector. Conversely, if $S \subseteq$ is an unauthorized sets of parties, then $\mathbf{e}_1^\mathsf{T}$ is not in the row-span of $\mathbf{M}$ (i.e., there does not exist $\boldsymbol{\omega}_S \in \mathbb{Z}_N^{|S|}$ where $\boldsymbol{\omega}_S^\mathsf{T} \mathbf{M}_S = \mathbf{e}_1^\mathsf{T}$).*

Remark 3.3 (One-Use Restriction). In this work, we construct a registered ABE scheme (Sect. 5) that supports any policy that can be described by a linear secret sharing scheme (Definition 3.2), with the restriction that each attribute is associated with at most one row of $\mathbf{M}$. This corresponds to policies $(\mathbf{M}, \rho)$ where the row-labeling function ρ is *injective*. As shown in Lewko et al. [30, §2.2], it is straightforward to extend a scheme with the one-use restriction into one where attributes can be used up to k times by expanding the public parameters and secret keys by a factor of k (i.e., split each attribute into k independent copies).

Remark 3.4 (Monotone Boolean Formulas). Our pairing-based registered ABE construction (Sect. 5) supports monotone access policies that can be described by any (one-use) linear secret sharing scheme. As a special case, this captures the class of monotone Boolean formulas. There are multiple ways to take a monotone Boolean formula and express it as a linear secret sharing scheme; we refer to [32, Appendix G] for one such approach.

4   Registered Attribute-Based Encryption

In this section, we introduce the notion of a registered attribute-based encryption scheme for a polynomial-size attribute space. Our definition is an adaptation of the notion of registration-based encryption (RBE) [18] to the more general attribute-based setting. We compare some features of our definition with RBE in the full version of this paper [24].

Definition 4.1 (Registered Attribute-Based Encryption). *Let λ be a security parameter. Let $\mathcal{U} = \{\mathcal{U}_\lambda\}_{\lambda \in \mathbb{N}}$ be a universe of attributes and $\mathcal{P} = \{\mathcal{P}_\lambda\}_{\lambda \in \mathbb{N}}$ be a set of policies on $\mathcal{U}$. Let $\mathcal{M} = \{\mathcal{M}_\lambda\}_{\lambda \in \mathbb{N}}$ be the message space. A registered attribute-based encryption scheme with attribute universe $\mathcal{U}$, policy space $\mathcal{P}$, and message space $\mathcal{M}$ consists of a tuple of efficient algorithms $\Pi_{\text{R-ABE}} = (\text{Setup}, \text{KeyGen}, \text{RegPK}, \text{Encrypt}, \text{Update}, \text{Decrypt})$ with the following properties:*

- Setup($1^\lambda, 1^{|\mathcal{U}|}$) $\rightarrow$ crs: *On input the security parameter λ and the size of the attribute universe $\mathcal{U}$, the setup algorithm outputs a common reference string crs.*
- KeyGen(crs, aux) $\rightarrow$ (pk, sk): *On input the common reference string crs, and a (possibly empty) state aux, the key-generation algorithm outputs a public key pk and a secret key sk.*
- RegPK(crs, aux, pk, S_{pk}) $\rightarrow$ (mpk, aux′): *On input the common reference string crs, a (possibly empty) state aux, a public key pk, and a set of attributes $S_{pk} \subseteq \mathcal{U}$, the registration algorithm deterministically outputs the master public key mpk and an updated state aux′.*
- Encrypt(mpk, P, μ) $\rightarrow$ ct: *On input the master public key mpk, an access policy $P \in \mathcal{P}$, and a message $\mu \in \mathcal{M}$, the encryption algorithm outputs a ciphertext ct.*
- Update(crs, aux, pk) $\rightarrow$ hsk: *On input the common reference string crs, a state aux, and a public key pk, the update algorithm deterministically outputs a helper decryption key hsk.*

- Decrypt(sk, hsk, ct) → $\mathcal{M} \cup \{\perp,$ GetUpdate$\}$: *On input the master public key* mpk, *a secret key* sk, *a helper decryption key* hsk, *and a ciphertext* ct, *the decryption algorithm either outputs a message* $\mu \in \mathcal{M}$, *a special symbol* $\perp$ *to indicate a decryption failure, or a special flag* GetUpdate *that indicates an updated helper decryption key is needed to decrypt.*

Correctness and Efficiency. We now define the correctness and efficiency requirements on a registered ABE scheme. At a high level, correctness says that if a user properly registers her public key along with a set of attributes, then she can use her secret key to decrypt all future ciphertexts ct encrypted under the resulting (and any subsequent) master public key, provided that her set of attributes satisfy the policy associated with the ciphertext. Notably, this should hold even if malicious users register (possibly-malformed) keys. In other words, as long as the key curator is semi-honest, an adversary cannot register "bad" keys to cause decryption to fail for an honest user. The main efficiency requirements we impose is that the size of the master public key and the size of each user's helper decryption key should be compact (i.e., polylogarithmic in the total number of users). We compare our notion with the RBE definition in the full version of this paper [24].

Registered ABE Security. The security requirement for a registered ABE scheme is analogous to the standard ABE security notion. Namely, semantic security should hold for a ciphertext associated with a policy P if the user only has keys registered to attribute sets $S_1, \ldots, S_k$ which do *not* satisfy the policy. In the security game, we allow the adversary the ability to register users with a set of attributes that *do* satisfy the challenge policy, provided the adversary does *not* know the user's secret key (i.e., they are generated honestly by the challenger). In addition, the adversary is allowed to register (arbitrary) public keys for attribute sets of its choosing, provided that none of them satisfy the challenge policy. We give the formal definition below:

Definition 4.2 (Security of Registered ABE). *Let* $\Pi_{\text{R-ABE}} =$ (Setup, KeyGen, RegPK, Encrypt, Update, Decrypt) *be a registered ABE scheme with attribute universe* $\mathcal{U}$, *policy space* $\mathcal{P}$, *and message space* $\mathcal{M}$. *For a security parameter* λ, *an adversary* $\mathcal{A}$, *and a bit* $b \in \{0,1\}$, *we define the following game between* $\mathcal{A}$ *and the challenger:*

- **Setup phase:** *The challenger samples the common reference string* crs ← Setup$(1^\lambda, 1^{|\mathcal{U}|})$. *It then initializes the auxiliary input* aux ← $\perp$, *the initial master public key* mpk ← $\perp$, *a counter* ctr ← 0 *for the number of honest-key-registration queries the adversary has made, an empty set of keys* $\mathcal{C}$ ← $\varnothing$ *(to keep track of corrupted public keys), and an empty dictionary mapping public keys to registered attribute sets* D ← $\varnothing$. *For notational convenience, if* pk ∉ D, *then we define* D[pk] := $\varnothing$. *to be the empty set. The challenger gives the* crs *to* $\mathcal{A}$.
- **Query phase:** *Adversary* $\mathcal{A}$ *can now issue the following queries:*

- **Register corrupted key query:** *In a corrupted-key-registration query, the adversary $\mathcal{A}$ specifies a public key* pk *and a set of attributes $S \subseteq \mathcal{U}$. The challenger registers the key by computing* $(\mathsf{mpk}', \mathsf{aux}') \leftarrow \mathsf{RegPK}(\mathsf{crs}, \mathsf{aux}, \mathsf{pk}, S)$. *The challenger updates its copy of the public key* $\mathsf{mpk} \leftarrow \mathsf{mpk}'$, *its auxiliary data* $\mathsf{aux} \leftarrow \mathsf{aux}'$, *adds* pk *to $\mathcal{C}$, and updates $D[\mathsf{pk}] \leftarrow D[\mathsf{pk}] \cup \{S\}$. It replies to $\mathcal{A}$ with* $(\mathsf{mpk}', \mathsf{aux}')$.

- **Register honest key query:** *In an honest-key-registration query, the adversary specifies a set of attributes $S \subseteq \mathcal{U}$. The challenger increments the counter* $\mathsf{ctr} \leftarrow \mathsf{ctr}+1$ *and samples* $(\mathsf{pk}_{\mathsf{ctr}}, \mathsf{sk}_{\mathsf{ctr}}) \leftarrow \mathsf{KeyGen}(\mathsf{crs}, \mathsf{aux})$, *and registers* $(\mathsf{mpk}', \mathsf{aux}') \leftarrow \mathsf{RegPK}(\mathsf{crs}, \mathsf{aux}, \mathsf{pk}_{\mathsf{ctr}}, S)$. *The challenger updates its public key* $\mathsf{mpk} \leftarrow \mathsf{mpk}'$, *its auxiliary data* $\mathsf{aux} \leftarrow \mathsf{aux}'$, *and* $D[\mathsf{pk}_{\mathsf{ctr}}] \leftarrow D[\mathsf{pk}_{\mathsf{ctr}}] \cup \{S\}$. *It replies to $\mathcal{A}$ with* $(\mathsf{ctr}, \mathsf{mpk}', \mathsf{aux}', \mathsf{pk}_{\mathsf{ctr}})$.

- **Corrupt honest key query:** *In a corrupt-honest-key query, the adversary specifies an index $1 \leq i \leq \mathsf{ctr}$. Let $(\mathsf{pk}_i, \mathsf{sk}_i)$ be the ith public/secret key the challenger samples when responding to the ith honest-key-registration query. The challenger adds pk_i to $\mathcal{C}$ and replies to $\mathcal{A}$ with* sk_i.

- **Challenge phase:** *The adversary $\mathcal{A}$ chooses two messages $\mu_0^*, \mu_1^* \in \mathcal{M}$ and an access policy $P^* \in \mathcal{P}$. The challenger replies with the challenge ciphertext* $\mathsf{ct}^* \leftarrow \mathsf{Encrypt}(\mathsf{mpk}, P^*, \mu_b^*)$.

- **Output phase:** *At the end of the game, algorithm $\mathcal{A}$ outputs a bit $b' \in \{0, 1\}$.*

Let $\mathcal{S} = \{S \in D[\mathsf{pk}] : \mathsf{pk} \in \mathcal{C}\}$ be the set of corrupted attributes. We say that an adversary $\mathcal{A}$ is admissible if the challenge policy P^* is not satisfied by any attribute set $S \in \mathcal{S}$. Note that it could be the case that P^* is satisfied by the attributes S from an honest key query (that was not subsequently corrupted). We say that a registered ABE scheme is secure if for all efficient and admissible adversaries $\mathcal{A}$, there exists a negligible function $\mathsf{negl}(\cdot)$ such that for all $\lambda \in \mathbb{N}$, we have that $|\Pr[b' = 1 \mid b = 0] - \Pr[b' = 1 \mid b = 1]| = \mathsf{negl}(\lambda)$ in the above security game.

Definition 4.3 (Bounded Registered ABE). *We say a registered ABE scheme $\Pi_{\mathsf{R\text{-}ABE}}$ is bounded if there is an a priori bound on the number of registered users in the system. In this setting, we modify* Setup *to takes as input an additional bound parameter 1^L which specifies the maximum number of registered users. In the correctness and security definitions, we allow the adversary to specify the bound 1^L at the beginning, and in the games themselves, the adversary can make up to L queries (the challenger answers subsequent registration queries with $\bot$).*

4.1 Slotted Registered Attribute-Based Encryption

In this section, we formally introduce the notion of a slotted registered ABE scheme which is the core building block underlying our pairing-based construction (Sect. 5) and obfuscation-based construction (Sect. 7). Then in Sect. 6, we show how to compile a slotted registered ABE scheme into a standard registered ABE scheme.

Definition 4.4 (Slotted Registration-Based Encryption). *Let λ be a security parameter. Let $\mathcal{U} = \{\mathcal{U}_\lambda\}_{\lambda \in \mathbb{N}}$ be a universe of attributes and $\mathcal{P} = \{\mathcal{P}_\lambda\}_{\lambda \in \mathbb{N}}$ be a set of policies on $\mathcal{U}$. Let $\mathcal{M} = \{\mathcal{M}_\lambda\}_{\lambda \in \mathbb{N}}$ be the message space. A slotted registered ABE scheme with attribute universe $\mathcal{U}$, policy space $\mathcal{P}$, and message space $\mathcal{M}$ is a tuple of efficient algorithms $\Pi_{\mathsf{sRBE}} = (\mathsf{Setup}, \mathsf{KeyGen}, \mathsf{IsValid}, \mathsf{Aggregate}, \mathsf{Encrypt}, \mathsf{Decrypt})$ with the following properties:*

- $\mathsf{Setup}(1^\lambda, 1^{|\mathcal{U}|}, 1^L) \to \mathsf{crs}$: *On input the security parameter λ, the size of the universe $\mathcal{U}$, and the number of slots L, the setup algorithm outputs a common reference string crs.*
- $\mathsf{KeyGen}(\mathsf{crs}, i) \to (\mathsf{pk}_i, \mathsf{sk}_i)$: *On input the common reference string crs, a slot index $i \in [L]$, the key-generation algorithm outputs a public key pk_i and a secret key sk_i for slot i.*
- $\mathsf{IsValid}(\mathsf{crs}, i, \mathsf{pk}_i) \to \{0, 1\}$: *On input the common reference string crs, a slot index $i \in [L]$, and a public key pk_i, the key-validation algorithm outputs a bit $b \in \{0, 1\}$ indicating whether pk_i is valid or not. This algorithm is deterministic.*
- $\mathsf{Aggregate}(\mathsf{crs}, (\mathsf{pk}_1, S_1), \ldots, (\mathsf{pk}_L, S_L)) \to (\mathsf{mpk}, \mathsf{hsk}_1, \ldots, \mathsf{hsk}_L)$: *On input the common reference string crs and a list of public keys and the associated attributes $(\mathsf{pk}_1, S_1), \ldots, (\mathsf{pk}_L, S_L)$, the aggregate algorithm outputs the master public key mpk and a collection of helper decryption keys $\mathsf{hsk}_1, \ldots, \mathsf{hsk}_L$. This algorithm is deterministic.*
- $\mathsf{Encrypt}(\mathsf{mpk}, P, \mu) \to \mathsf{ct}$: *On input the master public key mpk, an access policy $P \in \mathcal{P}$, and a message $\mu \in \mathcal{M}$, the encryption algorithm outputs a ciphertext ct.*
- $\mathsf{Decrypt}(\mathsf{sk}, \mathsf{hsk}, \mathsf{ct}) \to m$: *On input a decryption key sk, the helper decryption key hsk, and a ciphertext ct, the decryption algorithm outputs a message $\mu \in \mathcal{M} \cup \{\bot\}$. This algorithm is deterministic.*

Moreover, the above algorithms should satisfy the following properties:

- **Completeness:** *For all parameters $\lambda \in \mathbb{N}$, $L \in \mathbb{N}$, all attribute universes $\mathcal{U}$, and all indices $i \in [L]$,*

$$\Pr[\mathsf{IsValid}(\mathsf{crs}, i, \mathsf{pk}_i) = 1 : \mathsf{crs} \leftarrow \mathsf{Setup}(1^\lambda, 1^{|\mathcal{U}|}, 1^L);$$
$$(\mathsf{pk}_i, \mathsf{sk}_i) \leftarrow \mathsf{KeyGen}(\mathsf{crs}, i)] = 1.$$

- **Correctness:** *We say Π_{sRBE} is correct if for all security parameters $\lambda \in \mathbb{N}$, all attribute universes $\mathcal{U}$, all slot lengths $L \in \mathbb{N}$, all indices $i \in [L]$, if we sample $\mathsf{crs} \leftarrow \mathsf{Setup}(1^\lambda, 1^{|\mathcal{U}|}, 1^L)$, $(\mathsf{pk}_i, \mathsf{sk}_i) \leftarrow \mathsf{KeyGen}(\mathsf{crs}, i)$, then for all collections of public keys $\{\mathsf{pk}_j\}_{j \neq i}$ (which may be correlated with pk_i) where $\mathsf{IsValid}(\mathsf{crs}, j, \mathsf{pk}_j) = 1$, all messages $\mu \in \mathcal{M}$, all sets of attributes $S_1, \ldots, S_L \subseteq \mathcal{U}$, all policies $P \in \mathcal{P}$ where S_i satisfies policy P, the following holds:*

$$\Pr\left[\mathsf{Decrypt}(\mathsf{sk}_i, \mathsf{hsk}_i, \mathsf{ct}) = \mu\right] = 1,$$

where $(\mathsf{mpk}, \mathsf{hsk}_1, \ldots, \mathsf{hsk}_L) \leftarrow \mathsf{Aggregate}(\mathsf{crs}, (\mathsf{pk}_1, S_1), \ldots, (\mathsf{pk}_L, S_L))$, $\mathsf{ct} \leftarrow \mathsf{Encrypt}(\mathsf{mpk}, P, \mu)$, and the probability is taken over the randomness in Setup, KeyGen, and $\mathsf{Encrypt}$.

- **Compactness:** *There exists a universal polynomial* $\mathsf{poly}(\cdot, \cdot, \cdot)$ *such that the length of the master public key and individual helper secret keys output by* Aggregate *are* $\mathsf{poly}(\lambda, |\mathcal{U}|, \log L)$.
- **Security:** *Let* $b \in \{0, 1\}$ *be a bit. For an adversary* $\mathcal{A}$, *define the following security game between* $\mathcal{A}$ *and a challenger:*
  - **Setup phase:** *The adversary* $\mathcal{A}$ *sends a slot count* 1^L *to the challenger. The challenger then samples* $\mathsf{crs} \leftarrow \mathsf{Setup}(1^\lambda, 1^{|\mathcal{U}|}, 1^L)$ *and gives* crs *to* $\mathcal{A}$. *The challenger also initializes a counter* $\mathsf{ctr} \leftarrow 0$, *a dictionary* D, *and a set of slot indices* $\mathcal{C} \leftarrow \varnothing$.
  - **Pre-challenge query phase:** *Adversary* $\mathcal{A}$ *can now issue the following queries:*
    * **Key-generation query:** *In a key-generation query, the adversary specifies a slot index* $i \in [L]$. *The challenger responds by incrementing the counter* $\mathsf{ctr} \leftarrow \mathsf{ctr} + 1$, *sampling* $(\mathsf{pk}_{\mathsf{ctr}}, \mathsf{sk}_{\mathsf{ctr}}) \leftarrow \mathsf{KeyGen}(\mathsf{crs}, i)$ *and replies with* $(\mathsf{ctr}, \mathsf{pk}_{\mathsf{ctr}})$ *to* $\mathcal{A}$. *The challenger adds the mapping* $\mathsf{ctr} \mapsto (i, \mathsf{pk}_{\mathsf{ctr}}, \mathsf{sk}_{\mathsf{ctr}})$ *to the dictionary* D.
    * **Corruption query:** *In a corruption query, the adversary specifies an index* $1 \leq c \leq \mathsf{ctr}$. *In response, the challenger looks up the tuple* $(i', \mathsf{pk}', \mathsf{sk}') \leftarrow \mathsf{D}[c]$ *and replies to* $\mathcal{A}$ *with* sk'.
  - **Challenge phase:** *For each slot* $i \in [L]$, *adversary* $\mathcal{A}$ *must specify a tuple* $(c_i, S_i, \mathsf{pk}_i^*)$ *where either* $c_i \in \{1, \ldots, \mathsf{ctr}\}$ *to reference a challenger-generated key or* $c_i = \bot$ *to reference a key outside this set. The adversary also specifies a challenge policy* $P^* \in \mathcal{P}$ *and two messages* $\mu_0^*, \mu_1^* \in \mathcal{M}$. *The challenger responds by first constructing* pk_i *as follows:*
    * *If* $c_i \in \{1, \ldots, \mathsf{ctr}\}$, *then the challenger looks up the entry* $\mathsf{D}[c_i] = (i', \mathsf{pk}', \mathsf{sk}')$. *If* $i = i'$, *then the challenger sets* $\mathsf{pk}_i \leftarrow \mathsf{pk}'$. *Moreover, if the adversary previously issued a "corrupt identity" query on index* c_i, *then the challenger adds the slot index* i *to* $\mathcal{C}$. *Otherwise, if* $i \neq i'$, *then the experiment halts.*
    * *If* $c_i = \bot$, *then the challenger checks that* $\mathsf{IsValid}(\mathsf{crs}, i, \mathsf{pk}_i^*)$ *outputs* 1. *If not, the experiment halts. If the key is valid, the challenger sets* $\mathsf{pk}_i \leftarrow \mathsf{pk}_i^*$ *and adds the slot index* i *to* $\mathcal{C}$.
    The challenger computes $(\mathsf{mpk}, \mathsf{hsk}_1, \ldots, \mathsf{hsk}_L) \leftarrow \mathsf{Aggregate}(\mathsf{crs}, (\mathsf{pk}_1, S_1), \ldots, (\mathsf{pk}_L, S_L))$ *and replies with the challenge* $\mathsf{ct}^* \leftarrow \mathsf{Encrypt}(\mathsf{mpk}, P^*, \mu_b^*)$. *Note that because* Aggregate *is deterministic and can be run by* $\mathcal{A}$ *itself, there is no need to additionally provide* $(\mathsf{mpk}, \mathsf{hsk}_1, \ldots, \mathsf{hsk}_L)$ *to* $\mathcal{A}$. *Similarly, there is no advantage to allowing the adversary to select the challenge policy and messages after seeing the aggregated key.*
  - **Post-challenge query phase:** *Adversary* $\mathcal{A}$ *can now issue the following queries:*
    * **Corruption query:** *In a corruption query, the adversary specifies an index* $c \in \{1, \ldots, \mathsf{ctr}\}$. *In response the challenger looks up the tuple* $(i', \mathsf{pk}', \mathsf{sk}') \leftarrow \mathsf{D}[c]$ *and replies to* $\mathcal{A}$ *with* sk'. *Moreover, if the adversary registered a tuple of the form* (c, S, pk^*) *in the challenge phase for some choice of* $S \subseteq \mathcal{U}$ *and* pk^*, *then the challenger adds the slot index* $i' \in [L]$ *to* $\mathcal{C}$.

- **Output phase:** *At the end of the experiment, algorithm $\mathcal{A}$ outputs a bit $b' \in \{0, 1\}$, which is the output of the experiment.*

We say an adversary $\mathcal{A}$ is admissible if for all corrupted slot indices $i \in \mathcal{C}$, the set S_i does not satisfy P^* (i.e., the attributes associated with a corrupted slot does not satisfy the challenge policy). Finally, we say that a slotted registration-based encryption scheme is secure if for all polynomials $L = L(\lambda)$ and all efficient and admissible adversaries $\mathcal{A}$, there exists a negligible function $\mathsf{negl}(\cdot)$ such that for all $\lambda \in \mathbb{N}$,

$$|\Pr[b' = 1 : b = 0] - \Pr[b' = 1 : b = 1]| = \mathsf{negl}(\lambda)$$

in the above security experiment.

The security requirement in Definition 4.4 allows the adversary to issue additional corruption queries in a post-challenge query phase. However, as we show in the full version of this paper [24], it suffices to argue security in the simpler setting where there are no post-challenge queries. Security in the setting without post-challenge queries implies security in the setting with post-challenge queries.

5   Slotted Registered ABE from Pairings

In this section, we show how to construct a slotted registered ABE scheme for policies describable by a linear secret sharing scheme using composite-order bilinear maps.

5.1   Preliminaries: Composite-Order Pairing Groups

Our pairing-based construction of slotted registered ABE will rely on composite-order pairing groups [7]. We recall the formal definition below:

Definition 5.1 (Three-Prime Composite-Order Bilinear Group [7]). *A (symmetric) three-prime composite-order bilinear group generator is an efficient algorithm $\mathsf{CompGroupGen}$ that takes as input the security parameter λ and outputs a description $(\mathbb{G}, \mathbb{G}_T, p_1, p_2, p_3, g, e)$ of a bilinear group where p_1, p_2, p_3 are distinct primes, $\mathbb{G}$ and $\mathbb{G}_T$ are cyclic groups of order $N = p_1 p_2 p_3$, g is a generator of $\mathbb{G}$, and $e \colon \mathbb{G} \times \mathbb{G} \to \mathbb{G}_T$ is a non-degenerate bilinear map (called the "pairing"). We require that the group operation in $\mathbb{G}$ and $\mathbb{G}_T$ as well as the pairing operation be efficiently computable.*

Notation. Let $\mathbb{G}$ be a cyclic group with order $N = p_1 p_2 p_3$ and generator g. In the following, we will write $\mathbb{G}_1 = \langle g^{p_2 p_3} \rangle$ to denote the subgroup of $\mathbb{G}$ of order p_1. We define $\mathbb{G}_2$ and $\mathbb{G}_3$ analogously. By the Chinese Remainder Theorem, if g_1, g_2, g_3 are generators of $\mathbb{G}_1, \mathbb{G}_2, \mathbb{G}_3$, respectively, then $g_1 g_2 g_3 \in \mathbb{G}$ is a generator of $\mathbb{G}$, and moreover, every element $h \in \mathbb{G}$ can be *uniquely* written as $g_1^{x_1} g_2^{x_2} g_3^{x_3}$ where $x_1 \in \mathbb{Z}_{p_1}$, $x_2 \in \mathbb{Z}_{p_2}$, and $x_3 \in \mathbb{Z}_{p_3}$. In the following description, we will say $h \in \mathbb{G}$ has a non-trivial component in the $\mathbb{G}_i$ subgroup if $x_i \neq 0$.

Generalized subgroup assumptions. Security of our construction relies on several variants of the subgroup decision assumptions introduced by Lewko and Waters [31] for constructing adaptively-secure (hierarchical) identity-based encryption, and subsequently by Lewko et al. [30] for constructing adaptively-secure attribute-based encryption. The first two assumptions are special cases of the generalized subgroup decision assumption from Bellare et al. [5]. Lewko and Waters previously showed that all of the assumptions hold in the generic bilinear group model. Finally, we state a simple implication (Lemma 5.3) from [31] of the assumptions that will be useful in our security analysis.

Assumption 5.2 (Subgroup Decision Assumptions [31]). Let algorithm CompGroupGen be a three-prime composite-order bilinear group generator. Let $(\mathbb{G}, \mathbb{G}_T, p_1, p_2, p_3, g, e) \leftarrow \mathsf{CompGroupGen}(1^\lambda)$, $N = p_1 p_2 p_3$, $\mathcal{G} = (\mathbb{G}, \mathbb{G}_T, N, g, e)$, and $g_1 \xleftarrow{R} \mathbb{G}_1$, $g_2 \xleftarrow{R} \mathbb{G}_2$, and $g_3 \xleftarrow{R} \mathbb{G}_3$. We now define several pairs of distributions $\mathcal{D}_0, \mathcal{D}_1$ where each distribution $\mathcal{D}_b = (D, T_b)$ consists of a set of common components D and a challenge element T_b. We say that each assumption below holds with respect to CompGroupGen if for all efficient adversaries $\mathcal{A}$, there exists a negligible function $\mathsf{negl}(\cdot)$ such that for all $\lambda \in \mathbb{N}$,

$$|\Pr[\mathcal{A}(D, T_0) = 1] - \Pr[\mathcal{A}(D, T_1) = 1]| = \mathsf{negl}(\lambda).$$

Assumption 5.2a: Sample $r \xleftarrow{R} \mathbb{Z}_N$, and let

$$D = (\mathcal{G}, g_1, g_3), \qquad T_0 = g_1^r, \qquad T_1 = (g_1 g_2)^r.$$

Assumption 5.2b: Sample $s_{12}, s_{23}, r \xleftarrow{R} \mathbb{Z}_N$, and let

$$D = (\mathcal{G}, g_1, g_3, (g_1 g_2)^{s_{12}}, (g_2 g_3)^{s_{23}}), \qquad T_0 = (g_1 g_3)^r, \qquad T_1 = g^r.$$

Assumption 5.2c: Sample $\alpha, s, t_1, t_2, r \xleftarrow{R} \mathbb{Z}_N$, and let

$$D = (\mathcal{G}, g_1, g_2, g_3, g_1^\alpha g_2^{t_1}, g_1^s g_2^{t_2}), \qquad T_0 = e(g_1, g_1)^{\alpha s}, \qquad T_1 = e(g, g)^r.$$

Lemma 5.3 (Hardness of Factoring [31, Lemma 5]). *Let* CompGroupGen *be a composite-order bilinear group generator where Assumption 5.2b holds. Then, for all efficient adversaries $\mathcal{A}$, there exists a negligible function $\mathsf{negl}(\cdot)$ such that for all $\lambda \in \mathbb{N}$,*

$$\Pr \left[1 < \gcd(x, N) < N : \begin{array}{l} (\mathbb{G}, \mathbb{G}_T, p_1, p_2, p_3, g, e) \leftarrow \mathsf{CompGroupGen}(1^\lambda), \\ N \leftarrow p_1 p_2 p_3, \mathcal{G} \leftarrow (\mathbb{G}, \mathbb{G}_T, N, g, e), \\ g_1 \xleftarrow{R} \mathbb{G}_1, g_3 \xleftarrow{R} \mathbb{G}_3, s_{12}, s_{23} \xleftarrow{R} \mathbb{Z}_N \\ x \leftarrow \mathcal{A}(\mathcal{G}, g_1, g_3, (g_1 g_2)^{s_{12}}, (g_2 g_3)^{s_{23}}), \end{array} \right] = \mathsf{negl}(\lambda).$$

In words, given $(\mathcal{G}, g_1, g_3, (g_1 g_2)^{s_{12}}, (g_2 g_3)^{s_{23}})$, no efficient adversary can output a non-trivial factor of N.

5.2   Slotted Registered ABE from Composite-Order Pairing Groups

In this section, we show how to construct a slotted registered ABE scheme from composite-order pairing groups.

Construction 5.4 (Slotted Attribute-Based Registration-Based Encryption). Let CompGroupGen be a composite-order bilinear group generator, let $\mathcal{U} = \{\mathcal{U}_\lambda\}_{\lambda \in \mathbb{N}}$ be a (polynomial-size) attribute space, and let $\mathcal{P} = \{\mathcal{P}_\lambda\}_{\lambda \in \mathbb{N}}$ be a set of policies that can be described by a (one-use) linear secret sharing scheme (Definition 3.2 and Remark 3.3) over $\mathcal{U}$. We construct a slotted attribute-based registration-based encryption scheme $\Pi_{\mathsf{R\text{-}ABE}} = (\mathsf{Setup}, \mathsf{KeyGen}, \mathsf{IsValid}, \mathsf{Aggregate}, \mathsf{Encrypt}, \mathsf{Decrypt})$ with message space $\mathcal{M} = \mathbb{G}_T$, attribute space $\mathcal{U}$, and policy space $\mathcal{P}$ as follows:

– $\mathsf{Setup}(1^\lambda, 1^{|\mathcal{U}|}, 1^L)$: On input the security parameter λ, the size of the attribute space $\mathcal{U}$, and the number of slots L, the setup algorithm starts by sampling $(\mathbb{G}, \mathbb{G}_T, p_1, p_2, p_3, g, e) \leftarrow \mathsf{CompGroupGen}(1^\lambda)$. Let $\mathbb{G}_1, \mathbb{G}_2, \mathbb{G}_3$ be the subgroups of $\mathbb{G}$ of orders p_1, p_2, p_3, respectively. The setup algorithm now constructs the following quantities:

  • Let $N = p_1 p_2 p_3$ and let $\mathcal{G} = (\mathbb{G}, \mathbb{G}_T, N, g, e)$ be the (public) group description.

  • Sample generators $g_1 \xleftarrow{\mathrm{R}} \mathbb{G}_1$, $g_3 \xleftarrow{\mathrm{R}} \mathbb{G}_3$ and exponents $\alpha, \beta \xleftarrow{\mathrm{R}} \mathbb{Z}_N$. Let $h \leftarrow g_1^\beta$.

  • For each slot index $i \in [L]$, sample exponents $t_i, \delta_i \xleftarrow{\mathrm{R}} \mathbb{Z}_N$ and a slot blinding factor $\tau_i \xleftarrow{\mathrm{R}} \mathbb{Z}_N$. Construct the slot components as follows:

  $$A_i \leftarrow (g_1 g_3)^{t_i} \quad , \quad B_i \leftarrow g_1^\alpha A_i^\beta g_3^{\tau_i} \quad , \quad P_i \leftarrow (g_1 g_3)^{\delta_i}.$$

  Then, for each attribute $w \in \mathcal{U}$ and each slot $i \in [L]$, sample an exponent $u_{i,w} \xleftarrow{\mathrm{R}} \mathbb{Z}_N$, and for each $j \in [L]$ with $j \neq i$, sample a blinding factor $\gamma_{i,j,w} \xleftarrow{\mathrm{R}} \mathbb{Z}_N$. Construct the attribute components $U_{i,w}$ and $W_{i,j,w}$ as follows:

  $$U_{i,w} \leftarrow g_1^{u_{i,w}} \quad , \quad W_{i,j,w} \leftarrow A_i^{u_{j,w}} g_3^{\gamma_{i,j,w}}.$$

  • Finally, compute $Z \leftarrow e(g_1, g_1)^\alpha$ and output the common reference string

  $$\mathsf{crs} = \left(\mathcal{G}, Z, g_1, h, g_3, \{(A_i, B_i, P_i)\}_{i \in [L]}, \{U_{i,w}, W_{i,j,w}\}_{i \neq j, w \in \mathcal{U}}\right) \tag{5.1}$$

– $\mathsf{KeyGen}(\mathsf{crs}, i)$: On input the common reference string crs (with components given by Eq. (5.1)) and a slot index $i \in [L]$, the key-generation algorithm samples $r_i \xleftarrow{\mathrm{R}} \mathbb{Z}_N$ and computes

$$T_i \leftarrow g_1^{r_i} \quad , \quad Q_i \leftarrow P_i^{r_i} \quad , \quad R_i \leftarrow g_3^{r_i}.$$

Then for each $j \neq i$, it computes the cross terms $V_{j,i} \leftarrow A_j^{r_i}$. Finally, it outputs the public key pk_i and the secret key sk_i defined as follows:

$$\mathsf{pk}_i = (T_i, Q_i, R_i, \{V_{j,i}\}_{j \neq i}) \quad \text{and} \quad \mathsf{sk}_i = r_i.$$

Note that this particular key-generation algorithm does *not* depend on the set of attributes.

- IsValid(crs, i, pk$_i$): On input the common reference string crs (with components given by Eq. (5.1)), a slot index $i \in [L]$, and a purported public key pk$_i$ = $(T_i, Q_i, R_i, \{V_{j,i}\}_{j \neq i})$, the key-validation algorithm first affirms that each of the components in pk$_i$ is a valid group element (i.e., an element in $\mathbb{G}$). If so, it then checks

$$e(g_3, T_i) = 1 = e(g_1, R_i) \quad \text{and} \quad e(T_i, P_i) = e(g_1, Q_i)$$
$$\text{and} \quad e(R_i, P_i) = e(g_3, Q_i).$$

Next, for each $j \neq i$, the algorithm checks that

$$e(g_1, V_{j,i}) = e(T_i, A_j) \quad \text{and} \quad e(g_3, V_{j,i}) = e(R_i, A_j).$$

If all checks pass, it outputs 1; otherwise, it outputs 0.
- Aggregate(crs, (pk$_1$, S_1), ..., (pk$_L$, S_L)): On input the common reference string crs (with components given by Eq. (5.1)), a collection of L public keys pk$_i$ = $(T_i, Q_i, R_i, \{V_{j,i}\}_{j \neq i})$ together with their attribute sets $S_i \subseteq \mathcal{U}$, the aggregation algorithm starts by computing the attribute-independent public key $\hat{T}$ and the attribute-independent slot key $\hat{V}_i$ for each $i \in [L]$:

$$\hat{T} = \prod_{j \in [L]} T_j \quad , \quad \hat{V}_i = \prod_{j \neq i} V_{i,j}.$$

Next, for each attribute $w \in \mathcal{U}$, it computes the attribute-specific public key $\hat{U}_w$ and the attribute-specific slot key $\hat{W}_{i,w}$ for each $i \in [L]$:

$$\hat{U}_w = \prod_{j \in [L] : w \notin S_j} U_{j,w} \quad , \quad \hat{W}_{i,w} = \prod_{j \neq i : w \notin S_j} W_{i,j,w}$$

Finally, it outputs the master public key mpk and the slot-specific helper decryption keys hsk$_i$ where

$$\mathsf{mpk} = (\mathcal{G}, g_1, h, Z, \hat{T}, \{\hat{U}_w\}_{w \in \mathcal{U}}) \quad \text{and}$$
$$\mathsf{hsk}_i = (\mathsf{mpk}, i, S_i, A_i, B_i, \hat{V}_i, \{\hat{W}_{i,w}\}_{w \in \mathcal{U}}).$$

- Encrypt(mpk, $(\mathbf{M}, \rho), \mu$): On input the master public key mpk = $(\mathcal{G}, g_1, h, Z, \hat{T}, \{\hat{U}_w\}_{w \in \mathcal{U}})$, a policy $(\mathbf{M}, \rho)$ where $\mathbf{M} \in \mathbb{Z}_p^{K \times n}$ and $\rho \colon [K] \to \mathcal{U}$ is an injective row-labeling function, and a message $\mu \in \mathbb{G}_T$, the encryption algorithm starts by sampling a secret exponent $s \xleftarrow{R} \mathbb{Z}_N$ and $h_1, h_2 \xleftarrow{R} \mathbb{G}_1$ such that $h = h_1 h_2$. Then, it constructs the ciphertext components as follows:
  - **Message-embedding components:** First, let $C_1 \leftarrow \mu \cdot Z^s$ and $C_2 \leftarrow g_1^s$.
  - **Attribute-specific component:** Sample $v_2, \ldots, v_n \xleftarrow{R} \mathbb{Z}_N$ for the linear secret sharing scheme and let $\mathbf{v} = [s, v_2, \ldots, v_n]^{\mathsf{T}}$. For each $k \in [K]$, set $C_{3,k} \leftarrow h_2^{\mathbf{m}_k^{\mathsf{T}} \mathbf{v}} \hat{U}_{\rho(k)}^{-s}$, where $\mathbf{m}_k^{\mathsf{T}} \in \mathbb{Z}_p^n$ denotes the kth row of $\mathbf{M}$.
  - **Slot-specific component:** Set $C_4 \leftarrow h_1^s \hat{T}^{-s}$.

  It then outputs the ciphertext

$$\mathsf{ct} = ((\mathbf{M}, \rho), C_1, C_2, \{C_{3,k}\}_{k \in [K]}, C_4).$$

- Decrypt(sk, hsk, ct): On input the secret key sk $= r$, the helper key hsk $=$ $(\mathsf{mpk}, i, S_i, A_i, B_i, \hat{V}_i, \{\hat{W}_{i,w}\}_{w \in \mathcal{U}})$, where mpk $= (\mathcal{G}, g_1, h, Z, \hat{T}, \{\hat{U}_w\}_{w \in \mathcal{U}})$, and the ciphertext ct $= ((\mathbf{M}, \rho), C_1, C_2, \{C_{3,k}\}_{k \in [K]}, C_4)$ where $\mathbf{M} \in \mathbb{Z}_p^{K \times n}$ and $\rho \colon [K] \to \mathcal{U}$ is an injective row-labeling function, the decryption algorithm proceeds as follows:
  - If the set of attributes S_i is not authorized by $(\mathbf{M}, \rho)$, then the decryption algorithm outputs $\perp$.
  - Otherwise, let $I = \{k \in [K] : \rho(k) \in S_i\}$ be the indices of the rows of $\mathbf{M}$ associated with the attributes $S_i \subseteq \mathcal{U}$. Write the elements as $I = \{k_1, \ldots, k_{|I|}\}$.
  - Let $\mathbf{M}_{S_i}$ be the matrix formed by taking the subset of rows in $\mathbf{M}$ indexed by I. Since S_i is authorized, let $\boldsymbol{\omega}_{S_i} \in \mathbb{Z}_N^{|I|}$ be a vector such that $\boldsymbol{\omega}_{S_i}^\mathsf{T} \mathbf{M}_{S_i} = \mathbf{e}_1^\mathsf{T}$.
  - Then, compute and output the message μ computed as follows:

$$D_{\mathsf{slot}} = e(C_4, A_i) \cdot e(C_2, A_i^r \hat{V}_i)$$

$$D_{\mathsf{attrib}} = \prod_{1 \le j \le |I|} \left(e(C_{3,k_j}, A_i) \cdot e(C_2, \hat{W}_{i,\rho(k_j)}) \right)^{\omega_{S_i, j}}$$

$$\mu = C_1 \cdot D_{\mathsf{slot}} \cdot D_{\mathsf{attrib}} / e(C_2, B_i).$$

We will refer to D_{slot} as the *slot-specific* decryption component and D_{attrib} as the *attribute-specific* decryption component.

Correctness and Security Analysis. We provide the correctness and security analysis in the full version of this paper [24]. Taken together, we obtain the following corollary:

Corollary 5.5 (Slotted Registered ABE from Pairings). *Let λ be a security parameter, $L = L(\lambda)$ be the number of slots, and $\mathcal{M}, \mathcal{U}, \mathcal{P}$, be the message space, attribute space, and policy space from Construction 5.4, respectively. Assuming Assumption 5.2 holds with respect to* CompGroupGen, *Construction 5.4 is a secure slotted registered ABE scheme with the following efficiency properties:*

- *The size of the CRS is $L^2 \cdot |\mathcal{U}| \cdot \mathsf{poly}(\lambda)$.*
- *The size of the master public key* mpk *and each helper decryption key* hsk_i *for any slot $i \in [L]$ is $|\mathcal{U}| \cdot \mathsf{poly}(\lambda)$. Notably, this is independent of the number of slots (i.e., registered users).*
- *The size of a ciphertext associated with policy $P = (\mathbf{M}, \rho) \in \mathcal{P}$ is $|P| \cdot \mathsf{poly}(\lambda)$.*

6   From Slotted Registered ABE to Registered ABE

In this section, we show how to generically transform a slotted registered ABE scheme (Definition 4.4) to a standard registered ABE scheme (Definition 4.1). We refer to Sect. 2 for an overview of thhe construction.

Construction 6.1 (Slotted Registered ABE to Registered ABE).
Let λ be a security parameter. Let $\Pi_{\mathsf{sRBE}} = (\mathsf{sRBE.Setup}, \mathsf{sRBE.KeyGen},$
$\mathsf{sRBE.IsValid}, \mathsf{sRBE.Aggregate}, \mathsf{sRBE.Encrypt}, \mathsf{sRBE.Decrypt})$ be a slotted registered ABE scheme with attribute universe $\mathcal{U} = \{\mathcal{U}_\lambda\}_{\lambda \in \mathbb{N}}$, policy space $\mathcal{P} =$
$\{\mathcal{P}_\lambda\}_{\lambda \in \mathbb{N}}$, and message space $\mathcal{M} = \{\mathcal{M}_\lambda\}_{\lambda \in \mathbb{N}}$. We now construct a registered
ABE scheme $\Pi_{\mathsf{R\text{-}ABE}} = (\mathsf{Setup}, \mathsf{KeyGen}, \mathsf{RegPK}, \mathsf{Encrypt}, \mathsf{Update}, \mathsf{Decrypt})$ that
supports a bounded number of users and over the same attribute space $\mathcal{U}$, pol-
icy space $\mathcal{P}$, and message space $\mathcal{M}$ as follows. In the description, we adopt the
following conventions:

- Without loss of generality, we assume that the bound on the number of users
  $L = 2^\ell$ is a power of two. Rounding the bound to the next power of two incurs
  at most a factor of 2 overhead.
- The registered ABE scheme will internally maintain $\ell + 1$ slotted ABE
  schemes, where the kth scheme is a slotted scheme with 2^k slots (for $k \in [0, \ell]$).
- The auxiliary data $\mathsf{aux} = (\mathsf{ctr}, \mathsf{D}_1, \mathsf{D}_2, \mathsf{mpk})$ consists of the following compo-
  nents:
  - A counter ctr that keeps track of the number of registered users in the
    system.
  - A dictionary D_1 that maps a scheme index $k \in [0, \ell]$ and a slot index
    $i \in [2^k]$ to a pair (pk, S) which specifies the public key and attribute set
    currently assigned to slot i of scheme k.
  - A dictionary D_2 that maps a scheme index $k \in [0, \ell]$ and a user index
    $i \in [L]$ to the helper decryption key associated with scheme k and user i.
  - The current master public key $\mathsf{mpk} = (\mathsf{ctr}, \mathsf{mpk}_0, \dots, \mathsf{mpk}_\ell)$.
  If $\mathsf{aux} = \bot$, we parse it as $(\mathsf{ctr}, \mathsf{D}_1, \mathsf{D}_2, \mathsf{mpk})$ where $\mathsf{ctr} = 0$, $\mathsf{D}_1, \mathsf{D}_2 = \varnothing$, and
  $\mathsf{mpk} = (0, \bot, \dots, \bot)$. This corresponds to a fresh scheme with no registered
  users.

We construct our registered ABE scheme as follows:

- $\mathsf{Setup}(1^\lambda, 1^{|\mathcal{U}|}, 1^L)$: On input the security parameter λ, the attribute universe
  $\mathcal{U}$, and a bound on number of registrants $L = 2^\ell$, the setup algorithm runs
  the setup algorithm for $\ell + 1$ copies of the slotted RBE scheme. Specifically,
  for each $k \in [0, \ell]$, it samples $\mathsf{crs}_k \leftarrow \mathsf{sRBE.Setup}(1^\lambda, 1^{|\mathcal{U}|}, 1^{2^k})$ and outputs
  $\mathsf{crs} = (\mathsf{crs}_0, \dots, \mathsf{crs}_\ell)$.
- $\mathsf{KeyGen}(\mathsf{crs}, \mathsf{aux})$: On input the common reference string $\mathsf{crs} = (\mathsf{crs}_0, \dots, \mathsf{crs}_\ell)$
  and the auxiliary data $\mathsf{aux} = (\mathsf{ctr}, \mathsf{D}_1, \mathsf{D}_2, \mathsf{mpk})$, the key-generation algorithm
  generates a public/secret key-pair for each of the $\ell + 1$ underlying schemes.
  Specifically, for each $k \in [0, \ell]$, let $i_k \leftarrow (\mathsf{ctr} \bmod 2^k) + 1 \in [2^k]$ be a slot index
  for the kth scheme, and sample a key $(\mathsf{pk}_k, \mathsf{sk}_k) \leftarrow \mathsf{sRBE.KeyGen}(\mathsf{crs}_k, i_k)$.
  Output $\mathsf{pk} = (\mathsf{ctr}, \mathsf{pk}_0, \dots, \mathsf{pk}_\ell)$ and $\mathsf{sk} = (\mathsf{ctr}, \mathsf{sk}_0, \dots, \mathsf{sk}_\ell)$.
- $\mathsf{RegPK}(\mathsf{crs}, \mathsf{aux}, \mathsf{pk}, S_{\mathsf{pk}})$: On input the common reference string $\mathsf{crs} =$
  $(\mathsf{crs}_0, \dots, \mathsf{crs}_\ell)$, the auxiliary data $\mathsf{aux} = (\mathsf{ctr}_{\mathsf{aux}}, \mathsf{D}_1, \mathsf{D}_2, \mathsf{mpk})$, where $\mathsf{mpk} =$
  $(\mathsf{ctr}_{\mathsf{aux}}, \mathsf{mpk}_0, \dots, \mathsf{mpk}_\ell)$, a public key $\mathsf{pk} = (\mathsf{ctr}_{\mathsf{pk}}, \mathsf{pk}_0, \dots, \mathsf{pk}_\ell)$, and an associated set of attributes S_{pk}, the registration algorithm proceeds as follows:

- For each $k \in [0, \ell]$, let $i_k = (\mathsf{ctr_{aux}} \bmod 2^k) + 1 \in [2^k]$ be the slot index for the kth scheme.
- For each $k \in [0, \ell]$, check that $\mathsf{sRBE.IsValid}(\mathsf{crs}_k, i_k, \mathsf{pk}_k) = 1$. In addition, check that $\mathsf{ctr_{aux}} = \mathsf{ctr_{pk}}$. If any check fails, the algorithm halts and outputs the current auxiliary data aux and master public key mpk.
- Then for each $k \in [0, \ell]$, the registration algorithm updates $\mathsf{D}_1[k, i_k] \leftarrow (\mathsf{pk}, S_{\mathsf{pk}})$. In addition, if $i_k = 2^k$ (i.e., all of the slots in scheme k are filled), the registration algorithm additionally does the following:
  * Compute $\big(\mathsf{mpk}_k', \mathsf{hsk}_{k,1}', \ldots, \mathsf{hsk}_{k,2^k}'\big)$ as

$$\mathsf{sRBE.Aggregate}\big(\mathsf{crs}_k, \mathsf{D}_1[k, 1], \ldots, \mathsf{D}_1[k, 2^k]\big).$$

  * Update $\mathsf{D}_2[\mathsf{ctr} + 1 - 2^k + i, k] \leftarrow \mathsf{hsk}_{k,i}'$ for each $i \in [2^k]$.
  * If $i_k \neq 2^k$, $\mathsf{mpk}_k' = \mathsf{mpk}_k$ is unchanged.
- Define the new master public key $\mathsf{mpk}' = (\mathsf{ctr_{aux}} + 1, \mathsf{mpk}_0', \ldots, \mathsf{mpk}_\ell')$.
- Finally, the registration algorithm outputs the new master public key mpk' and auxiliary data $\mathsf{aux}' = (\mathsf{ctr_{aux}} + 1, \mathsf{D}_1, \mathsf{D}_2, \mathsf{mpk}')$.
- $\mathsf{Encrypt}(\mathsf{mpk}, P, \mu)$: On input the master public key $\mathsf{mpk} = (\mathsf{ctr}, \mathsf{mpk}_0, \ldots, \mathsf{mpk}_\ell)$, the access policy $P \in \mathcal{P}$, and a message $\mu \in \mathcal{M}$, the encryption algorithm computes $\mathsf{ct}_k \leftarrow \mathsf{sRBE.Encrypt}(\mathsf{mpk}_k, P, \mu)$ for each $k \in [0, \ell]$; if $\mathsf{mpk}_k = \bot$, then it sets $\mathsf{ct}_k \leftarrow \bot$. Then it outputs $\mathsf{ct} = (\mathsf{ctr}, \mathsf{ct}_0, \ldots, \mathsf{ct}_\ell)$.
- $\mathsf{Update}(\mathsf{crs}, \mathsf{aux}, \mathsf{pk})$: On input $\mathsf{crs} = (\mathsf{crs}_0, \ldots, \mathsf{crs}_\ell)$, the auxiliary data $\mathsf{aux} = (\mathsf{ctr_{aux}}, \mathsf{D}_1, \mathsf{D}_2, \mathsf{mpk})$, and a public key $\mathsf{pk} = (\mathsf{ctr_{pk}}, \mathsf{pk}_0, \ldots, \mathsf{pk}_\ell)$, the update algorithm outputs $\bot$ if $\mathsf{ctr_{pk}} \geq \mathsf{ctr_{aux}}$. Otherwise, for each $k \in [0, \ell]$, it sets $\mathsf{hsk}_k \leftarrow \mathsf{D}_2[\mathsf{ctr_{pk}} + 1, k]$ and replies with $\mathsf{hsk} = (\mathsf{hsk}_0, \ldots, \mathsf{hsk}_\ell)$.
- $\mathsf{Decrypt}(\mathsf{sk}, \mathsf{hsk}, \mathsf{ct})$: On input a secret key $\mathsf{sk} = (\mathsf{ctr_{sk}}, \mathsf{sk}_0, \ldots, \mathsf{sk}_\ell)$, a helper key $\mathsf{hsk} = (\mathsf{hsk}_0, \ldots, \mathsf{hsk}_\ell)$, and a ciphertext $\mathsf{ct} = (\mathsf{ctr_{ct}}, \mathsf{ct}_0, \ldots, \mathsf{ct}_\ell)$, the decryption algorithm outputs $\bot$ if $\mathsf{ctr_{ct}} \leq \mathsf{ctr_{sk}}$. Otherwise, it computes the largest index k on which ctr and ctr' differ (where bits are 0-indexed starting from the least significant bit). If $\mathsf{hsk}_k = \bot$, then the decryption algorithm outputs $\mathsf{GetUpdate}$. Otherwise, it outputs $\mathsf{sRBE.Decrypt}(\mathsf{sk}_k, \mathsf{hsk}_k, \mathsf{ct}_k)$.

We give the full analysis of Construction 6.1 in the full version of this paper [24]. Combining Construction 6.1 with Construction 5.4, we now obtain the following corollary:

Corollary 6.2 (Bounded Registered ABE from Pairings). *Let λ be a security parameter. Let $\mathcal{U} = \{\mathcal{U}_\lambda\}_{\lambda \in \mathbb{N}}$ be any (polynomial-size) attribute space, and let $\mathcal{P} = \{\mathcal{P}_\lambda\}_{\lambda \in \mathbb{N}}$ be a set of policies that can be described by a one-use linear secret sharing scheme over $\mathcal{U}$. Then, under Assumption 5.2, for every polynomial $L = L(\lambda)$, there exists a bounded registered ABE scheme with attribute universe $\mathcal{U}$, policy space $\mathcal{P}$, and supporting up to L users with the following properties:*

- *The size of the CRS and the size of the auxiliary data maintained by the key curator is $L^2 \cdot \mathsf{poly}(\lambda, |\mathcal{U}|, \log L)$.*
- *The running time of key-generation and registration is $L \cdot \mathsf{poly}(\lambda, |\mathcal{U}|, \log L)$.*

- The size of the master public key and the helper decryption keys are both $|\mathcal{U}| \cdot \mathsf{poly}(\lambda, \log L)$.
- The size of a ciphertext is $K \cdot \mathsf{poly}(\lambda, \log L)$, where K denotes the number of rows in the linear secret sharing matrix $\mathbf{M}$ associated with the access policy.

Remark 6.3 (Efficiency Preserving). Our transformation in Construction 6.1 preserves the efficiency of the underlying slotted registered ABE scheme with respect to the following properties:

- **Large universe:** If the underlying slotted registered ABE scheme supports a large universe (i.e., $|\mathcal{U}| = 2^{\omega(\log \lambda)}$), then the transformed scheme also supports a large universe. As discussed in the full version of this paper [24], we would formally model this by having the Setup algorithm take as input the *bit-length* of the attributes rather than the size of the attribute space in both the slotted scheme and the full scheme. Our obfuscation-based construction in Sect. 7 (Construction 7.1) supports a large universe.
- **Arbitrary number of users:** If the running time of Setup in the underlying slotted scheme is *polylogarithmic* in the bound on the number of users L, then the running time of Setup in the transformed scheme is also polylogarithmic in the number of users L. Note that if Setup runs in time that is polylogarithmic in L, the size of the CRS must also be polylogarithmic in L. In this case, we can set $L = 2^\lambda$ to support an arbitrary polynomial number of users. Formally, we would model this setting by having Setup take the bound L in *binary* rather than unary in both the slotted scheme and the full registered ABE scheme. While our pairing-based construction (Construction 5.4) does not support this notion, our obfuscation-based construction (Construction 7.1) does.

7   Registered ABE from Indistinguishability Obfuscation

In this section, we show how to build a registered ABE scheme that does *not* impose an a priori bound on the number of users in the system (in contrast to the pairing-based construction from Sect. 5 (Corollaries 5.5 and 6.2)) using indistinguishability obfuscation ($i\mathcal{O}$) [3,17], a somewhere statistically binding (SSB) hash function [25] and a pseudorandom generator (PRG). We refer to the full version of this paper [24] for formal definitions of these notions. Our approach is similar to but generalizes the RBE construction of Garg et al. [18] which uses $i\mathcal{O}$, SSB hash functions and public-key encryption.

Construction 7.1 (Slotted Registered ABE from iO). Let λ be a security parameter. Let $\mathsf{PRG} \colon \{0,1\}^\lambda \to \{0,1\}^{2\lambda}$ be a length-doubling pseudorandom function. Let $\ell_c = \ell_c(\lambda)$ be the attribute length and let $\mathcal{U} = \{0,1\}^{\ell_c}$ be the attribute space. Let $\mathcal{P} = \{\mathcal{P}_\lambda\}$ be a family of Boolean circuits on inputs of length ℓ_c. Let $\Pi_{\mathsf{SSB}} = (\mathsf{SSB.Setup}, \mathsf{SSB.Hash}, \mathsf{SSB.Open}, \mathsf{SSB.Verify})$ be a somewhere statistically binding hash function. We construct a slotted registered attribute-based encryption scheme $\Pi_{\mathsf{sRBE}} = (\mathsf{Setup}, \mathsf{KeyGen}, \mathsf{IsValid}, \mathsf{Aggregate}, \mathsf{Encrypt}, \mathsf{Decrypt})$ with message space $\mathcal{M} = \{0,1\}^\lambda$, attribute space $\mathcal{U}$, and policy space $\mathcal{P}$ as follows:

- Setup($1^\lambda, 1^{\ell_c}, L$): On input the security parameter λ, the bit-length ℓ_c of the attributes, and the number of users L (in *binary*), the setup algorithm sets $\ell_{\mathsf{blk}} = 2\lambda + \ell_c$ and samples a hash key $\mathsf{hk} \leftarrow \mathsf{SSB.Setup}(1^\lambda, 1^{\ell_{\mathsf{blk}}}, L, 1)$. It outputs $\mathsf{crs} \leftarrow \mathsf{hk}$.
- KeyGen(crs, i): On input the common reference string $\mathsf{crs} = \mathsf{hk}$, the key-generation algorithm samples a random seed $s \leftarrow \{0,1\}^\lambda$. It outputs the public key $\mathsf{pk} = \mathsf{PRG}(s)$ and the secret key $\mathsf{sk} = s$.
- IsValid($\mathsf{crs}, i, \mathsf{pk}_i$): On input the common reference string crs, an index i, and a public key pk, the validation algorithm outputs 1 if $\mathsf{pk} \in \{0,1\}^{2\lambda}$.
- Aggregate($\mathsf{crs}, (\mathsf{pk}_1, S_1) \ldots, (\mathsf{pk}_L, S_L)$): On input the common reference string $\mathsf{crs} = \mathsf{hk}$ and a collection of public keys pk_i along with their associated attributes $S_i \in \{0,1\}^{\ell_c}$, the aggregation algorithm computes the master public key

$$\mathsf{mpk} \leftarrow \left(\mathsf{hk}, \mathsf{SSB.Hash}\left(\mathsf{hk}, ((\mathsf{pk}_1, S_1), \ldots, (\mathsf{pk}_L, S_L))\right)\right).$$

Here we treat each pair (pk_i, S_i) as a binary string of length $\{0,1\}^{2\lambda + \ell_c}$, which is the length of an SSB hash block. Then, for each user $i \in [L]$, the aggregate algorithm computes

$$\pi_i \leftarrow \mathsf{SSB.Open}\left(\mathsf{hk}, ((\mathsf{pk}_1, S_1), \ldots, (\mathsf{pk}_L, S_L)), i\right),$$

which is the local opening of the SSB hash for index i, and sets the helper secret key to $\mathsf{hsk}_i \leftarrow (i, \mathsf{pk}_i, S_i, \pi_i)$. Finally, it outputs mpk and hsk_i for all $i \in [L]$.
- Encrypt(mpk, C, μ): On input the master public key $\mathsf{mpk} = (\mathsf{hk}, h)$, the ciphertext policy $C \in \mathcal{P}$ and a message $\mu \in \{0,1\}^\lambda$, the encryption algorithm sets $j = 0$ and defines the following program:

Constants: $\mathsf{mpk} = (\mathsf{hk}, h)$, Boolean circuit $C: \{0,1\}^{\ell_c} \to \{0,1\}$, message $\mu \in \{0,1\}^\lambda$, index $j \in [0, L+1]$
Inputs: index $i \in [L]$, public key $\mathsf{pk}_i \in \{0,1\}^{2\lambda}$, attribute $S_i \in \{0,1\}^{\ell_c}$, opening $\pi_i \in \{0,1\}^{\ell_{\mathsf{open}}}$, and secret key $\mathsf{sk}_i \in \{0,1\}^\lambda$.

1. If $\mathsf{SSB.Verify}(\mathsf{hk}, h, i, (\mathsf{pk}_i, S_i), \pi_i) = 1$ and $C(S_i) = 1$ and $\mathsf{pk}_i = \mathsf{PRG}(\mathsf{sk}_i)$ and $i > j$, output μ.
2. Otherwise, output $\perp$.

Fig. 1: Program $\mathsf{Embed}[\mathsf{mpk}, C, \mu, j]$.

Here we assume that the circuit $\mathsf{Embed}[\mathsf{mpk}, C, \mu, j]$ is padded to the maximum size of any program appearing in the proof (Fig. 1). The encryption algorithm then computes the obfuscated program $C' \leftarrow i\mathcal{O}(\mathsf{Embed}[\mathsf{mpk}, C, \mu, j])$ and outputs $\mathsf{ct} = C'$.
- Decrypt($\mathsf{sk}, \mathsf{hsk}, \mathsf{ct}$): On input the the secret key sk, the helper secret key $\mathsf{hsk} = (i, \mathsf{pk}_i, S_i, \pi_i)$, and a ciphertext $\mathsf{ct} = C'$, the decryption algorithm outputs $C'(i, \mathsf{pk}_i, S_i, \pi_i, \mathsf{sk})$.

We defer the correctness and security analysis of Construction 7.1 to the full version of this paper [24].

Acknowledgments. We thank the Eurocrypt reviewers for helpful feedback on the presentation. Susan Hohenberger is supported by NSF CNS-1908181, the Office of Naval Research N00014-19-1-2294, and a Packard Foundation Subaward via UT Austin. Brent Waters is supported by NSF CNS-1908611, a Simons Investigator award, and the Packard Foundation Fellowship. David J. Wu is supported by NSF CNS-2151131, NSF CNS-2140975, a Microsoft Research Faculty Fellowship, and a Google Research Scholar award.

References

1. Al-Riyami, S.S., Paterson, K.G.: Certificateless public key cryptography. In: Laih, C.-S. (ed.) ASIACRYPT 2003. LNCS, vol. 2894, pp. 452–473. Springer, Heidelberg (2003). https://doi.org/10.1007/978-3-540-40061-5_29

2. Barak, B., et al.: On the (Im)possibility of obfuscating programs. In: Kilian, J. (ed.) CRYPTO 2001. LNCS, vol. 2139, pp. 1–18. Springer, Heidelberg (2001). https://doi.org/10.1007/3-540-44647-8_1

3. Barak, B., et al.: On the (im)possibility of obfuscating programs. J. ACM **59**(2), 1–48 (2012)

4. Beimel, A.: Secure Schemes for Secret Sharing and Key Distribution. Ph.D. thesis, Technion (1996)

5. Bellare, M., Waters, B., Yilek, S.: Identity-based encryption secure against selective opening attack. In: Ishai, Y. (ed.) TCC 2011. LNCS, vol. 6597, pp. 235–252. Springer, Heidelberg (2011). https://doi.org/10.1007/978-3-642-19571-6_15

6. Boneh, D., Franklin, M.: Identity-based encryption from the Weil pairing. In: Kilian, J. (ed.) CRYPTO 2001. LNCS, vol. 2139, pp. 213–229. Springer, Heidelberg (2001). https://doi.org/10.1007/3-540-44647-8_13

7. Boneh, D., Goh, E.-J., Nissim, K.: Evaluating 2-DNF formulas on ciphertexts. In: Kilian, J. (ed.) TCC 2005. LNCS, vol. 3378, pp. 325–341. Springer, Heidelberg (2005). https://doi.org/10.1007/978-3-540-30576-7_18

8. Catalano, D., Fiore, D.: Vector commitments and their applications. In: Kurosawa, K., Hanaoka, G. (eds.) PKC 2013. LNCS, vol. 7778, pp. 55–72. Springer, Heidelberg (2013). https://doi.org/10.1007/978-3-642-36362-7_5

9. Chase, M.: Multi-authority attribute based encryption. In: Vadhan, S.P. (ed.) TCC 2007. LNCS, vol. 4392, pp. 515–534. Springer, Heidelberg (2007). https://doi.org/10.1007/978-3-540-70936-7_28

10. Chase, M., Chow, S.S.M.: Improving privacy and security in multi-authority attribute-based encryption. In: ACM CCS (2009)

11. Chen, L., Harrison, K., Soldera, D., Smart, N.P.: Applications of multiple trust authorities in pairing based cryptosystems. In: Davida, G., Frankel, Y., Rees, O. (eds.) InfraSec 2002. LNCS, vol. 2437, pp. 260–275. Springer, Heidelberg (2002). https://doi.org/10.1007/3-540-45831-X_18

12. Cocks, C.: An identity based encryption scheme based on quadratic residues. In: Honary, B. (ed.) Cryptography and Coding 2001. LNCS, vol. 2260, pp. 360–363. Springer, Heidelberg (2001). https://doi.org/10.1007/3-540-45325-3_32

13. Cong, K., Eldefrawy, K., Smart, N.P.: Optimizing registration based encryption. In: Paterson, M.B. (ed.) IMACC 2021. LNCS, vol. 13129, pp. 129–157. Springer, Cham (2021). https://doi.org/10.1007/978-3-030-92641-0_7

14. Datta, P., Komargodski, I., Waters, B.: Decentralized multi-authority ABE for DNFs from LWE. In: Canteaut, A., Standaert, F.-X. (eds.) EUROCRYPT 2021. LNCS, vol. 12696, pp. 177–209. Springer, Cham (2021). https://doi.org/10.1007/978-3-030-77870-5_7

15. Datta, P., Komargodski, I., Waters, B.: Decentralized multi-authority ABE for nc^1 from computational-bdh. IACR Cryptol. ePrint Arch. (2021)

16. Fiat, A., Shamir, A.: How to prove yourself: practical solutions to identification and signature problems. In: Odlyzko, A.M. (ed.) CRYPTO 1986. LNCS, vol. 263, pp. 186–194. Springer, Heidelberg (1987). https://doi.org/10.1007/3-540-47721-7_12

17. Garg, S., Gentry, C., Halevi, S., Raykova, M., Sahai, A., Waters, B.: Candidate indistinguishability obfuscation and functional encryption for all circuits. In: FOCS (2013)

18. Garg, S., Hajiabadi, M., Mahmoody, M., Rahimi, A.: Registration-based encryption: removing private-key generator from IBE. In: Beimel, A., Dziembowski, S. (eds.) TCC 2018. LNCS, vol. 11239, pp. 689–718. Springer, Cham (2018). https://doi.org/10.1007/978-3-030-03807-6_25

19. Garg, S., Hajiabadi, M., Mahmoody, M., Rahimi, A., Sekar, S.: Registration-based encryption from standard assumptions. In: Lin, D., Sako, K. (eds.) PKC 2019. LNCS, vol. 11443, pp. 63–93. Springer, Cham (2019). https://doi.org/10.1007/978-3-030-17259-6_3

20. Goyal, R., Vusirikala, S.: Verifiable registration-based encryption. In: Micciancio, D., Ristenpart, T. (eds.) CRYPTO 2020. LNCS, vol. 12170, pp. 621–651. Springer, Cham (2020). https://doi.org/10.1007/978-3-030-56784-2_21

21. Goyal, V.: Reducing trust in the PKG in identity based cryptosystems. In: Menezes, A. (ed.) CRYPTO 2007. LNCS, vol. 4622, pp. 430–447. Springer, Heidelberg (2007). https://doi.org/10.1007/978-3-540-74143-5_24

22. Goyal, V., Lu, S., Sahai, A., Waters, B.: Black-box accountable authority identity-based encryption. In: ACM CCS (2008)

23. Goyal, V., Pandey, O., Sahai, A., Waters, B.: Attribute-based encryption for fine-grained access control of encrypted data. In: ACM CCS (2006)

24. Hohenberger, S., Lu, G., Waters, B., Wu, D.J.: Registered attribute-based encryption. IACR Cryptol. ePrint Arch. (2022)

25. Hubácek, P., Wichs, D.: On the communication complexity of secure function evaluation with long output. In: ITCS (2015)

26. Jain, A., Lin, H., Sahai, A.: Indistinguishability obfuscation from well-founded assumptions. In: STOC (2021)

27. Jain, A., Lin, H., Sahai, A.: Indistinguishability obfuscation from LPN over $\mathbb{F}_p$, dlin, and prgs in nc^0. In: Dunkelman, O., Dziembowski, S. (eds.) EUROCRYPT 2022. Lecture Notes in Computer Science, vol. 13275, pp. 670–699. Springer, Cham (2022). https://doi.org/10.1007/978-3-031-06944-4_23

28. Kate, A., Goldberg, I.: Distributed private-key generators for identity-based cryptography. In: Garay, J.A., De Prisco, R. (eds.) SCN 2010. LNCS, vol. 6280, pp. 436–453. Springer, Heidelberg (2010). https://doi.org/10.1007/978-3-642-15317-4_27

29. Lai, R.W.F., Malavolta, G.: Subvector commitments with application to succinct arguments. In: Boldyreva, A., Micciancio, D. (eds.) CRYPTO 2019. LNCS, vol. 11692, pp. 530–560. Springer, Cham (2019). https://doi.org/10.1007/978-3-030-26948-7_19

30. Lewko, A., Okamoto, T., Sahai, A., Takashima, K., Waters, B.: Fully secure functional encryption: attribute-based encryption and (hierarchical) inner product encryption. In: Gilbert, H. (ed.) EUROCRYPT 2010. LNCS, vol. 6110, pp. 62–91. Springer, Heidelberg (2010). https://doi.org/10.1007/978-3-642-13190-5_4

31. Lewko, A., Waters, B.: New techniques for dual system encryption and fully secure HIBE with short ciphertexts. In: Micciancio, D. (ed.) TCC 2010. LNCS, vol. 5978, pp. 455–479. Springer, Heidelberg (2010). https://doi.org/10.1007/978-3-642-11799-2_27

32. Lewko, A., Waters, B.: Decentralizing attribute-based encryption. In: Paterson, K.G. (ed.) EUROCRYPT 2011. LNCS, vol. 6632, pp. 568–588. Springer, Heidelberg (2011). https://doi.org/10.1007/978-3-642-20465-4_31

33. Lin, H., Cao, Z., Liang, X., Shao, J.: Secure threshold multi authority attribute based encryption without a central authority. In: INDOCRYPT (2008)

34. Müller, S., Katzenbeisser, S., Eckert, C.: Distributed attribute-based encryption. In: Lee, P.J., Cheon, J.H. (eds.) ICISC 2008. LNCS, vol. 5461, pp. 20–36. Springer, Heidelberg (2009). https://doi.org/10.1007/978-3-642-00730-9_2

35. Paterson, K.G., Srinivasan, S.: Security and anonymity of identity-based encryption with multiple trusted authorities. In: Galbraith, S.D., Paterson, K.G. (eds.) Pairing 2008. LNCS, vol. 5209, pp. 354–375. Springer, Heidelberg (2008). https://doi.org/10.1007/978-3-540-85538-5_23

36. Rouselakis, Y., Waters, B.: Efficient statically-secure large-universe multi-authority attribute-based encryption. In: Böhme, R., Okamoto, T. (eds.) FC 2015. LNCS, vol. 8975, pp. 315–332. Springer, Heidelberg (2015). https://doi.org/10.1007/978-3-662-47854-7_19

37. Sahai, A., Waters, B.: Fuzzy identity-based encryption. In: Cramer, R. (ed.) EURO-CRYPT 2005. LNCS, vol. 3494, pp. 457–473. Springer, Heidelberg (2005). https://doi.org/10.1007/11426639_27

38. Shamir, A.: Identity-based cryptosystems and signature schemes. In: Blakley, G.R., Chaum, D. (eds.) CRYPTO 1984. LNCS, vol. 196, pp. 47–53. Springer, Heidelberg (1985). https://doi.org/10.1007/3-540-39568-7_5

39. Waters, B.: Dual system encryption: realizing fully secure IBE and HIBE under simple assumptions. In: Halevi, S. (ed.) CRYPTO 2009. LNCS, vol. 5677, pp. 619–636. Springer, Heidelberg (2009). https://doi.org/10.1007/978-3-642-03356-8_36

40. Waters, B., Wee, H., Wu, D.J.: Multi-authority ABE from lattices without random oracles. In: Kiltz, E., Vaikuntanathan, V. (eds.) TCC 2022. Lecture Notes in Computer Science, vol. 13747, pp. 651–679. Springer, Cham (2022). https://doi.org/10.1007/978-3-031-22318-1_23

41. Waters, B., Wu, D.J.: Batch arguments for NP and more from standard bilinear group assumptions. In: Dodis, Y., Shrimpton, T. (eds.) Advances in Cryptology - CRYPTO 2022, CRYPTO 2022. Lecture Notes in Computer Science, vol. 13508, pp. 433–463. Springer, Cham (2022). https://doi.org/10.1007/978-3-031-15979-4_15

Unbounded Quadratic Functional Encryption and More from Pairings

Junichi Tomida(✉) ⓘ

NTT Social Informatics Laboratories, Tokyo, Japan
junichi.tomida.vw@hco.ntt.co.jp

Abstract. We propose the first unbounded functional encryption (FE) scheme for quadratic functions and its extension, in which the sizes of messages to be encrypted are not a priori bounded. Prior to our work, all FE schemes for quadratic functions are bounded, meaning that the message length is fixed at the setup. In the first scheme, encryption takes $\{x_i\}_{i \in S_c}$, key generation takes $\{c_{i,j}\}_{i,j \in S_k}$, and decryption outputs $\sum_{i,j \in S_k} c_{i,j} x_i x_j$ if and only if $S_k \subseteq S_c$, where the sizes of S_c and S_k can be arbitrary. Our second scheme is the extension of the first scheme to partially-hiding FE that computes an arithmetic branching program on a public input and a quadratic function on a private input. Concretely, encryption takes a public input $\mathbf{u}$ in addition to $\{x_i\}_{i \in S_c}$, a secret key is associated with arithmetic branching programs $\{f_{i,j}\}_{i,j \in S_k}$, and decryption yields $\sum_{i,j \in S_k} f_{i,j}(\mathbf{u}) x_i x_j$ if and only if $S_k \subseteq S_c$. Both our schemes are based on pairings and secure in the simulation-based model under the standard MDDH assumption.

Keywords: functional encryption · unbounded · quadratic functions · arithmetic branching programs · pairings

1 Introduction

Functional encryption (FE) [10, 29] is a new cryptographic paradigm that allows a decrypter to learn a function value of the underlying message without revealing any other information and enables fine-grained access control over encrypted data. This is in contrast to traditional public-key encryption, which only provides all-or-nothing decryption. Concretely, an FE scheme that supports a function class $\mathcal{F}$ allows an owner of a master secret to issue a secret key SK for a function $f \in \mathcal{F}$. Decryption of a ciphertext CT for a message x with SK yields $f(x)$ and nothing else. Functional encryption has been extensively studied in the literature, with elegant constructions supporting various function classes, achieving different notions of security and from various assumptions, e.g., [1,8,12,17,18].

In this paper, we focus on the following FE system. Consider a database consisting of pairs of a unique public identifier i and an encrypted private attribute x_i (e.g., age, medical history, salary, etc.). An authority can issue a secret key SK that allows a user to compute an analysis f' using *a portion of* the encrypted

© International Association for Cryptologic Research 2023
C. Hazay and M. Stam (Eds.): EUROCRYPT 2023, LNCS 14006, pp. 543–572, 2023.
https://doi.org/10.1007/978-3-031-30620-4_18

data with respect to some identifier set S_k. In other words, the user given SK can learn $f'(\{x_i\}_{i \in S_k})$ if and only if $S_k \subseteq S_c$ from the encrypted database, where S_c is the set of all identifiers in the database. We consider that preventing decryption in the case $S_k \not\subseteq S_c$ is important since otherwise the decrypter may learn specific information on some private attribute, which is undesirable in many applications (for instance, even in the case where S_k is large and f' computes average, the decrypter can learn exact x_i if $S_k \cap S_c = \{i\}$). In both theory and practice, it is arguably desirable if the system satisfies the following properties:

1. the size of the database that can be encrypted is not a priori bounded;
2. the size of the encrypted database is linear in the number of records $|S_c|$; and
3. the system is based on standard assumption and does not rely on heavy cryptographic tools such as obfuscation [17] and multi-linear maps [16].

Most of the existing FE schemes do not satisfy item 1 since the size of messages to be encrypted is a priori fixed. To our knowledge, the exceptions are FE for Turing machines [7,11,22], unbounded FE for inner product [14,32], and FE for attribute-weighted sums [3,13]. However, since all the FE schemes for Turing machines (secure against unbounded collusion) rely on obfuscation, only a few FE schemes satisfy all the properties simultaneously. Furthermore, the output of the functions in these few FE schemes are all linear in $\{x_i\}_{i \in S_c}$. This naturally motivates the following question:

> *Can we construct an FE scheme for quadratic functions with all the properties?*

We basically use the term "unbounded" to describe the property of item 1, but crucially, it also implies that the system supports variable-length plaintext. Note that most FE schemes support only fixed-length plaintext, meaning that we always have $S_c = S_k = [n]$ for a fixed polynomial n. In fixed-length schemes, when encrypting messages shorter than the fixed length, it is necessary to do something like zero padding, and it is impossible to encrypt messages longer than the fixed length.

From an efficiency standpoint, the variable-length property is quite important in systems that may handle data of various lengths. Let us consider a case where a country introduces an FE system, and local governments use it to encrypt the database of their residents. It is natural for the number of residents in each district to be various sizes. At some point, local governments may annex their regions, and the population of the new region would exceed the system limit. In such a case, we have to re-deploy the encryption system with a larger limit if they are using a fixed-length FE scheme. This problem can be avoided by setting the system limit with a huge margin in the setup phase. However, this solution brings a significant overhead to the system since the lengths of all ciphertexts become at least linear in the fixed system limit even if most plaintexts to be encrypted in the system are much shorter than the fixed length!

In contrast, the ciphertext sizes of variable-length FE schemes are linear in the size $|S_c|$ of each database as specified in item 2. Hence, variable-length FE schemes can be much more efficient than fixed-length FE schemes in situations as described above. Furthermore, we do not need to care even the system limit if we can use an *unbounded* FE scheme. However, all previous FE schemes for quadratic functions are fixed-length [4,8,19,21,25,30,33], and no unbounded (or even no variable-length) schemes are known. Hence, the above question is not only of theoretical interest but also important from a practical viewpoint.

1.1 Our Results

We construct an unbounded (public-key) FE scheme for quadratic functions and its extension. Both schemes have semi-adaptive, simulation-based security under the matrix decisional Diffie-Hellman (MDDH) assumption in the random oracle model (ROM) and thus satisfy the three properties simultaneously. Note that achieving adaptive security in FE for quadratic functions is a long-standing open problem, and no quadratic FE scheme achieves adaptive security (except the scheme based on the generic group model). We also remark that we cannot use the ROM straightforwardly to extend the existing quadratic FE schemes to be unbounded, and we overcome many hurdles to obtain the current results. We elaborate on this later in the technical overview. We leave constructing unbounded quadratic FEs without the ROM as an interesting open problem.

The first scheme is unbounded FE for quadratic functions, that is, f' in the above context can be any quadratic function. More formally, the message space and the function space is specified as $\mathcal{X} = \{(x_1, x_2) \in 2^{[p]} \times \bigcup_{i \in [p]} \mathbb{Z}_p^i \mid |x_1| = |x_2|\}$, and $\mathcal{F} = \{(f_1, f_2) \in 2^{[p]} \times \bigcup_{i \in [p]} \mathbb{Z}_p^{i^2} \mid |f_1|^2 = |f_2|\}$, respectively, where p is an exponentially large prime[1], and $2^{[p]}$ denotes the set consisting of all subset of $[p]$. For $x = (S_c, \{x_i\}_{i \in S_c}) \in \mathcal{X}$ and $f = (S_k, \{c_{i,j}\}_{i,j \in S_k}) \in \mathcal{F}$, $f(x)$ is defined as

$$f(x) = \begin{cases} \sum_{i,j \in S_k} c_{i,j} x_i x_j & S_k \subseteq S_c \\ \bot & \text{otherwise} \end{cases}$$

where S_c is clear in the ciphertext. Observe that S_c can be an arbitrary subset of $[p]$ where p is an exponentially large prime, and thus the size of S_c is unbounded since encryption is a polynomial time algorithm.

Our unbounded quadratic FE scheme can be easily modified to a (bounded) variable-length quadratic FE scheme *without* random oracles. In the scheme, S_c and S_k must be subsets of a fixed poly-sized set $[n']$ instead of an exponentially large set $[p]$. We present a comparison of our quadratic FE schemes with previous schemes in Table 1.

The second scheme is inspired by the recent works of partially-hiding functional encryption [5,20,24,33], where a message consists of public input $\mathbf{u}$ and private input $\mathbf{x}$ while a secret key is associated with f' in NC1 or arithmetic branching programs (ABPs), and decryption yields $f(\mathbf{u}, \mathbf{x}) = \langle f'(\mathbf{u}), \mathbf{x} \otimes \mathbf{x} \rangle$. We extend this functionality to unbounded FE for quadratic functions. Assume

---

[1] Concretely, p is an order of bilinear groups that the scheme based on.

Table 1. Comparison among public-key functional encryption schemes for quadratic functions. Fixed-length schemes refer to [4,8,19,21,30,33]. In this table, n is the fixed vector length, S_c and S_k are the identifier sets, and n' is the upper bound of the vector length, i.e., S_c and S_k must be subsets of $[n']$ in the bounded scheme. RO stands for random oracles.

Scheme	|PK|	|CT|	|SK|	Variable-length	Unbounded	w/o RO
Fixed-length schemes	$O(n)$	$O(n)$	$O(n)$ or $O(1)$	×	×	✓
Ours (bounded)	$O(n')$	$O(|S_c|)$	$O(|S_k|)$	✓	×	✓
Ours (unbounded)	$O(1)$	$O(|S_c|)$	$O(|S_k|)$	✓	✓	×

that each database additionally has a public input $\mathbf{u}$ (e.g., the description of the database) with a fixed length n, while a secret key is associated with S_k and arithmetic branching program f'^2 the input and output lengths of which are n and $|S_k|^2$, respectively. Then, the decryption reveals $\sum_{i,j \in S_k} f'_{i,j}(\mathbf{u}) x_i x_j$ where $f'_{i,j}(\mathbf{u})$ is the (i,j)-th output of $f'(\mathbf{u})$. Formally, the message space and the function space is specified as $\mathcal{X} = \{(x_1, x_2, x_3) \in \mathbb{Z}_p^n \times 2^{[q]} \times \bigcup_{i \in [q]} \mathbb{Z}_p^i \mid |x_2| = |x_3|\}$, and $\mathcal{F} = \{(f_1, f_2) \in 2^{[q]} \times \bigcup_{i \in [q]} \mathcal{F}_{n,i^2}^{\mathsf{ABP}} \mid |f_1|^2 = \mathsf{OutLen}(f_2)\}$, respectively, where $q \in \mathbb{N}$ is an exponentially large number ($q = p - 1$ in our scheme), $\mathcal{F}_{n,n'}^{\mathsf{ABP}}$ denotes the set of all ABPs with the input and output lengths being n and n', respectively, and $\mathsf{OutLen}(f_2)$ denotes the output length of f_2. For $x = (\mathbf{u}, S_c, \{x_i\}_{i \in S_c}) \in \mathcal{X}$ and $f = (S_k, f') \in \mathcal{F}$, $f(x)$ is defined as

$$f(x) = \begin{cases} \sum_{i,j \in S_k} f'_{i,j}(\mathbf{u}) x_i x_j & S_k \subseteq S_c \\ \bot & \text{otherwise} \end{cases}$$

where $\mathbf{u}, S_c$ are clear in the ciphertext. We call this functionality ABP ∘ UQF.

By similar observation to [3], we can confirm that FE for ABP ∘ UQF subsumes many classes of FE: (unbounded) FE for inner product [1,32]; FE for quadratic functions [8]; attribute-based encryption for ABPs [26]; attribute-based inner product FE [2]; and attribute-based quadratic FE [33] as well as unbounded FE for quadratic functions (our first scheme)[3]. Hence, for instance, FE for ABP ∘ UQF allows the decryption of an encrypted database with description $\mathbf{u}$ and identifier set S_c in which it first checks whether $\mathbf{u}$ satisfies a NC1 predicate P and then outputs a quadratic function f' over the portion $\{x_i\}_{i \in S_k}$ of the private input of the database iff $\mathsf{P}(\mathbf{u}) = 1$ and $S_k \subseteq S_c$, because such computation can be expressed by ABPs.

Comparison with FE for Attribute-Weighted Sums. Although FE for ABP ∘ UQF is similar to FE for attribute-weighted sums [3] in that they can encrypt a database with unbounded length, and a secret key is associated with an ABP, their functionalities are essentially different as follows. The public input

---

[2] Note that ABPs are a stronger computational model than NC1 circuits.

[3] This does not mean that our results imply the listed schemes since we ignore the security requirement here and focus on only functionalities.

$\mathbf{u}$ is specific to a database in FE for ABP∘UQF while each record has the public input $\mathbf{u}_i$ in FE for attribute-weighted sums. In decryption with a secret key for an ABP f, the output of FE for ABP ∘ UQF is the weighted-sum of $x_i x_j$ for $i, j \in S_k$ with the weight being $f_{i,j}(\mathbf{u})$ while that of FE for attribute-weighted sums is the weighted-sum of x_i for $i \in S_c$ with the weight being $f(\mathbf{u}_i)$.

1.2 Technical Overview

For simplicity, we stick to the case using the SXDH assumption, which is the special case of the MDDH assumption in this overview.

Why the ROM does not Work Straightforwardly? Before diving into our construction, we first see why it is difficult to extend the existing quadratic FE schemes to be unbounded by the ROM. For all public-key quadratic FE schemes [8,19,21,30,33], a public key PK and a secret key SK for any quadratic function f consist of following elements:

$$\mathsf{PK} = ([\mathbf{A}_1]_1, [\mathbf{A}_2]_2, [\mathbf{B}]_1, \ldots), \quad \mathsf{SK} = ([\mathbf{D}]_i, \ldots)$$

where $\mathbf{A}_1, \mathbf{A}_2$ are (pseudo)random matrices in $\mathbb{Z}_p$ the sizes of which depend on the message length m, $\mathbf{B}, \mathbf{D}$ are some matrices in $\mathbb{Z}_p$, $i \in \{1, 2\}$, and $[\cdot]_i$ denotes element-wise exponentiation in the source group G_i. How to define these matrices and i depends on the scheme. The natural idea to make the scheme unbounded is to generate $[\mathbf{A}_1]_1, [\mathbf{A}_2]_2$ by hash functions $H_1 : \{0,1\}^* \to G_1$ and $H_2 : \{0,1\}^* \to G_2$ in an ad hoc way in encryption. In all the existing schemes, however, either $\mathbf{B}$ [19] or $\mathbf{D}$ [8,21,30,33] contains the entries of the form $v a_1 a_2 + c$, where a_1, a_2 are entries of $\mathbf{A}_1, \mathbf{A}_2$, respectively, and v, c are $\mathbb{Z}_p$ elements that are independent of both a_1 and a_2. It is not hard to see that neither $[v a_1 a_2 + c]_1$ nor $[v a_1 a_2 + c]_2$ can be computed efficiently even in symmetric pairings. Hence, this strategy makes encryption or key generation inefficient. Furthermore, such a construction will not become collusion resistant, that is, a user can generate a secret key for $S_{k,1}$ from secret keys for $S_{k,2}$ and $S_{k,3}$ such that $S_{k,1} \subseteq S_c$ but $S_{k,2}, S_{k,3} \nsubseteq S_c$ in a certain case [14].

Starting from Lin's Secret-Key FE Scheme. Since the known public-key quadratic FE schemes are not ROM-friendly as observed, we construct a new public-key quadratic FE scheme that is inspired by the secret-key quadratic FE scheme from pairings by Lin [25]. Her scheme builds on the public-key IPFE scheme from DDH by Abdalla *et al.* [1] (ABDP), which is described as follows:

Setup(1^λ): $\mathbf{w} \leftarrow \mathbb{Z}_p^m$, PK = $[\mathbf{w}]$, MSK = $\mathbf{w}$.
Enc(PK, $\mathbf{x} \in \mathbb{Z}^m$): $s \leftarrow \mathbb{Z}_p$, CT = (CT$_1$, CT$_2$) = $([s], [\mathbf{x} + s\mathbf{w}])$.
KeyGen(MSK, $\mathbf{c} \in \mathbb{Z}^m$): SK = $-\mathbf{c}^\top \mathbf{w}$.
Dec(CT, SK): SKCT$_1$ + $\mathbf{c}^\top$CT$_2$ = $-\mathbf{c}^\top \mathbf{w}[s] + \mathbf{c}^\top [\mathbf{x} + s\mathbf{w}]$ = $[\langle \mathbf{c}, \mathbf{x} \rangle]$.

Lin's quadratic FE scheme uses a clever interleaving of IPFE schemes. To compress the size of ABDP ciphertexts for quadratic terms, she uses function-hiding IPFE where a secret key hides the underlying vector as well as a ciphertext hides the message [9]. Decryption of components in this scheme yields a cipher-text of the ABDP IPFE scheme, while a secret key of the ABDP scheme is generated using another function-hiding IPFE. Finally, decryption of ABDP IPFE allows to recover the output. In more detail, let $\mathsf{iFE} = (\mathsf{iSetup}, \mathsf{iEnc}, \mathsf{iKeyGen}, \mathsf{iDec})$ be a function-hiding IPFE scheme based on pairings, which outputs a decryption value as an exponent of the target-group generator. Her quadratic FE scheme is informally described as follows (we omit the components of the scheme that are only used in the security proof):

$\mathsf{Setup}(1^\lambda)$: $\mathbf{w} = (w_1, \ldots, w_m), \widetilde{\mathbf{w}} = (\widetilde{w}_1, \ldots, \widetilde{w}_m) \leftarrow \mathbb{Z}_p^m$, $\mathsf{iMSK}' \leftarrow \mathsf{iSetup}(1^\lambda)$
  $\mathsf{MSK} = (\mathsf{iMSK}', \mathbf{w}, \widetilde{\mathbf{w}})$.
$\mathsf{Enc}(\mathsf{MSK}, \mathbf{x} \in \mathbb{Z}^m)$: $s \leftarrow \mathbb{Z}_p$, $\mathsf{iCT}' \leftarrow \mathsf{iEnc}(\mathsf{iMSK}', s)$, $\mathsf{iMSK} \leftarrow \mathsf{iSetup}(1^\lambda)$
  $\mathsf{iCT}_i \leftarrow \mathsf{iEnc}(\mathsf{iMSK}, (x_i, w_i))$, $\mathsf{iSK}_i \leftarrow \mathsf{iKeyGen}(\mathsf{iMSK}, (x_i, s\widetilde{w}_i))$.
  $\mathsf{CT} = (\mathsf{iCT}', \{\mathsf{iCT}_i, \mathsf{iSK}_i\}_{i \in [m]})$.
$\mathsf{KeyGen}(\mathsf{MSK}, \mathbf{c} = \{c_{i,j}\}_{i,j \in [m]} \in \mathbb{Z}^{m^2})$:
  $\mathsf{SK} = \mathsf{iSK}' \leftarrow \mathsf{iKeyGen}(\mathsf{iMSK}', \mathbf{c}^\top(\mathbf{w} \otimes \widetilde{\mathbf{w}}))$.
$\mathsf{Dec}(\mathsf{CT}, \mathsf{SK})$: $\sum_{i,j \in [m]} c_{i,j} \mathsf{iDec}(\mathsf{iCT}_i, \mathsf{iSK}_j) - \mathsf{iDec}(\mathsf{iCT}', \mathsf{iSK}') = [\langle \mathbf{c}, \mathbf{x} \otimes \mathbf{x} \rangle]_T$.

In decryption, we compute $\mathsf{iDec}(\mathsf{iCT}_i, \mathsf{iSK}_j) = [x_i x_j + s w_i \widetilde{w}_j]_T$, which can be seen as the (i, j)-th element of the ABDP ciphertext $[\mathbf{x} \otimes \mathbf{x} + s\mathbf{w} \otimes \widetilde{\mathbf{w}}]_T$, and $-\mathsf{iDec}(\mathsf{iCT}', \mathsf{iSK}') = [-s\mathbf{c}^\top(\mathbf{w} \otimes \widetilde{\mathbf{w}})]_T$, where $-\mathbf{c}^\top(\mathbf{w} \otimes \widetilde{\mathbf{w}})$ is an ABDP secret key for $\mathbf{c}$. Since $\mathbf{w} \otimes \widetilde{\mathbf{w}}$ only appears on the exponent, it looks uniformly distributed under the SXDH assumption.

Making Lin's Scheme Public-Key. We next show how to turn her scheme into a public-key scheme. Observe that her scheme is secret-key since it uses the function-hiding property of the secret-key IPFE. More specifically, encryption chooses fresh iMSK by itself while iMSK' is the part of MSK. This means that we would be able to make her scheme public-key if we can publicly encrypt s into iCT' in encryption, and at the same time, iSK' is still function-hiding so that the security proof goes well.

Fortunately, we already have slotted IPFE [27], which is a hybrid between public-key IPFE and a function-hiding IPFE and satisfies the above properties. Specifically, both message and key spaces of slotted IPFE are separated into two slots $\mathbb{Z}_p^{m_1}$ and $\mathbb{Z}_p^{m_2}$, and we can publicly encrypt all messages of the form $(\mathbf{x}_1, \mathbf{0})$ for $\mathbf{x}_1 \in \mathbb{Z}_p^{m_1}$ via slot encryption algorithm $\mathsf{iSlotEnc}$ while we need a master secret key to encrypt a message of the form $(\mathbf{x}_1, \mathbf{x}_2) \in \mathbb{Z}_p^{m_1} \times \mathbb{Z}_p^{m_2}$ for $\mathbf{x}_2 \neq \mathbf{0}$ via encryption algorithm iEnc. A secret key for $(\mathbf{y}_1, \mathbf{y}_2) \in \mathbb{Z}_p^{m_1} \times \mathbb{Z}_p^{m_2}$ is function-hiding with respect to $\mathbf{y}_2$, which is essential for the security proof.

Another nice property of (slotted) IPFE is that (slot) encryption and key generation can take a group element in G_1 and G_2 of pairing groups as input, respectively [26]. Thus, we can publish $[\mathbf{w}]_1$ and $[\widetilde{\mathbf{w}}]_2$ as a part of public key and use them to generate $\mathsf{iCT}_i, \mathsf{iSK}_i$ in encryption. It seems that the modified scheme is now public-key, but unfortunately, this is not the case. This is because, in the security proof of Lin's scheme, we argue that $[w_i \widetilde{\mathbf{w}}]_2$ looks random given PK, but it is not the case if $[\mathbf{w}]_1$ is included in PK. To circumvent this problem, we modify Lin's scheme to obtain a public-key scheme using a slotted IPFE scheme $\mathsf{iFE'} = (\mathsf{iSetup'}, \mathsf{iSlotEnc'}, \mathsf{iEnc'}, \mathsf{iKeyGen'}, \mathsf{iDec'})$ as follows (we again omit the components of the scheme that are only required for the proof of security):

$\mathsf{Setup}(1^\lambda)$: $\mathbf{w} = (w_1, \ldots, w_m) \leftarrow \mathbb{Z}_p^m$, $(\mathsf{iPK'}, \mathsf{iMSK'}) \leftarrow \mathsf{iSetup'}(1^\lambda)$
  $\mathsf{PK} = ([\mathbf{w}]_2, \mathsf{iPK'})$, $\mathsf{MSK} = \mathsf{iMSK'}$.
$\mathsf{Enc}(\mathsf{PK}, \mathbf{x} \in \mathbb{Z}^m)$: $\mathbf{s} = (s_1, \ldots, s_m) \leftarrow \mathbb{Z}_p^m$, $\mathsf{iCT'} \leftarrow \mathsf{iSlotEnc'}(\mathsf{iPK'}, [\mathbf{s}]_1)$
  $\mathsf{iMSK} \leftarrow \mathsf{iSetup}(1^\lambda)$
  $\mathsf{iCT}_i \leftarrow \mathsf{iEnc}(\mathsf{iMSK}, [(x_i, s_i)]_1)$, $\mathsf{iSK}_i \leftarrow \mathsf{iKeyGen}(\mathsf{iMSK}, [(x_i, w_i)]_2)$.
  $\mathsf{CT} = (\mathsf{iCT'}, \{\mathsf{iCT}_i, \mathsf{iSK}_i\}_{i \in [m]})$.
$\mathsf{KeyGen}(\mathsf{PK}, \mathsf{MSK}, \mathbf{c} = \{c_{i,j}\}_{i,j \in [m]} \in \mathbb{Z}^{m^2})$:
  $\mathsf{SK} = \mathsf{iSK'} \leftarrow \mathsf{iKeyGen'}(\mathsf{iMSK'}, [(\sum_{j \in [m]} c_{1,j} w_j, \ldots, \sum_{j \in [m]} c_{m,j} w_j)]_2)$.
$\mathsf{Dec}(\mathsf{CT}, \mathsf{SK})$: $\sum_{i,j \in [m]} c_{i,j} \mathsf{iDec}(\mathsf{iCT}_i, \mathsf{iSK}_j) - \mathsf{iDec'}(\mathsf{iCT'}, \mathsf{iSK'}) = [\langle \mathbf{c}, \mathbf{x} \otimes \mathbf{x} \rangle]_T$.

The above issue does not occur in this modified scheme, that is, we can argue that $[s_i \mathbf{w}]_2$ looks random under the SXDH assumption even if PK is given. Even better, this scheme is ROM-friendly in a sense that Enc and KeyGen are still efficient even if $[\mathbf{w}]_2$ is generated by hashing as $[w_i]_2 = H(i)$! Note that the ciphertext size of the above scheme is still linear in m since the ciphertext size of the slotted IPFE scheme is linear in m_1 and m_2, and $m_2 = 1$ is sufficient for the security proof.

How to Achieve the Partial Decryption. As discussed above, our goal is to allow an owner of a secret key with respect to S_k to decrypt the portion S_k of a ciphertext for S_c if and only if $S_k \subseteq S_c$. Our observation is that if the underlying slotted IPFE scheme $\mathsf{iFE'}$ is unbounded and allows the partial decryption, the entire quadratic FE scheme is also unbounded and allows the partial decryption. Intuitively, $\{\mathsf{iDec}(\mathsf{iCT}_i, \mathsf{iSK}_j)\}_{i,j \in S_c}$ in CT reveals only $\{[x_i x_j + s_i w_j]_T\}_{i,j \in S_c}$, and $\{[s_i w_j]_T\}_{i,j \in S_c}$ looks random under the SXDH assumption. Therefore, the decrypter can learn $[\sum_{i,j \in S_k} c_{i,j} x_i x_j]_T$ if and only if it can compute $[\sum_{i,j \in S_k} c_{i,j} s_i w_j]_T$. This is why the decryption condition of the quadratic FE scheme is reduced to that of the underlying slotted IPFE scheme. Thus, the remaining task is to construct an unbounded IPFE that allows the partial decryption armed with the *slotted* property, which is necessary to achieve simulation-based security of our unbounded quadratic FE schemes.[4]

The closest scheme to what we need is the public-key unbounded IPFE scheme by Tomida and Takashima [32], which is an unbounded IPFE allowing the partial decryption. However, their scheme is deficient in the two points. First, it is not slotted. Second, it can encode only a $\mathbb{Z}_p$ element for each identifier while we need to encode *a vector* consisting of group elements for each identifier in encryption and key generation[5]. This is why we construct a new unbounded

---

[4] We require only indistinguishability-based security for unbounded slotted IPFE to prove simulation-based security of unbounded quadratic FE schemes. Note that the slotted property with indistinguishability-based security basically implies simulation-based security, and thus our approach essentially follows previous quadratic FE schemes with simulation-based security [19, 21, 33].

[5] The second property is required for our unbounded quadratic FE from MDDH_k for $k > 1$ and FE for $\mathsf{ABP} \circ \mathsf{UQF}$.

slotted IPFE scheme, which is of independent interest. Recall that their scheme is a direct construction based on the DPVS framework [28], and its security analysis is rather complex. In contrast, our scheme is generically obtained from slotted IPFE and thus much simpler.

We construct the unbounded slotted IPFE (slotted uIPFE) scheme in two steps. First, we construct a predicate slotted IPFE (slotted pIPFE) from a slotted IPFE, which is a slotted variant of the predicate IPFE proposed in [4]. Then, we construct a slotted uIPFE from a slotted pIPFE.

Slotted pIPFE is an extension of slotted IPFE in which we can control decryption conditions by an inner product predicate. Specifically, the message space is separated in two slots $\mathbb{Z}_p^d \times G_1^{m_1}$ and $G_1^{m_2}$, and we can publicly encrypt all messages of the form $(\mathbf{u}, [\mathbf{x}_1]_1, [\mathbf{0}]_1)$ for $(\mathbf{u}, [\mathbf{x}_1]_1) \in \mathbb{Z}_p^d \times G_1^{m_1}$ while we need the master secret key to encrypt a message of the form $(\mathbf{u}, [\mathbf{x}_1]_1, [\mathbf{x}_2]_1)$ for $\mathbf{x}_2 \neq \mathbf{0}$. A secret key for $(\mathbf{v}, [\mathbf{y}_1]_2, [\mathbf{y}_2]_2) \in \mathbb{Z}_p^d \times G_2^{m_1} \times G_2^{m_2}$ is function-hiding with respect to $[\mathbf{y}_2]_2$, and decryption of these reveals $[\langle(\mathbf{x}_1, \mathbf{x}_2), (\mathbf{y}_1, \mathbf{y}_2)\rangle]_T$ if and only if $\langle\mathbf{u}, \mathbf{v}\rangle = 0$. The construction is almost the same as pIPFE in [4] except that we use a slotted IPFE as a building block instead of an IPFE.

We next define slotted uIPFE more formally. The message space consists of two slots $\{(x_1, x_2) \in 2^{[p]} \times \bigcup_{i \in [p]} (G_1^{m_1})^i \mid |x_1| = |x_2|/m_1\}$ and $G_1^{m_2}$, and we can publicly encrypt all messages of the form $(S_c, \{[\mathbf{x}_i]_1\}_{i \in S_c}, [\mathbf{0}]_1)$ while we need a master secret key to encrypt of the form $(S_c, \{[\mathbf{x}_i]_1\}_{i \in S_c}, [\mathbf{x}_0]_1)$ for $\mathbf{x}_0 \neq \mathbf{0}$ similarly to the other slotted FE schemes. A secret key for $(S_k, \{[\mathbf{y}_i]_2\}_{i \in S_k}, [\mathbf{y}_0]_2)$ is function-hiding with respect to $[\mathbf{y}_0]_2$, and decryption reveals $[\sum_{i \in S_k} \langle\mathbf{x}_i, \mathbf{y}_i\rangle + \langle\mathbf{x}_0, \mathbf{y}_0\rangle]_T$ if and only if $S_k \subseteq S_c$.

The high-level idea of the construction of slotted uIPFE is similar to the uIPFE scheme in [32]. For ease of exposition, let us ignore the second slot of uIPFE for now. Informally, slot encryption for $(S_c, \{[\mathbf{x}_i]_1\}_{i \in S_c})$ chooses $z \leftarrow \mathbb{Z}_p$ and encrypts $(\mathbf{u}_i, [\tilde{\mathbf{x}}_i]_1)$ by slot encryption of pIPFE for all $i \in S_c$, where $\mathbf{u}_i = (1, i)$ and $\tilde{\mathbf{x}}_i = (\mathbf{x}_i, z)$. Key generation for $(S_k, \{[\mathbf{y}_i]_2\}_{i \in S_k})$ chooses $a_i \leftarrow \mathbb{Z}_p$ so that $\sum_{i \in S_k} a_i = 0$ and computes a secret key of pIPFE for $(\mathbf{v}_i, [\tilde{\mathbf{y}}_i]_1)$ for all $i \in S_k$, where $\mathbf{v}_i = (i, -1)$ and $\tilde{\mathbf{y}}_i = (\mathbf{y}_i, a_i)$. Then, a decrypter can learn only $[\sum_{i \in S_c \cap S_k} \langle\mathbf{x}_i, \mathbf{y}_i\rangle + za_i]_T$ via decryption of pIPFE, where $za_i = 0$ only when $S_k \subseteq S_c$, and za_i looks random otherwise. Thus, we can recover $[\sum_{i \in S_k} \langle\mathbf{x}_i, \mathbf{y}_i\rangle]_T$ iff $S_k \subseteq S_c$. We defer how to obtain the slotted property to Sect. 4.

Put it All Together. Let uFE = (uSetup, uSlotEnc, uEnc, uKeyGen, uDec) be a slotted uIPFE scheme and $H : \{0,1\}^* \to G_2$ be a hash function. Then, our unbounded quadratic FE scheme qFE is informally given as follows:

Setup(1^λ): (PK, MSK) = (uPK, uMSK) $\leftarrow$ uSetup(1^λ)
Enc(PK, $(S_c, \{x_i\}_{i \in S_c})$): $s_i \leftarrow \mathbb{Z}_p$, uCT $\leftarrow$ uSlotEnc(uPK, $(S_c, \{s_i\}_{i \in S_c})$)
    iMSK $\leftarrow$ iSetup(1^λ), $[w_i]_2 = H(i)$
    iCT$_i$ $\leftarrow$ iEnc(iMSK, $[(x_i, s_i)]_1$), iSK$_i$ $\leftarrow$ iKeyGen(iMSK, $[(x_i, w_i)]_2$).
    CT = (uCT, $\{$iCT$_i$, iSK$_i\}_{i \in S_c}$).
KeyGen(PK, MSK, $(S_k, \{c_{i,j}\}_{i,j \in S_k})$): $[w_i]_2 = H(i)$
    SK = uSK $\leftarrow$ uKeyGen(uMSK, $(S_k, \{[\sum_{j \in S_k} c_{i,j} w_j]_2\}_{i \in S_k})$).

Dec(CT, SK):

$$\sum_{i,j \in S_k} c_{i,j} \text{iDec}(\text{iCT}_i, \text{iSK}_j) - \text{uDec}(\text{uCT}, \text{uSK}) = [\sum_{i,j \in S_k} c_{i,j} x_i x_j]_T.$$

Since the ciphertext size of slotted uIPFE is linear in $|S_c|$, that of the above quadratic FE scheme is also linear in $|S_c|$. The variable-length scheme without random oracles can be obtained by generating $[w_1]_2, \ldots, [w_{n'}]_2$ in the setup.

Security. Simulation-based security essentially asserts that a challenge ciphertext can be simulated without a challenge message, and secret keys can be simulated from corresponding decryption values. In our scheme, the simulation algorithms leverage the second slot of slotted uIPFE scheme uFE. Specifically, a simulated ciphertext is generated in the same manner as Enc except that uCT additionally encrypts $[1]_1$ (the generator of g_1) in the second slot, and $\text{iCT}_i, \text{iSK}_i$ encrypt $[(0, s_i)]_1, [(0, w_i)]_2$ instead of $[(x_i, s_i)]_1, [(x_i, w_i)]_2$, respectively. A simulated secret key for decryption value α is a secret key uSK of uFE that additional encodes $[-\alpha]_2$ if $S_k \subseteq S_c$ and $[0]_2$ otherwise in the second slot. Thanks to the slotted property, $-\text{uDec}(\text{uCT}, \text{uSK}) = [-\sum_{i,j \in S_k} c_{i,j} s_i w_j + \alpha]_T$ if $S_k \subseteq S_c$ in the above setting and the simulation goes well.

The indistinguishability between the real system and the simulated system can be proven by a series of hybrids similar to that used in Lin's secret-key quadratic FE scheme. Concretely, in the ℓ-th hybrid for $\ell \in S_c$, iCT_i and iSK_i is encrypting vectors $\mathbf{x}_i$ and $\widetilde{\mathbf{x}}_i$ where

$$\mathbf{x}_i = \begin{cases} (0, \ s_i) & (i \le \ell) \\ (x_i, s_i) & (i > \ell) \end{cases}, \quad \widetilde{\mathbf{x}}_i = (x_i, w_i)$$

However, this change is detectable by decrypting the challenge ciphertext, and we need to adjust the difference using the second slot of uFE in each hybrid. Concretely, we encode $[1]_1$ into the second slot of uCT in the challenge ciphertext and $[-\sum_{i \in S_c^\ell \cap S_h, j \in S_h} c_{i,j} x_i x_j]_2$ into the second slot of uSK iff $S_k \subseteq S_c$, where S_c^ℓ denotes the set consisting of the first ℓ elements of S_c. The indistinguishability between the $\ell - 1$-th hybrid and the ℓ-th hybrid can be proven similarly to the proof of Lin's scheme. Observe that, in the final hybrid, the view of the adversary basically corresponds to that in the simulated system.

Extension to FE for ABP∘UQF. The high-level idea to extend our unbounded quadratic FE to FE for ABP∘UQF is similar to the technique used when achieving unboundedness in quadratic FE. That is, we can basically obtain FE for ABP∘UQF by enhancing the unbounded uIPFE uFE so that it can compute ABPs on a public input and linear functions on a private input. A similar idea is also used in the construction of Wee's recent partially-hiding FE scheme [33]. We use a partially garbling scheme (PGS) for ABPs [23] for a building block.

We can formulate PGS for ABPs as follows. A garbling algorithm pgb takes an ABP $f : \mathbb{Z}_p^n \to \mathbb{Z}_p^{n'}$, a public input $\mathbf{u} \in \mathbb{Z}_p^n$, a private input $\mathbf{x} \in \mathbb{Z}_p^{n'}$, a random tape $\mathbf{t} \in \mathbb{Z}_p^{t-1}$ and outputs

$$\boldsymbol{\ell} = (\mathbf{u}'^\top \mathbf{L}_1 \mathbf{t}, \ldots, \mathbf{u}'^\top \mathbf{L}_m \mathbf{t}, x_1 + \mathbf{u}'^\top \mathbf{L}_{m+1} \mathbf{t}, \ldots, x_{n'} + \mathbf{u}'^\top \mathbf{L}_t \mathbf{t}) \in \mathbb{Z}_p^t$$

where $\mathbf{u}' = (\mathbf{u}, 1)$, the parameter t and matrices $\mathbf{L}_i \in \mathbb{Z}_p^{(n+1) \times (t-1)}$ are determined by f, and $m = t - n'$. The correctness of the PGS requires that we can reconstruct $\langle f(\mathbf{u}), \mathbf{x} \rangle$ given $\boldsymbol{\ell}$ together with f and $\mathbf{u}$. Furthermore, the reconstruction is linear in $\boldsymbol{\ell}$, that is, there exists $\mathbf{d}_{f,\mathbf{u}} \in \mathbb{Z}_p^t$ and we have $\langle \mathbf{d}_{f,\mathbf{u}}, \boldsymbol{\ell} \rangle = \langle f(\mathbf{u}), \mathbf{x} \rangle$. The PGS is secure if there is an efficient algorithm pgb^* that takes $(f, \mathbf{u}, \alpha, \mathbf{t})$ for $\alpha \in \mathbb{Z}_p$, and the output distributions of $\mathsf{pgb}(f, \mathbf{u}, \mathbf{x}; \mathbf{t})$ and $\mathsf{pgb}^*(f, \mathbf{u}, \langle f(\mathbf{u}), \mathbf{x} \rangle; \mathbf{t})$ are statistically close where the probability is taken over $\mathbf{t} \leftarrow \mathbb{Z}_p^{t-1}$.

Given the PGS for ABPs, we modify our unbounded quadratic FE scheme qFE to obtain FE for $\mathsf{ABP} \circ \mathsf{UQF}$ as follows. In encryption of $(\mathbf{u}, S_c, \{x_i\}_{i \in S_c})$, now uCT encrypts $r\mathbf{u}'$ with respect to identifier p in addition to $\{s_i\}_{i \in S_c}$ where $r \leftarrow \mathbb{Z}_p$ (recall that $S_c \subseteq [p-1]$ in FE for $\mathsf{ABP} \circ \mathsf{UQF}$). A secret key for (S_k, f) consists of a set $\{\mathsf{uSK}_h\}_{h \in [t]}$ of secret keys of slotted uIPFE where uSK_h encodes $[w_i]_2$ for $i \in S_k$ and $\mathbf{L}_h \mathbf{t}$ such that $\mathsf{uDec}(\mathsf{uCT}, \mathsf{uSK}_h)$ decrypts to the h-th element of $[\boldsymbol{\ell}]_T$ where

$$\boldsymbol{\ell} = (r\mathbf{u}'^\top \mathbf{L}_1 \mathbf{t}, \ldots, r\mathbf{u}'^\top \mathbf{L}_m \mathbf{t}, (s_i w_j + r\mathbf{u}'^\top \mathbf{L}_{\phi(i,j)} \mathbf{t})_{i,j \in S_k}) \in \mathbb{Z}_p^t \quad (1.1)$$

and $\phi : S_k \times S_k \to \{m+1, \ldots, t\}$ is a bijective function. Then, the decryption works as follows:

$$\sum_{i,j \in S_k} f_{i,j}(\mathbf{u}) \mathsf{iDec}(\mathsf{iCT}_i, \mathsf{iSK}_j) - \langle \mathbf{d}_{f,\mathbf{u}}, [\boldsymbol{\ell}]_T \rangle$$

$$= [\sum_{i,j \in S_k} f_{i,j}(\mathbf{u})(x_i x_j + s_i w_j)]_T - [\sum_{i,j \in S_k} f_{i,j}(\mathbf{u}) s_i w_j]_T = [\sum_{i,j \in S_k} f_{i,j}(\mathbf{u}) x_i x_j]_T$$

where the first equality follows from the correctness of the PGS.

The simulation algorithms of this extension scheme can be constructed in a similar manner to our unbounded quadratic FE scheme. A simulated ciphertext is the same as a normal ciphertext except that uCT encrypts $[\mathbf{0}]_1$ in the first slot and $[1]_1$ in the second slot, and $\mathsf{iCT}_i, \mathsf{iSK}_i$ encrypt $[(0, s_i)]_1, [(0, w_i)]_2$ instead of $[(x_i, s_i)]_1, [(x_i, w_i)]_2$, respectively. A simulated secret key for decryption value α is the same as a normal secret key except that the h-th element of $[\mathsf{pgb}^*(f, \mathbf{u}, -\alpha + \sum_{i,j \in S_k} f_{i,j}(\mathbf{u}) s_i w_j, \mathbf{t})]_2$ (if $S_k \subseteq S_c$) or 0 (if $S_k \not\subseteq S_c$) is encoded in the second slot of uSK_h, where $\mathbf{t}$ is a random vector in $\mathbb{Z}_p^{t-1}$. In this simulation, we have $\langle \mathbf{d}_{f,\mathbf{u}}, (\mathsf{uDec}(\mathsf{uCT}, \mathsf{uSK}_h)_{h \in [t]} \rangle = [-\alpha + \sum_{i,j \in S_k} f_{i,j}(\mathbf{u}) s_i w_j]_T$ if $S_k \subseteq S_c$, and thus the simulation works.[6]

The intuition for the indistinguishability between the real system and the simulated system is given as follows. The adversary in the real system can basically learn $\{[x_i x_j + s_i w_j]_T\}_{i,j \in S_c}$ from $\mathsf{iCT}_i, \mathsf{iSK}_i$ in the challenge ciphertext and $[\boldsymbol{\ell}]_T$ defined in Eq. (1.1) with respect to secret keys for $S_k \subseteq S_c$ from $\mathsf{uCT}, \mathsf{uSK}_h$. Under the SXDH, the adversary cannot detect the change if $\boldsymbol{\ell}$ is computed as

$$\boldsymbol{\ell} = (\mathbf{u}'^\top \mathbf{L}_1 \tilde{\mathbf{t}}, \ldots, \mathbf{u}'^\top \mathbf{L}_m \tilde{\mathbf{t}}, (s_i w_j + \mathbf{u}'^\top \mathbf{L}_{\phi(i,j)} \tilde{\mathbf{t}})_{i,j \in S_k})$$

---

[6] It is not hard to see that the security of the partially garbling scheme implies that $\langle \mathbf{d}_{f,\mathbf{u}}, \mathsf{pgb}^*(f, \mathbf{u}, \alpha; \mathbf{t}) \rangle = \alpha$ for all $\alpha \in \mathbb{Z}_p$.

where $\tilde{\mathbf{t}}$ is a random vector that is independent of $\mathbf{t}$ used in generating uSK_h. Then, due to the security of the PGS, ℓ reveals only $[\sum_{i,j \in S_k} f_{i,j}(\mathbf{u})s_i w_j]_T$. Again, $\{s_i w_j\}_{i,j \in S_c}$ looks random under the SXDH, and thus we have

$$\{\{[x_i x_j + s_i w_j]_T\}_{i,j \in S_c}, [\sum_{i,j \in S_k} f_{i,j}(\mathbf{u})s_i w_j]_T\}$$

$$\approx_c \{\{[s_i w_j]_T\}_{i,j \in S_c}, [\sum_{i,j \in S_k} f_{i,j}(\mathbf{u})(s_i w_j - x_i x_j)]_T\}$$

where the RHS basically corresponds to the view in the simulated system.

2 Preliminaries

2.1 Notations

For $m \in \mathbb{N}$, $[m]$ denotes a set $\{1, \ldots, m\}$. For vectors $\mathbf{v}_1, \ldots, \mathbf{v}_n$, $(\mathbf{v}_1, \ldots, \mathbf{v}_n)$ denotes the vector concatenation as row vectors *regardless of* whether each $\mathbf{v}_i$ is a row or column vector. For instance, for $\mathbf{v}_1 \in \mathbb{Z}_p^{m \times 1}, \mathbf{v}_2 \in \mathbb{Z}_p^{1 \times n}$, $(\mathbf{v}_1, \mathbf{v}_2) = (\mathbf{v}_1^\top || \mathbf{v}_2)$. For a matrix $\mathbf{A} = (a_{j,\ell})_{j,\ell}$ over $\mathbb{Z}_p$, $[\mathbf{A}]_i$ denotes a matrix over G_i whose (j, ℓ)-th entry is $g_i^{a_{j,\ell}}$, and we use this notation for vectors and scalars similarly. We use $\otimes$ for the Kronecker product. For a matrix $\mathbf{M} \in \mathbb{Z}_p^{a \times b}$ and vectors $\mathbf{a} \in \mathbb{Z}_p^a, \mathbf{b} \in \mathbb{Z}_p^b$, we denote a vector $\mathbf{m}$ such that $\langle \mathbf{a} \otimes \mathbf{b}, \mathbf{m} \rangle = \mathbf{a}^\top \mathbf{M} \mathbf{b}$ by $\mathsf{vec}(\mathbf{M})$. For families of distributions $X = \{X_\lambda\}_{\lambda \in \mathbb{N}}$ and $Y = \{Y_\lambda\}_{\lambda \in \mathbb{N}}$, we denote $X \approx_c Y$ and $X \approx_s Y$ as computational indistinguishability and statistical indistinguishability, respectively.

2.2 Basic Tools and Assumptions

We use cryptographic bilinear groups and the MDDH assumption [15].

Definition 2.1 (Arithmetic Branching Programs (ABPs)). An arithmetic branching program $f : \mathbb{Z}_p^n \to \mathbb{Z}_p$ is defined by a prime p, a directed acyclic graph (V, E), two special vertices $v_0, v_1 \in V$, and a labeling function $\sigma : E \to \mathcal{F}^{\mathsf{Affine}}$, where $\mathcal{F}^{\mathsf{Affine}}$ consists of all affine functions $g : \mathbb{Z}_p^n \to \mathbb{Z}_p$. The size of f is the number of vertices $|V|$. Given an input $\mathbf{x} \in \mathbb{Z}_p^n$ to the ABP, we can assign a $\mathbb{Z}_p$ element to edge $e \in E$ by $\sigma(e)(\mathbf{x})$. Let P be the set of all paths from v_0 to v_1. Each element in P can be represented by a subset of E. The output of the ABP on input $\mathbf{x}$ is defined as $\sum_{E' \in P} \prod_{e \in E'} \sigma(e)(\mathbf{x})$. We can extend the definition of ABPs for functions $f : \mathbb{Z}_p^n \to \mathbb{Z}_p^{n'}$ by evaluating each output in a coordinate-wise manner and denote such a function class by $\mathcal{F}_{n,n'}^{\mathsf{ABP}}$.

Note that we can convert any boolean formula, boolean branching program or arithmetic formula to an arithmetic branching program with a constant blow-up in the representation size. Thus, ABPs are a stronger computational model than all of the above.

2.3 Functional Encryption

We first define functional encryption (FE). In FE, the system can generate a secret key that is associated with a function f, and a ciphertext for a message x decrypts to $f(x)$ when it is decrypted by the secret key for f. Typically, FE is defined as the ciphertext for x entirely hides x. Recently, the more generalized notion called partially hiding FE [6] was introduced, where the ciphertext of x partially hides x. More precisely, x consists of the public part x_{pub} and the private part x_{priv}, and the ciphertext for x hides only x_{priv}. In this paper, we use several classes of partially hiding FE, which is formally defined as follows.

Definition 2.2 (Functional Encryption). Let $\mathcal{X} = \mathcal{X}_{\mathsf{pub}} \times \mathcal{X}_{\mathsf{priv}}$ be a message space. Let $\mathcal{F}$ be a function family such that, for all $f \in \mathcal{F}$, $f : \mathcal{X} \to \mathcal{Z}$. A (public-key) functional encryption (FE) scheme for $\mathcal{F}$, FE, consists of four algorithms.

$\mathsf{Setup}(1^{\lambda})$: It takes a security parameter 1^{λ} and outputs a public parameter PK
  and a master secret key MSK. The other three algorithms implicitly take PK
  as input.
$\mathsf{Enc}(x)$: It takes $x \in \mathcal{X}$ and outputs a ciphertext CT.
$\mathsf{KeyGen}(\mathsf{MSK}, f)$: It takes MSK and $f \in \mathcal{F}$, and outputs a secret key SK.
$\mathsf{Dec}(\mathsf{CT}, \mathsf{SK})$: It takes CT and SK, and outputs a decryption value $d \in \mathcal{Z}$ or a
  symbol $\perp$.

Correctness. FE is *correct* if it satisfies the following condition. For all $\lambda \in \mathbb{N}$, $x \in \mathcal{X}$, $f \in \mathcal{F}$, we have

$$\Pr\left[\mathsf{Dec}(\mathsf{CT}, \mathsf{SK}) = f(x) \,\middle|\, \begin{array}{l} \mathsf{PK}, \mathsf{MSK} \leftarrow \mathsf{Setup}(1^{\lambda}) \\ \mathsf{CT} \leftarrow \mathsf{Enc}(x) \\ \mathsf{SK} \leftarrow \mathsf{KeyGen}(\mathsf{MSK}, f) \end{array}\right] = 1.$$

Security. We define partially-hiding security for FE[7]. For a stateful PPT adversary $\mathcal{A}$ and $\lambda \in \mathbb{N}$, let

$$\mathsf{Adv}^{\mathsf{FE}}_{\mathcal{A},\mathsf{ph}}(\lambda) = \left| \Pr\left[\beta' = \beta \,\middle|\, \begin{array}{l} \beta \leftarrow \{0,1\}, \ \ \mathsf{PK}, \mathsf{MSK} \leftarrow \mathsf{Setup}(1^{\lambda}) \\ (x_{\mathsf{pub}}, x^0_{\mathsf{priv}}, x^1_{\mathsf{priv}}) \leftarrow \mathcal{A}(\mathsf{PK}) \\ \mathsf{CT} \leftarrow \mathsf{Enc}((x_{\mathsf{pub}}, x^{\beta}_{\mathsf{priv}})) \\ \beta' \leftarrow \mathcal{A}^{\mathsf{KeyGen}(\mathsf{MSK}, \cdot)}(\mathsf{CT}) \end{array}\right] - 1/2 \right| \quad (2.1)$$

Let q_k be a number of queries to KeyGen and f^{ℓ} be the ℓ-th function on which $\mathcal{A}$ queries KeyGen. We say $\mathcal{A}$ is *admissible* if $\mathcal{A}$'s queries satisfy the followings:

$$f^{\ell}((x_{\mathsf{pub}}, x^0_{\mathsf{priv}})) = f^{\ell}((x_{\mathsf{pub}}, x^1_{\mathsf{priv}})) \text{ for all } \ell \in [q_k].$$

FE is said to be *partially hiding* if, for all admissible PPT adversaries $\mathcal{A}$, we have $\mathsf{Adv}^{\mathsf{FE}}_{\mathcal{A},\mathsf{ph}}(\lambda) \le \mathsf{negl}(\lambda)$.

---

[7] We consider only selective (or semi-adaptive more precisely) security in this paper.

Next, we define a more generalized notion that we call slotted functional encryption. Slotted FE was first introduced in [27] for inner product functionality, which is called slotted inner product FE. We extend it to handle general functions since we use slotted FE schemes for other classes in this paper.

Before explaining the definition of slotted FE, let us recall the notion of function-hiding FE. In function-hiding FE, a secret key for f hides f as well as a ciphertext for x hides x. We usually consider the secret-key setting where encryption requires a master secret key for function-hiding FE. This is because an adversary can learn $f(x)$ for any x from a secret key for f in public-key FE, and it is difficult to achieve meaningful function-hiding security.

Slotted FE is a hybrid between public-key FE and function-hiding secret-key FE. In slotted FE, a private message space $\mathcal{X}_{\mathsf{priv}}$ consists of two spaces $\mathcal{X}_{\mathsf{priv1}}$ and $\mathcal{X}_{\mathsf{priv2}}$, that is, a message space consists of three spaces: $\mathcal{X} = \mathcal{X}_{\mathsf{pub}} \times \mathcal{X}_{\mathsf{priv1}} \times \mathcal{X}_{\mathsf{priv2}}$. For some default value $e \in \mathcal{X}_{\mathsf{priv2}}$, a user can publicly encrypt $(x_{\mathsf{pub}}, x_{\mathsf{priv}}, e) \in \mathcal{X}$ for all $(x_{\mathsf{pub}}, x_{\mathsf{priv}}) \in \mathcal{X}_{\mathsf{pub}} \times \mathcal{X}_{\mathsf{priv1}}$ while an owner of master secret key can encrypt all $x \in \mathcal{X}$. On the other hand, a function space $\mathcal{F}$ consists of two spaces $\mathcal{F}_{\mathsf{pub}}$ and $\mathcal{F}_{\mathsf{priv}}$. A secret key for $f = (f_{\mathsf{pub}}, f_{\mathsf{priv}}) \in \mathcal{F}_{\mathsf{pub}} \times \mathcal{F}_{\mathsf{priv}}$ hides f_{priv}. Intuitively, meaningful function-hiding security with respective to $\mathcal{F}_{\mathsf{priv}}$ can be achieved by the fact that the adversary can encrypt only messages of the form $(x_{\mathsf{pub}}, x_{\mathsf{priv}}, e) \in \mathcal{X}$. Slotted FE is formally defined as follows.

Definition 2.3 (Slotted Functional Encryption). Let $\mathcal{X} = \mathcal{X}_{\mathsf{pub}} \times \mathcal{X}_{\mathsf{priv1}} \times \mathcal{X}_{\mathsf{priv2}}$ be a message space. We sometimes denote $\mathcal{X}_{\mathsf{priv1}} \times \mathcal{X}_{\mathsf{priv2}}$ by $\mathcal{X}_{\mathsf{priv}}$. Let $\mathcal{F} = \mathcal{F}_{\mathsf{pub}} \times \mathcal{F}_{\mathsf{priv}}$ be a function family such that, for all $f \in \mathcal{F}$, $f : \mathcal{X} \to \mathcal{Z}$. A slotted functional encryption (SlotFE) scheme for $\mathcal{F}$, SlotFE, consists of five algorithms.

Setup(1^λ): It takes a security parameter 1^λ and outputs a public key PK and a master secret key MSK. The other four algorithms implicitly take PK as input.

Enc(MSK, x): It takes MSK and $x \in \mathcal{X}$ and outputs a ciphertext CT.

SlotEnc(x): It takes $x \in \mathcal{X}_{\mathsf{pub}} \times \mathcal{X}_{\mathsf{priv1}}$ and outputs a ciphertext CT.

KeyGen(MSK, f): It takes MSK and $f \in \mathcal{F}$, and outputs a secret key SK.

Dec(CT, SK): It takes CT and SK, and outputs a decryption value $d \in \mathcal{Z}$ or a symbol $\perp$.

Correctness. SlotFE is *correct* if it satisfies the following condition. For all $\lambda \in \mathbb{N}$, $x \in \mathcal{X}$, $f \in \mathcal{F}$, we have

$$\Pr\left[\mathsf{Dec}(\mathsf{CT}, \mathsf{SK}) = f(x) \;\middle|\; \begin{array}{l} \mathsf{PP}, \mathsf{MSK} \leftarrow \mathsf{Setup}(1^\lambda) \\ \mathsf{CT} \leftarrow \mathsf{Enc}(\mathsf{MSK}, x) \\ \mathsf{SK} \leftarrow \mathsf{KeyGen}(\mathsf{MSK}, f) \end{array}\right] = 1.$$

Slot-Mode Correctness. SlotFE is *slot-mode correct* with respect to a public element $e \in \mathcal{X}_{\mathsf{priv2}}$ if it satisfies the following condition. For all $\lambda \in \mathbb{N}$, $x \in$

$\mathcal{X}_{pub} \times \mathcal{X}_{priv1}$, the following distributions are identical:

$$\{(PK, MSK, CT) \mid (PK, MSK) \leftarrow \mathsf{Setup}(1^\lambda), \; CT \leftarrow \mathsf{Enc}(MSK, (x, e))\}$$
$$\{(PK, MSK, CT) \mid (PK, MSK) \leftarrow \mathsf{Setup}(1^\lambda), \; CT \leftarrow \mathsf{SlotEnc}(x)\}$$

Security. We define partially-hiding security for SlotFE. For a stateful PPT adversary $\mathcal{A}$ and $\lambda \in \mathbb{N}$, let

$$\mathsf{Adv}^{\mathsf{SlotFE}}_{\mathcal{A},\mathrm{ph}} = \left| \Pr\left[\beta' = \beta \; \middle| \; \begin{matrix} \beta \leftarrow \{0,1\}, \; PK, MSK \leftarrow \mathsf{Setup}(1^\lambda) \\ \beta' \leftarrow \mathcal{A}^{\mathsf{cO}(\beta,\cdot),\mathsf{kO}(\beta,\cdot)}(PK) \end{matrix} \right] - 1/2 \right| \quad (2.2)$$

where $\mathsf{cO}(\beta, \cdot)$ takes $(x_{\mathsf{pub}}, x^0_{\mathsf{priv}}, x^1_{\mathsf{priv}}) \in \mathcal{X}_{\mathsf{pub}} \times \mathcal{X}^2_{\mathsf{priv}}$ and returns $\mathsf{Enc}(MSK, (x_{\mathsf{pub}}, x^\beta_{\mathsf{priv}}))$, $\mathsf{kO}(\beta, \cdot)$ takes $(f_{\mathsf{pub}}, f^0_{\mathsf{priv}}, f^1_{\mathsf{priv}}) \in \mathcal{F}_{\mathsf{pub}} \times \mathcal{F}^2_{\mathsf{priv}}$ and returns $\mathsf{KeyGen}(MSK, (f_{\mathsf{pub}}, f^\beta_{\mathsf{priv}}))$. Let q_c, q_k be a number of queries to cO, kO, respectively. Let $x^{j,\beta} = (x^j_{\mathsf{pub}}, x^{j,\beta}_{\mathsf{priv}})$ for $j \in [q_c]$, and $f^{\ell,\beta} = (f^\ell_{\mathsf{pub}}, f^{\ell,\beta}_{\mathsf{priv}})$ for $\ell \in [q_k]$. We say $\mathcal{A}$ is *admissible* if $\mathcal{A}$'s queries satisfy the followings:

– $\mathcal{A}$ never queries cO after querying kO even once[8];
– $f^{\ell,0}(x^{j,0}) = f^{\ell,1}(x^{j,1})$ for all $j \in [q_c], \ell \in [q_k]$; and
– $f^{\ell,0}((x,e)) = f^{\ell,1}((x,e))$ for all $\ell \in [q_k], x \in \mathcal{X}_{\mathsf{pub}} \times \mathcal{X}_{\mathsf{priv1}}$ where e is the public element defined in slot-mode correctness[9].

SlotFE is said to be q_c-*partially hiding* if, for all admissible PPT adversaries $\mathcal{A}$ querying cO at most q_c times, we have $\mathsf{Adv}^{\mathsf{SlotFE}}_{\mathcal{A},\mathrm{ph}} \leq \mathsf{negl}(\lambda)$. When q_c can be any polynomial in λ, i.e., $q_c = \mathsf{poly}(\lambda)$, we call the scheme just *partially hiding*.

We define slotted FE for inner product over bilinear groups called slotted IPFE, which we extensively use in this paper. A concrete construction of slotted IPFE is found in [26, Appendix A].

Definition 2.4 (Slotted IPFE). Let $\mathbb{G} = (p, G_1, G_2, G_T, g_1, g_2, e)$ be bilinear groups, $\mathcal{X}_{\mathsf{pub}} = \emptyset, \mathcal{X}_{\mathsf{priv1}} = G_1^{m_1}, \mathcal{X}_{\mathsf{priv2}} = G_1^{m_2}, \mathcal{F}_{\mathsf{pub}} = G_2^{m_1}, \mathcal{F}_{\mathsf{priv}} = G_2^{m_2}$. A function family $\mathcal{F}^{\mathsf{IP}}_{m_1,m_2,\mathbb{G}} = \mathcal{F}_{\mathsf{pub}} \times \mathcal{F}_{\mathsf{priv}}$ consists of functions $f : \mathcal{X}_{\mathsf{pub}} \times \mathcal{X}_{\mathsf{priv1}} \times \mathcal{X}_{\mathsf{priv2}} \to G_T \cup \{\bot\}$. Each $f \in \mathcal{F}^{\mathsf{IP}}_{m_1,m_2,\mathbb{G}}$ is specified by $([\mathbf{y}_1]_2, [\mathbf{y}_2]_2) \in \mathcal{F}_{\mathsf{pub}} \times \mathcal{F}_{\mathsf{priv}}$ where $\mathbf{y}_i = \mathbb{Z}_p^{m_i}$ and defined as

$$f([\mathbf{x}_1]_1, [\mathbf{x}_2]_1) = [\langle \mathbf{x}_1, \mathbf{y}_1 \rangle + \langle \mathbf{x}_2, \mathbf{y}_2 \rangle]_T$$

where $\mathbf{x}_i \in \mathbb{Z}_p^{m_i}$. We refer to slotted FE (Definition 2.3) for $\mathcal{F}^{\mathsf{IP}}_{m_1,m_2,\mathbb{G}}$ as slotted IPFE. Note that when $m_1 = 0$, slotted IPFE corresponds to secret-key function-hiding IPFE.

---

[8] This condition implies selective security (or semi-adaptive security more precisely).
[9] In general, this condition is necessary since the adversary can publicly encrypt (x,e) for all $x \in \mathcal{X}_{\mathsf{pub}} \times \mathcal{X}_{\mathsf{priv1}}$ and decrypt the ciphertexts with its own secret keys. In this paper, however, we handle only function classes where this condition is always satisfied as long as the public parts of $f^{\ell,0}$ and $f^{\ell,1}$ are the same. Thus, we can ignore this condition in this paper.

We define FE for unbounded quadratic functions (UQF) and its extension to the combination with ABPs (ABP ∘ UQF). Our goal in this paper is to construct FE (not slotted FE) schemes for the two functionalities. We formally define the two functionalities as follows.

Definition 2.5 (Unbounded Quadratic Functional Encryption). Let $\mathbb{G} = (p, G_1, G_2, G_T, g_1, g_2, e)$ be bilinear groups, $\mathcal{X}_{\text{pub}} \times \mathcal{X}_{\text{priv}} = \{(x_1, x_2) \in 2^{[p]} \times \bigcup_{i \in [p]} \mathbb{Z}_p^i \mid |x_1| = |x_2|\}$ where $|x_1|$ denotes the cardinality of x_1, and $|x_2|$ denotes the length of x_2. Let $\mathcal{F} = \{(f_1, f_2) \in 2^{[p]} \times \bigcup_{i \in [p]} \mathbb{Z}_p^{i^2} \mid |f_1|^2 = |f_2|\}$. A function family $\mathcal{F}_{\mathbb{G}}^{\text{UQF}} = \mathcal{F}$ consists of functions $f : \mathcal{X}_{\text{pub}} \times \mathcal{X}_{\text{priv}} \to G_T \cup \{\bot\}$. Each $f \in \mathcal{F}_{\mathbb{G}}^{\text{UQF}}$ is specified by $(S_k, \mathbf{c}) \in \mathcal{F}$ where $S_k \subseteq [p], \mathbf{c} = (c_{i,j})_{i,j \in S_k} \in (\mathbb{Z}_p)^{S_k \times S_k}$ and defined as

$$f((S_c, \mathbf{x})) = \begin{cases} [\sum_{i,j \in S_k} c_{i,j} x_i x_j]_T & S_k \subseteq S_c \\ \bot & \text{otherwise} \end{cases}$$

where $S_c \subseteq [p], \mathbf{x} = (x_i)_{i \in S_c} \in \mathbb{Z}_p^{S_c}$. Note that S_c is the public input while $\mathbf{x}$ is a private input. We refer to FE for $\mathcal{F}_{\mathbb{G}}^{\text{UQF}}$ with the ciphertext-size being linear in $|S_c|$ as unbounded quadratic functional encryption.

Definition 2.6 (Functional Encryption for ABP ∘ UQF). Let $\mathbb{G} = (p, G_1, G_2, G_T, g_1, g_2, e)$ be bilinear groups, $q = p - 1$, $\mathcal{X}_{\text{pub}} \times \mathcal{X}_{\text{priv}} = \{((x_1, x_2), x_3) \in (\mathbb{Z}_p^n \times 2^{[q]}) \times \bigcup_{i \in [q]} \mathbb{Z}_p^i \mid |x_2| = |x_3|\}$ where $|x_2|$ denotes the cardinality of x_2, and $|x_3|$ denotes the length of x_3. Let $\mathcal{F} = \{(f_1, f_2) \in 2^{[q]} \times \bigcup_{i \in [q]} \mathcal{F}_{n,i^2}^{\text{ABP}} \mid |f_1|^2 = \text{OutLen}(f_2)\}$ where $|f_1|$ denotes the cardinality of f_1, and $\text{OutLen}(f_2)$ denotes the output length of f_2. A function family $\mathcal{F}_{n,\mathbb{G}}^{\text{ABP} \circ \text{UQF}} = \mathcal{F}$ consists of functions $f : \mathcal{X}_{\text{pub}} \times \mathcal{X}_{\text{priv}} \to G_T \cup \{\bot\}$. Each $f \in \mathcal{F}_{n,\mathbb{G}}^{\text{ABP} \circ \text{UQF}}$ is specified by $(S_k, f^{\text{ABP}}) \in \mathcal{F}$ where $S_k \subseteq [q], f^{\text{ABP}} \in \mathcal{F}_{n,|S_k|^2}^{\text{ABP}}$ and defined as

$$f((\mathbf{u}, S_c, \mathbf{x})) = \begin{cases} [\sum_{i,j \in S_k} f_{i,j}^{\text{ABP}}(\mathbf{u}) x_i x_j]_T & S_k \subseteq S_c \\ \bot & \text{otherwise} \end{cases}$$

where $\mathbf{u} \in \mathbb{Z}_p^n, S_c \subseteq [q], \mathbf{x} = (x_i)_{i \in S_c} \in \mathbb{Z}_p^{S_c}$ and $f_{i,j}^{\text{ABP}}(\mathbf{u})$ is the (i, j)-th element of $f^{\text{ABP}}(\mathbf{u})$. Note that $\mathbf{u}, S_c$ are the public inputs while $\mathbf{x}$ is a private input. We refer to FE for $\mathcal{F}_{n,\mathbb{G}}^{\text{ABP} \circ \text{UQF}}$ with the ciphertext-size being linear in $|S_c|$ and $|\mathbf{u}|$ as FE for ABP ∘ UQF.

Our scheme computes function values as an exponent of a group element where the discrete log problem is hard. Thus, we require the exponent to be in a polynomial range if the decrypter needs to obtain the function value as a $\mathbb{Z}_p$ element. Note that this restriction is common in all previous FE schemes for inner product or quadratic functions based on cyclic groups.

3   Predicate Slotted Inner Product Functional Encryption

In this section, we define a new primitive called predicate slotted IPFE and show how to construct it. We use it as a building block of our unbounded slotted IPFE scheme that we present in Sect. 4.

3.1   Definitions

Definition 3.1 (Predicate Slotted IPFE). Let $\mathbb{G}$ be bilinear groups, $\mathcal{X}_{\mathsf{pub}} = \mathbb{Z}_p^d, \mathcal{X}_{\mathsf{priv1}} = G_1^{m_1}, \mathcal{X}_{\mathsf{priv2}} = G_1^{m_2}, \mathcal{F}_{\mathsf{pub}} = \mathbb{Z}_p^d \times G_2^{m_1}, \mathcal{F}_{\mathsf{priv}} = G_2^{m_2}$. A function family $\mathcal{F}_{d,m_1,m_2,\mathbb{G}}^{\mathsf{PIP}} = \mathcal{F}_{\mathsf{pub}} \times \mathcal{F}_{\mathsf{priv}}$ consists of functions $f : \mathcal{X}_{\mathsf{pub}} \times \mathcal{X}_{\mathsf{priv1}} \times \mathcal{X}_{\mathsf{priv2}} \to G_T \cup \{\perp\}$. Each $f \in \mathcal{F}_{d,m_1,m_2,\mathbb{G}}^{\mathsf{PIP}}$ is specified by $((\mathbf{v}, [\mathbf{y}_1]_2), [\mathbf{y}_2]_2) \in \mathcal{F}_{\mathsf{pub}} \times \mathcal{F}_{\mathsf{priv}}$ where $\mathbf{v} \in \mathbb{Z}_p^d, \mathbf{y}_i \in \mathbb{Z}_p^{m_i}$ and defined as

$$f(\mathbf{u}, [\mathbf{x}_1]_1, [\mathbf{x}_2]_1) = \begin{cases} [\langle \mathbf{x}_1, \mathbf{y}_1 \rangle + \langle \mathbf{x}_2, \mathbf{y}_2 \rangle]_T & \text{if } \langle \mathbf{u}, \mathbf{v} \rangle = 0 \\ \perp & \text{if } \langle \mathbf{u}, \mathbf{v} \rangle \neq 0 \end{cases}$$

where $\mathbf{u} \in \mathbb{Z}_p^d, \mathbf{x}_i \in \mathbb{Z}_p^{m_i}$. We refer to slotted FE (Definition 2.3) for $\mathcal{F}_{d,m_1,m_2,\mathbb{G}}^{\mathsf{PIP}}$ as predicate slotted IPFE.

3.2   Predicate Slotted IPFE from Slotted IPFE

We construct a partially hiding slotted FE scheme for $\mathcal{F}_{d,m_1,m_2,\mathbb{G}}^{\mathsf{PIP}}$ from a partially hiding FE scheme for $\mathcal{F}_{kd+m_1,2m_2+1,\mathbb{G}}^{\mathsf{IP}}$ in a generic way. Note that k is a parameter for the MDDH$_k$ assumption.

Construction. Let iFE = (iSetup, iEnc, iSlotEnc, iKeyGen, iDec) be a partially hiding slotted FE scheme for $\mathcal{F}_{kd+m_1,2m_2+1,\mathbb{G}}^{\mathsf{IP}}$ with slot-mode correctness for $e = [0^{2m_2+1}]_1$. Then, our partially hiding slotted FE scheme pFE = (pSetup, pEnc, pSlotEnc, pKeyGen, pDec) for $\mathcal{F}_{d,m_1,m_2,\mathbb{G}}^{\mathsf{PIP}}$ with slot-mode correctness for $e = [0^{m_2}]_1$ is constructed as follows.

pSetup(1^λ): It outputs (pPK, pMSK) = (iPK, iMSK) $\leftarrow$ iSetup(1^λ).
pEnc(pMSK, $(\mathbf{u}, [\mathbf{x}_1]_1, [\mathbf{x}_2]_1)$): It outputs pCT as follows:

$$\mathbf{z} \leftarrow \mathbb{Z}_p^k, \ \tilde{\mathbf{x}}_1 = (\mathbf{z} \otimes \mathbf{u}, \mathbf{x}_1) \in \mathbb{Z}_p^{kd+m_1}, \ \tilde{\mathbf{x}}_2 = (\mathbf{x}_2, 0^{m_2}, 0) \in \mathbb{Z}_p^{2m_2+1}$$
$$\mathsf{iCT} \leftarrow \mathsf{iEnc}(\mathsf{iMSK}, ([\tilde{\mathbf{x}}_1]_1, [\tilde{\mathbf{x}}_2]_1)), \ \mathsf{pCT} = (\mathbf{u}, \mathsf{iCT}).$$

pSlotEnc($\mathbf{u}, [\mathbf{x}_1]_1$): It outputs pCT as follows:

$$\mathbf{z} \leftarrow \mathbb{Z}_p^k, \ \tilde{\mathbf{x}}_1 = (\mathbf{z} \otimes \mathbf{u}, \mathbf{x}_1) \in \mathbb{Z}_p^{kd+m_1}, \ \mathsf{iCT} \leftarrow \mathsf{iSlotEnc}([\tilde{\mathbf{x}}_1]_1), \ \mathsf{pCT} = (\mathbf{u}, \mathsf{iCT}).$$

pKeyGen(pMSK, $(\mathbf{v}, [\mathbf{y}_1]_2, [\mathbf{y}_2]_2)$): It outputs pSK as follows:

$$\mathbf{a} \leftarrow \mathbb{Z}_p^k, \ \tilde{\mathbf{y}}_1 = (\mathbf{a} \otimes \mathbf{v}, \mathbf{y}_1) \in \mathbb{Z}_p^{kd+m_1}, \ \tilde{\mathbf{y}}_2 = (\mathbf{y}_2, 0^{m_2}, 0) \in \mathbb{Z}_p^{2m_2+1}$$
$$\mathsf{iSK} \leftarrow \mathsf{iKeyGen}(\mathsf{iMSK}, ([\tilde{\mathbf{y}}_1]_1, [\tilde{\mathbf{y}}_2]_1)), \ \mathsf{pSK} = (\mathbf{v}, \mathsf{iSK}).$$

pDec(pCT, pSK): If $\langle \mathbf{u}, \mathbf{v} \rangle \neq 0$, it outputs $\bot$. Otherwise, outputs iDec(iCT, iSK).

Correctness. Since $\langle \mathbf{z} \otimes \mathbf{u}, \mathbf{a} \otimes \mathbf{v} \rangle = \langle \mathbf{z}, \mathbf{a} \rangle \cdot \langle \mathbf{u}, \mathbf{v} \rangle$, iDec(iCT, iSK) outputs $[\langle \widetilde{\mathbf{x}}_1, \widetilde{\mathbf{y}}_1 \rangle + \langle \widetilde{\mathbf{x}}_2, \widetilde{\mathbf{y}}_2 \rangle]_T = [\langle \mathbf{x}_1, \mathbf{y}_1 \rangle + \langle \mathbf{x}_2, \mathbf{y}_2 \rangle]_T$ if $\langle \mathbf{u}, \mathbf{v} \rangle = 0$. This follows from the correctness of iFE.

Slot-Mode Correctness. Thanks to slot-mode correctness of iFE, iSlotEnc($[\widetilde{\mathbf{x}}_1]_1$) and iEnc(iMSK, $([\widetilde{\mathbf{x}}_1]_1, [0^{2m_2+1}]_1)$) are identically distributed for all correctly generated (iMSK, iPK) and $\widetilde{\mathbf{x}}_1 \in \mathbb{Z}_p^{kd+m_1}$. Hence, pSlotEnc($\mathbf{u}, [\mathbf{x}_1]_1$) and pEnc(pMSK, $(\mathbf{u}, [\mathbf{x}_1]_1, [0^{m_2}]_1)$) are identically distributed for all correctly generated (pMSK, pPK), $\mathbf{u} \in \mathbb{Z}_p^d$, and $\mathbf{x}_1 \in \mathbb{Z}_p^{m_1}$.

Security. Due to space constraints, we present the security analysisn in the full verion [31].

4 Unbounded Slotted Inner Product Functional Encryption

In this section, we define a new primitive called unbounded slotted IPFE and show how to construct it. We use it as a building block of our FE schemes for unbounded quadratic functions (Sect. 5) and ABP ∘ UQF (Sect. 6).

4.1 Definitions

Definition 4.1 (Unbounded Slotted IPFE). Let $\mathbb{G}$ be bilinear groups, $\mathcal{X}_{\mathsf{pub}} \times \mathcal{X}_{\mathsf{priv1}} \times \mathcal{X}_{\mathsf{priv2}} = \{(x_1, x_2, x_3) \in 2^{[p]} \times \bigcup_{i \in [p]} (G_1^{m_1})^i \times G_1^{m_2} \mid |x_1| = |x_2|/m_1\}$, where $|x_1|$ denotes the cardinality of x_1, and $|x_2|$ denotes the length of x_2. Let $\mathcal{F}_{\mathsf{pub}} \times \mathcal{F}_{\mathsf{priv}} = \{((f_1, f_2), f_3) \in (2^{[p]} \times \bigcup_{i \in [p]} (G_2^{m_1})^i) \times G_2^{m_2} \mid |f_1| = |f_2|/m_1\}$. A function family $\mathcal{F}_{m_1,m_2,\mathbb{G}}^{\mathsf{UIP}} = \mathcal{F}_{\mathsf{pub}} \times \mathcal{F}_{\mathsf{priv}}$ consists of functions $f : \mathcal{X}_{\mathsf{pub}} \times \mathcal{X}_{\mathsf{priv}} \to G_T \cup \{\bot\}$. Each $f \in \mathcal{F}_{m_1,m_2,\mathbb{G}}^{\mathsf{UIP}}$ is specified by $((S_k, [\mathbf{y}]_2), [\mathbf{y}_0]_2) \in \mathcal{F}_{\mathsf{pub}} \times \mathcal{F}_{\mathsf{priv}}$ where $S_k \subseteq [p], \mathbf{y} = (\mathbf{y}_i)_{i \in S_k} \in (\mathbb{Z}_p^{m_1})^{S_k}, \mathbf{y}_0 \in \mathbb{Z}_p^{m_2}$ and defined as

$$f(S_c, [\mathbf{x}]_1, [\mathbf{x}_0]_1) = \begin{cases} [\sum_{i \in S_k} \langle \mathbf{x}_i, \mathbf{y}_i \rangle + \langle \mathbf{x}_0, \mathbf{y}_0 \rangle]_T & \text{if } S_k \subseteq S_c \\ \bot & \text{otherwise} \end{cases}$$

where $S_c \subseteq [p], \mathbf{x} = (\mathbf{x}_i)_{i \in S_c} \in (\mathbb{Z}_p^{m_1})^{S_c}, \mathbf{x}_0 \in \mathbb{Z}_p^{m_2}$. Note that S_c is the public input while $[\mathbf{x}]_1$ is a private input for the first slot, and $[\mathbf{x}_0]_1$ is a private input for the second slot. We refer to slotted FE (Definition 2.3) for $\mathcal{F}_{m_1,m_2,\mathbb{G}}^{\mathsf{UIP}}$ as unbounded slotted IPFE.

4.2 Unbounded Slotted IPFE from Predicate Slotted IPFE

Construction. Let k be the parameter of the MDDH$_k$ assumption. Let pFE = (pSetup, pEnc, pSlotEnc, pKeyGen, pDec) be a partially hiding slotted FE scheme for $\mathcal{F}_{2,m_1+k,1,\mathbb{G}}^{\mathsf{PIP}}$ with slot-mode correctness for $e = [0]_1$. Let iFE = (iSetup, iEnc, iSlotEnc, iKeyGen, iDec) be a partially hiding slotted FE scheme for $\mathcal{F}^{\text{IP}}_{k,m_2+1,\mathbb{G}}$ with slot-mode correctness for $e = [0^{m_2+1}]_1$. Then, our partially hiding slotted FE scheme uFE = (uSetup, uEnc, uSlotEnc, uKeyGen, uDec) for $\mathcal{F}^{\text{UIP}}_{m_1,m_2,\mathbb{G}}$ with slot-mode correctness for $e = [0^{m_2}]_1$ is constructed as follows.

uSetup(1^λ): It runs (pPK, pMSK) $\leftarrow$ pSetup(1^λ), (iPK, iMSK) $\leftarrow$ iSetup(1^λ), and outputs (uPK, uMSK) = ((pPK, iPK), (pMSK, iMSK)).

uEnc(uMSK, $(S_c, [\mathbf{x}]_1, [\mathbf{x}_0]_1)$): It chooses $\mathbf{z} \leftarrow \mathbb{Z}_p^k$ and outputs uCT as follows:

$$\mathbf{u}_i = (1, i), \ \widetilde{\mathbf{x}}_i = (\mathbf{x}_i, \mathbf{z}, 0), \ \text{pCT}_i \leftarrow \text{pEnc}(\text{pMSK}, (\mathbf{u}_i, [\widetilde{\mathbf{x}}_i]_1)) \text{ for } i \in S_c$$
$$\widetilde{\mathbf{x}}_0 = (\mathbf{z}, \mathbf{x}_0, 0), \ \text{iCT} \leftarrow \text{iEnc}(\text{iMSK}, [\widetilde{\mathbf{x}}_0]_1), \ \text{uCT} = (S_c, \{\text{pCT}_i\}_{i \in S_c}, \text{iCT}).$$

uSlotEnc($S_c, [\mathbf{x}]_1$): It chooses $\mathbf{z} \leftarrow \mathbb{Z}_p^k$ and outputs uCT as follows:

$$\mathbf{u}_i = (1, i), \ \widetilde{\mathbf{x}}_i = (\mathbf{x}_i, \mathbf{z}), \ \text{pCT}_i \leftarrow \text{pSlotEnc}(\mathbf{u}_i, [\widetilde{\mathbf{x}}_i]_1) \text{ for } i \in S_c$$
$$\text{iCT} \leftarrow \text{iSlotEnc}([\mathbf{z}]_1), \ \text{uCT} = (S_c, \{\text{pCT}_i\}_{i \in S_c}, \text{iCT}).$$

uKeyGen(uMSK, $(S_k, [\mathbf{y}]_2, [\mathbf{y}_0]_2)$): It chooses $\mathbf{a}_i \leftarrow \mathbb{Z}_p^k$ for all $i \in S_k$, sets $\mathbf{a}_0 = -\sum_{i \in S_k} \mathbf{a}_i$, and outputs uSK as follows:

$$\mathbf{v}_i = (i, -1), \ \widetilde{\mathbf{y}}_i = (\mathbf{y}_i, \mathbf{a}_i, 0), \ \text{pSK}_i \leftarrow \text{pKeyGen}(\text{pMSK}, (\mathbf{v}_i, [\widetilde{\mathbf{y}}_i]_2)) \text{ for } i \in S_k$$
$$\widetilde{\mathbf{y}}_0 = (\mathbf{a}_0, \mathbf{y}_0, 0), \ \text{iSK} \leftarrow \text{iKeyGen}(\text{iMSK}, [\widetilde{\mathbf{y}}_0]_2), \ \text{uSK} = (S_k, \{\text{pSK}_i\}_{i \in S_k}, \text{iSK}).$$

uDec(uCT, uSK): If $S_k \not\subseteq S_c$, it outputs $\perp$. Otherwise, outputs iDec(iCT, iSK) $+ \sum_{i \in S_k} \text{pDec}(\text{pCT}_i, \text{pSK}_i)$.

Correctness. Thanks to the correctness of iFE and pFE, uDec(uCT, uSK) outputs $[\sum_{i \in S_k}(\langle \mathbf{x}_i, \mathbf{y}_i \rangle + \langle \mathbf{z}, \mathbf{a}_i \rangle) + \langle \mathbf{x}_0, \mathbf{y}_0 \rangle + \langle \mathbf{z}, \mathbf{a}_0 \rangle]_T = [\sum_{i \in S_k} \langle \mathbf{x}_i, \mathbf{y}_i \rangle + \langle \mathbf{x}_0, \mathbf{y}_0 \rangle]_T$.

Slot-Mode Correctness. Thanks to slot-mode correctness of pFE, pSlotEnc($\mathbf{u}_i, [\widetilde{\mathbf{x}}_1]_1$) and pEnc(pMSK, $(\mathbf{u}_i, [(\widetilde{\mathbf{x}}_1, 0)]_1)$) are identically distributed for all correctly generated (pMSK, pPK), $\mathbf{u}_i \in \mathbb{Z}_p^2$, and $\widetilde{\mathbf{x}}_1 \in \mathbb{Z}_p^{m_1+k}$. Similarly, iSlotEnc($[\mathbf{z}]_1$) and iEnc(iMSK, $([(\mathbf{z}, 0^{m_2+1})]_1)$) are identically distributed for all correctly generated (iMSK, iPK) and $\mathbf{x} \in \mathbb{Z}_p^k$. Hence, uSlotEnc($S_c, [\mathbf{x}]_1$) and uEnc(uMSK, $(S_c, [\mathbf{x}]_1, [0^{m_2}]_1)$) are identically distributed for all correctly generated (uMSK, uPK), $S_c \subseteq [p]$, and $\mathbf{x} \in (\mathbb{Z}_p^{m_1})^{S_c}$.

4.3 Security Analysis

For security, we have the following theorem.

Theorem 4.1. *If pFE and iFE are IND-partially hiding, and the MDDH$_k$ assumption holds in $\mathbb{G}$, then uFE is IND-1-partially hiding.*

Proof. We prove Theorem 4.1 via a series of hybrid games $\mathsf{H}_1^\beta, \mathsf{H}_2^\beta, \mathsf{H}_f^\beta$. We show that $\mathsf{H}_s^\beta \approx_c \mathsf{H}_1^\beta \approx_c \mathsf{H}_2^\beta \approx_c \mathsf{H}_f^\beta$, where H_s^β for $\beta \in \{0,1\}$ is the original security game (described in Eq. (2.2)). Especially, the oracles cO and kO works as Fig. 1 in H_s^β. In the hybrid sequence, the behavior of the oracles is gradually changed. Each hybrid is defined as follows.

$\mathsf{cO}(\beta, \cdot)$	$\mathsf{kO}(\beta, \cdot)$
Input: $S_c \in \mathcal{X}_{\mathsf{pub}}, ([\mathbf{x}^0]_1, [\mathbf{x}^1]_1) \in \mathcal{X}_{\mathsf{priv1}}^2, ([\mathbf{x}_0^0]_1, [\mathbf{x}_0^1]_1) \in \mathcal{X}_{\mathsf{priv2}}^2$	Input: $(S_k, [\mathbf{y}]_2) \in \mathcal{F}_{\mathsf{pub}}, ([\mathbf{y}_0^0]_2, [\mathbf{y}_0^1]_2) \in \mathcal{F}_{\mathsf{priv}}^2$
$\mathbf{z} \leftarrow \mathbb{Z}_p^k, \; \mathbf{u}_i = (1, i)$	$\mathbf{a}_i \leftarrow \mathbb{Z}_p^k, \; \mathbf{a}_0 = -\sum_{i \in S_k} \mathbf{a}_i, \; \mathbf{v}_i = (i, -1)$
$\widetilde{\mathbf{x}}_i = (\mathbf{x}_i^\beta, \mathbf{z}, 0), \; \mathsf{pCT}_i \leftarrow \mathsf{pEnc}(\mathsf{pMSK}, (\mathbf{u}_i, [\widetilde{\mathbf{x}}_i]_1))$	$\widetilde{\mathbf{y}}_i = (\mathbf{y}_i, \mathbf{a}_i, 0), \; \mathsf{pSK}_i \leftarrow \mathsf{pKeyGen}(\mathsf{pMSK}, (\mathbf{v}_i, [\widetilde{\mathbf{y}}_i]_2))$
$\widetilde{\mathbf{x}}_0 = (\mathbf{z}, \mathbf{x}_0^\beta, 0), \; \mathsf{iCT} \leftarrow \mathsf{iEnc}(\mathsf{iMSK}, [\widetilde{\mathbf{x}}_0]_1)$	$\widetilde{\mathbf{y}}_0 = (\mathbf{a}_0, \mathbf{y}_0^\beta, 0), \; \mathsf{iSK} \leftarrow \mathsf{iKeyGen}(\mathsf{iMSK}, [\widetilde{\mathbf{y}}_0]_2)$
Output: $\mathsf{uCT} = (S_c, \{\mathsf{pCT}_i\}_{i \in S_c}, \mathsf{iCT})$	Output: $\mathsf{uSK} = (S_k, \{\mathsf{pSK}_i\}_{i \in S_k}, \mathsf{iSK})$.

Fig. 1. The behavior of cO and kO in H_s^β.

H_1^β: This game is the same as H_s^β except that
- for the query to cO, it chooses $\mathbf{z} \leftarrow \mathbb{Z}_p^k$ and sets $\widetilde{\mathbf{x}}_i, \widetilde{\mathbf{x}}_0^j$ as

$$\widetilde{\mathbf{x}}_i = (0^{m_1}, 0^k, 1), \quad \widetilde{\mathbf{x}}_0 = (0^k, 0^{m_2}, 1)$$

- for the ℓ-th query to kO on $(S_k^\ell, [\mathbf{y}^\ell]_2, ([\mathbf{y}_0^{\ell,0}]_2, [\mathbf{y}_0^{\ell,1}]_2))$, it chooses $\mathbf{a}_i^\ell \leftarrow \mathbb{Z}_p^k$ for $i \in S_k^\ell$ and sets $\mathbf{a}_0^\ell = -\sum_{i \in S_k^\ell} \mathbf{a}_i^\ell$ and

$$\widetilde{\mathbf{y}}_i^\ell = \begin{cases} (\mathbf{y}_i^\ell, \mathbf{a}_i^\ell, \langle \mathbf{x}_i^\beta, \mathbf{y}_i^\ell \rangle + \langle \mathbf{z}, \mathbf{a}_i^\ell \rangle) & (i \in S_c) \\ (\mathbf{y}_i^\ell, \mathbf{a}_i^\ell, 0) & (i \notin S_c) \end{cases}$$

$$\widetilde{\mathbf{y}}_0^\ell = (\mathbf{a}_0^\ell, \mathbf{y}_0^{\ell,0}, \langle \mathbf{z}, \mathbf{a}_0^\ell \rangle + \langle \mathbf{x}_0^\beta, \mathbf{y}_0^{\ell,\beta} \rangle)$$

H_2^β: This game is the same as H_1^β except the following: in each query to kO, it samples $t_i^\ell \leftarrow \mathbb{Z}_p$ for $i \in S_k^\ell \cup \{0\}$ so that $\sum_{i \in S_k^\ell \cup \{0\}} t_i^\ell = 0$ if $S_k^\ell \subseteq S_c$, and otherwise it just randomly samples $t_i^\ell \leftarrow \mathbb{Z}_p$ for $i \in (S_c \cap S_k^\ell) \cup \{0\}$. Then, it sets

$$\widetilde{\mathbf{y}}_i^\ell = \begin{cases} (\mathbf{y}_i^\ell, \mathbf{a}_i^\ell, \langle \mathbf{x}_i^\beta, \mathbf{y}_i^\ell \rangle + \underline{t_i^\ell}) & (i \in S_c) \\ (\mathbf{y}_i^\ell, \mathbf{a}_i^\ell, 0) & (i \notin S_c) \end{cases}, \quad \widetilde{\mathbf{y}}_0^\ell = (\mathbf{a}_0^\ell, \mathbf{y}_0^{\ell,0}, \underline{t_0^\ell} + \langle \mathbf{x}_0^\beta, \mathbf{y}_0^{\ell,\beta} \rangle)$$

H_f^β: This game is the same as H_2^β except the following: it sets

$$\widetilde{\mathbf{y}}_i^\ell = \begin{cases} (\mathbf{y}_i^\ell, \mathbf{a}_i^\ell, \langle \underline{\mathbf{x}_i^0}, \mathbf{y}_i^\ell \rangle + t_i^\ell) & (i \in S_c) \\ (\mathbf{y}_i^\ell, \mathbf{a}_i^\ell, 0) & (i \notin S_c) \end{cases}, \quad \widetilde{\mathbf{y}}_0^\ell = (\mathbf{a}_0^\ell, \mathbf{y}_0^{\ell,0}, t_0^\ell + \underline{\langle \mathbf{x}_0^0, \mathbf{y}_0^{\ell,0} \rangle})$$

Observe that the adversary does not obtain the information on β in H_f^β, and thus its advantage is 0. Due to the space constraints, the rest of the proof is given in the full version [31]. □

5 Unbounded Quadratic Functional Encryption

In this section, we present our FE scheme for unbounded quadratic functions defined in Definition 2.5.

5.1   Construction

Let k be the parameter of the $MDDH_k$ assumption. Let $uFE = (uSetup, uEnc, uSlotEnc, uKeyGen, uDec)$ be a partially hiding slotted FE scheme for $\mathcal{F}_{k,1,\mathbb{G}}^{UIP}$ with slot-mode correctness for $e = [0]_1$. Let $H : [p] \to G_2^k$ be a hash function modeled as a random oracle. Then, our partially hiding FE scheme $qFE = (qSetup, qEnc, qKeyGen, qDec)$ for $\mathcal{F}_{\mathbb{G}}^{UQF}$ is constructed as follows.

$qSetup(1^\lambda)$: It runs $(uPK, uMSK) \leftarrow uKeyGen(1^\lambda)$ outputs $(qPK, qMSK) = (uPK, uMSK)$.

$qEnc(S_c, \mathbf{x} = (x_i)_{i \in S_c})$: First, it defines vectors as follows:

$$[\mathbf{a}_i]_2 = H(i), \ \mathbf{z}_i \leftarrow \mathbb{Z}_p^k, \ \mathbf{b}_i = (x_i, \mathbf{z}_i, 0), \ \widetilde{\mathbf{b}}_i = (x_i, \mathbf{a}_i, 0)$$
$$\mathbf{d}_i = \mathbf{z}_i, \ \mathbf{d} = (\mathbf{d}_i)_{i \in S_c}.$$

Then, it outputs qCT as follows: let $iFE = (iSetup, iEnc, iSlotEnc, iKeyGen, iDec)$ be a partially hiding slotted FE scheme for $\mathcal{F}_{0,k+2,\mathbb{G}}^{IP}$ with slot-mode correctness for $e = [0^{k+2}]_1$, or equivalently standard function-hiding IPFE scheme with the vector length being $k + 2$.

$$(iPK, iMSK) \leftarrow iSetup(1^\lambda)$$
$$iCT_i \leftarrow iEnc(iMSK, [\mathbf{b}_i]_1), \ iSK_i \leftarrow iKeyGen(iMSK, [\widetilde{\mathbf{b}}_i]_2)$$
$$uCT \leftarrow uSlotEnc(S_c, [\mathbf{d}]_1), \ qCT = (iPK, \{iCT_i, iSK_i\}_{i \in S_c}, uCT)$$

$qKeyGen(qMSK, (S_k, \mathbf{c} = (c_{i,j})_{i,j \in S_k}))$ It outputs qSK as follows:

$$[\mathbf{a}_j]_2 = H(j), \ \widetilde{\mathbf{d}}_i = \sum_{j \in S_k} c_{i,j} \mathbf{a}_j, \ \widetilde{\mathbf{d}} = (\widetilde{\mathbf{d}}_i)_{i \in S_k}$$
$$uSK \leftarrow uKeyGen(uMSK, (S_k, [\widetilde{\mathbf{d}}]_2, [0]_2)), \ qSK = uSK$$

$qDec(qCT, qSK)$ If $S_k \not\subseteq S_c$, it outputs $\perp$. Otherwise, it outputs $[z]_T$ as follows:

$$[z_1]_T = \sum_{i,j \in S_k} c_{i,j} iDec(iCT_i, iSK_j), \ [z_2]_T = uDec(uCT, uSK)$$
$$[z]_T = [z_1 - z_2]_T.$$

Correctness. Due to the correctness of iFE and uEF, we have

$$z_1 = \sum_{i,j \in S_k} (c_{i,j} x_i x_j + c_{i,j} \langle \mathbf{z}_i, \mathbf{a}_j \rangle), \ z_2 = \sum_{i,j \in S_k} c_{i,j} \langle \mathbf{z}_i, \mathbf{a}_j \rangle$$

Hence, we have $z - \sum_{i,j \in S_k} c_{i,j} x_i x_j$.

5.2 Security

For security, we have the following theorem.

Theorem 5.1. *If* iFE *is IND-partially hiding,* uFE *is IND-1-partially hiding, and the* $MDDH_k$ *assumption holds in* $\mathbb{G}$*, then* qFE *is SIM-partially-hiding.*

Proof. First, we show our simulation algorithms. Note that our simulation algorithm for key key generation takes a G_2 element instead of a G_T element, which follows [21,33].

$qSetup^*(1^\lambda)$: It runs $(uPK, uMSK) \leftarrow uKeyGen(1^\lambda)$ outputs $(qPK^*, qMSK^*) = (uPK, uMSK)$.

$qEnc^*(qMSK^*, S_c)$: First, it defines vectors as follows:

$$[\mathbf{a}_i]_2 = H(i), \quad \mathbf{z}_i \leftarrow \mathbb{Z}_p^k, \quad \mathbf{b}_i = (0, \mathbf{z}_i, 0), \quad \widetilde{\mathbf{b}}_i = (0, \mathbf{a}_i, 0)$$
$$\mathbf{d}_i = \mathbf{z}_i, \quad \mathbf{d} = (\mathbf{d}_i)_{i \in S_c}.$$

Then, it outputs qCT^* as follows: let $iFE = (iSetup, iEnc, iSlotEnc, iKeyGen, iDec)$ be a partially hiding slotted FE scheme for $\mathcal{F}_{0,k+2,\mathbb{G}}^{\mathsf{IP}}$ with slot-mode correctness for $e = [0^{k+2}]_1$.

$(iPK, iMSK) \leftarrow iSetup(1^\lambda)$

$iCT_i \leftarrow iEnc(iMSK, [\mathbf{b}_i]_1), \quad iSK_i \leftarrow iKeyGen(iMSK, [\widetilde{\mathbf{b}}_i]_2)$

$uCT \leftarrow uEnc(uMSK, (S_c, [\mathbf{d}]_1, [1]_1)), \quad qCT^* = (iPK, \{iCT_i, iSK_i\}_{i \in S_c}, uCT)$

$qKeyGen^*(qMSK^*, (S_k, \mathbf{c} = (c_{i,j})_{i,j \in S_k}, S_c, [\alpha]_2 \text{ or } \perp))$: It outputs qSK^* as follows:

$$[\mathbf{a}_j]_2 = H(j), \quad \widetilde{\mathbf{d}}_i = \sum_{j \in S_k} c_{i,j} \mathbf{a}_j, \quad \widetilde{\mathbf{d}} = (\widetilde{\mathbf{d}}_i)_{i \in S_k}$$

$$uSK \leftarrow \begin{cases} uKeyGen(uMSK, (S_k, [\widetilde{\mathbf{d}}]_2, [-\alpha]_2)) & S_k \subseteq S_c \\ uKeyGen(uMSK, (S_k, [\widetilde{\mathbf{d}}]_2, [0]_2)) & \text{otherwise} \end{cases}, \quad qSK^* = uSK$$

We prove Theorem 5.1 via a series of hybrid games H_η for $\eta \in [s_{max}] \cup \{f\}$ where s_{max} is the maximum size of the challenge index set S_c. We show that $H_s \approx_c H_1 \approx_c \cdots \approx_c H_{s_{max}} \approx_c H_f$, where H_s is the real game. Each hybrid is defined as described in Fig. 2, where qEnc and qKeyGen are replaced with $\widetilde{qEnc}_\eta$ and $\widetilde{qKeyGen}_\eta$. They work as follows for $\eta \in [s_{max}]$.

$\widetilde{qEnc}_\eta(qMSK, \widetilde{\mathbf{x}})$: Let $S_c = (s_1, \ldots, s_{|S_c|})$. First, it defines vectors as follows:

$$[\mathbf{a}_i]_2 = H(i), \quad \mathbf{z}_i \leftarrow \mathbb{Z}_p^k$$
$$\mathbf{b}_i = \begin{cases} (0, \ \mathbf{z}_i, 0) & (i \leq s_\eta) \\ (x_i, \mathbf{z}_i, 0) & (i > s_\eta) \end{cases}, \quad \widetilde{\mathbf{b}}_i = (x_i, \mathbf{a}_i, 0) \tag{5.1}$$
$$\mathbf{d}_i = \mathbf{z}_i, \quad \mathbf{d} = (\mathbf{d}_i)_{i \in S_c} \tag{5.2}$$

H_s	H_η
$qPK, qMSK \leftarrow qSetup(1^\lambda)$	$qPK, qMSK \leftarrow qSetup(1^\lambda)$
$\widetilde{x} = (S_c, x) \leftarrow \mathcal{A}(1^\lambda, qPK)$	$\widetilde{x} = (S_c, x) \leftarrow \mathcal{A}(1^\lambda, qPK)$
$qCT \leftarrow qEnc(\widetilde{x})$	$qCT \leftarrow \widetilde{qEnc}_\eta(qMSK, \widetilde{x})$
$\beta \leftarrow \mathcal{A}^{qKeyGen(qMSK,\cdot)}(qCT)$	$\beta \leftarrow \mathcal{A}^{\widetilde{qKeyGen}_\eta(qMSK,\widetilde{x},\cdot)}(qCT)$

Fig. 2. Hybrids for qFE.

Then, it outputs qCT as follows:

$$(iPP, iMSK) \leftarrow iSetup(1^\lambda)$$

$$iCT_i \leftarrow iEnc(iMSK, [b_i]_1), iSK_i \leftarrow iKeyGen(iMSK, [\widetilde{b}_i]_2)$$

$$uCT \leftarrow \underline{uEnc(uMSK, (S_c, [d]_1, [1]_1))}, \quad qCT = (iPP, \{iCT_i, iSK_i\}_{i \in S_c}, uCT)$$

$\widetilde{qKeyGen}_\eta(qMSK, \widetilde{x}, (S_k, c))$: Let $S_{c,\eta} = (s_1, \ldots, s_\eta)$ where s_i is the i-th element of the challenge index set S_c. It outputs qSK as follows:

$$[a_j]_2 = H(j), \quad \widetilde{d}_i = \sum_{j \in S_k} c_{i,j} a_j, \quad \widetilde{d} = (\widetilde{d}_i)_{i \in S_k}$$

$$\widehat{d} = \begin{cases} -\sum_{\substack{i \in S_{c,\eta} \cap S_k \\ j \in S_k}} c_{i,j} x_i x_j & S_k \subseteq S_c \\ 0 & \text{otherwise} \end{cases}$$

$$uSK \leftarrow uKeyGen(uMSK, (S_k, [\widetilde{d}]_2, \underline{[\widehat{d}]_2})), \quad qSK = uSK$$

H_f is the same as $H_{s_{\max}}$ except that $\widetilde{qEnc}_\eta$ sets $\widetilde{b}_i = (\underline{0}, a_i, 0)$ in Eq. (5.1). Observe that the adversary's view in H_f is equivalent to that in the simulated game. Thanks to Lemmata 5.1 and 5.2, Theorem 5.1 holds. $\qquad\square$

Lemma 5.1. $H_{s_{\max}} \approx_c H_f$ *if iFE is IND-partially hiding.*

Proof. For all $i \in [|S_c|]$, let b_i^0 and $\widetilde{b}_i^0$ be b_i and $\widetilde{b}_i$ defined in $H_{s_{\max}}$. Similarly, let b_i^1 and $\widetilde{b}_i^1$ be b_i and $\widetilde{b}_i$ defined in H_f. Then, it is not hard to see that $\langle b_i^0, \widetilde{b}_j^0 \rangle = \langle b_i^1, \widetilde{b}_j^1 \rangle$ for all $i, j \in [|S_c|]$. Hence, the difference between $H_{s_{\max}}$ and H_f can be reduced to partially hiding security of iFE. $\qquad\square$

Lemma 5.2. *Let* $H_s = H_0$. *For* $\eta \in [s_{\max}]$, *we have* $H_{\eta-1} \approx_c H_\eta$ *if iFE and uFE are IND-partially hiding and the MDDH$_k$ assumption holds in* $\mathbb{G}$.

Proof. We define intermediate hybrids $\widehat{H}_{\eta,1}, \widehat{H}_{\eta,2}, \widehat{H}_{\eta,3}$ and prove that $H_{\eta-1} \approx_c \widehat{H}_{\eta,1} \approx_c \widehat{H}_{\eta,2} \approx_c \widehat{H}_{\eta,3} \approx_c H_\eta$. $\widehat{H}_{\eta,i}$ for $i \in \{1, 2, 3\}$ is the same as $H_{\eta-1}$ except that $\widetilde{qEnc}_{\eta-1}, \widetilde{qKeyGen}_{\eta-1}$ are replaced by $\widetilde{qEnc}_{\eta,i}, \widetilde{qKeyGen}_{\eta,i}$, respectively, which work as follows:

$\widehat{\mathsf{qEnc}}_{\eta,1}(\mathsf{qMSK}, \widetilde{\mathbf{x}})$: It is the same as $\widehat{\mathsf{qEnc}}_{\eta-1}$ except that it defines vectors as follows:

$$\mathbf{b}_i = \begin{cases} (0, \ \mathbf{z}_i, 0) & (i < s_\eta) \\ (0, \ \mathbf{0}, 1) & (i = s_\eta) \\ (x_i, \mathbf{z}_i, 0) & (i > s_\eta) \end{cases}, \quad \widetilde{\mathbf{b}}_i = (x_i, \mathbf{a}_i, \underline{\langle \mathbf{z}_{s_\eta}, \mathbf{a}_i \rangle + x_{s_\eta} x_i}) \tag{5.3}$$

$$\mathbf{d}_i = \begin{cases} \mathbf{0} & i = s_\eta \\ \mathbf{z}_i & i \neq s_\eta \end{cases}, \quad \mathbf{d} = (\mathbf{d}_i)_{i \in S_c} \tag{5.4}$$

$\widehat{\mathsf{qKeyGen}}_{\eta,1}(\mathsf{qMSK}, \widetilde{\mathbf{x}}, (S_k, \mathbf{c}))$: It is the same as $\widehat{\mathsf{qEnc}}_{\eta-1}$ except that, if and only if $S_k \subseteq S_c$, it defines uSK as follows:

$$\mathsf{uSK} \leftarrow \mathsf{uKeyGen}(\mathsf{uMSK}, (S_k, [\widetilde{\mathbf{d}}]_2, [\widehat{d} + \sum_{i \in S_k} c_{s_\eta, i} \langle \mathbf{z}_{s_\eta}, \mathbf{a}_i \rangle]_2))$$

where $c_{s_\eta, i} = 0$ if $s_\eta \notin S_k$.

$\widehat{\mathsf{qEnc}}_{\eta,2}(\mathsf{qMSK}, \widetilde{\mathbf{x}})$: It is the same as $\widehat{\mathsf{qEnc}}_{\eta,1}$ except that it defines vectors as follows:

$$\mathbf{r} = (r_i)_{i \in S_c} \leftarrow \mathbb{Z}_p^{S_c}, \quad \widetilde{\mathbf{b}}_i = (x_i, \mathbf{a}_i, \underline{r_i} + x_{s_\eta} x_i)$$

$\widehat{\mathsf{qKeyGen}}_{\eta,2}(\mathsf{qMSK}, \widetilde{\mathbf{x}}, (S_k, \mathbf{c}))$: Let $\mathbf{r} = (r_i)_{i \in S_c}$ be the random vector chosen in $\widehat{\mathsf{qEnc}}_{\eta,2}$. It is the same as $\widehat{\mathsf{qKeyGen}}_{\eta,1}$ except that, if and only if $S_k \subseteq S_c$, it defines uSK as follows:

$$\mathsf{uSK} \leftarrow \mathsf{uKeyGen}(\mathsf{uMSK}, (S_k, [\widetilde{\mathbf{d}}]_2, [\widehat{d} + \sum_{i \in S_k} c_{s_\eta, i} r_i]_2))$$

$\widehat{\mathsf{qEnc}}_{\eta,3}(\mathsf{qMSK}, \widetilde{\mathbf{x}})$: It is the same as $\widehat{\mathsf{qEnc}}_{\eta,2}$ except that it defines vectors as follows:

$$\mathbf{r} = (r_i)_{i \in S_c} \leftarrow \mathbb{Z}_p^{S_c}, \quad \widetilde{\mathbf{b}}_i = (x_i, \mathbf{a}_i, r_i + \underline{x_{s_\eta} x_i})$$

$\widehat{\mathsf{qKeyGen}}_{\eta,3}(\mathsf{qMSK}, \widetilde{\mathbf{x}}, (S_k, \mathbf{c}))$: Let $\mathbf{r} = (r_i)_{i \in S_c}$ be the random vector chosen in $\widehat{\mathsf{qEnc}}_{\eta,3}$. It is the same as $\widehat{\mathsf{qKeyGen}}_{\eta,2}$ except that, if and only if $S_k \subseteq S_c$, it defines uSK as follows:

$$\mathsf{uSK} \leftarrow \mathsf{uKeyGen}(\mathsf{uMSK}, (S_k, [\widetilde{\mathbf{d}}]_2, [\widehat{d} + \sum_{i \in S_k} c_{s_\eta, i} (r_i - \underline{x_{s_\eta} x_i})]_2))$$

Lemma 5.2 immediately follows from Lemmata 5.3 to 5.6. $\qquad\qquad\square$

Lemma 5.3. *For $\eta \in [s_{\mathsf{max}}]$, we have $\mathsf{H}_{\eta-1} \approx_c \widehat{\mathsf{H}}_{\eta,1}$ if iFE and uFE are IND-(1-)partially hiding.*

Proof. First, we consider the case of $\eta \geq 2$. Let $\mathbf{b}_i^0, \widetilde{\mathbf{b}}_i^0$ be $\mathbf{b}_i, \widetilde{\mathbf{b}}_i$ defined in $\mathsf{H}_{\eta-1}$, i.e., Eq. (5.1), and $\mathbf{b}_i^1, \widetilde{\mathbf{b}}_i^1$ be $\mathbf{b}_i, \widetilde{\mathbf{b}}_i$ defined in $\widehat{\mathsf{H}}_{\eta,1}$, i.e., Eq. (5.3). Then, it is not hard to see that we have $\langle \mathbf{b}_i^0, \widetilde{\mathbf{b}}_j^0 \rangle = \langle \mathbf{b}_i^1, \widetilde{\mathbf{b}}_j^1 \rangle$ for all $i, j \in S_c$. Thus, we can reduce the indistinguishability between the 0-side and 1-side to partially-hiding security of iFE.

Let $\mathbf{d}_i^0$ be $\mathbf{d}_i$ defined in $\mathsf{H}_{\eta-1}$, i.e., Eq. (5.2), and $\mathbf{d}_i^1$ be $\mathbf{d}_i$ defined in $\widehat{\mathsf{H}}_{\eta,1}$, i.e., Eq. (5.4). Then, for $\ell \in [q_k]$ where q_k is the number of queries to the key generation oracle, we have

$$\sum_{i \in S_k^\ell} \langle \mathbf{d}_i^0, \widetilde{\mathbf{d}}_i^\ell \rangle + \widehat{d} = \sum_{i \in S_k^\ell} \langle \mathbf{d}_i^1, \widetilde{\mathbf{d}}_i^\ell \rangle + \widehat{d} + \sum_{i \in S_k^\ell} c_{s_\eta, i} \langle \mathbf{z}_{s_\eta}, \mathbf{a}_i \rangle \qquad \text{if } S_k^\ell \subseteq S_c$$

where $c_{s_\eta, i} = 0$ if $s_\eta \notin S_k$. Thus, we can reduce the indistinguishability between the 0-side and 1-side to the partially function-hiding property of uFE.

Next, we consider the case of $\eta = 1$, which can be similarly proven to the case of $\eta \geq 2$. A main difference is that we need to first change $\mathsf{uSlotEnc}(S_c, [\mathbf{d}]_1)$ in qEnc to $\mathsf{uEnc}(\mathsf{uMSK}, (S_c, [\mathbf{d}]_1, [0]_1))$, which are identically distributed by the slot-mode correctness of uFE. The remaining proof is almost the same as the case of $\eta \geq 2$. □

Lemma 5.4. *Let q_r be the maximum number of queries to the random oracle H in the security game. For all $\eta \in [s_{\mathsf{max}}]$, we have $\widehat{\mathsf{H}}_{\eta,1} \approx_c \widehat{\mathsf{H}}_{\eta,2}$ if the $MDDH_k$ assumption holds in $\mathbb{G}$.*

Proof. We can construct an adversary $\mathcal{B}$ against an MDDH_k problem from a distinguisher $\mathcal{A}$ of the two hybrids as follows.

1. $\mathcal{B}$ obtains a $\mathcal{U}_{q_r, k}$-MDDH instance $(\mathbb{G}, [\mathbf{A}]_2, [\mathbf{k}_\delta]_2)$, where $\mathbf{A} \in \mathbb{Z}_p^{q_r \times k}$, $\mathbf{k}_0 = \mathbf{A}\mathbf{z}$, $\mathbf{k}_1 \leftarrow \mathbb{Z}_p^{q_r}$.
2. $\mathcal{B}$ simulates the random oracle H as follows: when H is queried on $i \in [p]$ as the j-th fresh query to H, it returns $[\mathbf{a}_i]_2$ where $\mathbf{a}_i$ is the j-th row of $\mathbf{A}$. $\mathcal{B}$ also defines k_i as the j-th entry of $\mathbf{k}_\delta$.
3. $\mathcal{B}$ runs $(\mathsf{uPK}, \mathsf{uMSK}) \leftarrow \mathsf{uSetup}(1^\lambda)$ and gives $\mathsf{qPK} = (\mathbb{G}, \mathsf{uPK})$ to $\mathcal{A}$. It sets $\mathsf{qMSK} = \mathsf{uMSK}$.
4. When $\mathcal{A}$ outputs $\widetilde{\mathbf{x}}$, $\mathcal{B}$ computes qCT in the same way as $\widehat{\mathsf{qEnc}}_{\eta,1}$ except that it defines $\widetilde{\mathbf{b}}_i = (x_i, \mathbf{a}_i, k_i + x_{s_\eta} x_i)$.
5. When $\mathcal{A}$ queries to the key generation oracle on $(S_k, \mathbf{c})$, $\mathcal{B}$ computes qSK in the same way as $\widehat{\mathsf{qKeyGen}}_{\eta,1}$ except that it computes uSK as $\mathsf{uSK} \leftarrow \mathsf{uKeyGen}(\mathsf{uMSK}, (S_k, [\mathbf{d}]_2, [\widehat{d} + \sum_{i \in S_k} c_{s_\eta, i} k_i]_2))$ if $S_k \subseteq S_c$.
6. $\mathcal{B}$ outputs what $\mathcal{A}$ outputs.

It is not hard to see that $\mathcal{A}$'s view corresponds to $\widehat{\mathsf{H}}_{\eta,1}$ if $\delta = 0$ and $\widehat{\mathsf{H}}_{\eta,2}$ otherwise. □

Lemma 5.5. *For $\eta \in [s_{\mathsf{max}}]$, $\widehat{\mathsf{H}}_{\eta,2}$ and $\widehat{\mathsf{H}}_{\eta,3}$ are identically distributed.*

Proof. For $i \in S_c$, by implicitly defining $r_i = r_i' - x_{s_\eta} x_i$ where $r_i' \leftarrow \mathbb{Z}_p$, it is obvious that $\mathcal{A}$'s views in $\widehat{\mathsf{H}}_{\eta,2}$ and $\widehat{\mathsf{H}}_{\eta,3}$ are identical since the distribution of r_i is not changed from the original definition. □

Lemma 5.6. *For* $\eta \in [s_{\max}]$, *we have* $\widehat{\mathsf{H}}_{\eta,3} \approx_c \mathsf{H}_\eta$ *if* iFE *and* uFE *are IND-(1-)partially hiding and the* $MDDH_k$ *assumption holds in* $\mathbb{G}$.

This lemma can be proven similarly to Lemmata 5.3 to 5.4.

5.3 Bounded Variable-Length Scheme Without Random Oracles

The scheme in Sect. 5.1 is easily modified into a bounded variable-length scheme that does not rely on random oracles. Note that the functionality of the scheme is the same as Definition 2.5 except that S_c and S_k is subsets of a fixed polynomial-sized set $[n']$ instead of $[p]$. The modification is simple: the setup algorithm randomly chooses $[\mathbf{a}_1]_2, \ldots, [\mathbf{a}_{n'}]_2$ from G_2^k and publish these. The encryption and key generation algorithms use them instead of computing by the hash function on the fly.

6 Functional Encryption for ABP ∘ UQF

In this section, we present our FE scheme for unbounded quadratic functions defined in Definition 2.6.

6.1 Partial Garbling Scheme for $\mathcal{F}_{n,n'}^{\mathsf{ABP}}$

We use the following partial garbling scheme for $\mathcal{F}_{n,n'}^{\mathsf{ABP}}$ [23] for the construction of our FE scheme.

Syntax. A partial garbling scheme for $\mathcal{F}_{n,n'}^{\mathsf{ABP}}$ consists of the four algorithms. Note that lgen and rec are deterministic algorithms while pgb and pgb* are probabilistic algorithms.

lgen(f): It takes $f \in \mathcal{F}_{n,n'}^{\mathsf{ABP}}$ and outputs $\mathbf{L}_1, \ldots, \mathbf{L}_t \in \mathbb{Z}_p^{(n+1) \times (t-1)}$ where t depends on f.

pgb($f, \mathbf{u}, \mathbf{x}; \mathbf{t}$): Let $\mathbf{u}'^{\top} = (\mathbf{u}, 1)$. It takes $f \in \mathcal{F}_{n,n'}^{\mathsf{ABP}}, \mathbf{u} \in \mathbb{Z}_p^n, \mathbf{x} \in \mathbb{Z}_p^{n'}$, and a random tape $\mathbf{t} \in \mathbb{Z}_p^{t-1}$. It then outputs

$$(\mathbf{u}'^{\top}\mathbf{L}_1\mathbf{t}, \ldots, \mathbf{u}'^{\top}\mathbf{L}_m\mathbf{t}, x_1 + \mathbf{u}'^{\top}\mathbf{L}_{m+1}\mathbf{t}, \ldots, x_{n'} + \mathbf{u}'^{\top}\mathbf{L}_t\mathbf{t}) \in \mathbb{Z}_p^t$$

where $m = t - n'$ and $(\mathbf{L}_1, \ldots, \mathbf{L}_t) = \mathsf{lgen}(f)$.

pgb*($f, \mathbf{u}, \mu; \mathbf{t}$): It takes $\mu \in \mathbb{Z}_p$ and $f, \mathbf{u}, \mathbf{t}$ as above and outputs

$$(\mathbf{u}'^{\top}\mathbf{L}_1\mathbf{t} + \mu, \mathbf{u}'^{\top}\mathbf{L}_2\mathbf{t}, \ldots, \mathbf{u}'^{\top}\mathbf{L}_t\mathbf{t}) \in \mathbb{Z}_p^t$$

where $(\mathbf{L}_1, \ldots, \mathbf{L}_t) = \mathsf{lgen}(f)$.

rec($f, \mathbf{u}$): It takes $f, \mathbf{u} \in \mathbb{Z}_p^n$ and outputs $\mathbf{d}_{f,\mathbf{u}} \in \mathbb{Z}_p^t$.

The concrete description of $\mathsf{lgen}, \mathsf{rec}$ that satisfies the following properties is found in [3, Appendix A]. We slightly modify the format of the output of lgen from [3] for convenience in our construction, but note that they are essentially the same.

Correctness. The garbling scheme is correct if for all $f \in \mathcal{F}_{n,n'}^{\mathsf{ABP}}, \mathbf{u} \in \mathbb{Z}_p^n, \mathbf{x} \in \mathbb{Z}_p^{n'}, \mathbf{t} \in \mathbb{Z}_p^{t-1}$, we have

$$\langle \mathsf{pgb}(f, \mathbf{u}, \mathbf{x}; \mathbf{t}), \mathsf{rec}(f, \mathbf{u}) \rangle = \langle f(\mathbf{u}), \mathbf{x} \rangle.$$

Security. The garbling scheme is secure if for all $f \in \mathcal{F}_{n,n'}^{\mathsf{ABP}}, \mathbf{u} \in \mathbb{Z}_p^n, \mathbf{x} \in \mathbb{Z}_p^{n'}$, the following distributions are statistically close:

$$\mathsf{pgb}(f, \mathbf{u}, \mathbf{x}; \mathbf{t}) \quad \text{and} \quad \mathsf{pgb}^*(f, \mathbf{u}, \langle f(\mathbf{u}), \mathbf{x} \rangle; \mathbf{t})$$

where the random tape is chosen over $\mathbf{t} \leftarrow \mathbb{Z}_p^{t-1}$.

Linearlity. Observe that pgb and pgb^* are an affine functions in $\mathbf{t}$ and μ, respectively. This means that $\mathbf{t}$ in pgb and μ in pgb^* can be group elements of order p.

6.2   Construction

Let k be the parameter of the MDDH_k assumption, n be the input length of arithmetic branching programs in $\mathcal{F}_{n,\mathbb{G}}^{\mathsf{ABP} \circ \mathsf{UQF}}$. Let $\mathsf{uFE} = (\mathsf{uSetup}, \mathsf{uEnc}, \mathsf{uSlotEnc}, \mathsf{uKeyGen}, \mathsf{uDec})$ be a partially hiding slotted FE scheme for $\mathcal{F}_{k(n+1),1,\mathbb{G}}^{\mathsf{UIP}}$ with slot-mode correctness for $e = [0]_1$. Let $(\mathsf{lgen}, \mathsf{pgb}, \mathsf{pgb}^*, \mathsf{rec})$ be a partial garbling scheme defined in the above. Let $H : [p] \to G_2^k$ be a hash function modeled as a random oracle. Then, our partially hiding FE scheme $\mathsf{aFE} = (\mathsf{aSetup}, \mathsf{aEnc}, \mathsf{aKeyGen}, \mathsf{aDec})$ for $\mathcal{F}_{n,\mathbb{G}}^{\mathsf{ABP} \circ \mathsf{UQF}}$ is constructed as follows.

$\mathsf{aSetup}(1^\lambda)$: It runs $(\mathsf{uPK}, \mathsf{uMSK}) \leftarrow \mathsf{uKeyGen}(1^\lambda)$ outputs $(\mathsf{aPK}, \mathsf{aMSK}) = (\mathsf{uPK}, \mathsf{uMSK})$.

$\mathsf{aEnc}(\mathbf{u}, S_c, \mathbf{x} = (x_i)_{i \in S_c})$: First, it defines vectors as follows:

$$[\mathbf{a}_i]_2 = H(i), \quad \mathbf{z}_i, \widetilde{\mathbf{z}} \leftarrow \mathbb{Z}_p^k, \quad \mathbf{b}_i = (x_i, \mathbf{z}_i, 0), \quad \widetilde{\mathbf{b}}_i = (x_i, \mathbf{a}_i, 0)$$

$$\mathbf{d}_i = \begin{cases} (\mathbf{z}_i, 0^{kn}) & (i \in S_c) \\ (\mathbf{u}, 1) \otimes \widetilde{\mathbf{z}} & (i = p) \end{cases}, \quad \mathbf{d} = (\mathbf{d}_i)_{i \in S_c \cup \{p\}}. \tag{6.1}$$

Then, it outputs aCT as follows: let $\mathsf{iFE} = (\mathsf{iSetup}, \mathsf{iEnc}, \mathsf{iSlotEnc}, \mathsf{iKeyGen}, \mathsf{iDec})$ be a partially hiding slotted FE scheme for $\mathcal{F}_{0,k+2,\mathbb{G}}^{\mathsf{IP}}$ with slot-mode correctness for $e = [0^{k+2}]_1$, or equivalently standard function-hiding IPFE scheme with the vector length being $k + 2$.

$(\mathsf{iPK}, \mathsf{iMSK}) \leftarrow \mathsf{iSetup}(1^\lambda)$

$\mathsf{iCT}_i \leftarrow \mathsf{iEnc}(\mathsf{iMSK}, [\mathbf{b}_i]_1), \quad \mathsf{iSK}_i \leftarrow \mathsf{iKeyGen}(\mathsf{iMSK}, [\widetilde{\mathbf{b}}_i]_2)$

$\mathsf{uCT} \leftarrow \mathsf{uSlotEnc}(S_c \cup \{p\}, [\mathbf{d}]_1), \quad \mathsf{aCT} = (\mathbf{u}, \mathsf{iPK}, \{\mathsf{iCT}_i, \mathsf{iSK}_i\}_{i \in S_c}, \mathsf{uCT})$

$$\tag{6.2}$$

aKeyGen(aMSK, $(S_k, f \in \mathcal{F}^{ABP}_{n,|S_k|^2})$): Let $\phi : S_k^2 \to \{m+1,\ldots,t\}$ be the bijective function defined as $\phi(\mu,\nu) = m + (\mu - 1)|S_k| + \nu$ (see Sect. 6.1 for how to define m, t). It outputs aSK as follows: first it computes $\mathbf{L}_1,\ldots,\mathbf{L}_t \leftarrow \mathsf{lgen}(f)$ and chooses $\mathbf{T} \leftarrow \mathbb{Z}_p^{(t-1)\times k}$. For $j \in [m], \mu, \nu \in S_k$, it defines

$$\widetilde{\mathbf{d}}_{j,i} = \begin{cases} \mathbf{0} & (i \in S_k) \\ \mathsf{vec}(\mathbf{L}_j\mathbf{T}) & (i = p) \end{cases}, \quad \widetilde{\mathbf{d}}_{\phi(\mu,\nu),i} = \begin{cases} \mathbf{0} & (i \in S_k\backslash\{\mu\}) \\ (\mathbf{a}_\nu, 0^{kn}) & (i = \mu) \\ \mathsf{vec}(\mathbf{L}_{\phi(\mu,\nu)}\mathbf{T}) & (i = p) \end{cases}$$

where $[\mathbf{a}_\nu]_2 = H(\nu)$. It then defines $\widetilde{\mathbf{d}}_j = (\widetilde{\mathbf{d}}_{j,i})_{i\in S_k\cup\{p\}}$ for $j \in [t]$. Finally it computes $\mathsf{uSK}_j \leftarrow \mathsf{uKeyGen}(\mathsf{uMSK}, (S_k \cup \{p\}, [\widetilde{\mathbf{d}}_j]_2, [0]_2))$ for all $j \in [t]$, and sets $\mathsf{aSK} = (f, \{\mathsf{uSK}_j\}_{j\in[t]})$.

aDec(aCT, aSK): Parse $\mathsf{aCT} = (\mathbf{u}, \mathsf{iPK}, \{\mathsf{iCT}_i, \mathsf{iSK}_i\}_{i\in S_c}, \mathsf{uCT})$ and $\mathsf{aSK} = (f, \{\mathsf{uSK}_j\}_{j\in[t]})$. If $S_k \not\subseteq S_c$, it outputs $\perp$. Otherwise, it computes $\mathbf{d}_{f,\mathbf{u}} = \mathsf{rec}(f, \mathbf{u})$ and outputs $[\delta]_T$ as follows:

$$[\delta_0]_T = \sum_{i,j\in S_k} f_{i,j}(\mathbf{u})\mathsf{iDec}(\mathsf{iCT}_i, \mathsf{iSK}_j), \quad [\delta_i]_T = \mathsf{uDec}(\mathsf{uCT}, \mathsf{uSK}_i)$$

$$[\delta]_T = [\delta_0 - \langle \mathbf{d}_{f,\mathbf{u}}, \boldsymbol{\delta}\rangle]_T$$

where $\boldsymbol{\delta} = (\delta_1,\ldots,\delta_t)$.

Correctness. Due to the correctness of iFE, uEF, we have

$$\delta_0 = \sum_{i,j\in S_k} (f_{i,j}(\mathbf{u})x_ix_j + f_{i,j}(\mathbf{u})\langle\mathbf{z}_i, \mathbf{a}_j\rangle), \quad \boldsymbol{\delta} = \mathsf{pgb}(f, \mathbf{u}, (\langle\mathbf{z}_i, \mathbf{a}_j\rangle)_{i,j\in S_k}; \mathbf{T}\widetilde{\mathbf{z}})$$

Hence, we have $\langle\mathbf{d}_{f,\mathbf{u}}, \boldsymbol{\delta}\rangle = \sum_{i,j\in S_k} f_{i,j}(\mathbf{u})\langle\mathbf{z}_i, \mathbf{a}_j\rangle$ and thus $z = \sum_{i,j\subset S_k} f_{i,j}(\mathbf{u})x_ix_j$, which follows from the correctness of the partial garbling scheme.

6.3   Security

For security, we have the following theorem.

Theorem 6.1. *If iFE is IND-partially hiding, uFE is IND-1-partially hiding, the partial garbling scheme is secure, and the MDDH$_k$ assumption holds in $\mathbb{G}$, then aFE is SIM-partially-hiding.*

Due to space constraints, we present the proof in the full version [31].

References

1. Abdalla, M., Bourse, F., De Caro, A., Pointcheval, D.: Simple functional encryption schemes for inner products. In: Katz, J. (ed.) PKC 2015. LNCS, vol. 9020, pp. 733–751. Springer, Heidelberg (2015). https://doi.org/10.1007/978-3-662-46447-2_33

2. Abdalla, M., Catalano, D., Gay, R., Ursu, B.: Inner-product functional encryption with fine-grained access control. In: Moriai, S., Wang, H. (eds.) ASIACRYPT 2020, Part III. LNCS, vol. 12493, pp. 467–497. Springer, Cham (2020). https://doi.org/10.1007/978-3-030-64840-4_16

3. Abdalla, M., Gong, J., Wee, H.: Functional encryption for attribute-weighted sums from k-Lin. In: Micciancio, D., Ristenpart, T. (eds.) CRYPTO 2020, Part I. LNCS, vol. 12170, pp. 685–716. Springer, Cham (2020). https://doi.org/10.1007/978-3-030-56784-2_23

4. Agrawal, S., Goyal, R., Tomida, J.: Multi-input quadratic functional encryption from pairings. In: Malkin, T., Peikert, C. (eds.) CRYPTO 2021, Part IV. LNCS, vol. 12828, pp. 208–238. Springer, Cham (2021). https://doi.org/10.1007/978-3-030-84259-8_8

5. Ananth, P., Jain, A., Lin, H., Matt, C., Sahai, A.: Indistinguishability obfuscation without multilinear maps: new paradigms via low degree weak pseudorandomness and security amplification. In: Boldyreva, A., Micciancio, D. (eds.) CRYPTO 2019, Part III. LNCS, vol. 11694, pp. 284–332. Springer, Cham (2019). https://doi.org/10.1007/978-3-030-26954-8_10

6. Ananth, P., Jain, A., Sahai, A.: Indistinguishability obfuscation without multilinear maps: IO from LWE, bilinear maps, and weak pseudorandomness. Cryptology ePrint Archive, Report 2018/615 (2018). https://eprint.iacr.org/2018/615

7. Ananth, P., Sahai, A.: Functional encryption for turing machines. In: Kushilevitz, E., Malkin, T. (eds.) TCC 2016, Part I. LNCS, vol. 9562, pp. 125–153. Springer, Heidelberg (2016). https://doi.org/10.1007/978-3-662-49096-9_6

8. Baltico, C.E.Z., Catalano, D., Fiore, D., Gay, R.: Practical functional encryption for quadratic functions with applications to predicate encryption. In: Katz, J., Shacham, H. (eds.) CRYPTO 2017, Part I. LNCS, vol. 10401, pp. 67–98. Springer, Cham (2017). https://doi.org/10.1007/978-3-319-63688-7_3

9. Bishop, A., Jain, A., Kowalczyk, L.: Function-hiding inner product encryption. In: Iwata, T., Cheon, J.H. (eds.) ASIACRYPT 2015, Part I. LNCS, vol. 9452, pp. 470–491. Springer, Heidelberg (2015). https://doi.org/10.1007/978-3-662-48797-6_20

10. Boneh, D., Sahai, A., Waters, B.: Functional encryption: definitions and challenges. In: Ishai, Y. (ed.) TCC 2011. LNCS, vol. 6597, pp. 253–273. Springer, Heidelberg (2011). https://doi.org/10.1007/978-3-642-19571-6_16

11. Boyle, E., Chung, K.-M., Pass, R.: On extractability obfuscation. In: Lindell, Y. (ed.) TCC 2014. LNCS, vol. 8349, pp. 52–73. Springer, Heidelberg (2014). https://doi.org/10.1007/978-3-642-54242-8_3

12. Brakerski, Z., Segev, G.: Function-private functional encryption in the private-key setting. In: Dodis, Y., Nielsen, J.B. (eds.) TCC 2015, Part II. LNCS, vol. 9015, pp. 306–324. Springer, Heidelberg (2015). https://doi.org/10.1007/978-3-662-46497-7_12

13. Datta, P., Pal, T.: (Compact) adaptively secure FE for attribute-weighted sums from k-Lin. In: Tibouchi, M., Wang, H. (eds.) ASIACRYPT 2021, Part IV. LNCS, vol. 13093, pp. 434–467. Springer, Cham (2021). https://doi.org/10.1007/978-3-030-92068-5_15

14. Dufour-Sans, E., Pointcheval, D.: Unbounded inner-product functional encryption with succinct keys. In: Deng, R.H., Gauthier-Umaña, V., Ochoa, M., Yung, M. (eds.) ACNS 2019. LNCS, vol. 11464, pp. 426–441. Springer, Cham (2019). https://doi.org/10.1007/978-3-030-21568-2_21

15. Escala, A., Herold, G., Kiltz, E., Ràfols, C., Villar, J.: An Algebraic Framework for Diffie–Hellman Assumptions. J. Cryptol. **30**(1), 242–288 (2015). https://doi.org/10.1007/s00145-015-9220-6
16. Garg, S., Gentry, C., Halevi, S.: Candidate multilinear maps from ideal lattices. In: Johansson, T., Nguyen, P.Q. (eds.) EUROCRYPT 2013. LNCS, vol. 7881, pp. 1–17. Springer, Heidelberg (2013). https://doi.org/10.1007/978-3-642-38348-9_1
17. Garg, S., Gentry, C., Halevi, S., Raykova, M., Sahai, A., Waters, B.: Candidate indistinguishability obfuscation and functional encryption for all circuits. In: 54th FOCS, pp. 40–49. IEEE Computer Society Press (2013). https://doi.org/10.1109/FOCS.2013.13
18. Garg, S., Gentry, C., Halevi, S., Zhandry, M.: Functional encryption without obfuscation. In: Kushilevitz, E., Malkin, T. (eds.) TCC 2016, Part II. LNCS, vol. 9563, pp. 480–511. Springer, Heidelberg (2016). https://doi.org/10.1007/978-3-662-49099-0_18
19. Gay, R.: A new paradigm for public-key functional encryption for degree-2 polynomials. In: Kiayias, A., Kohlweiss, M., Wallden, P., Zikas, V. (eds.) PKC 2020, Part I. LNCS, vol. 12110, pp. 95–120. Springer, Cham (2020). https://doi.org/10.1007/978-3-030-45374-9_4
20. Gay, R., Jain, A., Lin, H., Sahai, A.: Indistinguishability obfuscation from simple-to-state hard problems: new assumptions, new techniques, and simplification. In: Canteaut, A., Standaert, F.-X. (eds.) EUROCRYPT 2021, Part III. LNCS, vol. 12698, pp. 97–126. Springer, Cham (2021). https://doi.org/10.1007/978-3-030-77883-5_4
21. Gong, J., Qian, H.: Simple and efficient FE for quadratic functions. Cryptology ePrint Archive, Report 2020/1026 (2020). https://eprint.iacr.org/2020/1026
22. Ishai, Y., Pandey, O., Sahai, A.: Public-coin differing-inputs obfuscation and its applications. In: Dodis, Y., Nielsen, J.B. (eds.) TCC 2015, Part II. LNCS, vol. 9015, pp. 668–697. Springer, Heidelberg (2015). https://doi.org/10.1007/978-3-662-46497-7_26
23. Ishai, Y., Wee, H.: Partial garbling schemes and their applications. In: Esparza, J., Fraigniaud, P., Husfeldt, T., Koutsoupias, E. (eds.) ICALP 2014, Part I. LNCS, vol. 8572, pp. 650–662. Springer, Heidelberg (2014). https://doi.org/10.1007/978-3-662-43948-7_54
24. Jain, A., Lin, H., Matt, C., Sahai, A.: How to leverage hardness of constant-degree expanding polynomials over $\mathbb{R}$ to build $i\mathcal{O}$. In: Ishai, Y., Rijmen, V. (eds.) EURO-CRYPT 2019, Part I. LNCS, vol. 11476, pp. 251–281. Springer, Cham (2019). https://doi.org/10.1007/978-3-030-17653-2_9
25. Lin, H.: Indistinguishability obfuscation from SXDH on 5-linear maps and locality-5 PRGs. In: Katz, J., Shacham, H. (eds.) CRYPTO 2017, Part I. LNCS, vol. 10401, pp. 599–629. Springer, Cham (2017). https://doi.org/10.1007/978-3-319-63688-7_20
26. Lin, H., Luo, J.: Compact adaptively secure ABE from k-Lin: beyond NC^1 and towards NL. In: Canteaut, A., Ishai, Y. (eds.) EUROCRYPT 2020, Part III. LNCS, vol. 12107, pp. 247–277. Springer, Cham (2020). https://doi.org/10.1007/978-3-030-45727-3_9
27. Lin, H., Vaikuntanathan, V.: Indistinguishability obfuscation from DDH-like assumptions on constant-degree graded encodings. In: Dinur, I. (ed.) 57th FOCS, pp. 11–20. IEEE Computer Society Press (2016). https://doi.org/10.1109/FOCS.2016.11

28. Okamoto, T., Takashima, K.: Fully secure functional encryption with general relations from the decisional linear assumption. In: Rabin, T. (ed.) CRYPTO 2010. LNCS, vol. 6223, pp. 191–208. Springer, Heidelberg (2010). https://doi.org/10.1007/978-3-642-14623-7_11

29. O'Neill, A.: Definitional issues in functional encryption. Cryptology ePrint Archive, Report 2010/556 (2010). https://eprint.iacr.org/2010/556

30. Ryffel, T., Pointcheval, D., Bach, F.R., Dufour-Sans, E., Gay, R.: Partially encrypted deep learning using functional encryption. In: Wallach, H.M., Larochelle, H., Beygelzimer, A., d'Alché-Buc, F., Fox, E.B., Garnett, R. (eds.) NeurIPS 2019, pp. 4519–4530 (2019)

31. Tomida, J.: Unbounded quadratic functional encryption and more from pairings. Cryptology ePrint Archive, Report 2022/1124 (2022). https://eprint.iacr.org/2022/1124

32. Tomida, J., Takashima, K.: Unbounded inner product functional encryption from bilinear maps. In: Peyrin, T., Galbraith, S. (eds.) ASIACRYPT 2018, Part II. LNCS, vol. 11273, pp. 609–639. Springer, Cham (2018). https://doi.org/10.1007/978-3-030-03329-3_21

33. Wee, H.: Functional encryption for quadratic functions from k-Lin, revisited. In: Pass, R., Pietrzak, K. (eds.) TCC 2020, Part I. LNCS, vol. 12550, pp. 210–228. Springer, Cham (2020). https://doi.org/10.1007/978-3-030-64375-1_8

Multi-key and Multi-input Predicate Encryption from Learning with Errors

Danilo Francati[1]([✉]) [iD], Daniele Friolo[2] [iD], Giulio Malavolta[3],
and Daniele Venturi[2] [iD]

[1] Aarhus University, Aarhus, Denmark
dfrancati@cs.au.dk
[2] Sapienza University of Rome, Rome, Italy
[3] Max Planck Institute for Security and Privacy, Bochum, Germany

Abstract. We put forward two natural generalizations of predicate encryption (PE), dubbed *multi-key* and *multi-input* PE. More in details, our contributions are threefold.
- **Definitions.** We formalize security of multi-key PE and multi-input PE following the standard indistinguishability paradigm, and modeling security both against malicious senders (i.e., corruption of encryption keys) and malicious receivers (i.e., collusions).
- **Constructions.** We construct adaptively secure multi-key and multi-input PE supporting the conjunction of poly-many arbitrary single-input predicates, assuming the sub-exponential hardness of the learning with errors (LWE) problem.
- **Applications.** We show that multi-key and multi-input PE for expressive enough predicates suffices for interesting cryptographic applications, including non-interactive multi-party computation (NI-MPC) and matchmaking encryption (ME).

In particular, plugging in our constructions of multi-key and multi-input PE, under the sub-exponential LWE assumption, we obtain the first ME supporting *arbitrary policies* with unbounded collusions, as well as robust (resp. non-robust) NI-MPC for so-called *all-or-nothing* functions satisfying a non-trivial notion of reusability and supporting a constant (resp. polynomial) number of parties. Prior to our work, both of these applications required much heavier tools such as indistinguishability obfuscation or compact functional encryption.

Keywords: predicate encryption · non-interactive MPC · matchmaking encryption · LWE

1 Introduction

Predicate encryption (PE) [17,30,37] is a powerful cryptographic primitive that enriches standard encryption with fine-grained access control to the encrypted data. In PE, the ciphertext is associated to both a message m and an attribute[1]

---

[1] Sometimes, we also refer to x as the predicate input. Throughout the paper, we use the terms attribute and input interchangeably.

© International Association for Cryptologic Research 2023
C. Hazay and M. Stam (Eds.): EUROCRYPT 2023, LNCS 14006, pp. 573–604, 2023.
https://doi.org/10.1007/978-3-031-30620-4_19

x, whereas the secret key is associated to a predicate $\mathbb{P}$, in such a way that the decryption process reveals the message if and only if the attribute x satisfies the predicate $\mathbb{P}$ (i.e., $\mathbb{P}(x) = 1$). Typically, security of PE requires indistinguishability in the presence of *collusion attacks*, namely, for any pair of attributes (x^0, x^1) and for any pair of messages (m^0, m^1), ciphertexts corresponding to (x^0, m^0) and to (x^1, m^1) are computationally indistinguishable, even for an adversary possessing poly-many decryption keys $\mathsf{dk}_\mathbb{P}$, so long as $\mathbb{P}(x^0) = \mathbb{P}(x^1) = 0$ (otherwise it is easy to distinguish).

Recently, there has been a lot of progress in constructing PE supporting expressive predicates under standard assumptions [5, 12, 17, 30, 37, 38, 42, 43, 45, 46]. In particular, Gourbunov, Vaikuntanathan and Wee [30] give a construction of selectively secure PE (with unbounded collusions) for arbitrary predicates under the learning with errors (LWE) assumption. Moreover, under subexponential LWE, the same construction achieves adaptive security (this requires complexity leveraging).

1.1   Our Contributions

In this paper, we put forward two natural generalizations of PE which we dub *multi-key* PE and *multi-input* PE. Furthermore, we construct both multi-key PE and multi-input PE for a particular class of predicates, under the LWE assumption. As we show, the class of predicates our schemes can handle is powerful enough to yield interesting cryptographic applications, including matchmaking encryption (ME) [10, 11] for arbitrary policies and non-interactive multi-party computation (NI-MPC) [34] satisfying a weaker (but still non-trivial) notion of reusability. We elaborate on these contributions in Sect. 1.3.

Prior to our work, all of the above applications required much stronger tools such as indistinguishability obfuscation (iO) [13]. While recent work made significant progress towards basing iO on standard assumptions [35, 36], these constructions are fairly complex and still require a careful combination of multiple assumptions (i.e., learning parity with noise, the SXDH assumption on bilinear groups, and the existence of pseudorandom generators computable in constant depth). Furthermore, such constructions are not secure in the presence of a quantum attacker. Candidate constructions of *post-quantum* iO also exist [18, 28, 47], but they are based on problems whose hardness is less understood.

Multi-key PE. In multi-key PE, we consider an ensemble of predicates $\mathcal{P} = \{\mathbb{P}_v\}$ indexed by a value $v \in \mathcal{V}$ which is uniquely represented as a sequence $v = (v_1, \ldots, v_n) \in \mathcal{V}_1 \times \ldots \times \mathcal{V}_n$. A sender can encrypt a message under an input x using the public-key encryption algorithm $\mathsf{Enc}(\mathsf{mpk}, x, m)$. A trusted authority generates decryption keys dk_{v_i} (using the corresponding master secret key msk_i) for each $i \in [n]$, with the guarantee that, given the decryption keys $\mathsf{dk}_{v_1}, \ldots, \mathsf{dk}_{v_n}$, the receiver can decrypt successfully the ciphertext c (associated to plaintext m and attributes x), so long as $\mathbb{P}_v(x) = \mathbb{P}_{v_1, \ldots, v_n}(x) = 1$.

Security of multi-key PE says that, for any pair of attributes (x^0, x^1) and for any pair of messages (m^0, m^1), ciphertexts c associated to (x^0, m^0) and (x^1, m^1)

should be computationally indistinguishable even under unbounded collusions, where the latter essentially means that the adversary can obtain decryption keys for (poly-many) arbitrary values $v_1, \ldots, v_n$ which correspond to predicates indexed by any value $v = (v_1, \ldots, v_n)$ such that $\mathbb{P}_v(x^0) = \mathbb{P}_v(x^1) = 0$. This yields so-called CPA-1-sided security. The stronger notion of CPA-2-sided security additionally allows for predicates indexed by values v such that $\mathbb{P}_v(x^0) = \mathbb{P}_v(x^1) = 1$, so long as $m^0 = m^1$. These notions mimic the corresponding notions that are already established for standard PE.

Our first result is a construction of multi-key PE, from the sub-exponential LWE assumption, supporting conjunctions of arbitrary predicates, i.e. for predicates of the form $\mathbb{P}_v(x) = \mathbb{P}_{v_1}(x_1) \wedge \ldots \wedge \mathbb{P}_{v_n}(x_n)$, where $x = (x_1, \ldots, x_n)$ and $v = (v_1, \ldots, v_n)$.

Theorem 1 (Informal). *Assuming the sub-exponential hardness of LWE, there exists a CPA-1-sided adaptively secure multi-key PE scheme supporting conjunctions of $n = \mathsf{poly}(\lambda)$ arbitrary predicates with unbounded collusions.*

Multi-input PE. In multi-input PE, we consider predicates $\mathbb{P}$ with n inputs, i.e. predicates of the form $\mathbb{P}(x_1, \ldots, x_n)$. A trusted authority produces encryption keys ek_i which are associated to the i-th slot of an input for $\mathbb{P}$; namely, given a (possibly secret)[2] encryption key ek_i, a sender can generate a ciphertext c_i which is an encryption of message m_i under attribute x_i. At the same time, the authority can produce a decryption key $\mathsf{dk}_\mathbb{P}$ associated to an n-input predicate $\mathbb{P}$, with the guarantee that the receiver can successfully decrypt $c_1, \ldots, c_n$, and thus obtain $m_1, \ldots, m_n$, so long as $\mathbb{P}(x_1, \ldots, x_n) = 1$.

As for security, we consider similar flavors as CPA-1-sided and CPA-2-sided security for standard PE. Namely, for any pair of sequences of attributes $(x_1^0, \ldots, x_n^0)$ and $(x_1^1, \ldots, x_n^1)$ and for any pair of sequences of messages $(m_1^0, \ldots, m_n^0)$ and $(m_1^1, \ldots, m_n^1)$, ciphertexts $c_1, \ldots, c_n$ corresponding to either $(x_1^0, m_1^0), \ldots, (x_n^0, m_n^0)$ or $(x_1^1, m_1^1), \ldots, (x_n^1, m_n^1)$ should be computationally indistinguishable. Here, we additionally consider two cases:

- In the setting with no corruptions (a.k.a. the secret-key setting), all of the encryption keys ek_i are secret and cannot be corrupted (and thus all the senders are honest).
- In the setting with adaptive corruptions, the attacker can adaptively reveal some of the encryption keys ek_i (and thus corrupt a subset of the senders).

Naturally, for both of these flavors, one can define CPA-1-sided and CPA-2-sided security with or without collusions.

Our second result is a construction of multi-input PE, from the sub-exponential LWE assumption, supporting conjunctions of $n = \mathsf{poly}(\lambda)$ arbitrary predicates *with wildcards*, i.e. for predicates of the form $\mathbb{P}(x_1, \ldots, x_n) =$

---

[2] This is one of the differences between multi-key PE and multi-input PE: the former has a public-key encryption algorithm, whereas the latter could have a secret-key encryption algorithm.

$\mathbb{P}_1(x_1) \wedge \ldots \wedge \mathbb{P}_n(x_n)$ such that, for each $i \in [n]$, there exists a (public) wildcard input $x_i^\star$ for which $\mathbb{P}_i(x_i^\star) = 1$ for every i-th predicate $\mathbb{P}_i$.[3] Our multi-input PE construction retains its security only in the setting of no corruptions (i.e., the encryption keys ek_i are kept secret) and no collusions (i.e., the adversary only knows a single decryption key $\mathsf{dk}_\mathbb{P}$ for an adversarially chosen predicate $\mathbb{P}$).

Theorem 2 (Informal). *Assuming the sub-exponential hardness of LWE, there exists a CPA-1-sided adaptively secure multi-input PE scheme supporting conjunctions of $n = \mathsf{poly}(\lambda)$ arbitrary predicates with wildcards, without corruptions and without collusions.*

Our third result is a construction of multi-input PE, from the sub-exponential LWE assumption, supporting the same class of predicates as above but tolerating adaptive corruptions of up to $n-1$ parties. However, this particular scheme only supports predicates with constant arity.

Theorem 3 (Informal). *Assuming the sub-exponential hardness of LWE, there exists a CPA-1-sided adaptively secure multi-input PE scheme supporting conjunctions of $n = O(1)$ arbitrary predicates with wildcards, under $n-1$ adaptive corruptions and without collusions.*

Finally, we anticipate that all our constructions are transformations that leverage single-input PE schemes (e.g., [30]) and lockable obfuscation [31,48] as building blocks. Such transformations are general and achieve CPA-2-sided security if the underlying single-input PE schemes are CPA-2-sided secure. In particular, we obtain (*i*) CPA-2-sided secure multi-key PE with unbounded collusions for $n = \mathsf{poly}(\lambda)$, (*ii*) CPA-2-sided secure multi-input PE without corruptions and without collusions for $n = O(\log(\lambda))$,[4] and (*iii*) CPA-2-sided secure multi-input PE under $n-1$ corruptions and without collusions for $n = O(1)$. However, at the time of this writing, the LWE assumption is not sufficient for CPA-2-sided security. Indeed, even for single-input PE for arbitrary predicates, CPA-2-sided security implies iO [15]. The current state-of-the-art constructions of iO require much stronger assumptions compared to standard LWE.

1.2 Technical Overview

We now give a high level overview of our constructions. As explained above, both our multi-key and multi-input PE constructions handle conjunctions of arbitrary predicates, i.e., predicates of the form:

$$\mathbb{P}(x_1, \ldots, x_n) = \mathbb{P}_1(x_1) \wedge \ldots \wedge \mathbb{P}_n(x_n). \tag{1}$$

---

[3] Note that, in the setting with no corruptions, assuming the presence of a (single) wildcard $x_i^\star$ for each $\mathbb{P}_i$ does not affect the expressiveness and the security guarantees of multi-input PE. This is because the i-th sender can simply choose not to encrypt $x_i^\star$, which will not permit the receiver to evaluate $\mathbb{P}_i$ over $x_i^\star$.

[4] Note that, in case of no corruptions, our CPA-1-sided construction supports $n = \mathsf{poly}(\lambda)$. However, to achieve CPA-2-sided security we use complexity leveraging and this reduces n from $\mathsf{poly}(\lambda)$ to $O(\log(\lambda))$.

We start by explaining how to build multi-key PE for the above class of predicates by combining single-input PE and so-called lockable obfuscation [31, 48]. Informally, a lockable obfuscation scheme allows to obfuscate a circuit $\mathbb{C}$ under a lock y together with a message m, in such a way that evaluating the obfuscated circuit, on input x, returns m if $\mathbb{C}(x) = y$. As for security, an obfuscated circuit can be simulated in a virtual black-box (VBB) fashion whenever the lock is random and unknown to the adversary. Lockable obfuscation exists under the standard LWE assumption.

Then, we explain how to build multi-input PE (for the same class of predicates) by additionally using SKE and PKE. Here, we consider two settings: without corruptions (a.k.a. the secret-key setting) and with corruptions. The former assumes that all the encryption keys (each corresponding to an input) are secret. The latter is a stronger model that allows the adversary to leak one or more encryption keys (i.e., corruption of the senders). We achieve security in each setting by changing the way lockable obfuscation is used. In particular, part of the contribution of this paper is a new technique based on nested (lockable obfuscated) circuits that execute each other. This technique allows us to construct a multi-input PE that can handle adaptive corruptions. We provide a high-level overview in the remaining part of this section. For more details, we refer the reader to Sect. 4, Sect. 5, and the full version of this work [25].

Multi-key Predicate Encryption. An n-key PE allows a sender to encrypt a message m under an attribute x, by running $c \leftarrow_s \mathsf{Enc}(\mathsf{mpk}, x, m)$. Similarly to single-input PE, a receiver can correctly decrypt c if it has a decryption key for a predicate $\mathbb{P}_v$, within a family $\mathcal{P}$ of predicates indexed by values $v \in \mathcal{V}$, such that $\mathbb{P}_v(x) = 1$. The main difference between single-input PE and n-key PE is that in the latter the receiver must have n independent decryption keys $(\mathsf{dk}_{v_1}, \ldots, \mathsf{dk}_{v_n})$ that uniquely represent the predicate $\mathbb{P}_v(\cdot) = \mathbb{P}_{v_1, \ldots, v_n}(\cdot)$, i.e., the decryption key associated to a particular predicate is decomposed into n decryption keys. Each decryption key dk_{v_i} is generated by the authority via $\mathsf{KGen}(\mathsf{msk}_i, v_i)$ where $(\mathsf{msk}_1, \ldots, \mathsf{msk}_n)$ are the master secret keys generated during the setup. Hence, once obtained $(\mathsf{dk}_{v_1}, \ldots, \mathsf{dk}_{v_n})$ from the authority, the receiver can decrypt the ciphertext c (encrypted under attribute x) by executing $\mathsf{Dec}(\mathsf{dk}_{v_1}, \ldots, \mathsf{dk}_{v_n}, c)$. The message is returned if the predicate $\mathbb{P}_{v_1, \ldots, v_n}(x) = 1$, where $\mathbb{P}_{v_1, \ldots, v_n}(\cdot)$ is the predicate represented by the combination of the n decryptions keys $\mathsf{dk}_{v_1}, \ldots, \mathsf{dk}_{v_n}$. The security of n-key PE is analogous to that of single-input PE, where the validity of the adversary A is defined with respect to the (poly-many) tuples $(\mathsf{dk}_{v_1}, \ldots, \mathsf{dk}_{v_n})$ of n decryption keys that the adversary has access to. In particular, we consider the well-known notion of CPA-1-sided security, i.e., the attacker cannot distinguish between $\mathsf{Enc}(\mathsf{mpk}, x^0, m^0)$ and $\mathsf{Enc}(\mathsf{mpk}, x^1, m^1)$ so long as it only holds combinations of n decryption keys $(\mathsf{dk}_{v_1}, \ldots, \mathsf{dk}_{v_n})$ such that $\mathbb{P}_{v_1,\dots,v_n}(x^0) = \mathbb{P}_{v_1,\dots,v_n}(x^1) = 0$ (i.e., the adversary cannot decrypt the challenge ciphertext).[5]

As explained above, we focus on conjunctions of arbitrary predicates $\mathbb{P}_{v_1,\dots,v_n}(x) = \mathbb{P}_{v_1,\dots,v_n}(x_1,\dots,x_n) = \mathbb{P}_{v_1}(x_1) \wedge \cdots \wedge \mathbb{P}_{v_n}(x_n)$ as defined in Eq. (1); hence, $x = (x_1,\dots,x_n)$ and each dk_{v_i} identifies the i-th predicate of the conjunction (and, in turn, any tuple of n decryption keys uniquely identifies the global predicate). We build an n-key PE handling this class of predicates by extending the technique of Goyal et al. [31], that uses lockable obfuscation to transform any CPA secure attribute-based encryption (ABE) (recall that ABE schemes only guarantee the secrecy of the message) into a CPA-1-sided secure PE (i.e., secrecy of both message and attribute). Let $\mathsf{PE}_i = (\mathsf{Setup}_i, \mathsf{KGen}_i, \mathsf{Enc}_i, \mathsf{Dec}_i)$ for $i \in [n]$ be n single-input PE schemes, each with ciphertext expansion $\mathsf{poly}(\lambda) + |m_i|$ where $|m_i|$ is the message length supported by the i-th PE.[6] In a nutshell, our n-key PE scheme $\mathsf{kPE} = (\mathsf{Setup}, \mathsf{KGen}, \mathsf{Enc}, \mathsf{Dec})$ works as follows. The setup algorithm Setup simply executes Setup_i of each PE_i and outputs the master public key $\mathsf{mpk} = (\mathsf{mpk}_1,\dots,\mathsf{mpk}_n)$ and n master secret keys $(\mathsf{msk}_1,\dots,\mathsf{msk}_n)$. To generate a decryption key $\mathsf{dk}_{v_i} \leftarrow\!\!{}_\$ \mathsf{KGen}(\mathsf{msk}_i, v_i)$ (representing the i-th predicate $\mathbb{P}_{v_i}(\cdot)$ of the conjunction), the authority can use the key generation algorithm of the i-th PE, i.e., $\mathsf{dk}_{v_i} \leftarrow\!\!{}_\$ \mathsf{KGen}_i(\mathsf{msk}_i, \mathbb{P}_{v_i})$. To encrypt a message m under an input $x = (x_1,\dots,x_n)$, a sender samples a random lock y and encrypts it n times using $\mathsf{PE}_1,\dots,\mathsf{PE}_n$, i.e., $c \leftarrow\!\!{}_\$ \mathsf{Enc}_n(\mathsf{mpk}_n, x_n, \mathsf{Enc}_{n-1}(\mathsf{mpk}_{n-1}, x_{n-1}, \cdots, \mathsf{Enc}_1(\mathsf{mpk}_1, x_1, y)))$. Note that, for $n = \mathsf{poly}(\lambda)$, the final ciphertext will be of polynomial size since each underlying i-th PE scheme has $\mathsf{poly}(\lambda) + |m_i|$ ciphertext expansion where $|m_i|$ is the message length supported by i-th scheme.

The final ciphertext of the n-key PE kPE will be the obfuscation of the circuit $\mathbb{C}_c$ under the lock y together with the message m (i.e., $\widetilde{\mathbb{C}} \leftarrow\!\!{}_\$ \mathsf{Obf}(1^\lambda, \mathbb{C}_c, y, m)$), where $\mathbb{C}_c$, on input $(\mathsf{dk}_{v_1},\dots,\mathsf{dk}_{v_n})$, iteratively decrypts c and returns the last decrypted value, i.e., $y = \mathbb{C}_c(\mathsf{dk}_{v_1},\dots,\mathsf{dk}_{v_n}) = \mathsf{Dec}_1(\mathsf{dk}_{v_1}, \cdots, \mathsf{Dec}_n(\mathsf{dk}_{v_n}, c))$. Decryption is straightforward: the receiver simply executes $\widetilde{\mathbb{C}}$ using its n decryption keys.

The CPA-1-sided security of our construction follows by the CPA security (i.e., secrecy of the message) of $\mathsf{PE}_1,\dots,\mathsf{PE}_n$ and by the security of lockable obfuscation.[7] Intuitively, the proof works as follows. In order to be valid, an adversary A cannot hold a tuple of decryption keys $(\mathsf{dk}_{v_1},\dots,\mathsf{dk}_{v_n})$ such that $\mathbb{P}_{v_1,\dots,v_n}(x^b) = \mathbb{P}_{v_1,\dots,v_n}(x_1^b,\dots,x_n^b) = 1$, where $x^b = (x_1^b,\dots,x_n^b)$ is the

---

[5] Observe that the decryption keys can be interleaved. For example, starting from $(\mathsf{dk}_{v_1},\dots,\mathsf{dk}_{v_i},\dots\mathsf{dk}_{v_n})$ representing the predicate $\mathbb{P}_{v_1,\dots,v_i,\dots,v_n}$, the adversary can ask for an additional i-th decryption key $\mathsf{dk}_{v_i'}$ and rearrange the decryption keys as $(\mathsf{dk}_{v_1},\dots,\mathsf{dk}_{v_i'},\dots\mathsf{dk}_{v_n})$ in order to obtain the tuple representing a different predicate $\mathbb{P}_{v_1,\dots,v_i',\dots,v_n} \neq \mathbb{P}_{v_1,\dots,v_i,\dots,v_n}$.

[6] By leveraging hybrid encryption, we can transform any PE into one with $\mathsf{poly}(\lambda) + |m|$ ciphertext expansion, i.e., $\mathsf{Enc}'(\mathsf{mpk}, x, m) = \mathsf{Enc}(\mathsf{mpk}, x, s) \| \mathsf{PRG}(s) \oplus m$ where $s \leftarrow\!\!{}_\$ \{0,1\}^\lambda$.

[7] When we write CPA secure PE, without specifying 1-sided or 2-sided security, we refer to a PE scheme that guarantees only the secrecy of the message. CPA secure PE is the same as CPA secure ABE.

input chosen by A during the challenge phase, and b is the challenge bit. Since $\mathbb{P}_{v_1,\ldots,v_n}(x_1^b,\ldots,x_n^b)$ is a conjunction of arbitrary predicates (see Eq. (1)), this implies that there exists an $i \in [n]$ such that $\mathbb{P}_{v_i}(x_i^b) = 0$ for every i-th decryption key dk_{v_i} obtained by A. We can leverage this observation together with the CPA security of PE_i to do a first hybrid in which the challenger computes the i-th layer of the challenge ciphertext as $\mathsf{Enc}_i(\mathsf{mpk}_i, x_i^b, 0\ldots 0)$. Now, since the lock y is not encrypted anymore, we can use the security of lockable obfuscation to do a second hybrid in which the challenge ciphertext $\widetilde{\mathbb{C}}$ is simulated by using the simulator of lockable obfuscation. In this last hybrid, the challenge ciphertext does not depend on the bit b sampled by the challenger.

Despite we focused the discussion on CPA-1-sided security, we stress that the same construction achieves CPA-2-sided security if the underlying n single-input PE schemes $\mathsf{PE}_1,\ldots,\mathsf{PE}_n$ are CPA-2-sided secure, i.e., $\mathsf{Enc}(\mathsf{mpk}, x^0, m^0)$ and $\mathsf{Enc}(\mathsf{mpk}, x^1, m^1)$ are indistinguishable even when $\mathbb{P}_{v_1,\ldots,v_n}(x^0) = \mathbb{P}_{v_1,\ldots,v_n}(x^1) = 1$ and $m^0 = m^1$.

Multi-input Predicate Encryption. We now turn to the more challenging setting of multi-input PE.[8] Here, each of the n senders can use its corresponding encryption key to independently encrypt messages under different inputs for the predicate. For this reason, the setup algorithm of n-input PE outputs n encryption keys $(\mathsf{ek}_1,\ldots,\mathsf{ek}_n)$ and a master secret key msk. Each encryption key ek_i is given to the i-th sender and allows the latter to handle the i-th slot of a multi-input predicate. The i-th party encrypts a message m_i under an input x_i by using its encryption key ek_i, i.e., $c_i \leftarrow_{\$} \mathsf{Enc}(\mathsf{ek}_i, x_i, m_i)$. On the other hand, a receiver can use the decryption key $\mathsf{dk}_{\mathbb{P}}$ associated to an n-input predicate $\mathbb{P}$ (recall that $\mathsf{dk}_{\mathbb{P}}$ is generated by the authority via $\mathsf{KGen}(\mathsf{msk}, \mathbb{P})$) to execute $\mathsf{Dec}(\mathsf{dk}_{\mathbb{P}}, c_1,\ldots,c_n)$. Intuitively, the decryption algorithm returns $(m_1,\ldots,m_n)$ when $\mathbb{P}(x_1,\ldots,x_n) = 1$ where (m_i, x_i) are the message and the input associated to the i-th ciphertext c_i.

The CPA-1-sided security of n-input PE is similar to that of n-key PE, but adapted to the multi-input setting. Informally, an adversary A must not be able to distinguish between ciphertexts $(\mathsf{Enc}(\mathsf{ek}_i, x_i^0, m_i^0))_{i\in[n]}$ and $(\mathsf{Enc}(\mathsf{ek}_i, x_i^1, m_i^1))_{i\in[n]}$ where $(x_1^0,\ldots,x_n^0)$, $(x_1^1,\ldots,x_n^1)$ and $(m_1^0,\ldots,m_n^0)$, $(m_1^1,\ldots,m_n^1)$ are chosen by A. Naturally, this is subject to the usual validity condition, informally saying that A should not be able to decrypt (part of) the challenge ciphertext. This condition can assume different meanings depending on whether the encryption keys are all secret or some of them are public (or can be leaked). Because of this, we formalize security with and without corruptions. Throughout the rest of this section, we describe how CPA-1-sided security of n-input PE changes in these two settings, and give some intuition on our constructions for each setting.

Security in the Secret-Key Setting. Here, no corruptions are allowed and thus the encryption keys are all secrets. Hence, an adversary A playing the CPA-1-sided security game has adaptive oracle access to both the key generation

---

[8] Indeed, as we discuss in Remark 1, CPA-1-sided (resp. CPA-2-sided) secure multi-input PE for arbitrary predicates implies CPA-1-sided (resp. CPA-2-sided) secure multi-key PE.

oracle $\mathsf{KGen}(\mathsf{msk}, \cdot)$ and to n encryption oracles $\{\mathsf{Enc}(\mathsf{ek}_i, \cdot, \cdot)\}_{i \in [n]}$. The latter oracles allow A to generate ciphertexts (associated to the i-th input/sender) on adversarially chosen predicate inputs and messages. Since these ciphertexts are created independently, the adversary has the power to interleave part of the challenge ciphertext $(c_1^*, \ldots, c_n^*)$ with the ciphertexts obtained trough the encryption oracles. This has a huge impact on the security of the a n-input PE scheme and on the validity condition that A must satisfy. For example, during the challenge phase, A could choose two vectors of messages $(m_1^0, \ldots, m_n^0)$ and $(m_1^1, \ldots, m_n^1)$ and two vectors of predicate inputs $(x_1^0, \ldots, x_n^0)$ and $(x_1^1, \ldots, x_n^1)$ such that for every predicate $\mathbb{P}$ (submitted to oracle $\mathsf{KGen}(m, \cdot)$) we have $\mathbb{P}(x_1^0, \ldots, x_n^0) = \mathbb{P}(x_1^1, \ldots, x_n^1) = 0$. Although the vector $(c_1^*, \ldots, c_n^*)$ can not be directly decrypted, A could still be able to decrypt part of it by leveraging the encryption oracles. In more details, A could: (i) adversarially choose x_i' such that $\mathbb{P}(x_1^0, \ldots, x_i', \ldots x_n^0) = 1$ and $\mathbb{P}(x_1^1, \ldots, x_i', \ldots x_n^1) = 0$; (ii) submit (x_i', m_i') to oracle $\mathsf{Enc}(\mathsf{ek}_i, \cdot, \cdot)$ and obtain c_i'; and (iii) simply decrypt the vector $(c_1^*, \ldots, c_i', \ldots, c_n^*)$. When $b = 0$ (resp. $b = 1$), the adversary knows that the challenge ciphertext must (resp. must not) decrypt successfully. This allows it to easily win the CPA-1-sided security experiment of n-input PE. As a consequence, the condition defining when A is valid depends on both the queries submitted to $\mathsf{KGen}(\mathsf{msk}, \cdot)$ and to the oracles $\{\mathsf{Enc}(\mathsf{ek}_i, \cdot, \cdot)\}_{i \in [n]}$. More precisely, for every decryption key $\mathsf{dk}_{\mathbb{P}}$ corresponding to a predicate $\mathbb{P}$, for every vector of ciphertexts obtained by interleaving the challenge ciphertext $(c_1^*, \ldots, c_n^*)$ with the ciphertexts generated trough any of the n encryption oracles, we must have that $\mathbb{P}$ is not satisfied. This is formalized by the following condition: $\forall \mathbb{P} \in \mathcal{Q}_{\mathsf{KGen}}$, $\forall j \in [n]$, $\forall i_1 \in [k_1 + 1], \ldots, \forall i_n \in [k_n + 1]$, it holds that

$$
\begin{aligned}
\mathbb{P}(x_1^{(i_1,0)}, \ldots, x_{j-1}^{(i_{j-1},0)}, x_j^0, x_{j+1}^{(i_{j+1},0)}, \ldots, x_n^{(i_n,0)}) = \\
\mathbb{P}(x_1^{(i_1,1)}, \ldots, x_{j-1}^{(i_{j-1},1)}, x_j^1, x_{j+1}^{(i_{j+1},1)}, \ldots, x_n^{(i_n,1)}) = 0,
\end{aligned}
\tag{2}
$$

where $\mathcal{Q}_{\mathsf{KGen}}$ are the queries submitted to oracle $\mathsf{KGen}(\mathsf{msk}, \cdot)$, $(x_1^0, \ldots, x_n^0)$, $(x_1^1, \ldots, x_n^1)$ are the predicate inputs chosen by A during the challenge phase, and $\mathcal{Q}_i^b = \{x_i^{(1,b)}, \ldots, x_i^{(k_i,b)}, x_i^{(k_i+1,b)} = x_i^b\}$ is the ordered list composed of the k_i predicate inputs submitted to oracle $\mathsf{Enc}(\mathsf{ek}_i, \cdot, \cdot)$ and the challenge input x_i^b for $b \in \{0,1\}, i \in [n]$ (observe that $\mathcal{Q}_i^0$ and $\mathcal{Q}_i^1$ are identical except for the last element). The formal security definition appears in Sect. 4.

Construction in the Secret-Key Setting. We propose a construction of n-input PE for conjunctions of arbitrary predicates (see Eq. (1)) *with wildcards* from single-input PE, lockable obfuscation, and SKE. In particular, we start from single-input PE for arbitrary predicates. Actually, it will suffice that the underlying PE itself supports the predicates $\mathbb{P}(x_1, \ldots, x_n)$ as defined in Eq. (1), where we view $(x_1, \ldots, x_n)$ as a single input chosen by the sender. In addition, the predicate must have a (efficiently computable) wildcard input $(x_1^\star, \ldots, x_n^\star)$ such that $x_i^\star$ satisfies every i-th predicate of the conjunction, i.e., $\mathbb{P}_i(x_i^\star) = 1$. As we will describe next, the $n-1$ subset of wildcards $(x_1^\star, \ldots, x_{i-1}^\star, x_{i+1}^\star, \ldots, x_n^\star)$ will permit the i-th sender to put a "don't care" placeholder on the slots of the other senders. This will allow the construction to deal with multiple inputs without compromising the evaluation of the predicate.

The main intuition behind our construction is to evaluate the conjunction of the predicates inside lockable obfuscation in such a way that, as soon as one of the predicates (of the conjunction) is not satisfied, both the messages and the predicate inputs remain hidden (even if another predicate $\mathbb{P}_i$ is satisfied). To accomplish that, we need to create a link between the independently generated ciphertexts (each produced by different senders). This is done by leveraging an SKE scheme as follows.

In a nutshell, the i-th secret encryption key has the form $\mathsf{ek}_i = (\mathsf{mpk}, \mathsf{k}_i, \mathsf{k}_{i+1})$ where mpk is the master public key of the single-input PE, and k_i for $i \in [n]$ is a secret key for the SKE (we also let $\mathsf{ek}_{n+1} = \mathsf{k}_1$). In order to encrypt a message m_i under an input x_i, the i-th sender samples a random lock y_i and encrypts (y_i, k_{i+1}) via the single-input PE, using the input made by all the wildcards $x_j^\star$ except for the position $j = i$, where, instead, the sender places its real input x_i, i.e., $c_i^{(1)} \leftarrow\!\!\text{\tiny\$}\ \mathsf{Enc}(\mathsf{mpk}, (x_1^\star, \ldots, x_{i-1}^\star, x_i, x_{i+1}^\star, \ldots, x_n^\star), (y_i, \mathsf{k}_{i+1}))$. The final ciphertext c_i will be $c_i = (\widetilde{\mathbb{C}}_i, c_i^{(2)})$, where $c_i^{(2)} \leftarrow\!\!\text{\tiny\$}\ \mathsf{Enc}(\mathsf{k}_i, c_i^{(1)})$ and $\widetilde{\mathbb{C}}_i$ is the obfuscation of the circuit $\mathbb{C}_{c_i^{(2)}, \mathsf{k}_{i+1}}$ under the lock y_i and message m_i. Similarly to the case of multi-key PE, the latter circuit is responsible for the decryption. In particular, upon input the ciphertexts $(c_{i+1}^{(2)}, \ldots, c_n^{(2)}, c_1^{(2)}, \ldots, c_{i-1}^{(2)})$—note the order of the ciphertexts—and the decryption key $\mathsf{dk}_\mathbb{P}$ for $\mathbb{P}(x_1, \ldots, x_n)$, the circuit $\mathbb{C}_{c_i^{(2)}, \mathsf{k}_{i+1}}$ acts as follows:

1. Set $\mathsf{k} = \mathsf{k}_{i+1}$ where k_{i+1} is the secret key hardcoded into the circuit.
2. For $c_j^{(2)} \in \{c_{i+1}^{(2)}, \ldots, c_n^{(2)}, c_1^{(2)}, \ldots, c_{i-1}^{(2)}\}$ do:
   (a) Decrypt $c_j^{(2)}$ using the secret key k, i.e., $c_j^{(1)} = \mathsf{Dec}(\mathsf{k}, c_j^{(2)})$.
   (b) Decrypt $c_j^{(1)}$ using $\mathsf{dk}_\mathbb{P}$ in order to get (y_j, k_{j+1}). If $c_j^{(1)}$ decrypts correctly, k_{j+1} is the secret key used to encrypt the next ciphertext $c_{j+1}^{(2)}$.
   (c) Set $\mathsf{k} = \mathsf{k}_{j+1}$.
3. Compute $(y_i, \mathsf{k}_{i+1}) = \mathsf{Dec}(\mathsf{dk}_\mathbb{P}, \mathsf{Dec}(\mathsf{k}, c_i^{(2)}))$, where $c_i^{(2)}$ is the ciphertext hardcoded into the circuit.
4. Return y_i (note that if none of the decryptions fails then y_i is the lock used to obfuscate the circuit).

By the above description, decryption is immediate: Upon input $(c_i)_{i \in [n]}$, the receiver computes $m_i = \widetilde{\mathbb{C}}_i(c_{i+1}^{(2)}, \ldots, c_n^{(2)}, c_1^{(2)}, \ldots, c_{i-1}^{(2)}, \mathsf{dk}_\mathbb{P})$ where $c_i = (\widetilde{\mathbb{C}}_i, c_i^{(2)})$ and $\mathsf{dk}_\mathbb{P}$ is the decryption key of the underlying single-input PE for a predicate $\mathbb{P}(x_1, \ldots, x_n)$. We highlight that the combination of the SKE with the PE wildcards is what allows our construction to correctly implement the predicates of Eq. (1). This is because, when $c_i^{(1)}$ correctly decrypts under the key $\mathsf{dk}_\mathbb{P}$ (Item 2b), we are guaranteed that $\mathbb{P}_i(x_i) = 1$ (recall that x_i is the input of the i-th sender). In particular, the latter holds as, in any other slot, the i-th sender has used the wildcards. By repeating this argument, we can conclude that $\mathbb{P}(x_1, \ldots, x_n) = \mathbb{P}_1(x_1) \wedge \ldots \wedge \mathbb{P}_n(x_n)$ is satisfied if the execution of each $\mathbb{C}_{c_i^{(2)}, k_{i+1}}$ goes as expected. We refer the reader to the full version [25] for the formal construction.

As for security, we show that our construction satisfies CPA-1-sided security in the presence of *no collusions* (i.e., the adversary can submit a single query to the oracle KGen) if the underlying PE is CPA-1-sided secure, SKE is CPA secure, and the lockable obfuscation is secure. Roughly, the proof works as follows. Let $\mathbb{P}^*$ be the *only* predicate submitted to KGen by the adversary. Starting from A's validity condition, we infer that, for any choice of the challenge bit $b \in \{0,1\}$, then attacker A must maintain one of the following two conditions:

(i) either $\mathbb{P}_1^*(x_1^b) = \ldots = \mathbb{P}_n^*(x_n^b) = 0$ (i.e., all the predicates of the conjunctions are false);

(ii) or (if at least one predicate $\mathbb{P}_i^*$ is satisfied, i.e., $\mathbb{P}_i^*(x_i^b) = 1$) there exists $j \neq i$ such that, for every $x_j \in \mathcal{Q}_j^b$, it holds that $\mathbb{P}_j^*(x_j) = 0$ where $\mathcal{Q}_j^b$ is the ordered list composed of predicate inputs submitted to the oracle $\mathsf{Enc}(\mathsf{ek}_j, \cdot, \cdot)$ and the challenge input x_j^b (see Eq. (2)).[9]

When the first condition is satisfied, we can leverage the CPA-1-sided security of the single-input PE to show that the every lock y_i (encrypted using the PE), and every input x_i (encrypted in $c_i^{(2)}$), is completely hidden to the adversary. The latter allows us to use the security of lockable obfuscation to move to a hybrid experiment in which all the (obfuscated) circuits are simulated (including the messages).

On the other hand, when the second condition is satisfied, we can transition to a hybrid experiment (this time by leveraging the security of the underlying PE scheme) in which $\mathsf{Enc}(\mathsf{ek}_j, \cdot, \cdot)$ computes $c_j^{(1)}$ by encrypting the all-zero string (instead of (y_j, k_{j+1})). Thus, we can use the security of lockable obfuscation to move to another hybrid in which $\mathsf{Enc}(\mathsf{ek}_j, \cdot, \cdot)$ simulates all the obfuscations. At this point, the symmetric key k_{j+1} is not used anymore. Hence, we can use the security of SKE to transition to another hybrid in which $\mathsf{Enc}(\mathsf{ek}_{j+1}, \cdot, \cdot)$ computes $c_{j+1}^{(2)}$ by encrypting the all-zero string (instead of $c_{j+1}^{(1)}$ that, in turn, contains the lock y_{j+1} and the symmetric key k_{j+2}). After this hybrid, we can again use the security of lockable obfuscation to simulate all the obfuscations computed by $\mathsf{Enc}(\mathsf{ek}_{j+1}, \cdot, \cdot)$, and so on. By repeating these last two hybrids, we reach an experiment whose distribution does not depend on the challenge bit. The formal construction appears in the full version of this work [25].

We highlight that our scheme is not secure in the presence of collusions. In particular, the fact that the adversary can obtain a single decryption key $\mathsf{dk}_\mathbb{P}$ is crucial in order to get the validity condition (ii), i.e., for every $b \in \{0,1\}$ there exists a j such that for every predicate (submitted to $\mathsf{KGen}(\mathsf{msk}, \cdot)$) we have $\mathbb{P}_j(x_j^b) = 0$. In fact, in the case of collusions, the adversary can ask for two decryption keys $\mathsf{dk}_\mathbb{P}$ and $\mathsf{dk}_{\mathbb{P}'}$ such that for every $b \subset \{0,1\}$:

---

[9] If this condition is not satisfied, the adversary has obtained through the encryption oracles a set of ciphertexts that can be interleaved with one (or more) parts of the challenge ciphertext in order to satisfy the predicate $\mathbb{P}^*$.

$$\mathbb{P}_1(x_1^b) = 0 \text{ and } \mathbb{P}_2(x_2^b) = \ldots = \mathbb{P}_n(x_n^b) = 1$$
$$\mathbb{P}_1'(x_1^b) = 1 \text{ and } \mathbb{P}_2'(x_2^b) = \ldots = \mathbb{P}_n'(x_n^b) = 0.$$

Note that these are valid queries for the CPA-1-sided security experiment of n-input PE (the ciphertext cannot be decrypted). However, such a *unique* j for every predicate (as per condition (ii)) does not exist. When this happens, we are not able to conclude the proof by making a reduction to the security of single-input PE (the reduction will make an invalid set of queries to the KGen oracle of the single-input PE, making it invalid for the CPA-1-sided security of the single-input PE).[10]

Lastly, we stress that since we start from a single-input PE supporting conjunctions of arbitrary predicates *with wildcards*, we end up with an n-input PE for conjunctions of arbitrary predicates (see Eq. (1)) *with wildcards*. We highlight that wildcards do not play any role in the security proof of our secret-key construction. In other words, wildcards are required for functionality (correctness) and not for security. Indeed, in the secret-key setting (i.e., no corruptions), wildcards can be easily removed. This is because we can transform any secure multi-input PE for $\mathbb{P}(x_1, \ldots, x_n) = \mathbb{P}_1(x_1) \wedge \ldots \wedge \mathbb{P}_n(x_n)$ with a *single* wildcard $(x_1^\star, \ldots, x_n^\star)$ into a secure multi-input PE for the same class of predicates $\mathbb{P}(x_1, \ldots, x_n)$ *without the wildcard*. This can be done by requiring the senders not to encrypt the corresponding wildcard, i.e., for each $i \in [n]$, $\mathsf{Enc}(\mathsf{ek}_i, x_i^\star, m_i)$ outputs $\bot$ whenever $x_i = x_i^\star$. We stress that this only works in the case of no corruptions. In fact, as we will discuss later, in case of corruption, wildcards play a role in the security of our corruption-resilient multi-input PE scheme, e.g., an adversary can encrypt wildcards on its own using the leaked encryption keys.

Security Under Corruptions. Next, let us explain how to define security of multi-input PE in the presence of corruptions. Here, the adversary has the possibility to corrupt a subset of the senders and leak their encryption keys ek_i. We model this by introducing an additional corruption oracle $\mathsf{Corr}(\cdot)$ that, upon input an index $i \in [n]$, returns ek_i. Note that, once obtained ek_i, the adversary A has the possibility to produce arbitrary ciphertexts on any message and predicate input, without interacting with the challenger during the CPA-1-sided security game. As usual, the validity condition heavily depends on the queries submitted to both the encryption oracles and the corruption oracle. More precisely, the validity condition now says that, for every decryption key $\mathsf{dk}_\mathbb{P}$, for every vector of ciphertexts that can be obtained by interleaving the challenge ciphertext $(c_1^\star, \ldots, c_n^\star)$ with both the ciphertexts obtain trough any of the (uncorrupted) encryption oracles and the ones that A may autonomously produce by using the leaked encryption keys (trough oracle $\mathsf{Corr}(\cdot)$), we have that $\mathbb{P}$ is not satisfied. Hence, the validity condition is identical to that of the secret-key setting (see Eq. (2)), except that:

---

[10] As we discuss in the full version [25], our construction remains secure if we consider a weaker form of collusion in which the adversary can only obtain multiple decryption keys for predicates $\mathbb{P}$ such that there is a unique j *for all predicates* (submitted to KGen) that satisfies the validity condition (ii).

- If the i-th encryption key ek_i has been corrupted/leaked, then $\mathcal{Q}_i^b$ of Eq. 2 corresponds to the i-th predicate input space. This is because the adversary can produce a valid ciphertext on any input x_i.
- Else (i.e., the i-th encryption key ek_i is still secret), $\mathcal{Q}_i^b$ is defined as usual, i.e., it is the ordered list of predicate inputs submitted to oracle $\mathsf{Enc}(\mathsf{ek}_i, \cdot, \cdot)$ and challenge input x_i^b.

See Sect. 4 for the formal definition.

A Simple Attack. Before explaining our construction in details, let us show why the previous construction is not secure under corruptions. For simplicity, we focus on the 2-input setting. Suppose an adversary A has a single decryption key $\mathsf{dk}_\mathbb{P}$ for $\mathbb{P}(x_1, x_2) = \mathbb{P}_1(x_1) \wedge \mathbb{P}_2(x_2)$ and a vector of ciphertexts $(c_1^*, c_2^*) = ((\widetilde{\mathbb{C}}_1, c_1^{(2)}), (\widetilde{\mathbb{C}}_2, c_2^{(2)}))$ encrypted under the predicate input (x_1, x_2) such that $\mathbb{P}_1(x_1) = 0$ and $\mathbb{P}_2(x_2) = 1$. Note that this ciphertext should not decrypt under $\mathsf{dk}_\mathbb{P}$, since the conjunction of $\mathbb{P}_1$ and $\mathbb{P}_2$ evaluates to 0. If A can obtain ek_2, then it can easily determine the message m_2 (and thus the bit b). Indeed, once A gets $\mathsf{ek}_2 = (\mathsf{mpk}, \mathsf{k}_2, \mathsf{k}_1)$, it can compute a malicious ciphertext $\widetilde{c}_1^{(1)}$ (using the single-input PE) by encrypting $(\widetilde{y}, \mathsf{k}_2)$ (where $\widetilde{y}$ is a random lock) under the predicate input composed by (x_1', x_2') such that $\mathbb{P}_1(x_1') = 1$ and $\mathbb{P}_2(x_2') = 1$. Then, it can compute $\widetilde{c}_2^{(2)} \leftarrow_\$ \mathsf{Enc}(\mathsf{k}_1, \widetilde{c}_1^{(1)})$ and execute $\widetilde{\mathbb{C}}_2(\widetilde{c}_1^{(2)}, \mathsf{dk}_\mathbb{P})$ to get m_2. Note that by definition the execution of $\widetilde{\mathbb{C}}_2$ outputs the correct message, since $\mathbb{P}_1(x_1^*) \wedge \mathbb{P}_2(x_2) = 1$ and $\widetilde{c}_1^{(2)}$ contains the correct secret encryption key k_2, allowing the circuit to correctly end the computation. Also, note that this attack does not violate the validity condition. This is because $\mathbb{P}_1(x_1) = 0$, and A does not use the oracle $\mathsf{Enc}(\mathsf{ek}_1, \cdot, \cdot)$ at all. Hence, any interleaving of the ciphertexts will involve the predicate input x_1 that, in turn, will make the conjunction $\mathbb{P}(x_1, x_2') = \mathbb{P}_1(x_1) \wedge \mathbb{P}_2(x_2')$ unsatisfied for every choice of the input predicate x_2'.

In light of the above attack, we can identify what we need to do in order to extend our techniques to handle corruptions: First, following the proof of the previous construction, it is important to hide the (plain) single-input PE ciphertext that a particular sender produces (e.g., in the secret-key setting we re-encrypt $c_i^{(1)}$ using SKE). As we have described for the secret-key setting, this allows us to claim that everything remains hidden whenever one of the predicate $\mathbb{P}_i$ of the conjunction is not satisfied (even if a different $\mathbb{P}_j$ is satisfied).[11] Second, the leakage of one (or more) encryption keys should not allow to produce a malicious ciphertext on behalf of the uncorrupted senders (or simply decrypt the ciphertexts of other parties). Otherwise, the attacker can follow a strategy similar to the one above to break security.

---

[11] The secret-key construction achieves this by linking multiple PE ciphertexts via SKE, and including the secret key k_{i+1} into the PE ciphertext.

Construction Under Corruptions. In order to achieve the above properties, we propose a new technique based on nested (lockable obfuscated) circuits that can be executed one inside the other. This technique permits to make available secret information (e.g., secret keys) *only* during nested execution. For the sake of clarity, we first present our approach for the case of two inputs. As an initial attempt to deal with corruptions, we replace the SKE in our previous construction with a PKE, so that the encryption key ek_1 (resp. ek_2) is now composed of $(\mathsf{mpk}, \mathsf{sk}_1, \mathsf{pk}_1, \mathsf{pk}_2)$ (resp. $(\mathsf{mpk}, \mathsf{sk}_2, \mathsf{pk}_2, \mathsf{pk}_1)$) where $(\mathsf{sk}_i, \mathsf{pk}_i)$ is a secret/public key pair. Each $(\mathsf{sk}_i, \mathsf{pk}_i)$ is associated to the i-th sender (indeed, note that ek_i contains also the secret key sk_i). From the perspective of the first sender, in order to encrypt a message m_1 under the input x_1, it samples two random locks $(y_1^{\mathsf{in}}, y_1^{\mathsf{out}})$ and encrypts them (using the single-input PE) as before using the wildcard $x_2^\star$, i.e., $c_1^{(0)} \leftarrow_\$ \mathsf{Enc}(\mathsf{mpk}, (x_1, x_2^\star), (y_1^{\mathsf{in}}, y_1^{\mathsf{out}}))$.[12] At this point, the PE ciphertext $c_1^{(0)}$ is re-encrypted twice using pk_1 and pk_2, i.e., $c_1^{(i)} \leftarrow_\$ \mathsf{Enc}(\mathsf{pk}_i, c_1^{(i-1)})$ for $i \in [2]$. Intuitively, the two layers of PKE have the role of hiding the PE ciphertexts (that in turn contain the locks) even when the adversary leaks all encryption keys except one. The final ciphertext is composed by the two obfuscations $\widetilde{\mathbb{C}}_1^{\mathsf{out}}$, $\widetilde{\mathbb{C}}_1^{\mathsf{in}}$ of the circuits $\mathbb{C}_{\mathsf{sk}_1, c_1^{(2)}}^{\mathsf{out}}$, $\mathbb{C}_{\mathsf{sk}_1, c_1^{(2)}}^{\mathsf{in}}$, respectively. The former is obfuscated under the lock y_1^{out} and message m_1, whereas the latter is obfuscated under the lock y_1^{in} and message sk_1. The ciphertext produced by the second sender, is identical, except that it uses sk_2 (instead of sk_1) and that $c_2^{(0)}$ is computed using the predicate input $(x_1^\star, x_2)$ (instead of $(x_1, x_2^\star)$).

The crux of our nesting technique comes from the definition of the circuits $\mathbb{C}_{\mathsf{sk}_i, c_i^{(2)}}^{\mathsf{out}}$. More precisely, the outer circuit $\mathbb{C}_{\mathsf{sk}_1, c_1^{(2)}}^{\mathsf{out}}$ will take as input the obfuscation $\widetilde{\mathbb{C}}_2^{\mathsf{in}}$ of the inner circuit $\mathbb{C}_{\mathsf{sk}_2, c_2^{(2)}}^{\mathsf{in}}$ and a decryption key $\mathsf{dk}_{\mathbb{P}}$. Then, in order to securely check the conjunction inside the lockable obfuscation, $\mathbb{C}_{\mathsf{sk}_1, c_1^{(2)}}^{\mathsf{out}}$ will execute $\widetilde{\mathbb{C}}_2^{\mathsf{in}}(\mathsf{sk}_1, \mathsf{dk}_{\mathbb{P}})$. At this point, $\widetilde{\mathbb{C}}_2^{\mathsf{in}}$ has everything it needs to check the satisfiability of $\mathbb{P}_2(\cdot)$. It removes the PKE layers from $c_2^{(2)}$ by computing $c_2^{(0)} = \mathsf{Dec}(\mathsf{sk}_2, \mathsf{Dec}(\mathsf{sk}_1, c_2^{(2)}))$. Then, it decrypts the PE ciphertext $(y_2^{\mathsf{in}}, y_2^{\mathsf{out}}) = \mathsf{Dec}(\mathsf{dk}_{\mathbb{P}}, c_2^{(0)})$—observe that the decryption succeeds if $\mathbb{P}_2(x_2) = 1$— and returns y_2^{in}. By correctness of lockable obfuscation, if the computation of $\mathbb{C}_{\mathsf{sk}_2, c_2^{(2)}}^{\mathsf{in}}(\mathsf{sk}_1, \mathsf{dk}_{\mathbb{P}})$ goes as intended, then $\widetilde{\mathbb{C}}_2^{\mathsf{in}}(\mathsf{sk}_1, \mathsf{dk}_{\mathbb{P}})$ will output sk_2 (the message attached to the obfuscation). Once obtained sk_2, the computation of $\mathbb{C}_{\mathsf{sk}_1, c_1^{(2)}}^{\mathsf{out}}$ can continue and perform a similar computation to check the satisfiability of $\mathbb{P}_1(\cdot)$ except that, if the PE ciphertext $c_1^{(0)}$ decrypts correctly, it returns y_1^{out}. If all the decryptions (performed by $\mathbb{C}_{\mathsf{sk}_1, c_1^{(2)}}^{\mathsf{out}}$ and $\mathbb{C}_{\mathsf{sk}_2, c_2^{(2)}}^{\mathsf{in}}$) succeed, the execution of the obfuscation $\widetilde{\mathbb{C}}_1^{\mathsf{out}}$ of $\mathbb{C}_{\mathsf{sk}_1, c_1^{(2)}}^{\mathsf{out}}$ will output m_1. A symmetrical argument holds for $\mathbb{C}_{\mathsf{sk}_2, c_2^{(2)}}^{\mathsf{out}}$ and $\mathbb{C}_{\mathsf{sk}_1, c_1^{(2)}}^{\mathsf{in}}$, releasing m_2.

---

[12] Recall that wildcards must be efficiently computable.

We show that the above 2-input PE construction is CPA-1-sided secure under 1 corruption (i.e., one encryption key remains secret) and no collusions if the underlying single-input PE is CPA secure, PKE is CPA secure, and the lockable obfuscation is secure. The high level intuition is that sk_i remains unknown to the adversary if $\mathbb{P}_i(\cdot) = 0$ (unless the adversary invokes the oracle $Corr(i)$). This is reflected by the proof technique that is sketched below.

Let $dk_{\mathbb{P}^*}$ be the decryption key obtained by A for the predicate $\mathbb{P}^*(\cdot, \cdot) = \mathbb{P}_1^*(\cdot) \wedge \mathbb{P}_2^*(\cdot)$ (recall the presence of wildcards), and let $\mathcal{Q}_{Corr}$ be the queries submitted to the corruption oracle. Starting from the validity condition, we can infer that for any choice of the challenge bit $b \in \{0,1\}$ we have:

(i) either $\mathbb{P}_1^*(x_1^b) = \mathbb{P}_2^*(x_2^b) = 0$;
(ii) or (i.e., there exists an $i \in [2]$ such that predicate $\mathbb{P}_i$ is satisfied) $j \notin \mathcal{Q}_{Corr}$ such that $j \neq i$ and, for every $x_j \in \mathcal{Q}_j^b$, $\mathbb{P}_j^*(x_j) = 0$ (recall that $x_j^b \in \mathcal{Q}_j^b$). Observe that this second condition holds because of the following:
   - If there is $x_j \in \mathcal{Q}_j^b$ such that $\mathbb{P}_j^*(x_j) = 1$, A can use the corresponding ciphertext to decrypt the i-th part of the challenge ciphertext since $\mathbb{P}_i^*(x_i^b) = 1$.
   - If $j \in \mathcal{Q}_{Corr}$, A can simply use ek_j to encrypt a random message under the wildcard x_j^* (that always exists by design of our construction) and, again, decrypt the i-th part of the challenge ciphertext. Note that, contrarily from our secret-key construction, wildcards play an important role in the security of our multi-input PE construction under corruptions (if an encryption key ek_j gets leaked then a malicious adversary can always encrypt itself the j-th wildcards x_j^*, satisfying the j-th predicate $\mathbb{P}_j$). Hence, in the corruption setting, wildcards are used for both functionality and security.

By leveraging the above two conditions, the security of our scheme follows by using a similar argument to that of the secret-key setting. In particular, when the first condition is satisfied, we can show that the locks (y_1^{in}, y_1^{out}) and (y_2^{in}, y_2^{out}) (used to encrypt the challenge) are completely hidden. This, in turn, allows us to use the security of lockable obfuscation and simulate the obfuscations of $(\mathbb{C}^{out}_{sk_1, c_1^{(2)}}, \mathbb{C}^{in}_{sk_1, c_1^{(2)}})$, $(\mathbb{C}^{out}_{sk_2, c_2^{(2)}}, \mathbb{C}^{in}_{sk_2, c_2^{(2)}})$, and the corresponding messages.

On the other hand, when the second condition is satisfied, we can move to a hybrid (by leveraging the security of single-input PE) in which $Enc(ek_j, \cdot, \cdot)$ computes $c_j^{(0)}$ by encrypting the all-zero string (instead of (y_j^{in}, y_j^{out})). Then, we can use the security of lockable obfuscation to transition to another hybrid in which $Enc(ek_j, \cdot, \cdot)$ simulates all the obfuscations. At this point, the secret key sk_j of the uncorrupted j-th sender is not used anymore (recall that $j \notin \mathcal{Q}_{Corr}$). Hence, we can leverage the security of the PKE to remove the locks (y_i^{in}, y_i^{out}) chosen by the i-th sender (recall $i \neq j$). In more details, we do another hybrid in which the j-th PKE layer $c_i^{(j)}$ of the challenge ciphertext is an encryption of zeroes (instead of $c_i^{(j-1)}$ that, in turn, encrypts the locks (y_i^{in}, y_i^{out})). After this hybrid, we can again use the security of lockable obfuscation to simulate all the obfuscations (and the corresponding attached messages) that compose the i-th component of the ciphertext. The distribution of this last hybrid does not depend on the challenge bit b since all the ciphertexts are simulated by the simulator of the lockable obfuscation scheme.

To sum up, we can observe that encrypting $c_i^{(0)}$ (the PE ciphertext that contains the locks) with the public keys $(\mathsf{pk}_1, \mathsf{pk}_2)$ of both senders is crucial in order for our proof to work independently of which encryption key the adversary decides to leak. So long as at least one encryption key ek_i remains hidden, then there is a PKE layer that cannot be decrypted by the adversary. This allows the proof to go through.

Generalizing the Nesting Technique to $(n > 2)$ Inputs. By carefully modifying the definition of the outer and inner circuits, we can generalize the above technique to the case of $n > 2$. The structure of the encryption keys and of the encryption algorithm is similar to the case $n = 2$:

- Each encryption key ek_i is of the form $(\mathsf{mpk}, \mathsf{sk}_i, \mathsf{pk}_1, \ldots, \mathsf{pk}_n)$.
- To compute the i-th encryption of (x_i, m_i), the sender computes the initial PE ciphertext as $c_i^{(0)} \leftarrow_\$ \mathsf{Enc}(\mathsf{mpk}, (x_1^\star, \ldots, x_i, \ldots, x_n^\star), (y_i^{\mathsf{in}}, y_i^{\mathsf{out}}))$. Then, it re-encrypts n times the ciphertext $c_i^{(0)}$ using $(\mathsf{pk}_1, \ldots, \mathsf{pk}_n)$, i.e., $c_i^{(v)} \leftarrow_\$ \mathsf{Enc}(\mathsf{pk}_v, c_i^{(v-1)})$ for $v \in [n]$. As usual, the final ciphertext $c_i = (\widetilde{\mathbb{C}}_i^{\mathsf{out}}, \widetilde{\mathbb{C}}_i^{\mathsf{in}})$ is composed of the obfuscations of $\mathbb{C}_{\mathsf{sk}_i, c_i^{(n)}}^{\mathsf{out}}$ and $\mathbb{C}_{\mathsf{sk}_i, c_i^{(n)}}^{\mathsf{in}}$.

We now turn on the crucial point: the definition of the outer and inner circuits. Again, for the sake of clarity, we only describe the outer circuit $\mathbb{C}_{\mathsf{sk}_1, c_1^{(n)}}^{\mathsf{out}}$ and of the inner circuits $(\mathbb{C}_{\mathsf{sk}_2, c_2^{(n)}}^{\mathsf{in}}, \ldots, \mathbb{C}_{\mathsf{sk}_n, c_n^{(n)}}^{\mathsf{in}})$ generated by the corresponding senders. The remaining circuits are defined similarly. First off, the input space of these circuits is a follows:

- $\mathbb{C}_{\mathsf{sk}_1, c_1^{(n)}}^{\mathsf{out}}$ takes as input the $n-1$ obfuscations of the circuits $(\mathbb{C}_{\mathsf{sk}_2, c_2^{(n)}}^{\mathsf{in}}, \ldots, \mathbb{C}_{\mathsf{sk}_n, c_n^{(n)}}^{\mathsf{in}})$ and a decryption $\mathsf{dk}_\mathbb{P}$. These obfuscations are the inner circuits that needs to be executed in order to return the message m_1 attached to the obfuscation of $\mathbb{C}_{\mathsf{sk}_1, c_1^{(n)}}^{\mathsf{out}}$.
- On the other hand, $\mathbb{C}_{\mathsf{sk}_i, c_i^{(n)}}^{\mathsf{in}}$, for $i \in [n] \setminus \{1\}$, takes as input a tuple of n secret keys $(\mathsf{sk}_1, \ldots, \mathsf{sk}_n)$ (where some can be set to $\bot$), a decryption key $\mathsf{dk}_\mathbb{P}$, and the obfuscations of $(\mathbb{C}_{\mathsf{sk}_{i+1}, c_{i+1}^{(n)}}^{\mathsf{in}}, \ldots, \mathbb{C}_{\mathsf{sk}_n, c_n^{(n)}}^{\mathsf{in}})$. Intuitively, these obfuscations are the remaining inner circuits that we need to still execute in order to complete the nested execution.

Intuitively, the decryption of m_1 requires the nested execution of these circuits (starting from the outer one) in order to get all the secret keys required to decrypt the PE ciphertext. This is achieved as follows.

The outer circuit $\mathbb{C}^{\mathsf{out}}_{\mathsf{sk}_1, c_1^{(n)}}$ starts the nested execution by invoking the obfuscation of $\mathbb{C}^{\mathsf{in}}_{\mathsf{sk}_2, c_2^{(n)}}$ upon input $(\mathsf{sk}_1, \bot, \ldots, \bot)$, $\mathsf{dk}_{\mathbb{P}}$, and the remaining obfuscations of $(\mathbb{C}^{\mathsf{in}}_{\mathsf{sk}_3, c_3^{(n)}}, \ldots, \mathbb{C}^{\mathsf{in}}_{\mathsf{sk}_n, c_n^{(n)}})$. In turn, $\mathbb{C}^{\mathsf{in}}_{\mathsf{sk}_2, c_2^{(n)}}$ will do a similar thing: It executes the next obfuscated circuit $\mathbb{C}^{\mathsf{in}}_{\mathsf{sk}_3, c_3^{(n)}}$ upon input $(\mathsf{sk}_1, \mathsf{sk}_2, \bot, \ldots, \bot)$, $\mathsf{dk}_{\mathbb{P}}$, and the remaining obfuscations $(\mathbb{C}^{\mathsf{in}}_{\mathsf{sk}_4, c_4^{(n)}}, \ldots, \mathbb{C}^{\mathsf{in}}_{\mathsf{sk}_n, c_n^{(n)}})$. This process is repeated until $\mathbb{C}^{\mathsf{in}}_{\mathsf{sk}_n, c_n^{(n)}}$ is executed upon input $(\mathsf{sk}_1, \ldots, \mathsf{sk}_{n-1}, \bot)$ and $\mathsf{dk}_{\mathbb{P}}$. At this point, all the secret keys are know (observe that sk_n is hardcoded). From $c_n^{(n)}$, we can remove the n PKE layers, decrypt the PE ciphertext and, in turn, return y_n^{in} if the PE ciphertext decrypts correctly (i.e., $\mathbb{P}_n(\cdot)$ is satisfied). Once $\mathbb{C}^{\mathsf{in}}_{\mathsf{sk}_n, c_n^{(n)}}$ terminates, the secret key sk_n is released and $\mathbb{C}^{\mathsf{in}}_{\mathsf{sk}_{n-1}, c_{n-1}^{(n)}}$ performs the computation required to check if $\mathbb{P}_{n-1}(\cdot)$ is satisfied. Indeed, $\mathbb{C}^{\mathsf{in}}_{\mathsf{sk}_{n-1}, c_{n-1}^{(n)}}$ has been executed on input $(\mathsf{sk}_1, \ldots, \mathsf{sk}_{n-2}, \bot, \bot)$, it has sk_{n-1} harcoded, and the execution of $\mathbb{C}^{\mathsf{in}}_{\mathsf{sk}_n, c_n^{(n)}}$ has released sk_n. Hence, after the correct termination of $\mathbb{C}^{\mathsf{in}}_{\mathsf{sk}_n, c_n^{(n)}}$, all secret keys are known.

It may seems that this argument can be iterated. However, there is a problem. Even if $\mathbb{C}^{\mathsf{in}}_{\mathsf{sk}_{n-1}, c_{n-1}^{(n)}}$ correctly terminates, the circuit $\mathbb{C}^{\mathsf{in}}_{\mathsf{sk}_{n-2}, c_{n-2}^{(n)}}$ that invokes it does not have access to the secret key sk_n. This is because the latter circuit receives as input $(\mathsf{sk}_1, \ldots, \mathsf{sk}_{n-3}, \bot, \bot, \bot)$, it has sk_{n-2} hardcoded, and the circuit $\mathbb{C}^{\mathsf{in}}_{\mathsf{sk}_{n-1}, c_n^{(n)}}$ has returned sk_{n-1}. As a consequence, $\mathbb{C}^{\mathsf{in}}_{\mathsf{sk}_{n-2}, c_{n-2}^{(n)}}$ must re-run $\mathbb{C}^{\mathsf{in}}_{\mathsf{sk}_n, c_n^{(n)}}$ on input $(\mathsf{sk}_1, \ldots, \mathsf{sk}_{n-1}, \bot)$ in order to get sk_n and decrypt every PKE layer. This needs to be done at any level of the nested execution, yielding an asymptotic running time of $O(n^n)$. Hence, this technique only works assuming $n = O(1)$, i.e. for $O(1)$-input predicates. The formal construction is described in Sect. 5.2.

On Achieving CPA-2-Sided Secure Multi-input PE. Until now, we only focused the discussion on achieving CPA-1-sided security. Our multi-input constructions achieve CPA-2-sided security if the underlying single-input PE is CPA-2-sided secure (we highlight that, in our secret-key multi-input PE construction, we need to reduce the n-arity from $\mathsf{poly}(\lambda)$ to $O(\log(\lambda))$ since we use complexity leveraging). We just recall here that, already for the simple notion of single-input PE for arbitrary predicates, CPA-2-sided security implies iO [15].

1.3 Applications

Finally, we explore applications of multi-key and multi-input PE. This question is particularly relevant given the fact that we are only able to obtain multi-key and multi-input PE supporting conjunctions of arbitrary predicates (with wildcards). Luckily, we can show that this class of predicates is already expressive enough to yield interesting cryptographic applications which previously required much stronger assumptions. We refer the reader to the full version [25] for more details.

Matchmaking Encryption (ME). ME is a natural generalization of ABE in which both the sender and the receiver can specify their own attributes and access policies. Previous work showed how to obtain CPA-2-sided (i.e., mismatch and match) secure ME for arbitrary policies with unbounded collusions using iO [10,11], or for very restricted policies (i.e., for identity matching) using bilinear maps [20,26] (and ROM [10]). To this end, our CPA-1-sided secure multi-key PE scheme (from the sub-exponential LWE assumption) for conjunction of arbitrary predicates implies the weaker (and non-trivial) notion of CPA-1-sided secure ME (i.e., mismatch only). We stress that the seminal work of ME [10,11] defined ME in the setting of CPA-2-sided security (i.e., mismatch and match).

Non-interactive MPC (NI-MPC). NI-MPC [14,34] allows n parties to evaluate a function $f(v_1, \ldots, v_n)$ on their inputs using a single round of communication (i.e., each party sends a single message $c_i \leftarrow_s \mathsf{Enc}(\mathsf{crs}, \mathsf{ek}_i, v_i)$). This is achieved by assuming a trusted setup (that may depend on the function itself) that generates (possibly correlated) strings (e.g., common reference string crs and encryption keys ek_i) that can be later used by the parties to perform function evaluation. Security is formalized using an indistinguishability-based definition: an adversary A cannot distinguish between $(\mathsf{Enc}(\mathsf{crs}, \mathsf{ek}_i, v_i^0))_{i \in [n]}$ and $(\mathsf{Enc}(\mathsf{crs}, \mathsf{ek}_i, v_i^1))_{i \in [n]}$, so long as any combination of the messages known by the adversary (including the ones it can compute using the encryption key ek_i of a corrupted party) yields the same function's evaluation.[13] Previous works [14,29,32,33] showed that NI-MPC implies iO even if we consider very weak security models, like the non-reusable 1-robust (i.e., one malicious party) setting with $n = 2$ parties, or the reusable 0-robust (i.e., no malicious parties) setting with $n = \mathsf{poly}(\lambda)$ parties.[14]

We show that CPA-1-sided multi-input PE supporting predicates $\mathbb{P}(x_1, \ldots, x_n)$ tolerating k corruptions and no collusions implies k-robust NI-MPC for the following class of functions:

$$f_{\mathbb{P}}((x_1, m_1), \ldots, (x_n, m_n)) = \begin{cases} (m_1, \ldots, m_n) & \text{if } \mathbb{P}(x_1, \ldots, x_n) = 1 \\ \bot & \text{otherwise.} \end{cases}$$

The resulting NI-MPC satisfies a weaker notion of reusability without session identifiers (i.e., messages produced in different rounds can be interleaved by design) specifically tailored for all-or-nothing functions, which we name *CPA-1-sided reusability*. In a nutshell, CPA-1-sided reusable NI-MPC guarantees security even if the same setup is reused multiple times, so long as $f_{\mathbb{P}}$ outputs $\bot$ (i.e., $\mathbb{P}$ is not satisfied) for any combination of the honest messages and the ones the

---

[13] Note that security of NI-MPC for general functions is formalized by an indistinguishability-based definition [14,32]. This is because simulation-based NI-MPC implies virtual black-box (VBB) obfuscation that is known to be impossible for certain classes of functions [13].

[14] Reusable NI-MPC remains secure even when the same setup is used over multiple rounds. On the other hand, non-reusable NI-MPC does not permit to reuse the same setup, i.e., after each round the setup algorithm needs to be executed.

adversary can maliciously compute using the encryption key ek_i of a corrupted party.

By plugging in our results, we obtain either CPA-1-sided reusable $(n-1)$-robust NI-MPC with $n = O(1)$, or CPA-1-sided reusable 0-robust NI-MPC with $n = \mathsf{poly}(\lambda)$ where the predicate $\mathbb{P}$ of the function $f_{\mathbb{P}}$ is a conjunctions of arbitrary predicates (i.e., $\mathbb{P}(x_1, \ldots, x_n) = \mathbb{P}_1(x_1) \wedge \ldots \wedge \mathbb{P}_n(x_n)$) with wildcards under the LWE assumption. Note that a CPA-1-sided reusable NI-MPC for $f_{\mathbb{P}}$ where $\mathbb{P}(x_1, \ldots, x_n) = \mathbb{P}_1(x_1) \wedge \ldots \wedge \mathbb{P}_n(x_n)$ can be used to implement a voting protocol with message passing, i.e., only when each parties' vote x_i satisfies its dedicated set of requirements $\mathbb{P}_i(\cdot)$ (i.e., $\mathbb{P}_i(x_i) = 1$ for every $i \in [n]$) the messages are revealed to all the participants. Until this condition is not satisfied, everything remains secret.

We stress that, nonetheless CPA-1-sided reusability is a weakening of the standard reusability definition, our flavor of reusability is still non-trivial to achieve in the setting of general functions. This is because we can build null iO (and, in turn, witness encryption) [19,31,48] from CPA-1-sided reusable NI-MPC using the same constructions of iO from (standard) reusable NI-MPC, i.e., CPA-1-sided reusable (resp. CPA-1-sided non-reusable) 0-robust (resp. 1-robust) NI-MPC for $n = \mathsf{poly}(\lambda)$ parties (resp. $n = 2$ parties) and general functions implies null iO.

1.4   Relation with Witness Encryption (WE)

We observe that both multi-input and multi-key schemes imply witness encryption (WE) [27], if the former support arbitrary predicates (or any predicate that implements a desired NP relation). Brakerski et al. [19] have shown that n-input ABE (i.e., predicate inputs can be public), secure in the secret-key setting and without collusions, implies WE for NP and n-size witnesses. Similarly, we can build WE from multi-key ABE (i.e., a multi-key scheme where predicate inputs can be public) using a similar construction except that we substitute the multiple inputs with the multiple decryption keys of multi-key ABE. Unfortunately, we cannot use here our constructions of multi-key and multi-input since they only support conjunctions of arbitrary predicates (we stress that CPA-1-sided and CPA-2-sided security are not required for constructing WE).

We also observe that arbitrary predicates are not needed if we consider security under corruptions. Indeed, 2-input ABE for conjunctions of arbitrary predicates $\mathbb{P}(x_1, x_2) = \mathbb{P}_1(x_1) \wedge \mathbb{P}_2(x_2)$ *without wildcards* under 1 corruption and no collusions, implies WE for any relation. Even in this case, our $O(1)$-input scheme under corruptions fails to imply WE. This is because our construction supports conjunctions of arbitrary predicates *each one* having a wildcard (in other words, the wildcard is a trivial witness for any statement). We provide more details in the full version of this work [25].

From these observations, we can identify two plausible approaches that could lead to a construction of WE from standard assumptions: (i) enlarging the class of predicates of our secret-key n-input or n-key constructions, or (ii) supporting conjunctions of arbitrary predicates (without wildcards) in the setting of 2-input ABE with security under 1 corruption.

2   Related Work

Multi-input PE is a special case of multi-input FE [29]. It is well known that so-called compact FE (supporting arbitrary functions) implies multi-input FE [9,15], which in turn implies iO. Constructions of multi-input FE from standard assumptions, in turn, exist for restricted functions [1–4,6,7,16,21,22,24,39,44]. Multi-input PE can also be seen as stronger form of multi-input ABE [19], the difference being that the attributes are not private in the case of ABE. Previously to our work, all (provably secure) constructions of n-input ABE with $n > 2$ required iO (the only exception is the concurrent work of Agrawal et al. [8], which we discuss in the next paragraph).

The multi-input and multi-key settings have also been considered in the context of fully-homomorphic encryption [23,40,41].

Concurrent and Independent Work. The independent and concurrent work of Agrawal, Yadav, and Yamada [8] proposes two constructions of secret-key (i.e., no corruptions) 2-input key-policy ABE for NC^1 with unbounded collusions (recall that, in the ABE setting, only the secrecy of the messages is guaranteed, i.e., inputs can be public). The first construction is based on LWE and pairings, and it is provably secure in the generic group model. The second construction is based on function-hiding inner-product FE, a variant of the non-falsifiable KOALA knowledge assumption (which is proven to hold under the bilinear generic group model), and LWE. However, this second construction achieves a weaker selective flavor of security in which the adversary has to submit both the challenge and the decryption key queries before the setup phase. Additionally, they propose two heuristic constructions. The first is a 2-input ABE for P from lattices, and the second is a 3-input ABE for NC^1 from pairings and lattices. However, the security of these heuristic constructions remains unclear.

In comparison, our work directly focuses on the PE setting (i.e., CPA-1-sided security) and provides the first secret-key n-input PE that supports $n = \mathsf{poly}(\lambda)$ inputs, with (adaptive) CPA-1-sided security (i.e., secrecy of both inputs and messages) based solely on LWE. However, our construction only supports a restricted class of predicates (i.e., conjunctions of arbitrary predicates with wildcards) and it is secure only in the case of no collusions. Furthermore, differently from [8], we move away from the secret-key setting and propose a second construction of n-input PE (still for conjunctions of arbitrary predicates) that supports $n = O(1)$ inputs and can tolerate $n-1$ corruptions (i.e., up to $n-1$ encryption keys can be adaptively revealed by the adversary). Finally, we propose the notion of multi-key PE (not covered in [8]), and give the first construction of

CPA-1-sided secure n-key PE for $n = \mathsf{poly}(\lambda)$, with unbounded collusions and still supporting conjunctions of arbitrary predicates, based on LWE.

Regarding the techniques, we highlight that both our work and that of [8] introduce (albeit different) nesting techniques based on lockable obfuscation. In particular, the nesting technique of [8] permits to transform any secret-key n-input ABE into a secret-key n-input PE (achieving CPA-1-sided security). We stress that their approach only works in the secret-key setting. In contrast, we propose a different nesting technique which yields n-input PE for $n = O(1)$ while tolerating $n - 1$ corruptions. It is important to note that our nesting technique is not generic, but it is specifically tailored to work with the class of predicates considered in this work.

Turning to applications, we highlight that the multi-input schemes of [8] fail to imply ME, since their constructions are all in the secret-key setting (whereas ME requires a public-key encryption algorithm). As for NI-MPC, the constructions in [8] can be used to obtain a CPA-1-sided 0-robust reusable NI-MPC for all-or-nothing functions defined over arbitrary predicates, but only in the case of 2 parties (3 parties if we consider also the heuristic constructions).

3   Preliminaries

We assume the reader to be familiar with standard cryptographic notation and definitions. The preliminaries can be found in the full version [25].

4   Multi-key and Multi-input Predicate Encryption

We provide the formal definitions of multi-key PE and multi-input PE. In the full version [25], we build ME from multi-key PE and CPA-1-sided reusable robust NI-MPC for all-or-nothing functions from multi-input PE.

Multi-key PE. Formally, an n-key PE with message space $\mathcal{M}$, input space $\mathcal{X}$, and predicate space $\mathcal{P} = \{\mathbb{P}_{v_1,\dots,v_n}(x)\}_{(v_1,\dots,v_n)\in\mathcal{V}}$ indexed by $\mathcal{V} = \mathcal{V}_1 \times \dots \times \mathcal{V}_n$, is composed of the following polynomial-time algorithms:

$\mathsf{Setup}(1^\lambda)$: Upon input the security parameter 1^λ the setup algorithm outputs the master public key mpk and the n master secret key $(\mathsf{msk}_1, \dots, \mathsf{msk}_n)$.

$\mathsf{KGen}(\mathsf{msk}_i, v_i)$: Let $i \in [n]$. The randomized key generator takes as input the i-th master secret key msk_i and the i-th index $v_i \in \mathcal{V}_i$. The algorithm outputs the i-th secret decryption key dk_{v_i} for the predicate index v_i.

$\mathsf{Enc}(\mathsf{mpk}, x, m)$: The randomized encryption algorithm takes as the master public key mpk, an input $x \in \mathcal{X}$, and a message $m \in \mathcal{M}$. The algorithm produces a ciphertext c.

$\mathsf{Dec}(\mathsf{dk}_{v_1}, \dots, \mathsf{dk}_{v_n}, c)$: The deterministic decryption algorithm takes as input n secret decryption keys $(\mathsf{dk}_{v_1}, \dots, \mathsf{dk}_{v_n})$ for the n indexes $(v_1, \dots, v_n) \in \mathcal{V}$ and a ciphertext c. The algorithm outputs a message m.

$$\begin{array}{l}
\hline
\mathbf{G}^{\mathsf{CPA}\text{-}t\text{-}\mathsf{kPE}}_{\Pi,\mathsf{A}}(\lambda) \\
\hline
(\mathsf{mpk}, \mathsf{msk}_1, \ldots, \mathsf{msk}_n) \leftarrow\!\$\ \mathsf{Setup}(1^\lambda) \\
(m^0, m^1, x^0, x^1, \alpha) \leftarrow\!\$\ \mathsf{A}_0^{\mathsf{KGen}(\mathsf{msk}_1, \cdot), \ldots, \mathsf{KGen}(\mathsf{msk}_n, \cdot)}(1^\lambda, \mathsf{mpk}) \\
b \leftarrow\!\$\ \{0,1\}, c \leftarrow\!\$\ \mathsf{Enc}(\mathsf{mpk}, x^b, m^b) \\
b' \leftarrow\!\$\ \mathsf{A}_1^{\mathsf{KGen}(\mathsf{msk}_1, \cdot), \ldots, \mathsf{KGen}(\mathsf{msk}_n, \cdot)}(1^\lambda, c, \alpha) \\
\textbf{If } (b' = b)\textbf{: return } 1 \\
\textbf{Else: return } 0 \\
\hline
\end{array}$$

Fig. 1. Game defining CPA-t-sided security of n-key PE.

Correctness is intuitive: given the decryption keys $(\mathsf{dk}_{v_1}, \ldots, \mathsf{dk}_{v_n})$ for $(v_1, \ldots, v_n) \in \mathcal{V}$, the decryption algorithm returns the message m (encrypted under the input x) with overwhelming probability, whenever $\mathbb{P}_{v_1, \ldots, v_n}(x) = 1$. See [25] for the formal definition.

As for security, we adapt the standard CPA-1-sided and CPA-2-sided security of PE to the n-key setting. In particular, an adversary (with oracle access to $\mathsf{KGen}(\mathsf{msk}_i, \cdot)$ for $i \in [n]$) cannot distinguish between $\mathsf{Enc}(\mathsf{mpk}, x^0, m^0)$ and $\mathsf{Enc}(\mathsf{mpk}, x^1, m^1)$ except with non-negligible probability. When considering CPA-1-sided security, the adversary is valid only if it cannot decrypt the challenge ciphertext, i.e., it asks to the n key generation oracles indexes $(v_1, \ldots, v_n)$ such that $\mathbb{P}_{v_1, \ldots, v_n}(x^0) = \mathbb{P}_{v_1, \ldots, v_n}(x^1) = 0$. Analogously, the CPA-2-sided security captures the indistinguishability of $\mathsf{Enc}(\mathsf{mpk}, x^0, m^0)$ and $\mathsf{Enc}(\mathsf{mpk}, x^1, m^1)$ even when the adversary can decrypt the challenge ciphertext, i.e., $\mathbb{P}_{v_1, \ldots, v_n}(x^0) = \mathbb{P}_{v_1, \ldots, v_n}(x^1) = 1$ and $m^0 = m^1$. These security definitions are formalized below.

Definition 1 (CPA-1-sided and CPA-2-sided security of n-key PE). *Let $t \in [2]$. We say that a n-key PE Π is CPA-t-sided secure if for all valid PPT adversaries* $\mathsf{A} = (\mathsf{A}_0, \mathsf{A}_1)$:

$$\left| \mathbb{P}\left[\mathbf{G}^{\mathsf{CPA}\text{-}t\text{-}\mathsf{kPE}}_{\Pi,\mathsf{A}}(\lambda) = 1\right] - \frac{1}{2} \right| \leq \mathsf{negl}(\lambda),$$

where game $\mathbf{G}^{\mathsf{CPA}\text{-}t\text{-}\mathsf{kPE}}_{\Pi,\mathsf{A}}(\lambda)$ *is depicted in Fig. 1. Adversary* A *is called valid if* $\forall v_1 \in \mathcal{Q}_{\mathsf{KGen}(\mathsf{msk}_1, \cdot)}, \ldots, \forall v_n \in \mathcal{Q}_{\mathsf{KGen}(\mathsf{msk}_n, \cdot)}$, *we have*

> **Case $t = 1$:** $\mathbb{P}_{v_1, \ldots, v_n}(x^0) = \mathbb{P}_{v_1, \ldots, v_n}(x^1) = 0$.
>
> **Case $t = 2$:** *Either* $\mathbb{P}_{v_1, \ldots, v_n}(x^0) = \mathbb{P}_{v_1, \ldots, v_n}(x^1) = 0$
>
> *or* $\mathbb{P}_{v_1, \ldots, v_n}(x^0) = \mathbb{P}_{v_1, \ldots, v_n}(x^1) \wedge m^0 = m^1$.

Multi-input PE. Formally, an n-input PE with message space $\mathcal{M} = \mathcal{M}_1 \times \ldots \times \mathcal{M}_n$, input space $\mathcal{X} = \mathcal{X}_1 \times \ldots \times \mathcal{X}_n$, and predicate space $\mathcal{P}$, is composed of the following polynomial-time algorithms:

$\mathsf{Setup}(1^\lambda)$: Upon input the security parameter 1^λ the setup algorithm outputs the encryption keys $(\mathsf{ek}_1, \ldots, \mathsf{ek}_n)$ and the master secret key msk.

$\mathsf{KGen}(\mathsf{msk}, \mathbb{P})$: The randomized key generator takes as input the master secret key msk and a predicate $\mathbb{P} \in \mathcal{P}$. The algorithm outputs a secret decryption key $\mathsf{dk}_\mathbb{P}$ for predicate $\mathbb{P}$.

$\mathsf{Enc}(\mathsf{ek}_i, x_i, m_i)$: Let $i \in [n]$. The randomized encryption algorithm takes as input an encryption key ek_i, an input $x_i \in \mathcal{X}_i$, and a message $m_i \in \mathcal{M}_i$. The algorithm produces a ciphertext c_i linked to x_i.

$\mathsf{Dec}(\mathsf{dk}_\mathbb{P}, c_1, \dots, c_n)$: The deterministic decryption algorithm takes as input a secret decryption key $\mathsf{dk}_\mathbb{P}$ for predicate $\mathbb{P} \in \mathcal{P}$ and n ciphertexts $(c_1, \dots, c_n)$. The algorithm outputs n messages $(m_1, \dots, m_n)$.

Correctness states that ciphertexts $(c_1, \dots, c_n)$, each linked to an input x_i, correctly decrypt with overwhelming probability if $\mathbb{P}(x_1, \dots, x_n) = 1$. See the full version of this work [25] for the formal definition.

Security with and without Corruptions. The CPA-1-sided and CPA-2-sided security of n-input PE capture the infeasibility in distinguishing between ciphertexts $(\mathsf{Enc}(\mathsf{ek}_1, x_1^0, m_1^0), \dots, \mathsf{Enc}(\mathsf{ek}_n, x_n^0, m_n^0))$ and $(\mathsf{Enc}(\mathsf{ek}_1, x_1^1, m_1^1), \dots, \mathsf{Enc}(\mathsf{ek}_n, x_n^1, m_n^1))$. This is modeled by an adversary having oracle access to a key generation oracle $\mathsf{KGen}(\mathsf{msk}, \cdot)$ (allowing it to get decryption keys $\mathsf{dk}_\mathbb{P}$ on predicates of its choice) and n encryption oracles $\mathsf{Enc}(\mathsf{ek}_1, \cdot, \cdot), \dots, \mathsf{Enc}(\mathsf{ek}_n, \cdot, \cdot)$ (allowing it to get encryptions of arbitrary messages and inputs). Differently from the n-key setting, we consider different models of security with respect to whether the encryption keys are secret (i.e., no corruptions) or public/leaked (i.e., the adversary has the possibility to get one or more encryption keys of its choice). The corruption of an encryption key is captured by giving access to a corruption oracle $\mathsf{Corr}(\cdot)$ to the adversary that, on input $i \in [n]$, it returns ek_i. Intuitively, the knowledge of ek_i impacts the validity condition that the adversary must satisfy (e.g., the challenge ciphertext cannot be decrypted). Indeed, ek_i would allow the adversary to produce arbitrary i-th ciphertexts on arbitrary i-th inputs x_i and potentially decrypt part of the challenge ciphertext. Concretely, as for CPA-1-sided security, the validity of the adversary can be defined as follows:

- *No corruptions (a.k.a. the secret-key setting).* If all the encryption keys $(\mathsf{ek}_1, \dots, \mathsf{ek}_n)$ are secret the validity conditions of CPA-1-sided security is straightforward. It intuitively states that for every $\mathsf{dk}_\mathbb{P}$ (obtained through oracle $\mathsf{KGen}(\mathsf{msk}, \cdot)$) and any tuple of ciphertexts $(c_1, \dots, c_n)$ (each linked to an input x_i) obtained through the interleaving of part of the challenge ciphertext with the ciphertexts generated by invoking oracles $\{\mathsf{Enc}(\mathsf{ek}_i, \cdot, \cdot)\}_{i \in [n]}$, we must have that $\mathbb{P}(x_1, \dots, x_n) = 0$ (otherwise part of the challenge ciphertext can be decrypted).

$$\mathbf{G}^{\ell\text{-CPA-}t\text{-iPE}}_{\Pi,\mathsf{A}}(\lambda)$$

$(\mathsf{ek}_1, \ldots, \mathsf{ek}_n, \mathsf{msk}) \leftarrow\!\!\$\ \mathsf{Setup}(1^\lambda)$

$((m_i^0)_{i \in [n]}, (m_i^1)_{i \in [n]}, (x_i^0)_{i \in [n]}, (x_i^1)_{i \in [n]}, \alpha) \leftarrow\!\!\$\ \mathsf{A}_0^{\mathsf{KGen}(\mathsf{msk},\cdot),\mathsf{Corr}(\cdot),\{\mathsf{Enc}(\mathsf{ek}_j,\cdot,\cdot)\}_{j \in [n]}}(1^\lambda)$

$b \leftarrow\!\!\$\ \{0,1\}, c_1 \leftarrow\!\!\$\ \mathsf{Enc}(\mathsf{ek}_1, x_1^b, m_1^b), \ldots, c_n \leftarrow\!\!\$\ \mathsf{Enc}(\mathsf{ek}_n, x_n^b, m_n^b)$

$b' \leftarrow\!\!\$\ \mathsf{A}_1^{\mathsf{KGen}(\mathsf{msk},\cdot),\mathsf{Corr}(\cdot),\{\mathsf{Enc}(\mathsf{ek}_j,\cdot,\cdot)\}_{j \in [n]}}(1^\lambda, c_1, \ldots, c_n, \alpha)$

If $(b' = b)$: **return** 1

Else: **return** 0

Fig. 2. Game defining CPA-t-sided security of n-input PE in the ℓ-corruptions setting. Oracle $\mathsf{Corr}(j)$ returns ek_j for $j \in [n]$.

– *With corruptions.* If some of the encryption keys are known by the adversary (i.e., obtained through the corruption oracle $\mathsf{Corr}(\cdot)$) then the validity condition now changes according to which keys have been obtained. This is because the adversary can now autonomously compute arbitrary ciphertext (for a particular slot i) using the leaked i-th encryption key ek_i. Taking into account this observation, the validity of CPA-1-sided security *with corruptions* says that any tuple of ciphertexts $(c_1, \ldots, c_n)$ that can be obtained by interleaving part of the challenge ciphertexts with both the ones generated through oracles $\{\mathsf{Enc}(\mathsf{ek}_i, \cdot, \cdot)\}_{i \in [n]}$ and the ones that can be autonomously generated using the leaked encryption keys, we must have that $\mathbb{P}(x_1, \ldots, x_n) = 0$.

The validity of CPA-2-sided security (with and without corruptions) can be easily obtained by adapting the above discussion. Below, we provide the formal definition.

Definition 2 (ℓ-Corruptions CPA-1-sided and CPA-2-sided security of n-input PE). *Let $t \in [2]$. We say that an n-input PE Π is CPA-t-sided secure in the ℓ-corruptions setting if for all valid PPT adversaries $\mathsf{A} = (\mathsf{A}_0, \mathsf{A}_1)$:*

$$\left| \mathbb{P}\left[\mathbf{G}^{\ell\text{-CPA-}t\text{-iPE}}_{\Pi,\mathsf{A}}(\lambda) = 1 \right] - \frac{1}{2} \right| \leq \mathsf{negl}(\lambda),$$

where game $\mathbf{G}^{\ell\text{-CPA-}t\text{-iPE}}_{\Pi,\mathsf{A}}(\lambda)$ is depicted in Fig. 2. Let $\mathcal{Q}_i = \{x | \exists (x, m) \in \mathcal{Q}_{\mathsf{Enc}(\mathsf{ek}_i, \cdot, \cdot)}\}$ for $i \in [n] \setminus \mathcal{Q}_{\mathsf{Corr}}$ and $\mathcal{Q}_i = \mathcal{X}_i$ for $i \in \mathcal{Q}_{\mathsf{Corr}}$. Moreover, let $\mathcal{Q}_i^d$ (for $d \in \{0,1\}$) be the ordered list composed of the predicate inputs $\mathcal{Q}_i$ and the challenge input x_i^d, i.e., $\mathcal{Q}_i^d = \{x_i^{(1,d)}, \ldots, x_i^{(k_i,d)}, x_i^{(k_i+1,d)} = x_i^d\}$ where $k_i = |\mathcal{Q}_i|$ and $x^{(j,d)} \in \mathcal{Q}_i$ for $j \in [k_i]$.[15] Adversary A is called valid if $|\mathcal{Q}_{\mathsf{Corr}}| \leq \ell$ and

---

[15] Observe that $\mathcal{Q}_i^0$ and $\mathcal{Q}_i^1$ are identical except for the last element.

$\forall \mathbb{P} \in \mathcal{Q}_{\mathsf{KGen}}, \forall j \in [n], \forall i_1 \in [k_1 + 1], \dots, \forall i_n \in [k_n + 1]$, we have

Case $t = 1$: $\mathbb{P}(x_1^{(i_1,0)}, \dots, x_{j-1}^{(i_{j-1},0)}, x_j^0, x_{j+1}^{(i_{j+1},0)}, \dots, x_n^{(i_n,0)}) =$

$$\mathbb{P}(x_1^{(i_1,1)}, \dots, x_{j-1}^{(i_{j-1},1)}, x_j^1, x_{j+1}^{(i_{j+1},1)}, \dots, x_n^{(i_n,1)}) = 0.$$

Case $t = 2$: *Either*

$$\mathbb{P}(x_1^{(i_1,0)}, \dots, x_{j-1}^{(i_{j-1},0)}, x_j^0, x_{j+1}^{(i_{j+1},0)}, \dots, x_n^{(i_n,0)}) =$$

$$\mathbb{P}(x_1^{(i_1,1)}, \dots, x_{j-1}^{(i_{j-1},1)}, x_j^1, x_{j+1}^{(i_{j+1},1)}, \dots, x_n^{(i_n,1)}) = 0$$

or

$$\mathbb{P}(x_1^{(i_1,0)}, \dots, x_{j-1}^{(i_{j-1},0)}, x_j^0, x_{j+1}^{(i_{j+1},0)}, \dots, x_n^{(i_n,0)}) =$$

$$\mathbb{P}(x_1^{(i_1,1)}, \dots, x_{j-1}^{(i_{j-1},1)}, x_j^1, x_{j+1}^{(i_{j+1},1)}, \dots, x_n^{(i_n,1)}) \wedge m_j^0 = m_j^1.$$

Through the paper, for $t \in [2]$, we say that Π is CPA-t-sided secure in the ℓ-corruptions setting and *without collusions* if $|\mathcal{Q}_{\mathsf{KGen}}| = 1$ (i.e., the adversary asks for a single decryption key). If $|\mathcal{Q}_{\mathsf{Corr}}| = 0$ (i.e., no corruptions), we say that Π is CPA-t-sided secure in the *secret-key setting*. In case of both restrictions, we say that Π is CPA-t-sided secure in the *secret-key setting* and *without collusions* (i.e., $|\mathcal{Q}_{\mathsf{Corr}}| = 0$ and $|\mathcal{Q}_{\mathsf{KGen}}| = 1$).

Remark 1 (Relation with multi-key PE). In the full version of this work [25], we show that CPA-t-sided secure $(n+1)$-input PE tolerating 1 corruption, naturally implies CPA-t-sided secure n-key PE.[16] We stress that such a relation holds only if the $(n + 1)$-input PE supports arbitrary predicates. On the other hand, if we consider restricted classes of predicates (as studied in this work), the above implication does not to hold anymore, making multi-input and multi-key PE incomparable.[17]

Also, we discuss the relation between the multi-key and multi-input settings when considering a weaker definition of security. In particular, if we drop the secrecy of the predicate inputs, i.e., only the the messages remain secret (which is equivalent to ABE), then we can show that multi-key ABE implies multi-input ABE only in the presence of no corruptions.

5   Constructions

In this section, we give different constructions of multi-key and multi-input PE (see also Sect. 1.2) for predicates $\mathbb{P}(x_1, \dots, x_n) = \mathbb{P}_1(x_1) \wedge \dots \wedge \mathbb{P}_n(x_n)$.

---

[16] If we restrict the n-key PE's encryption algorithm to be secret-key (i.e., $\mathsf{Enc}(\mathsf{ek}, \cdot, \cdot)$ where ek is kept secret) then we can start from a secret-key $(n + 1)$-input PE, i.e., 0 corruptions.

[17] This is also reflected by the results achieved in this paper. For example, our multi-key PE construction for conjunctions of arbitrary predicates tolerates unbounded collusions whereas our multi-input PE constructions (for the same class of predicates with wildcards) are significantly more complex and are secure only in the case of no collusions.

$$\mathbb{C}_c(\mathsf{dk}_1, \ldots, \mathsf{dk}_n)$$

Initialize: $c_n = c$
For i **from** n **to** 1 **do:** $\mathsf{Dec}_i(\mathsf{dk}_i, c_i) = c_{i-1}$
return c_0

Fig. 3. Definition of the circuit $\mathbb{C}_c$ of Construction 1.

In particular, in Sect. 5.1 we give a construction of n-key PE from single-input PE and lockable obfuscation for $n = \mathsf{poly}(\lambda)$. This construction is secure against unbounded collusions.

In Sect. 5.2, we give a construction of $O(1)$-input PE, that is CPA-1-side secure without collusions and in the $(n-1)$-corruptions setting, from single-input PE, lockable obfuscation, and PKE. It leverages a new nesting execution technique of (lockable obfuscated) circuits. Our secret-key n-input PE construction for $n = \mathsf{poly}(\lambda)$ is deferred to full version [25].

Both multi-input constructions support conjunctions of arbitrary predicates with wildcards, i.e., for every $i \in [n]$, there exists (possibly unique) a wildcard $x_i^\star$ such that for every i-th predicate $\mathbb{P}_i$ we have $\mathbb{P}_i(x_i^\star) = 1$ (in [25] we discuss how to remove the wildcard when no corruptions are in place).

Also, our constructions are generic and achieve CPA-2-sided security if the underlying single-input PE is CPA-2-sided secure (our CPA-2-sided secure secret-key multi-input PE construction (see [25]) supports $n = O(\log(\lambda))$).

5.1 Multi-key PE from PE and Lockable Obfuscation

Construction 1. *Consider the following primitives:*

1. *For $i \in [n]$, a PE scheme $\mathsf{PE}_i = (\mathsf{Setup}_i, \mathsf{KGen}_i, \mathsf{Enc}_i, \mathsf{Dec}_i)$ with message space $\mathcal{M}_i$, input space $\mathcal{X}_i$, and predicate space $\mathcal{P}_i = \{\mathbb{P}_v(x)\}_{v \in \mathcal{V}_i}$ indexed by $\mathcal{V}_i$. Without loss of generality, we assume that PE_i has ciphertext space $\mathcal{Y}_i$, $\mathcal{M}_1 = \{0,1\}^{m(\lambda)}$, and $\mathcal{M}_i = \mathcal{Y}_{i-1}$ for every $i \in [n] \setminus \{1\}$. In order to do not incur into an exponential ciphertext growth (e.g., for $n = \mathsf{poly}(\lambda)$), each i-th PE scheme must have a ciphertext expansion of $\mathsf{poly}(\lambda) + |m_i|$ where $|m_i|$ is the length of the messages $m_i \in \mathcal{M}_i$ supported by the i-th PE scheme (this can be obtained generically from any PE scheme by leveraging hybrid encryption, i.e., $\mathsf{Enc}_i(\mathsf{mpk}, x, s) \| \mathsf{PRG}(s) \oplus m_i$ where $s \leftarrow_\$ \{0,1\}^\lambda$).*
2. *A lockable obfuscation scheme $\mathsf{LOBF} = (\mathsf{Obf}, \mathsf{Eval})$ with message space $\mathcal{M}$ for the family of circuits $\mathcal{C}_{n,s,d}(\lambda) = \{\mathbb{C}_c\}$ as defined in Fig. 3, where $n(\lambda)$, $s(\lambda)$, $d(\lambda)$ depends on the schemes $\mathsf{PE}_1, \ldots, \mathsf{PE}_n$ used, and the circuits $\mathcal{C}_{n,s,d}(\lambda)$.*

We build a n-key PE scheme Π with message space $\mathcal{M}$, input space $\mathcal{X} = \mathcal{X}_1 \times \ldots \times \mathcal{X}_n$, and predicate space $\mathcal{P} = \{\mathbb{P}_{v_1,\ldots,v_n}(x_1, \ldots, x_n) = \mathbb{P}_{v_1}(x_1) \wedge \ldots \wedge \mathbb{P}_{v_n}(x_n)\}_{(v_1,\ldots,v_n) \in \mathcal{V}}$ indexed by $\mathcal{V} = \mathcal{V}_1 \times \ldots \times \mathcal{V}_n$ (and $\mathbb{P}_{v_i} \in \mathcal{P}_i$ for $i \in [n]$), as follows:

Setup(1^λ): *Upon input the security parameter* 1^λ *the randomized setup algorithm outputs* $\mathsf{mpk} = (\mathsf{mpk}_1, \ldots, \mathsf{mpk}_n)$ *and* $\mathsf{msk}_1, \ldots, \mathsf{msk}_n$ *where* $(\mathsf{mpk}_i, \mathsf{msk}_i)$ $\leftarrow_\$ \mathsf{Setup}_i(1^\lambda)$ *for* $i \in [n]$.

KGen(msk_i, v_i): *Let* $i \in [n]$. *Upon input the* i-*th master secret key* msk_i *and the* i-*th predicate index* $v_i \in \mathcal{V}_i$, *the randomized key generator outputs* $\mathsf{dk}_{v_i} \leftarrow_\$$ $\mathsf{KGen}_i(\mathsf{msk}_1, \mathbb{P}_{v_i})$ *where* $\mathbb{P}_{v_i} \in \mathcal{P}_i$.

Enc(mpk, x, m): *Upon input the master public key* $\mathsf{mpk} = (\mathsf{mpk}_1, \ldots, \mathsf{mpk}_n)$, *an input* $x = (x_1, \ldots, x_n) \in \mathcal{X}$, *and a message* $m \in \mathcal{M}$, *the randomized encryption proceeds as follows:*

1. *Sample* $y \leftarrow_\$ \{0,1\}^{s(\lambda)}$ *and let* $c_0 = y$.
2. *For* $i \in [n]$, *compute* $c_i \leftarrow_\$ \mathsf{Enc}_i(\mathsf{mpk}_i, x_i, c_{i-1})$.

Finally, it outputs $c = \widetilde{\mathbb{C}}$ *where* $\widetilde{\mathbb{C}} \leftarrow_\$ \mathsf{Obf}(1^\lambda, \mathbb{C}_{c_n}, y, m)$.

Dec($\mathsf{dk}_{v_1}, \ldots, \mathsf{dk}_{v_n}, c$): *Upon input* n *decryption keys* $\mathsf{dk}_{v_1}, \ldots, \mathsf{dk}_{v_n}$ *and a ciphertext* $c = \widetilde{\mathbb{C}}$, *the deterministic decryption algorithm outputs* $m = \mathsf{Eval}(\widetilde{\mathbb{C}}, (\mathsf{dk}_{v_1}, \ldots, \mathsf{dk}_{v_n}))$.

Correctness follows from the correctness of the underlying schemes. We establish the following result whose proof is deferred to full version [25].

Theorem 4. *Let* $n = \mathsf{poly}(\lambda)$, $\mathsf{PE}_1, \ldots, \mathsf{PE}_n$ *and* LOBF *be as above. If* LOBF *is secure and*

1. *each* $\mathsf{PE}_1, \ldots, \mathsf{PE}_n$ *is CPA secure, then the* n-*key PE scheme* Π *from Construction 1 is CPA-1-sided secure (Definition 1).*
2. *each* $\mathsf{PE}_1, \ldots, \mathsf{PE}_n$ *is CPA-2-sided secure, then the* n-*key PE scheme* Π *from Construction 1 is CPA-2-sided secure (Definition 1).*

We stress that CPA secure single-input PE (see the above theorem) guarantees only the secrecy of the message (whereas predicate inputs can be public). This is equivalent to the notion of single-input ABE.

5.2   Multi-input PE from PE, Lockable Obfuscation and PKE

Corruption Setting. We present our construction of n-input PE that is CPA-1-sided secure in the $(n-1)$-corruptions setting without collusions. This construction handles constant-arity (i.e., $n \in O(1)$) since the decryption running time is $O(n^n)$. It is based on CPA secure single-input PE, lockable obfuscation, and PKE and it leverages the nested execution technique described in Sect. 1.2. Also, the same construction achieves CPA-2-sided security if the initial single-input PE is CPA-2-sided secure.

Construction 2 (n-input PE in the corruption setting). *Consider the following primitives:*

1. *A PE scheme* $\mathsf{PE} = (\mathsf{Setup}_1, \mathsf{KGen}_1, \mathsf{Enc}_1, \mathsf{Dec}_1)$ *with message space* $\mathcal{M}_1 = \{0,1\}^{m_3(\lambda)+m_4(\lambda)}$, *input space* $\mathcal{X}_1 = \mathcal{X}_{1,1} \times \ldots \times \mathcal{X}_{1,n}$, *and predicate space* $\mathcal{P}_1 = \{\mathbb{P}(x_1, \ldots, x_n)\} = \{\mathbb{P}_1(x_1) \wedge \ldots \wedge \mathbb{P}_n(x_n)\}$. *Without loss of generality, we assume that* PE *has ciphertext space* $\mathcal{Y}_1$ *and there exists a (single) wildcard input* $(x_1^\star, \ldots, x_n^\star) \in \mathcal{X}_1$ *such that* $\forall (\mathbb{P}_1(x_1) \wedge \ldots \wedge \mathbb{P}_n(x_n)) \in \mathcal{P}_1, \forall i \in [n], \mathbb{P}_i(x_i^\star) = 1$.

$$\mathbb{C}^{\mathsf{in}}_{c,\mathsf{sk},i}(\mathbb{C}_1,\ldots,\mathbb{C}_{n-2},\mathsf{sk}_1,\ldots,\mathsf{sk}_n,\mathsf{dk}_{\mathbb{P}})$$

Initialize:

$c_n = c, \mathsf{sk}'_i = \mathsf{sk}, \mathbb{C}_{n-1} = \bot, k = \bot, \forall j \in [n] \setminus \{i\}, \ \mathsf{sk}'_j = \mathsf{sk}_j$

If $\exists w \in [n-2]$ such that $\mathbb{C}_w \neq \bot$ and $\mathbb{C}_{w+1} = \bot$: $k = w$

end initialize.

If $k \neq \bot$ do: // If $k = \bot$, no circuit to execute.

    // Execute each circuit received in input in order to retrieve the related secret key.

    For $t \in [k]$ do:

        $\mathsf{Eval}_3(\mathbb{C}_t,(\mathbb{C}_{t+1},\ldots,\mathbb{C}_k,\overbrace{\bot,\ldots,\bot}^{n-2+t-k},\mathsf{sk}'_1,\ldots,\mathsf{sk}'_n,\mathsf{dk}_{\mathbb{P}})) = r$

        If $r = \bot$: return $\bot$

        Else: $\mathsf{sk}'_h = \overline{\mathsf{sk}}$ where $r = (\overline{\mathsf{sk}}, h)$ // Save the secret key returned by $\mathbb{C}_t$.

    end for.

end if.

// At this point, all secret keys are known.

For j from n to 1 do: $\mathsf{Dec}_{2,j}(\mathsf{sk}'_j, c_j) = c_{j-1}$

$\mathsf{Dec}_1(\mathsf{dk}_{\mathbb{P}}, c_0) = v$

If $v = \bot$: return $\bot$

Else: return y^{in}_i where $v = (y^{\mathsf{in}}_i, y^{\mathsf{out}}_i)$

$$\mathbb{C}^{\mathsf{out}}_{c,\mathsf{sk},i}(\mathbb{C}_1,\ldots,\mathbb{C}_{n-1},\mathsf{dk}_{\mathbb{P}})$$

Initialize: $c_n = c, \mathsf{sk}'_i = \mathsf{sk}, \forall j \in [n] \setminus \{i\}, \ \mathsf{sk}'_j = \bot$

// Execute each circuit received in input in order to retrieve the related secret key.

For t from 1 to $n-1$ do:

    $\mathsf{Eval}_3(\mathbb{C}_t,(\mathbb{C}_{t+1},\ldots,\mathbb{C}_{n-1},\overbrace{\bot,\ldots,\bot}^{t-1},\mathsf{sk}'_1,\ldots,\mathsf{sk}'_n,\mathsf{dk}_{\mathbb{P}})) = r$

    If $r = \bot$: return $\bot$

    Else: $\mathsf{sk}'_h = \overline{\mathsf{sk}}$ where $r = (\overline{\mathsf{sk}}, h)$ // Save the secret key returned by $\mathbb{C}_t$.

end for.

// At this point, all secret keys are known.

For j from n to 1 do: $\mathsf{Dec}_{2,j}(\mathsf{sk}'_j, c_j) = c_{j-1}$

$\mathsf{Dec}_1(\mathsf{dk}_{\mathbb{P}}, c_0) = v$

If $v = \bot$: return $\bot$

Else: return y^{out}_i where $v = (y^{\mathsf{in}}_i, y^{\mathsf{out}}_i)$

Fig. 4. Definitions of the circuits $\mathbb{C}^{\mathsf{in}}_{c,\mathsf{sk},i}$ and $\mathbb{C}^{\mathsf{out}}_{c,\mathsf{sk},i}$ supported by the lockable obfuscation schemes LOBF_3 and LOBF_4 of Construction 2.

2. *For $i \in [n]$, a PKE scheme $\mathsf{PKE}_{2,i} = (\mathsf{KGen}_{2,i}, \mathsf{Enc}_{2,i}, \mathsf{Dec}_{2,i})$ with message space $\mathcal{M}_{2,i}$. Without loss of generality, we assume that PKE_i has ciphertext space $\mathcal{Y}_{2,i}$ and secret-key space $\mathcal{K}_{2,i}$. Moreover, we assume that $\mathcal{M}_{2,1} = \mathcal{Y}_1$, and $\mathcal{M}_{2,i} = \mathcal{Y}_{2,i-1}$ for every $i \in [n] \setminus \{1\}$.*

3. *A lockable obfuscation scheme $\mathsf{LOBF}_3 = (\mathsf{Obf}_3, \mathsf{Eval}_3)$ with message space $\mathcal{M}_3 = (\mathcal{K}_{2,1} \cup \ldots \cup \mathcal{K}_{2,n}) \times \{0,1\}^{\lfloor \log_2(n) \rfloor + 1}$ for the family of circuits $\mathcal{C}_{n_3,s_3,d_3}(\lambda) = \{\mathbb{C}^{\mathsf{in}}_{c,\mathsf{sk},i}\}$ defined in Fig. 4, where $n_3(\lambda), s_3(\lambda), d_3(\lambda)$ depends on the schemes $\mathsf{PE}, \mathsf{PKE}_{2,1}, \ldots, \mathsf{PKE}_{2,n}$ used, and the circuits $\mathcal{C}^{\mathsf{in}}_{n_3,s_3,d_3}(\lambda)$.*

4. *A lockable obfuscation scheme $\mathsf{LOBF}_4 = (\mathsf{Obf}_4, \mathsf{Eval}_4)$ with message space $\mathcal{M}_4$ for the family of circuits $\mathcal{C}_{n_4,s_4,d_4}(\lambda) = \{\mathbb{C}^{\mathsf{out}}_{c,\mathsf{sk},i}\}$ defined in Fig. 4, where $n_4(\lambda), s_4(\lambda), d_4(\lambda)$ depends on the schemes $\mathsf{PE}, \mathsf{PKE}_{2,1}, \ldots, \mathsf{PKE}_{2,n}, \mathsf{LOBF}_3$ used, and the circuits $\mathcal{C}^{\mathsf{out}}_{n_4,s_4,d_4}(\lambda)$.*

We build a n-input PE scheme with message space $\mathcal{M} = \overbrace{\mathcal{M}_4 \times \ldots \times \mathcal{M}_4}^{n}$, input space $\mathcal{X} = \mathcal{X}_1$, and predicate space $\mathcal{P} = \mathcal{P}_1 = \{\mathbb{P}(x_1, \ldots, x_n)\} = \{\mathbb{P}_1(x_1) \wedge \ldots \wedge \mathbb{P}_n(x_n)\}$ with wildcard (i.e., there exists a (single) wildcard $(x_1^\star, \ldots, x_n^\star) \in \mathcal{X}$ such that $\forall(\mathbb{P}_1(x_1) \wedge \ldots \wedge \mathbb{P}_n(x_n)) \in \mathcal{P}$, $\forall i \in [n]$, $\mathbb{P}_i(x_i^\star) = 1$), as follows:

$\mathsf{Setup}(1^\lambda)$: Upon input the security parameter 1^λ the randomized setup algorithm outputs $(\mathsf{ek}_1, \ldots, \mathsf{ek}_n)$ and msk where $(\mathsf{mpk}, \mathsf{msk}) \leftarrow_\$ \mathsf{Setup}_1(1^\lambda)$, $\mathsf{ek}_i = (\mathsf{mpk}, \mathsf{sk}_i, \mathsf{pk}_1, \ldots, \mathsf{pk}_n)$, and $(\mathsf{sk}_i, \mathsf{pk}_i) \leftarrow_\$ \mathsf{KGen}_{2,i}(1^\lambda)$ for $i \in [n]$.

$\mathsf{KGen}(\mathsf{msk}, \mathbb{P})$: Upon input the master secret key msk and a predicate $\mathbb{P} \in \mathcal{P}$, the randomized key generator algorithm outputs $\mathsf{dk}_\mathbb{P} \leftarrow_\$ \mathsf{KGen}_1(\mathsf{msk}, \mathbb{P})$.

$\mathsf{Enc}(\mathsf{ek}_i, x_i, m_i)$: Let $i \in [n]$. Upon input an encryption key $\mathsf{ek}_i = (\mathsf{mpk}, \mathsf{sk}_i, \mathsf{pk}_1, \ldots, \mathsf{pk}_n)$, an input $x_i \in \mathcal{X}_{1,i}$, and a message $m_i \in \mathcal{M}_4$, the randomized encryption algorithm samples $(y_i^\mathsf{in}, y_i^\mathsf{out}) \leftarrow_\$ \{0,1\}^{s_3(\lambda)+s_4(\lambda)}$ and proceeds as follows:

1. Compute $c_i^{(0)} \leftarrow_\$ \mathsf{Enc}_1(\mathsf{mpk}, (x_1, \ldots, x_n), (y_i^\mathsf{in}, y_i^\mathsf{out}))$ where $x_j = x_j^\star$ for $j \in [n] \setminus \{i\}$.

2. For $j \in [n]$, compute $c_i^{(j)} \leftarrow_\$ \mathsf{Enc}_{2,j}(\mathsf{pk}_j, c_i^{(j-1)})$.

Finally, it outputs $c_i = (\widetilde{\mathbb{C}}_i^\mathsf{out}, \widetilde{\mathbb{C}}_i^\mathsf{in})$, where $\widetilde{\mathbb{C}}_i^\mathsf{out} \leftarrow_\$ \mathsf{Obf}_4(1^\lambda, \mathbb{C}_{c_i^{(n)}, \mathsf{sk}_i, i}^\mathsf{out}, y_i^\mathsf{out}, m_i)$ and $\widetilde{\mathbb{C}}_i^\mathsf{in} \leftarrow_\$ \mathsf{Obf}_3(1^\lambda, \mathbb{C}_{c_i^{(n)}, \mathsf{sk}_i, i}^\mathsf{in}, y_i^\mathsf{in}, (\mathsf{sk}_i, i))$.

$\mathsf{Dec}(\mathsf{dk}_\mathbb{P}, c_1, \ldots, c_n)$: Upon input a decryption key $\mathsf{dk}_\mathbb{P}$ for predicate $\mathbb{P} \in \mathcal{P}$, and n ciphertexts $(c_1, \ldots, c_n)$ such that $c_i = (\widetilde{\mathbb{C}}_i^\mathsf{out}, \widetilde{\mathbb{C}}_i^\mathsf{in})$ for $i \in [n]$. The deterministic decryption algorithm returns $(m_1, \ldots, m_n)$ where $m_i = \mathsf{Eval}_4(\widetilde{\mathbb{C}}_i^\mathsf{out}, (\widetilde{\mathbb{C}}_1^\mathsf{in}, \ldots, \widetilde{\mathbb{C}}_{i-1}^\mathsf{in}, \widetilde{\mathbb{C}}_{i+1}^\mathsf{in}, \ldots, \widetilde{\mathbb{C}}_n^\mathsf{in}, \mathsf{dk}_\mathbb{P}))$ for $i \in [n]$.

Correctness follows from the one of the underlying primitives (see also Fig. 4 for the definitions of $\mathbb{C}_{c,\mathsf{sk},i}^\mathsf{in}$ and $\mathbb{C}_{c,\mathsf{sk},i}^\mathsf{out}$). Moreover, decryption is polynomial time when $n \in O(1)$. Below, we establish the following result whose proof is deferred to full version [25].

Theorem 5. Let $n = O(1)$, PE, $\mathsf{PKE}_{2,1}, \ldots, \mathsf{PKE}_{2,n}$, LOBF_3, and LOBF_4 be as above. If each $\mathsf{PKE}_{2,i}$ (for $i \in [n]$) is CPA secure, both LOBF_3 and LOBF_4 are secure, and

1. PE is CPA secure without collusions, then the n-input PE scheme Π from Construction 2 is CPA-1-sided secure in the $(n-1)$-corruptions setting without collusions (Definition 2).
2. PE is CPA-2-sided secure without collusions, then the n-input PE scheme Π from Construction 2 is CPA-2-sided secure in the $(n-1)$-corruptions setting without collusions (Definition 2).

As for Theorem 4, CPA secure single-input PE (see the above theorem) guarantees only the secrecy of the message (whereas predicate inputs can be public). This is equivalent to the notion of single-input ABE.

Acknowledgements. The authors would like to thank the anonymous reviewers for useful feedback. The first author was supported by the Carlsberg Foundation under the Semper Ardens Research Project CF18-112 (BCM); the second and the fourth author were partially supported by project SERICS (PE00000014) under the NRRP MUR program funded by the EU - NGEU and by Sapienza University under the project SPECTRA; the third author was partially supported by the German Federal Ministry of Education and Research (BMBF) in the course of the 6GEM research hub under grant number 16KISK038 and by the Deutsche Forschungsgemeinschaft (DFG, German Research Foundation) under Germany's Excellence Strategy - EXC 2092 CASA - 390781972.

References

1. Abdalla, M., Benhamouda, F., Gay, R.: From single-input to multi-client inner-product functional encryption. In: Galbraith, S.D., Moriai, S. (eds.) ASIACRYPT 2019, Part III. LNCS, vol. 11923, pp. 552–582. Springer, Cham (2019). https://doi.org/10.1007/978-3-030-34618-8_19

2. Abdalla, M., Benhamouda, F., Kohlweiss, M., Waldner, H.: Decentralizing inner-product functional encryption. In: Lin, D., Sako, K. (eds.) PKC 2019, Part II. LNCS, vol. 11443, pp. 128–157. Springer, Cham (2019). https://doi.org/10.1007/978-3-030-17259-6_5

3. Abdalla, M., Catalano, D., Fiore, D., Gay, R., Ursu, B.: Multi-input functional encryption for inner products: function-hiding realizations and constructions without pairings. In: Shacham, H., Boldyreva, A. (eds.) CRYPTO 2018, Part I. LNCS, vol. 10991, pp. 597–627. Springer, Cham (2018). https://doi.org/10.1007/978-3-319-96884-1_20

4. Abdalla, M., Gay, R., Raykova, M., Wee, H.: Multi-input inner-product functional encryption from pairings. In: Coron, J.-S., Nielsen, J.B. (eds.) EUROCRYPT 2017, Part I. LNCS, vol. 10210, pp. 601–626. Springer, Cham (2017). https://doi.org/10.1007/978-3-319-56620-7_21

5. Agrawal, S., Freeman, D.M., Vaikuntanathan, V.: Functional encryption for inner product predicates from learning with errors. In: Lee, D.H., Wang, X. (eds.) ASIACRYPT 2011. LNCS, vol. 7073, pp. 21–40. Springer, Heidelberg (2011). https://doi.org/10.1007/978-3-642-25385-0_2

6. Agrawal, S., Goyal, R., Tomida, J.: Multi-input quadratic functional encryption from pairings. In: Malkin, T., Peikert, C. (eds.) CRYPTO 2021, Part IV. LNCS, vol. 12828, pp. 208–238. Springer, Cham (2021). https://doi.org/10.1007/978-3-030-84259-8_8

7. Agrawal, S., Goyal, R., Tomida, J.: Multi-input quadratic functional encryption: Stronger security, broader functionality. In: Kiltz, E., Vaikuntanathan, V. (eds.) TCC 2022, pp. 711–740. Springer, Cham (2023). https://doi.org/10.1007/978-3-031-22318-1_25

8. Agrawal, S., Yadav, A., Yamada, S.: Multi-input attribute based encryption and predicate encryption. In: Dodis, Y., Shrimpton, T. (eds.) CRYPTO 2022, pp. 590–621. Springer, Cham (2022). https://doi.org/10.1007/978-3-031-15802-5_21

9. Ananth, P., Jain, A.: Indistinguishability obfuscation from compact functional encryption. In: Gennaro, R., Robshaw, M. (eds.) CRYPTO 2015, Part I. LNCS, vol. 9215, pp. 308–326. Springer, Heidelberg (2015). https://doi.org/10.1007/978-3-662-47989-6_15

10. Ateniese, G., Francati, D., Nuñez, D., Venturi, D.: Match me if you can: matchmaking encryption and its applications. In: Boldyreva, A., Micciancio, D. (eds.) CRYPTO 2019, Part II. LNCS, vol. 11693, pp. 701–731. Springer, Cham (2019). https://doi.org/10.1007/978-3-030-26951-7_24

11. Ateniese, G., Francati, D., Nuñez, D., Venturi, D.: Match me if you can: matchmaking encryption and its applications. J. Cryptol. **34**(3), 1–50 (2021). https://doi.org/10.1007/s00145-021-09381-4

12. Attrapadung, N.: Dual system encryption via doubly selective security: framework, fully secure functional encryption for regular languages, and more. In: Nguyen, P.Q., Oswald, E. (eds.) EUROCRYPT 2014. LNCS, vol. 8441, pp. 557–577. Springer, Heidelberg (2014). https://doi.org/10.1007/978-3-642-55220-5_31

13. Barak, B., et al.: On the (im)possibility of obfuscating programs. In: Kilian, J. (ed.) CRYPTO 2001. LNCS, vol. 2139, pp. 1–18. Springer, Heidelberg (2001). https://doi.org/10.1007/3-540-44647-8_1

14. Beimel, A., Gabizon, A., Ishai, Y., Kushilevitz, E., Meldgaard, S., Paskin-Cherniavsky, A.: Non-interactive secure multiparty computation. In: Garay, J.A., Gennaro, R. (eds.) CRYPTO 2014. LNCS, vol. 8617, pp. 387–404. Springer, Heidelberg (2014). https://doi.org/10.1007/978-3-662-44381-1_22

15. Bitansky, N., Vaikuntanathan, V.: Indistinguishability obfuscation from functional encryption. In: Guruswami, V. (ed.) 56th FOCS, pp. 171–190. IEEE Computer Society Press (2015). https://doi.org/10.1109/FOCS.2015.20

16. Boneh, D., Lewi, K., Raykova, M., Sahai, A., Zhandry, M., Zimmerman, J.: Semantically secure order-revealing encryption: multi-input functional encryption without obfuscation. In: Oswald, E., Fischlin, M. (eds.) EUROCRYPT 2015, Part II. LNCS, vol. 9057, pp. 563–594. Springer, Heidelberg (2015). https://doi.org/10.1007/978-3-662-46803-6_19

17. Boneh, D., Waters, B.: Conjunctive, subset, and range queries on encrypted data. In: Vadhan, S.P. (ed.) TCC 2007. LNCS, vol. 4392, pp. 535–554. Springer, Heidelberg (2007). https://doi.org/10.1007/978-3-540-70936-7_29

18. Brakerski, Z., Döttling, N., Garg, S., Malavolta, G.: Factoring and pairings are not necessary for IO: circular-secure LWE suffices. In: ICALP 2022. Schloss Dagstuhl-Leibniz-Zentrum für Informatik (2022). https://doi.org/10.4230/LIPIcs.ICALP.2022.28

19. Brakerski, Z., Jain, A., Komargodski, I., Passelègue, A., Wichs, D.: Non-trivial witness encryption and null-iO from standard assumptions. In: Catalano, D., De Prisco, R. (eds.) SCN 2018. LNCS, vol. 11035, pp. 425–441. Springer, Cham (2018). https://doi.org/10.1007/978-3-319-98113-0_23

20. Chen, J., Li, Y., Wen, J., Weng, J.: Identity-based matchmaking encryption from standard assumptions. In: Agrawal, S., Lin, D. (eds.) ASIACRYPT 2022, pp. 394–422. Springer, Cham (2022). https://doi.org/10.1007/978-3-031-22969-5_14

21. Chotard, J., Dufour Sans, E., Gay, R., Phan, D.H., Pointcheval, D.: Decentralized multi-client functional encryption for inner product. In: Peyrin, T., Galbraith, S. (eds.) ASIACRYPT 2018. LNCS, vol. 11273, pp. 703–732. Springer, Cham (2018). https://doi.org/10.1007/978-3-030-03329-3_24

22. Ciampi, M., Siniscalchi, L., Waldner, H.: Multi-client functional encryption for separable functions. In: Garay, J.A. (ed.) PKC 2021, Part I. LNCS, vol. 12710, pp. 724–753. Springer, Cham (2021). https://doi.org/10.1007/978-3-030-75245-3_26

23. Clear, M., McGoldrick, C.: Multi-identity and multi-key leveled FHE from learning with errors. In: Gennaro, R., Robshaw, M. (eds.) CRYPTO 2015, Part II. LNCS, vol. 9216, pp. 630–656. Springer, Heidelberg (2015). https://doi.org/10.1007/978-3-662-48000-7_31

24. Datta, P., Okamoto, T., Tomida, J.: Full-hiding (unbounded) multi-input inner product functional encryption from the k-linear assumption. In: Abdalla, M., Dahab, R. (eds.) PKC 2018. LNCS, vol. 10770, pp. 245–277. Springer, Cham (2018). https://doi.org/10.1007/978-3-319-76581-5_9

25. Francati, D., Friolo, D., Malavolta, G., Venturi, D.: Multi-key and multi-input predicate encryption from learning with errors. Cryptology ePrint Archive (2022)

26. Francati, D., Guidi, A., Russo, L., Venturi, D.: Identity-based matchmaking encryption without random oracles. In: Adhikari, A., Küsters, R., Preneel, B. (eds.) INDOCRYPT 2021. LNCS, vol. 13143, pp. 415–435. Springer, Cham (2021). https://doi.org/10.1007/978-3-030-92518-5_19

27. Garg, S., Gentry, C., Sahai, A., Waters, B.: Witness encryption and its applications. In: Boneh, D., Roughgarden, T., Feigenbaum, J. (eds.) 45th ACM STOC, pp. 467–476. ACM Press (2013). https://doi.org/10.1145/2488608.2488667

28. Gay, R., Pass, R.: Indistinguishability obfuscation from circular security. In: Khuller, S., Williams, V.V. (eds.) STOC 2021: 53rd Annual ACM SIGACT Symposium on Theory of Computing, Virtual Event, Italy, 21–25 June 2021, pp. 736–749. ACM (2021). https://doi.org/10.1145/3406325.3451070

29. Goldwasser, S., et al.: Multi-input functional encryption. In: Nguyen, P.Q., Oswald, E. (eds.) EUROCRYPT 2014. LNCS, vol. 8441, pp. 578–602. Springer, Heidelberg (2014). https://doi.org/10.1007/978-3-642-55220-5_32

30. Gorbunov, S., Vaikuntanathan, V., Wee, H.: Predicate encryption for circuits from LWE. In: Gennaro, R., Robshaw, M. (eds.) CRYPTO 2015, Part II. LNCS, vol. 9216, pp. 503–523. Springer, Heidelberg (2015). https://doi.org/10.1007/978-3-662-48000-7_25

31. Goyal, R., Koppula, V., Waters, B.: Lockable obfuscation. In: Umans, C. (ed.) 58th FOCS, pp. 612–621. IEEE Computer Society Press (2017). https://doi.org/10.1100/FOCS.2017.62

32. Halevi, S., Ishai, Y., Jain, A., Komargodski, I., Sahai, A., Yogev, E.: Non-interactive multiparty computation without correlated randomness. In: Takagi, T., Peyrin, T. (eds.) ASIACRYPT 2017. LNCS, vol. 10626, pp. 181–211. Springer, Cham (2017). https://doi.org/10.1007/978-3-319-70700-6_7

33. Halevi, S., Ishai, Y., Jain, A., Kushilevitz, E., Rabin, T.: Secure multiparty computation with general interaction patterns. In: Sudan, M. (ed.) ITCS 2016, pp. 157–168. ACM (2016). https://doi.org/10.1145/2840728.2840760

34. Halevi, S., Lindell, Y., Pinkas, B.: Secure computation on the web: computing without simultaneous interaction. In: Rogaway, P. (ed.) CRYPTO 2011. LNCS, vol. 6841, pp. 132–150. Springer, Heidelberg (2011). https://doi.org/10.1007/978-3-642-22792-9_8

35. Jain, A., Lin, H., Sahai, A.: Indistinguishability obfuscation from well-founded assumptions. In: Khuller, S., Williams, V.V. (eds.) STOC 2021: 53rd Annual ACM SIGACT Symposium on Theory of Computing, Virtual Event, Italy, 21–25 June 2021, pp. 60–73. ACM (2021). https://doi.org/10.1145/3406325.3451093

36. Jain, A., Lin, H., Sahai, A.: Indistinguishability obfuscation from LPN over $\mathbb{F}_p$, DLIN, and PRGs in NC^0. In: Dunkelman, O., Dziembowski, S. (eds.) EUROCRYPT 2022, Part I. LNCS, vol. 13275, pp. 670–699. Springer, Heidelberg (2022). https://doi.org/10.1007/978-3-031-06944-4_23

37. Katz, J., Sahai, A., Waters, B.: Predicate encryption supporting disjunctions, polynomial equations, and inner products. In: Smart, N. (ed.) EUROCRYPT 2008. LNCS, vol. 4965, pp. 146–162. Springer, Heidelberg (2008). https://doi.org/10.1007/978-3-540-78967-3_9

38. Lewko, A., Okamoto, T., Sahai, A., Takashima, K., Waters, B.: Fully secure functional encryption: attribute-based encryption and (hierarchical) inner product encryption. In: Gilbert, H. (ed.) EUROCRYPT 2010. LNCS, vol. 6110, pp. 62–91. Springer, Heidelberg (2010). https://doi.org/10.1007/978-3-642-13190-5_4

39. Libert, B., Ţiţiu, R.: Multi-client functional encryption for linear functions in the standard model from LWE. In: Galbraith, S.D., Moriai, S. (eds.) ASIACRYPT 2019, Part III. LNCS, vol. 11923, pp. 520–551. Springer, Cham (2019). https://doi.org/10.1007/978-3-030-34618-8_18

40. López-Alt, A., Tromer, E., Vaikuntanathan, V.: On-the-fly multiparty computation on the cloud via multikey fully homomorphic encryption. In: Karloff, H.J., Pitassi, T. (eds.) 44th ACM STOC, pp. 1219–1234. ACM Press (2012). https://doi.org/10.1145/2213977.2214086

41. Mukherjee, P., Wichs, D.: Two round multiparty computation via multi-key FHE. In: Fischlin, M., Coron, J.-S. (eds.) EUROCRYPT 2016, Part II. LNCS, vol. 9666, pp. 735–763. Springer, Heidelberg (2016). https://doi.org/10.1007/978-3-662-49896-5_26

42. Okamoto, T., Takashima, K.: Fully secure functional encryption with general relations from the decisional linear assumption. In: Rabin, T. (ed.) CRYPTO 2010. LNCS, vol. 6223, pp. 191–208. Springer, Heidelberg (2010). https://doi.org/10.1007/978-3-642-14623-7_11

43. Okamoto, T., Takashima, K.: Adaptively attribute-hiding (hierarchical) inner product encryption. In: Pointcheval, D., Johansson, T. (eds.) EUROCRYPT 2012. LNCS, vol. 7237, pp. 591–608. Springer, Heidelberg (2012). https://doi.org/10.1007/978-3-642-29011-4_35

44. Tomida, J.: Tightly secure inner product functional encryption: multi-input and function-hiding constructions. In: Galbraith, S.D., Moriai, S. (eds.) ASIACRYPT 2019, Part III. LNCS, vol. 11923, pp. 459–488. Springer, Cham (2019). https://doi.org/10.1007/978-3-030-34618-8_16

45. Waters, B.: Functional encryption for regular languages. In: Safavi-Naini, R., Canetti, R. (eds.) CRYPTO 2012. LNCS, vol. 7417, pp. 218–235. Springer, Heidelberg (2012). https://doi.org/10.1007/978-3-642-32009-5_14

46. Wee, H.: Dual system encryption via predicate encodings. In: Lindell, Y. (ed.) TCC 2014. LNCS, vol. 8349, pp. 616–637. Springer, Heidelberg (2014). https://doi.org/10.1007/978-3-642-54242-8_26

47. Wee, H., Wichs, D.: Candidate obfuscation via oblivious LWE sampling. In: Canteaut, A., Standaert, F.-X. (eds.) EUROCRYPT 2021, Part III. LNCS, vol. 12698, pp. 127–156. Springer, Cham (2021). https://doi.org/10.1007/978-3-030-77883-5_5

48. Wichs, D., Zirdelis, G.: Obfuscating compute-and-compare programs under LWE. In: Umans, C. (ed.) 58th FOCS, pp. 600–611. IEEE Computer Society Press (2017). https://doi.org/10.1109/FOCS.2017.61

Broadcast, Trace and Revoke with Optimal Parameters from Polynomial Hardness

Shweta Agrawal[1], Simran Kumari[1], Anshu Yadav[1(✉)], and Shota Yamada[2]

[1] IIT Madras, Chennai, India
shweta@cse.iitm.ac.in, sim78608@gmail.com, anshu.yadav06@gmail.com
[2] AIST, Tokyo, Japan
yamada-shota@aist.go.jp

Abstract. A *broadcast, trace and revoke* system generalizes broadcast encryption as well as traitor tracing. In such a scheme, an encryptor can specify a list $L \subseteq N$ of revoked users so that (i) users in L can no longer decrypt ciphertexts, (ii) ciphertext size is independent of L, (iii) a pirate decryption box supports tracing of compromised users. The "holy grail" of this line of work is a construction which resists unbounded collusions, achieves all parameters (including public and secret key) sizes independent of $|L|$ and $|N|$, and is based on polynomial hardness assumptions. In this work we make the following contributions:

1. *Public Trace Setting:* We provide a construction which (i) achieves optimal parameters, (ii) supports embedding identities (from an exponential space) in user secret keys, (iii) relies on polynomial hardness assumptions, namely compact functional encryption (FE) and a key-policy attribute based encryption (ABE) with special efficiency properties, and (iv) enjoys adaptive security with respect to the revocation list. The previous best known construction by Nishimaki, Wichs and Zhandry (Eurocrypt 2016) which achieved optimal parameters and embedded identities, relied on indistinguishability obfuscation, which is considered an inherently subexponential assumption and achieved only selective security with respect to the revocation list.

2. *Secret Trace Setting:* We provide the first construction with optimal ciphertext, public and secret key sizes and embedded identities from any assumption outside Obfustopia. In detail, our construction relies on Lockable Obfuscation which can be constructed using LWE (Goyal, Koppula, Waters and Wichs, Zirdelis, Focs 2017) and two ABE schemes: (i) the key-policy scheme with special efficiency properties by Boneh et al. (Eurocrypt 2014) and (ii) a ciphertext-policy ABE for P which was recently constructed by Wee (Eurocrypt 2022) using a new assumption called *evasive and tensor* LWE. This assumption, introduced to build an ABE, is believed to be much weaker than lattice based assumptions underlying FE or iO – in particular it is required even for lattice based broadcast, without trace. Moreover, by relying on subexponential security of LWE, both our constructions can also support a *super-polynomial* sized revocation list, so

C. Hazay and M. Stam (Eds.): EUROCRYPT 2023, LNCS 14006, pp. 605–636, 2023.
https://doi.org/10.1007/978-3-031-30620-4_20

long as it allows efficient representation and membership testing. Ours is the first work to achieve this, to the best of our knowledge.

Keywords: Broadcast · Trace and Revoke · Revocable Predicate Encryption · Revocable Mixed Functional Encryption · Optimal Parameters

1   Introduction

Traitor Tracing. Traitor tracing (TT) schemes were first proposed by Chor, Fiat, and Naor [23] to enable content providers to trace malicious users who exploit their secret keys to construct illegal decryption boxes. More formally, a TT system is a public key encryption system comprising N users for some large polynomial N. Each user $i \in [N]$ is provided with a unique secret key sk_i for decryption, and there is a common public key pk which is used by the content distributor to encrypt content. If any collection of users attempts to create and sell a new decoding box that can be used to decrypt the content, then the tracing algorithm, given black-box access to any such pirate decoder, is guaranteed to output an index $i \in [N]$ of one of the corrupt users, which in turn allows to hold them accountable. The literature has considered both public and secret tracing, where the former requires knowledge of a secret key to run the trace procedure and the latter does not suffer from this restriction.

Broadcast Encryption. Broadcast Encryption [26] (BE) introduced by Fiat and Naor, is also an N user system which supports an encrypted broadcast functionality. In BE, a content provider can transmit a single ciphertext over a broadcast channel so that only an authorized subset $S \subseteq N$ of users can decrypt and recover the message. More formally, each user $i \in [N]$ is provided with a unique decryption key sk_i and a ciphertext ct_m for a message m also encodes an authorized list S so that sk_i decrypts ct_m if and only if $i \in S$. Evidently, public key encryption provides a trivial construction of BE with ciphertext of size $O(N)$ – thus, the focus in such schemes is to obtain short ciphertext, ideally logarithmic in N.

Broadcast, Trace and Revoke. Naor and Pinkas [43] suggested a meaningful interleaving of these two functionalities so that traitors that are identified by the TT scheme can be removed from the set of authorized users in a BE scheme. To capture this, they defined the notion of "Broadcast, Trace and Revoke" (or simply "Trace and Revoke", which we denote by TR) where the content provider in a broadcast encryption scheme includes a list L of revoked users in the ciphertext, and sk_i works to decrypt ct_L if $i \notin L$. Moreover, it is required that revocation remain compatible with tracing, so that if an adversary builds a pirate decoder that can decrypt ciphertexts encrypted with respect to L, then the tracing algorithm should be able to output a corrupt non-revoked user who participated in building the illegal decoder. Trace and revoke systems provide a functionality which is richer than a union of BE and TT, since the traitor traced by the latter must belong to the set of non-revoked users for the guarantee to be meaningful. As such, TT schemes have been challenging to construct even given TT and BE schemes.

The Quest for Optimal Parameters. All the above primitives have been researched extensively over decades, resulting in a long sequence of beautiful constructions, non-exhaustively [6, 14–17, 33, 34, 40, 44, 48]. A central theme in this line of work is to achieve optimal parameters, namely optimal sizes for the ciphertext, public key and secret key (and understanding tradeoffs thereof), while still supporting unbounded collusion resistance. Towards this, the powerful hammer of indistinguishability obfuscation (iO) [10] yielded the first feasibility results for traitor tracing [16] as well as trace and revoke [44] while multilinear maps [24, 27] led to the first construction for broadcast encryption [15]. Though there has been remarkable progress in the construction of iO from standard assumptions, with the breakthrough work of Jain, Lin and Sahai [38, 39] finally reaching this goal, iO is an inherently subexponential assumption [29] because the challenger is required to check whether two circuits are functionally equivalent, which can take exponential time in general. Indeed, all known constructions of iO assume subexponential hardness of the underlying algebraic assumptions. To address this limitation, a sequence of works [3, 18, 28, 29, 41] has sought to replace iO by polynomially hard assumptions such as functional encryption in different applications.

Optimal TT, BE and TR from Polynomial Assumptions: For traitor tracing, the first construction from standard assumptions was finally achieved by the seminal work of Goyal, Koppula and Waters [33] in the secret trace setting, from the Learning With Errors (LWE) assumption. For broadcast encryption, this goal was achieved by Agrawal and Yamada [6] from LWE and the bilinear GGM. In the standard model, Agrawal, Wichs and Yamada [5] provided a construction from a non-standard knowledge assumption on pairings, while Wee [48] provided a construction from a new assumption on lattices, called Evasive and Tensor LWE. For trace and revoke, the only construction without iO that achieves collusion resistance and optimal parameters is by Goyal, Vusirikala and Waters (GVW) [36] from *positional witness encryption* (PWE) which is a polynomial hardness assumption. However, their construction incurs an exponential loss in the security proof, requiring the underlying PWE to satisfy subexponential security. Moreover, although PWE is not an inherently subexponential assumption as are iO and witness encryption (WE), we do not currently know of any *constructions* of PWE that rely on standard polynomial hardness assumptions. In particular, [38, 39] do *not* imply PWE from polynomial hardness.

Pathway via Secret Tracing. Both the iO and PWE based constructions of TR [36, 44] achieve public tracing. Taking a lesson from TT, where optimal parameters were achieved from standard assumptions only in the secret trace setting [33], a natural approach towards optimal TR from better assumptions is to weaken the tracing algorithm to be secret key. This approach has been explored in a number of works – the current best parameters are achieved by Zhandry [51] who obtains the best known tradeoff in ciphertext, public key and secret key size. In particular, Zhandry [51] showed that all parameters can be of size $O(N^{1/3})$ by relying on the bilinear generic group model (GGM). Note that the generic group model is a strong assumption, and indeed a construction secure in this model cannot be considered as relying on standard assumptions, since several non-standard assumptions on pairings are secure in the GGM. Prior to [51], Goyal et al. [35] provided a construction from LWE and Pairings, but their overall parameters are significantly worse – while their ciphertext can be arbitrarily small, $O(N^\epsilon)$, their public key is $O(N)$ and secret key is $O(N^c)$ for some large constant c^1.

Thus, a central open question in TR is:

Can we construct collusion resistant Trace and Revoke with optimal parameters from concrete polynomial assumptions?

Embedding Identities. Traditionally, it was assumed that tracing the index $i \in [N]$ of a corrupt user is enough, and there is an external mapping, maintained by the content distributor or some other party which associates the number i to the identity of the user, i.e. name, national identity number and such, which is then used to ensure accountability. The work of Nishimaki, Wichs and Zhandry (henceforth NWZ) [44] argued that this assumption is problematic since it implies that a user must trust the content provider with her confidential information. Storing such a map is particularly worrisome in the setting of public tracing since the user either cannot map the recovered index to an actual person, or the index-identity map must be stored publicly.

NWZ provided an appealing solution to the above conundrum – they suggest that identifying information be embedded in the key of the user, so that if a coalition of traitors constructs a pirate decoder, the tracing algorithm can directly retrieve the identifying information from one of the keys that was used to construct the decoder and no one needs to keep any records associating users to indices. Notably, the identities can live in an *exponential* sized space, which introduces significant challenges in the tracing procedure. Indeed, handling an exponential space in the tracing procedure is the key contribution of NWZ. They also provided constructions of traitor tracing as well as trace and revoke with embedded identities, denoted by EITT and EITR respectively, from various assumptions.

1.1 Prior Work: Embedded Identity Trace and Revoke

In the *public* trace setting, the only work that achieves embedded identity trace and revoke (EITR) with full collusion resistance is that of NWZ. However, while it takes an important first step, the construction by NWZ suffers from the following drawbacks:

---

1 Zhandry [51] states that the secret size in [35] is $O(N^2)$ but in fact the exponent is much larger due to the usage of arithmetic computations in NC^1, which blows up the circuit size associated with the ABE secret keys.

1. *Reliance on Subexponential Hardness Assumption.* The construction relies on indistinguishability obfuscation [10], which appears to be an inherently subexponential assumption as discussed above.

2. *Selective Security in Revocation List:* Despite relying on adaptive security of functional encryption, the notion of security achieved by their construction is selective – the adversary must announce the revocation list before making any key requests or seeing the challenge ciphertext.

In the *secret* trace setting, the work of Kim and Wu [40] achieves EITR from the subexponential Learning With Errors (LWE) assumption. However, their construction incurs a ciphertext size that grows with the size of the revocation list. Additionally, while they can achieve adaptive security with respect to the revocation list, this is either by incurring an exponential loss in the security proof, or by assuming sub-exponential security for an ingredient scheme.

1.2 Our Results

In this work, we provide the first constructions with optimal parameters from polynomial assumptions, which additionally support embedded identities from an exponential space. We detail our contributions below.

Public Trace Setting. We provide a construction of Trace and Revoke with public tracing which overcomes the limitations of NWZ – (i) it relies on polynomial hardness assumptions, namely functional encryption and "special" attribute based encryption, both of which can be constructed using standard polynomial hardness assumptions [13,38,39] (ii) it enjoys adaptive security in the revocation list.

A detailed comparison with prior work is provided in Table 1.

Table 1. State of the art with Public Traceability.

Work	$|CT|$	$|SK|$	$|PK|$	Trace Space	Sel/Adp	Asspn	Identities
[44]	1	1	1	Exp	Selective	Subexp (iO)	Yes
[36]	1	1	1	Poly	Adaptive	Subexp (subexp PWE)	No
This	1	1	1	Exp	Adaptive	Poly (FE and Special ABE)	Yes

Our Assumptions. Functional Encryption (FE) and Attribute Based Encryption (ABE) are generalizations of Public Key Encryption. In FE, a secret key corresponds to a circuit C and a ciphertext corresponds to an input x from the domain of C. Given a function key sk_C and a ciphertext ct_x, the decryptor can learn $C(x)$ and nothing else. It has been shown that FE implies iO [8,12] albeit with exponential loss. The aforementioned work of Jain, Lin and Sahai [38,39] provides a construction of compact FE from polynomial hardness assumptions, namely LPN, PRG in NC_0 and pairings. ABE is a special case of FE in which the input can be divided into a public and private part (x, m) and the circuit C in the secret key sk_C is only evaluated on the public part x in the ciphertext $\mathsf{ct}_{x,m}$. The private message m is revealed by decryption if and only if $C(x) = 1$. While FE implies ABE in general, we require our underlying ABE to satisfy special efficiency properties, which is not generically implied by FE. However, the desired ABE can be instantiated using the construction of Boneh et al. [13] which is based on LWE.

Secret Trace Setting. In the secret trace setting, we achieve the optimal size of $O(\log N)$ for ciphertext, public and secret key by relying on Lockable Obfuscation (LO) [32,50] and two special ABE schemes – one, the key-policy scheme with special efficiency properties by Boneh et al. [13] which is based on LWE, and two, a ciphertext-policy ABE for P which was recently constructed by Wee [48] using the new evasive and tensor LWE assumptions. Along the way, we show that a small modification to the TR construction by Goyal et al. [35] yields a ciphertext of size $O(\log N)$ as against their original $O(N^\epsilon)$, from LWE and pairings. However, this construction retains the large public and secret keys of their construction, which depend at least linearly on N. Our results are summarized in Table 2.

Our Assumptions. We remark that while FE has now been constructed from standard assumptions [38,39], the reliance of these constructions on pairings makes it insecure in the post-quantum regime. From lattices, constructions of FE rely on strong, non-standard assumptions which are often subject to attack [1,4,25,30,37,49]. Hence, there is an active effort in the community [46–48] to construct advanced primitives from the hardness of weaker assumptions in the lattice regime. The new assumptions by Wee, also independently discovered by Tsabary [46], are formulated for designing ciphertext-policy ABE which is much weaker than FE since ABE is an all or nothing primitive in contrast to FE. As such, these are believed to be much weaker than lattice based assumptions that have been introduced in the context of FE or iO. In particular, based on the current state of art, evasive LWE is required even for broadcast encryption in the lattice regime, and is therefore necessary for the generalization of broadcast encryption studied in this work.

Super-polynomial Revoke List. Lastly, by relying on subexponential security of LWE, both our constructions can support a *super-polynomial* sized revocation list, so long as it allows efficient representation and membership testing. Ours is the first work to achieve this, to the best of our knowledge.

Table 2. State of the Art with Secret Traceability. The column $|\mathsf{CT}|$ captures the dependence of ciphertext size on N and L where N denotes the number of users and L denotes the length of the revocation list. Parameters that are logarithmic in N, L or polynomial in the security parameter are represented as 1. Here, $0 < a < 1$ and $\epsilon > 0$ can be chosen arbitrarily. c is a large constant.

Work	$|\mathsf{CT}|$	$|\mathsf{SK}|$	$|\mathsf{PK}|$	Trace Space	Asspn	Identities
[35]	N^ϵ	N^{poly}	N	Poly	LWE and Pairings	No
[51]	N^a	N^{1-a}	N^{1-a}	Poly	GGM Pairings	No
[40]	L	1	1	Exp	Subexp LWE	Yes
This	1	1	1	Exp	Evasive Tensor LWE	Yes
Modified [35]	1	N^c	N	Poly	LWE and Pairings	No

1.3   Technical Overview

We proceed to give an overview of our techniques. We begin by defining the notion of revocable predicate encryption (RPE) in both the public and secret setting, then describe the ideas used to instantiate this primitive. Finally we outline how to upgrade public/secret RPE to build trace and revoke with embedded identities with public/secret tracing.

Revocable Predicate Encryption. NWZ introduced the notion of revocable functional encryption (RFE) and used it to construct EITR with public tracing. Subsequently, Kim and Wu [40] adapted this notion to the secret key setting, under the name of revocable predicate encryption (RPE) and used it to construct EITR with secret tracing. In this work, we extend Kim and Wu's notion of RPE to the public key setting and use it to construct EITR with public tracing. Our notion of RPE in the public setting is similar to but weaker than RFE[2] – it only supports "all or nothing" decryption in contrast to RFE. This weaker notion nevertheless suffices to construct EITR and moreover admits constructions from weaker assumptions.

In RPE, the key generation algorithm takes as input the master secret key msk, a label $\mathsf{lb} \in \mathcal{L}$ and an attribute $x \in \mathcal{X}$. It outputs a secret key $\mathsf{sk}_{\mathsf{lb},x}$. The encryption algorithm takes as input the encryption key ek, a function f, a message $m \in \mathcal{M}$, and a revocation list $L \subseteq \mathcal{L}$. It outputs a ciphertext ct. Decryption recovers m if $f(x) = 1$ and $\mathsf{lb} \notin L$. In the public variant of RPE, ek is a public key, while in the secret variant, ek is a secret key. In the secret variant, the scheme is also required to support a public "broadcast" functionality, i.e. there exists a public encryption

---

[2] Syntactically, RPE is "ciphertext-policy" while RFE is "key-policy", i.e. the function is emdedded in the ciphertext in RPE as against the key in RFE.

algorithm that allows anyone to encrypt a message with respect to the "always-accept" policy, i.e. a policy that evaluates to true for all inputs. This is analogous to the primitive of "mixed FE" introduced by [33].

In terms of security, we require RPE to satisfy message hiding and function hiding. At a high level, message hiding stipulates that an adversary cannot distinguish between encryptions of (f, m_0) and (f, m_1) as long as every key query for (lb, x) satisfies $f(x) = 0$ or $\text{lb} \in L$. Function hiding stipulates that an adversary cannot distinguish between encryptions of (f_0, m) and (f_1, m) as long as every key query for (lb, x) satisfies $f_0(x) = f_1(x)$ or $\text{lb} \in L$.

Before we describe our constructions, we highlight the chief difficulties that are inherent to designing RPE:

1. *Independence of parameter sizes from* $|L|$. A key requirement in TR schemes is that the ciphertext size should be independent of the length of the revocation list L – this constraint must also be satisfied by the underlying RPE, in both the secret and public setting. In our work, we insist that even the public and secret keys satisfy $|L|$ independence. This constraint is inherited from broadcast encryption, and is challenging to satisfy. Further, note that L must be unbounded – its length cannot be fixed during setup, which introduces additional difficulties.

2. *Encrypted Computation.* While the revocation list L need not be hidden by the ciphertext, the function f^3 in the ciphertext is required to be hidden, as formalized by our function hiding requirement. Yet, this hidden function must participate in computing $f(x)$ where x is provided in the key. This requirement makes TR schemes worryingly close to collusion resistant functional encryption, an "obfustopia" primitive which we want to avoid in the secret trace setting.

Constructing Public Revocable Predicate Encryption. We proceed to describe the main ideas in constructing public RPE.

Overview of NWZ. The work of NWZ addresses the challenge of making the ciphertext size independent of $|L|$ by using a somewhere statistically binding (SSB) hash and hides the function f by using a functional encryption scheme, where f is encrypted in the ciphertext. However, they must additionally rely on iO – at a high level, this is because they require the *decryptor* to compute the SSB opening π and then run SSB verification on it (details of how SSB algorithms work are not relevant for this overview). In turn, the reason they need the decryptor to compute the opening π is because this needs both the set L and the label lb, which are available only to the decryptor – note that the encryptor has only L and the key generator has only lb. Now, since the decryptor has to compute π and run SSB verification, and since the program that computes SSB verification has some secrets, the decryptor is allowed to

---

[3] For the informed reader, this function encodes the "index" and function hiding corresponds to "index hiding" in the literature.

obtain obfuscation of this program. To implement this idea, they nest iO inside a compact FE scheme so that FE decryption outputs an iO which is then run by the decryptor on openings that it computes.

Trading iO *for* ABE. Above, note that the usage of iO is caused by the usage of SSB, which in turn is used to compress L. However, compression of a list has been achieved by much weaker primitives than iO in the literature of broadcast encryption – in particular, the construction of optimal broadcast encryption by Agrawal and Yamada uses the much weaker primitive of ABE (with special efficiency properties) to achieve this. However, ABE does not permit hiding anything other than a message, in particular, an ABE ciphertext cannot encrypt our function f since we desire f to participate in computation. ABE only permits computation on public values, and using ABE to encode f would force f to be public which we cannot allow.

In order to get around this difficulty, we leverage the power of functional encryption (FE), which permits encrypted computation and exactly fills the gap over ABE that we require. A natural candidate for RPE would be to simply use FE to encrypt f, L and m, and encode x and lb in the secret key for a functionality which tests that lb $\notin L$, that $f(x) = 1$ and outputs m if so. Indeed, this approach using FE is folklore, and was explicitly discussed by NWZ. Yet, they end up with a construction that additionally uses SSB, iO, a puncturable PRF and secret key encryption scheme because of the requirement of size independence from $|L|$ – we do not have candidates for FE with ciphertext size independent of the public attributes. In short, ABE gives us L compactness (in some cases by encoding L in the secret key [13] and in some cases by encoding L in the ciphertext [9]) but does not hide f, whereas FE gives the opposite.

Synthesis of ABE *and* FE. We address this conundrum by combining the two primitives in a way that lets us get the best of both. In particular, we use ABE to check that lb $\notin L$ and use FE to compute $f(x)$. Evidently, the two steps cannot be performed independently in order to resist mix and match attacks so we use nesting, i.e. we use FE to generate ABE ciphertexts. Here, care is required, because ABE encryption takes L as input and done naively, this strategy will again induce a size dependence on L. We address this challenge by using the special ABE by Boneh et al. [13] which enjoys succinct secret keys and encoding L in the ABE secret key. In more detail, we let the RPE encryption generate ABE.sk(C_L) for a circuit C_L which takes as input lb and checks that lb $\notin L$. Additionally, it generates an FE ciphertext for the function f and message m. The RPE key generator computes an FE key for a function which has (lb, x) hardwired and takes as input a function f, checks whether $f(x) = 1$ and if so, generates a fresh ABE ciphertext with attribute lb and message m. Thus the decryptor can first compute FE decryption to recover the ABE ciphertext ABE.ct(lb, m) and then use ABE decryption with ABE.sk(C_L) to output m if and only if lb $\notin L$. It is easy to verify that this construction achieves optimal parameters – this is because ABE has optimal parameters and we used FE only for a simple functionality that does not involve L.

Putting it All Together. The above description is over-simplified and ignores technical challenges such as how to leverage indistinguishability based security of FE, how to generate the randomness used for ABE encryption and such others – we refer the reader to Sect. 3 for details. However, even having filled in these details, we get only a selectively secure RPE. Substantial work and several new ideas are required for adaptive security, as we discuss next.

Adaptive Security. Next, we outline our ideas to achieve adaptive security, namely where the revocation list L is chosen adaptively by the adversary. Note that to avoid complexity leveraging, we are required to rely only on the selective security of the underling ABE – this creates multiple technical difficulties which are resolved by very carefully using specific algebraic properties of our ingredients.

Leveraging Late Generation of ABE. Our first observation is that full adaptive security of ABE may be unnecessary, since in our construction of RPE, the generation of the ABE instance is deferred until the generation of the challenge ciphertext, at which time the set of revoked users is known. This intuition turns out to be true, but via a complicated security proof as we outline next. Below, we consider the case of function hiding in the RPE ciphertext, the case of message hiding is similar.

Recall that function hiding says that two ciphertexts encoding (f_b, m, L), where $b \in \{0, 1\}$ should be indistinguishable so long as for any requested key $\mathsf{sk}_{\mathsf{lb}, x}$ it holds that $f_0(x) = f_1(x)$ or $\mathsf{lb} \in L$. Note that the adversary is permitted to query for keys that allow decryption of the ciphertexts, i.e. $f_0(x) = f_1(x) = 1$.

Embedding ABE CTs in FE keys. In order to use ABE security to prove RPE security, a first (by now standard) step is to use the "trapdoor technique" [7, 19,20], which allows us to hardwire ABE ciphertexts into FE secret keys. In the security game with the ABE challenger, the reduction submits the label lb associated with each RPE secret key as its challenge attribute and embeds the returned ABE ciphertext into the FE key. Here we immediately run into a difficulty, since in the RPE setting some ABE ciphertexts are decryptable by the adversary and we cannot leverage ABE security. Moreover, we cannot even hope to guess which keys will correspond to decryptable ABE ciphertexts since there are an unbounded polynomial number of key queries in the RPE security game. The same difficulty is faced by NWZ and is the main reason why their construction does not achieve adaptive security in the revocation list.

Polynomial Function Space Suffices for TR. To overcome this hurdle, we leverage the serendipitous fact that for the purpose of constructing TR, it suffices to construct RPE whose function space (recall that functions are encoded in the ciphertext) is only of polynomial size. This observation, which was implicitly present in [34], is abstracted and used explicitly in our proof. In particular, we can assume that the reduction algorithm knows the challenge functions (f_0, f_1) at the beginning of the game, since it can simply guess them. Now, given the secret key query (lb, x), the reduction checks whether $f_0(x) = f_1(x)$. If yes, then there is no need to use ABE security, for the ABE ciphertexts in this case will encode the same message, and will hence be independent of the challenge bit. On the other hand, if $f_0(x) \neq f_1(x)$, then we have by the admissibility condition that $\text{lb} \in L$, even when L is not known. In this case, the reduction can use the security of the ABE without any difficulty.

Additional Hurdles Stemming from ABE *Selective Security.* We now highlight another challenge in the proof. For concreteness, let us consider the second key query $(\text{lb}^{(2)}, x^{(2)})$, which we assume is a pre-challenge query, and assume that $f_0(x^{(2)}) \neq f_1(x^{(2)})$. Hence, by the above discussion, we are required to use ABE security for the ciphertexts with attribute $\text{lb}^{(2)}$. However, according to the selective definition, the reduction is required to choose the challenge attribute at the very start of the game, without even seeing the public parameters. At the same time, the reduction is required to simulate the ABE ciphertext for the first key query, before receiving the second key query from the adversary, that is, without seeing the ABE parameters, leading to an apparent impasse.

We address this issue by considering the following two cases separately: for the first query $(\text{lb}^{(1)}, x^{(1)})$, we have (1) $f_0(x^{(1)}) \neq f_1(x^{(1)})$ or (2) $f_0(x^{(1)}) = f_1(x^{(1)})$. In first case, it is tempting to think that one can simply use a hybrid argument to change the ABE ciphertext associated with each key query satisfying $f_0(x^{(i)}) \neq f_1(x^{(i)})$ for $i \in [2]$. However, this does not work as is, since the ABE ciphertext may leak information about the ABE public key. To address this, we rely on the pseudorandomness of ciphertexts in our ABE [13] due to which we are guaranteed that the ciphertext does not reveal any information about the public parameters, enabling the hybrid strategy above. To handle the second case, we change the way in which the ABE ciphertext for the first key is generated. In more detail, we stop hardwiring the the ABE ciphertext into the first key and instead generate it directly using ABE parameters. This removes the aforementioned problem since we no longer need to embed the ABE ciphertext or public key into the first FE key. To enable this idea, we introduce additional branch of trapdoor mode for the construction to separate the paths of computation for the cases $f_0(x) = f_1(x)$ and $f_0(x) \neq f_1(x)$. To handle post-challenge queries, we need to address additional challenges, which we do not describe here. We refer the reader to Sect. 3 for details.

Handling Super-polynomial Revocation List. Our construction (also the secret version, described next) organically supports super-polynomially large revocation list, something that was not known before, to the best of our knowledge. In more detail, let L be a list of super-polynomial size, such that L can be represented as a string of polynomial length and there exists a circuit C_L of polynomial size which takes as input some string lb and checks whether $\text{lb} \in L$ or not. Note that any super-polynomially large list must have efficient representation in order to even allow various algorithms to read it. Then, the key generation of [13] can naturally encode the circuit C_L as before and the construction works as before.

A subtlety that arises with super-polynomial L is that when we deal with post challenge key queries in the proof, we have to deal with the ABE queries in the order of key first and ciphertext later. With polynomial size L, this does not pose a problem because when the adversary chooses L, all the labels for which we use ABE security are in L and we can perform a hybrid argument over these labels. However, this is not possible for super polynomial L, which requires to rely on subexponentially secure LWE. Please see the full version of the paper [2] for details.

Instantiating Public RPE. Overall, armed with the above ideas, we get a public RPE from compact FE and efficient ABE supporting exponential sized identity space and adaptive security in the revocation list L. Currently, we only know how to instantiate our desired ABE from LWE [13], whereas FE can be instantiated in multiple different ways. A natural candidate would be the FE from standard assumptions [38,39] which relies on pairings, LPN and low depth PRG – in this case, our RPE will require the extra assumption of LWE. Another option is to instantiate FE with a post-quantum candidate [1,25,30,42,49] from non-standard strengthenings of LWE – this has the advantage that the ABE does not incur any extra assumption in the final construction. For super-polynomial L, we need subexponential hardness of LWE in either pathway to instantiation, as discussed above.

Alternative Construction Based on Laconic OT. Here, we sketch an alternative construction of RPE based on laconic OT (LOT) [22] that works when the number N of possible labels is polynomially bounded (i.e., the identity space is of polynomial size). Since LOT is known to be possible from various assumptions, this diversifies the assumptions that we need to rely on. The basic idea is to replace ABE with LOT. In more detail, the encryptor chooses LOT parameters instead of ABE parameters and computes the digest of the list of recipients (or equivalently, the list of revoked users), which is represented as a binary string of length N with 1 for non-revoked identities. The digest, whose size is independent of N, is then embedded into the FE ciphertext. Then, FE decryption yields LOT encryption of the message for the label $\mathsf{lb} \in [N]$, which is the label associated with the secret key, instead of ABE ciphertext. The LOT ciphertext is encrypted so that it can be decrypted only when the lb-th bit of the binary string representing the list of recipients is 1. We note that this idea does not extend for identities from exponentially large space and cannot therefore support embedded identities any more.

Revocable Predicate Encryption in Private Setting. For private revocable predicate encryption, our starting point is the work of Goyal et al. [35], who show how to combine "broadcast mixed FE" (called BMFE) together with ABE to achieve RPE (via a different abstraction which they call AugBE). They construct BMFE by adding the broadcast functionality to the primitive of mixed FE defined by [33]. They embed BMFE ciphertext into an ABE ciphertext to achieve RPE, where BMFE is constructed from LWE and ABE is instantiated using pairings.

Supporting Exponential Identity Space. To begin, we upgrade their notion of BMFE to support an exponential space of identities (which we refer to as labels) towards the goal of embedded identity trace and revoke. We refer to our notion as Revocable Mixed FE (denoted by RMFE) and construct it from LWE. Both [35] and our work start with a mixed FE scheme and add broadcast to it, but their construction builds upon the scheme based on constrained PRFs [21] while ours begins with the scheme based on Lockable Obfuscation (LO), also from [21]. Our construction of RMFE deviates significantly from theirs, and achieves significantly better secret key size – $O(\log N)$ as against $O(N)$ – in addition to supporting exponential instead of polynomial space. We describe this construction next.

Mixed FE. The notion of mixed FE was introduced by Goyal, Koppula and Waters in the context of traitor tracing [33]. Identifying and constructing this clever primitive is the key insight that enables [33] to construct traitor tracing with optimal parameters from LWE. Mixed FE is, as the name suggests, a mix of public and secret key FE. Thus, it has a secret as well as a public encryption procedure. The secret encryption procedure takes as input a function f and computes ct_f. This is decryptable by a key sk_x to recover $f(x)$. The adversary can make one query to the encryption oracle in addition to getting the challenge ciphertext for challenge (f_0, f_1). It can also make an unbounded number of key requests so long as $f_0(x) = f_1(x)$. The public encryption algorithm computes a ciphertext for the "always accept" function, i.e. a function which evaluates to 1 for any input x. It is required that the public ciphertext be indistinguishable from the secret ciphertext.

One of the constructions of mixed FE suggested by [21] uses a secret key FE scheme (SKFE) to construct the secret encryption algorithm and leverages the power of lockable obfuscation (LO) to construct the public encryption procedure. Recall that in a lockable obfuscation scheme [32,50] there exists an obfuscation algorithm Obf that takes as input a program C, a message m and a (random) "lock value" α and outputs an obfuscated program $\tilde{P}$. One can evaluate the obfuscated program on any input x to obtain as output m if $P(x) = \alpha$ and $\bot$ otherwise. Intuitively, the idea of [21] is to wrap the FE ciphertext using LO and to define the public key encryption algorithm as outputting a simulated version of the LO obfuscated circuit, which is publicly sampleable.

In more detail, the construction works as follows. The secret key for a user with input x is an SKFE secret key $\mathsf{SKFE.sk}(x)$. The secret ciphertext of MFE for function f is constructed as follows.

1. First, SKFE ciphertext $\mathsf{SKFE.ct}(H_{f,\alpha})$ is generated, where α is a freshly chosen random value and $H_{f,\alpha}$ is a circuit that takes as input x and outputs α if $f(x) = 0$ and 0 otherwise.
2. Then, LO with lock value α and any message $m \neq \bot$ is used to obfuscate the circuit $\mathsf{SKFE.Dec}(\mathsf{SKFE.ct}(H_{f,\alpha}), \cdot)$, namely the circuit that takes as input an SKFE secret key and decrypts the hardwired ciphertext using this.

The decryption result of MFE is defined as 1 if the evaluation result of the LO circuit on the given input SKFE secret key is $\perp$ and 0 otherwise. Correctness follows from correctness of SKFE and LO. In particular, if $f(x) = 0$, then SKFE decryption outputs α, which unlocks the LO to give m, otherwise $\perp$. By definition, MFE decryption will output 1 if LO outputs $\perp$ which happens when $f(x) = 1$, and 0 otherwise.

Revocable Mixed FE. RMFE augments MFE so that the encryption algorithms (both secret and public) now include a revocation list L and the secret key additionally includes a label lb. A secret key $\mathsf{sk}_{\mathsf{lb},x}$ decrypts a secret ciphertext $\mathsf{ct}_{f,L}$ to recover $f(x)$ if $\mathsf{lb} \notin L$ and 1 otherwise. For a public ciphertext ct_L, the output of decryption is always 1 regardless of which secret key is being used. For security, we need two properties: function hiding and mode hiding. For function hiding, we require that a secret ciphertext $\mathsf{ct}_{f_0,L}$ is indistinguishable from $\mathsf{ct}_{f_1,L}$ if for all queries, either $f_0(x) = f_1(x)$ or $\mathsf{lb} \in L$. For mode hiding, we require that a secret ciphertext $\mathsf{ct}_{f,L}$ is indistinguishable from a public ciphertext ct_L. Recall that L is not required to be hidden, but we require that the parameters do not depend on $|L|$.

To extend MFE to RMFE, we retain the idea of letting the secret ciphertext be an LO obfuscated circuit and public ciphertext be the simulated LO. To incorporate the list L, we must ensure that the LO lock value α is recovered only when $f(x) = 0$ and $\mathsf{lb} \notin L$. To do so, we consider two subsystems such that one system outputs partial decryption result α_1 only when $f(x) = 0$ and the second system outputs partial decryption result α_2 only when $\mathsf{lb} \notin L$ such that $\alpha = \alpha_1 + \alpha_2$. We must ensure that α_1 and α_2 are user specific decryption results to avoid collusion attacks.

Note that the second subsystem, which entails L, should be constructed so that the hardwired values inside the circuit do not depend on $|L|$, but still control access to the value α_2 depending on L. To satisfy these apparently conflicting requirements, we make use of the unique algebraic properties of the ABE construction by Boneh et al. [13], as described below. For the first subsystem, we use SKFE.

In more detail, our candidate scheme is as follows.

1. **Secret Key:** The RMFE secret key consists of $\mathsf{ABE.ct}(\mathsf{lb}, K)$ and $\mathsf{SKFE.ct}((x, K, R))$ where K and R are user specific random strings, lb is used as an attribute and K is the plaintext for ABE encryption.
2. **Ciphertext:** To generate RMFE ciphertext, the secret key encryption procedure is as follows:
   - It first generates $\mathsf{ABE.sk}(C_L)$, where C_L is a circuit that takes as input a label lb and outputs 1 only when $\mathsf{lb} \notin L$.
   - It also generates $\mathsf{SKFE.sk}(H_{f,\alpha})$, where $H_{f,\alpha}$ takes as input (x, K, R) and outputs $K \oplus \alpha$ if $f(x) = 0$ and R if $f(x) = 1$.
   - Now, consider the circuit $CC[\mathsf{ABE.sk}(C_L), \mathsf{SKFE.sk}(H_{f,\alpha})]$, which takes as an input the pair $(\mathsf{ABE.ct}, \mathsf{SKFE.ct})$, decrypts both ABE and SKFE ciphertexts using their respective keys, and then outputs the XOR between the decryption results.

– The final ciphertext is an LO of $CC[\mathsf{ABE}.\mathsf{sk}(C_L), \mathsf{SKFE}.\mathsf{Enc}(H_{f,K,\alpha})]$ with lock value α and any arbitrary message $m \neq \perp$.

By key compactness of [13], the size of $\mathsf{ABE}.\mathsf{sk}(C_L)$ is independent of $|L|$. A subtle point here is that ABE decryption is happening inside the LO and this depends on L. If the LO must process L, then the size of the LO and hence ciphertext blows up with L! Fortunately, the algebraic structure of the ABE scheme we use [13] again comes to our rescue. At a high level, ABE decryption can be divided into an "L-dependent" step which results in a short processed ciphertext, followed by an "L-independent" step. Importantly, the L-dependent step does not depend on the ABE secret key which is hardwired in the LO and hence inaccessible, and can hence be performed *outside* the LO by the decryptor! The resultant short processed ciphertext can then be provided as input to the LO preventing the problematic size blowup.

RMFE *Proof Overview.* Next we outline some of the ideas developed for the security proof. For ease of understanding, we limit ourselves to the simpler setting where the adversary does not have access to the encryption oracle. This restriction can be removed using combinatorial tricks, similar to [21]. For security, we must argue two properties – mode indistinguishability and function hiding. The former can be established by relying on security of SKFE and LO analogously to the MFE proof in [21]. Hence, we focus on function hiding for the rest of the overview, which is subtle and requires several new ideas.

For function hiding, we must make use of the security of ABE and SKFE. Intuitively, security of SKFE guarantees that the values encoded in SKFE ciphertexts and secret keys are hidden, beyond what is revealed by decryption.[4] First note that given a key for (lb, x) such that $f_0(x) = f_1(x)$, no information about the challenge bit is revealed by decryption, since the decryption results of SKFE are the same for both cases. The case with $f_0(x) \neq f_1(x)$ is more challenging. Let us assume $f_0(x) = 0$ and $f_1(x) = 1$. In this case, the decryption result of the challenge ciphertext is R or $K \oplus \alpha$ depending on the value of the challenge bit. Since both are random strings, it is tempting to conclude that they do not reveal any information of the challenge bit.

However, in reality, information about K is encoded in the ciphertext $\mathsf{ABE}.\mathsf{ct}(\mathsf{lb}, K)$ and creates a correlation which must be handled. Indeed, a computationally unbounded attacker can learn the challenge bit by breaking open the ABE ciphertext, recovering K and then correlating it with the decryption result of SKFE. Hence, security of ABE must play a role and fortunately, we show that security of ABE suffices to overcome this difficulty. Recall that our security definition of RMFE requires that if $f_0(x) \neq f_1(x)$, then it should hold that $\mathsf{lb} \in L$. This means that the ciphertext $\mathsf{ABE}.\mathsf{ct}(\mathsf{lb}, K)$ is computationally indistinguishable from $\mathsf{ABE}.\mathsf{ct}(\mathsf{lb}, 0)$, since the only ABE secret key available to the adversary is $\mathsf{ABE}.\mathsf{sk}(C_L)$. Now, in the adversary's view, both $K \oplus \alpha$ and R are random strings that are independent from other parameters. Therefore, the

---

[4] We note that we need message *and* function hiding security for the underlying SKFE, while [21] only needs message hiding security.

adversary cannot obtain any information of the challenge bit from the decryption result in this case as well. For more details, please see Sect. 4.

Comparison with the BMFE *by Goyal et al. [35].* We observe that both our RMFE as well as the BMFE by [35] rely solely on LWE. However, our secret key is ABE.ct(lb, K) and SKFE.ct((x, K, R)), which has optimal size, being clearly independent of N and L. In contrast their secret key depends linearly on N. We also observe that our RMFE can support an exponentially large space of identities, while their BMFE does not.

Combining RMFE *and* ABE *to get* RPE. Finally, we nest our RMFE inside an outer ABE scheme to obtain RPE. This step is very similar to [35], but we need to use a different ABE scheme. In particular, in the construction of RPE in [35], a key policy ABE (kpABE) is used to encrypt the message m with attributes as the RMFE ciphertext along with the list L. The RPE secret key for (x, lb) is a kpABE secret key for a the RMFE decryption circuit RMFE.Dec(RMFE.sk, $\cdot, \cdot$).

An obvious difficulty here is that encoding the attribute $(L, \text{RMFE.ct})$ in the ABE ciphertext can cause the ciphertext size to depend on the size of L. To avoid this blowup, [35] use a special kpABE which has the property that the ciphertext size is independent of the size of the attribute. They instantiate this kpABE with the scheme [9] which uses pairings[5]. However, we cannot use [9,45] because of the following two reasons:

1. First, the ABE scheme by [9] only supports NC_1. However, our circuit RMFE.Dec(RMFE.sk, $\cdot, \cdot$) does not fit into NC_1[6].
2. Furthermore, even if the above problem could be resolved, using [9] is problematic since their ABE has secret and public keys at least as large as $O(|L|)$. While the scheme of [35] also suffers from this blow-up, our goal is to obtain short keys, independent of $|L|$.

The first problem cannot be resolved even if we use the ABE schemes for circuits [13,31], since their ciphertext size also depends on $|L|$. To instantiate our ABE, we use recent construction of compact cpABE from evasive and tensor LWE [48], whose parameter sizes depend only on the input length of the circuit and are independent of its size. Armed with the above ideas, we suggest the following RPE:

1. The encryption algorithm of RPE, given m, f, L computes RMFE ciphertext encoding (f, L) and then computes cpABE.Enc(RMFE.Dec(RMFE.ct, $\cdot, L$), m).
2. The key generation algorithm RPE given (lb, x), computes RMFE secret key for (lb, x) and outputs cpABE.sk(RMFE.sk).

---

[5] In fact, one could instead use the kpABE constructed by [45]. This enjoys the same efficiency properties and is based on the standard DLIN assumption as against the q-type assumption of [9].

[6] The informed reader may wonder whether we can solve this issue by using preprocessing as in [35] but this does not work due to technical reasons.

Correctness of RPE follows from correctness of cpABE and RMFE while optimality of parameters follows from the efficiency of the underlying schemes. In particular, observe that all parameters are independent of $|L|$. Also note that evasive and tensor LWE are required only to instantiate cpABE with the desired efficiency. If future work standardizes the assumptions underlying the cpABE, our construction will inherit these assumptions. For more details, we refer the reader to the full version of the paper [2, Sect. 6].

Instantiating Secret RPE. Currently, the only two suitable ABE schemes that we know to instantiate our compiler are the LWE based kpABE by Boneh et al. [13] and the evasive and tensor LWE based cpABE by Wee [48]. These two ABEs give us a secret RPE scheme supporting exponential identities and with optimal parameters, from evasive and tensor LWE. Note that this construction does *not* achieve adaptive security in the revoke list. Nevertheless, it is the first construction of optimal RPE, even without embedded identities, from any assumption outside Obfustopia. Note that the usage of a non-standard assumption outside of obfustopia (in particular, only from lattice techniques) is somewhat inherent given that even broadcast encryption *without* tracing requires non-standard assumption if we instantiate it only from lattices. We are hopeful that future improvements in cpABE will yield a construction from completely standard assumptions.

Trace and Revoke with Optimal Ciphertext from LWE and Pairings. Along the way, we observe that the broadcast and trace construction provided by Goyal et al. [35], without embedded identities, can be easily modified to achieve at least optimal ciphertext size, from the same assumptions. At a high level, they construct a broadcast mixed FE from LWE with optimal ciphertext size and then nest this inside the kpABE by [9], which enjoys ciphertext size independent of the attribute length, and can support computation in NC_1. Since their BMFE decryption does not fit into NC_1, they preprocess the ciphertext so that part of the decryption is performed "outside", namely, they group $\log N$ matrix tuples into c groups of $(\log N)/c$ tuples each. Then they precompute all possible $2^{(\log N)/c} = N^{1/c}$ subset-products within each group. Due to this, BMFE decryption only needs to multiply together c of the preprocessed matrices, which can be done in NC_1 so long as c is constant. Unfortunately, this step increases their ciphertext size to $O(N^\epsilon)$ for any $\epsilon > 0$ though the BMFE ciphertext size was optimal.

We observe that they are "under-using" the ciphertext size independence of [9] – in particular, while the attribute length has indeed been blown up to $O(N^\epsilon)$, this does not affect the ciphertext size of [9]. Moreover, while the attribute must also be provided outside in the clear, this part can be compressed, i.e. the preprocessing which expands the attribute to size N^ϵ can be performed by the decryptor directly by grouping and multiplying matrices as described above, and there is no need for the encryptor to provide this expanded form. Thus, their scheme tweaked with this simple modification already achieves ciphertext of optimal size, though with large secret key $O(N^c)$ for some large constant c.

Trace and Revoke from Revocable Predicate Encryption. It remains to show how to construct the final goal of trace and revoke with embedded identities. As discussed earlier, we follow [40,44] and use the abstraction of RPE to build trace and revoke. However, to embed identities in our trace and revoke schemes, we deviate from these works and instead build upon ideas developed by [34] (henceforth GKW) in the context of traitor tracing.

Embedded Identity Traitor Tracing (EITT) by GKW. The work of Goyal, Koppula and Waters [34] provided an alternative approach for embedding identities in traitor tracing schemes. A well known approach for constructing Traitor Tracing systems suggested by Boneh, Sahai and Waters [11] is via the intermediate primitive of *Private Linear Broadcast Encryption* (PLBE), which allows to construct a tracing algorithm that performs a linear search over the space of users to recover the traitor. Since the number of users was polynomial, this algorithm could be efficient. However, if we allow arbitrary identities to correspond to user indices then the space over which this search must be performed becomes exponential even if the number of users is polynomial, and the trace algorithm is no longer efficient. The main new idea in NWZ that enables them to handle exponentially large identity spaces is to replace a linear search over indices by a clever generalization of binary search, which efficiently solves an "oracle jump problem" which in turn suffices for tracing.

Goyal, Koppula and Waters (GKW) provided an alternate route to the problem of embedding identities. Instead of using PLBE and generalizing the search procedure, they instead extend the definition of PLBE to support embedded identities, denoted by EI-PLBE, and then used this to get a full fledged EITT scheme. This approach has the notable advantage that even if the space of identities is exponential, it can use the fact that the number of users is only *polynomial* and hence rely on only *selective* security of the underlying primitives. In particular, they demonstrate a "nested" tracing approach, where the tracing algorithm works in two steps: first, it outputs a set of indices that correspond to the users that are traitors, and then it uses each index within this set to recover the corresponding identity. Additionally, GKW provide a sequence of (increasingly stronger) TT primitives with embedded identities, namely, indexed EITT, bounded EITT and finally unbounded EITT where unbounded EITT satisfies the most general notion of embedded identity traitor tracing. They also provide generic transformations between these notions, which allows to focus on the weakest notion for any new instantiation.

Embedded Identity Trace and Revoke (EITR). We adapt the approach of GKW and show how to use their nested approach to trace embedded identities even in the more challenging setting of trace and revoke. As in their case, this lets us use polynomial hardness assumptions in obtaining EITR, in contrast to NWZ. We also define indexed, bounded and unbounded EITR and provide transformations between them. Our definitions as well as transformations are analogous to GKW albeit care is required to incorporate the revoke list L in each step and adapt the definitions and proofs of security accordingly. We then construct indexed EITR using RPE, and obtain unbounded EITR via our generic conversions.

We note that our framework unifies the approaches of Kim and Wu [40] who used the framework of RPE in the context of TR and that of GKW who used the framework of El-PLBE in the context of TT, to obtain EITR. This unification yields a clean abstraction which can be used for both public and secret key settings. We believe this framework is of independent interest. We refer the reader to Sects. 7, 8, 9 and 10 in the full version [2] for details. An overview of our constructions is provided in Fig. 1.

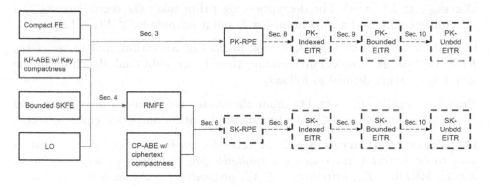

Fig. 1. Overview of our constructions. Solid lines represent the implications shown by our work and are based on new techniques. Dashed lines represent the implications that are new but based on techniques developed in [34]. The constructions in dashed boxes are provided in the respective sections of the full version of our paper [2].

Organization of the paper. We define RPE in Sect. 2 and construct public-key RPE in Sect. 3. We provide our construction of RMFE in Sect. 4. Due to space constraints, our construction of secret-key RPE using RMFE is deferred to the full version [2]. We also refer the reader to the full version [2] for preliminaries, definitions of indexed-EITR, bounded-EITR and unbounded-EITR and conversions between them [2, Sect. 8, Sect. 9, Sect. 10], and the mechanism for supporting super-polynomial sized revocation list [2, Sect. 11].

2 Revocable Predicate Encryption

We define revocable predicate encryption (RPE), in both public and secret key setting. Since the two notions differ only in the encryption algorithm, we present them here in a unified way.

Definition 2.1. A RPE scheme for an attribute space $\mathcal{X} = \{\mathcal{X}_\lambda\}_{\lambda \in [N]}$, a function family $\mathcal{F} = \{\mathcal{F}_\lambda\}_{\lambda \in [N]}$ where $\mathcal{F}_\lambda = \{f : \mathcal{X}_\lambda \to \{0,1\}\}$, a label space

$\mathcal{L} = \{\mathcal{L}_\lambda\}_{\lambda \in [\mathbb{N}]}$ and a message space $\mathcal{M} = \{\mathcal{M}_\lambda\}_{\lambda \in [\mathbb{N}]}$ has the following probabilistic polynomial time algorithms:

Setup$(1^\lambda) \rightarrow$ (mpk, msk). The setup algorithm takes the security parameter λ as input and it outputs a master public key mpk and a master secret key msk.

KeyGen(msk, lb, x) $\rightarrow$ sk$_{\text{lb},x}$[7]. The key generation algorithm takes as input the master secret key msk, a label lb $\in \mathcal{L}_\lambda$ and an attribute $x \in \mathcal{X}_\lambda$. It outputs a secret key sk$_{\text{lb},x}$.

Enc(ek, f, m, L) $\rightarrow$ ct. The encryption algorithm takes as input the encryption key ek, a function f, a message $m \in \mathcal{M}_\lambda$, and a revocation list $L \subseteq \mathcal{L}_\lambda$. It outputs a ciphertext ct.

Dec(sk$_{\text{lb},x}$, ct, L) $\rightarrow m'$. The decryption algorithm takes the secret key sk$_{\text{lb},x}$, a ciphertext ct, and a revocation list L and it outputs $m' \in \mathcal{M}_\lambda \cup \{\bot\}$.

In *public-key RPE*, we take ek = mpk in the Enc algorithm, and in *secret-key RPE*, we take ek = msk. Furthermore, there is an additional algorithm in the secret key setting defined as follows:

Broadcast(mpk, m, L) $\rightarrow$ ct. On input the master public key, a message m, and a revocation list $L \subseteq \mathcal{L}_\lambda$, the broadcast algorithm outputs a ciphertext ct.

Definition 2.2 (Correctness). *A revocable predicate encryption scheme is said to be correct if there exists a negligible function* negl$(\cdot)$ *such that for all* $\lambda \in \mathbb{N}$, *label* lb $\in \mathcal{L}_\lambda$, *attributes* $x \in \mathcal{X}_\lambda$, *predicates* $f \in \mathcal{F}_\lambda$ *such that* $f(x) = 1$, *all messages* $m \in \mathcal{M}_\lambda$ *and any set of revoked users* $L \subseteq \mathcal{L}_\lambda$ *such that* lb $\notin L$, *if we set* (mpk, msk) $\leftarrow$ Setup(1^λ) *and* sk$_{\text{lb},x}$ $\leftarrow$ KeyGen(msk, lb, x), *then the following holds*

$$\Pr[\text{ Dec}(\text{sk}_{\text{lb},x}, \text{ct}, L) = m] \geq 1 - \text{negl}(\lambda),$$

for ct $\leftarrow$ Enc(ek, f, m, L) *(Encryption correctness) and* ct $\leftarrow$ Broadcast(mpk, m, L) *(Broadcast correctness).*

Security. In the following security definitions, we assume for simplicity that the adversary does not make key queries for same input (lb, x) more than once.

Definition 2.3 (q-query Message Hiding). *Let* $q(\cdot)$ *be any fixed polynomial. A RPE scheme satisfies q-query message hiding property if for every PPT adversary* $\mathcal{A}$, *there exists a negligible function* negl$(\cdot)$ *such that for every* $\lambda \in \mathbb{N}$, *all messages* $m \in \mathcal{M}_\lambda$ *and any subset of revoked users* $L \subseteq \mathcal{L}_\lambda$, *the following holds*

$$\Pr\left[\beta' = \beta : \begin{array}{l} (\text{mpk}, \text{msk}) \leftarrow \text{Setup}(1^\lambda); \\ (f, m_0, m_1, L) \leftarrow \mathcal{A}^{\text{KeyGen}(\text{msk},\cdot,\cdot), \text{Enc}(\text{ek},\cdot,\cdot,\cdot)}(\text{mpk}); \\ \beta \leftarrow \{0,1\}; \text{ct}_\beta \leftarrow \text{Enc}(\text{ek}, f, m_\beta, L); \\ \beta' \leftarrow \mathcal{A}^{\text{KeyGen}(\text{msk},\cdot,\cdot), \text{Enc}(\text{ek},\cdot,\cdot,\cdot)}(\text{ct}_\beta) \end{array}\right] \leq \frac{1}{2} + \text{negl}(\lambda)$$

where $\mathcal{A}$ *can make at most* $q(\lambda)$ *queries to the encryption oracle* Enc(ek, $\cdot, \cdot, \cdot$), *and* $\mathcal{A}$ *is admissible if and only if for all the key queries* (lb, x) *to the* KeyGen(msk, $\cdot, \cdot$) *oracle, either* $f(x) = 0$ *or* lb $\in L$.

---

[7]   We want to point out that the secret key sk$_{\text{lb},x}$ does not hide the corresponding label lb and attribute x and we assume these to be included in the secret key.

Definition 2.4 (q-query Selective Message Hiding). *This is the same as the Definition 2.3 except that* $\mathcal{A}$ *outputs the revocation list* L *in the beginning of the game, before the* Setup *algorithm is run.*

Definition 2.5 (q-query Very Selective Message Hiding). *This is the same as the Definition 2.4 except that* $\mathcal{A}$ *outputs all the key queries* (lb, x) *to the* KeyGen$(\mathsf{msk}, \cdot, \cdot)$ *oracle in the beginning of the game, before the* Setup *algorithm is run.*

Definition 2.6 (q-query Function Hiding). *Let* $q(\cdot)$ *be any fixed polynomial. A* RPE *scheme satisfies* q-*query function hiding property if for every PPT adversary* $\mathcal{A}$, *there exists a negligible function* $\mathsf{negl}(\cdot)$ *such that for every* $\lambda \in \mathbb{N}$, *all messages* $m \in \mathcal{M}_\lambda$ *and any subset of revoked users* $L \subseteq \mathcal{L}_\lambda$, *the following holds*

$$
\Pr\left[\beta' = \beta : \begin{array}{l} (\mathsf{mpk}, \mathsf{msk}) \leftarrow \mathsf{Setup}(1^\lambda); \\ (f_0, f_1, m, L) \leftarrow \mathcal{A}^{\mathsf{KeyGen}(\mathsf{msk},\cdot,\cdot),\mathsf{Enc}(\mathsf{ek},\cdot,\cdot,\cdot)}(\mathsf{mpk}); \\ \beta \leftarrow \{0,1\}; \mathsf{ct}_\beta \leftarrow \mathsf{Enc}(\mathsf{ek}, f_\beta, m, L); \\ \beta' \leftarrow \mathcal{A}^{\mathsf{KeyGen}(\mathsf{msk},\cdot,\cdot),\mathsf{Enc}(\mathsf{ek},\cdot,\cdot,\cdot)}(\mathsf{ct}_\beta) \end{array}\right] \leq \frac{1}{2} + \mathsf{negl}(\lambda)
$$

where $\mathcal{A}$ *can make at most* $q(\lambda)$ *queries to the encryption oracle* $\mathsf{Enc}(\mathsf{ek}, \cdot, \cdot, \cdot)$, *and* $\mathcal{A}$ *is admissible if and only if for all the key queries* (lb, x) *to the* KeyGen$(\mathsf{msk}, \cdot, \cdot)$ *oracle, either* $f_0(x) = f_1(x)$ *or* $\mathsf{lb} \in L$.

Definition 2.7 (q-query Selective Function Hiding). *This is the same as the Definition 2.6 except that* $\mathcal{A}$ *outputs the revocation list* L *in the beginning of the game, before the* Setup *algorithm is run.*

The following security notion is defined only for secret-key RPE scheme.

Definition 2.8 (q-query Selective Broadcast Security). *Let* $q(\cdot)$ *be any fixed polynomial. A* RPE *scheme satisfies* q-*query selective broadcast security if there exists a negligible function* $\mathsf{negl}(\cdot)$ *such that for every PPT adversary* $\mathcal{A}$, *for every* $\lambda \in \mathbb{N}$, *all messages* $m \in \mathcal{M}_\lambda$ *and any subset of revoked users* $L \subseteq \mathcal{L}_\lambda$, *the following holds*

$$
\Pr\left[\beta' = \beta : \begin{array}{l} L \leftarrow \mathcal{A}(1^\lambda); \\ (\mathsf{mpk}, \mathsf{msk}) \leftarrow \mathsf{Setup}(1^\lambda); \\ f, m \leftarrow \mathcal{A}^{\mathsf{KeyGen}(\mathsf{msk},\cdot,\cdot),\mathsf{Enc}(\mathsf{msk},\cdot,\cdot,\cdot)}(\mathsf{mpk}); \\ \beta \leftarrow \{0,1\}; \mathsf{ct}_0 \leftarrow \mathsf{Enc}(\mathsf{msk}, f, m, L); \\ \mathsf{ct}_1 \leftarrow \mathsf{Broadcast}(\mathsf{mpk}, m, L); \\ \beta' \leftarrow \mathcal{A}^{\mathsf{KeyGen}(\mathsf{msk},\cdot,\cdot),\mathsf{Enc}(\mathsf{msk},\cdot,\cdot,\cdot)}(\mathsf{ct}_\beta) \end{array}\right] \leq \frac{1}{2} + \mathsf{negl}(\lambda)
$$

where $\mathcal{A}$ *can make at most* $q(\lambda)$ *queries to the encryption* $\mathsf{Enc}(\mathsf{msk}, \cdot, \cdot, \cdot)$ *oracle and* $\mathcal{A}$ *is admissible if and only if* $f(x) = 1, \forall x \in \mathcal{X}_\lambda$.

Remark 2.9. In the *public-key* RPE scheme, the adversary $\mathcal{A}$ can itself simulate the encryption oracle $\mathsf{Enc}(\mathsf{ek}, \cdot, \cdot, \cdot)$, as $\mathsf{ek} = \mathsf{mpk}$ in this setting. Therefore, in public-key setting, we refer to the security definitions without imposing the q-query bound on the encryption oracle.

Remark 2.10. We note that when the message space is binary, function space $\mathcal{F}_\lambda$ is polynomially small and q is a constant, the weaker security definitions where adversary outputs the challenge function f, the challenge message m and the SK-Enc query functions $\{\bar{f}_i\}_{i \in [q]}$ at the beginning of the game, before the Setup(1^λ) algorithm is run, is equivalent to the definitions where the adversary outputs $f, m, \{\bar{f}_i\}_{i \in [q]}$ adaptively. First, the functions can be guessed with polynomial loss. Furthermore, if we restrict the message space to be binary, we can guess the challenge message as well. To extend the message space, we can encrypt each bit by parallel systems.

3   Public-key RPE from FE and LWE

In this section we provide our construction of a public key RPE scheme RPE = (RPE.Setup, RPE.KeyGen, RPE.Enc, RPE.Dec) for an attribute space $\mathcal{X} = \{\mathcal{X}_\lambda\}_\lambda$, a function family $\mathcal{F} = \{\mathcal{F}_\lambda\}_\lambda$ where $\mathcal{F}_\lambda = \{f : \mathcal{X}_\lambda \rightarrow \{0,1\}\}$, a label space $\mathcal{L} = \{\mathcal{L}_\lambda\}_\lambda$ and a message space $\mathcal{M} = \{\mathcal{M}_\lambda\}_\lambda$ from polynomial hardness assumptions. We assume that $|\mathcal{F}_\lambda|$ and $|\mathcal{M}_\lambda|$ are bounded by some polynomial in λ. The restriction on $|\mathcal{F}_\lambda|$ is sufficient for our purpose and the restriction on $|\mathcal{M}_\lambda|$ can be removed by running the scheme in parallel.

Our construction uses the following building blocks:

1. A Sel-INDr secure key-policy ABE scheme kpABE = (kpABE.Setup, kpABE.Enc, kpABE.KeyGen, kpABE.Dec) for circuit class $\mathcal{C}_{\ell(\lambda),d(\lambda)}$ with parameter succinctness and key compactness ([2, Theorem 2.18]). Here $\ell(\lambda)$ is the input length and is the length of labels in our setting and the depth of the circuit is $d(\lambda) \in \omega(\log \lambda)$ to support unbounded revocation list. The message space of the scheme kpABE is $\mathcal{M} = \{\mathcal{M}_\lambda\}_\lambda$ and $\mathcal{CT}_{\mathsf{kpABE}}$ denotes the ciphertext space. We assume that uniform sampling from $\mathcal{CT}_{\mathsf{kpABE}}$ is efficiently possible without any parameter.
2. A (fully) compact, selectively secure, public-key functional encryption scheme FE = (FE.Setup, FE.Enc, FE.KeyGen, FE.Dec) that supports polynomial sized circuits. We assume that the message space is sufficiently large so that it can encrypt an ABE master public key, a (description of) function $f \in \mathcal{F}_\lambda$, a PRF key, two secret keys of SKE, and a trit mode $\in \{0,1,2\}$.
3. A PRF $F : \{0,1\}^\lambda \times \mathcal{X} \rightarrow \{0,1\}^t$ where t is the length of the randomness used in kpABE encryption ([2, Def. 2.1]).
4. A symmetric key encryption schemes SKE = (SKE.KeyGen, SKE.Enc, SKE.Dec) with pseudorandom ciphertexts ([2, Def. 2.3]). We let $\mathcal{CT}_{\mathsf{SKE}}$ denote the ciphertext space of SKE.[8] We assume that uniform sampling from $\mathcal{CT}_{\mathsf{SKE}}$ is efficiently possible without any parameter.

We describe our construction below.

---

[8] We note that we use the same ciphertext space for simplicity even though messages with different lengths are going to be encrypted. To have the same ciphertext space, we can, for example, pad short messages to be some fixed length, which is possible when the message length is bounded by some polynomial.

RPE.Setup(1^λ) $\rightarrow$ (RPE.mpk, RPE.msk). The setup algorithm does the following:
- Generate (FE.mpk, FE.msk) $\leftarrow$ FE.Setup(1^λ).
- Output RPE.mpk = FE.mpk and RPE.msk = FE.msk.

RPE.KeyGen(RPE.msk, lb, x) $\rightarrow$ RPE.sk$_{\text{lb},x}$. The key generation algorithm does the following:
- Sample random values $\gamma_1, \gamma_2, \delta \leftarrow \mathcal{CT}_{\text{SKE}}$.
- Construct a circuit Re-Enc[lb, $x, \gamma_1, \gamma_2, \delta$] which has the label lb, attribute x, γ_1, γ_2 and δ hardwired, as defined in Fig. 2.
- Compute FE.sk$_{\text{lb},x}$ $\leftarrow$ FE.KeyGen(FE.msk, Re-Enc[lb, $x, \gamma_1, \gamma_2, \delta$]).
- Output RPE.sk$_{\text{lb},x}$ = FE.sk$_{\text{lb},x}$.

RPE.Enc(RPE.mpk, f, m, L) $\rightarrow$ RPE.ct. The encryption algorithm does the following:
- Parse RPE.mpk = FE.mpk.
- Sample a PRF key $K \leftarrow \{0,1\}^\lambda$.
- Generate (kpABE.mpk, kpABE.msk) $\leftarrow$ kpABE.Setup(1^λ).
- Compute FE.ct $\leftarrow$ FE.Enc(FE.mpk, (kpABE.mpk, $f, m, K, 0, \bot, \bot$)).
- Construct a circuit C_L, with revocation list L hardwired defined as follows:
  On input a label lb $\in \mathcal{L}_\lambda$,

$$C_L(\text{lb}) = 1 \text{ if and only if lb} \notin L. \tag{3.1}$$

  Compute kpABE.sk$_L$ $\leftarrow$ kpABE.KeyGen(kpABE.msk, C_L).
- Output RPE.ct = (kpABE.mpk, kpABE.sk$_L$, FE.ct).

RPE.Dec(RPE.sk$_{\text{lb},x}$, RPE.ct, L) $\rightarrow m'$. The decryption algorithm does the following:
- Parse RPE.ct = (kpABE.mpk, kpABE.sk$_L$, FE.ct) and RPE.sk$_{\text{lb},x}$ = FE.sk$_{\text{lb},x}$.
- Compute ct$'$ = FE.Dec(FE.sk$_{\text{lb},x}$, FE.ct).
- Construct circuit C_L from L and compute m' = kpABE.Dec(kpABE.mpk, kpABE.sk$_L$, C_L, ct$'$, lb).
- Output m'.

Correctness and Security. We prove that our construction of RPE satisfies correctness and both function hiding and message hiding security via the following theorems.

Theorem 3.1. *Suppose FE and kpABE schemes are correct. Then the above construction satisfies the encryption correctness (Definition 2.2).*

Theorem 3.2. *Assume that F is a secure PRF, SKE is correct and secure, FE and kpABE are secure as per Definition [2, Def. 2.6] and [2, Def. 2.15], respectively. Furthermore, assume $|\mathcal{F}_\lambda| \leq \text{poly}(\lambda)$ and $|\mathcal{M}_\lambda| \leq \text{poly}(\lambda)$. Then the RPE constructed above is function hiding (Definition 2.6).*

Function Re-Enc[lb, $x, \gamma_1, \gamma_2, \delta$]

Hardwired values: A label lb, an attribute x, and SKE ciphertexts γ_1, γ_2, and δ.

Inputs: A kpABE master public key kpABE.mpk, a function $f \in \mathcal{F}_\lambda$, a message $m \in \mathcal{M}_\lambda$, a PRF key K, a trapdoor mode mode $\in \{0, 1, 2\}$ and SKE keys SKE.key$_1$ and SKE.key$_2$.

Output : A kpABE ciphertext.

1. Parse the input as (ABE.mpk, f, m, K, mode, SKE.key$_1$, SKE.key$_2$).
2. Set $\tilde{m} = \begin{cases} m & \text{if } f(x) = 1 \\ 0 & \text{if } f(x) = 0. \end{cases}$
3. Compute kpABE.ct$_{\text{lb}}$ = kpABE.Enc(kpABE.mpk, lb, $\tilde{m}$; $F(K, (\text{lb}, x))$).
4. Compute flag = SKE.Dec(SKE.key$_2$, δ).
5. Compute out$_i$ = SKE.Dec(SKE.key$_i$, γ_i) for $i \in \{1, 2\}$.
6. If mode = 0, output kpABE.ct$_{\text{lb}}$.
7. If mode = 1, output out$_1$.
8. If mode = 2, output $\begin{cases} \text{out}_2 & \text{if flag} = 1 \\ \text{kpABE.ct}_{\text{lb}} & \text{if flag} = 0. \end{cases}$

Fig. 2. Function to compute kpABE ciphertexts depending on various conditions.

Theorem 3.3. *Assume that F is a secure PRF, SKE is correct and secure, FE and kpABE are secure as per Definitions [2, Def. 2.6] and [2, Def. 2.15], respectively. Furthermore, assume $|\mathcal{F}_\lambda| \le \text{poly}(\lambda)$ and $|\mathcal{M}_\lambda| \le \text{poly}(\lambda)$. Then the construction for RPE satisfies message hiding property as defined in Definition 2.3.*

Due to space constraints, we provide the proofs in the full version.

Efficiency. Here we argue that our construction achieves optimal parameters. Namely, we show that the size of each parameter is independent of $|L|$. For details, please see the full version.

3.1   Alternate Construction Using LOT

The construction is similar to the above except that we use LOT in place of ABE, which brings in the following changes in the KeyGen, Enc, and Dec algorithms:

- We use LOT = (LOT.crsGen, LOT.Hash, LOT.Send, LOT.Receive) instead of kpABE.
- The function in Fig. 2, for which FE key is generated now takes as input LOT objects crs and digest, instead of kpABE.mpk and computes LOT.ct$_{\text{lb}}$ = LOT.Send(crs, digest, lb, 0, $\tilde{m}$; $F(K, (\text{lb}, x))$), instead of kpABE.ct$_{\text{lb}}$.

- The encryption algorithm changes as follows:
RPE.Enc(RPE.mpk, f, m, L) → RPE.ct. The encryption algorithm does the
following:
  - Parse RPE.mpk = FE.mpk and sample a PRF key $K \leftarrow \{0, 1\}^\lambda$.
  - Generate crs ← LOT.crsGen(1^λ).
  - Compute (digest, $\hat{D}$) ← LOT.Hash(crs, D), where D is a binary vector of
    length N (the no. of users) and is 1 at positions corresponding to non-
    revoked labels, i.e. $D[\text{lb}'] = 1$ iff lb' $\notin L$.
  - Compute FE.ct ← FE.Enc(FE.mpk, (crs, digest, $f, m, K, 0, \bot, \bot$)).
  - Output RPE.ct = (crs, FE.ct).
- The algorithm for decryption also changes accordingly as follows:
RPE.Dec(RPE.sk$_{\text{lb},x}$, RPE.ct, L) → m'. The decryption algorithm does the fol-
lowing:
  - Parse RPE.ct = (crs, FE.ct) and RPE.sk$_{\text{lb},x}$ = FE.sk$_{\text{lb},x}$.
  - Define D from L as described in the encryption algorithm and compute
    (digest, $\hat{D}$) ← LOT.Hash(crs, D).
  - Compute LOT.ct' = FE.Dec(FE.sk$_{\text{lb},x}$, FE.ct).
  - Compute $m' = $ LOT.Receive$^{\hat{D}}$(crs, LOT.ct', lb).
  - Output m'.

We provide the proofs for correctness and security in the full version.

4 Revocable Mixed Functional Encryption

4.1 Definition

A revocable mixed functional encryption (RMFE) scheme with input domain
$\mathcal{X} = \{\mathcal{X}_\lambda\}_{\lambda \in [\mathbb{N}]}$, a function family $\mathcal{F} = \{\mathcal{F}_\lambda\}_{\lambda \in [\mathbb{N}]}$ where $\mathcal{F}_\lambda = \{f : \mathcal{X}_\lambda \to \{0, 1\}\}$,
a label space $\mathcal{L} = \{\mathcal{L}_\lambda\}_{\lambda \in [\mathbb{N}]}$ has the following syntax.

Setup(1^λ) → (mpk, msk). The setup algorithm takes as input the security parameter λ and outputs a master public key mpk and a master secret key msk.

KeyGen(msk, lb, x) → sk$_{\text{lb},x}$. The key generation algorithm takes as input the
master secret key msk, a label lb $\in \mathcal{L}_\lambda$ and an input $x \in \mathcal{X}_\lambda$. It outputs a
secret key sk$_{\text{lb},x}$.

PK-Enc(mpk, L) → ct. The public key encryption algorithm takes as input the
master public key mpk and a revocation list $L \subseteq \mathcal{L}_\lambda$ and outputs a ciphertext
ct.

SK-Enc(msk, f, L) → ct. The secret key encryption algorithm takes as input the
master secret key msk, a function $f \in \mathcal{F}_\lambda$ and a revocation list $L \subseteq \mathcal{L}_\lambda$, and
outputs a ciphertext ct.

Dec(sk$_{\text{lb},x}$, L, ct) → $\{0, 1\}$. The decryption algorithm takes the secret key sk$_{\text{lb},x}$,
a revocation list $L \subseteq \mathcal{L}_\lambda$ and a ciphertext ct and outputs a bit.

Definition 4.1 (Correctness). *A RMFE scheme is said to be correct if there exists negligible functions* $\mathsf{negl}_1(\cdot), \mathsf{negl}_2(\cdot)$ *such that for all* $\lambda \in \mathbb{N}$, *the following holds*

$$\Pr\left[\ \mathsf{Dec}(\mathsf{sk}_{\mathsf{lb},x}, L, \mathsf{ct}) = 1 : \begin{array}{c} (\mathsf{mpk}, \mathsf{msk}) \leftarrow \mathsf{Setup}(1^\lambda); \\ \mathsf{sk}_{\mathsf{lb},x} \leftarrow \mathsf{KeyGen}(\mathsf{msk}, \mathsf{lb}, x); \\ \mathsf{ct} \leftarrow \mathsf{PK\text{-}Enc}(\mathsf{mpk}, L) \end{array}\ \right] \geq 1 - \mathsf{negl}_1(\lambda).$$

$$\mathsf{lb} \notin L \Rightarrow \Pr\left[\ \mathsf{Dec}(\mathsf{sk}_{\mathsf{lb},x}, L, \mathsf{ct}) = f(x) : \begin{array}{c} (\mathsf{mpk}, \mathsf{msk}) \leftarrow \mathsf{Setup}(1^\lambda); \\ \mathsf{sk}_{\mathsf{lb},x} \leftarrow \mathsf{KeyGen}(\mathsf{msk}, \mathsf{lb}, x); \\ \mathsf{ct} \leftarrow \mathsf{SK\text{-}Enc}(\mathsf{msk}, f, L) \end{array}\ \right] \geq 1 - \mathsf{negl}_2(\lambda).$$

Security. Here we define the security requirements of RMFE scheme.

Definition 4.2 (q-query Mode Hiding). *Let* $q(\cdot)$ *be any fixed polynomial. A RMFE scheme satisfies q-query mode hiding security if for every PPT adversary* $\mathcal{A}$, *there exists a negligible function* $\mathsf{negl}(\cdot)$ *such that for every* $\lambda \in \mathbb{N}$,

$$\Pr\left[\ \beta' = \beta : \begin{array}{c} (\mathsf{mpk}, \mathsf{msk}) \leftarrow \mathsf{Setup}(1^\lambda); \\ f, L \leftarrow \mathcal{A}^{\mathsf{KeyGen}(\mathsf{msk}, \cdot, \cdot), \mathsf{SK\text{-}Enc}(\mathsf{msk}, \cdot, \cdot)}(\mathsf{mpk}); \\ \beta \leftarrow \{0, 1\}; \mathsf{ct}_0 \leftarrow \mathsf{SK\text{-}Enc}(\mathsf{msk}, f, L); \\ \mathsf{ct}_1 \leftarrow \mathsf{PK\text{-}Enc}(\mathsf{mpk}, L); \\ \beta' \leftarrow \mathcal{A}^{\mathsf{KeyGen}(\mathsf{msk}, \cdot, \cdot), \mathsf{SK\text{-}Enc}(\mathsf{msk}, \cdot, \cdot)}(\mathsf{ct}_\beta) \end{array}\ \right] \leq \frac{1}{2} + \mathsf{negl}(\lambda)$$

where $\mathcal{A}$ *can make at most* $q(\lambda)$ *queries to the* $\mathsf{SK\text{-}Enc}(\mathsf{msk}, \cdot, \cdot)$ *oracle and is admissible only if for all the key queries* (lb, x) *to the* $\mathsf{KeyGen}(\mathsf{msk}, \cdot, \cdot)$ *oracle,* $f(x) = 1$.

Definition 4.3 (q-query Selective Function Hiding). *Let* $q(\cdot)$ *be any fixed polynomial. A RMFE scheme satisfies q-query selective function hiding security if for every PPT adversary* $\mathcal{A}$, *there exists a negligible function* $\mathsf{negl}(\cdot)$ *such that for every* $\lambda \in \mathbb{N}$,

$$\Pr\left[\ \beta' = \beta : \begin{array}{c} L \leftarrow \mathcal{A}(1^\lambda); \\ (\mathsf{mpk}, \mathsf{msk}) \leftarrow \mathsf{Setup}(1^\lambda); \\ (f_0, f_1) \leftarrow \mathcal{A}^{\mathsf{KeyGen}(\mathsf{msk}, \cdot, \cdot), \mathsf{SK\text{-}Enc}(\mathsf{msk}, \cdot, \cdot)}(\mathsf{mpk}); \\ \beta \leftarrow \{0, 1\}; \mathsf{ct}_\beta \leftarrow \mathsf{SK\text{-}Enc}(\mathsf{msk}, f_\beta, L); \\ \beta' \leftarrow \mathcal{A}^{\mathsf{KeyGen}(\mathsf{msk}, \cdot, \cdot), \mathsf{SK\text{-}Enc}(\mathsf{msk}, \cdot, \cdot)}(\mathsf{ct}_\beta) \end{array}\ \right] \leq \frac{1}{2} + \mathsf{negl}(\lambda)$$

where $\mathcal{A}$ *can make at most* $q(\lambda)$ *queries to the* $\mathsf{SK\text{-}Enc}(\mathsf{msk}, \cdot, \cdot)$ *oracle and for all the key queries* (lb, x) *to the* $\mathsf{KeyGen}(\mathsf{msk}, \cdot, \cdot)$ *oracle, either* $f_0(x) = f_1(x)$ *or* $\mathsf{lb} \in L$.

Remark 4.4. We note that when the function space $\mathcal{F}_\lambda$ is polynomially small and q is a constant, a variant of Definition 4.3 where the adversary outputs the challenge functions (f_0, f_1) and the SK-Enc query functions $\{\bar{f}_i\}_{i \in [q]}$ at the beginning of the game, before the $\mathsf{Setup}(1^\lambda)$ algorithm is run, is equivalent to Definition 4.3 where the adversary adaptively outputs the challenge functions (f_0, f_1) and can make SK-Enc queries adaptively, with polynomial loss. Similar comment also applies to Definition 4.2. We will use these simplifications in the security proofs.

4.2   Construction

In this section we give a construction of 1-query secure RMFE scheme, with input space $\mathcal{X} = \{\mathcal{X}_\lambda\}_\lambda$, a function family $\mathcal{F} = \{\mathcal{F}_\lambda\}_\lambda$ where $\mathcal{F}_\lambda = \{f : \mathcal{X}_\lambda \to \{0,1\}\}$ and a label space $\mathcal{L} = \{\mathcal{L}_\lambda\}_\lambda$. We assume that the size of $|\mathcal{F}_\lambda|$ is bounded by some polynomial in λ, which will suffice for our purpose.

Our scheme uses the following building blocks:

1. A 2-bounded semi-adaptive simulation based function-message private ([2, Def. 2.11]) SKFE scheme SKFE = (SKFE.Setup, SKFE.KeyGen, SKFE.Enc, SKFE.Dec) that supports the function class $\mathcal{F}$. This can be instantiated from one-way functions ([2, Lemma 2.12]).
2. A key-policy ABE scheme kpABE = (kpABE.Setup, kpABE.Enc, kpABE.KeyGen, kpABE.Dec) for the circuit class $\mathcal{C}_{\ell(\lambda),d(\lambda)}$ with message space $\{0,1\}^\lambda$ satisfying Sel-IND security ([2, Def. 2.14]) and efficiency properties described in [2, Theorem 2.18]. We set $\ell(\lambda) = \ell_{\mathsf{lb}} + \log(\lambda) + 1$ and $d(\lambda) = \omega(\log\lambda)$, where ℓ_{lb} is the label length.[9] This can be instantiated from the LWE assumption ([2, Theorem 2.18]).
3. A lockable obfuscation scheme LO = (LO.Obf, LO.Eval) with lock space $\{0,1\}^\lambda$ that supports circuits of the form CC defined in Fig. 3. As we will analyze later, the circuit is of fixed polynomial size in λ and $|f|$, where $|f|$ is the description size of the function $f \in \mathcal{F}$. This can be instantiated from the LWE assumption ([2, Theorem 2.25].).

Below we describe our construction of a 1-query secure RMFE scheme RMFE = (RMFE.Setup, RMFE.KeyGen, RMFE.PK-Enc, RMFE.SK-Enc, RMFE.Dec).

RMFE.Setup(1^λ) → (RMFE.mpk, RMFE.msk). The setup algorithm does the following:
- Generate SKFE.msk ← SKFE.Setup(1^λ).
- Generate (kpABE.mpk, kpABE.msk) ← kpABE.Setup(1^λ).
- Output
  RMFE.mpk = kpABE.mpk and RMFE.msk = (SKFE.msk, kpABE.mpk, kpABE.msk).

RMFE.KeyGen(RMFE.msk, lb, x) → RMFE.sk$_{\mathsf{lb},x}$. The key generation algorithm does the following:
- Parse RMFE.msk = (SKFE.msk, kpABE.mpk, kpABE.msk).
- For all $j \in [\lambda], b \in \{0,1\}$, sample $K_{j,b}, R_{j,b} \leftarrow \{0,1\}^\lambda$.
  Denote $K = \{K_{j,b}\}_{j\in[\lambda],b\in\{0,1\}}$ and $R = \{R_{j,b}\}_{j\in[\lambda],b\in\{0,1\}}$.
- Compute

$$\mathsf{SKFE.ct} \leftarrow \mathsf{SKFE.Enc}(\mathsf{SKFE.msk}, (x, K, R)).$$

- For all $j \in [\lambda], b \in \{0,1\}$, compute

$$\mathsf{kpABE.ct}_{\mathsf{lb},j,b} \leftarrow \mathsf{kpABE.Enc}(\mathsf{kpABE.mpk}, (\mathsf{lb}, j, b), K_{j,b}).$$

---

[9] Concretely, we can choose $d(\lambda) = \Theta(\log\lambda \log\log\lambda)$ for example.

- Output $\mathsf{RMFE.sk}_{\mathsf{lb},x}$ = $(\mathsf{SKFE.ct}, \mathsf{kpABE.mpk}, \{(\mathsf{lb}, j, b), \mathsf{kpABE}.$ $\mathsf{ct}_{\mathsf{lb},j,b}\}_{j\in[\lambda],b\in\{0,1\}})$.

$\mathsf{RMFE.PK\text{-}Enc}(\mathsf{RMFE.mpk}, L) \to \mathsf{RMFE.ct}$. The public key encryption algorithm does the following:
- Computes a simulated code $\mathsf{RMFE.ct} \leftarrow \mathsf{LO.Sim}(1^\lambda, 1^{|\mathsf{CC}|})^{10}$.
- It outputs $\mathsf{RMFE.ct}$ as the ciphertext.

$\mathsf{RMFE.SK\text{-}Enc}(\mathsf{RMFE.msk}, f, L) \to \mathsf{RMFE.ct}$. The secret key encryption algorithm does the following:
- Parse $\mathsf{RMFE.msk} = (\mathsf{SKFE.msk}, \mathsf{kpABE.mpk}, \mathsf{kpABE.msk})$, and sample a tag $\mathbf{z} \leftarrow \{0,1\}^\lambda$ and a lock value $\alpha \leftarrow \{0,1\}^\lambda$.
- For   all $j \in [\lambda]$, compute $\mathsf{kpABE.sk}_{L,j,z_j} \leftarrow \mathsf{kpABE.KeyGen}(\mathsf{kpABE.msk}, C_{L,j,z_j})$, where the function C_{L,j,z_j} has L, j and z_j hardwired and is defined as follows :
  On input $(\mathsf{lb}, i, b) \in \mathcal{L}_\lambda \times [\lambda] \times \{0,1\}$,

$$C_{L,j,z_j}(\mathsf{lb}, i, b) = \begin{cases} 1 & \text{if } (\mathsf{lb} \notin L) \wedge (i = j) \wedge (b = z_j) \\ 0 & \text{otherwise.} \end{cases} \quad (4.1)$$

- Compute $\mathsf{SKFE.sk} \leftarrow \mathsf{SKFE.KeyGen}(\mathsf{SKFE.msk}, P_{f,\mathbf{z},\alpha})$, where the function $P_{f,\mathbf{z},\alpha}$ has $f, \mathbf{z}, \alpha$ hardwired and is defined as follows :
  On input $x \in \mathcal{X}_\lambda, K = \{K_{j,b}\}_{j\in[\lambda],b\in\{0,1\}}, R = \{R_{j,b}\}_{j\in[\lambda],b\in\{0,1\}}$,

$$P_{f,\mathbf{z},\alpha}(x, K, R) = \begin{cases} \bigoplus_j K_{j,z_j} \oplus \alpha & \text{if } f(x) = 0 \\ \bigoplus_j R_{j,z_j} & \text{if } f(x) = 1. \end{cases} \quad (4.2)$$

- Construct function $\mathsf{CC}[\mathsf{SKFE.sk}, \{\mathsf{kpABE.sk}_{L,j,z_j}\}_{j\in[\lambda]}]$, with $\mathsf{SKFE.sk}$ and $\{\mathsf{kpABE.sk}_{L,j,z_j}\}_{j\in[\lambda]}$ hardwired and is defined as in Fig. 3.
- Output $\mathsf{RMFE.ct} \leftarrow \mathsf{LO.Obf}(\mathsf{CC}[\mathsf{SKFE.sk}, \{\mathsf{kpABE.sk}_{L,j,z_j}\}_{j\in[\lambda]}], \alpha)$.

$\mathsf{RMFE.Dec}(\mathsf{RMFE.sk}_{\mathsf{lb},x}, \mathsf{RMFE.ct}, L) \to \{0,1\}$. The decryption algorithm does the following:
- Parse $\mathsf{RMFE.sk}_{\mathsf{lb},x}$ = $(\mathsf{SKFE.ct}, \mathsf{kpABE.mpk}, \{(\mathsf{lb}, j, b), \mathsf{kpABE.ct}_{\mathsf{lb},j,b}\}_{j\in[\lambda],b\in\{0,1\}})$
  and $\mathsf{RMFE.ct} = \widetilde{\mathsf{CC}}$, where $\widetilde{\mathsf{CC}}$ is regarded as an obfuscated circuit of LO.
- For all $j \in [\lambda], b \in \{0,1\}$, compute

$$\mathsf{kpABE.off}_{\mathsf{lb},j,b} \leftarrow \mathsf{kpABE.Dec}^{\mathsf{off}}(\mathsf{kpABE.mpk}, C_{L,j,b}, (\mathsf{lb}, j, b)).$$

- Compute

$$y = \mathsf{LO.Eval}\big(\widetilde{\mathsf{CC}}, (\mathsf{SKFE.ct}, \{\mathsf{kpABE.ct}_{\mathsf{lb},j,b}, \mathsf{kpABE.off}_{\mathsf{lb},j,b}\}_{j\in[\lambda],b\in\{0,1\}})\big).$$

- Output 1 if $y = \bot$, else output 0.

Remark 4.5. We note that by performing the part of the ABE decryption that uses $C_{L,j,b}$, outside of CC , we do not need to provide $C_{L,j,b}$ (or L) as input to CC. Instead, we provide $\{\mathsf{kpABE.off}_{\mathsf{lb},j,b}\}_{j\in[\lambda],b\in\{0,1\}}$ whose size is independent of the size of $C_{L,j,b}$ (and thus that of L). This helps us in getting succinct ciphertext.

---

[10] Here, CC represents the maximum possible size of $\mathsf{CC}[\cdot, \cdot]$ circuit defined in Fig. 3.

Function $\mathsf{CC}[\mathsf{SKFE.sk}, \{\mathsf{kpABE.sk}_{L,j,z_j}\}_{j\in[\lambda]}]$

Hardwired values: A SKFE secret key SKFE.sk and kpABE keys $\{\mathsf{kpABE.sk}_{L,j,z_j}\}_{j\in[\lambda]}$.

Inputs: A SKFE ciphertext SKFE.ct and kpABE ciphertexts $\{\mathsf{kpABE.ct}_{\mathsf{lb},j,b}, \mathsf{kpABE.off}_{\mathsf{lb},j,b}\}_{j\in[\lambda],b\in\{0,1\}}$.

Output : A binary string $\alpha^* \in \{0,1\}^\lambda$.

1. For all $j \in [\lambda]$, compute $m_j = \mathsf{kpABE.Dec}^{\mathsf{on}}(\mathsf{kpABE.sk}_{L,j,z_j}, \mathsf{kpABE.ct}_{\mathsf{lb},j,z_j}, \mathsf{kpABE.off}_{\mathsf{lb},j,z_j})$.
   Let $M_0 = \bigoplus_j m_j$
2. Compute $M_1 = \mathsf{SKFE.Dec}(\mathsf{SKFE.sk}, \mathsf{SKFE.ct})$.
3. Output $M_1 \oplus M_0$.

Fig. 3. Compute and Compare function CC

Correctness and Security. We prove the correctness and security via the following theorems.

Theorem 4.1. *Suppose* kpABE, LO *and* SKFE *are correct and* LO *is secure , then the above construction of* RMFE *satisfies correctness as defined in Definition 4.1.*

Theorem 4.2. *Assume that* SKFE *and* LO *are secure as per Definitions [2, Def. 2.11] and [2, Def. 2.24], respectively. Furthermore, assume* $|\mathcal{F}_\lambda| \leq \mathrm{poly}(\lambda)$ *Then the* RMFE *construction satisfies 1-query mode hiding security as per Definition 4.2.*

Theorem 4.3. *Assume* SKFE *is secure ([2, Def. 2.11]),* kpABE *satisfies* Sel-IND *security ([2, Def. 2.14]). Furthermore, assume* $|\mathcal{F}_\lambda| \leq \mathrm{poly}(\lambda)$. *Then, the* RMFE *construction satisfies 1-query function hiding as defined in Definition 4.3.*

Due to space constraints, we prove these theorems in the full version.

Efficiency. Here we argue that our construction achieves optimal parameters. Namely, we show that the sizes of the parameters are independent of $|L|$. For details, please see the full version.

Acknowledgements. We thank the reviewers of Eurocrypt 2023 for helpful comments, especially for suggesting the alternative construction of RPE based on FE and laconic OT. This work was supported in part by the DST "Swarnajayanti" fellowship, Cybersecurity Center of Excellence, IIT Madras, National Blockchain Project and the Algorand Centres of Excellence programme managed by Algorand Foundation. Any opinions, findings, and conclusions or recommendations expressed in this material are those of the author(s) and do not necessarily reflect the views of sponsors. The fourth author was partially supported by JST AIP Acceleration Research JPMJCR22U5 and JSPS KAKENHI Grant Number 19H01109, Japan.

References

1. Agrawal, S.: Indistinguishability obfuscation without multilinear maps: new techniques for bootstrapping and instantiation. In: Eurocrypt (2019). https://doi.org/10.1007/978-3-030-17653-2_7
2. Agrawal, S., Kumari, S., Yadav, A., Yamada, S.: Trace and revoke with optimal parameters from polynomial hardness. Cryptology ePrint Archive (2022). https://eprint.iacr.org/2022/1347.pdf
3. Agrawal, S., Maitra, M.: Fe and iO for turing machines from minimal assumptions. In: Beimel, A., Dziembowski, S. (eds.) Theory of Cryptography. TCC 2018. LNCS, vol. 11240. Springer, Cham (2018). https://doi.org/10.1007/978-3-030-03810-6_18
4. Agrawal, S., Pellet-Mary, A.: Indistinguishability obfuscation without maps: attacks and fixes for noisy linear FE. In: Eurocrypt (2020)
5. Agrawal, S., Wichs, D., Yamada, S.: Optimal broadcast encryption from LWE and pairings in the standard model. In: TCC (2020). https://doi.org/10.1007/978-3-030-64375-1_6
6. Agrawal, S., Yamada, S.: Optimal broadcast encryption from pairings and LWE. In: EUROCRYPT (2020). https://doi.org/10.1007/978-3-030-45721-1_2
7. Ananth, P., Brakerski, Z., Segev, G., Vaikuntanathan, V.: From selective to adaptive security in functional encryption. In: CRYPTO (2015). https://doi.org/10.1007/978-3-662-48000-7_32
8. Ananth, P., Jain, A.: Indistinguishability obfuscation from compact functional encryption. In: CRYPTO (2015). https://doi.org/10.1007/978-3-662-47989-6_15
9. Attrapadung, N., Libert, B., de Panafieu, E.: Expressive key-policy attribute-based encryption with constant-size ciphertexts. In: Catalano, D., Fazio, N., Gennaro, R., Nicolosi, A. (eds.) PKC 2011. LNCS, vol. 6571, pp. 90–108. Springer, Heidelberg (2011). https://doi.org/10.1007/978-3-642-19379-8_6
10. Barak, B., et al.: On the (Im)possibility of obfuscating programs. In: CRYPTO (2001). https://doi.org/10.1007/3-540-44647-8_1
11. Bethencourt, J., Sahai, A., Waters, B.: Ciphertext-policy attribute-based encryption. In: IEEE Symposium on Security and Privacy, pp. 321–334 (2007). https://doi.org/10.1109/SP.2007.11
12. Bitansky, N., Vaikuntanathan, V.: Indistinguishability obfuscation from functional encryption. In: FOCS (2015)
13. Boneh, D., et al.: Fully key-homomorphic encryption, arithmetic circuit ABE and compact garbled circuits. In: EUROCRYPT (2014). https://doi.org/10.1007/978-3-642-55220-5_30
14. Boneh, D., Gentry, C., Waters, B.: Collusion resistant broadcast encryption with short ciphertexts and private keys. In: CRYPTO (2005). https://doi.org/10.1007/11535218_16
15. Boneh, D., Waters, B., Zhandry, M.: Low overhead broadcast encryption from multilinear maps. In: CRYPTO (2014). https://doi.org/10.1007/978-3-662-44371-2_12
16. Boneh, D., Zhandry, M.: Multiparty key exchange, efficient traitor tracing, and more from indistinguishability obfuscation. Algorithmica **79**(4), 1233–1285 (2017). https://doi.org/10.1007/978-3-662-44371-2_27
17. Boyen, X., Waters, B.: Anonymous hierarchical identity-based encryption (without random oracles). In: CRYPTO (2006). https://doi.org/10.1007/11818175_17
18. Brakerski, Z., Komargodski, I., Segev, G.: Multi-input functional encryption in the private-key setting: stronger security from weaker assumptions. In: Fischlin, M.,

Coron, J.-S. (eds.) EUROCRYPT 2016. LNCS, vol. 9666, pp. 852–880. Springer, Heidelberg (2016). https://doi.org/10.1007/978-3-662-49896-5_30

19. Brakerski, Z., Segev, G.: Function-private functional encryption in the private-key setting. J. Cryptol. **31**(1), 202–225 (2018). https://doi.org/10.1007/s00145-017-9255-y

20. Caro, A.D., Iovino, V., Jain, A., O'Neill, A., Paneth, O., Persiano, G.: On the achievability of simulation-based security for functional encryption. In: CRYPTO (2013). https://doi.org/10.1007/978-3-642-40084-1_29

21. Chen, Y., Vaikuntanathan, V., Waters, B., Wee, H., Wichs, D.: Traitor-tracing from LWE made simple and attribute-based. In: TCC (2018). https://doi.org/10.1007/978-3-030-03810-6_13

22. Cho, C., Döttling, N., Garg, S., Gupta, D., Miao, P., Polychroniadou, A.: Laconic oblivious transfer and its applications. In: CRYPTO (2017). https://doi.org/10.1007/978-3-319-63715-0_2

23. Chor, B., Fiat, A., Naor, M.: Tracing traitors. In: CRYPTO (1994). https://doi.org/10.1007/3-540-48658-5_25

24. Coron, J., Lepoint, T., Tibouchi, M.: Practical multilinear maps over the integers. In: CRYPTO (2013). https://doi.org/10.1007/978-3-642-40041-4_26

25. Devadas, L., Quach, W., Vaikuntanathan, V., Wee, H., Wichs, D.: Succinct LWE sampling, random polynomials, and obfuscation. In: TCC (2021). https://doi.org/10.1007/978-3-030-90453-1_9

26. Fiat, A., Naor, M.: Broadcast encryption. In: Stinson, D.R. (ed.) CRYPTO (1993). https://doi.org/10.1007/3-540-48329-2_40

27. Garg, S., Gentry, C., Halevi, S.: Candidate multilinear maps from ideal lattices. In: EUROCRYPT (2013). https://doi.org/10.1007/978-3-642-38348-9_1

28. Garg, S., Pandey, O., Srinivasan, A.: Revisiting the cryptographic hardness of finding a Nash equilibrium. In: CRYPTO (2016). https://doi.org/10.1007/978-3-662-53008-5_20

29. Garg, S., Pandey, O., Srinivasan, A., Zhandry, M.: Breaking the sub-exponential barrier in Obfustopia. In: EUROCRYPT (2017). https://doi.org/10.1007/978-3-319-56617-7_6

30. Gay, R., Pass, R.: Indistinguishability obfuscation from circular security. In: STOC (2021). https://doi.org/10.1145/3406325.3451070

31. Gorbunov, S., Vaikuntanathan, V., Wee, H.: Attribute based encryption for circuits. In: STOC (2013). https://doi.org/10.1145/2488608.2488677

32. Goyal, R., Koppula, V., Waters, B.: Lockable obfuscation. In: FOCS (2017). https://doi.org/10.1109/FOCS.2017.62

33. Goyal, R., Koppula, V., Waters, B.: Collusion resistant traitor tracing from learning with errors. In: STOC (2018). https://doi.org/10.1145/3188745.3188844

34. Goyal, R., Koppula, V., Waters, B.: New approaches to traitor tracing with embedded identities. In: TCC (2019). https://doi.org/10.1007/978-3-030-36033-7_6

35. Goyal, R., Quach, W., Waters, B., Wichs, D.: Broadcast and trace with n^ϵ ciphertext size from standard assumptions. In: Crypto (2019). https://eprint.iacr.org/2019/636

36. Goyal, R., Vusirikala, S., Waters, B.: Collusion resistant broadcast and trace from positional witness encryption. In: PKC (2019). https://doi.org/10.1007/978-3-030-17259-6_1

37. Jain, A., Lin, H., Lou, P., Sahai, A.: Polynomial-time cryptanalysis of the subspace flooding assumption for post-quantum IO. In: EUROCRYPT (2023)

38. Jain, A., Lin, H., Sahai, A.: Indistinguishability obfuscation from well-founded assumptions. In: STOC (2021). https://doi.org/10.1145/3406325.3451093

39. Jain, A., Lin, H., Sahai, A.: Indistinguishability obfuscation from LPN over large fields, DLIN, and constant depth PRGs. In: EUROCRYPT (2022). https://doi.org/10.1007/978-3-031-06944-4_23

40. Kim, S., Wu, D.J.: Collusion resistant trace-and-revoke for arbitrary identities from standard assumptions. In: ASIACRYPT (2020). https://doi.org/10.1007/978-3-030-64834-3_3

41. Komargodski, I., Segev, G.: From minicrypt to Obfustopia via private-key functional encryption. J. Cryptol. **33**(2), 406–458 (2020). https://doi.org/10.1007/978-3-319-56620-7_5

42. Lin, H., Pass, R., Seth, K., Telang, S.: Output-compressing randomized encodings and applications. In: TCC (2016). https://doi.org/10.1007/978-3-662-49096-9_5

43. Naor, M., Pinkas, B.: Efficient trace and revoke schemes. Int. J. Inf. Secur. **9**(6), 411–424 (2010). https://doi.org/10.1007/s10207-010-0121-2

44. Nishimaki, R., Wichs, D., Zhandry, M.: Anonymous traitor tracing: how to embed arbitrary information in a key. In: EUROCRYPT (2016). https://doi.org/10.1007/978-3-662-49896-5_14

45. Takashima, K.: Expressive attribute-based encryption with constant-size ciphertexts from the decisional linear assumption. In: SCN (2014). https://doi.org/10.1007/978-3-319-10879-7_17

46. Tsabary, R.: Candidate witness encryption from lattice techniques. In: Crypto (2022)

47. Vaikuntanathan, V., Wee, H., Wichs, D.: Witness encryption and null-IO from evasive LWE. In: Asiacrypt (2022)

48. Wee, H.: Optimal broadcast encryption and CP-ABE from evasive lattice assumptions. In: Eurocrypt (2022). https://doi.org/10.1007/978-3-031-07085-3_8

49. Wee, H., Wichs, D.: Candidate obfuscation via oblivious LWE sampling. In: Canteaut, A., Standaert, F.-X. (eds.) EUROCRYPT 2021. LNCS, vol. 12698, pp. 127–156. Springer, Cham (2021). https://doi.org/10.1007/978-3-030-77883-5_5

50. Wichs, D., Zirdelis, G.: Obfuscating compute-and-compare programs under LWE. In: FOCS (2017). https://doi.org/10.1109/FOCS.2017.61

51. Zhandry, M.: New techniques for traitor tracing: Size $N^{1/3}$ and more from pairings. In: CRYPTO (2020). https://doi.org/10.1007/978-3-030-56784-2_22

Traitor Tracing with $N^{1/3}$-Size Ciphertexts and $O(1)$-Size Keys from k-Lin

Junqing Gong[1,2(✉)], Ji Luo[3(✉)] [iD], and Hoeteck Wee[4(✉)]

[1] East China Normal University, Shanghai, China
jqgong@sei.ecnu.edu.cn
[2] Shanghai Qi Zhi Institute, Shanghai, China
[3] Paul G. Allen School of Computer Science & Engineering,
University of Washington, Seattle, USA
luoji@cs.washington.edu
[4] NTT Research, Sunnyvale, USA
wee@di.ens.fr

Abstract. We present a pairing-based traitor tracing scheme for N users with

$$|\mathsf{pk}| = |\mathsf{ct}| = O(N^{1/3}), \quad |\mathsf{sk}| = O(1).$$

This is the first pairing-based scheme to achieve $|\mathsf{pk}| \cdot |\mathsf{sk}| \cdot |\mathsf{ct}| = o(N)$. Our construction relies on the (bilateral) k-Lin assumption, and achieves private tracing and full collusion resistance. Our result simultaneously improves upon the sizes of pk, ct in Boneh–Sahai–Waters [Eurocrypt '06] and the size of sk in Zhandry [Crypto '20], while further eliminating the reliance on the generic group model in the latter work.

1 Introduction

Traitor tracing schemes [13] enable a content distributor to generate secret keys for different users, any of whom can decrypt some protected content (e.g., a cable TV stream). However, if any group of "traitors" get together and publish some program capable of decrypting the content, then it is possible to use this program to "trace" and identify at least one of the traitors and therefore hold them accountable. We would like to design traitor tracing schemes with short parameters, namely short public key pk, ciphertext overhead ct and secret key sk that depend minimally on the total number of users N.

J. Gong—Partially supported by National Natural Science Foundation of China (62002120), Innovation Program of Shanghai Municipal Education Commission (2021-01-07-00-08-E00101) and the "Digital Silk Road" Shanghai International Joint Lab of Trustworthy Intelligent Software (22510750100). Part of this work was done while visiting NTT Research.

J. Luo—Partially supported by NSF grants CNS-1936825 (CAREER), CNS-2026774, a JP Morgan AI Research Award, a Cisco Research Award, and a Simons Collaboration on the Theory of Algorithmic Fairness. Part of this work was done during an internship at NTT Research.

ⓒ International Association for Cryptologic Research 2023
C. Hazay and M. Stam (Eds.): EUROCRYPT 2023, LNCS 14006, pp. 637–668, 2023.
https://doi.org/10.1007/978-3-031-30620-4_21

In this work, we focus on pairing-based traitor tracing schemes, where the most efficient schemes achieve $|\mathsf{pk}| \cdot |\mathsf{sk}| \cdot |\mathsf{ct}| = \Theta(N)$, with the classic result of Boneh, Sahai, and Waters (BSW) [6] achieving $|\mathsf{pk}| = |\mathsf{ct}| = O(N^{1/2})$, $|\mathsf{sk}| = O(1)$ as well as a recent work by Zhandry [30] achieving $|\mathsf{pk}| = |\mathsf{ct}| = |\mathsf{sk}| = O(N^{1/3})$.

In view of the state of the art for pairing-based traitor tracing, Zhandry put forth the following conjecture, which captures the community's intuition about the optimal trade-offs for pairing-based traitor tracing:

> For any $a, b, c \geq 0$ such that $a + b + c = 1$, there exists a pairing-based traitor tracing scheme with $|\mathsf{pk}| = O(N^a), |\mathsf{sk}| = O(N^b)$, $|\mathsf{ct}| = O(N^c)$.

He also proved the conjecture for (1) $b = 0, c \geq a$ and (2) $b, c \geq a$ [30]. In light of this conjecture, we consider two open problems in this work. The first is a special case of Zhandry's conjecture:

> Does there exist a traitor tracing scheme with
> $|\mathsf{pk}| = O(N^{2/3}), |\mathsf{ct}| = O(N^{1/3}), |\mathsf{sk}| = O(1)$ from pairings?

Such a scheme would inherit the short ciphertexts and short keys of the aforementioned pairing-based schemes in [6,30]. We note that minimizing secret key size is important in settings where the decryption devices have limited long-term cryptographic storage, and perhaps even more important than minimizing ciphertext overhead, since the total ciphertext size is often dominated by the size of the payload (megabytes) and not the ciphertext overhead coming from the traitor tracing scheme (kilobytes).

The next question challenges the optimality of Zhandry's conjecture:

> Does there exist a traitor tracing scheme with
> $|\mathsf{pk}| \cdot |\mathsf{sk}| \cdot |\mathsf{ct}| = O(N^{1-\delta})$ for some $\delta > 0$ from pairings?

An affirmative answer would indicate that the trade-off suggested in Zhandry's conjecture is far from optimal, and more importantly, that our intuition about pairing-based traitor tracing is in fact flawed!

Traitor Tracing Beyond Pairings. Before we go on to describe our results, we note that from LWE (or obfuscation), we have "optimal" traitor tracing schemes achieving $|\mathsf{pk}| + |\mathsf{sk}| + |\mathsf{ct}| = \mathrm{poly}(\log N)$ [9,12,19]. Nonetheless, we believe there is still tremendous value in obtaining better pairing-based schemes. From a theoretical perspective, we want (i) good traitor tracing from different assumptions; (ii) to understand what's the best parameters we can get from pairings, as also considered in [30]; and (iii) to develop new tracing techniques, and indeed, the LWE-based schemes with $\mathrm{poly}(\log N)$ parameters rely crucially on ideas first developed in earlier pairing-based schemes. From a practical perspective, pairing-based cryptographic schemes are more widely deployed than lattice-based ones (e.g., in blockchain-type applications, and with better libraries, etc.) and for moderately small values of N that arise in applications, could potentially achieve better concrete efficiency than the asymptotically more efficient LWE-based schemes.

Scheme	|pk|	|ct|	|sk|	Assumption	Tracing
folklore + IBE [30]	1	N	1	IBE	public
BN08 [5] *†	1	κ	$N^2\kappa^2$	IBE	private
BP08 [4] *	1	κ	$N^2\kappa$	IBE	private
BSW06 [6]	$\sqrt{N}$	$\sqrt{N}$	1	composite	private
BW06 [8]	$\sqrt{N}$	$\sqrt{N}$	$\sqrt{N}$	composite	public
PLBE + W20 [29]	$\sqrt{N}$	$\sqrt{N}$	1	bi-k-Lin	public
Z20 [30]	$\sqrt[3]{N\kappa^4}$	$\sqrt[3]{N\kappa^4}$	$\sqrt[3]{N\kappa^4}$	GGM	private
this work (§ 3)	$\sqrt[3]{N\kappa}$	$\sqrt[3]{N\kappa}$	κ	bi-k-Lin	private

Fig. 1. Comparison with prior pairing-based traitor tracing schemes for N users, where size L means $\Theta(L)$ group elements plus $O(L)$ bits. Here, κ denotes the statistical security parameter, with statistical error $2^{-\Omega(\kappa)}$. In the "**Assumption**" column, "bi-k-Lin" (bilateral k-Lin) is a strengthening of the k-Linear assumption in prime-order groups (equivalent to k-Linear for symmetric bilinear groups), "composite" stands for assumptions in composite-order symmetric bilinear groups (e.g., subgroup membership assumption), and "GGM" stands for generic group model. * IBE is used to compress pk [30]. † Threshold elimination compiler [30] is applied.

1.1 Our Results

We answer both open problems in the affirmative: we present a pairing-based traitor tracing scheme for N users with

$$|\mathsf{pk}| = |\mathsf{ct}| = O(N^{1/3}), \quad |\mathsf{sk}| = O(1).$$

This is the first pairing-based scheme to achieve $|\mathsf{pk}| \cdot |\mathsf{sk}| \cdot |\mathsf{ct}| = o(N)$. Our construction relies on the (bilateral) k-Lin assumption, and achieves private tracing and full collusion resistance. Our result simultaneously improve upon the sizes of pk, ct in [6] and the size of sk in [30], while further eliminating the reliance on the generic group model (GGM) in the latter work. As in Zhandry's work, the $O(\cdot)$ terms hides factors polynomial in the security parameter. See Fig. 1 for comparison with prior works.

1.2 Technical Overview

We proceed to provide a brief overview of our scheme and a technical comparison with Zhandry's construction [30]. In this overview, for any positive integer N, we define $[N] = \{1, 2, \ldots, N\}$ and $[0, N] = \{0, 1, \ldots, N\}$. Note that $[0] = \emptyset$.

Recap: PLBE and BSW Traitor Tracing. An N private linear broadcast encryption (N-PLBE) [6] is a type of anonymous broadcast encryption where we can revoke decryption capabilities for the first z users. In particular,

– key generation produces a key sk for each user identity $i \in [N]$;

- encryption takes as input a private index $z \in [0, N]$ and a message m to produce a ciphertext ct;
- decryption returns m if $i > z$, or equivalently, $i \notin [z]$.

The security requirements for PLBE are as follows:

- message-hiding: the message m is hidden given unauthorized keys;
- index-hiding: encryptions of $(z-1, m)$ and (z, m) are computationally indistinguishable given all secret keys for identities $i \neq z$.

Starting from an N-PLBE, BSW traitor tracing scheme [6] with identity space $[N]$ works as follows:

- The public key and secret keys are the same as for PLBE;
- An encryption of m is a PLBE encryption of m with $z = 0$.

Correctness is straight-forward: every secret key satisfies $i > 0$, or equivalently, $i \notin [0] = \emptyset$, and is authorized to recover m.

Given a decoder D with distinguishing advantage ε, we can identify a traitor $i^* \in [N]$ with probability negligibly close to 1 as follows: for $i = 0, 1, \ldots, N$, revoke the decryption capabilities of the first i users by feeding the decoder PLBE encryption of (i, m). We know that the advantage of D is ε for $i = 0$ (by the fact that decoder is "good") and negligible for $i = N$ (by message-hiding). Therefore, there exists $i^* \in [N]$ such that there is a significant drop –at least roughly ε/N– in the distinguishing advantage of the decoder from $i^* - 1$ to i^*; index-hiding ensures that i^* is a traitor.

The state of the art for N-PLBE achieves parameter sizes

$$|\mathsf{pk}| = O(N^{1/2}), \quad |\mathsf{ct}| = O(N^{1/2}), \quad |\mathsf{sk}| = O(1)$$

from the bilateral k-Lin, via functional encryption for quadratic functions [3,29]. The resulting traitor tracing scheme achieves the same parameter sizes.

Our Starting Point: Revocable PLBE. We will explain our traitor tracing scheme using a generalization of PLBE which we refer to as (N_1, N_2) revocable private linear broadcast encryption $((N_1, N_2)$-rPLBE). In an (N_1, N_2)-rPLBE,

- key generation takes as input a user identity $(i_1, i_2) \in [N_1] \times [N_2]$ to produce a key sk;
- encryption takes as input a private index $z \in [0, N_1]$, a private set $S \subseteq [N_1] \times [N_2]$ of size at most N_2, and a message m to produce a ciphertext ct;
- decryption returns m if $(i_1, i_2) \notin ([z] \times [N_2]) \cup S$.

This allows us to revoke the decryption capability of the first $z \cdot N_2$ users as well as additional (at most) N_2 users in the set S. We call them *index-revocation* and *set-revocation*, respectively. Accordingly, the security requirements for rPLBE are generalized as follows:

- message-hiding: the message m is hidden given only unauthorized keys.

- index-hiding: encryptions of $(z-1, S, m)$ and (z, S, m) are indistinguishable, even given secret keys for all identities in $\{(i_1, i_2) \in [N_1] \times [N_2] : i_1 \neq z\} \cup S$.
- set-hiding: encryptions of (z, S_0, m) and (z, S_1, m) with $S_0 \subset S_1$ are indistinguishable, even given secret keys for all identities $(i_1, i_2) \notin S_1 \setminus S_0$.

Note that PLBE corresponds to the special case $N_2 = 1$ and $S = \emptyset$ during encryption. In this case, the identity is of the form $(i_1, 1)$; index-hiding reduces to that for PLBE; set-hiding becomes dummy since we always have $S_0 = S_1 = \emptyset$.

Tracing Using rPLBE. Starting from an (N_1, N_2)-rPLBE, we build a traitor tracing scheme with identity space $[N_1] \times [N_2]$ as follows:

- The public key and secret keys are the same as for rPLBE;
- An encryption of m is a rPLBE encryption of m with $z = 0, S = \emptyset$.

Correctness is straight-forward.

Given a decoder D with distinguishing advantage ε, our goal is to identify a traitor $(i_1^*, i_2^*) \in [N_1] \times [N_2]$ with probability negligibly close to 1. The tracing strategy proceeds in two steps:

Step 1: Identifying i_1^* via Index-Revocation. For $i_1 = 0, 1, \ldots, N_1$, we revoke the decryption capabilities of the first $i_1 \cdot N_2$ users by feeding the decoder rPLBE encryptions of $(i_1, \emptyset, m)$. As with BSW traitor tracing with PLBE, there exists $i_1^* \in [N_1]$ such that there is a significant drop –at least roughly ε/N_1– in the distinguishing advantage of the decoder from $i_1^* - 1$ to i_1^*, upon which we know that one of the users in $\{i_1^*\} \times [N_2]$ is a traitor by index-hiding security (applied to $z = i_1^*, S = \emptyset$).

Step 2: Identifying i_2^* via Set-Revocation. Next, for $i_2 = 0, \ldots, N_2$, we revoke the decryption capabilities of the first i_2 users in $\{i_1^*\} \times [N_2]$ by feeding the decoder rPLBE encryptions of $(i_1^*-1, S_{i_1^*, i_2}, m)$ and $(i_1^*, S_{i_1^*, i_2}, m)$, where $S_{i_1^*, i_2}$ is $\{(i_1^*, j) : j \in [i_2]\}$, and define ε_{i_2} to be the difference between the distinguishing advantages for the two ciphertext distributions. We begin with the following bounds on ε_0 and ε_{N_2} (corresponding to $i_2 = 0$ and $i_2 = N_2$ respectively):

(1) $\varepsilon_0 \gtrsim \varepsilon/N_1$. This follows from Step 1 and the fact that $S_{i_1^*, 0} = \emptyset$.
(2) ε_{N_2} is negligible. This follows from applying index-hiding to $z = i_1^*$ and $S = S_{i_1^*, N_2}$, and holds even when the adversary gets the secret keys for all possible identities since $\{(i_1, i_2) \in [N_1] \times [N_2] : i_1 \neq i_1^*\} \cup S_{i_1^*, N_2} = [N_1] \times [N_2]$.

Therefore, there exists $i_2^* \in [N_2]$ such that $\varepsilon_{i_2^*} - \varepsilon_{i_2^*-1} \gtrsim \varepsilon/N_1 N_2$. By set-hiding applied to $z = i_1^* - 1, S_0 = S_{i_1^*, i_2^*-1}, S_1 = S_{i_1^*, i_2^*}$ and $z = i_1^*, S_0 = S_{i_1^*, i_2^*-1}$, $S_1 = S_{i_1^*, i_2^*}$, the user (i_1^*, i_2^*) must be a traitor. Note that, for Step 2, we always have $|S| \leq N_2$.

Implementing Set-Revocation and Set-Hiding. For set-revocation, we will need to relax the syntax for (N_1, N_2)-rPLBE as follows (following "mixed functional encryption" in [19]):

- encrypting to arbitrary sets S requires knowledge of msk;
- encrypting to $S = \emptyset$ only requires mpk.

As a result of this relaxation, our traitor tracing scheme only achieves private tracing, as is also the case in [19] and in Zhandry's work [30].

One-Ciphertext Security. Consider the following construction for set-revocation (i.e., ignoring the index-revocation) for N_2 users (cf. Step 2 of our tracing) based on any negated-IBE scheme where a key for id $\in \{0,1\}^\kappa$ can decrypt a ciphertext for id$' \in \{0,1\}^\kappa$ iff id $\neq$ id$'$.

- The public key consists of N_2 independent public keys for negated-IBE $\mathsf{mpk}_1, \ldots, \mathsf{mpk}_{N_2}$.
- The secret key for user i_2 is a random $u_{i_2} \leftarrow \{0,1\}^\kappa$, together with a negated-IBE key for u_{i_2} w.r.t. mpk_{i_2}. This means that u_{i_2} is perfectly hidden from the decoder if user i_2 is honest.
- To encrypt to $S \subseteq [N_2]$, we provide N_2 negated-IBE ciphertexts for identities $r_1, \ldots, r_{N_2}$ w.r.t. $\mathsf{mpk}_1, \ldots, \mathsf{mpk}_{N_2}$ respectively, where $r_{i_2} \leftarrow \{0,1\}^\kappa$ if $i_2 \notin S$, and $r_{i_2} = u_{i_2}$ if $i_2 \in S$.

Correctness is straight-forward: $\Pr[r_{i_2} \neq u_{i_2} : r_{i_2} \leftarrow \{0,1\}^\kappa] = 1 - 2^{-\kappa}$. Set-hiding for a single ciphertext follows from the fact that (1) if the adversary does not see the key for user i_2, then u_{i_2} is statistically random and (2) we always have N_2 negated-IBE ciphertexts (which hides $|S|$).

Multi-ciphertext Security via Threshold Broadcast. In order to achieve set-hiding for multiple ciphertexts, as is necessary for tracing, we adopt Zhandry's "threshold broadcast" technique. We will rely on an *approximated* version of negated-IBE where id $\neq$ id$'$ (i.e., $\mathsf{wt}(\mathsf{id} \oplus \mathsf{id}') > 0$) is replaced with $\mathsf{wt}(\mathsf{id} \oplus \mathsf{id}') \geq 2\kappa/5$ where $\mathsf{wt}(\cdot)$ corresponds to Hamming weight. To revoke a user $i_2 \in S$ while preserving set-hiding, we will sample r_i from a carefully-designed distribution of bit-strings close to u_i in Hamming distance, where the distribution depends adaptively on the adversary (cf. Lemma 1 in Sect. 3.2); for this reason, we will require adaptive security w.r.t. id.

Instantiating rPLBE: Warm-Up. Next, we translate the problem of building an (N_1, N_2)-rPLBE to a problem about functional encryption, specifically, that of attribute-based functional encryption (AB-FE) [1]. In AB-FE, a ciphertext is associated with a private attribute z and a public attribute x, a key with a function f and a predicate P, and decryption returns $f(z)$ if $P(x)$ is true. Specifically, an (N_1, N_2)-rPLBE implementing threshold-broadcast-based set-revocation (sketched above) would follow from AB-FE for

$$f_{i_1}^{\mathsf{comp}}(\overbrace{j_1, m}^{z}) = \begin{cases} m, & \text{if } i_1 > j_1; \\ 0, & \text{otherwise;} \end{cases}$$

$$P_{i_2,u}^{\text{tbe}}(\overbrace{r_1,\ldots,r_{N_2}}^{x}) = \begin{cases} 1, & \text{if } \text{wt}(r_{i_2} \oplus u) \geq 2\kappa/5; \\ 0, & \text{otherwise;} \end{cases}$$

where $f_{i_1}^{\text{comp}}$ implements index-revocation and index-hiding, and $P_{i_2,u}^{\text{tbe}}$, set-revocation. Recall that set-hiding relies on the distribution of $r_1,\ldots,r_{N_2}$.

The recent work of Abdalla, Catalano, Gay, and Ursu (ACGU) [1] presented an AB-FE scheme based on the k-Lin assumption for the setting where f corresponds to inner product and P corresponds to read-once span programs. It is easy to see that we can implement $f_{i_1}^{\text{comp}}$ as an inner product over vectors of length $O(N_1)$, and $P_{i_2,u}^{\text{tbe}}$ as a read-once span program of size $O(N_2\kappa)$. Combined with the ACGU result, we obtain an (N_1, N_2)-rPLBE with

$$|\text{pk}| = O(N_1 + N_2\kappa), \quad |\text{ct}| = O(N_1 + N_2\kappa), \quad |\text{sk}| = O(N_2\kappa).$$

The parameter sizes are essentially the sum of those for (i) inner product FE for vectors of length $\ell = N_1$, namely $|\text{pk}| = |\text{ct}| = O(\ell), |\text{sk}| = O(1)$, and (ii) ABE for read-once span programs of size $s = N_2\kappa$, namely $|\text{pk}| = |\text{ct}| = |\text{sk}| = O(s)$.

Instantiating rPLBE: Ours. We present an (N_1, N_2)-rPLBE based on (bilateral) k-Lin achieving shorter parameters

$$|\text{pk}| = O(\underline{N_1^{1/2}} + N_2\kappa), \quad |\text{ct}| = O(\underline{N_1^{1/2}} + N_2\kappa), \quad |\text{sk}| = O(\underline{\kappa}),$$

we highlight the improvements by underlines. Setting $N_1 = N^{2/3}, N_2 = N^{1/3}$ yields our main result. We achieve shorter parameters as follows:

- To reduce the dependency on N_1 in pk, ct to $N_1^{1/2}$, we implement $f_{i_1}^{\text{comp}}$ using quadratic functions over inputs of length $N_1^{1/2}$, following [3,6].
- To reduce $|\text{sk}|$ to $O(\kappa)$, we observe that the span program computing $P_{i_2,u}^{\text{tbe}}$ is κ-local, that is, it depends only on κ bits of its input and show that for such span programs, the ABE key size can be decreased to $O(\kappa)$.

To put these two pieces together, we combine the ACGU construction which only supports linear functions over the private attribute z with techniques from functional encryption for quadratic functions [29].

Achieving Adaptive Security from k-Lin. We need an additional idea to achieve adaptive security w.r.t. r's, which is necessary for our traitor tracing strategy. The challenge lies in the fact that current techniques for realizing ABE adaptive security from the k-Lin assumption via dual system encryption methodology [27] rely on the guarantee (provided by the ABE security game) that the predicate P is never satisfied to switch the secret key distribution in the security proof. In the AB-FE security game, this guarantee goes away. To address this challenge, we observe that it suffices to construct AB-FE secure under a selective choice of z and an adaptive choice of x, since z (ignoring the payload m) comes from a polynomial-size domain. When a key query for f, P comes along, we will decide whether to switch the secret key distribution depending on $f(z)$. More precisely, the security experiment requires that an adversary selectively specifies z_0, z_1, we only switch the secret key distribution (to a "semi-functional" key) if $f(z_0) \neq f(z_1)$, for which $P(x)$ must be false.

Comparison with Zhandry's $O(N^{1/3})$ Scheme. We provide a simplified overview of Zhandry's traitor tracing scheme [30]. The first step is a traitor tracing scheme for $N_1 N_2$ users with parameters:

$$|\mathsf{pk}| = O(N_2), \quad |\mathsf{ct}| = O(N_2 \kappa), \quad |\mathsf{sk}| = O(N_1 + N_2 \kappa).$$

The underlying scheme is a variant of an (N_1, N_2)-rPLBE, which is adaptively secure in the generic group model.[1]

Observe that the total parameter size for this scheme is $O(N_1 + N_2)$, similar to that based on ACGU, whereas we achieve total parameter size $O(N_1^{1/2} + N_2)$. The construction uses ideas from mixed bit matching encryption [18] (MBME), which can be instantiated from inner product predicate encryption.[2] In contrast, we crucially rely on techniques from quadratic FE to achieve the square-root dependency on N_1.

The second step in [30] is to amplify this to a traitor tracing scheme for $N_1 N_2 N_3$ users with parameters:

$$|\mathsf{pk}| = O(N_2), \quad |\mathsf{ct}| = O(N_2 \kappa + N_3), \quad |\mathsf{sk}| = O(N_1 + N_2 \kappa).$$

Setting $N_1 = N_2 = N_3 = N^{1/3}$ yields a traitor tracing scheme for N users with $|\mathsf{pk}| = |\mathsf{ct}| = |\mathsf{sk}| = O(N^{1/3})$.

Note that in addition to achieving better parameters and assumptions, our approach also streamlines Zhandry's approach, eliminating the use of MBME and risky tracing [18] and the second step above. Moreover, our scheme supports partially public tracing, in the sense that we can publicly identify a prefix

---

[1] In a bit more detail, the construction starts with a variant of $(O(1), N_2)$-rPLBE with parameters

$$|\mathsf{pk}| = O(N_2), \quad |\mathsf{ct}| = O(N_2 \kappa), \quad |\mathsf{sk}| = O(1),$$

which yields a "$1/N_1$-risky" traitor tracing scheme for $N_1 N_2$ users following [18]. That is, tracing succeeds with probability $1/N_1$. This is then amplified to a standard traitor tracing scheme with a blow-up in sk.

[2] In MBME, ciphertexts are associated with $(z_1, \ldots, z_\ell) \in \{0,1\}^\ell$ and keys with $(y_1, \ldots, y_\ell) \in \{0,1\}^\ell$ and decryption is possible iff

$$\bigwedge_{i=1}^\ell z_i \vee y_i = 1.$$

Security requires both attribute and function hiding. MBME for ℓ-bit vectors can be instantiated from attribute-hiding function-hiding inner product predicate encryption for $O(\ell)$-dimensional vectors, since

$$\bigwedge_{i=1}^\ell z_i \vee y_i = 1 \iff \sum_{i=1}^\ell (1 - z_i)(1 - y_i) \stackrel{?}{=} 0.$$

$i_1^* \in [N_1]$ specifying a subset of $N_2 = N^{1/3}$ identities, one of which must be a traitor (via PLBE). This could be useful in applications where identity prefixes constitute important information, like country of origin or name of company.

Nonetheless, we stress that our results do not completely subsume those in [30]. In particular, the latter achieves some parameter trade-offs that we do not immediately achieve using our techniques, for instance, $|\mathsf{pk}| = O(1)$, $|\mathsf{sk}| = O(N), |\mathsf{ct}| = O(1)$ or $|\mathsf{pk}| = O(N^{1/4}), |\mathsf{sk}| = O(1), |\mathsf{ct}| = O(N^{3/4})$. Also, we do not present any broadcast-and-trace schemes.

1.3   Discussion

Open Problems. We conclude with several open problems:

- Combined with Zhandry's conjecture which asserts that we should be able to achieve full range of parameters with the same $|\mathsf{pk}| \cdot |\mathsf{sk}| \cdot |\mathsf{ct}|$, our result raises the tantalizing possibility of a pairing-based traitor tracing scheme with total parameter size $O(N^{2/9})$. In fact, it seems entirely plausible to have a pairing-based traitor tracing scheme with total parameter size $O(N^{1/4})$.
- Can we extend our techniques to broadcast with tracing following [20]? Or to public tracing with smaller parameters than in [6]? For public tracing from pairings, we conjecture that BSW is essentially optimal, namely we need $\min(|\mathsf{ct}|, |\mathsf{pk}| \cdot |\mathsf{sk}|) = \Omega(\sqrt{N})$.

Organization. We provide preliminaries in Sect. 2. Our traitor tracing based on AB-FE is given out in Sect. 3. We develop the AB-FE scheme required by the traitor tracing in Sect. 4.

2   Preliminaries

Notations. We denote by $s \leftarrow S$ the fact that s is picked uniformly at random from a finite set S. We use $\approx_s$ to denote two distributions being statistically indistinguishable, and $\approx_c$ to denote two distributions being computationally indistinguishable. We use lower-case boldfaced letters to denote *row* vectors and upper-case boldfaced letters to denote matrices. We use $\mathbf{e}_i$ to denote the ith elementary row vector (with 1 at the i'th position and 0 elsewhere, and the total length of the vector specified by the context). For any positive integer N, we use $[N]$ to denote $\{1, 2, \ldots, N\}$ and $[0, N]$ to denote $\{0, 1, \ldots, N\}$.

2.1   Prime-Order Bilinear Groups

A group generation algorithm $\mathcal{G}$ takes as input the security parameter 1^λ and outputs a description $\mathbb{G} := (p, \mathbb{G}_1, \mathbb{G}_2, \mathbb{G}_T, e)$, where p is a prime, $\mathbb{G}_1$, $\mathbb{G}_2$ and $\mathbb{G}_T$ are cyclic groups of order p, and $e : \mathbb{G}_1 \times \mathbb{G}_2 \rightarrow \mathbb{G}_T$ is a non-degenerate bilinear map. We require that the group operations in $\mathbb{G}_1$, $\mathbb{G}_2$, $\mathbb{G}_T$ and the bilinear map e be computable in deterministic polynomial time in λ. Let $g_1 \in \mathbb{G}_1$,

$g_2 \in \mathbb{G}_2$, and $g_T = e(g_1, g_2) \in \mathbb{G}_T$ be the respective generators. We employ the *implicit representation* of group elements: for a matrix $\mathbf{M}$ over $\mathbb{Z}_p$, we define $[\mathbf{M}]_1 := g_1^{\mathbf{M}}, [\mathbf{M}]_2 := g_2^{\mathbf{M}}, [\mathbf{M}]_T := g_T^{\mathbf{M}}$, where exponentiation is carried out component-wise. Also, given $[\mathbf{A}]_1, [\mathbf{B}]_2$, we let $e([\mathbf{A}]_1, [\mathbf{B}]_2) = [\mathbf{AB}]_T$. We recall the matrix Diffie–Hellman (MDDH) assumption in $\mathbb{G}_1$ [14]:

Assumption 1 (MDDH$_{k,\ell}^d$). *Let $k, \ell, d \in \mathbb{N}$. We say that the* MDDH$_{k,\ell}^d$ *assumption holds in $\mathbb{G}_1$ if for all p.p.t. adversary $\mathcal{A}$,*

$$\mathsf{Adv}_{\mathcal{A}}^{\mathrm{MDDH}_{k,\ell}^d}(\lambda) := \big| \Pr[\mathcal{A}(1^\lambda, \mathbb{G}, [\mathbf{A}]_1, \boxed{[\mathbf{SA}]_1}) = 1]$$
$$- \Pr[\mathcal{A}(1^\lambda, \mathbb{G}, [\mathbf{A}]_1, \boxed{[\mathbf{C}]_1}) = 1] \big|$$

is negligible in λ, where $\mathbb{G} := (p, \mathbb{G}_1, \mathbb{G}_2, \mathbb{G}_T, e) \leftarrow \mathcal{G}(1^\lambda)$, $\mathbf{A} \leftarrow \mathbb{Z}_p^{k \times \ell}$, $\mathbf{S} \leftarrow \mathbb{Z}_p^{d \times k}$, $\mathbf{C} \leftarrow \mathbb{Z}_p^{d \times \ell}$.

The MDDH assumption in $\mathbb{G}_2$ can be defined analogously. Escala *et al.* [14] showed that

$$k\text{-Lin} \Rightarrow \mathrm{MDDH}_{k,k+1}^1 \Rightarrow \mathrm{MDDH}_{k,\ell}^d \quad \forall k, d \geq 1.$$

When $\ell \leq k$, the MDDH$_{k,\ell}^d$ assumption holds unconditionally.

Assumption 2 (bilateral MDDH$_{k,\ell}^d$). *Let $k, \ell, d \in \mathbb{N}$. We say that the bilateral* MDDH$_{k,\ell}^d$ *assumption holds in $\mathbb{G}_1, \mathbb{G}_2$ if for all p.p.t. adversary $\mathcal{A}$,*

$$\mathsf{Adv}_{\mathcal{A}}^{\mathrm{biMDDH}_{k,\ell}^d}(\lambda) := \big| \Pr[\mathcal{A}(1^\lambda, \mathbb{G}, [\mathbf{A}]_1, \boxed{[\mathbf{SA}]_1}, [\mathbf{A}]_2, \boxed{[\mathbf{SA}]_2}) = 1]$$
$$- \Pr[\mathcal{A}(1^\lambda, \mathbb{G}, [\mathbf{A}]_1, \boxed{[\mathbf{C}]_1}, [\mathbf{A}]_2, \boxed{[\mathbf{C}]_2}) = 1] \big|$$

is negligible in λ, where $\mathbb{G} := (p, \mathbb{G}_1, \mathbb{G}_2, \mathbb{G}_T, e) \leftarrow \mathcal{G}(1^\lambda)$, $\mathbf{A} \leftarrow \mathbb{Z}_p^{k \times \ell}$, $\mathbf{S} \leftarrow \mathbb{Z}_p^{d \times k}$, $\mathbf{C} \leftarrow \mathbb{Z}_p^{d \times \ell}$.

The bilateral MDDH assumption is a strengthening of the MDDH assumption for asymmetric bilinear groups. It cannot hold for $k = 1$ for reasons similar to why DDH cannot hold in symmetric bilinear groups. An implication similar to that due to Escala *et al.* [14] holds:

$$\text{bilateral } k\text{-Lin} \Rightarrow \text{bilateral } \mathrm{MDDH}_{k,k+1}^1 \Rightarrow \text{bilateral } \mathrm{MDDH}_{k,\ell}^d \quad \forall k \geq 2, d \geq 1.$$

By the implication, we will work with (bilateral) MDDH$_{k,k+1}^1$. This is sufficient for deriving our results based on (bilateral) k-Lin.

2.2 Traitor Tracing

We follow the definition in [30]. A traitor tracing scheme with key space $\mathcal{K}$ consists of four p.p.t. algorithms:

- $\mathsf{Gen}(1^\lambda, 1^N) \to (\mathsf{pk}, \mathsf{tk}, \{\mathsf{sk}_i\}_{i\in[N]})$: The key generation algorithm takes the security parameter 1^λ and the number 1^N of users as input. It outputs a public key pk, a tracing key tk, and secret keys $\{\mathsf{sk}_i\}_{i\in[N]}$ (one for each user).
- $\mathsf{Enc}(\mathsf{pk}) \to (\mathsf{ct}, k)$: The encapsulation algorithm takes pk as input and outputs a ciphertext ct and an encapsulated key $k \in \mathcal{K}$.
- $\mathsf{Dec}(\mathsf{pk}, \mathsf{sk}_i, \mathsf{ct}) \to k$: The decapsulation algorithm takes $\mathsf{pk}, \mathsf{sk}_i, \mathsf{ct}$ as input and outputs a decapsulated key k.
- $\mathsf{Trace}^D(\mathsf{pk}, \mathsf{tk}, 1^{1/\varepsilon}) \to i^*$: The tracing algorithm takes pk, tk, and the error parameter $1^{1/\varepsilon}$ as input. It has oracle access to a decoder D and outputs a traitor identity $i^* \in [N]$ or $\perp$.

Correctness. We require that for all $c \in \mathbb{N}$, there exists a negligible function $\varepsilon(\lambda)$ such that for all $\lambda \in \mathbb{N}$, $N \in [\lambda^c]$, $i \in [N]$,

$$\Pr\left[\begin{array}{c}(\mathsf{pk}, \mathsf{tk}, \{\mathsf{sk}_i\}_{i\in[N]}) \leftarrow \mathsf{Gen}(1^\lambda, 1^N) \\ (\mathsf{ct}, k) \leftarrow \mathsf{Enc}(\mathsf{pk})\end{array} : \mathsf{Dec}(\mathsf{pk}, \mathsf{sk}_i, \mathsf{ct}) = k\right] \geq 1 - \varepsilon(\lambda).$$

Tracing Security. The scheme is secure if for all $\varepsilon(\lambda) > 0$ such that $1/\varepsilon(\lambda)$ is polynomially bounded, all efficient adversary $\mathcal{A}$ wins the following game with negligible probability:

- Launch $\mathcal{A}(1^\lambda)$ and receive 1^N from it. Run $(\mathsf{pk}, \mathsf{tk}, \{\mathsf{sk}_i\}_{i\in[N]}) \leftarrow \mathsf{Gen}(1^\lambda, 1^N)$ and send pk to $\mathcal{A}$.
- $\mathcal{A}$ adaptively queries keys for $i_q \in [N]$. Upon this query, send sk_{i_q} to $\mathcal{A}$. This stage can be repeated as many times as $\mathcal{A}$ wants. Let T be the set of i_q's for which the key is queried.
- $\mathcal{A}$ outputs a decoder D. Run $i^* \leftarrow \mathsf{Trace}^D(\mathsf{pk}, \mathsf{tk}, 1^{1/\varepsilon(\lambda)})$. $\mathcal{A}$ wins if

$$\Pr\left[b \leftarrow \{0,1\}, k_0 \leftarrow \mathcal{K}, (\mathsf{ct}, k_1) \leftarrow \mathsf{Enc}(\mathsf{pk}) : D^*(\mathsf{ct}, k_b) = b\right] - \frac{1}{2} \geq \varepsilon(\lambda)$$

and $i^* = \perp$, or if $i^* \notin T \cup \{\perp\}$.

Note that tracing security implies standard semantic security, cf. [30, Remark 3].

2.3   Attribute-Based Functional Encryption

An attribute-based functional encryption (AB-FE) for

function class $\mathcal{F} = \{f : \mathcal{Z} \to \{0,1\}^*\}$ and predicate $P : \mathcal{X} \times \mathcal{Y} \to \{0,1\}$

consists of four p.p.t. algorithms:

- $\mathsf{Setup}(1^\lambda, \mathcal{F}, \mathcal{Z}, \mathcal{X}, \mathcal{Y}) \to (\mathsf{mpk}, \mathsf{msk})$: The set-up algorithm takes the security parameter 1^λ and the domains $\mathcal{F}, \mathcal{Z}, \mathcal{X}, \mathcal{Y}$ as input, and outputs a master public/secret key pair $(\mathsf{mpk}, \mathsf{msk})$.

- KeyGen(mpk, msk, f, y) → sk: The key generation algorithm takes mpk, msk, $f \in \mathcal{F}$, $y \in \mathcal{Y}$ as input, and outputs a secret key sk.
- Enc(mpk, z, x) → ct: The encryption algorithm takes mpk, $z \in \mathcal{Z}$, $x \in \mathcal{X}$ as input, and outputs a ciphertext ct.
- Dec(mpk, sk, f, y, ct, x) → d: The decryption algorithm takes mpk, sk, f, y, ct, x as input and outputs $d \in \{0, 1\}^*$.

Correctness. For all $\lambda \in \mathbb{N}$, $\mathcal{F}$, $\mathcal{Z}$, $\mathcal{X}$, $\mathcal{Y}$, $f \in \mathcal{F}$, $y \in \mathcal{Y}$, $z \in \mathcal{Z}$, $x \in \mathcal{X}$ such that $P(x, y) = 1$, we require

$$\Pr\left[\begin{array}{c} (\mathsf{mpk}, \mathsf{msk}) \leftarrow \mathsf{Setup}(1^\lambda, \mathcal{F}, \mathcal{Z}, \mathcal{X}, \mathcal{Y}) \\ \mathsf{sk} \leftarrow \mathsf{KeyGen}(\mathsf{mpk}, \mathsf{msk}, f, y) : \mathsf{Dec}(\mathsf{mpk}, \mathsf{sk}, f, y, \mathsf{ct}, x) = f(z) \\ \mathsf{ct} \leftarrow \mathsf{Enc}(\mathsf{mpk}, z, x) \end{array}\right] = 1.$$

Our scheme will be based on pairing, for which we require f to take values in $\mathbb{Z}_p$ and relax the correctness requirement so that Dec only needs to output $[f(z)]_T$.

Indistinguishability Security with Adaptive x and Semi-adaptive z. For all p.p.t. stateful $\mathcal{A}$, we require

$$\Pr\left[\begin{array}{c} b \leftarrow \{0, 1\} \\ (\mathcal{F}, \mathcal{Z}, \mathcal{X}, \mathcal{Y}) \leftarrow \mathcal{A}(1^\lambda) \\ (\mathsf{mpk}, \mathsf{msk}) \leftarrow \mathsf{Setup}(1^\lambda, \mathcal{F}, \mathcal{Z}, \mathcal{X}, \mathcal{Y}) \\ (z_0, z_1) \leftarrow \mathcal{A}(\mathsf{mpk}) \\ x \leftarrow \mathcal{A}^{\mathsf{KeyGen}(\mathsf{mpk}, \mathsf{msk}, \cdot, \cdot)}() \\ \mathsf{ct} \leftarrow \mathsf{Enc}(\mathsf{mpk}, z_b, x) \\ : \quad \mathcal{A}^{\mathsf{KeyGen}(\mathsf{mpk}, \mathsf{msk}, \cdot, \cdot)}(\mathsf{ct}) = b \end{array}\right] - \frac{1}{2}$$

to be negligible, where for each query (f_q, y_q) made to KeyGen by $\mathcal{A}$, it is required that $f_q(z_0) = f_q(z_1)$ or $P(x, y_q) = 0$.

We also consider a strengthened notion with partially adaptive z, where part of z_0, z_1 can be chosen with x, after querying arbitrarily many keys.

3 Building Traitor Tracing

We define threshold broadcast, private linear broadcast encryption (TB-PLBE), a certain kind of AB-FE, and use it to construct our traitor tracing scheme. We provide a construction for AB-FE that can be instantiated to TB-PLBE in Sect. 4; the instantiation can be found in Sect. 4.5.

3.1 TB-PLBE

We define TB-PLBE as an AB-FE (Sect. 2.3) for the function class

$$\mathcal{Z} = [0, N_1] \times \mathbb{Z}_p, \qquad \mathcal{F}_{N_1}^{\mathsf{comp}} = \left\{ f_{i_1}^{\mathsf{comp}} : [0, N_1] \times \mathbb{Z}_p \to \mathbb{Z}_p \mid i_1 \in [N_1] \right\},$$

$$\forall i_1 \in [N_1], \quad f_{i_1}^{\mathrm{comp}}(j_1, m) = \begin{cases} m, & \text{if } i_1 > j_1; \\ 0, & \text{otherwise;} \end{cases}$$

and the predicate

$$\mathcal{X} = (\{0,1\}^\kappa)^{N_2}, \qquad \mathcal{Y} = [N_2] \times \{0,1\}^\kappa,$$

$$P_{N_2,\kappa}^{\mathrm{tbe}}\big((r_1,\dots,r_{N_2}),(i_2,u)\big) = \begin{cases} 1, & \text{if } \mathsf{wt}(r_{i_2} \oplus u) \geq 2\kappa/5; \\ 0, & \text{otherwise.} \end{cases}$$

In Setup, the functionality $(\mathcal{F}_{N_1}^{\mathrm{comp}}, \mathcal{Z}, \mathcal{X}, \mathcal{Y})$ is represented by $(1^{N_1}, 1^{N_2})$. In KeyGen and Dec, the function $f_{i_1}^{\mathrm{comp}}$ is represented by i_1. We need a TB-PLBE secure under adaptively chosen $j_1, r_1, \dots, r_{N_2}$ and semi-adaptively chosen m (cf. Sect. 2.3). We will present a construction of TB-PLBE in Sect. 4 that is secure under adaptively chosen $r_1, \dots, r_{N_2}$ and selectively chosen j_1, m based on bi-k-Lin; the fact that $N_1 = \mathrm{poly}(\lambda)$ implies security against adaptively chosen j_1 by a standard guessing argument.

Remark 1 (relation with rPLBE). We will build traitor tracing from TB-PLBE directly in Sect. 3.2. For completeness, we briefly sketch how to implement (N_1, N_2)-rPLBE (with set-revocation suitable for our tracing algorithm) as outlined in Sect. 1.2 from TB-PLBE which is a AB-FE for $\mathcal{F}_{N_1}^{\mathrm{comp}}$ and $P_{N_2,\kappa}^{\mathrm{tbe}}$:

- The public key are the same as TB-PLBE; the secret key for user $(i_1, i_2) \in [N_1] \times [N_2]$ consists of a TB-PLBE key for $(i_1; i_2, u_{i_1,i_2})$ where u_{i_1,i_2} is fresh for each user.
- An encryption of (z, S, m) where $S \subseteq \{i_1^*\} \times [N_2]$ is a TB-PLBE encryption of $(z; (r_1, \dots, r_{N_2}), m)$ where we sample r_{i_2} uniformly for $(i_1^*, i_2) \notin S$ but sample r_{i_2} according to the distribution $\rho_{i_1^*,i_2}$ for $(i_1^*, i_2) \in S$ described in Sect. 3.2.

Revocation mechanisms are as follows:

- The index-revocation for z relies on the function $\mathcal{F}_{N_1}^{\mathrm{comp}}$ of TB-PLBE: $i_1 > z$ iff $(i_1, i_2) \notin [z] \times [N_2]$; index-hiding follows from the security of TB-PLBE, namely z is hidden.
- The set-revocation S relies on the predicate $P_{N_2,\kappa}^{\mathrm{tbe}}$ and property of the distribution ρ_{i_1,i_2}: this ensures that $\mathsf{wt}(r_{i_2} \oplus u_{i_1^*,i_2}) < 2\kappa/5$ for all $(i_1^*, i_2) \in S$. However, set-hiding require an additional property of those distributions: distributions ρ_{i_1,i_2} are quite close to random distribution without the knowledge of u_{i_1,i_2}. See Lemma 1 for the two properties of ρ_{i_1,i_2}.

Note that we need the knowledge of u_{i_1,i_2} for finding ρ_{i_1,i_2} (see algorithm Learn in Lemma 1), therefore the encryption need secret key when $S \neq \emptyset$ for tracing (Step 2).

3.2   Traitor Tracing from TB-PLBE

Traitor Tracing Scheme. Let TBPLBE be a TB-PLBE scheme as defined in Sect. 3.1. Our traitor tracing scheme works as follows:

- Gen$(1^\lambda, 1^N)$ sets κ to be any $\omega(\log \lambda)$ function that is polynomially bounded by λ, and $N_1 = N^{2/3}\kappa^{2/3}$, $N_2 = N^{1/3}\kappa^{-1/3}$. Treating the identity space $[N]$ as $[N_1] \times [N_2]$, the algorithm samples $u_{i_1,i_2} \leftarrow \{0,1\}^\kappa$ for all $i_1 \in [N_1]$ and $i_2 \in [N_2]$, runs

$$(\mathsf{tpmpk}, \mathsf{tpmsk}) \leftarrow \mathsf{TBPLBE.Setup}(1^\lambda, 1^{N_1}, 1^{N_2}),$$

$$\mathsf{tpsk}_{i_1,i_2} \leftarrow \mathsf{TBPLBE.KeyGen}(\mathsf{tpmsk}, i_1, (i_2, u_{i_1,i_2})),$$

$$\mathsf{sk}_{i_1,i_2} \leftarrow (\mathsf{tpsk}_{i_1,i_2}, i_1, (i_2, u_{i_1,i_2})), \qquad \forall i_1 \in [N_1], i_2 \in [N_2],$$

and outputs

$$\mathsf{pk} = \mathsf{tpmpk}, \quad \mathsf{tk} = \{u_{i_1,i_2}\}_{i_1 \in [N_1], i_2 \in [N_2]}, \quad \{\mathsf{sk}_{i_1,i_2}\}_{i_1 \in [N_1], i_2 \in [N_2]}.$$

- Enc(pk) samples $m \leftarrow \mathbb{Z}_p$ and $r_{j_2} \leftarrow \{0,1\}^\kappa$ for $j_2 \in [N_2]$. It runs

$$\mathsf{tpct} \leftarrow \mathsf{TBPLBE.Enc}(\mathsf{tpmpk}, (0, m), (r_1, \ldots, r_{N_2}))$$

and outputs $\mathsf{ct} = (\mathsf{tpct}, r_1, \ldots, r_{N_2})$ and $k = [m]_\mathrm{T}$. (Here, j_1 is set to 0.)
- Dec$(\mathsf{sk}_{i_1,i_2}, \mathsf{ct})$ first parses sk_{i_1,i_2} into $(\mathsf{tpsk}_{i_1,i_2}, i_1, (i_2, u_{i_1,i_2}))$ and ct into $(\mathsf{tpct}, r_1, \ldots, r_{N_2})$. It outputs

$$\mathsf{TBPLBE.Dec}(\mathsf{tpsk}_{i_1,i_2}, i_1, (i_2, u_{i_1,i_2}), \mathsf{tpct}, (r_1, \ldots, r_{N_2})).$$

- Trace$^D(\mathsf{pk}, \mathsf{tk}, 1^{1/\varepsilon})$ is described later.

Correctness. The correctness follows from that of TB-PLBE scheme with the fact that (i) $0 = j_1 < i_1$ for all $i_1 \in [N_1]$; and (ii) $\mathsf{wt}(r_{i_2} \oplus u_{i_1,i_2}) \geq 2\kappa/5$ with probability $1 - 2^{-\Omega(\kappa)}$ for all $i_1 \in [N_1]$ and $i_2 \in [N_2]$.

Distributions and Lemma for Tracing. Given $\rho = \sigma_1 \cdots \sigma_t \in \{0, 1, \star\}^t$ for $t \leq \kappa$, we associated ρ with a distribution and write $r \leftarrow \rho$ for

$$r = s_1 \cdots s_\kappa, \quad \begin{cases} s_i = \sigma_i, & \text{if } i \leq t \text{ and } \sigma_i \in \{0,1\}; \\ s_i \leftarrow \{0,1\}, & \text{if } i > t \text{ or } \sigma_i = \star. \end{cases}$$

Our tracing algorithm follows the description in the technical overview, except $u^*_{i_1,i_2}$ is sampled from ρ_{i_1,i_2} instead of being fixed. The distributions ρ_{i_1,i_2} are found iteratively. We rely on the following result:

Lemma 1 (implicit in [30, Sect. 8.1]). *There is an algorithm* Learn$^B(u, 1^{1/\delta})$ *that given* $u \in \{0,1\}^\kappa$, $\delta > 0$, *and oracle access to a randomized algorithm* B *with bit output, makes* poly$(\kappa, 1/\delta)$ *calls to* B *and runs in additional time* poly$(\kappa, 1/\delta)$. *Its output* $\rho \in \{0, 1, \star\}^\kappa$ *satisfies the following conditions:*

- *Each symbol of ρ is either the corresponding symbol in u, or is $\star$.*
- *The number of $\star$'s in ρ is no greater than $2\kappa/5$.*

Moreover, for all B and $\delta > 0$,

$$\Pr\left[\begin{matrix} u \leftarrow \{0,1\}^\kappa \\ \rho \leftarrow \mathsf{Learn}^B(u, 1^{1/\delta}) \end{matrix} : \Pr_{r\leftarrow\rho}[B(r)=1] \geq \Pr_{r\leftarrow\{0,1\}^\kappa}[B(r)=1] - \delta\right] = 1 - 2^{-\Omega(\kappa)}.$$

The proof can be found in the full version [16]. We remark that [15,25] solves the same problem using similar techniques in incomparable parameter regimes that are insufficient for our application.

Tracing Algorithm. Given a decoder D and a distribution $\mathcal{D}$ over traitor tracing ciphertexts and encapsulated keys, we write

$$\varepsilon_D(\mathcal{D}) = \Pr\left[b \leftarrow \{0,1\}, k_0 \leftarrow \mathcal{K}, (\mathsf{ct}, k_1) \leftarrow \mathcal{D} : D(\mathsf{ct}, k_b) = b\right] - \frac{1}{2}.$$

Recall that $\mathcal{K}$ is the key space, cf. Sect. 2.2. For brevity, we represent $\mathcal{D}$ by $(j_1; r_1, \ldots, r_{N_2})$ used in TB-PLBE.

The algorithm $\mathsf{Trace}^D(\mathsf{pk}, \mathsf{tk}, 1^{1/\varepsilon})$ works as follows:

1. Let $\xi_1 = \frac{\varepsilon}{10N_1}$. Compute estimations $\hat\varepsilon_{i_1}$ of ε_{i_1} within additive error ξ_1 for $i_1 = 0, \ldots, N_1$, where

$$\varepsilon_{i_1} = \varepsilon_D(i_1; r_1, \ldots, r_{N_2}), \qquad r_1, \ldots, r_{N_2} \leftarrow \{0,1\}^\kappa.$$

   Recall that $\varepsilon_D(\cdots)$ is defined by the probability of an efficient experiment minus $\frac{1}{2}$. Perform $\lceil(\kappa \log 2 + \log(4N_1 + 4))/(2\xi_1^2)\rceil$ independent trials of that experiment and set $\hat\varepsilon_{i_1}$ to be the empirical frequency minus $\frac{1}{2}$.
2. Pick any $i_1^* \in [N_1]$ such that $\hat\varepsilon_{i_1^*-1} - \hat\varepsilon_{i_1^*} \geq 3\xi_1$. If there is no such i_1^*, the algorithm Trace aborts.
3. For every $t < N_2$ and values of $\rho_{i_1^*,1}, \ldots, \rho_{i_1^*,t}$ (to be found later in Step 4), define $B[\rho_{i_1^*,1}, \ldots, \rho_{i_1^*,t}](r)$, which has the values of ρ's hardwired, as

$$b \leftarrow \{0,1\}, \quad b' \leftarrow \{0,1\}, \quad k_0 \leftarrow \mathcal{K}, \quad m \leftarrow \mathbb{Z}_p, \quad k_1 = [m]_\mathsf{T},$$
$$u_{i_1^*,1}^* \leftarrow \rho_{i_1^*,1}, \ldots, u_{i_1^*,t}^* \leftarrow \rho_{i_1^*,t},$$
$$r_{t+1} = r, \quad r_{t+2} \leftarrow \{0,1\}^\kappa, \ldots, r_{N_2} \leftarrow \{0,1\}^\kappa,$$
$$R = (u_{i_1^*,1}^*, \ldots, u_{i_1^*,t}^*, r_{t+1}, \ldots, r_{N_2}),$$
$$\text{output } D\big(\mathsf{TBPLBE.Enc}(\mathsf{tpmpk}, (i_1^* + b', m), R), R, k_b\big) \oplus b \oplus b' \oplus 1.$$

4. Let $\delta = \frac{\varepsilon}{540N_1N_2}$. For $i_2 = 1, \ldots, N_2$, run

$$\rho_{i_1^*,i_2} \leftarrow \mathsf{Learn}^{B[\rho_{i_1^*,1}, \ldots, \rho_{i_1^*,i_2-1}]}(u_{i_1^*,i_2}, 1^{1/\delta}).$$

5. Let $\xi_2 = \frac{\varepsilon}{180 N_1 N_2}$. Estimate $\hat{\varepsilon}_{i_1^*, i_2, 0}, \hat{\varepsilon}_{i_1^*, i_2, 1}$ of $\varepsilon_{i_1^*, i_2, 0}, \varepsilon_{i_1^*, i_2, 1}$ within additive error ξ_2 for $i_2 = 0, \ldots, N_2$, where

$$\varepsilon_{i_1^*, i_2, b'} = \varepsilon_D(i_1^* - 1 + b'; u_{i_1^*, 1}^*, \ldots, u_{i_1^*, i_2}^*, r_{i_2+1}, \ldots, r_{N_2}),$$

$$u_{i_1^*, 1}^* \leftarrow \rho_{i_1^*, 1}, \ldots, u_{i_1^*, i_2}^* \leftarrow \rho_{i_1^*, i_2}, \quad r_{i_2+1} \leftarrow \{0,1\}^\kappa, \ldots, r_{N_2} \leftarrow \{0,1\}^\kappa.$$

They are computed with $\lceil (\kappa \log 2 + \log(8N_2 + 8))/(2\xi_2^2) \rceil$ independent trials.
6. Pick any $i_2^* \in [N_2]$ such that $(\hat{\varepsilon}_{i_1^*, i_2^*-1, 0} - \hat{\varepsilon}_{i_1^*, i_2^*-1, 1}) - (\hat{\varepsilon}_{i_1^*, i_2^*, 0} - \hat{\varepsilon}_{i_1^*, i_2^*, 1}) \geq 5\xi_2$. If there is no such i_2^*, the algorithm Trace aborts.
7. Output (i_1^*, i_2^*) as a traitor.

Tracing Security. We prove the following theorem.

Theorem 1. *Assuming* TBPLBE *being a TB-PLBE secure under adaptively chosen* $j_1, r_1, \ldots, r_{N_2}$ *and semi-adaptively chosen* m *(cf. Sect. 2.3), our traitor tracing scheme is secure (cf. Sect. 2.2).*

Our proof uses the following lemmas which will be proved later:

Lemma 2. *Assuming* TBPLBE *being a TB-PLBE secure under adaptively chosen* $j_1, r_1, \ldots, r_{N_2}$ *and semi-adaptively chosen* m, *in the tracing security game,* $\varepsilon_{N_1} \leq \frac{\varepsilon(\lambda)}{2}$ *with probability* $1 - \lambda^{-\omega(1)}$.

Lemma 3. *Assuming* TBPLBE *being a TB-PLBE secure under adaptively chosen* $j_1, r_1, \ldots, r_{N_2}$ *and semi-adaptively chosen* m, *in the tracing security game,* $\varepsilon_{i_1^*, N_2, 0} - \varepsilon_{i_1^*, N_2, 1} \leq \frac{\varepsilon(\lambda)}{20 N_1}$ *with probability* $1 - \lambda^{-\omega(1)}$, *where* i_1^* *is the index found in Step 2 of* Trace.

It should be noted that in the tracing security game, $\varepsilon_{N_1}, \varepsilon_{i_1^*, N_2, 0}, \varepsilon_{i_1^*, N_2, 1}$ depend on the random coins of $\mathcal{A}$, and more importantly, those used to set up the traitor tracing scheme in the security game, so they are random variables (not constants) even when $\mathcal{A}, \varepsilon, \lambda$ are fixed. Therefore, $\varepsilon_{N_1} \geq \frac{\varepsilon(\lambda)}{2}$ and $\varepsilon_{i_1^*, N_2, 0} - \varepsilon_{i_1^*, N_2, 1} \leq \frac{\varepsilon(\lambda)}{20 N_1}$ are events (i.e., probabilistic) and the above lemmas bound their probabilities.

Lemma 2 corresponds to the claim in the introduction that ε_{N_1} is negligible, and Lemma 3, $\varepsilon_{i_1^*, N_2, 0} - \varepsilon_{i_1^*, N_2, 1}$. They are indeed negligible with overwhelming probability, but we only need the weakened version as stated in those lemmas.

Proof (Theorem 1). It suffices to prove the following three claims:

- Claim 1: The probability (of the conjunction event) that $\varepsilon_0 \geq \varepsilon(\lambda)$ and Trace aborts at Step 2 is $\lambda^{-\omega(1)}$.[3]
- Claim 2: The probability that Trace aborts at Step 6 is $\lambda^{-\omega(1)}$.
- Claim 3: Let i_1^* and i_2^* be the indices found in Steps 2 and 6, then $\mathsf{sk}_{i_1^*, i_2^*}$ is queried by the adversary in the tracing security game with probability $1 - 2^{-\Omega(\kappa)} \mathrm{poly}(N)$ (i.e., user (i_1^*, i_2^*) is not honest).[4]

---

[3] As $\kappa = \omega(\log \lambda)$ and $N = \mathrm{poly}(\lambda)$, any statistical error $2^{-\Omega(\kappa)}$ is absorbed by $\lambda^{-\omega(1)}$ when combined with a computational argument, and thus omitted in such case.

[4] Claim 3 does not care about whether $\varepsilon_0 \geq \varepsilon(\lambda)$.

Let GoodEst be the event that all estimations are within the prescribed additive errors:

$$|\hat{\varepsilon}_{i_1} - \varepsilon_{i_1}| \leq \xi_1 \qquad \text{for all } i_1 = 0, \ldots, N_1,$$
$$|\hat{\varepsilon}_{i_1^*, i_2, b'} - \varepsilon_{i_1^*, i_2, b'}| \leq \xi_2 \qquad \text{for all } i_2 = 0, \ldots, N_2 \text{ and } b' = 0, 1.$$

By the Chernoff bound, the union bound, and how the numbers of trials are set, we have $\Pr[\mathsf{GoodEst}] \geq 1 - 2^{-\kappa}$. We proceed to prove the claims.

Proof of Claim 1. By Lemma 2 and our choice of ξ_1, with probability $1 - \lambda^{-\omega(1)}$,

$$\max_{i_1 \in [N_1]} \{\varepsilon_{i_1-1} - \varepsilon_{i_1}\} \geq \frac{1}{N_1} \sum_{i_1 \in [N_1]} (\varepsilon_{i_1-1} - \varepsilon_{i_1}) = \frac{\varepsilon_0 - \varepsilon_{N_1}}{N_1} \geq \frac{\varepsilon(\lambda) - \frac{\varepsilon(\lambda)}{2}}{N_1} = 5\xi_1,$$

when $\varepsilon_0 \geq \varepsilon(\lambda)$. Then, GoodEst implies

$$\max_{i_1 \in [N_1]} \{\hat{\varepsilon}_{i_1-1} - \hat{\varepsilon}_{i_1}\} \geq 5\xi_1 - 2\xi_1 = 3\xi_1.$$

This proves Claim 1.

Proof of Claim 2. GoodEst implies

$$\varepsilon_{i_1^*-1} - \varepsilon_{i_1^*} \geq \hat{\varepsilon}_{i_1^*-1} - \hat{\varepsilon}_{i_1^*} - 2\xi_1 = \xi_1.$$

Note that $\varepsilon_{i_1^*, 0, b'} = \varepsilon_{i_1^*-1+b'}$. Together with Lemma 3 and our choice of ξ_1, ξ_2, with probability $1 - \lambda^{-\omega(1)}$,

$$\max_{i_2 \in [N_2]} \{(\varepsilon_{i_1^*, i_2-1, 0} - \varepsilon_{i_1^*, i_2-1, 1}) - (\varepsilon_{i_1^*, i_2, 0} - \varepsilon_{i_1^*, i_2, 1})\}$$
$$\geq \frac{1}{N_2} \left((\varepsilon_{i_1^*, 0, 0} - \varepsilon_{i_1^*, 0, 1}) - (\varepsilon_{i_1^*, N_2, 0} - \varepsilon_{i_1^*, N_2, 1})\right) \geq \frac{\xi_1 - \frac{\varepsilon(\lambda)}{20 N_1}}{N_2} = 9\xi_2.$$

Again with GoodEst, we have

$$\max_{i_2 \in [N_2]} \{(\hat{\varepsilon}_{i_1^*, i_2-1, 0} - \hat{\varepsilon}_{i_1^*, i_2-1, 1}) - (\hat{\varepsilon}_{i_1^*, i_2, 0} - \hat{\varepsilon}_{i_1^*, i_2, 1})\} \geq 9\xi_2 - 4\xi_2 = 5\xi_2.$$

This proves Claim 2.

Proof of Claim 3. Let GoodLearn be the event that for all $i_2 \in [N_2]$ such that $\mathsf{sk}_{i_1^*, i_2}$ is not queried by the adversary,

$$\Pr_{r \leftarrow \rho_{i_1^*, i_2}} [B[\rho_{i_1^*, 1}, \ldots, \rho_{i_1^*, i_2-1}](r) = 1] \geq \Pr_{r \leftarrow \{0,1\}^\kappa} [B[\rho_{i_1^*, 1}, \ldots, \rho_{i_1^*, i_2-1}](r) = 1] - \delta.$$

Note that if $\mathsf{sk}_{i_1^*, i_2}$ is not queried, then $u_{i_1^*, i_2}$ is independent of the tracing security game until Learn is invoked with it, and therefore, Lemma 1 applies. By a union bound over Lemma 1, we have $\Pr[\mathsf{GoodLearn}] = 1 - 2^{-\Omega(\kappa)} \mathrm{poly}(N)$.

Following the definition of B (with $t = i_2 - 1$) in Step 3 of Trace and that of $\varepsilon_{i_1^*, i_2 - 1, b'}$ in Step 5, and applying the law of total probability over b',

$$\Pr_{r \leftarrow \{0,1\}^\kappa} \left[B[\rho_{i_1^*, 1}, \ldots, \rho_{i_1^*, i_2 - 1}](r) = 1 \right]$$

$$= \frac{1}{2} \Pr \left[D\big(\mathsf{TBPLBE.Enc}(\mathsf{tpmpk}, (i_1^* + 0, m), R), R, k_b\big) \oplus b \oplus 0 \oplus 1 = 1 \right]$$

$$+ \frac{1}{2} \Pr \left[D\big(\mathsf{TBPLBE.Enc}(\mathsf{tpmpk}, (i_1^* + 1, m), R), R, k_b\big) \oplus b \oplus 1 \oplus 1 = 1 \right]$$

$$= \frac{1}{2} \Pr \left[D\big(\mathsf{TBPLBE.Enc}(\mathsf{tpmpk}, (i_1^*, m), R), R, k_b\big) = b \right]$$

$$+ \frac{1}{2} \big(1 - \Pr \left[D\big(\mathsf{TBPLBE.Enc}(\mathsf{tpmpk}, (i_1^* + 1, m), R), R, k_b\big) = b \right] \big)$$

$$= \frac{1}{2} \varepsilon_{i_1^*, i_2 - 1, 0} + \frac{1}{2} \big(1 - \varepsilon_{i_1^*, i_2 - 1, 1} \big).$$

Similarly, considering $t = i_2$ and $\varepsilon_{i_1^*, i_2, b'}$,

$$\Pr_{r \leftarrow \rho_{i_1^*, i_2}} \left[B[\rho_{i_1^*, 1}, \ldots, \rho_{i_1^*, i_2 - 1}](r) = 1 \right] = \frac{1}{2} \varepsilon_{i_1^*, i_2, 0} + \frac{1}{2} \big(1 - \varepsilon_{i_1^*, i_2, 1} \big).$$

Therefore,

$$\Pr_{r \leftarrow \rho_{i_1^*, i_2}} \left[B[\rho_{i_1^*, 1}, \ldots, \rho_{i_1^*, i_2 - 1}](r) = 1 \right] - \Pr_{r \leftarrow \{0,1\}^\kappa} \left[B[\rho_{i_1^*, 1}, \ldots, \rho_{i_1^*, i_2 - 1}](r) = 1 \right]$$

$$= \frac{-1}{2} \big((\varepsilon_{i_1^*, i_2 - 1, 0} - \varepsilon_{i_1^*, i_2 - 1, 1}) - (\varepsilon_{i_1^*, i_2, 0} - \varepsilon_{i_1^*, i_2, 1}) \big).$$

GoodLearn thus implies that for all $i_2 \in [N_2]$ such that $\mathsf{sk}_{i_1^*, i_2}$ is not queried by the adversary,

$$(\varepsilon_{i_1^*, i_2 - 1, 0} - \varepsilon_{i_1^*, i_2 - 1, 1}) - (\varepsilon_{i_1^*, i_2, 0} - \varepsilon_{i_1^*, i_2, 1}) \leq 2\delta.$$

Together with GoodEst, for all $i_2 \in [N_2]$ such that $\mathsf{sk}_{i_1^*, i_2}$ is not queried by the adversary,

$$(\hat{\varepsilon}_{i_1^*, i_2 - 1, 0} - \hat{\varepsilon}_{i_1^*, i_2 - 1, 1}) - (\hat{\varepsilon}_{i_1^*, i_2, 0} - \hat{\varepsilon}_{i_1^*, i_2, 1}) \leq 2\delta + 4\xi_2 < 5\xi_2,$$

i.e., except with probability $2^{-\Omega(\kappa)} \operatorname{poly}(N)$, such i_2 cannot be chosen as i_2^* by Trace. This proves Claim 3 and thus Theorem 1. $\qquad \square$

Proving Lemmas. To prove Lemma 2 and Lemma 3, we will use the following trick of advantage sign correction:

Lemma 4 ([7, Exercise 2.22(a)]). *Suppose the tuple of a distinguisher D and two distributions $\mathcal{D}_0, \mathcal{D}_1$ follows some joint distribution. Let*

$$\varepsilon := \Pr_{x \leftarrow \mathcal{D}_0} [D(x) = 1] - \Pr_{x \leftarrow \mathcal{D}_1} [D(x) = 1]$$

be the signed advantage of D against $\mathcal{D}_0, \mathcal{D}_1$, which itself is a random variable (because $D, \mathcal{D}_0, \mathcal{D}_1$ are randomized). Consider

$$\tilde{b} \leftarrow \{0,1\}, \quad \tilde{x} \leftarrow \mathcal{D}_{\tilde{b}}, \quad \tilde{c} \leftarrow D(\tilde{x}), \quad \tilde{D}(x) := \tilde{c} \oplus \tilde{b} \oplus D(x),$$

$$\tilde{\varepsilon} := \Pr_{x \leftarrow \mathcal{D}_0}[\widetilde{D}(x) = 1] - \Pr_{x \leftarrow \mathcal{D}_1}[\widetilde{D}(x) = 1],$$

then $\mathbb{E}[\tilde{\varepsilon}] = \mathbb{E}[\varepsilon^2]$.

In our reduction algorithm, ε in Lemma 4 is the signed advantage of the decoder D against certain ciphertext distributions $(\mathcal{D}_0, \mathcal{D}_1)$ used by Trace, and we want to prove that ε is negligible with overwhelming probability. However, if we directly use D as *the* distinguisher, depending on the sampling of $D, \mathcal{D}_0, \mathcal{D}_1$, the realization of ε could be positive or negative, causing cancellation in $\mathbb{E}[\varepsilon]$, the advantage of the reduction algorithm. The $\tilde{\ }$ components estimate the sign of ε with one trial, and $\widetilde{D}$ is an attempted correction of D, which is *the* distinguisher used by the reduction algorithm and immune from cancellation.

We are now ready to present our proofs.

Proof (Lemma 2). Let $\mathcal{A}$ be an efficient adversary against tracing security. We construct the following efficient $\mathcal{B}$ against TB-PLBE security:

- $\mathcal{B}$ launches $\mathcal{A}$, receives 1^N from it, picks κ, N_1, N_2 as specified by the traitor tracing scheme, samples

$$m_0 \leftarrow \mathbb{Z}_p, \quad m_1 \leftarrow \mathbb{Z}_p, \quad u_{i_1,i_2} \leftarrow \{0,1\}^\kappa \quad \text{for } i_1 \in [N_1], i_2 \in [N_2],$$

  sends $1^{N_1}, 1^{N_2}, m_0, m_1$ to TB-PLBE game, and receives back tpmpk. It sends pk = tpmpk to $\mathcal{A}$. Here, m_0, m_1 sent to TB-PLBE game are part of the challenge plaintexts.
- When, and only when, $\mathcal{A}$ queries for sk_{i_1,i_2}, the adversary $\mathcal{B}$ queries TB-PLBE game and sends the key to $\mathcal{A}$.
- When $\mathcal{A}$ outputs a decoder D, the adversary $\mathcal{B}$ samples $r_1, \ldots, r_{N_2} \leftarrow \{0,1\}^\kappa$, sends N_2, N_2 as the rest of the challenge plaintexts and $r_1, \ldots, r_{N_2}$ as the challenge attribute, and receives back tpct.
- $\mathcal{B}$ samples and computes

$$\tilde{m}_0, \tilde{m}_1 \leftarrow \mathbb{Z}_p, \quad \tilde{b} \leftarrow \mathbb{Z}_p, \quad \tilde{r}_1, \ldots, \tilde{r}_{N_2} \leftarrow \{0,1\}^\kappa,$$
$$\widetilde{\mathsf{tpct}} \leftarrow \mathsf{TBPLBE.Enc}\big(\mathsf{tpmpk}, (N_1, \tilde{m}_{\tilde{b}}), (\tilde{r}_1, \ldots, \tilde{r}_{N_2})\big),$$
$$\tilde{c} \leftarrow D(\widetilde{\mathsf{tpct}}, \tilde{r}_1, \ldots, \tilde{r}_{N_2}, [\tilde{m}_1]_{\mathrm{T}}),$$
$$c \leftarrow D(\mathsf{tpct}, r_1, \ldots, r_{N_2}, [m_1]_{\mathrm{T}}).$$

It outputs $\tilde{c} \oplus \tilde{b} \oplus c$.

By Lemma 4, the advantage of $\mathcal{B}$ is $\mathbb{E}[\varepsilon_{N_1}^2]$, which must be $\lambda^{-\omega(1)}$ by TB-PLBE security. It follows that in the tracing security game with $\mathcal{A}$,

$$\Pr\left[\varepsilon_{N_1} \geq \frac{\varepsilon(\lambda)}{2}\right] \leq \Pr\left[\varepsilon_{N_1}^2 \geq \frac{(\varepsilon(\lambda))^2}{4}\right]$$

$$= \frac{4}{(\varepsilon(\lambda))^2} \cdot \frac{(\varepsilon(\lambda))^2}{4} \cdot \Pr\left[\varepsilon_{N_1}^2 \geq \frac{(\varepsilon(\lambda))^2}{4}\right]$$

$$\leq \frac{(\varepsilon(\lambda))^2}{4} \cdot \mathbb{E}[\varepsilon_{N_1}^2] = \lambda^{-\omega(1)}.$$

$\square$

Proof (Lemma 3). The reduction is similar to that in the previous proof, with the following changes:

- The selective part of the challenge plaintexts are m, m.
- After $\mathcal{A}$ outputs D, the reduction computes $1/\varepsilon(\lambda)$, runs Trace to obtain i_1^* and $\rho_{i_1^*,i_2}$'s, samples $u_{i_1^*,i_2}^* \leftarrow \rho_{i_1^*,i_2}$ for $i_2 \in [N_2]$, and sends $i_1^* - 1, i_1^*$ as the challenge plaintexts and $u_{i_1^*,1}^*, \ldots, u_{i_1^*,N_2}^*$ as the challenge attribute.
- The $\widetilde{}$ components sampled by the reduction are

$$
\begin{aligned}
\widetilde{m} &\leftarrow \mathbb{Z}_p & &\text{instead of } \widetilde{m}_0, \widetilde{m}_1, \\
\widetilde{u}_{i_1^*,i_2}^* &\leftarrow \rho_{i_1^*,i_2} & &\text{instead of } \widetilde{r}_{i_2}, \\
(i_1^* - 1 + \widetilde{b}, \widetilde{m}) \text{ in } \widetilde{\mathsf{tpct}} & & &\text{instead of } (N_1, \widetilde{m}_{\widetilde{b}}).
\end{aligned}
$$

We verify the constraints of TB-PLBE. The constraints of sk_{i_1,i_2} for all $i_1 \neq i_1^*$ and all i_2 are satisfied as

$$
f_{i_1}(i_1^* - 1, m) = f_{i_1}(i_1^*, m) = \begin{cases} m, & \text{if } i_1 > i_1^*; \\ 0, & \text{if } i_1 \leq i_1^* - 1. \end{cases}
$$

The constraint of $\mathsf{sk}_{i_1^*,i_2}$ for each i_2,

$$
0 = P\big((u_{i_1^*,1}^*, \ldots, u_{i_1^*,N_2}^*), (i_2, u_{i_1^*,i_2}^*)\big) = \begin{cases} 1, & \text{if } \mathsf{wt}(u_{i_1^*,i_2}^* \oplus u_{i_1^*,i_2}) \geq 2\kappa/5; \\ 0, & \text{otherwise}; \end{cases}
$$

holds with probability $1 - 2^{-\Omega(\kappa)}$ by Lemma 1 and a standard Chernoff bound.

The reduction checks the constraints (for both non-$\widetilde{}$ and $\widetilde{}$ values) and aborts if any of them is violated. By the analysis above, the probability of aborting is $2^{-\Omega(\kappa)} \mathrm{poly}(N) = \lambda^{-\omega(1)}$, which we denote by ε'. By Lemma 4, the reduction algorithm has advantage $\mathbb{E}[(\varepsilon_{i_1^*,N_2,0} - \varepsilon_{i_1^*,N_2,1})^2] - \varepsilon'$, which is $\lambda^{-\omega(1)}$ by TB-PLBE security. Let C be a polynomial upper bound[5] of $\frac{20N_1}{\varepsilon(\lambda)}$, then

$$
\begin{aligned}
&\Pr\left[\varepsilon_{i_1^*,N_2,0} - \varepsilon_{i_1^*,N_2,1} \geq \frac{\varepsilon(\lambda)}{20N_1}\right] \\
&\leq \Pr\left[(\varepsilon_{i_1^*,N_2,0} - \varepsilon_{i_1^*,N_2,1})^2 \geq \frac{1}{C^2}\right] \\
&= C^2 \cdot \frac{1}{C^2} \cdot \Pr\left[(\varepsilon_{i_1^*,N_2,0} - \varepsilon_{i_1^*,N_2,1})^2 \geq \frac{1}{C^2}\right] \\
&\leq C^2\big(\mathbb{E}[(\varepsilon_{i_1^*,N_2,0} - \varepsilon_{i_1^*,N_2,1})^2] - \varepsilon' + \varepsilon'\big) = \lambda^{-\omega(1)}.
\end{aligned}
$$

$\square$

---

[5] N_1 is a random variable due to the random coins of $\mathcal{A}$, so it is impossible to write N_1 outside probability or expectation. For non-uniform security we may assume N_1 is fixed for every λ, yet it is better to present the more general proof.

4 Building Attribute-Based Functional Encryption

This section builds TB-PLBE scheme promised in Sect. 3.1. At the core is an attribute-based functional encryption (AB-FE) for predicate $P : \mathcal{X} \times \mathcal{Y} \to \{0,1\}$ and quadratic function class

$$\mathcal{F}_{\ell_1,\ell_2}^{\text{quad}} = \{ f_{\mathbf{f}}^{\text{quad}} : \mathbb{Z}_p^{\ell_1} \times \mathbb{Z}_p^{\ell_2} \to \mathbb{Z}_p, (\mathbf{z}_1, \mathbf{z}_2) \mapsto (\mathbf{z}_1 \otimes \mathbf{z}_2) \mathbf{f}^{\mathsf{T}} \mid \mathbf{f} \in \mathbb{Z}_p^{\ell_1 \ell_2} \} \quad (1)$$

with $\mathcal{Z} = \mathbb{Z}_p^{\ell_1} \times \mathbb{Z}_p^{\ell_2}$, called AB-QFE. We combine a slightly tweaked version of the FE scheme for quadratic functions (QFE) in [29] and a compatible attribute-based key encapsulation mechanism (AB-KEM) for P. In the following sections, we first introduce the two building blocks in Sect. 4.1 and Sect. 4.2; for generality, we will work with general AB-KEM in Sect. 4.3 where we build our AB-QFE scheme and describe AB-KEM for a certain P (i.e., local (read-once) monotone span program) in Sect. 4.4 needed for traitor tracing in Sect. 3. We show how to instantiate our AB-QFE to get TB-PLBE in Sect. 4.5.

4.1 Building Block: Functional Encryption for Quadratic Functions

A functional encryption scheme for function class $\mathcal{F} = \{f : \mathcal{Z} \to \{0,1\}^*\}$ consists of four p.p.t. algorithms:

- Setup$(1^\lambda, \mathcal{F}, \mathcal{Z}) \to$ (mpk, msk): The set-up algorithm takes the security parameter 1^λ and the domains $\mathcal{F}, \mathcal{Z}$ as input, and outputs a master public/secret key pair (mpk, msk).
- KeyGen(mpk, msk, f) $\to$ sk: The key generation algorithm takes mpk, msk, and a function $f \in \mathcal{F}$ as input, and outputs a secret key sk.
- Enc(mpk, z) $\to$ ct: The encryption algorithm takes mpk and function input $z \in \mathcal{Z}$ as input, and outputs a ciphertext ct.
- Dec(mpk, sk, f, ct) $\to d$: The decryption algorithm takes mpk, sk, f, ct as input and outputs $d \in \{0,1\}^*$.

Correctness. For all $\lambda \in \mathbb{N}$, $\mathcal{F}$, $\mathcal{Z}$, $f \in \mathcal{F}$, $z \in \mathcal{Z}$, we require

$$\Pr\left[\begin{array}{l} (\mathsf{mpk}, \mathsf{msk}) \leftarrow \mathsf{Setup}(1^\lambda, \mathcal{F}, \mathcal{Z}) \\ \mathsf{sk} \leftarrow \mathsf{KeyGen}(\mathsf{mpk}, \mathsf{msk}, f) \quad : \quad \mathsf{Dec}(\mathsf{mpk}, \mathsf{sk}, f, \mathsf{ct}) = f(z) \\ \mathsf{ct} \leftarrow \mathsf{Enc}(\mathsf{mpk}, z) \end{array} \right] = 1.$$

Semi-adaptive Simulation Security. For all p.p.t. stateful $\mathcal{A}$, there exists p.p.t. stateful $(\widetilde{\mathsf{Setup}}, \widetilde{\mathsf{KeyGen}}, \widetilde{\mathsf{Enc}})$ such that

$$\left\{ \begin{array}{c} (\mathcal{F}, \mathcal{Z}) \leftarrow \mathcal{A}(1^\lambda) \\ (\mathsf{mpk}, \mathsf{msk}) \leftarrow \mathsf{Setup}(1^\lambda, \mathcal{F}, \mathcal{Z}) \\ z \leftarrow \mathcal{A}(\mathsf{mpk}) \\ \mathsf{ct} \leftarrow \mathsf{Enc}(\mathsf{mpk}, z) \\ \textbf{output} \quad \mathcal{A}^{\mathsf{KeyGen}(\mathsf{mpk},\mathsf{msk},\cdot)}(\mathsf{ct}) \end{array} \right\} \approx_c \left\{ \begin{array}{c} (\mathcal{F}, \mathcal{Z}) \leftarrow \mathcal{A}(1^\lambda) \\ \widetilde{\mathsf{mpk}} \leftarrow \widetilde{\mathsf{Setup}}(1^\lambda, \mathcal{F}, \mathcal{Z}) \\ z \leftarrow \mathcal{A}(\widetilde{\mathsf{mpk}}) \\ \widetilde{\mathsf{ct}} \leftarrow \widetilde{\mathsf{Enc}}() \\ \textbf{output} \quad \mathcal{A}^{\widetilde{\mathsf{KeyGen}}(\cdot,\cdot)}(\widetilde{\mathsf{ct}}) \end{array} \right\},$$

where for each query $f_q \in \mathcal{F}$ made by $\mathcal{A}$, we supply $\widetilde{f_q(z)}$ to KeyGen.

QFE. A functional encryption scheme for quadratic functions (QFE) is an FE computing
$$(\mathbf{z}_1, \mathbf{z}_2, \mathbf{u}) \mapsto (\mathbf{z}_1 \otimes \mathbf{z}_2)\mathbf{f}^\top + \mathbf{u}\mathbf{v}^\top$$
where $\mathbf{z}_1 \in \mathbb{Z}_p^{\ell_1}$, $\mathbf{z}_2 \in \mathbb{Z}_p^{\ell_2}$, $\mathbf{u} \in \mathbb{Z}_p^{\ell_3}$ are the function input, and $\mathbf{f} \in \mathbb{Z}_p^{\ell_1 \ell_2}$, $\mathbf{v} \in \mathbb{Z}_p^{\ell_3}$ are specified by the function. In this work, we consider QFE implemented using pairing. We let KeyGen, Dec take $(\mathbf{f}, [\mathbf{v}]_2)$ instead of $(\mathbf{f}, \mathbf{v})$ as the description of the function, let Enc take $(\mathbf{z}_1, \mathbf{z}_2, [\mathbf{u}]_1)$ instead of $(\mathbf{z}_1, \mathbf{z}_2, \mathbf{u})$, and only require that Dec output $[(\mathbf{z}_1 \otimes \mathbf{z}_2)\mathbf{f}^\top + \mathbf{u}\mathbf{v}^\top]_T$. We also let the simulator take the function output encoded in $\mathbb{G}_2$ when simulating a key, which will be convenient for the security proof of AB-FE for quadratic functions.

IPFE. Our construction of QFE is similar to that in [29] and uses an inner-product function encryption (IPFE) scheme which is an FE for $\mathbf{u} \mapsto \mathbf{u}\mathbf{v}^\top$, where $\mathbf{u} \in \mathbb{Z}_p^{\ell_4}$ is the function input and $\mathbf{v} \in \mathbb{Z}_p^{\ell_4}$ is specified by the function. Again, in a group-based scheme, KeyGen, Dec takes $[\mathbf{v}]_2$, Enc takes $[\mathbf{u}]_1$, Dec outputs $[\mathbf{u}\mathbf{v}^\top]_T$, and $\widetilde{\text{KeyGen}}$ takes $[\mathbf{u}\mathbf{v}^\top]_2$. The IPFE in [2] is first proved to be semi-adaptively simulation-secure in [28]. Its parameter sizes are (ignoring constants)
$$|\mathsf{mpk}| = \ell_4|\mathbb{G}_1|, \qquad |\mathsf{ct}| = \ell_4|\mathbb{G}_1|, \qquad |\mathsf{sk}| = |\mathbb{G}_2|.$$

Construction. Suppose k_2-Lin holds in $\mathbb{G}_2$ and bilateral k_{12}-Lin holds. Let IPFE be a semi-adaptively simulation-secure IPFE. Our QFE is as follows:

- Setup$(1^\lambda, 1^{\ell_1}, 1^{\ell_2}, 1^{\ell_3})$ samples $\mathbf{A}_1 \leftarrow \mathbb{Z}_p^{k_{12} \times \ell_1}$, $\mathbf{A}_2 \leftarrow \mathbb{Z}_p^{k_2 \times \ell_2}$, sets the IPFE dimension to $\ell_4 = k_2\ell_1 + k_{12}\ell_2 + \ell_3$, runs $(\mathsf{impk}, \mathsf{imsk}) \leftarrow \mathsf{IPFE.Setup}(1^\lambda, 1^{\ell_4})$, and outputs
$$\mathsf{mpk} = ([\mathbf{A}_1]_1, [\mathbf{A}_1]_2, [\mathbf{A}_2]_2, \mathsf{impk}), \qquad \mathsf{msk} = \mathsf{imsk}.$$

- KeyGen$(\mathsf{mpk}, \mathsf{msk}, \mathbf{f}, [\mathbf{v}]_2)$ outputs
$$\mathsf{sk} = \mathsf{isk} \leftarrow \mathsf{IPFE.KeyGen}(\mathsf{imsk}, [(\mathbf{A}_1 \otimes \mathbf{I}_{\ell_2})\mathbf{f}^\top, \ (\mathbf{I}_{\ell_1} \otimes \mathbf{A}_2)\mathbf{f}^\top, \ \mathbf{v}]_2).$$

- Enc$(\mathsf{mpk}, \mathbf{z}_1, \mathbf{z}_2, [\mathbf{u}]_1)$ samples $\mathbf{s}_1 \leftarrow \mathbb{Z}_p^{k_{12}}$, $\mathbf{s}_2 \leftarrow \mathbb{Z}_p^{k_2}$, run
$$\mathsf{ict} \leftarrow \mathsf{IPFE.Enc}(\mathsf{impk}, [-\mathbf{s}_1 \otimes \mathbf{z}_2, \ -(\mathbf{s}_1\mathbf{A}_1 + \mathbf{z}_1) \otimes \mathbf{s}_2, \ \mathbf{u}]_1)$$
and outputs
$$\mathsf{ct} = ([\mathbf{s}_1\mathbf{A}_1 + \mathbf{z}_1]_1, [\mathbf{s}_2\mathbf{A}_2 + \mathbf{z}_2]_2, \mathsf{ict}).$$

- Dec$(\mathsf{mpk}, \mathsf{sk}, \mathbf{f}, [\mathbf{v}]_2, \mathsf{ct})$ outputs
$$[\underbrace{(\mathbf{s}_1\mathbf{A}_1 + \mathbf{z}_1)}_{\text{in ct}} \otimes \underbrace{(\mathbf{s}_2\mathbf{A}_2 + \mathbf{z}_2)}_{\text{in ct}} \cdot \mathbf{f}^\top]_T$$
$$\cdot \ \mathsf{IPFE.Dec}(\mathsf{impk}, \mathsf{isk}, [(\mathbf{A}_1 \otimes \mathbf{I}_{\ell_2})\mathbf{f}^\top, \ (\mathbf{I}_{\ell_1} \otimes \mathbf{A}_2)\mathbf{f}^\top, \ \mathbf{v}]_2, \mathsf{ict}).$$

The correctness is analogous to [29], we defer the details to the full version [16]. Its parameter sizes are (ignoring constants)

$$|\mathsf{mpk}| = \ell_1|\mathbb{G}_1| + (\ell_1 + \ell_2)|\mathbb{G}_2| + |\mathsf{impk}| = (\ell_1 + \ell_2 + \ell_3)|\mathbb{G}_1| + (\ell_1 + \ell_2)|\mathbb{G}_2|,$$
$$|\mathsf{ct}| = \ell_1|\mathbb{G}_1| + \ell_2|\mathbb{G}_2| + |\mathsf{ict}| = (\ell_1 + \ell_2 + \ell_3)|\mathbb{G}_1| + \ell_2|\mathbb{G}_2|,$$
$$|\mathsf{sk}| = |\mathsf{isk}| = |\mathbb{G}_2|.$$

Security. We have the following theorem. The proof is analogous to that for QFE in [29], we defer the details to the full version [16].

Theorem 2. *Assume* IPFE *is semi-adaptively simulation-secure, k_2-Lin holds in $\mathbb{G}_2$, and bilateral k_{12}-Lin holds, our QFE scheme achieves semi-adaptive simulation security.*

4.2 Building Block: Attribute-Based Key Encapsulation Mechanism

We define attribute-based key encapsulation mechanism (AB-KEM) with syntactical properties compatible for constructing AB-FE for quadratic functions. Fix the source groups $\mathbb{G}_1, \mathbb{G}_2$ and the target group $\mathbb{G}_T$, an AB-KEM for predicate $P : \mathcal{X} \times \mathcal{Y} \to \{0, 1\}$ consists of four p.p.t. algorithms:

- Setup($1^\lambda, \mathcal{X}, \mathcal{Y}$) $\to$ (mpk, $[\mathbf{A}]_2$): The set-up algorithm takes the security parameter 1^λ and the domains $\mathcal{X}, \mathcal{Y}$ as input, and outputs a master public key mpk and a public matrix $[\mathbf{A}]_2$ with $\mathbf{A} \in \mathbb{Z}_p^{\ell_3 \times \ell_5}$.
- KeyGen(mpk, $\mathbf{k}, y$) $\to$ sk: The key generation algorithm takes mpk, a vector $\mathbf{k} \in \mathbb{Z}_p^{\ell_5}$, and $y \in \mathcal{Y}$ as input, and outputs a secret key sk.
- Enc(mpk, $\mathbf{s}, x$) $\to$ ct: The encapsulation algorithm takes a vector $\mathbf{s} \in \mathbb{Z}_p^{\ell_3}$ and $x \in \mathcal{X}$ as input, and outputs a ciphertext ct.
- Dec(mpk, sk, y, ct, x) $\to$ d: The decapsulation algorithm takes mpk, sk, y, ct, x as input, and outputs an encapsulated key d.

Correctness. For all $\lambda \in \mathbb{N}$, $\mathcal{X}, \mathcal{Y}$, $\mathbf{k} \in \mathbb{Z}_p^{\ell_5}$, $\mathbf{s} \in \mathbb{Z}_p^{\ell_3}$, $x \in \mathcal{X}$, $y \in \mathcal{Y}$ such that $P(x, y) = 1$, we require

$$\Pr\left[\begin{array}{c} (\mathsf{mpk}, [\mathbf{A}]_2) \leftarrow \mathsf{Setup}(1^\lambda, \mathcal{X}, \mathcal{Y}) \\ \mathsf{sk} \leftarrow \mathsf{KeyGen}(\mathsf{mpk}, \mathbf{k}, y) \; : \; \mathsf{Dec}(\mathsf{mpk}, \mathsf{sk}, y, \mathsf{ct}, x) = [\mathbf{s}\mathbf{A}\mathbf{k}^\top]_T \\ \mathsf{ct} \leftarrow \mathsf{Enc}(\mathsf{mpk}, \mathbf{s}, x) \end{array}\right] = 1.$$

Adaptive Indistinguishability. For all p.p.t. stateful $\mathcal{A}$, we require

$$\Pr\left[\begin{array}{c} (\mathcal{X}, \mathcal{Y}) \leftarrow \mathcal{A}(1^\lambda) \\ (\mathsf{mpk}, [\mathbf{A}]_2) \leftarrow \mathsf{Setup}(1^\lambda, \mathcal{X}, \mathcal{Y}) \\ \mathbf{s} \leftarrow \mathbb{Z}_p^{\ell_3} \\ x \leftarrow \mathcal{A}^{\mathsf{NewKey}_{\mathrm{kem}}(\cdot)}([\mathbf{s}\mathbf{A}]_2) \\ \mathsf{ct} \leftarrow \mathsf{Enc}(\mathsf{mpk}, \mathbf{s}, x) \\ : \; \mathcal{A}^{\mathsf{NewKey}_{\mathrm{kem}}(\cdot)}(\mathsf{ct}) = 1 \end{array}\right] - \Pr\left[\begin{array}{c} (\mathcal{X}, \mathcal{Y}) \leftarrow \mathcal{A}(1^\lambda) \\ (\mathsf{mpk}, [\mathbf{A}]_2) \leftarrow \mathsf{Setup}(1^\lambda, \mathcal{X}, \mathcal{Y}) \\ \mathbf{s} \leftarrow \mathbb{Z}_p^{\ell_3} \\ x \leftarrow \mathcal{A}^{\mathsf{NewKey}_{\$}(\cdot)}([\mathbf{s}\mathbf{A}]_2) \\ \mathsf{ct} \leftarrow \mathsf{Enc}(\mathsf{mpk}, \mathbf{s}, x) \\ : \; \mathcal{A}^{\mathsf{NewKey}_{\$}(\cdot)}(\mathsf{ct}) = 1 \end{array}\right]$$

to be negligible under the constraint that $P(x, y_q) = 0$ for all query y_q made by $\mathcal{A}$, where $\mathsf{NewKey}_{\mathsf{kem}}(y_q)$ and $\mathsf{NewKey}_{\$}(y_q)$ run

$$\mathbf{k}_q \leftarrow \mathbb{Z}_p^{\ell_5}, \quad \mathsf{sk}_q \leftarrow \mathsf{KeyGen}(\mathsf{mpk}, \mathbf{k}_q, y_q), \quad \begin{cases} \mathsf{kem}_q \leftarrow [\mathbf{s}\mathbf{A}\mathbf{k}_q^\top]_2, & \text{in } \mathsf{NewKey}_{\mathsf{kem}}; \\ \mathsf{kem}_q \leftarrow \mathbb{G}_2, & \text{in } \mathsf{NewKey}_{\$}; \end{cases}$$

and return $(\mathsf{sk}_q, [\mathbf{A}\mathbf{k}_q^\top]_2, \mathsf{kem}_q)$ to $\mathcal{A}$. The security notion requires that the encapsulated key be pseudorandom even when encoded in $\mathbb{G}_2$, which is stronger than the usual requirement for KEM. This strengthening is for security reduction from AB-FE.

Remark 2. Our formalization basically captures the setting with one key per instance for polynomially many instances and requires that master secret key have special structure. In more detail, mpk here is the public parameter shared among all instances and $\mathbf{k}$ is the master secret key. We will show a concrete construction for local (read-once) monotone span programs in Sect. 4.4. The construction can be generalized to support a broader class of predicates (see Remark 3).

4.3   AB-FE for Quadratic Functions

We present our AB-FE for quadratic functions (AB-QFE) as defined in (1). In Setup, the functionality $\mathcal{F}_{\ell_1, \ell_2}^{\mathrm{quad}}$ is represented by $(1^{\ell_1}, 1^{\ell_2})$; in KeyGen and Dec, the function $f_{\mathbf{f}}^{\mathrm{quad}}$ is represented by $\mathbf{f}$ where $\mathbf{f} \in \mathbb{Z}_p^{\ell_1 \ell_2}$. In this section, we consider general P, as defined in (1) and Sect. 4.2, and provide concrete instance for our use.

Construction. Let QFE be the QFE scheme and ABE an AB-KEM for predicate P. Our AB-QFE for P works as follows:

- $\mathsf{Setup}(1^\lambda, 1^{\ell_1}, 1^{\ell_2}, \mathcal{X}, \mathcal{Y})$ runs

$$(\mathsf{qmpk}, \mathsf{qmsk}) \leftarrow \mathsf{QFE.Setup}(1^\lambda, 1^{\ell_1}, 1^{\ell_2}, 1^{\ell_3}),$$
$$(\mathsf{abmpk}, [\mathbf{A}]_2) \leftarrow \mathsf{ABE.Setup}(1^\lambda, \mathcal{X}, \mathcal{Y}),$$

and outputs

$$\mathsf{mpk} = (\mathsf{abmpk}, \mathsf{qmpk}) \quad \text{and} \quad \mathsf{msk} = ([\mathbf{A}]_2, \mathsf{qmsk}).$$

- $\mathsf{KeyGen}(\mathsf{mpk}, \mathsf{msk}, \mathbf{f}, y)$ samples $\mathbf{k} \leftarrow \mathbb{Z}_p^{\ell_5}$, runs

$$\mathsf{absk} \leftarrow \mathsf{ABE.KeyGen}(\mathsf{abmpk}, \mathbf{k}, y), \quad \mathsf{qsk} \leftarrow \mathsf{QFE.KeyGen}(\mathsf{qmsk}, \mathbf{f}, [\mathbf{A}\mathbf{k}^\top]_2),$$

and outputs

$$\mathsf{sk} = (\mathsf{absk}, \mathsf{qsk}, [\mathbf{A}\mathbf{k}^\top]_2).$$

- $\mathsf{Enc}(\mathsf{mpk}, \mathbf{z}_1, \mathbf{z}_2, x)$ samples $\mathbf{s} \leftarrow \mathbb{Z}_p^{\ell_3}$, runs

$$\mathsf{abct} \leftarrow \mathsf{ABE}.\mathsf{Enc}(\mathsf{abmpk}, \mathbf{s}, x), \quad \mathsf{qct} \leftarrow \mathsf{QFE}.\mathsf{Enc}(\mathsf{qmpk}, \mathbf{z}_1, \mathbf{z}_2, [\mathbf{s}]_1),$$

and outputs

$$\mathsf{ct} = (\mathsf{abct}, \mathsf{qct}).$$

- $\mathsf{Dec}(\mathsf{mpk}, \mathsf{sk}, \mathbf{f}, y, \mathsf{ct}, x)$ checks whether $P(x, y) = 0$ and aborts if so. Otherwise, $P(x, y) = 1$, it runs

$$d_{\mathsf{ABE}} \leftarrow \mathsf{ABE}.\mathsf{Dec}(\mathsf{abmpk}, \mathsf{absk}, y, \mathsf{abct}, x),$$
$$d_{\mathsf{QFE}} \leftarrow \mathsf{QFE}.\mathsf{Dec}(\mathsf{qmpk}, \mathsf{qsk}, \mathbf{f}, [\mathbf{A}\mathbf{k}^\top]_2, \mathsf{qct}),$$

and outputs $d_{\mathsf{QFE}} d_{\mathsf{ABE}}^{-1}$.

Correctness. When $P(x, y) = 1$, the correctness follows from those of ABE and QFE which imply that

$$d_{\mathsf{QFE}} = [(\mathbf{z}_1 \otimes \mathbf{z}_2)\mathbf{f}^\top + \mathbf{s}\mathbf{A}\mathbf{k}^\top]_\mathsf{T}, \quad d_{\mathsf{ABE}} = [\mathbf{s}\mathbf{A}\mathbf{k}^\top]_\mathsf{T}.$$

Efficiency. Our scheme inherits the efficiency from the building blocks:

$$|\mathsf{mpk}| = |\mathsf{abmpk}| + |\mathsf{qmpk}|, \quad |\mathsf{ct}| = |\mathsf{abct}| + |\mathsf{qct}|, \quad |\mathsf{sk}| = |\mathsf{absk}| + |\mathsf{qsk}| + \ell_3 |\mathbb{G}_2|.$$

Here, ℓ_3 depends on the assumption used by AB-KEM.

Security. We have the following theorem.

Theorem 3. *Assuming* QFE *is semi-adaptively simulation-secure as defined in Sect. 4.1 and* ABE *achieves security as defined in Sect. 4.2, our AB-QFE scheme achieves security as defined in Sect. 2.3.*

Let $(\mathbf{z}_{0,1}, \mathbf{z}_{0,2}, \mathbf{z}_{1,1}, \mathbf{z}_{1,2})$ be the semi-adaptive challenge message, x be the adaptive challenge attribute and $(\mathbf{f}_q, y_q)$ be the q-th query. We prove Theorem 3 via the following game sequence where we write $\eta_{q,b} = (\mathbf{z}_{b,1} \otimes \mathbf{z}_{b,2})\mathbf{f}_q^\top$ for $b \in \{0, 1\}$.

- G_0 is the real game, where the keys and the challenge ciphertext are

$$\mathsf{mpk} = (\mathsf{abmpk}, \mathsf{qmpk}),$$
$$\mathsf{ct} = (\mathsf{ABE}.\mathsf{Enc}(\mathsf{abmpk}, \mathbf{s}, x), \underbrace{\mathsf{QFE}.\mathsf{Enc}(\mathsf{qmpk}, \mathbf{z}_{b,1}, \mathbf{z}_{b,2}, [\mathbf{s}]_1)}_{\mathsf{qct}}),$$
$$\mathsf{sk}_q = (\mathsf{ABE}.\mathsf{KeyGen}(\mathsf{abmpk}, \mathbf{k}_q, y_q), \underbrace{\mathsf{QFE}.\mathsf{KeyGen}(\mathsf{qmpk}, \mathbf{f}_q, [\mathbf{A}\mathbf{k}_q^\top]_2)}_{\mathsf{qsk}_q}, [\mathbf{A}\mathbf{k}_q^\top]_2).$$

- G_1 is identical to G_0, except we use the simulator for QFE to generate QFE components:

$$\mathsf{mpk} = (\mathsf{abmpk}, \widetilde{\mathsf{qmpk}}), \quad \mathsf{qct} = \widetilde{\mathsf{QFE}.\mathsf{Enc}}(),$$

$$\text{qsk}_q = \boxed{\text{QFE.}\widetilde{\text{KeyGen}}}\left(\mathbf{f}_q, [\mathbf{A}\mathbf{k}_q^\top]_2, \boxed{[\eta_{q,b} + \mathbf{s}\mathbf{A}\mathbf{k}_q^\top]_2}\right).$$

We have $\mathsf{G}_0 \approx_c \mathsf{G}_1$ by semi-adaptive simulation security of QFE.

- G_2 is identical to G_1, except we change $\mathbf{s}\mathbf{A}\mathbf{k}_q^\top$ in qsk_q to uniformly random $\mu_q \leftarrow \mathbb{Z}_p$ if $\eta_{q,0} \neq \eta_{q,1}$:

$$\text{qsk}_q = \begin{cases} \text{QFE.}\widetilde{\text{KeyGen}}(\mathbf{f}_q, [\mathbf{A}\mathbf{k}_q^\top]_2, [\eta_{q,b} + \mathbf{s}\mathbf{A}\mathbf{k}_q^\top]_2), & \text{if } \eta_{q,0} = \eta_{q,1}; \\ \text{QFE.}\widetilde{\text{KeyGen}}(\mathbf{f}_q, [\mathbf{A}\mathbf{k}_q^\top]_2, [\eta_{q,b} + \boxed{\mu_q}]_2), & \text{if } \eta_{q,0} \neq \eta_{q,1}. \end{cases}$$

We have $\mathsf{G}_1 \approx_c \mathsf{G}_2$ by adaptive security of AB-KEM. Roughly speaking, the reduction algorithm receives abmpk, $[\mathbf{A}]_2$, $[\mathbf{s}\mathbf{A}]_2$, and abct from the AB-KEM game. To answer an AB-QFE key query from the adversary, if $\eta_{q,0} = \eta_{q,1}$, the reduction algorithm samples $\mathbf{k}_q \leftarrow \mathbb{Z}_p^{\ell_5}$ and computes sk_q using abmpk, $[\mathbf{A}]_2$, $[\mathbf{s}\mathbf{A}]_2$, $\mathbf{k}_q$, $\mathbf{f}_q$. Otherwise, it queries the AB-KEM game to obtain absk_q, $[\mathbf{A}\mathbf{k}_q^\top]_2$, kem_q, where kem_q is either $[\mathbf{s}\mathbf{A}\mathbf{k}_q^\top]_2$ or random, and computes sk_q with $[\eta_{q,b}]_2 \cdot \text{kem}_q$ as the third argument to QFE.$\widetilde{\text{KeyGen}}$.

The advantage is 0 in G_2. To see this, note that b only appears in G_2 as

$$\left(\{\eta_{q,b}\}_{\eta_{q,0}=\eta_{q,1}}, \{\eta_{q,b} + \mu_q\}_{\eta_{q,0}\neq\eta_{q,1}}\right) \equiv \left(\{\eta_{q,0}\}_{\eta_{q,0}=\eta_{q,1}}, \{\tilde{\mu}_q\}_{\eta_{q,0}\neq\eta_{q,1}}\right),$$

thus completely hidden.

4.4   AB-KEM for Local (Read-Once) Monotone Span Programs

We describe AB-KEM for local (read-once) monotone span program [10,11]; we redo the scheme and proof in order to fit our syntax and security notion as well as pursue optimal size.

Preliminaries. An m-local (read-once) monotone span program (roMSP) with input length n is specified by $(\mathbf{M}, \rho)$, where $\mathbf{M} \in \mathbb{Z}_p^{m \times t}$ and $\rho : [m] \to [n]$ is injective.[6] The predicate for roMSPs of input length n is

$$P_{n,m}^{\text{roMSP}}(x, (\mathbf{M}, \rho)) = \begin{cases} 1, & \text{if } \mathbf{e}_1 \in \text{span}\{\mathbf{m}_j \mid x_{\rho(j)} = 1\}; \\ 0, & \text{otherwise}; \end{cases}$$

where $x \in \{0,1\}^n$ and $\mathbf{m}_j$ is the jth row of $\mathbf{M}$. We say x is accepted by $(\mathbf{M}, \rho)$ for $P(x, (\mathbf{M}, \rho)) = 1$. It is also worth noting that by the tight equivalence between monotone span programs and linear secret sharing schemes (LSSS) [22], m-local roMSPs are equivalent to LSSS where at most m parties have a share and the size of each party's share is at most one.

---

[6] It is important that we do *not* assume ρ is the identity map by enlarging $\mathbf{M}$, so that we capture key size dependency in m, the locality. The scheme will be instantiated for κ-local roMSPs ($\kappa \ll n$), which is crucial for the efficiency of our application.

Construction. The AB-KEM for local roMSPs, denoted by ABQFEMSP, is as follows:

- Setup($1^\lambda, 1^n$) samples

$$\mathbf{A} \leftarrow \mathbb{Z}_p^{k_{12} \times (k_{12}+1)}, \quad \mathbf{B} \leftarrow \mathbb{Z}_p^{k_2 \times (k_2+1)}, \quad \mathbf{W}_i \leftarrow \mathbb{Z}_p^{(k_{12}+1) \times (k_2+1)} \text{ for } i \in [n],$$

and outputs

$$\mathsf{mpk} = \left([\mathbf{A}]_1, \{[\mathbf{A}\mathbf{W}_i]_1\}_{i \in [n]}, [\mathbf{B}]_2, \{[\mathbf{B}\mathbf{W}_i^\top]_2\}_{i \in [n]}\right) \quad \text{and} \quad [\mathbf{A}]_2.$$

- KeyGen($\mathsf{mpk}, \mathbf{k}, (\mathbf{M}, \rho)$) samples $\mathbf{r} \leftarrow \mathbb{Z}_p^{k_2}$ and $\mathbf{T}' \leftarrow \mathbb{Z}_p^{(t-1) \times (k_{12}+1)}$, sets $\mathbf{T} = \begin{pmatrix} \mathbf{k} \\ \mathbf{T}' \end{pmatrix}$, and outputs

$$\mathsf{sk} = \left([\mathbf{r} \cdot \mathbf{B}]_2, \{[\mathbf{m}_j \mathbf{T} + \mathbf{r} \cdot \mathbf{B}\mathbf{W}_{\rho(j)}^\top]_2\}_{j \subset [m]}\right).$$

- Enc($\mathsf{mpk}, \mathbf{s}, x$) outputs

$$\mathsf{ct} = \left([\mathbf{s} \cdot \mathbf{A}]_1, \{[\mathbf{s} \cdot \mathbf{A}\mathbf{W}_i]_1\}_{x_i=1}\right).$$

- Dec($\mathsf{mpk}, \mathsf{sk}, (\mathbf{M}, \rho), \mathsf{ct}, x$) checks whether $P_{n,m}^{\mathrm{roMSP}}(x, (\mathbf{M}, \rho)) = 0$ and aborts if so. Otherwise, it finds $\beta_1, \ldots, \beta_n \in \mathbb{Z}_p$ such that $\sum_{x_{\rho(j)}=1} \beta_{\rho(j)} \mathbf{m}_j = \mathbf{e}_1$, and outputs

$$\prod_{x_{\rho(j)}=1} \frac{[\beta_{\rho(j)} \cdot \overbrace{(\mathbf{m}_j \mathbf{T} + \mathbf{r}\mathbf{B}\mathbf{W}_{\rho(j)}^\top)}^{\mathsf{sk}}) \cdot (\overbrace{\mathbf{s}\mathbf{A}}^{\mathsf{ct}})^\top]_{\mathrm{T}}}{[\beta_{\rho(j)} \cdot \underbrace{\mathbf{r}\mathbf{B}}_{\mathsf{sk}} \cdot (\underbrace{\mathbf{s}\mathbf{A}\mathbf{W}_{\rho(j)}}_{\mathsf{ct}})^\top]_{\mathrm{T}}}.$$

The correctness is straight-forward (cf. [10], more details can be found in the full version [16]). The parameter sizes of the scheme are (ignoring constants)

$$|\mathsf{mpk}| = n|\mathbb{G}_1| + n|\mathbb{G}_2|, \quad \ell_3 = \ell_5 = 1, \quad |\mathsf{ct}| = \mathsf{wt}(x)|\mathbb{G}_1|, \quad |\mathsf{sk}| = m|\mathbb{G}_2|,$$

where $n, m, \mathsf{wt}(x)$ are the length of x, the locality of the span program (number of rows of $\mathbf{M}$), and the Hamming weight of x.

Security. We have the following theorem. The proof basically follows that in [10] and we defer the details to the full version [16].

Theorem 4. *Assume k_2-Lin holds in $\mathbb{G}_2$ and bilateral k_{12}-Lin holds, our AB-KEM for local roMSPs achieves security defined in Sect. 4.2.*

Remark 3. Our construction is basically a concrete instantiation of [10] and the proof is adapted from it. The adaptation can be generalized to support predicate encoding: only step $\mathsf{G}_4^0 \equiv \mathsf{G}_4^1$ relies on the so-called α-privacy of predicate encoding, other steps, which are irrelevant to the predicate, remain unchanged. Thanks to versatile instantiations of predicate encoding (cf. Appendix A in [10]), this allows us to cover AB-KEM (and thus AB-FE) for arithmetic branching program. Furthermore, many existing dual-system ABE schemes in prime-order pairing groups [17,21,23,24] can be fit into this definition with slight tweaks.

4.5   Threshold Broadcast, Private Linear Broadcast Encryption

Putting together Sects. 4.3 and 4.4, we readily have an AB-FE for

$$\mathcal{F}_{\ell_1,\ell_2}^{\mathrm{quad}} \quad \text{and} \quad P_{n,m}^{\mathrm{roMSP}} \tag{2}$$

with

$$|\mathsf{mpk}| = O(\ell_1 + \ell_2 + n), \quad |\mathsf{ct}| = O(\ell_1 + \ell_2 + n), \quad |\mathsf{sk}| = O(m).$$

We can obtain a TB-PLBE scheme (for message space $\mathbb{Z}_p$) as an AB-FE for

$$\mathcal{F}_{N_1}^{\mathrm{comp}} \quad \text{and} \quad P_{N_2,\kappa}^{\mathrm{tbe}} \tag{3}$$

as defined in Sect. 3.1 by applying the following efficiently computable mappings that reduce (3) to (2) so that

$$\ell_1 = \ell_2 = N_1^{1/2} \quad \text{and} \quad n = 2\kappa N_2, \; m = \kappa.$$

This gives our TB-PLBE with shorter parameters:

$$|\mathsf{mpk}| = O(N_1^{1/2} + \kappa N_2), \quad |\mathsf{ct}| = O(N_1^{1/2} + \kappa N_2), \quad |\mathsf{sk}| = O(\kappa).$$

Below, we first describe the mappings in general. In **Setting Parameters for Efficiency**, we choose the optimal parameters achieving the desired efficiency.

Function Part. For any $n_1, n_2 \in \mathbb{N}$ satisfying $n_1 n_2 = N_1$, we can perform $\mathcal{F}_{N_1}^{\mathrm{comp}} \mapsto \mathcal{F}_{n_1,n_2}^{\mathrm{quad}}$. For this, we follow [3, Sect. 6.1] and define

$$\eta_z : \quad [0,N_1] \times \mathbb{Z}_p \to \mathbb{Z}_p^{n_1} \times \mathbb{Z}_p^{n_2}, \quad (j_1, m) \mapsto \begin{cases} (m\mathbf{e}_{j_{11}}, \mathbf{e}_{j_{12}}), & \text{if } j_1 < N_1; \\ (\mathbf{0}, \mathbf{0}), & \text{if } j_1 = N_1; \end{cases}$$

$$\eta_f : \quad [N_1] \to \mathbb{Z}_p^{n_1 n_2}, \quad i_1 \mapsto \sum_{0 \leq j_1 < i_1} \mathbf{e}_{j_{11}} \otimes \mathbf{e}_{j_{12}},$$

where $j_{11} \in [n_1]$, $j_{12} \in [n_2]$ satisfy $(j_{11} - 1)n_2 + (j_{12} - 1) = j_1$ for $j_1 \in [0, N_1 - 1]$. Note that, for notation convenience, j_1 is the input of η_z and also serves as a general index in the description of η_f. It is straightforward to verify that

$$f_{i_1}^{\mathrm{comp}}(j_1, m) = \mathcal{F}_{\eta_f(i_1)}^{\mathrm{quad}}(\eta_z(j_1, m)).$$

This follows from the fact that

$$\langle \mathbf{e}_{j_{11}} \otimes \mathbf{e}_{j_{12}}, \mathbf{e}_{j_{11}'} \otimes \mathbf{e}_{j_{12}'} \rangle = \begin{cases} 1 & \text{if } j_1 = j_1'; \\ 0 & \text{if } j_1 \neq j_1'; \end{cases}$$

where j_{11}', j_{12}' are defined analogous to j_{11}, j_{12}.

Predicate Part. We will perform $P^{\text{tbe}}_{N_2,\kappa} \mapsto P^{\text{roMSP}}_{2\kappa N_2,\kappa}$. For this, we define

$$\eta_x: \quad (\{0,1\}^\kappa)^{N_2} \to \{0,1\}^{2\kappa N_2}, \quad (r_1,\ldots,r_{N_2}) \mapsto (r_1,\bar{r}_1,\ldots,r_{N_2},\bar{r}_{N_2}),$$

$$\eta_y: \quad [N_2] \times \{0,1\}^\kappa \to \{\kappa\text{-local roMSP with input length } 2\kappa N_2\},$$

$$(i_2,u) \mapsto (\mathbf{M},\rho) \text{ with } \mathbf{M} = \begin{pmatrix} \mathbf{m}_1 \\ \vdots \\ \mathbf{m}_\kappa \end{pmatrix} \in \mathbb{Z}_p^{\kappa \times 2\kappa/5}$$

$$\text{where} \quad \mathbf{m}_\theta = (1,\theta,\theta^2,\cdots,\theta^{2\kappa/5-1}),$$
$$\rho(\theta) = 2(i_2-1)\kappa + u_\theta\kappa + \theta, \quad \forall\theta \in [\kappa].$$

The construction of η_y is simply Shamir's secret sharing [26]. We show that

$$P^{\text{tbe}}_{N_2,\kappa}((r_1,\ldots,r_{N_2}),(i_2,u)) = P^{\text{roMSP}}_{2\kappa N_2,\kappa}(\eta_x(r_1,\ldots,r_{N_2}),\eta_y(i_2,u))$$

by proving that $\text{wt}(r_{i_2} \oplus u) \geq 2\kappa/5$ if and only if $\eta_x(r_1,\ldots,r_{N_2})$ is accepted by $\eta_y(i_2,u)$. To see this, first note that

$$(\eta_x(r_1,\ldots,r_{N_2}))_{\rho(\theta)} = (\overbrace{r_1,\bar{r}_1,\ldots,r_{i_2-1},\bar{r}_{i_2-1}}^{2(i_2-1)\kappa \text{ bits}},r_{i_2},\bar{r}_{i_2},\ldots)_{2(i_2-1)\kappa+u_\theta\kappa+\theta}$$

$$= (r_{i_2},\bar{r}_{i_2})_{u_\theta\kappa+\theta} = \begin{cases} (r_{i_2})_\theta, & \text{if } u_\theta = 0; \\ (\bar{r}_{i_2})_\theta, & \text{if } u_\theta = 1; \end{cases}$$

$$= (r_{i_2})_\theta \oplus u_\theta.$$

By the Vandermonde determinant, any $2\kappa/5$ vectors among $\mathbf{e}_1$ and $\mathbf{m}_\theta$'s are linearly independent, and therefore,

$$\eta_y(i_2,u) \text{ accepts } \eta_x(r_1,\ldots,r_{N_2}) \iff |\{\theta \mid (\eta_x(r_1,\ldots,r_{N_2}))_{\rho(\theta)} = 1\}| \geq 2\kappa/5$$
$$\iff |\{\theta \mid (r_{i_2})_\theta \oplus u_\theta = 1\}| \geq 2\kappa/5$$
$$\iff \text{wt}(r_{i_2} \oplus u) \geq 2\kappa/5.$$

Transformation. Given those mappings and an AB-FE ABQFEMSP for $\mathcal{F}^{\text{quad}}_{n_1,n_2}$ and $P^{\text{roMSP}}_{2\kappa N_2,\kappa}$, our TBPLBE for $\mathcal{F}^{\text{comp}}_{N_1}$ and $P^{\text{tbe}}_{N_2,\kappa}$ works as follows for $n_1 n_2 = N_1$:

- Setup$(1^\lambda,1^{N_1},1^{N_2},1^\kappa)$ is

$$\text{ABQFEMSP.Setup}(1^\lambda,1^{n_1},1^{n_2},1^{2\kappa N_2});$$

- KeyGen$(\text{tpmsk},i_1,i_2,u_{i_1,i_2})$ is

$$\text{ABQFEMSP.KeyGen}(\text{tpmsk},\eta_f(i_1),\eta_y(i_2,u_{i_1,i_2}));$$

- Enc$(\text{tpmpk},j_1,m,r_1,\ldots,r_{N_2})$ is

$$\text{ABQFEMSP.Enc}(\text{tpmpk},\eta_z(j_1,m),\eta_x(r_1,\ldots,r_{N_2}));$$

- Dec = ABQFEMSP.Dec.

Setting Parameters for Efficiency. By definition, $\mathsf{wt}(\eta_x(r_1, \ldots, r_{N_2})) = \kappa N_2$ and the roMSP $\eta_y(i_2, u)$ is always κ-local. We have TB-PLBE with parameter sizes (ignoring constants)

$$|\mathsf{tpmpk}| = (n_1 + n_2 + \kappa N_2)|\mathbb{G}_1| + (n_1 + n_2 + \kappa N_2)|\mathbb{G}_2|,$$
$$|\mathsf{tpct}| = (n_1 + n_2 + \kappa N_2)|\mathbb{G}_1| + n_2|\mathbb{G}_2|,$$
$$|\mathsf{tpsk}| = \kappa|\mathbb{G}_2|,$$

where $n_1 n_2 = N_1$ and $N_1 N_2 = N$. By setting

$$n_1 = n_2 = N^{1/3}\kappa^{1/3} \quad \text{and} \quad N_2 = N^{1/3}\kappa^{-2/3},$$

we obtain

$$|\mathsf{tpmpk}| = |\mathsf{tpct}| = N^{1/3}\kappa^{1/3}|\mathbb{G}_1| + N^{1/3}\kappa^{1/3}|\mathbb{G}_2|, \qquad |\mathsf{tpsk}| = \kappa|\mathbb{G}_2|.$$

Security. We will need our TB-PLBE to be secure under adaptively chosen $j_1, r_1, \ldots, r_{N_2}$ and semi-adaptively chosen m. The scheme we obtain is already adaptive in $r_1, \ldots, r_{N_2}$ and semi-adaptive in j_1, m. Since $j_1 \in [0, N_1]$ is within a polynomial range, by a standard guessing argument, the scheme is also adaptive in j_1, at a loss of $\frac{1}{N_1+1}$.

References

1. Abdalla, M., Catalano, D., Gay, R., Ursu, B.: Inner-product functional encryption with fine-grained access control. In: Moriai, S., Wang, H. (eds.) ASIACRYPT 2020. LNCS, vol. 12493, pp. 467–497. Springer, Cham (2020). https://doi.org/10.1007/978-3-030-64840-4_16
2. Agrawal, S., Libert, B., Stehlé, D.: Fully secure functional encryption for inner products, from standard assumptions. In: Robshaw, M., Katz, J. (eds.) CRYPTO 2016. LNCS, vol. 9816, pp. 333–362. Springer, Heidelberg (2016). https://doi.org/10.1007/978-3-662-53015-3_12
3. Baltico, C.E.Z., Catalano, D., Fiore, D., Gay, R.: Practical functional encryption for quadratic functions with applications to predicate encryption. In: Katz, J., Shacham, H. (eds.) CRYPTO 2017. LNCS, vol. 10401, pp. 67–98. Springer, Cham (2017). https://doi.org/10.1007/978-3-319-63688-7_3
4. Billet, O., Phan, D.H.: Efficient traitor tracing from collusion secure codes. In: Safavi-Naini, R. (ed.) ICITS 2008. LNCS, vol. 5155, pp. 171–182. Springer, Heidelberg (2008). https://doi.org/10.1007/978-3-540-85093-9_17
5. Boneh, D., Naor, M.: Traitor tracing with constant size ciphertext. In: Ning, P., Syverson, P.F., Jha, S. (eds.) ACM CCS 2008, pp. 501–510. ACM Press, October 2008. https://doi.org/10.1145/1455770.1455834
6. Boneh, D., Sahai, A., Waters, B.: Fully collusion resistant traitor tracing with short ciphertexts and private keys. In: Vaudenay, S. (ed.) EUROCRYPT 2006. LNCS, vol. 4004, pp. 573–592. Springer, Heidelberg (2006). https://doi.org/10.1007/11761679_34
7. Boneh, D., Shoup, V.: A Graduate Course in Applied Cryptography. Draft (2015). version 0.2. https://toc.cryptobook.us/

8. Boneh, D., Waters, B.: A fully collusion resistant broadcast, trace, and revoke system. In: Juels, A., Wright, R.N., De Capitani di Vimercati, S. (eds.) ACM CCS 2006. pp. 211–220. ACM Press, October/November 2006. https://doi.org/10.1145/1180405.1180432

9. Boneh, D., Zhandry, M.: Multiparty key exchange, efficient traitor tracing, and more from indistinguishability obfuscation. In: Garay, J.A., Gennaro, R. (eds.) CRYPTO 2014. LNCS, vol. 8616, pp. 480–499. Springer, Heidelberg (2014). https://doi.org/10.1007/978-3-662-44371-2_27

10. Chen, J., Gay, R., Wee, H.: Improved dual system ABE in prime-order groups via predicate encodings. In: Oswald, E., Fischlin, M. (eds.) EUROCRYPT 2015. LNCS, vol. 9057, pp. 595–624. Springer, Heidelberg (2015). https://doi.org/10.1007/978-3-662-46803-6_20

11. Chen, J., Gong, J., Kowalczyk, L., Wee, H.: Unbounded ABE via bilinear entropy expansion, revisited. In: Nielsen, J.B., Rijmen, V. (eds.) EUROCRYPT 2018. LNCS, vol. 10820, pp. 503–534. Springer, Cham (2018). https://doi.org/10.1007/978-3-319-78381-9_19

12. Chen, Y., Vaikuntanathan, V., Waters, B., Wee, H., Wichs, D.: Traitor-tracing from LWE made simple and attribute-based. In: Beimel, A., Dziembowski, S. (eds.) TCC 2018. LNCS, vol. 11240, pp. 341–369. Springer, Cham (2018). https://doi.org/10.1007/978-3-030-03810-6_13

13. Chor, B., Fiat, A., Naor, M.: Tracing traitors. In: Desmedt, Y.G. (ed.) Advances in Cryptology — CRYPTO 1994. LNCS, vol. 839, pp. 257–270. Springer, Heidelberg (1994). https://doi.org/10.1007/3-540-48658-5_25

14. Escala, A., Herold, G., Kiltz, E., Ràfols, C., Villar, J.: An algebraic framework for Diffie-Hellman assumptions. In: Canetti, R., Garay, J.A. (eds.) CRYPTO 2013. LNCS, vol. 8043, pp. 129–147. Springer, Heidelberg (2013). https://doi.org/10.1007/978-3-642-40084-1_8

15. Etesami, O., Mahloujifar, S., Mahmoody, M.: Computational concentration of measure: Optimal bounds, reductions, and more. In: Chawla, S. (ed.) 31st SODA, pp. 345–363. ACM-SIAM, January 2020. https://doi.org/10.1137/1.9781611975994.21

16. Gong, J., Luo, J., Wee, H.: Traitor tracing with $N^{1/3}$-size ciphertexts and $O(1)$-size keys from k-Lin. Cryptology ePrint Archive, Report 2023/256 (2023). https://eprint.iacr.org/2023/256

17. Gong, J., Wee, H.: Adaptively secure ABE for DFA from k-Lin and more. In: Canteaut, A., Ishai, Y. (eds.) EUROCRYPT 2020. LNCS, vol. 12107, pp. 278–308. Springer, Cham (2020). https://doi.org/10.1007/978-3-030-45727-3_10

18. Goyal, R., Koppula, V., Russell, A., Waters, B.: Risky traitor tracing and new differential privacy negative results. In: Shacham, H., Boldyreva, A. (eds.) CRYPTO 2018. LNCS, vol. 10991, pp. 467–497. Springer, Cham (2018). https://doi.org/10.1007/978-3-319-96884-1_16

19. Goyal, R., Koppula, V., Waters, B.: Collusion resistant traitor tracing from learning with errors. In: Diakonikolas, I., Kempe, D., Henzinger, M. (eds.) 50th ACM STOC, pp. 660–670. ACM Press, June 2018. https://doi.org/10.1145/3188745.3188844

20. Goyal, R., Quach, W., Waters, B., Wichs, D.: Broadcast and trace with N^{ε} ciphertext size from standard assumptions. In: Boldyreva, A., Micciancio, D. (eds.) CRYPTO 2019. LNCS, vol. 11694, pp. 826–855. Springer, Cham (2019). https://doi.org/10.1007/978-3-030-26954-8_27

21. Ishai, Y., Wee, H.: Partial garbling schemes and their applications. In: Esparza, J., Fraigniaud, P., Husfeldt, T., Koutsoupias, E. (eds.) ICALP 2014. LNCS, vol. 8572, pp. 650–662. Springer, Heidelberg (2014). https://doi.org/10.1007/978-3-662-43948-7_54

22. Karchmer, M., Wigderson, A.: On span programs. In: Proceedings of Structures in Complexity Theory, pp. 102–111 (1993)
23. Kowalczyk, L., Wee, H.: Compact adaptively secure ABE for NC^1 from k-Lin. In: Ishai, Y., Rijmen, V. (eds.) EUROCRYPT 2019. LNCS, vol. 11476, pp. 3–33. Springer, Cham (2019). https://doi.org/10.1007/978-3-030-17653-2_1
24. Lin, H., Luo, J.: Succinct and adaptively secure ABE for ABP from k-Lin. In: Moriai, S., Wang, H. (eds.) ASIACRYPT 2020. LNCS, vol. 12493, pp. 437–466. Springer, Cham (2020). https://doi.org/10.1007/978-3-030-64840-4_15
25. Mahloujifar, S., Mahmoody, M.: Can adversarially robust learning leverage computational hardness? CoRR abs/1810.01407 (2018). http://arxiv.org/abs/1810.01407
26. Shamir, A.: How to share a secret. Commun. Assoc. Comput. Mach. **22**(11), 612–613 (1979)
27. Waters, B.: Dual system encryption: realizing fully secure IBE and HIBE under simple assumptions. In: Halevi, S. (ed.) CRYPTO 2009. LNCS, vol. 5677, pp. 619–636. Springer, Heidelberg (2009). https://doi.org/10.1007/978-3-642-03356-8_36
28. Wee, H.: Attribute-hiding predicate encryption in bilinear groups, revisited. In: Kalai, Y., Reyzin, L. (eds.) TCC 2017. LNCS, vol. 10677, pp. 206–233. Springer, Cham (2017). https://doi.org/10.1007/978-3-319-70500-2_8
29. Wee, H.: Functional encryption for quadratic functions from k-Lin, revisited. In: Pass, R., Pietrzak, K. (eds.) TCC 2020. LNCS, vol. 12550, pp. 210–228. Springer, Cham (2020). https://doi.org/10.1007/978-3-030-64375-1_8
30. Zhandry, M.: New techniques for traitor tracing: size $N^{1/3}$ and more from pairings. In: Micciancio, D., Ristenpart, T. (eds.) CRYPTO 2020. LNCS, vol. 12170, pp. 652–682. Springer, Cham (2020). https://doi.org/10.1007/978-3-030-56784-2_22

Author Index

C. Hazay and M. Stam (Eds.): EUROCRYPT 2023, LNCS 14006, pp. 669–670, 2023.
https://doi.org/10.1007/978-3-031-30620-4

Printed in the United States
by Baker & Taylor Publisher Services